Genealogical Records of Descendants of John and Anthony Emery, of Newbury, Mass., 1590-1890

GENEALOGICAL RECORDS

OF

DESCENDANTS OF

JOHN AND ANTHONY EMERY,

OF

NEWBURY, MASS,

1590-1890.

COMPILED BY

REV. RUFUS EMERY.

"Fidelis et Suavis."

EMERY CLEAVES ·
SALEM, MASS
1890

PRINTED BY
SALEM PRESS PUBLISHING AND PRINTING CO.
The Salem Press
1891

PREFACE.

This book is not an exhaustive Genealogy of the Emery Family in America, but a compilation and arrangement of such records as have been collected by the Genealogical Committee or furnished by other members of the family interested in this work, relating to the descendants of John and Anthony Emery, brothers, who came from Romsey, Hampshire, England, in 1635, and settled in Newbury the same year.

Many of the descendants of the two brothers are not to be found in this volume because their records have not been received and in many instances it has been impossible to obtain them, either because they had been destroyed or because the possessors had no interest in such a work.

There are in this country many bearing the name who are not descended from the Newbury emigrants; their ancestors having come to America subsequent to the coming of John and Anthony of Newbury, and there are others, descendants of the two brothers, who through lack of knowledge or want of interest are unable to trace any relationship to them.

It was the intention of the compiler not to publish the book till a larger part of the gaps in the record had been filled, but at the Annual Reunion held in Boston in September, 1889, the desire was general that such records as were in the hands of the committee should be arranged and published, and they were instructed by a unanimous vote that these should be printed before the next Reunion.

Great care has been taken to avoid errors but with the utmost attention perfect accuracy is impossible. The records are oftentimes conflicting and the compiler has been compelled to put down dates and facts which seemed to have the greatest probability.

There are many subjects of interest which, if time and the limits of this book allowed, might have been presented, such as the "Origin and History of the name," the "Coat of Arms" and the "Ancestors of John Emery of Romsey," but must find a place in a supplemental volume if such is desired by those interested in the Family History.

The thanks of the compiler are due to all the members of the Genealogical Committee and all others who have been engaged in this work, and who have aided either by records or the means of procuring them, particularly to John S. Emery and Thomas J. Emery of Boston for unflagging zeal and generous aid, to Edwin Emery of New Bedford, Mass., and Lieut. Jonas Aden Emery, U. S. A., Sackett's Harbor, N. Y., for their great assistance in reading and correcting the manuscript of this work

RUFUS EMERY.

INTRODUCTORY NOTE.

By Rev. Samuel Hopkins Emery, First President of the
Emery Family Association.

This bulky volume took its rise in a family meeting of the
Emerys, called by the following circular:

We, the undersigned, moved by what seems to us a becoming interest in
the Emery name and family, invite all like-minded, who bear that name or who,
once bearing it and valuing it, have married into other families, to assemble
for a pleasant family reunion in "Ould Newberrie," whence so many of us
sprang on Wednesday, Sept 3, 1879, gathering as near nine o'clock in the
morning, as possible, at the Merrimack House, in Newburyport, whence those
inclined can proceed in barges to places of interest to the Emerys in the old
town, returning for dinner to the Merrimack House, sometime in the after-
noon.

The only expense of the meeting will be one dollar for the dinner and fifty
cents for the barge and a small assessment to meet the cost of calling the meeting

Hoping the members of the Emery family will gladly and in large numbers
respond to this call, we remain,

Yours very truly,

Samuel Hopkins Emery, Taunton,
  Mass,
Rufus Emery, Newburgh, New York,
Samuel M Emery, Newburyport,
  Mass.,
George Edwin Emery, Lynn, Mass,
George Freeman Emery, Boston,
  Mass,
George Francis Emery, Boston,
  Mass,
Henry Emery Lowell, Mass

Isaac M Emery, Kennebunkport, Me,
Smith F. Emery, Centre Harbor,
  N H,
John Chamberlin Emery, Montpelier,
  Vt,
Joseph Faulkner Emery, Philadel-
  phia, Pa,
Joseph Welch Emery, Quincy, Ill,
Charles Francis Emery, Kansas City,
  Mo.,
And sixteen others.

More than a hundred responded to this call and it was a very
enthusiastic meeting. The following officers were appointed:

President, Rev. SAMUEL HOPKINS EMERY, of Taunton, Mass
Secretary, GEORGE FRANCIS EMERY, Esq., of Boston, Mass.
Treasurer, Rev SAMUEL M. EMERY, of Newburyport, Mass.

The above-named officers and THOMAS C. AMORY, Esq., of Boston, Mass., Rev. RUFUS EMERY, of Newburgh, N. Y., THOMAS J. EMERY, Esq., of Boston, Mass , Messrs. JOHN S. EMERY and WILLIAM G. EMERY of Boston, CALEB J. EMERY of Newton and HENRY EMERY, of Lowell, were chosen an Executive Committee.

Prayer was offered by Rev. Samuel M. Emery, of Newburyport.

The day was spent in visiting the landing place of John and Anthony Emery at Parker river, and the localities where they first settled, not forgetting the burial places of the dead, where, with bowed heads, religious services were held. The dinner at the Merrimack House was followed by addresses and reminiscences from various members of the family present. It was voted, with entire unanimity to hold another meeting the next year.

A second meeting was held in Newburyport, Sept. 9, 1880.

The morning was spent in visiting the farm of Rev. Samuel M. Emery at West Newbury, on the Artichoke and Merrimack rivers, formerly owned by John, jr., son of John Emery, senior, and which has been in the family ever since.

Dinner was served at the Merrimack House.

The meeting was called to order by the President, Rev. Samuel H. Emery, of Taunton.

Rev. Rufus Emery, of Newburgh, N. Y., read a paper on the Romsey emigrants, John and Anthony Emery. He also stated what had been accomplished during the year in gathering genealogical material.

Hon. Thomas C. Amory, of Boston, read a paper upon the early history of the name, tracing the history of the family in England.

Hon. Charles Emery Stevens, of Worcester, read an essay upon the Emery coat of arms.

A vote of thanks to the above-named gentlemen was passed, for their interesting and instructive papers.

Officers for the ensuing year were chosen as follows:

President, Rev SAMUEL HOPKINS EMERY, of Taunton, Mass.

Secretary, THOMAS J. EMERY, Esq., of Boston, Mass.

Treasurer, Rev. SAMUEL M. EMERY, of Newburyport, Mass.

The above-named officers and Messrs. George Francis Emery, John S. Emery, Thomas C. Amory, William G. Emery, George Freeman Emery, all of Boston, and Rev Rufus Emery, of Newburgh, N Y, Caleb J. Emery, of Newton, Henry Emery, of Lowell, George E Emery, of Lynn, were appointed an Executive Committee.

Rev. Rufus Emery was chosen historian of the family, to be assisted by Josiah Emery, of Williamsport, Pa., George E. Emery, of Lynn, Mass, John S Emery, of Boston, Edwin Emery, of New Bedford, Mass, and Rev Enville J. Emery, of West Swanzey, N. H.

Voted, to meet next year, in Dover Point, N. H., where Anthony Emery settled.

A third meeting was held at the Dover Point House, Dover Point, N. H, Sept. 8, 1881.

The meeting was opened with prayer by the President.

A paper on the life and labors of Elder Joshua Emery, of Berwick, Me., prepared by Rev. Enville J. Emery, was read by Rev. Rufus Emery.

Edwin Emery read a paper upon Col. Caleb Emery of Sanford, Me

A poem by Eva L. Emery was then read.

A committee, of which Rev. Rufus Emery was chairman, presented a resolution of respect and sympathy for the President of the United States, dangerously sick, which was adopted, and followed with prayer by Rev. George F. Clark, of Mendon.

Mayor Murphy of Dover, extended the congratulations of the city to the family. United States Senator Rollins, also, of New Hampshire, being present, expressed his interest in the object of the meeting.

Rev. Rufus Emery gave an account of the life of Anthony Emery, whose house was once in this part of Dover and whose place of settlement had been visited by some of the family in the morning.

The president of the family meeting, declining a reelection, Rev. Rufus Emery, of Newburgh, N. Y., was chosen President.

Treasurer and Secretary, Thomas J. Emery, Esq., of Boston.

Executive and Genealogical Committees same as last year, with the addition of Rev. George F Clark to the latter committee.

The singing of Auld Lang Syne closed the meeting.

A fourth meeting was held in Fraternity Hall, Newburyport, Sept. 6, 1882.

The meeting was opened with prayer by Rev. S. H. Emery, of Taunton.

The President, Rev. Rufus Emery, delivered an address. He also read a poem, written for the occasion, by Mrs. Eva L. Dye, formerly Emery, of Ohio.

The Genealogical Committee made a report.

The officers of last year were reelected, with the addition to the Executive Committee of George A. Emery, Saco, Me., George H. Emery, Concord, N. H., John C. Emery, Montpelier, Vt., and Josiah Emery, Williamsport, Pa Dinner was served with the usual after-dinner speeches. It was voted to meet in 1883.

The fifth meeting was held in Newburyport, Sept. 12, 1883.

It was opened with prayer by Rev. S H. Emery, of Taunton.

The officers of the preceding year were reelected with the addition of Lewis Emery, jr, of Bradford, Pa., to the Executive Committee.

A poem, written by Brainerd P. Emery, was read by the President.

The time of the meeting was principally occupied with the report of the Genealogical Committee and discussion of matters relating thereto.

Voted, that the time and place of the next meeting be left with the Executive Committee.

As usual, there was a dinner, with after-dinner speeches.

No meeting was held in 1884. The Executive Committee decided Boston was the most convenient place in which to hold family meetings. Accordingly the sixth meeting was held in the Meionaon, Tremont Temple, Boston, Thursday, Sept. 10, 1885.

The attendance was unusually large, something like two hundred. Prayer was offered by Rev. Ira Emery, of China, Me.

Hon. George F Emery, of Portland, Me , delivered an address.

Hon. Charles Emery Stevens, of Worcester, read a paper on Noah Emery, of Exeter, N H.

A poem by Mrs. E. Emery Dye was read by the President, and a hymn, composed by Mrs. Emery Tilton, was sung

The officers of preceding year were reelected, with addition of Emery Cleaves, of Boston, Mass., Charles W. Emery, Canterbury, N H., to the Genealogical Committee; and William H. Emery, of Boston, Noah Emery, Bangor, Me., Samuel H. Emery, jr., Concord, Mass , Mark P. Emery, Portland, Me., to the Executive Committee.

An excellent dinner was provided, followed by speeches.

The seventh meeting was held in the Meionaon, Tremont Temple, Boston, Sept. 13, 1886.

Prayer by Rev. S. Hopkins Emery, of Taunton.

Genealogical matters occupied most of the time of the meeting

The officers of preceding years were re-appointed, with addition to the Executive Committee of George W. Emery, Marshfield, Mass., Thomas B. Emery, Greensboro', Ohio, Matthew G. Emery, Washington, D. C., Francis F. Emery, Boston, Stephen A. Emery, Newton, Mass.

As usual, an excellent dinner with speeches.

The eighth meeting was held in Boston, Sept. 14, 1887, in the same place, opened with prayer by Rev. Charles M. Emery, of Portland, Me.

A hymn, written by Miss Mabel S. Emery, of Lynn, was sung.

The address was delivered by Rev. S. Hopkins Emery, of Taunton, who also read a poem by Miss Eleanor S. Deane, of Taunton, as, also, a hymn by Miss Ann D. Reed, of Taunton, which was sung.

A change in officers was made by appointing those who had been members of the Executive Committee, residents in other states, as Vice Presidents, adding to their number Hon. Hannibal Hamlin, of Bangor, Me

S. Hopkins Emery was appointed a committee of one to bear friendly greetings to the Boynton Family, in session in another part of the Temple He returned, bringing with him a kind response from the Boyntons.

An excellent dinner, as usual, was served, followed by speaking

The ninth meeting was held in Boston, Sept. 12, 1888. Prayer by Rev. S H. Emery, of Taunton.

A telegram of greeting was sent to the Perry family in Reholoth, who returned a friendly answer. A poem by Mrs. D. A. Green, of Medford, was read. Dinner, as usual, with speaking.   No essential change in officers

The tenth meeting was held in Boston, Sept. 18, 1889, opened with prayer by Rev. Charles M. Emery, of Portland, Me

Poems written by Miss Ellen H. Butler, of Portland, Me , and George W. Emery, of Minneapolis, Minn., were read by the President, who also reported, for the Genealogical Committee, satisfactory progress, and on motion of Rev. S H Emery, the thanks of the family were cordially extended to this committee for their good work

Dinner, with after speaking, as usual. No change in officers.

The eleventh meeting was held in Boston, Sept 18, 1890, in the usual place.

After an interesting opening address by President Rufus Emery, prayer was offered by Rev. George F. Clark, of West Acton, Mass.

Edwin Emery, of New Bedford, read a paper on the origin and significance of the family name. Both papers were considered of great value and were requested for publication in a supplement to the forthcoming book. Readers, who should detect errors in the book were desired to send notice of the same at once to the chairman of the publication committee, Rev. Rufus Emery, Newburgh, N. Y.

A poem by Mrs Eva Emery Dye, of Oregon City, O., was read by the President, sent by the writer from her western home.

Dinner and the after-dinner speaking had their usual interest

Officers of the Association were unanimously chosen for 1890–91, as follows :

President, Rev. RUFUS EMERY, Newburgh, N. Y.

Vice Presidents, Hon. HANNIBAL HAMLIN, Bangor, Me., Rev. S. HOPKINS EMERY, Taunton, Mass., Hon. MATTHEW G. EMERY, Washington, D. C., Hon LEWIS EMERY, jr., Bradford, Pa.. Hon. CHARLES T. EMERY, Toledo, Ohio. Hon. GEORGE W. EMERY, Sea View, Mass.. Hon. GEORGE F. EMERY, Portland, Me., Hon. CHARLES E. EMERY, Brooklyn, N. Y

Secretary and Treasurer, THOMAS J. EMERY, Esq., Boston, Mass.

Executive Committee, PRESIDENT and SECRETARY, and Messrs. JOHN S. EMERY, WILLIAM H. EMERY, HIRAM EMERY, FRANCIS F. EMERY, all of Boston, EMERY CLEAVES, of Salem, Mass., MARK P. EMERY, of Portland, Me.

Genealogical Committee, PRESIDENT and SECRETARY, and Messrs. JOHN S EMERY, Boston, EDWIN EMERY, New Bedford, EMERY CLEAVES, Salem, GEORGE F. CLARK, West Acton, CHARLES E. STEVENS, Worcester, CHARLES W. EMERY, Canterbury, N. H., Lieut. JONAS A. EMERY, U. S A., Sackett's Harbor, N. Y., and Miss JANE T. EMERY, South Berwick, Me.

PART I.

JOHN EMERY, SEN. AND HIS DESCENDANTS.

1 JOHN EMERY, sen., son of John and Agnes Emery of Romsey, Hants, England, was born in England, Sept 29, 1598; he sailed from Southampton, April 3, 1635, with his brother Anthony in the ship James of London, William Cooper, Master, their wives and one or two children each probably with them; he landed in Boston, June 3, 1635, and went soon after to Newbury where John, sen., had a town grant of half an acre for a house lot John Emery was fined Dec. 22, 1637, by the town, twenty shillings for inclosing ground not laid out, or owned by the town, contrary to a town order, and on Feb. 1, 1638, the town granted him that part of ground which was already inclosed He was made freeman June 2. 1641, and recorded as one of the ninety-one freeholders of the town Dec 2, 1642, in the same year he was appointed with three others to make a valuation of all the property in the town, for the purpose of proportioning each man's share in the new division On March 16, 1663, John Emery was presented to the Court at Ipswich by Henry Jaques, Constable of Newbury, for entertaining travellers and Quakers May 5, 1663, his presentment for entertaining Quakers was referred unto next Court. The next Court fined him four pounds, costs and fees for entertaining strangers. The evidence given in the case was "yt two men quakers wi entertained very kindly to bed and table & John Emmerie shok ym by ye hand and bid ym welcome" Also, "that the witness heard John Emery and his wife say that he had entertained quakers and that he would not put them from his house and used argument for the lawfulness of it" John Emery in May, 1663, petitioned the General Court for the remission of his fine His petition was signed by the selectmen of the town and fifty of the citizens The fine was not remitted.

He was also prominent in the case of Lieut Robert Pike, refusing to recognize the authority of the Court to deprive him and his neighbors of the right of petition In the famous ecclesiastical difficulties John Emery was a member of the Woodman party.

April 10, 1644, he had a grant from the town of twenty-two acres and five rods being his own and Henry Palmer's portion of "Divident" land in the great field beyond the new town He was selectman, 1661, fence viewer, 1666; grand juryman in the same year, jury of trials in 1672, appointed to carry votes to Salem in 1676. He married, first, in England, Mary ———. who died in Newbury, April, 1649 He married, second, Mrs. Mary Webster (*née* Shatswell) widow

of John Webster of Ipswich, Oct. 29, 1650   He died in Newbury,
Mass., Nov. 3, 1683.   His wife died April 28, 1694.   He made his
will May 1, 1680, proved Nov. 27, 1683, in which he mentions his
age as eighty-three years   The inventory of his estate was taken the
same day, amounting to 263 pounds, 11 shillings.   His wife made
her will Aug., 1693, proved June 11, 1696.

Children

  2   i   JOHN,[2] b in England, about 1628.
  3   ii   ANN, b in England about 1631.
  4   iii   EBENEZER, daughter, b in Newbury, Sept. 16, 1648.
  5   iv   JONATHAN, b in Newbury, May 13, 1652.

2 JOHN[2] EMERY, jun. (*John[1]*), son of John Emery, sen., and his
first wife, came with his father to Newbury in 1635 , married Mary
Webster daughter of John and Mary (Shatswell) Webster, Oct. 2,
1648.   Selectman. 1670–1673 ; jury of trials, 1675–1676 ; chosen to
carry votes to Salem 1675–1676 , chosen to serve on jury of trials at
Ipswich , tything-man, 1679 , way-warden, 1679.   In 1642 he had laid
out to him fourscore acres over the Artichoke or Raspberry River.
Forty acres of this land was a grant of the town of Newbury to John
Emery, sen., and by him given to his son in consideration of love
and affection.   The remaining forty acres were bought of Archelaus
Woodman for thirty pounds, being a town grant to him.   This tract
of land has been in possession of the name since it was laid out to
John Emery, jun. ; and now, included in the farm of the late Eliphalet Emery, Esq., of West Newbury, is owned by his daughter, Mrs.
Mary Hale Emery.   In 1679, March 3, " the town of (Newbury)
granted John Emery, jun., twelve acres of land on the west side of
Artichoke River, provided he build and maintain a corn mill to grind
the town's corn from time to time and to build it within one year and
a half after the date hereof."   This mill is now known as Curzons Mills,
Newburyport, Mass.   John Emery, jun., was a signer of the petition
in the case of Lieut. Robert Pike, and a member of the Woodman
party in the church difficulties.   He is styled Sergeant on the records.
He was made freeman May 30, 1660 ; made his will Aug. 3, 1693.
His wife died Feb. 3. 1709.

Children, born in Newbury :

  6   i   MARY,[3] b. June 24, 1652
  7   ii   HANNAH, b April 26, 1654.
  8   iii   JOHN, b Sept 12, 1656, d July 14, 1730.
  9   iv   BETHIA, b Oct 15, 1658.
10   v   SARAH, b Feb 26, 1660.
11   vi   JOSEPH, b March 23, 1663 ; d in Andover, Mass , Sept. 22,
            1721
12   vii   STEPHEN b. Sept. 6, 1666.
13   viii   ABIGAIL, b Jan 16, 1668.
14   ix   SAMUEL, b Dec 20, 1670.
15   x   JUDITH, b Feb. 5, 1673
16   xi   LYDIA, b Feb. 19, 1675
17   xii   ELIZABETH, b. Feb. 8, 1680.
18   xiii   JOSIAH, b. Feb 28, 1681, m. Abigail, dau of Dr Caleb and
            Ruth (Morse) Moody, Nov 25, 1714 He died March 16, 1718.
            She m., 2nd, Jno Stickney, jr ; 3d, Capt. William Johnson;
            4th, Joseph Swasey.

3 ANN[2] EMERY (*John*[1]), daughter of John Emery, sen., and his first wife, married James Ordway (born 1620, died after 1702), Nov. 23, 1648. She died March 31, 1687.
Children, born in Newbury:

19 i   EPHRAIM,[3] b April 25, 1650.
20 ii   JAMES, b. April 16, 1651
21 iii EDWARD, b Sept 14, 1653.
22 iv   SARAH, b Sept 14, 1656
23 v   JOHN, b. Nov. 17, 1658
24 vi   ISAAC, b Dec. 4, 1660, d. at the age of eight years.
25 vii JANE, b Nov 12, 1663.
26 viii HANNANIAH, b Dec 2, 1665.
27 ix   ANN, b. Feb 12, 1670
28 x   MARY, b April 5, 1671.

4 EBENEZER[2] EMERY (*John*[1]), daughter of John Emery, sen., and his first wife, married John Hoag, April 21, 1669 John Hoag was born in England, or Wales, in 1643, and came to America with his father's family when about seven years old The rest of the family returned, but John, being bound out as an apprentice, was obliged to remain. He was opposed to the Salem witchcraft. After the children were grown up all the family became Quakers. John Hoag died 1728, aged 85
Children, born in Newbury:

29 i   JOHN,[3] b Feb 20, 1670.
30 ii   JONATHAN, b. Oct. 28, 1671, m Martha Goodwin.
31 iii JOSEPH, b Jan 10, 1677.
32 iv   HANNAH, b. Jan. 3, 1683
33 v   JUDITH, b April 20, 1687.

5 JONATHAN[2] EMERY (*John*[1]), son of John, sen., and Mrs. Mary (Webster) Emery, made freeman April 19, 1691 ; married Mary Woodman, daughter of Mr. Edward Woodman, Nov. 29, 1676. He was pressed at Newbury, Dec. 3, 1675, as a soldier for King Philip's War and was at the great Narragansett fight Dec 19, 1675, and wounded in the shoulder. His will was made Feb. 6, 1722–23 ; proved Oct 7, 1723. Amount of inventory, two hundred and two pounds, two shillings ten pence He died in Newbury, Sept. 29, 1723. His wife died Sept. 13, 1723.
Children, born in Newbury:

34 i   MARY,[3] b Sept 25, 1677
35 ii   JOHN, b ———, 1678
36 iii JONATHAN, b Feb. 2, 1680.
37 iv   DAVID, b. Sept 28, 1682
38 v   ANTHONY, b Nov 13, 1684; m. Hannah Plummer, 1711; d. April 6, 1766, without issue His wife d April 6, 1760, æ. 77 years.
39 vi   STEPHEN, b Jan. 13, 1687, d Dec. 19, 1688.
40 vii SARAH, b Dec 18, 1688; m. Ambrose Berry, June 3, 1728
41 viii STEPHEN, b June 24, 1693.
42 ix   EDWARD, b Nov 10, 1694
43 x   JAMES, bapt. April 10, 1698.

6 MARY[3] EMERY (*John,*[2] *John*[1]), daughter of John, jun., and Mary (Webster) Emery, born 1652; married Samuel Sawyer, son of Wil-

liam and Ruth Sawyer, March 18, 1670-71. He was made freeman
May 12, 1675 , died Feb. 11, 1718.
Children, born in Newbury :

44   i   MARY,⁴ b. Jan 20, 1672.
45   ii   SAMUEL, b June 5, 1674.
46   iii   JOHN, b March 15, 1676.
47   iv   JOSHUA.
48   v   HANNAH, b Jan 12, 1679
49   vi   JOSIAH, b Jan. 20, 1681.
50   vii   JOHN, b. Feb 23 1683.
51   viii   A DAUGHTER, b. March 7, 1685.
52   ix   BENJAMIN, b. Oct 27, 1686.

7 HANNAH³ EMERY (*John,² John¹*), daughter of John, jun., and
Mary (Webster) Emery, born 1654 , married, Nov. 18, 1673, Richard
Bartlett, son of Richard and Abigail Bartlett, born Feb. 21, 1649.
Children :

53   i   HANNAH,⁴ b Nov 8, 1674.
54   ii   RICHARD, b Oct 20, 1676
55   iii   JOHN, b Sept 23, 1678.
56   iv   SAMUEL b July 8, 1680
57   v   DANIEL, b Aug. 8, 1682.
58   vi   JOSEPH, b Nov 18, 1686.
59   vii   SAMUEL, b May 2, 1689
60   viii   STEPHEN, b. April 21, 1691.
61   ix   THOMAS, b July 14, 1695
62   x   MARY, b. Sept 15, 1697

8 JOHN³ EMERY (*John,² John¹*), son of John, jun., and Mary
(Webster) Emery, married Mary Sawyer (daughter of William and
Ruth Sawyer, born July 29, 1660) June 13, 1683 ; Mary Sawyer
Emery died Nov 3, 1699. He married, second, Abigail Bartlett,
May 27, 1700 ; and, third, May March, Dec 7, 1723.
Children, born in Newbury :

63   i   MARY⁴, b Dec 29, 1684, m Jonathan Wiggins, Nov. 9, 1703.
64   ii   JOHN, b Sept 29 1686.
65   iii   JOSIAH, b. Dec. 19, 1688 , d March 16, 1718.
66   iv   DANIEL, b June 15, 1693.
67   v   LYDIA b April 29, 1698
68   vi   SAMUEL, b Oct 25, 1699.
69   vii   RUTH.
70   viii   HANNAH.

9 BETHIA³ EMERY (*John,² John¹*), daughter of John Emery, jun., and
Mary (Webster) Emery, born 1658 ; married Henry Bodwell, May 4,
1681. Henry Bodwell was pressed from Newbury, Aug., 1676, to go
against the Indian enemy. He was one of the survivors of the battle
of Bloody Brook , had his left arm broken by a musket ball ; being a
man of great strength and courage, he seized his gun in his right hand
and, swinging it around his head, forced his way through the Indians
by whom he was surrounded. He was a renowned hunter and marks-
man and a terror to the hostile Indians   He is said on one occasion,
to have shot an Indian on the opposite side of the Merrimack, who,
thinking himself at a safe distance, was making insulting gestures.

Children :

71	i	BETHIA,[4] b June 2, 1682.
72	ii	MARY, b April 1, 1684
73	iii	HENRY and JOSIAH, twins, b Jan 27, 1685, both died the same year
74	iv	ABIGAIL, b Jan 15, 1686.
75	v	HENRY, b Nov 6, 1688
76	vi	JAMES, b. Jan. 16, 1691
77	vii	DANIEL, b Feb 14, 1693.
78	viii	SARAH, b Dec. 1, 1694
79	ix	HANNAH, b Sept 1, 1696
80	x	JUDITH, b April 4, 1698.
81	xi	RUTH, b Dec. 2, 1699.
82	xii	CHILD, b. July 10, 1701.

10 SARAH[3] EMERY (*John,*[2] *John*[1]), daughter of John, jun , and Mary (Webster) Emery, married Isaac Bailey, June 13, 1683. She died April 1, 1694. He married, second, Rebecca Bartlett, Sept. 5, 1700.

Children, born in Newbury :

83	i	ISAAC,[4] b. Dec 30, 1683, m Sarah Titcomb.
84	ii	JOSHUA, b. Oct 30, 1685.
85	iii	DAVID, b Dec 12, 1687, m Experience Putnam
86	iv	JUDITH, b Feb 11, 1690, m James Ordway
87	v	SARAH, b Feb 11, 1692.

11 JOSEPH[3] EMERY (*John,*[2] *John*[1]), son of John, jun., and Mary (Webster) Emery, married Elizabeth Merrill, daughter of Abraham and Abigail (Webster) Merrill, Oct 2, 1693. He died in Andover, Mass , Sept 22, 1721. Abigail Webster was the daughter of Mrs. Mary Webster, the second wife of John Emery, sen.

Children, born in Andover :

88	i	JOSEPH,[4] b April 9, 1696.
89	ii	ELIZABETH, b Sept 28, 1698
90	iii	MARY.
91	iv	SARAH, m William Russell
92	v	ABIGAIL, b Nov , 1705
93	vi	HANNAH, b ———; d unm , 1746.

12 ENSIGN STEPHEN[3] EMERY (*John,*[2] *John*[1]), son of John, jun., and Mary (Webster) Emery, married Nov. 29, 1692, Ruth, daughter of Henry and Anna (Knight) Jaques (born April 14, 1672). Millwright and planter. He died Feb. 1, 1746-7. His wife died Jan. 9, 1764.

Children, born in Newbury :

94	i	ANNA,[4] b Oct 10, 1693
95	ii	SARAH, b Jan 1, 1696
96	iii	RUTH, b June 6, 1698
97	iv	MARY, b Dec 15, 1700
98	v	JUDITH, b Feb 25, 1703.
99	vi	ABIGAIL, b May 4, 1705.
100	vii	ELIZABETH, b Feb 2, 1708.
101	viii	STEPHEN, b July 16, 1710.

102 ix HANNAH, b. April 23, 1712; d., unm., 1772
103 x   MIRIAM, b Nov 22, 1714
104 xi LYDIA, b July 29, 1717 (see No 257).

13 ABIGAIL[3] EMERY (*John,[2] John[1]*), daughter of John, jun. and Mary (Webster) Emery; married Henry Ingalls, Jan. 6, 1688. Children, born in Andover :

105 i   HENRY,[4] b April 2, 1689.
106 ii   MARY, b. Feb 25, 1691
107 iii ABIGAIL, b. Jan. 15, 1693
108 iv   FRANCIS, b Dec. 20, 1694
109 v   JOSEPH, b. April 17, 1697

14 REV. SAMUEL[3] EMERY (*John,[2] John[1]*), son of John, jun. and Mary (Webster) Emery ; graduated at Harvard College, 1691.   He went to Wells, Me , previous to 1698, probably as chaplain to the garrison stationed there.   In the town records of 1698, he is mentioned as a minister of the town.   March 17, 1701, the town voted to settle Mr Emery as their regular minister and " to give him yearly 45 pounds to be paid one half in good merchantable provisions as follows · Wheat at five shillings a bushel , Indian corn at three shillings a bushel , rye at three shillings a bushel ; pork at three pence a pound ; beef at two pence a pound ; and to cut and bring to his house twenty-five cords of fire wood and that he should have the use of the ministerial land " A church was organized Oct. 29, 1701. Mr Emery was ordained Oct. 29, 1701, the churches of Newbury, Dover, Portsmouth and York being invited to assist   In 1716, the people being poor in consequence of the war, Mr Emery relinquished all that was due, being a large part of the amount allowed him as salary   After this his people raised his salary to eighty pounds, and directed all mill rents to be paid to him and built a study for his use   The latter years of his life were disturbed by some troublesome matters.   He was charitable and of a quiet temperament, performing his duty without ostentation, with zeal and courage fulfilling in an eminent degree the apostolic precept, " as much as in you lieth live peaceably with all men."

Rev Samuel Emery married Tabitha Littlefield, daughter of Francis Littlefield, jun., of Wells.   He died at Biddeford, Me , Dec 28, 1724.   Mrs Emery died April 27, 1736.

Children, born in Wells :

110 i   SAMUEL,[4] b Aug 14. 1698.
111 ii   MARY, b Dec 7, 1699 , m John Fairfield
112 iii HANNAH, b Feb 10, 1701 , m. Ira Littlefield.
113 iv   SARAH, b Dec. 29, 1702
114 v   TABITHA, b. March 23, 1704.
115 vi   REV STEPHEN, b. Aug 3, 1707.
116 vii IRENE, b March 4, 1710
117 viii JOHN, b March 2, 1715 , d , unm., 1736

15 JUDITH[3] EMERY (*John,[2] John[1]*), daughter of John, jun. and Mary (Webster) Emery , married Abel Huse, son of Abel and Mary (Sears) Huse, born Feb. 19, 1665. He died in Newbury, March 11, 1758, aged 93.

Children, born in Newbury ·

118   i   JOHN,⁴ b Oct 31, 1694
119   ii ABEI, b Nov. 18, 1696
120   iii STEPHEN, b Nov 16, 1702; grad of Harvard College, 1726, m
              Mrs Judith Emery, widow of Daniel Emery (d Sept 5,
              1736). Dr. Huse removed to Haverhill, Mass , m. Sarah
              Clement, Jan 2, 1785
121   iv SAMUEL, b March 30, 1705.
122   v   JUDITH, b Feb 13, 1709, m John Holman.
123   vi SARAH, b Jan 29, 1712, m Caleb Kimball.
124   vii MARY, b March 16, 1716; m Enoch Davis, May 8, 1760.

16 LYDIA³ EMERY (*John,² John¹*), daughter of John, jun., and Mary
(Webster) Emery; married Joseph Brown, 1696.
  Children :

125   i   JOSEPH,⁴ b. Nov. 1, 1699.
126   ii FRANCIS, b Jan 23, 1702
127   iii ELIZABETH, b June 8, 1716; m. Ebenezer Little; d in Camp-
              ton, N. H., Nov. 13, 1795

17 ELIZABETH³ EMERY (*John², John¹*), daughter of John, jun., and
Mary (Webster) Emery, married John Kelly, jun., Nov. 6, 1696
(born June 17, 1668; died Nov. 3, 1735).
  Children :

128   i   JOHN,⁴ b Oct 8, 1697
129   ii   ELIZABETH, bapt. Oct 1, 1699, m Stephen Morse.
130   iii JUDITH, bapt March 29, 1702
131   iv   RICHARD, b March 8, 1704
132   v   STEPHEN, b July 9, 1706, d young
133   vi   MARY, b Dec. 31, 1708, m Samuel Sawyer, July 9, 1729
134   vii HANNAH, b. March 2, 1711
135   viii LYDIA, b May 31, 1713
136   ix   DANIEL, b May 9, 1716.
137   x   SARAH, b. Oct. 6, 1718
138   xi   MOSES, b. July 20, 1721, d. young

20 JAMES³ ORDWAY (*Ann,² John¹*), son of James and Ann
(Emery) Ordway; married Tirzah Bartlett, widow of Thomas Bart-
lett and daughter of William and Joanna (Bartlett) Titcomb, born
in Newbury, Feb 21, 1658. He married, second, Sarah Clark of
Rowley, May, 1696.
  Children :

139   i   A CHILD,⁴ b Oct 16, 1691, d Jan 10, 1696.
140   ii LYDIA, b July 12, 1693, d young
141   iii LYDIA, b. July 14, 1696.
142   iv JOANNA, b. May 22, 1697
143   v   JOHN, b June 22, 1699
144   vi MARY, b. April 28, 1703.

21 EDWARD³ ORDWAY (*Ann,² John¹*), son of James and Ann
(Emery) Ordway; married Mary Wood, Dec. 12, 1678.
  Children ·

145   i   JOANNA,⁴ b. Nov. 28, 1685.
146   ii RACHEL, b. Jan 14, 1688
147   iii JACOB, b Jan 14, 1690
148   iv ISAIAH, b Jan 28, 1692.
149   v   DANIEL, b Jan., 1694.

23 John[3] ORDWAY (*Ann*,[2] *John*[1]), son of James and Ann (Emery) Ordway, married Mary Godfrey, daughter of Peter and Mary (Browne) Godfrey, Dec. 5, 1681.
Children:

    150　i　MARY,[4] b Sept 18, 1682
    151　ii　JOHN, b Oct 29, 1684.
    152　iii　JAMES, b July 4, 1687
    153　iv　PETER, b. Sept 15, 1691
    154　v　HANNAH, b Nov 29, 1693, d young.
    155　vi　HANNAH, b March 6, 1695.
    156　vii　STEPHEN, b. April 8, 1697.
    157　viii　ANN, b May, 1699
    158　ix　NATHAN, b April 28, 1703

26 HANNANIAH[3] ORDWAY (*Ann*,[2] *John*[1]), son of James and Ann (Emery) Ordway, married ———
Children.

    159　i　REBECCA,[4] b Dec. 29, 1690
    160　ii　ABIGAIL, b Aug. 2, 1693.
    161　iii　NATHANIEL, b July 3, 1695
    162　iv　JOANNA, b. April 15, 1698.
    163　v　ELIZABETH, b Feb 15, 1702

35 JOHN[3] EMERY (*Jonathan*,[2] *John*[1]), son of Jonathan and Mary (Woodman) Emery, married Hannah Morse, daughter of Joshua and Joanna Morse, Feb 1705, second, Rebecca Walker, Nov. 8, 1733. He died Aug 24, 1759. First wife died Oct. 4, 1732. Second wife died Oct 19, 1753.
Children:

    164　i　HANNAH,[4] b. Jan 19, 1706, m Edward Holman, May 19, 1726.
    165　ii　JOSHUA, b March 21, 1709
    166　iii　DAVID, b Jan 24, 1710
    167　iv　SARAH, b Dec 5, 1711; m David Chase, Nov 24, 1729.
    168　v　ANTHONY, b Sept 5 1713
    169　vi　JOHN, b. June 30, 1715
    170　vii　MEHETABLE, b Oct 12, 1718
    171　viii　JUDITH, b Jan 10, 1722, m Samuel Smith, Dec 2, 1742
    172　ix　MARY, b Dec 8, 1726.

36 JONATHAN[3] EMERY (*Jonathan*,[2] *John*[1]), son of Jonathan and Mary (Woodman) Emery, married Ruth Richardson, daughter of Caleb and Mary (Ladd) Richardson (born in Newbury, Dec. 4, 1683; died in Plaistow, N. H, Sept. 18, 1749)
Children, born in Newbury:

    173　i　CALEB,[4] b 1706
    174　ii　RUTH, b Aug 25 1709; m Nathan Smith, Nov. 19, 1730.
    175　iii　ANN, b April 7, 1711
    176　iv　JONATHAN, b Jan 27, 1714
    177　v　HUMPHREY, b April 15, 1715.
    178　vi　SYLVANUS, b April 7, 1717.

41 STEPHEN[3] EMERY (*Jonathan*,[2] *John*[1]), son of Jonathan and Mary (Woodman) Emery, married Lydia Jackman, Feb. 25, 1715. He made his will Oct. 5, 1761, proved June 21, 1762.
Children:

179 i REBECCA,[4] b Nov. 21, 1715
180 ii MEHETABLE, b Aug 1, 1718, m. Nathan Morse
181 iii STEPHEN, b Nov. 12, 1719.
182 iv JOHN, b Nov 23, 1721
183 v MOSES, b April 27, 1724
184 vi DANIEL, b Jan. 1, 1727.
185 vii BENJAMIN, b July 14, 1734
186 viii EDMOND, b April 5 1737, was in Capt Beniah Young's Co,
Col. Bagley's regiment at Fort William Henry, Aug 9, 1756,
and his name appears on the muster roll of Capt Young's
Co, Feb 8, 1757

42 EDWARD[3] EMERY (*Jonathan,*[2] *John*[1]), son of Jonathan and Mary
(Woodman) Emery; married, Dec. 19, 1719, Sarah Sibley (born
March 27, 1699), daughter of Samuel Sibley. He removed from Newbury to Contoocook, N H, in 1733. He was an influential citizen
and often selected to transact public business. He was a member of the
Committee to locate the town and also of one to prepare and arrange
for the ordination of Rev Phineas Stevens. The council which settled
Mr. Stevens met at Mr Emery's house. His bill for services was twenty-six shillings, for use of his house, one pound eleven shillings The
materials for the entertainment were five bushels of wheat, sixteen
pounds of pork, two pounds of sugar, " Cranberrys, cabbage and tur-
nips " In 1756 he, with Ezekiel Flanders, was killed by the Indians,
while hunting at Newfound Lake.
Children:

187 i SARAH,[4] b Nov 5, 1720, m Moses Burbank
188 ii SAMUEL, b. Dec. 14, 1722.
189 iii WILLIAM, b Jan 6, 1725
190 iv MARY, b Aug 6, 1727, m Nathaniel Danforth, jun, before
1761
191 v ANTHONY, b. Dec 6 1730, d Dec. 20, 1730
192 vi DAVID, b May 9, 1732, d Jan 21, 1735
193 vii DAVID, b Aug, 1736, d Aug 7, 1737.
194 viii EDWARD, b March 10, 1740.

43 JAMES[3] EMERY (*Jonathan,*[2] *John*[1]), son of Jonathan and Mary
(Woodman) Emery; married Ruth Watson of Haverhill, Mass., in Haverhill Dec. 10, 1719 He was a farmer and lived in Haverhill till
about 1725, when he moved to Dracut, Mass. The record of baptism
of James Emery is from the records of the First Church of Newbury.
The records of birth and death of himself and wife are not known He
was probably born in Newbury, early in 1698 It is probable that she
was born in Haverhill and that she died in Dracut.

He died in Dracut before April 4, 1763, having made his will May
3, 1762, at which time he stated that he was "now Inlisted a soldier
in his Majeste's Service"

On March 30, 1757, he presented a petition to the General Court of
Massachusetts in which he stated that his son Ambrose, a minor, "Inlisted himself into His Magestic's Service in the Expedition Carrying
on against Crown Point, in the year 1756, under the command of Capt.
Butterfield, and after he was dismissed [discharged] at Lake George,
as he was returning home, he was taken sick at Glasgo, and not able
to travel, and when tidings thereof was brought to your Petitioner he

sent a man and horse to fetch his son home, which occasioned considerable charge to your Petitioner, according to the account herewith exhibited." He asked that he be remunerated. He was given three pounds, nine shillings and eight pence.

Children:

195 i   DAVID,[4] b. Oct 1, 1720, at Haverhill, Mass , was living in Dracut, March 3, 1743–44.
196 ii   JONATHAN, b Nov 23, 1722 at Haverhill, Mass
197 iii EZEKIEL, b July 6, 1724, at Haverhill, Mass , d unm , before May 3, 1762
198 iv   ANTHONY, b 1726
199 v   JAMES d in Dracut, Mass., Nov 1755.
200 vi   MOSES is said to have followed the sea as captain of a vessel.
201 vii MARY was living May 4, 1792, in Dracut   She never married.
202 viii JOHN, b 1786 in Dracut, soldier in the French War, enlisted in Capt Wm Peabody's Co., Col Ichabod Plaisted's Reg Killed in battle with Indians near Fort William Henry, Sept 18, 1756
203 ix   AMBROSE, b Feb 25, 1738–39, in Dracut
204 x   EDWARD, b July 26, 1741, in Dracut
205 xi   NATHANIEL, b March 8, 1743–44, in Dracut, married Mrs Phebe Clough of Dracut He was a farmer and lived in Dracut He married for his second wife, Patience——— They lived in Anson, Me He was a soldier in the service of the Americans in the Revolution He was in Capt Henry Elkins's Co., Nov. 23, 1775   In March, 1777, he volunteered for three years under Capt Josiah Jenkins in Col Brewer's Regt He was transferred to Capt Sewall's Co , of Col Ebenezer Sprout's Regt , from which he was discharged at the expiration of his term of service He was in the battles of Hubbardstown, Bemis Heights, the surrender of Burgoyne, the assault and capture of Stony Point and Monmouth, N J He was at Valley Forge during the winter of 1777–78 There is no record of children by either marriage

45 SAMUEL[4] SAWYER (*Mary,[3] John,[2] John[1]*), son of Samuel and Mary (Emery) Sawyer; married in Newbury, Dec 17, 1702, Abigail, daughter of Joseph and Martha (Moores) Goodridge (born Sept. 17, 1675). He died April 21, 1723. His wife died Oct. 14, 1722.

Children

206 i   SAMUEL,[5] b June 4, 1705.
207 ii   MARTHA, b Feb 11, 1707, m Edmund Hale May 16, 1728.
208 iii ABIGAIL, b May 26, 1709
209 iv   JOSEPH, b April 8, 1711.
210 v   MARY, b. Oct 3, 1712.
211 vi   EDMUND, b Nov 6, 1714
212 vii JACOB, b June 4, 1716

49 JOSIAH[4] SAWYER (*Mary,[3] John,[2] John[1]*), son of Samuel and Mary (Emery) Sawyer , married Jan. 22, 1708, Tirzah, daughter of Thomas and Tirzah (Titcomb) Bartlett.

Children :

213 i   JOSIAH,[5] b April 12, 1709.
214 ii   TIRZAH, b Nov 7, 1713
215 iii ISRAEL, b Oct 9, 1717.
216 iv   GIDEON, b Dec 15 1719
217 v   JAMES, b May 12, 1722

50 John[4] Sawyer (*Mary*,[3] *John*,[2] *John*[1]), son of Samuel and Mary (Emery) Sawyer, married Mary Merrill, Dec. 25, 1700. She died Feb. 21, 1708. He married, second, Sarah, widow of Samuel Sibley of Salem, 1711.

Children, by his first wife

218   i   Judith,[2] b Oct 16, 1701
219   ii   John, b April 5, 1704.

Children, by his second wife:

220   iii   Lydia, b. March 29, 1712
221   iv   Eunice, b Jan 21, 1715, m in 1736, Joshua Woodman
222   v   Lois, b July 21, 1718

52 Benjamin[4] Sawyer (*Mary*,[3] *John*,[2] *John*[1]), son of Samuel and Mary (Emery) Sawyer, married Elizabeth———.
Children:

223   i   Benjamin,[2] b March 2 1716.
224   ii   Elizabeth, b. Sept 2, 1718

53 Hannah[4] Bartlett (*Hannah*,[3] *John*,[2] *John*[1]) daughter of Richard and Hannah (Emery) Bartlett; married John Ordway.
Children:

225   i   Nehemiah,[2] b
226   ii   Hannah, b.

54 Richard[4] Bartlett (*Hannah*.[3] *John*,[2] *John*[1]), son of Richard and Hannah (Emery) Bartlett; married Margaret Woodman, daughter of Edward Woodman, April 12, 1699
Children:

227   i   Richard[5], b. June 27 1700.
228   ii   Joseph, b. Feb. 18, 1702

55 John[4] Bartlett (*Hannah*,[3] *John*,[2] *John*[1]), son of Richard and Hannah (Emery) Bartlett; married Mary Ordway.
Child:

229   i   Hannah[5], m Richard Kelly (131), son of John and Elizabeth (Emery) Kelly (17).

57 Daniel[4] Bartlett (*Hannah*,[3] *John*,[2] *John*[1]) son of Richard and Hannah (Emery) Bartlett, married ———.
Children:

230   i   John[5]
231   ii   Daniel.
232   iii   Stephen.

58 Joseph[4] Bartlett (*Hannah*,[3] *John*[2], *John*[1]), son of Richard and Hannah (Emery) Bartlett; married ———
He was pressed and sent to Haverhill and quartered at the house of Capt Simon Wainwright. When the Indians made an attack on the

town Aug. 29, 1708, he was captured and taken to Canada. He was a prisoner four years two months and nine days. He returned to Newbury, Nov. 8, 1712. He died in 1754 at sixty-eight.

Children:

233 i JOSEPH [5]
234 ii GERSHOM.
235 iii RICHARD
236 iv MATTHIAS.
237 v ELIZABETH
238 vi MARY
239 vii HANNAH
240 viii SARAH.
241 ix MARY
242 x LYDIA

59 SAMUEL[4] BARTLETT(*Hannah*,[3] *John*,[2] *John*[1]), son of Richard and Hannah (Emery) Bartlett; married ———.

Child:

243 i JOSHUA.[5]

60 STEPHEN[4] BARTLETT (*Hannah*,[3] *John*,[2] *John*[1]), son of Richard and Hannah (Emery) Bartlett; married Hannah Webster, Dec. 18, 1712.

Children:

244 i STEPHEN [5]
245 ii JOSEPH.
246 iii SIMEON.
247 iv JOSIAH, b in Amesbury, Mass , Nov , 1729; studied medicine under Dr Ordway of Amesbury, finished his medical education in 1750 and at the age of twenty-one began the practice of medicine in Kingston, N H Representative from Kingston in 1765, chosen delegate to the Continental Congress, Aug. 23, 1775, reelected to the same office, Jan 23, 1776 He was the first to vote for and the second to sign the Declaration of Independence Delegate to the Congress at Yorktown March 14, 1778, Chief Justice of Common Pleas in 1779, Justice of the Superior Court in 1782, Chief Justice in 1788, member of the convention which adopted the Federal Constitution, Senator to Congress, 1789, President of New Hampshire, 1790–93, first Governor of the state, 1793 He died May, 1795, at sixty six. He married Hannah Webster, who died 1789.
248 v LEVI
249 vi HANNAH

61 THOMAS[4] BARTLETT (*Hannah*,[3] *John*,[2] *John*[1]), son of Richard and Hannah (Emery) Bartlett; married Hannah Moody, daughter of Cutting and Judith (Little) Moody.

Children:

250 i CUTTING [5]
251 ii EDMUND.
252 iii ABIGAIL
253 iv PARKER
254 v JUDITH

62 MARY[4] BARTLETT (*Hannah,*[3] *John*[2], *John*[1]), daughter of Richard and Hannah (Emery) Bartlett, married——Hill.
Children.

255 i NEHEMIAH [5]
256 ii JOSIAH

64 JOHN[4] EMERY (*John,*[3] *John,*[2] *John*[1]), son of John and Mary (Sawyer) Emery; married Mehetable, daughter of Henry and Ann (Longfellow) Short, Dec. 30, 1714. Mrs Ann (Longfellow) Short was the second wife of Henry Short, widow of William Longfellow and daughter of Henry Sewall and Jane Dummer. Lieut. John Emery died June 30, 1750, aged sixty-four. His wife died June 11, 1773, aged sixty-eight
Children:

257 i MOSES,[5] b Oct 12, 1715. See No. 104
258 ii ANNA, b. Nov 21, 1716, m Woodbridge Brown, son of Rev.
      W Brown of Abington Mass
259 iii JOSIAH, b March 16, 1718, d Dec 8, 1729
260 iv MARY, b. Jan 25, 1720.
261 v JOHN, b Feb 24, 1722, d Aug 1, 1736.
262 vi MEHITABLE, b March 23, 1725, d June 29, 1739.
263 vii SARAH, b Dec 15, 1726
264 viii JANE, b Aug 4, 1729, d June 19 1736
265 ix JOSIAH, b Oct 29, 1731, d June 4, 1736.
266 x DANIEL b Dec 7, 1733
267 xi SAMUEL, b July 26, 1737.

66 DANIEL[4] EMERY (*John,*[3] *John,*[2] *John*[1]), son of John and Mary (Sawyer) Emery; married Hannah, daughter of Jacob Tappan, Nov. 26, 1718, made his will Jan. 2, 1728–29; proved Feb. 3, 1728–29. He gave sixty pounds for the use of the ministry, of which ten pounds was for Communion plate twenty pounds more for the first Church which should be gathered at Chester, N. H., and a minister ordained; twenty pounds for Nottingham, N H., twenty pounds to the Parish in which he belonged, twenty-five pounds to Mr. Tufts, fifty pounds to his kinsman in College, and one thousand pounds to his brothers and sisters, besides providing liberally for his widow.

Mrs. Hannah (Tappan) Emery died Oct 15, 1719, aged twenty. He married, second, Mrs. Judith Knight widow of Mr John Knight, Nov. 29, 1723, died Jan. 28, 1728–29 aged thirty-six. Mrs. Judith Emery married, third, Mr. Stephen Huse, July 30, 1729 and died Sept. 5, 1736.

Children, born in Newbury.

268 i SAMUEL,[5] b Oct 11, 1719, probably died young
269 ii MARY, b Nov. 10, 1724, probably died young.

67 LYDIA[4] EMERY (*John,*[3] *John,*[2] *John*[1]), daughter of John and (Mary Sawyer) Emery; married Edward Dean of Ipswich, son of Philemon Dean, May 29, 1716. He died in 1716 She married, second, Thomas Bancroft of Reading, Mass, Oct 31, 1717, who died Feb 24, 1748. She married, third, Joseph Damon, June 11, 1750 and died in 1784.

Children, born in Reading:

270 I MARY,[5] b Aug 14, 1718
271 II THOMAS, b Sept 26, 1721; d 1763.
272 III MOSES, b Sept 7, 1723, d 1797
273 IV LYDIA, b March 4, 1725-6
274 V ABIGAIL, b March 14, 1728
275 VI DANIEL, b. Dec 1, 1730
276 VII SUSANNAH, b Dec 14, 1733, m.———Chase.
277 VIII JOSEPH, b. Nov. 10, 1735; d 1825
278 IX ELIZABETH, b May 28, 1738; m. Samuel Woodman in Newbury, March 25, 1761
279 X HANNAH, b May 25, 1741, m ———Gale of Sutton, Mass.

69 RUTH[4] EMERY (*John,*[3] *John,*[2] *John*[1]), daughter of John and Mary (Sawyer) Emery, married Ezekiel Hale in 1711. Mrs Ruth Hale died Nov 27, 1735. He married, second, Sarah (Poor) Spofford, Oct 31, 1736.
Children:

280 I[5]
281 II
282 III
283 IV
284 V
285 VI
286 VII
287 VIII

70 HANNAH[4] EMERY (*John,*[3] *John,*[2] *John*[1]), daughter of John and Mary (Sawyer) Emery, married Samuel Chase (son of Aquila and Ann (Follansbee) Chase, b. in Newbury, Mass., May 13, 1690), Dec. 8, 1713. He was killed by falling from his horse, July 24, 1743. His widow married, second, James Shute of Rowley, Mass., 1762, and died Oct. 6, 1776.
Children, born in Newbury, Mass:

288 I FRANCIS,[5] b Aug 15, 1715
289 II AMOS, b Jan 9, 1718
290 III HANNAH, b March 23, 1721.
291 IV MARY, b Aug 15, 1724, d young
292 V ANN, b Oct 23, 1727; m Amos Pillsbury, 2nd, Thomas Noyes.
293 VI SAMUEL,   } b Oct 22, 1729,   } went to Kennebunk, Me
294 VII BENJAMIN,
295 VIII MARY, b Dec 24, 1731
296 IX BETTY, b Oct 9, 1739, m Stephen Noyes, March 23, 1758
297 X JOHN, b March 25, 1740, m Ruth Hills, dau. of Moses Hills.

75 HENRY[4] BODWELL, JUN (*Bethia,*[3] *John,*[2] *John*[1]), son of Henry and Bethia (Emery) Bodwell, born in Andover, Mass., Nov. 6, 1688; married in 1726 Ann ———
Children:

298 I ANN,[5] b Feb 25, 1727.
299 II HENRY, b July 26, 1729, m Mary Robinson, daughter of Joseph and Mehetable[6] (Eames) Robinson He was the grandfather of the late Joseph Robinson Bodwell, Governor of Maine, who died in Hallowell, Maine, Dec 15, 1887
300 III PHEBE, b Feb 15, 1731
301 IV BETHIA, b. May 25, 1734

302 v   JOSHUA, b Oct 4, 1736.
303 vi   MARY, b July 21, 1740
304 vii WILLIAM, b March 1743; d. young.
305 viii WILLIAM, b. May 18, 1747.

77 DANIEL[4] BODWELL (*Bethia,*[3] *John,*[2] *John*[1]), son of Henry and Bethia (Emery) Bodwell; married Elizabeth Parker, of Haverhill, Mass.

Children.

306 i   TIFTIN [5]
307 ii   DANIEL.
308 iii JOHN
309 iv   ELIZABETH
310 v   RUTH.
311 vi   ABIGAIL, m Nathaniel Ladd, and lived in Norwich and Coventry, Conn.
312 vii SAMUEL
313 viii MARY.
314 ix   PARKER.

84 JOSHUA[4] BAILEY (*Sarah,*[3] *John,*[2] *John*[1]), son of Isaac and Sarah (Emery) Bailey; married Sarah, daughter of Stephen and Sarah (Atkinson) Coffin.

Children:

315 i   STEPHEN,[5] b 1708, d 1797.
316 ii   JOSHUA b 1712, d 1786
317 iii REV ABNER, b 1716, m Mary Baldwin, d 1798
318 iv   MAJOR ENOCH, b. 1720; m Abigail Fry, d. 1756.
319 v   SARAH, b 1722, m Edward Tappan
320 vi   JUDITH, b 1724, m Stephen Little.
321 vii ABIGAIL, b 1724, m Moses Little
322 viii GEN. JACOB, b. 1726, m Prudence Noyes, d 1816
323 ix   JOHN, b 1729, m. Annis Chase

88 JOSEPH[4] EMERY (*Joseph,*[3] *John,*[2] *John*[1]), son of Joseph and Elizabeth (Merrill) Emery, married Abigail Merrill, daughter of Abraham and Abigail (Bartlett) Merrill (born in Newbury, Mass, May 5, 1701); published in Amesbury, Mass., June 6, 1730; lived in Andover till 1769 when he removed to Pembroke, N. H., where he died July 12, 1776, aged 80. His wife died Jan. 18, 1736. He married second, Abigail Long, daughter of Shubal and Hannah (Merrill) Long, published in Newbury Aug. 17, 1738.

Children, by first wife:

324 i   ELIZABETH.[5]
325 ii   DAUGHTER, name unknown
326 iii JACOB.

Child, by second wife:

327 iv   JOSEPH, b. June 3, 1739.

89 ELIZABETH[4] EMERY (*Joseph,*[3] *John,*[2] *John*[1]), daughter of Joseph and Elizabeth (Merrill) Emery, married Robert Pease of Andover, Mass. She was his third wife. He died Nov. 17, 1766.

Children, born in Enfield, Conn.:

328   i   ELIZABETH,[5] b. 1718.
329   ii   HANNAH, b 1720.
330   iii   ABIGAIL, b 1722
331   iv   ROBERT, b Dec 19, 1724.
332   v   EMERY, b 1727
333   vi   JANE, b. 1729, m Thomas Buck.
334   vii   ANN, b. 1730
335   viii BATHSHEBA, b 1732
336   ix   MARY, born in Somers, Conn , July 3, 1734
337   x   ABIAL, b in Somers, Jan 24, 1736.
338   xi   NOAH, b in Somers, June 28, 1739

90 MARY[4] EMERY (*Joseph,*[3] *John,*[2] *John*[1]), daughter of Joseph and Elizabeth (Merrill) Emery ; married Joseph Parker, Dec. 31, 1722. Child :

339   i   JOSEPH [5]

92 ABIGAIL[4] EMERY (*Joseph,*[3] *John,*[2] *John*[1]), daughter of Joseph and Elizabeth (Merrill) Emery ; married Abiel Frye.
Children :

340   i   ABIGAIL,[5] b Feb. 19, 1733, d young.
341   ii   ABIEL, b Nov 3, 1734
342   iii   Hon SIMON, b Sept 29, 1737, d Oct 1822 Member of the
            Mass House of Representatives, Senate or Council for nearly
            twenty years, Justice of the Court of Common Pleas in York
            Co , and Chief Justice of the same court in the Co. of Oxford
343   iv   ABIGAIL, b. Nov 16, 1740.
344   v   SARAH
345   vi   MAJOR ISAAC, b Feb 6, 1748.

94 ANNA[4] EMERY (*Stephen,*[3] *John,*[2] *John*[1]), daughter of Stephen and Ruth (Jaques) Emery, married, April 10, 1711, Tristram Little, son of Joseph and Mary (Coffin) Little (born April 7, 1688). She died Oct. 4, 1755
Children :

346   i   MARY,[5] b March 17, 1713
347   ii   STEPHEN, b March 31, 1715, d Nov 11, 1716
348   iii   ANNA, b Aug 4, 1716
349   iv   JUDITH, b Sept 22, 1720, d unm Feb 11, 1796.
350   v   SARAH, b Aug 8, 1724, d Nov 26, 1736
351   vi   ABIGAIL, b Nov 21, 1730, d Aug. 20, 1736.

95 SARAH[4] EMERY (*Stephen,*[3] *John,*[2] *John*[1]), daughter of Stephen and Ruth (Jaques) Emery, married May 21, 1719, Richard Dole (born Dec 31, 1689), son of William and Mary (Brocklebank) Dole. Children, born in Newbury :

352   i   SARAH,[5] b. March 12, 1720
353   ii   RICHARD, b March 1, 1721 ; d young.
354   iii   RICHARD, b April 23, 1722 ; d. young.
355   iv   MOSES
356   v   ABIGAIL, b. April 14, 1727.
357   vi   MARY
358   vii   STEPHEN, b July 7, 1741

96 RUTH[4] EMERY (*Stephen,*[3] *John,*[2] *John*[1]), daughter of Stephen and Ruth (Jaques) Emery, married William Moulton, April 24, 1716.

Children :

- 359 i RUTH [5]
- 360 ii ANNE
- 361 iii STEPHEN
- 362 iv MARY
- 363 v WILLIAM.
- 364 vi JONATHAN
- 365 vii JUDITH
- 366 viii ELIZABETH
- 367 ix DAVID
- 368 x JAMES.

97 MARY[4] EMERY (*Stephen,*[3] *John,*[2] *John*[1]), daughter of Ensign Stephen and Ruth (Jaques) Emery, married Jan. 5, 1727, Thomas Noyes, jun., son of Col. Thomas and Elizabeth (Greenleaf) Noyes, born Oct. 2, 1679 His wife died June 14, 1735. He married, second Mrs. Elizabeth Ilsley, July 24, 1740. He died July 10, 1758 All his children were by his first wife.

Children, born in Newbury ·

- 369 i CHILD,[2] b Oct. 30 and d Nov. 12, 1727
- 370 ii THOMAS, b April 12, 1729.
- 371 iii STEPHEN, b Jan 18, 1731
- 372 iv MOSES, b. June 13, 1735, d Aug 10, 1735

98 JUDITH[4] EMERY (*Stephen,*[3] *John,*[2] *John*[1]), daughter of Stephen and Ruth (Jaques) Emery, married, Dec 29, 1720, Capt. Daniel Hale (born Feb. 22, 1696-7) Capt Hale commanded a company in Col. Samuel Waldo's Mass Regt in the Expedition against Louisburg in 1745, and was killed at the head of his company in the trenches before that fortification, May 21, 1745.

Children .

- 373 i DANIEL,[2] b Feb 15, 1722, in Rowley, Mass., m., 1st, Edna Pickard, 2nd, Kezia Plummer , 3rd, Priscilla Brown
- 374 ii EBENEZER, b March 2, 1724-5, in Rowley, Mass , m —— Mion
- 375 iii SARAH P
- 376 iv DAVID, b Sept. 30, 1729, in Newbury, Mass , m Mehetable Eastman
- 377 v AMOS, b Aug. 25, 1732, in Newbury, Mass , d Jan. 24, 1735-6
- 378 vi JUDITH, b July 10, 1738, in Newbury, Mass, m Oliver Hale
- 379 vii ABIGAIL, b July 1, 1741, in Newbury, Mass., m Moses Jaques.

99 ABIGAIL[4] EMERY (*Stephen,*[3] *John,*[2] *John*[1]) daughter of Stephen and Ruth (Jaques) Emery ; married Gideon Bartlett, Dec 16, 1725.

Children :

- 380 i MARY,[2] d. young.
- 381 ii GIDEON, d. young
- 382 iii ELIPHALET, d young.
- 383 iv STEPHEN
- 384 v MAHALA.
- 385 vi GIDEON
- 386 vii ELIPHALET
- 387 viii MARY
- 388 ix ABIGAIL.

2

100 ELIZABETH[4] EMERY (*Stephen,*[3] *John,*[2] *John*[1]), daughter of Stephen and Ruth (Jaques) Emery, married Caleb Moody, son of Deacon Caleb and Ruth (Morse) Moody. She died Sept. 14, 1754, aged 47 years

Children, born in Newbury :

    389 i   MARY.[5]
    390 ii ELIZABETH.
    391 iii CALEB, b July 29, 1727
    392 iv JOSHUA
    393 v   HANNAH.
    394 vi SARAH
    395 vii STEPHEN.
    396 viii

101 STEPHEN[4] EMERY (*Stephen,*[3] *John,*[2] *John*[1]), son of Stephen and Ruth (Jaques) Emery, married Hannah Rolfe, daughter of Henry and Hannah (Tappan) Rolfe, May 5, 1732   Stephen Emery was commissioned Ensign of a company of Foot by William Shirley, May 21, 1746 ; Colonel of the Seventh Regiment of militia by Francis Bernard, Esq , March 23, 1767, and by Thomas Hutchinson, Esq , Colonel of the Second Division of the Second Regiment in the town of Newbury and Rowley in 1771. Col. Stephen Emery died in Newbury (West Newbury) Sept. 16, 1795, aged 85. His wife died at the same place Jan. 10, 1779, aged 71

Children, born in Newbury :

    397 i   STEPHEN,[5] b Jan 18, 1732-33
    398 ii BENJAMIN, b May 14, 1735, d May 13, 1736
    399 iii HANNAH, b Oct 25, 1737, d Nov. 7, 1737
    400 iv BENJAMIN, b Dec 10, 1738.
    401 v   JOSEPH, b Sept 19, 1740, d Oct. 6, 1740
    402 vi NATHANIEL, b Aug 23, 1741
    403 vii HANNAH, b. Feb 12, 1744
    404 viii MARY, b May 12, 1746, d , unm , May 21, 1803
    405 ix ELIPHALET, b July 20, 1748, educated for a physician   He is
             said to have been a surgeon in a privateer which sailed from
             Newburyport   He d Oct 15, 1773, aged 26
    406 x   ELIZABETH, b July 30 1750
    407 xi ENOCH, b April 13, 1752, d , unm , Jan. 30, 1760

103 MIRIAM[4] EMERY (*Stephen,*[3] *John,*[2] *John*[1]), daughter of Stephen and Ruth (Jaques) Emery, married John Moody, Oct. 18, 1750. She was his second wife. His first wife was Hannah Tappan, daughter of Peter and Sarah (Greenleaf) Tappan, born 1710.

Children :

    408 i   JACOB [5]
    409 ii EBENEZER, m Lydia Bartlett.
    410 iii ANNA, b. Nov. 21, 1756.

104 LYDIA[4] EMERY (*Stephen,*[3] *John,*[2] *John*[1]), daughter of Stephen and Ruth (Jaques) Emery ; married, March 24, 1738. Moses (257) Emery, son of John and Mehetable (Short) Emery (born Oct. 12, 1715) He died April 11, 1789, aged 73. His wife died July 11, 1800, aged 82 (see No 257).

Children, born in Newbury ·

411   i   LYDIA,' b Feb 17, 1738-9
412   ii   MARY, b April 14, 1741
413   iii   JOHN, b March 12, 1743
414   iv   MOSES, b Jan. 31, 1745
415   v   JOSIAH, b May 17, 1747
416   vi   NATHAN, b May 31, 1750; d unm
417   vii   SARAH, b July 13, 1753
418   viii   ANN, b May 13, 1756
419   ix   AMOS, b April 24, 1758 (see No 410).
420   x   MICHAEL, b Aug 5, 1764

106 MARY[4] INGALLS (*Abigail*,[3] *John*,[2] *John*[1]), daughter of Henry and Abigail (Emery) Ingalls, married Ephraim Farnum of Concord, N. H., Nov 12, 1728.
Children :

421   i   EPHRAIM,[5] b. Sept 21, 1733
422   ii   BENJAMIN, b March 21, 1739, m Anna Merrill

108 FRANCIS[4] INGALLS (*Abigail*,[3] *John*,[2] *John*[1]), son of Henry and Abigail (Emery) Ingalls, married Lydia Ingalls (his cousin), Nov. 19, 1719
Children.

423   i   FRANCIS,[5] b Aug 26, 1721
424   ii   ISAIAH, b. June 6, 1723

109 JOSEPH[4] INGALLS (*Abigail*,[3] *John*,[2] *John*[1]), son of Henry and Abigail (Emery) Ingalls, married Phebe Farnum, Dec. 29, 1720
Children ·

425   i   JOSEPH,[5] b 1721, d Feb 20, 1721-2
426   ii   JOSEPH, b. Aug 9, 1723

110 SAMUEL[4] EMERY (*Rev. Samuel*,[3] *John*,[2] *John*[1]), son of Rev. Samuel and Tabitha (Littlefield) Emery, married Bathsheba Hill. He probably lived for a time in Wells and afterwards removed to Falmouth.
Children :

427   i   SAMUEL.°
428   ii   STEPHEN, bapt in Wells, Me , July 4, 1735.
429   iii   JOHN
430   iv   MOSES
431   v   BATHSHEBA, bapt in Wells, Me., Dec. 30,1730, m Paul Thorndyke, June 13, 1761
432   vi   SARAH, bapt in Wells, Me , April 8, 1732
433   vii   HANNAH.

113 SARAH[4] EMERY (*Rev Samuel*,[3] *John*,[2] *John*[1]), daughter of Rev Samuel and Tabitha (Littlefield) Emery, married, Sept. 16, 1725, Nathaniel, son of Nicholas Gilman (born March 2, 1704).

She married, second, Hon. John Phillips, one of the founders of Phillips Exeter Academy. He was the son of Rev. Samuel and Hannah (White) Phillips. Mrs Sarah Phillips died Oct., 1765. The children were all by her first husband
Children .

434   ı   TABITHA,[5] b. July 21, 1726
435   ıı   SARAH, b 1727, d. 1729
436   ııı   NATHANIEL, b 1730, d. 1746
437   ıv   SARAH, b. Sept 5, 1733, d. 1735.
438   v   ELIZABETH, b Dec 14, 1735, d 1736
439   vı   JOANNA, b 1737.

115 REV. STEPHEN[4] EMERY (*Rev. Samuel,*[3] *John,*[2] *John*[1]), son of Rev Samuel and Tabitha (Littlefield) Emery ; was graduated at Harvard College, 1730 ; ordained at Nottingham, N H., 1741, driven out by the Indians in 1748 From Nottingham he removed to Exeter, N. H., afterwards to Chatham, Cape Cod, where he was installed and passed the remainder of his life. He was minister at Chatham thirty-three years during which period he admitted to the church one hundred and thirty-five and baptized six hundred and eighty-one persons. He married Hannah, daughter of Rev Benjamin Allen of Falmouth, Oct. 8, 1742. He died May 24, 1782 She died June 7, 1799

Children ·

440   ı   TABITHA,[5] b. Dec., 1743, at Cape Elizabeth
441   ıı   HANNAH, b Oct , 1745, at Nottingham, N. H
442   ııı   JOHN, b March 28, 1747, at Nottingham, N H.
443   ıv   STEPHEN, b March 23, 1749, at Exeter, N. H
444   v   SAMUEL, b Feb 22, 1751, at Chatham, was graduated at Harvard College, 1774, m Mary Appleton, dau of Nath. Appleton, d in 1838. His wife d March 13, 1824, s *p*

116 IRENE[4] EMERY (*Rev Samuel,*[3] *John,*[2] *John*[1]), daughter of Rev. Samuel and Tabitha (Littlefield) Emery ; married, in 1730, Rev. Thomas Prentice (born in Cambridge, Nov 9, 1702), was graduated at Harvard College, 1726. She died in 1745. He was a minister in Arundel, now Kennebunkport, Me , 1730 ; installed as the colleague of Rev H Abbot in Charlestown, Oct. 31, 1739 After the burning of Charlestown, June 17, 1775, Mr. Prentice returned to Cambridge, his native place, where he died June 17, 1782.

Children

445   ı   IRENE,[5] b. in Arundel, Me., 1737, d in Cambridge, Mass , April 29, 1791, unm , æt. 54.
446   ıı   MARY, m James Frost of Cambridge, Mass , Dec 1, 1768 He d July 22, 1770 She m , 2nd, Nehemiah Rand of Charlestown She d in Lyndeboro, N. H , m 1791 He m , 2nd, Margaret Prentice sister of his first wife
447   ııı   LUCY, b Aug. 18, 1740, d young
448   ıv   MARGARET, b Aug. 9, 1742 m Nehemiah Rand, Oct 21, 1791.
449   v   THOMAS, b June 9, 1745 ; d young

118 JOHN[4] HUSE (*Judith,*[3] *John,*[2] *John*[1]), son of Abel and Judith (Emery) Huse, married Sarah Tappan, daughter of Jacob and Sarah (Kent) Tappan, Oct 25, 1716 She died May 4, 1730. He married, second, Sarah Hopkinson, Oct. 22, 1730

Children .

450   ı   MARTHA[5], b July 14, 1717, m Wm Jenkins, March 4, 1735
451   ıı   SARAH, b Dec 20, 1718, m Nicholas Johnson, March 23, 1737.

452 III HANNAH, b Jan 31, 1720.
453 IV MARY, b Dec 26, 1721, m Daniel March, April 6, 1742
454 V ABIGAIL, b Nov 26, 1723, m Moses Hule, April 20, 1742

119 ABEL[4] HUSE (*Judith,*[3] *John.*[2] *John*[1]), son of Abel and Judith (Emery) Huse ; married, first, Elizabeth Little, April 29, 1729 ; second, Hannah Farley, of Ipswich, 1739.
Child

455 I ELIZABETH,[5] b July 14, 1730, d young

121 SAMUEL[4] HUSE (*Judith,*[3] *John,*[2] *John*[1]), son of Abel and Judith (Emery) Huse, married Mary Marick, July 14, 1726. Lived in Methuen.
Children ·

456 I ABEL,[5] b. Aug 14, 1727, m Mary Whittier, Oct 30, 1772; removed to Derryfield, N H
457 II MARY, b Aug 10, 1729, m Aaron Chamberlin and removed to Derryfield, N. H.
458 III JUDITH, b. Jan 8, 1732, m John Pettingell, Dec. 27, 1753, d. in 1830, æt 98
459 IV LYDIA, b Dec 28, 1733, m John Morse, Nov. 1, 1753
460 V ABIGAIL, b Aug 26, 1736
461 VI ANNL, b. Jan. 18, 1739, m John Griffin, Feb 18, 1759.
462 VII SAMUEL, b. March 7, 1741, m Elizabeth Austin, April 28, 1763
463 VIII MOSES, b Dec 4, 1743, m Elizabeth Barton, March 28, 1769, and d Feb 3, 1814.

128 JOHN[4] KELLY(*Elizabeth,*[3] *John,*[2] *John*[1]), son of John and Elizabeth (Emery) Kelly, married Hannah, daughter of Capt William Somes of Gloucester, Mass. He lived in Newbury, Mass., until middle life when he removed to Atkinson, N H, where he died April 27, 1783
Children .

464 I JOHN,[5] b Oct 15, 1724, m Hannah Hale of West Newbury, Mass , d Dec 18, 1807 His wife d Nov 27, 1811, æt 85
465 II PRUDENCE, b Nov 1 1726, m Capt John Knight, resided in Atkinson, N H , and had ten children.
466 III HANNAH, b Nov. 12 1728, d. unm
467 IV ELIZABETH, b May 8, 1732
468 V JUDITH, b May 26, 1734
469 VI MOSES, b March 5, 1738–9, m Lydia Sawyer, Nov 10, 1757, high sheriff of Hillsborough Co., N. H., for thirty years Lived in Hopkinton and Goffstown, N. H , and d. Aug 2, 1824.
470 VII STEPHEN, b March 16, 1740
471 VIII JOSHUA, b Feb 13, 1743, m Deborah Page of Atkinson, N. H , removed to Conway, N H , where he d. in 1822
472 IX WILLIAM, b Oct 31, 1744, graduated Harvard College, 1767; ordained in Warren, N. H., m Lavinia Bayley, dau of Rev. Abner Bayley of Salem, N H , and d May 18, 1818.

131 RICHARD[4] KELLY (*Elizabeth,*[3] *John,*[2] *John*[1]), son of John and Elizabeth (Emery) Kelly, married Hannah Bartlett, lived in West Amesbury (now Merrimack), Mass., where he was a prominent and much respected citizen. He died June 8, 1771.

Children :

473   i   HANNAH,⁵ b Oct 21, 1726, m Bartholomew Heath.
474   ii   ELIZABETH, b Dec 28, 1728 m. Capt. John Sawyer of West
           Amesbury (now Merrimack).
475   iii MARY, b Nov. 19, 1730; m , 1st, William Moulton, 2nd, Dea.
           John Hoyt
476   iv   STEPHEN, b Aug 28, 1732, d. Nov. 4, 1736.
477   v   RICHARD, b. Nov 29, 1734, d March 14, 1750
478   vi   JOHN, b. Oct 22, 1736, m Elizabeth Hoyt and d March 9,
           1821
479   vii JUDITH, b Nov 17, 1737, m Joseph Sawyer, resided in
           Hampstead and Warner, N H
480   viii STEPHEN, b Nov 4, 1740, m Lois Sargent.
481   ix   ESTHER, b April 20, 1743, d July 29, 1743
482   x   MOSES, b Aug 12, 1748, d March 15, 1749–50

134 HANNAH⁴ KELLY (*Elizabeth,³ John,² John¹*), daughter of John
and Elizabeth (Emery) Kelly , married Stephen Bailey of West Newbury, Mass., July 9, 1729.
   Children :

483   i   STEPHEN,⁵ b. 1735, d. Dec 3, 1771.
484   ii   ENOCH
485   iii JOSHUA, b. 1739, d Jan 7, 1806
486   iv   AMOS.
487   v   SARAH

135 LYDIA⁴ KELLY (*Elizabeth,³ John,² John¹*), daughter of John
and Elizabeth (Emery) Kelly ; married John Morse.
   Children :

488   i   LYDIA,⁵ d in infancy.
489   ii   MARY b March 28, 1736; m Abner Chase of West Amesbury.
490   iii JOHN, b.1738, m Dorothy, dau. of Timothy Morse.
491   iv   LYDIA, b 1740, m Samuel Sawyer, 2nd, Joseph Chase
492   v   TIMOTHY, b 1743, m Hannah Smith of Ipswich and lived
           there
493   vi   SARAH, b 1745, m Daniel Harriman and lived in Plaistow,
           N. H
494   vii JONATHAN, b. Oct 17, 1747, m Mary Moody, 2nd, Judith Brown,
           and lived in Newburyport, Mass
495   viii DANIEL, b April 17, 1750, m Mary Challis
496   ix   ELIZABETH, b 1752, m Nicholas Short of Newbury.
497   x   JUDITH, b 1754, d. 1756
498   xi   AMOS, b. 1759, d 1775

136 DANIEL⁴ KELLY (*Elizabeth,³ John,² John¹*). son of John and
Elizabeth (Emery) Kelly, married Mary Smith of Newbury , resided
in West Amesbury, Mass.
   Children

499   i   ELIZABETH,⁵ b Nov 15, 1735, m Stephen Bartlett and lived
           in Bath, N H
500   ii   MERCY, b. Sept 10, 1737, d Oct 17, 1747.
501   iii MARY, b May 31, 1739, d July 31, 1739
502   iv   LYDIA, b Aug 15, 1740, d Oct 19, 1747
503   v   MARY, b June 3, 1742, d Oct 20, 1747
504   vi   DEBORAH, b. Jan 4, 1744, d Oct 29, 1747.
505   vii MOSES, b Sept 4, 1745, d. Oct. 30, 1747
506   viii DANIEL, b May 13, 1747, m Mary Webster of Kingston, N H.

137 Sarah[4] Kelly (*Elizabeth*,[3] *John*,[2] *John*[1]), daughter of John and Elizabeth (Emery) Kelly, married Amos Clark
Children :

507 i   Judith,[2] b. Oct. 5, 1740
508 ii   Thomas, b March 7, 1743
509 iii   Moses, b March 25, 1746
310 iv   Priscilla, b March 13, 1748
311 v   Amos, b Oct 22, 1751
312 vi   Anna, d Jan 18, 1752
513 vii   Jonathan, } b March 31, 1754, { d young.
514 viii Elizabeth, }
315 ix   Jonathan, b April 30, 1756

165 Joshua[4] Emery (*Jonathan*,[3] *Jonathan*,[2] *John*[1]), son of John and Hannah (Morse) Emery, married Sarah Smith, March 28, 1728. She died Oct. 25, 1752. He married, second, Sarah Short, Aug 29, 1754.
Children, born in Haverhill, Mass ·

516 i   John,[5] b Jan 6, 1728-9
317 ii   Hannah, b March 28, 1733, m John Johnson of New Salem, N H , died *s p*
518 iii Sarah, b March 29, 1735, m William Woodbury of Salem, N H , April 16 1761
519 iv   Joshua, b Feb 1, 1738-9.
520 v   Benjamin, b Aug 11, 1740
521 vi   Molly, b July 3, 1742.

By second wife

522 vii Moses, b July 13, 1760

166 David[4] Emery (*John*,[3] *Jonathan*,[2] *John*[1]), son of John and Hannah (Morse) Emery; married Abigail Chase, Jan. 27, 1732 She died Aug. 29, 1753 He married, second, Mrs. Mary Hale, Dec. 30, 1756. She died Sept. 12, 1778, aged 66 He died Oct 29, 1778, aged 69.
Children .

523 i   David,[5] b Jan 23, 1734, d Feb., 1734
524 ii   John, b. Jan 16, 1735
525 iii Abigail, b June 2, 1737, m Ephraim Boynton, Feb 19, 1756.
526 iv   Hannah, b Feb 5, 1739
527 v   Martha, b March 1, 1741, m Nathaniel Bailey, Aug. 6, 1761.
528 vi   Sarah, b June 24, 1744, m Enoch Noyes, Oct 30, 1765
529 vii Moses, b June 13, 1747
530 viii Thomas, b Sept 4, 1750

167 Sarah[4] Emery (*John*,[3] *Jonathan*,[2] *John*[1]), daughter of John and Hannah(Morse) Emery, married David Chase, Nov 24, 1729, son of Aquila Chase, born Oct. 20, 1710
Children .

531 i   David,[2] b Dec. 1, 1730
532 ii   Joshua, b Oct 21, 1733
533 iii Anthony, b Dec 6, 1735
534 iv   Tristram, b. Jan. 23, 1737.
535 v   Simeon

168 Anthony[4] Emery (*John*,[3] *Jonathan*,[2] *John*[1]), son of John and Hannah (Morse) Emery, graduated at Harvard College 1736, married

Abigail Leavitt, May 10, 1738 , was the first physician in Chelmsford, Mass ; removed to Hampton, N H , where he passed a very active, useful and honorable life. He had an extensive medical practice and fine farm and carried on quite a trade in West India goods. He was Auditor of Selectmen accounts at Hampton. 1753–62 Selectman, 1757; moderator, 1766 , surgeon during the siege of Louisburg, being commissioned by Sir William Pepperrell, Feb. 10, 1745 ; enlisted in the Expedition against Crown Point under Sir William Johnson as surgeon in Col Jos Blanchard's Regiment and was commissioned as Lieutenant in Capt. John Moore's Co , discharged Dec 5, 1755. In this expedition he was detailed to serve as an associate of John Hale. He was one of the grantees of the town of Andover, N. H , and built the first saw-mill in that town. He died at Hampton, Aug. 19, 1781. His wife died Nov. 22, 1799.

Children :

536	i	JOHN,[5] b 1739, d April 11, 1756.
537	ii	SARAH, b. Dec 31, 1740
538	iii	WILLIAM, b. April 16, 1742
539	iv	JOSEPH, b 1744.
540	v	THOMAS, b 1746, d. young
541	vi	CLEMENT, b 1748, m. Mary Page, April 23, 1771, lived in Orford, N H , d in Andover
542	vii	THOMAS, b Jan. 5, 1750, bapt. Nov. 10, 1751
543	viii	NATHANIEL, b 1751
544	ix	MOLLY, b. 1753, d. July 27, 1755
545	x	WILLARD, b 1756, d May 7, 1756
546	xi	WILLARD, b July 16, 1759

172 MARY[4] EMERY (*John*,[3] *Jonathan*[2] *John*[1]), daughter of John and Hannah (Morse) Emery , married William Smith, son of Capt. James and Elizabeth (Moody) Smith, May 20, 1747.

Child

547	i	HANNAH [5]

173 CALEB[4] EMERY (*Jonathan*,[3] *Jonathan*,[2] *John*[1]), son of Jonathan and Ruth (Richardson) Emery ; married Abigail Simons, in Haverhill, July 23, 1730.

Children .

548	i	ABIGAIL,[5] b July 25, 1731, in Amesbury, prob m. Ebenezer Hackett in Newbury, March 26, 1752
549	ii	PRUDENCE, b June 27, 1733, in Amesbury.
550	iii	CALEB, b May 13, 1736, in Amesbury
551	iv	SYLVANUS, b March 11, 1742, in Plaistow, N H
552	v	AMOS, b 1750
553	vi	JOEL, b 1753
554	vii	EUNICE, b ——, m Timothy Corliss, son of Timothy and Sarah (Hutchins) Corliss of Weare, N H (b Nov 28, 1726); he d in 1810, she d Dec 21, 1821
555	viii	LOIS, b ——, m Nathaniel Corliss, brother of Timothy (b. in 1738), lived in South Weare and Sandwich, N H Each family had eleven children

175 ANN[4] EMERY (*Jonathan*,[3] *Jonathan*,[2] *John*[1]), daughter of Jonathan and Ruth (Richardson) Emery ; married Joseph Heath, jun., in Haverhill, Mass., April 14, 1732 ; lived in Plaistow, N. H.

Children .

556   i   PRISCILLA,⁵ b March 4, 1733.
557   ii   JOSEPH, b Nov 20, 1735, d. Sept 18, 1749
558   iii   HANNAH, b Nov 24, 1737
559   iv   SYLVANUS, b Sept 27, 1739.
560   v   ANNE, b July 26, 1741.
561   vi   MOSES, b May 7, 1743.
562   vii   JONATHAN, b. Feb 22, 1744.
563   viii   ABIGAIL, b Dec 26, 1746.
564   ix   ASA, b July 29, 1748
565   x   ABRAHAM, } b March 24, 1753; { d March 26, 1753
566   xi   ISAAC,
567   xii   ISAAC, b Sept. 9, 1754.

177 HUMPHREY⁴ EMERY (*Jonathan,³ Jonathan,³ John¹*), son of Jonathan and Ruth (Richardson) Emery, married Sarah Heath, in Haverhill, Mass., March 14, 1737–8, removed to Dunbarton, N H, settled and on a farm near the town of Bow, now called the Emery farm.

Children

568   i   ENOCH,⁵ b July 10, 1738; d. July 26, 1745.
569   ii   NOAH, b July 16, 1739, said to have been drowned in a brook. See Appendix A.
570   iii   FRANCES, b July 21, 1741.
571   iv   RUTH, b June 10, 1743
572   v   HUMPHREY, b May 18, 1746
573   vi   JOANNA, b May 18, 1748, prob d young
574   vii   LYDIA, b June 10 1750
575   viii   ENOCH b March 10, 1752
576   ix   RICHARDSON, b March 10, 1753
577   x   JOANNA, b March 17, 1755

181 STEPHEN⁴ EMERY (*Stephen,³ Jonathan,² John¹*), son of Stephen and Lydia (Jackman) Emery, married Deliverance Styles (born in Boxford, Feb 21, 1722–3) daughter of John and Eleanor (Peal) Styles. Oct. 20, 1743. He was a soldier in the expedition against Canada in the company of Capt Israel Gerrish and died soon after his return home in 1758.

Children ·

578   i   DAVID,⁵ bapt July, 1744 See Appendix B
579   ii   STEPHEN, b Feb. 22, 1745, bapt. March 2, 1746, d. young
580   iii   STEPHEN, b April 10, 1748
581   iv   JOHN, b Sept 9, 1750
582   v   JESSE, b April 13, 1753
583   vi   REBECCA, b. June 18, 1755

182 JOHN⁴ EMERY (*Stephen,³ Jonathan,² John¹*), son of Stephen and Lydia (Jackman) Emery, married in Boxford, Mass., Dec. 18, 1753, Abigail Styles, daughter of John and Eleanor (Peal) Styles (born in Boxford, Feb 8, 1727–8).

Children.

584   i   LYDIA ⁵ b June 30, 1755
585   ii   ABIGAIL, b May 13, 1757
586   iii   MOLLY, b Oct 25, 1759
587   iv   JUDITH, b Nov. 29, 1761, d in Newbury, Mass., April 2, 1845.
588   v   DANIEL, bapt in Newbury, Feb 26, 1764.
589   vi   JOHN, b in Newbury, Nov 1, 1768

185 BENJAMIN[4] EMERY (*Stephen,*[3] *Jonathan,*[2] *John*[1]), son of Stephen and Lydia (Jackman) Emery, married Sarah Samson, July 8, 1753

Children

> 590 ı Moses,[5] b Oct. 5, 1754
> 591 ıı SARAH, b Jan 3, 1757, m. Jonathan Page of Atkinson, N H

188 SAMUEL[4] EMERY (*Edward,*[3] *Jonathan,*[2] *John*[1]), son of Edward and Sarah (Sibley) Emery, married Elizabeth Woodwell, 1746.

Children:

> 592 ı ELIZABETH[5]
> 593 ıı MARY, b in Hopkinton, May 22, 1751

189 WILLIAM[4] EMERY (*Edward,*[3] *Jonathan,*[2] *John*[1]), son of Edward and Sarah (Sibley) Emery, married Mary Chase, Aug 4, 1749, daughter of Nathan and Judith (Sawyer) Chase (born in West Newbury, Mass., Nov. 1, 1729). See Appendix C.

Child.

> 594 ı JUDITH,[5] b July, 1753

196 JONATHAN[4] EMERY (*James,*[3] *Jonathan,*[2] *John*[1]), son of James and Ruth (Watson) Emery, married Jerusha Barron, daughter of John and Hannah Barron of Dracut, Mass (born Aug 4, 1735). He entered the intention of their marriage with the town clerk of Dracut, Dec. 7, 1753 He lived in Dracut, Mass., Winthrop, Me., and Fairfield, Me., and was probably the first settler in the last-named town. He settled there in 1771 at Emery Hill, on the west side of the Kennebec, and was a carpenter and farmer. He was very benevolent. His home was a stopping place for travellers and all were welcome. He invariably declined to receive pay. In 1775, when Arnold was making his famous expedition into Canada, he made his headquarters at Jonathan Emery's house for two weeks while his boats and baggage were being transported over the carrying-place to avoid the rapids of the Kennebec. Jonathan Emery assisted in repairing Arnold's boats. He was an Indian scout for eight years, in revenge, it is said, for the murder of his brother John He was an intimate friend of Rev Paul Coffin His wife died in Fairfield, Me, in 1781 He afterwards married a widow by the name of Whitten. He died in Fairfield in June, 1807. His second wife died there about 1810.

Children:

> 595 ı DAVID,[5] b in Dracut, Mass, Sept 24, 1754
> 596 ıı JERUSHA, b in Dracut, Mass
> 597 ııı HANNAH, b in Dracut, Mass
> 598 ıv JOHN, b in Dracut, Mass
> 599 v THANKFUL b in Dracut Mass, Sept 10, 1763
> 600 vı JAMES b in Dracut, Mass, 1766, m Polly Wheelen of Canaan, Me, Jan. 1, 1801 (b 1769) He d in Fairfield, Me, Nov 22, 1831 His wife d there Oct 4, 1848, *s p*
> 601 vıı BRIGGS II, b in Dracut. Mass, Nov. 11, 1767
> 602 vııı JONES b in Winthrop, Me, 1770 or 1771
> 603 ıx SAMUEL, b in Fairfield, Me, June 15, 1773
> 604 x RACHEL b in Fairfield Me in Jan. or Feb 1777

198 ANTHONY[4] EMERY (*James*,[3] *Jonathan*.[2] *John*[1]), son of James and Ruth (Watson) Emery, born probably in Dracut, Mass , married ———— ———— He was living in Dracut, Feb 11, 1760, and in Conway, N. H., March 21, 1771, and was there as late as April 24, 1789. He was a farmer.

Children :

605 i SAMUEL,' born in Conway, N H , 1775
606 ii JOHN
607 iii JAMES
608 iv NAOMI.

203 AMBROSE[4] EMERY (*James*,[3] *Jonathan*.[2] *John*[1]). son of James and Ruth (Watson) Emery ; married Mrs Catherine Foster of Pelham, N. H He entered the intention of marriage with the town clerk of Dracut, July 17, 1762 He was a farmer and lived in Dracut. He married for his second wife Rebecca Yocum of Pennsylvania She was born in 1746 They lived at Philadelphia and Thompsontown, Pa., and also in Mifflin Co. and Greene Co , Pa. He was a soldier in the British service in the French and Indian War, and was mustered into service Oct. 11, 1756 in Capt. Jonathan Butterfield's company. He was in the Crown Point expedition and was reported on one of the muster-rolls of his company as " killed or taken " This was a mistake, but he was wounded by an arrow. He was in the Boston "Tea Party " His home was within hearing of the battle of Brandywine and in one of the winter camps of General Washington's army, and his wife Rebecca cooked the soldiers' rations. He died near Jefferson, Greene Co., Pa , in 1824 She died there in 1843.

Children by first marriage, born in Dracut, Mass.

609 i SARAH,[5] b March 14, 1762
610 ii RUTH, b Feb 2, 1764
611 iii DANIEL, b Nov 2, 1765, d there Dec. 25, 1765
612 iv LYDIA, b April 12, 1769

Children by second marriage, born in Philadelphia :

613 v JOHN, b Oct 4, 1771
614 vi CHARLES, d there in childhood
615 vii JAMES, d there in childhood
616 viii ELIZABETH, d. there in childhood.
617 ix SAMUEL, b March 8, 1779
618 x CLEMENTINE, b Nov 17, 1784
619 xi REBECCA, b 1786, d unm in Greene Co , Ind , in Sept , 1869.
620 xii JONAS, b July 23, 1788
621 xiii AMBROSE, b Nov 23, 1790
622 xiv NATHAN'L, b 1792, m Elizabeth Botts in Greene Co , Pa , 1816; lived in Greene Co , Pa, and Cochecton Co , O ; farmer, d s p in Carlisle, O , 1845 His wife d a few years later
623 xv JESSE, b 1794

204 EDWARD[4] EMERY (*James*[3] *Jonathan*,[2] *John*[1]), son of James and Ruth (Watson) Emery ; married Mrs. Eunice McKie, *née* Smith, widow of Capt. McKie and daughter of Robert Smith of London, England. She was born in Queen's Square, London, between 1724 and 1730. Captain McKie brought his wife Eunice and two sons to Salem, Mass. He was afterwards lost at sea with his vessel It is said that Robert Smith belonged to the nobility of England. He was very wealthy and left a large fortune to his heirs. Edward Emery was a farmer and lived in Fairfield, Me , where he settled in 1771. He died in Fairfield, Me. His wife died in Vassalboro, Me.

Children :

624 i   ROBERT S,[5] ⎫
625 ii   EUNICE,   ⎬ b July 15, 1764
626 iii DAVID   ⎭
627 iv   EDWARD
628 v   PRISCILLA, b in Fairfield, Me , Aug 10, 1771

260 MARY[5] EMERY (*John* [4] *John*,[3] *John*,[2] *John*[1]). daughter of John and Mehetable (Short) Emery , married Bernard Currier of Amesbury, Mass . Oct. 23, 1739, son of Richard and Dorothy Currier (born in Amesbury, April 15, 1719).

Children :

629 i   MEHETABLE,[6] b June 27, 1740.
630 ii   STEPHEN, b Nov 16, 1741
631 iii MARY, b Sept 10. 1743
632 iv   ANNE, b July 8, 1745
633 v   STEPHEN, b Sept 13, 1747
634 vi   RICHARD, b. Sept 13, 1749
635 vii ANNA, b. Dec. 6, 1754.

263 SARAH[5] EMERY (*John*,[4] *John*,[3] *John*,[2] *John*[1]). daughter of John and Mehetable (Short) Emery , married Henry Adams of Newbury, Nov. 20, 1746.

Children :

636 i   ANNE,[6] b April 2, 1747
637 ii   JOHN, b Oct 4, 1748
638 iii ENOCH, b July 11, 1752
639 iv   NATHAN, b May 1, 1755
640 v   SARAH b Feb 3, 1757
641 vi   PAUL, b March 23, 1762
642 vii MEHETABLE, b Jan 12, 1764.

266 DANIEL[5] EMERY (*John*,[4] *John*,[3] *John*,[2] *John*[1]), son of John and Mehetable (Short) Emery , married Sarah Brocklebank in 1757. Child .

643 i   JOHN,[6] b Jan 22, 1758

267 SAMUEL[5] EMERY (*John*,[4] *John*,[3] *John*,[2] *John*[1]), son of John and Mehetable (Short) Emery , married Ruth Annis. daughter of Christopher Annis, Nov. 25, 1760; died in West Newbury, Aug 10, 1805 His wife died March 20, 1800, aged 62

Children, born in Newbury :

644 i   SARAH,[6] b Sept 21, 1762, d in West Newbury, Oct 4, 1838, unm
645 ii   MEHETABLE, b. Aug 25, 1764
646 iii DANIEL, b July 25, 1766, d in West Newbury, Jan 18, 1841, æt 74

647 ɪv ANNE, b Sept 20, 1768, d Sept 10, 1778
648 v   HANNAH, b April 2 1771, d unm Aug 26, 1857
649 vɪ MOSES, b April 17, 1773
650 vɪɪ POLLY, b Jan. 7, 1777, d unm Sept 8, 1854, æt. 77

270 MARY[5] BANCROFT (*Lydia,*[4] *John,*[3] *John,*[2] *John*[1]), daughter of Thomas and Lydia (Emery-Dean) Bancroft, married Samuel, son of Thomas and Mary (Herbert) Nichols (born 1714), Jan. 21, 1736.
Child:

651 ɪ SARAH,[6] b 1739

273 LYDIA[5] BANCROFT (*Lydia,*[4] *John,*[3] *John,*[2] *John*[1]), daughter of Thomas and Lydia (Emery-Dean) Bancroft, married Aug. 24, 1742, Jonathan Noyes of Newbury, Mass.
Child.

652 ɪ JOSEPH,[6] served in the Revolutionary War and was Captain of Marines on the brig Palace He was commissioned Lieutenant in the 11th Mass. Bay Regt , Jan 1, 1777

274 ABIGAIL[5] BANCROFT (*Lydia,*[4] *John,*[3] *John,*[2] *John*[1]), daughter of Thomas and Lydia (Emery-Dean) Bancroft, married Joseph Parker, Oct 26, 1748. He died in Hopkinton, June 5, 1765. She married, second, Jonathan Amsden ; third, Joseph Dudley ; died in Princeton, Mass , aged 79.
Children :

653 ɪ   JACOB.[6]
654 ɪɪ AMOS
655 ɪɪɪ ABIGAIL, m Mark Collins
656 ɪv NEHEMIAH
657 v   JOHN.

288 FRANCIS[5] CHASE (*Hannah,*[4] *John*[3], *John,*[2] *John*[1]), son of Samuel and Hannah (Emery) Chase ; married Sarah Pike. He died Aug. 30, 1806. Lived in Newton, N. H.
Children :

658 ɪ   HANNAH,[6] b. Sept 22, 1738, m Joseph Welch
659 ɪɪ   SAMUEL, b Oct 23, 1739, m Mary Stewart, lived in Litchfield, N. H , d 1816
660 ɪɪɪ AMOS, b July 6, 1741, m Hannah Carleton, lived in Unity, N H
661 ɪv   FRANCIS, b July 4, 1743, m. Sarah Hubbard, lived in Unity, N. H
662 v   JOSEPH, b Feb. 5, 1745, m Elizabeth Darrah, lived in Litchfield, N. H , d 1829
663 vɪ   ABNER, b Nov 19, 1746, m Joanna Moody, lived in Unity, N H
664 vɪɪ SIMEON, b Aug 26, 1748; m Dolly Parker , lived in Litchfield, N. H , d 1839
665 vɪɪɪ SARAH, b July 24, 1750, m Reuben Currier; lived in Unity, N H
666 ɪx   DANIEL, b May 21, 1753, m Hannah Eaton, lived in Newton, N. H , d Aug. 1, 1802
667 x   BETTY, b Oct 27, 1758, m Richard Whittier , lived in Canaan, N H , d 1828

668 xi MOLLY, b Feb 12, 1760, m Jonathan Carleton in Canaan,
          N H., and d 1830
669 xii MOSES, b. March 2, 1763, m his cousin Mary Noyes, dan. of
          Stephen and Betsey (Chase) Noyes lived in Plaistow,
          N. H., d Feb 15, 1853

289 AMOS[5] CHASE (*Hannah*,[4] *John*,[3] *John*,[2] *John*[1]), son of Samuel
and Hannah (Emery) Chase ; married Sarah Cole and died in Saco,
Me , March 2, 1808
   Children ·

   670 i   SAMUEL,[6] b 1742.
   671 ii   REUBEN, b 1744
   672 iii SARAH, b 1747
   673 iv   HANNAH, b 1749.
   674 v   BETTY, b 1751
   675 vi   AMOS, b 1752
   676 vii JOSEPH, b 1754
   677 viii JOHN, b 1757
   678 ix   OLIVER, b 1759
   679 x   DANIEL, b 1762
   680 xi   MARY, b 1761
   681 xii ABNER, b 1768

293 SAMUEL[5] CHASE(*Hannah*,[4] *John*,[3] *John*,[2] *John*[1]), son of Samuel
and Hannah (Emery) Chase ; married Sarah Stewart, daughter of
Robert Stewart of Amesbury, Mass., and was killed by falling from
an apple tree Oct 31, 1769. His wife married, second, Major Thomas
Noyes and died Jan. 15, 1813, aged 80   (See No. 370.)
   Children

   682 i   MARY,[6] b Feb , 1753, m Moody Smith, 1774.
   683 ii   ANNA, b Aug 7, 1755, m Wm. Bailey, 1778, d in Bradford,
             Mass , 1818
   684 iii ROBERT, b April 10, 1757, m Lydia Bodwell
   685 iv   BENJAMIN, b 1758, m Alice Bartlett
   686 v   SARAH, b 1760, m Joshua Bailey, 1780
   687 vi   SAMUEL, b 1763, d unm April 19, 1782, æt 18
   688 vii ELIZABETH, b 1765 ; d at 10 years of age
   689 viii HANNAH, b April 21 1768, m Maj Samuel Bailey, Dec 17,
             1791, he d in West Newbury.
   690 ix   AMOS, b May 5, 1770, m Judith Little in Haverhill, West
             Parish

324 ELIZABETH [5]EMERY (*Joseph*,[4] *Joseph*,[3] *John*,[2] *John*[1]), daughter
of Joseph and Abigail (Merrill) Emery , married Samuel Eames of
Haverhill, Mass
   Child .

   691 i   NABBY,[6] b in Haverhill, April 23, 1758

326 REV JACOB[5] EMERY (*Joseph*,[4] *Joseph*,[3] *John*,[2] *John*[1]), son of
Joseph and Abigail (Merrill) Emery ; graduated at Harvard College
in 1761 ; succeeded Rev. Aaron Whittemore as pastor of the Congregational Society of Pembroke, N. H. , ordained Aug 3, 1768, holding his office for seven years. In March, 1775, he sought a dissolu-
tion of the pastoral relation on account of poor health.   In that
year, after relinquishing his parish, he was elected as delegate to a

convention of the state, at Exeter, to consider the state of the
country In this convention. Mr. Emery was member of a committee to prepare and set forth a proclamation for a day of fasting
and prayer. He was a member of the House in the session beginning Dec. 18, 1776. In going from Exeter to his home in Pembroke,
he was taken ill and suffered much. He died in Pembroke, N H ,
March 16, 1777, aged 39 He married Elizabeth Cushing, daughter
of Rev. James Cushing of Haverhill, Mass.
Children.

692   i   JACOB,[6] b April 12, 1770
693   ii   THOMAS, b ———, d unm. in Farmington, Me , 1825.
694   iii   JAMES C , b June 17, 1773.

327 JOSEPH[5] EMERY (*Joseph,*[4] *Joseph,*[3] *John,*[2] *John*[1]), son of
Joseph and Abigail (Long) Emery, married Hannah Stickney,
June 2, 1763, who was born in Boxford, Mass., June 27, 1738,
daughter of Joseph and Hannah (Goodridge) Stickney. They re-
moved from Andover to Pembroke. N H , May 16, 1769. He died
Nov 4, 1821 His wife died Feb. 1, 1834, aged 97
Children

695   i   JOSEPH,[6] b Dec 19, 1764, in Andover
696   ii   SAMUEL, b Aug 18, 1766, in Andover
697   iii   HANNAH, b Feb 19, 1775, in Pembroke, N. H
698   iv   JACOB, b March 24, 1777, in Pembroke, N H
699   v   NABBY, b March 6 1780, in Pembroke, N H
            Also six children who died in infancy, one of whom was
            Jacob, b. July 18, 1768

331 ROBERT[5] PEASE (*Elizabeth,*[4] *Joseph,*[3] *John,*[2] *John*[1]), son of
Robert and Elizabeth(Emery) Pease , married Hannah Sexton of Somers, Sept 4, 1746. He married, second, Submit Davis He removed to
Blandford, Mass., 1780, lived there for a short time, lost his property
by depreciation of Continental money which he received in pay for
his farm and returned to Somers, Conn , where he died in 1805.
Children :

700   i   ROBERT,[6] b Sept 3, 1749, in Somers
701   ii   HANNAH, b Aug. 29, 1751, in Somers
702   iii   ABIA, b 1753
703   iv   STEPHEN, b July 4, 1755.
704   v   ABNER, b Nov 9, 1757
705   vi   ERASTUS, b 1759.
706   vii   ALPHEUS, b April 16, 1762
707   viii CHARLES, b 1764
708   ix   SARAH, b Sept 28, 1766, d young.
709   x   HANNAH, b. Nov. 29, 1769.
710   xi   MIRIAM, b. Sept. 25, 1771.

332 EMERY[5] PEASE (*Elizabeth,*[4] *Joseph,*[3] *John,*[2] *John*[1]), son of
Robert and Elizabeth (Emery), Pease ; married Mary Horton Jan. 9,
1755 , lived in Somers where he died in 1796 aged 69. He was Justice
of the Peace and one of the first to answer the call to defend the
liberty of his country. He marched to Boston at the first alarm at
the head of seventy volunteers from his town and was more or less
engaged as Captain during the Revolutionary War.

Children, born in Somers

```
711  i    DAVID,⁶ b Aug 24, 1755
712  ii   EMERY, Aug 26, 1757
713  iii  AUGUSTUS, b July 19, 1759
714  iv   SYLVANUS, b Oct 3, 1761
715  v    MARY, b Jan 19, 1764
716  vi   ELIZABETH, b. Aug 7, 1766; m Elam Hale, 1798.
717  vii  GAIUS, b Dec 1, 1768
718  viii MARGARET b June 1, 1772
719  ix   MATILDA, b April 24, 1774
720  x    INDEPENDENCE, b Aug 27, 1776, m Gen David Mack
```

335 BATHSHEBA⁵ PEASE (*Elizabeth,⁴ Joseph,³ John,² John¹*), daughter of Robert and Elizabeth (Emery) Pease; married Joseph Hunt. Children.

```
721  i    PETER⁶ m Molly Pease
722  ii   BATHSHEBA, b 1768, m Jan 14, 1790, Stephen Parsons.
723  iii  ANNA, b ———, m Stephen Richardson
724  iv   ELEANOR, b ———, m Issachar Jones
```

337 COL. ABIAL⁵ PEASE (*Elizabeth,⁴ Joseph,³ John,² John¹*), son of Robert and Elizabeth (Emery) Pease; married Esther Cooley, May 12, 1757, daughter of Eliakim and Griswold (Beckwith) Cooley, born Oct. 15, 1729. Col. Pease settled in Somers where he died, 1806, aged 70. He was an officer in the Revolutionary War.

Child

```
725  i    ESTHER,⁶ b Feb 6, 1763, m Seth Dwight
```

338 NOAH⁵ PEASE (*Elizabeth,⁴ Joseph,³ John,² John¹*), son of Robert and Elizabeth (Emery) Pease, married Mary Ward in 1762. He married, second, Mrs Dorcas Arnold, widow of Samuel Arnold, and daughter of Dea John Hubbard, of Ellington, Conn. Lieut Pease was a farmer He died July 20, 1818.

Children, born in Somers.

```
726  i    GILES,⁶ b April 13, 1763
727  ii   NOAH, b Sept 30, 1765, d young
728  iii  HANNAH, b July 17, 1769, m Calvin Pitkin of Somers
```

346 MARY⁵ LITTLE (*Anna,⁴ Stephen,³ John,² John¹*), daughter of Tristram and Anna (Emery) Little; married Capt. Michael Dalton, Feb. 5, 1734. He died March 1, 1770, aged 61 years His widow married Patrick Tracy, and died Dec. 10, 1791.

Children

```
729  i    MARY,⁶ b Dec 2, 1734, d. Nov 18, 1736
730  ii   MICHAEL, b Nov. 1, 1736, d young
731  iii  TRISTRAM, b May 28, 1738, grad H C at seventeen years of
          age and studied law, inherited a fortune from his father and
          had a large landed property in West Newbury  He enter-
          tained as guests, Washington, John Adams, Louis Philippe
          and Talleyrand, was warden of St Paul's Church, New-
          buryport; speaker of the Mass House of Rep, Senator of
          Mass and of the U S in the first Congress after the adop-
          tion of the Federal Constitution  He possessed great per-
          sonal beauty, graceful and accomplished manners and was
          a diligent and finished scholar  He m Ruth Hooper  He d
          in Boston May 30, æt 79  They had three daughters and
          two sons none of whom attained their majority
```

348 Anna[5] Little (*Anna,*[4] *Stephen,*[3] *John,*[2] *John*[1]), daughter of Tristram and Anna (Emery) Little ; married Stephen Sewall. Dec. 27, 1739 and died Feb. 16, 1796.   He was a schoolmaster in Newburyport and died in 1795

Children :

    732 i   John,[6] b Oct 11, 1740, d. at Surinam, S A., Sept. 1, 1766
    733 ii   Sarah, b Aug 18, 1743; d. Nov. 7, 1745
    734 iii Sarah, b Nov. 2, 1746.
    735 iv Anna, b Sept. 25, 1749.

352 Sarah[5] Dole (*Sarah,*[4] *Stephen,*[3] *John,*[2] *John*[1]), daughter of Richard and Sarah (Emery) Dole ; married James Knight, May 22, 1740

Children :

    736 i   Daniel [6]
    737 ii   James

356 Abigail[5] Dole (*Sarah,*[4] *Stephen,*[3] *John,*[2] *John*[1]), daughter of Richard and Sarah (Emery) Dole , married John Plummer, April 4, 1751

Children :

    738 i   Ruth [6]
    739 ii   Sarah.
    740 iii Anna

357 Mary[5] Dole (*Sarah,*[4] *Stephen,*[3] *John,*[2] *John*[1]), daughter of Richard and Sarah (Emery) Dole ; married Stephen Ilsley, Nov. 24, 1747.

Children :

    741 i   Richard [6]
    742 ii   Jonathan.
    743 iii William.

370 Thomas[5] Noyes (*Mary,*[4] *Stephen,*[3] *John,*[2] *John*[1]), son of Thomas and Mary (Emery) Noyes ; married Elizabeth Morse, daughter of Dea. Stephen and Elizabeth Morse, Jan. 4, 1753.   She died May 15, 1793. He married, second, Sarah Chase, Dec. 9, 1794, and died Nov. 29, 1801. See No. 293.

Children :

    744 i   Thomas,[6] b. March 20, 1754, grad of Harvard College, 1777;
                studied for the ministry but was never ordained; d. unm.
                Aug 9, 1797
    745 ii   Stephen, b July 13, 1758, d unm June 20, 1796.
    746 iii Moses, b Jan 15, 1773; d Oct 10, 1778

371 Stephen[5] Noyes (*Mary,*[4] *Stephen.*[3] *John,*[2] *John*[1]), son of Thomas and Mary (Emery) Noyes , married Susannah, daughter of Lieut. Joseph Chase, June 15, 1756.   She died Feb. 11, 1758. He married, second, Betty Chase, daughter of Samuel and Hannah (Emery) Chase, March 28, 1758. He died Sept. 15, 1815. Betty, his wife, died Aug. 5, 1812.

Children :

747   i   SUSANNAH,[6] b April 6, 1759   m. in 1783,——Moody, d Nov
          23, 1803
748   ii MOSES, b Dec 13, 1760, d Dec 20, 1760
749   iii SAMUEL, b June 29, 1762, d. unm Aug 26, 1839.
750   iv MARY, b March 23, 1767, m Moses Chase of Plaistow, N H.,
          April 17, 1788, d Feb 15, 1853
751   v   BETTY, b July 30, 1770, d unm Nov 6, 1862
752   vi STEPHEN, b Aug. 7 1775, m Jane Little, dau of Edmund and
          Sarah (Hale) Knight, pub April 3, 1804   She died July 6,
          1816   He m, 2d, Ruth Ayer of Haverhill, Mass, 1818
          She d Jan 8, 1847   He m, 3rd, Fanny Ayer Hills, widow
          of Thomas Hills, first town clerk of West Newbury, Mass.
          She d June 1, 1867.   He d Jan 19, 1867.

391 CALEB[5] MOODY (*Elizabeth*,[4] *Stephen*,[3] *John*,[2] *John*[1]), son of
Caleb and Elizabeth (Emery) Moody, married Dorothy Sargent, 1754.
He died July 24, 1793   His wife died March 18, 1826, aged 89.
   Children :

753   i   MOSES S,[6] b. March 20, 1757, m 1st, Susan Brown, 2nd, Sally
           Dean; 3rd, Ruth Ordway, d Jan 1, 1818, s p
754   ii   JOSHUA, b Sept 11, 1759, never married
755   iii SAMUEL, b July 14, 1762
756   iv   CALEB, b Jan 4, 1765, d Jan, 1784, æ 19
757   v   STEPHEN, b Jan 21 1767, m Fanny Coffin, d April ?1 1842
758   vi   DOLLY, b April 2, 1769, m. Joshua Brown, d. Sept, 1863, æt.
           94
759   vii ELIZABETH, b Nov 8, 1771, m Joseph Ridgeway, d Feb. 20,
           1860, æt 88
760   viii SALLY, b Dec. 13, 1773, m Josiah Bartlett, d. Feb 20, 1862.
761   ix   JOSEPH,   } b Nov 11, 1777, { d young
762   x   BENJAMIN, }   { d in Epsom, N H., Feb. 28,
                                         1820
763   xi   JOSEPH, b. May 13, 1781, d at St. Pierre, Martinique, May 7,
           1805

397 STEPHEN[5] EMERY (*Stephen*,[4] *Stephen*,[3] *John*,[2] *John*[1]), son of
Stephen and Hannah (Rolfe) Emery, married Sarah Moody, Nov 6,
1760   She died Nov 6, 1777, aged 36   He married, second, Sarah
Bartlett, who died July 23, 1791.   He died April 16, 1799, aged 67.
   Children, born in Newbury

764   i   STEPHEN,[6] b July 8 1761.
765   ii   ENOCH, b March 16, 1763
766   iii ELIZABETH, b Dec 7 1764, d May 11, 1778
767   iv   HANNAH, b Dec. 20, 1765.
768   v   MOODY, b. June 20, 1769
769   vi   NATHANIEL, b July 24, 1772, m Mary Quimby, Nov. 27, 1799,
           d Aug 23, 1812, s p

400 BENJAMIN[5] EMERY (*Stephen*,[4] *Stephen*,[3] *John*,[2] *John*[1]), son of
Stephen and Hannah (Rolfe) Emery : married Sarah Bailey. March
12, 1761 ; removed to Rumford (now Concord, N. H.), before 1766,
Jan. 21, 1766, he was elected constable at the first legal meeting of
the freeholders and inhabitants of the parish of Concord.   In 1775,
he was captain of militia, and in the Revolutionary War commanded
a company at the battle of White Plains, N. Y ; in 1776, signed the
" Association Test, " in 1777, one of the committee of safety ; dele-

gate in 1788 to the Convention that ratified the Constitution; was
selectman, 1770, 1771, 1775 1782, 1791–93.   She died Nov 2, 1819.
He married, second, Sarah——, who died in 1827.

Children, born in Concord·

```
770   i    SUSAN,⁵ b  April 15, 1762
771   ii   BENJAMIN, b  Jan 3, 1764; d  June 4, 1785.
772   iii  SARAH, b  Feb 25, 1766
773   iv   ISAAC, b  Nov 28, 1768
774   v    ELIZABETH, b  April 30, 1771
775   vi   RUTH, b  Aug 30, 1773; d  Dec. 3, 1801
776   vii  ELIPHALET, b  Aug 14, 1775
777   viii ENOCH, b  May 23 1778, d  April 3, 1802
778   ix   CHARLES, b  July 22, 1780
779   x    JOHN, b  Jan 24, 1783, d  March 20, 1783
780   xi   BENJAMIN, b. April 9, 1786; d  unm
```

402 LIEUT. NATHANIEL⁵ EMERY (*Stephen,*⁴ *Stephen.*³ *John,*² *John¹*),
son of Stephen and Hannah (Rolfe) Emery, commissioned Ensign of
second Military company of Newbury, by Gov. Thomas Hutchinson,
Jan 12, 1772, appointed second lieutenant of a company drafted from
Newbury and Rowley, Mass, Sept 30, 1776.   Upon the Lexington
alarm he went as private in the company of Thomas Noyes, 3d, to Cambridge, Mass   Married Sarah Short, daughter of Mr. Nicholas Short
of Newbury, Mass, Nov. 11, 1777.   She died Dec. 22, 1783, aged 30.
He married, second, Abigail Longfellow, May 21, 1795.   She died in
West Newbury, Mass., Dec 9, 1843, aged 97.

Children, born in Newbury·

```
781   i    SARAH⁶ b  Aug 10, 1779
782   ii   ELIPHALET, b  Sept 15, 1781
783   iii  CAPT NICHOLAS, b  Dec. 16, 1783, m. Sarah Robinson and
           d. s. p., Oct. 7, 1826.  His wife d  March 18, 1816, æt 76
```

403 HANNAH⁵ EMERY (*Stephen,*⁴ *Stephen,*³ *John,*² *John¹*), daughter
of Stephen and Hannah (Rolfe) Emery: married Paul Little, May 20,
1762. She died at Casco, Me., Sept. 4, 1777.

Children.

```
784   i    HANNAH,⁵ b  May, 1763 (see No 764)
785   ii   PAUL, b  Aug 8, 1767, m  Mary Osgood
```

406 ELIZABETH⁵ EMERY(*Stephen,*⁴ *Stephen,*³ *John.*² *John¹*), daughter of Stephen and Hannah (Rolfe) Emery; married Rev Moses Hale
(born Feb 19, 1749, son of Rev Moses Hale of Newbury, Mass, and
Mehetable Dummer) Dec 28, 1775, in Newbury Newtown (now West
Newbury).   Rev. Moses Hale graduated at Harvard College, 1771;
ordained at Boxford, Mass, Dec 28, 1778, and died there May 25,
1786   His wife died April 24, 1785.

Children.

```
786   i    ELIZABETH,⁶ b  Nov. 5, 1776, bapt  Nov 10, 1776.
787   ii   MOSES, b. Sept. 26, 1778, bapt. Sept. 27, 1778.
788   iii  STEPHEN b  Dec 6, 1780, bapt  Dec 8, 1780
789   iv   SARAH, b  Dec 4, 1782, bapt  Dec 8. 1782
790   v    MARY, b  April 17, 1785, bapt  May 8, 1785, d. in West New-
           bury, March 16, 1819
```

408 JACOB[5] MOODY (*Miriam,*[4] *Stephen,*[3] *John,*[2] *John*[1]), son of John Moody and Miriam (Emery) Moody ; married Susannah Noyes.
　　Children :

　　　791　i　　JOHN,[6] m. Mary Sargent.
　　　792　ii　 EBENEZER.

410 ANNA[5] MOODY (*Miriam,*[4] *Stephen,*[3] *John,*[2] *John*[1]), daughter of John and Miriam (Emery) Moody ; married Amos Emery, son of Moses and Lydia (Emery) Emery.　He died Oct. 21, 1810.　His wife died Nov. 19, 1818.
　　Children, born in Newbury :

　　　793　i　　HANNAH,[6] b. Feb. 19, 1785.
　　　794　ii　 ANNA, b. Dec. 6, 1786.
　　　795　iii　EBENEZER, b. March 20, 1789 ; d. unm. in West Newbury, July 9, 1864, æt. 75.
　　　796　iv　LYDIA, b. April 16, 1791 ; d. unm. in West Newbury, Dec. 16, 1874, æt. 83.
　　　797　v　 MIRIAM, b. April 13, 1793 ; d. unm. in West Newbury, March 2, 1878, æt. nearly 85.
　　　798　vi　MOSES, b. Feb. 4, 1795 ; m. Ella Maria Taylor in Amesbury, Mass., Dec. 14, 1821, and d. Feb. 1, 1822.
　　　799　vii　AMOS, b. May 5, 1797 ; d. unm. in West Newton, Jan. 1, 1836, æt. 38.
　　　800　viii JACOB M., b. June 22, 1799.

411 LYDIA[6] EMERY* (*Moses,*[5] *John,*[4] *John,*[3] *John,*[2] *John*[1]), daughter of Moses and Lydia (Emery) Emery ; married Eliphalet Coffin, Jan. 17, 1760 ; died in Newbury, May 12, 1823, aged 84.
　　Children :

　　　801　i　　LYDIA.[7]
　　　802　ii　 HANNAH, d. unm.
　　　803　iii　JOHN.
　　　804　iv　HEZEKIAH.
　　　805　v　 HANNAH.
　　　806　vi　MOSES.
　　　807　vii　NATHAN.

412 MARY[6] EMERY (*Moses,*[5] *John,*[4] *John,*[3] *John,*[2] *John*[1]), daughter of Moses and Lydia (Emery) Emery ; married David Bachelder of Rye, N. H.
　　Children :

　　　808　i　　MARY.[7]
　　　809　ii　 LYDIA.
　　　810　iii　ANNA.
　　　811　iv　RHODA.
　　　812　v　 REUBEN.
　　　813　vi　DOROTHY, d. unm.
　　　814　vii　MOSES.
　　　815　viii ABIGAIL.

413 JOHN[6] EMERY (*Moses,*[5] *John,*[4] *John,*[3] *John,*[2] *John*[1]), son of Moses and Lydia (Emery) Emery ; married Elizabeth Woodman,

---

* Lydia Emery is the fifth generation on her mother's side and the sixth on her father's side.　The paternal line is followed in her descendants.

Oct. 1, 1767, daughter of John and Anna (Adams) Woodman (born March 29, 1744), who died in West Newbury, Mass., Jan. 28, 1791 He married, second, Sarah Platts in Boxford, Mass., June 10, 1796.
Children :

816   i   JOHN,[7] b March 16, 1769, d unm.
817   ii   LYDIA, b April 18, 1771, d unm
818   iii   JUDITH, b May 31, 1773, d unm
819   iv   SAMUEL, b Aug 10, 1775
820   v   NATHAN, b Nov , 1777, d unm
821   vi   BETSEY, b. March 3, 1780.
822   vii   MARY, b Dec. 30, 1783

414 MOSES[6] EMERY (*Moses,[5] John,[4] John,[3] John,[2] John[1]*), son of Moses and Lydia (Emery) Emery ; married, in Newbury, Ruth Bodwell of Methuen. Mass., who was born Feb. 13, 1750   He was the third settler in Bakerstown, Me , now Minot, and built the first sawmill in the place.   His wife was eminent for her courage and piety.
Children .

823   i   OLIVE,[7] b Sept 18, 1767.
824   ii   RUTH, b May 29, 1769
825   iii   MOSES, b. Sept 20, 1772
826   iv   NATHAN, b Aug 5, 1780
827   v   MARY, b March 18, 1785
828   vi   STEPHEN, b. April 29, 1790

415 JOSIAH[6] EMERY (*Moses,[5] John,[4] John,[3] John,[2] John*),[1] son of Moses and Lydia (Emery) Emery, married Rebecca Woodman, 1770, daughter of John and Anna (Adams) Woodman (born July 10, 1746), sister to Elizabeth, who married John Emery. She died Jan. 5, 1788   He married, second, Mrs Elizabeth (Meader) Morrison, widow of Samuel Morrison, Oct. 13, 1791, who died July, 1837, aged 70.
Children :

829   i   MOSES,[7] b Feb 2, 1772, at Epping, N H
830   ii   NATHAN, b Dec 6 1773, at Epping, N H
831   iii   ANN (NANCY), b July 8, 1775, in Sanbornton, N H
832   iv   MOLLY (POLLY), b March 21, 1777, in Sanbornton, N. H.
833   v   LYDIA, b Nov 8, 1778,   "   "   " "
834   vi   REBECCA, b Nov 9, 1780,   "   "   " "
835   vii   SARAH (SALLY), b Aug 26, 1782,   "   "   " "
836   viii   BETTY (BETSEY), b May 3, 1784, m. Simon D Sanborn, Feb.
         6, 1817.
837   ix   AN INFANT

417 SARAH[6] EMERY (*Moses,[5] John,[4] John,[3] John,[2] John[1]*), daughter of Moses and Lydia (Emery) Emery, married Ezekiel Merrill, June 1, 1773   He was a soldier in the Revolutionary War and at the capture of Burgoyne ; removed to Auburn, Me   He was born in Newbury, Mass , Dec 9, 1748, and died in Auburn, Me., March 16, 1830 His wife died March 4, 1848, aged 95.
Children :

838   i   ROGER,[7] b June 2, 1774, in Newbury.
839   ii   MOSES, b Oct. 1, 1775, in Newbury
840   iii   SARAH, b March 10, 1777, in Pelham, N. H
841   iv   ANNA M , b. Aug 26, 1779, in Pelham, N. H

842   v   MARY, b Feb. 3, 1781, in Pelham, N. H
843   vi   EZEKIEL, b Nov 15, 1782, m Pelham, N. II
844   vii LYDIA, b March 19, 1785, "   "   "   "
845   viii SUSAN, b July 13, 1790, in Andover, Me.

418 ANN⁶ EMERY (*Moses,*⁵ *John,*⁴ *John,*³ *John,*² *John*¹), daughter of Moses and Lydia (Emery) Emery, married Abel Merrill, Jan. 4, 1776. He was the son of John and Ruth (Hale) Merrill (born in Newbury, July 4, 1752)   He died in West Newbury, Mass , July 1, 1834, aged 82. His wife died in the same place, May 28, 1840, aged 84.

Children.

846   i   JOHN,⁷ b Nov 15, 1776 , d. unm.
847   ii   SUSANNAH, b Nov. 17, 1778.
848   iii NATHAN, b April 3, 1781, d. unm.
849   iv   SARAH, b June 13, 1793
850   v   LYDIA E., b. April 4, 1801.

420 MICHAEL⁶ EMERY (*Moses,*⁵ *John,*⁴ *John,*³ *John,*² *John*¹), son of Moses and Lydia (Emery) Emery, married, 1804, Mrs. Sarah Worthen Sargent (born Nov , 1764, daughter of Joseph Worthen of Amesbury, Mass.), published in Amesbury, Mass , Aug 18, 1804. She died March 1, 1814. He married, second, Lydia Hoyt Sargent, widow of Jonathan Sargent, March 23, 1815. She died May 15, 1849, aged 82. He died Oct. 27, 1842, aged 78. Being incapacitated from manual labor by a lame wrist, he became a teacher and taught school in Sanbornton, N. H , for some years He, in company with William Little, started the carriage business in 1800.

Children:

851   i   JOHN SARGENT,⁷ b Dec 2, 1805, in Newbury.
852   ii   JOSEPH, b. Sept 19, 1807, in Amesbury

427 SAMUEL⁵ EMERY (*Samuel,*⁴ *Rev Samuel,*³ *John,*² *John*¹), son of Samuel and Bathsheba (Hill) Emery, married Margaret Dalzel, June 28, 1758.

Children:

853   i   SAMUEL⁶
854   ii   FOREST, b Jan.17, 1781; d. Jan. 24, 1845.
855   iii STEPHEN.
856   iv   MARY

434 TABITHA⁵ GILMAN (*Sarah,*⁴ *Rev. Samuel,*³ *John,*² *John*¹), daughter of Nathaniel and Sarah (Emery) Gilman, married Samuel son of John and Elizabeth (Hale) Gilman, 1743.

Children.

857   i   SARAH,⁶ b June 17, 1743 , m Capt Josiah Gilman, Nov. 30,
            1763, d. July 26, 1785
858   ii   PHILLIPS, b Aug 23, 1746, d Dec 27, 1780, unm.

440 TABITHA⁵ EMERY(*Rev Stephen,*⁴ *Rev Samuel* ³ *John,*² *John*¹), daughter of Rev. Stephen and Hannah (Allen) Emery ; married David Gilman, Dec. 8, 1763.

Children :

   859   i   SUSANNAH,[6] b. 1764
   860   ii   SAMUEL, b. 1768
   861   iii ABIGAIL, b. 1770.
   862   iv HANNAH, b. 1776

441 HANNAH[5] EMERY (*Rev. Stephen,*[4] *Rev. Samuel,*[3] *John,*[2] *John*[1]), daughter of Rev. Stephen and Hannah (Allen) Emery ; married John Ward Gilman of Exeter, N. H , Dec 3, 1767. She died June 22, 1802. He was elected lieutenant of a company that marched from Exeter to Bunker Hill, appointed postmaster by Washington and retained the office forty years ; died June 16, 1823.

Children .

   863   i   STEPHEN,[6] b. Aug 27, 1768; sea captain; d , unm , Oct 9, 1849
   864   ii   WARD, b. Dec 18, 1769
   865   iii JANE,   } b. July 16 1773,   } d April 3, 1778
   866   iv   ALLEN,   }
   867   v   DEBORAH HARRIS, b. May 26, 1775, d , unm , in Exeter, N H.
   868   vi   JOHN, b April 8, 1777; d April 11, 1777.
   869   vii HANNAH, b May 6, 1778, d , unm , Aug. 15, 1850
   870   viii JANE, b July 22 1780, d. in Exeter, N H , Nov. 2, 1835
   871   ix   JOHN, b Aug 15, 1782 married, lived and died in New Orleans, La , Sept 10, 1822
   872   x   SAMUEL, b Jan 4, 1785; unm followed the sea
   873   xi   JOSEPH, b. March 4, 1789, d Aug. 18, 1805
   874   xii ELIZABETH, b. May 29, 1791, d , unm , March 10, 1858

442 JOHN[5] EMERY (*Rev Stephen,*[4] *Rev. Samuel,*[3] *John,*[2] *John*[1]), son of Rev. Stephen and Hannah (Allen) Emery ; married Mercy Crowell, Nov 28, 1782. John Emery is borne as ensign on the rolls of Capt Abijah Bangs' company, Colonel Dike's regiment for five days' service in November, 1776 , as second lieutenant in same company, Dec 1, 1776 , also in the same company as second lieutenant, commissioned as such Feb 1, 1777 ; among the officers of that regiment who engaged to tarry on Dorchester Heights in March, 1777 , and on roll of Capt Benjamin Godfrey's company, Col Z. Winslow's regiment, for six days in September, 1778, at Bedford and Falmouth.

Children :

   875   i   STEPHEN,[6] b Aug 21, 1783
   876   ii   JOHN, b March 15, 1785 , d , unm , June 29, 1820.
   877   iii SAMUEL, b March 18, 1787
   878   iv   BENJAMIN, d in infancy
   879   v   BETSEY, b Sept. 26, 1789
   880   vi   JOSEPH, b April 4, 1791, d June 23, 1818.

443 STEPHEN[5] EMERY (*Rev Stephen,*[4] *Rev Samuel,*[3] *John,*[2] *John*[1]), son of Rev. Stephen and Hannah (Allen) Emery ; married Ann Knox of Boston, daughter of Thomas Knox , died Nov. 16, 1801. His wife died December, 1801.

Children :

   881   i   ANN,[6] b Jan 7, 1778 , m ———— Hitchborn, d. Oct. 1801.
   882   ii   MARY, b Oct 13, 1779; d , unm , Oct 28, 1819

883　lu　Hannah　b. July 11, 1782; d , unm., Jan 2, 1802
884　iv　Thomas K , b Jan. 28, 1784, m Mary H Parker, d. 1815,
　　　　s. p
885　v　Stephen, b Dec 20, 1785, d , unm , May 2, 1815
886　vi　Samuel, b Jan 15, 1787; m Elizabeth Blanchard of Salem,
　　　　Mass.; d. March 24, 1882, æt. 95.

516 John[5] Emery (*Joshua,[4] John,[3] Jonathan,[2] John[1]*), son of Joshua and Sarah (Smith) Emery ; married Abigail Webster, in Haverhill, Jan. 24, 1751-2. He died in Haverhill, Jan. 7, 1764. His widow married, second, Thomas Webster, Oct. 14, 1766, and had : Thomas, born Aug 10, 1767 , Amos, born Jan. 30, 1770; Daniel, born July 27, 1771.

Children .

887　i　John,[6] b Jan 28, 1753, in Plaistow, N H
888　ii　Samuel, b. Oct. 25 1754, in Plaistow, N H.
889　iii　Joshua, b. March 14, 1757. in Haverhill, Mass
890　iv　Moses, b. April 1, 1759, in Haverhill, Mass.

519 Joshua[5] Emery (*Joshua,[4] John,[3] Jonathan,[2] John[1]*), son of Joshua and Sarah (Smith) Emery ; married Hannah Currier of Haverhill, May 5, 1763. She died Feb. 9, 1769. He married, second, Rachel Currier, Aug. 29, 1770. He died Sept. 14, 1784.

Children :

891　i　Abigail,[6] b. Feb. 29, 1768, in Haverhill, Mass
892　ii　Smith, b Aug 16 1771, in Haverhill, Mass
893　iii　Hannah, b Feb 25 1773, d 1795, in Haverhill, Mass.
894　iv　Joshua, b Sept 16, 1774, in Haverhill, Mass
895　v　Rachel, b Feb 11, 1777
896　vi　Sarah, b Nov. 26, 1778, m. —— Rowell of Bow, N H
897　vii　John, b Sept. 25, 1780
898　viii　Isablila, b July 14, 1782.
899　ix　Mary b April 9, 1784

520 Benjamin[5] Emery (*Joshua,[4] John,[3] Jonathan,[2] John[1]*), son of Joshua and Sarah (Smith) Emery , married Mary Rawlins (Rollins), Sept. 23, 1762, daughter of Benjamin and Martha (Wheeler) Rawlins. Major Benjamin Emery died in Atkinson, N. H , Jan. 28, 1817, aged 76. His wife died in the same place, Nov. 17, 1824, aged 80.

Children :

900　i　Sarah,[6] b July 9, 1765
901　ii　Mary, b. Aug 22, 1766
902　iii　Martha (Patty), b July 22, 1770
903　iv　Benjamin Rawlins, b March 27, 1775 , m Ruth Webster of
　　　　Haverhill, Mass , Dec 27, 1798 His wife d in Atkinson,
　　　　N. H , July 3, 1848, æt 70 years He d at the same
　　　　place, Aug 1, 1834. They had an adopted daughter, Ruth
　　　　E Webster

521 Mary[5] Emery (*Joshua,[4] John,[3] Jonathan,[2] John[1]*), daughter of Joshua and Sarah (Smith) Emery ; married James Merrill of Plaistow, N. H , March 15, 1759.

Children .

904 i   JAMES,[6] b Feb 26, 1760, at Atkinson, N. H., d , unm , Jan 21, 1839
905 ii   JOHN, b April 6, 1761; m Elizabeth Gordon and lived in Derry, N H
906 iii   NATHANIEL, b March 3, 1762, at Atkinson, N H
907 iv   JOSHUA, b. Feb 13 1764
908 v   SARAH, b Nov 6, 1768, m Evan Jones, Jan 28, 1789, lived in Methuen, Mass.
909 vi   RUTH, b June 27, 1771, d , unm., Jan 6, 1833
910 vii   EMERY, b Aug 24 1772
911 viii JESSE, b July 18, 1774, m ———— Clark, lived in Bradford, Vt.
912 ix   SAMUEL, b Feb 11, 1776
913 x   HEZEKIAH, b Sept 10, 1782, m. Betsey Orr, lived in Atkinson, N H.
914 xi   CALEB, b May 22, 1784, grad Dart. Coll , 1808; m ———— Underhill, d Dec 19, 1841.
915 xii AMOS, b June 22, 1786; m , 1st, Sarah ————, 2nd, E. Kimball; lived in Atkinson, N H.

522 MOSES[5] EMERY (*Joshua*,[4] *John*,[3] *Jonathan*,[2] *John*[1]), son of Joshua and his second wife, Sarah (Short) Emery; married Abiah Bradley, Jan. 26, 1784. He died in Haverhill, Mass., Sept. 13, 1839. She died Sept 13, 1840, aged 75.

Children, born in Haverhill :

916 i   SALLY,[6] b March 26, 1797, m , 1st, ————Emerson, 2d,———— Howe.
917 ii   MOSES G. J , b April 28, 1799
918 iii ELIZA, b. May 7, 1801.

524 JOHN[5] EMERY (*David*,[4] *John*,[3] *Jonathan*,[2] *John*[1]), son of David and Abigail (Chase) Emery; married Edna Noyes, daughter of Ephraim and Abigail (Platts) Noyes, April 7, 1756.

Children :

919 i   EPHRAIM,[6] b Feb 20, 1758
920 ii   HANNAH, b Sept 30, 1760, d young
921 iii DAVID, b. April 20, 1763

526 HANNAH[5] EMERY (*David*,[4] *John*,[3] *Jonathan*,[2] *John*[1]), daughter of David and Abigail (Chase) Emery; married Daniel Hills, May 10, 1757.

Children :

922 i   DANIEL,[6] b May 12, 1758
923 ii   ABIGAIL, b March 7, 1760.
924 iii DAVID, b June 4, 1761
925 iv   TIMOTHY, b. Jan 27, 1764.
926 v   HANNAH, b. July 16, 1768.
927 vi   JOHN, b June 15, 1770

529 MOSES[5] EMERY (*David*,[4] *John*,[3] *Jonathan*,[2] *John*[1]), son of David and Abigail (Chase) Emery ; married Sarah Hale, Sept. 27, 1770.

Children, born in Newbury ·

928 i   TAPPAN,[6] b. ————, d May 14, 1777
929 ii   ABIGAIL, b Jan 27, 1778, m. Jeremiah Jewett, July 15, 1797.
930 iii JOHN, b April 5, 1775
931 iv   TAPPAN, b ————
932 v   JACOB, b Oct 23, 1779
933 vi   MOSES, b. Aug. 29, 1782.

530 THOMAS[5] EMERY (*David,[4]John,[3] Jonathan,[2] John[1]*), son of David and Abigail (Chase) Emery; graduated Harvard College 1768, married Ruth March, Oct 10, 1770 He died in Newbury (now West Newbury) Nov 21, 1770 His widow married, second, John White, 3d, May 7, 1772 They lived in Haverhill, N. H

Child :

934 i THOMAS,[6] b Jan 25, 1771 (see No 786)

537 SARAH[5] EMERY(*Dr. Anthony,[4] John,[3]Jonathan,[2] John[1]*), daughter of Dr. Anthony and Abigail (Leavitt) Emery, married Col., afterwards Gen., Jonathan Moulton. Sept. 11, 1776 He died Sept. 18, 1787. His widow married, second, Rev. Benjamin Thurston and died Oct. 24, 1817.

Children :

935 i SALLY,[6] b June 13, 1779.
936 ii EMERY, b May 21 1782
937 iii JOHN WASHINGTON, b Sept 20, 1783
938 iv NATHANIEL THAYER, bapt Aug 5, 1787

538 WILLIAM[5] EMERY(*Dr. Anthony,[4] John,[3]Jonathan,[2] John[1]*), son of Dr Anthony and Abigail (Leavitt) Emery, married Joanna Elkins, 1763 He died in Andover, N. H., May 31, 1825, aged 88.

Children, born in Andover, N. H :

939 i WILLARD,[6] b May 15. 1768
940 ii JOSEPH, b Nov 10, 1770
941 iii ANTHONY, b Aug 8, 1773
942 iv WILLIAM, b Jan 24, 1779
943 v POLLY, b April 30, 1782.
944 vi HENRY, b Sept 25, 1788.

539 DR JOSEPH[5] EMERY (*Dr Anthony,[4] John,[3] Jonathan,[2] John[1]*), son of Dr. Anthony and Abigail (Leavitt) Emery, was the first physician of Fryeburg, Me., married Mary Fessenden, sister of Rev. William Fessenden, of Cambridge, Mass, first minister of Fryeburg (born in Cambridge, Nov 11, 1748; graduated Harvard College, 1768, settled in Fryeburg, Me , 1774), married, second, Sarah Clement of Dunbarton, N. H. Dr. Emery died in Andover, N. H., Sept. 9, 1814

Children :

945 i A DAUGHTER [6]
946 ii SARAH, m , Nov 8, 1814, Rev Daniel Dana, D.D , of Newburyport, Mass

542 THOMAS[5] EMERY (*Dr Anthony,[4] John,[3] Jonathan,[2] John[1]*), son of Dr Anthony and Abigail (Leavitt) Emery, baptized Nov. 10, 1751, married Dolly Sargent (born in Candia, N. H., March 22. 1754, and died in London, N H , March 16, 1833). He died Aug 10, 1834.

Children :

947 i SUSANNAH,[6] b July 12, 1774.
948 ii SALLY, b May 12, 1776
949 iii JOHN, b June 16, 1781.
950 iv HANNAH, b March 29, 1786, d , unm , Apr 24, 1847

951   v   JOSHUA, b May 16, 1788
952   vi   ANTHONY, b Oct 16, 1798, m Belinda Brown and d. Aug 10, 1850 *s p*

543 NATHANIEL[5] EMERY (*Dr. Anthony,*[4] *John,*[3] *Jonathan,*[2] *John*[1]), son of Dr. Anthony and Abigail (Leavitt) Emery; married Mary Perkins of Hampton, settled in Andover, N H, April 1, 1777; removed to Loudon and died there.
Children

953   i   JOHN,[6] b Nov 20, 1778
954   ii   MOLLY, b Aug 27, 1781.
955   iii   JOSIAH, b Jan 27 1784.
956   iv   JAMES b Aug. 26, 1786; d young
957   v   ABIGAIL, b Oct 19, 1787; m John Scribner of Andover, N H
958   vi   SALLY, b Aug 9, 1790
959   vii   JAMES, b. May 9, 1792
960   viii   NANCY, b July 1, 1795
961   ix   JONATHAN.
962   x   HANNAH

546 WILLARD[5] EMERY (*Dr. Anthony,*[4] *John,*[3] *Jonathan,*[2] *John*[1]), son of Dr Anthony and Abigail (Leavitt) Emery, married Sarah Perkins of Rye, N. H; died at Hampton, N H, March 29, 1827. His wife died Dec. 18, 1835, aged 73
Children :

963   i   NABBY,[6] b July 12, 1785, m —— Nudd
964   ii   WILLARD, b Oct 28, 1788. See Appendix E
965   iii   ANTHONY, b Feb 6, 1789.
966   iv   POLLY, b May 6, 1791, m —— Monson
967   v   SARAH, b. Sept 29, 1799.

550 CALEB[5] EMERY (*Caleb,*[4] *Jonathan,*[3] *Jonathan,*[2] *John*[1]), son of Caleb and Abigail (Simons) Emery, married Susannah Worthley. He was in the Revolutionary War under Gen. Sullivan and also served in the French and Indian Wars, Selectman of Dunbarton, N. H., 1769.
Children :

968   i   JESSE[6], b July 17, 1759
969   ii   ANNE, b. July 2, 1761, m James Brown
970   iii   MOLLY, or MARY, b July 1, 1764, m Abraham Jones; 2d, Amos Jones
971   iv   DANIEL, b Dec 31, 1766
972   v   MEHITABLE, b May 24, 1768, m. Josiah Brown
973   vi   ABIGAIL, b June 3, 1771
974   vii   CALEB, b Jan 13, 1773
975   viii   JONATHAN, b Aug 27, 1775
976   ix   JOHN, b Oct 6, 1777
977   x   DAVID, b. Feb 4, 1780, d young.

551 SYLVANUS[5] EMERY (*Caleb,*[4] *Jonathan,*[3] *Jonathan,*[2] *John*[1]). son of Caleb and Abigail (Simons) Emery, married ——Pope.
Children :

978   i   SYLVANUS[6]
979   ii   TWIN INFANTS who died
980   iii   HANNAH
981   iv   SALLY

982 v   BETSEY [6]
983 vi   LOUISA
984 vii RUTH
985 viii POLLY
986 ix   TAMAR
987 x   EUNICE

552 AMOS[5] EMERY (*Caleb,*[4] *Jonathan,*[3] *Jonathan,*[2] *John*[1]), son of
Caleb and Abigail (Simons) Emery; married Anna Foote, published
in Dunbarton, N. H., March, 1772.

Children:

988 i   ANNE,[6] d unm
989 ii   CALEB, b. 1776
990 iii SAMUEL, b Jan. 31, 1781

553 JOEL[5] EMERY (*Caleb,*[4] *Jonathan,*[3] *Jonathan,*[2] *John*[1]), son of
Caleb and Abigail (Simons) Emery; married Love Ladd, daughter of
Trueworthy and Lydia (Harriman) Ladd (born in Kingston, N. H,
Jan. 2, 1761) He was born in Goffstown, N H, April 28, 1753, moved
from Goffstown to Tunbridge, Vt; was there in June, 1832. In April,
1775, enlisted in Capt Samuel Richards' Co., Col. John Stark's Regi-
ment; was in the battle of Bunker Hill, reenlisted in Col. Stark's
Regiment

Children, born in Goffstown, N. H. :

991 i   LYDIA,[6] b April 21, 1779; m. James Giles, d. in Tunbridge,
          Vt
992 ii   JAMES, b Jan. 26, 1781, m. ———— Metcalf.
993 iii JOHN, b Sept 19, 1785
994 iv   JOEL b Oct 10, 1787
995 v   BETSEY, b Nov 13, 1789, m ———— Kimball.
996 vi   MARY, b Oct 10, 1795, d 1872
997 vii JONATHAN b Dec 11, 1797.
998 viii SEAVEL, b Jan 15, 1801
999 ix   IRA, b Aug 19, 1804.

556 PRISCILLA[5] HEATH(*Ann,*[4] *Jonathan,*[3] *Jonathan,*[2] *John*[1]), daughter of Joseph, jr., and Ann (Emery) Heath, married Moses Fol-
lansbee.

Children, born in Plaistow, N. H. :

1000 i   MOSES,[6] b Sept 17, 1752
1001 ii   RACHEL, b Oct 10, 1754
1002 iii JOHN, b Jan. 2, 1756
1003 iv   ANN, b July 21, 1758.
1004 v   WILLIAM, b Sept 22, 1760
1005 vi   SUSANNAH, b Oct. 17, 1762.

572 HUMPHREY[5] EMERY (*Humphrey,*[4] *Jonathan,*[3] *Jonathan,*[2] *John*[1]),
son of Humphrey and Sarah (Heath) Emery, married Patty Reed,
who died in 1827. He died in Bartlett, N. H, Jan 19, 1829.

Children, born in Bartlett, N. H. :

1006 i   ESTHER[6], b Sept 18, 1783
1007 ii   PETER, b ————, teacher in N H, brick-maker in Fredonia,
           N Y removed to New Madrid, Ky.
1008 iii SYLVANUS
1009 iv   RUTH

1010   v   ABIGAIL, b ——; m —— Penny and removed to Kentucky.
1011   vi   SARAH
1012   vii POLLY, m , 1st, —— Messie, 2d, Charles Hill of Shelburn,
            N H , d , s p , at Gorham, N H , 1852

575 ENOCH[5] EMERY (*Humphrey*,[4] *Jonathan*,[3] *Jonathan*,[2] *John*[1]),
son of Humphrey and Sarah (Heath) Emery, married Rachel Tyrrell.
Children ·

1013   i   WILLIAM[6]
1014   ii   STEPHEN, b. March 28, 1774
1015   iii   JACOB, m Rosannah Emery, had one child.
1016   iv   SAMUEL, b Nov 13, 1783, in Bartlett, N H   See No 1006
1017   v   NATHANIEL, b May 7, 1789, in Bartlett, N. H.
1018   vi   HUMPHREY
1019   vii   JOHN, b 1793.
1020   viii ENOCH, b July 18, 1794, in Bartlett, N H , m Louisa Rumery
1021   ix   BETSEY
1022   x   JENNIE
1023   xi   POLLY, m Russell Emery

576 RICHARDSON[5] EMERY (*Humphrey*,[4] *Jonathan*,[3] *Jonathan*,[2]
John[1]), son of Humphrey and Sarah (Heath) Emery; married Jane
Swan, of Irish descent who was born at sea when the mother was en
route from Ireland to America   Richardson Emery married for his
second wife Mrs. Winchester, a widow of Plattsburg, N. Y   He was
a farmer and died on his farm in the town of Peru. Clinton Co., N. Y.
He was a soldier in the service of the Americans in the Revolution and
was in Capt. Abijah Smith's Co. for N. Y. He enlisted in this company out of Col. Enoch Hale's Regt. of Militia on Sept 21, 1776.

Children, first marriage (none by second marriage), born in Massachusetts .

1024   i   SARAH,[6] b , d young
1025   ii   WILLIAM, b about 1777
1026   iii   HANNAH
1027   iv   SARAH
1028   v   MARTHA.
1029   vi   RUSSELL
1030   vii   NATHANIEL
1031   viii JANE
1032   ix   ROBERT

580 STEPHEN[5] EMERY (*Stephen*,[4] *Stephen*,[3] *Jonathan*,[2] *John*[1]),
son of Stephen and Deliverance (Styles) Emery, married Lydia Kimball. He married, second, Eliza W. Roberts who died Aug. 24, 1816,
aged 46 He died March 7, 1846, aged 98. He enlisted in March, 1775,
as a minute man in Capt Wm. Perley's Co. of Col. James Frye's
Regiment. On the day of the battle of Lexington, he turned out in
pursuit of the British on their retreat from Concord to Boston   He
is said to have been in the battle of Bunker Hill. Enlisted for eight
months in the same company, discharged Dec 31, 1775, was in
Capt. Wilde's Co in the battle at the surrender of Burgoyne.

Children, born in Winchendon, Mass , except first and second .

1033   i   BETSEY,[6] b Aug 29, 1769, in Wenham, Mass
1034   ii   SALLY, b Jan 26, 1777 in Boxford, Mass , m —— Foster
1035   iii LYDIA, b. March 31, 1779.
1036   iv   STEPHEN, b Feb 18, 1781

1037 v   JOHN, b. March 7, 1783; d. Sept. 26, 1859.
1038 vi   NANCY, b. April 4, 1785; m. Edward Bickford; d. 1878.
1039 vii   OLIVER, b. March 4, 1787; d., unm., Sept., 1857.
1040 viii   LUCY, b. 1807.
1041 ix   OLIVE, b. 1816; d., unm., Sept., 1858.

581 JOHN⁵ EMERY (*Stephen*,⁴ *Stephen*,³ *Jonathan*,² *John*¹), son of Stephen and Deliverance (Styles) Emery, went from Topsfield, Mass., to Rindge, N. H., 1771; married Elizabeth Perkins in Topsfield. He was one of the fifty-four men who went to Cambridge at the time of the Lexington Fight, April 19, 1775; signed the test June 1, 1776. He marched for Ticonderoga, May 6, 1777, and in Aug. 8, 1778, was a volunteer to reinforce Gen. Sullivan at Newport, R. I. He was unpretending in manner and upright in character; died March 26, 1839, aged 88; she died May 27, 1839, aged 90 years.

Children, except first two, born in Rindge:

1042 i   FRANCIS,⁶ b. Aug. 14, 1770, in Topsfield, Mass.
1043 ii   DANIEL, b. July 5, 1772, in Boxford, Mass.
1044 iii   JOHN, b. Oct. 14, 1774.
1045 iv   ISAAC, b. March 25, 1776; removed to N. Y. and d. there.
1046 v   STEPHEN, b. May 13, 1778.
1047 vi   BETSEY, b. April 25, 1782; d., unm., Sept. 1, 1844.
1048 vii   OLIVE, b. Sept. 26, 1784; d., unm., Aug. 26, 1855.
1049 viii   ENOS, b. Oct. 23, 1791.
1050 ix   JONAS, d. in Boston.

582 JESSE⁵ EMERY (*Stephen*,⁴ *Stephen*,³ *Jonathan*,² *John*¹), son of Stephen and Deliverance (Styles) Emery; married Ruth Dwinnell of Boxford, Mass., Feb. 16, 1776. They lived in Londonderry, N. H. She died in Newry, Me., aged 96. He was in the battle of Bunker Hill; He afterwards (March, 1777,) reënlisted for three years in Capt. Carr's Co. of Col. Phinney's Regt. He served out his time and reënlisted for the war; was in the battle of Monmouth, N. J., and others. He died in Londonderry, March 18, 1812.

Children:

1051 i   JESSE.⁶
1052 ii   HANNAH.
1053 iii   SALLY.
1054 iv   REBECCA.
1055 v   DAVID, d. at twenty-one years of age.
1056 vi   EUNICE, b. Sept. 2, 1795.
1057 vii   STEPHEN.
1058 viii   CHARLOTTE.

588 DANIEL⁵ EMERY (*John*,⁴ *Stephen*,³ *Jonathan*,² *John*¹), son of John and Abigail (Styles) Emery; settled in Sutton, N. H., and married Mary Jones (born about 1768). He died in Wilmot, N. H., Aug. 29, 1850. His wife died Nov. 12, 1849. He enlisted for three years in March, 1781, under Capt. Eleazar Frye in Col. Henry Dearborn's N. H. Regt. (the first). He joined his company at a place called Soldiers' Fortune near West Point.

Children:

1059 i   JOHN,⁶ d. when eighteen years of age.
1060 ii   DANIEL.

1061 iii EZRA
1062 iv   JUDITH, b in 1804
1063 v   TIMOTHY, b in 1808

590 MOSES[5] EMERY(*Benjamin,[4] Stephen,[3] Jonathan,[2] John[1]*), son of Benjamin and Sarah (Samson) Emery, married Abigail Knight, Aug. 20, 1778, who died Jan. 16, 1779, aged 25, and, second, Mehetable Ingalls, Dec. 5, 1780.

Children by second wife:

1064 i   ABIGAIL [6]
1065 ii   BETSEY (Elizabeth), b May 10, 1783
1066 iii SALLY, b in Atkinson, N H, in 1784
1067 iv   RHODA, b in Atkinson, N. H, in 1785.
1068 v   JESSE.

594 JUDITH[5] EMERY(*William,[4] Edward,[3] Jonathan,[2] John[1]*), daughter of William and Mary (Chase) Emery, married Cutting Moulton Nov. 25, 1784. She was his second wife His first wife was Mary Merrill Children, except first three, born in Parsonsfield, Me. ·

1069 i   WILLIAM,[6] b July 2, 1785, in Newbury, Mass
1070 ii   JOHN, b Nov 5, 1786 in Newbury, Mass
1071 iii CUTTING, b June 14, 1788, in Newbury, Mass
1072 iv   POLLY, b Sept 7, 1789, lived in Parsonsfield, and d there April 7, 1856
1073 v   JOSEPH, b Nov 6, 1791.
1074 vi   DAVID, b July 27, 1793
1075 vii JUDITH, b Oct. 8, 1794, lived in Newburyport, Mass and d there
1076 viii NATHAN, b. Feb 21, 1796.

595 DAVID[5] EMERY (*Jonathan,[4] James,[3] Jonathan,[2] John[1]*), son of Jonathan and Jerusha (Barron) Emery, married Abigail Goodwin (born 1763, died 1838). There is no record of his marriage as the town of Fairfield was not incorporated in 1788. His intention of marriage is on record dated April 5, 1782; "David Emery and Abigail Goodwin both of Kennebeck River without the boundaries of any town, but in the county of Lincoln, intend marriage." Enlisted Sept., 1775, under Capt Scott in Arnold's expedition against Canada, went as far as Dead River, returned under Col Enos and joined the army at Boston, served at the siege of Boston and vicinity till March, 1777, when he enlisted at Winslow, Me. (Kennebeck Co), for three years under Capt Josiah Jenkins. Col. Sam. Brewer's Mass. Reg, joined the army at Ticonderoga, N Y.; served two years; transferred to Valley Forge, Penn. to the command of Major Caleb Gibbs as one of Gen. Washington's Life Guards, discharged at Morristown, N. J, March, 1780; died in Fairfield, Me., Nov 18, 1830

Children, born in Fairfield, Me.

1077 i   JOHN [6]
1078 ii   BENJAMIN, b June 13, 1784
1079 iii JONATHAN, b Jan 3, 1786
1080 iv   CYNTHIA, b 1793, d, unm æt 72
1081 v   CALEB, b Jan 1, 1794, m Emily Chase
1082 vi   JERUSHA, m Moses S Wyman
1083 vii MILES, b Nov 29, 1799
1084 viii RACHEL, b 1800, m Isaac Chase
1085 ix   NEHEMIAH
1086 x   SUSANNAH, b 1809 d, unm, at 60.

596 JERUSHA[5] EMERY (*Jonathan,*[4] *James,*[3] *Jonathan,*[2] *John*[1]), daughter of Jonathan and Jerusha (Barron) Emery ; married John Abbot. She married, second,——Swan.

Children :

1087 i JOHN,[6] } 1st marriage.
1088 ii BUTLER, }
1089 iii
1090 iv
1091 v } 2nd marriage.
1092 vi
1093 vii

597 HANNAH[5] EMERY (*Jonathan,*[4] *James,*[3] *Jonathan,*[2] *John*[1]), daughter of Jonathan and Jerusha (Barron) Emery ; married Reuben Wyman.

Children :

1094 i REUBEN.[6]
1095 ii RODNEY,—: supposed to have been lost at sea.
1096 iii SOPHIA,
1097 iv HANNAH.

598 JOHN[5] EMERY (*Jonathan,*[4] *James,*[3] *Jonathan,*[2] *John*[1]), son of Jonathan and Jerusha (Barron) Emery ; married Alice Ballard of Vassalboro, Me., March 10, 1791. He died, 1836. His wife died March, 1856.

Children :

1098 i JAMES[6].
1099 ii SOPHIA, b. May 28, 1792.

599 THANKFUL[5] EMERY (*Jonathan,*[4] *James,*[3] *Jonathan,*[2] *John*[1]), daughter of Jonathan and Jerusha (Barron) Emery ; died in Clinton, Me., Oct. 10, 1837, aged 74. Married, first, David Pearson, July 22, 1785 (born in Berwick, England, July 5, 1745, died Oct. 30, 1799) ; second, Rev. Mephibosbeth Cain, Jan. 14, 1802 (born in Hingham, May 22, 1766 ; died Jan. 29, 1849).

Children :

1100 i JANE[6], b. Feb. 14, 1786.
1101 ii SUSANNAH, b. Sept. 16, 1787; d. April 16, 1796.
1102 iii DAVID, JR., b. March 28, 1789.
1103 iv MELINDA, b. May 12, 1791.
1104 v RACHEL, b. May 27, 1793.
1105 vi WILLIAM, b. April 10, 1795; d. March 4, 1801.
1106 vii DEIDAMIA, b. July 10, 1799.
1107 viii LOUISA, b. Oct. 4, 1802; d. Dec. 24, 1804; b. and d. in Clinton, Me.
1108 ix LOUISA, b. Dec. 1, 1804, in Clinton, Me.
1109 x

601 BRIGGS H[5]. EMERY (*Jonathan,*[4] *James,*[3] *Jonathan,*[2] *John*[1]), son of Jonathan and Jerusha (Barron) Emery ; removed to Fairfield, Me., in 1771, and married, 1795, Sally, daughter of Daniel and Lydia (Porter) Farnham, of Andover, Mass. (born June 27, 1774), Died in Fairfield, Me., June 10, 1840. His wife died April 27, 1852.

Children, born in Fairfield ·

1110　i　SAMUEL,[6] b. Nov 15, 1795
1111　ii　BRIGGS H., b April 11, 1797, d , nnm , June 30, 1819.
1112　iii　BENJAMIN FARNHAM, b April 8, 1799
1113　iv　JOSEPH, b Oct 24, 1801
1114　v　ALBEN, b Dec 27, 1803
1115　vi　JOHN ABBOT, b July 28, 1807, d , umn., May 4, 1885; merchant of Bath, Me
1116　vii　SARAH J., b April 2, 1810, m John Davis.
1117　viii　CHARLES, b Dec 17, 1812, d , umn., Nov. 6, 1834, in Bath, Me
1118　ix　OBED, b Nov 23, 1815
1119　x　WILLIAM HENRY, b March 7, 1818, m. Mary Gifford

602 JONES[5] EMERY (*Jonathan,*[4] *James,*[3] *Jonathan.*[2] *John*[1]), son of Jonathan and Jerusha (Barron) Emery; married Alice Johnston. Lived and died at Medford Ferry, Me.

Children :

1120　i　RUTH [6]
1121　ii　RACHEL
1122　iii　HIRAM, supposed to have died at sea
1123　iv　RODNEY.
1124　v　VALENTINE
1125　vi　WILLIAM KING.
1126　vii　THANKFUL C , b Oct 8, 1817
1127　viii　HARRIET, unm
1128　ix　FRANCES
1129　x　GEORGE W.
1130　xi　PAUL JONES
1131　xii　JOSEPH D

603 SAMUEL[5] EMERY (*Jonathan,*[4] *James,*[3] *Jonathan,*[2] *John*[1]), son of Jonathan and Jerusha (Barron) Emery, married Deidamia Johnston, sister of Alice Johnston, wife of Jones Emery (born in Vassalboro, Me , April 2, 1783), Feb , 1801. He died in Fairfield, Me., March 7, 1839. His wife died there Feb. 20, 1851.

Children, born in Fairfield :

1132　i　WILLIAM,[6] b Nov 20, 1801
1133　ii　BUTLER A b Jan 15, 1803
1134　iii　LOUISA CAIN, b Nov 4, 1804, m James Sands in Oldtown, Me , Oct 1, 1845 He was b in Buxton, Me , April 20, 1806. They live at Somerset Mills, Me., and have no children
1135　iv　JOHN J , b Aug 28, 1806
1136　v　LUCY J , b March 18, 1808.
1137　vi　SAMUEL, b May 22, 1810
1138　vii　GEORGE B , b Sept. 27, 1811
1139　viii　DEIDAMIA P , b June 7, 1813
1140　ix　DARIUS B , b June 16, 1815
1141　x　THANKFUL C , b April 23, 1817
1142　xi　PAULINA, b Dec 3, 1818
1143　xii　BRIGGS H , b Aug 25, 1820
1144　xiii　THOMAS J , b. March 7, 1823.
1145　xiv　PARTHENIA D , b Feb 8, 1825.
1146　xv　AUGUSTUS F., b. April 4, 1828, unm , lives in Benezette, Pa.

604 RACHEL[5] EMERY (*Jonathan,*[4] *James,*[3] *Jonathan,*[2] *John*[1]), daughter of Jonathan and Jerusha (Barron) Emery, born in Fairfield,

4

Me.; married in Skowhegan, Me., John Durrell. He died in Skowhegan, Me., April, 1835. She died there in Nov. 5, 1857.

Children, all born in Fairfield, Me., except last two :

1147 i DRUSILLA,[6] m. John Mills.
1148 ii OBED.
1149 iii PARTHENIA, b. 1802; m. Daniel Wells.
1150 iv HARRIET, m. Rev. Elihu Whipley; lived in Etna, Me.; he d. there. She d. there about 1876, s. p.
1151 v RACHEL P., b. Sept. 1, 1806; m. Daniel Wells.
1152 vi JOHN SULLIVAN, d. unm. in Oldtown, Me., 1834.
1153 vii BARRON E. H., b. Sept. 1, 1806.
1154 viii ELKANAH H., b. June 7, 1812
1155 ix SAMUEL E., m. Olive Kimball, in Clinton, Me. She was b. in Clinton. He d. in Hartland, Me., 1856, s. p.
1156 x BELINDA, d. unm. in Fairfield, Me.
1157 xi GEORGE W., b. July 3, 1818, in Skowhegan, Me.
1158 xii MARCIA O., b. in Skowhegan, Me.

605 SAMUEL[5] EMERY (*Anthony,*[4] *James,*[3] *Jonathan,*[2] *John*[1]), son of Anthony; married Sally Densmon; died in 1855. His wife died in 1857.

They removed from New Hampshire to Canada near Fort Erie; he was captured in 1814 for furnishing supplies to the American army and lodged in Fort Erie from which he escaped in a row-boat under fire from the fort. Later, he with his family settled at Sodus Point on Lake Ontario, then removed to Ohio where he died.

Children :

1159 i EBENEZER,[6] b. about 1797, Conway, N. H.
1160 ii ELSIE, b. about 1799, Conway, N. H.
1161 iii SALLY, b. about 1801. Conway, N. H.
1162 iv GILBERT, b. about 1804, Conway, N. H.
1163 v LEWIS, b. July 4, 1806, Conway, N. H.
1164 vi SOPHIA, b. about 1809, Canada.
1165 vii JOHN, b. about 1811, Canada.

606 JOHN[5] EMERY (*Anthony,*[4] *James,*[3] *Jonathan,*[2] *John*[1]), son of Anthony; was a tanner and currier.

Child :

1166 i JONAS S.,[6] a minister.

613 JOHN[5] EMRIE (*Ambrose,*[4] *James,*[3] *Jonathan,*[2] *John*[1]), son of Ambrose and his second wife Rebecca (Yocum) Emery; married Margaret Ross in Newmarket, O., March, 1800 (b. Tyrone Co., Ireland). Theirs was the first marriage in Highland Co., O. He was a farmer; lived in Hillsboro, Highland Co., O., and died there Dec. 22, 1852. His wife died in New Market, O. He was a soldier in the war of 1812. He always spelled his name " Emrie " and his descendants have followed his method.

Children :

1167 i JAMES ST. CLAIR,[6] b. March 3, 1801, Hillsboro, O.
1168 ii JEHU AMBROSE, b. March 1, 1803, Newmarket, O.
1169 iii JOHN, died in infancy, Hillsboro, O.
1170 iv FRANCES ELINOR, b. May 18, 1807, Hillsboro, O.

1171 v   JESSE, d. in infancy, Hillsboro, O
1172 vi   SARAH HARE, b June 29, 1810, Hillsboro, O
1173 vii JONAS REECE. b. April 24, 1812, Hillsboro, O.
1174 viii SAMUEL, b May 18, 1814, d unm in New Market, O., 1836.
1175 ix   MARY ANN, b May 5, 1816; d unm in Athens, O , 1870.

617 SAMUEL[5] EMERY (*Ambrose*,[4] *James*,[3] *Jonathan*,[2] *John*[1]), son of Ambrose and his second wife Rebecca (Yocum) Emery; married Sarah Anderson, daughter of Richard and Mary Anderson, Cumberland Township, Greene Co., Pa , April 7, 1808 (b. Greene Co., Pa., 1791); lived in 1815 in Greene Co , Pa., then near New Market, O., where he died April 5, 1856. His wife died April 6, 1881, in New Market.

Children :

1176 i   CLEMENTINE,[6] b. April 14, 1809, Pa. ⎫
1177 ii   AMBROSE, b Dec. 26, 1810, Pa.   ⎪
1178 iii MARY, b. Nov 28, 1812, Pa   ⎬ Greene Co
1179 iv   REBECCA, b Jan. 16, 1815, Pa .   ⎭ m. David Ashmore in
            Highland Co , O , Aug 5, 1883.   They live in New Market,
            O   No children
1180 v   ISABEL, b. May 23, 1817, New Market, Ohio
1181 vi   JOHN, b March 27, 1819, New Market, Ohio.
1182 vii ELIZABETH, b March 17, 1821, New Market, Ohio.
1183 viii SAMUEL, jr , b March 7, 1823, New Market, Ohio
1184 ix   SARAH, b April 13, 1825, New Market, Ohio
1185 x   NANCY, b July 20, 1827; d June 25, 1828, New Market, Ohio.
1186 xi   RICHARD ANDERSON, b April 21, 1829, New Market, Ohio
1187 xii JAMES M , b June 19, 1832, d Feb. 5, 1849, New Market,
            Ohio

618 CLEMENTINE[5] EMERY (*Ambrose*,[4] *James*,[3] *Jonathan*,[2] *John*[1]), daughter of Ambrose and his second wife Rebecca (Yocum) Emery; married Samuel Kennedy, Feb. 11, 1813 (b in Hagerstown, Md , 1785; d. in Clarksville, Pa , July 5, 1824). She died in Cross Plains, Ind., Oct. 30, 1862 , married in Greene Co., Pa.

Children, born Greene Co., Pa. :

1188 i   REBECCA,[6] b Sept 2, 1815
1189 ii   CATHARINE, b March 12, 1817
1190 iii RACHEL, b Jan 12, 1819
1191 iv   ELIZABETH, b March 3, 1822.
1192 v   EMERY, b April 14, 1824

620 JONAS[5] EMERY (*Ambrose*,[4] *James*,[3] *Jonathan*,[2] *John*[1]), son of Ambrose and his second wife Rebecca (Yocum) Emery; married Susan Morris (daughter of Asa and Susan (Herred) Morris of Rahway, N. J Susan Herred was the widow of Gen Herred and daughter of Solomon Hunt), born in Woodbridge, N. J , Feb. 4, 1787. Lived in Greene Co., Pa., and died June 13, 1857. His wife died June 17, 1879.

Children, born in Greene Co., Pa. :

1193 i   ELIZABETH,[6] b Feb 11, 1810, d March 5, 1830, unm , in Greene
            Co , Pa
1194 ii   PHŒBE, b. Aug 10, 1811
1195 iii REBECCA, b Feb 28, 1813.
1196 iv   CATHARINE, b Feb 28, 1815.

1197   v   PERMELIA, b. Dec 16, 1816
1198   vi CASSANDRA, b Aug 10, 1818, m Thomas Horner in Greene Co ,
           Pa , Oct 7, 1857   He was b in Luzerne Tp , Fayette Co ,
           Pa , Oct 14, 1809   They live at Rice's Landing, Greene
           Co , Pa , and have no children
1199   vii CLEMENTINE, b Aug 10, 1820, d young.
1200   viii JAMES, b Jan 20, 1823
1201   ix JONAS, jr , b Jan 10, 1825
Two children died in infancy.

621 AMBROSE[5] EMERY (*Ambrose,[4] James,[3] Jonathan,[2] John[1]*), son
of Ambrose and his second wife Rebecca (Yocum) Emery, married
Mary Anderson, sister of Sarah, who married Samuel Emery, 1812,
in Greene Co., Pa   They removed to Coshocton Co., O., and next
to Greene Co , Ind., in 1848.   He was a farmer and died near Scotland, Ind., July 8, 1873.   His wife died March 21, 1870.
   Children .
   1202   i   JOHN,[6] b Dec 22, 1812, in Greene Co , Pa.
   1203   ii   SARAH, b Oct 24, 1814.   Teacher, unm ; lives near Scotland,
               Ind.
   1204   iii ELIZABETH, b Nov. 12, 1816, d unm April 30, 1843, in Coshoc-
               ton Co , O
   1205   iv   RICHARD A , b. March 29, 1818; d. Dec. 25, 1827, in Greene Co ,
               Pa
   1206   v   REBECCA, b Sept 16, 1820
   1207   vi   AMBROSE, jr , b July 7, 1822
   1208   vii WILLIAM S , b Aug. 17, 1824.
   1209   viii MARY ANN, b July 29, 1826.
   1210   ix   CLEMENTINE, b Feb 8, 1829
   1211   x   NATHANIEL, b April 2, 1831, in Coshocton Co , O.
   1212   xi   JONAS, b Sept 4, 1834, d in the Field Hospital on the field of
               Antietam, Sept 27, 1862   He was wounded during the battle
               Sept. 17, 1862, but before his removal from near "Bloody
               Lane" received a mortal wound   Enlisted, April, 1861, pri-
               vate in Co D , 14th Reg Ind Inf., mustered in June 7, 1861 ;
               was in the battles of Cheat Mountain, Green Brier, Hanging
               Rock, Bloomery Furnace, Winchester, Fort Royal, Harri-
               son's Landing and Antietam   Teacher   3470 Ind Section,
               Antietam Nat Cem   He was never married
   1213   xii JESSE, b. Sept 4, 1834, d unm Oct 11, 1852, in Greene Co , Pa.

623 JESSE[5] EMERY (*Ambrose,[4] James,[3] Jonathan,[2] John[1]*), son of
Ambrose and his second wife Rebecca (Yocum) Emery, married Hannah Simonton.   Farmer ; lived in Knox Co., O. , died near Mount Vernon.
   Children :
   1214   i   JAMES,[6] m and had several children; died in Knox Co , O
   1215   ii WILLIAM BOTTS, d in Ill from falling from a building, unm.
   1216   iii JONAS, m , d in Knox Co , O
   1217   iv SARAH ANN, m David Sutton, lived in Licking Co , O.
   1218   v   PERMELIA, m David Waldreth; lived in Knox Co , O.

624 ROBERT S.[5] EMERY (*Edward,[4] James,[3] Jonathan,[2] John[1]*), son
of Edward and Eunice (McKie) Emery : married Temperance Mathews
(born in Cape Cod, Mass , Sept. 6, 1778 , died June 16, 1855) of Vassalboro, Me., April 30, 1801.   He died May 23, 1825.   His widow
married George Arnold,

Children.

<pre>
1219   i   JAMES,⁶ b May 11, 1802, in Fairfield, Me
1220   ii   MELINDA, b Aug 2, 1803 in Clinton, Me
1221   iii EUNICE S , b May 19, 1805, in Vassalboro, Me
1222   iv   ISAIAH, b 1808, in Vassalboro, Me
1223   v   GEORGE A , b May 15, 1810, in Vassalboro, Me
1224   vi   HAMILTON, b Aug 9, 1811, in Vassalboro, Me
1225   vii THANKFUL M., b Aug 23, 1814, in Vassalboro, Me
</pre>

625 EUNICE⁵ EMERY (*Edward,*⁴ *James,*³ *Jonathan,*² *John¹*), daughter of Edward and Eunice (McKie) Emery, married Thomas Myrick of Fairfield. Me. , lived in Burnham and Patten, Me. She died in Patten, Me.

Children, born in Burnham, Me :

<pre>
1226   i   EDWARD,⁶ m , and had two children
1227   ii   SIMEON, d unm
1228   iii EZRA, m and had ten children
1229   iv   VIANNA, m Abner Dodge and had five children.
1230   v   LOUISIANA, d. unm
1231   vi   KIMBALL, d unm
1232   vii THOMAS, jr , b Feb 29, 1812, m and had one child, d March,
             1885
1233   viii JOHN W., married Louisa Soper of Oldtown, Me , d. in Patten,
             Me   Widow lives in Patten
1234   ix   FANNIE M , m Asa Kneeland
1235   x   ROSILLA, d. unm
1236   xi   EMILY, m Henry Buzzell and had four children.
1237   xii ELIZA J , b 1813, m H F Heald, live in Lawrence, Mass ; no
             children
</pre>

626 DAVID⁵ EMERY (*Edward,*⁴ *James,*³ *Jonathan,*² *John¹*), son of Edward and Eunice (McKie) Emery, married Mary Cooly in Clinton, Me., June 8, 1802 ; lived and died in Fairfield, Me. ; died 1858.

Children :

<pre>
1238   i   JOSEPH C ,⁶ b April 14, 1803, in Frankfort, Me , left home
             young. Parents never heard from him
1239   ii   PRISCILLA, b Feb 24, 1805, in Frankfort, Me
1240   iii REBECCA, b April 13, 1807, in Unity, Me., m ——Whitcomb,
             and lived in Fairfield, Me
1241   iv   BETSEY S., b Jan 15, 1809, in Unity, Me , m Thomas Cannon
             and lives in Fairfield, Me.
1242   v   MILBURY b April 1, 1812, d April 27, 1812, in Fairfield, Me.
1243   vi   AVIS S , b June 29, 1814, in Fairfield, Me ; m
1244   vii WILLIAM F , b April 7, 1817, d May 4, 1817, in Fairfield, Me.
1245   viii FRANCIS C , b April 23, 1818 in Fairfield, Me
1246   ix   DAVID, b Aug 12, 1820, in Fairfield, Me was a soldier in the
             War with Mexico
1247   x   ASA S , b March 15, 1823, in Fairfield, Me.
1248   xi   MARY ANN, b June 24, 1827, in Fairfield, Me , m ——Hopkins
             of Bangor, Me They live in North Bend, Neb
</pre>

627 EDWARD⁵ EMERY (*Edward,*⁴ *James,*³ *Jonathan,*² *John¹*), son of Edward and Eunice (McKie) Emery, married —— Myrick ; lived at Sherman Mills, Aroostook Co., Me , and died there.

Children :

<pre>
1249   i   AMBROSE.⁶
1250   ii   DANIEL.
1251   iii RUFUS.
</pre>

1252 iv NANCY.
1253 v   SARAH.
1254 vi JOHN.
1255 vii CLARISSA.

628 PRISCILLA[5] EMERY (*Edward,*[4] *James,*[3] *Jonathan,*[2] *John*[1]), daughter of Edward and Eunice (McKie) Emery; married Peter Pushor, March 27, 1794; lived at Twenty-five-mile Pond, Me.; his wife died in Fairfield, Me.; he died in Plymouth, Me.

Children:

1256 i   ABRAM.[6]
1257 ii AMOS.
1258 iii DAVID, d. young unm.
1259 iv EUNICE, m. Adney Bolton. She d. in Frankfort, Me., *s. p.*
1260 v   MARGARET.
1261 vi INFANT, d. in infancy.

640 SARAH[5] ADAMS (*Sarah,*[4] *John,*[3] *John,*[2] *John*[1]), daughter of Henry and Sarah (Emery) Adams; married Samuel Northend (born July 10, 1757), June 2, 1780. He died Dec. 30, 1824. She died April, 1839.

Children:

1262 i   ELIZABETH,[6] b. April 1, 1781; m. John Kent; d. Sept. 28, 1856.
1263 ii SAMUEL, b. 1783; d. 1802.
1264 iii JOHN, b. May 18, 1785.

643 JOHN[6] EMERY (*Daniel,*[5] *John,*[4] *John,*[3] *John,*[2] *John*[1]), son of Daniel and Sarah (Brocklebank) Emery; married Susannah Bartlett of Walpole, N. H., a granddaughter of Gov. Josiah Bartlett of New Hampshire (born Oct. 20, 1756).

Children:

1265 i   DANIEL,[7] b. Oct. 6, 1782, in Newbury, Mass.; m.; d. in Lyndon, Vt., *s p.*, March 21, 1859.
1266 ii   LYDIA HALE, b. Aug. 19, 1784.
1267 iii JOHN, b. July 15, 1788.
1268 iv   GEORGE REED, b. July 22, 1791.
1269 v   ALPHIA BARTLETT, b. Sept. 10, 1793.
1270 vi   HENRIETTA, b. July 10, 1796.
1271 vii JOSIAH BARTLETT, b. April 1, 1798.
1272 viii SAMUEL, b. Nov. 14, 1800; studied law and d., 1822.

645 MEHETABLE[6] EMERY (*Samuel,*[5] *John,*[4] *John,*[3] *John,*[2] *John*[1]), daughter of Samuel and Ruth (Annis) Emery; married Ezekiel Little, Esq., of Boston, May 24, 1801 (born July 28, 1762); graduated from Harvard College, 1784; teacher in public schools in Boston; author of an arithmetic; died March 21, 1840.

Children:

1273 i   RUTH,[7] b. May 16, 1802; d. May 16, 1802.
1274 ii ANN POOR, b. Nov. 21, 1806.

649 MOSES[6] EMERY (*Samuel,*[5] *John,*[4] *John,*[3] *John,*[2] *John*[1]), son of Samuel and Ruth (Annis) Emery; married, first, Caroline Smith, daughter of Dr. Smith of Newburyport, Mass. She died May 10, 1817, aged 40. He married, second, Sarah Moseley Stewart, daughter of Rev. Joseph and Sarah Moseley Stewart, Jan. 4, 1825. She died Oct. 7, 1875.

Child :

1275 ı   CAROLINE SMITH,[7] b. ——, d Jan 8, 1828, aged 12 years.

692 JACOB[6] EMERY (*Rev. Jacob,[5] Joseph,[4] Joseph,[3] John,[2] John[1]*), son of Rev Jacob and Elizabeth (Cushing) Emery ; married Hannah Noyes, April 11, 1799.
Children :

1276 ı   ANN WAINWRIGHT,[7] b. Jan. 25, 1800; d , unm , Dec. 31, 1877, aged 77.
1277 ıı   ELIZABETH C , b April 16, 1801; d Oct. 25, 1803
1278 ııı   HANNAH, b June 8. 1803
1279 ıv   MARY, b Dec 18, 1806
1280 v   BENJAMIN N , b Feb 17, 1809.
1281 vı   JACOB, b Feb 5, 1811

694 JAMES C[6] EMERY (*Rev. Jacob,[5] Joseph,[4] Joseph,[3] John,[2] John[1]*), son of Rev Jacob and Elizabeth (Cushing) Emery, died Dec. 22, 1849 , married Olive Pettingall, Nov 26, 1801 (born 1769 ; died Nov. 28, 1836).
Children :

1282 ı   SUSAN,[7] b Sept 21, 1802
1283 ıı   SETH, b April 1, 1804
1284 ııı   JAMES, b. June 24, 1806 , d. young

695 JOSEPH[6] EMERY (*Joseph,[5] Joseph,[4] Joseph,[3] John,[2] John[1]*), son of Joseph and Hannah (Stickney) Emery ; married Dorcas Holt, Sept. 16, 1787 He died June 8, 1830. She died Sept. 17, 1850.
Children :

1285 ı   PHŒBE,[7] b. April 19, 1788.
1286 ıı   SALLY, b Feb. 14, 1790.
1287 ııı   DORCAS.
1288 ıv   JOSEPH, b Sept 9, 1793, d Dec 24, 1796
1289 v   HANNAH, b July 5, 1795
1290 vı   NABBY, b Sept 10, 1797.
1291 vıı   JOSEPH, b. Sept. 13, 1799
1292 vııı   FANNY, b Sept. 21, 1801 , d Nov 4, 1802
1293 ıx   MELINDE, b June 18, 1805, d. July 10, 1827.

696 SAMUEL[6] EMERY (*Joseph,[5] Joseph,[4] Joseph,[3] John,[2] John[1]*), son of Joseph and Hannah (Stickney) Emery ; married Mary Mc-Connell, Nov. 13, 1798. He died March 12, 1812. His wife died Jan 25, 1858.
Children :

1294 ı   CLARISSA,[7] b May 29, 1800
1295 ıı   ANNA, b Sept 19, 1802; d. March 9, 1804
1296 ııı   ANNE, b June 2, 1804
1297 ıv   MARY B , b May 18, 1808
1298 v   SAMUEL MCCONNELL, b. May 6, 1811; d Aug 14, 1852

697 HANNAH[6] EMERY (*Joseph,[5] Joseph,[4] Joseph,[3] John,[2] John[1]*), daughter of Joseph and Hannah (Stickney) Emery ; married Hall Burgin in Pembroke, N H , Dec 24, 1801, son of Ede and Elizabeth (Bryant) Burgin
Children, born in Allenstown, N. H. ·

1299 i   JOHN YOUNG,[7] b. July 3, 1806; d., unm., Nov. 11, 1836, at Jackson, Clarke Co., Ala., while on a visit through the southern states.
1300 ii   HALL JACKSON, b. Sept. 2, 1809; d., unm., Aug. 9, 1872.
1301 iii MARY LOUISA, b. Jan. 26, 1811.

698 JACOB[6] EMERY (*Joseph,*[5] *Joseph,*[4] *Joseph,*[3] *John,*[2] *John*[1]), son of Joseph and Hannah (Stickney) Emery; married Jane Gault, daughter of Matthew Gault (a Revolutionary soldier), 1804. She was born March 27, 1786. He died Feb. 5, 1870. His wife died April 28, 1862. He was a man of honor and integrity, respected by all.

Children :

1302 i   SOPHIA,[7] b. Dec. 21, 1805.
1303 ii   JOHN BROWN, b. June 5, 1807.
1304 iii CHARLES LONG, b. July 20, 1811.
1305 iv ELIZABETH, b. April 28, 1813.
1306 v   SAMUEL, b. Oct. 18, 1815.
1307 vi MATTHEW GAULT, b. Sept. 28, 1818.
1308 vii JOSEPH STICKNEY, b. Sept. 30, 1820.
1309 viii HALL BURGIN, b. Oct. 20, 1822.
1310 ix MARY JANE, b. Feb. 22, 1825; d., in Baltimore, July 28, 1867, unm.

699 NABBY[6] EMERY (*Joseph,*[5] *Joseph,*[4] *Joseph,*[3] *John,*[2] *John*[1]), daughter of Joseph and Hannah (Stickney) Emery; married William Haseltine, May 19, 1803.

Children, born in Suncook, N. H. :

1311 i   WILLIAM,[7] b. Feb. 4, 1806; d. May 10, 1808.
1312 ii   SALLY EMERY, b. Jan. 5, 1808; d. Oct. 3, 1842.
1313 iii WILLIAM, b. Oct. 9, 1809.
1314 iv CAROLINE, b. Dec. 28, 1811; d. Sept. 14, 1842.
1315 v   HANNAH BURGIN, b. May 23, 1814.
1316 vi ABBY EMERY, b. Nov. 27, 1815; m. S. Sherman of Salem, N. H., Oct. 6, 1842; d. Nov. 11, 1844.
1317 vii MOSES B., b. Sept. 18, 1818; d., in Ohio, Aug. 19, 1870.
1318 viii MARY K., b. April 27, 1824 (see No. 1307).

764 STEPHEN[6] EMERY (*Stephen,*[5] *Stephen,*[4] *Stephen,*[3] *John,*[2] *John*[1]), son of Stephen and Sarah (Moody) Emery, born in Newbury, Mass., July 8, 1761; married Hannah Little, daughter of Paul and Hannah (Emery) Little, May 4, 1783.

Children, born in Newbury, Mass. :

1319 i   POLLY,[7] b. Oct. 18, 1783.
1320 ii   STEPHEN, b. Aug. 7, 1786; d., unm., June 7, 1834.
1321 iii SARAH, b. Dec. 29, 1788.
1322 iv PAUL, b. Sept. 28, 1794; d., unm., Washington, D. C., Aug. 16, 1837.
1323 v   EDWARD, b. Feb. 3, 1801.

765 ENOCH[6] EMERY (*Stephen,*[5] *Stephen,*[4] *Stephen,*[3] *John,*[2] *John*[1]), son of Stephen and Sarah (Moody) Emery; married Sarah Sargent (born June, 1766; died Nov., 1848, aged 82). He died May 20, 1846, aged 83.

Children :

1324 i   ELIZABETH,[7] b Feb 17 1785
1325 ii   SARAH b Oct 12 1786
1326 iii EDMUND SAWYER, b Jan 28, 1789, d , 1810, at sea
1327 iv   HANNAH, b March 21, 1791
1328 v   MOODY, b May 9, 1793, d., 9 years old.
1329 vi   MARY, b Aug 7, 1795 d , unm , in Newmarket, N H
1330 vii ENOCH, b June 26, 1797
1331 viii NATHANIEL, d young
1332 ix   SUSAN, b Aug 2, 1800
1333 x   STEPHEN, b 1803, d young.
1334 xi   CATHERINE, b May 18, 1805.
1335 xii MOODY, b Feb 8, 1807
1336 xiii STEPHEN MOODY, b Dec 26, 1809, graduate of Dartmouth
           College, 1836; Dartmouth Medical School, 1842 , m Lucy
           Ann Augusta Hosmer, daughter of Capt Jacob and Catherine
           (Wellington) Hosmer, Nov 22, 1838.   She was b July 16,
           1809, and d in Fisherville, April 8, 1878   Settled in Fish-
           erville, N H (Boscawen), where he died, s p , Nov., 1881,
           ranked high in his profession and was active in town affairs
           and often elected to office.

767 HANNAH[6] EMERY (*Stephen*,[5] *Stephen*,[4] *Stephen*,[3] *John*,[2] *John*[1]),
daughter of Stephen and Sarah (Moody) Emery ; married Samuel
Moody, April 25, 1790 , died June 15, 1801
    Children :

    1337 i   CHARLES,[7] b Feb 2, 1791, d , unm., Feb 21, 1875, æt 84
    1338 ii   HANNAH, b. Nov 22, 1792.
    1339 iii SALLY, b April, 1795
    1340 iv   ELIZA, b. April 21, 1797

768 MOODY[6] EMERY (*Stephen*,[5] *Stephen*,[4] *Stephen*,[3] *John*,[2] *John*[1]),
son of Stephen and Sarah (Moody) Emery , married Abigail Pres-
cott, daughter of Philemon Prescott, Oct 18, 1795.
    Children :

    1341 i   GEORGE,[7] b. Aug 15, 1797, m Mary R Foote Dec 11, 1822,
                d. Nov 11, 1868   He died in West Newbury, Mass , Dec.
                29, 1864, prominent in town affairs and respected by all.
    1342 ii   RUFUS, b Aug 15, 1797; drowned in the Merrimac River, Nov
                13, 1819
    1343 iii ELIZABETH, b Dec 23, 1801
    1344 iv   SAMUEL MOODY, b April 10, 1804
    1345 v   EUNICE MARY, b April 16, 1808, d Feb 17, 1832

770 SUSAN[6] EMERY (*Benjamin*,[5] *Stephen*,[4] *Stephen*,[3] *John*,[2] *John*[1]),
daughter of Benjamin and Sarah (Bailey) Emery ; married Jona-
than Bradley, son of Lieut. Timothy Bradley.   She died July 27,
1793   He married, second, Mrs Lucretia Cook.
    Children :

    1346 i   RUTH [7]
    1347 ii   CLARISSA, m ——— Bachelder , had one son
    1348 iii ISAAC, m ; had children , all died young.

772 SARAH[6] EMERY (*Benjamin*,[5] *Stephen*,[4] *Stephen*,[3] *John*,[2] *John*[1]),
daughter of Benjamin and Sarah (Bailey) Emery ; married Philbrick
Bradley.   She died Nov 8, 1801   He married, second, ———
His second wife died June 29, 1833.

Children :

```
1349   i     JOHN,⁷ b  Dec  25, 1783
1350   ii    LUCY, b  May 27, 1785
1351   iii   ABIGAIL, b  Feb  13, 1787
1352   iv    SOPHIA, b. Nov  4, 1788
1353   v     SARAH, b  Dec  11, 1791
1354   vi    SABRA, b  April 27, 1793
1355   vii   ROBERT, b  June 1, 1794
1356   viii  ENOCH, b  April 24, 1796
1357   ix    PHILBRICK, b  Aug  13, 1798.
1358   x     SUSANNAH, b  July 29, 1800.
```

773 ISAAC⁶ EMERY (*Benjamin,⁵ Stephen,⁴ Stephen,³ John,² John¹*), son of Benjamin and Sarah (Bailey) Emery, married Esther Tay. He died March 30, 1848, aged 80   He was for many years the well-known landlord of a public house and a member of the legislature of New Hampshire and held many other offices.

Children :

```
1359   i     HARRIET,⁷ b  Aug  16, 1796 , d  Aug. 16, 1796.
1360   ii    HARRIET, b  Nov. 28, 1798 , d  Nov  22, 1830
1361   iii   SUSAN, b  Feb  4, 1801, d  Dec  30, 1830
1362   iv    SARAH B , b  July 19, 1803; m  John Miller, d  Feb  14. 1876
1363   v     ALBERT GALLATIN, b  Aug. 20, 1805, m  Abigail Clough, d.,
              1877.
1364   vi    ISAAC, b. Aug  22, 1807.
1365   vii   ESTHER, b  Aug  1, 1811, m  Newton E  Johnson, d. 1852
1366   viii  TIMOTHY W , b  Dec  21, 1813
1367   ix    ELIZA A , b  Dec  18. 1816, m  David M  Bradley; d. 1862.
1368   x     MARY, b  July 19, 1819 , d  Sept  24, 1828
1369   xi    CLARA E , b  Jan  21, 1821, m  Josiah S  Locke
1370   xii   NANCY A., b  Aug  14, 1824; d. Nov  24, 1859.
```

774 ELIZABETH⁶ EMERY (*Benjamin,⁵ Stephen,⁴ Stephen,³ John,² John¹*), daughter of Benjamin and Sarah (Bailey) Emery ; married David George, jr., Aug 30, 1789. He died April 21, 1838, aged 70. His wife died Aug 6, 1827.

Children :

```
1371   i     DAVID BAILEY,⁷ b  April 12, 1790
1372   ii    CHARLES HENRY, b  Aug  11, 1792
1373   iii   DOLLY, b  May 23, 1794
1374   iv    ELIZABETH, b  May 10, 1797
1375   v     HANNAH, b  July 29, 1800
1376   vi    RUTH EMERY, b  Aug  14, 1802.
1377   vii   SARAH, b  Feb  27, 1806.
1378   viii  MATTHEW OLIVER, b  June 30, 1809
1379   ix    GRACE LOW, b. Aug  14, 1812
```

776 ELIPHALET⁶ EMERY (*Benjamin,⁵ Stephen,⁴ Stephen,³ John,² John¹*), son of Benjamin and Sarah (Bailey) Emery ; married, April 4, 1804, Betsey Walker, daughter of Judge Timothy and Esther (Burbeen) Walker (born April 15, 1780) He died Sept. 16, 1825, and she died Aug 23, 1834.

Children :

```
1380   i     ESTHER W ,⁷ b  Oct  1, 1806
1381   ii    JOHN LANGDON, b  Sept  25, 1809.
```

778 CHARLES[6] EMERY (*Benjamin,*[5] *Stephen,*[4] *Stephen,*[3] *John,*[2] *John*[1]), son of Benjamin and Sarah (Bailey) Emery ; married, Oct. 25, 1805. Polly (Mary) Walker, daughter of Judge Timothy and Esther (Burbeen) Walker (born March 22, 1786). He died in Concord, N H , Oct. 9, 1811. His widow married, second, Hon F. W. Fisk, March 1, 1813.

Children :

   1382   i   MARY W ,[7] b May 2, 1807, d in infancy
   1383   ii   CHARLES LIVERMORL, b Aug 8, 1808, d , in Texas, unm
   1384   iii   CLARISSA W., b Oct 30, 1810.

781 SARAH[6] EMERY (*Nathaniel,*[5] *Stephen,*[4] *Stephen,*[3] *John,*[2] *John*[1]), daughter of Lieut Nathaniel and Sarah (Short) Emery . married Nathaniel Noyes of Salisbury, N H., son of Rev Nathaniel and Sarah (Hale) Noyes, Feb. 6, 1809 , published in Newbury, Mass , Nov. 25, 1808.

Children :

   1385   i   SARAH,[7] d in infancy.
   1386   ii   MARY EMERY, b Sept 19, 1811
   1387   iii   NATHANIEL EMERY, b April, 1813
   1388   iv   SARAH, d. young.

782 ELIPHALET[6] EMERY (*Nathaniel,*[5] *Stephen,*[4] *Stephen,*[3] *John,*[2] *John*[1]), son of Nathaniel and Sarah (Short) Emery ; married Sarah Hale, daughter of Rev. Moses and Elizabeth (Emery) Hale, April 4, 1820. He was prominent in town affairs, representative to general court several terms and interested in all things relating to the public welfare. He died in West Newbury, April 20, 1869. His wife died March 4, 1865

Children :

   1389   i   MARY HALE,[7] b Sept 24, 1821 (see No 1344).
   1390   ii   SARAH NOYES, b June 15, 1824, d Jan 18, 1834

785 PAUL[6] LITTLE (*Hannah,*[5] *Stephen,*[4] *Stephen,*[3] *John,*[2] *John*[1]), son of Paul and Hannah (Emery) Little ; married Mary Osgood, daughter of Abraham Osgood, April 22, 1792, who was born April 22, 1772, and died Sept. 16, 1819. He died in Windham, Me., Jan 5, 1849, where he lived.

Children .

   1391   i   JOSIAH,[7] b April 7, 1793, m , 1st, Barbara M. Merrill, 2nd, Elizabeth Craque His first wife d. 1843, his second wife d. in Lynn, Mass , Sept , 1880
   1392   ii   MARY, b Oct 4, 1798, d , unm , Sept 12, 1869
   1393   iii   MOSES, b March 5, 1801, m Eliza Webb, who died Oct 13, 1847 He lived in Windham and died there, Sept 12, 1843

786 ELIZABETH[6] HALE (*Elizabeth,*[5] *Stephen,*[4] *Stephen,*[3] *John,*[2] *John*[1]), daughter of Rev. Moses and Elizabeth (Emery) Hale , married Thomas Emery, son of Thomas[6] and Ruth (March) Emery, Nov. 27, 1796. She died from the effects of a severe burn May 29, 1803. He married, second, Mrs. Margaret Coffin, widow of Joseph Coffin of Newbury, daughter of Robert Sutherland of Portland, Me , who

was a native of Scotland, Nov. 27, 1806. He died April 11, 1860.
His second wife died Sept. 7, 1861.

Children :

1394   i   FLAVIUS,[7] b. Nov. 2, 1797 (see 1343).
1395   ii   CHARLES, b. June 20, 1800; m. Mary E. George.
1396   iii MOSES HALE, b. Feb. 15, 1803; d., in West Newbury, June 9, 1873.

787 MOSES[6] HALE (*Elizabeth,[5] Stephen,[4] Stephen,[3] John,[2] John[1]*),
son of Rev. Moses and Elizabeth (Emery) Hale ; married Susan Tappan of Newbury, Mass., March 12, 1804. She died Aug. 30, 1817 ;
married, second, Austice Jaques, daughter of Nathaniel Jaques, Esq.,
of Ipswich, Mass., Feb. 13, 1821. He died in Newburyport, Mass.,
Oct. 14, 1843. Shipmaster.

Children :

1397   i   ELIZABETH,[7] b. Jan. 10, 1805; d. young.
1398   ii   ELIZABETH, b. Dec. 6, 1806; m. Daniel Putnam of Boston,
              May 8, 1832.
1399   iii   LYDIA, b. Mar. 31, 1810; d. Feb., 1811.
1400   iv   LYDIA TAPPAN, b. Dec. 22, 1811; married Pemberton Hale, Sept.
              9, 1845; died in Salem, Mass.
1401   v   MOSES, b. June 5, 1814; m. Lydia E. Jaques, Aug. 19, 1851; d.
              in Newburyport, Mass., Dec. 5, 1859.
1402   vi   SUSAN, b. Feb. 23, 1816; d. Aug. 30, 1817.
1403   vii   CAPT. NATHANIEL, b. Jan. 19, 1823; m. Eliza P. Witham of
              Annisquam, Mass., April 14, 1851; d. in London, Eng., Jan.
              6, 1863.
1404   viii CAPT. GEORGE WILLIAM, b. Jan. 8, 1825; m. Elizabeth B.
              Cheney, dau. of James Cheney of Newburyport, Mass., Feb.
              7, 1850.
1405   ix   CAPT. CHARLES, b. June 27, 1827; m. Mary B. Huse, dau. of
              William Huse of Newburyport, Mass.
1406   x   ELIPHALET EMERY, b. Nov. 6, 1830; m. in London, Eng., Han-
              nah Tappan of Newburyport, Mass., April 18, 1856.
1407   xi   CHILD, b. June 9; d. June 10, 1836.

788 STEPHEN[6] HALE (*Elizabeth,[5] Stephen,[4] Stephen,[3] John,[2] John[1]*),
son of Rev. Moses and Elizabeth (Emery) Hale, married Nancy How,
Dec. 6, 1808 ; graduated at Harvard College, 1802, Unitarian clergyman and teacher. He died in West Newbury, Mass., Oct. 4, 1844.
His wife died in Claremont, N. H., March 19, 1829.

Children :

1408   i   ELIZABETH EMERY,[7] b. in Dorchester, Mass., Sept. 30, 1809; d.
              unm. in West Newbury, Feb. 13, 1879.
1409   ii   NANCY, b. Sept. 16, 1813; m. Ferdinand Gori; d. Dec. 17,
              1841.
1410   iii   SUSAN, b. Oct. 13, 1815; m. Plummer Burpee, Nov. 26, 1844.

793 HANNAH[7] EMERY (*Amos,[6] Moses,[5] John,[4] John,[3] John,[2] John[1]*),
daughter of Amos and Anna (Moody) Emery ; married Robert How-
ell. Oct. 6, 1814. He died Aug. 19, 1849, aged 62. She died July 5,
1859, aged 74.

Children :

1411   i   A SON.[8]
1412   ii   AMOS EMERY, b. March 18, 1817.
1413   iii ANN MOODY, b. April 17, 1819; d. April 1, 1838.
1414   iv   MARY E., b. July 15, 1821.

794 ANNA[7] EMERY (*Amos,[6] Moses,[5] John,[4] John,[3] John,[2] John[1]*), daughter of Amos and Anna (Moody) Emery, married Edmund Worth. Oct 6, 1814; she was his second wife His first wife was Mary Morse, who died Nov 14, 1812 His second wife died May 7, 1871. He died Feb 6, 1858, aged 83.

Children:

    1415 i SARAH,[5] b Aug 28, 1820, d April, 1847.
    1416 ii LYDIA, d when 27 years of age

800 JACOB M[7] EMERY (*Amos,[6] Moses,[5] John,[4] John,[3] John,[2] John[1]*), son of Amos and Anna (Moody) Emery; married Jane R. Emerson, Dec. 6, 1826, who was born Oct. 11, 1798, in Dunbarton, N H., died in West Newbury, Aug. 16, 1886. He died Nov. 30, 1872, aged 73.

Children:

    1417 i MARGARET ANN,[8] b Sept 19, 1827, d Oct 4, 1827
    1418 ii MOSES AVERY, b March 18, 1829, d unm. Dec 6, 1851, æt. 22.
    1419 iii EBENEZER b Feb 28, 1831
    1420 iv JOHN MOODY, b Dec 17, 1832
    1421 v MARGARET JANE, b June 16, 1836
    1422 vi MARY ELLEN, b July 10, 1845, d., unm., April 22, 1885.

801 LYDIA[7] COFFIN (*Lydia,[6] Moses[5] John,[4] John,[3] John,[2] John[1]*), daughter of Eliphalet and Lydia (Emery) Coffin; married Oliver Hale, son of Oliver and Judith (Hale) Hale.

Children:

    1423 i LYDIA[8]
    1424 ii SARAH
    1425 iii OLIVER.
    1426 iv JUDITH
    1427 v ELIPHALET.
    1428 vi BETSEY.
    1429 vii SILAS

803 JOHN[7] COFFIN (*Lydia,[6] Moses,[5] John,[4] John,[3] John,[2] John[1]*), son of Eliphalet and Lydia (Emery) Coffin, married Lois Sargent.

Children.

    1430 i THOMAS[8]
    1431 ii ELIPHALET
    1432 iii HANNAH.

804 HEZEKIAH[7] COFFIN (*Lydia,[6] Moses,[5] John,[4] John,[3] John,[2] John[1]*), son of Eliphalet and Lydia (Emery) Coffin, married Anna Hale

Children:

    1433 i WILLIAM.[8]
    1434 ii ENOCH.

806 MOSES[7] COFFIN (*Lydia,[6] Moses,[5] John,[4] John,[3] John,[2] John[1]*) son of Eliphalet and Lydia (Emery) Coffin; married Mary Jones.

Children

1435 i   EMERY [8]
1436 ii   FREDERICK JAMES.
1437 iii   ELIZABETH.

807 NATHAN[7] COFFIN (*Lydia*,[6] *Moses*,[5] *John*,[4] *John*,[3] *John*,[2] *John*[1]), son of Eliphalet and Lydia (Emery) Coffin ; married Eunice Coffin.

Children :

1438 i   CHARLES [8]
1439 ii   NATHAN EMERY
1440 iii   JOHN D.

808 MARY[7] BACHELDER (*Mary*,[6] *Moses*,[5] *John*,[4] *John*,[3] *John*,[2] *John*[1]), daughter of David and Mary (Emery) Bachelder ; married Jeremiah Elkins.

Children :

1441 i   BETSEY.[8]
1442 ii   MARY.
1443 iii   DAVID
1444 iv   LYDIA
1445 v   HENRY

810 ANNA[7] BACHELDER (*Mary*,[6] *Moses*,[5] *John*,[4] *John*,[3] *John*,[2] *John*[1]), daughter of David and Mary (Emery) Bachelder ; married Levi Lane.

Children :

1446 i   JEREMIAH [8]
1447 ii   MARY ANN.
1448 iii   SARAH
1449 iv   EMERY.
1450 v   RHODA
1451 vi   DAVID EMERY.

812 REUBEN[7] BACHELDER (*Mary*,[6] *Moses*,[5] *John*,[4] *John*,[3] *John*,[2] *John*[1]), son of David and Mary (Emery) Bachelder , married Betsey Tilton.

Child :

1452 i   DAVID [8]

814 MOSES[7] BACHELDER (*Mary*,[6] *Moses*,[5] *John*,[4] *John*,[3] *John*,[2] *John*[1]), son of David and Mary (Emery) Bachelder ; married Abigail Drake.

Child .

1453 i   JOSIAH [8]

819 SAMUEL[7] EMERY (*John*,[6] *Moses*,[5] *John*,[4] *John*,[3] *John*,[2] *John*[1]), son of John and Elizabeth (Woodman) Emery ; married Ruby Woodward, Feb. 4, 1808. who was born Sept. 1, 1774, and died Feb 13, 1856. He died Feb 10, 1810

Child :

1454 i   JAMES WOODWARD,[8] b Nov 30, 1808.

821 BETSEY[7] EMERY (*John,*[6] *Moses,*[5] *John,*[4] *John,*[3] *John,*[2] *John*[1]), daughter of John and Elizabeth (Woodman) Emery, married Christopher S Kimball.
Children:

    1455 i ELIZA WOODWARD [8]
    1456 ii MARY EMERY.

822 MARY[7] EMERY (*John,*[6] *Moses,*[5] *John,*[4] *John,*[3] *John,*[2] *John*[1]), daughter of John and Elizabeth (Woodman) Emery; married John Webster.
Children:

    1457 i A SON [8]
    1458 ii A SON.

823 OLIVE[7] EMERY (*Moses,*[6] *Moses,*[5] *John,*[4] *John,*[3] *John,*[2] *John*[1]), daughter of Moses and Ruth (Bodwell); married Ezekiel Loring
Children:

    1459 i NATHAN [8]
    1460 ii ROXANNA.
    1461 iii OLIVE.
    1462 iv STEPHEN.
    1463 v MARY ANN.
    1464 vi CHAUNCEY
    1465 vii WELLINGTON.
    1466 viii CLARISSA.

824 RUTH[7] EMERY (*Moses,*[6] *Moses,*[5] *John,*[4] *John,*[3] *John,*[2] *John*[1]), daughter of Moses and Ruth (Bodwell) Emery, married John Dunning, who was born Feb. 1, 1766; died Sept 12, 1852.
Children.

    1467 i RUTH,[8] b Aug 11, 1789, m Feb 1, 1809, William Harris, jr.; d June 11, 1821
    1468 ii SALLY, b Sept 1, 1791, m Ephraim Harris, Mar 7, 1823
    1469 iii OLIVE, b Dec 9, 1793, m Joseph Strout, Feb 28, 1817.
    1470 iv REBECCA, b. June 15, 1796, m Jabez Waterman
    1471 v JOHN, b Sept 29, 1798, m Sarah J Moody, 2nd, Eliza Briggs. He d in Aug., 1873
    1472 vi ABIGAIL, b Jan 14, 1801, m Nathaniel Brackett, Sept.5, 1842
    1473 vii ISAAC, b. June 21, 1802, m , 1st, Rachel R Gay, 2nd, Lavinia Clark, Feb. 15, 1848. Methodist local preacher.

825 MOSES[7] EMERY (*Moses,*[6] *Moses,*[5] *John,*[4] *John,*[3] *John,*[2] *John*[1]), son of Moses and Ruth (Bodwell) Emery. He was the first male child born in Minot, Me , and by virtue of this received a grant of land of fifty acres. He was a Methodist local preacher beginning when he was about fifty years of age. He married Susannah Woodward He died at Livermore Falls, Me , Nov. 4, 1861.
Children:

    1474 i MOSES,[8] b. July 16, 1794.
    1475 ii SUSANNAH, b Jan 9, 1797
    1476 iii ABIGAIL, b Oct 15, 1799
    1477 iv EUNICE, b Nov 20, 1802

1478 v   IRENE, b. Aug. 2, 1805.
1479 vi ELIZA ANN, b. July 23, 1809.
1480 vii NATHAN ADDISON, b. Oct. 25, 1813; killed accidentally, April, 1839.
1481 viii MARY ANN, b. July 23, 1816; d. July 16, 1840.
1482 ix SARAH STOWELL, b. Sept. 22, 1819, in Minot, Me.; m. Samuel A. Bailey, Sept. 18, 1843. He d. Aug. 12, 1850. She m., 2nd, Richardson Moffat, Esq. (ship builder of Boston), Oct. 18, 1853, in Portland, Me. They resided in Berlin, Wis., 1854–1857, when they returned to East Boston. During the war she was in the soldiers' hospital in Annapolis, Md., and in other places, and afterwards organized and successfully taught a school for colored children in New Castle, Del. In all relations of life she was active, faithful and devoted. She d. in East Boston, Mass., May 22, 1887.

826 NATHAN[7] EMERY (*Moses*,[6] *Moses*,[5] *John*,[4] *John*,[3] *John*,[2] *John*[1]), son of Moses and Ruth (Bodwell) Emery. When sixteen years old he became interested in the subject of religion under the preaching of Rev. Jesse Lee ; elected class leader at sixteen ; at nineteen he was licensed to preach ; he entered the itinerant service in Maine ; was ordained deacon at Union, Me., in 1802. The principal part of his ministerial labors was performed in Conn., New York and Ohio. Under his ministry in 1816 the first Sunday School was established in the old Sands Street Church in Brooklyn, N. Y. In 1821 he bought in Waterville, Ohio, a farm and cultivated it. He had not the advantages of early training, but by incessant labor, he became a good classical student and eloquent preacher. He was familiarly called Father Emery. The prominent traits of his character were good sense, great zeal and a deep and uniform piety. He died May 27, 1849, aged 69. He married in Middletown, Conn., Clarissa Frothingham, in 1806, who died Dec. 18, 1845.

Child :

1483 i   MARY,[8] m. Lineheart; 2nd, ——— Pierce.

827 MARY[7] EMERY (*Moses*,[6] *Moses*,[5] *John*,[4] *John*,[3] *John*,[2] *John*[1]), daughter of Moses and Ruth (Bodwell) Emery ; died March 4, 1848 ; married Ebenezer Emerson, March 11, 1804. He was born July 17, 1771 ; died Aug. 7, 1842.

Children :

1484 i   CLARISSA F.,[8] b. Sept. 26, 1805.
1485 ii   OLIVE E., b. Feb. 21, 1808.
1486 iii EMERY, b. Oct. 15, 1810.
1487 iv   MARIA A., b. July 20, 1813.
1488 v   NATHAN, b. Jan. 30, 1816.
1489 vi   ALBION, b. Nov. 23, 1819.
1490 vii RICHARD HENRY, b. Nov. 2, 1822.
1491 viii JENNETT L., b. Jan. 25, 1826; d. Jan. 2, 1857.

828 STEPHEN[7] EMERY (*Moses*,[6] *Moses*,[5] *John*,[4] *John*,[3] *John*,[2] *John*[1]), son of Moses and Ruth (Bodwell) Emery. He fitted for college under many obstacles and hindrances and contrary to the will of his father ; graduated at Bowdoin college, 1814 ; taught the Academy at Hallowell, Me., teaching a singing school and day school and

reciting in college at the same time; studied law at Portland, Me.,
admitted to the bar, June, 1819, and settled at Paris, Me. Judge of
Probate for Oxford Co., Me., for several years, Attorney General
of Maine, chairman of the Board of Education; member of Executive
Council and judge of District Court   He married Jan. 15, 1815,
Sarah Stowell, daughter of Daniel Stowell, one of the early settlers
of Paris, Me. She was born March 26, 1792, and died Nov. 18,
1822. He married, second, Jennett, daughter of John and Jennett
B Loring, Feb. 7, 1825 (born July 25, 1800, died Sept. 29, 1858).
Children

1492	i	SARAH T,[8] b. Nov 2, 1815
1493	ii	GEORGE F, b Nov 10, 1817
1494	iii	STEPHEN, b 1822, died in infancy
1495	iv	JENNETT, b May 16, 1828
1496	v	ELLEN VESTA, b Sept 14, 1835
1497	vi	STEPHEN ALBERT, b Oct 14, 1841

829 DEA. MOSES[7] EMERY (*Josiah*,[6] *Moses*,[5] *John*,[4] *John*,[3] *John*,[2]
John[1]), son of Josiah and Rebecca (Woodman) Emery, married
Mrs. Hannah (Woodman) Morrison, Nov 12, 1794   He was a member
of the Congregational Church of Sanbornton, N. H., from May 3,
1807, till the time of his death, Sept 10, 1850. His wife died July
11, 1837, aged 70 years.
Children :

1498	i	ELIZABETH,[8] b. Jan 13, 1796
1499	ii	HANNAH b May 25, 1799, d, unm, March 17, 1861.
1500	iii	WOODMAN, b Nov 4, 1802.

830 NATHAN[7] EMERY (*Josiah*,[6] *Moses*,[5] *John*,[4] *John*,[3] *John*,[2]
John[1]), son of Josiah and Rebecca (Woodman) Emery; married
Betsey McCrillis, 1798 (born Aug 8, 1780, died in Lowell, Mass.,
Aug. 6, 1852, aged 72). He died Feb 19, 1850, aged 76. "He was
one of the best specimens of the productions of New England,— the
honored head of a large and enterprising family, a pillar in society
and a true member of the church of God."
Children.

1501	i	JOHN TAYLOR GILMAN,[8] b Jan. 10, 1799
1502	ii	DAVID, b May 24, 1800
1503	iii	JOSIAH, b Nov. 30, 1801
1504	iv	CHARLES, b Dec 25, 1803; mate of a vessel, d of yellow fever in Havana Nov, 1824, unm
1505	v	NATHAN, b Feb 19, 1806.
1506	vi	SUSAN, b Dec 28, 1807; d June 11, 1811
1507	vii	NANCY, b Sept 13, 1809
1508	viii	ALVAN, b March 17, 1811
1509	ix	JOSEPH WOODMAN, b Jan 15, 1813
1510	x	HENRY, b Nov. 5, 1814
1511	xi	MARTHA, } b Sept 2, 1816
1512	xii	MARY, }
1513	xiii	ELIZABETH, b Jan 24, 1819, d Nov 22, 1821.
1514	xiv	MOSES, b April 21, 1820
1515	xv	ENOCH, b Aug 31, 1822
1516	xvi	SAMUEL, b June 17, 1827.

831 ANN[7] EMERY (*Josiah*,[6] *Moses*,[5] *John*,[4] *John*,[3] *John*,[2] *John*[1]), daughter of Josiah and Rebecca (Woodman) Emery ; married Ede Taylor, Dec. 12, 1793 ; died April 9, 1847, aged 72. He was born April 27, 1767, and died in Lebanon, N. H., April 5, 1846, aged 79.

Children :

1517	i	AGNES MOORE,[8] b. May 23, 1795 ; m. Benjamin Whidden, April 2, 1831 (b. in Canterbury, N. H., Aug. 5, 1791 ; d. Jan., 1873, aged 81). His wife d. June 5, 1871.
1518	ii	REBECCA WOODMAN, b. May 1, 1796.
1519	iii	MARY (POLLY), b. Oct. 12, 1797.
1520	iv	RACHEL MOORE, b. March 11, 1799.
1521	v	NANCY, b. July 11, 1800.
1522	vi	CHARLOTTE, b. Dec. 21, 1801 ; m. Freeman Lane, May 14, 1833 ; d. *s. p.*
1523	vii	ELECTA, b. Nov. 23, 1803 ; d. May 25, 1812.
1524	viii	ELIZA CROCKETT, b. Nov. 8, 1806.
1525	ix	SALLY HUSE, b. Dec. 13, 1808.
1526	x	IRENE B., b. June 5, 1811.
1527	xi	ELECTA, b. March 29, 1813 ; d. Nov. 29, 1832.
1528	xii	MIRANDA, b. Dec. 5, 1815 ; d. June 17, 1829.
1529	xiii	JOSIAH EMERY, b. Feb. 3, 1819 ; maker of edged tools in Nashua, N. H. ; d. June 10, 1848 ; m. Susan H. Manser, Nov. 21, 1847.

832 MOLLY[7] EMERY (*Josiah*,[6] *Moses*,[5] *John*,[4] *John*,[3] *John*,[2] *John*[1]), daughter of Josiah and Rebecca (Woodman) Emery ; married John P. Hayes, Jan. 21, 1796.

Children :

1530	i	WILLIAM,[8] b. Nov. 9, 1796.
1531	ii	REBECCA W., b. July 23, 1798.
1532	iii	BRADSTREET MOODY, b. March, 1800.
1533	iv	JOHN PLUMMER, b. Oct. 24, 1803.
1534	v	ROSINA, b. 1804 ; d., in Sanbornton, N. H., Nov. 23, 1829, unm.
1535	vi	MARY P., b. 1807 ; d., in Hennepin, Ill., 1838.
1536	vii	ELIZA ANN, b. April 15, 1810.
1537	viii	ABIGAIL W., b. March, 1812.
1538	ix	SALLY EMERY, b. Nov. 30, 1813.
1539	x	JOSIAH EMERY, b. July 6, 1817.

833 LYDIA[7] EMERY (*Josiah*,[6] *Moses*,[5] *John*,[4] *John*,[3] *John*,[2] *John*[1]), daughter of Josiah and Rebecca (Woodman) Emery ; married Jeremiah Hackett, Nov. 15, 1798.

Children :

1540	i	MARY (POLLY),[8] b. March, 1800.
1541	ii	NANCY, b. Dec. 31, 1802.
1542	iii	MAHALA.
1543	iv	EMERY.
1544	v	BETSEY EMERY, b. Aug. 18, 1807.
1545	vi	ASA, d., unm.
1546	vii	SUSAN.

834 REBECCA[7] EMERY (*Josiah*,[6] *Moses*,[5] *John*,[4] *John*,[3] *John*,[2] *John*[1]), daughter of Josiah and Rebecca (Woodman) Emery ; married Jonathan Morrison, Oct. 28, 1798.

Children :

1547   i   ELIZABETH MEADER,⁸ b Aug 12, 1799, d young.
1548   ii   JONATHAN, b Dec 15, 1800; d Oct. 6, 1815.
1549   iii ELIZA MEADER, b Nov. 14, 1802.
1550   iv   JOSIAH EMERY, b. April 30, 1804
1551   v   ABIGAIL LIBBY, b March 4, 1806
1552   vi   JUDITH LANE, b March 2, 1808.
1553   vii AMOS EMERY, b. Aug. 2, 1811.
1554   viii HANNAH WOODMAN, b July 21, 1814, m., 1st, George Teel,
             2nd, M N Hawks.
1555   ix   REBECCA ANN, b. June 28, 1817.
1556   x   JONATHAN EASTMAN, b Feb 11, 1820

835 SARAH⁷ EMERY (*Josiah,⁶ Moses,⁵ John,⁴ John,³ John,² John¹*),
daughter of Josiah and Rebecca (Woodman) Emery; married Joseph Huse, Nov. 5, 1805. She died June 27, 1855. He died Jan.
24, 1856.
Children :

1557   i   RACHEL,⁸ b Nov 3, 1806
1558   ii   DANIEL MORRISON, b. Dec 8, 1808
1559   iii WILLIAM BRILR, b. June 23, 1810
1560   iv   WOODMAN EMERY, b. April 12, 1815, m Sarah J Rogers; d.
             Aug 14, 1846
1561   v   EBENEZER B , b. June 11, 1820

838 ROGER⁷ MERRILL (*Sarah,⁶ Moses,⁵ John,⁴ John,³ John,²
John¹*), son of Ezekiel and Sarah (Emery) Merrill; married, in
Bethel, Me., March 1, 1803, Sarah Freeland, youngest daughter of
Dr. James Freeland of Sutton, Mass. (born Aug 27, 1782 ; died in
Brunswick, Me., Dec. 3, 1855). He removed to Brunswick, Me., and
engaged in lumbering on the Androscoggin, and died suddenly Feb.
17, 1849.
Children :

1562   i   CAPT MOSES EMERY,⁸ b Dec 2, 1803, grad West Point, 1826,
             killed at the battle of Molino del Rey, Mexico, Sept. 8, 1847,
             m Louisa Slaughter of Culpepper Co , Va
1563   ii   JAMES FREELAND, d in infancy
1564   iii SARAH FREELAND, b Aug 10, 1806; d Aug. 18, 1820.
1565   iv   ANGELINE, b Aug 7, 1808, m George Earle, Nov 18, 1829.
1566   v   JAMES FREELAND, b Oct 20, 1810, d Nov 12, 1816
1567   vi   SAMUEL RAWSON, b Nov 23, 1813; m at Stevens' Point, Wis.,
             June 1, 1860, Anna C Emmons of Rochester, N Y , who
             lived in Juneau, Wis , where he died Dec 17, 1881
1568   vii FRANCES FREELAND, b Oct 4, 1817, m , in Brunswick, Me ,
             Oct 7, 1844, Warren Rundlett of Alna, Me   She died in
             Brunswick, Me , April 14, 1884
1569   viii ARABELLA, b Nov. 10, 1819.
1570   ix   LEONARD PARKER, b.. Sept. 27, 1821, grad. Bowdoin College,
             1842 , was a lawyer; abandoned his practice and entered the
             merchant service and died in New Orleans, La , Oct 31,
             1870   He m Catherine Kent Newman of Brunswick, Me.,
             Oct 27, 1851, left two sons
1571   x   SARAH FREELAND, b Aug 28, 1823; d Aug 16, 1844
1572   xi   LYDIA STONE, b. Sept 4, 1826 , m , in Louisville, Ky., June 29,
             1853, William Rhodes of Cincinnati, O , removed to St.
             Paul, Minn , 1857, where he died Feb. 14, 1882, aged 56

839 MOSES[7] MERRILL (*Sarah*,[6] *Moses*,[5] *John*,[4] *John*,[3] *John*,[2] *John*[1]), son of Ezekiel and Sarah (Emery) Merrill ; married Dorothy Bragg, May 1, 1810 (born 1782 ; died in Andover, Me., June 16, 1848, aged 66).

Children :

    1573 i   MARY FRYE,[8] b. June, 1811 ; m. Caleb Franklin Poore, Dec. 20, 1827 ; d. July 16, 1857.

    1574 ii   SARAH EMERY, b. Sept. 2, 1812 ; d. Sept. 8, 1812.

    1575 iii MOSES GILMAN, b. Oct. 25, 1813 ; m. Sarah ——— ; d. in Lawrence, Mass.

    1576 iv SARAH EMERY, b. Aug. 25, 1815 ; m. Jeremiah Barker ; d. May, 1854.

    1577 v   JOHN CALVIN, b. July 17, 1817 ; m. Araminta P. Jones, dau. of Benjamin and Jannette (Allen) Jones, b. in Turner, Me., March 14, 1828 ; d. May 24, 1884.

840 SARAH[7] MERRILL (*Sarah*,[6] *Moses*,[5] *John*,[4] *John*,[3] *John*,[2] *John*[1]), daughter of Ezekiel and Sarah (Emery) Merrill ; married Peregrine Bartlett, one of the first settlers in Bethel, Me.

    Children :

    1578 i   NATHAN,[8] b. Aug. 3, 1793 ; d. May 25, 1801, Bethel, Me.

    1579 ii   RUBY, b. March 11, 1796 ; m. Aaron Mason, May 3, 1817.

    1580 iii FREEBORN, b. Oct. 14, 1797 ; d., unm., in La.

    1581 iv MARIA, b. Sept. 30, 1799 ; m. David H. Farnham of Rumford, Me.

    1582 v   SALINA, b. March 28, 1802.

    1583 vi EZEKIEL MERRILL, b. Apr. 20, 1804.   Physician ; settled in the west.

    1584 vii ELIJAH, } b. Jan. 26, 1806 ; { d. March 11, 1806.

    1585 viii ELISHA, } b. Jan. 26, 1806 ; { d. Feb. 13, 1806.

    1586 ix MARINA, b. Feb. 7, 1807 ; m. Bart Bartlett.

    1587 x   STEPHEN, b. July 9, 1809 ; m. ——— Stevens.

    1588 xi SOLON, b. Nov. 22, 1810 ; lived in N. Y.

    1589 xii LUNA EMELINE, b. March 19, 1814 ; d. March 2, 1817.

    1590 xiii SOCRATES PLATO, } b. Jan. 1, 1816 ; { d. Feb. 20, 1817.

    1591 xiv SYLVANUS PORTER, } b. Jan. 1, 1816 ; { d. Nov. 11, 1832.

    There were five other children who died in infancy.

841 ANNA MOODY[7] MERRILL (*Sarah*,[6] *Moses*,[5] *John*,[4] *John*,[3] *John*,[2] *John*[1]), daughter of Ezekiel and Sarah (Emery) Merrill ; died in Andover, Me., Nov. 27, 1848 ; married Samuel Poor (son of Benjamin and Phebe (Varnum) Poor), born May 3, 1767 ; died Feb. 4, 1820. She married, second, Abner Rawson and, third, Daniel Gould.   Her children were all by the first husband.

    Children :

    1592 i   SAMUEL,[8] b. March 22, 1800 ; m. Asenath Farnham, b. 1802, and d. Aug. 26, 1863 ; he d. in Andover, Me., May 26, 1867.

    1593 ii   JAMES VARNUM, b. May 21, 1803, at Andover, Me. ; m. Rachel Hamilton.

    1594 iii BENJAMIN, b. in Andover, Me., Sept. 26, 1804 ; m. Catherine, daughter of John Montgomery.

842 MARY[7] MERRILL (*Sarah*,[6] *Moses*,[5] *John*,[4] *John*,[3] *John*,[2] *John*[1]), daughter of Ezekiel and Sarah (Emery) Merrill ; married Dr.

Sylvanus Poor of Andover, Me , Feb 18, 1802, who was born March 7, 1768. She died suddenly July 17, 1841.

Children :

1595 i LAURA,[8] b. Dec 5, 1802, d Oct 27, 1880, at Bolton, Mass , m Rev. Thomas Treadwell Stone, D D , in 1825, son of Solomon and Hepzibah Treadwell Stone, b in Waterford, Me., Feb 9, 1801 graduated Bowdoin College, 1820

1596 ii SYLVANUS, b Feb. 23, 1805, m , 1st, Jan 22, 1834, Eliza Fox, d Jan 23, 1867, 2nd, Lovicy Cole, widow of Amos Chipman, b April 4, 1819

1597 iii JOHN ALFRED, b Jan 6, 1809, a prominent railroad and business man of Portland, Me , m , 1st, Elizabeth A Hill, 2nd, Elizabeth Orr; 3rd, Margaret Gwynne, d at Portland, Me , Sept 5, 1871

1598 iv ELBRIDGE, b May 6, 1811 , m , 1st, Susan Bragg, Jan. 20, 1834 , 2nd, Huldah Ellen Hale, Nov 25, 1877.

1599 v HENRY VARNUM, b Dec 8, 1812, grad. Bowdoin College, 1835, m. Mary Wild Pierce, Sept 7, 1841, dau of Dr John Pierce of Brookline, Mass , and has had seven children three sons, four daughters.

1600 vi MARY PALMER, b Dec 15, 1814; d 1818

1601 vii MARTHA LAURENS, b Feb. 1, 1818, m William Henry Talbot, Sept. 9, 1846

843 EZEKIEL[7] MERRILL (*Sarah,[6] Moses,[5] John,[4] John,[3] John,[2] John[1]*), son of Ezekiel and Sarah (Emery) Merrill , married Phebe V. Farrington, daughter of John and Phebe (Poor) Farrington, June 1, 1809.

Children :

1602 i EZEKIEL EMERY,[8] b. Jan 22, 1811, m Hannah Abbot Frost, Dec 11, 1834

1603 ii HENRY PUTNAM, b Nov 3. 1814, m , in Canada, 2nd, Barbara Drum and had two daughters

1604 iii PHEBE VARNUM, b Feb 3, 1813; m Daniel Cary Dresser, Feb 18, 1836

1605 iv SARAH FARRINGTON, b Nov 15, 1818; m Whitman W Hobbs

1606 v JOHN FARRINGTON, b April 11, 1821;

1607 vi MARTHA SWAN b March 10, 1827 , m., 1st Samuel Allen, Oct. 4, 1853, 2nd, Nathan Dresser, Dec 14, 1858

1608 vii LYDIA TALBOT, b. Oct 14, 1832, m William A Morehead

844 LYDIA[7] MERRILL (*Sarah,[6] Moses.[5] John,[4] John,[3] John,[2] John[1]*), daughter of Ezekiel and Sarah (Emery) Merrill , married Isaac Winslow Talbot, March 13, 1812, son of David and Esther (Winslow) Talbot ; lived in Turner, Me. He died July 8, 1856. She died Aug. 29, 1875.

Children :

1609 i ISAAC WINSLOW,[8] b May 4, 1813; d unm

1610 ii JOSEPH EMERY, b Aug. 11, 1817, m Martha V Stevens, March 1, 1842

1611 iii EZEKIEL MERRILL, b April 23, 1823, m , 1st Nancy Whitman, July 13, 1848, 2nd, Marella Vermilyea, Dec. 30, 1856

845 SUSAN[7] MERRILL (*Sarah,[6] Moses,[5] John,[4] John,[3] John,[2] John[1]*), daughter of Ezekiel and Sarah (Emery) Merrill , married Nathan Adams, March 17, 1817. He died at Rumford, Me., Jan 26, 1850. She died at Wilton, Me., May 1, 1868.

Children :

1612   i   MILTON,[8] b. April 15, 1818; d. Sept. 7, 1819.
1613   ii   JOHN MILTON, b. Sept. 22, 1819; m., 1st, Sept. 16, 1851, So-
               phia E. Preble, widow of Edward E. Preble, only son of
               Com. Edward Preble, U. S. N. They separated in 1862.
               He m., 2nd, Apr. 16, 1867, Adela Sophronia Hobbs; was
               admitted to the Bar in 1864; Lieut Col. on the staff of Gov.
               Hubbard; County Supervisor of Schools; Reporter of the
               decisions of the Supreme Court; Manager of the *Eastern
               Argus;* and, in 1866, became its sole proprietor and editor-
               in-chief. In 1876 and 1877 he was a member of the Maine
               Legislature from Deering, Me.
1614   iii   CHARLES, b. July 10, 1821; d. Nov. 14, 1845.

847 SUSANNAH[7] MERRILL (*Ann,[6] Moses,[5] John,[4] John,[3] John,[2] John[1]*), daughter of Abel and Ann (Emery)Merrill; married Simeon Welch, May 26, 1799, son of Col. Joseph and Hannah (Chase) Welch (born July 24, 1772).

Children :

1615   i   SUSANNAH,[8] b. in Plaistow, N. H., April 22, 1800; m. Col. War-
               ren Porter, Oct. 9, 1823.
1616   ii   JOHN, d. young.
1617   iii   JOHN, b. 1803; d. young.
1618   iv   HANNAH CHASE, b. 1805.
1619   v   SUSANNA MOODY, b. 1809.
1620   vi   SARAH MERRILL, b. 1810.
1621   vii   MATILDA, b. March 29, 1812.
1622   viii RICHARD, b. May 31, 1814.
1623   ix   CATHARINE, b. July 23, 1819.

849 SARAH[7] MERRILL (*Ann,[6] Moses,[5] John,[4] John,[3] John,[2] John[1]*), daughter of Abel and Ann (Emery) Merrill; married Stephen Chase of West Newbury; lived in Plaistow, N. H.

Children :

1624   i   MARY ANNA.[8]
1625   ii   LYDIA ADALINE.
1626   iii   ALFRED.
1627   iv   WARREN, d. on the passage from West Indies.
1628   v   FLAVIUS, d. unm.
1629   vi   MELVINA.
1630   vii   HORACE.
1631   viii CHARLOTTE.
1632   ix   MILTON.

850 LYDIA EMERY[7] MERRILL (*Ann,[6] Moses,[5] John,[4] John,[3] John,[2] John[1]*), daughter of Abel and Ann (Emery) Merrill; married John Poor, May 19, 1825. He died Oct. 12, 1866, aged 73. She died Jan. 17, 1884.

Children :

1633   i   JOHN MERRILL,[8] b. Aug. 14, 1829.
1634   ii   ABEL MERRILL, b. Nov. 12, 1832.
1635   iii   MOSES, b. June 8, 1834.
1636   iv   LYDIA.
1637   v   MARY MALVINA.
1638   vi   HANNAH.
1639   vii   MARTHA.

851 JOHN SARGENT[7] EMERY (*Michael*,[6] *Moses*,[5] *John*,[4] *John*,[3] *John*,[2] *John*[1]), son of Michael and Sarah (Worthen–Sargent) Emery, married, first, Jane Wilson Page, Dec 14, 1831, who died Aug. 7, 1843, aged 35; married, second, Susan Breck Haseltine (born Feb. 2, 1811), Jan. 28, 1844.

Children:

    1640 i   CHARLES W,[8] b. May 17, 1837; killed in action May 5, 1862, at Williamsburg, Va.
    1641 ii   SARAH JANE, b Aug., 1839, m Alex C. Ordway, Nov, 1877.
    1642 iii FREDERICK A, b July 28, 1847.
    1643 iv JULIA M, b Dec 17, 1848
    1644 v   ANNIE BARTLETT, b March 19, 1851
    1645 vi RICHARD S., b. July 6, 1852, m. Elizabeth Carleton, Nov. 26, 1874
    1646 vii MARY LOUISA, b May 10 1854, d Nov 17, 1854.
    1647 viii SUSAN HASELTINE, b Oct. 4, 1857, unm

852 DEA. JOSEPH[7] EMERY (*Michael*,[6] *Moses*,[5] *John*,[4] *John*,[3] *John*,[2] *John*[1]), son of Michael and Sarah (Worthen–Sargent) Emery, married Judith A Lane, daughter of Joseph H. and Polly (Lane) Lane (born Nov. 17, 1817), May 25, 1843. He died May 6, 1883.

Child:

    1648 i   LYDIA LOUISA,[8] b. April 30, 1844; m. Horatio N March, son of Joshua and Hannah S Thompson March (b May 12, 1831), June 4, 1873

854 FOREST[6] EMERY (*Samuel*,[5] *Samuel*,[4] *Rev Samuel*,[3] *John*,[2] *John*[1]), son of Samuel and Margaret (Dalzel) Emery; married Mary Adams, daughter of Capt. Richard Adams of York, Me. (born Oct. 14, 1777), died Jan. 24, 1845

Children:

    1649 i   SARAH,[7] b June 27, 1802, m Benj Stewart of Wells, Me
    1650 ii   MARY, b Dec 6, 1803 m Eben Blaisdell of York.
    1651 iii HANNAH, b Oct. 2, 1805.
    1652 iv ELIZA, b Feb 5, 1808· m Elisha Littlefield of Wells
    1653 v   JAMES, b July 29, 1810
    1654 vi STEPHEN, b Sept 26, 1811
    1655 vii HEPZIBAH, b March 26, 1814; m Bernard McCann.
    1656 viii ANN, b. May 7, 1817
    1657 ix ABIGAIL, b. July 14, 1819

864 WARD[6] GILMAN (*Hannah*,[5] *Rev Stephen*,[4] *Rev. Samuel*,[3] *John*,[2] *John*[1]), son of John Ward and Hannah (Emery) Gilman, married Hannah, daughter of Mark Seavy of Rye, N. H., 1797 (born June 2, 1771; died March 12, 1868). He died Dec. 14, 1821.

Children:

    1658 i   HANNAH EMERY,[7] b Feb 27, 1798, m Gideon Colcord Lyford of Exeter, N H,, Sept 9, 1821
    1659 ii   JOHN WARD, b April 25, 1799, lost at sea
    1660 iii MARK SEAVY, b. Aug. 25, 1800, m Hannah Esty of Nashua, N H, May 22, 1832.
    1661 iv WILLIAM, b March 31, 1802, d. Oct. 3, 1802.
    1662 v   WILLIAM, } b Oct 9, 1803, { d Jan. 20, 1805
    1663 vi MARY, } { m May 13, 1828, C W Brewster, editor of *Portsmouth Journal* and author of "Rambles about Portsmouth."

866 ALLEN[6] GILMAN (*Hannah,*[5] *Rev. Stephen,*[4] *Rev. Samuel,*[3] *John,*[2] *John*[1]), son of John W. and Hannah (Emery) Gilman; married, first, Pamelia Augusta Dearborn, second, Eleanor Brewer, died April 7, 1846. He was the first mayor of Bangor, Me.

Children:

1664　ı　PAMELIA AUGUSTA SOPHIA,[7] m, 1822, Col Greenleave Dearborn, U S A, who d Sept 9, 1846
1665　ıı　CHARLES, b June 30, 1807, m Annette M Dearborn, Jan 20, 1822, d July 24, 1849.
1666　ııı　JOSEPH, b Sept 18, 1809; m Sabina P Hodsdon, July 9, 1833
1667　ıv　SAMUEL ALLEN, b, 1811.
1668　v　WILLIAM ABBOT
1669　vı　ELIZABETH, b 1815, d. 1815
1670　vıı　HENRY, b 1817
1671　vııı　EMELINE HURST, b. 1820, m., 1843, Leonard Jones.

875 STEPHEN[6] EMERY (*John,*[5] *Rev Stephen,*[4] *Rev. Samuel,*[3] *John,*[2] *John*[1]), son of John and Mercy (Crowell) Emery; married Betsey Ryder, Nov. 20, 1807.

Children:

1672　ı　JOHN,[7] b June 6, 1808
1673　ıı　MARY, b June 28, 1810, m John Witherill of Wellfleet, Mass., Dec. 13, 1832, d. Aug 28, 1863
1674　ııı　PRISCILLA, b. Oct. 30, 1812, m, 1st, David Taylor, 2nd, A Gilmore, 3d, E Baker She d July 11, 1864, s p.
1675　ıv　BETSEY, b Nov 29, 1814; m Capt Eben Harding, Jan 27, 1837, d Aug 26 1885
1676　v　STEPHEN, b April 17, 1817.
1677　vı　ALATHINA, b April 19, 1819
1678　vıı　SARAH, b Feb 4, 1821, m Capt Kimball Eldredge, Oct. 7, 1841, d May 12, 1869
1679　vııı　CYRUS, b July 8, 1827

877 SAMUEL[6] EMERY (*John,*[5] *Rev. Stephen,*[4] *Rev. Samuel,*[3] *John,*[2] *John*[1]), son of John and Mercy (Crowell) Emery, married Jerusha Chase, 1808; died Feb 5, 1850

Children.

1680　ı　CAROLINE,[7] b. July 29, 1808, m Elisha Mayo of Orleans, Mass, May 30, 1826
1681　ıı　MERCY, b. Nov. 4, 1809, d. May 15, 1810
1682　ııı　JOSEPH, b Oct 27, 1811.
1683　ıv　HANNAH, b Sept 28, 1813, d, unm, Feb 15, 1885
1684　v　MEROY, b July 8, 1817, m Capt Eli Nickerson May 9, 1839.
1685　vı　JERUSHA, b Oct 25, 1819; m John Charter, Oct. 25, 1866, d. Sept 2, 1887.
1686　vıı　SAMUEL, b July 6, 1822; d, unm, June 3, 1853.
1687　vııı　JULIA ANN, b Sept 4, 1824; m Payson Crowell, July 5, 1852.

879 BETSEY[6] EMERY (*John,*[5] *Rev. Stephen,*[4] *Rev. Samuel,*[3] *John,*[2] *John*[1]), daughter of John and Mercy (Crowell) Emery; married Dr. Daniel Clifford, Feb., 1812, died Sept. 26, 1866.

Children:

1688　ı　SAMUEL D,[7] b Nov 20, 1812
1689　ıı　BENJAMIN F, b Dec 13, 1813, m Betsey Harding
1690　ııı　WILLIAM D., b. Dec. 20, 1815.
1691　ıv　BETSEY, b Oct 21 1822.

1692 v   DANIEL, b March 5, 1825.
1693 vi RUTH H , b March 13, 1827

887 JOHN[6] EMERY (*John,[5] Joshua,[4] John,[3] Jonathan,[2] John[1]*), son of John and Abigail (Webster) Emery, married Abiah Page of Haverhill, Mass , May 6, 1779. He died Jan. 28, 1823.
Children:

1694 1   ABIGAIL,[7] b June 13, 1780, m. Benjamin Morse of Lowell, Mass ; d Sept 10, 1830.
1695 11   JOHN, b Oct 8, 1785, d , unm , Jan. 4, 1816.
1696 111 SAMUEL, b. Nov 9, 1788
1697 1v   ABIAH, b Feb 5, 1792; m ——— Morse, d., *s. p.*, Dec. 19, 1815
1698 v   RICHARD, b Nov. 23, 1794.
1699 vi   ELIZA, b. April 15, 1799, m. John Young.

889 JOSHUA[6] EMERY (*John,[5] Joshua,[4] John,[3] Jonathan,[2] John[1]*), son of John and Abigail (Webster) Emery; married Ruth Nott in Walpole, N H , Jan 21, 1781. He died Jan. 6, 1832.
Children:

1700 1   ABIGAIL, b Jan 15, 1782
1701 11   MARY, b May 6, 1784
1702 111 HANNAH, b April 16, 1786, d July 9, 1788
1703 1v   PHŒBE, b March 23, 1788.
1704 v   HANNAH, b May 29, 1790.
1705 vi   SAMUEL, b July 14, 1792
1706 vii MOSES, b June 17, 1794
1707 viii CYNTHIA, b. July 22, 1795.

890 MOSES[6] EMERY (*John,[5] Joshua,[4] John,[3] Jonathan,[2] John[1]*), son of John and Abigail (Webster) Emery, married, 1787, Mary, daughter of Capt. Stephen Webster. He died in Lisbon, N. H , Feb 11, 1849. His wife died Aug 16, 1831. He prepared for Harvard College, entered the army during the war, became a manufacturer of buckles; removed to Lisbon, N. H., in 1850, was clerk of the proprietors of unsettled land in the township for twenty-two years, justice of the peace; prominent in town affairs and an influential member and worker of the Methodist Society. His impartial decisions in matters of controversy were well known and widely acknowledged.
Children:

1708 1   MARY,[7] b. Jan 18, 1789, Haverhill, Mass., d , unm , in Lisbon, N. H., July 25, 1834.
1709 11   ABIGAIL W , b June 4, 1791, Dover, N H
1710 111 STEPHEN, b March 9, 1794, Dover, N H , d , unm , in Lisbon, N H , Oct 23 1838
1711 1v   LUCY, b Aug 24, 1798, Hopkinton, N. H
1712 v   MOSES, b July 6, 1801, Lisbon, N H.

892 SMITH[6] EMERY (*Joshua,[5] Joshua,[4] John,[3] Jonathan,[2] John[1]*), son of Joshua and Rachel (Currier) Emery, married Rhoda Burroughs in Alstead, N. H.
Children

1713 1   WILLARD, b Aug 19, 1796, d April 9, 1844.
1714 11   JOHN WINSLOW, b March 30, 1798

1715 iii SMITH, b Feb 7, 1800
1716 iv SANFORD, b Aug 6, 1805.
1717 v RHODA, b Oct., 1808
1718 vi ANNA, b Sept 24, 1811
1719 vii BELINDA, b Dec 25, 1814
1720 viii ARNOLD S , b. March 10, 1817
1721 ix PAMELIA, b July 13, 1819; d Oct. 22, 1839
1722 x LUCY, b Oct 8, 1826.

894 JOSHUA[6] EMERY (*Joshua,[5] Joshua,[4] John,[3] Jonathan,[2] John[1]*), son of Joshua and Rachel (Currier) Emery; married Elizabeth Welch, daughter of Col Joseph and Hannah (Chase) Welch, Feb. 1, 1801. He was steward of Andover Theological Seminary for many years and died June 28, 1854, aged 80. His wife died Sept. 4, 1868, aged 92.

Children :

1723 i JOSEPH WELCH,[7] b Aug. 31, 1802
1724 ii FRANCIS WELCH ROBERTS, b May 31, 1804.
1725 iii JOSHUA, b. Aug. 5, 1807.
1726 iv SEWALL NORTON, b Feb 23, 1810
1727 v SAMUEL HOPKINS, b Aug. 22, 1815
1728 vi JUSTIN EDWARDS, b Nov 30 1818, d Nov 4, 1821, in Andover.

897 JOHN[6] EMERY (*Joshua.[5] Joshua,[4] John,[3] Jonathan,[2] John[1]*), son of Joshua and Rachel (Currier) Emery, married Harriet Humphrey, June 18, 1807. He was a merchant in Boston.

Children :

1729 i MARGARET L ,[7] b June 8, 1808, d Aug. 27, 1809
1730 ii MARGARET L . b. March 10, 1810
1731 iii JOHN L , b. May 1, 1812 , d March 15, 1816
1732 iv HENRY A , b Oct 2, 1814 , d Dec 20, 1815.
1733 v HARRIET E , b Aug 14, 1816

905 NATHANIEL[6] MERRILL (*Mary.[5] Joshua.[4] John.[3] Jonathan,[2] John[1]*), son of James and Mary (Emery) Merrill, married Mary Little, daughter of Benjamin and Hepzibah (Poor) Little, July 17, 1789.

Children :

1734 i MARY EMERY [7]
1735 ii MEHETABLE EMERY.

906 JOSHUA[6] MERRILL (*Mary,[5] Joshua,[4] John,[3] Jonathan ,[2] John[1]*), son of James and Mary (Emery) Merrill; married Mehetable Dow, daughter of Abraham and Susannah (Hoyt) Dow, of Salem, N. H.

Children :

1736 i JOHN JOHNSON,[7] b Sept 2, 1792, m Dec. 25, 1813, Betsey Eaton.
1737 ii HANNAH, b April 2, 1794; m Capt Bucket Bradley of West Haverhill, Mass
1738 iii ABRAHAM DOW, b March 7, 1796.
1739 iv MEHETABLE, b Nov 1, 1797 , m Leonard Emerson of Haverhill, Mass

917 MOSES GILL J [6] EMERY (*Moses,[5] Joshua,[4] John,[3] Jonathan,[2]*

John[1]), son of Moses and Abiah (Bradley) Emery; baptized by Rt. Rev. Edward Bass, first bishop of Mass., Jan 12, 1800; married Frances G. Brewster, daughter of Dr Royal Brewster of Buxton, Me., and granddaughter of Rev. Paul Coffin; she was born June 19, 1806.

Child.

1740   i   ANNIE P[7] b in Haverhill, Mass, Feb 23, 1842.

919 EPHRAIM[6] EMERY (*John,[5] David,[4] John,[3] Jonathan,[2] John[1]*), son of John and Edna (Noyes) Emery, died in West Newbury, Mass., Nov. 29, 1827; married Mary Russell (born June 19, 1765) Sept. 17, 1785. Enlisted as fifer April 19, 1775, at the Lexington alarm; entered the service in William Rogers' Company, Col. Baldwin's Regt., April 27, 1775; Sergeant in Capt. Pillsbury's company, Col Wigglesworth's Regiment, 1777; promoted Ensign Jan. 1, 1778, promoted Lieut. in the 13th Regiment, Col. Smith, April 10, 1778; acted as Adjutant from 1781 until appointed paymaster to the Sixth Regiment, 1783, was in the assault on Stony Point, July 16, 1779; in the battle of White Plains, Oct. 28, 1776; at West Point, N. Y., and in Sullivan's Rhode Island campaign, 1778. Commissioned Lieutenant and Paymaster in Tupper's (6th) Regiment, 1783, after the war appointed, in 1799, captain in the United States Army, 14th Regiment, which was disbanded in 1800, and was successively Captain, Brigade Major and Inspector in the state militia in the county of Essex   Member of the Cincinnati   His widow died in Newbury, March 3, 1843.

Children:

1741   i   MARY,[7] b March 27, 1786
1742   ii   JOHN, b March 1, 1788, d, unm, March 25, 1869
1743   iii   THOMAS, b Sept 7, 1791
1744   iv   HANNAH, b June 1, 1801, m Joseph Brown; d May 15, 1860
              He died Dec 4, 1876

921 DAVID[6] EMERY (*John,[5] David,[4] John,[3] Jonathan,[2] John[1]*), son of John and Edna (Noyes) Emery, married Betty Little, Aug. 22, 1785   He died Oct. 21, 1785   His widow married Moses Coleman of Byfield, Dec. 5, 1787. He was in the army during the Revolutionary war till after the battle of Brooklyn, when, his term of service having expired, he returned home. He enlisted in the company of Captain Silas Andrews in 1776, and went to Rhode Island, he served as fifer under Captain Noyes in Col. Wade's regiment, from 1779 to 1780, and from July to Oct., 1780, he was in Capt Mighill's company, Col. Wade's regiment, West Point. Mrs. Coleman died Sept 12, 1857.

Child:

1745   i   DAVID,[7] b in Newbury, Mass, Dec. 22, 1785.

930 JOHN[6] EMERY (*Moses,[5] David,[4] John.[3] Jonathan,[2] John[1]*), son of Moses and Sarah (Hale) Emery, married Sarah Fellows, Jan. 14, 1796, in Dunbarton, N H.

Children

1746 i SARAH,[7] b. Sept., 1797.
1747 ii JOHN, b. Oct. 11, 1799.
1748 iii TAPPAN, b. March 10, 1802.
1749 iv ISAAC, b. Feb. 22, 1804; m. Sarah Hosum, May 19, 1832; d. s. p.
1750 v NANCY, b. April 15, 1806.
1751 vi BETSEY, b. May 2, 1808.
1752 vii MOSES, b. June 10, 1810.
1753 viii SUSAN, b. Aug. 1, 1815.

932 JACOB[6] EMERY (*Moses,*[5] *David,*[4] *John,*[3] *Jonathan,*[2] *John*[1]), son of Moses and Sarah (Hale) Emery ; married Lydia Noyes, daughter of Joseph and Abigail Noyes (born Sept. 23, 1782), Nov., 1804. She died Dec. 10, 1858. Comb manufacturer. He died Dec. 6, 1858.
Children :

1754 i HARRIET,[7] b. Jan. 11, 1806.
1755 ii CLEMENTINE, b. June 24, 1807.
1756 iii MARY ELIZABETH, b. June 22, 1809.
1757 iv CATHARINE, b. June 15, 1812.
1758 v LYDIA ANN, b. July 18, 1814.
1759 vi RUFUS KING, b. Nov. 15, 1816.
1760 vii ELIZA T., b. June 18, 1819.
1761 viii CALVIN, b. Nov. 21, 1821.

933 MOSES[6] EMERY (*Moses,*[5] *David,*[4] *John,*[3] *Jonathan,*[2] *John*[1]), son of Moses and Sarah (Hale) Emery ; married Betsey Follansbee, Sept. 24, 1803.
Children :

1762 i LUCIAN A.,[7] b. Jan. 10, 1804.
1763 ii CHARLES H., b. April 15, 1806; d. young.
1764 iii BETSEY C., b. Dec. 11, 1808; d. young.
1765 iv BETSEY F., b. Dec. 19, 1810.
1766 v LUCY, b. Oct. 20, 1812; d. young.
1767 vi CHARLES H., b. May 9, 1814.
1768 vii MOSES H., b. Feb. 6, 1816.
1769 viii HARRIET K., b. Jan. 9, 1819.
1770 ix NEHEMIAH F., b. Dec. 29, 1821.
1771 x LUTHER M., b. July 7, 1824; d. Aug. 24, 1854, unm.
1772 xi DAVID F., b. Jan. 8, 1828.

935 SALLY[6] MOULTON (*Sarah,*[5] *Anthony,*[4] *John,*[3] *John,*[2] *John*[1]), daughter of Gen. Jonathan and his second wife, Sarah (Emery) Moulton ; married Rev. Huntington Porter of Rye, N. H., March 30, 1797; died Jan. 2, 1835.
Children :

1773 i MARIA,[7] b. Feb. 12, 1798.
1774 ii ELIPHALET, b. April 25, 1800.
1775 iii OLIVER, b. March 3, 1802.
1776 iv LOUISA, b. May 18, 1803.
1777 v MARTHA RUGGLES, b. June 11, 1805.
1778 vi SUSAN SARGENT, b. April 12, 1807.
1779 vii SARAH EMERY, b. June 2, 1809.
1780 viii OLIVIA, b. Feb. 15, 1811.
1781 ix HUNTINGTON, b. Dec. 4, 1812.
1782 x EMERY MOULTON, b. April 1, 1815.
1783 xi CHARLES HENRY, b. Aug. 7, 1816; d. young.

1784 xii CHARLES HENRY, }
1785 xiii WILLIAM HENRY, } b. Sept. 19, 1817.
1786 xiv ELVIRA, b Jan 11, 1820

936 EMERY[6] MOULTON (*Sarah*,[5] *Dr. Anthony*,[4] *John*,[3] *Jonathan*,[2] *John*[1]), son of Gen. Jonathan and his second wife Sarah (Emery) Moulton, was married, died in Lynn, 1850.
 Child :

1787 i OTIS[7]

937 JOHN WASHINGTON[6] MOULTON (*Sarah*,[5] *Dr. Anthony*,[4] *John*,[3] *John*,[2] *John*[1]), son of Gen. Jonathan and his second wife (Sarah Emery) Moulton ; was married ; died Jan. 24, 1821.
 Children :

1788 i AMELIA[7]
1789 ii AMANDA, b 1826, m. Rev. —— Bacon of New Haven, Conn.
1790 iii SON, died young

938 NATHANIEL THAYER[6] MOULTON (*Sarah*,[5] *Dr. Anthony*,[4] *John*,[3] *Jonathan*,[2] *John*[1]), son of Gen. Jonathan and his second wife Sarah (Emery) Moulton, died Dec. 6, 1870 ; married Lydia D Holbrook, May 11, 1809, who died Dec. 2, 1870.
 Children :

1791 i ANGELINE,[7] b. Sept. 27, 1810; m Jona L Pierce of Milwaukee, Wis, March 3, 1832, d May 23, 1883
1792 ii SARAH EMERY, b June 15, 1812, d Oct 13, 1826.
1793 iii MARTHA CLARK, b. July 24, 1815, m. Alfred M Stearns, April 26, 1842
1794 iv HARRIETT NEWELL, b Feb 26, 1818, m Henry Nowell of Portsmouth, N H, May 9, 1843
1795 v CLAUDIUS BUCHANAN, b. July 19, 1820, m Frances Manson of Portsmouth, N H
1796 vi CORDELIA, b April 26, 1822, m. Daniel F. Jones of Boston, Mass, June 4, 1844.
1797 vii NATH THAYER, JR, b. Feb 28, 1824, m Lucretia Shaw of Portsmouth, N. H
1798 viii JOHN EMERY, b June 25, 1826, d Sept 3, 1826
1799 ix EMELINE LYDIA, b Jan 19, 1828, d. Oct. 18, 1828.
1800 x ARABELLA PORTER, b. Feb. 11, 1832

939 WILLARD[6] EMERY (*William*,[5] *Dr. Anthony*,[4] *John*,[3] *Jonathan*[2] *John*[1]), son of William and Joanna (Elkins) Emery ; married, Nov. 15, 1792, Sarah Cilley, who was born in Epping, N. H., Aug. 6, 1770, and died in Andover, N H., Dec. 12, 1847.
 Children :

1801 i WILLIAM,[7] b March 31, 1794, (see 960)
1802 ii JONATHAN, b July 22, 1796
1803 iii ABIGAIL, b Feb 10, 1801
1804 iv SARAH, b. June 13, 1805.
1805 v POLLY, b March 27, 1809
1806 vi HORATIO GATES, b. July 2, 1812

940 JOSEPH[6] EMERY (*William*,[5] *Dr* *Anthony*,[4] *John*,[3] *Jonathan*,[2]

John[1]), son of William and Joanna (Elkins) Emery) ; married Dolly Blake (born Jan., 1777 , died June 17, 1835), March 13, 1800 , died May, 1852.

Children, born in Andover, N H. :

```
1807  i    JOHN,[7] b March 30, 1804
1808  ii   JOSEPH, jr., b. Nov 29, 1805
1809  nl   DOLLY, b Dec 23, 1807.
1810  iv   WILLIAM BLAKE, b  May 16, 1816.
1811  v    MARY, b. Jan 18, 1822
```

941 ANTHONY[6] EMERY (*William,[5] Dr. Anthony,[4] John,[3] Jonathan,[2] John[1]*), son of William and Joanna (Elkins) Emery ; died Oct. 30, 1846 ; married Abigail Cilley (born Jan. 4, 1773), Nov. 17, 1796, who died July 21, 1858

Children, born in Andover, N. H. :

```
1812  i    JOHN,[7] b. Sept , 1797, d Sept 16, 1805.
1813  ii   WILLARD, b March 13, 1804.
1814  iii  JOHN, b  Oct , 1806, d , unm., 1871; school teacher.
```

942 WILLIAM[6] EMERY (*William,[5] Dr. Anthony,[4] John,[3] Jonathan,[2] John[1]*), son of William and Joanna (Elkins) Emery ; died Oct 12, 1848 ; married Ruth Brown, Nov. 7, 1802, who died Feb. 28, 1861.

Children, born in Andover, N. H. :

```
1815  i    ABIGAIL,[7] b Dec 15, 1803; d 1809
1816  ii   JOSEPH, b Aug 15, 1806, d. May 6, 1807.
1817  iii  WILLIAM, b April 14. 1808, d Sept 22, 1809.
1818  iv   JOSEPH, b Nov. 15, 1809.
```

943 POLLY[6] EMERY (*William[5], Dr. Anthony,[4] John,[3] Jonathan,[2] John[1]*), daughter of William and Joanna (Elkins) Emery , died Feb. 4, 1872 ; married James Marston, sen. (son of Paul Smith Marston), Dec. 4, 1806, who was born Feb. 8, 1783 , died April 26, 1809.

Children :

```
1819  i    JAMES, JR ,[7] b Aug. 25, 1810.
1820  ii   WILLIAM SMITH, b Dec. 8, 1819, m. Vienna S Catton of Ef-
            fingham, N H , April 3, 1858
```

944 HENRY[6] EMERY (*William,[5] Dr. Anthony,[4] John,[3] Jonathan,[2] John[1]*), son of William and Joanna (Elkins) Emery; married Susannah Rowe (born in Kingston, N H), Feb. 25, 1813, daughter of Jacob and Molly (Burns) Rowe of Hampton Falls, N H He was killed by the cars at Fellows Crossing, East Andover, N. H., June 13, 1849

Children :

```
1821  i    MARY,[7] b Aug 24, 1815, d March 4, 1820
1822  ii   WILLARD A , b Dec 9, 1817, d March 12, 1820.
1823  iii  WILLARD ANDREW, b Jan. 28, 1821.
1824  iv   MARY ANN, b. Feb. 22, 1823, m Moses H Atwood, d April
            11, 1872, s  p
1825  v    ABBIE, b April 13, 1825 m Nason W. Case, Nov 19, 1856
```

947 SUSANNAH[6] EMERY (*Thomas,[5] Dr. Anthony,[4] John,[3] Jona-*

than,[2] *John*[1]), daughter of Thomas and Dolly (Sargent) Emery; married Thomas Brown, Dec. 17, 1799. She died Nov 19, 1820.
Children.

1826	i	IRA,[7] b March 21. 1802.
1827	ii	ELIZA B., b. May 21, 1804.
1828	iii	BELINDA, b Aug 2, 1806
1829	iv	THOMAS F , b. Feb 14, 1809

948 SALLY[6] EMERY (*Thomas,*[5] *Dr. Anthony,*[4] *John,*[3] *Jonathan,*[2] *John*[1]), daughter of Thomas and Dolly (Sargent) Emery; married Levi Staniels. She died in Loudon, N. H., Feb. 18, 1854.
Children :

1830	i	ASA [7]
1831	ii	ELDRIDGE.
1832	iii	DAVID.
1833	iv	DOLLY
1834	v	SUSAN
1835	vi	EMERY T.

949 JOHN[6] EMERY (*Thomas,*[5] *Dr Anthony,*[4] *John,*[3] *Jonathan,*[2] *John*[1]), son of Thomas and Dolly (Sargent) Emery, married Betsey Burpee of Boscawen, N. H., 1807. His wife died and he married in 1810, Abigail Osborne of Loudon, N. H., who was born July 19, 1787; died Oct. 8, 1831.
Children ·

1836	i	MARY,[7] b 1808, m Cutting G Stevens, May, 1830; d. in Lowell, Mass , May 24, 1879, s p.
1837	ii	JACOB O , b March 12, 1812
1838	iii	BETSEY, b Feb 6, 1815

951 JOSHUA[6] EMERY (*Thomas,*[5] *Dr Anthony,*[4] *John,*[3] *Jonathan,*[2] *John*[1]), son of Thomas and Dolly (Sargent) Emery; married, first, —— Chamberlin; second, Betsey Abbot, third, Eliza Eastman, and died Jan. 21, 1870.
Children.

1839	i	JOHN C ,[7] b Aug 25, 1816, d , unm., in Montpelier, Vt.
1840	ii	WILLIAM, b Aug 31 1819, d in London, N H
1841	iii	ELIZABETH, b. Jan 28, 1822, d. when 11 years of age.
1842	iv	THOMAS S , b Jan 24, 1824, d. when 22 years of age.
1843	v	CHARLES E , b Oct 9, 1827, d when 22 years of age.
1844	vi	ROBERT A , b June 18, 1831 d when 35 years of age.
1845	vii	ELLEN M., b Dec 18, 1843, teacher and unm. at the South

953 JOHN[6] EMERY (*Nathaniel,*[5] *Dr Anthony,*[4] *John,*[3] *Jonathan,*[2] *John*[1]), son of Nathaniel and Mary (Perkins) Emery; died in Boston, 1834   Merchant in Portsmouth, N H , lost his property by fire in that place; stationed at Fort Independence, Boston Harbor, during the war of 1812, died of consumption contracted by exposure while on duty. Married Jane Kimball (born in Concord, N. H , May 19, 1780 , died in Boston, Sept 4, 1861), 1800
Children ·

1846	i	HULDAH P ,[7] b. Feb 2, 1803
1847	ii	MARY K., b June 13, 1804

1848 iii HARRIET M., b. March 25, 1806.
1849 iv   JOHN, JR., b. June 5, 1808.
1850 v   SOPHRONIA, b. May 25, 1812.
1851 vi   ASA K., b. July 4, 1816.
1852 vii LUCRETIA L., b. Oct. 12, 1818.
1853 viii SARAH J., b. Oct. 5, 1820.

954 MOLLY[6] EMERY (*Nathaniel*,[5] *Dr. Anthony*,[4] *John*,[3] *Jonathan*,[2] *John*[1]), daughter of Nathaniel and Mary (Perkins) Emery ; married John T. Leavitt, of Chichester, N. H.

Children :

1854 i   SOPHIA,[7] ⬤ Aug. 11, 1818.
1855 ii   J. WARREN.
1856 iii ADELINE.
1857 iv   BENJ. F.
1858 v   GEORGE W., b. July 2, 1812.
1859 vi   HAMILTON.
1860 vii SOPHIA ANN.

955 JOSIAH[6] EMERY (*Nathaniel*,[5] *Dr. Anthony*,[4] *John*,[3] *Jonathan*,[2] *John*[1]), son of Nathaniel and Mary (Perkins) Emery ; married, first, Betsy Osgood ; second, Nancy Sanborn, of Pembroke, N. H. He died in Dover, N. H., July, 1837.

Children :

1861 i   SHERBURNE,[7] d. in infancy.
1862 ii   OLIE, d. 17 years of age.
1863 iii CHARLES OSGOOD, d. 17 years of age.
1864 iv   NATHANIEL.
1865 v   MARY, d. 9 years of age.
1866 vi   CHASE, d. young.
1867 vii ELIZA PERKINS, b. Feb., 1812.
1868 viii SHUAH BLAKE, b. Nov., 1814.
1869 ix   JOSIAH, b. Jan. 13, 1818.
1870 x   MARY JANE, d. 17 years of age.
1871 xi   SARAH ANN, b. in Dover, N. H.
1872 xii NANCY, d. 22 years of age.
1873 xiii ELIZABETH.

958 SALLY[6] EMERY (*Nathaniel*,[5] *Dr. Anthony*,[4] *John*,[3] *Jonathan*,[2] *John*[1]), daughter of Nathaniel and Mary (Perkins) Emery ; married Moses Morse of Loudon, 1815 (born April 13, 1788 ; died Nov. 22, 1880). His wife died Feb. 24, 1872.

Children :

1874 i   HARRIS E.,[7] b. April 1, 1816.
1875 ii   ALVAH L., b. Oct. 16, 1818 ; d. in Loudon, N. H., Oct. 7, 1839.
1876 iii JULIANN P., b. May 10, 1825.

960 NANCY[6] EMERY (*Nathaniel*,[5] *Dr. Anthony*,[4] *John*,[3] *Jonathan*,[2] *John*[1]), daughter of Nathaniel and Mary (Perkins) Emery ; married July 4, 1822, William Emery of Andover, N. H., son of Willard and Sarah (Cilley) Emery. He died in Franklin, N. H., March 13, 1860. His wife died in Lebanon, N. H., July, 1871.

Children, born in Andover :

1877 i   ELIZA FELLOWS,[7] b. March 28, 1825.
1878 ii   CAROLINE DEARBORN, b. May 14, 1828.
1879 iii NANCY JANE, b. June 29, 1834.

968 Jesse[6] Emery (*Caleb,*[5] *Caleb,*[4] *Jonathan,*[3] *Jonathan,*[2] *John*[1]), son of Caleb and Susannah (Worthley) Emery, the first male child born in the town; married, first, Hannah Corlis (born July 10, 1765), daughter of Jeremiah (the first town clerk of Weare) and Mary (Ordway) Corlis He married, second, about 1814, Betsey Elizabeth, daughter of Timothy and Elizabeth (Shattuck) Wyman of Hillsborough, N. H. He removed to Henniker, where he died July 10, 1838 He was a man of ingenuity and skill, a manufacturer of clocks and spinning wheels. His second wife, born March 13, 1777, died Jan. 30, 1850.

Child :

1880 i   Ruth,[7] b Sept. 8, 1786, m Daniel Colby.

971 Daniel[6] Emery (*Caleb,*[5] *Caleb,*[4] *Jonathan,*[3] *Jonathan,*[2] *John*[1]), son of Caleb and Susannah (Worthley) Emery; married Elizabeth Straw and lived in Henniker, N. H.

Children :

1881 i   Polly (Mary),[7] b Oct 27, 1790; m , Aug 1, 1824, —— Wilkins; d. March 16, 1877
1882 ii   David, b Aug 14, 1792
1883 iii   Levi, b. June 13, 1794.
1884 iv   John, b Nov 24, 1799

973 Abigail[6] Emery (*Caleb,*[5] *Caleb,*[4] *Jonathan,*[3] *Jonathan,*[2] *John*[1]), daughter of Caleb and Susannah (Worthley) Emery; married Jonathan Hoag. He married, second, Phœbe Hoag

Children :

1885 i   Israel,[7] b 1795
1886 ii   Anna, b. 1799, m Samuel Osborne.
1887 iii   Joseph, b. 1809.

974 Caleb[6] Emery (*Caleb,*[5] *Caleb,*[4] *Jonathan,*[3] *Jonathan,*[2] *John*),[1] son of Caleb and Susannah (Worthley) Emery; married Polly Harriman.

Children :

1888 i   Molly (Mary),[7] b. 1805, d , unm
1889 ii   Sally, b. 1808, m. William Cheney.
1890 iii   William, m 1st, Mary Peaslee, 2d, Mary McNealley
1891 iv   John G , b 1809

976 John[6] Emery (*Caleb,*[5] *Caleb,*[4] *Jonathan,*[3] *Jonathan,*[2] *John*[1]), son of Caleb and Susannah (Worthley) Emery, married, Nov. 26, 1801, Sally Noyes (born April 14, 1785) who died in 1863. He removed to Washington, Vt., and died, 1819.

Children :

1892 i   John [7]
1893 ii   Sally.
1894 iii   Clarissa.
1895 iv   Caleb
1896 v   Elvira
1897 vi   Daniel.
1898 vii   Ira.

6

978 SYLVANUS[6] EMERY (*Sylvanus,[5] Caleb,[4] Jonathan,[3] Jonathan,[2] John[1]*), son of Sylvanus and ——— (Pope) Emery; married Abigail Knowles and removed to Sandwich, N. H. He died Aug. 13, 1851. His wife died April 4, 1854.

Children :

  1899 i   NATHANIEL,[7] b. 1807; m. Lois Greenleaf.
  1900 ii SAMUEL, b. 1809; went from home when a boy; never heard
              from.
  1901 iii ABIJAH, b. 1811; m. Abigail Greenleaf.
  1902 iv MARK.
  1903 v   ABIGAIL, b. 1818; d. 1862.
  1904 vi ARVILLA, b. 1821.
  1905 vii JOHN, b. 1824; d. 1865.

989 CALEB[6] EMERY (*Amos,[5] Caleb,[4] Jonathan,[3] Jonathan,[2] John[1]*), son of Amos and Anna (Foote) Emery; married Eleanor Heath (born May 12, 1776) of Bow, N. H., 1803, who died at Lyman, N. H., Feb. 24, 1878. He emigrated with his wife from Dunbarton, N. H., to Lyman in 1809; called by his townsmen to discharge nearly all the various offices and services required in town affairs, having been town clerk for twenty-eight years; selectman, representative and justice of the peace for thirty years, and during all preserving a reputation above reproach. He died Jan. 21, 1842.

Children :

  1906 i   SOLOMON, H.,[7] b. Nov. 11, 1803.
  1907 ii HORACE, b. Aug. 6, 1805.
  1908 iii EDWARD, d. young.
  1909 iv CYNTHIA E., b. Feb. 13, 1808.
  1910 v   ANN, b. 1810.
  1911 vi BETSEY, b. 1815; d. July 19, 1839.
  1912 vii EDWARD, b. Jan. 18, 1818.
  1913 viii GEORGE W., b. June, 1821; d., in Lyman, 1847.
  1914 ix ELEANOR VESTA, b. 1825; d., unm., in Bartlett, Vt.
  1915 x   MARY C., b. 1827.

990 SAMUEL[6] EMERY (*Amos,[5] Caleb,[4] Jonathan,[3] Jonathan,[2] John[1]*), son of Amos and Anna (Foote) Emery; married Polly (Mary) Flanders, in Bath, N. H., March 16, 1809; died in Munroe, N. H., July 10, 1856.

Children :

  1916 i   CHELLIS,[7] b. June 27, 1810, Munroe, N. H.
  1917 ii FRANCIS F., b. Sept. 25, 1817.
  1918 iii WARREN S., b. Sept. 28, 1831.
  1919 iv WALTER H., b. April 25, 1834.

993 JOHN[6] EMERY (*Joel,[5] Caleb,[4] Jonathan,[3] Jonathan,[2] John[1]*), son of Joel and Love (Ladd) Emery; married Rhoda, daughter of Peter and Prudence (French) Gale (born Feb. 1, 1788).

Children :

  1920 i   ORLINZO.[7]
  1921 ii CLARISSA.

994 JOEL[6] EMERY (*Joel,[5] Caleb,[4] Jonathan,[3] Jonathan,[2] John[1]*), son of Joel and Love (Ladd) Emery; married May 7, 1814, Lucy Goddard (daughter of Samuel and Mary Goddard, born in Royalton, Vt., Feb. 17, 1797). He died Feb. 13, 1860 His wife died Oct. 10, 1878

Children :

```
1922  i    SILAS,7 b  Sept  26, 1816
1923  ii   NANCY, b  Nov  28, 1818
1924  iii  ISAAC, b. May 16, 1821.
1925  iv   LOVE ANN, b  Sept. 1, 1823; m. Samuel Turner, Jan. 15  1854
1926  v    GARDNER, b  Feb 8, 1826, d , unm , Nov 18, 1848
1927  vi   CAROLINE, b  Jan  1, 1828, d. young
1928  vii  LEONARD, b  July 16, 1829
1929  viii CAROLINE L  b  Aug 18, 1831; m Ezra Briggs, Aug  30, 1858
1930  ix   EDSON, b. July 26. 1833, m Jennie Gay, May 20, 1866
1931  x    PHILO, b. July 2, 1836, soldier in the Union Army, wounded
           in the battle of the Wilderness, May 5, 1864, d in Armory
           Square Hospital, Washington, D  C , June 9, 1864, unm
```

999 IRA6 EMERY (*Joel,*5 *Caleb,*4 *Jonathan,*3 *Jonathan,*2 *John*1), son of Joel and Love (Ladd) Emery, married Betsey Richardson of Bethel, Vt., Aug. 1, 1830.

Children :

```
1932  i    EZRA H ,7 b  June 6, 1831
1933  ii   EMELINE T , b  Sept  5  1832
1934  iii  JANE G , b  Sept  22, 1834
1935  iv   GEORGE, b  Sept 12, 1836, d  July 8, 1840.
1936  v    LYMAN S ,  b  Jan  3, 1839
1937  vi   IRA, b  May 23, 1840
1938  vii  GEORGE S., b  Dec. 17, 1843
1939  viii ALONZO, b  March 31, 1845
1940  ix   ELIZA, b  Sept  23, 1846.
1941  x    ELLEN, b  Oct , 1850; m. Thomas J  Lazier of Claremont,
           N  H
```

1006 ESTHER6 EMERY (*Humphrey,*5 *Humphrey,*4 *Jonathan,*3 *Jonathan,*2 *John*1), daughter of Humphrey and Patty (Reed) Emery, married Samuel, son of Enoch and Rachel (Tyrrell) Emery, died in Gorham, N. H., Nov 17, 1845. His wife died Nov 26, 1841

Children, born in Shelburne, N. H.

```
1942  i    JOEL,7 b  June 7, 1807, d  in Oxford, Me , June, 1828.
1943  ii   FREEMAN, b. 1809, died young
1944  iii  ABIGAIL, b  Sept. 17, 1813.
1945  iv   SAMUEL F., b  March 20, 1826.
```

1008 SYLVANUS6 EMERY (*Humphrey,*5 *Humphrey,*4 *Jonathan,*3 *Jonathan,*2 *John*1), son of Humphrey and Patty (Reed) Emery, married Susan Rodgers

Children .

```
1946  i    DOLLY 7 b  Jan  4, 1795   See No  1019
1947  ii   DANIEL
1948  iii  BARZILLAI
1949  iv   THOMAS
1950  v    HUBBARD.
1951  vi   GILBERT, b. Aug. 7, 1818
1952  vii  ROBERT.
1953  viii STEPHEN
1954  ix   REUBEN.
```

1009 RUTH[6] EMERY (*Humphrey,*[5] *Humphrey,*[4] *Jonathan,*[3] *Jonathan,*[2] *John*[1]), daughter of Humphrey and Patty (Reed) Emery ; married Peter Emery, who died at Swanton, Vt., in 1806. She married, second, James Morgan who was born April 1, 1764 and died in Fredonia, N. Y., Sept. 13, 1857. His wife died in Kenedy, Dec. 17, 1862.
Children :

1955 i   NOAH,[7] b. Jan. 1, 1795, Bartlett, N. H.
1956 ii SILAS, b. 1804; was given to a Mr. Hall; was known as Silas Hall, went to Michigan and was never heard from.
1957 iii THOMAS, b. 1801, removed South and all trace of him is lost.
1958 iv JONAS, b. March 8, 1807.

By second marriage :

1959 v   SARAH MORGAN, b. July 20, 1817.
1960 vi EMILY MORGAN, b. Jan. 23, 1819.

1011 SARAH[6] EMERY (*Humphrey,*[5] *Humphrey,*[4] *Jonathan,*[3] *Jonathan*[2], *John*[1]), daughter of Humphrey and Patty (Reed) Emery ; married Enoch Emery. He died in Bethel, Vt., Nov., 1843. His wife died in Albany, Me., Dec., 1849.
Children :

1961 i   HUMPHREY,[7] d. in Bethel, Vt., April, 1876, unm.
1962 ii AMOS, b. 1804; d. unm. in Albany, Me., Aug. 11, 1865.
1963 iii PETER, b. March 28, 1811, in Guildhall, Vt.

1013 WILLIAM[6] EMERY (*Enoch,*[5] *Humphrey,*[4] *Jonathan,*[3] *Jonathan*[2], *John*[1]), son of Enoch and Rachel (Tyrrell) Emery.
Children :

1964 i   JOSEPH.[7]
1965 ii WILLIAM.
1966 iii ALICE.

1014 STEPHEN[6] EMERY (*Enoch,*[5] *Humphrey,*[4] *Jonathan,*[3] *Jonathan*[2], *John*[1]), son of Enoch and Rachel (Tyrrell) Emery ; married Dolly Rogers in Bartlett, N. H., 1796.
Children :

1967 i   ISAAC,[7] b. Aug. 23, 1798.
1968 ii SAMUEL, b. Sept. 30, 1799; m. Betsey Copp of Jackson, N. H.
1969 iii BETSEY, b. Sept. 9, 1801; d. seventeen years of age.
1970 iv JOSHUA, b. Oct. 12, 1803.
1971 v   WILLIAM, b. May 25, 1810; m., 1st, Lucy D. Allen; 2nd, Harriet C. R. (Blanchard) Adams, widow of Samuel Adams. He d. in S. Gray, Me., April 11, 1883.
1972 vi LYDIA, b. March 22, 1812.

1017 NATHANIEL[6] EMERY (*Enoch,*[5] *Humphrey,*[4] *Jonathan,*[3] *Jonathan*[2], *John*[1]), son of Enoch and Rachel (Tyrrell) Emery ; married Deborah Rogers (born Nov. 27, 1784). He died Dec. 29, 1820. His wife died Oct. 1, 1877.
Children :

1973 i   DOLLY,[7] b. April 25, 1807.
1974 ii HANNAH, b. Oct. 7, 1809; d. June 15, 1882.
1975 iii IRA, b. July 30, 1811; m.; d. June 13, 1879.
1976 iv JONATHAN, b. March 30, 1814.
1977 v   JANE, b. March 27, 1817; d. July 18, 1817.
1978 vi MARTHA B., b. May 15, 1821.

1019 John[6] Emery (*Enoch,[5] Humphrey,[4] Jonathan,[3] Jonathan,[2] John[1]*), son of Enoch and Rachel (Tyrrell) Emery; married Dolly Emery, daughter of Sylvanus and Susan (Rodgers) Emery (born Jan. 4, 1795). He died July 1, 1868. His wife died Jan 10, 1870.
Children:

    1979 i   Henderson S.,[7] b. Nov. 28, 1816; d. Oct. 19, 1857.
    1980 ii   Susan, b. Oct. 30, 1821.
    1981 iii Thomas R., b. May 29, 1826; m. Elizabeth J. Emery, April 18, 1852.
    1982 iv   Mary J. E., b. Nov. 8, 1831.

1020 Enoch[6] Emery (*Enoch,[5] Humphrey,[4] Jonathan,[3] Jonathan,[2] John[1]*), son of Enoch and Rachel (Tyrrell) Emery; married Louisa Rumery (born in Shelburne, N. H., April 21, 1793).
Children:

    1983 i   Rachel,[7] b. Aug. 11, 1826.
    1984 ii   Joel, b. Feb. 1, 1830.
    1985 iii Judith Ann, b. June 10, 1833.
    1986 iv   Charles, b. April 7, 1837.

1021 Betsey[6] Emery (*Enoch,[5] Humphrey,[4] Jonathan,[3] Jonathan,[2] John[1]*), daughter of Enoch and Rachel (Tyrrell) Emery; married George Nicholson.
Children:

    1987 i   Christopher.[7]
    1988 ii   George.
    1989 iii Nathaniel.
    1990 iv   Eliza.

1022 Jennie[6] Emery[6] (*Enoch[5], Humphrey,[4] Jonathan,[3] Jonathan,[2] John[1]*), daughter of Enoch and Rachel (Tyrrell) Emery; married Thomas Cole.
Children:

    1991 i   Rachel.[7]
    1992 ii   Enoch.
    1993 iii John.

1025 William[6] Emery (*Richardson,[5] Humphrey,[4] Jonathan,[3] Jonathan,[2] John[1]*), son of Richardson and Jane (Swan) Emery, farmer; married Margaret Aseltine (died in Brandon, N. Y.), lived in Swanton, Vt., and Schuyler Falls, N. Y. He was run over by an ox cart and killed in Brandon, Franklin Co., N. Y., aged 72.
Children:

    1994 i   Jane,[7] b. in Swanton, Vt.
    1995 ii   Richardson, b. Feb. 24, 1804, in Swanton, Vt.
    1996 iii   Maria, b. in Swanton, Vt.
    1997 iv   Theophilus Mansfield, b. March 6, 1808, in Swanton, Vt.
    1998 v   Mandana, b. in Clinton Co., N. Y., 1810.
    1999 vi   Nathaniel, b. 1812. at "the Gore," Schuyler Falls, N. Y.
    2000 vii   William, jr., b. 1822, at "the Gore, Schuyler Falls, N. Y.
    2001 viii Sabrina.
    2002 ix   Elizabeth.
    2003 x   Martha, d. unm. in Brandon, N. Y.

1026 Hannah[6] Emery (*Richardson*,[5] *Humphrey*,[4] *Jonathan*,[3] *Jonathan*,[2] *John*[1]), daughter of Richardson and Jane (Swan) Emery; died Feb. 18, 1879; married Rev. Edward Gould (born in Vermont, Aug., 1792) in Clinton Co., N. Y., 1816. He was a Methodist minister and lived in St. Lawrence Co., N. Y., and died in Michigan; known as the Sleeping Preacher and in his later years as Father Gould.
  Children :

    2004 i   Charlotte E.,[7] b. in Schuyler Falls, N. Y., Sept. 12, 1818.
    2005 ii   Mary, lives in Chicago, unm.
    2006 iii George.
    2007 iv   Uriah, was m. twice; lived in Texas.
    2008 v   Edward, Union soldier (spy); d. in service in hospital, Paducah, Ky., unm.
    2009 vi   John, drowned in Black Brook, Clinton Co., N. Y., unm.
    2010 vii Hannah.
    2011 viii Jacob, m. ———— Ladd; res. Gibsonville, Cal.

1027 Sarah[6] Emery (*Richardson*,[5] *Humphrey*,[4] *Jonathan*,[3] *Jonathan*,[2] *John*[1]), daughter of Richardson and Jane (Swan) Emery; married Uriah Ayer (born in Connecticut) in Schuyler Falls, N. Y.; farmer; lived and died in Schuyler Falls.
  Children, all born in Schuyler Falls :

    2012 i   Darius,[7] Town Supt. of public schools; supervisor of town; sheriff of Clinton Co., N. Y.
    2013 ii   Joseph, d. unm.
    2014 iii Seba, m. ———— Johnson of Schuyler Falls.
    2015 iv   Florinda, m. and d.
    2016 v   Elizabeth, m. Oscar Hudson.
    2017 vi   Martha, d. unm.

1028 Martha[6] Emery (*Richardson*,[5] *Humphrey*,[4] *Jonathan*,[3] *Jonathan*,[2] *John*[1]), daughter of Richardson and Jane (Swan) Emery; married Charles Hazen in Schuyler Falls, N. Y. Farmer; lived and died in Schuyler Falls.
  Children, born in Schuyler Falls :

    2018 i   Nathan,[7] m. Jane Deforest; res. Nebraska.
    2019 ii   Valentine, m.; res. Nebraska.

1029 Russell[6] Emery (*Richardson*,[5] *Humphrey*,[4] *Jonathan*,[3] *Jonathan*,[2] *John*[1]), son of Richardson and Jane (Swan) Emery; married probably Polly, daughter of Enoch and Rachel (Tyrrell) Emery (see No. 1023). He died in Chateaugay, Franklin Co., N. Y., aged 70.
  Children :

    2020 i   Sophronia,[7] m. and d.
    2021 ii   Daniel, m. and d.
    2022 iii Almira, m. and d.
    2023 iv   Enoch, b. July 31, 1815.

1030 Nathaniel[6] Emery (*Richardson*,[5] *Humphrey*,[4] *Jonathan*,[3] *Jonathan*,[2] *John*[1]), son of Richardson and Jane (Swan) Emery; married Lydia ————. He died in West Peru, Clinton Co., N. Y., aged 65.
  Children :

2024	i	CINDERELLA [7]
2025	ii	HANNAH
2026	iii	ALVAH, m , d s p in Plattsburg N. Y , 1887
2027	iv	ROBERT lives in Dorr, Allegan Co , Mich , unm
2028	v	MARTHA, b June 5, 1807
2029	vi	SAMUEL

1033 BETSEY[6] EMERY (*Stephen,*[5] *Stephen,*[4] *Stephen*[3] *Jonathan,*[2] *John*[1]), daughter of Stephen and Lydia (Kimball) Emery; married, May 20, 1800, Isaac, son of Pelatiah Cummins of Winchendon, Mass. (born Jan 23, 1767) He removed to Winchendon in 1817. He died Feb 24, 1843, aged 77.

Children.

2030	i	A SON,[7] who d. young
2031	ii	ELIZA, b Aug. 31, 1804, m Dea Levi Prentice, who d July 27, 1877
2032	iii	GEORGE, b June 22, 1806, m , 1st, Seba Whitney, 2nd, Miranda Morse
2033	iv	ALONZO, b. Jan 17, 1808, d Sept 17, 1824
2034	v	A SON, who d at 3 years of age.
2035	vi	ISAAC, b Dec 13, 1810; m Eliza T Wood
2036	vii	LYDIA, b 1812, m Andsen Beard, d March 16, 1861

1036 STEPHEN[6] EMERY (*Stephen,*[5] *Stephen,*[4] *Stephen,*[3] *Jonathan,*[2] *John*[1]), son of Stephen and Lydia (Kimball) Emery, graduated at Dartmouth College 1808, lawyer in Gloucester and West Cambridge, Mass. lived in Cambridge, Lyndeboro, N H., and Orange, Mass , married Rhoda W. Nason, April 8, 1816 · died in Orange, Mass , May 2, 1863. His wife died Jan 25, 1866.

Children :

2037	i	SAMUEL DEXTER,[7] b May 1, 1817, Cambridge , d Sept 15, 1817
2038	ii	MARY ANN WHITEMORE, b April 7, 1818, Lyndeboro
2039	iii	ALMIRA KIMBALL, b Aug. 20, 1820, Cambridge , m John Turner, Nov 22, 1839.
2040	iv	OLIVER PARSONS, b June 17, 1822, in Gardner, Mass , m Eliza Munn in 1867
2041	v	JAMES WEBSTER, b Sept 8, 1826, m , 1st, Julia C Ward, Oct 8, 1862, 2nd, Mary L Humes.
2042	vi	ALZINA CUMMINS, b. Aug. 8, 1827, m. W. M. Raymond, 1850.

1042 FRANCIS[6] EMERY (*John,*[5] *Stephen,*[4] *Stephen,*[3] *Jonathan,*[2] *John*[1]), son of John and Elizabeth (Perkins) Emery, married Eunice Philbrick (daughter of James and Eunice (Hale) Philbrick), Jan 18, 1796 (born May 13, 1771) ; resided a few years in Grafton, Vt., and subsequently in Winchendon, Mass. He died Jan. 31, 1843. His wife died Oct. 13, 1856.

Children, except first two, born in Winchendon :

2043	i	GRATA P ,[7] b. Oct. 17, 1796, Grafton, Vt.; d. Oct 13, 1801
2044	ii	ELIZABETH P , b Aug 23, 1798, Grafton, Vt.
2045	iii	JOHN W , b Nov 20, 1799
2046	iv	EUNICE H , b. April 30, 1803
2047	v	LUCRETIA P , b Feb 24, 1805, m Hubbard Moore July 12, 1832, d. May 6, 1873 He d Feb 20, 1874
2048	vi	LOUISA F., b. Oct 3, 1807; m. Horace Chaffin, April 3, 1834.
2049	vii	SARAH S., b. Aug 26, 1809.
2050	viii	MARY, b. Oct 16, 1811; d Oct 31, 1813

1043 Daniel[6] Emery (*John,[5] Stephen,[4] Stephen,[3] Jonathan,[2] John[1]*), son of John and Elizabeth (Perkins) Emery; married Betsey Curtice (daughter of Abner and Ruth (Hale) Curtice, born July 14, 1772). He was a manufacturer of nest-boxes in Rindge, N. H., till 1806, when he removed to Jaffrey. In 1825, he removed to Pennsylvania and engaged in agriculture; was postmaster for several years; died in Mehoopany, Wyoming county, Pa., 1855. His wife died in Jaffrey, N. H., 1848.

Children:

2051	i	Pamelia,[7] b. Nov. 1, 1794; d., unm., in Ware, Mass.
2052	ii	Prentice Burr, b. July 17, 1797; d. in New Jersey; physician.
2053	iii	Alvah, b. June 11, 1799; m. and d., *s. p.*
2054	iv	Ambrose, b. Nov. 12, 1802.
2055	v	Cynthia.
2056	vi	Daniel, b. Jan. 16, 1809.
2057	vii	Sophia, m. Jonathan Ayres.

1044 John[6] Emery (*John,[5] Stephen,[4] Stephen,[3] Jonathan,[2] John[1]*), son of John and Elizabeth (Perkins) Emery; married Deborah Towne, daughter of Dea. Francis Towne. He died June 7, 1838. She died Oct. 14, 1832.

Children:

2058	i	Charles Pinckney,[7] b. Oct. 15, 1808; d., unm., April 5, 1853.
2059	ii	Francis Towne, b. June 24, 1811.
2060	iii	Elizabeth P., b. June 10, 1815; m. Walter Brooks, 1857; d. Aug., 1870.
2061	iv	Deborah, b. Dec., 1820.

1046 Capt. Stephen[6] Emery (*John,[5] Stephen,[4] Stephen,[3] Jonathan,[2] John[1]*), son of John and Elizabeth (Perkins) Emery; married, first, Feb. 15, 1804, Betsey Wood, daughter of Isaac Wood, sen., (born Sept. 10, 1785; died March 2, 1807); second, May 30, 1810, Polly Ingalls, daughter of Jonathan Ingalls (born March 28, 1785; died May 20, 1826); third, July 19, 1827, Hepsie Buswell, daughter of John Buswell (died March 7, 1858). He died Jan. 13, 1874, aged 95, being five years older than any other person living in Rindge at the time.

Children:

2062	i	Derostus Wood,[7] b. Feb. 22, 1807.
2063	ii	Albert L., b. March 5, 1811.
2064	iii	Augustus C., b. Sept. 27, 1813.
2065	iv	Eliza, b. May 31, 1816; d. Sept. 16, 1816.
2066	v	Eliza, b. Feb. 21, 1819.
2067	vi	Infant, } b. July, 1823; } d. the same month.
2068	vii	Infant, }	
2069	viii	Stephen B., b. Sept. 1, 1828; d., in Rindge, N. H., Dec. 17, 1847.
2070	ix	Elizabeth, or Hepsibath, b. April 23, 1833; d. May 24, 1836.
2071	x	Caroline M., b. June 26, 1834; d. April 22, 1836.
2072	xi	Ellen, b. Jan. 7, 1836; d., unm., Sept. 30, 1864.

1049 Enos[6] Emery (*John,[5] Stephen,[4] Stephen,[3] Jonathan,[2] John[1]*), son of John and Elizabeth (Perkins) Emery; married Zipporah Hale, daughter of David Hale, April 22, 1817. She died of smallpox, Sept. 14, 1848. He died Feb. 20, 1867. He resided in Keene, Groton and Ashburnham.

Children :

2073 i MARY JANE,[7] b. Jan 23, 1818, m. George B Lane, June 15, 1839
2074 ii WILLIAM H , b March 27, 1821; m. Mary A. Lane
2075 iii CHARLES H , b March 29, 1823
2076 iv PASCAL P , b. July 21, 1825

1057 STEPHEN[6] EMERY (*Jesse,[5] Stephen.[4] Stephen,[3] Jonathan,[2] John[1]*), son of Jesse and Ruth (Dwinnell) Emery; married Margaret Chase, 1816, in Londonderry. N. H. (born April, 1796), died in Curtis Corners, Leeds, Me.

Children :

2077 i DAVID.[7]
2078 ii ELIZA
2079 iii SARAH M., b Sept 7, 1821.
2080 iv MARY
2081 v GEORGE, m. Matilda or Lydia Eames
2082 vi ROSANNAH.
2083 vii LUCINDA
2084 viii JOHN, b Feb. 15, 1834
2085 ix CLARK, b. April 9, 1837.

1060 DANIEL[6] EMERY (*Daniel,[5] John,[4] Stephen,[3] Jonathan.[2] John[1]*), son of Daniel and Mary (Jones) Emery, married Rebecca Chase. He died in Wilmot, N. H., Jan., 1882. His wife died Aug. 24, 1882, aged 84.

Children :

2086 i TILTON E.[7]
2087 ii MATTHEW P
2088 iii HARRIET J., m William Hubbard, d *s p.*

1061 EZRA[6] EMERY (*Daniel,[5] John,[4] Stephen,[3] Jonathan,[2] John[1]*), son of Daniel and Mary (Jones) Emery; married Jane Dole. March 17, 1825 He died at Dunbar, N. H., July 26, 1833, aged 30. His wife died Oct. 8, 1877.

Children ·

2089 i MARY JANE,[7] d young.
2090 ii WILLIAM G
2091 iii NANCY G
2092 iv SARAH W
2093 v JAMES, m Jane McKenzie.
2094 vi JOHN, m Frances Backs in of Danbury, N H.
2095 vii MASON N., d. in 1863, nineteen years of age
2096 viii MAY W , m John Carsei of Salisbury, N. H , who d in 1883.

1062 JUDITH[6] EMERY (*Daniel,[5] John,[4] Stephen,[3] Jonathan,[2] John[1]*), daughter of Daniel and Mary (Jones) Emery; married Eben White, June 4, 1823. She died in Wilmot, N. H., Oct. 1, 1850. He died May 14, 1861

Children :

2097 i MARY,[7] b 1823
2098 ii LIZZIE JANE, b. July 16, 1825.

2099 iii LYSIAS E., b. May 31, 1827.
2100 iv   DAVID H., b. Nov. 7, 1829; d. young.
2101 v   MOSES E., b. Nov. 14, 1834; Union soldier in 3d N. H. Vols.,
           wounded in the retreat from Fort Wagner; d. in N. Y. from
           his wounds, Aug. 22, 1863.
2102 vi   M. HELEN, b. July 30, 1837.
2103 vii ADDIE J., b. May 23, 1840.
2104 viii LORENZO N., b. Sept. 6, 1844; d. young.

1063 TIMOTHY[6] EMERY (*Daniel,*[5] *John,*[4] *Stephen,*[3] *Jonathan,*[2]
John[1]), son of Daniel and Mary (Jones) Emery; married Fanny
Jones who died in Merrimack, Wisconsin, Feb. 28, 1876, aged 68.
He died Sept. 26, 1886, aged 77.

Children :

2105 i   ANNIE,[7] d. 1852, æt. nineteen.
2106 ii LAVINIA.

1064 ABIGAIL[6] EMERY (*Moses,*[5] *Benjamin,*[4] *Stephen,*[3] *Jonathan,*[2]
John[1]), daughter of Moses and his second wife Mehetable (Ingalls)
Emery; married Benjamin Emerson, jr., of Hampstead, N. H., Feb.
22, 1803.

Children :

2107 i   MARY.[7]
2108 ii MOSES.

1065 ELIZABETH[6] EMERY (*Moses,*[5] *Benjamin,*[4] *Stephen,*[3] *Jonathan,*[2]
John[1]), daughter of Moses and his second wife Mehetable (Ingalls)
Emery; married John Emerson, Nov. 15, 1804. He died June 5,
1848. She died May 10, 1875.

Children, born in Hampstead, N. H. :

2109 i   JESSE EMERY,[7] b. Oct. 24, 1805.
2110 ii ALFRED, b. Oct. 10, 1807; m., 1st, Susan E. Perry in 1838; 2nd,
          Mary Gauson in 1841; 3rd, Lucretia A. Butler in 1855.
2111 iii JOHN WEBSTER, b. Nov. 24, 1810.
2112 iv ROBERT HENRY, b. Oct. 26, 1816.
2113 v   ELIZABETH, b. July 14, 1821; d. July 12, 1845.
2114 vi MARY, b. Aug. 24, 1823.

1066 SARAH[6] (SALLY) EMERY (*Moses,*[5] *Benjamin,*[4] *Stephen,*[3] *Jonathan,*[2] *John*[1]), daughter of Moses and his second wife Mehetable (Ingalls) Emery; died in Haverhill, Mass., March 10, 1868; married
Nathan Currier of Atkinson, N. H. (born in Salem, N. H., Nov.,
1787, and died April 17, 1845). Lived in Salem, N. H.

Children :

2115 i   DUDLEY W.,[7] b. March 24, 1813.
2116 ii   MEHETABLE E., b. April 5, 1815.
2117 iii ALPHEUS, b. Jan. 23, 1817.
2118 iv   SARAH, b. March 30, 1819.
2119 v   ABIGAIL, b. March 19, 1821.
2120 vi   RHODA E., b. July 10, 1823.
2121 vii ELIZABETH R., b. Aug. 9, 1825.
2122 viii HARRIET, b. Sept. 27, 1829.
2123 ix   FANNY N., b. Nov. 24, 1833.

1067 Rhoda[6] Emery (*Moses*,[5] *Benjamin*,[4] *Stephen*,[3] *Jonathan*,[2] *John*[1]), daughter of Moses and his second wife Mehetable (Ingalls) Emery, married Benjamin Wilson (born in Pelham, N. H., Feb 14, 1803); died in Chester, N H   Lived in Atkinson.

Children :

2124 i   Mehetable Emery,[7] b in Atkinson, April 8, 1828, d. in Chester, N H., June 7, 1859
2125 ii Andrew Jackson, b. in Salem, March 24, 1830, d in Chester, N H, Oct 15, 1852
2126 iii Elizabeth Ingalls, b in Salem, April 15, 1832; m Lucien Kent in Chester, N. H, Sept 13, 1855, who died April 1, 1880
2127 iv Benj Franklin, b May 19, 1840, in Salem
2128 v   Charles Albert, b April 19, 1843, in Chester, m. Mary E Abbot; d May 27, 1871

1068 Jesse[6] Emery (*Moses*,[5] *Benjamin*,[4] *Stephen*,[3] *Jonathan*,[2] *John*[1]), son of Moses and his second wife Mehetable (Ingalls) Emery, married Sarah B. Welch

Children :

2129 i   David,[7] b Dec. 11, 1816
2130 ii Benj Emerson, b April 16 1818
2131 iii Abigail Page, b April 16, 1822

1069 William[6] Moulton (*Judith*,[5] *William*,[4] *Edward*,[3] *Jonathan*,[2] *John*[1]), son of Cutting and Judith (Emery) Moulton ; married in 1804, Mary Pearl (born 1784).

Children .

2132 i   Clarissa,[7] b. Sept. 26, 1805.
2133 ii Samuel, b June 11, 1807
2134 iii Cutting, b April 19, 1810
2135 iv William Emery b March 19 1813
2136 v   Judith, b July 19, 1817
2137 vi Catharine, b. Dec 11, 1820

1070 John[6] Moulton (*Judith*,[5] *William*,[4] *Edward*,[3] *Jonathan*,[2] *John*[1]), son of Cutting and his second wife Judith (Emery) Moulton, married Hannah Foster of Parsonsfield, Me. Lived in Saccarappa, Me.

Children

2138 i   Abigail [7]
2139 ii   Eliza
2140 iii Lucy
2141 iv   Joseph
2142 v   George
2143 vi   John
2144 vii Lydia.
2145 viii William

1071 Cutting[6] Moulton (*Judith*,[5] *William*,[4] *Edward*,[3] *Jonathan*,[2] *John*[1]), son of Cutting and his second wife Judith (Emery) Moulton ; married Lydia Lord. He died March 22, 1854   His wife died Oct. 8, 1881.

Children :

```
2146   i    LYDIA B.,⁷ m. ——— Wentworth.
2147   ii   SARAH L., m. ——— Libby.
2148   iii  PATIENCE, m. ——— Pray.
2149   iv   ALMIRA, m. ——— Smith.
2150   v    ORINDA, m. ——— Shorey.
2151   vi   EMERY B.
2152   vii  MARY F., m. ——— Ravel.
2153   viii JAMES W.
2154   ix   JOHN L.
2155   x    ALBERT N.
2156   xi   SUSAN E., m. ——— Doe.
```

1073 JOSEPH⁶ MOULTON (*Judith,*⁵ *William,*⁴ *Edward,*³ *Jonathan,*²
John¹), son of Cutting and his second wife Judith (Emery) Moulton ;
married Ruth Messer of Newport, N. H., 1815. She died in 1841.
He married, second, Polly Barker, April 13, 1843 ; removed to An-
trim, N. H., and died, 1864. She died in 1872.
Children :

```
2157   i    SALOME W.,⁷ b. March 5, 1817.
2158   ii   MARTHA J., b. Feb. 20, 1821.
2159   iii  LUCETTA, b. June 25, 1826.
2160   iv   LUCRETIA, b. Dec. 4, 1828.
2161   v    REV. JOSEPH, b. Aug. 12, 1834.
```

1074 DAVID⁶ MOULTON (*Judith,*⁵ *William,*⁴ *Edward,*³ *Jonathan,*²
John¹), son of Cutting and his second wife Judith (Emery) Moulton ;
married Mary Weatherbee, May 5, 1817. He died Oct. 1, 1868,
aged 75. Lived in Oak Grove, Dodge Co., Wis.
Children :

```
2162   i    MARTHA J.,⁷ b. March 14, 1818.
2163   ii   LORENZO M., b. Oct. 29, 1819.
2164   iii  ALMON, b. Nov. 21, 1821.
2165   iv   SOBIESKI, b. Sept. 10, 1823.
2166   v    ABEL, b. Nov. 27, 1825.
2167   vi   HENRY, b. Oct. 14, 1827.
2168   vii  DAVID, b. Feb. 26, 1830.
2169   viii FRANKLIN B., b. Feb. 15, 1835.
2170   ix   AMOS, b. March 1, 1836.
```

1076 NATHAN⁶ MOULTON (*Judith,*⁵ *William,*⁴ *Edward,*³ *Jonathan,*²
John¹), son of Cutting and his second wife Judith (Emery) Moulton ;
married Mary Edgerly of Tamworth, N. H., Nov., 1829. Lived in
Parsonsfield, Me., and died Dec. 20, 1874.
Children :

```
2171   i    LORENZO,⁷ b. Oct. 7, 1830.
2172   ii   MARTHA J., b Sept. 5, 1833.
2173   iii  MARY A., b. Oct. 23, 1834.
2174   iv   ELI, b. Dec. 22, 1836.
2175   v    HANNAH E., b. April 22, 1839.
```

1077 JOHN⁶ EMERY (*David,*⁵ *Jonathan,*⁴ *James,*³ *Jonathan,*²*John¹*),
son of David and Abigail (Goodwin) Emery ; married Abigail Brown
in Clinton, Me., Oct. 18, 1805 ; lived in Waterville ; farmer. She was
born Jan. 10, 1787, and died in Waterville, Jan. 26, 1851. He died
in Waterville, Nov. 24, 1860.

Children, all born in Waterville :

2176   i   Avis,[7] b 1807
2177   ii   Lauretta, m Rev Thomas M Brown of Clinton, Me. He d. She lives in Goliad, Goliad Co , Tex
2178   iii   David
2179   iv   Sumner
2180   v   Abigail, m Daniel Blackstone; they live in Boston
2181   vi   Reuben
2182   vii   Nathaniel G.
2183   viii   Eveline, b. April 29, 1824; m Othniel Smith, Nov 8, 1870, farmer, they live in Canaan, Me , s p.
2184   ix   A Son, d. in infancy
2185   x   A Daughter, d in infancy

1078 Benjamin[6] Emery (*David*,[5] *Jonathan*,[4] *James*,[3] *Jonathan*,[2] *John*[1]), son of David and Abigail (Goodwin) Emery, married Mary Whidden in Canaan, Me., 1808 (born in Canaan, Aug 4, 1786), where he lived till 1826, then in Skowhegan ; later in Bangor, and lastly in Upper Stillwater ; died there April 28, 1871. His wife died May 2, 1873.

Children, born in Canaan :

2186   i   Orra,[7] b Oct. 15, 1809
2187   ii   Rachel, b April 29 1811.
2188   iii   Harrison, b Nov. 29, 1812
2189   iv   Samuel I , b Sept 30, 1814
2190   v   Esther Ellen, b. Sept 29, 1816; m Colonel John Pooler of Skowhegan, Me (b in Skowhegan, Me , Oct 13, 1802), in Bangor, Me , March 27, 1851, merchant, and colonel in the state militia, d in Bangor, June 5, 1860 His widow m . 2nd, Joseph Metcalf in Orono, Me , Jan 15, 1873, b. in Lisbon, Me , Feb 22, 1807; farmer
2191   vi   Benjamin Watson, b July 9, 1819.
2192   vii   Nehemiah N , b July 29, 1821, m Cleora A Sampson (b in Dover, Me , March 25, 1832) of Milo, Me , Oct 2, 1852, in South Hadley Falls, Mass Union soldier, discharged for disability, workman in National Armory, Springfield, Mass , d in Stratford, Conn , June 20, 1874, s p.
2193   viii   Lorenzo Dow, b. May 2, 1824
2194   ix   Miles, b Oct. 13, 1826 , m Mary Elizabeth Taylor (b in Ohio) in Drytown, Cal , removed from Bangor, Me , to Cal , 1851 , merchant and miner, d March 23, 1873, s p , in Drytown
2195   x   Joslph B , b in Skowhegan, Me , Oct. 15, 1828 , went to California via Cape Horn, 1853, spent five years in gold mines; in 1858 settled in Oakland, Douglass Co , Oregon, and engaged in business, in 1882 removed to Portland Ore , postal clerk on the Columbia River Steamship Mail Line from Portland to Astoria. U S mail agent for eight years, unm
       Orinda, an adopted daughter of Benjamin and Mary (Whidden) Emery, b Aug 16, 1830, in Skowhegan, Me ; m Albert Webb of Sangerville, Me , Jan 4, 1856. They had one child named Stanley F , b Oct. 30, 1857, in S Sangerville, Me , where they live

1079 Jonathan[6] Emery (*David*,[5] *Jonathan*,[4] *James*,[3] *Jonathan*,[2] *John*[1]), son of David and Abigail (Goodwin) Emery : married Hannah Cheney of Vermont (born in Lunenburg, Vt., 1786), in Fairfield, Me., 1810, lived in Canaan and died in Harmony, Me., Dec. 17, 1863. His wife died Oct., 1848. Farmer; soldier in the war of 1812.

Children, born in Canaan, Me.:

2196 i SYLVIA C.,[7] b. Jan. 3, 1814.
2197 ii COLUMBUS W., b. Sept. 21, 1815.
2198 iii JONATHAN E., b. April 27, 1817.
2199 iv ISRAEL, b. Jan. 10, 1820; d. July 10, 1820.
2200 v SARAH ANN, b. July 8, 1821; m., 1st, William Ellis in Brunswick, Me., Jan. 30, 1849 (b. Sept. 23, 1799, and d. in Brunswick, Me., Sept 17, 1858); 2nd, George E. Bevers, 1879, in Hancock. Minn. He was b. in Jacksonville, Ill., Jan. 25, 1834. No children.
2201 vi MARY ANN, b. May 24, 1823; d. in St. Albans, Me., unm., æt. 18.
2202 vii ISABELLA, b. Dec. 16, 1826; d. Jan. 28, 1827.
2203 viii MARCIA I,
2204 ix EMILY ORA, b. June 6, 1829.
2205 x ELVIRA, b. May 7, 1830; d. young.
2206 xi CAROLINE ELIZABETH, b. May 7, 1831.
2207 xii LEVI FRANKLIN, b. June 21, 1833.

1081 CALEB[6] EMERY (David,[5] Jonathan,[4] James,[3] Jonathan,[2] John[1]), son of David and Abigail (Goodwin) Emery; married —— Lowe; second, Oct. 24, 1819, Emily Chase, daughter of Isaac and Bridget (Delano) Chase. She was born in Fairfield, Me., Oct. 25, 1804.

Children, by his second wife, born in Fairfield, Me.:

2208 i ALONZO KING,[7] b. Nov. 1, 1823.
2209 ii FRANKLIN, b. Aug. 4, 1825.
2210 iii CAROLINE, b. July 19, 1827; m. James McNellie.
2211 iv JOSHUA, b. March 3, 1830; lumberman.
2212 v EMELINE, b. March 4, 1836; m., 1st, Watson Lord; 2nd, Adelbert Nichols,
2213 vi CALEB G., b. Sept. 28, 1838.
2214 vii EBEN TRIPP, b. Aug. 1, 1840.
2215 viii MELVILLE, b. Aug., 1842.
2216 ix AMY FRANCES, b. Feb. 4, 1845.

1082 JERUSHA[6] EMERY (David,[5] Jonathan,[4] James,[3] Jonathan,[2] John[1]), daughter of David and Abigail (Goodwin) Emery; married Moses S. Wyman; lived in Kendall's Mills, Me., and died in Fairfield, Me. She died in Kendall's Mills, 1866.

Children, born in Fairfield:

2217 i CHARLES SUMNER,[7] b. Oct. 10, 1816; m. Melinda Cayford.
2218 ii INCREASE KENDALL, b. March 8, 1819.
2219 iii WILLIAM HARRISON, b. March 3, 1821; lives in St. Paul, Minn.; unm.
2220 iv RACHEL CHASE, b. Aug. 10, 1823; d. in Lowell, Mass., unm., July 15, 1843.
2221 v AMANDA SAWYER, m. Alden Blackwell. She d. s. p.
2222 vi BUTLER EMERY, d. in Philadelphia, Pa.; m., 1st, Jane Rose; 2nd, Malinda Sylons.
2223 vii EMILY MAYNARD, m. John D. Robbins; live in Augusta, Me.
2224 viii HENRY GULIFER, m.; d. in California.

1083 MILES[6] EMERY (David,[5] Jonathan,[4] James,[3] Jonathan,[2] John[1]), son of David and Abigail (Goodwin) Emery; married Mary Delia Nedeau, in Tobigue, Victoria, N. B., March 17, 1832 (born in St. Andrews, Quebec, Canada, Oct. 7, 1817). Lived in Fort Kent, Me. He died Oct. 10, 1884. Lumberman.

Children, born in Fort Kent :

2225 i   MILES,[7] jr , b Nov 28 1832; d in Ft Kent, unm , Oct. 17,
           1862, carpenter
2226 ii   RAPHILE, b July 17, 1835
2227 iii LOUISA, b Dec 27, 1836
2228 iv   DANIEL, b Nov 12, 1838
2229 v   CHARLES, b Jan 18, 1840; lives in Mason, Bayfield Co , Wis ;
           lumberman , unm
2230 vi   SUSAN, b June 4, 1842
2231 vii SOPHIA, b May 10 1844
2232 viii CRYSTY ANN, b Jan 23, 1846
2233 ix   HARRIET, b Dec 7, 1847, d Dec 16, 1853, in Ft Kent
2234 x   ELIZALETH, b Feb 5, 1849.
2235 xi   DAVID C , b. March 8, 1852
2236 xii MARTHA, b April 5, 1854, m William Chase, in Patten, Me ,
           Jan 31, 1879
2237 xiii WILLIAM, b May 21, 1856
2238 xiv ELLEN, b Aug 3, 1858 resides in Bangor, Me ; unm
2239 xv   RUTH H , b July 5, 1860.

1084 RACHEL[6] EMERY (*David,[5] Jonathan,[4] James,[3] Jonathan,[2] John[1]*), daughter of David and Abigail (Goodwin) Emery , died March 15, 1887, married, in Fairfield, Me., Dec. 1, 1825, Isaac Chase (born in Sidney, Me , May 15, 1800) , brother of Emily Chase, who married Caleb Emery, No. 1081

Children, born in Fairfield, Me :

2240 i   ORRA ANN,[7] b. Sept. 7, 1826
2241 ii   ALBERT B , b Feb 11, 1828.
2242 iii EMILY EMERY, b May 21, 1830
2243 iv   BENJAMIN F , b April 27, 1832, went to Cal.
2244 v   SARAH S , b Feb 17, 1835
2245 vi   REV JOHN WESLEY, b May 6, 1837

1085 NEHEMIAH[6] EMERY (*David,[5] Jonathan,[4] James,[3] Jonathan,[2] John[1]*), son of David and Abigail (Goodwin) Emery , married, first, Nancy Carpenter, in Lincoln, Me ; second, —— Adams, in Lincoln, Me. , merchant in Lincoln, Me

Children, born in Lincoln, Me. :

By first wife .

2246 i   WILLIAM HENRY CRAWFORD [7]

By second wife ·

2247 ii   ALVANUS, d. in Lincoln, Me , æt 16.
2248 iii AUGUSTUS, d young.
2249 iv   NANCY d young

1098 JAMES[6] EMERY (*John,[5] Jonathan,[4] James,[3] Jonathan,[2] John[1]*), son of John and Alice (Ballard) Emery , married and lived in St John, N B.

Children

2250 i   SON [7]
2251 ii   SON.
2252 iii SON
2253 iv   DAUGHTER

1099 SOPHIA[6] EMERY (*John*,[5] *Jonathan* [4] *James*,[3] *Jonathan*,[2] *John*[1]), daughter of John and Alice (Ballard) Emery ; married Isaac Holt ; lived in Benton, Me., and died there April 2, 1889, aged 98. He was born March 6, 1791. She died Aug. 2, 1828.

Children :

2254	i	JACKSON,[7] b. Nov. 30, 1814 ; d. Nov. 16, 1835.
2255	ii	OBADIAH, b. Oct. 19, 1816.
2256	iii	MARY ACHSHA, b. Oct. 16, 1818.
2257	iv	WILLIAM AMES, b. Oct. 31, 1820 ; d. in Florida.
2258	v	JAMES EMERY, d.
2259	vi	ISAAC JONES, b. Dec. 15, 1822 ; d. Dec. 29, 1883.
2260	vii	ESTERIA LOUISA, b. Sept. 9, 1825.
2261	viii	SARAH ADALINE, b. Nov. 29, 1827.

1108 LOUISA[6] CAIN (*Thankful*,[5] *Jonathan*,[4] *James*,[3] *Jonathan*,[2] *John*[1]), daughter of Mephibosheth and Mrs. Thankful (Emery) Pearson Cain ; married Richard Wells of Vienna, Me., Dec. 7, 1825 ; lived in Clinton, Me., and died there Aug. 7, 1879. She died there Nov. 27, 1886.

Children, born in Clinton, Me. :

2262	i	RUBY S.,[7] b. June 17, 1827 ; d. Feb. 12, 1828.
2263	ii	GEORGE N., b. July 11, 1828 ; m. Philena Bigelow of Starks, Me., Oct. 12, 1854. He d. Iowa, Dec. 16, 1878.
2264	iii	MEPHIBOSHETH, b. Nov. 19, 1829 ; d. Dec. 29, 1829.
2265	iv	GIDEON, b. Nov. 13, 1830 ; d. Aug. 28, 1831.
2266	v	RICHARD M., b. Sept. 17, 1832 ; m. Leora J. Nicholls, of Searsport, Me., March 13, 1873.
2267	vi	GIDEON M., b. Aug. 19, 1833 ; m. Caroline Woodsum of Clinton, Me., Jan. 1862.
2268	vii	THANKFUL C., b. Sept. 17, 1834 ; m. Ezra McIntire of Bloomfield, Me., Feb. 2, 1856.
2269	viii	MEPHIBOSHETH C., b. Oct. 17, 1835 ; m. Jane Shillinglan of Neponset, Ill., 1855.
2270	ix	WILLIAM E., b. Jan. 26, 1837.
2271	x	DAVID P , b. June 14, 1838 ; d. Sept. 1, 1838.
2272	xi	RACHEL L., b. Nov. 6, 1839 ; m. Elias Drake of Milo, Me., April 10, 1859. She d. in Clinton, Sept. 15, 1862.
2273	xii	SARAH E., b. July 11, 1841 ; m. Elias Drake of Milo, Me., Aug. 25, 1867.
2274	xiii	DANIEL, b. Dec. 19, 1842 ; d. Jan. 6, 1843.
2275	xiv	RUBY V., b. Dec. 26, 1845 ; m. Benjamin Drake of Worcester, Mass., Jan. 20, 1870.

1110 SAMUEL[6] EMERY (*Briggs H.*,[5] *Jonathan*,[4] *James*,[3] *Jonathan*,[2] *John*[1]), son of Briggs H. and Sally (Farnham) Emery ; married Abiah Judkins in Fairfield, Me., May 28, 1820 (born in Fayette, Me., Nov. 30, 1796) ; enlisted in July, 1862, as private in company "C," 19th Reg. Me. Vol. Inf. ; mustered into United States service Aug. 25, 1862. He was familiarly known throughout his brigade as "Uncle Sam." On the march his rifle and knapsack were frequently carried in the sutler's wagon while he busied himself saving rifles, belts and clothing which the other soldiers threw away.

He was too old and crippled to do a soldier's duty, and was discharged, but reënlisted in the invalid corps, and was a guard over prisoners of war, at the time of his death in Augusta, Me., May 1, 1865. His record is one of which his descendants may well be proud.

His is an example of American patriotism   He was an old man exempt from military duty, but went to the front, faced the enemy in the battles of Fredericksburg and Falmouth and in other desperate engagements, and was in the service when he died at the age of seventy   His widow died in Fairfield, Me , Sept. 26, 1866.

Children, born in Fairfield, Me. ·

2276   i   BENJAMIN F ,[7] b March 14, 1821 ; miner in California; d., unm , in Glen Haven, N Y , March 24, 1856
2277   ii   ADONIRAM J , b April 5, 1823 ; d March 6, 1825.
2278   iii MARY JANE, b June 22, 1824 , d July 30, 1825
2279   iv   ZERI J , b. July 3, 1826.
2280   v   CHARLES H , b June 15, 1828, miner in Cal ; enlisted in company "L", 1st Reg Cal. Cav., April 1, 1863, Sen Corporal of his company , drowned in Sacramento river, Sept 6, 1863
2281   vi   INFANT SON, b and d June, 1830
2282   vii ANDREW J , b Aug 19, 1831
2283   viii EDWIN ALLEN, b May 7, 1834
2284   ix   ABIGAIL J., b. July 23, 1835.

1112 BENJAMIN FARNHAM[6] EMERY (*Briggs H ,[5] Jonathan,[4] James,[3] Jonathan,[2] John[1]*), son of Briggs H. and Sally (Farnham) Emery, married, first, in Bath, Me., Oct. 12, 1829, Mary Ann Leavitt (born in Brentwood, N. H , Jan. 20, 1810 ; died in Bath, Oct 28 1831) , married, second, in Bath, May 16, 1839, Lucinda W. Noyes (born in Freeport, Me , June 1, 1812)   Wool merchant ; died in Bath, Dec. 21, 1873.   His wife died Dec 25, 1883

Children, born in Bath :

2285   i   MARY ANN LEAVITT,[7] b Oct 2, 1830, d Jan 29, 1831.
2286   ii   ANN MARY, b Feb 22, 1840.
2287   iii SARAH AUGUSTA, b Aug 27, 1841 m Isaac Rogers, Dec. 1, 1859 in Bath, Me   He was born in Bath, Oct. 9, 1834 , res in Bath, *s p*
2288   iv   CHARLES DAVIS, b. Sept. 1, 1843.
2289   v   BRIGGS HALLOWELL, b Sept 14, 1845
2290   vi   HELEN LUCINDA, b March 28, 1849.
2291   vii BENJAMIN F , JR , b Nov 28, 1851, m Emma B Carlton, Nov 21, 1877, in Whitefield, Me , d Feb 8, 1880, *s p* , she m , 2nd, John Bailey
2292   viii ADA FRANCES, b. Nov. 13, 1853, m John H. Owens, Nov. 18, 1880, in Boston, Mass (b in Meriden, Conn , Sept 20, 1848) ; farmer ; they reside at Jamaica Plain, Mass , *s p*

1113 JOSEPH[6] EMERY (*Briggs H.,[5] Jonathan,[4] James,[3] Jonathan,[2] John[1]*), son of Briggs H. and Sally (Farnham) Emery ; died Oct 18, 1852 ; married, first, in Fairfield, June 28, 1828, Susanna Gordon (born in Salem, N. H., June 23, 1808 , died in Fairfield, Feb 24, 1837) ; married, second, Nov 28, 1839, Mrs Deidamia P. Tyler (born in Fairfield, June 7, 1813, daughter of Samuel and Deidamia (Johnson) Emery , died Nov. 30, 1850).

Children, born in Fairfield :

2293   i   MARY ANN,[7] b April 27, 1829
2294   ii   SUSAN J., b Nov. 12, 1830
2295   iii JAMES F , b. July 18, 1832
2296   iv   CHARLES B., b. Oct. 4, 1834.

By second marriage :

2297 v MELVILLE D., b. July 28, 1842.
2298 vi SARAH M., b. Aug. 31, 1848.
2299 vii LOTTIE L., b. Sept. 21, 1850.

1114 ALBEN[6] EMERY (*Briggs H.,*[5] *Jonathan,*[4] *James,*[3] *Jonathan,*[2] *John*[1]), son of Briggs H. and Sally (Farnham) Emery; married in Fairfield, Dec. 29, 1831, Betsey Ellis Tobey (born in Fairfield, June 30, 1813). Wool merchant; lived in Fairfield, Me., till 1851, when he moved to Waterville, Me., and died Jan. 29, 1873.

Children born in Fairfield, Me. :

2300 i ALBERT PORTER,[7] b. April 19, 1833.
2301 ii ALBEN FRANKLIN, b. Nov. 3, 1834.
2302 iii CHARLES MELVIN, b. July 6, 1836; m. Fannie Isabel Barrell, dau. of Dea. Elijah and Adaline (Stockbridge) Barrell of Green, Me., July 5, 1868 (b. Nov. 17, 1839); taught school every winter from 1854 to 1864; was graduated at Waterville Coll. (now Colby University) 1863, and from Newton Theo. Institution, 1868; clerk in Paymaster General's Office, Washington, D. C., 1864-5; ordained pastor of Baptist Church in Thomaston, Me., Sept. 29, 1868, and was pastor in Thomaston, Greene, Fairfield and Freeport, Me.; chaplain of Maine State Prison, secretary of Maine Baptist Educational Society four years and financial agent of Hebron Academy. Lives in Portland, Me.
2303 iv LAURA ELLEN, b. July 8, 1838; d., unm., in Waterville, Me., Oct. 9, 1886. Teacher of high rank and attainment in the public schools. Graduate of Waterville Academy.
2304 v WILLIAM H., b. March 27, 1840.
2305 vi FLORETTA, b. July 21, 1842; d. in Waterville, Me., Jan. 17, 1852.
2306 vii VIRA CHANDLER, b. Jan. 7, 1845; d. in Waterville, Jan. 19, 1852.
2307 viii JAMES HIRAM, b. April 16, 1847; m., 1st, in Waterville, Eliz. S., dau. of William and Varila (Fuller) Dyer, May 13, 1874 (b. May 13, 1847; d. Sept. 21, 1876); m., 2nd, Myra A., dau. of Ruel M. and Emily A. Gifford in Winslow, Me., Nov. 2, 1880 (b. March 31, 1854); wool merchant in Chicago, Ill.
2308 ix LINDA ABBOT, b. April 15, 1849; m. Henry T. Hanson in Waterville, Me., May 7, 1883 (b. in Boston, Mass., Dec. 16, 1849).
2309 x EDWARD BYRON, b. April 26, 1851; d. in Fairfield, Nov. 28, 1851.
2310 xi IDA MAY, b. Dec. 29, 1852; d. Dec. 21, 1879; m. Robert T. Albertson, son of Alanson and Rhena Albertson of N. Y. City, Dec. 4, 1878, in Waterville, Me. (b. in Kinderhook. N. Y.).

1116 SARAH J.[6] EMERY (*Briggs H.,*[5] *Jonathan,*[4] *James,*[3] *Jonathan,*[2] *John*[1]), daughter of Briggs H. and Sally (Farnham) Emery; married in Fairfield, Me., Sept. 12, 1843, John Davis; died in California. She died in Fairfield, Dec. 1, 1847.

Child :

2311 i JOHN HENRY,[7] b. in Fairfield, Me.; soldier in the Union Army; d. in Hospital in Augusta, Me., unm.

1118 OBED[6] EMERY (*Briggs H.,*[5] *Jonathan,*[4] *James,*[3] *Jonathan,*[2] *John*[1]), son of Briggs H. and Sally (Farnham) Emery; married, Aug. 28, 1851, Louise E. Atwood (born Feb. 29, 1824, in Fairfield). Farmer and stock raiser in Fairfield, Me.

Children, born in Fairfield :

2312   i   VIRGIL PARIS,[7] b March 24, 1853.
2313   ii   CORA LOUISE, b Dec 26, 1855, unm.
2314   iii HENRY CHESTER, b. Nov 30, 1859, m. Florence M. Randall,
            Nov. 30, 1887.

1119 WILLIAM H [6] EMERY (*Briggs H.,*[5] *Jonathan,*[4] *James,*[3] *Jonathan,*[2] *John*[1]), son of Briggs H and Sally (Farnham) Emery ; married in Fairfield, Feb. 10, 1847, Mary Gifford (born April 10, 1828). He died March 30, 1855, in Fairfield.

Children, born in Fairfield :

2315   i   CLARENCE PERCY,[7] b Dec. 31, 1847
2316   ii   CHELSEA B , b Dec 14, 1849
2317   iii VIRTURA ANN, b April 23, 1853

1120 RUTH[6] EMERY (*Jones,*[5] *Jonathan,*[4] *James,*[3] *Jonathan,*[2] *John*[1]), daughter of Jones and Alice (Johnston) Emery, married M. McDuff, lived in Lagrange, Me. She is dead.

Seven children, Nos. 2318 to 2324. Names unknown.

1121 RACHEL[6] EMERY (*Jones,*[5] *Jonathan,*[4] *James,*[3] *Jonathan,*[2] *John*[1]), daughter of Jones and Alice (Johnston) Emery, married Geo W. Farrar ; lived in Oldtown, Me. She is dead.

Seven children, Nos. 2325 to 2331. Names unknown.

1123 RODNEY[6] EMERY (*Jones,*[5] *Jonathan,*[4] *James,*[3] *Jonathan,*[2] *John*[1]), son of Jones and Alice (Johnston) Emery, married ———. Soldier in the Second Regt Me. Vol. Inf., and lived in Medford, Me , where he died.

Four children, Nos. 2332 to 2335. Names unknown.

1124 VALENTINE[6] EMERY (*Jones,*[5] *Jonathan,*[4] *James,*[3] *Jonathan,*[2] *John*[1]), son of Jones and Alice (Johnston) Emery ; married ———.

Three children, Nos 2336 to 2338. Names unknown.

1125 WILLIAM K.[6] EMERY (*Jones,*[5] *Jonathan,*[4] *James,*[3] *Jonathan,*[2] *John*[1]), son of Jones and Alice (Johnston) Emery ; married ———; lives in Mass.

Seven children, Nos. 2339 to 2345. Names unknown.

1126 THANKFUL C.[6] EMERY (*Jones,*[5] *Jonathan,*[4] *James,*[3] *Jonathan,*[2] *John*[1]), daughter of Jones and Alice (Johnston) Emery ; married in Clinton, Me , April 10, 1842, Aaron Eldridge (born Aug. 22, 1812 ; died in Dayton, Me., May 1, 1879). She died in Medford, Me., July 29, 1885.

Children, born in Clinton, Me.:

2346   i   IRA S ,[7] b April 30, 1843, soldier in the Union Army in 4th
            Maine Battery, d. in the Hospital, Baltimore, Md , Nov. 25,
            1862, unm.
2347   ii   RANSOM, b March 1, 1846
2348   iii FRANCES A , b Feb 24, 1848 ; d Nov 13, 1848.
2349   iv   JONES EMERY, b Dec 3, 1849.
2350   v   WILLIAM M., b. Nov 9, 1851, unm , farmer in Dexter, Me.

2351　vi　Richard F., b. April 27, 1854; unm.; dealer in live stock in
　　　　　　Clinton.
2352　vii　George W., b. March 11, 1856; d. April 19, 1856.
2353　viii　Joseph V., b. April 9, 1859; d. Dec. 16, 1859.
2354　ix　Aaron M., b. Sept. 14, 1860; m. Eliz. Galusha in Clinton, Me.,
　　　　　　Aug. 22, 1880; farmer in Clinton.

1128 Frances[6] Emery (*Jones*,[5] *Jonathan*,[4] *James*,[3] *Jonathan*,[2]
John[1]), daughter of Jones and Alice (Johnston) Emery; married
R. Fritts or Fitts. Lived in Medford, Me.
　　Four children, Nos. 2355 to 2358. Names unknown.

1129 George W.[6] Emery (*Jones*,[5] *Jonathan*,[4] *James*,[3] *Jonathan*,[2]
John[1]), son of Jones and Alice (Johnston) Emery; married——;
lives in Vermont.
　　Three children, Nos. 2359 to 2361. Names unknown.

1130 Paul Jones[6] Emery (*Jones*,[5] *Jonathan*,[4] *James*,[3] *Jonathan*,[2]
John[1]), son of Jones and Alice (Johnston) Emery; married Fidelia
Rollins of Sebec, Me.; live in Clinton, Me. He was a Union soldier.
　　Children :

2362　i　Emma P.[7]
2363　ii　Daughter.
2364　iii　Son.

1131 Joseph D.[6] Emery (*Jones*,[5] *Jonathan*,[4] *James*,[3] *Jonathan*,[2]
John[1]), son of Jones and Alice (Johnston) Emery; married——;
live in Medford, Me.
　　Children :

2365　i　A daughter,[7] m. —— Harthorn.
2366　ii　A daughter, m. J. G. Daggit.
　　Six other children, Nos. 2367 to 2372. Names unknown.

1132 William[6] Emery (*Samuel*,[5] *Jonathan*,[4] *James*,[3] *Jonathan*,[2]
John[1]), son of Samuel and Deidamia (Johnston) Emery; married,
Dec. 1, 1833, in Clinton, Me., Julia Ann Reynolds (born in Clinton,
June 6, 1813). He died in Fairfield, Jan. 17, 1866. She married, sec-
ond, in Augusta, Me., Nov. 16, 1872, John H. Weeks.
　　Children :

2373　i　William Gardiner,[7] b. Nov. 11, 1834, in Clinton, Me.
2374　ii　Lucy Jane, b. Dec. 7, 1836, in Clinton, Me.; m. Geo. Packard,
　　　　　　Nov. 28, 1854, in Augusta, Me.; farmer. He d., *s. p.*, in Fair-
　　　　　　field, Me., April 19, 1855. She d. in N. H., Sept. 22, 1857.
2375　iii　Daniel Webster, b. Oct. 24, 1839, in Phippsburg, Me.
2376　iv　Esther Davis, b. July 4, 1841, in Phippsburg, Me.
2377　v　Freeman Henry, b. Nov. 8, 1844; m. Josephine Robinson (b.
　　　　　　Feb. 10, 1862), in Clearfield, Pa., Dec. 25, 1880; enrolled as
　　　　　　private in Co. "C", 19th Regt. Me. Vol. Inf., July 30, 1862;
　　　　　　wounded at Gettysburg; transferred to Co. "F", 11th Regt.
　　　　　　V. R. C.; appointed Corporal of Color Guard of his Regt.
　　　　　　July 18, 1864; discharged July 8, 1865. Res. in Phillips-
　　　　　　burgh, Pa.
2378　vi　George Evans, b. Aug. 19, 1846, in Phippsburg, Me.
2379　vii　Mary Emma, b. Oct. 1, 1849, in Phippsburg, Me.

2380   viii MATILDA HELEN, b May 21, 1852; m. Preston Eldridge in
         Bellows Falls, Vt., May 21, 1873 (b. in Clinton, Me , May
         8, 1841); d in Seward, Neb , June 30, 1878, s p
2381   ix HOLLIS CAMPBELL, b Jan 3, 1854 in Augusta, Me
2382   x   CHARLES, b. Oct. 3, 1856, in Fairfield, Me.

1133 BUTLER ABBOT[6] EMERY (*Samuel,[5] Jonathan,[4] James,[3] Jona-
than,[2] John[1]*), son of Samuel and Deidamia (Johnston) Emery, mar-
ried in Fairfield. Me , Apr. 14, 1834, Mary Gibson (born in Fairfield,
Oct. 24, 1815). He died Feb. 23, 1873, in Fairfield. Lumberman.
His widow lives in Fairfield
   Children, born in Fairfield :

2383   i   MATILDA,[7] b. Jan 26, 1835, d , unm , Aug 24, 1851, in Fairfield
2384   ii ISRAEL MANUEL, b Oct. 4, 1836, lives at Walnut Creek, Contra
          Costa Co , Cal , unm
2385   iii JANE HELEN, b Dec. 21, 1837, d Dec 6, 1842, in Fairfield.
2386   iv PHŒBE ANN, b June 26, 1841
2387   v   MARY HELEN, b Dec. 19, 1846; d., unm., Dec. 10, 1869

1135 JOHN J.[6] EMERY (*Samuel,[5] Jonathan,[4] James,[3] Jonathan,[2]
John[1]*), son of Samuel and Deidamia (Johnston) Emery; married,
March 20, 1833, in Fairfield, Miranda S Deering (born in Gorham,
Oct. 14, 1814), of Gorham, Me. Selectman of Fairfield, Me , nine
years. Representative, 1850 , lived in Fairfield and Waterville, Me ,
and Turner's Falls, Mass.
   Children, born in Fairfield, Me. :

2388   i   ZENORA A ,[7] b April 7, 1834.
2389   ii   ERASTUS F , b Aug 20, 1835.
2390   iii MARTHA E , b April 12, 1837
2391   iv   SAMUEL D , b Nov 18, 1838
2392   v   MARY F., b. Aug 24, 1840 , unm
2393   vi   JOHN WARD, b. March 19, 1843.
2394   vii MIRANDA S , b Nov 22, 1844, d July 29, 1845.
2395   viii FANEUIL HALL, b March 29, 1846
2396   ix   HOWARD G , b April 2, 1848; d. June 14, 1869, unm
2397   x   KATE I , b Nov 13, 1849
2398   xi   LESLIE A , b April 22, 1852
2399   xii FLORENCE M , b. March 7, 1854; m. Franklin A Packard, Sept.
           17, 1883, in Boston, Mass.
2400   xiii JESSIE F , b in Waterville, March 4, 1856. Prin of Teachers
           Training School, Pawtucket, R I. , unm

1136 LUCY[6] JOHNSTON EMERY (*Samuel,[5] Jonathan,[4] James,[3] Jonathan,[2] John[1]*), daughter of Samuel and Deidamia (Johnston) Emery ;
married, April 21, 1831, Elisha Parkhurst, of Unity. Me. (born June
26, 1766 , died, in Unity, Sept. 30, 1859). She died March 17, 1836.
   Children :

2401   i   MARY LOUISA[7] b April 2, 1832, d Feb 27, 1833
2402   ii HON ELISHA EMERY, b Jan 26, 1834, in Dresden, Me.
2403   iii SAMUEL BUTLER, b. Aug 6, 1835, in Dresden, Me.

1137 SAMUEL[6] EMERY (*Samuel,[5] Jonathan,[4] James,[3] Jonathan,[2]
John[1]*), son of Samuel and Deidamia (Johnston) Emery , married
in Phippsburg, June 12, 1838, Frances A. Oliver, (born in Phipps-
burg, Me., May 7, 1821) , soldier in Company " D," Twenty-first
Regiment, Maine Vol Inf. in the war of the Rebellion and died in
Chelsea, Me., Feb. 16, 1889.

Children :

 2404 i PAULINA D.,[7] b. Jan. 6, 1840, in Phippsburg.
 2405 ii AUGUSTUS F., b. March 19, 1843, in Phippsburg.
 2406 iii RICHARD O., b. May 17, 1845, in Fairfield.
 2407 iv ALWILDA E., b. Aug. 31, 1847, in Fairfield.
 2408 v THOMAS L., b. Oct. 13, 1849, in Phippsburg.
 2409 vi ESTHER L., b. April 1, 1855, in Phippsburg.

1138 GEORGE BEAL[6] EMERY (*Samuel*,[5] *Jonathan*,[4] *James*,[3] *Jonathan*,[2] *John*[1]), son of Samuel and Deidamia (Johnston) Emery ; married, first, in Dresden, Me., April 22, 1834, Abigail Hondlett (born in Dresden, Me., Jan. 31, 1812; died in Fairfield, April 27, 1867). He married, second, Mrs. Caroline H. Wyman (*née* Fogg), Dec. 9, 1869 (born in Buckston, Me.) ; carpenter and lumberman in Fairfield.

Children, born in Fairfield :

 2410 i PRESTON M.,[7] b. March 24, 1836.
 2411 ii ANNE E., b. Jan. 19, 1838.
 2412 iii WILLIAM H., b. Nov. 5, 1839; m. Ellen C. Lawrence, in Fairfield, March 24, 1867 (born in Fairfield, July 5, 1846); enlisted in Co. "C," 19th Regt. Maine Vol. Inf., June 25, 1862; appointed corporal; promoted sergeant; promoted second lieutenant Dec. 29, 1863; first lieutenant Jan. 10, 1864; in action first and second battles of Fredericksburg, Gettysburg, Buell's Station, Wilderness, Mine Run and other battles; wounded at Gettysburg and also in another battle; postmaster of Fairfield sixteen years; register of deeds for Somerset Co., Me.
 2413 iv GEORGE F., b. Nov. 8, 1841.
 2414 v MARIA A., b. April 12, 1843.
 2415 vi PARTHENIA H., b. Jan. 14, 1845; m. Ed. C. Lowe, Nov. 26, 1870, in Waterville, Me. (b. in Waterville, 1839); druggist in Westboro, Mass.
 2416 vii ELIJAH B., b. June 21, 1846.
 2417 viii JANE A., b. April 17, 1848.
 2418 ix WILLIS C., b. Dec. 15, 1853.

1139 DEIDAMIA P.[6] EMERY (*Samuel*,[5] *Jonathan*,[4] *James*,[3] *Jonathan*,[2] *John*[1]), daughter of Samuel and Deidamia (Johnston) Emery ; married, first, in Dixmont, Me., Feb. 21, 1835, Fred. Tyler, who died June 18, 1836, *s. p.* ; second, in Fairfield, Nov. 28, 1839, Joseph Emery, son of Briggs H. and Sally (Farnham) Emery.

Children :

 2419 i
 2420 ii } (see Nos. 2297–2299.)
 2421 iii

1140 DARIUS[6] BALLARD EMERY (*Samuel*,[5] *Jonathan*,[4] *James*,[3] *Jonathan*,[2] *John*[1]), son of Samuel and Deidamia (Johnston) Emery ; married in Blythe Island, Wayne County, Ga., Jan. 16, 1867, Winifred P. Smith (born in Hayward County, N. C., June 29, 1835). He was a bridge-builder ; lived in Brunswick, Ga., and died in Wayne County, Ga., Aug. 20, 1882. His wife died in Waycross, Ga., Jan. 4, 1878.

Children, born in Brunswick, Ga. :

 2422 i THOMAS S.,[7] b. March 2, 1868 ; d. July, 1869.
 2423 ii NELLIE PAULINE, b. Feb. 8, 1870 ; teacher in Georgia.
 2424 iii MABEL R., b. Oct. 25, 1873.
 2425 iv KATE, b. Aug. 9, 1875.

1141 THANKFUL CAIN[6] EMERY (*Samuel,[5] Jonathan,[4] James,[3] Jonathan,[2] John[1]*), daughter of Samuel and Deidamia (Johnston) Emery; married in Oldtown, Me, March 16, 1837, Richard Burnham (born in Scarboro, Me., Aug. 25, 1813) ; lumberman.
Children, born in Oldtown

2426	i	JOSEPHINE A ,[7] b Dec 13, 1837
2427	ii	CHARLOTTE FRANCES, b Jan 16, 1840, d., in Oldtown, Aug 29, 1841
2428	iii	RICHARD DARIUS, b Aug 31, 1842, first corporal, Co " E," 7th Regt Me Vol Inf ; enlisted 1861, d , unm , in Oldtown, Me , Jan. 17, 1882
2429	iv	SARAH FRANCES, b June 4, 1844
2430	v	INFANT DAUGHTER. b and d , 1848
2431	vi	HORACE MANN, b Oct 16, 1849

1142 PAULINA[6] EMERY (*Samuel,[5] Jonathan,[4] James,[3] Jonathan,[2] John[1]*), daughter of Samuel and Deidamia (Johnston) Emery, married in Fairfield, Me., May 24, 1835. John Deering (born in Scarboro, Me., Oct. 19, 1806), lived in Fairfield and died there, Jan. 9, 1859.
Children, born in Fairfield :

2432	i	ELLEN,[7] b June 7, 1837
2433	ii	CHARLES SAWYER, b April 1, 1839.
2434	iii	ISABEL FRANCES, b April 23, 1841; unm.
2435	iv	ARIANNA, b March 28, 1844
2436	v	MARY LOUISA, b. June 30, 1853, unm.

1143 BRIGGS H.[6] EMERY (*Samuel,[5] Jonathan,[4] James,[3] Jonathan,[2] John[1]*), son of Samuel and Deidamia (Johnston) Emery, married, in Fairfield, Oct. 13, 1847, Sarah Marshall Woodsum (born in Waterborough, Me., April 7, 1826). He was accidentally killed in California, while engaged in mining, March 3, 1857. His widow married, second, Jesse B Nye. Dec. 14, 1857.
Child, born in Fairfield :

2437	i	WALTER SCOTT,[7] b June 3, 1850, d March 30, 1857

1144 THOMAS JEFFERSON[6] EMERY (*Samuel,[5] Jonathan,[4] James,[3] Jonathan,[2] John[1]*), son of Samuel and Deidamia (Johnston) Emery, married. in Fairfield. Oct 28, 1856, Julia Maria Poor (born in Belfast, Me , March 5. 1838), civil engineer; lives in Waterville, Me
Children :

2438	i	CARRIE M ,[7] b Oct. 16, 1859, d March 10, 1860. in Fairfield
2439	ii	HERBERT LINCOLN, b. March 16, 1861, in Fairfield, m Sarah Leslie Davies in Sidney, Me , Dec. 5, 1883 (b in Sidney, Jan 11. 1859), merchant in Farmington. Me , *s p*
2440	iii	FANNY ADELE, b. in Fairfield, Dec. 15, 1863, d April 28, 1877, in Waterville.
2441	iv	CHARLES POOR, b Jan 14, 1875, drowned in Waterville, July 30, 1886

1145 PARTHENIA DURRELL[6] EMERY (*Samuel,[5] Jonathan,[4] James,[3] Jonathan,[2] John[1]*), daughter of Samuel and Deidamia (Johnston) Emery; married Robert Hannah and died in Boston, Mass., Feb 14, 1850.
Children .

2442 i CHILD,[7] d. young.
2443 ii CHILD, d. young.

1147 DRUSILLA[6] DURRELL (*Rachel*,[5] *Jonathan*,[4] *James*,[3] *Jona-than*,[2] *John*[1]), daughter of John and Rachel (Emery) Durrell; married John Mills (born in Clinton, Me.); lived in Clinton and Skowhegan, Me.; both died in Skowhegan.
Children :
2444 i OBED.[7]
2445 ii RACHEL, m. Captain Cutler, U. S. Volunteers. She d. in Lewiston, Me., *s. p.*
2446 iii SYLVIA, b. in Skowhegan.
2447 iv BOARDMAN.
2448 v FAREWELL, d. in California.
2449 vi OLIVER, soldier in an Ill. Regt., in the war of the Rebellion.
2450 vii AMANDA, d. in Lewiston, Me.

1148 OBED[6] DURRELL (*Rachel*,[5] *Jonathan*,[4] *James*,[3] *Jonathan*,[2] *John*[1]), son of John and Rachel (Emery) Durrell; married Betsey Starkey; merchant and lived in Vassalboro, Detroit, Bangor and Old-town, Me.; representative to Maine legislature two terms. He died in Oldtown, Me. She died in Vassalboro, Me.
Children :
2451 i GEORGE,[7] orderly of General McClellan's bodyguard; cashier.
2452 ii HELEN A., d. young.

1149 PARTHENIA[6] DURRELL (*Rachel*,[5] *Jonathan*,[4] *James*,[3] *Jona-than*,[2] *John*[1]), daughter of John and Rachel (Emery) Durrell; married Daniel Wells (born in Clinton, Me., Feb. 17, 1804). She died, 1830.
Child :
2453 i ZENOBIA,[7] b. June 26, 1826; m. Harford Merrow, 1847. He was b. In Waterville, Me., 1818; lives in Hartland, Me., *s. p.*

1151 RACHEL P.[6] DURRELL (*Rachel*,[5] *Jonathan*,[4] *James*,[3] *Jona-than*,[2] *John*[1]), daughter of John and Rachel (Emery) Durrell; married in Palmyra, Me., July, 1831, Daniel Wells. She died in Clinton, Jan. 12, 1866; lived in Clinton, Me.
Child, born in Clinton :
2454 i ROYAL,[7] b. Feb. 16, 1833; m. Martha B. Pratt, May 13, 1855 (b. in Clinton, Feb. 26, 1836); farmer in Pishon's Ferry, Me.

1153 BARRON E. H.[6] DURRELL (*Rachel*,[5] *Jonathan*,[4] *James*,[3] *Jona-than*,[2] *John*[1]), son of John and Rachel (Emery) Durrell; married Judith Currier. Mill owner and merchant. Lived in Carmel, Salem, Dexter, Hodgdon and Houlton, Me.
Children :
2455 i ALBERT,[7] accidentally killed when five years of age.
2456 ii MARY,[7] m. Benj. Bassey, M.D., of Houlton, Me.

1154 ELKANAH H.[6] DURRELL (*Rachel*,[5] *Jonathan*,[4] *James*,[3] *Jona-than*,[2] *John*[1]), son of John and Rachel (Emery) Durrell; married, March 30, 1838, Susan Parker.
Children, born in Skowhegan :

2457 i   Parthenia,[7] b. Feb. 13, 1840, m Stetson Bowman, Sept 13, 1860
2458 ii Samuel, b July 3, 1842; m George Littlefield, Nov 23, 1867
2459 iii Adaline P , b March 5, 1845; m Simeon Sawyer, Dec 18, 1868.
2460 iv Flora L , b Oct. 31, 1854, m Hiram Warner, Dec 30, 1880
2461 v   Clara, b Jan. 27, 1861, m Charles Green, Feb 26, 1879

1157 George W.[6] Durrell (*Rachel,*[5] *Jonathan,*[4] *James,*[3] *Jonathan,*[2] *John*[1]), son of John and Rachel (Emery) Durrell, married Sept., 1843, Rose A. Cleveland (born Nov. 19, 1821, died Sept. 3, 1883). Children, born in Skowhegan

2462 i   Helen A.,[7] b. June 23, 1844, m Herbert T Jewett
2463 ii   Lucia S , b. April 20, 1347, m Eugene L Williams, Oct 31, 1875 in Providence, R 1 , where he is a merchant, *s p*
2464 iii John S , b. May 19, 1848; m Ida M Fletcher, Sept 6, 1871
2465 iv   Mary B , b. Jan 2, 1851, m Horace E Parlin, Nov 26, 1872, R R engineer, Bangor, Me
2466 v   Rose E , b June 15, 1852, m. Augustus J Sawyer, June 24, 1872
2467 vi   James C , b Oct 15 1854, m Elizabeth M Whitney, July 16, 1874
2468 vii George A , b Oct 5, 1856, d Sept , 1861
2469 viii Stephen C , b Oct 18, 1858, m. Flora A Bacon, May 7, 1886, Providence, *s p*
2470 ix   Elmer E , b. April 5, 1860, m. Harriet F Moses, Sept. 17, 1884. Clerk in Minneapolis, Minn , *s. p.*

1158 Marcia O [6] Durrell (*Rachel,*[5] *Jonathan,*[4] *James,*[3] *Jonathan*[2] *John*[1]), daughter of John and Rachel (Emery) Durrell ; married Levi Parker who died on a steamer from Panama, 1849. She died in Skowhegan.
Children :

2471 i   Ruby,[7] m John Elwood Wyman , 2nd, Arthur Mathews
2472 ii Elvira, m. William Hall, a lawyer. They live in Richmond, Me

1162 Gilbert[6] Emery (*Samuel,*[5] *Anthony,*[4] *James,*[3] *Jonathan,*[2] *John*[1]), son of Samuel and Sally (Densmon) Emery; married at Sodus Point, N. Y , ———.
Child ·

2473 i   William [7]

1163 Lewis[6] Emery (*Samuel,*[5] *Anthony,*[4] *James,*[3] *Jonathan,*[2] *John*[1]), son of Samuel and Sally (Densmon) Emery : married in Lyons, N Y., Nov. 28, 1826, Maria Gilson (born Feb. 2, 1809). With his father, in 1817, he removed to Ohio and was apprenticed to a woolen manufacturer and learned the trade ; returned to Sodus Point, N Y , and after marriage settled in Junius, N Y. , removed to Alloway, Wayne Co., N. Y , in 1829 ; to Villanova, Chaut. Co., N Y., in 1832 , and afterwards to Cherry Creek, followed his trade from 1826 to 1840 when he contracted to build several miles of the Erie R R , and 1841, he built two miles of the Erie Canal and in both instances failed to get his pay ; later he removed to Michigan and established a woolen manufactory at Jonesville, Hillsdale Co.. and carried on a large and profitable business ; in 1848 he built a second factory and bought a large farm near Hillsdale ; in 1864 sold his factory and his farm and settled in Hillsdale, where he died, Aug. 21, 1886.

Children :

2474   i   SARAH JANE,[7] b. Dec. 12, 1827, in Junius, N. Y.; m. Wesley Lockwood; d. 1853.
2475   ii CLARISSA, b. Aug. 22, 1829, in Junius, N. Y.; d. 1835.
2476   iii MARIA, b. Sept. 25, 1831, in Alloway, N. Y.; d. 1853, Hillsdale, Mich.
2477   iv GRANGER G., b. in Villanova, Chaut. Co., N. Y., July 22, 1833; d. 1847.
2478   v   OLIVER G., b. in Villanova, Chaut. Co., N. Y., Aug. 22, 1835.
2479   vi DAVID, b. in Cherry Creek, Chaut. Co., N. Y., Sept. 7, 1837.
2480   vii LEWIS, JR., b. in Cherry Creek, Chant. Co., N. Y., Aug. 10, 1839.

1167 JAMES ST. CLAIR[6] EMRIE (*John*,[5] *Ambrose*,[4] *James*,[3] *Jonathan*,[2] *John*[1]), son of John and Margaret (Ross) Emrie; married in New York City, Ann Skedmore. Tanner and sailor; U. S. soldier during the Mexican War; settled in California where he probably died.

Child :

2481   i   LYDIA,[7] b. in New York City.

1168 JUDGE JEHU[6] AMBROSE EMRIE (*John*,[5] *Ambrose*,[4] *James*,[3] *Jonathan*,[2] *John*[1]), son of John and Margaret (Ross) Emrie; married in Hillsboro, O., April 2, 1825, Harriet Stout (born in Flemingsburg, Ky., Feb. 23, 1805). Cabinet maker; hotel keeper; merchant; government officer in the Internal Revenue Service; lived in Hillsboro, O., and Cochran, and Anrora, Ind. Mayor of Aurora four years and filled other public offices; called Judge from having been judge of Probate Court of Dearborn Co., Ind.; died in Aurora, March 24, 1875. His wife died July 12, 1881.

Children :

2482   i   MARGARET ANN,[7] b. Dec. 31, 1825.
2483   ii SARAH JANE, b. Oct. 4, 1827; d. Nov. 2, 1842, in Aurora, Ind.
2484   iii JOHN STOUT, b. June 23, 1831.
2485   iv MARY LOUISA, b. Nov. 13, 1833.
2486   v   JAMES SAMUEL, b. April 8, 1836; d. Aug. 28, 1836.
2487   vi GEORGE SMITH, b. April 11, 1839, in Aurora, Ind.
2488   vii CURTIS KELSEY, b. Aug. 21, 1841, in Aurora, Ind.

1170 FRANCES ELINOR[6] EMRIE (*John*,[5] *Ambrose*,[4] *James*,[3] *Jonathan*,[2] *John*[1]), daughter of John and Margaret (Ross) Emrie; married Robert Holliday; lived near Logansport, Ind.

Children :

2489   i   CREIGHTON.[7]
2490   ii ROBERT.
2491   iii JAMES.
2492   iv MARGARET.
2493   v   MARY ANN.

1172 SARAH HARE[6] EMRIE (*John*,[5] *Ambrose*,[4] *James*,[3] *Jonathan*,[2] *John*[1]), daughter of John and Margaret (Ross) Emrie; married, Jan. 6, 1831, Benjamin Chaney (born 1806; died Aug. 6, 1884).

Children, born in Hillsboro :

```
2494   i    MARGARET 7
2495   ii   BENJAMIN FRANKLIN
2496   iii  SALLY MARY, m Geo W Boies, who was in the U. S. N. seven
            years, County Clerk of Highland Co , O
2497   iv  ⎫
2498   v   ⎪
2499   vi  ⎬ Names unknown
2500   vii ⎪
2501   viii⎭
2502   ix   ORISSA BELLE.
```

1173 HON. JONAS REECE⁶ EMRIE (*John*,⁵ *Ambrose*,⁴ *James*,³ *Jonathan*,² *John*¹), son of John and Margaret (Ross) Emrie ; married, first, Nov. 12, 1835, Rebecca Edwards Marshall (born in N J , March 12, 1816 , died Jan. 26, 1846)   He married, second, in Cincinnati, O., Nov. 18, 1847, Emma Longwell   Printer, editor, lawyer ; member of the Ohio Senate, 1848 , Judge of the Probate Court of Highland Co., 1851–1854 ; elected Representative to U. S Congress, 1854 ; in company with his brother, Benjamin Chaney, edited and published the *Hillsboro Gazette* 1839–1841 , was editor and publisher of this paper 1841–1848 and 1854–1856 ; leader in organizing the Hillsboro Female College ; removed in 1857 to Mound City, Ill. , conducted the *Emporium* newspaper and engaged in mercantile business.   Police magistrate of the city, Township Treasurer of shools ; Master in Chancery of Pulaski Co., Ill. ; widely known as Judge Emrie, a lawyer of integrity and ability, a citizen of influence and virtue, a gentleman of intelligence and high social standing ; died in Mound City, June 5, 1869   His widow died Nov. 11, 1873

Children, by first wife, born in Hillsboro .

```
2503   i    JOHN MARSHALL,⁷ b Nov 7, 1836
2504   ii   LLEWELLYN REECE, b Nov  11, 1838, m. Sarah Carter in Pad-
            ucah, Ky , 1863   Union soldier, printer and editor , d in
            Mound City, May 8, 1863, s p
2505   iii  CLARA ESTHER, b Oct 13, 1840
2506   iv   MARY REBECCA, b April 6, 1842.
2507   v    SARAH LUVENIA, b March 4, 1844 : m William Sprague of Al-
            leghany City, Pa., in Mound City, Ill , Dec 26, 1865 (b. in
            Pittsburg, Pa , April 23, 1836), served in U. S N three years
            of the Rebellion as first Asst Engineer on U S Gunboat,
            Red Rover , received an honorable discharge at the time of
            his marriage
2508   vi   MARGARET EDWARDS, b. Jan 15, 1846, d. in infancy.
```

Children by second marriage :

```
2509   vii  ELLA E., b. Sept 9, 1848, in Hillsboro, O
2510   viii FRANCES A , b April 8, 1850, in Hillsboro, O
2511   ix   OLLIE M , b Sept 24, 1853, d in infancy
2512   x    JUSTIN R , b , 1855, in Hillsboro.
2513   xi   HARRIET BANKS, b Feb 7, 1856, d in Mound City, 1858.
2514   xii  LELIA LINCOLN, b. Feb 22, 1861, in Mound City
2515   xiii JAY REECE, b., 1864, in Mound City, Ill
```

1176 CLEMENTINE⁶ EMERY (*Samuel*,⁵ *Ambrose*,⁴ *James*,³ *Jonathan*,² *John*¹), daughter of Samuel and Sarah (Anderson) Emery ; married

March 31, 1836, Daniel Emry (born in Sugar Valley, Pa., Sept. 2, 1806), who was of German descent and not related to his wife's family; lived near New Market, O. His wife died April 29, 1841. He died May 3, 1848.

Children, born in New Market:

2516　i　FRANCIS M.,[7] b. March 10, 1838.
2517　ii　NANCY, b. Oct. 6, 1839.

1177 AMBROSE[6] EMERY (*Samuel*,[5] *Ambrose*,[4] *James*,[3] *Jonathan*,[2] *John*[1]), son of Samuel and Sarah (Anderson) Emery; married, in Hillsboro, O., July 9, 1835, Sarah Mullinix (born in Charleston, W. Va., March 12, 1817). Farmer.

Children, born near Danville, O.:

2518　i　CLEMENTINE,[7] b. March 26, 1836.
2519　ii　MARY ANN, b. May 14, 1837.
2520　iii　SARAH CATHARINE, b. Oct. 1, 1838.
2521　iv　SAMUEL C., b. Jan. 9, 1841; d. Nov. 30, 1856.
2522　v　NANCY E., b. March 17, 1844.
2523　vi　NATHANIEL, b. June 10, 1846; d. July 8, 1861.
2524　vii　WILLIAM GADDES, b. Sept. 26, 1848.
2525　viii　MARGARET JANE, b. Sept. 17, 1851.
2526　ix　JOHN WESLEY, b. March 6, 1854.
2527　x　GEORGE W., b. Feb. 26, 1859; d. Nov. 8, 1863.

1178 MARY[6] EMERY (*Samuel*,[5] *Ambrose*,[4] *James*,[3] *Jonathan*,[2] *John*[1]), daughter of Samuel and Sarah (Anderson) Emery; married, March 22, 1844, in Highland Co., O., George Morris. She died Sept. 7, 1846, in Paulding Co., O. He was born March 3, 1822.

Child:

2528　i　DAVID HENRY,[7] b. near New Market, O., March 7, 1845.

1180 ISABEL[6] EMERY (*Samuel*,[5] *Ambrose*,[4] *James*,[3] *Jonathan*,[2] *John*[1]), daughter of Samuel and Sarah (Anderson) Emery; married John Kinner (born Sept. 30, 1808), Nov. 24, 1850; lived in Defiance and Arthur, O., and died Sept. 29, 1889.

Children:

2529　i　SAMUEL P.,[7] b. June 21, 1852, in Higgensport, O.; d. in Paulding Co., O., Jan. 28, 1874, unm.
2530　ii　JOHN H., b. Aug. 21, 1854, in Higgensport; m. Cora E. Hall, Nov. 6, 1887.
2531　iii　JACKSON D., b. Nov. 13, 1856, in New Market, O.
2532　iv　AMBROSE M., b. July 10, 1858, in New Market, O.; m. Katie Boutwell, Nov. 20, 1870; farmer in Arthur.

1181 JOHN[6] EMERY (*Samuel*,[5] *Ambrose*,[4] *James*,[3] *Jonathan*,[2] *John*[1]), son of Samuel and Sarah (Anderson) Emery; married, near New Market, O., March 25, 1852, Barbara Emry (born March 27, 1833), niece of Daniel Emry (who married Clementine, No. 1176).

Children, born near New Market, O.:

2533　i　DR. WILLIAM H.,[7] b. March 10, 1853.
2534　ii　SAMUEL N., b. Sept. 19, 1854; d. July 30, 1860.
2535　iii　JESSE R., b. June 26, 1856.
2536　iv　AMBROSE W., b. March 11, 1858; d. Oct. 2, 1861.

2537 v SARAH I , b June 24, 1860, d May 29, 1861.
2538 vi NANCY A., b April 22, 1862, m., in Mt Sterling, O , W. H
        Snyder, Sept 23, 1888 (b in Mt Sterling, March 10, 1841),
        merchant in Mt Sterling
2539 vii PHŒBE E , b Feb 23, 1864
2540 viii ORISSA J , b Nov 28, 1866
2541 ix MAGNOLIA E , b Feb 13, 1874
2542 x CORA E , b June 1, 1876

1182 ELIZABETH⁶ EMERY (*Samuel,⁵ Ambrose,⁴ James,³ Jonathan,² John¹*), daughter of Samuel and Sarah (Anderson) Emery , married George Rex (born April 6, 1813, in Westmoreland, Pa), Dec 30, 1848   She was his second wife   The first wife was her cousin, Elizabeth Kennedy. Lived in Cross Plains, Versailles and Rexville, Ind.; Alexandria, Canton and Palmyra, Mo ; enlisted in the Union army at Kahoka, Mo , Dec. 4, 1861; served as hospital steward till his death in Palmyra, Mo., Sept. 21, 1863 ; she served as matron in the U. S. hospitals from June, 1861, to May, 1863.
Children :

2543 i SARAH SAMANTHA,⁷ b Aug 25, 1850, in Versailles Ind
2544 ii REBECCA OLIVE, b Sept. 25, 1852 in Rexville, Ind
2545 iii SAMUEL WATSON, b Oct 16, 1854, in Versailles, Ind , d March
        8, 1862, in Alexandria, Mo
2546 iv JOHN EMERY, b Dec 7, 1856, in Ashton, Mo , bookkeeper,
        Denver, Col , unm
2547 v NANCY ISABEL, b Jan 22, 1859, in Ashton Mo
2548 vi JAMES ISADORE, b Oct 4, 1861, in Clark City, Mo

1183 SAMUEL⁶ EMERY, JR (*Samuel,⁵ Ambrose,⁴ James,³ Jonathan,² John¹*), son of Samuel and Sarah (Anderson) Emery ; married, in Danville, O., July, 1850, Harriet Chaplain   He died in Missouri, Nov. 22, 1872 ; wagon maker and farmer.
Children, born in Danville :

2549 i NANCY SOPHIA,⁷ b April, 1851, m Noah Workman, of Prince-
        ton, O
2550 ii JOHN FRANK, b April 15, 1854
2551 iii WILLIAM SHANNON, b Nov.. 1858
2552 iv SARAH B , b Jan 29, 1864

1184 SARAH⁶ EMERY (*Samuel,⁵ Ambrose,⁴ James,³ Jonathan,² John¹*), daughter of Samuel and Sarah (Anderson) Emery ; married, Jan 12, 1862, Patrick H. Hobbs (born in Hillsboro, O., April 15, 1826) ; lives in Folsom, O.
Children, born in Sugartree Ridge, O. :

2553 i SARAH ISABEL ⁷ b Sept 3, 1863, unm
2554 ii MARY ELIZABETH, b Nov 11, 1864, d Dec 8, 1865

1186 RICHARD ANDERSON⁶ EMERY (*Samuel,⁵ Ambrose,⁴ James,³ Jonathan,² John¹*), son of Samuel and Sarah (Anderson) Emery ; married, Dec. 15, 1850, Mary Ann Larrick (born in Belfast, O , April 2, 1830). Farmer ; lives at Winkle, O.
Children :

2555 i SARAH ELLEN,⁷ b. Sept 29 1852, in New Market.
2556 ii JAMES FRANK, b. Nov 10, 1854, in New Market.

2557   iii   OLIVER SYLVESTER, b. Sept. 26, 1857, in Sugartree Ridge, O.;
                unm.
2558   iv   MARY ELIZABETH, b. May 2, 1863, in Buford, O.; unm.
2559   v   MARTHA JANE, b. Oct. 1, 1866, in Sugartree Ridge; unm.

1188 REBECCA[6] KENNEDY (*Clementine,[5] Ambrose,[4] James,[3] Jonathan,[2] John[1]*), daughter of Samuel and Clementine (Emery) Kennedy;
married in Cross Plains, Ind., July 12, 1849, James McGee (born in
Winchester, W. Va., May 14, 1817; died March 16, 1881); merchant.
Resides in Cross Plains.
    Children, born in Cross Plains:

2560   i   MARY A.,[7] b. May 1, 1850; m. Sam. Johnson, Feb. 16, 1881.
2561   ii   ISABEL CLEMENTINE, b. Oct. 5, 1851; d. Nov. 20, 1866.
2562   iii   SARAH ELIZABETH, b. Aug. 9, 1853; m. Dr. R. H. Miller, Nov.
                28, 1878.
2563   iv   ELIZA CATHERINE, b. Jan. 11, 1856; m. N. H. Conyers, Nov.
                27, 1879.
2564   v   JAMES A. K., b. Dec. 8, 1859; unm.

1189 CATHARINE[6] KENNEDY (*Clementine,[4] Ambrose,[4] James,[3] Jonathan,[2] John[1]*), daughter of Samuel and Clementine (Emery) Kennedy; married, Oct. 14, 1838, Joseph Arford (born March 26, 1814).
Farmer.   Resides in Friendship, Ind.
    Children:

2565   i   REBECCA E.,[7] b. Aug. 25, 1839, in Greene Co., Pa.; m. W. H.
                Howell, Dec. 24, 1868.
2566   ii   PHŒBE, b. Nov. 9, 1840, in Greene Co., Pa.; unm.
2567   iii   SUSANNA M , b. Oct. 14, 1842, in Greene Co., Pa.; m. W. W.
                Palmer, Oct. 16, 1864.
2568   iv   SAMUEL K., b. May 31, 1844; enlisted at Farmer's Retreat, Ind.,
                Aug., 1862, in Co. "B," 83rd Regt., Ind. Vol. Inf.; mustered
                in U. S. Service, Aug. 11, 1862; d. on steamer Sioux City, at
                Young's Point, La., Jan. 19, 1863; unm.
2569   v   JAMES R., b. March 16, 1846, Ripley Co., Ind.; m. Mary E. Hig-
                bee, March 14, 1867; enlisted as private in 2nd Ind. Battery,
                Oct. 9, 1864; in battle of Nashville; discharged in Indianap-
                olis, July 3, 1865.
2570   vi   MORDICA M., b. Feb. 12, 1848; d. Feb. 26, 1848, Ripley Co.,
                Ind.
2571   vii   JOHN K., b. April 7, 1851; m. Virginia Pate, Jan. 18, 1874.
2572   viii   CLEMENTINE, b. July 24, 1853, in Ripley Co., Ind.; m. Fred
                Tegner, Aug. 6, 1873.
2573   ix   LOUIS G., b. March 26, 1855, in Ripley Co., Ind.; unm.

1190 RACHEL[6] KENNEDY (*Clementine,[5] Ambrose,[4] James,[3] Jonathan,[2] John[1]*), daughter of Samuel and Clementine (Emery) Kennedy;
married in Highland Co., O., May 22, 1844, Louis Gibler.
    Children, born in Highland Co., O.:

2574   i   SOBISCA J.,[7] b. March 24, 1845; m. W. L. Anderson, May 27,
                1880.
2575   ii   ORLANDO, b. Nov. 25, 1846; m. Sarah Vaughn, Sept. 30, 1873.
2576   iii   JOSEPH A., b. Sept. 16, 1851; d. Sept. 13, 1881; unm.
2577   iv   OLIVE E., b. May 2, 1859; m. Robert C. Vance, Oct. 23, 1881.

1191 ELIZABETH[6] KENNEDY (*Clementine,[5] Ambrose,[4] James,[3] Jonathan,[2] John[1]*), daughter of Samuel and Clementine (Emery) Kennedy;

married March 18, 1844, George Rex, and died July 18, 1848, in Boone Co., Ky.

Children ·

2578 i WILLIAM H.,[7] b March 7, 1845, Aurora, Ind ; m Mary E Ivie, Dec 31 1875, stock raiser and farmer; private in Co "F," 21st Mo Inf , June 8, 1861, corporal in 1861, in battles of Iuka, Holly Springs, Corinth and others in '62, discharged for disability in Nov , '62, reenlisted as private in Co "C," 3rd Mo Cav , Feb. 4, 1864, mustered out at New Orleans, La., July 27, 1865.

2579 ii SAMUEL, d in infancy

2580 iii LOUISA T , b Nov 7, 1847, d in Alexandria, Mo, March 8, 1862.

1192 EMERY[6] KENNEDY (*Clementine,[5] Ambrose,[4] James,[3] Jonathan,[2] John[1]*), son of Samuel and Clementine (Emery) Kennedy, married, in Gallatin Co , Ky., Dec. 29, 1851, Mary Roberts; enrolled as a private in Co. "B," 30th Kentucky Mounted Infantry, Aug. 12, 1863 , mustered in the United States Service, Feb. 19, 1864, at Frankfort, Ky.; mustered out, April 18, 1865 ; died in Cincinnati, O., May 21, 1882.

Children, born in Gallatin Co , Ky

2581 i CLEMENTINE E ,[7] b Aug 19, 1853 lives in Cincinnati, O ; unm

2582 ii GEORGE R., b Sept. 27, 1855, m Sarah Scroggin, Feb 25, 1886 (b May 13, 1865), in Owentown, Ky

2583 iii JAMES, d in infancy

2584 iv REBECCA M , b Aug 7, 1859 , d in Cross Plains, Ind , unm , May 26, 1881.

2585 v THOMAS

1194 PHŒBE[6] EMERY (*Jonas,[5] Ambrose,[4] James,[3] Jonathan,[2] John[1]*), daughter of Jonas and Susan (Morris) Emery ; married, in Greene Co , Pa , March 23, 1833, Joseph Millikin (born in Greene Co. and died Sept. 14, 1854). She died May 8, 1836.

Child :

2586 i MARY A [7] b in Cumberland township, Greene Co , Pa , March 16, 1834, m Samuel Crea, in Greene Co , Feb 10, 1877 (b. July 27, 1833, farmer in Toulon, Stark Co.. Ill.), *s p*

1195 REBECCA[6] EMERY (*Jonas,[5] Ambrose,[4] James,[3] Jonathan,[2] John[1]*), daughter of Jonas and Susan (Morris) Emery ; married, Dec., 1832, in Greene Co , Pa , Thomas Lucas, where he was born, 1812 , farmer , sheriff of Greene Co. He died in Reneck, Mo., 1867 She died at Clear Springs, Texas Co., Mo , Sept 20, 1884.

Children, born in Carmichaels, Greene Co , Pa. :

2587 i MARY,[7] b. 1833 ; m William Ashburn.

2588 ii PHŒBE E , b. Sept 18, 1836, m James J Flynn in Greene Co , Pa , March 11, 1866 He was born in Meath Co., Ireland, June 5, 1831, merchant in Pittsburgh, Pa ; died there May 31, 1870. Res Peck, Kan ; *s p*

2589 iii MARTHA, b March 14, 1838, m Adam Seese.

2590 iv THOMAS BENTON, b May 7, 1840, is married and lives in Judson, Mo.

2591 v   SOLOMON M., b. March 12, 1842; m.; deputy sheriff of Greene
          Co., Pa.
2592 vi CASSANDRA M., b. Sept. 1, 1847; m. Geo. Edw. Howe.
2593 vii JONAS EMERY, b. April 28, 1850; unm.
2594 viii JAMES LINDSEY, b. June 12, 1856; d. in Ackworth, Iowa, March
          14, 1875; unm.

1196 CATHARINE[6] EMERY (*Jonas,*[5] *Ambrose,*[4] *James,*[3] *Jonathan,*[2]
John[1]), daughter of Jonas and Susan (Morris) Emery ; married, first,
in Pa., Oct., 1834, George Litzenburgh (born in Washington Co., Pa.,
Dec. 25, 1808 ; lived in Greene Co., Pa. ; died in Licking Co.. O.,
April 16, 1844). She married. second, in Pa., Sept. 28. 1847, Swan
Lucas. He was a brother of Thomas Lucas who married Rebecca
Emery April 27, 1805. He was the widower of Pamelia Emery and
died in Warren Co., Ia., Nov. 12, 1881.

Children, by first husband, born in Greene Co., Pa.

2595 i   CHARLOTTE,[7] b. Sept. 1, 1835; d. in Knox Co., O., May 24, 1841.
2596 ii JOHN, b. Sept. 12, 1838; Union soldier; killed in battle, Oct.
          4, 1862; unm.
2597 iii SUSAN E., m. —— Sarazin and lives in St. Louis, Mo.

Children, by second husband :

2598 iv MARTHA PAMELIA, b. in Tyler Co., W. Va., March 14, 1848; d.
          in Warren Co , Iowa, June 12, 1865; unm.
2599 v   BENJAMIN FRANKLIN, b. in Tyler Co., W. Va., July 26, 1850;
          m. Lillian Elvira Haynes in Warren Co., Iowa, Nov. 26, 1874
          (b. in Ohio, Sept. 5, 1855); farmer; lives in Indianola, Iowa.
2600 vi WILLIAM PIERCE, b. in Tyler Co., W. Va., June 27, 1852; m.
          Effie Maria Bundy in Warren Co., Iowa, Jan 18, 1874 (b. in
          Warren Co., April 25, 1858); lives in Indianola, Iowa; farmer.
2601 vii MARY CATHARINE, b. in Greene Co., Pa., Oct. 15, 1854; m.
          George A. Bundy, brother of Effie Maria Bundy, in Warren
          Co., Ia., March 20, 1873; live in Atkinson, Neb.

1197 PAMELIA[6] EMERY (*Jonas,*[5] *Ambrose,*[4] *James,*[3] *Jonathan,*[2]
John[1]), daughter of Jonas and Susan (Morris) Emery ; married in
Greene Co., Pa., Sept. 26, 1833, Swan Lucas. She died in Greene
Co., Jan. 17, 1847.

Children :

2602 i   JAMES,[7] b. Jan. 6, 1840; enlisted in Co. "I" 8th Regt. Pa. Re-
          serve Corps in May, 1861. Killed in the battle of the Wilder-
          ness, May 6, 1864.
2603 ii SUSANNAH, b. May 6, 1842; m. James Dabley in Washington
          Co., Pa., Dec. 19, 1865; d. Dec. 26, 1867.
2604 iii SARAH, m. John Crawford, and lives in Indianola, Iowa.
2605 iv JONAS EMERY, banker in Central City, Neb., Union soldier.
2606 v   THOMAS, farmer in Central City, Neb., Union soldier.
2607 vi CHARLES, banker in Central City, Neb., Union soldier.

1200 JAMES[6] EMERY (*Jonas,*[5] *Ambrose,*[4] *James,*[3] *Jonathan,*[2]
John[1]), son of Jonas and Susan (Morris) Emery ; married in Greene
Co., Pa., Aug. 31, 1851, Margaret Ann Major. She was born in
Washington Co., Pa., Nov. 8, 1828.

Children, born in Washington Co., Pa. :

2608 i   JONAS WILLIAM,[7] b. Aug. 4, 1852.

2609 ii SUSAN CECELIA, b. March 8, 1854, d Nov. 14, 1875, unm.
2610 iii CELENA, b. Sept. 21, 1855
2611 iv JAMES C , b April 30, 1857, d , unm., Sept 4, 1883
2612 v BENJ FRANKLIN b Jan 31, 1860, merchant in Cannousburgh, Pa , unm
2613 vi EBEN, b Aug 6, 1862; clerk in store in Pittsburgh, Pa ; num
2614 vii CORA PATTERSON, b April 17, 1865, unm
2615 viii ELLA MAY, b. Aug 17, 1869, unm
2616 ix LUCY RODGERS, b June 3, 1871.
2617 x LESTER, b June 13, 1873

1201 JONAS[6] EMERY, JR. (*Jonas,[5] Ambrose,[4] James,[3] Jonathan,[2] John[1]*), son of Jones and Susan (Morris) Emery, married Mary C. Seaton (born in Greene Co., Pa., April 20, 1828).   Resides in Whiteley, Pa
Children, born in Greene Co , Pa. :

2618 i SARAH ELIZABETH,[7] b Jan 31, 1854
2619 ii MARGARET ELLEN, b Nov 25, 1861.

1202 JOHN[6] EMERY (*Ambrose,[5] Ambrose,[4] James,[3] Jonathan,[2] John[1]*), son of Ambrose and Mary (Anderson) Emery, married, first, in Coshocton Co , O., Dec. 25, 1834, Alcinda Hayes (born in Fauquier Co , Va , July 24, 1813 ; died in Scotland, Ind , May 18, 1859) , second, in Greene Co , Ind , Dec. 22, 1859, Mrs. Alletta Ann Wells (*née* Burgess) He died in Koleen, Ind., May 10, 1888. He was thoroughly educated and from choice made teaching his calling ; taught in Ohio and in the public schools of Indiana for more than thirty years Justice of the Peace and the legal authority of his townsmen, a man of wide information and universally respected and honored.
Children :

2620 i MARY,[7] b. Oct. 23, 1835, in Pike Township, Coshocton Co , O
2621 ii SARAH A D , b Sept 25 1837, in same place.
2622 iii CHARLES ANDERSON, b March 14, 1839, in same place.
2623 iv HARRIET E , b Nov 19, 1841, in same place
2624 v THOMAS B , b Nov 16, 1844, in same place, Union soldier in Co. "E," 97th Regt Ind Inf , mustered in Oct 16 1862, was in the Vicksburg Campaign and battle of Jackson, Miss , d in Camp Sherman on Big Black River, Aug 28, 1863
2625 vi WILLIAM AMBROSE, b May 15, 1847, in Pike Tp , Coshocton Co , O
2626 vii DAVIS BENJ , b Sept 9, 1850, in Greene Co , Ind.
2627 viii ELLEN R , b Oct 23, 1854, in Greene Co , Ind
2628 ix LORENZO NELSON, b 1860, in Greene Co , Ind ; d 1861
2629 x CLEMENTINE PAMELIA, b 1864, in Greene Co , Ind.
2630 xi WALTER M , b 1867, in Greene Co , Ind , farmer.
2631 xii SCHUYLER C , b 1869, in Greene Co , Ind
2632 xiii SUSAN VIOLA, b 1870, in Greene Co , Ind
2633 xiv NATHANIEL, b 1872, d 1876 in Greene Co , Ind.

1206 REBECCA[6] EMERY (*Ambrose,[5] Ambrose,[4] James,[3] Jonathan,[2] John[1]*), daughter of Ambrose and Mary (Anderson) Emery ; married in Coshocton Co., Oct 14, 1841, Benj. John Meredith (born in Coshocton Co., O , Oct. 12, 1822) , removed from Ohio to Ind., 1848. She died in Cincinnati, Ind., Feb. 23, 1890.

8

Children :

2634　i　AMBROSE EMERY,[7] b. Oct. 10, 1842, in Coshocton Co., O.
2635　ii　WILLIAM ADAMS DAVIS, b. Oct. 27, 1846, in Coshocton Co., O.
2636　iii　DR. SAMUEL GILBERT, b. Dec. 18, 1851, in Greene Co., Ind.
2637　iv　JOHN WALTER JONAS, b. June 2, 1855, in Greene Co., Ind.
2638　v　FRED. ALONZO LORENZO, b. Jan. 31, 1858, in Greene Co., Ind.
2639　vi　SARAH J. CELESTINE, b. Feb. 18, 1862, in Greene Co., Ind.; m. Jan. 11, 1883, in Greene Co., Ind., Jacob Floyd (b. in Greene Co., Feb. 5, 1859; carpenter; res. Hobbieville, Ind., s. p.).

1207 AMBROSE[6] EMERY, JR. (*Ambrose,*[5] *Ambrose,*[4] *James,*[3] *Jonathan,*[2] *John*[1]), son of Ambrose and Mary (Anderson) Emery; married in Coshocton Co., Ohio, May 10, 1847, Ann V. Hayes (born in Fauquier Co., Va., Nov. 28, 1825; died Nov. 16, 1886). Teacher and farmer. He died Nov. 22, 1856.

Children, born in Greene Co., Ind. :

2640　i　CATHARINE,[7] b. April 30, 1849.
2641　ii　ELIZABETH, b. Nov. 9, 1851; d. unm.
2642　iii　ELIZA A., b. Dec. 25, 1853.
2643　iv　LAVINIA F., b. Dec. 28, 1855.

1208 WILLIAM SPENCER[6] EMERY (*Ambrose,*[5] *Ambrose,*[4] *James,*[3] *Jonathan,*[2] *John*[1]), son of Ambrose and Mary (Anderson) Emery; married in Bloomfield, Ind., June 17, 1847, Marcia Hill (born April 29, 1825). Union soldier, Sergeant in Co. "E", 59th Regt. Ind. Inf., died in hospital, St. Louis, Mo., Aug. 28, 1862; gallant soldier; teacher.

Children, born in Greene Co., Ind. :

2644　i　WILLIAM NOBLE,[7] b. May 4, 1848.
2645　ii　JOHN WESLEY, b. Dec. 6, 1849, in Bloomfield.
2646　iii　SAMUEL RICHARD, b. March 4, 1851; d. March 17, 1863.
2647　iv　SARAH ANN, b. July 3, 1853; d. Oct. 10, 1854.
2648　v　MARY MABEL, b. Feb. 10, 1855; d. Feb. 2, 1882, unm.
2649　vi　CLEMENTINE JOSEPHINE, b. Nov. 30, 1857.
2650　vii　LITTLE BERRY, b. Sept. 25, 1859.
2651　viii　MINA MARCIA, b. Sept. 23, 1862.

1209 MARY ANN[6] EMERY (*Ambrose,*[5] *Ambrose,*[4] *James,*[3] *Jonathan,*[2] *John*[1]), daughter of Ambrose and Mary (Anderson) Emery; married in Coshocton Co., O., Nov. 26, 1846, Daniel Ashcraft (born in Dresden, O., Sept. 9, 1823). Farmer.

Children, born in Owensburg, Ind. :

2652　i　WILLIAM JASPER,[7] b. Aug. 21, 1848.
2653　ii　DANIEL BOONE, b. July 8, 1851.
2654　iii　AMBROSE WAYNE, b. June 12, 1854.
2655　iv　MARY ELIZ., b. June 28, 1857.
2656　v　SARAH, b. April 20, 1860; d. May 7, 1865.
2657　vi　SEYMOUR, b. Jan. 16, 1863.
2658　vii　ROBERT, b. April 25, 1866; d. Nov. 11, 1866.
2659　viii　AGNES, b. Aug. 14, 1868; m. Charles Fox, July 4, 1889.
2660　ix　NOAH, b. March 25, 1872.

1210 CLEMENTINE[6] EMERY (*Ambrose,*[5] *Ambrose,*[4] *James,*[3] *Jonathan,*[2]

John[1]), daughter of Ambrose and Mary (Anderson) Emery, married, first, in Greene Co , Ind., Eli Adams (born in Tennessee, May 10, 1810 , died Nov. 16, 1862 , farmer). She married, second, April 1, 1866, C. A. Meredith (born in Coshocton Co., O., Aug 9, 1827 , died Sept 13, 1866). She died Oct. 18, 1866

Child :

2661   i   HARRIET ERELDA,[7] b Feb 9, 1853, in Greene Co , Ind

1211 NATHANIEL[6] EMERY (*Ambrose*,[5] *Ambrose*,[4] *James*,[3] *Jonathan*,[2] *John*[1]), son of Ambrose and Mary (Anderson) Emery ; married in Greene Co , Ind , Nov. 15. 1855, Susan McWhirter (born Sept. 28, 1835) , farmer. Soldier in Co. " G," 149th Regt. Ind. Inf , enlisted at Terre Haute, Ind , Feb 5, 1865 , mustered in at Indianapolis, Ind., Feb. 22, 1865 , discharged on account of disability incurred in the line of duty, May 15, 1865.

Children, born in Greene Co , Ind. :

2662   i   JONES ADEN,[7] b Nov 8, 1856.
2663   ii   MARY ELIZ , b Sept 7, 1858, d July 14, 1878, unm.
2664   iii JESSE WALKER, b April 16, 1861
2665   iv   CHARLES SIGEL, b Jan 5, 1863
2666   v   INFANT SON, b. Dec 21, 1864, d Dec. 24, 1864
2667   vi   HARVEY NATHANIEL, b Jan 18, 1869.
2668   vii ROBERT LUCAS, b Jan 7, 1872; d. May 21, 1878.
2669   viii LILLY VICTORIA, b Aug 10, 1874.

1219 JAMES[6] EMERY (*Robert S.*,[5] *Edward*,[4] *James*,[3] *Jonathan*,[2] *John*[1]), son of Robert S and Temperance (Matthews) Emery ; married, first, in Philadelphia, Pa , Amanda Fowler (born in England, died in Augusta, Me.) ; second, Nancy Hall of Bowdoinham, Me. (born in Bowdoinham, Aug 18, 1823). He died April 22, 1883. James Emery followed the seas over thirty years, three years of this time on a man-of-war and the rest of the time on a merchantman, was first mate part of the time, and captain of a merchantman several years.

Children, born in Vassalboro. Me.

2670   i   JAMES E ,[7] b Dec 1, 1841; m Cynthia H Tobey, 1859.
2671   ii   ELIZA J , b. Dec 4, 1842
2672   iii GEORGE H , b July 1, 1844, d., unm , May 4, 1867, sailor and
             soldier in service of U S
2673   iv   ISADORE, b. April 13, 1855, m in Augusta, Me , Dec 18, 1884,
             Alexander J Cameron (b in Aberdeen, Scotland, Sept 15,
             1852, bookbinder in Augusta).

1220 MELINDA[b] EMERY (*Robert S.*,[5] *Edward*,[4] *James*,[3] *Jonathan*,[2] *John*[1]), daughter of Robert S and Temperance (Matthews) Emery ; married, Nov , 1835, Thaddeus Snell (born in Vassalboro, Me., 1799, died June 28, 1881). She died Sept 14, 1884.

Children :

2674   i   HOWARD H ,[7] b June 27, 1836, in Augusta, Me ; farmer in
             Riverside, Me. , unm
2675   ii   HORACE, b July 26, 1838, in Augusta, Me
2676   iii HANNAH R , b Nov 19, 1841, in Vassalboro, Me , unm
2677   iv   HESTER J , b March 25, 1844, in Vassalboro, Me , unm

1221 EUNICE S.[6] EMERY (*Robert S.*,[5] *Edward*,[4] *James*,[3] *Jonathan*,[2] *John*[1]), daughter of Robert S. and Temperance (Matthews) Emery; married in 1829, Edward Snell (died in Riverside, Me., 1857). She died there April 1, 1886.

Children, born in Vassalboro, Me. :

2678 i   CYNTHIA R.,[7] b. Sept. 10, 1830; unm., in Riverside, Me.
2679 ii CHARLES E., b. June 15, 1832; d. Feb., 1833.
2680 iii HELEN M., b. Dec. 27, 1833.
2681 iv ANNE H., b. April 28, 1836; unm., in Riverside, Me.
2682 v CAROLINE H., b. July 15, 1839; unm., in Riverside, Me.

1222 ISAIAH[6] EMERY (*Robert S.*,[5] *Edward*,[4] *James*,[3] *Jonathan*,[2] *John*[1]), son of Robert and Temperance (Matthews) Emery; married in Augusta, Me., March 17, 1831, Sabrina Babcock (born in Augusta, Mar. 12, 1812; died in China, Me., May 22, 1853). He died June 14, 1854. Was in the Aroostook war, 1839.

Children, born in Augusta :

2683 i   ROBERT S.,[7] b. March 16, 1832; d. in Lincoln, Me., June 14, 1854; unm.
2684 ii LAFAYETTE, b. in 1834; d. in infancy.
2685 iii AMANDA F., b. Dec. 8, 1836.
2686 iv JAMES S., b. Feb. 16, 1839; m. Susan Louisa Hatch, Nov. 29, 1883; enlisted in U. S. N., Aug. 1, 1864; was on the U. S. steamer Ino, Wilkes Squadron and the East Gulf Squadron, U. S. ship San Jacinto.
2687 v EUNICE S., b. June 27, 1841.
2688 vi GEORGE A., b. April 21, 1843.
2689 vii MERCY S. STACKPOLE, b. April, 1845; d. in Oct., 1845.
2690 viii FRANKIE (daughter), b. Oct. 11, 1852.
2691 ix ALBERT L., b. March 15, 1855, in China, Me.

1223 GEORGE A.[6] EMERY (*Robert S.*,[5] *Edward*,[4] *James*,[3] *Jonathan*,[2] *John*[1]), son of Robert S. and Temperance (Matthews) Emery; married in Fairfield, Me., Dec. 2, 1832, Mary Libby (born in Gardiner, Me., May 26, 1816). Farmer; lived in Fairfield, Me., 1816–1850; removed to Lycoming Co., Pa., and afterward to Lock Haven, Pa.

Children, born in Fairfield, Me. :

2692 i   GEORGE MELVIN,[7] b. Feb. 22, 1834; lumberman and commercial traveller; mustered into U. S. service in company "D," 1st Regt. Pa. Cav., Aug. 11, 1861; promoted sergeant Sept. 25, 1862; mustered out Sept. 9, 1864; also served in 15th Regt. Pa. Reserve Corps; engaged at Cedar Mountain, Shepherdstown and other battles.
2693 ii JOHN CLEVELAND, b. Aug. 18, 1836.
2694 iii THANKFUL B., b. Oct. 16, 1838; d. Nov. 12, 1838.
2695 iv BENJAMIN LIBBY, b. May 2, 1840.
2696 v ORLANDO H., b. June 29, 1842.
2697 vi COL. JAMES MANLEY, b. Jan 1, 1845.
2698 vii SILAS WRIGHT, b. Sept. 1, 1846; accidentally killed in a saw mill in Tangascootac, Pa., April 8, 1859.
2699 viii JOSEPH LIBBY, b. March 2, 1848.

1224 HAMILTON[6] EMERY (*Robert S.*,[5] *Edward*,[4] *James*,[3] *Jonathan*,[2] *John*[1]), son of Robert S. and Temperance (Matthews) Emery; married Oct. 16, 1834, Emily Buck of Fairfield, Me. (born in Fairfield Jan. 18, 1816; died Sept. 30, 1888). He died Jan. 18, 1843.

Children, born in Fairfield, Me. :

2700　i　ALBERT,[7] b May 3, 1836; d. Dec. 31, 1887.
2701　ii　JANE E , b. Aug. 14, 1838.
2702　iii　JOHN H , b Jan 31, 1840
2703　iv　FANNIE E , b Jan 26, 1842; m Joseph Foster, May 24, 1882, in Vassalboro, Me.

1247 ASA S.[6] EMERY (*David,[5] Edward,[4] James,[3] Jonathan,[2] John[1]*), son of David and Mary (Cooly) Emery ; married Alma Ann Philbrick (born Sept 11, 1832 ; died Nov 27, 1871), daughter of Samuel Philbrick of Skowhegan, Me. She was in the eighth generation in lineal descent from the "Emigrant" Thomas Philbrick who came to America between 1630 and 1636.
Child .

2704　i　DAUGHTER [7]

1249 AMBROSE[6] EMERY (*Edward,[5] Edward,[4] James,[3] Jonathan,[2] John[1]*), son of Edward and ——— (Myrick) Emery ; lives in Enfield, Me
Child :

2705　i　EDWARD [7]

1256 ABRAM[6] PUSHOR (*Priscilla,[5] Edward.[4] James,[3] Jonathan,[2] John[1]*), son of Peter and Priscilla (Emery) Pushor ; married Martha St. Clair of Prince Edward's Island. He died in Plymouth, Me., 1883
Children :

2706　i　PETER,[7] lives in Bath, Me.
2707　ii　ANN,[7] m ———Trueworthy and lives in Newport, Me

1257 AMOS[6] PUSHOR (*Priscilla,[5] Edward,[4] James,[3] Jonathan,[2] John[1]*), son of Peter and Priscilla (Emery) Pushor; married Mahala Rogers of Cambridge, Me.
Child .

2708　i　SON [7]

1260 MARGARET[6] PUSHOR (*Priscilla,[5] Edward,[4] James,[3] Jonathan,[2] John[1]*), daughter of Peter and Priscilla (Emery) Pushor , married in Hartland, Me., in 1816, Uriah Spearin (born April 7, 1793). He died in 1865. She died Dec. 9, 1865.
Children .

2709　i　JOSEPH [7]
2710　ii　DAVID, lives in Plymouth, Me
2711　iii　WILLIAM W., lived in Tunbridge, Vt
2712　iv　WALDO.
2713　v　JOHN.
2714　vi　BETSEY, m William Richards
2715　vii　RACHEL
2716　viii　PRISCILLA, b May 30, 1825 , m Nathan W Crookson, June 17, 1842; live in Pittsfield, Me

1266 LYDIA HALE[7] EMERY (*John,[6] Daniel,[5] John,[4] John,[3] John,[2]*

John¹), daughter of John and Susannah (Bartlett) Emery ; married Benjamin Smith ; removed to Ohio, 1827 ; died Aug. 6, 1867.
Children, born in Danville, Vt. :

    2717 i   STEPHEN,⁸ b. May 20, 1806.
    2718 ii   ELVIRA, b. May 5, 1808.
    2719 iii SUSAN, b. Nov. 13, 1809.
    2720 iv   EMILY, b. May 29, 1816.
    2721 v   ISAAC, b. May 1, 1818.
    2722 vi   BENJAMIN, b. Oct. 19, 1821.

1267 DR. JOHN⁷ EMERY (*John,⁶ Daniel,⁵ John,⁴ John,³ John,²
John¹*), son of John and Susannah (Bartlett) Emery ; married, first, in Harpersfield, O., July 4, 1816, Elizabeth Wheeler (born in Harpersfield, Dec. 7, 1796) ; second, in Talmage, O., June 6, 1830, Ann Walcott (born in Farmington, Conn., May 16, 1797 ; died in Byron, O., July 21, 1881). He was paymaster in the war of 1812, and died in Swanton, Ohio, Nov. 2, 1862.
Children, by first wife, born in Harpersfield :

    2723 i   SUSAN,⁸ b. Sept. 9, 1817; d. Sept. 9, 1817.
    2724 ii   JOHN, b. May 7, 1819; d. Sept. 2, 1819.
    2725 iii AARON W., b. Dec. 17, 1821; d. Dec. 17, 1821.
    2726 iv   MARGARET, b. Oct. 20, 1823.
    2727 v   SAMUEL, b. Jan. 2, 1826.
    2728 vi   SOLON, b. Dec. 10, 1827; d. Aug. 16, 1828.

By second wife :

    2729 vii   ELIZABETH, b. July 17, 1831, in Wadsworth, O.
    2730 viii HENRIETTA, b. April 22, 1833.
    2731 ix   JOHN W., b. March 4, 1835; m. Emma E. Shepler, Jan. 14, 1866.
    2732 x   RUSH, b. May 2, 1838, in Swanton, O.

1269 ALPHIA BARTLETT⁷ EMERY (*John,⁶ Daniel,⁵ John,⁴ John,³
John,² John¹*), daughter of John and Susannah (Bartlett) Emery ; married Dec. 5, 1816, in Lyndon, Vt., Harlow Bailey, who was born in Winstead, Conn., June 19, 1792 ; died in Madison, O., Feb. 11, 1880.
Children, born in Madison, except the first :

    2733 i   JOHN EMERY,⁸ b. Sept. 30, 1817, in Burke, Vt.
    2734 ii   ALANSON, b. Oct. 23, 1821; m. F. E. Bond, Oct. 23, 1862.
    2735 iii CAROLINE E., b. Dec. 17, 1823.
    2736 iv   HARLOW, b. Aug. 7, 1826; d. Oct. 18, 1844.
    2737 v   DANIEL EMERY, b. May 18, 1830.
    2738 vi   EDWIN JOSIAH BARTLETT, b. Feb 10, 1835; d. Aug. 31,1837.

1270 HENRIETTA⁷ EMERY (*John,⁶ Daniel,⁵ John,⁴ John,³ John,²
John¹*), daughter of John and Susannah (Bartlett) Emery ; died Oct. 19, 1825 ; married William Beach.
Children :

    2739 i   SAMUEL.⁸
    2740 ii ERASMUS.

1271 JOSIAH BARTLETT⁷ EMERY (*John,⁶ Daniel,⁵ John,⁴ John,³
John,² John¹*), son of John and Susannah (Bartlett) Emery. Phy-

sician in Carrolton, Carrol Co., O. ; died in Ridgeville Corners, Henry Co , O., Feb. 24, 1884 ; married, 1821, Lucinda Goold (born July 31, 1806). She died Nov. 7, 1861.

Children :

2741 1 ROBERT G ,[3] b Sept 24, 1825.
2742 11 DANIEL, b March 23 1827.
2743 111 SUSANNAH, b Nov. 5, 1828
2744 IV SAMUEL, b Oct 27, 1830
2745 v MARGARET A , b July 29, 1832
2746 VI JOSIAH B , b. July 19, 1834
2747 VII LUCINDA, b Oct 26, 1836
2748 VIII WILLIAM G , b Nov 24, 1837.
2749 IX JAMES A , b Oct. 30, 1840.
2750 x JOHN G , b Feb 4, 1843
2751 XI JOSEPH S , b Dec 29, 1844
2752 XII HENRIETTA E , b. Jan 4, 1848; d Aug. 26, 1861

1274 ANN POOR[7] LITTLE (*Mehetable,*[6] *Samuel.*[5] *John,*[4] *John* [3] *John,*[2] *John*[1]), daughter of Ezekiel and Mehetable (Emery) Little , married Jan. 18, 1837, Rev. Jesse Page. She died Dec. 8, 1846. He died Mar. 2, 1888 ; was a graduate of Dartmouth College, 1831 , Andover Theological Seminary, 1835 , ordained Sept. 9, 1835 ; had charge of churches in North Andover and Atkinson, N. H.

Children :

2753 1 MARY ANN,[8] Nov 30, 1839
           Three sons died in infancy.

1278 HANNAH[7] EMERY (*Jacob,*[6] *Rev. Jacob,*[5] *Joseph.*[4] *Joseph,*[3] *John.*[2] *John*[1]), daughter of Jacob and Hannah (Noyes) Emery , married Dec. 25, 1828, John B. Paine (born Sept. 4, 1803 , died Aug. 9, 1881, aged 77).

Children :

2754 1 JOHN KELLY,[8] b Dec 12, 1829
2755 11 ELIZABETH ANN, b Dec 23, 1831, d April 29, 1855
2756 111 CHARLES LEWIS, b May 12, 1834 , d June 10, 1840
2757 IV RUFUS HOSMER, b. April 8, 1836
2758 v WILLIAM DRAPER, b March 17, 1838 , m Mary Springer
2759 VI MARY SARGENT, b Feb 1, 1841, d. Feb 13, 1859
2760 VII JOSEPH HARVEY, b July 2, 1843, d Nov 9, 1860
2761 VIII CHARLES HENRY, b. Oct. 7, 1848

1279 MARY[7] EMERY (*Jacob,*[6] *Rev Jacob,*[5] *Joseph,*[4] *Joseph,*[3] *John,*[2] *John*[1]), daughter of Jacob and Hannah (Noyes) Emery ; married Stephen Chickering of Pembroke, N. H., Oct., 1831. She died March 30, 1863.

Children :

2762 1 JOHN,[8] b. June 25, 1832, d Oct 18, 1851.
2763 11 JACOB EMERY, b. Aug 30, 1833
2764 111 MARY ANN, b May 23, 1835, d Sept 6, 1853
2765 IV CHARLES, b Nov 12, 1836, d Nov 13, 1836
2766 v JESSE, b Jan 23, 1838, d Feb 22, 1860
2767 VI EDWIN, b July 5, 1839.
2768 VII BETSIE, b July 10, 1841.
2769 VIII JABEZ, b Feb 20, 1843
2770 IX EBEN BAILEY, b Aug. 10, 1845, d April 20, 1866
2771 x SARAH HAZELTINE, b Sept 7, 1849

1280 BENJAMIN N.[7] EMERY (*Jacob,[6] Rev. Jacob,[5] Joseph,[4] Joseph,[3] John,[2] John[1]*), son of Jacob and Hannah (Noyes) Emery; married Hannah T. Hayes (born March 31, 1814). He died April 1, 1873.

Children :

   2772 i   THOMAS,[8] b. June 7, 1837; m. Sarah Adams.
   2773 ii CHARLES, b. June 17, 1840.

1281 JACOB[7] EMERY (*Jacob,[6] Rev. Jacob,[5] Joseph,[4] Joseph,[3] John,[2] John[1]*), son of Jacob and Hannah (Noyes) Emery; married July 13, 1841, Mary Smith (born in Candia, N. H., Jan. 7, 1816).

Children :

   2774 i   MARY ETTA,[8] b. June 5, 1842.
   2775 ii GEORGE S., b. Dec. 5, 1847; m. Hannah E. Sargent of Orford, N. H., May 31, 1879.

1282 SUSAN[7] EMERY (*James C.,[6] Rev. Jacob.[5] Joseph,[4] Joseph,[3] John,[2] John[1]*), daughter of James C. and Olive (Pettingill) Emery; married William B. Paine.

Children :

   2776 i   WILLIAM H.,[8] b. May 17, 1828.
   2777 ii CHARLES EMERY, b. Jan. 29, 1830.
   2778 iii JAMES EMERY, b. April 11, 1832.
   2779 iv HARRIET MARIA, b. Oct. 10, 1834.
   2780 v   ALBERT DRAPER, b. Sept. 7, 1838; enlisted in 5th Wis. Regt.; was twice taken prisoner; was eleven months in Castle Thunder, Richmond, and exchanged when almost starved to death.
   2781 vi JOHN CUSHING, b. June 1, 1840; was killed in battle on the Little Blue, Oct., 1864; corporal of Co. "M," 11th Kansas.
   2782 vii SUSAN LORINDA, b. Sept. 2, 1843.

1283 SETH[7] EMERY (*James C.,[6] Rev. Jacob,[5] Joseph,[4] Joseph,[3] John,[2] John[1]*), son of James C. and Olive (Pettingill) Emery; born April 1, 1804; married Lorinda H. Ames, May 1, 1834.

Children :

   2783 i   SUSAN M.,[8] b. June 10, 1835.
   2784 ii JAMES R., b. July 15, 1837.
   2785 iii HARLAN P., b. March 19, 1839.
   2786 iv AUGUSTUS P., b. May 22, 1842.
   2787 v   LAURA J., b. Jan. 4, 1850.
   2788 vi MILTON G., b. Feb. 19, 1852.

1285 PHŒBE[7] EMERY (*Joseph,[6] Joseph,[5] Joseph,[4] Joseph,[3] John,[2] John[1]*), daughter of Joseph and Dorcas (Holt) Emery; married Charles K. Williams, Dec. 11, 1817; died Oct. 18, 1818.

Child :

   2789 i   CHILD,[8] d. in infancy.

1286 SALLY[7] EMERY (*Joseph,[6] Joseph,[5] Joseph,[4] Joseph,[3] John,[2] John[1]*), daughter of Joseph and Dorcas (Holt) Emery; married John Buss, 1810.

Children :

2790　i　SARAH [8]
2791　ii　ELVIRA
2792　iii　ELIZABETH.
　　　　There was probably another dau , Ella Appleton, who m
　　　　Stephen Webster.

1287 DORCAS[7] EMERY (*Joseph*,[6] *Joseph*,[5] *Joseph*,[4] *Joseph*,[3] *John*,[2] *John*[1]), daughter of Joseph and Dorcas (Holt) Emery ; married John Parker (born May 20, 1783). She was his second wife and died September, 1852. His first wife died in 1824.
　Children :

2793　i　ESTHER MELANDE,[8] b　June, 1827, d　Sept 3, 1829
2794　ii　EMILY, b. May 22, 1829
2795　iii　JOSEPH E , b　Nov , 1830; d　Aug., 1835
2796　iv　ESTHER M., b. Aug., 1832

1289 HANNAH[7] EMERY (*Joseph*,[6] *Joseph*,[5] *Joseph*,[4] *Joseph*,[3] *John*,[2] *John*[1]), daughter of Joseph and Dorcas (Holt) Emery ; married Dec　22, 1824, Stephen Bates　He died in Pembroke, N. H., Sept. 20, 1872, aged 88.　His wife died May 6, 1883, aged 87.
　Children .

2797　i　CHARLES T ,[8] b　Sept 17, 1825, in Dunstable, Mass.
2798　ii　STEPHEN A , b　March 20, 1829
2799　iii　ANNE M., b. Feb. 2, 1835, d , unm , Sept 4, 1870

1290 NABBY (ABIGAIL)[7] EMERY (*Joseph*,[6] *Joseph*,[5] *Joseph*,[4] *Joseph*,[3] *John*,[2] *John*[1]), daughter of Joseph and Dorcas (Holt) Emery ; married Charles K. Williams ; died Jan. 1, 1860.
　Children :

2800　i　CHARLES,[8] b　Sept　16, 1826; m , 1st, Orinthea Greer; 2nd, Elizabeth Buss.
2801　ii　PHŒBE ANN, b. June 1, 1829.

1291 JOSEPH[7] EMERY (*Joseph*,[6] *Joseph*,[5] *Joseph*,[4] *Joseph*,[3] *John*,[2] *John*[1]), son of Joseph and Dorcas (Holt) Emery ; married Hannah Merrill of Epping, N　H., Feb. 16, 1829.
　Children :

2802　i　JOSEPH M ,[8] b　April 27, 1831
2803　ii　NATHANIEL B., b　April 19, 1834.
2804　iii　SARAH E , b　May 13, 1841. m. James W Hall, d　June, 1888, s p

1294 CLARISSA[7] EMERY (*Samuel*,[6] *Joseph*,[5] *Joseph*,[4] *Joseph*,[3] *John*,[2] *John*[1]), daughter of Samuel and Mary (McConnell) Emery ; married Feb　20, 1820, Samuel Gault (born June 9, 1797).
　Children :

2805　i　SAMUEL EMERY,[8] b　Oct　27, 1822, d. Dec. 15, 1858.
2806　ii　MARY ANN, b. Oct 25, 1829.

1302 SOPHIA[7] EMERY (*Jacob*,[6] *Joseph*,[5] *Joseph*,[4] *Joseph*,[3] *John*,[2] *John*[1]), daughter of Jacob and Jane (Gault) Emery , married Norris Cochran of Pembroke, N. H., Nov. 24, 1825.　He died Oct. 4, 1880. His wife died May 6, 1876.　Cattle drover and lumber dealer.

Children :

2807	i	DAUGHTER,[8] b. and d. Oct. 27, 1826.
2808	ii	EVANDER, b. Sept. 25, 1828 ; d. Jan. 12, 1830.
2809	iii	IRAD, b. Jan. 23, 1831.
2810	iv	ELIZABETH JANE, b. April 7, 1833.
2811	v	HANNAH BURGIN, b. Sept. 6, 1835.
2812	vi	NORRIS, JR., b. Nov. 27. 1838.
2813	vii	JACOB EMERY, b. Feb. 21, 1841 ; d. July 27, 1841.
2814	viii	SARAH HASELTINE, b. Feb. 12, 1845.

1303 JOHN BROWN[7] EMERY (*Jacob,*[6] *Joseph,*[5] *Joseph,*[4] *Joseph,*[3] *John,*[2] *John*[1]), son of Jacob and Jane (Gault) Emery ; married, first, Sept. 8, 1831, Mary A. McGrath, daughter of Richard and Mary McGrath (born in Baltimore, Md., Aug. 10, 1810 ; died, *s, p.,* Nov. 6, 1870) ; second, Oct. 24, 1871, Mary Virginia Nichols (born in Georgetown, D. C., Aug. 10, 1836 ; died in Baltimore, 1890), daughter of Samuel T. and Sarah Nichols.

Children :

2815	i	JOHN B.,[8] b. Aug. 3, 1872.
2816	ii	JENNIE, b. Aug. 29, 1874.
2817	iii	JESSIE, b. March 18, 1877.
2818	iv	HALL B., b. Aug. 8, 1879.

1304 CHARLES LONG[7] EMERY (*Jacob,*[6] *Joseph,*[5] *Joseph,*[4] *Joseph,*[3] *John,*[2] *John*[1]), son of Jacob and Jane (Gault) Emery ; married March 7, 1841, Elizabeth Watts of Baltimore, Md. He died in 1860.
Children :

2819	i	JACOB,[8] b. April 3, 1843 ; d. Aug. 25, 1864.
2820	ii	GEORGE W., b. Feb. 26, 1847 ; d. Dec. 5, 1865.
2821	iii	CHARLES L.. b. Nov. 9, 1849.
2822	iv	SOPHIA C., b. Aug. 30, 1852 ; d. 1870.
2823	v	HARRIET V., b. March 17, 1855 ; d. Oct. 6, 1874.
2824	vi
2825	vii

1305 ELIZABETH[7] EMERY (*Jacob,*[6] *Joseph,*[5] *Joseph,*[4] *Joseph,*[3] *John,*[2] *John*[1]), daughter of Jacob and Jane (Gault) Emery ; married Rodney M. Farnum, May 15, 1834 ; he died in Washington, D. C., 1862.
Children :

2826	i	JANE E.,[8] b. March 15, 1836, in Bow, N. H. ; m. John W. Rogers, May 31, 1855.
2827	ii	CHARLES R., b. Oct. 29, 1837 ; d. Feb. 27, 1841.
2828	iii	JACOB E., b. May 19, 1839 ; d. June 26, 1839.
2829	iv	JOHN, b. May 21, 1840 ; d. Feb. 23, 1841.
2830	v	CHARLES R., b. March 18, 1843 ; d. Sept. 29, 1843.
2831	vi	MARY S., b. Jan. 27, 1847.
2832	vii	JOHN E., b. Oct. 14, 1848.
2833	viii	NORRIS C., b. Aug. 23, 1850.
2834	ix	MATTHEW H., b. Sept. 17, 1852 ; d. July 13, 1853.
2835	x	WILLIAM G., b. May 9, 1855 ; d. July 24, 1855.
2836	xi	ELIZABETH JANE, b. July 29, 1857 ; d. June 30, 1859.

1306 SAMUEL[7] EMERY (*Jacob,*[6] *Joseph,*[5] *Joseph,*[4] *Joseph,*[3] *John,*[2] *John*[1]), son of Jacob and Jane (Gault) Emery ; married Mary G. Watts of Baltimore, Md., 1839. Dealer in brown stone and coal.
Children :

2837 i   ELIZABETH JANE,[8] b Nov 5, 1841
2838 ii   MARY JULIEI, b March 27, 1844
2839 iii HARRIET LOUISA, b Dec 2, 1846, d Dec. 13, 1846.
2840 iv   JOHN HALE, b Sept 3, 1848.
2841 v   SAMUEL, b July 20, 1851, m Amanda Sailor
2842 vi   SALLIE ARMITAGE, b Aug 12, 1860; d July 26, 1862
2843 vii JAMES ARMITAGE, b Aug 26, 1867

1307 MATTHEW GAULT[7] EMERY (*Jacob*,[6] *Joseph*,[5] *Joseph*,[4] *Joseph*,[3] *John*,[2] *John*[1]), son of Jacob and Jane(Gault) Emery; married, first, Dec 3, 1844, Juliet Day Weston of Va (born March 4 1825; died March 3, 1853) , second, April 3, 1854, Mary K Haseltine, No. 1318 (born April 27, 1854), daughter of Wm. and Nabby (Emery) Haseltine of Pembroke, N H Mr Emery is a merchant in Washington, D C ; was last mayor of the city and now president of 2nd National Bank. A business man of strict integrity, deeply interested in the prosperity of his city and supporter of all enterprises benefiting society and the church.

Children :

2844 i   CLARA KATE,[8] b March 15, 1851; m Gen S S Henkle, July
                 21, 1880
2845 ii   MATTHEW G , b Feb 18, 1855
2846 iii JULILI HASELTINE b Jan 21, 1858
2847 iv   WILLIAM R , b March 25, 1864, d April 25, 1864
2848 v   MARY ABBIE, b Oct 17, 1866

1308 JOSEPH STICKNEY[7] EMERY (*Jacob*,[6] *Joseph*,[5] *Joseph*,[4] *Joseph*,[3] *John*,[2] *John*[1]), son of Jacob and Jane (Gault) Emery , married, first, in San Francisco, Nov. 27, 1853, Mary Adele Andres of N. Y. ; second, Ella Andreas.

Children ·

2849 i   JOSEPH.[8]
2850 ii   JOHN
2851 iii ABBIE.
2852 iv   FANNY, m Fred E Fair of Oakland, Cal
2853 v   HENRY
2854 vi   SON, b 1879

1309 HALL BURGIN[7] EMERY (*Jacob*,[6] *Joseph*,[5] *Joseph*,[4] *Joseph*,[3] *John*,[2] *John*[1]), son of Jacob and Jane (Gault) Emery; married June 15, 1854, Ellen Osgood (born July 7, 1834 ; died May 27, 1859), daughter of John S. Osgood. Esq. , second, Sallie B. Head (born April 25, 1826 , died Sept 2, 1869), daughter of Col John Head of Hooksett, N. H. He died in Suncook, N. H , Sept 14, 1886.

Child :

2855 i   ORVILLE,[8] b. April 26, 1857, d. Feb 22, 1858

1319 POLLY (MARY)[7] EMERY (*Stephen*,[6] *Stephen*,[5] *Stephen*,[4] *Stephen*,[3] *John*,[2] *John*[1]), daughter of Stephen and Hannah (Little) Emery ; married Aug. 9, 1802, David Ordway of West Newbury, Mass. (born Sept , 1778; died Oct., 1847) His wife died Oct. 21, 1819.

Children :

2856 i   HANNAH MOODY,[8] b. Nov. 15. 1803.
2857 ii   MARY MALVINA, b. Aug. 12, 1806; m. John Sargent; d., *s. p.*,
           1838.
2858 iii WARREN, b. May 17, 1810.

1321 SARAH[7] EMERY (*Stephen*,[6] *Stephen*,[5] *Stephen*,[4] *Stephen*,[3] *John*,[2] *John*[1]), daughter of Stephen and Hannah (Little) Emery; married Nov. 2, 1807, Richard Rand of Rye, N. H. (died April 14, 1845). His wife died March 20, 1865.
   Children :

2859 i   HANNAH LITTLE,[8] b. 1808.
2860 ii   SARAH EMERY, b. Jan. 12, 1822.

1323 EDWARD[7] EMERY (*Stephen*,[6] *Stephen*,[5] *Stephen*,[4] *Stephen*,[3] *John*,[2] *John*[1]), son of Stephen and Hannah (Little) Emery; married Mrs. Sarah Quimby in West Newbury, Mass., March 22, 1836.
   Children :

2861 i   HANNAH L.,[8] b. 1836.
2862 ii   STEPHEN, b. 1838.

1324 ELIZABETH[7] EMERY (*Enoch*,[6] *Stephen*,[5] *Stephen*,[4] *Stephen*,[3] *John*,[2] *John*[1]), daughter of Enoch and Sarah (Sargent) Emery; married Amos Pickard, Feb. 16, 1815.
   Children :

2863 i   JEREMIAH,[8] b. Aug. 4, 1817.
2864 ii   ENOCH EMERY, b. Aug. 18, 1818.
2865 iii JOSEPH, b. July 22, 1820.
2866 iv   JOHN D., b. March 22, 1822.
2867 v   ELLIS W., b. Dec. 31, 1823.
2868 vi   MEHETABLE D., b. Dec. 3, 1826.

1325 SARAH[7] EMERY (*Enoch*,[6] *Stephen*,[5] *Stephen*,[4] *Stephen*,[3] *John*,[2] *John*[1]), daughter of Enoch and Sarah (Sargent) Emery; married Reuben Fellows of Canterbury, N. H., Aug. 10, 1810.
   Children :

2869 i   EMILY MERRILL,[8] b. 1811; m. Jesse Haley, Aug. 25, 1833.
2870 ii   SARAH ANN. b. Nov. 12, 1812; d. 1850.
2871 iii   ELIZABETH EMERY, b. Nov. 14, 1814; m. Joseph M. Foster,
            Oct. 16, 1837.
2872 iv   ENSIGN SARGENT, b. Nov. 21, 1816; m. Abbie J. Weston, April
            13, 1840.
2873 v   MARY HALE, b. Sept. 1, 1818; m. Jonathan B. Foster, Dec. 5,
            1839.
2874 vi   MOSES AUGUSTUS, b. Dec. 18, 1820; d. July 10, 1822.
2875 vii   MOSES AUGUSTUS, b. Nov. 13, 1822.
2876 viii SUSAN EMERY, b. Jan. 26, 1825.
2877 ix   REUBEN LYMAN, b. Sept. 8, 1827.
2878 x   AUGUSTA CAROLINE, b. Dec. 4, 1829; d. Oct., 1846.

1327 HANNAH[7] EMERY (*Enoch*,[6] *Stephen*,[5] *Stephen*,[4] *Stephen*,[3] *John*,[2] *John*[1]), daughter of Enoch and Sarah (Sargent) Emery; married May 16, 1811, Jacob Smith of Dunbarton, N. H. (born Aug. 8, 1785; died July 26, 1863). His wife died May 2, 1873.
   Children :

2879   i   EDMUND EMERY,[8] b June 22, 1812.
2880   ii   LUCINDA A , b Dec 1, 1813; d in Dunbarton, N. H , Feb. 15, 1824.
2881   iii   ABIGAIL, b July 27. 1815
2882   iv   JACOB B , b. Oct 30, 1817.
2883   v   SARAH EMERY, b June 26 1819
2884   vi   ISRAEL NEWELL, b in Canterbury, N H , April 9, 1822, m , 1st, Cornelia Bates of North Brookfield, April 21, 1842, 2nd, Julia Collins of Newton, Mass , July 19, 1855 Graduate of Berkshire Med Coll , Mass ; practised medicine in Lake Providence, La., Haverhill, Mass , and Saginaw City, Mich , d March 29, 1883, s p
2885   vii   HANNAH b Feb 11, 1824; d June 2, 1826
2886   viii GEORGE O , b in Dunbarton, N H , Dec 16, 1825 , graduated in medicine, Woodstock, Vt , d in Saginaw City, Mich., s p. Assistant Surg on 53rd Reg Ill Vol , m. Malinda Lunt of Bradford, Mass
2887   ix   CHARLES C., b Feb 22, 1829
2888   x   ALMIRA P , b Feb 22, 1831
2889   xi   LORANY, b Dec 22, 1833, d March. 1849. unm
2890   xii   DAVID G , b Nov 26, 1835, d Oct 29, 1869, unm.

1330 ENOCH[7] EMERY (*Enoch,[6] Stephen,[5] Stephen,[4] Stephen,[3] John,[2] John[1]*), son of Enoch and Sarah (Sargent) Emery, married Oct. 1, 1818, Abigail Prichard (born Jan. 7, 1791, died Sept. 21, 1879). He died Oct. 1, 1879

Children .

2891   i   ELIZA ANN,[8] b Aug 25, 1819
2892   ii   MOSES MOODY, b. Dec 9, 1821
2893   iii   APPHIA MARIA, b May 18, 1824, d. in Stewartstown, N H , Feb 15, 1852
2894   iv   MARY, b Jan 22 1827, d in Oskaloosa, Ia , Jan 10, 1858
2895   v   CHARLES SARGENT, b July 22, 1830, m Sarah N. Garland, April 5, 1856.
2896   vi   DANIEL, b. March 27, 1833.

1332 SUSAN[7] EMERY (*Enoch,[6] Stephen,[5] Stephen,[4] Stephen,[3] John,[2] John[1]*), daughter of Enoch and Sarah (Sargent) Emery; married Dr. Sanborn of New Market, N. H

Four children, Nos. 2897 to 2900. Names unknown.

1334 CATHARINE[7] EMERY (*Enoch,[6] Stephen,[5] Stephen,[4] Stephen,[3] John,[2] John[1]*), daughter of Enoch and Sarah (Sargent) Emery , married ——Kelsey.

Two children, Nos. 2901 to 2902. Names unknown.

1335 MOODY[7] EMERY (*Enoch,[6] Stephen,[5] Stephen,[4] Stephen,[3] John,[2] John[1]*), son of Enoch and Sarah (Sargent) Emery; married Susan Whidden, May 17, 1831.

Children :

2903   i   HANNAH,[8] b. June 1, 1832
2904   ii   STEPHEN MOODY, b Nov. 21, 1837.

1338 HANNAH[7] MOODY (*Hannah,[6] Stephen,[5] Stephen,[4] Stephen,[3] John,[2] John[1]*), daughter of Samuel and Hannah (Emery) Moody; married Paul Pearson Downer, March 28, 1811.

Children :

2905 i   SAMUEL M.,[8] b. Jan. 2, 1812; d. Oct. 8, 1839.
2906 ii   THOMAS P., b. Feb. 24, 1813.
2907 iii DOLLY S., b. Nov. 10, 1814; m. William Page, Nov., 1833.
2908 iv   NANCY M., b. Aug. 4, 1816; m. Joseph Pickett, Nov., 1839.
2909 v   MOSES N., b. July 28, 1818; m. Sarah E. Kelsey.
2910 vi   JOSEPH S., b. Dec. 19, 1820.
2911 vii HANNAH M., b. March 10, 1823; m. Otto Herman, Sept., 1846;
           d. May 11, 1847.
2912 viii ELIZABETH S., b. June 29, 1826; d. Feb. 28, 1831.
2913 ix   JAMES R., b. Oct. 25, 1831.

1339 SALLY[7] MOODY (*Hannah,[6] Stephen,[5] Stephen,[4] Stephen,[3] John,[2] John[1]*), daughter of Samuel and Hannah (Emery) Moody ; married Hon. Moses Newell of West Newbury.

Children :

2914 i   REBECCA,[8] b. July 27, 1816; d. Aug. 28, 1827.
2915 ii   JOSEPH, b. June 12, 1819; m. Betsey Moody, Oct., 1845; d.
           May 28, 1884.
2916 iii MOSES, b. Dec. 4, 1820; d. Feb. 9, 1821.
2917 iv   MOSES, b. Sept. 16, 1822; m. Catharine Hill, Jan. 7, 1864; d.
           July 9, 1868.
2918 v   SARAH ELIZABETH, b. May 29, 1824; d. Jan. 21, 1827.
2919 vi   REBECCA, b. Dec. 4, 1827; m. Hannibal E. Chase, Dec. 20, 1864.
           He d. April 19, 1884.
2920 vii JOHN, b. March 31, 1830; m. Judith Hill, 1867.
2921 viii SAMUEL, b. May 22, 1833; m. Mary L. Marshall, May 1, 1867.
2922 ix   CHARLES, b. April 4, 1836; m. Frederica Boyden, April, 1858;
           d. June 23, 1858.
2923 x   RICHARD, b. April 17, 1839; m. Lydia Poor, May 29, 1863.

1340 ELIZA[7] MOODY (*Hannah,[6] Stephen,[5] Stephen,[4] Stephen,[3] John,[2] John[1]*), daughter of Samuel and Hannah (Emery) Moody ; married Aug. 31, 1820, Obadiah Smith, of New Hampton, N. H. (born May, 1787; died June 2, 1853).

Children, born in New Hampton :

2924 i   MARY MOONEY,[8] b. July 12, 1821; m. Rev. James Calley, March
           23, 1848.
2925 ii   FRANCES MOODY, b. Dec. 29, 1822; m. George Hoyt, April 25,
           1852.
2926 iii SAMUEL MOODY, b. June 19, 1824; d., unm., Feb. 21, 1850.
2927 iv   ROXANNA, b. Nov. 18, 1825; m. James F. Briggs, Feb. 10, 1851.
2928 v   SARAH ELIZABETH, b. Sept. 22, 1828; m. Charles G. Cheney,
           Oct. 25, 1851.
2929 vi   HENRY HARRISON, b. Oct. 21, 1840; d., unm., March 28, 1862.

1343 ELIZABETH[7] EMERY (*Moody,[6] Stephen,[5] Stephen,[4] Stephen,[3] John,[2] John[1]*), daughter of Moody and Abigail (Prescott) Emery ; married, Nov. 1, 1826, Capt. Flavius Emery, son of Thomas and Elizabeth (Hale) Emery, shipmaster ; died in Newburyport, Mass., March 5, 1830. His widow died in Newburgh, N. Y., July 15, 1880.

Children :

2930 i   RUFUS,[8] b. July 25, 1827.
2931 ii   FLAVIUS, b. June 22, 1829; d. Feb. 22, 1830.

1344 REV. SAMUEL MOODY[7] EMERY (*Moody,[6] Stephen,[5] Stephen,[4]*

Stephen,[3] *John,*[2] *John*[1]), son of Moody and Abigail (Prescott) Emery ; educated at Phillips Academy, Exeter, N H , was graduated at Harvard College, 1830 ; taught school in Northfield, Mass , and Portsmouth, N H ; ordained Deacon in the ministry of the Protestant Episcopal Church by the Rt Rev. Alexander V. Griswold, in Trinity church, Boston, July 12, 1835 ; became assistant to Rev. William Jarvis, rector of Trinity church, Portland, Conn ; advanced to the priesthood, Dec 12, 1835 ; elected rector of the parish April 23, 1837 , received the degree of D. D. from Trinity College, Hartford, Conn. , resigned the rectorship of the parish, Aug., 1870 , removed to Newburyport, Mass , had charge of St James Church, Amesbury, several years , died in West Newbury, Aug 16, 1883, aged 80 ; interested in the public schools of his native town ; married Mary Hale Emery, daughter of Eliphalet and Sarah (Hale) Emery, of West Newbury, Nov 17, 1841.

Children, born in Portland, except the first .

2932 i   SARAH NOYES,[8] b. Sept 6, 1842, in West Newbury, Mass
2933 ii   MARY ELIZABETH, b. March 19, 1846
2934 iii LOUISA JANE, b July 29, 1849
2935 iv   SAMUEL ELIPHALET, b April 10 1852 , D D S , in Newburyport.
2936 v   ABBY PRESCOTT, b. Oct 11, 1854, d Nov 11, 1855
2937 vi   FRANCES JARVIS, b. April 18, 1857.
2938 vii GEORGIANA, b Oct 15, 1859

1346 RUTH[7] BRADLEY (*Susan,*[6] *Benjamin,*[5] *Stephen,*[4] *Stephen,*[3] *John,*[2] *John*[1]), daughter of Jonathan and Susan (Emery) Bradley , married John George.

Children :

2939 i   PAUL ROLFE,[8] b April 25, 1807.
2940 ii   SUSAN, b Feb. 25, 1809, d June 4, 1832
2941 iii CLARISSA B , b Sept 3, 1811, m. Hamilton E Perkins, May 14, 1833

1364 ISAAC[7] EMERY (*Isaac,*[6] *Benjamin,*[5] *Stephen,*[4] *Stephen,*[3] *John,*[2] *John*[1]), son of Isaac and Esther (Tay) Emery , married Eliza Eastman ; died Jan. 31, 1879

Child .

2942 i   ALFRED E ,[8] b April 21, 1841.

1366 TIMOTHY W.[7] EMERY (*Isaac,*[6] *Benjamin,*[5] *Stephen,*[4] *Stephen,*[3] *John,*[2] *John*[1]), son of Isaac and Esther (Tay) Emery , married, first, Comfort Potter ; second, Ann Bickford ; died May 29, 1875.

Children, by first wife ·

2943 i   ELVIRA B.,[8] b Dec , 1841, m Rev Charles L Little
2944 ii   ELBRIDGE, b Aug. 18, 1845, m Clara Saunders.
2945 iii ESTHER J., b Jan. 9, 1851, m Sidney E. Gates.

1380 ESTHER W.[7] EMERY (*Eliphalet,*[6] *Benjamin,*[5] *Stephen,*[4] *Stephen,*[3] *John,*[2] *John*[1]), daughter of Eliphalet and Betsey (Walker) Emery married Capt. Ebenezer Towle, April 11, 1827.

Children :

2946   i   GEORGE SANBORN,[8] b. April 25, 1828.
2947   ii   ESTHER, b. May 25, 1831.
2948   iii SUSAN, b. Dec. 12, 1832.
2949   iv   CHARLES, b Dec. 5, 1834.
2950   v   SARAH, b. Dec. 13, 1837.
2951   vi   ELIZABETH, b. July 10, 1844.
2952   vii MARY, b. May 25, 1848; d. Aug. 1, 1848.

1384 CLARISSA WALKER[7] EMERY (*Charles,[6] Benjamin,[5] Stephen,[4] Stephen,[3] John,[2] John[1]*), daughter of Charles and Mary (Walker) Emery; married Horatio Hill, April 25, 1830; died Sept. 19, 1839.
  Child :
  2953   i   SARAH ELIZABETH;[8] m. Enoch G. Hook, of Chicago, Ill., June, 1855.

1386 MARY EMERY[7] NOYES (*Sarah,[6] Nathaniel,[5] Stephen,[4] Stephen,[3] John,[2] John[1]*), daughter of Nathaniel and Sarah (Emery) Noyes; married, Oct. 15, 1832, Hon. Alfred Kittredge (born in Canterbury, N. H., Oct. 22, 1805), son of Jonathan Kittredge. He was a lawyer; graduated from Dartmouth College, 1827; admitted to Essex Bar, 1831; representative from Haverhill, Mass., 1840–41; member Mass. Senate, 1844–45; editor *Haverhill Gazette*, 1869–77; strong in his convictions, outspoken in his opinions, a good citizen and an upright magistrate; died May 1, 1877.
  Child :
  2954   i   SARAH NOYES,[8] b. July 30, 1833.

1395 CHARLES[7] EMERY (*Thomas,[6] Thomas,[5] David,[4] John,[3] Jonathan,[2] John[1]*), son of Thomas and Elizabeth (Hale) Emery; married Mary E. George, daughter of Joseph George of Newburyport, Mass., Feb. 21, 1829. They had two children: Margaret E., born Aug. 27, 1831; married Charles Bevan, June, 1853, and died July 7, 185-, and had two children, Charles and Harriet. Charles Thomas, born March 4, 1833, enlisted in the Union Army, taken prisoner and died at Andersonville, Sept. 25, 1864. Charles Emery died May 24, 1849. His widow married, second, Freeman P. Greenough of Newburyport, June 8, 1862, and died in 1890.

1412 AMOS EMERY[7] HOWELL (*Hannah,[6] Amos,[5] Moses,[4] John,[3] John,[2] John[1]*), son of Robert and Hannah (Emery) Howell; married Joanna Fogg.
  Children :
  2955   i   EDWIN HARRIS.[8]
  2956   ii   HENRY B.
  2957   iii WINSLOW E.

1414 MARY E.[7] HOWELL (*Hannah,[6] Amos,[5] Moses,[4] John,[3] John,[2] John[1]*), daughter of Robert and Hannah (Emery) Howell; married, 1846, Edward Libby (born Oct. 7, 1819). She died June 27, 1887.
  Children :
  2958   i   ROBERT H.[8]
  2959   ii   FRANCES ANN.
  2960   iii CHARLES EDWIN.

1419 Ebenezer[8] Emery (*Jacob M*,[7] *Amos*,[6] *Moses*,[5] *John*,[4] *John*,[3] *John*,[2] *John*[1]), son of Jacob M and Jane R. (Emerson) Emery; married Mary Jane Short, Aug 24, 1865. He died June 1, 1869.

Children:

2961   i   Clara Lincoln[9]
2962   ii   Walter Plummer

1420 John Moody[8] Emery (*Jacob M*,[7] *Amos*,[6] *Moses*,[5] *John*,[4] *John*,[3] *John*,[2] *John*[1]), son of Jacob M and Jane R (Emerson) Emery, married Roxanna Slack, Oct. 17, 1854

Children:

2963   i   Roxie Jane,[9] b Aug 28, 1855, m Will Merrill Carlton, April 1, 1876
2964   ii   William Slack, b Feb 10, 1861
2965   iii Annie May, b May 1, 1865, d Aug 15, 1866

1454 James W[8] Emery (*Samuel*,[7] *John*,[6] *Moses*,[5] *John*,[4] *John*,[3] *John*,[2] *John*[1]), son of Samuel and Ruby (Woodward) Emery; was graduated from Dartmouth College, 1830, read law with Hon Ichabod Bartlett of Portsmouth, and became his partner; representative to the state legislature several years, superintendent of the Portsmouth and Concord Railroad, president of the Union Railway Company, of Cambridge, Mass; married Martha E, daughter of Andrew W. Bell of Portsmouth, N. H., Aug. 15, 1837.

Children:

2966   i   Edward Andrew,[9] b Jan 22, 1839, d Dec 12, 1839
2967   ii   Frederick C, b Dec 17 1840, d Jan. 14, 1859
2968   iii Woodward, b Sept. 5, 1842
2969   iv   Manning, b. May 9, 1844
2970   v   Caroline Bell, b Oct 19, 1847.
2971   vi   Octavia Bell, b Jan 9, 1850
2972   vii Alice Christine, b. Jan. 29, 1852, d May 26, 1856

1474 Moses[8] Emery (*Moses*,[7] *Moses*,[6] *Moses*,[5] *John*,[4] *John*,[3] *John*,[2] *John*[1]), son of Moses and Susannah (Woodward) Emery, married Sarah Cutts Thornton Nov. 27, 1823 His boyhood was spent in hardy toil at home, but an irrepressible desire for a liberal education pushed him forward in spite of adverse influences and obstacles, and finally crowned his self-supporting efforts with success. His impulse in this direction was stimulated by the kindred example of his uncle Stephen, who procured for him the use of Latin books, the mastery of which he achieved without instruction in hours of rest and by the glimmer of candle-light. In the autumn of 1813 he pursued a brief academic course at Bridgton Academy, which was cut short by a mandate to return to his accustomed field of labor. In 1814 having occasion to visit Bowdoin College whence his uncle was about to graduate, he was induced by him to offer himself for examination for admission. He passed the ordeal successfully and was granted a year's leave of absence His father, taken by surprise, a Methodist clergyman at Brooklyn, procured for him through his brother Nathan the position of cashier in a dry goods house in New York City. But on reaching his majority he returned to college, trudging his way from Boston on foot. He was admitted to the sophomore class, graduated in 1818, having become a proficient in mathematical and classical studies, the love of which was ever afterward a constant guest. The money for defraying his college expenses was earned principally by teaching at Brunswick, Buckfield and Hebron Academy. In 1821 he was admitted to the bar at Wiscasset where he studied with Judge Bailey, who took him into co-partnership. But in 1825 having married Sarah C. a daughter of Marshall Thornton, he removed to Saco, his subsequent home. His professional life brought him in competition with John Holmes, the Shepleys, Daniel Goodenow, John Fairfield, Nathan Clifford and N. D. Appleton, and with them he shared the honors and emoluments of success. His career was characterized by untiring industry, accompanied by a will and zeal in behalf of his clients which would brook no defeat, if in any way victory was attainable by honorable methods. But his moral convictions, sometimes disturbed by application of the rigid rules of the common law, led him to become early enamored with equity practice, his success in which is sufficiently attested by the fact that in a list of nineteen cases, some of which involved important principles and large amounts, he lost but two. For many years he was the honored President of the York County Bar.

Up to Webster's 7th of March speech he was an ardent Whig ; after that he affiliated with the Republican party. But his taste was professional rather than political, although he once came within three hundred votes of an election to Congress in a strong Democratic district, but without any solicitation on his part. In 1836–37, then in the legislature, he, its draftsman, successfully engineered the enactment of the charter of the Portland, Saco and Portsmouth Railroad Company in the face of a powerful opposition.

Of the cause of education he was a prominent champion, and for a long period was President of the Board of Trustees of Thornton Academy. In the temperance reform he was a conspicuous pioneer ; as a member of the Unitarian denomination and as a citizen he was always in the front rank of those who strove for the elevation of the people, and for the material prosperity of the community in which he closed a long and honorable career, May 12, 1881.

Children, born in Saco, Me. :

2973　i　THORNTON CUTTS,[9] b. Nov. 16, 1824 ; m., Jan. 1, 1849, Abby Little Bailey ; she d. May 10, 1858, at Emery's Crossing (Middle Yuba), Cal.

2974　ii　ANNE PAINE, b. Feb. 25, 1827 ; d. June 11, 1842.

2975　iii　CHARLES CARROLL, b. May 31, 1830.

2976　iv　SIDNEY HAMDEN, b. Sept. 27, 1832 ; d. Sept. 13, 1833.

2977　v　SARAH GENNETT, b. Sept. 6, 1834 ; d. Nov. 8, 1835.

2978　vi　MOSES, b. Sept. 15, 1837 ; d. Sept 4, 1838.

2979　vii　GEORGE ADDISON, b. Nov. 14, 1839 ; was graduated at Bowdoin Coll., 1863 ; read law with his father ; admitted to the York County Bar, 1866 ; representative to the legislature of Maine ; judge of the Municipal Court of Saco, where he is an honored citizen.

1475 SUSANNAH[3] EMERY (Moses,[7] Moses,[6] Moses,[5] John.[4] John,[3] John,[2] John[1]), daughter of Moses and Susannah (Woodward) Emery ; married Asa W. Soulé, 1815.

Children :

    2980   i   Clarissa,[9] b. 1818.
    2981   ii   Persis, b in Gloucester, Me , Aug 23, 1820
    2982   iii Maria Louisa, b in Garland, Me , July 12, 1823

1476 Abigail[8] Emery (*Moses,*[7] *Moses,*[6] *Moses,*[5] *John,*[4] *John,*[3] *John,*[2] *John*[1]), daughter of Moses and Susannah (Woodward) Emery; married Abial Lapham, 1818, died Dec. 2, 1872. He died in Anoka, Minn , Jan , 1883
Children, born in Minot, Me. :

    2983   i   Laura,[9] b 1822
    2984   ii   Julia, b May 1, 1824 , m George Campbell, March 8, 1841.
    2985   iii David, b. Oct. 18,1827
    2986   iv   George, b. 1831.

1477 Eunice[8] Emery (*Moses,*[7] *Moses,*[6] *Moses,*[5] *John,*[4] *John,*[3] *John,*[2] *John*[1]), daughter of Moses and Susannah (Woodward) Emery , married David Lapham ; died March 22, 1854.
    Children :

    2987   i   Eliza Ann,[9] b June 1, 1829
    2988   ii   Lucy Ellen, b July 12, 1833
    2989   iii Albert Barnard, b April 4, 1837 , d. Sept , 1839
    2990   iv   Mary Emery, b March 12, 1841.

1478 Irene[8] Emery (*Moses,*[7] *Moses,*[6] *Moses,*[5] *John,*[4] *John,*[3] *John,*[2] *John*[1]), daughter of Moses and Susannah (Woodward) Emery ; married, first, Benjamin Waterman, Dec. 28, 1824, second, William French, 1844.
    Children :

    2991   i   Edwin R ,[9] b Nov. 26, 1827; m , 1st, Abbie Sweet, Jan , 1852 , 2nd, Jennie McDowell, May, 1858
    2992   ii   Emily J, b May 20, 1831 , m John Morrill, May, 1857.
    2993   iii Maria A., b Jan 10, 1834 , m. Nelson A Hatch, 1852
    2994   iv   Sarah E , b Dec 4, 1837 , m. William F Sawyer, Nov. 25, 1871
    2995   v   Addison E.

1479 Eliza Ann[8] Emery (*Moses,*[7] *Moses,*[6] *Moses,*[5] *John,*[4] *John,*[3] *John,*[2] *John*[1]), daughter of Moses and Susannah (Woodward) Emery , married Albert F. Barnard, July 16, 1835. She died Aug. 14, 1853
    Child :

    2996   i   Charles A ,[9] b May 7, 1842; m. Ellen A Hunt, Aug 14, 1879 Grad Wes Univ , Middletown, Conn , 1863 Author of pamphlet "Forms for complaint relating to prevention of cruelty to animals "

1480 Nathan Addison[8] Emery (*Moses,*[7] *Moses,*[6] *Moses,*[5] *John*[4] *John,*[3] *John,*[2] *John*[1]), son of Moses and Susannah (Woodward) Emery ; married Nov. 19, 1835, Chloe Packard of Minot, Me
    Child :

    2997   i   Addie E ,[9] b July 8, 1839, m , 1st, Sept 25, 1884, Job Carr at Olympia, Washington , 2nd, June 23, 1888, John W Wood at Oakland, Cal.

1487 MARIA A.[8] EMERSON (*Mary,*[7] *Moses,*[6] *Moses,*[5] *John,*[4] *John,*[3] *John,*[2] *John*[1]), daughter of Ebenezer and Mary (Emery) Emerson; married William Osgood, Nov. 23, 1842.

Children :

   2998 i   AUGUSTA.[9]
   2999 ii   GEORGE E.
   3000 iii NATHAN P.

1492 SARAH J.[8] EMERY (*Stephen,*[7] *Moses,*[6] *Moses,*[5] *John,*[4] *John,*[3] *John,*[2] *John*[1]), daughter of Stephen and Sarah (Stowell) Emery; married Hon. Hannibal Hamlin, Dec. 10, 1833 ; died April 17, 1855.

Hon. Hannibal Hamlin fitted for college ; served in a printing-office as a compositor one year ; admitted to the bar, 1833, and continued the practice of law in Hampden, Me., till 1848 ; member of the state legislature, 1836–40 and 1847 ; speaker of the House, 1837, 1839–40 ; representative to Congress, 1843–7 ; U. S. senator, 1848–1856 ; governor of Maine 1856 ; again senator 1857–61 ; Vice President of the U. S. 1861–65 ; collector of the port of Boston, 1865–6 ; U. S. senator, 1869–1881 ; regent of the Smithsonian Institution, 1861–5, and again in 1876. (See No. 1496.)

Children :

   3001 i   GEORGE E.,[9] b. Sept. 30, 1835 ; d. July 14, 1844.
   3002 ii   CHARLES, b. Sept. 13, 1837.
   3003 iii CYRUS, b. April 26, 1839 ; d. Aug. 28, 1867 ; union soldier, brevet major general, lawyer in New Orleans ; wife d. soon after marriage.
   3004 iv SARAH J., b. Jan. 7, 1842.

1493 GEORGE F.[8] EMERY (*Stephen,*[7] *Moses,*[6] *Moses,*[5] *John,*[4] *John,*[3] *John,*[2] *John*[1]), son of Stephen and Sarah (Stowell) Emery; married, Sept. 7, 1841, Abby Eliza Appleton (born Feb. 15, 1822). Graduated Bowdoin College, 1836 ; admitted to the bar, 1838 ; Register of Probate for six years in Oxford Co., Me. ; clerk of U. S. Circuit Court, 1848 to 1876 ; Nov., 1877, removed from Portland to Boston and became president of the Post Publishing Co. Pension agent under President Buchanan, 1857–61 ; returned to Portland and resumed his law practice, 1881.

Children :

   3005 i   JOHN APPLETON,[9] b. Oct. 7, 1842.
   3006 ii   GEORGE FREEMAN, b. April 29, 1845 ; d. Dec. 20, 1873.
   3007 iii FRANK WILSON, b. Aug. 9, 1849 ; d. July 20, 1880.
   3008 iv HANNIBAL HAMLIN, b. Jan. 7, 1853.
   3009 v   SARAH ELLEN, b. Sept. 12, 1856.
   3010 vi SUSAN APPLETON, b. July 29, 1861 ; m. Henry H. Furbish, Sept. 20, 1883.

1495 JENNETT[8] EMERY (*Stephen,*[7] *Moses,*[6] *Moses,*[5] *John,*[4] *John,*[3] *John,*[2] *John*[1]), daughter of Stephen and his second wife Jennett (Loring) Emery; married, Dec. 19, 1849, Rev. Nathaniel Butler (born Oct. 19, 1824), clergyman ; he has had charges in Eastport, Auburn, Bangor, Rockland, Hallowell, Vassalboro and Camden, Me., Leavenworth, Kan., and Alton, Ill.

Children :

3011　ı　JEANNIE EMERY,[9] b Oct 31, 1850
3012　ıı　NATHANIEL. JR . b May 22, 1853, graduate of Colby University,
　　　　　Watervılle, Me , class of 1873
3013　ııı　ELLEN HAMLIN, b Oct 22 1860.
3014　ıv　ANNA PAYNE, b Aug. 24, 1862

1496 ELLEN VESTA[8] EMERY (*Stephen*,[7] *Moses*,[6] *Moses*,[5] *John*,[4]
John,[3] *John*,[2] *John*[1]), daughter of Stephen and his second wife Jennett
(Loring) Emery, married Hon. Hannibal Hamlin, Sept. 25, 1856.
Children ·

3015　ı　HANNIBAL E ,[9] b Aug 22, 1858
3016　ıı　FRANK, b. Sept 26, 1862.

1497 STEPHEN ALBERT[8] EMERY (*Stephen*,[7] *Moses*,[6] *Moses*,[5] *John*,[4]
John,[3] *John*,[2] *John*[1]), son of Stephen and his second wife Jennett
(Loring) Emery; married Lydia Arabella Lord, Oct. 24, 1867. Pro-
fessor of music in the Boston Conservatory.
Children, except last, born in Malden, Mass..

3017　ı　STEPHEN,[9] b Dec. 24, 1868
3018　ıı　CHARLES A L , b Feb 9, 1870.
3019　ııı　SIDNEY S , b May 5, 1871.
3020　ıv　MORITZ H , b Nov. 19, 1875
3021　v　ERNESTINE, b Sept 24, 1877, in Newton Centre, Mass.

1498 ELIZABETH[8] EMERY (*Moses*,[7] *Josiah*,[6] *Moses*,[5] *John*,[4] *John*,[3]
John,[2] *John*[1]), daughter of Moses and Hannah (Woodman-Morri-
son) Emery; married Joshua Merrick, of New Hampton, Oct. 7,
1823 ; died May 3, 1837.
Child :

3022　ı　JOSHUA M.[9]

1500 WOODMAN[8] EMERY (*Moses*,[7] *Josiah*,[6] *Moses*,[5] *John*,[4] *John*,[3]
John[1]), son of Moses and Hannah (Woodman-Morrison) Emery;
married Oct. 31, 1824, Fanny Taylor (born Aug. 23, 1803) daughter
of John and Susanna (Thompson) Taylor , removed from Sanbornton to Dover, N. H , Aug 6, 1851, and from Dover to Madbury,
N. H., Dec. 7, 1857. He died Jan. 24, 1875.
Children :

3023　ı　MARTHA,[9] b Feb. 25, 1829.
3024　ıı　HORACE, b May 10, 1831, d , in Sanbornton, N. H., Sept 15,
　　　　　1835
3025　ııı　JOHN W , b Sept 9, 1838

1502 DAVID[8] EMERY (*Nathan*,[7] *Josiah*,[6] *Moses*,[5] *John*,[4] *John*,[3]
John,[3] *John*[1]), son of Nathan and Betsey (McCrillis) Emery; mar-
ried, first, Mahala Hoyt (died Aug. 7, 1877), second, ———
——.
Six children, Nos. 3026 to 3031.

3026　ı　JOHN HOYT [9]

1503 JOSIAH[8] EMERY(*Nathan*,[7] *Josiah*,[6] *Moses*,[5] *John*,[4] *John*,[3] *John*,[2]
John[1]), son of Nathan and Betsey (McCrillis) Emery; married Julia

Ann Beecher, daughter of Hon. John Beecher, Feb. 12, 1830.   She died July 25, 1871.   Educated at Kimball Union Academy ; entered Dartmouth College, 1819 ; left, 1821 ; taught five years in New York state ; entered junior class, Union College, 1826 ; graduated, 1828 ; principal of Wellsboro Academy, 1828–30 ; practised law in Wellsboro, 1831–71 ; removed to Williamsport, Pa., 1871 ; was district attorney, commissioner of bankruptcy and commissioner of draft ; frequent writer in various publications.

Children, born in Wellsboro :

    3032   i   MARY C.,[9] b. Nov. 27, 1830.
    3033   ii   CHARLES D., b. May 17, 1833.
    3034   iii   MARTHA P., b. Feb. 16, 1838 ; educated at Dickinson Seminary ;
                    went south as a teacher ; returned north at beginning of the
                    war ; m. Judge Charles S. Bundy of Washington, D. C.,
                    Dec. 19, 1867.
    3035   iv   EVA VANDERBILT, b. Feb. 15, 1840.
    3036   v   ELIZABETH, b. May 24, 1842.
    3037   vi   JOHN BEECHER, b. Dec. 28, 1843.
    3038   vii   WILLIAM V., b. Oct. 29, 1845.
    3039   viii CLARA B., b. June 6, 1848.
    3040   ix   ANNIE, b. Jan. 30, 1851 ; d. Dec. 15, 1851.
    3041   x   GEORGE, b. Feb. 28, 1852 ; d. Sept. 17, 1862.
    3042   xi   FRANK B., b. Sept. 15, 1855 ; m. Rose Holden, Nov. 18, 1879.

1505 NATHAN[8] EMERY (*Nathan,[7] Josiah,[6] Moses,[5] John,[4] John,[3] John,[2] John[1]*), son of Nathan and Betsey (McCrillis) Emery ; married, first, Mary Peverly ; second, Louise Bradley of Canterbury, N. H. Both died *s. p.*

1507 NANCY[8] EMERY (*Nathan,[7] Josiah,[6] Moses,[5] John,[4] John,[3] John,[2] John[1]*), daughter of Nathan and Betsey (McCrillis) Emery ; married Freeman Webster of Boscawen, N. H. (born Aug. 12, 1809).

Children :

    3043   i   ELIZABETH EMERY,[9] b. April 27, 1845.
    3044   ii   CLARA, b. April 9, 1851.

1508 ALVAN[8] EMERY (*Nathan,[7] Josiah,[6] Moses,[5] John,[4] John,[3] John,[2] John[1]*), son of Nathan and Betsey (McCrillis) Emery ; settled in Michigan and afterward in Central Illinois ; married, first, Susan Hayes ; second, Henrietta Ward of Lowell, Mass.   He died in prison, in Cataba, Ala., Oct. 8, 1864.

Six children :   Nos. 3045–3050.

1509 JOSEPH WOODMAN[8] EMERY (*Nathan,[7] Josiah,[6] Moses,[5] John,[4] John,[3] John,[2] John[1]*), son of Nathan and Betsey (McCrillis) Emery ; married, first, March, 1838, Frances Rosalinda Leland, Upton, Mass. (born Jan. 11, 1818 ; died, in Canterbury, N. H., Sept. 17, 1853) ; second, Frances Ann Sanborn, Feb. 16, 1854. He died Nov. 21, 1882.

Children :

    3051   i   CHARLES,[9] b. Feb., 1839 ; d. Sept. 29, 1841, in Canterbury,
                  N. H.
    3052   ii   ELLEN SOPHIA, b. Aug. 30, 1842, in Upton, Mass ; unm.
    3053   iii BETSEY, b. March 3, 1844, in Upton, Mass.
    3054   iv   MARY JANE, b. May 14, 1847 ; d. in Austin, Ill., Feb. 2, 1864.

3035   v   CHARLES WOODMAN, b Oct 5, 1851, in Upton, Mass
3056   vi   CLARENCE F , b Sept., 1856, in Clinton, Ill
3057   vii   FRANCES ROSALINDA, b Aug , 1862, in Macon Co , Ill., d
          March 13, 1870

1510 HENRY[8] EMERY (*Nathan,[7] Josiah,[6] Moses,[5] John,[4] John,[3]
John,[2] John[1]*), son of Nathan and Betsey (McCrillis) Emery, married, June 5, 1843, Betsey A Martin of Wolfboro, N. H.(born April 1, 1818).

Children :

3058   i   ELMIRA L ,[9] b April 3, 1844 ; m , Dec 17, 1870, Addison L
          Nute (b in Wolfboro, N. H , July 10, 1846, d June 27, 1880).
3059   ii   ANGELINE, b July 14, 1846, d. Aug. 8, 1846
3060   iii   WILLIAM C , b March 24, 1847.
3061   iv   MARIA M , b Oct 7, 1851.

1514 MOSES[8] EMERY (*Nathan,[7] Josiah,[6] Moses,[5] John.[4] John,[3]
John.[2] John[1]*), son of Nathan and Betsey (McCrillis) Emery, married Rebecca Haynes.

Seven children : Nos. 3062–3068.

1515 ENOCH[8] EMERY (*Nathan,[7] Josiah,[6] Moses,[5] John,[4] John,[3]
John,[2] John[1]*), son of Nathan and Betsey (McCrillis) Emery, married, first, Mary Moore ; second, Lydia Whiteside ; connected with the press in Lowell, Mass , and editor of the Peoria (Ill.) *Transcript* He died June 20, 1882.

Four children : Nos 3069–3072.

1516 SAMUEL[8] EMERY (*Nathan,[7] Josiah,[6] Moses,[5] John,[4] John,[3]
John,[2] John[1]*), son of Nathan and Betsey (McCrillis) Emery ; married, first, Lydia Coombs of Lowell, Mass ; second, Mittie Clough of Canterbury, N. H., lived in Lowell, Mass., Clinton and Peoria, Ill. He died in Canterbury, Sept. 10, 1873.

Children :

3073   i   MARY MAUD,[9] b Feb 19, 1869, in Ill.
3074   ii   ABBIE JOSEPHINE, b. July 23, 1870, in Canterbury, N H
3075   iii   MITTIE LOUISA, b. Jan , 1872, in Peoria, Ill.

1518 REBECCA W.[8] TAYLOR (*Ann,[7] Josiah [6] Moses,[5] John,[4] John,[3]
John,[2] John[1]*), daughter of Ede and Ann (Nancy Emery) Taylor, married, April 17. 1831, Roswell Surtland (born Oct 8, 1801).

Children, born in Lebanon, N. H. :

3076   i   NAOMI R ,[9] b April 4, 1832
3077   ii   FREEMAN L , b July 23, 1835
3078   iii   WILLIAM A , b Oct 16, 1837

1519 MARY (POLLY)[8] TAYLOR (*Ann,[7] Josiah,[6] Moses,[5] John,[4]
John,[3] John,[2] John[1]*), daughter of Ede and Ann (Nancy Emery) Taylor, married Jonathan C. Smith, Aug 29, 1816, who died Nov. 19, 1853. She died Sept., 1875.

Children :

3079   i   EDE,⁹   } b. June, ——; } d. June 18, 1817.
3080   ii   ELVAH,
3081   iii MARY A., b. Jan. 17, ——; d. June 30, 1819.
3082   iv   CELESTIA, b. July 15, 1820; m., Feb. 4, 1840, Elbert Goodale
            (b. Nov. 16, 1816); d. Dec. 17, 1863.
3083   v   HANNAH INGALLS, b. Oct. 2, 1822; m., July 20, 1846, Peter S.
            Morton (b. Feb 2, 1822); d. Jan. 5, 1865.
3084   vi   SHADRACH TAYLOR, b. March 5, 1825; m. Marenda T. Wad-
            leigh, Aug. 2, 1845.
3085   vii JONATHAN ALBERT, b. Nov. 18, 1827; m. Mrs. Harriet (Styles)
            Ingalls, July 24, 1858.
3086   viii ALONZO FRANK, b. May 24, 1830; m. Jerusha S. Newton, Sept.
            19, 1854.
3087   ix   ELECTA TAYLOR, b. Jan. 28, 1832; m.. Nov. 30, 1857, Gustavus
            Emmons, who was killed at the battle of Gettysburg, July,
            1863.
3088   x   MARY BRACKETT JOHNSON, b. Feb. 26, 1836; m. Samuel Hodge,
            Dec. 4, 1854; d. April 19, 1867.
3089   xi   ELBERT GOODALE, b. March 16, 1840; Union soldier in N. H.
            regiments during the war; m. Mary Ann Hanniford, July 4,
            1870.

1520 RACHEL MOORE⁸ TAYLOR (*Ann,*⁷ *Josiah,*⁶ *Moses,*⁵ *John,*⁴
*John,*³ *John,*² *John¹*), daughter of Ede and Ann (Nancy Emery)
Taylor; married Trueworthy S. Gordon, Dec. 1, 1819.
   Children :

3090   i   SARAH A. K.,⁹ b. April 8, 1821; m. Jona. R. Pike, Aug. 25,
            1847.
3091   ii   EDE TAYLOR, b. May 13, 1822; d. Nov. 20, 1853.
3092   iii LUCIEN S., b. June 5, 1827; m. Amanda M. Harris, Aug. 18,
            1852.
3093   iv   ELIPHALET S., b. Sept. 10, 1831.

1521 NANCY⁸ TAYLOR (*Ann,*⁷ *Josiah,*⁶ *Moses,*⁵ *John,*⁴ *John,*³ *John,*²
John¹), daughter of Ede and Ann (Nancy Emery) Taylor; married
Nov. 17, 1822, Calvin Ingalls of Canterbury, N. H. (born July 7,
1799; died July 16, 1855); she died Feb., 1874.
   Children :

3094   i   NATHANIEL P.,⁹ b. Dec. 30, 1823.
3095   ii   JOSEPH, b. July 21, 1825; m. Elizabeth R. Lucas, Aug. 9, 1848.
3096   iii CHARLES M., b. Jan. 4, 1827.
3097   iv   GORDON S., b. July 11, 1829.
3098   v   ANDREW J., b. March 30, 1831.
3099   vi   IRENE T., b. April 26, 1833.
3100   vii RICHMOND J., b. Jan. 29, 1835; m. Aaron Lord, Nov. 16, 1854.
3101   viii CHARLOTTE L., b. March 27, 1838.
3102   ix   ANNIE C., b. Jan. 20, 1843.

1524 ELIZA CROCKETT⁸ TAYLOR (*Ann,*⁷ *Josiah,*⁶ *Moses,*⁵ *John,*⁴
*John,*³ *John,*² *John¹*), daughter of Ede and Ann (Nancy Emery) Tay-
lor; married, June 8, 1826, Jonathan E. Cilley (born July 26, 1800).
She died in Dover, March 5, 1848.
   Children :

3103   i   ELIZABETH A.,⁹ b. March 14, 1827.
3104   ii   ANN T., b. July 2, 1830; m. G. H. Monroe, July 2, 1848.

3105 iii HORACE LYMAN, b Feb 16, 1833, m Myra Tibbetts
3106 iv ORPAN GEORGE, b April 4 1840, grad Dart Med Coll , 1867,
           Surgeon Gen of Mass , under Gov Butler, m. Mary Jane
           Haines, Feb 26, 1868.

1525 SALLY HUSE[8] TAYLOR (*Ann*,[7] *Josiah*,[6] *Moses*,[5] *John*,[4] *John*,[3]
John,[2] *John*[1]), daughter of Ede and Ann (Nancy Emery) Taylor ;
married May 29, 1832, Horace Lyman Plaisted (born July 1, 1810)
Children ·

3107 i   PHŒBE E ,[9] b Aug 10, 1836
3108 ii   CLARINDA T , b Dec 22, 1838
3109 iii HORACE S , b. May 10, 1840
3110 iv   DANIEL E , b Nov. 23, 1843

1526 IRENE B [8] TAYLOR (*Ann*,[7] *Josiah*,[6] *Moses*,[5] *John*,[4] *John*,[3]
John,[2] *John*[1]), daughter of Ede and Ann (Nancy Emery) Taylor ,
married Feb 23, 1835, Christopher S Mason (born May 23, 1811).
Children .

3111 i   MARTHA ANN,[9] b April 13, 1846
3112 ii FRANK TAYLOR, b Oct 28, 1850

1530 WILLIAM[8] HAYES (*Molly*,[7] *Josiah*,[6] *Moses*,[5] *John*,[4] *John*,[3]
John,[2] *John*[1]), son of John P and Molly (Emery) Hayes, married
May 24, 1821, Lydia Sanborn , noted school teacher , removed in 1854
to Milo, Bureau Co., Ill. ; died Feb., 1881.
Children :

3113 i   JEREMIAH,[9] b June 22, 1822, m Mary A Dearborn in North-
           field, N H , Nov 15, 1843
3114 ii   JOHN MOODY, b 1829, grad Dart. Coll. 1851, Prof Greek,
           Lombard University, Galesburgh, Ill , d Sept , 1856
3115 iii MARY PLUMMER, b Jan , 1833, m George Lombard of Han-
           over, N H , farmer
3116 iv   AMOS WALTON, b 1835, d Nov , 1866

1531 REBECCA W [8] HAYES (*Molly*,[7] *Josiah*,[6] *Moses*,[5] *John*,[4] *John* [3]
John,[2] *John*[1]). daughter of John P. and Molly (Emery) Hayes , married Elisha Durkee of Hanover, N H., Sept 21, 1825 ; lived in Syca-
more, Ill , and Olathe, Kan , where he died. She died Jan., 1877.
Children

3117 i   MARY ELIZ ,[9] b Sept 12, 1826, m. Jesse Alden, Sept 12 1847
3118 ii   SAMULL THOMPSON, b March 31, 1837, Hanover, N H , m
           Laura Ann Dow of Mayfield, Ill , Sept 12, 1860   Teacher in
           Cal
3119 iii SILAS WHIDDEN, b March 31, 1837, in Hanover, N. H , m.
           Louisa Emeline Withing, Nov , 1858

1532 BRADSTREET MOODY[8] HAYES (*Molly*,[7] *Josiah*,[6] *Moses*,[5] *John*,[4]
John,[3] *John*,[2] *John*[1]), son of John P and Molly (Emery) Hayes , died
in Milo, Ill., 1832. Physician and farmer
Child ·

3120 i BYRON [9]

1533 JOHN PLUMMER[8] HAYES (*Molly*,[7] *Josiah*,[6] *Moses*,[5] *John*,[4] *John*,[3]

John,[2] *John*[1]), son of John P. and Molly (Emery) Hayes; clergyman
in M. E. Church in Ill., for thirty years; agent of A. B. S. 1864–1871;
married, first, Julia Ann Patterson of Ky., June 1, 1829 (died Dec. 3,
1833); second, Betsey Carpenter of Norton, Mass., Oct. 7, 1834
(died April 23, 1852); third, Sarah C. Gardner, Providence, R. I.,
Sept. 2, 1853.

Children :

 3121 i JOHN P.,[9] b. Aug. 12, 1830; soldier in the Union Army; d. in
     Texas.
 3122 ii JONATHAN B., b. Feb. 3, 1833; went south; d. at Memphis,
     Tenn.

1536 ELIZA ANN[8] HAYES (*Molly,*[7] *Josiah,*[6] *Moses,*[5] *John,*[4] *John,*[3]
John,[2] *John*[1]), daughter of John P. and Molly (Emery) Hayes; married July 4, 1833, Aaron Morse of Hopkinton, N. H. (died Aug. 9,
1849).

Children :

 3123 i MARTHA HALL,[9] b. May 8, 1834; m. Lewis Dow (artist in Cal.)
     Dec. 25, 1866.
 3124 ii GEORGE, b. April 12, 1842; music teacher.

1537 ABIGAIL W.[8] HAYES (*Molly,*[7] *Josiah,*[6] *Moses,*[5] *John,*[4] *John,*[3]
John,[2] *John*[1]), daughter of John P. and Molly (Emery) Hayes; died
July 1, 1838; married William Henry Mead of Meredith, N. H., May
1, 1833.

Child :

 3125 i ASA LEWIS,[9] went west and died.

1538 SALLY EMERY[8] HAYES (*Molly,*[7] *Josiah,*[6] *Moses,*[5] *John,*[4] *John,*[3]
John,[2] *John*[1]), daughter of John P. and Molly (Emery) Hayes; married Francis D. Slade of Hanover, N. H., June 9, 1840; died May,
1882.

Children :

 3126 i HORACE TOPLIFT,[9] b. Feb. 24, 1844; d. Nov. 2, 1865.
 3127 ii MARY ESTHER, b. Dec. 2, 1849; m. Chas. H. Woodbury of West
     Lebanon, N. H., July 17, 1872.

1539 JOSIAH EMERY[8] HAYES (*Molly,*[7] *Josiah,*[6] *Moses,*[5] *John,*[4] *John,*[3]
John,[2] *John*[1]), son of John P. and Molly (Emery) Hayes; died April,
1881. Colonel in the War of the Rebellion; merchant; state treasurer, Kansas.

Children :

 3128 i CHARLES.[9]
 3129 ii EMMA.
 3130 iii ARTHUR.
 3131 iv HOLLEY.

1540 MARY (POLLY)[8] HACKETT (*Lydia,*[7] *Josiah,*[6] *Moses,*[5] *John,*[4]
John,[3] *John,*[2] *John*[1]), daughter of Jeremiah and Lydia (Emery)
Hackett; married Stephen Gale at Gilmanton, N. H., Jan. 7, 1822.
 Child :

3132 i Charles W ,⁹ m Jane E Long of Rockland, Me ; officer in Mass.
State Prison twenty-five years

1541 Nancy⁸ Hackett (*Lydia,*⁷ *Josiah,*⁶ *Moses,*⁵ *John,*⁴ *John,*³ *John,*² *John¹*), daughter of Jeremiah and Lydia (Emery) Hackett, married Sewall Batchelder, Gilmanton, N. H., April 12, 1828.
Children :

3133 i George A ,⁹ b. May 5, 1829, in Boston, Mass.
3134 ii Hattie, b Dec. 23, 1833

1542 Mahala⁸ Hackett (*Lydia,*⁷ *Josiah,*⁶ *Moses,*⁵ *John,*⁴ *John,*³ *John,*² *John¹*) daughter of Jeremiah and Lydia (Emery) Hackett; married, first, William Goss who was drowned ; second, John Goss ; third, M Merrill ; died Oct., 1870.
Children :

3135 i Julia A ,⁹ b Jan , 1827, m , 1st, Stephen Bryer in Guilford,
N H . Nov 2, 1847, 2nd. Hiram S Twombly, July 3, 1880
3136 ii Asa, b Nov 26, 1831, m L Smith, d in Dover, N H , 1862.
3137 iii Lydia J , b in Guilford, N H , m H S Twombly; d in
Dover, N H , 1869
3138 iv Abby M , b. 1846, m. George Greenleaf who d. in the army, 1871.

1543 Emery⁸ Hackett (*Lydia,*⁷ *Josiah,*⁶ *Moses,*⁵ *John,*⁴ *John,*³ *John,*² *John¹*), son of Jeremiah and Lydia (Emery) Hackett ; married June 26, 1836, Mehetable R. Durgin (born Aug. 13, 1818 ; died Dec 6, 1859). He is known as Hackett Emery.
Children :

3139 i John A ,⁹ b March 28, 1837
3140 ii Charles P , b Nov 25 1838; d in infancy.
3141 iii Eliza J , b Jan 30, 1841, m J L. Bryant, 1857
3142 iv Nellie M , b April 30, 1843, m.. J. N. Staples, June 8, 1866
3143 v Addie A , b Feb 17, 1845, d unm
3144 vi Nathan E , b March 4, 1847.
3145 vii Arthur E , b. March 28, 1849
3146 viii Clara, b Nov 14, 1851, married George P Davis, Dec. 24,
1877
3147 ix Lizzie M , b April 20, 1853; d. unm
3148 x Fannie E., b Sept. 19, 1855, m Fred F Chauncey, July 29,
1875

1544 Betsey Emery⁸ Hackett (*Lydia,*⁷ *Josiah,*⁶ *Moses,*⁵ *John,*⁴ *John,*³ *John,*² *John¹*), daughter of Jeremiah and Lydia (Emery) Hackett ; married William Finney of Plymouth, Mass., at Boston, Jan 2, 1830.
Children ·

3149 i William H ,⁹ b Aug 9, 1832, in Gilmanton, N. H., m Sarah
B Edmonds of Charlestown, Mass , Oct 15, 1855.
3150 ii Elizabeth E , b Jan 2, 1835, in Plymouth, Mass ; m. James
H Allen of Medford, Mass , Sept 20, 1855
3151 iii Alfred C , b. Aug 20, 1841, in Boston, Mass. , Union soldier,
Corp in Co E , 5th Mass Vols
3152 iv Charles E , b Nov 8, 1842, m Susan M Leonard of Plymouth, Mass , April 6, 1862

1546 Susan⁸ Hackett (*Lydia,*⁷ *Josiah,*⁶ *Moses,*⁵ *John,*⁴ *John,*³

John², *John¹*), daughter of Jeremiah and Lydia (Emery) Hackett; married Lemuel Crosby.

Children :

   3153 i   EDWIN F.,[9] m. Emma Shirley.
   3154 ii GEORGE L.
   3155 iii ANNE E., m. ——Huntington.
   3156 iv SUSAN H., m. William Lamox.
   3157 v WILLIAM, d. young.
   3158 vi CHARLES, d. young.

1547 ELIZABETH M.[8] MORRISON (*Rebecca*,[7] *Josiah*,[6] *Moses*,[5] *John*,[4] *John*,[3] *John*,[2] *John¹*), daughter of Jonathan and Rebecca (Emery) Morrison ; married B. Walton in Lynn, Mass., May 1, 1823 ; died 1861.

Children :

   3159 i   ELIZA MALVINA,[9] m. William Smith.
   3160 ii ELLEN MARIA, m. George Smith.
   3161 iii JONATHAN B., d. unm.
   3162 iv JOSEPH WILLIAM, d. unm.

1550 JOSIAH E.[8] MORRISON (*Rebecca*,[7] *Josiah*,[6] *Moses*,[5] *John*,[4] *John*,[3] *John*,[2] *John¹*), son of Jonathan and Rebecca (Emery) Morrison ; married Mehetable George, June 4, 1832.

Children :

   3163 i   SAMUEL L.,[9] b. Jan. 21, 1834.
   3164 ii JOSIAH GEORGE, b. Sept. 18, 1839.

1551 ABIGAIL L.[8] MORRISON (*Rebecca*,[7] *Josiah*,[6] *Moses*,[5] *John*,[4] *John*,[3] *John²*, *John¹*), daughter of Jonathan and Rebecca (Emery) Morrison ; married Samuel Lunt, Feb. 7, 1828.

Children :

   3165 i   ABBIE ELIZABETH.[9]
   3166 ii SAMUEL, d. in the war of the Rebellion.

1552 JUDITH L.[8] MORRISON (*Rebecca*,[7] *Josiah*,[6] *Moses*,[5] *John*,[4] *John*,[3] *John*,[2] *John¹*), daughter of Jonathan and Rebecca (Emery) Morrison ; married Amos Walton, Sept. 11, 1825.

Children :

   3167 i   SARAH W.,[9] m. James Leavitt.
   3168 ii ABBIE L., m. John Woods.
   3169 iii FEDORA ELIZ., m. O. H. P. Fander.
   3170 iv SAMUEL, d. unm.

1553 AMOS E.[8] MORRISON (*Rebecca*,[7] *Josiah*,[6] *Moses*,[5] *John*,[4] *John*,[3] *John*,[2] *John¹*), son of Jonathan and Rebecca (Emery) Morrison ; married Lucinda Bean, Aug. 19, 1837.

Children :

   3171 i   JULIA ANN,[9] b. Nov. 10, 1838 ; d. Jan. 10, 1840.
   3172 ii EDWIN CHAPIN, b. July 4, 1845 ; d. Oct. 12, 1870.
   3173 iii MARY ELLEN, b. April 24, 1851.

1555 REBECCA ANN[8] MORRISON (*Rebecca*,[7] *Josiah*,[6] *Moses*,[5] *John*,[4]

John,[3] *John,*[2] *John*[1]), daughter of Jonathan and Rebecca (Emery) Morrison, married Nathaniel Jones, May 1, 1837.

Children.

3174	i	NATHANIEL PERKINS,[9] d young
3175	ii	CHARLES WILLIAM, d young
3176	iii	CHARLES CARROL, d young.
3177	iv	WALTER CARROL, d young.
3178	v	GRANVILLE MORRISON, d young.
3179	vi	ANN REBECCA, d young
3180	vii	ALICE MAY, b May 6, 1860

1556 JONATHAN E.[8] MORRISON (*Rebecca,*[7] *Josiah,*[6] *Moses,*[5] *John,*[4] *John,*[2] *John,*[2] *John*[1]), son of Jonathan and Rebecca (Emery) Morrison, married, first, Mary N. Page, Nov. 5, 1843; second, Mary A. Sylvester, Feb. 11, 1873.

Children:

3181	i	HERBERT E.,[9] b Aug 26, 1844
3182	ii	MARY G. GERTRUDE, b March 28, 1846

By second wife

3183	iii	WALTER J., b Feb 11, 1874.

1557 RACHEL[8] HUSE (*Sarah,*[7] *Josiah,*[6] *Moses,*[5] *John,*[4] *John,*[3] *John,*[2] *John*[1]), daughter of Joseph and Sarah (Emery) Huse, married Oct. 29, 1837, Daniel Demerritt.

Children.

3184	i	SARAH E.,[9] b Feb 11, 1840
3185	ii	JOSEPH b Sept 17, 1841, d, unm, March 22, 1871, a soldier in the 13th Vt Regt
3186	iii	DANIEL, b July 3, 1843. d May 10, 1854.
3187	iv	ARTHUR, b April 17, 1845

1558 DANIEL M.[8] HUSE (*Sarah,*[7] *Josiah,*[6] *Moses,*[5] *John,*[4] *John,*[3] *John,*[2] *John*[1]), son of Joseph and Sarah (Emery) Huse; married Eliza Dudley, Nov 25, 1830; died Sept 3, 1883. His wife died Jan. 18, 1888.

Children.

3188	i	LOVINA A.,[9] b Sept 3, 1834, m Morrell Moore
3189	ii	SARAH EMILY, b Sept 1, 1840, m B W Plummer.
3190	iii	ANN ELIZA, b Jan 3, 1845, m G F Blanchard

1559 WILLIAM B.[8] HUSE (*Sarah,*[7] *Josiah,*[6] *Moses,*[5] *John,*[4] *John,*[3] *John,*[2] *John*[1]), son of Joseph and Sarah (Emery) Huse; married Fanny Plummer, Dec. 15, 1833.

Children:

3191	i	LUTHER PLUMMER,[9] b May 4, 1835; m Eliz Hale, Dec 25, 1866
3192	ii	WARREN DANIEL, b Dec 25, 1836, m Irene Goodwin, March 6, 1859
3193	iii	LAURA ANN, b Nov 2, 1838, m Isaac Blake, June 17, 1860
3194	iv	WILLIAM SANBORN, b July 13, 1840, m Clara French, Aug 12, 1869
3195	v	LEONARD, b May 7, 1842, d. in La, May 30, 1863. Union soldier
3196	vi	FANNY, b June 12, 1845, m. Simeon Drake, March 24, 1868
3197	vii	MARY ELLEN, b. Aug 6, 1847. Teacher.

1561 EBENEZER B.[8] HUSE (*Sarah,*[7] *Josiah,*[6] *Moses,*[5] *John,*[4] *John,*[3] *John,*[2] *John*[1]), son of Joseph and Sarah (Emery) Huse; married Lydia Fisk, June 5, 1844.

Child:

3198   ALMA R.,[9] b. Sept. 29, 1845; m. George E. Moody, March 8, 1866.

1642 FREDERICK A.[8] EMERY (*John Sargent,*[7] *Michael,*[6] *Moses,*[5] *John,*[4] *John,*[3] *John,*[2] *John*[1]), son of John Sargent and his second wife Susan B. (Haseltine) Emery; married, March 25, 1885, Clara E. LaFayette (born in Waterboro, Me., April 14, 1854).

Child:

3199   i   ANNE GRACE,[9] b. June 10, 1886, in Boston.

1644 ANNIE B.[8] EMERY (*John Sargent,*[7] *Michael,*[6] *Moses,*[5] *John,*[4] *John,*[3] *John,*[2] *John*[1]), daughter of John Sargent and his second wife Susan B. (Haseltine) Emery; married Luther C. Richardson of Pelham, N. H., Dec. 25, 1876; she died Jan. 17, 1882.

Children:

3200   i   CHESTER AUGUSTUS,[9] b. Oct. 17, 1877.
3201   ii   MABEL ANN, b. March 21, 1879.
3202   iii   MARION LOUISA, b. May 18, 1880.
3203   iv   MAXWELL C., b. Nov. 2, 1881.

1651 HANNAH[7] EMERY (*Forest,*[6] *Samuel,*[5] *Samuel,*[4] *Rev. Samuel,*[3] *John,*[2] *John*[1]), daughter of Forest and Mary (Adams) Emery; married Jotham Welch of Sanford, Me., published Jan. 14, 1827.

Children, born in Sanford:

3204   i   MARY ABIGAIL,[8] b. March 19, 1831; d. June 11, 1832.
3205   ii   ABBIE ANNIS, b. March 2, 1834.
3206   iii   STEPHEN EMERY, b. May 11, 1836; m. Octavia E. Lane, 1861, in Boothbay, Me.; had several children.
3207   iv   MARY, b. April 26, 1839; m. C. W. Tripp; d. Dec. 7, 1884.
3208   v   ANN E., b. Aug. 13, 1841; m. Nov. 11, 1865, Hiram S. Pinkham.

1653 JAMES[7] EMERY (*Forest,*[6] *Samuel,*[5] *Samuel,*[4] *Rev. Samuel,*[3] *John,*[2] *John*[1]), son of Forest and Mary (Adams) Emery; married Mrs. Mary Ann Auld, widow of William Auld, and daughter of Robert Getchell of Wells, Me., Dec. 3, 1840. He died Feb. 5, 1852.

Children, born in Wells:

3209   i   MARY ANN,[8] b. Aug. 27, 1841; m. Brackett Hall of N. Berwick, Me.
3210   ii   SAMUEL, b. Oct. 25, 1843.
3211   iii   URSULA JANE, b. Oct. 10, 1845; m. Alonzo Hubbard of Wells.
3212   iv   LYDIA LORD, b. April 19, 1848; m. Rufus Hubbard.

1654 STEPHEN[7] EMERY (*Forest,*[6] *Samuel,*[5] *Samuel,*[4] *Rev. Samuel,*[3] *John,*[2] *John*[1]), son of Forest and Mary (Adams) Emery; married, first, Keziah Eaton; second, Olive Eaton, Nov. 19, 1840.

Children:

3213   i   MARY,[8] b. Dec. 14, 1837, in Wells; m. John D. Lawrence, of Kittery, Me.
3214   ii   JAMES, b. Jan. 29, 1839, in Wells.

3215 iii AFFA E , b May 29, 1841, in Wells
3216 iv FOREST, b Jan 13, 1843, in Belmont, Me.
3217 v   OSCAR L , b. Nov 19, 1845 in Wells. Burned to death
3218 vi NOAH, b Oct 9, 1847, in Wells
3219 vii OSCAR L , b Dec 6 1849
3220 viii KEZIAH E , b Dec. 10, 1852.
3221 ix FOREST H , b May 15 1857, in Kittery, Me
3222 x   FLORA A , b July 17, 1859.
3223 xi JOHN L , b Jan 17, 1864

1672 JOHN[7] EMERY (*Stephen,*[6] *John,*[5] *Rev Stephen,*[4] *Rev Samuel,*[3] *John,*[2] *John*[1]), son of Stephen and Betsey (Ryder) Emery ; married first, Jan 10, 1832, Almira Harding, who died Aug 9, 1843 ; second, Mary Attwood, Feb 1, 1844.
Children :

3224 i   ORZELIA, b Oct 21, 1834 ; m Capt Rufus Hours April 1, 1856
3225 ii JOHN ANSON, b Nov 16, 1837
3226 iii MINERVA FRANCES, b Feb 10, 1839, m Capt. Bassett J Smith,
           May 6, 1860, d Sept 12, 1879
3227 iv EDSON, b Nov 4, 1841 ; d April 13, 1871, unm
3228 v   RUFUS b. Aug. 3, 1843
3229 vi ERASTUS, b Aug 7, 1846.
3230 vii BENJAMIN VALENTINE, b Feb 14, 1848
3231 viii MARY ATTWOOD, b Dec 26, 1852
3232 ix CARRIE LUELLA, b Oct 27, 1855
3233 x   ALMIRA HARDING, b Dec 17, 1857.

1676 STEPHEN[7] EMERY (*Stephen*[6] *John,*[5] *Rev. Stephen,*[4] *Rev Samuel,*[3] *John,*[2] *John*[1]), son of Stephen and Betsey (Ryder) Emery , married Rebecca T Harding, Feb. 28, 1840.
Children :

3234 i   GEORGE NEWELL,[8] b May 12, 1841.
3235 ii STEPHEN AMBROSE, b July 2, 1844
3246 iii REBECCA H , b July 14, 1849
2237 iv LUCY ANNA, b Sept 14, 1851
3238 v   JOSHUA, b Feb 13, 1858
3239 vi ROBERT, b. July 8, 1862

1677 ALATHINA[7] EMERY (*Stephen,*[6] *John,*[5] *Rev. Stephen,*[4] *Rev. Samuel,*[3] *John,*[2] *John*[1]), daughter of Stephen and Betsey (Ryder) Emery ; married Eben Taylor, Jan. 28, 1840
Children .

3240 i   LYSANDER,[8] b Nov 5, 1840, m Sarah S Tripp, Aug. 25, 1864
8241 ii ALATHINA EMERY, b Nov. 5, 1847, m. Richard F. Smith, Sept.
           19, 1866
3242 iii LUELLA, b Jan 22, 1852, m Horace E Durgin, Feb 20, 1877
3243 iv MELINDA S., b. Oct. 21, 1858, m. L. Frank Berkley, Nov. 5,
           1876.
3244 v   E AUGUSTINE, b Dec 1, 1861 ; m Nellie Lawton, Sept. 10,
           1885

1679 CYRUS[7] EMERY (*Stephen,*[6] *John,*[5] *Rev. Stephen,*[4] *Rev. Samuel,*[3] *John,*[2] *John*[1]), son of Stephen and Betsey (Ryder) Emery ; married Louisa Cahoon, of Hardwick, Mass., March 23, 1848 ; died March 30, 1873.

Children :

3245　i　ELNORA,[8] b. June 29, 1849 ; m., 1st, George Ryder, Dec. 16, 1869 ;
　　　　　2nd, Chester Cahoon, March 28, 1884.
3246　ii　HENRY, b. April 28, 1853.
3247　iii　LOUISA MAY, b. Nov. 10, 1855.
3248　iv　WALTER, b. Nov. 13, 1857 ; m. Nettie Doane, Dec. 14, 1883.
3249　v　ELMER E., ⎱ b. June 29, 1860; ⎰ m. Nettie B. Nickerson, Dec.
　　　　　　　　　　　　　　　　　　　　　　22, 1886.
3250　vi　EDNA, ⎰ ⎱ d. June, 1873.
3251　vii　NELSON, b. July 15, 1862.
3252　viii　NETTIE L., b. Aug. 9, 1864 ; m. Zephaniah Nickerson, Jan. 26,
　　　　　1886.
3253　ix　TRUMAN, b. Aug. 1, 1867.

1682 JOSEPH[7] EMERY (*Samuel,*[6] *John,*[5] *Rev. Stephen,*[4] *Rev. Samuel,*[3] *John,*[2] *John*[1]), son of Samuel and Jerusha (Chase) Emery ; married Martha Harding, Jan. 16, 1834 ; died Jan. 30, 1879. He was a successful sea captain, having been on the sea for forty years, during which time he never met with an accident nor lost more than one man ; made the first trip from Japan to San Francisco after the treaty was signed. His wife died in Medford, Mass., May 20, 1887.

Children :

3254　i　MARCELIA,[8] b. March 1, 1838.
3255　ii　EDWIN FRANCIS, b. Dec. 26, 1839 ; d. Sept. 15, 1859.
3256　iii　BENJ. OSGOOD, b. Feb. 26, 1843.

1688 SAMUEL D.[7] CLIFFORD (*Betsey,*[6] *John,*[5] *Rev. Stephen,*[4] *Rev. Samuel,*[3] *John,*[2] *John*[1]), son of Dr. Daniel and Betsey (Emery) Clifford ; married, first, Jan. 15, 1837, Louisa C. Burrows, who died July 30, 1840 ; second, Rebecca Beane of Barnstable, Mass., March 25, 1845.

Children :

3257　i　SAMUEL D.,[8] b. July 21, 1840 ; d. Oct. 10, 1840.
3258　ii　OPHELIA M., ⎱ b. Jan. 21, 1846; ⎰
3259　iii　CORDELIA A. E., ⎰ ⎱ d. Sept. 3, 1847.
3260　iv　CORDELIA A. E., b. June 4, 1848 ; m., 1st, Martin L. Bearse, Feb.
　　　　　20, 1872 ; 2nd, Lucian M. Gagh, Nov. 29, 1885.
3261　v　MARY E., b. Feb. 4, 1850 ; m. Reuben A. Tripp, Nov. 18, 1869.
3262　vi　SAMUEL D., b. Jan. 16, 1856 ; d. April 10, 1858.
3263　vii　ELLA B., b. Feb. 17, 1861.
3264　viii　SAMUEL D., b. Oct. 17, 1865.

1690 WILLIAM D.[7] CLIFFORD (*Betsey,*[6] *John,*[5] *Rev. Stephen,*[4] *Rev. Samuel,*[3] *John,*[2] *John*[1]), son of Dr. Daniel and Betsey (Emery) Clifford ; married Lucy A. Bartlett, June 11, 1845. He died in Ware, Mass.

Children :

3265　i　LUCY H.,[8] b. July 1, 1848 ; m. Alonzo Bearse, Nov. 27, 1866.
　　　　　He d. March 31, 1886.
3266　ii　MARY E. B., b. Nov. 10, 1853 ; m. Silas Albee, Nov. 1, 1871.
3267　iii　SARAH C., b. Dec. 11, 1855 ; m. Joseph P. Sumpter, Oct. 17,
　　　　　1877.

1691 BETSEY[7] CLIFFORD (*Betsey,*[6] *John,*[5] *Rev. Stephen,*[4] *Rev.*

Samuel,[3] John,[2] John[1]), daughter of Dr. Daniel and Betsey (Emery) Clifford, married Issachar B Barnes, Feb 4, 1844.

Children:

    3268   i   LOUISA C ,[8] b. Sept 18, 1844, m Nathan Downey, Aug 11, 1861.
    3269   ii   WILLIAM E , b 1846, m Clara Small, 1866
    3270   iii ISSACHER B , b. Dec 10, 1849, m. Sallie A. Kelley, Jan. 15, 1874.
    3271   iv   DANIEL P C , b Aug 6, 1851, m Anne P White, Nov 4, 1880
    3272   v   EDGAR V., b. Oct 5, 1856; lost at sea, March 6, 1868.

1692 DANIEL[7] CLIFFORD (*Betsey,*[6] *John,*[5] *Rev. Stephen,*[4] *Rev. Samuel,*[3] *John,*[2] *John*[1]), son of Dr. Daniel and Betsey (Emery) Clifford; married Angeline T. Baxter, Dec. 3, 1857 He died May 21, 1885. His wife died 1881. Lived in Chatham and Hyannis, Mass.

Children :

    3273   i   ANGELINE P ,[8] b Nov. 14, 1860, m George L. Thacher, jr.,
                  June 24, 1880.
    3274   ii   CORA M , b Dec 22 1863; d Feb 1, 1865
    3275   iii FRANK L , b June 6, 1866
    3276   iv   BESSIE E , b July 22, 1868, m Wm L Drew, Aug 1, 1885
    3277   v   KATE R., b. Jan 22, 1870, m Frederick W. Bunker Aug 26,
                  1886
    3278   vi   MINNIE R , b Dec. 25, 1872.
    3279   vii AMY S , b Oct 31, 1875 , d July 8, 1877.
    3280   viii MAY T , b July 5, 1877

1693 RUTH H [7] CLIFFORD (*Betsey,*[6] *John,*[5] *Rev. Stephen,*[4] *Rev. Samuel,*[3] *John,*[2] *John*[1]), daughter of Dr. Daniel and Betsey (Emery) Clifford; married George W. Nickerson, Dec. 3, 1844.

Children :

    3281   i   BETSEY FRANKLIN,[8] b Aug. 4, 1845, m Hiram P. Harriman,
                  lawyer and judge at Barnstable, Mass
    3282   ii   GEORGE WILLIAM, b July 14, 1847, m. Maria G. Knowles,
                  July 22, 1869
    3283   iii EDGAR VERNON, b Oct 9, 1849, d. April 27, 1856.

1696 SAMUEL[7] EMERY (*John,*[6] *John,*[5] *Joshua,*[4] *John,*[3] *Jonathan,*[2] *John*[1]), son of John and Abiah (Page) Emery, married, Feb. 22, 1814, Elizabeth Wolfe Young, grand-niece of General Wolfe (died Jan. 1, 1860); removed to Franklin Furnace, O , 1831, and Tivoli, Peoria Co , Ill , 1836. She died March, 1863.

Children :

    3284   i   ABIAH PAGE,[8] m Robert McConnell.
    3285   ii   JOHN, b Dec 28, 1816, in Orford, N H ; m Eliza Dana, have
                  eight children
    3286   iii ELIZA YOUNG, b. May 29, 1820.
    3287   iv   RUBY M , b. Nov. 21, 1829.
    3288   v   SAMUEL B.

1698 RICHARD[7] EMERY (*John,*[6] *John,*[5] *Joshua,*[4] *John,*[3] *Jonathan,*[2] *John*[1]), son of John and Abiah (Page) Emery, married Betsey Hardy of Groton, Conn He was an itinerant minister of the Methodist Episcopal Church ; began preaching at sixteen years of age ; ordained deacon, June 4, 1814 , elder, June 5, 1816 , died in Wethersfield, Conn , Jan. 7, 1821. His wife died in Craftsbury, Vt., March, 1845.

10

Children, born in Craftsbury:

3289 i EMELINE B.,[8] b. Oct. 17, 1818.
3290 ii BETSEY, b. June 15, 1820; d. July 11, 1821.

1700 ABIGAIL[7] EMERY (*Joshua,*[6] *John,*[5] *Joshua,*[4] *John,*[3] *Jonathan,*[2] *John*[1]), daughter of Joshua and Ruth (Nott) Emery; married Jan. 11, 1804, John Mather of Rockingham, N. H. (born Feb. 22, 1780); lived in Essex, N. Y.

Children:

3291 i CORNELIA,[8] b. Aug. 22, 1804; d. 1831.
3292 ii ABIGAIL WEBSTER, b. Jan. 5, 1806.
3293 iii ELISHA, b. Sept. 25, 1807; m. Betsey Potter; d. June 17, 1833, *s. p.*
3294 iv ISRAEL, b. Dec. 3, 1808.
3295 v JOSHUA EMERY, b. Nov. 24, 1810.
3296 vi JOHN ROYCE, b. Oct. 3, 1812; d. 1842.
3297 vii RUTH PHŒBE, b. April 13, 1814.
3298 viii MARY CYNTHIA. b. March 27, 1816; d. March, 1839.
3299 ix SAMUEL, b. June 13, 1818.
3300 x SARAH, b. April 13, 1820; d. May 14, 1820.
3301 xi JONATHAN, b. June 1, 1821.
3302 xii CAROLINE, b. July 14, 1823; d. 1842.
3303 xiii ROSWELL HUNT, b. July 6, 1825; d. 1842.

1701 MARY[7] EMERY (*Joshua,*[6] *John,*[5] *Joshua,*[4] *John,*[3] *Jonathan,*[2] *John*[1]), daughter of Joshua and Ruth (Nott) Emery; married, Jan. 17, 1802, Jonathan Royce (born Oct. 19, 1780); removed to Illinois.

Children:

3304 i LOIS,[8] b. July 12, 1803.
3305 ii SARAH, b. July 2, 1805.
3306 iii MARY, b. July 11, 1807.
3307 iv PHŒBE, b. Aug. 20, 1809; m. Israel Mather (3294), Jan. 1, 1830; d. Jan. 30, 1835.
3308 v ORLEAN, b. Sept. 2, 1811.
3309 vi HANNAH, b. June 22, 1813; m. Israel Mather (3294), Jan. 8, 1837.
3310 vii HEPZIBAH, b. June 15, 1815; m. William King; d. Jan. 3, 1888, *s. p.*
3311 viii ABIGAIL, b. June 24, 1817; m. Alex. Fortune.
3312 ix MARIA, b. March 27, 1820; m. E. P. Mack.
3313 x JONATHAN, b. May 9, 1822.
3314 xi CHARLOTTE ELIZA, b. Feb. 26, 1824; m. J. Hobson.
3315 xii ABNER, b. June 13, 1826.

1703 PHŒBE[7] EMERY (*Joshua,*[6] *John,*[5] *Joshua,*[4] *John,*[3] *Jonathan,*[2] *John*[1]), daughter of Joshua and Ruth (Nott) Emery; married Bela Frink, Feb. 10, 1825.

Child:

3316 i SARAH JANE,[8] m. ——— Copeland.

1704 HANNAH[7] EMERY (*Joshua,*[6] *John,*[5] *Joshua,*[4] *John,*[3] *Jonathan,*[2] *John*[1]), daughter of Joshua and Ruth (Nott) Emery; married, Dec. 7, 1815, Joshua Shepard, jr. (born Nov. 12, 1788); lived in New Hampshire; removed to Michigan. He died Sept. 21, 1830. His wife died April 1, 1860.

Children :

```
3317   i    CHAUNCEY,⁸ b  May 3, 1817.
3318   ii   LUCY MARY, b  Sept  29, 1819, d  March 11, 1824
3319   iii  WILLIAM MATHER, b. Sept 14, 1822
3320   iv   JOSHUA NORMAN, b  Nov 5, 1825
3321   v    JAMES HARVEY, b  Nov 20, 1827.
3322   vi   SARAH.
3323   vii  MARY.
```

1705 SAMUEL⁷ EMERY (*Joshua,⁶ John,⁵ Joshua,⁴ John,³ Jonathan,² John¹*), son of Joshua and Ruth (Nott) Emery, married, Jan 2, 1820, Catharine Shepard of Alstead, N. H. (born Aug. 19, 1795, died July 27, 1854). He died 1854.

Children

```
3324   i    SON,⁸ d  in infancy
3325   ii   ELIZA  b  June 26, 1822
3326   iii  HARRIET  b  Feb 19, 1824
3327   iv   EDWIN, b  Nov 21, 1825
3328   v    JOSHUA SHEPARD, b  Dec  21, 1827.
3329   vi   BREWSTER PALMER, b  Aug 19, 1830.
3330   vii  PERSIS, b  Aug. 14, 1832, d  at South Richland, N  Y , Aug  1,
            1870
3331   viii ALBERT HAMILTON, b  June 21, 1834
3332   ix   CYRUS FARNSWORTH, b  July 4, 1836, d  in New York, July
            16, 1865
3333   x    LOTTIE A.
```

1706 MOSES⁷ EMERY (*Joshua,⁶ John,⁵ Joshua,⁴ John,³ Jonathan,² John¹*), son of Joshua and Ruth (Nott) Emery; married, first, in Surry, N. H , Jan 19. 1815, Catharine Winchester (born in Jaffrey, N. H., April 26, 1794) , second, Lydia Sprague Stowell (born in Hingham, Mass., May 4, 1797 ; died Feb. 17, 1861).   He died in Lakeville, Mass., Nov. 26, 1860.

Children

```
3334   i    WILLIAM WINCHESTER,⁸ b. in Rockingham, N.H., Nov. 23, 1815.
3335   ii   MOSES WEBSTER, b  in Walpole, N. H , April 15, 1818.
3336   iii  CYNTHIA WINCHESTER, b  in Surry, N  H., April 3, 1820.
3337   iv   SARAH FRANCES WINCHESTER, b  May 12, 1821
3338   v    JOHN DEXTER PRATT, b  in East Bridgewater, Mass , Nov  22,
            1828
3339   vi   LUCY STOWELL, b. in Middleton, Mass , July 20, 1830
```

1707 CYNTHIA⁷ EMERY (*Joshua,⁶ John,⁵ Joshua,⁴ John,³ Jonathan,² John¹*), daughter of Joshua and Ruth (Nott) Emery, married Samuel Hall, Dec. 2, 1819.

Samuel Hall and Samuel Emery, his brother-in-law, removed from Walpole, N. H. to Mexico, N. Y., in 1820, being three weeks on the way   Their conveyance was a long ox sled drawn by two yoke of oxen, carrying their families and household goods.

Children .

```
3340   i    ALMIRA ⁸
3341   ii   CYNTHIA.
3342   iii  EMERY
3343   iv   PHŒBE
3344   v    ——— ; d  unm.
3345   vi   ——— ; d. unm.
```

1709 ABIGAIL W.[7] EMERY (*Moses*,[6] *John*,[5] *Joshua*,[4] *John*,[3] *Jonathan*,[2] *John*[1]), daughter of Moses and Mary (Webster) Emery ; married, Sept. 4, 1813, Ebenezer Cushman ; clothier ; lived in Warren, N. H. (born June 24, 1787).

Children :

3346   i   MARY W.,[8] b. June 5, 1814.
3347   ii   FRANCIS A., b April 22, 1816.
3348   iii   MOSES E., b. Dec. 15, 1818.
3349   iv   ABIGAIL E., b. July 8, 1822 ; m. Eluathan Searles ; d. May 16, 1843.
3350   v   FANNY, b. Aug. 22, 1827 ; d. Aug., 1875.
3351   vi   REBECCA, b. March 23, 1830 ; d. June, 1881.
3352   vii   CHARLES W., b. May 11, 1834.
3353   viii GEORGE F., b. Jan. 17, 1837.

1711 LUCY[7] EMERY (*Moses*,[6] *John*,[5] *Joshua*,[4] *John*,[3] *Jonathan*,[2] *John*[1]), daughter of Moses and Mary (Webster) Emery ; married, 1827, Elisha Andross.

Children :

3354   i   MOSES E.,[8] b. 1829 ; d. num.
3355   ii   CLARISSA, b. 1834 ; m. Wilson Dexter.
3356   iii   LUCY, b. 1837.
3357   iv   ELISHA, b. 1839.

1712 MOSES[7] EMERY (*Moses*,[6] *John*,[5] *Joshua*,[4] *John*,[3] *Jonathan*,[2] *John*[1]), son of Moses and Mary (Webster) Emery ; married Eunice English of Lyme, N. H., 1825 ; fitted for Dartmouth College under his uncle Stephen P. Webster ; did not enter college, but turned his attention to agriculture ; member of the M. E. Church ; an upright and respected citizen ; died in Lisbon, July 25, 1861. His wife died Oct. 4, 1875.

Children, born in Lisbon, N. H. :

3358   i   HARVEY WEBSTER,[8] b. Nov. 8, 1827.
3359   ii   MARY ELIZABETH, b. Sept. 7, 1830.
3360   iii   JOHN ENGLISH, b. Aug. 16, 1832 ; d. Sept. 20, 1832.
3361   iv   FANNY JANE, b. July 8, 1833 ; d. July 7, 1834.
3362   v   SAMUEL, b. May 1, 1835.
3363   vi   MOSES, b. March 12, 1837.
3364   vii   CHARLES WESLEY, b. Aug. 30, 1840.

1715 SMITH[7] EMERY (*Smith*,[6] *Joshua*,[5] *Joshua*,[4] *John*,[3] *Jonathan*,[2] *John*[1]), son of Smith and Rhoda (Burroughs) Emery ; married Maria Howe in Plymouth, Vt.

Children :

3365   i   JOHN SMITH,[8] b. Aug. 22, 1824 ; m., 1st, Lucinda Wylie, Feb. 22, 1849, who d. Oct. 16, 1875 ; 2nd, Mrs. Amelia E. Crooker (*née* Smith).
3366   ii   ALFRED J.
3367   iii   MARIA L.
3368   iv   RHODA E.
3369   v   EMELINE L., m. Howard Sickles.
3370   vi   JOSEPH, m. ; has two children. Resides in Adrian, Mich.
3371   vii   OLIVE, m. Horatio Reed.
3372   viii ANN ELIZA, m., 1st, ——— ; 2nd, ——— Balwin ; 3rd, ——— Newman Holmes. Resides in Lake City, Minn.

3373 ix WILLIAM H
3374   x HELEN MARY, m ———— Simmons Resides in Harper, Kansas
3375 xi SARAH E
3376 xii HATTIE, d young
3377 xiii CHARLES, d young
3378 xiv EVA
3379 xv JULIA.
3380 xvi HATTIE.

1716 SANFORD[7] EMERY (*Smith*,[6] *Joshua*,[5] *Joshua*,[4] *John*,[3] *Jonathan*,[2] *John*[1]). son of Smith and Rhoda (Burroughs) Emery; married, first, Isabel Warner, 1832; second, Chloe Beebe, April 8, 1852.
Children:

3381   i EDSON F ,[8] b March 20, 1835, d Sept 3, 1884.
3382   ii SANFORD, JR , b. Nov. 9, 1839, d. March 17, 1864.
3383   iii JAMES F , b Jan 30, 1843, m. Emma Haywood
3384   iv WILLIAM F , b Jan 30, 1849.
3385   v ISABELLA C., b Feb 18, 1853, m Frank D Parker, M D ,
            June 23, 1887
3386   vi LAURA A , b April 1, 1855.
3387   vii ARTHUR R., b. April 5, 1856.

1723 JOSEPH WELCH[7] EMERY (*Joshua*,[6] *Joshua*,[5] *Joshua*,[4] *John*,[3] *Jonathan*,[2] *John*[1]), son of Joshua and Elizabeth (Welch) Emery; married Nancy Low Faulkner of Boston, July 1, 1832.   He was a large real-estate owner in Philadelphia Pa., and Camden, N. J., and a successful business man   He died May 1, 1865.
Children, born in Philadelphia:

3388   i JOSEPH FAULKNER,[8] b Sept 17, 1834
3389   ii ELIZABETH ANN, b Aug 9, 1840
3390   iii MARY FAULKNER, b May 24, 1842; d Sept 20, 1867.
3391   iv WOLCOTT JABEZ, b Nov 14, 1845; d Aug 17, 1849
3392   v AARON WELCH, b. Dec 16, 1848, d Aug 27, 1866.
3393   vi FRANCIS WELCH, b April 20, 1851, d. May 18, 1851

1724 FRANCIS WELCH ROBERTS[7] EMERY (*Joshua*,[6] *Joshua*,[5] *Joshua*,[4] *John*,[3] *Jonathan*,[2] *John*[1]), son of Joshua and Elizabeth (Welch) Emery, married, first, Sophronia Faulkner of Boston, July 2, 1829, who died Dec. 21, 1837: second, Mary Baker Wolcott of Bedford, Mar. 26, 1839, who died Sept. 6, 1847, third, May, 1848 Susan Ward of West Brookfield, Mass (died in Neponset, 1875). He was a large contractor and builder of Music Hall and other buildings in Boston, a man of great executive ability, generous impulses, highly esteemed and beloved. He died in Glasgow, Scotland, Feb 15, 1860
Children:

3394   i FRANCIS FAULKNER,[8] b in Roxbury, Mass , March 26, 1830.
3395   ii SOPHRONIA FAULKNER, b. in Roxbury, Mass., Oct , 1831, d.
            Dec 21, 1833
3396   iii ELIZABETH WELCH, b in Roxbury, Mass , 1834, d May 6, 1841
3397   iv AARON FAULKNER, b in Roxbury, Mass , March 27, 1836.
3398   v SOPHRONIA FAULKNER, b and d in Bedford, Mass , 1839.
3399   vi MARY WOLCOTT, b in Bedford, April 12, 1841.
3400   vii JULIA REED, b and d in Bedford, Mass.
3401   viii JULIA REED, b in Boston, May, 1847
3402   ix ANDREW C , b in Boston, Oct 9, 1849; d. July 9, 1851
3403   x GEORGE DEANE, b in Boston, 1852.

1725 Rev. Joshua[7] Emery (*Joshua*,[6] *Joshua*,[5] *Joshua*,[4] *John*,[3] *Jonathan*,[2] *John*[1]), son of Joshua and Elizabeth (Welch) Emery ; prepared for Amherst College at Phillips Academy, Andover, Mass. ; graduated in 1831 ; student in theology in Andover Theological Seminary ; pastor of first Congregational Church, Weymouth, Mass., for thirty-five years ; resigned from loss of voice in 1873 ; married, May 19, 1835, Harriet Peabody of Salem (born in Salem, July 6, 1812) daughter of Jacob Peabody, the "honest auctioneer." He died in Kansas City, Mo., April 24, 1882.

Children :

3404 i   HARRIET PEABODY,[8] b. July 23, 1836, in Fitchburg, Mass.
3405 ii   JOSHUA, b. June 1, 1840, in Weymouth, Mass.
3406 iii CHARLES FRANCIS, b. March 10, 1849, in Weymouth, Mass.
3407 iv   MARGARET, b. Sept. 2, 1850; d. Sept. 1, 1852.

1726 Sewall Norton[7] Emery (*Joshua*,[6] *Joshua*,[5] *Joshua*,[4] *John*,[3] *Jonathan*,[2] *John*)[1], son of Joshua and Elizabeth (Welch) Emery ; married Martha Baker of Boston, June 5, 1836, who died Jan. 17, 1882.   He died in Boston, Oct. 27, 1843.

Children :

3408 i   JUSTIN EDWARDS,[8] b. May 17, 1840, in Boston; d. Feb. 17, 1862.
3409 ii   MARTHA ANN, b. July, 1841, in Boston, Mass. ; d. Nov. 7, 1845.

1727 Samuel Hopkins[7] Emery (*Joshua*,[6] *Joshua*,[5] *Joshua*[4], *John*,[2] *Jonathan*,[2] *John*[1]), son of Joshua and Elizabeth (Welch) Emery ; fitted for college at Phillips Academy, Andover, Mass. ; entered the sophomore class, Amherst College ; graduated, 1834 ; declined the office of professor in the New York Deaf and Dumb Institution ; studied theology in the Andover Theological Seminary ; ordained and installed pastor of the Winslow church, Taunton, Mass., Nov. 23, 1837 ; called to Bedford, Mass. ; recalled to Taunton ; in 1855 called to the first Congregationalist church, Quincy, Ill., remaining fourteen years ; supplied the New England church in Chicago, the Richmond St. church, Providence, R. I., Olivet church, Bridgeport, Conn., and the church in North Middleton, Mass. ; minister at large in Taunton eleven years ; author of "The Ministry of Taunton" and "History of No. Middleboro Church ;" registrar of the Genealogical Association of Illinois ; hospital chaplain during the war of the Rebellion and known as the "soldier's friend ;" member of the N. E. Gen. and Hist. Soc. ; Chicago Hist. Soc. ; President of the Old Colony Hist. Soc. ; representative to the Mass. Legislature, 1890 ; married Julia, daughter of William Reed of Taunton, Mass., March 7, 1838.

Children :

3410 i   WILLIAM REED,[8] b. June 5, 1839, in Taunton, Mass; d. June 9, 1852.
3411 ii   SAMUEL HOPKINS, b. Aug. 3, 1840, in Taunton.
3412 iii FRANCIS WOLCOTT, b. April 24, 1842, in Bedford, Mass.
3413 iv   JOSEPH WELCH, b. Nov. 10, 1850, in Taunton, Mass.

1730 Margaret L.[7] Emery (*John*,[6] *Joshua*,[5] *Joshua*,[4] *John*,[3]

Jonathan,[2] John[1]), daughter of John and Harriet (Humphrey) Emery; married Charles Butrick, Feb 5, 1846, died Dec. 27, 1878.
Child

3414　i　CHARLES D ,[8] b Sept. 1, 1847, in Somerville, Mass ; d May 1, 1877.

1733 HARRIET E [7] EMERY (*John,[6] Joshua,[5] Joshua,[4] John,[3] Jonathan,[2] John[1]*), daughter of John and Harriet (Humphrey) Emery; married Henry Seaver, Jan. 7, 1844.
Children, born in Boston :

3415　i　HARRIET C ,[8] b Jan 21, 1845, d. the same day.
3416　ii　HENRY H., b July 15, 1846

1740 ANNIE P.[7] EMERY (*Moses G. J ,[6] Moses,[5] Joshua,[4] John,[3] Jonathan,[2] John[1]*), daughter of Moses G. J , and Frances G (Brewster) Emery, married Daniel B. Hallett, Esq , of Boston, June 9, 1869
Child :

3417　i　DANIEL EMERY,[8] b. July 29, 1876.

1741 MARY[7] EMERY (*Ephraim,[6] John,[5] David,[4] John,[3] Jonathan,[2] John[1]*), daughter of Ephraim and Mary (Russell) Emery; married Captain John Remick who died Oct. 31, 1837. She died June 4, 1848.
Children :

3418　i　ISAAC RUSSELL [8]
3419　ii　JOHN E , b. March, 1812
3420　iii　SARAH BARTLETT EMERY, b 1817
3421　iv　MARY RUSSELL, b. April 14, 1819

1743 THOMAS[7] EMERY (*Ephraim,[6] John,[5] David,[4] John,[3] Jonathan,[2] John[1]*), son of Ephraim and Mary (Russell) Emery ; married Mary Hoyt, April 14, 1818 , died Nov. 12, 1840.
Children, born in West Newbury, Mass :

3422　i　EPHRAIM RUSSELL,[8] b Oct 8, 1818
3423　ii　THOMAS GALE, b Jan 17, 1820, d young
3424　iii　GEORGE WASHINGTON, b. Sept 10, 1821, m. Mary E Carroll.
3425　iv　SARAH JANE, b July 21, 1823
3426　v　BENJ FRANKLIN, b June 29, 1825.
3427　vi　JUDITH KIMBALL, b Oct 31, 1830.

1745 DAVID[7] EMERY (*David,[6] John,[5] David,[4] John,[3] Jonathan,[2] John[1]*), son of David and Betty (Little) Emery, married, April 22, 1812, Sarah Smith (born July 11, 1787), daughter of James and Prudence (Little) Smith. He was an innkeeper ; major in the militia and noted for his fine bearing and distinguished horsemanship. He died Jan , 1869. His wife died Aug. 28, 1879.
Child :

3428　i　SARAH ANNA,[8] b. Nov. 29, 1821, in Newburyport, Mass , author of "Three Generations" and "Recollections of a Nonogenarian"

1746 SARAH[7] EMERY (*John,[6] Moses,[5] David,[4] John,[3] Jonathan,[2] John[1]*), daughter of John and Sarah (Fellows) Emery, married

George Hosum, April, 1821, who died April 30, 1881, aged 81.   She died March 25, 1887.

Children, born in West Newbury :

   3429   i   SARAH,[8] b July 29, 1828 , m Eben C. Bailey.
   3430   ii   LYDIA ANN, b April, 1830

1747 JOHN[7] EMERY (*John*,[6] *Moses*,[5] *David*,[4] *John* [3] *Jonathan*,[2] *John*[1]), son of John and Sarah (Fellows) Emery, married Mehetable Grant, April 13, 1827.   Comb maker.

Children, born in West Newbury :

   3431   i   GUSTAVUS BYRON,[8] b April 15, 1828
   3432   ii   JOHN GILMAN, b May 3, 1830 , d. Oct. 3, 1830
   3433   iii MARY ESTHER, b Aug 23, 1833

1748 TAPPAN[7] EMERY (*John* [6] *Moses*,[5] *David*,[4] *John*,[3] *Jonathan*,[2] *John*[1]), son of John and Sarah (Fellows) Emery ; married Lydia Williams Colby, Aug. 12, 1833 ; died in Merrimacport, Mass , Feb 14, 1887, aged 84.

Children :

   3434   i   CHARLES,[8] b June 23, 1834.
   3435   ii   IRA TAPPAN, } b Dec 25, 1839 ; { d. June 8, 1851
   3436   iii LYDIA IRENE, }

1750 NANCY[7] EMERY (*John*,[6] *Moses*,[5] *David*,[4] *John*,[3] *Jonathan*,[2] *John*[1]), daughter of John and Sarah (Fellows) Emery, married Anson W. Noyes of West Newbury, Nov. 6, 1824, and died Feb. 16, 1887

Children :

   3437   i   ADDISON BROWN,[8] b Aug 8, 1825
   3438   ii   THOMAS CHASE, b Nov 23, 1827
   3439   iii SALLY ANN WHITTIER, b. Dec 28, 1830

1751 BETSEY[7] EMERY (*John*,[6] *Moses*,[5] *David*,[4] *John*,[3] *Jonathan*,[2] *John*[1]), daughter of John and Sarah (Fellows) Emery ; married in Amesbury, March 3, 1830, Thomas Sargent Currier of Amesbury, Mass   She died in 1887.

Children :

   3440   i   THOMAS FLORIAN,[8] b Nov 10, 1833, in West Newbury.
   3441   ii   SUSAN ELIZ , b Oct 21, 1835 in West Newbury
   3442   iii HORACE HAMILTON, b May 23, 1838, in Amesbury
   3443   iv   SARAH REBECCA, b June 23, 1847, in Amesbury

1752 MOSES[7] EMERY (*John*,[6] *Moses* [5] *David*,[4] *John*,[3] *Jonathan*,[2] *John*[1]), son of John and Sarah (Fellows) Emery ; married July 10, 1835, Harriet L. Pillsbury (born Aug. 11, 1813, in Charlestown, Mass).

Children, born in Charlestown, Mass. :

   3444   i   HARRIET,[8] b Sept 23, 1837 , d. March 16, 1843.
   3445   ii   MOSES A , b Jan. 5, 1843

1753 SUSAN[7] EMERY (*John*,[6] *Moses*,[5] *David*,[4] *John*,[3] *Jonathan*,[2]

John[1]), daughter of John and Sarah (Fellows) Emery; married Nov. 1, 1844, Nathan Huntington (born Oct. 8, 1818).
Children :

        3446   i   Louisa[8] b July 10, 1847
        3447   ii   Susan Emely, b Nov 27, 1849
        3448   iii Sarah Fellows, b July 5, 1850
        3449   iv   Nathan, b Dec 15, 1852.
        3450   v   Nettie, b March 9, 1856
        3451   vi   Emery, b May 26, 1860

1754 Harriet[7] Emery (*Jacob*,[6] *Moses*,[5] *David*,[4] *John*,[3] *Jonathan*,[2] *John[1]*), daughter of Jacob and Lydia (Noyes) Emery, married Benjamin Edwards, Oct. 23, 1824; died Dec 25, 1881
Children :

        3452   i   Benj ,[8] b Dec 25, 1825
        3453   ii   George A , b Oct 4. 1828   d in W Newbury, July 4, 1843.
        3454   iii Charles H , b Aug 5, 1832
        3455   iv   Harriet E , b Sept 1, 1834.
        3456   v   Lydia A , b Jan 1, 1836
        3457   vi   Sarah G , b. June 4, 1840

1755 Clementine[7] Emery (*Jacob*.[6] *Moses*,[5] *David*,[4] *John*,[3] *Jonathan*,[2] *John[1]*), daughter of Jacob and Lydia (Noyes) Emery, married Albert Grant, May 11, 1836. He died Sept 6, 1849   His widow married, second, Joseph Brown, Dec. 25, 1866, who died Dec., 1876.
Children :

        3458   i   Eliza Tappan,[8] b March 3, 1837, d May 19, 1844
        3459   ii   Susan Eliz , b March 7, 1839, d Apr 27, 1861
        3460   iii Lucy Ann, b. Feb 18, 1843, d Feb 5, 1866.

1756 Mary Elizabeth[7] Emery (*Jacob*,[6] *Moses*,[5] *David*,[4] *John*,[3] *Jonathan*.[2] *John[1]*), daughter of Jacob and Lydia (Noyes) Emery ; married Rev Josiah H Tilton of Limerick, Me , Nov. 2, 1839   She died Jan. 15, 1842   He married, second, Eliza T. Emery, sister of his first wife, July 26, 1843.
Child

        3461   i   Mary Abbie,[8] b Oct 7, 1841.

1757 Catharine[7] Emery (*Jacob*,[6] *Moses*,[5] *David*,[4] *John*,[3] *Jonathan*,[2] *John[1]*), daughter of Jacob and Lydia (Noyes) Emery, married Charles P Coffin of Newburyport, Mass., June 2, 1834. He died June 29, 1874.
Children :

        3462   i   Frances Lane[8] b Nov 6 1837; d Nov 21, 1839
        3463   ii   Charles M , b May 18, 1839.
        3464   iii John G , b May 4, 1843
        3465   iv   Samuel F , b Dec 27, 1851

1758 Lydia Ann[7] Emery (*Jacob*,[6] *Moses*,[5] *David*,[4] *John*,[3] *Jonathan*,[2] *John[1]*), daughter of Jacob and Lydia (Noyes) Emery ; married, May 1, 1834, Samuel Durgin (born Jan. 13, 1811, died Dec. 12, 1886).
Children :

3466   i   LUCY C.,⁸ b. March 6, 1835
3467   ii   HENRY F., b. Sept. 12, 1837, d. Oct 5, 1838.
3468   iii LYDIA A., b Jan. 12, 1839, m. Samuel W Bailey, March 5,
             1868
3469   iv   ABBIE F., }b Nov 5, 1841, {
3470   v   ELLEN L , }   { m John Odiorne, April 5, 1864
3471   vi   SAMUEL W , b Oct 5, 1850; d July 11, 1866
3472   vii MARY L . b May 16, 1852, m John C. Chase, Oct. 21, 1871.

1759 RUFUS KING⁷ EMERY (*Jacob*,⁶ *Moses*,⁵ *David*,⁴ *John*,³ *Jona-*
than,² *John¹*), son of Jacob and Lydia (Noyes) Emery, married Mary
Bradley, Dec. 30, 1842, died Jan. 15, 1865.
   Child :

3473   i   FRANCIS BERNETT,⁸ b Jan 29, 1848

1760 ELIZA T.⁷ EMERY (*Jacob*,⁶ *Moses*,⁵ *David*,⁴ *John*,³ *Jonathan*,²
John¹), daughter of Jacob and Lydia (Noyes) Emery, married Rev.
J. H Tilton, July 26, 1843
   Children :

3474   i   GEORGE LEWIS,⁸ b. Sept. 10, 1846, in South Gardiner, Mass.,
             d Sept. 14, 1848
3475   ii   JULIA GERTRUDE, b July 18, 1851, in Holden, Mass
3476   iii JACOB EMERY, b Jan 12, 1854, in Lynn, Mass., d Sept. 24,
             1854
3477   iv   ALFRED LEROY, b. Jan. 4, 1856, in Lynn, Mass., d. Jan 22,
             1856.

1761 CALVIN⁷ EMERY (*Jacob*,⁶ *Moses*,⁵ *David*,⁴ *John*,³ *Jonathan*,²
John¹), son of Jacob and Lydia (Noyes) Emery, married, first,
Nov. 26, 1846, Waita Todd, who died June 25, 1853, second, July
26. 1854, Mary Todd, who died July 20, 1858 ; third, Clara Shannon,
Nov 24, 1859.
   Children, born in West Newbury :

3478   i   SARAH WAITA,⁸ b Sept. 7, 1857, d. April 1, 1858.
3479   ii   CLARA A , b Feb 25, 1861

1762 LUCIAN ALEXANDER⁷ EMERY(*Moses*,⁶ *Moses*,⁵ *David*,⁴ *John*,³
Jonathan,² *John¹*), son of Moses and Betsey (Follansbee) Emery;
married Eliza Stanwood, April, 1827, and died June 6, 1865.
   Children :

3480   i   ELIZA H ,⁸ b Feb. 1, 1829, m. H. Webster, Nov. 29, 1853, who
             grad Dartmouth College, 1844
3481   ii   LUCIAN H , b. Dec 1. 1831, m. Mary V. Rundlett, Nov 29,
             1854   She d July 19, 1871.

1769 HARRIET K ⁷ EMERY (*Moses*,⁶ *Moses*,⁵ *David*,⁴ *John*,³ *Jona-*
than,² *John¹*), daughter of Moses and Betsey (Follansbee) Emery;
married Hayden Brown.
   Children, born in West Newbury

3482   i   HARRIET EMERY,⁸ b Sept 11, 1844, d. Feb 14, 1864
3483   ii   LUCY HILLS, b. April 14, 1849, d. Aug 20, 1849.
3484   iii HORACE, b Aug 31, 1851, graduate of Harvard College, 1872;
             d July 5, 1883
3485   iv   GILMAN WELD, b. April 5, 1857.

1770 NEHEMIAH F [7] EMERY (*Moses*,[6] *Moses*,[5] *David*,[4] *John*,[3] *Jonathan*,[2] *John*[1]); son of Moses and Betsey (Follansbee) Emery; married Mary Ann Wyatt, April 29, 1844, and died April 14, 1890.
Children

    3486   i   GRACE L ,[8] b Sept. 26, 1845.
    3487   ii   MARY W , b April 7. 1850
    3488   iii THOMAS H , b May 1, 1855
    3489   iv   HARVEY DWIGHT, b July 11, 1860

1772 DAVID FRANCIS[7] EMERY (*Moses*,[6] *Moses*,[5] *David*,[4] *John*,[3] *Jonathan*,[2] *John*[1]), son of Moses and Betsey (Follansbee) Emery, married Mary N. Wyatt, July 3, 1853.
Children :

    3490   i   CLARA E ,[8] b Dec. 13, 1853, in Warren, R. I
    3491   ii   HARRY B , b Nov 26, 1857 in Newburyport, Mass
    3492   iii EDWARD K , b July 17, 1861, in Philadelphia, Pa.
    3493   iv   ANNA B., b May 26, 1866, in Philadelphia, Pa.

1801 WILLIAM[7] EMERY (*Willard*,[6] *William*,[5] *Dr Anthony*,[4] *John*,[3] *Jonathan*,[2] *John*[1]), son of Willard and Sarah (Cilley) Emery , married, July 4, 1822, Nancy (Perkins) Emery of Loudon, N H. (died in Lebanon, N H., July, 1871). He died in Franklin, N. H , March 13, 1860 , farmer
Children, born in Andover, Me. ·

    3494   i   ELIZA FELLOWS,[8] b March 28, 1825
    3495   ii   CAROLINE DEARBORN b May 14, 1828
    3496   iii NANCY JANE, b June 29, 1834

1802 JONATHAN[7] EMERY(*Willard*,[6] *William*,[5] *Dr Anthony*,[4] *John*,[3] *Jonathan*,[2] *John*[1]), son of Willard and Sarah (Cilley) Emery ; married, first, March 13, 1818, Nancy Weare Rowe (born Jan. 10, 1799 ; died March 20, 1844), daughter of Jacob Rowe; second, Sept. 23, 1845, Eliza Weare (born June 9, 1811), daughter of Timothy Weare. He died March, 1879 ; farmer.
Children, born in Andover, N. H :

    3497   i   ELBRIDGE GERRY,[8] b May 15, 1818
    3498   ii   JOHN ROWE b Sept 15, 1821
    3499   iii WILLARD HENRY, b July 5, 1824
    3500   iv   SARAH FRANCES, b June 26, 1826, teacher
    3501   v   JACOB ROWE, b July 28, 1828
    3502   vi   ANN JANNLIE, b Oct 5, 1832, d Jan 11, 1866
    3503   vii LAURLTIA M , b Jan 25, 1839, d June 19, 1843.
    3504   viii MARTHA VICTORIA b Mar. 9, 1843.
    3505   ix   JOSIAH WEARE, b Jan 5, 1849, in Flora B Bacon, May 29, 1879

1803 ABIGAIL[7] EMERY (*Willard*,[6] *William*,[5] *Dr. Anthony*,[4] *John*,[3] *Jonathan*,[2] *John*[1]), daughter of Willard and Sarah (Cilley) Emery ; married, first, Col. Joshua L Weare, Feb 23, 1825   He died Dec. 17, 1847   She married, second, Rev. Peter Clark, July 13, 1848, who died in Gilmanton, N H , Nov. 25, 1865   Colonel Weare was a farmer and inn-keeper in East Andover, Me.
Children .

3506   i   CYRUS,³ b. Sept. 3, 1827; d. March 17, 1851; teacher.
3507   ii MARY AUGUSTA, b. March 18, 1832; d. Oct. 9, 1833.
3508   iii MARY JOSEPHINE, b. June 13, 1837; d. May 3, 1840.

1804 SARAH⁷ EMERY (*Willard,⁶ William,⁵ Dr. Anthony,⁴ John,³ Jonathan,² John¹*), daughter of Willard and Sarah (Cilley) Emery; married, Watson Dickerson, son of Moses and Sally (Kinsman) Dickerson, May 14, 1829. He married, second, ———— Daniels. She died Sept. 9, 1868.
Child :

3509   i   FRANK.⁸

1805 POLLY⁷ EMERY (*Willard,⁶ William,⁵ Dr. Anthony,⁴ John,³ Jonathan,² John¹*), daughter of Willard and Sarah (Cilley) Emery; married Col. Jacob Rowe, March 20, 1834; died May 3, 1868.
Children :

3510   i   ELBRIDGE GERRY,⁸ b. May 30, 1836; d. June 4, 1852; student.
3511   ii ELLEN JOSEPHINE, b. Feb. 25, 1840; m. Frank Hersey.

1806 HORATIO GATES⁷ EMERY (*Willard,⁶ William,⁵ Dr. Anthony,⁴ John,³ Jonathan,² John¹*), son of Willard and Sarah (Cilley) Emery; married Jane Taylor Brown at Auburn, N. Y., daughter of Samuel Brown of Andover, N. H.
Children, born in Milton, Mass. :

3512   i   MARY ANGELINE,⁸ b. Sept. 26, 1837.
3513   ii   SARAH REBECCA, b. June 10, 1840.
3514   iii SUSAN JANE, b. Aug. 4, 1842; d. May 6, 1845.
3515   iv   HENRY DEARBORN, b. Feb. 27, 1845; d. April 30, 1845.
3516   v   JANE AUGUSTA, b. March 26, 1848; d. Sept. 26, 1848.
3517   vi   FRANK HARVEY, b. Sept. 1, 1850.
3518   vii ALICE EVA, b. June 18, 1853.

1807 JOHN⁷ EMERY (*Joseph,⁶ William,⁵ Dr. Anthony,⁴ John,³ Jonathan,² John¹*), son of Joseph and Dolly (Blake) Emery; married first, April, 1825, Sally Fifield of Andover, Me. (born in Poultney, Vt.; died at Holderness, N. H., Dec., 1856). He married, second, Mary S. Clement, March 6, 1858.
Children :

3519   i   MARY ELIZABETH,⁸ b. Jan. 7, 1826, in Andover.
3520   ii HIRAM F., b. Oct., 1829, in Holderness, N. H.
3521   iii JOHN, JR., b. Nov. 22, 1830, in Holderness, N. H.
3522   iv CALEB C., b. Jan., 1834.
3523   v   WILLIAM, b. Jan., 1843, in Plymouth, N. H.

1808 JOSEPH⁷ EMERY, JR. (*Joseph,⁶ William,⁵ Dr. Anthony,⁴ John,³ Jonathan,² John¹*), son of Joseph and Dolly (Blake) Emery; married, at New Chester (now Hill), N. H., Nov. 24, 1829, Mary Ann Gordon (born in Sanbornton, N. H., Feb. 25, 1806.) He died Nov. 28, 1835. His widow married, second, Jesse Graves, Esq., Nov. 24, 1842, who died Aug. 2, 1844; third, Ahira Barney of Grafton, N. H., and died Oct. 6, 1854.
Children, born in Andover, N. H. :

3524 i HORACE,[8] b Sept 18, 1830.
3525 ii HANNAH JANE, b Jan. 9, 1834.

1809 DOLLY[7] EMERY (*Joseph,[6] William,[5] Dr Anthony,[4] John,[3] Jonathan,[2] John[1]*), daughter of Joseph and Dolly (Blake) Emery; married Joseph Ayers Rowe, farmer, Oct. 29, 1829, who died April 17, 1885.
Children, born in Andover, N. H

3526 i JOSEPH AYERS,[8] b March 8, 1831; d May 3, 1868
3527 ii EMILY ANN, b March 13, 1837; m Andrew J Scribner, April 10, 1869
3528 iii FRANK PIERCE, b Nov 17, 1840, d. Jan 11, 1863.

1810 WILLIAM[7] BLAKE EMERY (*Joseph,[6] William,[5] Dr. Anthony,[4] John,[3] Jonathan,[2] John[1]*), son of Joseph and Dolly (Blake) Emery, married Dolly C. Dresser (born in Sutton, N H), Jan. 10, 1843. Farmer, selectman, town clerk, tax collector of Andover.
Children, born in Andover, N H.:

3529 i ELLEN MARIA,[8] b. March 7, 1847.
3530 ii LUCY JANE, b Aug. 18, 1849

1813 CAPT. WILLARD[7] EMERY (*Anthony,[6] William,[5] Dr Anthony,[4] John,[3] Jonathan,[2] John[1]*), son of Anthony and Abigail (Cilley) Emery; died in Ipswich, Mass.. July 21, 1871; married Sarah Hobart, March 13, 1825 (born in Hebron, N H., June 25, 1805; died in East Andover, N. H., May 12, 1858). Farmer and trader.
Children:

3531 i INFANT,[8] b and d 1826
3532 ii GEO EDWIN, b March 27, 1828, in Andover
3533 iii CYRUS HOBART, b Aug. 10, 1832, d Feb 12, 1833, in Andover.
3534 iv ADELAIDE LOUISE, b Nov 1, 1839, in Franklin, N H

1818 JOSEPH[7] EMERY (*William,[6] William,[5] Dr. Anthony,[4] John,[3] Jonathan,[2] John[1]*), son of William and Ruth (Brown) Emery, married Ruth M A. Stevens, April 16, 1846.
Children, born in Andover, N. H..

3535 i ROSTO R,[8] b Oct 7, 1847.
3536 ii ALPHONSO, b Nov. 9, 1851

1819 JAMES[7] MARSTON, JR. (*Polly,[6] William,[5] Dr. Anthony,[4] John,[3] Jonathan,[2] John[1]*), son of James and Polly (Emery) Marston married at Hill, N. H, Betsy Tucker, May 27, 1832.
Children:

3537 i MARY ELIZ,[8] b. March 9, 1833.
3538 ii CAROLINE, b June 4, 1838
3539 iii ARVILLA, b Aug 6, 1844, m Samuel A Tuttle

1837 JACOB O[7] EMERY (*John,[6] Thomas,[5] Dr. Anthony,[4] John,[3] Jonathan,[2] John[1]*), son of John and Abigail (Osborn) Emery; married Mary Hilton of Sandwich, N. H, 1844.
One child 3540. Name unknown.

1838 Betsey[7] Emery (*John,[6] Thomas,[5] Dr. Anthony,[4] John,[3] Jonathan,[2] John[1]*), daughter of John and Abigail (Osborn) Emery ; married Samuel Stickney of Lowell, Mass.

Children :

    3541   i   Abbie Osborn,[8] b. Oct 26, 1844
    3542   ii   Fred W , b June 17, 1853.

1846 Huldah P.[7] Emery (*John,[6] Nathaniel,[5] Dr Anthony,[4] John,[3] Jonathan,[2] John[1]*), daughter of John and Jane (Kimball) Emery ; married John Wilson at Dunbarton, N. H., Jan. 20, 1823.

Children, born in Pembroke, N. H :

    3543   i   Eliza A ,[8] b Dec 1, 1824.
    3544   ii   John E , b Sept. 13, 1826
    3545   iii Harriet M , b Feb 4, 1828

1847 Mary K.[7] Emery (*John,[6] Nathaniel,[5] Dr. Anthony,[4] John,[3] Jonathan,[2] John[1]*), daughter of John and Jane (Kimball) Emery ; married in Boston, David F. Bradlee, Oct. 5, 1821.

Children :

    3546   i   Mary Kimball,[8] b Sept 23 1823 , d Feb , 1825
    3547   ii   David Henry, b July 30, 1826 , d. July 29, 1868
    3548   iii Mary Jane, b Dec 17, 1828
    3549   iv   John Emery, b. July 19, 1831
    3550   v   Sarah Fulton, b. Sept. 4, 1838.
    3551   vi   Ellen Maria, b. May 2, 1842
    3552   vii Charles Horace, b Aug 18, 1844

1848 Harriet M [7] Emery (*John,[6] Nathaniel,[5] Dr. Anthony,[4] John,[3] Jonathan,[2] John[1]*), daughter of John and Jane (Kimball) Emery ; married —— Stone in Boston.

Child :

    3553   i   Mary [8]

1849 John[7] Emery, jr (*John,[6] Nathaniel,[5] Dr. Anthony,[4] John,[3] Jonathan,[2] John[1]*), son of John and Jane (Kimball) Emery ; married Mercy Daniels of Boston.

Children :

    3554   i   Walter.[8]
    3555   ii   Martha
    3556   iii Henry

1850 Sophronia[7] Emery (*John,[6] Nathaniel,[5] Dr Anthony,[4] John,[3] Jonathan,[2] John[1]*), daughter of John and Jane (Kimball) Emery , married Peter Man of Boston.

Children :

    3557   i   Samuel [8]
    3558   ii   Sophronia.
    3559   iii Sarah.

1851 Asa K [7] Emery (*John,[6] Nathaniel,[5] Dr. Anthony,[4] John,[3] Jonathan,[2] John[1]*), son of John and Jane (Kimball) Emery ; married Mary C. Lord in Dunbarton, N. H.

Child

3560 1   MARY [8]

1852 LUCRETIA L [7] EMERY (*John*,[6] *Nathaniel*,[5] *Dr. Anthony*,[4] *John*,[3] *Jonathan*,[2] *John*[1]), daughter of John and Jane (Kimball) Emery : married G W. Man.
Children .

3561 1   G W [8]
3562 ii   SARAH J
3563 iii HELEN MARIA.

1853 SARAH J [7] EMERY (*John*,[6] *Nathaniel*,[5] *Dr. Anthony*,[4] *John*,[3] *Jonathan*,[2] *John*[1]), daughter of John and Jane (Kimball) Emery ; married A. E. Newton. May 27, 1845.
Children :

3564 1   SARAH ADELAIDE,[8] b Jan 18, 1848.
3565 ii   CHARLES ALONZO, b Feb. 18, 1850
3566 iii ELIZABETH J , b. Oct. 6, 1852

1864 NATHANIEL[7] EMERY (*Josiah*,[6] *Nathaniel*,[5] *Dr. Anthony*,[4] *John*,[3] *Jonathan*,[2] *John*[1]), son of Josiah and Betsey (Osgood) Emery; married, at Grandville, Mich., Mary L Arnold, March 6, 1842, who died April 2, 1857.   He died July 27, 1856.
Children

3567 1   EMELINE B ,[8]   } b. March 17, 1843
3568 ii   ELIZABETH B ,   }
3569 iii JOSEPH B , b Oct. 30, 1844 ; d Sept 15, 1847.
3570 iv   BENJAMIN F., b. May 26, 1846
3571 v   MARY A , b Dec 11, 1847.
3572 vi   ABBY O , b March 29, 1850 ; m G Marshall McCray, Oct 6, 1877.

1867 ELIZA PERKINS[7] EMERY (*Josiah*,[6] *Nathaniel*,[5] *Dr Anthony*,[4] *John*,[3] *Jonathan*,[2] *John*[1]), daughter of Josiah and Betsey (Osgood) Emery , married Andrew Lynn of Portsmouth, N. H. (died in Boston, 1877).
Children .

3573 1   ANDREW JACKSON,[8] b July. 1836
3574 ii   ANN ELIZA, b Sept , 1838 , m James B Gunning , d May, 1865 He d July, 1877
3575 iii ELLEN JANE b Aug , 1840 , m John M. Clark, Feb., 1869.
3576 iv   AUBELLA EMERY, b Nov , 1844
3577 v   ALBERT CLARENCE, b July, 1848
3578 vi   CLARA AMANDA, b Sept , 1851.
3579 vii EMMA ANETTA, b Feb , 1856

1868 SHUAH BLAKE[7] EMERY (*Josiah*,[6] *Nathaniel*,[5] *Dr. Anthony*,[4] *John*,[3] *Jonathan*,[2] *John*[1]), daughter of Josiah and Betsey (Osgood) Emery , married, Oct. 1, 1833, Horatio D. Page (born in Raymond, N. H , died April 13, 1871).
Children :

3580 1   ELIZABETH FRANCES,[8] b March 29, 1835
3581 ii   HARRIET AMANDA, b. 1838 , d Jan , 1850.

3582 iii SHUAH ELLEN, b. June 28, 1841.
3583 iv   LAURA FARNSWORTH, b. Sept. 9, 1847.
3584 v   FOREST EMERY, b. Feb. 1, 1858; m. Agnes E. Gould.

1869 JOSIAH[7] EMERY (*Josiah,*[6] *Nathaniel,*[5] *Dr. Anthony,*[4] *John,*[3]
Jonathan,[2] *John*[1]), son of Josiah and Betsey (Osgood) Emery ; married in Lowell, Mass., Louisa J. Woodbury of Salem, N. H.
Children :

3585 i   LOUISA ADELAIDE,[8] b. Sept. 26, 1841, in Lowell; d. March 26, 1843.
3586 ii   MARIA ELIZABETH, b. July 13, 1843, in Lowell; d. Sept. 15, 1870.
3587 iii AMELIA FRANCES, b. July 31, 1845.
3588 iv   GEORGE FOREST, b. June 17. 1849, in Newburyport, Mass.
3589 v   JULIA ADELAIDE,   } b. March 28, 1852, { d. July 29, 1888.
3590 vi   LOUISA FLORENCE,   } in Newburyport; {
3591 vii LAURENS CLINTON, b. April 20, 1855, in Newburyport.
3592 viii WILLIAM FORBES, b April 27, 1857, in Newburyport.
3593 ix   CHARLES ALBERT, b. May 12, 1862; d. June 27, 1863, in Newburyport.
3594 x   JOSIAH, JR., b. Nov. 21, 1864; d. same day.

1871 SARAH ANN[7] EMERY (*Josiah,*[6] *Nathaniel,*[5] *Dr. Anthony,*[4]
John,[3] *Jonathan,*[2] *John*[1]), daughter of Josiah and Betsey (Osgood)
Emery ; married, Jan. 22, 1851, Charles Hayes of Dover, N. H. (born in Barrington, N. H., Aug. 30, 1822).
Children, born in Dover, N. H. :

3595 i   ETTA,[8] b. Nov. 22, 1851.
3596 ii   LAURA, b. Dec. 13, 1853.
3597 iii WALTER, b. Jan. 22, 1862.

1873 ELIZABETH[7] EMERY (*Josiah,*[6] *Nathaniel,*[5] *Dr. Anthony,*[4]
John,[3] *Jonathan,*[2] *John*[1]), daughter of Josiah and Betsey (Osgood)
Emery ; married Elbridge Smith of Dover, June 14, 1860 (born in Puling, Vt., Nov. 26, 1832).
Children :

3598 i   FREDERICK EMERY,[8] b. May 11, 1862; m. Lottie O. Sanderson, Sept. 1, 1886.
3599 ii   HARRY R., b. Dec. 21, 1867.
3600 iii MARY A. B., b. May 30, 1870; d. Sept. 30, 1876.

1874 HARRIS E.[7] MORSE (*Sally,*[6] *Nathaniel,*[5] *Dr Anthony,*[4] *John,*[3]
Jonathan,[2] *John*[1]), son of Moses and Sally (Emery) Morse ; married Sarah Ann Eaton, Oct. 16, 1842.
Children, born in Loudon :

3601 i   MARY ADELAIDE,[8] b. April 16, 1844; d. Nov. 11, 1844.
3602 ii   SARAH ABBIE, b. Aug. 22, 1847; m. James M. Bachelder of Pittsfield, N. H.
3603 iii HARRIS FRANK, b. March 9, 1849; m. Ida M. Ladd of Manchester, N. H.
3604 iv   MARY EMMA, b. Dec. 1, 1851; m. Charles K. Scribner of Laconia, N. H.
3605 v   ALVA L., b. May 14, 1860; m. Della M. Prichard of Loudon, N. H.

1876 JULIANN P.[7] MORSE (*Sally,*[6] *Nathaniel,*[5] *Dr Anthony,*[4] *John,*[3] *Jonathan,*[2] *John*[1]), daughter of Moses and Sally (Emery) Morse ; married Charles H. Walker in London, Jan. 1, 1847, chomœopathi physician.
Children :

3606　i　CHARLES A ,[8] b Oct 13, 1847; m , at Campton, N H., May 23, 1873, Elizabeth Mitchell.
3607　ii　JULIA ARABELLA, b Feb 18, 1859, in Manchester, N H.; m. Ed O Punchard, Oct 2, 1873
3608　iii　HENRIETTA P., b June 8, 1862, in Chelsea, Mass

1878 CAROLINE DEARBORN[7] EMERY (*Nancy,*[6] *Nathaniel,*[5] *Dr. Anthony,*[4] *John,*[3] *Jonathan,*[2] *John*[1]), daughter of William and Nancy (Emery) Emery, married Dec. 21, 1848, Albert M. Shaw (born in Poland, Me., May 3, 1819).
Children :

3609　i　WILLIAM FRANCIS,[8] b Sept 21, 1849. in Brunswick, Me.
3610　ii　MARY ESTELLE, b Sept 6, 1852, in Franklin, N H
3611　iii　ALBERT ONSLOW, b Jan 3, 1865, in Lebanon, N H

1879 NANCY JANE[7] EMERY (*Nancy,*[6] *Nathaniel,*[5] *Dr. Anthony,*[4] *John,*[3] *Jonathan,*[2] *John*[1]), daughter of William and Nancy (Emery) Emery, married in Lebanon, N. H , July 15, 1860, Richard Whitney Cragin (born in Weston, Vt., Nov. 20, 1827).
Children, born in Lebanon, N. H :

3612　i　GEORGE,[8] b April 10, 1861
3613　ii　LENA BELLA, b Dec 24, 1866

1882 DAVID[7] EMERY (*Daniel,*[6] *Caleb,*[5] *Caleb,*[4] *Jonathan,*[3] *Jonathan,*[2] *John*[1]), son of Daniel and Elizabeth (Straw) Emery, married Dec. 27, 1832, Lydia Flint of Hillsboro, N. H.; died March 9, 1875.
Children :

3614　i　DANIEL F ,[8] b Aug 7, 1834.
3615　ii　LEANDER, b Feb 23, 1839

1883 LEVI[7] EMERY (*Daniel,*[6] *Caleb,*[5] *Caleb,*[4] *Jonathan,*[3] *Jonathan,*[2] *John*[1]), son of Daniel and Elizabeth (Straw) Emery; married Sarah Hildreth in Henniker, N. H., 1815.
Children :

3616　i　LOVILLA,[8] b Dec 16, 1820.
3617　ii　ABIJAH H., b. Dec 29, 1822.
3618　iii　HORACE S , b. May 7, 1826.
3619　iv　MARTHA M., b Sept 23, 1829.
3620　v　ELSA J , b Jan 15, 1833
3621　vi　LEWIS L., b Oct. 21, 1834, m Frances M Russell

1884 JOHN[7] EMERY (*Daniel,*[6] *Caleb,*[5] *Caleb,*[4] *Jonathan,*[3] *Jonathan,*[2] *John*[1]), son of Daniel and Elizabeth (Straw) Emery : married, first, Jane Sweetzer of Bennington, Vt , 1820, who died, 1862. He married, second, 1863, Betsey Colby of Sutton and died in Antrim, N. H., Sept. 17, 1880.
Children :

11

3622 i   AURELIA,⁵ b March 28 1824.
3623 ii   MARTHA J , b May 3, 1827.

1885 ISRAEL⁷ HOAG (*Abigail*,⁶ *Caleb*,⁵ *Caleb*,⁴ *Jonathan*,³ *Jonathan*,² *John¹*), son of Jonathan and Abigail (Emery) Hoag ; married
Abigail Breed (died June 23, 1884). He died Dec., 1882.
     Children :
     3624 i   MARTHA B ,⁸ b 1824, d 1845
     3625 ii   MARY P , b 1828, d 1838
     3626 iii CHARLES E , b 1842

1887 JOSEPH⁷ HOAG (*Abigail*,⁶ *Caleb*,⁵ *Caleb*,⁴ *Jonathan*,³ *Jonathan*,² *John¹*), son of Jonathan and Abigail (Emery) Hoag ; married,
Alice Buxton.
     Children :
     3627 i   JONATHAN,⁸ b 1839 m Clara Sargent.
     3628 ii   ANN, b 1840, m W L Dean
     3629 iii MARY, b. 1843, m. Nathan Morrison

1890 WILLIAM⁷ EMERY (*Caleb*,⁶ *Caleb*,⁵ *Caleb*,⁴ *Jonathan*,³ *Jonathan*,² *John¹*), son of Caleb and Polly (Harriman) Emery ; married,
first, Mary Peasley ; second, Mary Neally. He died Aug 10, 1874.
     Children :
     3630 i   MARY ANN,⁸ m John Colburn
     3631 ii   LYDIA, b. 1848 , m Charles Colburn.

1891 JOHN G ⁷ EMERY (*Caleb*,⁶ *Caleb*,⁵ *Caleb*,⁴ *Jonathan*,³ *Jonathan*,² *John¹*), son of Caleb and Polly (Harriman) Emery ; married,
Oct. 19, 1848, Sarah Piper of Bradford, N H .
     Children :
     3632 i   JOHN,⁸ b 1849, in Weare
     3633 ii   CHARLES, b 1851, in Henniker.

1901 ABIJAH⁷ EMERY (*Sylvanus*,⁶ *Sylvanus*,⁵ *Caleb*,⁴ *Jonathan*,³
Jonathan,² *John¹*), son of Sylvanus and Abigail (Knowles) Emery,
married Abigail Greenleaf of Barnard, Vt.(died, 1869). He died 1877.
     Children .
     3634 i   EUGENE,⁸ b 1850
     3635 ii   NYSIN, b 1858.

1902 MARK⁷ EMERY (*Sylvanus*,⁶ *Sylvanus*,⁵ *Caleb*,⁴ *Jonathan*,³
Jonathan,² *John¹*), son of Sylvanus and Abigail (Knowles) Emery ,
married Simena S. Silver of Bow, N. H. , died, 1870.
     Children :
     3636 i   LEWIS F ,⁸ b March 20, 1840, in Thornton, N H
     3637 ii   MARK F., b. Feb 11, 1842, in Weare, N H , d at Fort Jefferson
                in the war of the Rebellion, 1862
     3638 iii MARIA D , b. April 6, 1844, in Weare, N H
     3639 iv   SAMUEL F P , b March 29, 1846, in Hookset, N. H.
     3640 v   CHARLES F , b March 19, 1848; m Mattie Harvey.
     3641 vi   GEORGE W., b March 19, 1850, in Hookset, N H
     3642 vii EDWIN H , b March 19, 1853, in Allenstown, N H ,; served five
                years in the U S army, discharged, Jan 1, 1881.

3643   viii MARY L , b 1856
3644   ix   HORACE K , b. 1859.
3645   x   WILLIE O , b. 1861

1906 SOLOMON H [7] EMERY (*Caleb*,[6] *Amos*,[5] *Caleb*,[4] *Jonathan*,[3] *Jonathan*,[2] *John*[1]), son of Caleb and Eleanor (Heath) Emery ; married Fanny Day (born in Littleton, N. H , Dec. 10, 1803 ; died in Brighton, Ill., Jan 6, 1876) Representative to the legislature 1855–56 ; removed to Illinois, 1861.
Children, born in Lyman, N. H .

3646   i   GEORGE H ,[8] b Nov 6, 1827.
3647   ii   MARY F , b March 22, 1830.
3648   iii HENRY D N , b Dec 12, 1831, d Feb. 11, 1882.
3649   iv   ANN E , b Dec 3, 1835
3650   v   JOHN C., b. Nov 3, 1838, enlisted Aug 9, 1861, reënlisted,
           wounded at Chicamauga, Ga , d at Chattanooga, Jan , 1844,
           from wounds received at Kenesaw Mountain, Ga.

1907 HORACE[7] EMERY (*Caleb*,[6] *Amos*,[5] *Caleb*,[4] *Jonathan*,[3] *Jonathan*,[2] *John*[1]), son of Caleb and Eleanor (Heath) Emery , married Mary Cheney of Derby, Vt., Sept. 1, 1843
Children, born in Lyman

3651   i   MARY E ,[8] b June 25, 1844, m. Cornelius J Houghton, April
           22, 1866
3652   ii   SARAH, b 1846; d. in Lyman, 1847
3653   iii SAMUEL C., b Dec 18, 1848, m. Kittie M Peters, June 17,
           1879
3654   iv   JULIA H , b Nov 22, 1851.

1909 CYNTHIA E.[7] EMERY (*Caleb*,[6] *Amos*,[5] *Caleb*,[4] *Jonathan*,[3] *Jonathan*,[2] *John*[1]), daughter of Caleb and Eleanor (Heath) Emery , married in Derby, Vt , Jan., 1836, Elijah M. Davis who died in 1843.
Child :

3655   i   ELLEN,[8] d. 1852

1910 ANN[7] EMERY (*Caleb*,[6] *Amos*,[5] *Caleb*,[4] *Jonathan*,[3] *Jonathan*,[2] *John*[1]), daughter of Caleb and Eleanor (Heath) Emery , married Lewis Blake.
Children :

3656   i   GEORGE B [8]
3657   ii   ADRIANA

1912 EDWARD[7] EMERY (*Caleb*,[6] *Amos*,[5] *Caleb*,[4] *Jonathan*,[3] *Jonathan*,[2] *John*[1]), son of Caleb and Eleanor (Heath) Emery ; married Julia Pierce of Derby, Vt , June 29, 1851. Selectman in his town twelve years
Children, born in Lyman :

3658   i   NELLIE D ,[8] b May 26, 1852; d Sept. 12, 1854
3659   ii   WILLIE E , b July 17, 1855, m Maria Lang, March 3, 1879.
3660   iii EDWIN C., b. Feb 27, 1858.

1915 MARY C.[7] EMERY (*Caleb*,[6] *Amos*,[5] *Caleb*,[4] *Jonathan*,[3] *Jona-

than,[2] John[1]), daughter of Caleb and Eleanor (Heath) Emery; married Asa M. Berry of Wakefield, N. H., March 30, 1852; died in Barnett, Vt., Oct. 15, 1873.

Children, born in Boston:

3661 i   FLORENCE ADA,[8] b. Jan. 14, 1853.
3662 ii   HELEN C., b. June 4, 1857.
3663 iii ELIZ. GERTRUDE, b. May 1, 1863.

1916 CHELLIS[7] EMERY (*Samuel,[6] Amos,[5] Caleb,[4] Jonathan,[3] Jonathan,[2] John[1]*), son of Samuel and Mary (Flanders) Emery; married Martha H. Cross of Lyman, Nov. 29, 1832.

Children:

3664 i   JOHN C.,[8] b. Nov. 9, 1833, in Lyman.
3665 ii   WILLIAM H., b. July 6, 1840, in Franklin; m. Helen E. Green, July, 1865.
3666 iii SAMUEL H., b. May 6, 1852, in Albany, Vt.; m. Helen E. Pelton, Dec. 24, 1873.

1918 WARREN S.[7] EMERY (*Samuel,[6] Amos,[5] Caleb,[4] Jonathan,[3] Jonathan,[2] John[1]*), son of Samuel and Mary (Flanders) Emery; married, first, Elvira C. Whitcomb of Bethlehem, N. H., May 27, 1869; second, Julia E. McDonnald of Providence, R. I., Oct. 28, 1874. He died in East Burke, Vt., Dec. 4, 1881. Clergyman.

Children:

3667 i   ALVA W.,[8] b. in Providence, R. I., Nov. 10, 1872; d. in Natick, R. I., Sept. 25, 1877.
3668 ii   FLORENCE E., b. in Natick, R. I., Sept. 20, 1876; d. Oct. 5, 1877.
3669 iii ADRIAN D., b. in Natick, R. I., Jan. 30, 1878.
3670 iv   JULIA, b. March 6, 1879.

1919 WALTER H.[7] EMERY (*Samuel,[6] Amos,[5] Caleb,[4] Jonathan,[3] Jonathan,[2] John[1]*), son of Samuel and Mary (Flanders) Emery; married Eliza Hutton of Monroe, N. H., March 15, 1858.

Children, born in Monroe, N. H.:

3671 i   EVELYN,[8] b. March 22, 1859.
3672 ii   ALFRED, b. May 11, 1861; m. Emma Walter, Dec. 20, 1882.
3673 iii   E. BELLE, b. July 21, 1863; m. David Knowlton, Dec. 20, 1882.
3674 iv   JOHN S., b. April 9, 1865.
3675 v   W. CLEMENT, b. May 7, 1867.
3676 vi   NELLIE, b. Nov. 5, 1869.
3677 vii   BERTHA, b. March 4, 1875.
3678 viii CHARLES, b. March 28, 1877.

1922 SILAS[7] EMERY (*Joel,[6] Joel,[5] Caleb,[4] Jonathan,[3] Jonathan,[2] John[1]*), son of Joel and Lucy (Goddard) Emery; married Catharine M. Littlefield, Nov. 11, 1849; died Feb. 17, 1884.

Children:

3679 i   MARY E.,[8] b. March 15, 1851; m. Lewis C. Williams, Sept. 9, 1872.
3680 ii   ALMA A., b. Oct. 18, 1853; m. John W. Allen, April 29, 1884.
3681 iii CARRIE E., b. April 7, 1859; m. Harry A. Pearsons, July 3, 1879.

1923 NANCY[7] EMERY (*Joel,[6] Joel,[5] Caleb,[4] Jonathan,[3] Jonathan,[2]*

John[1]), daughter of Joel and Lucy (Goddard) Emery; married March 12, 1849, Jasper Lyman (born Oct. 5, 1824) son of Orange and Mary (Smith) Lyman.

Children:

    3682   i   FLORENCE,[8] b Nov 13, 1851, d Oct. 14, 1868.
    3683   ii   FRANCIS, b. Oct 13, 1853
    3684   iii LUCY E., b. Aug 19, 1857
    3685   iv   EDWARD B, b Feb 17, 1861

1924 ISAAC[7] EMERY (*Joel*,[6] *Joel*,[5] *Caleb*,[4] *Jonathan*,[3] *Jonathan*,[2] *John*[1]), son of Joel and Lucy (Goddard) Emery, married Alice Austin, March 9, 1854.

Children:

    3686   i   HATTIE,[8] b Jan 5, 1855, d Aug., 1862.
    3687   ii   GARDNER, b Aug 3, 1857
    3688   iii ELLEN M, b Sept 23, 1859
    3689   iv   AUSTIN C, b June 13, 1863.

1928 LEONARD[7] EMERY (*Joel*,[6] *Joel*,[5] *Caleb*,[4] *Jonathan*,[3] *Jonathan*,[2] *John*[1]), son of Joel and Lucy (Goddard) Emery, married Mary Smith, May 8, 1864 (born in Tunbridge, Vt.). He died May 24, 1884. Lived in Tunbridge, Vt.

Children.

    3690   i   CARRIE L,[8] b March 6, 1869.
    3691   ii   ANNA A., b. Aug 31, 1872.

1932 EZRA H.[7] EMERY (*Ira*,[6] *Joel*,[5] *Caleb*,[4] *Jonathan*,[3] *Jonathan*,[2] *John*[1]), son of Ira and Betsey (Richardson) Emery; married Lucy Ann Davis of Greensboro, Vt., May 17, 1859; died in the army at Baton Rouge, La., Oct. 4, 1863.

Child:

    3692   i   SAMUEL D.,[8] b July 10, 1860

1933 EMELINE TEMPLE[7] EMERY (*Ira*,[6] *Joel*,[5] *Caleb*,[4] *Jonathan*,[3] *Jonathan*,[2] *John*[1]), daughter of Ira and Betsey (Richardson) Emery; married Dec. 13, 1849, Nathan Noyes of Tunbridge, Vt, who died in Gaysville, Vt. His widow married, second, Robert C. West of Gaysville, and died in Stockbridge, Vt., Oct 20, 1879.

Children, born in Tunbridge:

    3693   i   ORIN BURBANK,[8] b Sept 24, 1850, d., in Gaysville, Oct. 21.
                 1865
    3694   ii   OSCAR ALMON, b Nov 11, 1851
    3695   iii ALONZO EMERY, b. July 3, 1857, m. Henrietta Aurelia Swift,
                 Sept 24, 1881
    3696   iv   ELLEN JANE, b July 28, 1861, d., in Brattleboro, Vt, Sept
                 14, 1876

1934 JANE G.[7] EMERY (*Ira*,[6] *Joel*,[5] *Caleb*,[4] *Jonathan*,[3] *Jonathan*,[2] *John*[1]), daughter of Ira and Betsey (Richardson) Emery; married Chester J. Morse, of Rochester, Vt, April 10, 1854 (born Nov. 11, 1828, died March 6, 1883).

Children:

3697 i ORAMEL,[8] b. July 17, 1857, in Bethel, Vt.; m. Cora Gifford, March 11, 1879.
3698 ii JENNIE E., b. Aug. 7, 1860, in Rochester, Vt.; m. Clarence E. Dearing.
3699 iii VEASEY L., b. March 31, 1863.
3700 iv EMELINE, b. Nov. 9, 1864.
3701 v CHARLES, b. Sept. 29, 1866, in Rochester, Vt.
3702 vi ELLA H., b. March 5, 1874, in Stockbridge, Vt.

1936 LYMAN S.[7] EMERY (*Ira,*[6] *Joel,*[5] *Caleb,*[4] *Jonathan,*[3] *Jonathan,*[2] *John*[1]), son of Ira and Betsey (Richardson) Emery; married Harriet E. Morse, of Royalton, Vt., Sept. 8, 1864.

Children, born in Washington, D. C.:

3703 i ALICE G.,[8] b. Feb. 17, 1868.
3704 ii HERBERT, b. Oct. 16, 1871.
3705 iii BESSIE, b. July 19, 1878.
3706 iv ISADORE, b. March 5, 1884.

1937 IRA[7] EMERY (*Ira,*[6] *Joel,*[5] *Caleb,*[4] *Jonathan,*[3] *Jonathan,*[2] *John*[1]), son of Ira and Betsey (Richardson) Emery; married Ellen Morse, of Bethel, Vt., March 3, 1861. Killed in the battle of Gettysburg, July 3, 1863.

Child:

3707 i BELLE.[8]

1938 GEORGE S.[7] EMERY (*Ira,*[6] *Joel,*[5] *Caleb,*[4] *Jonathan,*[3] *Jonathan,*[2] *John*[1]), son of Ira and Betsey (Richardson) Emery; married Abby Moxley, of Tunbridge, Vt., May 1, 1867.

Children:

3708 i INA.[8]
3709 ii CLARA.
3710 iii FRANK.
3711 iv FRED.

1939 ALONZO[7] EMERY (*Ira,*[6] *Joel,*[5] *Caleb,*[4] *Jonathan,*[3] *Jonathan,*[2] *John*[1]), son of Ira and Betsey (Richardson) Emery; married Angeline Leach, of Bethel, Vt., Dec. 24, 1872.

Children, born in Bethel, Vt.:

3712 i CLARENCE E.,[8] b. Aug. 7, 1875.
3713 ii SUSAN JOSEPHINE, b. Feb. 2, 1877.

1940 ELIZA[7] EMERY (*Ira,*[6] *Joel,*[5] *Caleb,*[4] *Jonathan,*[3] *Jonathan,*[2] *John*[1]), daughter of Ira and Betsey (Richardson) Emery; married Smith J. Merrill, of Randolph, Vt. She died Feb., 1887.

Children:

3714 i MABEL.[8]
3715 ii GERTRUDE.
3716 iii BESSIE.
3717 iv ALICE.
3718 v JANE.

1944 ABIGAIL[7] EMERY (*Esther,*[6] *Humphrey,*[5] *Humphrey,*[4] *Jona-*

than,[3] *Jonathan,*[2] *John*[1]), daughter of Samuel and Esther (Emery) Emery, married Curtis Willey.

Children ·

3719   i   WELLINGTON,[8] Union soldier, d., in the army, 1861
3720   ii CLINTON.
3721   iii LYDIA
3722   iv ESTHER
3723   v   BETSEY.
3724   vi NANCY
3725   vii ROSA, d young.

1945 SAMUEL F[7] EMERY (*Esther,*[6] *Humphrey,*[5] *Humphrey,*[4] *Jonathan,*[3] *Jonathan,*[2] *John*[1]), son of Samuel and Esther (Emery) Emery; married, at Pinkham Grant, N. H , Almira McCarter (born in Jackson, N. H., March 11, 1824). He died June 29, 1884.

Children, born in Gorham, N. H.:

3726   i   HIRAM,[9] b Dec 29, 1846.
3727   ii   OSCAR, b Dec 5, 1848
3728   iii SARAH F b Sept. 8, 1853.
3729   iv   ELLA, b Sept 10, 1858

1950 HUBBARD[7] EMERY (*Sylvanus,*[6] *Humphrey,*[5] *Humphrey,*[4] *Jonathan,*[3] *Jonathan,*[2] *John*[1]), son of Sylvanus and Susan (Rogers) Emery, married ———.

Children :

3730   i   JULIA[8]
3731   ii   LUCINDA.
3732   iii DANIEL
3733   iv   DAVID
3734   v   MARY
3735   vi   WARREN
3736   vii SOLOMON
3737   viii ELIZABETH
3738   ix   CHARLOTTE
3739   x   JOSEPH.
3740   xi   HENRY.
3741   xii DIANTHA.

1951 GILBERT[7] EMERY (*Sylvanus,*[6] *Humphrey,*[5] *Humphrey,*[4] *Jonathan,*[3] *Jonathan,*[2] *John*[1]), son of Sylvanus and Susan (Rogers) Emery, married Nancy Littlefield, of Madison, N. H.

Children, born in Bartlett, N. H .

3742   i   DORCAS,[8] b. 1843, d 1863
3743   ii   STEPHEN E , b 1844, m Margaret Dana, 1865.
3744   iii SAMUEL E., b 1848, d. 1851
3745   iv   ALPHENIA, b 1852 , m Henry Abbot, 1870
3746   v   SOPHRONIA, b 1854, m O Dana, 1878
3747   vi   GILBERT, b 1857, m Eliza B. Jackson, 1880

1955 NOAH[7] EMERY (*Ruth,*[6] *Humphrey,*[5] *Humphrey,*[4] *Jonathan,*[3] *Jonathan,*[2] *John*[1]), son of Peter and Ruth (Emery) Emery, married Irene Loomis Morgan, the daughter of his stepfather, Feb. 14, 1818; died in Kennedy, Chautauqua Co , N Y., Oct 8, 1869. His widow died Feb. 1, 1876, aged 81.

Children :

```
3748  i     ALMIRA,8 b. July 30, 1819.
3749  ii    ANCELINE, b. July 5, 1820.
3750  iii   ABBIE, b. Oct. 15, 1823.
3751  iv    AMELIA, b. Sept. 14, 1825.
3752  v     ALTON WASHINGTON, m. Sarah A. Burnett, April 9, 1874.
3753  vi    ALVINA D., b. Dec. 18, 1827.
3754  vii   AMANDA, b. March 19, 1830; m. J. Bill, Dec. 28, 1863.
3755  viii  ELIZABETH, b. July 28, 1832.
3756  ix    LODEMA, b. Sept. 2, 1834.
3757  x     SARAH SIBLEY, b. Nov. 5, 1836.
3758  xi    ORETT JANE, b. Sept. 2, 1839.
3759  xii   MORGAN, b. Feb. 5, 1842; member of Co. "G," 9th N. Y. Cav.;
            killed at the battle of Meadow Bridge, Va., May 12, 1864.
3760  xiii  GEORGE WELLINGTON, b. Jan. 22, 1845; d. Sept. 18, 1851.
```

1958 JONAS[7] EMERY (*Ruth,[6] Humphrey,[5] Humphrey,[4] Jonathan,[3] Jonathan,[2] John[1]*), son of Peter and Ruth (Emery) Emery ; married Lucette Wood, who died 1877. He was a lawyer and died June 26, 1885.

Children :

```
3761  i     RUTH MORGAN,8 b. July 5, 1827.
3762  ii    THOMAS, b. Aug. 18, 1829.
3763  iii   SAMANTHA ANN, b. April 27, 1831.
3764  iv    JAMES M., b. May, 1832.
3765  v     MADISON RILEY, b. March 1, 1834.
3766  vi    WILLIAM HENRY, b. Oct. 1, 1838; d. Oct. 4, 1838.
3767  vii   CURTIS J., b. June 30, 1841.
```

1959 SARAH[7] MORGAN (*Ruth,[6] Humphrey,[5] Humphrey,[4] Jonathan,[3] Jonathan,[2] John[1]*), daughter of James and Mrs. Ruth (Emery) Morgan ; married Oct. 22, 1836, at Fredonia, N. Y., Jabez Reed Normand of Paris Hill, Oneida Co., N. Y. (born Oct. 28, 1811 ; died at Dunkirk, N. Y., April 24, 1868).

Children :

```
3768  i     FRANKLIN FREEMAN,8 b. July 6, 1837.
3769  ii    KATHARINE EMERY, b. Dec. 9, 1840; Prin. of public school,
            Dunkirk, N. Y.
3770  iii   ESTHER, b. June 12, 1843.
3771  iv    HOBART, b. March 31, 1845.
```

1960 EMILY[7] MORGAN (*Ruth,[6] Humphrey,[5] Humphrey,[4] Jonathan,[3] Jonathan,[2] John[1]*), daughter of James and Mrs. Ruth (Emery) Morgan ; married Daniel Fletcher, May 22, 1845.

Children :

```
3772  i     DAVID JAMES,8 b. March 17, 1846.
3773  ii    SARAH KATHARINE, b. Nov. 27, 1847.
3774  iii   CHARLES NELSON, b. March 4, 1850.
3775  iv    RUTH BELLE, b. April 17, 1857.
```

1963 PETER[7] EMERY (*Sarah,[6] Humphrey,[5] Humphrey,[4] Jonathan,[3] Jonathan,[2] John[1]*), son of Enoch (son of Enoch and Rachel (Tyrrell) Emery) and Sarah (Emery) Emery ; married Hannah Upton, widow of Cyrus Moore, Nov. 29, 1846.

Children, born in Albany, Me. :

3776 i NOAH R ,⁸ b Jan 2, 1851.
3777 ii FRANCIS H , b May 31, 1856, m. Winnie F. Farmer, July 2, 1884.

1967 ISAAC⁷ EMERY (*Stephen,*⁶ *Enoch,*⁵ *Humphrey,*⁴ *Jonathan,*³ *Jonathan,*² *John*¹), son of Stephen and Dolly (Rogers) Emery , married Susan Nute.
Children ·

3778 i STEPHEN ⁸
3779 ii JOEL.
3780 iii SAMUEL.
3781 iv JOSHUA.

1970 JOSHUA⁷ EMERY (*Stephen,*⁶ *Enoch.*⁵ *Humphrey.*⁴ *Jonathan,*³ *Jonathan.*² *John*¹), son of Stephen and Dolly (Rogers) Emery , married, in 1827, Hannah, daughter of Stephen and Esther (Wentworth) Emery, who died in Canaan, Vt., April 12, 1876.
Children :

3782 i JOHN PITMAN,⁸ b June 23. 1828
3783 ii GEORGE CASS, b May 20, 1830, d Jan 1855, unm
3784 iii STEPHEN WENTWORTH, b Feb 17, 1832
3785 iv LOUISA LUCRETIA, b Aug. 6, 1834.
3786 v WARREN DANA, b Nov 12, 1837
3787 vi ELIZ HANNAH, b April 20, 1839
3788 vii ELSIE ANN, b Jan 29, 1846
3789 viii HARRIET ADELINE, b. July 19, 1849; m John Flanders, May 15, 1867.

1973 DOLLY⁷ EMERY (*Nathaniel,*⁶ *Enoch,*⁵ *Humphrey,*⁴ *Jonathan,*³ *Jonathan,*² *John*¹), daughter of Nathaniel and Deborah (Rogers) Emery , married Hayes D. Copp.
Children .

3790 i JEREMIAH B ,⁹ b. Sept 7, 1832
3791 ii NATH E , b Jan , 1834, m Lizzie Pray, July 1, 1883
3792 iii HANNAH SYLVIA b Nov 18, 1838, m , 1st, Benj Potter, Nov. 18, 1858, 2d, Edwin M Hanson, Aug 16, 1883
3793 iv DANIEL S , b Aug 14, 1849, m Lizzie Drew of Oberlin, O , Dec. 18, 1874.

1976 JONATHAN⁷ EMERY (*Nathaniel,*⁶ *Enoch,*⁵ *Humphrey,*⁴ *Jonathan,*³ *Jonathan,*² *John*¹) son of Nathaniel and Deborah (Rogers) Emery ; married ———.
Child :

3794 i CHARLES EDWARD ⁸

1978 MARTHA B ⁷ EMERY (*Nathaniel,*⁶ *Enoch,*⁵ *Humphrey,*⁴ *Jonathan,*³ *Jonathan,*² *John*¹), son of Nathaniel and Deborah (Rogers) Emery ; married Nov 14, 1844, in Portland, Me., George Vining of Templeton, Mass , who died June 1, 1875.
Children, born in Templeton, Mass :

3795 i FANNIE,⁸ } b July 23, 1846.
3796 ii MARTHA, }
3797 iii GEORGE LUTHER, b Oct 6, 1851; m Fannie A Balcom, Oct 2, 1877.

1979 Henderson S.[7] Emery (*John,*[6] *Enoch,*[5] *Humphrey,*[4] *Jona-than,*[3] *Jonathan,*[2] *John*[1]), son of John and Dolly (Emery) Emery, married Hannah Bailey; died Oct. 19, 1857.

Children

3798	i	Mary Abby [8]
3799	ii	Dolly Ann
3800	iii	Susan Ann.
3801	iv	Emily
3802	v	Olive
3803	vi	Elmer.

1980 Susan[7] Emery (*John,*[6] *Enoch,*[5] *Humphrey,*[4] *Jonathan,*[3] *Jonathan,*[2] *John*[1]), daughter of John and Dolly (Emery) Emery; married Joseph Littlefield.

Children:

3804	i	John [8]
3805	ii	Martha Jane
3806	iii	Henderson.
3807	iv	Reuben

1982 Mary J E.[7] Emery (*John,*[6] *Enoch,*[5] *Humphrey,*[4] *Jonathan,*[3] *Jonathan,*[2] *John*[1]) daughter of John and Dolly (Emery) Emery; married Uriah Burbank of Bartlett, N. H., Oct. 8, 1849.

Children.

3808	i	James M ,[8] b Jan , 1850
3809	ii	Fanny S , b. Aug , 1852; m , 1st, Frank Lord, 2d, John Hayes
3810	iii	Orson, d 4 years of age
3811	iv	Mary Susan, b May 19, 1859
3812	v	Julia A , b 1862, d 22 years of age
3813	vi	Alva Maria, b 1864, d Dec 28, 1884.
3814	vii	Frank Uriah, b Oct 6, 1867
3815	viii	Henry William, b. June 16, 1871.

1994 Jane[7] Emery (*William* [6] *Richardson,*[5] *Humphrey,*[4] *Jonathan,*[3] *Jonathan,*[2] *John*[1]), daughter of William and Margaret (Aseltine) Emery; married John Winters, and died aged 50.

Children:

3816	i	Silas [8]
3817	ii	Melissa.
3818	iii	George.
3819	iv	Lorenzo

1995 Richardson[7] Emery (*William,*[6] *Richardson,*[5] *Humphrey,*[4] *Jonathan,*[3] *Jonathan,*[2] *John*[1]), son of William and Margaret (Aseltine) Emery, married, first, in Vermont, May 14. 1831, Deidamia Reynolds, who died Dec. 4, 1838; second, June 24, 1839, in Canton, N. Y., Electa Reynolds (born March 28, 1810), sister to Deidamia. They had eight children, five boys and three girls, all of whom died in infancy, except one son and a daughter. He died at Kekoski, Dodge Co , Wis., Sept. 5, 1888.

Children, by first wife:

3820	i	Electa,[8] m and had one son, Oscar Hanson
3821	ii	Ann Eliza, d when two weeks old

The sons all d in infancy.

Children by second wife :

3822 iii GEORGE M ,[8] entered the 3rd Wis. Reg 1863, d , unm , in hospital, 1864
3823 iv DAUGHTER, unm.

1996 MARIA[7] EMERY (*William,*[6] *Richardson,*[5] *Humphrey,*[4] *Jonathan,*[3] *Jonathan,*[2] *John*[1]), daughter of William and Margaret (Aseltine) Emery , married William Wilkison. She lives in Potsdam, N. Y. He died there.

Children, three sons and three daughters, Nos. 3824 to 3829.

1997 THEOPHILUS MANSFIELD[7] EMERY (*William,*[6] *Richardson,*[5] *Humphrey,*[4] *Jonathan,*[3] *Jonathan,*[2] *John*[1]), son of William and Margaret (Aseltine) Emery , married, first, Hannah Bruce Coolidge (born in Peru, N. Y., died in Schuyler Falls, N Y, Oct. 30, 1872) ; second, in Morrisonville, N. Y., Mrs. Lucette Weston, widow of Rev. Z N. Weston of Plattsburgh, N. Y. (died 1888). Ordained minister Methodist Episcopal Church, at Keeseville, N. Y , May 31, 1846.

Children ·

3830 i   RICHARD H ,[8] b March 29, 1833, in Swanton, Vt
3831 ii CAROLINE M d at 5 years of age.
3832 iii
3833 iv } INFANTS, d young
3834 v
3835 vi SANFORD H , d at 8 years of age

1998 MANDANA[7] EMERY (*William,*[6] *Richardson,*[5] *Humphrey,*[4] *Jonathan,*[3] *Jonathan,*[2] *John*[1]), daughter of William and Margaret (Aseltine) Emery ; married her cousin Shedrick Aseltine, and died in Brandon, N. Y., 1887.

Children :

3836 i   FILO,[8] a son, m. and d.
3837 ii   LESTER
3838 iii NATHAN
3839 iv   CORNELIA
3840 v   FAYETTE
3841 vi   HAROLD.
3842 vii ANSON.
3843 viii HENRY

1999 NATHANIEL[7] EMERY (*William,*[6] *Richardson,*[5] *Humphrey,*[4] *Jonathan,*[3] *Jonathan,*[2] *John*[1]), son of William and Margaret (Aseltine) Emery ; married Nancy Garlick ; lives in Potsdam, N. Y.

Children, born in Brandon, N. Y..

3844 i   CHARLES[8]
3845 ii GEORGE
3846 iii MARTHA.
3847 iv MARY
3848 v   SARAH HELEN
3849 vi HENRY MUNSON.

2000 WILLIAM[7] EMERY JR. (*William,*[6] *Richardson,*[5] *Humphrey,*[4] *Jonathan,*[3] *Jonathan,*[2] *John*[1]), son of William and Margaret (Aseltine) Emery ; married July 22, 1844, in Brandon, N. Y., where they lived, Rosanna Witherell (born in Vermont, Dec. 12, 1827 ; died May 24, 1871).   He was a Union soldier in active service two and a half years ; died in the service on Staten Island, N. Y., Nov. 3, 1864.

Children, born in Brandon, N. Y.:

3850   i   LOUISA,[8] b. Sept. 29, 1845; m. Edwin Noyes, March 22, 1866; d. Sept. 25, 1866.
3851   ii   HANNAH, b. June 24, 1847.
3852   iii   JEWETT, b. June 6, 1849; m. Sarah Freeman, in Minn.; d. 1885.
3853   iv   MONROE, b. April 3, 1851; farmer; unm.; lives in Yakima, Washington.
3854   v   ALBERT W., b. Jan. 16, 1853.
3855   vi   ALONZO, b. Nov. 28, 1855; d. April 2, 1860.
3856   vii   PASCHAL, b. Jan. 27, 1857.
3857   viii   NEWELL, } b. Jan. 5, 1859; { farmer; unm.; lives in Marion,
3858   ix   NEWTON, }   South Dakota.
3859   x   WILBERT, } b. Dec. 12, 1861; {
3860   xi   WILBER, }   d. Sept. 28, 1862.
3861   xii   ANNA, } b. July 13, 1862; {
3862   xiii   ANNETTE, }   d. July 27, 1862.

2001 SABRINA[7] EMERY (*William,*[6] *Richardson,*[5] *Humphrey,*[4] *Jonathan,*[3] *Jonathan,*[2] *John*[1]), daughter of William and Margaret (Aseltine) Emery ; married Warren Aseltine ; had eight children ; lived and died in Brandon, N. Y., aged about 55 years.

2002 ELIZABETH[7] EMERY (*William,*[6] *Richardson,*[5] *Humphrey,*[4] *Jonathan,*[3] *Jonathan,*[2] *John*[1]), daughter of William and Margaret (Aseltine) Emery ; married Ira Chase ; had eight children ; died in Fort Jackson, N. Y., aged about 60 years.

2004 CHARLOTTE E.[7] GOULD (*Hannah,*[6] *Richardson,*[5] *Humphrey,*[4] *Jonathan,*[3] *Jonathan,*[2] *John*[1]), daughter of Edward and Hannah (Emery) Gould ; married, first, Allen Smith.   He died in South Carolina. She married, second, Leander Cadwell, of Redford, N. Y., and died in Redford, Feb. 18, 1879.

Children, by first marriage, born in Schuyler Falls, N. Y.:

3863   i   EMELINE LAVINA,[8] b. Dec. 17, 1837.
3864   ii   HANNAH J., b. Oct. 4, 1841.

2006 GEORGE[7] GOULD (*Hannah,*[6] *Richardson,*[5] *Humphrey,*[4] *Jonathan,*[3] *Jonathan,*[2] *John*[1]), son of Edward and Hannah (Emery) Gould ; married Jeannette Torrence ; had six children ; farmer ; died in Vinton, Iowa.

2010 HANNAH[7] GOULD (*Hannah,*[6] *Richardson,*[5] *Humphrey,*[4] *Jonathan,*[3] *Jonathan,*[2] *John*[1]), daughter of Edward and Hannah (Emery) Gould ; married and has six children ; lives in Au Sable Forks, Clinton Co., N. Y.

2023 ENOCH[7] EMERY (*Russell,*[6] *Richardson,*[5] *Humphrey,*[4] *Jonathan,*[3] *Jonathan,*[2] *John*[1]), son of Russell Emery ; married Alzina Canfield , died in Schuyler Falls, N. Y., Nov. 15, 1888 ; farmer.   She lives in Schuyler Falls.

Children :

```
3865   i     HULDAH,8 lives in Schuyler Falls; unm.
3866   ii    SON, living in Cadyville, N  Y
3867   iii   SON, living in Cadyville, N  Y
3868   iv    SON, living in Cadyville, N. Y
3869   v     ALMOND, living in Schuyler Falls, N  Y ; soldier in the war
             of the Rebellion
3870   vi    SON, d
3871   vii   RUSSELL was a soldier, killed in battle by Indians near Chey-
             enne, Wyoming
```

2024 CINDERELLA[7] EMERY (*Nathaniel*,[6] *Richardson*,[5] *Humphrey*,[4] *Jonathan*,[3] *Jonathan*,[2] *John*[1]), daughter of Nathaniel and Lydia(——) Emery ; married Anson Wescot in Peasleyville, N. Y., where she died.

Children .

```
3872   i     JAMES 8
3873   ii    BENJAMIN
3874   iii   ABIGAIL.
3875   iv    OLIVE
3876   v     LYDIA
3877   vi    NATHANIEL.
```

2025 HANNAH[7] EMERY (*Nathaniel*,[6] *Richardson*,[5] *Humphrey*,[4] *Jonathan*,[3] *Jonathan*,[2] *John*[1]), daughter of Nathaniel and Lydia Emery , married Daniel Ferris.   She died ——.

Children :

```
3878   i     EMERY 8
3879   ii    ALVAH.
3880   iii   ELINOR.
3881   iv    KATE
3882   v     MARY
3883   vi    SEYMOUR.
3884   vii   JOHN.
```

2028 MARTHA[7] EMERY (*Nathaniel*,[6] *Richardson*,[5] *Humphrey*,[4] *Jonathan*,[3] *Jonathan*,[2] *John*[1]), daughter of Nathaniel and Lydia Emery ; married Jan. 17, 1825, William Bowles (born May 23, 1803).   She died December 8, 1887.

Children :

```
3885   i     JOHN V R ,8 b May 4, 1827 ; d Oct. 19, 1887
3886   ii    ROBERT, b June 13, 1830, burned to death in a starch factory.
3887   iii   LYDIA, b Sept 5, 1835, in Brandon, N  Y
3888   iv    WILLIAM, JR , b. Feb 9, 1838 ; m Levisa Adams, 1862, d Jan
             17, 1889
3889   v     BEISLY, b Oct 9, 1839, Peasleyville, N. Y.
3890   vi    SAMUEL, b June 15, 1841
3891   vii   HANNAH, b Sept 1, 1844, d in Brandon, N. Y., in 1863
3892   viii  JANE S., b June 3, 1848, in Bangor, N. Y.
```

2029 SAMUEL[7] EMERY (*Nathaniel*,[6] *Richardson*,[5] *Humphrey*,[4] *Jonathan*,[3] *Jonathan*,[2] *John*[1]), son of Nathaniel and Lydia Emery ; married ; lives in Saranac, N. Y. ; farmer.

Children :
3893 i   CORNELIA,[8] d. in Brandon, N. Y.
3894 ii   EZEKIEL.

2045 JOHN W.[7] EMERY (*Francis,[6] John,[5] Stephen,[4] Stephen,[3] Jonathan,[2] John[1]*), son of Francis and Eunice (Philbrick) Emery ; married, first, Sept. 24, 1823, Sarah F. Bassett (born June 17, 1801 ; died May 9, 1830) ; second, Almira Jones. He died Dec. 6, 1866.
Children :
3895 i   SARAH JANE,[8] b. Sept. 30, 1824.
3896 ii   JUSTIN THEODORE, b. Feb. 17, 1826.
3897 iii MARIA ELIZABETH, b. April 21, 1827.

2046 EUNICE HALE[7] EMERY (*Francis,[6] John,[5] Stephen,[4] Stephen,[3] Jonathan,[2] John[1]*), daughter of Francis and Eunice (Philbrick) Emery ; married, first, May 17, 1832, Milo M. Stone, who died July 16, 1834 ; second, George French.
Child :
3898 i   CHILD,[8] d. young.

2049 SARAH S.[7] EMERY (*Francis,[6] John,[5] Stephen,[4] Stephen,[3] Jonathan,[2] John[1]*), daughter of Francis and Eunice (Philbrick) Emery ; married Hosby Shed, July 3, 1838. She died Dec. 9, 1873.
Child :
3899 i   SARAH ANNA.[5]

2054 AMBROSE[7] EMERY (*Daniel,[6] John,[5] Stephen,[4] Stephen,[3] Jonathan,[2] John[1]*), son of Daniel and Betsey (Curtice) Emery ; married Mary Godding, daughter of Henry Godding ; died in Amherst, N. H., April 12, 1840.
Children :
3900 i   GEORGE.[8]
3901 ii   MARTHA ANN; m. John Durant.

2055 CYNTHIA[7] EMERY (*Daniel,[6] John,[5] Stephen,[4] Stephen,[3] Jonathan,[2] John[1]*), daughter of Daniel and Betsey (Curtice) Emery ; married Levi Joslin of Rindge, N. H.
Children :
3902 i   LEVI.[8]
3903 ii   JUDSON.

2056 DANIEL[7] EMERY (*Daniel,[6] John,[5] Stephen,[4] Stephen,[3] Jonathan,[2] John[1]*), son of Daniel and Betsey (Curtice) Emery ; married, Sept. 20, 1829, Susannah Pierce (born Jan. 31, 1807), daughter of Lieut. Stephen and Drusilla (Patterson) Pierce. He died March 31, 1858.
Children :
3904 i   CHARLES AUGUSTUS,[8] b. April 21, 1831.
3905 ii   SIDNEY PATTERSON, b. Feb. 28, 1835.
3906 iii WILLIAM CHILDS, b. June 23, 1836.
3907 iv   CAROLINE FRANCES, b. July 5, 1838; d. May 7, 1840.

3908   v   EDWARD FRANKLIN, b April 28, 1841
3909   vi FREDERICK PIERCE, b April 29 1843, d. May 12, 1844
3910   vii SARAH EMMA, b April 7, 1845
3911   viii ABBIE SUSAN, b Oct. 16, 1847, d Aug 24, 1848
3912   ix HERBERT, b Feb. 3, 1851, drowned at Salisbury Beach, Mass ,
            Aug. 30, 1876

2059 FRANCIS TOWNE[7] EMERY (*John*,[6] *John*,[5] *Stephen*,[4] *Stephen*,[3] *Jonathan*,[2] *John*[1]), son of John and Deborah (Towne) Emery, married, Nov. 5, 1844, Mary Smith (born Jan 29, 1818 , died March 21, 1887) He died July 22, 1886.
Children :

3913   i   CHARLES HORACE,[8] b. Nov. 16, 1845
3914   ii   WARHAM R , b. March 17 1848
3915   iii FRANCIS FREDERICK, b. July 22, 1858.

2061 DEBORAH[7] EMERY (*John*,[6] *John*,[5] *Stephen*,[4] *Stephen*,[3] *Jonathan*,[2] *John*[1]), daughter of John and Deborah (Towne) Emery ; married Jacob Newell, of Jaffrey, N. H , member of Co. "F," 16th N H. Vols., and died in army April 5, 1863.
Children :

3916   i   GEORGE A ,[8] b June 19, 1850
3917   ii   HENRY O , b Feb 8, 1856, d young.
3918   iii FRANCIS H , b April 8, 1857, d young

2062 DEROSTUS WOOD[7] EMERY (*Stephen*,[6] *John*,[5] *Stephen*,[4] *Stephen*,[3] *Jonathan*,[2] *John*[1]), son of Stephen and Betsey (Wood) Emery ; married Mary Pierce, daughter of Benjamin and Judith (Metcalf) Pierce (born Aug. 2, 1805).
Children :

3919   i   GEORGE A ,[8] b March 28, 1828, m , 1st, Martha L Bass, May 20,
            1854 (d June 21, 1863), 2nd, Mary E Stearns, June 5, 1864
3920   ii   JULIA AUGUSTA, b Sept. 24, 1830, m., Charles F. Stearns,
            Sept 24, 1851
3921   iii DEROSTUS P , b March 27, 1832
3922   iv   JANE E , b Feb 13, 1835; m Rodney A. Hubbard
3923   v   WARREN W , b Feb. 12, 1837, m.,1st, Caroline Lake, 2nd, Abbie
            S Lake.
3924   vi   ALBERT A , b July 7. 1842, m Mary Ann Wilder, Nov , 1866
3925   vii MARIANNA, b. Sept 18, 1847 m Wm B Robbins, Sept. 18,
            1872

2063 ALBERT[7] L. EMERY (*Stephen*,[6] *John*,[5] *Stephen*,[4] *Stephen*,[3] *Jonathan*,[2] *John*[1]), son of Stephen and Betsey (Wood) Emery , married Dec. 25, 1841, Sarah Jane Capps (born Sept. 24, 1825). He died Aug. 6, 1881.
Children .

3926   i   ELIZA JANE,[8] b Nov. 19, 1851.
3927   ii   CHARLES ALBERT, b Jun 11, 1855

2064 AUGUSTUS C [7] EMERY (*Stephen*,[6] *John*,[5] *Stephen*,[4] *Stephen*,[3] *Jonathan*,[2] *John*[1]), son of Stephen and Betsey (Wood) Emery , married Pamelia Woodworth (born March 4, 1832).
Child :

3928   i   HERBERT W.,[8] b. Jan 21, 1868.

2075 CHARLES H.[7] EMERY (*Enos,*[6] *John,*[5] *Stephen,*[4] *Stephen,*[3] *Jonathan,*[2] *John*[1]), son of Enos and Zipporah (Hale) Emery ; married Oct. 11, 1848, Eliza M. Lane, daughter of Elias and Anna (Jones) Lane (born June 25, 1823).

Child :

3929   i   LIZZY M.,[8] b. June 28, 1857.

2076 PASCAL P.[7] EMERY (*Enos,*[6] *John,*[5] *Stephen,*[4] *Stephen,*[3] *Jonathan,*[2] *John*[1]), son of Enos and Zipporah (Hale) Emery ; married, Nov. 27, 1850, Marilla J. Lane, daughter of Elias and Anna (Jones) Lane (born July 1, 1827).

Children :

3930   i   ETTA E.,[8] b. Sept. 2, 1856; d. Nov. 3, 1878.
3931   ii   FLORA J., b. April 17, 1861; d. Aug. 9, 1861.
3932   iii   CARRIE J., b. Feb. 23, 1863.

2077 DAVID[7] EMERY (*Stephen,*[6] *Jesse,*[5] *Stephen,*[4] *Stephen,*[3] *Jonathan,*[2] *John*[1]), son of Stephen and Margaret (Chase) Emery ; married Betsey Foster.

Child :

3933   i   VALORA.[8]

2078 ELIZA[7] EMERY (*Stephen,*[6] *Jesse,*[5] *Stephen,*[4] *Stephen,*[3] *Jonathan,*[2] *John*[1]), daughter of Stephen and Margaret (Chase) Emery ; married J. D. Smith.

Children :

3934   i   LLEWELLYN.[8]
3935   ii   LUSETTA.
3936   iii   ADDIE.
3937   iv   LORIN.

2079 SARAH M.[7] EMERY (*Stephen,*[6] *Jesse,*[5] *Stephen,*[4] *Stephen,*[3] *Jonathan,*[2] *John*[1]), daughter of Stephen and Margaret (Chase) Emery ; married Otis H. Abbot of Grafton, Me.

Children, born in Upton, Mass. :

3938   i   LOIS M.,[8] b. March 18, 1841; m. John Akers of Errol, N. H.
3939   ii   ENOCH, b. Dec. 18, 1844; m. Louisa Ford.
3940   iii   VALORA A., b. Aug. 25, 1846; m. Leonidas West.
3941   iv   MARTHA L., b. Aug. 23, 1849; m. Ingalls F. Evans.
3942   v   HARRY M., b. May 27, 1864.

2080 MARY[7] EMERY (*Stephen,*[6] *Jesse,*[5] *Stephen,*[4] *Stephen,*[3] *Jonathan,*[2] *John*[1]), daughter of Stephen and Margaret (Chase) Emery ; married Isaac King.

Children :

3943   i   EMILY RUTH.[8]
3944   ii   DELPHINA A.
3945   iii   SARAH A.
3946   iv   AMOS S.
3947   v   MARY, drowned when two years old.
3948   vi   GEORGE W.
3949   vii   THERSIA M., m. Horatio Wight.

2082 ROSANNAH[7] EMERY (*Stephen*,[6] *Jesse*,[5] *Stephen*[4] *Stephen*,[3] *Jonathan*[2] *John*[1]), daughter of Stephen and Margaret (Chase) Emery; married William H. Estes.
Children:

3950   i   ELLA[8]
3951   ii   ESMER
3952   iii
3953   iv

2083 LUCINDA[7] EMERY (*Stephen*,[6] *Jesse*,[5] *Stephen*,[4] *Stephen*,[3] *Jonathan*,[2] *John*[1]), daughter of Stephen and Margaret (Chase) Emery, married Milton York.

3954   i   FRANK[8]
3955   ii   FRED
3956   iii   LILLA
3957   iv   NELLIE.

2084 JOHN[7] EMERY (*Stephen*,[6] *Jesse*,[5] *Stephen*,[4] *Stephen*,[3] *Jonathan*,[2] *John*[1]), son of Stephen and Margaret (Chase) Emery; married first, Sept. 25, 1858, Asenath W. Littlehale of Newry, Me. (born March 26, 1842, died Dec 19, 1879), second, March 1, 1881, Altora L. Harper of Errol, N. H. (born in Wilton. Me., Sept. 24, 1839).
Children.

3958   i   CORA A.,[8] b. Aug. 18, 1859, m Charles C Bennett.
3959   ii   IDA L , b April 5, 1862
3960   iii   ESMA L , b April 15, 1864.

2085 CLARK[7] EMERY (*Stephen*,[6] *Jesse*,[5] *Stephen*,[4] *Stephen*,[3] *Jonathan*,[2] *John*[1]), son of Stephen and Margaret (Chase) Emery; married Nancy Barker, March 28, 1863, in Newry, Me.
Children·

3961   i   ULYSSES S ,[8] b. Sept 10, 1865
3962   ii   MARIETTA, b Dec 8, 1869, d young

2086 TILTON ELKINS[7] EMERY (*Daniel*,[6] *Daniel*,[5] *John*,[4] *Stephen*,[3] *Jonathan*,[2] *John*[1]), son of Daniel and Rebecca (Chase) Emery, married Hannah E. Bancroft, June 11, 1857; died Feb. 26, 1887.
Child·

3963   i   NELLIE GERTRUDE,[8] b June 16, 1860

2087 MATTHEW P.[7] EMERY (*Daniel*,[6] *Daniel*,[5] *John*,[4] *Stephen*,[3] *Jonathan*,[2] *John*[1]), son of Daniel and Rebecca (Chase) Emery, married Elnorah Messer of Wilmot, N. H.
Children·

3964   i   MASON WHIPPLE.[8]
3965   ii   MICAJAH.
3966   iii   ARTHUR TILTON
3967   iv   ADDIE MARIA
3968   v   NETTIE ELNORAH.
3969   vi   CADY J.
3970   vii   LILLIE ESTHER.

12

2090 WILLIAM G.[7] EMERY (*Ezra*,[6] *Daniel*,[5] *John*,[4] *Stephen*,[3] *Jonathan*,[2] *John*[1]), son of Ezra and Jane (Dole) Emery; married Lucy A. Hodgdon of Tremont, Me.; died in Eden, Me., Dec. 3, 1880.
Children :

    3971   i   ELLA F.[8]
    3972   ii   ANNA L.
    3973   iii WILLIAM A.
    3974   iv   EDDIE E.
    3975   v   GUY W.

2091 NANCY G.[7] EMERY (*Ezra*,[6] *Daniel*,[5] *John*,[4] *Stephen*,[3] *Jonathan*,[2] *John*[1]), daughter of Ezra and Jane (Dole) Emery, married Nelson Stevens of Sunapee, N. H.
Children :

    3976   i   EDWIN [8]
    3977   ii   CHARLES.
    3678   iii MATTIE.

2092 SARAH W.[7] EMERY (*Ezra*,[6] *Daniel*,[5] *John*,[4] *Stephen*,[3] *Jonathan*,[2] *John*[1]), daughter of Ezra and Jane (Dole) Emery, married Frank W. Flanders of Danbury, N. H.
Children :

    3979   i   ALICE [8]
    3980   ii   ELLA.
    3981   iii EMMA.
    3982   iv   GRACE.

2098 LIZZIE J.[7] WHITE (*Judith*,[6] *Daniel*,[5] *John*,[4] *Stephen*,[3] *Jonathan*,[2] *John*[1]), daughter of Eben and Judith (Emery) White; married, Oct 25, 1857, in Hoosick Falls, N Y, Aaron White, who died Jan 27, 1865. His widow married, second, 1865, John Cary.
Child, by first husband :

    3983   i   HARRY E [8]

2099 LYSIAS E.[7] WHITE (*Judith*,[6] *Daniel*,[5] *John*,[4] *Stephen*,[3] *Jonathan*,[2] *John*[1]), son of Eben and Judith (Emery) White, married Mary H Graves of Bellows Falls, Vt., June 2, 1857.
Children :

    3984   i   FRANK F.,[8] b July 12, 1858, d July 17, 1876
    3985   ii   HENRY H , b July 11, 1860, m Mary Whalen of Houston, Tex.,
                Oct 5, 1889
    3986   iii CHARLES C , b March 1, 1862; m Cora E Sutton, Oct. 6,
                1883.
    3987   iv   IDA J., b Jan. 10, 1864, m Fred R. Shaw, Dec. 13, 1882
    3988   v   GEORGE G., b. June 11, 1868.

2102 M. HELEN[7] WHITE (*Judith*,[6] *Daniel*,[5] *John*,[4] *Stephen*,[3] *Jonathan*,[2] *John*[1]), daughter of Eben and Judith (Emery) White; married Cyrus N. Corning of Concord, N. H., Oct. 29, 1854.
Children :

    3989   i   WILLIE N.,[8] d June, 1862
    3990   ii   JESSIE N.

2103 ADDIE J [7] WHITE (*Judith*,[6] *Daniel*,[5] *John*,[4] *Stephen*,[3] *Jonathan*,[2] *John*[1]), daughter of Eben and Judith (Emery) White; married Eben M. Davis of Hill, N H., who was killed in Vineland, N. J., by the caving in of a well, Jan. 30, 1865.
Child :
3991 i GEORGIA H.[8]

2106 LAVINIA[7] EMERY (*Timothy*,[6] *Daniel*,[5] *John*,[4] *Stephen*,[3] *Jonathan*,[2] *John*[1]), daughter of Timothy and Fanny (Jones) Emery ; married James Marcy.
Child .
3992 i ARTHUR [8]

2109 JESSE EMERY[7] EMERSON (*Elizabeth*,[6] *Moses*,[5] *Benjamin*,[4] *Stephen*,[3] *Jonathan*,[2] *John*[1]), son of John and Elizabeth (Emery) Emerson, married Mary E Morrison, Oct , 1834. He died Oct. 12, 1871.
Children :
3993 i ALFRED P.,[8] b. July 26, 1841.

2111 JOHN WEBSTER[7] EMERSON (*Elizabeth*,[6] *Moses*,[5] *Benjamin*,[4] *Stephen*,[3] *Jonathan*,[2] *John*[1]), son of John and Elizabeth (Emery) Emerson ; married Abigail J. Page, July, 1834. Prominent in the affairs of his town.
Children :
3994 i ELIZABETH,[8] b. Nov. 11, 1835. In Hampstead, N H
3995 ii SUSAN, b. March 23, 1840, in Youngstown, N Y
3996 iii JOHN WEBSTER, b Dec 4, 1841, in Youngstown, N Y
3997 iv FRED, b Jan 2, 1845, in Youngstown, N Y
3998 v MARIA, b Sept 27, 1849, in Youngstown, N Y
3999 vi MARION, b. Jan. 19, 1853, in Bennington, Vt.

2112 ROBERT HENRY[7] EMERSON (*Elizabeth*,[6] *Moses*,[5] *Benjamin*,[4] *Stephen*,[3] *Jonathan*,[2] *John*[1]), son of John and Elizabeth (Emery) Emerson ; married, first, Nov., 1843, Cyrene S. Wheeler, who died Aug. 29, 1852 ; second, Oct. 25, 1853, Sarah S. Carlton, who died Jan. 19, 1855 ; third, Nov. 30, 1855, Mary P. Eastman. He died in Chelsea, Mass., June 8, 1883.
Children :
4000 i CHILD,[8] d in infancy.
4001 ii CHILD, d. in infancy
4002 iii SARAH ALMIRA, b Oct 4, 1854
4003 iv SON, b. July 23, 1869; d Oct., 1869

2114 MARY[7] EMERSON (*Elizabeth*,[6] *Moses*,[5] *Benjamin*,[4] *Stephen*,[3] *Jonathan*,[2] *John*[1]), daughter of John and Elizabeth (Emery) Emerson ; married John C. Bradley of Danville, N. H., Nov. 14, 1844.
Children :
4004 i ALBERT [8]
4005 ii ELIZABETH, b July 19, 1852, d Feb 21, 1855
4006 iii MARY
4007 iv CHARLES H , b. March 3, 1863.

2115 Dudley W.[7] Currier (*Sarah,*[6] *Moses,*[5] *Benjamin,*[4] *Stephen,*[3] *Jonathan,*[2] *John*[1]), son of Nathan and Sarah (Emery) Currier ; married in Salem, N. H., Rebecca Noyes, April 21, 1840 ; died in Bridgeport, Conn., Nov. 9, 1873.

Children :

    4008   i   Alice Wheeler,[8] b. Aug. 31, 1841 ; m. Nathaniel Jewett Jones.
    4009   ii   Levi Wheeler, b. June 27, 1845 ; m. Sarah L. Ayer, Sept. 5,
                  1876.
    4010   iii Abbie Frances, b. May 21, 1849 ; m. Theodore Constright,
                  Sept. 19, 1871.
    4011   iv   Willis Dudley, b. Aug. 20, 1855 ; d. Nov. 8, 1861.

2116 Mehetable E.[7] Currier (*Sarah,*[6] *Moses,*[5] *Benjamin,*[4] *Stephen,*[3] *Jonathan,*[2] *John*[1]), daughter of Nathan and Sarah (Emery) Currier ; married, in Methuen, N. H., Dec. 31, 1839, Ezra M. Bartlett of Plymouth, N. H.

Children :

    4012   i   Ezra Sargent,[8] b. March 14, 1842 ; killed at Port Hudson,
                  July 14, 1863.
    4013   ii   Alonzo Henry, b. May 29, 1846 ; d. Aug. 25, 1848.
    4014   iii Leroy Alphonso, b. April 10, 1858.
    4015   iv   Ellen Luetta, b. Sept. 23, 1859.

2117 Alpheus[7] Currier (*Sarah,*[6] *Moses,*[5] *Benjamin,*[4] *Stephen,*[3] *Jonathan,*[2] *John*[1]), son of Nathan and Sarah (Emery) Currier ; married in Plymouth, N. H., Sarah J. Bartlett, April 15, 1841 (died Nov. 24, 1871).

Children :

    4016   i   Horace Gilbert,[8] b. May 9, 1847 ; m. Emma M. Buffum, Sept.
                  1, 1874.
    4017   ii   Zelia Jeannette, b. Feb. 3, 1855.

2118 Sarah[7] Currier (*Sarah,*[6] *Moses,*[5] *Benjamin,*[4] *Stephen,*[3] *Jonathan,*[2] *John*[1]), daughter of Nathan and Sarah (Emery) Currier ; married Richard H. Ayer, of Haverhill, Mass., Jan. 26, 1842.

Children :

    4018   i   Annette,[8] b. June 13, 1843 ; m. Hazen Littlefield, April 19,
                  1866.
    4019   ii   Sarah L., b. May 10, 1846 ; m. Levi Wheeler Currier, Sept. 5,
                  1876.
    4020   iii Abbie A., b. Sept. 12, 1848 ; m. George H. Sargent, Sept., 1872.
    4021   iv   Hazen, b. Nov. 7, 1852.
    4022   v   George Davis, b. Aug. 24, 1860.

2119 Abigail[7] Currier (*Sarah,*[6] *Moses,*[5] *Benjamin,*[4] *Stephen,*[3] *Jonathan,*[2] *John*[1]), daughter of Nathan and Sarah (Emery) Currier ; married, Nov. 25, 1847, Edward A. Sargent, in Haverhill, Mass. She died March 14, 1877.

Children :

    4023   i   Charles.[8]
    4024   ii   Harry.
    4025   iii Carrie.
    4026   iv   William.
    4027   v   Minnie.

2120 RHODA E.[7] CURRIER (*Sarah*,[6] *Moses*,[5] *Benjamin*,[4] *Stephen*,[3] *Jonathan*,[2] *John*[1]), daughter of Nathan and Sarah (Emery) Currier; married, in New York, Dec. 14, 1849, Daniel Moulton, of Gilmanton, N. H.

Children ·

4028 i   EMMA A ,[8] b April 6, 1852, d 1871.
4029 ii   ALVIN D , b April 12, 1855
4030 iii NETTIE A , b July 31, 1861; m. Samuel Young, Dec 25, 1888

2121 ELIZABETH R [7] CURRIER (*Sarah*,[6] *Moses*,[5] *Benjamin*,[4] *Stephen*,[3] *Jonathan*,[2] *John*[1]), daughter of Nathan and Sarah (Emery) Currier, married Levi Taylor, of Atkinson, N. H., May 1, 1849 , died in Haverhill, Mass , Oct. 7, 1862.

Children :

4031 i   LEVI LE FOREST HAYDEN,[8] b 1853.
4032 ii   HENRY, b 1856, d
4033 iii EZRA WILLIAM B , b. 1858.

2122 HARRIET[7] CURRIER (*Sarah*,[6] *Moses*,[5] *Benjamin*,[4] *Stephen*,[3] *Jonathan*,[2] *John*[1]), daughter of Nathan and Sarah (Emery) Currier; married George G. Davis, Dec. 23, 1851 ; died in Haverhill, Mass., Aug. 31, 1876.

Children .

4034 i   FRED H ,[8] b. June, 1855 , m Ida M. Edgerly, April, 1876
4035 ii   LIZZIE W , b May 30, 1858; d May 26, 1880.
4036 iii GEORGE IRA, b Oct 7, 1868.

2123 FANNIE N.[7] CURRIER (*Sarah*,[6] *Moses*,[5] *Benjamin*,[4] *Stephen*,[3] *Jonathan*,[2] *John*[1]), daughter of Nathan and Sarah (Emery) Currier ; married, in Haverhill, Mass., Oct. 27, 1858, George L. Moulton, of Gilmanton, N H.

Children .

4037 i   EDWIN H ,[8] b Sept 29, 1861, m Gertrude F Amazeen, Nov 27, 1883.
4038 ii   ALINE C , b March 28, 1865.
4039 iii GEORGE WILLIS, b July 24, 1867
4040 iv   FANNIE MAUD, b Nov 16, 1870.

2127 BENJAMIN FRANKLIN[7] WILSON (*Rhoda*,[6] *Moses*,[5] *Benjamin*,[4] *Stephen*,[3] *Jonathan*,[2] *John*[1]), son of Benjamin and Rhoda (Emery) Wilson ; married Anna A. Abbot, in Chester, N. H., July 4, 1867

Children :

4041 i   FANNIE M ,[8] b June 11, 1869.
4042 ii   ROSA BRITE, b May 5, 1872.
4043 iii HATTIE MAY, b May 21 1874.
4044 iv   IRA FRANK, b July 11, 1876.

2129 DAVID[7] EMERY (*Jesse*,[6] *Moses*,[5] *Benjamin*,[4] *Stephen*,[3] *Jonathan*,[2] *John*[1]), son of Jesse and Sarah B (Welch) Emery , married June 2, 1844, Ann E Merrill (born in Haverhill, Mass., Feb. 15, 1825 , died in Atkinson, N. H., Feb , 1890).

Children .

4045　ı　ABBY F ,[8] b　ın Haverhill, Mass, May 28, 1847.
One child, name unknown.

2130 BENJAMIN EMERSON[7] EMERY(*Jesse,*[6] *Moses,*[5] *Benjamın,*[4] *Ste-phen,*[3] *Jonathan,*[2] *John*[1]), son of Jesse and Sarah B (Welch) Emery ; married, June 21, 1841, ın Haverhill, Mass., Elızabeth H Poor (born in Haverhill, Oct 6 1821).
Children, born ın Haverhill :

4046　ı　HARRIET FRANCES,[8] b Sept. 20, 1843.
4047　ıı　SUSAN PERLLY, b May 17, 1854.
4048　ııı　ALBERT EMERSON, b. Dec 21, 1857.

2131 ABIGAIL PAGE[7] EMERY (*Jesse,*[6] *Moses,*[5] *Benjamın,*[4] *Stephen,*[3] *Jonathan,*[2] *John*[1]), daughter of Jesse and Sarah B (Welch) Emery ; married, June 30, 1846, Fred G. Nason (born March 21, 1821).
Children :

4049　ı　LOWELL H ,[8] b April 6. 1847.
4050　ıı　ABBIF J , b Dec 14, 1849.
4051　ıı　SUSAN E , b Dec 4, 1852
4052　ıv　LILLIE E , b Jan 14, 1855
4053　v　CHARLOTTE M , b April 6, 1860

2176 AVIS[5] EMERY (*John,*[6] *David,*[5] *Jonathan,*[4] *James,*[3] *Jonathan,*[2] *John*[1]), daughter of John and Abigail (Brown) Emery , married Luther Burrell, who died ın 1882　She died Feb 15, 1888
Six children, Nos. 4054–4059.　Names unknown.

2178 DAVID[7] EMERY (*John,*[6] *David,*[5] *Jonathan,*[4] *James,*[3] *Jonathan* [2] *John*[1]), son of John and Abigail (Brown) Emery , married ; drowned ın Fairfield, Me., April 12, 1846.
Children :

4060　ı　AUGUSTUS,[8] Unıon soldier, died in the service.
4061　ıı　CHARLES
4062　ııı　SON, lıvıng ın the west.

2179 SUMNER[7] EMERY (*John,*[6] *David,*[5] *Jonathan,*[4] *James,*[3] *Jonathan,*[2] *John*[1]), son of John and Abigail (Brown) Emery ; married four times and lives with fourth wife ın Benton, Me. ; farmer.
Ten children, Nos 4063–4072.

4063　ı　SUMNER,[8] Union soldier

2180 ABIGAIL[7] EMERY (*John,*[6] *David,*[5] *Jonathan,*[4] *James,*[3] *Jonathan,*[2] *John*[1]), daughter of John and Abigail (Brown) Emery ; married Daniel Blackstone, who was a Unıon soldier , lives ın Boston.
Thirteen children, Nos. 4073–4085.

4073　ı　GEORGE O ,[8] Unıon soldier.
4074　ıı　CHARLES H , Unıon soldier

2181 REUBEN[7] EMERY (*John,*[6] *David,*[5] *Jonathan,*[4] *James,*[3] *Jonathan,*[2] *John*[1]), son of John and Abigail (Brown) Emery ; married Mahala Sımpson, and dıed in Waterville, aged sixty years.

Six children, three sons and three daughters, Nos. 4086-4091.

4086 i   NATHANIEL S.,[8] lives in Waterville.

2186 ORRA[7] EMERY (*Benjamin,[6] David,[5] Jonathan,[4] James,[3] Jonathan,[2] John[1]*), daughter of Benjamin and Mary (Whidden) Emery; married in Skowhegan, Me , Nov 3, 1836, Benjamin Fitzgerald (born in Fairfield, Feb. 19, 1809 , died April 14, 1885).
Children, born in Canaan, Me. :

4092 i   WILSON C.,[8] b March 4, 1838
4093 ii   PAULINA N , b Jan 31, 1840
4094 iii MARY E , b. March 9, 1842
4095 iv   ANN SALOME, b. May 17, 1844
4096 v   BURKE L , b Aug 25, 1847
4097 vi   VARA ELLEN, b April 27, 1855

2187 RACHEL[7] EMERY (*Benjamin,[6] David,[5] Jonathan,[4] James,[3] Jonathan,[2] John[1]*), daughter of Benjamin and Mary (Whidden) Emery; married, April 4, 1833, in Skowhegan, Me., William Libby (born in Gray, Me., May 16, 1804 ; died in Vineland, Wis., April 30, 1873) She died in Vineland, Wis , June 11, 1874.
Children, born in Canaan, Me. :

4098 i   BENJAMIN EMERY,[8] b March 22, 1834.
4099 ii   ORRA, b Dec 19, 1835 m Mantheno Kimball, June 4, 1856.
4100 iii EDWIN, b May 15 1838 , d June 4, 1865, unm.
4101 iv   JOHN F , b Dec 22, 1842
4102 v   ESTHER, b April 20, 1844.

2188 HARRISON[7] EMERY (*Benjamin,[6] David,[5] Jonathan,[4] James,[3] Jonathan,[2] John[1]*), son of Benjamin and Mary (Whidden) Emery; married in Bangor, Me., Jan 5, 1842, Nancy Stiles (born in Athens, Me , Aug. 10, 1823). Farmer in Glenburn, Me. :
Children :

4103 i   CHARLES H ,[8] b Sept 6, 1843, in Bangor, Me.
4104 ii   WILLIAM F , b. Nov. 22, 1844, in Bangor, Me ; m Ellen A. Graffam in Bangor, Me , Nov. 23, 1869, farmer in Glenburn
4105 iii GEORGE F , b June 29, 1847, in Bangor, Me , unm.
4106 iv   MILES E , b Dec 16, 1849, in Bangor, Me.
4107 v   LEONARD C., b March 2, 1852, in Bangor, Me ; unm.
4108 vi   JOSEPH A , b May 12, 1854, in Glenburn, Me , unm.
4109 vii WILLIS S., b Dec 20, 1856, in Glenburn, Me.; unm.
4110 viii MARY E , b. April 18, 1859, in Glenburn, Me.
4111 ix   ADDIE L , b June 27, 1861, in Glenburn, Me. , unm
4112 x   HATTIE B., b. Oct 9, 1863, in Glenburn, Me ; d , unm., Feb 8, 1889
4113 xi   MELVIN T , b March 5, 1866, in Glenburn, Me , unm
4114 xii LEVI S., b June 17, 1868, in Glenburn, Me , d Aug. 3, 1874

2189 DR. SAMUEL I [7] EMERY (*Benjamin,[6] David,[5] Jonathan,[4] James,[3] Jonathan,[2] John[1]*), son of Benjamin and Mary (Whidden) Emery ; married Olive Merrill Aug. 23, 1843, in Glenburn, Me.
Children, born in Glenburn :

4115 i   EDGAR NELSON,[8] b. Aug 27, 1844; m. Ella R Johnston in Arcadia, Wis , Nov 15, 1874 She was b at West Bend, Wis , July 7, 1855

4116 ii   CHARLES M , b. Jan 29, 1848 , d , unm , in Glenburn, Jan 28, 1876.

4117 iii   EMMA MARY, b. May 18, 1850; d., unm., in Glenburn, Oct 2, 1883.

4118 iv   ANDREW MERRILL, b Jan 21, 1853

4119 v   SOPHIA OLIVE, b March 23, 1855; school teacher, d , unm., Sept 22, 1878

4120 vi   CHAPIN SAMUEL, b April 16 1859

4121 vii   WALTER W., b. April 18, 1861, unm

4122 viii   HOSEA B., b. Feb. 8, 1867, uum.

2191 BENJAMIN WATSON[7] EMERY (*Benjamin,*[6] *David,*[5] *Jonathan,*[4] *James,*[3] *Jonathan,*[2] *John*[1]), son of Benjamin and Mary (Whidden) Emery ; married, Feb 13, 1849, Emily Merrill (born in Albany, Me , Jan. 9, 1826), sister of Olive Merrill, wife of Dr. Samuel I. Emery. Farmer in Glenburn, Me., and Sparta, Wis. He died in Sparta, Wis., April 23, 1889.

Children :

4123 i   EVA JOSEPHINE,[8] b Jan 21, 1854, in Glenburn, Me , m. in Cal , Sept 30, 1882, Charles French (b. in Hallowell Me., Sept. 22, 1847)

4124 ii   MINA CELIA, b Aug 4, 1856, in Glenburn· unm in Cal.

4125 iii   BYRON WATSON, b Aug 8, 1859, in Glenburn, Me

4126 iv   NELLIE FRANCES, b Aug 11, 1862, in Glenburn , unm in Cal

4127 v   FRED ARTEMAS, b. Sept 23, 1866, in Sparta, Wis unm

4128 vi   CONY BOYNTON, b. March 13, 1870, in Sparta, Wis , unm. in Cal

2193 LORENZO DOW[7] EMERY (*Benjamin,*[6] *David,*[5] *Jonathan,*[4] *James,*[3] *Jonathan,*[2] *John*[1]), son of Benjamin and Mary (Whidden) Emery ; married, in Orono, Aug. 27, 1858, Mary A. Inman (born in Orono, Me , Oct. 2, 1838, died in Lewiston, Me., May 26, 1880). Millman in Lowell.

Children :

4129 i   MARCIE ANNA H ,[8] b March 5, 1860, in Orono, Me

4130 ii   BENJAMIN S , b. March 28, 1862, m. in Nashua, N. H., Jan 15, 1883, Jennie A. Donnelly (b. in Elgin, Canada, Nov 22, 1859).

4131 iii   GEORGE D , b. March 3, 1864, d Jan 9, 1869, in Orono

4132 iv   COBURN D , b April 5, 1866, in Bangor, Me ; unm.

4133 v   ABBOTT L , b Dec 2, 1868, in Orono, Me , unm

4134 vi   JOSEPH B , b July 27, 1876, in Orono, Me

4135 vii   ALICE MARY, b Jan 3, 1880, in Lewiston, Me.; d Feb 18, 1880.

2196 SYLVIA C.[7] EMERY (*Jonathan,*[6] *David,*[5] *Jonathan,*[4] *James,*[3] *Jonathan, John*[1]), daughter of Jonathan and Hannah (Cheney) Emery , married in Canaan, Me., June 6, 1836, Ephraim Evans (born in China, Me., Oct. 28, 1809 ; died May 1, 1878 ; architect and builder).

Children, born in Levant, Me.:

4136 i   GEORGE,[8] b Sept. 9, 1840, d Aug. 12, 1847.

4137 ii   LEVI, b April 18, 1847: unm

4138 iii   LORENZO A , b March 1, 1853, unm

2197 COLUMBUS W [7] EMERY (*Jonathan,*[6] *David,*[5] *Jonathan,*[4] *James,*[3] *Jonathan,*[2] *John*[1]), son of Jonathan and Hannah (Cheney) Emery , married in East New Portland, Me., July 22, 1849, Sophia Hutchins (born in New Portland, Me., Nov. 29, 1823). Lived in Harmony and Pittsfield, Me. He died in Pittsfield, Me., Dec. 29, 1879.

Children, born in Harmony:

    4139   i   CHENEY H.,[8] b. April 30, 1850
    4140   ii   CYNTHIA P , b Aug 5, 1853
    4141   iii JAMES H , b March 29, 1855, d in Pittsfield, Me., Sept 1, 1875, unm
    4142   iv   COLUMBUS J , b Jan 6, 1860, d in infancy.
    4143   v   MARCIA C , b Aug 22, 1861, unm
    4144   vi   LURA BELLE, b July 13, 1864, unm
    4145   vii FRVENA S., b. May 17, 1870, in Pittsfield, Me , unm.

2198 JONATHAN E [7] EMERY (*Jonathan,*[6] *David,*[5] *Jonathan,*[4] *James,*[3] *Jonathan,*[2] *John*[1]), son of Jonathan and Hannah (Cheney) Emery; married in St Albans, Me., Jan. 1, 1842, Mary Elizabeth Leathers (born in Leeds, Me , May 18, 1823 , died in Parkham, Me., May 4, 1858). He died in Bangor, Me., March 15, 1853.

Children:

    4146   i   MARY A ,[8] b Oct. 12, 1843, in St Albans, Me
    4147   ii   CORREN EVLRETTE, b March 31, 1846, in St Albans, Me
    4148   iii EMMA A , b Oct 6, 1850, in Bangor, Me
    4149   iv   CARO ELIZABETH, b Oct 28, 1852, in Bangor, Me

2203 MARCIA I.[7] EMERY (*Jonathan,*[6] *David,*[5] *Jonathan,*[4] *James,*[3] *Jonathan,*[2] *John*[1]), daughter of Jonathan and Hannah (Cheney) Emery , married, first, David Leavitt in Bangor, Me., 1853 ; civil engineer in Red Wing, Minn. Second, Alonzo Hurd, merchant. He died March, 1859.

Children:

    4150   i   WALTER C ,[8] b. 1854, in Patten, Me ; lawyer, unm.
    4151   ii   OLIN P , b 1863, merchant, unm

2204 EMILY O.[7] EMERY (*Jonathan,*[6] *David,*[5] *Jonathan,*[4] *James,*[3] *Jonathan,*[2] *John*[1]), daughter of Jonathan and Hannah (Cheney) Emery, married in Harmony, Me., Nov. 19, 1847, John Warmlight (born in Birmingham, Eng., April 3, 1816 ; farmer in Harmony, Me.). She died in Minneapolis, Minn., April 23, 1880.

Children, born in Harmony, Me.:

    4152   i   MARY ANN,[8] b March 4, 1849.
    4153   ii   EPHRAIM, b Sept. 23, 1850, d Sept. 22, 1851.
    4154   iii ALBERT HOWARD, b July 17, 1852, m Dec 25, 1876, Elizabeth A Weeks (b in Jefferson, Me , April, 1852, d in Lewiston, Me , Dec 10, 1877), proprietor of the Los Angeles Tank Line Oil Co.

2206 CAROLINE ELIZABETH[7] EMERY (*Jonathan,*[6] *David,*[5] *Jonathan,*[4] *James,*[3] *Jonathan,*[2] *John*[1]), daughter of Jonathan and Hannah (Cheney) Emery; married, first, in Bangor, Me , Dec 14, 1854, James T Chamberlain (born in Bangor, Dec. 14, 1827 ; died in Red Wing, Minn., May 28, 1862 . county treasurer of Goodhue county, Minn.) , second, Rev. S. R. Thorpe, Dec. 25, 1862 (born in Batavia,

N. Y., Feb. 14, 1820 ; Methodist Episcopal cleigyman ; professor of
Greek and mathematics in Hamlin University, Red Wing, Minn. ;
died in Red Wing, July 19, 1866).
Children.

    4155 i   FRANCIS ASBURY,[8] b April 20, 1856, in Bangor, Me
    4156 ii   CARRIE LOUISE, b. April 22, 1859, in Red Wing, Minn
    4157 iii JAMES RUGGLES,   } b. April 20, 1864, in Red Wing, Minn.,
    4158 iv SAMUEL SKIDMORE, }   unm

2207 LEVI FRANKLIN[7] EMERY (*Jonathan,*[6] *David,*[5] *Jonathan,*[4]
James,[3] *Jonathan,*[2] *John*[1]), son of Jonathan and Hannah (Cheney)
Emery ; married Sarah Chase (daughter of his aunt Rachel Chase) in
Fairfield, Me., Feb. 23, 1865 ; real estate dealer in Minneapolis,
Minn.
Child.

    4159 i   LIEWELLYN VICTOR,[8] b May 13, 1868 ; unm ; banker

2208 ALONZO KING[7] EMERY (*Caleb,*[6] *David,*[5] *Jonathan,*[4] *James,*[3]
Jonathan,[2] *John*[1]), son of Caleb and Emily G. (Chase) Emery , mar-
ried ——— ———.
Child ·

    4160 i   ELEAZER,[8] merchant.

2217 CHARLES SUMNER[7] WYMAN (*Jerusha,*[6] *David,*[5] *Jonathan,*[4]
James,[3] *Jonathan,*[2] *John*[1]), son of Moses S and Jerusha (Emery)
Wyman ; married Melinda Cayford.
Child :

    4161 i   FRANCIS [8]

2218 INCREASE KENDALL[7] WYMAN (*Jerusha,*[6] *David,*[5] *Jonathan,*[4]
James,[3] *Jonathan,*[2] *John*[1]), son of Moses S. and Jerusha (Emery)
Wyman ; married Augusta Runnels.
Children :

    4162 i   EMMA.[8]
    4163 ii FRANK.

2222 BUTLER EMERY[7] WYMAN (*Jerusha,*[6] *David,*[5] *Jonathan,*[4]
James,[3] *Jonathan,*[2] *John*[1]), son of Moses S. and Jerusha (Emery)
Wyman , married, first, Jane Rose ; second, Melinda Sylons of Lock
Haven, Pa. ; and third, ——— ———. He died in Philadelphia, Pa.
Child, by first wife :

    4164 i   FRED [8]

2226 RAPHILE[7] EMERY (*Miles,*[6] *David,*[5] *Jonathan,*[4] *James,*[3] *Jonathan,*[2] *John*[1]), son of Miles and Mary D. (Nedeau) Emery ; married
June 1, 1858, Anchemes Plurde (born in St. Pascal, Can., Jan. 1,
1841).
Children ·

    4165 i   DAN,[8] b March 21, 1859, in Fort Kent, m , 1889
    4166 ii CHRISTY, b. June 24, 1861, in Middle St. Francis, N. B., unm.

4167 iii ARMINE, b July 10, 1863, in Fort Kent; unm.
4168 iv   MARY, b May 10, 1865, in Fort Kent, unm
4169 v   MILES, b April 20, 1867, in Fort Kent. d. June 19, 1867
4170 vi   EILEN, b May 30, 1869, in Fort Kent; d. Nov. 30, 1869, at Glazier Lake, N B
4171 vii SUSAN, b. March 20, 1871, in Glazier Lake, N B , d June 15, 1875
4172 viii EDWARD, b Aug. 10, 1873, in Glazier Lake, N. B ; d Jan 6, 1885.
4173 ix   DAVID, b June 20, 1875, in Glazier Lake, N B
4174 x   JERY, b. April 6, 1877, in Glazier Lake, N. B
4175 xi   JANF, b Oct 6, 1880, in Glazier Lake, N B
4176 xii RAPHILE, JR , b. Oct. 7, 1883, in Middle St. Francis, N. B.

2227 LOUISA[7] EMERY (*Miles,*[6] *David,*[5] *Jonathan,*[4] *James,*[3] *Jonathan,*[2] *John*[1]), daughter of Miles and Mary D. (Nedeau) Emery; married Nov. 13, 1854, William Hafford, carpenter, son of John Hafford (born July 26, 1830).

Children, born in Fort Kent:

4177 i   ELIZABETH,[8] b Nov. 22, 1855.
4178 ii   SUSAN, b Nov 18, 1857, d in St Francis, N. B , May 12, 1859.
4179 iii CHARLES, b March 28, 1860, carpenter ; unm
4180 iv   ISABELLA, b July 26, 1862; d July 29, 1862
4181 v   JOANNA, b June 5, 1863, m. Wm. Murphy, June 28, 1882, d. April 22, 1883, s p
4182 vi   PERCY ELLSWORTH, b May 7, 1866, d. Sept 11, 1870.
4183 vii ROSANNA, b Jan 21, 1869
4184 viii MARTHA, b May 11, 1872, unm
4185 ix   WILLIAM, JR , b Sept 20, 1874.
4186 x   MARK, b Sept 21, 1878.

2228 DANIEL[7] EMERY (*Miles,*[6] *David,*[5] *Jonathan,*[4] *James,*[3] *Jonathan,*[2] *John*[1]), son of Miles and Mary D. (Nedeau) Emery, married Dariety Underwood.

Three children, all dead : Nos. 4187 to 4189.

2230 SUSAN[7] EMERY (*Miles,*[6] *David,*[5] *Jonathan,*[4] *James,*[3] *Jonathan,*[2] *John*[1]), daughter of Miles and Mary D. (Nedeau) Emery ; married Charles Pelletier and died Dec. 5, 1886.

Children :

4190 i   CYNTHIA,[8] b in Fort Kent.
4191 ii   MARY ADELINE, b in Fort Kent; unm.
4192 iii SOPHIA, b in Fort Kent , d there.
4193 iv   HENRY, b in Fort Kent, April 7, 1868.
4194 v   JOHN, b. Jan. 1, 1870, in Glazier Lake, N B.
4195 vi   CHARLES, JR , b in Fort Kent, d there.
4196 vii CORA MAY, b in Fort Kent; d there
4197 viii ELIZABETH, b 1875 , m Stephen Giles of Patten, Me

2231 SOPHIA[7] EMERY (*Miles,*[6] *David,*[5] *Jonathan,*[4] *James,*[3] *Jonathan,*[2] *John*[1]), daughter of Miles and Mary D. (Nedean) Emery; married May 20, 1863, Charles Tarrio (born in Isle Verte, Can., April 8, 1830).

Children :

4198 i   FRANK,[8] b May 26, 1864, in St. Francis, N B., d. July 26, 1864.

4199 ii   Dennis, b. Nov. 16, 1865, in St. Francis, N. B.; m.
4200 iii Charles, b. Jan. 4, 1868, in St. Francis, N. B.; uum.
4201 iv   Hattie, b. May 21, 1870, in St. Francis, N. B.; m. Peter Mo-
            rin, Oct. 22, 1888.
4202 v   Hangess, b. July 30, 1872, in St. Francis, N. B.
4203 vi   Leona, b. March 11, 1874; in Caribou, Me.; d. Dec. 15, 1879.
4204 vii Betzaby, b. July 20, 1876. in Caribou, Me.
4205 viii Malanda, b. March 7, 1878, in Caribou, Me.; d. March 10,
            1878.
4206 ix   Adeline, b. Nov. 7, 1881, in Caribou, Me.
4207 x   Ulysses, b. Aug. 20, 1884, in Caribou, Me.

2232 Crysty Ann[7] Emery (*Miles,[6] David,[5] Jonathan,[4] James,[3] Jon-athan,[2] John[1]*), daughter of Miles and Mary D. (Nedeau) Emery; married, first, Angus Campbell, in Middle St. Francis. N. B., 1867; second, Heron Jackson, Sept., 1881.   She died May 10, 1888.

Children, by first husband:

4208 i   John,[8] b. Jan 15, 1870, in St. Francis, N. B.
4209 ii   Susan, b. in St. Francis, N. B.
4210 iii Annie, b. in Calais, Me.

Six children by second husband: Nos. 4211–4216.

2234 Elizabeth[7] Emery (*Miles,[6] David,[5] Jonathan,[4] James,[3] Jon-athan,[2] John[1]*), daughter of Miles and Mary D. (Nedeau) Emery; married Nathaniel Ross in St. Francis, N. B., 1867.   She died May, 1869.

Children :

4217 i   Jennie,[8] b. 1867; m. James Meonet, Portage Lake.
4218 ii   Mary Adeline, b. 1868; d. young.

2235 David C.[7] Emery (*Miles,[6] David,[5] Jonathan,[4] James,[3] Jona-than,[2] John[1]*), son of Miles and Mary D. (Nedeau) Emery; married in Katahdin Iron Works, Me., Dec. 19, 1885, Mary Baleau (born in East Waterville, Me., Aug. 5, 1868).   Lumberman.

Children, born in Katahdin Iron Works :

4219 i   Charles Henry,[8] b. Sept. 13, 1886.
4220 ii   John William, b. April 18, 1888.

2237 William[7] Emery (*Miles,[6] David,[5] Jonathan,[4] James,[3] Jona-than,[2] John[1]*), son of Miles and Mary D. (Nedeau) Emery; married in Sherman, Me., May 20, 1886, Jennie M. Chase (born in Patten, Me., April 8, 1867), daughter of William Chase, husband of Martha Emery.

Child:

4221 i   Charles M.,[8] b. Sept. 24, 1886, in Bangor, Me.

2239 Ruth H.[7] Emery (*Miles,[6] David,[5] Jonathan,[4] James,[3] Jona-than,[2] John[1]*), daughter of Miles and Mary D. (Nedeau) Emery; mar-ried in Bangor, Nov. 17, 1886, Samuel E. Harvey (born in N. Bucks-port, Me., Dec. 20, 1865; sea captain).

Child:

4222 i   Fannie Ethel,[8] b. Dec. 15, 1887, in N. Bucksport, Me.

2240 ORRA ANN[7] CHASE (*Rachel,*[6] *David,*[5] *Jonathan,*[4] *James,*[3] *Jonathan,*[2] *John*[1]), daughter of Isaac and Rachel (Emery) Chase; married Benjamin Hatch, in Fairfield. She died Dec., 1862.
Children, born in Fairfield

```
4223   i    ETTA C ,8 m —— Haywood
4224   ii   VERA, m —— Elliott
4225   iii  BARTLETT, unm
```

2241 ALBERT B.[7] CHASE (*Rachel,*[6] *David,*[5] *Jonathan,*[4] *James,*[3] *Jonathan,*[2] *John*[1]), son of Isaac and Rachel (Emery) Chase; married in Portland, Me., Frances Noble, farmer in Sidney, Neb.
Children:

```
4226   i    ELLA A ,8 m William Priest. Oct  11, 1876
4227   ii   GERTRUDE E , m  Charles McNellie, in Lewiston, Me , 1877,
              and d  May 4, 1878
4228   iii  JOSIE, d æt  6 years
4229   iv   BENJAMIN W , farmer in Sidney, unm
4230   v    JOSIE MAY, m  Eugene S  Gifford, of Fairfield, Me ; lives in
              Skowhegan
4231   vi   ALBERT LAMONT, unm
4232   vii  MINNIE EVELYN, unm
```

2242 EMILY E.[7] CHASE (*Rachel,*[6] *David,*[5] *Jonathan,*[4] *James,*[3] *Jonathan,*[2] *John*[1]), daughter of Isaac and Rachel (Emery) Chase; married George B. Cain. She is Grand Superintendent, Juvenile Temples, Grand Lodge of Maine Independent Order of Good Templars. They were married in Fairfield, Sept. 13, 1849.
Children:

```
4233   i    ALBERT M.,8 m. Anna Hill, of Waterville, Me.
4234   ii   LLEWELLYN B , b  Jan. 29, 1862 , unm
```

2244 SARAH S [7] CHASE (*Rachel,*[6] *David,*[5] *Jonathan,*[4] *James,*[3] *Jonathan,*[2] *John*[1]), daughter of Isaac and Rachel (Emery) Chase. See No. 2207.

2245 REV. JOHN WESLEY[7] CHASE (*Rachel,*[6] *David,*[5] *Jonathan,*[4] *James,*[3] *Jonathan,*[2] *John*[1]), son of Isaac and Rachel (Emery) Chase, married in Fairfield, Nov. 22, 1860, Margaret C. Nolan (born in Cape Cod, Mass , June 5, 1842 , died in Fairfield, Sept 28, 1889) Rev. John Wesley Chase was a civil engineer, but spent the last fourteen years of his life as clergyman of the Methodist Episcopal church. He died Dec. 27, 1876.
Children, born in Fairfield:

```
4235   i    ALICE W ,8 b  Sept 4, 1861, m  in Fairfield, Mch 22, 1876,
              James L  Keith
4236   ii   FRANK L , b  in Somer's Falls, Mass , Feb. 9, 1867 , unm  in
              Fairfield
4237   iii  CHARLES WESLEY, b  Dec 6, 1869 , d  Dec 19 1869
4238   iv   CHARLES WILBOR, b  Feb 20, 1871 , civil engineer, unm
4239   v    GEORGE EMERY, b  June 9, 1874.
```

2279 ZERI J [7] EMERY (*Samuel,*[6] *Briggs H.,*[5] *Jonathan,*[4] *James,*[3] *Jonathan,*[2] *John*[1]), son of Samuel and Abiah (Judkins) Emery ; mar-

ried March 7, 1850, Rosanna Whitcomb (born May 28, 1830 ; died Feb. 3, 1886). He died April 26, 1884. Farmer.
Children, born in Fairfield, Me. :

    4240 i   ELLEN A.,[9] b. Dec. 6, 1850.
    4241 ii   ABBIE, b. Jan. 2, 1853; d. Jan. 3, 1853.
    4242 iii ANNIE, b April 23, 1854; d. Sept. 9, 1868.
    4243 iv   GEORGE W., b. May 10, 1857; d. Feb. 1, 1874.
    4244 v   HUGH M., b. Oct. 3, 1860; d. Nov. 15, 1861.

2282 ANDREW J.[7] EMERY (*Samuel,[6] Briggs H.,[5] Jonathan,[4] James,[3] Jonathan,[2] John[1]*), son of Samuel and Abiah (Judkins) Emery ; married in Skowhegan, Nov. 3, 1860, Mary S. Gray (born in Starks, Me., Feb. 13, 1839). He went around the " Horn " in 1849-50 ; spent two years in the gold mines of California ; returned to Fairfield, 1860 ; removed to Iowa, 1867 ; afterwards settled in Minneapolis, Minn., where he was accidentally killed by falling from a roof, Dec. 3, 1879 ; street commissioner and assessor in Minneapolis.
Children, born in Fairfield, Me. : .

    4245   i   FLORENCE M.,[8] b. June 28, 1863 ; d., in Minn., July 8, 1871.
    4246   ii   ELWOOD A., b. Jan. 10, 1865; unm. ; student in Institute of
                Technology at Boston. Graduate of State University of
                Minn., 1887.
    4247   iii ERNEST G., b. Oct. 11, 1872, in Minn.; d. Aug. 18, 1873.

2283 EDWIN ALLEN[7] EMERY (*Samuel,[6] Briggs H.,[5] Jonathan,[4] James,[3] Jonathan,[2] John[1]*), son of Samuel and Abiah (Judkins) Emery ; married in Canaan, Me., May 21, 1854, Mary Ann Ricker (born in Canaan, May 16, 1833) ; enlisted in Co. " E," 7th Regt. Maine Volunteer Infantry, being one of the first soldiers enrolled in his town after the news of the attack on Fort Sumter was received ; served in the Peninsula battles ; honorably discharged for disability contracted in the line of duty, from which he died, in Fairfield, Dec. 25, 1862. His widow lives in Canaan.
Children :

    4248   i   FRANK EDWIN,[8] b. May 31, 1855, in Fairfield.
    4249   ii   LYDIA ABBY, b. April 16, 1857, in Fairfield.
    4250   iii HANNAH ABIAH, b. Jan. 15, 1859, in The Forks, Me.
    4251   iv   WALTER SAMUEL, b. June 26, 1861, in Fairfield.

2284 ABIGAIL J.[7] EMERY (*Samuel,[6] Briggs H.,[5] Jonathan,[4] James,[3] Jonathan,[2] John[1]*), daughter of Samuel and Abiah (Judkins) Emery ; married April 22, 1860, George W. Brooks (born at The Forks, Me., Jan. 10, 1838). Farmer in Bath.
Children :

    4252   i   NELLIE G.,[8] b. Aug. 1, 1861, in Fairfield.
    4253   ii   MABEL V., b. Jan. 1, 1867, in Fairfield ; unm.
    4254   iii FLORENCE ADA, b. July 29, 1873, in Bath, Me.

2286 ANN MARY[7] EMERY (*Benjamin F.,[6] Briggs H.,[5] Jonathan,[4] James,[3] Jonathan,[2] John[1]*), daughter of Benjamin F. and Lucinda (Noyes) Emery ; married Hiram L. Chase, Dec. 2, 1862. Merchant.
Children, born in Bath, Me. :

4255 i SARAH ADDIE,[9] b. Nov. 3, 1863; unm.
4256 ii WALTER EMERY, b. April 18, 1865; m. Elizabeth Bishop Morse, Sept. 28, 1887; councilman of Bath, Me.; merchant.

2288 CHARLES DAVIS[7] EMERY (*Benjamin F.,[6] Briggs H.,[5] Jonathan,[4] James,[3] Jonathan,[2] John[1]*), son of Benjamin F. and Lucinda (Noyes) Emery; married, Dec. 3, 1867, Fannie Maud Coombs (born Oct. 27, 1846). Wool merchant. Councilman of Bath.

Children, born in Bath:

4257 i MAUD ELENORA,[8] b. May 14, 1868; unm.
4258 ii FLORENCE GERTRUDE, b. Jan. 16, 1870; unm.
4259 iii EDWARD DEXTER, b. June 2, 1872.
4260 iv BRENDA FRANCES, b. Aug. 27, 1882.

2289 BRIGGS HALLOWELL[7] EMERY (*Benjamin F.,[6] Briggs H.,[5] Jonathan,[4] James,[3] Jonathan,[2] John[1]*), son of Benjamin F. and Lucinda (Noyes) Emery; married in Lynn, Mass., Nov. 26, 1866, Nancy E. Robbins (born in Brimfield, Mass., April 17, 1849). Railroad conductor. Soldier in 1st Regt. Maine Volunteer Cavalry, in the war of the Rebellion. He enlisted as private in Co. "K," 1st Regt. Maine Volunteer Cavalry, Dec. 25, 1863; mustered into service, Jan. 1, 1864; was in Dahlgren raid, Sheridan's raid, battles of Wilderness, Dinwiddie Court House, capture of Petersburg and others; discharged at Petersburg, Va., Aug. 1, 1865.

Children:

4261 i GILBERT E.,[8] b. April 10, 1868, in Lynn; drowned in Cumberland, Me., April 12, 1871.
4262 ii JOSEPHINE A., b. April 12, 1871, in Cumberland.
4263 iii GRACE E., b. Sept. 8, 1875, in Auburn, Me.
4264 iv ADA MAY, b. May 14, 1884, in South Braintree, Mass.

2290 HELEN LUCINDA[7] EMERY (*Benjamin F.,[6] Briggs H.,[5] Jonathan,[4] James,[3] Jonathan,[2] John[1]*), daughter of Benjamin F. and Lucinda (Noyes) Emery; married, June 19, 1873, Moses M. Judkins (born in Kingston, N. H., Feb. 28, 1829, farmer; in Brunswick, Me.).

Children, all but last born in Jamaica Plains, Mass.:

4265 i PRESTON WILLIAMS,[8] b. April 20, 1874.
4266 ii ALICE, b. Aug. 8, 1877.
4267 iii MARY, b. Oct. 14, 1879.
4268 iv BERTHA, b. June 30, 1881.
4269 v ETHEL, b. June 20, 1884.
4270 vi OTIS WELD, b. Oct. 13, 1888, in Brunswick, Me.

2293 MARY ANN[7] EMERY (*Joseph,[6] Briggs H.,[5] Jonathan,[4] James,[3] Jonathan,[2] John[1]*), daughter of Joseph and Susannah (Gordon) Emery; married in Fairfield, Me., Dec. 6, 1849, Thomas Agry, of Bath (born Sept. 5, 1821; died in South Boston, Mass., Jan. 11, 1879; carriage maker).

Children, all but first born in Bath:

4271 i WILLIAM H.,[8] b. Oct. 4, 1850, in Fairfield, Me.
4272 ii SUSAN E., b. March 23, 1852; d. Aug. 13, 1854.
4273 iii EMMA G., b. March 26, 1854; d. Aug. 31, 1855.

4274 iv HARRIET E., b. Oct. 14, 1856; d. Feb. 23, 1867.
4275 v   SARAH H , b. April 23, 1858.
4276 vi JOHN E., b. July 28, 1860; d. in Boston, May 12, 1886; unm.
4277 vii CARRIE V., b. Sept. 9, 1862.

2294 SUSAN J.[7] EMERY (*Joseph*,[6] *Briggs H.*,[5] *Jonathan*,[4] *James*,[3] *Jonathan*,[2] *John*[1]), daughter of Joseph and Susannah (Gordon) Emery ; married, Nov. 27, 1851, in Waterville, Me., Lorenzo M. Davis (born March 26, 1831 ; carriage maker).

Children :

4278 i   LUCY A.,[8] b. Nov. 2, 1853, in Waterville, Me. ; m. W. F. Bow-
          man, April 30, 1876.
4279 ii EMMA V., b. June 2, 1855, in Fairfield.
4280 iii EVA MADORA, b. June 2, 1855, in Fairfield; m. Horace A. To-
          zier, Dec., 1881.
4281 iv OSCAR M. H., b. Aug. 21, 1863, in Fairfield; m. Hattie F. Getch-
          el, June 26, 1886.
4282 v   HATTIE S., b. June 4, 1866, in Fairfield; unm.

2295 JAMES F. EMERY[7] (*Joseph*,[6] *Briggs H.*,[5] *Jonathan*,[4] *James*,[3] *Jonathan*,[2] *John*[1]), son of Joseph and Susannah (Gordon) Emery ; married, in Great Pond, Me., April 14, 1866, Hattie A. Lord (born in Greenfield, Me., July 9, 1844). Lumberman and postmaster in Great Pond.

Child :

4283 i   FLORENCE PERCY,[8] b. Aug. 1, 1869; unm.

2296 CHARLES B.[7] EMERY (*Joseph*,[6] *Briggs H.*,[5] *Jonathan*,[4] *James*,[3] *Jonathan*,[2] *John*[1]), son of Joseph and Susannah (Gordon) Emery ; married, first, ——— ——— ; second, ——— ——— ; third, ——— ———.

Six children, Nos. 4284–4289.

4284 1   CHARLES.[8]

2297 MELVILLE DARIUS[7] EMERY (*Joseph*,[6] *Briggs H.*,[5] *Jonathan*,[4] *James*,[3] *Jonathan*,[2] *John*[1]), son of Joseph and his second wife, Mrs. Deidamia P. (Tyler) Emery ; married in S. Norridgewock, Me., April 24, 1867, Mary Elizabeth Haynes (born Oct. 21, 1848) ; enlisted as private in Co. " B," 21st Regt. Maine Volunteer Infantry, Sept. 10, 1862 ; was wounded at Port Hudson, May 27, 1863 ; discharged Aug. 25, 1863. Farmer.

Children, born in Fairfield :

4290 1   EDWARD JAMES,[8] b. Jan. 30, 1868; unm.
4291 ii LENA ALICE, b. June 18, 1874.

2298 SARAH MELISSA[7] EMERY (*Joseph*,[6] *Briggs H.*,[5] *Jonathan*,[4] *James*,[3] *Jonathan*,[2] *John*[1]), daughter of Joseph and his second wife, Mrs. Deidamia P. (Tyler) Emery ; married, Nov. 10, 1869, Edgar Williams of Great Pond (born Feb. 20, 1842 ; farmer).

Children, born in Fairfield :

4292 1   PERCY FULLER,[8] b. June 28, 1874.
4293 ii FRANK PERRY, b. Nov. 4, 1875.

4294 iii HENRY L., b. Dec. 15, 1877.
4295 iv CHARLES MORRILL, b. March 2, 1879.
4296 v ELLA MAY, b. May 16, 1880.
4297 vi LULU LUCINDA, b. Dec. 15, 1882.
4298 vii EDNA ESTELLE, b. Feb. 21, 1887.
4299 viii SARAH A., b. Jan. 8, 1889.

2299 LOTTIE LOUISA[7] EMERY (*Joseph*,[6] *Briggs II.*,[5] *Jonathan*,[4] *James*,[3] *Jonathan*,[2] *John*[1]), daughter of Joseph and his second wife, Mrs. Deidamia P. (Tyler) Emery; married, Nov. 18, 1871, Albert Porter Noble (born in Fairfield, April 13, 1839; painter). He was a soldier in the Union army from Oct., 1861, to Aug., 1865; served three years in Co. " B," 13th Regt. Me. Vol. Inf.; reënlisted in the 30th Regt. Me. Vet. Vol.; wounded at Sabine Cross Roads.

Children, born in Fairfield:

4300 i WALTER EMERY,[8] b. April 19, 1873.
4301 ii GRACE MAY, b. Oct. 26, 1875.

2300 ALBERT PORTER[7] EMERY (*Alben*,[6] *Briggs II.*,[5] *Jonathan*,[4] *James*,[3] *Jonathan*,[2] *John*[1]), son of Alben and Betsey Ellis (Tobey) Emery; married, Oct. 8, 1868, Mary Albertson of New York City (born in Kinderhook, N. Y., Dec. 19, 1838), daughter of Alanson and Rhena Albertson. Wool merchant in Waterville, Me.

Child:

4302 i GRACE E.,[8] b. July 21, 1871, in New York City.

2301 ALBEN FRANKLIN[7] EMERY (*Alben*,[6] *Briggs II.*,[5] *Jonathan*,[4] *James*,[3] *Jonathan*,[2] *John*[1]), son of Alben and Betsey Ellis (Tobey) Emery; married, Aug. 13, 1862, Emily Frances Burrill (born Nov. 20, 1842), daughter of Benj. C. and Rebecca (Osborn) Burrill. Wool merchant, Elmhurst, Ill.

Children:

4303 i NELLIE PORTER,[8] b. July 8, 1864, in New Haven, Conn.; m. Frederick Bates, M.D.
4304 ii ARTHUR PERCY, b. March 8, 1869, in Augusta, Me.; bookkeeper; unm.
4305 iii BESSIE MAY, b. June 9, 1874, in Augusta, Me.; d. in Elmhurst, Ill., Jan., 1889.
4306 iv MARY ELIZABETH, b. Jan. 20, 1884, in Elmhurst, Ill.

2304 WILLIAM H.[7] EMERY (*Alben*,[6] *Briggs H.*,[5] *Jonathan*,[4] *James*,[3] *Jonathan*,[2] *John*[1]), son of Alben and Betsey Ellis (Tobey) Emery; married, Oct. 6, 1863, Mary Adelia Tobey (born Jan. 6, 1843), daughter of Samuel and Nancy Tobey of Waterville, Me.; removed from Augusta, Me., to Oak Park, 1869; hide broker in Chicago; lives in Elmhurst, Ill. Member of the school board eleven years and president of it five years.

Children:

4307 i JOHN TOBEY,[8] b. in Waterville, Me., July 22, 1864; unm; merchant in Chicago.
4308 ii HERBERT PORTER, b. in Augusta, May 27, 1868; d. Nov. 19, 1868.
4309 iii IDA ADELIA, b. Feb. 15, 1870, in Oak Park, Ill.

13

4310   iv   WILLIAM H., b. Feb. 4, 1876, in Oak Park, Ill.
4311   v   GRACE, b. Jan. 15, 1880, in Oak Park, Ill.

2312 VIRGIL PARIS[7] EMERY (*Obed,*[6] *Briggs H.,*[5] *Jonathan,*[4] *James,*[3] *Jonathan,*[2] *John*[1]), son of Obed and Louise E. (Attwood) Emery; married in Lewiston, Me., Nov. 16, 1876, Elizabeth M. Harding of Bath, Me. (born in Bath, March 22, 1853). Grocer and member of the city council of Bath, Me.
Child :

4312   i   CLARENCE H.,[8] b. April 7, 1887, in Bath.

2314 HENRY CHESTER[7] EMERY (*Obed,*[6] *Briggs H.,*[5] *Jonathan,*[4] *James,*[3] *Jonathan,*[2] *John*[1]), son of Obed and Louise E. (Attwood) Emery; married in China, Me., Nov. 30, 1887, Florence M. Randall (born in China). Farmer in Fairfield, Me.
Child :

4313   i   MAURICE CARLTON,[8] b. in Fairfield, Nov. 10, 1889.

2316 CHELSEA B.[7] EMERY (*William H.,*[6] *Briggs H*[5] *Jonathan,*[4] *James,*[3] *Jonathan,*[2] *John*[1]), son of Wm. H. and Mary (Gifford) Emery; married in Durant, Iowa, Oct. 8, 1873, Emma J. Hedges (born in Wolcott, N. Y., May 18, 1854). Farmer in Geneva, Neb.
Children :

4314   i   DAVID H.,[8] b. in Durant, Iowa, Aug. 12, 1874.
4315   ii   FLORENCE F., b. in Geneva, Neb., Aug. 17, 1881.
4316   iii   FAYE B., b. in Geneva, Neb., May 28, 1887.
4317   iv   HAROLD BLISS, b. in Geneva, Neb., July 11, 1889.

2317 VIRTURA ANN[7] EMERY (*William H.,*[6] *Briggs H.,*[5] *Jonathan,*[4] *James,*[3] *Jonathan,*[2] *John*[1]), son of William H. and Mary (Gifford) Emery; married in Durant, Iowa, Feb. 23, 1881, William Henry Bartlett (born in Winchester, N. H., Feb. 4, 1839 ; farmer in Victor, Iowa).
Children, born in Victor:

4318   i   HARRY LEAH,[8] b. Dec. 16, 1882.
4319   ii   WILLIAM EMERY, b. Aug. 25, 1887.

2347 RANSOM[7] ELDRIDGE (*Thankful C.,*[6] *Jones,*[5] *Jonathan,*[4] *James,*[3] *Jonathan,*[2] *John*[1]), son of Aaron and Thankful C. (Emery) Eldridge; married in Manchester, N. H., June 15, 1867, Maria W. McKenny. Dealer in live stock, Clinton, Me.
Children, born in Clinton :

4320   i   LAFOREST R.,[8] b. Aug. 24, 1868.
4321   ii   PERLEY E., b. April 3, 1872.

2349 JONES EMERY[7] ELDRIDGE (*Thankful C.,*[6] *Jones,*[5] *Jonathan,*[4] *James,*[3] *Jonathan,*[2] *John*[1]), son of Aaron and Thankful C. (Emery) Eldridge; married in Canaan, Me., June 25, 1879, Clara E. Marr (died Feb. 2, 1884). Dealer in live stock. He died Aug. 17, 1887.
Children, born in Clinton, Me. :

4322 i   INA ALBERTA,⁸ b. March 6, 1880.
4323 ii   CLARA EVELINE, b April 4, 1882
4324 iii BERTIE C , b Jan 12, 1884

2373 WILLIAM GARDINER⁷ EMERY (*William*,⁶ *Samuel*,⁵ *Jonathan*,⁴ *James*,³ *Jonathan*,² *John*¹), son of William and Julia A (Reynolds) Emery ; married in Nova Scotia, Sept. 15, 1862, Mary Ells. Millwright ; died in Tionesta, Pa., July, 1877.

Children

4325 i   HELEN ⁸
4326 ii   ARTHUR, lives in Boston

2375 DANIEL WEBSTER⁷ EMERY (*William*,⁶ *Samuel*,⁵ *Jonathan*,⁴ *James*,³ *Jonathan*,² *John*¹), son of William and Julia A. (Reynolds) Emery ; married in Fairfield, Me , Aug 31, 1864, Rose Bowman Lawrence(born Nov 12, 1844). He enlisted as private in Co "F," 3d Regt. Me Vol. Inf., May 28, 1861 ; mustered into U. S service as corporal, June 3, 1861 ; promoted sergeant, Sept. 11, 1861 ; commissioned first lieutenant, Aug 19, 1862, and mustered out with his regiment, June 28, 1864 , was in the following battles : First Bull Run, Siege of Yorktown, Williamsburg, Seven Pines, Fair Oaks, Peach Orchard, Glendale, Malvern Hill, Georgetown, White Oak Swamp, Monocacy, Manassas, or Second Bull Run, Chantilly, Fredericksburg and Chancellorsville ; wounded in the knee at Fair Oaks and in the side at Chancellorsville.

Children :

4327 i   WALTER HOWARD,⁸ b July 21, 1865, in Augusta, Me
4328 ii   ERNEST WEBSTER, b Dec 19, 1872, in Fairfield
4329 iii CRESWELL ALTON, b. Sept 1, 1882, in Pittston, Me.

2376 ESTHER DAVIS⁷ EMERY (*William*,⁶ *Samuel*,⁵ *Jonathan*,⁴ *James*,³ *Jonathan*,² *John*¹), daughter of William and Julia A (Reynolds) Emery : married in Fairfield, Me , Dec. 7, 1865, Josiah Gifford (born Sept 14, 1836).

Children, born in Curwinsville, Pa. :

4330 i   MATILDA HELEN,⁸ b Oct 15, 1870.
4331 ii   NELLIE BURT, b. May 22, 1875
4332 iii BLANCHE B , b Sept 14, 1878
4333 iv   HARRY EDWARD, b Oct 20, 1880
4334 v   EVA GERTRUDE, b April 20, 1882
4335 vi   MAUD S., b. May 20, 1887

2378 GEORGE EVANS⁷ EMERY (*William*,⁶ *Samuel*,⁵ *Jonathan*,⁴ *James*,³ *Jonathan*,² *John*¹), son of William and Julia A (Reynolds) Emery , married in Wiscasset, Me , March 6, 1882, Alma Cutten (born July 24, 1860). He enlisted in Company "B," 30th Regt Me. Vol. Inf., Nov. 1, 1863 , mustered into service, Dec 18, 1863 , engaged at Sabine Cross Roads, Pleasant Hill, Cane River, Mansura Plain, Deep Bottom and Cedar Creek ; mustered out Aug. 19, 1865 ; millman in Randolph.

Children :

4336 i   FRANK CUTTEN,⁸ b April 2, 1883, in Wiscasset.

4337 11 IDA CORAVINA, b Feb 25, 1885, in Pittston, Me
4338 111 THEODORE EVANS, b Oct 4, 1888, in Randolph, Me.

2379 MARY EMMA[7] EMERY (*William*,[6] *Samuel*,[5] *Jonathan*,[4] *James*,[3] *Jonathan*,[2] *John*[1]), daughter of William and Julia A (Reynolds) Emery, married in Fairfield, Me, March 23, 1865, Orlando F Eldridge (born in Hartland, Me., Aug 3, 1843, machinist in Newport, Me.).
Children

4339 1   CHARLES H.,[8] b. May 16, 1866, in Canaan, Me, unm, machinist
4340 11 MANLY F, b Dec 25, 1868, d June 27 1876, in Fairfield, Me
4341 111 JENNIE M, b March 30, 1870

2381 HOLLIS CAMPBELL[7] EMERY (*William*,[6] *Samuel*,[5] *Jonathan*,[4] *James*,[3] *Jonathan*,[2] *John*[1]), son of William and Julia A. (Reynolds) Emery, married, first, Sarah Taylor, in Augusta, where she died; second, in Wild Rose, Wis, May 6, 1880, Maggie A Patterson (born in New York City, Feb. 2, 1852)   Farmer in Grand Rapids, Wis.
Children

4342 1   BENJAMIN F [8]
4343 11 A DAUGHTER
4344 111 LLOYD WALTON, b Jan 4, 1882, in Saratoga, Wis
4345 1v FRED EARL, b July 30, 1885, in Saratoga, Wis

2382 CHARLES FREMONT[7] EMERY (*William*,[6] *Samuel*,[5] *Jonathan*,[4] *James*,[3] *Jonathan*,[2] *John*[1]), son of William and Julia A. (Reynolds) Emery; married in Pittsfield, Me, Nov. 28, 1878, Hattie B. Smith (born June 11, 1860), millman in Wiscasset, Me
Children:

4346 1   LULU M,[8] b Aug. 4, 1880, in Princeton, Minn
4347 11 LEE E, b. July 13, 1885, in Wiscasset, Me.

2386 PHŒBE ANN[7] EMERY (*Butler A*,[6] *Samuel*,[5] *Jonathan*,[4] *James*,[3] *Jonathan*,[2] *John*[1]), daughter of Butler A and Mary (Gibson) Emery, married, Sept. 6, 1867, Edwin Bradbury (born May 21, 1839, died March 25, 1874; lumberman).
Children, born in Fairfield, Me. ·

4348 1   HARRY EVENDER,[8] b Feb 26, 1869
4349 11 ADDIE MAY, b Jan 3, 1871; d Oct 6, 1877.

2388 ZENORA A.[7] EMERY (*John J.*,[6] *Samuel*,[5] *Jonathan*,[4] *James*,[3] *Jonathan*,[2] *John*[1]). daughter of John J and Miranda S. (Deering) Emery, married, in Londonderry, N. H, Feb. 11, 1854, A. L M. Atwood (born in New Hampshire, April 17, 1835, carpenter)   He was a soldier in the 18th Wis. Vol. Inf., and was in the battle of Pittsburg Landing: died on a steamer on Mississippi River, May 14, 1862. His widow married, second, in Linwood, Wis., Oct. 27, 1862, Ezra Lanphere (born in Murray, N. Y., July 1, 1839, farmer in Barron county, Wis.).
Children, by first wife:

4350 1   CHARLES F,[8] b Sept 13, 1856, in Waterville, Me.
4351 11 WALTER L, b Oct 28, 1858, in Waushara Co., Wis.

By second wife :

4352 iii MARY ALICE, b Jan 1, 1866, in Sergel, Wis.
4353 iv MIRANDA JANE, b Sept 30, 1869, in Lynn, Wis ; unm
4354 v EVELYN, b July 7, 1872, in Bloomer, Wis., d Feb 26, 1885
4355 vi ELLEN, b June 1, 1876, in Bloomer, Wis

2389 ERASTUS F [7] EMERY (*John J.*,[6] *Samuel*,[5] *Jonathan*,[4] *James*,[3] *Jonathan*,[2] *John*[1]), son of John J. and Miranda S (Deering) Emery, married, Oct 24, 1861, Livona Smith of Oldtown, Me He served in the 1st Regt. Me Heavy Art , from Aug , 1862, to March 25, 1865, when he was taken prisoner in front of Petersburg, Va.; confined in Libby prison four days and paroled at the end of the war.

Children, born in Oldtown :

4356 i FRED L ,[8] b Dec. 24, 1864, unm
4357 ii MABEL, b May 20, 1867, m Clinton F. Smith, Dec 21, 1886

2390 MARTHA E [7] EMERY (*John J.*,[6] *Samuel*,[5] *Jonathan*,[4] *James*,[3] *Jonathan*,[2] *John*[1]), daughter of John J. and Miranda S. (Deering) Emery, married George W. Dyer of Gorham, Me , March 12, 1863 , they live in Boston

Children, born in Gorham, Me :

4358 i EDITH H ,[8] b Feb 2, 1864, unm
4359 ii HOWARD N , b March 8, 1866, unm

2391 SAMUEL D [7] EMERY (*John J.*,[6] *Samuel*,[5] *Jonathan*,[4] *James*,[3] *Jonathan*,[2] *John*[1]), son of John J. and Miranda S. (Deering) Emery, married Harriet A. Edson of Amherst, Mass., July 7, 1866 He enlisted as a private in Company " B," 14th Regt Mass. Vol. Inf., May, 1861 , mustered into the service July 5, 1861, discharged as sergeant Dec 4, 1863 , reenlisted the same day as private, Company " B," 1st Regt. Mass. Heavy Art ; discharged as sergeant July 31, 1865. At the time of his second enlistment he received a veteran sergeant's warrant, dated back to 1862, for good conduct as a soldier and promptness in performing street military duty.

Children, born in Turner's Falls, Mass

4360 i LINWOOD B ,[8] b Sept 16, 1867, unm
4361 ii HATTIE A , b July 2, 1873
4362 iii SAMUEL D , JR , b Nov 4, 1876
4363 iv ARTHUR G , b Oct 14, 1881
4364 v ERVIN B , b. Aug 31, 1884.

2393 JOHN WARD[7] EMERY (*John J.*,[6] *Samuel*,[5] *Jonathan*,[4] *James*,[3] *Jonathan*,[2] *John*[1]), son of John J and Miranda S (Deering) Emery, married Ella Bowman of Turner's Falls, Mass , Nov 18, 1869. He was a Union soldier , served in the 26th Regt Mass. Vol. Inf , from Sept , 1861, to the close of the war

Children, born in Turner's Falls, Mass. .

4365 i LILIAN M ,[8] b. Nov. 13, 1870 , unm.
4366 ii WALTER G , b Oct 25, 1876
4367 iii ERNEST S , b July 19, 1878
4368 iv ETHEL G , b April 5, 1882.

2395 FANEUIL HALL[7] EMERY (*John J.*,[6] *Samuel,*[5] *Jonathan,*[4] *James,*[3] *Jonathan,*[2] *John*[1]), son of John J. and Miranda S (Deering) Emery; married Ida M. Breed of Lowell, Mass., Oct. 18, 1871. He enlisted in Company "A," 20th Regt Me Vol. Inf, in July, 1862, and served to the close of the war with distinction, receiving a corporal's warrant for good behavior ; died Oct 28, 1883.

Child .

4369   i   ALBERT,[8] b Jan 26, 1874, in Vassalboro, Me.

2397 KATE I.[7] EMERY (*John J.*,[6] *Samuel,*[5] *Jonathan,*[4] *James,*[3] *Jonathan,*[2] *John*[1]), daughter of John J and Miranda S. (Deering) Emery ; married Benjamin F. Stevens of Waterville, Me., June 3, 1868.

Children

4370   i   GEORGE W ,[8] b Feb 17, 1869, in St Augustine, Fla., unm
4371   ii   FLORENCE J , b Dec 7, 1871, in St. Augustine, Fla ; unm.
4372   iii   ISABEL G , b. April 7, 1874, in Coltewah, Tenn
4373   iv   GUY H , b June 19, 1877, in Cleveland, Tenn
4374   v   ANGIE M , b. Aug 2, 1884, in Lewiston, Me.
4375   vi   ROY FOSTER, b July 24, 1886, in Lewiston, Me.

2398 LESLIE A [7] EMERY (*John J.,*[6] *Samuel,*[5] *Jonathan,*[4] *James,*[3] *Jonathan,*[2] *John*[1]), son of John J. and Miranda S. (Deering) Emery, married Evelyn M Dunbar of Turner's Falls, Mass , Nov. 18, 1880. Mason and contractor of note and possessed remarkable talent. His first notable work was in connection with the Hoosac Tunnel ; later, was engaged in rebuilding the city of St John, N B , after the great fire , contractor in the Boston and New Haven water works, also in the Washington aqueduct , died in Dorchester, Mass., April 21, 1889.

Children .

4376   i   GRACE G ,[8] b. Aug 26, 1881, in Turner's Falls, Mass.
4377   ii   WILLARD D , b June 23, 1883, in Boston, Mass.; d Feb 9, 1886.

2402 HON. ELISHA EMERY[7] PARKHURST (*Lucy J.,*[6] *Samuel,*[5] *Jonathan,*[4] *James,*[3] *Jonathan,*[2] *John*[1]). son of Elisha and Lucy J. (Emery) Parkhurst , married in Unity, Me , Nov 6, 1853, Sarah Chase Small (born March 26, 1835).   Town clerk and selectman of Maysville Centre, Me. ; chaplain of Maine State Grange four years ; member of board of agriculture three years; trustee of Maine State Agricultural College three years ; representative in Maine legislature, 1877–78, and senator, 1883 and 1885.

Children .

4378   i   IDELLA MARSETT,[8] b Oct 12, 1855 in Unity, Me , m Albert N' Cross, Jan 9, 1889, in Lynn, Mass
4379   ii   DANIEL VINCENT, b Oct 14, 1868, in Maysville. Me , unm.
4380   iii PERCY ELISHA, b Aug 12, 1870, in Maysville, Me. , unm

2403 SAMUEL BUTLER[7] PARKHURST (*Lucy J ,*[6] *Samuel,*[5] *Jonathan,*[4] *James,*[3] *Jonathan,*[2] *John*[1]), son of Elisha and Lucy J (Emery) Parkhurst; married, in Freedom, Me., July 8, 1856, Abbie L. Moody (born in Unity, April 2, 1839).   He died in Albion, Me., Sept. 14,

1875   His widow married, second, in Winslow, Me , Jan 9, 1881, Harry C Newhall.

Children, born in Unity :

4381 i   EMERY L ,[8] b June 11, 1857; m —— ——, July 23, 1888.
4382 ii   LUEPIA E , b Sept 5, 1862, m C H. Richardson, Feb 9, 1880, in Winslow, Me
4383 iii EMMA F., b March 7, 1872.

2404 PAULINA D.[7] EMERY (*Samuel*,[6] *Samuel*,[5] *Jonathan*,[4] *James*,[3] *Jonathan*,[2] *John*[1]), daughter of Samuel and Frances A (Oliver) Emery, married, April 29, 1857, Ezekiel Oliver (born in Phippsburg, May 8, 1822 ; dam builder).

Children, born in Phippsburg, Me. :

4384 i   ABBIE J.,[8] b Sept 5, 1858, m Alpheus E Purington, Jan 1, 1880
4385 ii   FRANKLIN A , b. April 7, 1860, d Nov. 4, 1861
4386 iii   ANGELIA F , b March 18, 1863, m Franklin G. Purington, sea captain, Sept. 25, 1884, in Bath, Me.
4387 iv   INFANT SON, b Aug. 18, 1864, d Sept. 23, 1864.
4388 v   DESPER W , b Feb 15, 1866, unm , engineer.
4389 vi   LILIAN R , b Feb 28, 1867, d Jan 7, 1872
4390 vii   VINCENT M , b Sept 11, 1868, d Sept 12, 1869.
4391 viii NETTIE M , b May 9, 1871, d Sept 15, 1871
4392 ix   HERMAN V., b Oct. 13, 1873, d Sept. 13, 1874.
4393 x   PAULINA B , b Jan. 13, 1875.
4394 xi   INFANT SON,   } b Jan 10, 1880, { d Jan 11, 1880
4395 xii   INFANT DAUGHTER, }
4396 xiii GRACE N , b April 23, 1881, d Aug 9, 1881.

2405 AUGUSTUS F.[7] EMERY (*Samuel*,[6] *Samuel*,[5] *Jonathan*,[4] *James*,[3] *Jonathan*,[2] *John*[1]); son of Samuel and Frances A (Oliver) Emery; married, Oct. 1, 1863, Rose A. Jewell (born in Bath, Me., Jan. 30, 1842) Mustered into Co. "A," 3rd Regt. Me. Vol. Inf , June 5, 1861 ; reenlisted at Brandy Station, Va , Feb 8, 1864 ; transferred to 17th Regt. Me. Vol Inf., June 4, 1864, and to the 1st Regt. Me. Heavy Art., June 5, 1865 ; wounded Dec. 13, 1862, at Fredericksburg ; July 2, 1863, at Gettysburg and June 16, 1864, at Petersburg ; mustered out of service Sept. 20, 1865   Mechanic in South Boston.

Children :

4397 i   HATTIE M.,[8] b June 12, 1866, in Phippsburg, Me ; unm
4398 ii HARRY D. BIBBER, b. March 13, 1876, in Bath, Me

2406 RICHARD O [7] EMERY (*Samuel*,[6] *Samuel*,[5] *Jonathan*,[4] *James*,[3] *Jonathan*,[2] *John*[1]), son of Samuel and Frances A. (Oliver) Emery ; married in Richmond, Me., June 3, 1871, Sarah Johnson Hall (born in Dresden, Me , May 22, 1847). Soldier in Co "D," 21st Regt. Me Vol. Inf. , wounded at the siege of Port Hudson.

Children :

4399 i   MARY H ,[8] b March 12, 1872, in Springfield Mass.
4400 ii HERMAN H , b Feb 28, 1873 in Springfield, Mass , d Sept. 27, 1873
4401 iii FLORALE EDNA, b. June 2, 1874, in Springfield, Mass
4402 iv FLORENCE L , b March 11, 1878, in Dresden, Me.
4403 v   FRANCES H , b Dec 10, 1882, in Richmond, Me.
4404 vi GRACE M , b June 14, 1885, in Phippsburg, Me

2407 ALWILDA E.[7] EMERY (*Samuel,*[6] *Samuel,*[5] *Jonathan,*[4] *James,*[3] *Jonathan,*[2] *John*[1]), daughter of Samuel and Frances A (Oliver) Emery ; married in Phippsburg, Me , June 18, 1864, Thomas R. Marr (born Feb. 20, 1838 ; served at life-saving station, Fort Popham, 1883–4).

Children, born in Phippsburg ·

    4405 i   JAMES R ,[8] b May 23, 1865, d Sept 11, 1866.
    4406 ii   IDA BLANCHE, b. Dec 3, 1867, m. Benj F. White, Oct 16,
                  1887, in Hallowell Me
    4407 iii EFFIE PAULINA, b. July 25, 1884, d Dec 25, 1884.

2408 THOMAS L [7] EMERY (*Samuel,*[6] *Samuel,*[5] *Jonathan,*[4] *James,*[3] *Jonathan,*[2] *John*[1]), son of Samuel and Frances A (Oliver) Emery ; married, Aug. 9, 1874, Sarah Ellen Rook (born April 16,1851). Master mariner.

Children, born in Phippsburg :

    4408 i   GERTRUDE P ,[8] b Jan 25, 1876
    4409 ii   LILIAN A , b Dec 27, 1878

2409 ESTHER L [7] EMERY (*Samuel,*[6] *Samuel,*[5] *Jonathan,*[4] *James,*[3] *Jonathan,*[2] *John*[1]), daughter of Samuel and Frances A. (Oliver) Emery ; married in Bath, Me , Feb. 19, 1877, John Hilton Jordan (born in Dresden, Me , Sept. 24, 1857 , U S. mail carrier).

Children, born in Bath ·

    4410 i   NELLIE SAVAGE,[8] b July 2, 1877 , d. May 8, 1882.
    4411 ii   JAMES SAVAGE, b April 29 1883

2410 PRESTON M [7] EMERY (*George B.,*[6] *Samuel,*[5] *Jonathan,*[4] *James,*[3] *Jonathan,*[2] *John*[1]), son of George B and Abigail (Hondlett) Emery ; married, Aug. 21, 1864, Ann S. Kelley (born in Unity, Me., Sept 8, 1836). Enlisted in Co. "B" 13th Regt. Me Vol Inf., Nov. 9, 1861 , promoted second lieutenant, Aug 20, 1863 , first lieutenant Co. "H," 30th Regt Me. Vol. Inf ,1865 ; in action at Mustang Island, Tex , Fort Esperanza, Sabine Cross Roads, La , Pleasant Hill, La., Cane River and Mansura Plain ; joined Gen Sheridan in Oct., 1864, and remained with his command until Lee's surrender. Lumberman in Fairfield

Children born in Fairfield, Me. ·

    4412 i   MABEL A ,[8] b June 27, 1865 teacher; unm.
    4413 ii   MAUD L b Feb 16, 1868, teacher; unm
    4414 iii EUGENE H , b May 1, 1870, unm.
    4415 iv   CARRIE E , b July 30, 1873
    4416 v   JENNIE ADELIA, b Oct 10, 1876.

2411 ANNE E [7] EMERY (*George B.,*[6] *Samuel,*[5] *Jonathan,*[4] *James,*[3] *Jonathan,*[2] *John*[1]), daughter of George B. and Abigail (Hondlett) Emery ; married Dec 26, 1861, Weston A. Curtis (born in Jefferson, Me., May 14, 1835). Mechanic in Westborough, Mass.

Children .

    4417 i   WALTER,[8] b Feb 18, 1863; d March 4, 1863, in New Castle, Me.
    4418 ii   WILLIAM E , b Feb 19, 1866, in New Castle Me., unm , clerk.
    4419 iii EDITH REBECCA, b Aug 16, 1873, in Westborough, Mass.

2413 GEORGE F.[7] EMERY (*George B.*,[6] *Samuel*,[5] *Jonathan*,[4] *James*,[3] *Jonathan*,[2] *John*[1]), son of George B. and Abigail (Hondlett) Emery; married, first, in Westborough, Mass., April 13, 1865, Sarah E. Belknap (born Sept. 2, 1841). He married, second, ———— and lives in Aroyo, Colorado.

Children, born in Westborough:

 4420 i   ARTHUR LOWELL,[8] b. April 5, 1869; unm.; student at Cornell University.
 4421 ii GEORGE HENRY, b. Sept. 28, 1871.
 4422 iii CLARENCE BELKNAP, b. May 22, 1874.
 4423 iv EDWARD WINSLOW, b. Sept. 23, 1876.

2414 MARIA A.[7] EMERY (*George B.*,[6] *Samuel*,[5] *Jonathan*,[4] *James*,[3] *Jonathan*,[2] *John*[1]), daughter of George B. and Abigail (Hondlett) Emery; married, Sept. 11, 1864, George E. Mayo (born in Waterville, Me., Jan. 23, 1843; mechanic in Worcester, Mass.).

Children, born in Fairfield:

 4424 i   LENA F.,[8] b. Aug. 11, 1866; d. Aug. 15, 1866.
 4425 ii HARRY C., b. June 18, 1868; unm.
 4426 iii SILAS ILSLEY, b. July 8, 1872.

2416 ELIJAH B.[7] EMERY (*George B.*,[6] *Samuel*,[5] *Jonathan*,[4] *James*,[3] *Jonathan*,[2] *John*[1]), son of George B. and Abigail (Hondlett) Emery; married in Shrewsbury, Mass., Dec. 25, 1871, Sarah Eliz. Stone (born July 9, 1850). Mechanic in Westborough, Mass.

Children, born in Westborough:

 4427 i   ETHELINE MARION,[8] b. Dec. 17, 1873.
 4428 ii NATHAN STONE, b. Jan. 24, 1876.
 4429 iii HELEN GERTRUDE, b. Dec. 23, 1882.

2417 JANE A.[7] EMERY (*George B.*,[6] *Samuel*,[5] *Jonathan*,[4] *James*,[3] *Jonathan*,[2] *John*[1]), daughter of George B. and Abigail (Hondlett) Emery; married, Sept. 15, 1869, Daniel Webster Allen (born Aug. 5, 1845). Member of the Executive Council of Maine, 1889–90. Merchant.

Children, born in Fairfield, Me.:

 4430 i   EVERETT L.,[8] b. Aug. 20, 1873; d. Dec. 6, 1875.
 4431 ii BLANCHE, b. Feb. 13, 1879; d. Jan. 9, 1881.

2418 WILLIS C.[7] EMERY (*George B.*,[6] *Samuel*,[5] *Jonathan*,[4] *James*,[3] *Jonathan*,[2] *John*[1]), son of George B. and Abigail (Hondlett) Emery; married in Unity, Me., June 22, 1875, Nellie F. Nye (born Jan. 9, 1856). Superintendent of a canning establishment in Anson, Me.

Child:

 4432 i   ROY RROWN,[8] b. Dec. 19, 1881, in N. Anson, Me.; d. in Fairfield, May 30, 1883.

2426 JOSEPHINE A.[7] BURNHAM (*Thankful C.*,[6] *Samuel*,[5] *Jonathan*,[4] *James*,[3] *Jonathan*,[2] *John*[1]), daughter of Richard and Thankful C. (Emery) Burnham; married, first, in Ogdensburg, N. Y., Aug. 24, 1860, Lyman Lord; who died June 9, 1869; second, in Boston, May 22, 1880, Frederick S. Crosby.

Children :

    4433   i   WALTER A.,[8] b Aug 1, 1862, m. Ada E. Crosby, March 10,
            1886, in Boston

2429 SARAH FRANCES[7] BURNHAM (*Thankful C.*,[6] *Samuel*,[5] *Jonathan*,[4] *James*,[3] *Jonathan*,[2] *John*[1]), daughter of Richard and Thankful
C. (Emery) Burnham, married in Lowell, Mass., Nov. 26, 1866, Edw.
S. Tukey (born in Fairfield; died in Jersey City, N. J., April 11,
1889). She died in Boston, May 27, 1884.
    Children, born in Fairfield, Me. :

    4434   i   LOUISE B.,[8] b May 27, 1869 ; d in Boston April 26, 1882
    4435   ii BERTHA, d in Fairfield, Me
    4436   iii ANNIE, d in Fairfield, Me
    4437   iv BERTRAND D , b. Aug 7, 1875.

2431 HORACE MANN[7] BURNHAM (*Thankful C.*,[6] *Samuel*,[5] *Jonathan*,[4] *James*,[3] *Jonathan*,[2] *John*[1]), son of Richard and Thankful C
(Emery) Burnham; married in Orono, Me , May 13, 1877, Rowena
Williams (born in Skowhegan, May 25, 1848, died in Oldtown, Feb.
4, 1884) ; second, in Orono, Me Oct 20, 1888, Ada M White (born
in Greenfield, Me , May 13, 1864). Druggist in Oldtown, Me.
    Children, born in Oldtown, Me. :

    4438   i   AGNES R ,[8] b May 26, 1878
    4439   ii EDITH MAUD,⎫ b March 15, 1880, ⎰d April 30, 1880.
    4440   iii EDNA MAY,⎭   ⎱d Sept 4, 1882
    4441   iv BERTHA W., b. June 15, 1881.
    4442   v   ISA, b. Oct 20, 1883

2432 ELLEN[7] DEERING (*Paulina*,[6] *Samuel*,[5] *Jonathan*,[4] *James*,[3]
Jonathan,[2] *John*[1]), daughter of John and Paulina (Emery) Deering ;
married, Nov. 27, 1860, Prince Edward Gifford (born Sept. 5, 1829 ;
died in Washington, April 12, 1887). Lumberman.
    Children, born in Fairfield ·

    4443   i   ELLA BELLE,[8] b Oct. 15, 1861, m. George Burbeck, Jan. 1,
            1881, in Oakland, Cal
    4444   ii EDWARD JOHN, b June 24, 1863; d., unm , Feb. 27, 1887.
            Killed in R R accident
    4445   iii INFANT DAUGHTER, b May 8, 1876, d May 9, 1876, in Lock Ha-
            ven, Pa.

2433 CHARLES SAWYER[7] DEERING (*Paulina*,[6] *Samuel*,[5] *Jonathan*,[4]
James,[3] *Jonathan*,[2] *John*[1]), son of John and Paulina (Emery) Deering ;
married, first, Sept. 22, 1867, Abbie L. Flood (born in Clinton, Me.,
April 9, 1850 ; died March 13, 1874) , second, in Plankington, South
Dakota, Aug. 17, 1884, Addie F. Steiner, who was born in Oceola,
Ohio, Aug. 28, 1860. Mustered into U. S. service, Co " B," 13th
Regt. Me Vol. Inf., Nov. 28, 1861 ; on duty at Ship Island, Miss., Fort
St. Philip, La , and on several raids into the country in 1862 ; on pro-
vost duty in New Orleans in 1863 ; at the surrender of Fort Esper-
anza ; commissioned second lieutenant 10th Regt. U. S Heavy Artil-
lery, Feb. 29. 1864 ; at the front in the Red River Campaign, Sabine
Cross Roads, Pleasant Hill and other battles , mustered out of U. S.

service as Brevet 1st Lieut., at Baton Rouge, La., Feb. 22, 1867.
Furniture dealer in Plankington, Dak. President of Farmers' National
Insurance Co.
Children ·

    4446   i   CHARLES O ,⁸ b. March 4. 1874; d May 4, 1874, in Fairfield, Me.
    4447   ii MARIE PAULINA, b. Oct. 6, 1889, in Plankington, S. Dak

2435 ARIANNA⁷ DEERING (*Paulina,⁶ Samuel,⁵ Jonathan,⁴ James,³
Jonathan,² John¹*), daughter of John and Paulina (Emery) Deering;
married, May 7, 1871, Abner L. Hoxie (born May 8, 1836 ; farmer).
Children ·

    4448   i   CARO LEAH,⁸ b Sept 25, 1873, in Fairfield.
    4449   ii   CHARLES DEERING, b in Skowhegan, April 28, 1877, d in
                Skowhegan, Aug 15, 1877
    4450   iii RAYMOND AUBREY, b Oct 20, 1878, in Skowhegan

2478 OLIVER G.⁷ EMERY (*Lewis,⁶ Samuel,⁵ Anthony,⁴ James,³ Jon-
athan,² John¹*), son of Lewis and Maria (Gilson) Emery ; married
Ellen Stebbens, Aug., 1856.   Farmer in North Dakota.
Children :

    4451   i   ARTHUR CLIFFORD,⁸ b Feb , 1859
    4452   ii   FANNIE ELLEN, b Aug 10, 1861, m. Wm A. Morgan, Dec. 14,
                1887
    4453   iii HERBERT LEWIS, b Aug 31, 1863, farmer.
    4454   iv   ERNEST OLIVER, b March 28, 1874, d. March, 1878.

2479 DAVID⁷ EMERY (*Lewis,⁶ Samuel,⁵ Anthony,⁴ James,³ Jonathan,² John¹*), son of Lewis and Maria (Gilson) Emery , married Angeline S Edwards, Sept. 7, 1858.   Representative in Penn Legislature two years   Producer and refiner of petroleum.   Resides at
Titusville, Pa.
Children :

    4455   i   MORSMAN A ,⁸ b Aug., 1863; d. Dec , 1863
    4456   ii   EVA LENA, b Aug 21, 1866
    4457   iii VERNA MAY, b March 14, 1870
    4458   iv   FRED DAVID, b Jan , 1877, d. March, 1879

2480 HON LEWIS⁷ EMERY, JR (*Lewis,⁶ Samuel,⁵ Anthony,⁴
James,³ Jonathan,² John¹*), son of Lewis and Maria (Gilson) Emery ,
married, Dec 29, 1863, Elizabeth A Caldwell.   Representative in
the House two years and senator eight years, Pa. Legislature.   Producer and refiner of petroleum , merchant ; farmer.
Children, born in Bradford, Pa. :

    4459   i   CLARA LOUISE,⁸ b July 20 1865, d. Aug. 12, 1866
    4460   ii   DELEVAN, b Sept 26, 1867, unm.
    4461   iii GRACE ELIZABETH, b Jan. 27, 1874.
    4462   iv   EARL CALDWELL, b Dec. 12, 1875
    4463   v   LEWIS, JR , b Aug. 27, 1878.

2482 MARGARET ANN⁷ EMRIE (*Jehu A.,⁶ John,⁵ Ambrose,⁴ James,³
Jonathan,² John¹*), daughter of Judge Jehu A. and Harriet (Stout)
Emrie , married in Aurora, Ind., June 30, 1844, James A. Kelsey

(born in Addison Co , Vt , Sept. 28, 1817 , died May 7, 1868). He was
a Union scout in Virginia during the three months service without
rank or pay ; served three years in Co " D," 3rd Regt. Ind. Vol. Cav. ;
mustered in as senior sergeant of his company, Aug. 22, 1861 ; promoted second lieutenant, Dec 31, 1862 , first lieutenant, March 7,
1863 ; mustered out, Aug. 22, 1864. Commission merchant. She
died in Paradise, Ill , March 9, 1866.

Children, born in Aurora.

4464 i   HELEN,[8] b April 30, 1845
4465 ii   EDWARD, b March 3, 1847, d Feb 25, 1849
4466 iii DOUGLAS, b Jan 19, 1848, d March 3, 1852.
4467 iv   ANNA, b Jan 27, 1851
4468 v   CHARLES A , b June 13, 1853.
4469 vi   HARRIET, b Aug 5, 1856.
4470 vii MARY, b Sept 19, 1858 m. Sampson J. Powell, 1879.

2484 CAPT. JOHN STOUT[7] EMRIE (*Jehu A ,[6] John,[5] Ambrose,[4]
James,[3] Jonathan,[2] John[1]*), son of Jehu A and Harriet (Stout) Emrie , married in Golconda, Ill., Sept. 22, 1859, Mary E Scranton
(born in Rising Sun, Ind., Sept. 23, 1835). Pilot and captain on
the Ohio and Mississippi rivers, between Cincinnati and New Orleans,
for thirty years ; served in the U S. Navy during the war of the Rebellion , piloted the gun-boat "Moose" in the Cumberland river division to Fort Pillow, also piloted the gun-boat "Hastings" to Fort
Pillow, having on board the senate committee sent to investigate the
massacre , also served on the gun-boat "Fairy" and naval transport
"Volunteer." He died Dec. 28, 1889.

Children :

4471 i   ALMON,[8] b July 1, 1860, in Cochran, Ind , m 1889, skilled ma-
           chinist
4472 ii   JULIET, b. Dec. 15, 1861, in Cochran, Ind ; m Aug 21, 1888,
           Levi F Jackson, who d in Boone Co., Ky , Sept 22, 1889
4473 iii HERBERT, b May 3, 1871, Aurora, Ind

2485 MARY LOUISE[7] EMRIE (*Jehu A ,[6] John,[5] Ambrose,[4] James,[3]
Jonathan,[2] John[1]*), daughter of Jehu A. and Harriet (Stout) Emrie ;
married, May 7, 1854, Edward F. Sibley (born in Canandaigua, N. Y.,
March 3, 1829), who is postmaster in Cando, Towner Co., North Dakota , editor and publisher ; county judge of Towner Co.

Children :

4474 i   EVA MAY,[8] b March 4, 1863, in Cochran, Ind , d in Lawrence-
           burg, Ind , April 3, 1877
4475 ii   EDWIN, b Oct 17, 1866, d in Aurora, Ind , Dec. 18, 1866
4476 iii ARCHIBALD, b Nov 18, 1868, in Aurora. Ind., unm
4477 iv   MAUD, b May 29, 1872, in Lawrenceburg, Ind

2487 GEORGE SMITH[7] EMRIE (*Jehu A.,[6] John,[5] Ambrose,[4] James,[3]
Jonathan,[2] John[1]*), son of Jehu A and Harriet (Stout) Emrie ; married, Aug. 8, 1861, Clara Louise Arnold (born June 10. 1841, in Ed-
enburg, Germany). Printer.

Children .

4478 i   HARRY,[8] b. June 22, 1862, in Cochran, Ind. ; unm ; druggist and
           jeweller

4479 ii FRANK, b April 27, 1864; d Nov. 19, 1864, in Aurora, Ind.
4480 iii CLARA LOUISE, b Feb 16, 1868, in Aurora; unm

2488 CURTIS KELSEY[7] EMRIE (*Jehu A*,[6] *John*,[5] *Ambrose*,[4] *James*,[3] *Jonathan*,[2] *John*[1]), son of Jehu A and Harriet (Stout) Emrie; married, Nov. 26, 1865, Mary L Kemple (born in Wheeling, W. Va, June 6, 1847) Enlisted April 16, 1861, for three months, in the 16th Regt Ind. Inf. ; when the call for three months' service was filled, his regiment tendered their services for one year and were accepted; mustered out as senior sergeant of Co " I," of his regiment, at Washington, D C , May 14, 1862 , reenlisted in Company " B," 4th Regt. Ind. Cav , May 1, 1863 ; mustered out as sergeant major of his regiment, at Edgefield, Tenn , July 28, 1865 , commissioned first lieutenant of Aurora Guards, 12th Regt Ind Legion, Sept. 11, 1862 Printer.

Children, born in Aurora :

4481 i CAREY CURTIS,[8] b Oct 26, 1866, unm
4482 ii MARY LUCINDA, b Dec 23, 1873.

2495 BENJ F [7] CHANEY (*Sarah H.*,[6] *John*,[5] *Ambrose*,[4] *James*,[3] *Jonathan*,[2] *John*[1]), son of Benjamin and Sarah H (Emrie) Chaney ; married, first, Maggie A Pike, daughter of Col. S. Pike(who during his lifetime owned and controlled twenty-six newspapers) She died, 1867. He married, second, in Hillsboro, O., Sarah H. McFadden (born in Rushville, O). Merchant.

Child

4483 i MARGUERITE FLORENCE,[8] b in Hillsboro, m Wm H Yeazell, June 27, 1888, in Hillsboro, live in Columbus, O.

2502 ORISSA BELLE[7] CHANEY(*Sarah H* ,[6] *John*,[5] *Ambrose*,[4] *James*,[3] *Jonathan*,[2] *John*[1]), daughter of Benjamin and Sarah H. (Emrie) Chaney , married Henry C. Mader, of Greenfield, O (born in Heidelberg, Germany, 1843) , she died Dec., 1871.

Child

4484 i ORISSA MAUD.[8] b. Dec , 1871.

2503 JOHN MARSHALL[7] EMRIE (*Jonas R.*,[6] *John*,[5] *Ambrose*,[4] *James*,[3] *Jonathan*,[2] *John*[1]), son of Hon. Jonas Rand and Rebecca E. (Marshall) Emrie ; married in Mound City, Ill , 1866, Lydia Tucker, who died in Mound City. He died in Belton, Texas, Jan. 9, 1886.

Children, born in Mound City:

4485 i WALTER EDWARDS,[8] d in infancy.
4486 ii ROSA LUVENIA, d. in infancy.

2505 CLARA ESTHER[7] EMRIE (*Jonas R.*,[6] *John*,[5] *Ambrose*,[4] *James*,[3] *Jonathan*,[2] *John*[1]), daughter of Hon Jonas R and Rebecca E. (Marshall) Emrie , married in Cochran, Ind.. March 8, 1862, Dr T. L. A. Greve of Cincinnati, O. (born in St. Michaelis, Holstein, Germany, April 2, 1830). She died in Cincinnati, O , Jan. 4, 1873.

Child :

4437   i   CHARLES THEODORE,[8] b   in Cincinnati, Jan 3 1863, graduate
of Hillsboro High School, 1878, A B , Harvard College, 1884;
LL B , Cincinnati Law School, 1885, attorney-at-law, Cincinnati.

2506 MARY REBECCA[7] EMRIE (*Jonas R ,*[6] *John,*[5] *Ambrose,*[4]
James,[3] *Jonathan,*[2] *John*[1]), daughter of Hon Jonas R and Rebecca
E. (Marshall) Emrie , married in Mound City, Ill., April 5, 1863,
John A. Waugh (born in Mercer Co , Pa., March 30, 1835). He was
bookkeeper at the Navy Yard at Mound City during the Rebellion ;
bookkeeper, Cairo, Ill.
Children, born in Mound City :

4488   i   WALTER REECE,[8] b June 1, 1864, d Dec. 13, 1876.
4489   ii   BERTHA EDWARDS, b Dec 4, 1870
4490   iii WILLIAM J , b Sept 26, 1878, d Feb 29, 1880.

2509 ELLA E [7] EMRIE (*Jonas R.,*[6] *John,*[5] *Ambrose,*[4] *James,*[3]
Jonathan,[2] *John*[1]), daughter of Hon. Jonas R and his second wife,
Emma (Longwell) Emrie , married in Mound City, Ill., 1870, James
H Speer , died in San Antonio, Tex.. July 28, 1889.
Child ·

4491   i   ARTHUR,[8] b. 1871, in San Antonio, Tex

2510 FRANCES A [7] EMRIE (*Jonas R.,*[6] *John,*[5] *Ambrose,*[4] *James,*[3]
Jonathan,[2] *John*[1]), daughter of Hon. Jonas R and his second wife,
Emma (Longwell) Emrie , married in Mound City, Ill., Nov. 30, 1865.
Thomas Wilson Carrico (born in Hardin Co , Ky , June 26, 1840).
Union soldier.   Architect ; contractor and builder in San Antonio,
Tex.
Children ·

4492   i   CLARA BOIES,[8] b Nov. 5, 1868, in Mound City, Ill.
4493   ii   CORA BELLE, b Dec 3, 1871, in Mound City, Ill
4494   iii EMMA LAVINIA b. Oct 3, 1873, in Cairo, Ill
4495   iv   THOMAS WILSON, JR., b Nov 13, 1876, in Austin, Tex
4496   v   LELIA JAY, b April 16, 1879, in Austin, Tex
4497   vi   FRANK ALBERT, b Sept. 16, 1887, in San Antonio, Tex.

2512 JUSTIN R [7] EMRIE (*Jonas R.,*[6] *John,*[5] *Ambrose,*[4] *James,*[3]
Jonathan,[2] *John*[1]), son of Hon Jonas R. and his second wife, Emma
(Longwell) Emrie , married Mary Emma Alcot in Vincennes, Ind.,
June 1, 1881. Railroad conductor in the Republic of Mexico , killed
by his train at Soldad, Mex., Nov. 11, 1887.   She was born April 14,
1861.
Child :

4498   i   WALTER JUSTIN,[8] b in Vincennes, June 1, 1883, d July 31,
1883.

2514 LELIA LINCOLN[7] EMRIE (*Jonas R ,*[6] *John,*[5] *Ambrose,*[4]
James,[3] *Jonathan,*[2] *John*[1]), daughter of Hon. Jonas R and his second wife, Emma (Longwell) Emrie ; graduate of Pittsburg High
school , married in San Antonio, Tex., Oct. 18, 1887, George Willis

Johnson of Springfield, Ill. (born in Springfield, Nov. 16, 1851; civil engineer).

Child ·

4499   i   FRANCES VIOLET,[8] b. Sept. 20, 1888, in San Antonio, Tex

2515 JAY REECE EMRIE[7] (*Jonas R.,*[6] *John,*[5] *Ambrose,*[4] *James,*[3] *Jonathan*[2] *John*[1]), son of Hon. Jonas R. and his second wife, Emma (Longwell) Emrie, married in San Antonio, Tex, June 15, 1887, Sarah Marguerite Kinahan. Builder.

Child :

4500   1   JUSTINE REECE,[8] b. April 2, 1888, in San Antonio, Tex

2516 FRANCIS M[7] EMRY (*Clementine,*[6] *Samuel,*[5] *Ambrose,*[4] *James,*[3] *Jonathan,*[2] *John*[1]), son of Daniel and Clementine (Emery) Emry, married in Mt. Vernon, O., Jan 1, 1862, Eveline Shaver (born near Danville, O, April 15, 1839) Farmer.

Children, all born near New Market, O. :

4501   i   CORA MAY,[8] b. Oct 26, 1862, unm.
4502   ii   WILLIAM EDWIN, b Nov 6, 1864
4503   iii   FRANK MELVIN, b Nov 2, 1868; unm.
4504   iv   CHARLES CLIFFORD, b. Nov 12, 1871; unm.

2517 NANCY[7] EMRY (*Clementine,*[6] *Samuel,*[5] *Ambrose,*[4] *James,*[3] *Jonathan,*[2] *John*[1]), daughter of Daniel and Clementine (Emery) Emry, married, Oct 9, 1834, Alexander S. Nesbit, Highland Co., O. (born in Clermont Co., Oct. 2, 1862). She died in Adams Co , O., April 30, 1874

Children, all born near Beasley's Fork, Adams Co., O. :

4505   i   SAMUEL EDWIN,[5] b Feb 27, 1864, unm   Teacher.
4506   ii   DANIEL E , b July 1, 1866, unm   Farmer.
4507   iii   MARY E , b May 28, 1868, unm
4508   iv   ALEXANDRIA CLEMENTINE, b Aug. 5, 1870, unm
4509   v   INEZ ELLEN, b. Sept 29, 1872

2518 CLEMENTINE[7] EMERY (*Ambrose,*[6] *Samuel,*[5] *Ambrose,*[4] *James,*[3] *Jonathan,*[2] *John*[1]), daughter of Ambrose and Sarah (Mullinix) Emery; married, July 5, 1855, Isaac M. Davidson (born in Hollowtown, O., July 17, 1836).

Children :

4510   1   MATILDA F ,[8] b March 15, 1856, in Danville, O.
4511   ii   SARAH M., b Oct. 15, 1858, in Princeton, O , m Albert S. Rhoads, Aug 24, 1884
4512   iii   WILLIAM E , b Nov 25, 1861, in Princeton, O , m Julia Agnes Newton, March 17, 1889   Farmer
4513   iv   NANCY C , b. Jan 28, 1864, in Princeton, O.

2519 MARY ANN[7] EMERY (*Ambrose,*[6] *Samuel,*[5] *Ambrose,*[4] *James,*[3] *Jonathan,*[2] *John*[1]), daughter of Ambrose and Sarah (Mullinix) Emery; married, Sept. 4, 1856, George Leinegar (born in Merteshem, France, Dec. 31, 1834; soldier in Co. " B," 60th Ohio Inf. and in Co. "B," 2d Ohio H. Art.; mechanic in Wilmington, Ohio).

Child

4514   i   MARGARET,[8] b. April 11, 1859, in Danville; d March 28, 1862.

2520 SARAH CATHARINE[7] EMERY (*Ambrose*,[6] *Samuel*,[5] *Ambrose*,[4] *James*,[3] *Jonathan*,[2] *John*[1]), daughter of Ambrose and Sarah (Mullinix) Emery, married, Sept. 8, 1861. John Hibler (born in Lynchburg, O., Jun. 8, 1836, farmer).

Children, born in Danville

4515   i   IDA E [8] b   June 24 1862
4516   ii   CLEMENTINA, b Jan 8, 1864
4517   iii ROSA A , b July 29, 1869
4518   iv   SARAH L , b. Dec 30, 1876
4519   v   EMERY O , b Sept. 7, 1880

2522 NANCY E.[7] EMERY (*Ambrose*,[6] *Samuel*,[5] *Ambrose*,[4] *James*,[3] *Jonathan*,[2] *John*[1]), daughter of Ambrose and Sarah (Mullinix) Emery; married, Aug. 31, 1862, Ellis Davidson, farmer (born in Hollowtown, O , April 29, 1842), brother of Isaac Davidson who married Clementine Emery.

Children ·

4520   i   EDWARD M ,[8] b Oct 1, 1863, in Hollowtown.
4521   ii   EVA L , b March 15, 1865, in Danville.
4522   iii   MARY M , b May 7, 1867, in Hollowtown
4523   iv   SARAH L , b Feb 16, 1869, in Keosauqua, Ia , unm
4524   v   ELVIRA E , b March 30, 1871, in Hollowtown
4525   vi   JOHN A , b April 11, 1873, in Hollowtown
4526   vii   GEORGE E , b March 24, 1875, in Danville.
4527   viii LOTTIE G , b July 27, 1877, in Danville
4528   ix   LEONARD D , b May 19 1880, in Danville.
4529   x   AMANDA R , b July 2, 1882, in Danville
4530   xi   ESTHER E , b April 14, 1885, in Danville
4531   xii   RAYMOND O , b May 12, 1887, in Danville.

2524 WILLIAM GADDES[7] EMERY (*Ambrose*,[6] *Samuel*,[5] *Ambrose*,[4] *James*,[3] *Jonathan*,[2] *John*[1]), son of Ambrose and Sarah (Mullinix) Emery, married, in Hollowtown, Oct. 14, 1869, Mary M. Pringle (born Oct 16, 1851).   Farmer.

Children, born near Danville

4532   i   AMBROSE M ,[8] b Oct 14, 1871.
4533   ii   PHILIP A , b Nov 29, 1872
4534   iii SARAH C , b July 19, 1875
4535   iv   ELMA JANE, b March 1, 1879
4536   v   ALICE J , b Oct 4, 1884

2525 MARGARET JANE[7] EMERY (*Ambrose*,[6] *Samuel*,[5] *Ambrose*,[4] *James*,[3] *Jonathan*,[2] *John*[1]), daughter of Ambrose and Sarah (Mullinix) Emery, married, Dec. 30, 1868, William L Marconnette (born in Hollowtown, O , Oct. 11, 1844).   She died Sept. 11, 1879.

Children, born in Hollowtown, except the first :

4537   i   OLLIE BELLE,[8] b Sept 29, 1869, in Danville
4538   ii   AMBROSE, b March 7, 1871, d April 2, 1871
4539   iii SAMUEL, b Feb 29, 1872
4540   iv   ICY DORA, b May 15 1874
4541   v   JOHN, b. March 4, 1876.

2526 JOHN WLSLEY[7] EMERY (*Ambrose,*[6] *Samuel,*[5] *Ambrose,*[4] *James,*[3] *Jonathan,*[2] *John*[1]), son of Ambrose and Sarah (Mullinix) Emery; married in Wilmington, Clinton Co., O , Aug 1, 1878, Margaret Leinegar (born in Merteshem, France, Jan. 1, 1858). Farmer. Children, born near Danville, O. .

```
4542  i    LEWIS E ,⁸ b  April 26, 1879
4543  ii   WILLIAM G , b  March 18, 1881.
4544  iii  SARAH C., b  Dec 28, 1882
4545  iv   MARY E , b  March 5, 1887
4546  v    ROSA A , b. March 18, 1889.
```

2528 DAVID HENRY[7] MORRIS (*Mary,*[6] *Samuel,*[5] *Ambrose,*[4] *James,*[3] *Jonathan,*[2] *John*[1]), son of George and Mary (Emery) Morris; married Sarah Ellen Scammyhorn near Belfast, O., died Sept. 2, 1879, in Paulding Co , O.
Children:

```
4547  i   LEONA,⁸ b. 1869, in Anglaze Township, Paulding Co., O ; unm
4548  ii  ANNA MAY, b  1873, in same place.
```

2531 JACKSON D.[7] KINNER (*Isabel,*[6] *Samuel,*[5] *Ambrose,*[4] *James,*[3] *Jonathan,*[2] *John*[1]), son of John and Isabel (Emery) Kinner ; married, Dec 25, 1877, in Arthur, O., Ida Karnes (born in Defiance, O , Oct. 19, 1862). Merchant in Arthur.
Children, born in Paulding Co , O. :

```
4549  i    GUY E ,⁸ b  Nov  23, 1878
4550  ii   IDA MABEL, b  Jan 26, 1883.
4551  iii  DORA C., b. Jan. 21, 1886.
4552  iv   NELLIE MAY, b  July 16, 1887.
4553  v    JOHN F , b. Oct. 8, 1889
```

2533 DR WILLIAM H.[7] EMERY (*John,*[6] *Samuel,*[5] *Ambrose,*[4] *James,*[3] *Jonathan,*[2] *John*[1]), son of John and Barbara (Emry) Emery, married in New Petersburg, O , Sept. 24, 1878, Cora R Oates, daughter of Lemuel Oates (born April 1, 1863). Teacher Graduate of Ohio Med. Col., Cincinnati, March, 1880. Practised in Mt. Sterling, O. ; died there Jan. 30, 1890.
Children, born in Mt. Sterling :

```
4554  i   INFZ,⁸ b  May 9, 1881, d  June 4, 1882.
4555  ii  RENA O , b. July 21, 1885
```

2535 JESSE R.[7] EMERY (*John*[6] *Samuel,*[5] *Ambrose,*[4] *James,*[3] *Jonathan,*[2] *John*),[1] son of John and Barbara (Emry) Emery, married near Danville, O., Feb. 6, 1879, Icy D. Wood, daughter of John Wood (born in Danville , died in Rapid City, S. Dak., Aug. 25, 1885).
Children, born in Hamilton, O. .

```
4556  i    LLOYD H ,⁸ b  April 14, 1880
4557  ii   HERBERT M , b  Aug 16, 1881.
4558  iii  EARL C , b. Nov  2, 1882
4559  iv   MYRTLE, b  May 3, 1883
```

2543 SARAH SAMANTHA[7] REX (*Elizabeth,*[6] *Samuel,*[5] *Ambrose,*[4]

14

James,[3] *Jonathan,*[2] *John*[1]), daughter of George and Elizabeth (Emery) Rex; married in Castle Rock, Col., Jan. 27, 1879, David Henry Wood (born in Dubuque, Ia., Nov. 7, 1845). She served in the United States Hospital from Jan., 1861, to May, 1863.

Children, born in Kiowa, Col. :

4560 i   DELA ALICE[8], b Nov 9, 1879
4561 ii GRACE ANN, b. Sept 26, 1885.

2544 REBECCA OLIVE[7] REX (*Elizabeth,*[6] *Samuel,*[5] *Ambrose,*[4] *James,*[3] *Jonathan,*[2] *John*[1]), daughter of George and Elizabeth (Emery) Rex, married in Kiowa, Col, Oct. 25, 1884, Julius A Hooker (born in Big Flats, Chemung county, N. Y., May 18, 1846, farmer). She died in Denver, Col., Jan. 19, 1889.

Child

4562 i   OLIVER WOLCOTT,[8] b Dec 24, 1888, in Denver.

2547 NANCY ISABELLA[7] REX (*Elizabeth,*[6] *Samuel,*[5] *Ambrose,*[4] *James,*[3] *Jonathan,*[2] *John*[1]), daughter of George and Elizabeth (Emery) Rex, married in Centreville, Ia , July 2, 1878, Mark Samuel Ward (born in Maquoketa, Ia , March 13, 1854 ; jeweller). Children .

4563 i   RALPH SARGENT,[8] b May 20, 1879, in Unionville, Mo
4564 ii NELLIE HORTENSE, b Aug 29. 1885, in Denver, Col

2548 JAMES I.[7] REX (*Elizabeth,*[6] *Samuel,*[5] *Ambrose,*[4] *James,*[3] *Jonathan,*[2] *John*[1]), son of George and Elizabeth (Emery) Rex , married in Centreville, Ia . Sept. 4, 1885, Caroline Matilda Kreugar (born in Germany. Nov. 26, 1866). Bookkeeper.

Child :

4565 i   IDA CLARA,[8] b June 17, 1886, in Denver, d. July 9, 1886.

2555 SARAH ELLEN[7] EMERY (*Richard A.,*[6] *Samuel,*[5] *Ambrose,*[4] *James,*[3] *Jonathan,*[2] *John*[1]), daughter of Richard A. and Mary Ann (Larrick) Emery, married in Hillsboro, O., Oct. 21, 1877, Moses Vance.

Children, born in Hillsboro :

4566 i   HARLEY,[8] b. Aug 5, 1878
4567 ii   NELLY, b Aug 8, 1880
4568 iii FRANK, b Sept 17, 1882
4569 iv   ANNA, b Nov 4, 1884
4570 v   LOUETTA, b. Feb 14, 1886

2556 JAMES FRANK[7] EMERY (*Richard A.,*[6] *Samuel,*[5] *Ambrose,*[4] *James,*[3] *Jonathan,*[2] *John*[1]), son of Richard A. and Mary Ann (Larrick) Emery : married in Hollowtown, O , Feb. 2, 1878, Ann Fender. Children, born in New Market, O. ·

4571 i   EFFIE B.,[8] b. Dec. 2, 1878
4572 ii PERRY O., b. May 19, 1881.

2587 MARY[7] LUCAS (*Rebecca,*[6] *Jonas,*[5] *Ambrose,*[4] *James,*[3] *Jona-*

than,[2] *John*[1]), daughter of Thomas and Rebecca (Emery) Lucas ; married in Greene county, Pa , Nov. 11, 1852, William Ashburn (born in the same county, July 15, 1830 ; burned to death in Parkersburgh, W Va., April 2, 1880 ; millwright and carpenter).

Children :

4573   i   MARTHA JANE,[9] b Sept. 17, 1853, in Greene Co , Pa , dressmaker, unm
4574   ii   EPHRAIM COLMAN, b Nov 12, 1855, in Greene Co , Pa ; drowned July 31, 1870, in the Ohio River at Parkersburgh, in attempting to rescue a comrade
4575   iii   HANNAH REBECCA, b Jan 18, 1863, in Washington Co , Pa ; m Sept 22, 1886, Edward J Savage in Marietta, O (b in Augusta Co , Va , Aug 23, 1861) She was a school-teacher before marriage
4576   iv   JAMES, b Sept 17, 1872, in Parkersburgh
4577   v   LOUISIANA, b March 15, 1874, in Parkersburgh, d March 20, 1874.

2589 MARTHA C.[7] LUCAS (*Rebecca*,[6] *Jonas*,[5] *Ambrose*,[4] *James*,[3] *Jonathan*,[2] *John*[1]), daughter of Thomas and Rebecca (Emery) Lucas, married in Greene county, Pa., Aug 9, 1861, Adam Seese (born in Somerset county, Pa., April 30, 1834 , farmer).

Children, born in Woodford county, Ill. ·

4578   i   THOMAS,[8] b Aug 10, 1865, unm ; farmer.
4579   ii   JAMES L , b Nov 9, 1867, unm , farmer.
4580   iii   MARY R , b Oct 16, 1870, unm
4581   iv   AYRES B , b March 1, 1873.
4582   v   BERTHA E , b July 17, 1875
4583   vi   CHARLES E , b Sept 17, 1878
4584   vii   FLORENCE L , b July 22, 1881.

2592 CASSANDRA M [7] LUCAS (*Rebecca*,[6] *Jonas*,[5] *Ambrose*,[4] *James*,[3] *Jonathan*,[2] *John*[1]), daughter of Thomas and Rebecca (Emery) Lucas; married in Indianola, Ia , Dec. 20, 1870, George E Howe (born in Wilson's Station, Clinton county, O., Nov. 28, 1847 ; farmer).

Children :

4585   i   AUBIN J.,[8] b. May 1, 1872, in Indianola, Ia
4586   ii   BURT L , b Oct 2, 1873, in Indianola, Ia
4587   iii   MINNIE M , b Sept 18, 1881, in London, Sumner Co , Kan.

2599 BENJAMIN FRANKLIN[7] LUCAS (*Catharine*,[6] *Jonas*,[5] *Ambrose*,[4] *James*,[3] *Jonathan*,[2] *John*[1]), son of Swan and Mrs. Catharine (Litzenburgh) Lucas ; married in Warren county, Ia., Nov. 26, 1874, Lilian Elvira Haynes (born in Ohio, Sept. 5, 1855). Farmer.

Children .

4588   i   HUEY ELVIRA,[8] b Sept 22, 1876, in Warren Co , Ia
4589   ii   LAURA HAYNES, b Oct 19, 1878, in Warren Co , Ia
4590   iii   CLARA ALMA, b. Jan 28, 1882, in Warren Co , Ia
4591   iv   MAY LULU, b. Nov 15, 1883, in Madison Co., Ia.
4592   v   ACHSA EVELYN, b. April 12, 1887, in Warren Co , Ia.

2600 WILLIAM PIERCE[7] LUCAS (*Catharine*,[6] *Jonas*,[5] *Ambrose*,[4] *James*,[3] *Jonathan*,[2] *John*[1]), son of Swan and Mrs. Catharine (Litzen-

burgh) Lucas; married in Warren county, Ia., Jan. 18, 1874, Effie Maria Bundy (born April 25, 1858). Farmer.
  Children :

    4593   i   John Swan,⁸ b Oct 18, 1875
    4594   ii   Edward Alzo, b April 4, 1879
    4595   iii Harry Patterson, b. Oct. 5, 1888, d Dec 24, 1889.

  2608 Jonas William⁷ Emery (*James,⁶ Jonas,⁵ Ambrose,⁴ James,³ Jonathan,² John¹*), son of James and Margaret Ann (Major) Emery ; married Ella A. Welsh in East Bethlehem, Pa , April 16, 1884. Farmer and commercial traveller.
  Children :

    4596   i   Joseph Welsh,⁸ b Aug 26, 1885 in E. Bethlehem, Pa.
    4597   ii   Helen Caroline, b. Oct 20, 1887.

  2618 Sarah Elizabeth⁷ Emery (*Jonas,⁶ Jonas,⁵ Ambrose,⁴ James,³ Jonathan,² John¹*), daughter of Jonas and Mary C. (Seaton) Emery , married Dec. 28, 1870, L L Garard (born Sept. 28, 1850).
  Children :

    4598   i   Sudie,⁸ b Jan 10, 1872
    4599   ii   Frank Leslie, b May 28, 1874.
    4600   iii Lilian, b Nov 24, 1876; d Dec 23, 1876
    4601   iv   Holly Holmes, b Nov 22, 1877.
    4602   v   Walter, b. May 2, 1880, d Aug 30, 1881.

  2619 Margaret E.⁷ Emery (*Jonas,⁶ Jonas,⁵ Ambrose,⁴ James,³ Jonathan,² John¹*), daughter of Jonas and Mary C (Seaton) Emery ; married, Sept. 19, 1885, William F. Robinson (born Sept. 2, 1858).
  Child .

    4603   i   Vera,⁸ b. March 3, 1887, in McPherson, Kan

  2620 Mary⁷ Emery (*John,⁶ Ambrose,⁵ Ambrose,⁴ James,³ Jonathan,² John¹*), daughter of John and Alcinda (Hayes) Emery , married in Greene county, Ind., Oct. 23, 1855, Walter Hayes (born in Ohio. Nov 3, 1834 ; farmer and postmaster)
  Children, born in Scotland, Greene county, Ind. :

    4604   i   Harriet Rebecca,⁸ b Sept 13, 1856.
    4605   ii   John P., b Dec 24, 1858
    4606   iii William Jonas, b. Nov 21, 1861
    4607   iv   Sarah D , b April 28, 1864, m John Reed, March 17, 1887.
    4608   v   Elizabeth, B , b. Dec. 5, 1866, d. Sept. 26, 1873.
    4609   vi   Charles D., b Nov 26, 1869, d Sept 28, 1872.
    4610   vii Alice A , b March 22, 1873, d May 18, 1874
    4611   viii Ellen P , b. July 17, 1875

  2621 Sarah A. D.⁷ Emery (*John,⁶ Ambrose,⁵ Ambrose,⁴ James,³ Jonathan,² John¹*), daughter of John and Alcinda (Hayes) Emery ; married James W Ault in Greene county, Ind , Dec. 17, 1857. He was a Union soldier from 1861 to 1865 ; was at Fort Donelson, Shiloh, Corinth, Stone River, Perryville, Chicamauga, Resaca, Atlanta, Jonesborough, Frankville and Nashville. She died in Koleen, Ind., July 25, 1878.

Children :

4612 i   JOHN WALTER,[8] b May 12, 1859, in Scotland, Ind , m
4613 ii MARY E , b Oct 18, 1866, in Scotland, Ind , m Solomon Hol-
          der, 1882.
4614 iii URSULA ANN, b April 30, 1869, m Koleen, Ind.
4615 iv MARGARET L , b 1871
4616 v   ELIZABETH, b 1873
4617 vi CHARLES D , b July 17, 1878

2622 CHARLES ANDERSON[7] EMERY (*John,*[6] *Ambrose,*[5] *Ambrose,*[4]
James,[3] *Jonathan,*[2] *John*[1]), son of John and Alcinda (Hayes) Em-
ery ; married, first, in Greene county, Ind., Feb. 18, 1866, Sarah Jane
Stalcup (born 1844 ; died May 13, 1870) ; second, in Bloomfield, Ind.,
Nov. 17, 1871, Martha Victoria Quillen (born in Greene county, Ind ,
Nov. 11, 1852).   Union soldier in Company "H," 1st Iowa Cavalry,
from 1861 to 1864, when he was honorably discharged. Farmer.
Children, born in Greene county, Ind :

4618 i   ANNA ARABELLA [8]
4619 ii   LUCIAN ALBERT, b Oct 15, 1872, d. Dec. 11, 1872.
4620 iii LILLIAN MAY, b Sept. 7, 1873, d Sept 11, 1873.
4621 iv   MARY ROSETTA, b Oct 8, 1874
4622 v   WILLIAM HENRY, b Feb 24, 1877
4623 vi   HARVEY LYCURGUS, b. Sept 18, 1880.
4624 vii AMOS ELMORE, b April 5, 1883
4625 viii ERNEST VANE, b. Sept. 21, 1886

2623 HARRIET ELIZA[7] EMERY (*John,*[6] *Ambrose,*[5] *Ambrose,*[4]
James,[3] *Jonathan,*[2] *John*)[1], daughter of John and Alcinda (Hayes)
Emery ; married in Greene county, Ind , Feb. 28, 1861, John C. Mar-
tindale (born in Cincinnati, Ind , Jan. 9, 1840 ; farmer)
Children, born near Cincinnati, Greene Co , Ind :

4626 i   ALFRED FRANKLIN,[8] b Sept 9, 1862; unm
4627 ii   ALCINDA, b March 4, 1864 ; d in New York Township, Cald-
           well Co , Mo , Nov. 2, 1882, unm
4628 iii HENRY THOMAS, b June 19, 1867, unm.
4629 iv   MARIA, b Oct 25, 1869; unm
4630 v   MARY, b May 13, 1872 , unm
4631 vi   SARAH ANN, b. June 5, 1877
4632 vii JOHN WILLIAM, b. July 10, 1880.

2625 WILLIAM AMBROSE[7] EMERY (*John,*[6] *Ambrose,*[5] *Ambrose,*[4]
James,[3] *Jonathan,*[2] *John*[1]), son of John and Alcinda (Hayes) Emery ;
married in Greene county, Ind., Nov 18, 1869, Mary Catharine ——
(born in Kentucky, July 29, 1849) , lived near Scotland, Ind., until
1879, when he removed to Bonanza, Caldwell Co., Mo.
Children :

4633 i   RHODA FLORENCE,[8] b Oct 20, 1870 in Scotland, Ind
4634 ii   JOHN WILLIAM, b May 21, 1872, in Scotland, Ind
4635 iii FLORA ELLEN, b March 9, 1875, in Scotland, Ind
4636 iv   MARY HARRIET, b Aug. 2, 1876, in Scotland, Ind
4637 v   JONAS DUANE, b Feb 9, 1878, in Scotland, Ind
4638 vi   MELINDA JANE, b. Feb. 15, 1880, in Bonanza, Mo
4639 vii ANNA STELLA, b. Jan 12, 1882, in Bonanza, Mo.
4640 viii WALLACE ALEXANDER, b June 4, 1885, in Bonanza, Mo.
4641 ix   OLIVE CATHARINE, b Jan 4, 1887, in Bonanza, Mo.
4642 x   BENJAMIN FRANKLIN, b Aug 8, 1888, in Bonanza, Mo

2626 Davis Benjamin[7] Emery (*John*,[6] *Ambrose*,[5] *Ambrose*,[4] *James*,[3] *Jonathan*,[2] *John*[1]), son of John and Alcinda Hayes (Emery) ; married in Greene county, Ind., Jan 29, 1876, Charity J. Sanders (born in Ohio, March 20, 1859)   Farmer.

Children, born in Koleen, Ind. :

    4643   i   Ada E ,[8] b Oct 24 1878
    4644   ii   John W , b. Sept 16 1881.
    4645   iii   Jonas N , b Feb 9, 1883
    4646   iv   Davis B , jr , b June 20, 1885

2627 Ellen R.[7] Emery (*John*,[6] *Ambrose*,[5] *Ambrose*,[4] *James*,[3] *Jonathan*,[2] *John*[1]), daughter of John and Alcinda (Hayes) Emery ; married in Greene Co., Ind , Feb. 6, 1873, Barnard J. Lynch (born Nov. 19, 1853).   She died Dec. 26, 1888.

Children, born near Koleen, Ind. :

    4647   i   Orum,[8] b March 6, 1874
    4648   ii   Nathaniel, b July 18, 1875, d. young.
    4649   iii   Noah D , b Dec 2, 1876
    4650   iv   Annias, b Oct 28, 1878, d. young
    4651   v   Sibyl, b Feb 29, 1880
    4652   vi   Mary D , b Jan 31, 1882
    4653   vii   Stephen Grover Cleveland, ⎱ b May 25, 1885.
    4654   viii Thomas A Hendricks,   ⎰
    4655   ix   Emery, b Dec 19, 1887, d Dec 22, 1887.

2634 Ambrose Emery[7] Meredith (*Rebecca*,[6] *Ambrose*,[5] *Ambrose*,[4] *James*,[3] *Jonathan*,[2] *John*[1]), son of Benjamin J and Rebecca (Emery) Meredith ; married in Greene Co , Ind , Jan. 22, 1862, Hester Jane Dugger (born Sept 12, 1839) ; died Sept 22, 1874.

Children, born near Cincinnati, Ind. :

    4656   i   William Marion.[8] b April 4, 1863; unm , farmer
    4657   ii   Jonas Emery, b July 20, 1866, m. S E Goodman, Sept. 20,
                 1888
    4658   iii   Otis Homer, b. Dec. 15, 1871.

2635 William A D [7] Meredith (*Rebecca*,[6] *Ambrose*,[5] *Ambrose*,[4] *James*,[3] *Jonathan*,[2] *John*[1]), son of Benjamin J and Rebecca (Emery) Meredith ; married in Greene Co , Ind , March 7, 1872, Saluda Jane Carmichael (born Aug. 1, 1849)   Teacher : farmer, notary public

Children, born in Cincinnati, Ind. ·

    4659   i   Charles Landis,[8] b Jan 18, 1874; d May 3, 1875.
    4660   ii   Mary Olive, b Oct 23, 1876
    4661   iii   Ernest Adolphus, b Nov 5, 1878

2636 Dr Samuel G.[7] Meredith (*Rebecca*,[6] *Ambrose*,[5] *Ambrose*,[4] *James*,[3] *Jonathan*,[2] *John*[1]), son of Benjamin J. and Rebecca (Emery) Meredith , married, first, in Monroe Co , Ind , Sept 16, 1874, Mary C Walker (born in Monroe Co , Ind., Nov. 12, 1852 , died in Cincinnati, Ind , Aug 24, 1875) ; second, March 28, 1878, Rachel Pethtel (born in Noble Co., O., Jan. 23, 1857)   Teacher , graduate of Eclectic Medical College, Cincinnati, O., 1868 ; surgeon and physician.

Children :

4662 i EDGAR FRANCIS,[8] b June 13, 1875, in Cincinnati, Ind.
4663 ii OSCAR ORLANDO, b Jan 9, 1880, same place
4664 iii HERMA JANE, b Jan 15, 1887, in N. Y. Township, Caldwell Co , Mo.
4665 iv FOREST LEE, b Nov 4, 1888, in N. Y. Township.

2637 JOHN WALTER JONAS[7] MEREDITH (*Rebecca,*[6] *Ambrose,*[5] *Ambrose,*[4] *James,*[3] *Jonathan,*[2] *John*[1]), son of Benjamin J. and Rebecca (Emery) Meredith; married in Cincinnati, Ind , March 9. 1879, Sarah Cullison (born June 1, 1856). Teacher in the public schools of Greene Co., Ind.
Children, born in Cincinnati, Ind.:
4666 i PAULINA IRVINE,[8] b Feb 15, 1880.
4667 ii CLARENCE, b. July 26, 1882; d Aug 17, 1884.

2638 FRED ALONZO LORENZO[7] MEREDITH (*Rebecca,*[6] *Ambrose,*[5] *Ambrose,*[4] *James,*[3] *Jonathan,*[2] *John*[1]), son of Benjamin J and Rebecca (Emery) Meredith; married in Monroe Co , Ind , March 7, 1878, Mary Catharine Carmichael (born in Cincinnati, Ind., April 19, 1860). Farmer.
Children, born in Cincinnati, Ind :
4668 i ISIS ROSALIE[8] b. March 11, 1879.
4669 ii ESTA MAUD, b. April 11, 1881
4670 iii CHRISTA CLAUD, b. Aug 25, 1883.
4671 iv BENJAMIN JOHN, b Jan. 5, 1887

2640 CATHARINE[7] EMERY (*Ambrose,*[6] *Ambrose,*[5] *Ambrose,*[4] *James,*[3] *Jonathan,*[2] *John*[1]), daughter of Ambrose and Ann V. (Hayes) Emery; married in Greene Co , Ind , Nov. 29, 1867, Emit Dagley (born in Elmore Township, Davies Co , Ind., May 30, 1847; farmer). He was a soldier in Co. "H," 31st Ind. Inf.
Children, born in Cincinnati, Ind. ·

4672 i NORA F ,[8] b Sept. 12, 1868
4673 ii OSCAR EDMUND, b April 15, 1870, teacher.
4674 iii EMMA JANE, b March 15, 1872
4675 iv MIRANDA B , b May 27, 1874
4676 v HOMER L , b April 4, 1876
4677 vi ALGIE ESTA, b April 5, 1881.
4678 vii HARLEY CLEVELAND, b March 5, 1887.

2642 ELIZA ANN[7] EMERY (*Ambrose,*[6] *Ambrose,*[5] *Ambrose,*[4] *James,*[3] *Jonathan,*[2] *John*[1]), daughter of Ambrose and Ann V (Hayes) Emery; married in Greene Co., Ind., Oct. 4, 1869, Alfred Westmoreland (born in Bear's Creek, Washington Co , Ind., Aug. 13, 1848). She died March 22, 1871.
Child :
4679 i ORAL,[8] b. March 20, 1871, d Oct 19, 1874

2643 LAVINIA F.[7] EMERY (*Ambrose,*[6] *Ambrose,*[5] *Ambrose,*[4] *James,*[3] *Jonathan,*[2] *John*[1]), daughter of Ambrose and Ann V. (Hayes) Emery; married in Greene Co., Ind.. June 10, 1884, Hezekiah Collins (born Dec 10, 1861).
Children, born in Cincinnati, Ind. :

4680   i   ADA P[8], b July 29, 1885
4681   ii   WAD F , b April 17, 1888.

2644 WILLIAM NOBLE[7] EMERY (*William S ,[6] Ambrose,[5] Ambrose,[4] James,[3] Jonathan,[2] John[1]*), son of William S. and Marcia (Hill) Emery; married Sept. 20, 1870, Jemima Seaton Dowden (born in Scotland, Ind., May 3, 1855). Farmer and sawyer.
Children, born in Greene Co., Ind. :

4682   i   CHARLES WADE,[8] b Sept 23, 1871.
4683   ii   JOHN SPENCER, b Nov 11, 1873.
4684   iii EDGAR WAYNE, b Oct 10, 1877.
4685   iv   STELLA MAY, b March 8, 1881

2645 JOHN WESLEY[7] EMERY (*William S ,[6] Ambrose,[5] Ambrose,[4] James,[3] Jonathan,[2] John[1]*), son of William S and Marcia (Hill) Emery: married in Greene Co , Ind., April 14, 1873, Lavinia Jane Ault, (born at White Oak Spring, Greene Co., Ind., June 10, 1853). Nurseryman.
Children, born in Greene Co., Ind. :

4686   i   WILLIAM HORACE,[8] b Feb 6, 1874
4687   ii   MARCIA FIDELIA, b. March 6, 1876, m Martin Co , Ind.
4688   iii MARY JOSEPHINA, b July 11, 1878 , d Jan 13, 1880
4689   iv   CLARENCE, b March 4, 1880, d Nov 11, 1880
4690   v   SAMUEL CONNELL, b. July 3, 1883 ; d. March 10, 1884
4691   vi   IDA BELLE, b. March 22, 1884.
4692   vii MINA MABEL, b Oct 10, 1887.

2649 CLEMENTINE JOSEPHINE[7] EMERY (*William S ,[6] Ambrose,[5] Ambrose,[4] James,[3] Jonathan,[2] John[1]*), daughter of William S. and Marcia (Hill) Emery; married in Greene Co., Ind., June 2, 1878, John Thomas Jamison (born at White Oak Spring, Aug. 29, 1857).
Children .

4693   i   HENRY ISAAC,[8] b March 13, 1879, in Benton Co , Ark.
4694   ii   ERASTUS, b July 26, 1884, in Lawrence Co , Ind.

2650 LITTLE BERRY[7] EMERY (*William S ,[6] Ambrose,[5] Ambrose,[4] James,[3] Jonathan,[2] John[1]*), son of William S and Marcia (Hill) Emery, married in Greene Co., Ind., Sept. 23, 1878, Sarah J. Wright (born Aug. 10, 1857) Carpenter and mason.
Children, born in Greene Co , Ind .

4695   i   ONAS ADEN,[8] b March 23, 1879
4696   ii   FLORA ELLEN, b. March 7, 1881.

2651 MINA MARCIA[7] EMERY (*William S ,[6] Ambrose,[5] Ambrose,[4] James,[3] Jonathan,[2] John[1]*), daughter of William S. and Marcia (Hill) Emery ; married March 19, 1880, Erastus Dobbins (born in Owensburg, Ind , Dec. 5, 1854; proprietor of Indian Springs Hotel, Martin Co , Ind).
Children, born in Greene Co., Ind. .

4697   i   OSCAR,[8] b. Dec 12, 1882 , d March 10, 1883.
4698   ii   EMERY, b March 18, 1884

2652 WILLIAM JASPER[7] ASHCRAFT (*Mary Ann,*[6] *Ambrose,*[5] *Ambrose,*[4] *James,*[3] *Jonathan,*[2] *John*[1]), son of Daniel and Mary Ann (Emery) Ashcraft; married Jan 20, 1869, Margaret Florence Dobbins (born April 7, 1853) ; removed to Osage Mission, Neosho Co., Kan., 1884. Farmer.

Children :

4699	i	DANIEL BENTON,[8] b Jan 16, 1871, in Dresden, Ind
4700	ii	LAURA ANN, b May 30, 1873, in Dresden, Ind
4701	iii	MARY FRANCES, b Sept 5, 1875, in Dresden, Ind.
4702	iv	WILLIAM ODUS WAYNE, b. Sept 30, 1877, in Dresden, Ind.
4703	v	ELSIE DICKSON, b. April 14, 1880, in Dresden, Ind
4704	vi	CHARLES LESLIE, b Feb 28, 1883, in Dresden, Ind.
4705	vii	HOMER HENDRICKS. b July 14, 1885, in Osage Mission, Kan.
4706	viii	GORDIE ELLEN, b. Jan. 29, 1888, in Osage Mission, Kan

2653 DANIEL BOONE[7] ASHCRAFT (*Mary Ann,*[6] *Ambrose,*[5] *Ambrose,*[4] *James,*[3] *Jonathan,*[2] *John*[1]), son of Daniel and Mary Ann (Emery) Ashcraft; married July 10, 1879. Hannah Inman (born in Dover Hill, Martin Co., Ind., Aug. 11, 1847). A man of talent; public school teacher in Greene Co., Ind., and Harrison Co , Ia.

Child :

| 4707 | i | DELLA BOONE,[8] b July 12, 1880, in Dresden, Ind |

2654 AMBROSE WAYNE[7] ASHCRAFT (*Mary Ann,*[6] *Ambrose,*[5] *Ambrose,*[4] *James,*[3] *Jonathan,*[2] *John*[1]) son of Daniel and Mary Ann (Emery) Ashcraft; married March 8, 1877. Sarah Adaline McKinzie (born March 8, 1862). Farmer and school teacher.

Children, born in Greene Co , Ind :

4708	i	BERTHA IONA,[8] b. Feb 17, 1878.
4709	ii	MYRTLE JOY, b. Oct. 28, 1879
4710	iii	MAMIE, b Sept. 9, 1881.
4711	iv	BLANCH, b Oct 10, 1883
4712	v	QUINCY KELSO, b Aug 24, 1885
4713	vi	Z. GUSTAVUS, b Oct 6, 1887

2655 MARY E.[7] ASHCRAFT (*Mary Ann,*[6] *Ambrose.*[5] *Ambrose,*[4] *James,*[3] *Jonathan,*[2] *John*[1]), daughter of Daniel and Mary Ann (Emery) Ashcraft, married in Koleen, Ind , Sept. 19, 1878, Bloomer Duane Hibbets (born in Gallia Co , O., April 22, 1853; farmer and school teacher).

Children, born in Greene Co., Ind. :

4714	i	DANIEL BOONE,[8] b. March 30, 1880.
4715	ii	HOMER DUANE, b June 14, 1883; d. Aug. 22, 1884
4716	iii	VICTOR GUY, b Dec. 19, 1887

2657 SEYMOUR[7] ASHCRAFT (*Mary Ann,*[6] *Ambrose,*[5] *Ambrose,*[4] *James,*[3] *Jonathan,*[2] *John*[1]), son of Daniel and Mary Ann (Emery) Ashcraft) ; married Barthena Adams in Lyons, Ind., Dec. 30, 1888. Farmer and school teacher.

Child :

| 4717 | i | EDITH,[8] b. July 6, 1889, in Lyons, Ind |

2661 HARRIET E.[7] ADAMS (*Clementine,*[6] *Ambrose,*[5] *Ambrose,*[4]

James,[3] *Jonathan*,[2] *John*[1]), daughter of Eli and Clementine (Emery) Adams; married March 19, 1872, Morris Robert Barker (born Aug. 1, 1837; farmer)

Children born in Greene Co., Ind.:

    4718 i   LAURA AGNES[8], b Feb 13, 1873
    4719 ii   REBECCA EILEN, b May 14, 1875.
    4720 iii WILLIAM ALBERT, b June 6, 1877
    4721 iv   STELLA MAY, b Aug 6, 1882.

2662 JONAS ADEN[7] EMERY (*Nathaniel*,[6] *Ambrose*,[5] *Ambrose*,[4] *James*,[3] *Jonathan*,[2] *John*[1]), son of Nathaniel and Susan (McWhirter) Emery; married Sept 12, 1882, Emma Gainev (born in Bloomfield, Ind, Jan. 4, 1859). Graduate of U. S. Military Academy, West Point, N. Y., 1881, now first lieutenant of the 11th Regt., U. S. Inf. Children.

    4722 i   AMBROSE ROBERT,[8] b July 26, 1883, in Bloomfield, Ind.
    4723 ii   JESSIE MAY, b March 2, 1885, in Fort Sully, S. Dak.
    4724 iii NATHANIEL WILLIAM, b July 14, 1889, in Madison Barracks,
                 N. Y.

2664 JESSE WALKER[7] EMERY (*Nathaniel*,[6] *Ambrose*,[5] *Ambrose*,[4] *James*,[3] *Jonathan*,[2] *John*[1]), son of Nathaniel and Susan (McWhirter) Emery; married April 1, 1884, Julia Anna O'Donald (born Oct 15, 1866). Farmer.

Children.

    4725 i   NELLIE MAUD,[8] b Nov 19, 1884
    4726 ii   GRACE MAY, b. March 8, 1886, d in Boston, Col, Sept 30,
                 1887
    4727 iii LILLY PEARL, b July 18, 1888, in Meade Co, Kan.
    4728 iv   JONAS NATHANIEL, b. Feb 17, 1890, in Sterling, Kan

2665 CHARLES SIGEL[7] EMERY (*Nathaniel*,[6] *Ambrose*,[5] *Ambrose*,[4] *James*,[3] *Jonathan*,[2] *John*[1]), son of Nathaniel and Susan (McWhirter) Emery; married in Greene Co., Ind, Oct 12, 1887, Minerva Jane Hardesty (born in Greene Co, Ind., Oct. 12, 1868). Farmer. Children, born in Scotland, Ind..

    4729 i   JONAS,[8] b Dec. 25, 1888
    4730 ii   FRANCES MAY, b Jan 10, 1890.

2671 ELIZA J.[7] EMERY (*James*,[6] *Robert S*,[5] *Edward*,[4] *James*,[3] *Jonathan*,[2] *John*[1]), daughter of James and his second wife Nancy (Hall) Emery; married in Augusta, Me., Dec 13, 1867, Edwin A. Getchell (born in Hallowell, Me., Feb. 5, 1841; druggist).

Child:

    4731 i   BERNARD EMERY,[8] b. June 10, 1874, in Augusta, Me

2675 HORACE[7] SNELL (*Melinda*,[6] *Robert S.*,[5] *Edward*,[4] *James*,[3] *Jonathan*,[2] *John*[1]), son of Thaddeus and Melinda (Emery) Snell; married in Gloucester, Mass., Oct., 1874, Emma J Anderson of Bowdoinham, Me. (born in Richmond, Me, 1854). Railroad station agent.

Children, born in Bowdoinham, Me..

4732 i   STEPHEN C.,⁸ b Mav 12, 1876
4733 ii   ETHEL, b Nov 23, 1877
4734 iii MILDRED, b Aug. 20, 1884.

2680 HELEN M ⁷ SNELL (*Eunice S.,⁶ Robert S.,⁵ Edward,⁴ James,³ Jonathan², John¹*), daughter of Edward and Eunice S. (Emery) Snell ; married in Boston, Jan . 1868, Albert P. Saben (born in Augusta, Me , April 19, 1836 , farmer).
Child :

4735 i   CAROLINE S ,⁸ b. April 12, 1873, in Vassalboro, Me

2685 AMANDA F ⁷ EMERY (*Isaiah,⁶ Robert S ,⁵ Edward,⁴ James,³ Jonathan,² John¹*), daughter of Isaiah and Sabrina (Babcock) Emery ; married in Newburgh, Me , Dec. 9. 1873, John Bradley (born in Newburgh, May 26, 1847; farmer).
Child .

4736 i   LINDA MAY,⁸ b. May 2, 1875 ; d Oct 1, 1875.

2687 EUNICE SNELL⁷ EMERY (*Isaiah,⁶ Robert S.,⁵ Edward,⁴ James,³ Jonathan,² John¹*), daughter of Isaiah and Sabrina (Babcock) Emery ; married in Skowhegan, Me , May 2, 1864, Wingate W. Bradbury, jr., of Athens, Me. (born in Athens, Me , Feb. 18, 1843 , Union soldier in the war of the Rebellion). She was a school teacher and died Oct. 27, 1870.
Child .

4737 i   EUNICE,⁸ b April, 1865 ; d in infancy.

2688 GEORGE ARNOLD⁷ EMERY (*Isaiah,⁶ Robert S ,⁵ Edward,⁴ James,³ Jonathan,² John¹*), son of Isaiah and Sabrina (Babcock) Emery) , married in Falmouth, Me , Aug. 5, 1865, Rebecca Frances Dougherty of Gray, Me. (born Sept. 12, 1845). He enlisted in Co. "A," 1st Battalion, 17th Regt U. S Inf., was in the battles of Malvern Hill and Gains's Farm , enlisted in the U. S N. under the name of George Arnold and served on the gunboats Iron Age and Nancemond ; discharged Sept. 12, 1864. He afterwards proved to the government that his name was George Arnold Emery. Carpenter in Gray, Me.
Children, born in Gray Corner, Me..

4738 i   FRED WALLACE,⁸ b March 16. 1866, mechanic in Boston.
4739 ii   MARTHA ANN, b June 30, 1868, unm
4740 iii JAMES ALBERT, b Aug 5, 1870
4741 iv ESTHER DOUGHERTY, b Sept 3, 1872.
4742 v   GEORGE WALKER BLAINE, b April 21, 1886

2690 FRANKIE⁷ EMERY (*Isaiah,⁶ Robert S ,⁵ Edward,⁴ James,³ Jonathan,² John¹*), daughter of Isaiah and Sabrina (Babcock) Emery ; married in Manistee, Mich., Dec. 16, 1884, Henry Rock (born in Mitchell, Canada).
Children :

4743 i   DAISY EMMA,⁸ b April 27, 1887, in Manistee, Mich.
4744 ii   A DAUGHTER, b Nov. 28, 1889, in Manistee, Mich.

2691 ALBERT L [7] EMERY (*Isaiah,*[4] *Robert S.,*[5] *Edward,*[4] *James,*[3] *Jonathan,*[2] *John*[1]), son of Isaiah and Sabrina (Babcock) Emery, married in West Branch, Ia, Nov. 21, 1875, Emma A. Bennett (born in Durham, Me., Sept. 26, 1848). Albert L. Emery's mother died when he was an infant; his nurse was a Mrs Jepson who wanted him called Jepson but his father would not consent   After his father's death, Mrs. Jepson, without the knowledge or consent of his relatives, took the child from Maine to Iowa and he was called by her name, and to please her he was married under that name but his real name is Emery. His descendants will be recorded under the name of Emery-Jepson.

Children, born in West Branch, Ia :

    4745   i   GEORGE DELMONT,[8] b Aug 22, 1876
    4746   ii   RALPH WILSON, b Sept 30, 1878, drowned Aug. 30, 1881.
    4747   iii   FRANKIE ELIZ , b Sept. 21, 1880.
    4748   iv   WORTH EMERY, b Sept 21, 1882
    4749   v   PERCY F , b Aug 19, 1885
    4750   vi   KATE LAVONA, b. March 2, 1888, in Elsinore, Cal.

2693 JOHN CLEVELAND[7] EMERY (*George A ,*[6] *Robert S.,*[5] *Edward,*[4] *James,*[3] *Jonathan,*[2] *John*[1]), son of George A. and Mary (Libby) Emery; married, in Lock Haven, Pa., Sept. 3. 1863, Maria C. Clark (born in Parkham. Me , March 2, 1845)   Lumberman.

Children .

    4751   i   EMMA A ,[8] b Jan. 18, 1865, in Lock Haven Pa., m. Ivory G.
                  Littlefield, Feb 22, 1886, in Haverhill, Mass
    4752   ii   NETTIE A , b   March 16, 1868, in Benezette, Pa ; m. Willard
                  Langley in Haverhill, April 29, 1886
    4753   iii   JOHN C., JR., b. Sept. 22, 1869, in Hix Run, Pa ; d. in Lock
                  Haven, Aug. 9, 1870.
    4754   iv   MARY A , b May 8, 1871, in Lock Haven, Pa , m Frank W.
                  Eastman, March 6, 1889, in Bradford, Mass.
    4755   v   GEORGE M , b March 30, 1874, in Lock Haven, Pa.
    4756   vi   MYRA B , b Jan 13, 1880, in Lock Haven, Pa.
    4757   vii   LEROY R., b Feb 12, 1888, in Haverhill, Mass.

2695 BENJAMIN LIBBY[7] EMERY (*George A.,*[6] *Robert S ,*[5] *Edward,*[4] *James,*[3] *Jonathan,*[2] *John*[1]), son of George A. and Mary (Libby) Emery; married, first, in Benezette, Pa , Dec 25, 1867, Annie C Freeman (born in Emporium, Pa , April 30, 1847; died in Lock Haven, Pa.. July 26, 1884) ; second, in Osceola, Pa , July 6, 1886, Jennie E. McGhee (born in Salona, Pa , April 14, 1848). Corporal in Co. "D," 1st Pa. Cav , Aug 11, 1861 ; wounded at Cedar Mountain, Va., Aug. 9, 1862 ; discharged at Alexandria, Va., Dec. 24, 1862. Lumberman

Children :

    4758   i   FRANKLIN WEYMOUTH,[8] b April 26, 1870, in Emporium, Pa.
    4759   ii   ANNIE L , b. Oct 3, 1871, in Emporium, Pa
    4760   iii   MAUD M , b. Oct 25, 1874, in Emporium, Pa
    4761   iv   ORLANDO H , b Dec 12, 1876, in Emporium, Pa.
    4762   v   MIRIAM MILDRED, b May 3, 1879, in Lock Haven, Pa.
    4763   vi   BESSIE R , b. Jan 3, 1888, in Lock Haven, Pa.

2696 ORLANDO H.[7] EMERY (*George A.,*[6] *Robert S.,*[5] *Edward,*[4] *James,*[3] *Jonathan,*[2] *John*[1]), son of Geo. A. and Mary (Libby) Emery ;

married in North East, Pa., April 28, 1869, Mary E. Pearsall (born in Caledonia, Pa , Aug. 8, 1846). Soldier in Co. "D," 1st Pa Cav. ; promoted sergeant, May 30, 1863 , was in both battles of Bull Run, the whole of the Peninsula campaign and the three days' fight at Gettysburg , wounded at Gettysburg where he was on duty at Gen. Mead's headquarters, serving as dispatch carrier. As a soldier he exhibited great courage and daring. The O H. Emery Sons of Veterans were named in his honor He was tendered a captaincy which he declined on account of ill health He died in Oleana, Pa , Feb 25, 1882.

Children :

 4764 i GEORGIANA,[8] b. March 2, 1870, in Lock Haven, Pa.
 4765 ii CAROLINE M , b. May 22. 1871, in St Mary's, Pa
 4766 iii FREDERICK B , b March 28, 1875, in Lock Haven, Pa.

2697 COL. JAMES M [7] EMERY (*George A.*,[6] *Robert S.*,[5] *Edward*,[4] *James*,[3] *Jonathan*,[2] *John*[1]), son of George A and Mary (Libby) Emery, married in Florence, Pa Oct 28, 1875. Luella Clark (born in Cincinnati, O , Sept. 20, 1855). Soldier in Co. "D," and Co. "A," 3d Pa Art., served on various gunboats in Va.; captured at Smithfield, Va , Feb. 1, 1864 , confined in Libby prison, Belle Isle and Andersonville prisons , exchanged March 25, 1865 , discharged as Corporal Co. "A," 3d Pa. Art., June 16, 1865. Aide de camp on the staff of Gov. Sherman of Iowa with rank of Lieut. Col. General agent N. Y Life Ins. Co. for South Dak , publisher of *Le Mars Sentinel* Major 6th Regt Iowa N. G , clerk of House Committee on Territories, Congress, 1889–90

Children, born in Le Mars, Ia :

 4767 i MARY L ,[8] b Aug 4, 1876
 4768 ii CLARK MANLY, b. April 23, 1878.

2699 JOSEPH LIBBY[7] EMERY (*George A.*,[6] *Robert S.*,[5] *Edward*,[4] *James*,[3] *Jonathan*,[2] *John*[1]), son of George A. and Mary (Libby) Emery , married in Emporium, Pa , March 15, 1871, Jennie C. Freeman (born Jan. 7, 1851). Lumberman

Children:

 4769 i RUEL F ,[8] b Jan 11, 1872, in Lock Haven, Pa
 4770 ii SILAS W , b March 27, 1874, in Lock Haven, Pa
 4771 iii JOSEPH L , JR , b Aug 7, 1876, in Sinnamahoning, Pa.
 4772 iv SUSAN PEARL, b Jan 4, 1879, in Westport, Pa
 4773 v REGINALD A , b Aug 9, 1881 in Westport, Pa
 4774 vi RUBY HANNAH, b. May 12, 1884, in Westport, Pa.
 4775 vii SAMUEL J , b Sept 22, 1886, in Westport, Pa
 4776 viii LUELLA AGNES, b Jan 16, 1889, in Westport, Pa.

2700 ALBERT[7] EMERY (*Hamilton*,[6] *Robert S.*,[5] *Edward*,[4] *James*,[3] *Jonathan*,[2] *John*[1]), son of Hamilton and Emily (Buck) Emery ; married April 2, 1854, Joanna Bragg of Winslow, Me. (born Nov 8, 1835). City marshal of Wakefield and Deputy Sheriff of Dixon Co., Neb He died in Wakefield, Neb., Dec 31, 1887.

Children :

4777   ı   HORACE E.,[8] b April 8, 1856, ın Vassalboro, Me., m. Mary
            Pierce, Nov 16, 1879
4778   ıı   WARREN A , b Oct 16, 1864, ın Benton, Me.

2701 JANE E [7] EMERY (*Hamilton*,[6] *Robert S.*,[5] *Edward*,[4] *James*,[3]
Jonathan,[2] *John*[1]), daughter of Hamilton and Emily (Buck) Emery ;
married March 29, 1853, Edward R. Bragg of Winslow, Me (born
Feb. 7, 1825, mechanic)
Children, born ın Winslow, Me. ;

4779   i   ALMIRA,[8] b Dec 22, 1854, d March 19, 1867.
4780   ıı   MARY A , b Jan 30, 1858, d. Feb 28, 1858.
4781   ııı FRED H , b May 19, 1868, grad Portland Coll , 1889

2702 JOHN H [7] EMERY (*Hamilton*,[6] *Robert S* ,[5] *Edward*,[4] *James*,[3]
Jonathan,[2] *John*[1]), son of Hamilton and Emily (Buck) Emery ; mar-
ried, first, Dec. 25. 1860, Deborah Bragg (born ın Winslow, Me., Nov.
8, 1835, twın sıster of Joanna (Bragg) Emery and sıster of Edward R.
Bragg who marrıed Jane E Emery, dıed June 4, 1874) , second, Oct.
14, 1877, Fannıe O. Whıte (born ın Greenfield, Me., Sept 18, 1853).
Blacksmith
Children, born in Winslow, Me. :

4782   ı   LESTER M ,[8] b June 10, 1863
4783   ıı   STEPHEN H., b Oct 22, 1864, lıves ın Provıdence, R. I.
4784   ııı NETTIE F., b. Aug 9, 1867.
4785   ıv   EMILY F , b. Aug 25, 1871, d in North Vassalboro, Me., Aprıl
            1, 1874
4786   v   CHARLES JOHN, b Oct 21, 1878

2718 ELVIRA[8] SMITH (*Lydıa H.*,[7] *John*,[6] *Daniel*,[5] *John*,[4] *John*,[3]
John,[2] *John*[1]), daughter of Benj. and Lydıa Hale (Emery) Smith ;
marrıed in Madison, O., Sept. 1, 1831, Caleb Strong Stratton (born
ın Northfield, Mass., May 30, 1802 ; dıed in Unıonville, O., Sept. 12,
1842).
Children, born ın Unionvılle, O. ·

4787   ı   CHARLES,[9] b Sept 16, 1832, d. Aug 8, 1836
4788   ıı   ELIZA JANE, b Feb 6, 1834, d in Oberlin, O , July 12, 1854
4789   ııı ASA STRONG, b Sept 16, 1836, m Sarah Glezen, Dec 19,
            1866   Union soldier
4790   ıv   LYDIA ALMIRA, b Aug 10, 1839, m Rev. J. E Smith, Sept.
            9, 1870.
4791   v   EMILY, b May 27, 1842

2719 SUSAN[8] SMITH (*Lydıa H.*,[7] *John*,[6] *Danıel*,[5] *John*,[4] *John*,[3]
John,[2] *John*[1]), daughter of Benjamın and Lydıa Hale (Emery) Smith ,
marrıed John G. Croxton, merchant ın Madison, O , March 24. 1831.
Children, except first two, born ın Magnolıa, Ohio:

4792   i   WILLIAM BALEMAN,[9] b ın Carrollton, O , Jan 12, 1832; m.
            Carrıe Anderman ın New Phıla , O , Oct 17, 1859
4793   ıı   HENRIETTA EMERY b at Yellow Creek, O , Aug 29, 1834; m.
            I II Barnhıll at Magnolıa, O , Dec 20, 1853.
4794   ııı JOSEPHINE, b Jan 27, 1837, d 1840
4795   ıv   JOHN G., b March 18, 1839, m Gertrude Baıley, Nov 11, 1868.
4796   v   BENJ F , b Dec 14, 1841, m. Clara Deardeff, Jan. 7, 1867, ın
            Canal Dover, O , where he d. Aug 29, 1880.

4797   vi   SAMUEL W , b. March 25, 1845, m Electa Miller, June 17, 1869
4798   vii ALICE E , b Aug. 31, 1850, m George Hopkins, Nov. 13, 1873.

2720 EMILY[8] SMITH (*Lydia H ,*[7] *John,*[6] *Daniel,*[5] *John,*[4] *John,*[3] *John,*[2] *John*[1]), daughter of Benjamin and Lydia Hale (Emery) Smith ; married Aug 31, 1841, at Madison, O , Enoch N. Bartlett (born in Bath, N. Y., July 4, 1813 ; graduate of Oberlin Coll).
Children ·

4799   i   JULIA E ,[9] b. 1843, in Farmington, O , d in Madison Co , O., 1844
4800   ii   GEORGE W , b Sept 3, 1845, in Farmington, O
4801   iii JOSEPH E , b in Olivet, Mich , Oct 5, 1848, graduate of Leipsic, 1869   Musician
4802   iv   HORACE M , b in Olivet, Mich , April 7, 1859

2726 MARGARET[8] EMERY (*John,*[7] *John,*[6] *Daniel,*[5] *John,*[4] *John,*[3] *John,*[2] *John*[1]), daughter of John and Elizabeth (Wheeler) Emery ; married Nov. 14, 1848, E. C. Moore, and died in Maumee, O., Nov. 29, 1849.
Child :
4803   i   J H ,[9] soldier in Co. "A," 14th Ohio Vol.

2727 SAMUEL[8] EMERY (*John,*[7] *John,*[6] *Daniel,*[5] *John,*[4] *John,*[3] *John,*[2] *John*[1]), son of John and Elizabeth (Wheeler) Emery ; married in Maumee O , June 4, 1848, Henrietta Reese
Children, born in Maumee, O , except the ninth :

4804   i   CHLOE A ,[9] b March 2, 1849 ; m C. A Bassett, Nov 13, 1873
4805   ii   MARGARET E , b Feb 28, 1851, m W H. Irving, Sept 3, 1874.
4806   iii AMANDA L , b Dec. 20, 1852, d Sept 20, 1854
4807   iv   JAMES S , b March 5, 1855, m Ella Custis, Feb. 28, 1878.
4808   v   CHARLES S , } b March 14, 1857, } m Mary B Shepard, June
4809   vi   GEORGE W., }   }   24, 1883.
4810   vii AMANDA E , b Oct 17, 1859, m L J Fuke, Sept. 12, 1882.
4811   viii HARVEY R , b Jan 17, 1861, m Sept , 1889, Dora B. Lautzenheiser
4812   ix   IDA E , b Nov. 15, 1863, Swanton, O
4813   x   EDWIN W , b May 4, 1867

2729 ELIZABETH[8] EMERY (*John,*[7] *John,*[6] *Daniel,*[5] *John,*[4] *John,*[3] *John,*[2] *John*[1]), daughter of John and his second wife Ann (Wolcott) Emery ; married at Swanton, O , June 6, 1854, John Adam Simon (born in Keidenheim, Rhine Bavaria, Germany, May 20, 1819 , died at Byron, O., Feb. 22, 1885).
Children, born in Byron :

4814   i   FLORA E ,[9] b July 6, 1863
4815   ii   CATHARINE O , b Feb 20, 1867
4816   iii PHILIP WOLCOTT, b Oct , 1873

2730 HENRIETTA[8] EMERY (*John,*[7] *John,*[6] *Daniel,*[5] *John,*[4] *John,*[3] *John,*[2] *John*[1]), daughter of John and his second wife Ann (Wolcott) Emery , married at Byron, O., Sept. 22, 1868, Albert Elliot (born in Coshocton, O., Dec. 27, 1839).

Children, born in Defiance, O. :

4817 1   SAMUEL E.,[9] b July 1, 1869
4818 11 FLORA BELLE, b Sept 17, 1871.
4819 111 ALBERT WOLCOTT, b March 11, 1874.

2732 RUSH[8] EMERY (*John,*[7] *John,*[6] *Daniel,*[5] *John,*[4] *John,*[3] *John,*[2] *John*[1]), son of John and his second wife, Ann (Wolcott) Emery; married Nettie Hart, of Iowa City, Ia., June 25, 1866. He died at Terre Haute, Ind , Sept. 6, 1872.

Children .

4820 1 NELSON H.[9]
4821 ii EDWARD.

2733 JOHN EMERY[8] BAILEY (*Alphia B ,*[7] *John,*[6] *Daniel,*[5] *John,*[4] *John,*[3] *John,*[2] *John*[1]), son of Harlow and Alphia B. (Emery) Bailey; married Eliza Naomi Church, Oct 18, 1838.

Children :

4822 1   ANTOINETTE [9] b June 16, 1841, d Sept 11, 1860.
4823 ii GERTRUDE, b Feb 4, 1843, m John G Crotchet, Nov , 1868.
4824 111 AGNES, b Sept 9, 1850, m., Oct 25, 1871, H H Marvin

2735 CAROLINE E.[8] BAILEY (*Alphia B ,*[7] *John* [6] *Daniel,*[5] *John,*[4] *John,*[3] *John,*[2] *John*[1]), daughter of Harlow and Alphia B. (Emery) Bailey , married March 17, 1845, J. F. Blair (born Aug. 30, 1820).

Children .

4825 1 CORWIN,[9] b March 14, 1848, m Celestia M Pierce, July 10, 1874
4826 11 EMERY, b Oct 31, 1855
4827 111 NETTIE B b Dec , 1861, m D A Strong, Oct 2, 1878.
4828 1v STELLA, b May 6, 1865.

2737 DANIEL EMERY[8] BAILEY (*Alphia B.,*[7] *John,*[6] *Daniel,*[5] *John,*[4] *John,*[3] *John,*[2] *John*[1]), son of Harlow and Alphia B. (Emery) Bailey ; married Feb 23, 1854, Mary Ann Donnelly, of New York (born Nov. 28, 1836) President of the Lumber Stowage and Transfer Co , Buffalo, N. Y.

Children .

4829 1 EVA CAROLINE,[9] b Feb 28, 1855; d Dec 25, 1874.
4830 11 HARLOW WARD, b Sept 4, 1864.

2741 ROBERT G [8] EMERY(*Josiah B.,*[7] *John,*[6] *Daniel,*[5] *John,*[4] *John,*[3] *John,*[2] *John*[1]), son of Josiah B and Lucinda (Goold) Emery , married, first, Feb. 29, 1852, Jerusha E. White (died in Ridgeville, Henry Co , O., May 21, 1858) , second, April 20, 1859, Emily Eugenia Palmer (born in Defiance, O , Jan. 12, 1840). Hospital steward in Co. " G, ' 68th Ohio Vols. , was in the battles of Fort Donelson and Pittsburg Landing Physician He died in Florida, O., March 26, 1885, aged 59.

Children, born in Ridgeville :

4831 1 LUCINDA JERUSHA,[9] b. Nov. 30, 1852.
4832 11 ERASMUS GEORGE, b Oct 16, 1855
4833 111 WILLIAM BARTLETT, b. June 9, 1857, d. April 17, 1859.

4834 iv INFANT SON, b. and d. May 4, 1860.
4835 v WILLIAM GOOLD, b. July 1, 1862; m. Sarah E. Richholt.
4836 vi DANIEL BARTLETT, b. May 26, 1865; d. July 30, 1866.
4837 vii BARTLETT JOSEPH, b. Aug. 11, 1867.

2746 JOSIAH BARTLETT[8] EMERY, JR. (*Josiah B.*,[7] *John*,[6] *Daniel*,[5] *John*,[4] *John*,[3] *John*,[2] *John*[1]), son of Josiah B. and Lucinda (Goold) Emery; married in Carroll Co., O., Sept. 27, 1855, Mary Harper (born in Rockcurry, Ireland, July 15, 1835). He died in Ridgefield Corner, O., June 17, 1861.

Children, born in Henry Co., O.:

4838 i JOHN THOMAS,[9] b. July 9, 1856.
4839 ii DANIEL ALANSON, b. June 18, 1858; lawyer in Ottumwa, Ia., and 2nd Lieut. in Iowa N. G.
4840 iii EMILY JANE, b. Jan. 4, 1861; d. Feb. 16, 1861.

2751 JOSEPH STRAIN[8] EMERY (*Josiah B.*,[7] *John*,[6] *Daniel*,[5] *John*,[4] *John*,[3] *John*,[2] *John*[1]), son of Josiah B. and Lucinda (Goold) Emery; married in Leipsic, Putnam Co., O., March 11, 1869, M. L. Lowery (born Sept. 29, 1851); enlisted in the U. S. Navy, 1864, for two years; served on the iron clad "Mound City." Farmer.

Children, born in Ridgeville Corner, O.:

4841 i MYRTLE EUGENIA,[9] b. Aug. 10, 1872.
4842 ii ANNA MAY, b. Aug. 12, 1877.

2754 JOHN KELLY[8] PAINE (*Hannah*,[7] *Jacob*,[6] *Rev. Jacob*,[5] *Joseph*,[4] *Joseph*,[3] *John*,[2] *John*[1]), son of John B. and Hannah (Emery) Paine; married, first, Aug. 11, 1853, Laura E. Bosworth; second, in Sandwich, Ill., Jan. 17, 1864, Mrs. Harriet Harrison.

Children:

4843 i ANNA LAURA.[9]
4844 ii CORA ELIZABETH.
4845 iii JOHN.
4846 iv HATTIE ADA.
4847 v GRACE MAY.
4848 vi GEORGE HAY.
4849 vii JESSIE KATE.

2757 RUFUS HOSMER[8] PAINE (*Hannah*,[7] *Jacob*,[6] *Rev. Jacob*,[5] *Joseph*,[4] *Joseph*,[3] *John*,[2] *John*[1]), son of John B. and Hannah (Emery) Paine; married, Sept. 1, 1859, Mary A. V. Aldrich; enlisted in Co. "A," New Hampshire Heavy Artillery, at Fort Constitution, Portsmouth Harbor, July 17, 1863, and stationed at Fort Bayard, near Washington, July, 1864.

Children:

4850 i JESSE RUFUS,[9] b. July 12, 1860.
4851 ii ELIZABETH ANN, b. Oct. 4, 1861.
4852 iii MARY NELLIE, b. July 12, 1864.
4853 iv CLARA LOCKE, b. May 3, 1869; d. Nov. 28, 1872.
4854 v CLARA, b. May 3, 1873; d. Aug. 25, 1875.

2761 CHARLES HENRY[8] PAINE (*Hannah*,[7] *Jacob*,[6] *Rev. Jacob*,[5] *Joseph*,[4] *Joseph*,[3] *John*,[2] *John*[1]), son of John B. and Hannah (Emery)

15

Paine, married, June 1, 1873, Emma Edgerly. Manufacturer of spring beds.

Children, born in Suncook, N. H. :

4855　ɪ　LOU GRACE,[9] b Aug 9 1879
4856　ɪɪ　CHARLES CHENEY, b March 22, 1883

2767 EDWIN[8] CHICKERING (*Mary*,[7] *Jacob*,[6] *Rev. Jacob*,[5] *Joseph*,[4] *Joseph*,[3] *John*,[2] *John*[1]), son of Stephen and Mary (Emery) Chickering; married, May 2, 1868, Lucia S Holt.

Children .

4857　ɪ　JESSE ELMER,[9] b April 3, 1874, d June 15, 1875
4858　ɪɪ　MARY ELLA, b Dec 7, 1876.

2774 MARY ETTA[8] EMERY (*Jacob*,[7] *Jacob*,[6] *Rev. Jacob*,[5] *Joseph*,[4] *Joseph*,[3] *John*,[2] *John*[1]), daughter of Jacob and Mary (Smith) Emery; married B F. French.

Children :

4859　ɪ　CHARLES F [9]
4860　ɪɪ　MARY LOVETTA.

2776 WILLIAM H [8] PAINE (*Susan P.*,[7] *James C*,[6] *Rev. Jacob*,[5] *Joseph*,[4] *Joseph*,[3] *John*,[2] *John*[1]). son of William B and Susan P. (Emery) Paine; married, first, Sept. 29, 1858, Harriet A Wheeler, who died Feb 12, 1861, second, Aug 10, 1865, Catharine Jones. Inventor of a measure for ascertaining the change of length of metals under strain, the steel tape line; straight wire; the roller grip and devices used in connection with the cable (rope) traction used on the New York and Brooklyn bridge; made the first chain measurement across the Nevada mountains in 1853; served as aid de-camp, acting as topographical engineer, on the staffs of Gens. McDowell, Pope, Hooker and Meade, assistant engineer during the construction of the New York and Brooklyn bridge, and connected with many other engineering works.

Children :

4861　ɪ　HATTIE LAWRENCE [9]
4862　ɪɪ　KATHREEN LYMAN.

2777 CHARLES EMERY[8] PAINE (*Susan P*,[7] *James C*,[6] *Rev. Jacob*,[5] *Joseph*,[4] *Joseph*,[3] *John*,[2] *John*[1]), son of William B. and Susan P. (Emery) Paine, married, May 25, 1857, Ann Eliza Sickles Enlisted in the 2nd Kansas Vols. , was in many battles under Gen Lyon; later was in the 11th Regt. Vols in Missouri and on the plains, doing good service in command of escort trains.

Children ·

4863　ɪ　CHARLES [9]
4864　ɪɪ　WILLIAM HENRY, b May 15, 1861.
4865　ɪɪɪ　EDWIN CHARLES, b. Dec 11, 1868
4866　ɪᴠ　SUSIE, d young
4867　ᴠ　CLARENCE A., b Jan., 1874.

2778 JAMES EMERY[8] PAINE (*Susan P.*,[7] *James C.*,[6] *Rev. Jacob*,[5]

Joseph,[4] *Joseph,*[3] *John,*[2] *John*[1]), son of William B. and Susan P. (Emery) Paine; married Jannett Jamison.
Children:

4868 i   HOWARD [9]
4869 ii   JANNETT.
4870 iii   JOHN
4871 iv   ROBERT.
4872 v   HENRY.

2779 HARRIET MARIA[8] PAINE (*Susan P*,[7] *James C*,[6] *Rev. Jacob,*[5] *Joseph,*[4] *Joseph,*[3] *John,*[2] *John*[1]), daughter of William B. and Susan P. (Emery) Paine; married, first, James D. Marsh; second, Winfield Scott.
Child:

4873 i   A DAUGHTER [9]

2782 SUSAN LORINDA[8] PAINE (*Susan P.,*[7] *James C.,*[6] *Rev. Jacob,*[5] *Joseph,*[4] *Joseph,*[3] *John,*[2] *John*[1]), daughter of William B. and Susan P. (Emery) Paine, married, first, Stanley Price; second, D. Muzzy.
Child:

4874 i   A DAUGHTER.[9]

2793 ESTHER M [8] PARKER (*Dorcas,*[7] *Joseph,*[6] *Joseph* [5] *Joseph,*[4] *Joseph,*[3] *John,*[2] *John*[1]), daughter of John and Dorcas (Emery) Parker, married Thomas R. Holt of Pembroke, N. H, Nov., 1856.
Children:

4875 i   FLORA J ,[9] b Aug , 1857; m Dr Roscoe Hill, Oct. 29, 1884.
4876 ii   THOMAS P , b May, 1860
4877 iii   EMERY, b April, 1864.
4878 iv   SADIE, b. July, 1866; d Nov , 1871.

2798 STEPHEN A.[8] BATES (*Hannah,*[7] *Joseph,*[6] *Joseph,*[5] *Joseph,*[4] *Joseph,*[3] *John,*[2] *John*[1]), son of Stephen and Hannah (Emery) Bates; married, May 28, 1871, Catharine Scammell.
Children:

4879 i   STEPHEN EMERY,[9] b Feb 17, 1872.
4880 ii   CHARLES F., b Oct 2, 1873
4881 iii   MARY A , b. Dec 22, 1875
4882 iv   GEORGE E , b Sept 30, 1878.
4883 v   LAURENCE C., b Sept 25, 1880.
4884 vi   ALONZO, b July 13, 1883
4885 vii   JOHN W., b Aug. 29, 1885

2801 PHŒBE ANN[8] WILLIAMS (*Nabby,*[7] *Joseph,*[6] *Joseph,*[5] *Joseph,*[4] *Joseph,*[3] *John,*[2] *John*[1]), daughter of Charles K. and Nabby (Emery) Williams; married, Dec. 31, 1849, Philips Sargent of Allenstown, N. H.
Child:

4886 i   ELLEN F.,[9] b. Oct. 5, 1850.

2802 JOSEPH M.[8] EMERY (*Joseph,*[7] *Joseph,*[6] *Joseph,*[5] *Joseph,*[4] *Jo-*

seph,[3] *John*,[2] *John*[1]), son of Joseph and Hannah (Merrill) Emery; married, Feb. 21, 1856, Martha E. Hall of Epsom, N. H.

Children :

4887 i   ANNA M.,[9] b. March 20, 1859.
4888 ii HARRIET A., b. June 20, 1867; m. James W. Hall of Epsom, N. H.; d. in Lynn, Mass., s. p.

2803 NATHANIEL B.[8] EMERY (*Joseph*,[7] *Joseph*,[6] *Joseph*,[5] *Joseph*,[4] *Joseph*,[3] *John*,[2] *John*[1]), son of Joseph and Hannah (Merrill) Emery; married, Nov. 10, 1859, Abbie H. Sargent of Allenstown, N. H.

Children :

4889 i   FRED P.,[9] b. April 11, 1865.
4890 ii   ELSIE S., b. April 4, 1869; d. Nov. 12, 1871.
4891 iii NATHANIEL M., b. April 16, 1873.

2806 MARY ANN[8] GAULT (*Clarissa*,[7] *Samuel*,[6] *Joseph*,[5] *Joseph*,[4] *Joseph*,[3] *John*,[2] *John*[1]), daughter of Samuel and Clarissa (Emery) Gault; married, Nov. 8, 1860; Hiram D. Smith (born Nov. 19, 1827).

Children :

4892 i   CLARA MAY,[9] b. March 31, 1864.
4893 ii   ANNIE FRANCES, b. April 27, 1867.
4894 iii EMERY GAULT, b. Jan. 26, 1869.

2809 IRAD[8] COCHRAN (*Sophia*,[7] *Jacob*,[6] *Joseph*,[5] *Joseph*,[4] *Joseph*,[3] *John*,[2] *John*[1]), son of Norris and Sophia (Emery) Cochran; married Lizzie Pope.

Children :

4895 i   JULIET.[9]
4896 ii IRAD.

2810 ELIZABETH JANE[8] COCHRAN (*Sophia*,[7] *Jacob*,[6] *Joseph*,[5] *Joseph*,[4] *Joseph*,[3] *John*,[2] *John*[1]), daughter of Norris and Sophia (Emery) Cochran; married, Feb. 20, 1859, Horace H. Towne (born Dec. 18, 1828).

Children :

4897 i   DAUGHTER,[9] b. May 16, 1861, in Chicago, Ill.
4898 ii   FRANK EMERY, b. March 4, 1863, in Chicago, Ill.
4899 iii JENNIE COCHRAN, b. Feb. 11, 1867, in Chicago, Ill.
4900 iv   NORRIS COCHRAN, b. July 7, 1869; d. Nov. 2, 1870.
4901 v   SOPHIA ADELIA, b. April 6, 1877, in Oakland, Cal.

2811 HANNAH B.[8] COCHRAN (*Sophia*,[7] *Jacob*,[6] *Joseph*,[5] *Joseph*,[4] *Joseph*,[3] *John*,[2] *John*[1]), daughter of Norris and Sophia (Emery) Cochran; married, Nov. 24, 1859, Alonzo Osgood of Suncook, N. H. (born Aug. 4, 1831).

Child :

4902 i   ELLEN,[9] b. Feb. 23, 1867, in Rockford, Ill.; m. Fred. Carr Lyford.

2812 NORRIS[8] COCHRAN, JR. (*Sophia*,[7] *Jacob*,[6] *Joseph*,[5] *Joseph*,[4] *Joseph*,[3] *John*,[2] *John*[1]), son of Norris and Sophia (Emery) Cochran; married, June 12, 1866, Sarah J. Whitehouse (born Nov. 11, 1843).

Children :

4903   i   LIZZIE SOPHIA,⁹ b. Oct. 24, 1869, in Clarence, Ia.
4904   ii   ANNA MABEL, b. Aug., 1879, in Chicago, Ill.
4905   iii   NORRIS WHITEHOUSE, b. Dec. 3, 1884, in Chicago, Ill.

2814 SARAH H.⁸ COCHRAN (*Sophia,*⁷ *Jacob,*⁶ *Joseph,*⁵ *Joseph,*⁴ *Joseph,*³ *John,*² *John¹*), daughter of Norris and Sophia (Emery) Cochran; married, May 2, 1867, James F. Longmaid (born in Chichester, N. H., April 24, 1835).
Children, born in Pembroke, N. H. :

4906   i   A DAUGHTER,⁹ b. March 3, 1868; d. same day.
4907   ii   A DAUGHTER, b. March 3, 1869; d. same day.
4908   iii   GRACE SOPHIA, b. April 7, 1870.
4909   iv   LIZZY COCHRAN, b. Nov. 30, 1872.
4910   v   ABBY BAILEY, b. Nov. 16, 1874.

2821 CHARLES LONG⁸ EMERY, JR. (*Charles L.,*⁷ *Jacob,*⁶ *Joseph,*⁵ *Joseph,*⁴ *Joseph,*³ *John,*² *John¹*), son of Charles L. and Elizabeth (Watts) Emery; married, Feb. 26, 1878, Sarah L. Ridgeley.
Children :

4911   i   ELMER,⁹ b. Nov. 21, 1880.
4912   ii   SYLVESTER, b. Oct. 30, 1881; d. June 25, 1882.
4913   iii   FRANK R., b. April 15, 1883; d. Aug. 5, 1883.
4914   iv   NORRIS, b. Oct. 7, 1884; d. Jan. 3, 1885.
4915   v   SAMUEL WADE, b. Dec. 31, 1885.

2831 MARY S.⁸ FARNUM (*Elizabeth,*⁷ *Jacob,*⁶ *Joseph,*⁵ *Joseph,*⁴ *Joseph,*³ *John,*² *John¹*), daughter of Rodney M. and Elizabeth (Emery) Farnum; married, April 5, 1866, Earle S. Smith of Manchester, N. H. (born in New Ipswich, N. H., Oct. 12, 1826).
Children :

4916   i   MARY ELIZABETH,⁹ b. Feb. 4, 1867; d. May 10, 1868.
4917   ii   EMERY SEARL, b. Oct. 27, 1868; d. Feb. 15, 1869.
4918   iii   EDGAR EARLE, b. Oct. 16, 1880; d. Jan. 16, 1882.

2832 JOHN E.⁸ FARNUM (*Elizabeth,*⁷ *Jacob,*⁶ *Joseph,*⁵ *Joseph,*⁴ *Joseph,*³ *John,*² *John¹*), son of Rodney M. and Elizabeth (Emery) Farnum; married, July 23, 1879, Minnie L. Knight of Oakland, Cal. Cashier of First National Bank of Pasadena, Los Angeles Co., Cal.
Children :

4919   i   ELSIE ELIZA,⁹ b. Feb. 14, 1881.
4920   ii   EMERY KNIGHT, b. Nov. 16, 1882.
4921   iii   FREDERICK ALLEN, b. Sept. 7, 1887.

2833 NORRIS C.⁸ FARNUM (*Elizabeth,*⁷ *Jacob,*⁶ *Joseph,*⁵ *Joseph,*⁴ *Joseph,*³ *John,*² *John¹*), son of Rodney M. and Elizabeth (Emery) Farnum; married, first, Dec. 22, 1872, Jessie M. Gettings of Washington, D. C. (died April 7, 1883) ; second, April 29, 1886, Rachel Trahern of Stockton, Cal. (born in Washington, D. C., April 9, 1851).
Children :

4922   i   NORRIS C.,⁹ b. Dec. 14, 1874; d. June 25, 1878.
4923   ii   JESSIE M., b. March 23, 1877.

4924 iii RODNEY E , b. Jan. 11, 1879.
4925 iv CLARK G., b. Jan. 27, 1882; d. July 4, 1882.

2837 ELIZABETH JANE[8] EMERY (*Samuel,*[7] *Jacob,*[6] *Joseph,*[5] *Joseph,*[4] *Joseph,*[3] *John,*[2] *John*[1]), daughter of Samuel and Mary G. (Watts) Emery ; married, Dec. 27, 1864, Edward Burrough of Baltimore, Md.

Children :

4926 i SALLIE EMERY,[9] b. Oct. 9, 1865.
4927 ii ELIZABETH JULIET, b. Nov. 13, 1867.
4928 iii EDWARD H., b. Nov. 19, 1870; d. March 25, 1886.
4929 iv FRANK.

2838 MARY JULIET[8] EMERY (*Samuel,*[7] *Jacob,*[6] *Joseph,*[5] *Joseph,*[4] *Joseph,*[3] *John,*[2] *John*[1]), daughter of Samuel and Mary G. (Watts) Emery ; married, June 6, 1865, Horace Burrough of Baltimore, Md.

Children, born in Baltimore, Md. :

4930 i EDWARD EMERY,[9] b. March 6, 1866; d. Dec. 10, 1867.
4931 ii HORACE, b. April 24, 1868.
4932 iii EMERY ARMITAGE, b. Nov. 25, 1871; d. Aug. 24, 1873.
4933 iv IRAD COCHRAN, b. Jan. 5, 1875.

2840 JOHN H.[8] EMERY (*Samuel,*[7] *Jacob,*[6] *Joseph,*[5] *Joseph,*[4] *Joseph,*[3] *John,*[2] *John*[1]), son of Samuel and Mary G. (Watts) Emery ; married, June, 1875, Catharine Trego.

Children :

4934 i JOHN RALPH,[9] b. July 9, 1876.
4935 ii WALLACE.

2845 MATTHEW GAULT[8] EMERY, JR. (*Matthew G.,*[7] *Jacob,*[6] *Joseph,*[5] *Joseph,*[4] *Joseph,*[3] *John,*[2] *John*[1]), son of Matthew G. and his second wife Mary K. (Haseltine) Emery ; married, Sept. 20, 1882, Helen Lawson Simpson of Hudson, N. Y., daughter of Joel T. and Sarah B. Simpson. Graduate of Princeton College, 1879, and the Law Department of Columbian University ; a lawyer of brilliant intellect, thorough education and great ability. He died Oct. 10, 1887.

Child :

4936 i RUTH,[9] b. March 12, 1886, in Washington, D. C.

2846 JULIET H E EMERY (*Matthew G.,*[7] *Jacob,*[6] *Joseph,*[5] *Joseph,*[4] *Joseph,*[3] *John,*[2] *John*[1]), daughter of Matthew G. and his second wife Mary K. (Haseltine) Emery ; married, Oct. 27, 1886, William Van Zandt Cox of Zanesville, O., son of Col. Thomas J. Cox, U. S. Vol.; graduate of Ohio Wesleyan University, 1874 ; admitted to the Bar by Superior Court of Ohio, 1877 ; clerk, Ohio Senate, 1877–78 ; secretary of American Commission to the International Fisheries Exhibition, London, 1883–4 ; financial officer of the Smithsonian Institution at the World's Exposition at New Orleans, 1884–5 ; representative of the Smithsonian Institution at the Industrial Exposition, Minneapolis, 1887, and the Ohio Centennial, Marietta, O., 1888 ; chief clerk, U. S. National Museum, Washington, D. C.

Child :

4937   ı   EMERY,[9] b May 23, 1888, in Washington *

2856 HANNAH MOODY[8] ORDWAY (*Mary,*[7] *Stephen,*[6] *Stephen,*[5] *Stephen,*[4] *Stephen,*[3] *John,*[2] *John*[1]), daughter of David and Mary (Emery) Ordway, married Moses Carr of West Newbury, Mass. Children, born in West Newbury :

4938   ı   HORATIO F ,[9] b. Aug 19, 1825, m R E Flanders, Dec 2, 1849
4939   ıı   MARY E , b Feb 26, 1827, m Albert H. Knight, Sept. 3, 1848
4940   ııı   HARRIET MARIA, b. Nov. 21, 1828, d. same day
4941   ıv   MARY ELIZ , b Jan 19, 1830.
4942   v   HANNAH JANE, b Nov 22, 1831, m E D Chase, July 28, 1853.
4943   vı   MOSES F., b April 16, 1834, m Addie M Smith, April 30, 1865
4944   vıı   CHARLOTTE J , b July 1 1836
4945   vııı   JOHN C , b March 5, 1838, m Mary S. Morse

2858 WARREN[8] ORDWAY (*Mary,*[7] *Stephen,*[6] *Stephen,*[5] *Stephen,*[4] *Stephen,*[3] *John,*[2] *John*[1]), son of David and Mary (Emery) Ordway, married, July 3, 1834, Caroline Greenleaf Foote of Haverhill, Mass. (born Aug. 2, 1811). Shoe manufacturer
Children, born in Bradford, Mass.

4946   ı   GEORGE W ,[9] b May 8, 1835; m , 1st, H M. Richmond, 2nd, Abby A Fiske
4947   ıı   ENOCH FOOTE, b Sept. 21, 1836.
4948   ııı   CAROLINE F , b Dec. 9, 1838; m Walter Everett, Sept 3, 1863
4949   ıv   MARY E , b June 26, 1841, m Major Enoch Carter, April 4, 1864
4950   v   DAVID LEIGHTON, b Aug 5, 1844, d , unm , in Florence, Italy, March 16, 1869
4951   vı   ELLEN B , b Dec 31, 1846; d Nov 14, 1860
4952   vıı   HERBERT I , b Nov. 21, 1851, m Sarah Alice Fitts, June 12, 1878

2859 HANNAH L [8] RAND (*Sarah,*[7] *Stephen,*[6] *Stephen,*[5] *Stephen,*[4] *Stephen,*[3] *John,*[2] *John*[1]), daughter of Richard and Sarah (Emery) Rand, married, March 22, 1827, Jonathan Corliss (died Nov. 9, 1879). She died May 13, 1861.
Children, born in Amesbury, Mass. ·

4953   ı   WILLIAM H ,[9] b March 24, 1828; m Carrie Bede, April 13, 1857, d May 5, 1872
4954   ıı   HANNAH L , b. Sept 8, 1829, d July 5, 1831
4955   ııı   SARAH E , b Aug 24, 1832, d. Feb 9, 1834
4956   ıv   HANNAH L , b Aug 12, 1834, m C T P Wadleigh, June 1, 1851
4957   v   JONATHAN M , b July 16, 1838; d May 28, 1841
4958   vı   SARAH E HANSON, b Feb 19, 1842, m Thomas H Bowman, Nov 21, 1867, d Nov 15, 1868

2860 SARAH E [8] RAND (*Sarah,*[7] *Stephen,*[6] *Stephen,*[5] *Stephen,*[4] *Stephen,*[3] *John,*[2] *John*[1]), daughter of Richard and Sarah (Emery)

*Another child Hazel Van Zandt, son of William Van Zandt and Juliett H (Emery) Cox, born in Washington, D C , Feb 14, 1890

Rand ; married, March 3, 1844, John F. Merrill.   She died April 9, 1873.

Children, born in Haverhill, Mass.:

4959   i   SARAH E.,[9] b. Oct. 31, 1844.
4960   ii   ANN OLIVIA, b. Sept. 18, 1846.
4961   iii GEORGE WARREN, b. Sept. 7, 1848 ; m. Eugenia T. Robinson, April 27, 1876.
4962   iv   MARY E., b. May 26, 1858.
4963   v   FRANK O., b. Nov. 16, 1860.

2861 HANNAH L.[8] EMERY (*Edward,*[7] *Stephen,*[6] *Stephen,*[5] *Stephen,*[4] *Stephen,*[3] *John,*[2] *John*[1]), daughter of Edward and Mrs. Sarah (Quimby) Emery ; married, Nov., 1854, George H. Poor.   She died March 14, 1866.

Child :

4964   i   GEORGE EMERY,[9] b. May 1, 1860.

2863 JEREMIAH[8] PICKARD (*Elizabeth,*[7] *Enoch,*[6] *Stephen,*[5] *Stephen,*[4] *Stephen,*[3] *John,*[2] *John*[1]), son of Jeremiah and Elizabeth (Emery) Pickard ; married, March 7, 1853, Jane E. Parrot ; died Aug. 13, 1864.

Children :

4965   i   JOHN.[9]
4966   ii   SARAH E.
4967   iii JANNETTE A.
4968   iv   FRANCES E.

2864 ENOCH EMERY[8] PICKARD (*Elizabeth,*[7] *Enoch,*[6] *Stephen,*[5] *Stephen,*[4] *Stephen,*[3] *John,*[2] *John*[1]), son of Jeremiah and Elizabeth (Emery) Pickard ; married, Jan. 11, 1848, Mary Jane Small.

Children :

4969   i   JOHN,[9] b. 1849.
4970   ii   JANE, b. 1851.
4971   iii MARY E., b. 1853.
4972   iv   FRANCES H., b. 1854.
4973   v   LOUISA M., b. 1856.
4974   vi   WARREN D., b. 1859.
4975   vii GRACE S., b. 1863.

2865 JOSEPH[8] PICKARD (*Elizabeth,*[7] *Enoch,*[6] *Stephen,*[5] *Stephen,*[4] *Stephen,*[3] *John,*[2] *John*[1]), son of Jeremiah and Elizabeth (Emery) Pickard ; married, Jan. 5, 1853, Lucy M. Towle.

Children :

4976   i   WALTER A.,[9] b. 1853.
4977   ii   GEORGE A., b. 1855.
4978   iii ALVIN N., b. 1857.
4979   iv   CHARLES, b. 1861.

2866 JOHN D.[8] PICKARD (*Elizabeth,*[7] *Enoch,*[6] *Stephen,*[5] *Stephen,*[4] *Stephen,*[3] *John,*[2] *John*[1]), son of Jeremiah and Elizabeth (Emery) Pickard ; married, Jan. 22, 1853, Mary Crowley.   He died July 19, 1872.

Children :

4980   i   JULIA E.,[9] b. 1854.
4981   ii   BERTHA, b. 1862.

4982 iii CHARLES, b. 1865.
4983 iv LILIAN.
4984 v CORA.

2867 ELLIS W.[8] PICKARD (*Elizabeth,*[7] *Enoch,*[6] *Stephen,*[5] *Stephen,*[4] *Stephen,*[3] *John,*[2] *John*[1]), son of Jeremiah and Elizabeth (Emery) Pickard; married, April, 1846, Sarah Glines.
Children:

4985 i ELIZABETH.[9]
4986 ii FRANK O., b. 1848.
4987 iii JANE M., b. 1850.
4988 iv CARRIE, b. 1854.
4989 v NANCY, b. 1856.
4990 vi SUSAN.
4991 vii ETTA.
4992 viii MARY E.
4993 ix CHARLES H.

2868 MEHETABLE D.[8] PICKARD (*Elizabeth,*[7] *Enoch,*[6] *Stephen,*[5] *Stephen,*[4] *Stephen,*[3] *John,*[2] *John*[1]), daughter of Jeremiah and Elizabeth (Emery) Pickard; married, Nov., 1860, True Harvey.
Child:

4994 i EDWIN S.,[9] b. March, 1863.

2876 SUSAN E.[8] FELLOWS (*Sarah,*[7] *Enoch,*[6] *Stephen,*[5] *Stephen,*[4] *Stephen,*[3] *John,*[2] *John*[1]), daughter of Reuben and Susan (Emery) Fellows; married, April 8, 1849, James Dearborn.
Children:

4995 i ALLAH J.,[9] b. 1850.
4996 ii ALVAH J., b. 1851; m. C. Wesley Carter, Jan. 24, 1872.
4997 iii SUSAN, b. 1854.

2879 EDMUND EMERY[8] SMITH (*Hannah,*[7] *Enoch,*[6] *Stephen,*[5] *Stephen,*[4] *Stephen,*[3] *John,*[2] *John*[1]), son of Jacob and Hannah (Emery) Smith; married in Bradford, N. H., Feb., 1838, Elvira Ashby. He died in Detroit, Mich., Aug. 30, 1881.
Children:

4998 i SARAH ADALINE,[9] b. Sept. 6, 1839; m. Frank K. Leach, April 5, 1864.
4999 ii FREEMAN, b. Feb. 8, 1842; d. Jan. 14, 1852.
5000 iii ANGELINE. b. Sept. 30, 1845; d. April 28, 1875.
5001 iv CHARLES E., b. April 29, 1848.
5002 v EMMA J., b. March 19, 1853; m. Spencer Hulbert.
5003 vi FRANK E., b. March 29, 1859.

2881 ABIGAIL[8] SMITH (*Hannah,*[7] *Enoch,*[6] *Stephen,*[5] *Stephen,*[4] *Stephen,*[3] *John,*[2] *John*[1]), daughter of Jacob and Hannah (Emery) Smith; married in Bradford, N. H., May 3, 1838, Dea. Nehemiah Colby (born Feb., 1802; died June 15, 1864).
Children, born in Bradford, N. H. :

5004 i ELLEN MARIA,[9] b. July 12, 1840; m. Col. W. C. Cogswell, March 22, 1860.
5005 ii SARAH M., b. April 1, 1842; m. Dr. P. H. Wheeler, June 5, 1866.
5006 iii HANNAH E., b. Aug. 7, 1845; d. Dec. 3, 1845.

2882 Jacob B.[8] Smith (*Hannah,*[7] *Enoch,*[6] *Stephen,*[5] *Stephen,*[4] *Stephen,*[3] *John,*[2] *John*[1]), son of Jacob and Hannah (Emery) Smith ; married, first, May 1, 1837, Letitia Gregg of New Boston, N. H. (died 1847) ; second, 1849, Mary Ann Parshley (died 1872) ; third, Charlotte Kimball (died 1883). Teacher ; chairman of selectmen of Strafford during the war ; member of the state legislature ; chairman of the board of education ; died in Strafford, Dec. 30, 1888.
Children :

    5007 i   James G.,[9] b. 1841 ; d., unm., 1857.
    5008 ii   Charles B., b. 1843 ; m. Sarah W. Kimball of Dover, 1864.
    5009 iii Letitia Jane G., b. 1847 ; m. Hiram D. Berry, 1870 ; d. 1877.
    5010 iv Mary E , b. 1855 ; m. Frank McDuffee, 1876.
    5011 v   Emma J., b. 1858 ; m. Fred Hurd.

2883 Sarah Emery[8] Smith (*Hannah,*[7] *Enoch,*[6] *Stephen,*[5] *Stephen,*[4] *Stephen,*[3] *John,*[2] *John*[1]), daughter of Jacob and Hannah (Emery) Smith ; married in North Brookfield, Mass., June 10, 1856, Lieut. John Goodson (born in North Carolina, Dec. 15, 1818 ; died in Detroit, Mich., May 8, 1887).
Children :

    5012 i   John Franklin,[9] b. Feb. 14, 1857.
    5013 ii   Abby Bell, b. July 15, 1859 ; d. in Saginaw City, Mich., Feb. 16, 1867.

2887 Charles C.[8] Smith (*Hannah,*[7] *Enoch,*[6] *Stephen,*[5] *Stephen,*[4] *Stephen,*[3] *John,*[2] *John*[1]), son of Jacob and Hannah (Emery) Smith ; graduated at Dartmouth College ; assistant surgeon, 24th Mich. Vol. ; representative in Michigan legislature ; married at Redford, Mich., March 4, 1856, Mary House (born Feb. 28, 1832).
Children, born in Redford, Mich. :

    5014 i   Nellie A.,[9] b. Oct. 5, 1857 ; m. E. L. Small, Sept. 18, 1876.
    5015 ii   Charles Newell, b. Nov. 14, 1859 ; m. Mary Lobdell, June 3, 1886.
    5016 iii Kittie,   } b. Dec. 17, 1862 ; { d. March 27, 1863.
    5017 iv Freddie, }   { d. Aug. 17, 1864.
    5018 v   Elmira Bell, b. April 8, 1865.
    5019 vi Eddie G., b. March, 1872 ; d. Nov. 30, 1873.

2888 Almira P.[8] Smith (*Hannah,*[7] *Enoch,*[6] *Stephen,*[5] *Stephen,*[4] *Stephen,*[3] *John,*[2] *John*[1]), daughter of Jacob and Hannah (Emery) Smith ; married, Sept. 1, 1853, Daniel Fifefield.
Child :

    5020 i   Fannie.[9]

2891 Eliza Ann[8] Emery (*Enoch,*[7] *Enoch,*[6] *Stephen,*[5] *Stephen,*[4] *Stephen,*[3] *John,*[2] *John*[1]), daughter of Enoch and Abigail (Prichard) Emery ; married, June, 1844, Timothy C. Rolfe.
Children :

    5021 i   Timothy Emery,[9] } b. July 17, 1845 ; } m. Jennie Woodward,
    5022 ii   Eliza Jane,   }   } Oct., 1876.
    5023 iii Enoch Emery, b. April 3, 1848.
    5024 iv Henry, b. Jan. 31, 1850.
    5025 v   George, b. Dec. 2, 1851.

5026   vi   MARY LYDIA. b Feb. 17 1854.
5027   vii MARTHA, b June 10, 1857
5028   viii WALTER, b May 24, 1859.

2892 MOSES MOODY[8] EMERY (*Enoch*,[7] *Enoch*,[6] *Stephen*,[5] *Stephen*,[4] *Stephen*,[3] *John*,[2] *John*[1]), son of Enoch and Abigail (Prichard) Emery; married Judith G. Moore.
Children:

5029   i   CHARLES MOODY,[9] b July 24, 1843, m Emma Rachel Robinson, d at Guilford Village, N H , Jan 20, 1885   Teacher in the public schools; graduate of Concord Commercial College; licensed to preach May 29, 1879, became a candidate for ordination Sept. 10, 1879; ordained Sept 26 1879; pastor of the Alton Corner Free Baptist Church from Dec 7, 1879, to Nov 20, 1882, pastor of the Free Will Baptist Church at Guilford Village till his death, clerk of the Belmont quarterly meeting for five years
5030   ii ABBIE, b. March 4, 1846
5031   iii MILLARD FILLMORE, b July 27, 1850

2896 DANIEL[8] EMERY (*Enoch*,[7] *Enoch*[6] *Stephen*,[5] *Stephen*,[4] *Stephen*,[3] *John*,[2] *John*[1]), son of Enoch and Abigail (Prichard) Emery, married, first, Nov. 12, 1856, Mary J. Fuller (died Jan. 19, 1874) ; second, March, 1875, —— Hubbard.
Children:

5032   i   HATTIE ELIZA,[9] b Nov 1, 1858, d Aug , 1875.
5033   ii SARAH FRANCES, b May 31, 1861.

2903 HANNAH[8] EMERY (*Moody*,[7] *Enoch*,[6] *Stephen*,[5] *Stephen*,[4] *Stephen*,[3] *John*,[2] *John*[1]), daughter of Moody and Susan (Whidden) Emery ; married, Dec. 27, 1857, Charles L. French.
Children:

5034   i   GEORGIA H ,[9] b Feb 1, 1861.
5035   ii NELLIE L , b Aug 14, 1864
5036   iii ANDREW T., b. Aug 27, 1866
5037   iv AUGUSTUS H., b July 18, 1873

2904 STEPHEN MOODY[8] EMERY (*Moody*,[7] *Enoch*,[6] *Stephen*,[5] *Stephen*,[4] *Stephen*,[3] *John*,[2] *John*[1]), son of Moody and Sarah (Whidden) Emery ; married, Nov. 26, 1873, Alvira Livingstone.
Child.

5038   i   VINETTA,[9] b Oct 29, 1879

2930 RUFUS[8] EMERY (*Elizabeth*,[7] *Moody*,[6] *Stephen*,[5] *Stephen*,[4] *Stephen*,[3] *John*,[2] *John*[1]), son of Capt. Flavius and Elizabeth (Emery) Emery , married, in Portland, Conn., Nov., 1858, Adelaide Brainerd, daughter of Erastus Brainerd, Esq.   Graduate of Trinity College, Hartford, Conn , 1854 ; instructor in Episcopal Academy, Cheshire, Conn., 1854–55 , tutor in Trinity College, 1855–57 ; studied at Berkeley Divinity School, Middletown, Conn. ; ordained deacon, May 26, 1858 , took charge of Trinity church, Southport, Conn , July 18, 1858 ; admitted to the order of priest, in St. John's church, Stamford, Conn., April 27, 1859 ; resigned the rectorship of Trinity church,

July 31, 1870 ; elected rector of Calvary church, Stonington, Conn.,
March 16, 1871 ; resigned in Sept , 1872 ; elected rector of St. Paul's
church, Newburgh, N. Y , Sept., 1872.　Member of Webster Historical Society, Boston and Newburgh Bay Historical Society ; corresponding member of the Old Colony Historical Society, Taunton,
Mass. , member of Newbury Historical Society, Newbury, Mass.
　　Children, born in Southport, Conn.:

　　　5039　1　　CORINNE BRAINERD,[9] b Jan 22, 1860; d Jan. 25, 1860.
　　　5040　11　ANNIE ELIZABETH, b July 10, 1861, d. Aug 5, 1864.
　　　5041　111　BRAINERD PRESCOTT, b March 25, 1865.

　　2942 ALFRED E.[8] EMERY (*Isaac.[7] Isaac,[6] Benjamin,[5] Stephen,[4] Stephen,[3] John,[2] John[1]*), son of Isaac and Eliza (Eastman) Emery ; married Annie E Stark.
　　Children .

　　　5042　1　　ANNE K ,[9] b Feb. 10, 1866
　　　5043　11　MARY S , b June 12, 1870
　　　5044　111　ARTHUR B , b Oct 12, 1872.

　　2964 WILLIAM SLACK[9] EMERY (*John Moody,[8] Jacob M.,[7] Amos,[6]
Moses,[5] John,[4] John,[3] John,[2] John[1]*), son of John Moody and Rox-
anna (Slack) Emery , married, July 6, 1884, Elizabeth A. Young.
　　Children :

　　　5045　1　　JOHN WARREN,[10] b April 20, 1885
　　　5046　11　WILLIAM EDWARD, b April 25, 1887.

　　2968 WOODWARD[9] EMERY (*James W.,[8] Samuel,[7] John.[6] Moses,[5]
John,[4] John,[3] John,[2] John[1]*), son of James W. and Martha E. (Bell)
Emery ; married, Dec. 5, 1878, Ann P. Jones.
　　Children :

　　　5047　1　　ARTHUR WOODWARD,[10] b Nov 16, 1879, d. Oct. 5, 1880.
　　　5048　11　FREDERICK INGERSOL, b. July 27, 1881

　　2969 MANNING[9] EMERY (*James W.,[8] Samuel,[7] John,[6] Moses,[5]
John,[4] John,[3] John,[2] John[1]*), son of James W. and Martha E. (Bell)
Emery , married, Aug. 3, 1875, Maria Haven Ladd (born April 1,
1848), daughter of Alexander H and Elizabeth W. (Jones) Ladd.
He was a soldier in Co. " K," 44th Mass. Inf.
　　Children .

　　　5049　1　　ELIZABETH LADD,[10] b. June 7, 1876, in Portsmouth, N. H.
　　　5050　11　MANNING, JR., b. Aug 7, 1878, in Cambridge, Mass
　　　5051　111　RUTH, b June 7, 1880, in Cambridge, Mass.

　　2970 CAROLINE BELL[9] EMERY (*James W.,[8] Samuel,[7] John,[6] Mo-
ses,[5] John,[4] John,[3] John,[2] John[1]*), daughter of James W. and Martha
E. (Bell) Emery ; married, June 4, 1867, Edwin Farnham.
　　Children :

　　　5052　1　　EDWIN EMERY,[10] b July 31. 1868
　　　5053　11　LYDIA RAGUET, b. Sept. 22, 1869
　　　5054　111　BENJAMIN ARMSTRONG, b Nov., 1870, d Dec 25, 1875.
　　　5055　1v　SON, b. 1871; d in infancy.

2975 CHARLES CARROLL[9] EMERY (*Moses,*[8] *Moses,*[7] *Moses,*[6] *Moses,*[5] *John,*[4] *John,*[3] *John,*[2] *John*[1]), son of Moses and Sarah Cutts (Thornton) Emery; married, Sept. 9, 1857, Anna Caldwell.
Children, born in Lawrence, Kan.:

    5056 i   JOHN CARROLL,[10] b. Jan. 16, 1860.
    5057 ii   FRANK WOODWARD, b. April 24, 1863.
    5058 iii EUGENE THORNTON, b. Jan. 9, 1866.

2980 CLARISSA[9] SOULE (*Susan,*[8] *Moses,*[7] *Moses,*[6] *Moses,*[5] *John,*[4] *John,*[3] *John,*[2] *John*[1]), daughter of Asa and Susan (Emery) Soule; married, first, Sept. 3, 1838, Samuel S. Luke, of Portland, Me. (died in Cuba, Feb. 22, 1841); second, July 9, 1843, Rev. John Gierlow, Ph.D. (born in Copenhagen, Denmark); teacher of languages; ordained to the priesthood of the Protestant Episcopal Church, 1858, in La Grange, Tex.
Children:

    5059 i   LAURIN LOUISA,[10] b. Oct. 8, 1839; m. S. F. King, at Gold Hull, Nev.
    5060 ii   JOHN CHRISTIAN, b. March 16, 1844; d. Oct. 2, 1848.
    5061 iii CIDLI, b. Feb. 23, 1846; d. Jan. 15, 1847.
    5062 iv META, b. Feb. 17, 1848.
    5063 v   MINNA, b. Aug. 23, 1850; d. Feb. 8, 1852.
    5064 vi EDWARD H., b. June 8, 1854; d. Dec. 4, 1855.

2981 PERSIS[9] SOULE (*Susan,*[8] *Moses,*[7] *Moses,*[6] *Moses,*[5] *John,*[4] *John,*[3] *John,*[2] *John*[1]), daughter of Asa and Susan (Emery) Soule; married Barak E. Matthews (died Feb. 5, 1884).
Children:

    5065 i   DAVID T.,[10] b. March 20, 1846; d. June 2, 1846.
    5066 ii   SARAH, b. Sept. 3, 1847; d. Sept. 5, 1847.
    5067 iii ELLA E., b. Sept. 10, 1848; m. C. A. Tripp, Aug. 29, 1870.
    5068 iv IMOGENE, b. Feb. 5, 1852; d. Feb. 6, 1880.
    5069 v   CAROLINE J., b. Aug. 24, 1854; d. April 3, 1864.
    5070 vi MARY E., b. Dec. 10, 1858; d. March 7, 1859.
    5071 vii MELVILLE L., b. Oct. 6, 1861.

2982 MARIA L.[9] SOULE (*Susan,*[8] *Moses,*[7] *Moses,*[6] *Moses,*[5] *John,*[4] *John,*[3] *John,*[2] *John*[1]), daughter of Asa and Susan (Emery) Soule; married by Rev. Moses Emery, her grandfather, in Minot, Me., July 27, 1845, to Rev. F.A. Crafts.
Children:

    5072 i   FREDERICK HENRY,[10] b. Sept. 12, 1846; m. Blanch E. Bowes, Nov. 24, 1881.
    5073 ii   WILBUR FISK, b. Jan. 12, 1850; m. Sarah J. Timanus, May 1, 1874.
    5074 iii ALBERT B., b. Sept. 4, 1851; m. Jennie Louisa Blake, Oct. 1, 1881.
    5075 iv GEORGE EMERY, b. Aug. 18, 1858; m. Rose R. Carter, Nov. 27, 1882.
    5076 v   ADDIE LOUISA, b. Sept. 17, 1860; m. Alfred E. Barr, Sept. 17, 1883.

2984 JULIA[9] LAPHAM (*Abigail,*[8] *Moses,*[7] *Moses,*[6] *Moses,*[5] *John,*[4] *John,*[3] *John,*[2] *John*[1]), daughter of Abial and Abigail (Emery) Lapham; married, March 8, 1841, George Campbell.

Children :

5077 i   ELLEN M.,[10] b July 5, 1842; m Edmond Barker, Feb 24, 1863.
5078 ii SEWALL M , b March 29. 1845, d July 8, 1875
5079 iii GEORGE F , b Nov 27, 1848, d Aug 6, 1867.
5080 iv FRED E , b Aug 21, 1855, m Edna Record, Nov 18, 1876.
5081 v   WILLARD L , b Jun 8, 1862; m. Pollie Cole, May 1, 1883
5082 vi HATTIE M., b May 20, 1864, m Sumner Foss, May 15, 1886.

2985 DAVID[9] LAPHAM (*Abigail*,[8] *Moses*,[7] *Moses*,[6] *Moses*,[5] *John*,[4] *John*,[3] *John*,[2] *John*[1]), son of Abial and Abigail (Emery) Lapham; married, first, in Boston, Mass , Dec. 21, 1853, Elizabeth W. Whitehouse; second, in Anoka, Minn , Oct. 24, 1867, Judith Coleman. He died Sept 30, 1880, aged 80.

Children, born in Anoka, Minn :

5083 i   FRANK M ,[10] b Oct 2, 1854
5084 ii NELLIE J , b Jan 18, 1859
5085 iii FRED S , b Feb 3, 1863
5086 iv VICTOR M , b March 16, 1869.
5087 v   BERTIE A , b Jan., 1874.

2986 GEORGE[9] LAPHAM (*Abigail*,[8] *Moses*,[7] *Moses*,[6] *Moses*,[5] *John*,[4] *John*,[3] *John*,[2] *John*[1]), son of Abial and Abigail (Emery) Lapham; married, in Minneapolis, Minn , 1866, Sarah Cates.

Children, born in Anoka, Minn.:

5088 i   HARRY,[10] b. Oct 16, 1867
5089 ii EVA, b April, 1871.

2987 ELIZA ANN[8] LAPHAM (*Eunice*,[7] *Moses*,[6] *Moses*,[5] *Moses*,[4] *John*,[3] *John*[2] *John*[1]), daughter of David and Eunice (Emery) Lapham; married, Feb. 2, 1848. George Thomas Gould (died Feb. 8, 1852).

Child .

5090 i   GEORGE MILBURY,[9] b Nov. 8, 1848. Physician, Philadelphia, Pa. Author.

3002 CHARLES[9] HAMLIN (*Sarah J.*,[8] *Stephen*,[7] *Moses*,[6] *Moses*,[5] *John*.[4] *John*,[3] *John*,[2] *John*[1]), son of Hon. Hannibal and Sarah J. (Emery) Hamlin; married, Nov 28, 1860, Sarah Purington Thompson , served during the war of the Rebellion and left the service Brevet Brigadier General. Representative in Maine Legislature ; speaker of the House ; Commissioner of Bankruptcy. Lawyer.

Children .

5091 i   CHARLES E ,[10] b Oct. 11, 1861.
5092 ii ADDISON, b March 30, 1863.
5093 iii CYRUS, b Aug 18, 1869
5094 iv EDWIN T , b June 6, 1872.

3004 SARAH J [9] HAMLIN (*Sarah J*,[8] *Stephen*,[7] *Moses*,[6] *Moses*,[5] *John*,[4] *John*,[3] *John*,[2] *John*[1]), daughter of Hon. Hannibal and Sarah J. (Emery) Hamlin; married George A. Batchelder , died June 28, 1878.

Child ·

5095 i   ARTHUR.[10]

3011 JEANNIE EMERY[9] BUTLER (*Jennett,*[8] *Stephen,*[7] *Moses,*[6] *Moses,*[5] *John,*[4] *John,*[3] *John,*[2] *John*[1]), daughter of Rev. Nathaniel and Jennett (Emery) Butler; married, Jan. 21, 1874, George F. Wood, of Camden, Me.

Children:

  5096 i   FREDERICK TAYLOR,[10] b. Dec. 19, 1874.
  5097 ii ERNEST HOSMER, b. Sept. 3, 1887.

3012 NATHANIEL[9] BUTLER, JR. (*Jennett,*[8] *Stephen,*[7] *Moses,*[6] *Moses,*[5] *John,*[4] *John,*[3] *John,*[2] *John*[1]), son of Rev. Nathaniel and Jennett (Emery) Butler; married at Highland Park, Ill., April 28, 1881, Florence R. Sheppard (born in Chicago, July 19, 1861). Graduate of Colby University, Waterville, Me., 1873; Principal of Highland College for Women, Highland Park, Ill., 1884; Professor of English Literature in the University of Chicago and of Latin in the University of Illinois, Champaign, Ill.

Children:

  5098 i   SHEPPARD EMERY,[10] b. July 9, 1883.
  5099 ii ALBERT NATHANIEL, b. Jan. 16, 1888.

3022 JOSHUA M.[9] MERRICK (*Elizabeth,*[8] *Moses,*[7] *Josiah,*[6] *Moses,*[5] *John,*[4] *John,*[3] *John,*[2] *John*[1]), son of Joshua and Elizabeth (Emery) Merrick; married, April 1, 1847, Abigail B. Morrison.

Children:

  5100 i   HORACE B.,[10] b. May 10, 1849; d. in San Francisco, Cal., March 9, 1872.
  5101 ii ELIZA E., b. Sept. 13, 1856; d. in Boston, Nov. 3, 1877.

3023 MARTHA[9] EMERY(*Woodman,*[8] *Moses,*[7] *Josiah,*[6] *Moses,*[5] *John,*[4] *John,*[3] *John,*[2] *John*[1]), daughter of Woodman and Fanny (Taylor) Emery; married, Dec. 22, 1859, Jonathan Jenkins of Madbury, N. H.

Children:

  5102 i   MELVIN,[10] b., 1860; d. Jan. 20, 1864.
  5103 ii HORACE W., b. Feb. 8, 1864.
  5104 iii HERBERT T., b. Feb. 13, 1867.

3025 JOHN W.[9] EMERY (*Woodman,*[8] *Moses,*[7] *Josiah,*[6] *Moses,*[5] *John,*[4] *John,*[3] *John,*[2] *John*[1]), son of Woodman and Fanny (Taylor) Emery; married, March 24, 1864, Eveline F. Pinkham of Madbury.

Child:

  5105 i   FANNY T.,[10] b. July 17, 1865.

3032 MARY C.[9] EMERY (*Josiah,*[8] *Nathan,*[7] *Josiah,*[6] *Moses,*[5] *John,*[4] *John,*[3] *John,*[2] *John*[1]), daughter of Josiah and Julia Ann (Beecher) Emery; married, first, Dec. 27, 1854, J. M. Ruckman; second, June 6, 1865, G. S. Ransom of Williamsport, Pa., Principal of Wellsboro Academy; teacher of Mathematics in Huntsville Female Seminary, Huntsville, Ala.; at the beginning of the war returned north.

Children:

  5106 i   ANNIE EMERY,[10] b. April 23, 1856; d., in Ala., Nov. 16, 1860.
  5107 ii WILLIAM E., b. Feb. 12, 1869.

3033 Charles D.[9] Emery (*Josiah*,[8] *Nathan*,[7] *Josiah*,[6] *Moses*,[5] *John*,[4] *John*,[3] *John*,[2] *John*[1]), son of Josiah and Julia Ann (Beecher) Emery, studied law; admitted to the Bar in Williamsport, Pa.; married, March 18, 1858, Lavinia D. Evans of Philadelphia. Acting Consul at Callao, S. A. He died at Seattle, Washington Territory, April 26, 1881.

Children, born in Williamsport :

    5108   i   Rachel Evans,[10] b. June 16, 1859.
    5109   ii   Mary Ruckman, b Nov 1, 1861; m James D. Lowman of
                   Seattle
    5110   iii David Evans, b June 20, 1864.
    5111   iv   Fanny Evans, b Jan 1, 1867

3035 Eva Vanderbilt[9] Emery (*Josiah*,[8] *Nathan*,[7] *Josiah*,[6] *Moses*.[5] *John*,[4] *John*,[3] *John*,[2] *John*[1]), daughter of Josiah and Julia Ann (Beecher) Emery, married, Dec 26, 1861, Rev. E. J. Gray, D D., President of Dickinson Seminary, Williamsport, Pa.

Children :

    5112   i   William E. [10] b Feb 7, 1863, in Lewisburgh, Pa
    5113   ii   Edith, b Dec 15, 1870, in Frostburgh Md , d young.
    5114   iii Grace b May 6, 1873 in Baltimore, Md., d. June 29, 1873.
    5115   iv   Eva C., b July 29, 1876, in Williamsport, Pa
    5116   v   Edward P , b July 16, 1877, in Williamsport, Pa

3036 Elizabeth[9] Emery (*Josiah*,[8] *Nathan*,[7] *Josiah*,[6] *Moses*,[5] *John*,[4] *John*,[3] *John*,[2] *John*[1]), daughter of Josiah and Julia Ann (Beecher) Emery; graduate of Dickinson Seminary; married, Feb. 10, 1863, Joshua A. Knapp (born Jan., 1837 ; died at Emporium, Pa , May 7, 1869). Mrs. Knapp, in 1880, went as missionary to the Indians under the auspices of the Episcopal Church and became Principal of Hope School, Springfield, Dakota.

Children, born at Emporium :

    5117   i   Anson D.,[10] b Aug 12, 1865
    5118   ii   Joshua A., b. Nov 9, 1868, d Aug 12, 1869.

3037 John Beecher[9] Emery (*Josiah*,[8] *Nathan*,[7] *Josiah*,[6] *Moses*,[5] *John*,[4] *John*,[3] *John*,[2] *John*[1]), son of Josiah and Julia Ann (Beecher) Emery ; married, Sept. 30, 1868, Helen A. Otto of Williamsport, Pa. (born in Reading. Pa., March 1, 1846). He enlisted in Co. "I," 45th Pa Vols ; was in the battles of Innes Island, Hilton Head, S C., in the Army of the Potomac at the second battle of Bull Run, at South Mountain and Antietam ; promoted Corporal for meritorious conduct at Antietam , in all the engagements of Bermuda, 9th Corps , in operations in Kentucky, Mississippi, and later in the Army of the Potomac from Cold Harbor to Petersburg ; captured Dec. 14, 1863, at Flat Gap, Clinch Mt , E. Tenn ; in prison at Belle Isle, Richmond, from Jan 14, 1863, to April 2, 1864 , returned on release and remained with the Army of the Potomac till Dec. 3, 1864 ; declined commission of 1st Lieut , Co. "G," 45th Reg. Vols , Dec , 1863   Clerk in Northern Central R. R Office ; Superintendent and General Manager of West Branch Lumber Co. ; solicitor for Penn. R. R.

Children, born in Williamsport :

5119 i FRANK OTTO,[10] b. Aug. 24, 1869.
5120 ii JULIA, b June 15, 1872.

3038 WILLIAM V [9] EMERY (*Josiah*,[8] *Nathan*,[7] *Josiah*,[6] *Moses*,[5] *John*,[4] *John*,[3] *John*,[2] *John*[1]), son of Josiah and Julia Ann (Beecher) Emery; married Emily J. Leas, daughter of E B. Leas. Engaged in the Bellefont Nail Works.
Children, born in Williamsport.

5121 i WILLIAM LEAS,[10] b. June 30, 1874
5122 ii MARY STEWART, b April 20, 1880

3039 CLARA BEECHER[9] EMERY (*Josiah*,[8] *Nathan*,[7] *Josiah*,[6] *Moses*,[5] *John*,[4] *John*,[3] *John*,[2] *John*[1]), daughter of Josiah and Julia Ann (Beecher) Emery: married, May 13, 1879, John H. Price, jr., of Westport, Pa. He died June 7, 1884

Child :

5123 i CLARENCE EMERY,[10] b May 31, 1884

3043 ELIZABETH EMERY[9] WEBSTER (*Nancy*,[8] *Nathan*,[7] *Josiah*,[6] *Moses*,[5] *John*,[4] *John*,[3] *John*,[2] *John*[1]), daughter of Freeman and Nancy (Emery) Webster, married, Aug. 8, 1876, Fred. Wm. Widmer (born Aug 22, 1838).
Children.

5124 i ALICE WEBSTER,[10] b May 18. 1877, d Oct 2, 1881
5125 ii MARY ETIZ, b Sept 13, 1878; d Nov. 9, 1878
5126 iii FRED EMERY, b Jan 24, 1880.
5127 iv JAMIE, b May 9, 1881, d June 18, 1881.
5128 v EDITH WEBSTER, b Nov 1, 1884

3044 CLARA[9] WEBSTER (*Nancy*,[8] *Nathan*,[7] *Josiah*,[6] *Moses*.[5] *John*,[4] *John*,[3] *John*,[2] *John*[1]), daughter of Freeman and Nancy (Emery) Webster : married, Aug. 13, 1872, Lewis E. Hastings.
Children :

5129 i MARION WEBSTER,[10] b. Aug 25, 1873.
5130 ii MAY E , } b. Oct. 25, 1877.
5131 iii PAUL E , }

3053 BETSEY McC.[9] EMERY (*Joseph W.*,[8] *Nathan*.[7] *Josiah*,[6] *Moses*,[5] *John*,[4] *John*,[3] *John*,[2] *John*[1]), daughter of Joseph W and Frances R. (Leland) Emery, married, April, 1871, Henry S. Balcom (born in Watertown, N Y., April 28, 1847).
Children :

5132 i MARY L.,[10] b March, 1872
5133 ii GEORGE W , b Jan , 1874.
5134 iii WILLIAM T , b 1875.
5135 iv FLORA L , b Jan , 1877
5136 v LUCY E , b Nov 10, 1878
5137 vi NELLIE T., b. Aug 17, 1880.
5138 vii TENIE S., b. Dec. 3, 1881.
5139 viii ELLA M , b. Dec 18, 1888

3055 CHARLES W.[9] EMERY (*Joseph W.*,[8] *Nathan*,[7] *Josiah*,[6] *Moses*,[5]

16

John,[4] *John*,[3] *John*,[2] *John*[1]), son of Joseph W. and Frances R. (Leland) Emery ; graduate of Pennacook Academy, Fisherville, N. H., 1871 ; Dartmouth College, 1875 ; studied law in Concord, N. H. ; married in Canterbury, N. H., Feb. 27, 1883, Caroline Elizabeth Foster (born in Providence, R. I., Oct. 16, 1848).

Child :

5140 i NATHAN,[10] b. Dec. 9, 1883 ; d. Feb. 28, 1885, in Canterbury, N. H.

3056 CLARENCE F.[9] EMERY (*Joseph W.*,[8] *Nathan*,[7] *Josiah*,[6] *Moses*,[5] *John*,[4] *John*,[3] *John*,[2] *John*[1]), son of Joseph W. and his second wife Frances Ann (Sanborn) Emery ; married, Aug. 22, 1880, Eleanor Mowlin (born in Dearborn Co., Ill., Aug. 4, 1863).

Children, born in Austin, Ill. :

5141 i ALVIN,[10] b. June 27, 1881.
5142 ii LEWIS, b. Sept. 18, 1882.
5143 iii MAY, b. Jan. 22, 1884.
5144 iv WALTER, b. Oct. 17, 1885.
5145 v EMMA, b. Nov. 27, 1886 ; d. Aug. 9, 1887.
5146 vi INFANT SON, b. June 12, 1888 ; d. June 15, 1888.
5147 vii INFANT SON, b. June 2, 1889.

3206 STEPHEN EMERY[8] WELCH (*Hannah*,[7] *Forest*,[6] *Samuel*,[5] *Samuel*,[4] *Rev. Samuel*,[3] *John*,[2] *John*[1]), son of Jotham and Hannah (Emery) Welch ; married in Boothbay, Me., 1861, Octavia E. Lane.

Five children, Nos. 5148–5152.

5148 i ADDIE,[9] drowned in Boothbay Harbor, Me. ; aged 19.
5149 ii EDITH M.
5150 iii LEWIS EMERY.

3207 MARY[8] WELCH (*Hannah*,[7] *Forest*,[6] *Samuel*,[5] *Samuel*,[4] *Rev. Samuel*,[3] *John*,[2] *John*[1]), daughter of Jotham and Hannah (Emery) Welch ; married C. W. Tripp.

Children :

5153 i LOUISA JANE,[9] b. Oct. 19, 1862 ; d. Sept. 12, 1887.
5154 ii NETTIE PEARL, b. Oct. 29, 1868 ; d. Sept. 30, 1877.

3208 ANN E.[8] WELCH (*Hannah*,[7] *Forest*,[6] *Samuel*,[5] *Samuel*,[4] *Rev. Samuel*,[3] *John*,[2] *John*[1]), daughter of Jotham and Hannah (Emery) Welch ; married Hiram S. Pinkham.

Children :

5155 i BURK LESLIE,[9] b. May 20, 1868 ; d. March 8, 1871.
5156 ii EDITH PEARL, b. Jan. 28, 1872 ; m., June 6, 1889, Marriner Card, of Clinton, Mass.
5157 iii ERNEST LEROY, b. Aug. 22, 1875.

3214 JAMES[8] EMERY (*Stephen*,[7] *Forest*,[6] *Samuel*,[5] *Samuel*,[4] *Rev. Samuel*,[3] *John*,[2] *John*[1]), son of Stephen and Keziah (Eaton) Emery ; married, first, Sarah Jenkins of Kittery ; second, Nellie Moore of Portsmouth, N. H.

Children, by first wife :

5158 i   LOUIE M.⁹
5159 ii   STEPHEN N.

By second wife:

5160 iii WINNIFRED E.
5161 iv   ISADORE F.
5162 v   LOUIE M.

3215 AFFA E.⁸ EMERY (*Stephen*,⁷ *Forest*,⁶ *Samuel*,⁵ *Samuel*,⁴ *Rev. Samuel*,³ *John*,² *John*¹), daughter of Stephen and his second wife Olive (Eaton) Emery; married Joseph Blaisdell of York.
Child:

5163 i   IDA F.⁹

3218 NOAH⁸ EMERY (*Stephen*,⁷ *Forest*,⁶ *Samuel*,⁵ *Samuel*,⁴ *Rev. Samuel*,³ *John*,² *John*¹), son of Stephen and second wife Olive (Eaton) Emery; married Abbie E. Faye.
Children:

5164 i   CHESTER H.,⁹ b. March 7, 1869.
5165 ii   CHARLES H., b. Oct. 26, 1870.
5166 iii   CORA O., b. Feb. 8, 1873.
5167 iv   JOSEPH E., b. July 17, 1875.
5168 v   MILLARD G., b. Feb. 20, 1878.
5169 vi   LOUIE M., b. May 1, 1880.
5170 vii   WILLARD M., b. March 18, 1882.
5171 viii ANNIE B., b. Aug. 1, 1884.

3219 OSCAR L.⁸ EMERY (*Stephen*,⁷ *Forest*,⁶ *Samuel*,⁵ *Samuel*,⁴ *Rev. Samuel*,³ *John*,² *John*¹), son of Stephen and his second wife Olive (Eaton) Emery; married, Dec. 31, 1870, Josie E. Hayden of Lanesville, Mass.
Children:

5172 i   OSCAR L.,⁹ b. Nov. 27, 1871.
5173 ii   WILLIE H., b. Feb. 1, 1874.
5174 iii   JENNIE D., b. March 3, 1877.
5175 iv   JOSIE E., b. Aug. 30, 1879.
5176 v   BLANCHARD M., b. May 2, 1882.
5177 vi   STEPHEN E., b. Feb. 7, 1886.

3220 KEZIAH⁸ EMERY (*Stephen*,⁷ *Forest*,⁶ *Samuel*,⁵ *Samuel*,⁴ *Rev. Samuel*,³ *John*,² *John*¹), daughter of Stephen and his second wife Olive (Eaton) Emery; married John Parrott of Kittery, Me.
Children:

5178 i   BERTIE.⁹
5179 ii   CHILD, d. young.

3221 FOREST H.⁸ EMERY (*Stephen*,⁷ *Forest*,⁶ *Samuel*,⁵ *Samuel*,⁴ *Rev. Samuel*,³ *John*,² *John*¹), son of Stephen and his second wife Olive (Eaton) Emery; married, June 1, 1880, Nellie L. Emery of Brockton, Mass., daughter of John and Mary E. (Hobart) Emery.
Child:

5180 i   LEROY FOREST,⁹ b. Oct. 2, 1883.

3225 JOHN ANSON[8] EMERY(*John*[7], *Stephen,*[6] *John,*[5] *Rev. Stephen,*[4] *Rev. Samuel,*[3] *John,*[2] *John*[1]), son of John and Almira (Harding) Emery; married, Oct. 15, 1872, Mary T. Morrison of Alleghany City, Pa. Graduate of Amherst College, 1869.

Children :

5181　i　HANNAH GRAY,[9] b. March 2, 1876.
5182　ii　JOHN ANSON, b. May 16, 1877.

3228 RUFUS[8] EMERY (*John,*[7] *Stephen,*[6] *John,*[5] *Rev. Stephen,*[4] *Rev. Samuel,*[3] *John,*[2] *John*[1]), son of John and Almira (Harding) Emery; married, in 1866, Roxanna Cook of Provincetown, Mass.

Children :

5183　i　RUFUS FRANKLIN,[9] b. Sept. 27, 1869.
5184　ii　IDA NOYES, b. June, 1872.

3234 GEORGE NEWELL[8] EMERY (*Stephen,*[7] *Stephen,*[6] *John,*[5] *Rev. Stephen,*[4] *Rev. Samuel,*[3] *John,*[2] *John*[1]), son of Stephen and Rebecca T. (Harding) Emery; married, April 9, 1864, Phœbe W. Rogers of Chatham.

Children :

5185　i　WINNIFRED NEWELL,[9] b. June 11, 1866.
5186　ii　MARY WILMAN, b. July 17, 1876.

3254 MARCELIA[8] EMERY (*Joseph,*[7] *Samuel,*[6] *John,*[5] *Rev. Stephen,*[4] *Rev. Samuel,*[3] *John,*[2] *John*[1]), daughter of Joseph and Martha (Harding) Emery; married, Oct. 3, 1859, George H. Wiggin.

Children :

5187　i　LOIS H.,[9] b. Dec. 10, 1860, in Philadelphia, Pa.
5188　ii　ELLA F., b. Feb. 5, 1863, in Chelsea, Mass.
5189　iii　JESSIE E., b. Sept. 20, 1869, in Somerville, Mass.

3256 BENJ. OSGOOD[8] EMERY (*Joseph,*[7] *Stephen,*[6] *John,*[5] *Rev. Stephen,*[4] *Rev. Samuel,*[3] *John,*[2] *John*[1]), son of Joseph and Martha (Harding) Emery; married, June 27, 1867, Emma Daggett. He died in Boston, May 24, 1888.

Child :

5190　i　FLORENCE MAY,[9] b. Oct. 9, 1872; d. April 17, 1873.

3286 ELIZA YOUNG[8] EMERY (*Samuel,*[7] *John,*[6] *John,*[5] *Joshua,*[4] *John,*[3] *Jonathan,*[2] *John*[1]), daughter of Samuel and Elizabeth Wolfe (Young) Emery; married, Jan., 1841, H. M. Weed (died May 10, 1867).

Five children, Nos. 5191–5195.

5191　i　EDGAR EMERY.

3287 RUBY M.[8] EMERY (*Samuel,*[7] *John,*[6] *John,*[5] *Joshua,*[4] *John,*[3] *Jonathan,*[2] *John*[1]), daughter of Samuel and Elizabeth Wolfe (Young) Emery; married, first, in Tivoli, Ill., April 7, 1847, Dr. M. B. Vanpetten (died Jan. 6, 1871, in Farmington, Ill.); second, in Peoria, Ill., June 23, 1882, William Stevenson (born July 28, 1817, in Hannibal, N. Y.).

Children, born in Tivoli, Ill. :

5196　i　ELIZ. Y.,[9] b. Feb. 9. 1848; m. George Robinson.
5197　ii　S. EMERY, b. Dec. 2, 1849; m. Carrie Waughop; d. Nov. 13, 1877.
5198　iii　JOHN B., b. Aug. 6, 1852; m. Nancy A. Buchanan, Nov. 4, 1876.
5199　iv　MATTHEW B., b. May 4, 1854; m. Jennie Buchanan, Aug. 18, 1875.
5200　v　MARY J., b. June 27, 1856; m. B. Frank Traxler, Nov. 1, 1877.
5201　vi　RUBY M., b. Sept. 6, 1859; m. James W. Henry, May 24, 1880.
5202　vii　EDWIN M., b. Feb. 17, 1863; m. Lulu D. Young, Aug. 31, 1887.
5203　viii　PRINCE, b. Nov. 11, 1865.

3288 SAMUEL B.[8] EMERY (*Samuel*,[7] *John*,[6] *John*,[5] *Joshua*,[4] *John*,[3] *Jonathan*,[2] *John*[1]), son of Samuel and Elizabeth Wolfe (Young) Emery; married, in Tivoli, Ill., Dec. 25, 1845, Sarah E. Parkhurst. Children, born in Tivoli, Ill. :

5204　i　JOSEPHINE,[9] b. Nov. 2, 1846; m. Walker N. Hitchcock, Sept. 30, 1868; d. March 28, 1874.
5205　ii　ANN ABIAH, b. Sept. 24, 1855; m. W. J. Smith, Feb. 8, 1875; d. May 4, 1877.
5206　iii　SAMUEL, b. July 8, 1860; d. April 9, 1861.
5207　iv　LAVINIA G., b. June 22, 1862; m. Henry L. Young, Dec. 23, 1886.
5208　v　NELLIE YOUNG, b. Jan. 21, 1866; d. Nov. 20, 1881.

3289 EMELINE B.[8] EMERY (*Rev. Richard*,[7] *John*,[6] *John*,[5] *Joshua*,[4] *John*,[3] *Jonathan*,[2] *John*[1]), daughter of Rev. Richard and Betsey (Harding) Emery; married, April 7, 1840, Charles Marston of Orford, N. H.

Children :

5209　i　ELLEN,[9] b. Jan. 10, 1841.
5210　ii　JEREMIAH, b. Aug. 17, 1846; m. Ida Williams, Aug. 29, 1877.
5211　iii　LIZZIE, b. June 6, 1848; m. William Clark, Sept. 27, 1871.

3292 ABIGAIL WEBSTER[8] MATHER (*Abigail*,[7] *Joshua*,[6] *John*,[5] *Joshua*,[4] *John*,[3] *Jonathan*,[2] *John*[1]), daughter of John and Abigail (Emery) Mather; married Calvin Royce ; died Oct. 4, 1889.

Children :

5212　i　HORACE MATHER,[9] b. Sept. 4, 1828; m. Fanny Emerson, July 14, 1866.
5213　ii　WILLIAM WEBSTER, b. Jan. 5, 1831; m. Alice Sturtevant, Feb. 1, 1882.
5214　iii　CAMILLA ABIGAIL, b. Aug. 14, 1833; m. Gardner Walker, June 26, 1853.
5215　iv　PHŒBE MATHER, b. April 2, 1836; m. John Fortune, July 8, 1863.
5216　v　MARY CYNTHIA, b. Oct. 14, 1840; d. Feb. 5, 1842.
5217　vi　CAROLINE RUTH, b. March 12, 1843; m. Parker Torrance, April 5, 1865.
5218　vii　CORDELIA ELLEN, b. March 14, 1847; m. Edward Mather, Oct. 1, 1884.

3294 ISRAEL[8] MATHER (*Abigail*,[7] *Joshua*,[6] *John*,[5] *Joshua*,[4] *John*,[3] *Jonathan*,[2] *John*[1]), son of John and Abigail (Emery) Mather; married, first, in Essex, N. Y., Jan. 1, 1830, Phœbe, daughter of Polly

Emery and Jonathan Royce; second, in Napierville, DuPage Co., Ill., Hannah, sister of his first wife.   He died April 2, 1866.
Children:

5219   i   ADELINE ELIZA,[9] b. Aug. 5, 1837; m. E. B. McKinney.
5320   ii   MARY, b. May 6, 1839; m. Fred Chambers, May 6, 1875.
5221   iii   JOHN DEWITT, b. Feb. 17, 1841; m. Ella S. Warne, Nov. 1, 1865.
5222   iv   PHŒBE H., b. Oct. 26, 1842; m. C. A. Porter, Nov. 14, 1872.
5223   v   EMERY CLINTON, b. Feb. 14, 1845; m. Mary Jane Monk, Jan. 1, 1868.
5224   vi   SARAH MARIA, b. June 24, 1847; m. George Roberts, Dec., 1880.
5225   vii   JONATHAN ROYCE, b. Oct. 9, 1849; m. Nellie Ketcham.
5226   viii CAROLINE J. EMMA, b. May 15, 1852.
5227   ix   JESSIE BENTON FREMONT, b. April 9, 1856; m. George Colman, Aug., 1883.
5228   x   MARTHA ELIZ., b. March 28, 1859; m. J. Montague, Feb. 6, 1880.

3295 JOSHUA   EMERY[8] MATHER (*Abigail,*[7] *Joshua,*[6] *John,*[5] *Joshua,*[4] *John,*[3] *Jonathan,*[2] *John*[1]), son of John and Abigail (Emery) Mather; married Maria Frisbee.
Children:

5229   i   SARAH ABIGAIL,[9] m. Jonathan Royce.
5230   ii   JAMES J.
5231   iii   JOSHUA EMERY.
5232   iv   RUTH PHŒBE, m. Daniel Safford.
5233   v   SAMUEL, m., 1st, Emily Auger; 2nd, Mary ——.
5234   vi   ABRAM.

3296 JOHN R.[8] MATHER (*Abigail,*[7] *Joshua,*[6] *John,*[5] *Joshua,*[4] *John,*[3] *Jonathan,*[2] *John*[1]), son of John and Abigail (Emery) Mather; married, June 11, 1836, Mrs. Betsey (Potter) Mather, widow of Elisha Mather.   He died, 1842.
Children:

5235   i   MARY JANE,[9] b. May 31, 1837; m. Newell T. Knowlton, July 22, 1853.
5236   ii   STEPHEN P., b. July 5, 1839; m. Julia A. Conger, May 1, 1859.
5237   iii   JOHN R., b. April 4, 1842; m. Amy S. Brasted, April 11, 1866.

3297 RUTH PHŒBE[8] MATHER (*Abigail,*[7] *Joshua,*[6] *John,*[5] *Joshua,*[4] *John,*[3] *Jonathan,*[2] *John*[1]), daughter of John and Abigail (Emery) Mather; married L. Whitney Safford.
Children:

5238   i   PAMELIA M.,[9] b. March 14, 1839; m. Charles Stafford, Sept. 18, 1862.
5239   ii   ABIGAIL E., b. July 16, 1841; m. Henry S. Barrett, Feb. 12, 1867.
5240   iii   DANIEL H., b. Sept. 15, 1843; m. Abbie Stafford, Oct. 15, 1870.
5241   iv   SALLY W., b. Oct. 27, 1845; m. Miron O. Brasted, Oct. 3, 1871.
5242   v   LOUISA L., b. Jan. 12, 1848; m. March 30, 1871, George Sprague.
5243   vi   EDWARD E., b. Jan. 31, 1852.

3299 SAMUEL[8] MATHER (*Abigail,*[7] *Joshua,*[6] *John,*[5] *Joshua,*[4] *John,*[3]

Jonathan,[2] *John*[1]), son of John and Abigail (Emery) Mather; married, first, Emily Auger; second, Mary ———.

Children:

   5244 i   MARY.[9]
   5245 ii ABRAM S.

3304 LOIS[8] ROYCE (*Mary,*[7] *Joshua,*[6] *John,*[5] *Joshua,*[4] *John,*[3] *Jonathan,*[2] *John*[1]), daughter of Jonathan and Mary (Emery) Royce; married Henry Ingalls.

Children:

   5246 i   SAMUEL,[9] b. Feb. 8, 1825; d. Dec. 29, 1852.
   5247 ii MARY A., b. April 3, 1827; d. Dec. 29. 1873.
   5248 iii HENRY INGALLS, JR., b. Jan. 18, 1829; d. 1871.
   5249 iv HANNAH, b. June 10, 1831.
   5250 v JONATHAN R , b. March 8. 1833; d. Oct. 8, 1847.
   5251 vi PHŒBE R., b. Dec. 10, 1834; d. Feb. 20, 1836.
   5252 vii LOIS M., b. Jan. 1, 1837.
   5253 viii LEWIS, b. Oct. 26, 1839.
   5254 ix ABNER E., ⎱ b. May 8, 1840; ⎰ d. Dec. 15, 1863.
   5255 x ANDREW E., ⎰   ⎱
   5256 xi GEORGE I., b. Nov. 25, 1844.
   5257 xii FRANKLIN T., b. Sept. 29, 1846.

3305 SARAH[8] ROYCE (*Mary,*[7] *Joshua,*[6] *John,*[5] *Joshua,*[4] *John,*[3] *Jonathan,*[2] *John*[1]), daughter of Jonathan and Mary (Emery) Royce; married John Shelden.

Children:

   5258 i   JONATHAN W.,[9] b. Nov. 30, 1830; m. July 25, 1858, Maria Noble; d. July 8, 1865.
   5259 ii SARAH P., b. Nov. 19, 1832; m. Dec. 15, 1852, Henry Kimball.
   5260 iii GEORGE W., b. Dec. 4, 1833; m. Dec. 5, 1855, Amanda Noble.
   5261 iv ABIGAIL P., b. Nov. 5, 1835; m. April 10, 1855, William McDonald.
   5262 v ROBERT W., b. May 22, 1838; m. March 18, 1860, Margaret Thomas.
   5263 vi ABNER W., b. Oct. 10, 1840; d. Feb. 12, 1841.
   5264 vii CHARLES W., b. Jan. 6, 1843; m. Sept. 10, 1864, Celia Roche.
   5265 viii CAROLINE E., b. June 18, 1847; m. Nov. 15, 1862, John T. Potts.

3306 MARY[8] ROYCE (*Mary,*[7] *Joshua,*[6] *John,*[5] *Joshua,*[4] *John,*[3] *Jonathan,*[2] *John*[1]), daughter of Jonathan and Mary (Emery) Royce; married, April 29, 1830, Andrew W. Lott (born May 23, 1805; died March 8, 1853). She died Feb. 1, 1859.

Children:

   5266 i   MARY ADELAIDE,[9] b. Aug 29, 1831.
   5267 ii SARAH CORNELIA, b. May 18, 1833.
   5268 iii MARTIN ALBERT, b. March 11, 1834.
   5269 iv EDWIN R., b. Aug. 22, 1836.
   5270 v BENAGER A., b. March 13, 1838.
   5271 vi MARTHA M., b. June 2, 1841.
   5272 vii ELIZABETH E., b. June 11, 1844; m., March, 1860, W. H. Conger.
   5273 viii JULIA, b. July 12, 1847.
   5274 ix JONATHAN E., b. June 29, 1849; m., Sept. 30, 1868, Mary L. Sprague.

3326 HARRIET[8] EMERY (*Samuel,*[7] *Joshua,*[6] *John,*[5] *Joshua,*[4] *John,*[3] *Jonathan,*[2] *John*[1]), daughter of Samuel and Catharine (Shepard) Emery; married, June 15, 1847, Horace Skinner (born Sept. 27, 1820).

Children :

    5275 i   HATTIE ELIZA,[9] b. Dec. 13, 1852; d. Sept. 26, 1881.
    5276 ii   FRANK WOODWARD, b. June, 1858.
    5277 iii MARY, b. Aug. 8, 1861; d. April, 1862.
    5278 iv   CYRUS ALFRED, b. Dec. 7, 1865.

3327 EDWIN[8] EMERY (*Samuel,*[7] *Joshua,*[6] *John,*[5] *Joshua,*[4] *John,*[3] *Jonathan,*[2] *John*[1]), son of Samuel and Catharine (Shepard) Emery; married, first, July 27, 1859, Marian Viola Lindsay (born July 27, 1830; died Feb. 20, 1865) ; second, Lucy Hitchcock Aiken (born June 13, 1837).

Children :

    5279 i   WALTER JAMES,[9] b. July 19, 1860; d. June 7, 1870.

By second marriage :

    5280 ii   WILLIS AIKEN, b. Nov. 12, 1867.
    5281 iii MARTHA ELIZA, b. Dec. 20, 1871.
    5282 iv   CHARLES FERDINAND, b. Dec. 26, 1876.

3328 JOSHUA SHEPARD[8] EMERY (*Samuel,*[7] *Joshua,*[6] *John,*[5] *Joshua,*[4] *John,*[3] *Jonathan,*[2] *John*[1]), son of Samuel and Catharine (Shepard) Emery; married, first, Dec. 19, 1855, Lydia M. Heath (born March, 1838; died April 6, 1864) ; second, April 19, 1865, Mrs. Amelia P. Dodge (born Sept. 15, 1830).

Children :

    5283 i   ELLEN AMELIA,[9] b. June 14, 1858.
    5284 ii   FRANK HEATH,   }
    5285 iii FANNIE LOUISE, } b. July 23, 1860.

3329 BREWSTER P.[8] EMERY (*Samuel,*[7] *Joshua,*[6] *John,*[5] *Joshua,*[4] *John,*[3] *Jonathan,*[2] *John*[1]), son of Samuel and Catharine (Shepard) Emery; married, Dec. 30, 1857, Annie Maria Foster (born in Volney, Oswego Co., N. Y., Nov. 9, 1839).

Children :

    5286 i   SAMUEL FOSTER,[9] b. Nov. 25, 1859.
    5287 ii   WINNIFRED MILLICENT, b. May 3, 1864; d. Aug. 1, 1865.
    5288 iii ALLAN FABER, b. Aug. 26, 1866.
    5289 iv   WALTER HERBERT, b. June 27, 1872.
    5290 v   MILTON DWIGHT, b. Oct. 24, 1876.

3331 ALBERT II.[8] EMERY (*Samuel,*[7] *Joshua,*[6] *John,*[5] *Joshua,*[4] *John,*[3] *Jonathan,*[2] *John*[1]), son of Samuel and Catharine (Shepard) Emery; married, March 3, 1875, Mrs. Fannie B. Myers (born Sept. 1, 1839). Mechanical inventor and civil engineer of great ability and reputation. He designed and constructed the 400-ton government hydraulic testing machine, now at the United States arsenal, Watertown, Mass., which is described as the "world-famous testing machine" and as " one of the greatest pieces of engineering work ever done."

He is also the inventor of powerful guns and scales of great accuracy. At the fair of the "Massachusetts Charitable Mechanics' Association" for 1881, held in Boston, but one award was made which was a grand medal of honor to A. H. Emery. The medal was provided by the fair association but awarded by the American Academy of Arts and Sciences for the " exhibit most conducive to human welfare."

Child :

5291 i ALBERT H., JR.,[9] b. Aug. 25, 1876.

3333 LOTTIE A.[8] EMERY (*Samuel*,[7] *Joshua*,[6] *John*,[5] *Joshua*,[4] *John*,[3] *Jonathan*,[2] *John*[1]), daughter of Samuel and Catharine (Shepard) Emery ; married John Twitchell.

Child :

5292 i EARL,[9] b. Oct. 29, 1879.

3335 MOSES WEBSTER[8] EMERY (*Moses*,[7] *Joshua*,[6] *John*,[5] *Joshua*,[4] *John*,[3] *Jonathan*,[2] *John*[1]), son of Moses and Cynthia (Winchester) Emery ; married, Dec. 28, 1844, Martha Coolee of Norwich, Conn.

Children :

5293 i WILLIAM W.,[9] b. Oct. 4, 1845.
5294 ii CYNTHIA W., b. Dec. 31, 1847.
5295 iii ROSWELL WEBSTER, b. June 27, 1850.

3338 JOHN D. P.[8] EMERY (*Moses*,[7] *Joshua*,[6] *John*,[5] *Joshua*,[4] *John*,[3] *Jonathan*,[2] *John*[1]), son of Moses and his second wife Lydia S. (Sprague) Emery ; married, Dec. 25, 1850, Susan H. Morey (born in Deer Isle, Me.).

Children :

5296 i CHARLES FRANCIS,[9] b. July 18, 1851, in East Stoughton, Mass.
5297 ii DEXTER E., b. June 29, 1853, in East Stoughton, Mass.
5298 iii ALICE EUGENIE, b. Jan., 1857, in Bridgewater, Mass.
5299 iv GEORGE BARNARD, d. in infancy.

3339 LUCY STOWELL[8] EMERY (*Moses*,[7] *Joshua*,[6] *John*,[5] *Joshua*,[4] *John*,[3] *Jonathan*,[2] *John*[1]), daughter of Moses and his second wife Lydia (Sprague) Emery ; married, Feb. 4, 1849, Edward Brown (born May 23, 1824).

Children :

5300 i EDWARD EMERY,[9] b. Dec. 4, 1849, in Raynham, Mass.
5301 ii LUCY J., b. Nov. 24, 1851, in Raynham, Mass.
5302 iii HERBERT F., b. Aug. 25, 1855, in East Bridgewater, Mass.
5303 iv LYDIA ELLA, b. Oct. 13, 1861, in Lakeville, Mass.
5304 v ALBERT BISHOP, b. Dec. 3, 1863, in Lakeville, Mass.

3346 MARY W.[8] CUSHMAN (*Abigail W.*,[7] *Moses*,[6] *John*,[5] *Joshua*,[4] *John*,[3] *Jonathan*,[2] *John*[1]), daughter of Ebenezer and Abigail W. (Emery) Cushman ; married James W. Morey, a Methodist minister. She died Feb. 14, 1848.

Child :

5305 i MARY FRANCES,[9] m. Chauncey Loring of Barre, Vt. ; d. in that place.

3347 FRANCIS A.[8] CUSHMAN(*Abigail W.*,[7] *Moses*,[6] *John*,[5] *Joshua*,[4] *John*,[3] *Jonathan*,[2] *John*[1]), son of Ebenezer and Abigail W. (Emery) Cushman; married, first, Dec. 4, 1842, Harriet Smart, of Rumney, N. H. (died Feb., 1884); second, Feb. 22, 1886, Mrs. Kate Leverett, of Plymouth, N. H.

Children :

    5306 i   MARY ELLEN,[9] b. Aug. 12, 1848 ; m. Ward M. Amsden, in Lebanon, N. H., Sept. 14, 1872.
    5307 ii   HARRIET A., b. Dec. 17, 1858.

3348 MOSES EMERY[8] CUSHMAN (*Abigail W.*,[7] *Moses*,[6] *John*,[5] *Joshua*,[4] *John*,[3] *Jonathan*,[2] *John*[1]), son of Ebenezer and Abigail W. (Emery) Cushman; married, Sept. 15, 1845, Rebecca P. Hale, of Orford, N. H. (born May 24, 1825 ; died Dec. 24, 1880).

Child :

    5308 i   ADA L.,[9] b. Dec. 9, 1847.

3352 CHARLES W.[8] CUSHMAN (*Abigail W.*,[7] *Moses*,[6] *John*,[5] *Joshua*,[4] *John*,[3] *Jonathan*,[2] *John*[1]), son of Ebenezer and Abigail W. (Emery) Cushman; married Sarah Stearns (died Feb., 1878).

Children :

    5309 i   STELLA,[9] m. Ira Gilley, of Carrol City, Ia.
    5310 ii   LIZZIE, m. Charles Buck.
    5311 iii MAY.
    5312 iv CHARLES.

3353 GEORGE F.[8] CUSHMAN (*Abigail W.*,[7] *Moses*,[6] *John*,[5] *Joshua*,[4] *John*,[3] *Jonathan*,[2] *John*[1]), son of Ebenezer and Abigail W. (Emery) Cushman; married, April 5, 1864, L. M. Parker.

Children :

    5313 i   HENRY O.,[9] b. Aug. 25, 1865.
    5314 ii   CHARLES P., b. Jan. 9, 1867.
    5315 iii NELLIE M., b. May 9, 1873.
    5316 iv JAMES M., b. Nov. 29, 1875.

3358 COL. HARVEY WEBSTER[8] EMERY (*Moses*,[7] *Moses*,[6] *John*,[5] *Joshua*,[4] *John*,[3] *Jonathan*,[2] *John*[1]), son of Moses and Eunice (English) Emery ; married, Aug., 1853, Mary J. Dow, daughter of Rev. James Dow. Graduate of Norwich Military Academy, June, 1853 ; principal of Danville Academy and Morganstown Female Seminary ; admitted to the Bar and removed to Portage City, Wis. ; representative to Wisconsin legislature, 1861 ; elected Lieut. Col. of the 5th Wis. He was in the battle of Williamsburg, where he displayed coolness, judgment and decision, his regiment winning the honors of the day, General McClellan causing Williamsburg to be inscribed on their banners ; also in the succeeding battles, till near the close of the seven days' retreat, when he was compelled by ill health to retire to Fortress Monroe. At the expiration of his furlough, he hastened from Fortress Monroe to reinforce the army at the last battle of Bull Run, where he distinguished himself by courage and sound judgment. As a teacher, scholar and soldier, he honored himself, his town, his na-

tive and adopted states and his country. Died in Lisbon, N. H.,
Oct. 13, 1862.

Children:

    5317 i   EVELYN,[9] b. Aug. 19, 1859, in Portage City, Wis.
    5318 ii   HATTIE MAY, b. May 5, 1861.

3359 MARY ELIZABETH[8] EMERY (*Moses*,[7] *Moses*,[6] *John*,[5] *Joshua*,[4]
John,[3] *Jonathan*,[2] *John*[1]), daughter of Moses and Eunice (English)
Emery; married, Feb. 19, 1850, Ora O. Kelsea (died in Topeka, Kan.,
July 29, 1871). He was commissioned by the government captain of
Co. " H," 8th Ohio Regiment; afterward appointed colonel, and later
was in the secret service of the government, earning an excellent mil-
itary record.

Child:

    5319 i   ORA CARLOS,[9] b. Feb. 13, 1854.

3362 SAMUEL[8] EMERY (*Moses*,[7] *Moses*,[6] *John*,[5] *Joshua*,[4] *John*,[3]
Jonathan,[2] *John*[1]), son of Moses and Eunice (English) Emery; married, Oct. 13, 1865, Rebecca E. Ash, of Lisbon, N. H. He fitted for
college at Newbury Seminary; entered Wesleyan University, Middletown, Conn., where he distinguished himself for scholarship; compelled by ill health to leave before the completion of his college course;
spent some time in teaching in the Southern States; returned North
before the war; correspondent for newspapers in New Hampshire.
Farmer; postmaster.

Child:

    5320 i   HARVEY D.,[9] b. Sept. 18, 1873.

3363 MOSES[8] EMERY (*Moses*,[7] *Moses*,[6] *John*,[5] *Joshua*,[4] *John*,[3] *Jonathan*,[2] *John*[1]), son of Moses and Eunice (English) Emery; married,
Feb. 7, 1869, Lucena M. Howe. Farmer.

Children:

    5321 i   CLARA MAY,[9] b. July 6, 1870.
    5322 ii   NELLIE BLANCH, b. May 21, 1872.
    5323 iii NINA C., b. Oct. 12, 1882.

3366 ALFRED J.[8] EMERY (*Smith*,[7] *Smith*,[6] *Joshua*,[5] *Joshua*,[4] *John*,[3]
Jonathan,[2] *John*[1]), son of Smith and Maria (Howe) Emery; married
Charlotte Chandler, daughter of Daniel Chandler. Resides in Dun-
dee, N. Y.

Children:

    5324 i   CHARLES.[9]
    5325 ii   LIZZIE.
    5326 iii ROBERT.

3367 MARIA L.[8] EMERY (*Smith*,[7] *Smith*,[6] *Joshua*,[5] *Joshua*,[4] *John*,[3]
Jonathan,[2] *John*[1]), daughter of Smith and Maria (Howe) Emery;
married Daniel Chandler.

Children:

    5327 i   ALFRED.[9]
    5328 ii   JULIA.
    5329 iii EMMA.

5330   iv   ELLA, m. Shelley S. Emery.
5331   v   FLORA.
5332   vi   LILLIAN.
5333   vii   MARIE.

3368 RHODA E.[8] EMERY (*Smith*,[7] *Smith*,[6] *Joshua*,[5] *Joshua*,[4] *John*,[3] *Jonathan*,[2] *John*[1]), daughter of Smith and Maria (Howe) Emery; married Aaron Aldrich, of Clarendon, Vt.

Children:

5334   i   EDGAR.[9]
5335   ii   JAMES D.
5336   iii   SHELLEY S., m. Ella Chandler.
5337   iv   LILLIE, m. W. W. Brown.

3374 HELEN MARY[8] EMERY (*Smith*,[7] *Smith*,[6] *Joshua*,[5] *Joshua*,[4] *John*,[3] *Jonathan*,[2] *John*[1]), daughter of Smith and Maria (Howe) Emery; married —— ——.

Children:

5338   i   TIMMONS.[9]
5339   ii   ANN ELIZA.
5340   iii   ALFRED MYRON.

3375 SARAH E.[8] EMERY (*Smith*,[7] *Smith*,[6] *Joshua*,[5] *Joshua*,[4] *John*,[3] *Jonathan*,[2] *John*[1]), daughter of Smith and Maria (Howe) Emery; married Norman Townsend.

Children:

5341   i   IDA.[9]
5342   ii   MINNIE.
5343   iii   BERTHA.

3381 EDSON F.[8] EMERY (*Sanford*,[7] *Smith*,[6] *Joshua*,[5] *Joshua*,[4] *John*,[3] *Jonathan*,[2] *John*[1]), son of Sanford and Isabella (Warner) Emery; married, first, April 14, 1860, Cornelia J. Coon; second, Oct. 28, 1878, Georgiana Lowry. He died Sept. 3, 1884.

Children, by first wife:

5344   i   ANNA M.,[9] b. Feb. 14, 1861; m., Oct. 28, 1877, John Clark White; have a son, John Emery White.
5345   ii   ELLA P., b. Feb. 7, 1863; m., Nov. 29, 1887, J. Bull Rouse.
5346   iii   GEORGE S., b. Nov. 23, 1864.
5347   iv   EDSON F., JR., b. Aug. 7, 1872.

3384 WILLIAM F.[8] EMERY (*Sanford*,[7] *Smith*,[6] *Joshua*,[5] *Joshua*,[4] *John*,[3] *Jonathan*,[2] *John*[1]), son of Sanford and Isabella (Warner) Emery; married, 1880, Ada Prior.

Child:

5348   i   ELLA P.,[9] b. 1881.

3386 LAURA A.[8] EMERY (*Sanford*,[7] *Smith*,[6] *Joshua*,[5] *Joshua*,[4] *John*,[3] *Jonathan*,[2] *John*[1]), daughter of Sanford and his second wife, Chloe (Beebe) Emery; married, March 31, 1881, William G. Stanton, attorney and counselor-at-law, Buffalo, N. Y.

Child:

5349   i   SANFORD E.,[9] b. June 28, 1883.

3387 ARTHUR R.[8] EMERY (*Sanford,*[7] *Smith,*[6] *Joshua,*[5] *Joshua,*[4] *John,*[3] *Jonathan,*[2] *John*[1]), son of Sanford and his second wife Chloe (Beebe) Emery; married, April, 1887, Ella M. Bentley.
Children:

5350　i　LAURA B.[9]
5351　ii　INFANT.

3388 JOSEPH F.[8] EMERY (*Joseph W.,*[7] *Joshua,*[6] *Joshua,*[5] *Joshua,*[4] *John,*[3] *Jonathan,*[2] *John*[1]), son of Joseph W. and Nancy L. (Faulkner) Emery; married July 17, 1862, Mary Matilda Grace.
Children:

5352　i　FLORENCE MATILDA.[9] b. May 3, 1863; d. Oct. 17, 1863.
5353　ii　EDWARD WELCH, b. Jan. 10, 1865.
5354　iii　JOSEPH FAULKNER, b. Oct. 27, 1867.

3394 FRANCIS F.[8] EMERY (*Francis W. R.,*[7] *Joshua,*[6] *Joshua,*[5] *Joshua,*[4] *John,*[3] *Jonathan,*[2] *John*[1]), son of Francis W. R. and Sophronia (Faulkner) Emery; married in Boston, Mass., Sept. 18, 1855, Caroline Sweetser Jones, daughter of Frederick and Maria (Sweetser) Jones. Member of the firm of F. Jones & Co., Boston.
Children:

5355　i　MARIA SWEETSER,[9] b. Aug. 22, 1856, in Boston.
5356　ii　FRANCIS F., b. May 24, 1860, in Boston.
5357　iii　EDWARD STANLEY, b. Dec. 28, 1864, in Boston.
5358　iv　FREDERICK JONES, b. July 5, 1870, in Newton, Mass.; d. May 17, 1872.

3397 AARON FAULKNER[8] EMERY (*Francis W. R.,*[7] *Joshua,*[6] *Joshua,*[5] *Joshua,*[4] *John,*[3] *Jonathan,*[2] *John*[1]), son of Frances W. R. and his second wife, Mary Baker (Wolcott) Emery; married Jan. 23, 1862, Virginia W. Comstock of Quincy, Ill.
Children, born in Newton, Mass.:

5359　i　ALICE FAULKNER,[9] b. Nov. 19, 1862.
5360　ii　SARAH WHITE, b. March 15, 1865.
5361　iii　CAROLINE SWEETSER, b. May 12, 1873.
5362　iv　ALLEN COMSTOCK, b. March 17, 1875.

3399 MARY WOLCOTT[8] EMERY (*Francis W. R.,*[7] *Joshua,*[6] *Joshua,*[5] *Joshua,*[4] *John,*[3] *Jonathan,*[2] *John*[1]), daughter of Francis W. R. and his third wife, Susan (Ward) Emery; married, in Boston, Mass., Feb. 16, 1859, Arthur W. Cowdrey, M.D., of Acton, Mass.
Children:

5363　i　MAUD HELEN,[9] b. Jan. 14, 1869.
5364　ii　HELEN W., b. Dec. 23, 1871.

3404 HARRIET P.[8] EMERY (*Rev. Joshua,*[7] *Joshua,*[6] *Joshua,*[5] *Joshua,*[4] *John,*[3] *Jonathan,*[2] *John*[1]), daughter of Rev. Joshua and Harriet (Peabody) Emery; married, March 30, 1857, William Aug. Herrick, (born in Boxford, Mass., Jan. 6, 1831; lawyer in Boston). He died in Boston, Aug. 24, 1885.
Children:

5364a   i   WILLIAM HALE,[9] b. Aug. 10, 1860; d. in Colorado Springs, Nov. 9, 1887.
5364b   ii PERCY MANNING, b. Aug. 16, 1862.
5364c   iii MARGARET EMERY, b. July 10, 1864.
5364d   iv ROBERT WELCH, b. April 12, 1868.
5364e   v   AGNES PEABODY, b. Feb. 15, 1873.
5364f   vi ELIZABETH HARRIET, b. May 24, 1878.

3405 JOSHUA[8] EMERY (*Rev. Joshua,*[7] *Joshua,*[6] *Joshua,*[5] *Joshua,*[4] *John,*[3] *Jonathan,*[2] *John*[1]), son of Rev. Joshua and Harriet (Peabody) Emery; married, first, Carrie E. Kellogg of Boston (died Dec. 15, 1879); second, Emily L. Trimingham, April 10, 1882, in Chicago, Ill. He is a member of the firm of Hatch and Emery, Chicago.
Children:

5365   i   HARRIET P.[9] b. Aug. 18, 1863.
5365a   ii ADELE WELCH, b. March 18, 1876; d. June 19, 1876.

3406 CHARLES FRANCIS[8] EMERY (*Rev. Joshua,*[7] *Joshua,*[6] *Joshua,*[5] *Joshua,*[4] *John,*[3] *Jonathan,*[2] *John*[1]), son of Rev. Joshua and Harriet (Peabody) Emery; married, in 1873, Kittie S. Chester of New London, Conn.
Children:

5366   i   AUGUSTUS BACHELDER,[9] b. May 7, 1875, in Kansas City, Mo.
5366a   ii   FLORENCE CHESTER, b. Sept. 28, 1881.
5366b   iii EDITH PALMER, b. Jan. 7, 1883.
5366c   iv   JOSHUA, b. April 28, 1884; d. Jan. 3, 1886.
5366d   v   A SON, b. Nov. 1, 1886.

3411 SAMUEL HOPKINS[8] EMERY (*Rev. Samuel H.,*[7] *Joshua,*[6] *Joshua,*[5] *Joshua,*[4] *John,*[3] *Jonathan,*[2] *John*[1]), son of Rev. Samuel H. and Julia (Reed) Emery; married Aug. 15, 1865, Mary McClure, daughter of A. W. McClure, D.D. He received an Honorary A.M. from Amherst College; LL.B. from Harvard University. Presided for some years over the Concord School of Philosophy. At present is business manager of large paper works in the city of Quincy, Illinois.
Child:

5367   i   CONSTANCE,[9] b. June 2, 1866.

3412 FRANCIS WOLCOTT[8] EMERY (*Rev. Samuel H.,*[7] *Joshua,*[6] *Joshua,*[5] *Joshua,*[4] *John,*[3] *Jonathan,*[2] *John*[1]), son of Rev. Samuel H. and Julia (Reed) Emery; married July 15, 1869, Eliza Ann Sproat of Taunton, Mass. He manages a large farm of 1500 acres in Dakota. Served through the entire four years' war of the Rebellion in the Union army, spending nine months in Andersonville prison.
Children:

5368   i   SON,[9] b. and d. March 25, 1871.
5369   ii   ALLAN SPROAT, b. March 2, 1873; d. July 27, 1873.
5370   iii ALICE SPROAT, b. Feb. 22, 1879.

3413 JOSEPH WELCH[8] EMERY (*Rev. Samuel H.,*[7] *Joshua,*[6] *Joshua,*[5] *Joshua,*[4] *John,*[3] *Jonathan,*[2] *John*[1]), son of Rev. Samuel H, and Julia (Reed) Emery; married April 14, 1879, Effie Stillwell of Hannibal, Mo.

Children, born in Quincy, Ill. :

5371   i   RALPH HOPKINS,[9] b. Jan. 27, 1881; d. April 29, 1881.
5372   ii MARGUERITA DUNCAN, b. Sept. 13, 1882; d. Nov. 18, 1882.

3420 SARAH B.[8] REMICK (*Mary,*[7] *Ephraim,*[6] *John,*[5] *David,*[4] *John,*[3] *Jonathan,*[2] *John,*[1]) daughter of Capt. John and Mary (Emery) Remick; married Lewis F. Emery of Lowell, Mass. (died April 25, 1876). She died Aug. 15, 1858.

Children:

5373   i   MARY ALLISON,[9] d. Nov. 28, 1847.
5374   ii LEWIS RUSSELL, b. Nov. 2, 1848.

3421 MARY R.[8] REMICK (*Mary,*[7] *Ephraim,*[6] *John,*[5] *David,*[4] *John,*[3] *Jonathan,*[2] *John*[1]), daughter of Capt. John and Mary (Emery) Remick; married, in 1846, James Howard of Lowell, Mass. She died March 12, 1880.

Children:

5375   i   MARY ALICE,[9] b. Aug. 4. 1849; m., Jan. 30, 1875, Capt. Field-
              ing Pope Meigs of Washington, D. C., who d. March 27,
              1882.
5376   ii CLARA, b. Nov. 8, 1851.

3422 EPHRAIM R.[8] EMERY (*Thomas,*[7] *Ephraim,*[6] *John,*[5] *David,*[4] *John,*[3] *Jonathan,*[2] *John*[1]), son of Thomas and Mary (Hoyt) Emery; married Dec. 5, 1852, Abby Parker Foote (born Dec. 23, 1824).

Children:

5377   i   MARY HOYT,[9] b. Jan. 23, 1854, in West Newbury, Mass.
5378   ii   WILLIAM RUSSELL, b. Nov. 9, 1855, in Woburn, Mass.
5379   iii CHARLES EUSTICE, b. Sept 15, 1857, in Woburn, Mass.
5380   iv   SOPHIA ADELAIDE, b. Aug. 18, 1859, in Woburn, Mass.; d. Oct.
              22, 1874.

3425 SARAH J.[8] EMERY (*Thomas,*[7] *Ephraim,*[6] *John,*[5] *David,*[4] *John,*[3] *Jonathan,*[2] *John*[1]), daughter of Thomas and Mary (Hoyt) Emery; married June 7, 1865, Lewis G. Farrington (born Dec. 17, 1819).

Children:

5381   i   MARY EMERY.[9]
5382   ii   GEORGE W.
5383   iii LEWIS GILMAN.

3426 BENJAMIN F. EMERY[8] (*Thomas,*[7] *Ephraim,*[6] *John,*[5] *David,*[4] *John,*[3] *Jonathan,*[2] *John*[1]), son of Thomas and Mary (Hoyt) Emery; married Mary Frances Colby who died in April, 1879.

Children:

5384   i   SARAH JANE,[9] b. Jan. 19, 1855, in West Newbury, Mass.
5385   ii GEORGE F., b. June, 1864, in Lynn, Mass.

3427 JUDITH K.[8] EMERY (*Thomas,*[7] *Ephraim,*[6] *John,*[5] *David,*[4] *John,*[3] *Jonathan,*[2] *John*[1]), daughter of Thomas and Mary (Hoyt)

Emery; married William, son of Lewis and Mary (Farrington) Gilman of Springfield.

Children:

5386 i   MARY EMERY.[9]
5387 ii ROSE ANNA.

3430 LYDIA ANN[8] HOSUM (*Sarah*[7], *John*,[6] *Moses*,[5] *David*,[4] *John*,[3] *Jonathan*,[2] *John*[1]), daughter of George and Sarah (Emery) Hosum; married, first, May 2, 1852, Paul S. Davis, who died Feb., 16, 1879; second, Oct., 1886, Moses B. Merrill, who died Feb. 13, 1888.

Children:

5388 i   SARAH E.,[9] b. July 25, 1854; m. Dec. 28, 1876, Frank E. Bailey.
5389 ii GEORGE H., b. Aug 19, 1857; m. June 11, 1879, Mary L. Tupper.

3431 GUSTAVUS BYRON[8] EMERY (*John*,[7] *John*,[6] *Moses*,[5] *David*,[4] *John*,[3] *Jonathan*,[2] *John*[1]), son of John and Mehetable (Grant) Emery; married ———— ————.

Child:

5390 i   MARY ESTHER,[9] m. Aug. Hutchinson.

3434 CHARLES[8] EMERY (*Tappan*,[7] *John*,[6] *Moses*,[5] *David*,[4] *John*,[3] *Jonathan*,[2] *John*[1]), son of Tappan and Lydia Williams (Colby) Emery; married Hannah Chamberlain of Epsom, N. H.

Children:

5391 i   CLARENCE.[9]
5392 ii MOSES.
5393 iii OSCAR.
5394 iv MONROE.
5395 v   CHARLES.
5396 vi ANNE GERTRUDE.

3436 LYDIA IRENE EMERY[8] (*Tappan*,[7] *John*,[6] *Moses*,[5] *David*,[4] *John*,[3] *Jonathan*,[2] *John*[1]), daughter of Tappan and Lydia Williams (Colby) Emery; married, April 3, 1872, Charles E. Williams.

Child:

5397 i   EMERY DEAN,[9] b. June 18, 1874.

3440 THOMAS F.[8] CURRIER (*Betsey*,[7] *John*,[6] *Moses*,[5] *David*,[4] *John*,[3] *Jonathan*,[2] *John*[1]), son of Thomas S. and Betsey (Emery) Currier; married in Abington, Mass., Jan. 9, 1862, Lucinda F. Reed.

Children:

5398 i   MARY WHITTIER,[9] b. April 20, 1865.
5399 ii SUSAN ELIZABETH, b. March 22, 1869.
5400 iii MARTHA, b. Feb. 22, 1871.
5401 iv THOMAS FRANKLIN, b. Feb. 26, 1873.

3441 SUSAN ELIZABETH[8] CURRIER (*Betsey*,[7] *John*,[6] *Moses*,[5] *David*,[4] *John*,[3] *Jonathan*,[2] *John*[1]), daughter of Thomas S. and Betsey

(Emery) Currier; married in Amesbury, Mass, John James Bailey, who died April 10, 1868.

Children:

5402　i　GRACE H,[9] b March 25, 1864
5403　ii　JAMES LESLIE, b. March 21, 1866; d. in Brookfield, Mass, Jan 12, 1888.

3442 HORACE H.[8] CURRIER (*Betsey,*[7] *John,*[6] *Moses,*[5] *David,*[4] *John,*[3] *Jonathan,*[2] *John*[1]), son of Thomas S. and Betsey (Emery) Currier, married in Chelsea, Mass. Oct 23, 1872, Ann Maria Allen (died in Boston, 1875). He died Oct. 18, 1879.

Children:

5404　i　AllEN CURRIER,[9] b July 22, 1873, in Boston.
5405　ii　HORACE, b July 28, 1875.

3443 SARAH R[8] CURRIER (*Betsey,*[7] *John,*[6] *Moses,*[5] *David,*[4] *John,*[3] *Jonathan,*[2] *John*[1]), daughter of Thomas S and Betsey (Emery) Currier, married Moses M. Ordway, died Jan. 28, 1878.

Children:

5406　i　EDITH,[9] b July 27, 1872
5407　ii　LOUIS P, b. Oct 22, 1877

3445 MOSES A.[8] EMERY (*Moses,*[7] *John,*[6] *Moses,*[5] *David,*[4] *John,*[3] *Jonathan.*[2] *John*[1]), son of Moses and Harriet (Pillsbury) Emery; married in Westboro, Mass., Nov. 11, 1862, Lydia A Basford (born Oct. 27, 1842).

Children:

5408　i　MOSES,[9] b. Aug. 13, 1863, in Westboro, Mass
5409　ii　GEORGE A, b July 29, 1865, in Westboro Mass.
5410　iii　ANNA M, b July 18, 1867, in Southboro, Mass.
5411　iv　HERBERT A, b July 5, 1871, in Southboro, Mass
5412　v　FREDERICK S, b. Sept 8, 1881, in Southboro, Mass

3446 LOUISA[8] HUNTINGTON (*Susan,*[7] *John,*[6] *Moses,*[5] *David,*[4] *John,*[3] *Jonathan,*[2] *John*[1]), daughter of Nathan and Susan (Emery) Huntington; married, Dec. 10, 1871, Luther G. Morrison.

Children:

5413　i　AGNES L,[9] b Dec 30, 1874
5414　ii　HENRY L, b March 8, 1876.
5415　iii　ALLAN C, b. April 9, 1877.
5416　iv　ADA S, b March 2, 1879
5417　v　ROBERT H., b Feb. 3, 1884

3447 SUSAN EMERY[8] HUNTINGTON (*Susan,*[7] *John,*[6] *Moses,*[5] *David,*[4] *John.*[3] *Jonathan,*[2] *John*[1]), daughter of Nathan and Susan (Emery) Huntington; married, Sept. 3, 1873, Melvin J. Clement.

Children.

5418　i　RALPH H.,[9] b. July 3, 1884.
5419　ii　CLARA M, b Dec 9, 1885

3452 BENJAMIN[8] EDWARDS (*Harriet,*[7] *Jacob,*[6] *Moses,*[5] *David,*[4] *John,*[3] *Jonathan,*[2] *John*[1]), son of Benjamin and Harriet (Emery)

17

Edwards; married, Nov. 11, 1847, Mary E. Brown; died Dec. 1, 1862.

Children :

    5420 i   BENJAMIN G.,⁹ b. Dec. 9, 1848; m. April 15, 1868, Augusta Sargent.
    5421 ii MARY B., b. July 20, 1850; m. June 5, 1873, Woodbury Knight.
    5422 iii HATTIE, b. Aug. 9, 1852.
    5423 iv GEORGE, b. May 18, 1855.
    5424 v MARTHA, b. May 3, 1857; m. Jan. 13, 1887, Granville J. Williams.

3454 CHARLES H.⁸ EDWARDS (*Harriet*,⁷ *Jacob*,⁶ *Moses*,⁵ *David*,⁴ *John*,³ *Jonathan*,² *John*¹), son of Benjamin and Harriet (Emery) Edwards; married Louisa Paine.

Child :

    5425 i   LYDIA A.⁹

3455 HARRIET E.⁸ EDWARDS (*Harriet*,⁷ *Jacob*,⁶ *Moses*,⁵ *David*,⁴ *John*,³ *Jonathan*,² *John*¹), daughter of Benjamin and Harriet (Emery) Edwards; married James H. Durgin; died May 15, 1858.

Child :

    5426 1   M. LIZZIE.⁹

3456 LYDIA A.⁸ EDWARDS (*Harriet*,⁷ *Jacob*,⁶ *Moses*,⁵ *David*,⁴ *John*,³ *Jonathan*,² *John*¹), daughter of Benjamin and Harriet (Emery) Edwards; married Thomas S. Ruddock (born Sept. 20, 1835).

Children :

    5427 1   AUSTIN EDWARDS,⁹ b. Oct. 7, 1863.
    5428 ii HATTIE E., b. Dec. 13, 1872.
    5429 iii AGNES, b. Aug. 12, 1874.

3475 JULIA G.⁸ TILTON (*Eliza T.*,⁷ *Jacob*,⁶ *Moses*,⁵ *David*,⁴ *John*,³ *Jonathan*,² *John*¹), daughter of Rev. J. H. and Eliza T. (Emery) Tilton; married Nov. 29, 1880, Gordon A. McGregor of Boston.

Children :

    5430 1   GORDON MERCER,⁹ b. June 10, 1882, in Hyde Park, Mass.
    5431 ii MILTON EMERY, b. Sept. 10, 1884.

3479 CLARA A.⁸ EMERY (*Calvin*,⁷ *Jacob*,⁶ *Moses*,⁵ *David*,⁴ *John*,³ *Jonathan*,² *John*¹), daughter of Calvin and his third wife Clara (Shannon) Emery; married Jan. 15, 1880, Moses M. Jaques.

Children :

    5432 i   MARY E.,⁹ b. June 29, 1881, in West Newbury.
    5433 ii EMILY S., b. Feb. 7, 1883, in Groveland, Mass.

3485 GILMAN W.⁸ BROWN (*Harriet K.*,⁷ *Moses*,⁶ *Moses*,⁵ *David*,⁴ *John*,³ *Jonathan*,² *John*¹), son of Hayden and Harriet K. (Emery) Brown; married Henrietta B. Little of Atkinson, N. H. (died Nov. 8, 1887).

Children :

5434 ı   HARRIET LITTLE,[9] b Dec 18, 1885
5435 ıı HAYDEN LITTLE, b Nov. 8, 1887

3495 CAROLINE D.[8] EMERY (*William,*[7] *Willard,*[6] *William.*[5] *Dr.
Anthony,*[4] *John,*[3] *Jonathan,*[2] *John*[1]), daughter of William and Nancy
Perkins (Emery) Emery, married Dec. 21, 1848, Albert M. Shaw
(born in Poland, Me., May 3, 1819).
   Children:
      5436 ı   WILLIAM FRANCIS,[9] b Sept 21, 1849, in Brunswick, Me.
      5437 ıı   MARY ESTELLE, b Sept 6, 1852. in Franklin, N H
      5438 ııı ALBERT ONSLOW, b Jan 3, 1865, in Lebanon, N H

3496 NANCY JANE[8] EMERY (*William,*[7] *Willard,*[6] *William,*[5] *Dr.
Anthony,*[4] *John,*[3] *Jonathan,*[2] *John*[1]), daughter of William and Nancy
Perkins (Emery) Emery, married July 15, 1860, Richard W. Cragin
(born in Weston, Vt, Nov. 20, 1827).
   Children, born in Lebanon, N. H.:
      5439 ı   GEORGE EMERY,[9] b April 10, 1861.
      5440 ıı LENA BELLA, b Dec 24, 1866.

3497 ELBRIDGE GERRY[8] EMERY (*Jonathan,*[7] *Willard,*[6] *William,*[5]
Dr. Anthony,[4] *John,*[3] *Jonathan,*[2] *John*[1]), son of Jonathan and Nancy
Weare (Rowe) Emery, married April 8, 1869, Mary Saline Shaw,
died Dec 26, 1877, at East Andover, N H. Teacher and farmer.
   Children:
      5441 ı   CLARA JEANNETT,[9] b July 24, 1870
      5442 ıı ETHEL, b. Nov. 17, 1873

3498 JOHN ROWE[8] EMERY (*Jonathan,*[7] *Willard,*[6] *William,*[5] *Dr.
Anthony,*[4] *John,*[3] *Jonathan,*[2] *John*[1]), son of Jonathan and Nancy
Weare (Rowe) Emery; married June 3, 1851, Esther White of North
Londonderry, N H (born Feb. 12, 1829, died May 7, 1885). Far-
mer
   Children.
      5443 ı   NELSON WHITE,[9] b Sept 4, 1853.
      5444 ıı LIZZY, b Oct. 9, 1862.

3504 MARTHA V [8] EMERY (*Jonathan,*[7] *Willard,*[6] *William,*[5] *Dr.
Anthony,*[4] *John,*[3] *Jonathan,*[2] *John*[1]), daughter of Jonathan and Nancy
Weare (Rowe) Emery, married Oct. 23, 1861, Hiram Fellows Emery.
   Children, born in Pine Island, Minn.:
      5445 ı   WILLARD H ,[9] b June 10, 1863.
      5446 ıı   NETTIE ESTELLE, b. Oct 4, 1866.
      5447 ııı GEORGE ERNEST, b. Oct. 26, 1868.

3519 MARY ELIZABETH[8] EMERY (*John,*[7] *Joseph,*[6] *William,*[5] *Dr.
Anthony,*[4] *John,*[3] *Jonathan,*[2] *John*[1]), daughter of John and Sally
(Fifield) Emery, married March 19, 1850, Edmund Moulton (born in
Ellsworth, N H , April 15, 1816).
   Children, born in Ellsworth.
      5448 ı   SARAH MARIA,[9] b May 13, 1851.
      5449 ıı MARY ELLEN, b Nov 2, 1852.

5450   iii   KATIE ROSANA, b. July 25, 1855.
5451   iv   EMMA ESTELLE, b. Feb. 2, 1857.
5452   v   NAPOLEON BRYANT, b. May 1, 1859.

3520 HIRAM F.[8] EMERY (*John*,[7] *Joseph*,[6] *William*,[5] *Dr. Anthony*,[4] *John*,[3] *Jonathan*,[2] *John*[1]), son of John and Sally (Fifield) Emery ; married, first, Oct. 29, 1852, Mary Ellen Bryant (born in Canterbury, N. H., Feb. 23, 1832 ; died Aug. 30, 1854) ; second, Oct. 14, 1855, Mrs. Mahala Marian Sackett Soule (died at Pine Island, Minn.) ; third, Oct. 23, 1861, Martha V. Emery.

Children :

5453   i   ELLEN MARIA,[9] b. April 10, 1854; d. Sept. 8, 1854, in Andover, N. H.
5454   ii   CLARA ELLEN, b. Aug. 21, 1857, in Orinoco, Minn.
5455   iii   WILLARD HAMILTON, b. June 10, 1863, in Pine Island, Minn.
5456   iv   NETTIE ESTELLE, b. Oct. 4, 1866, in Pine Island, Minn.
5457   v   GEORGE ERNEST, b. Oct. 26, 1868.

3521 JOHN[8] EMERY, JR. (*John*,[7] *Joseph*,[6] *William*,[5] *Dr. Anthony*,[4] *John*,[3] *Jonathan*,[2] *John*[1]), son of John and Sally (Fifield) Emery ; married Oct. 25, 1858, Paulina Cocagne (born in Cape Vincent, N. Y.).

Children, born in Orinoco, Minn. :

5458   i   JOHN FRANKLIN,[9] b. March 21, 1859.
5459   ii   LOUISA LANE, b. Sept. 9, 1863.
5460   iii   MARY ALMEDA, b. May 24, 1867.

3522 CALEB C.[8] EMERY (*John*,[7] *Joseph*,[6] *William*,[5] *Dr. Anthony*,[4] *John*,[3] *Jonathan*,[2] *John*[1]), son of John and Sally (Fifield) Emery ; married May 8, 1867, Helen May George (born in Hamilton, Butler Co., O.).

Child :

5461   i   CLARA EDITH,[9] b. Jan. 21, 1869, in Orinoco, Minn.

3532 GEORGE EDWIN[8] EMERY (*Capt. Willard*,[7] *Anthony*,[6] *William*,[5] *Dr. Anthony*,[4] *John*,[3] *Jonathan*,[2] *John*[1]), son of Capt. Willard and Sarah (Hobart) Emery ; married Nov. 4, 1851, Mary Elizabeth Bachelder, daughter of Dea. Josiah Bachelder of Andover (born Nov. 11, 1829) ; Lieutenant in New Hampshire Militia ; Justice of the Peace in Mass. ; alderman of Lynn, Mass., four years ; member of New England Historical and Genealogical Society ; New Hampshire Historical Society ; Essex Institute, Salem, Mass. ; corresponding member of Wisconsin Historical Society ; Essex Agricultural Soc., Mass. ; Temperance Alliance ; Exeter Natural History Society.   Historian, poet, essayist.

Children, born in Lynn, Mass. :

5462   i   MARY ELLA BRYANT,[9] b. Dec. 27, 1855.
5463   ii   MABEL S., b. Feb. 22, 1859.
5464   iii   LIZZIE GENEVIEVE, b. May 5, 1861; d. in Exeter, N. H., Jan. 21, 1875.
5465   iv   ANNIE GERTRUDE, b. June 14, 1863.

3534 ADELAIDE LOUISA[8] EMERY (*Capt. Willard*,[7] *Anthony*,[6] *Wil-*

liam,[5] *Dr. Anthony*,[4] *John*,[3] *Jonathan*,[2] *John*[1]), daughter of Capt. Willard and Sarah (Hobart) Emery; married Nov. 24, 1860, Addison Gage of Lynn, Mass. (born July 24, 1837), son of Dennison Gage.
Children, born in Lynn :

5466 i BELLE ADELAIDE,[9] b. July 16, 1861; d. Jan. 2, 1862.
5467 ii LOUIE EVELYN, b. Nov. 16, 1862.
5468 iii FRANK DENNISON, b. Sept. 26, 1864; d. Nov. 10, 1865.
5469 iv CHARLES ALBERT, b. Aug. 15, 1866.
5470 v GEORGE ALBION, } b. March 27, 1876.
5471 vi ERNEST LESLIE, }

3564 SARAH ADELAIDE[8] NEWTON (*Sarah J*,[7] *John*,[6] *Nathaniel*,[5] *Dr. Anthony*,[4] *John*,[3] *Jonathan*,[2] *John*[1]), daughter of A. E. and Sarah J. (Emery) Newton; married J. T. Trowbridge, author and poet.
Children :

5472 i GRACE EVELYN,[9] b. July 24, 1874.
5473 ii EDITH VANELIA, b. Aug. 1, 1876.
5474 iii ARTHUR TOWNSEND, b. Aug. 28, 1883.

3567 EMELINE B.[8] EMERY (*Nathaniel*,[7] *Josiah*,[6] *Nathaniel*,[5] *Dr. Anthony*,[4] *John*,[3] *Jonathan*,[2] *John*[1]), daughter of Nathaniel and Mary L. (Arnold) Emery; married Sept. 13, 1866, John Calder. She died May 1, 1878.
Children :

5475 i MARY C.,[9] } b. May 1, 1867; { d. Aug. 22, 1867.
5476 ii JOHN C., } { d. Aug. 16, 1867.

3568 ELIZABETH B.[8] EMERY (*Nathaniel*,[7] *Josiah*,[6] *Nathaniel*,[5] *Dr. Anthony*,[4] *John*,[3] *Jonathan*,[2] *John*[1]), daughter of Nathaniel and Mary L. (Arnold) Emery; married Ophir R. Goodus, Nov. 13, 1864. She died March 14, 1876.
Children :

5477 i BERTIE M.,[9] b. June 25, 1867.
5478 ii RABBIE O., b. Sept. 4, 1868; d. Dec. 5, 1884.
5479 iii PEARL L., b. Aug. 17, 1871; d. July 14, 1872.

3570 BENJAMIN F.[8] EMERY (*Nathaniel*,[7] *Josiah*,[6] *Nathaniel*,[5] *Dr. Anthony*,[4] *John*,[3] *Jonathan*,[2] *John*[1]), son of Nathaniel and Mary L. (Arnold) Emery; married Aug. 13, 1876, Ada M. A. Goffin. Merchant, Grant Rapids, Mich.
Children :

5480 i FRANK L.,[9] b. May 24, 1877.
5481 ii RALPH T., b. Jan. 14, 1879.

3671 MARY A.[8] EMERY (*Nathaniel*,[7] *Josiah*,[6] *Nathaniel*,[5] *Dr. Anthony*,[4] *John*,[3] *Jonathan*,[2] *John*[1]), daughter of Nathaniel and Mary L. (Arnold) Emery; married Nov. 16, 1870, James Roys.
Children :

5482 i FRED B.,[9] b. Sept. 21. 1871.
5483 ii FRANK M., b. April 23, 1876; d. Aug. 17, 1876.
5484 iii ABBY E., b. Feb. 6, 1879.

3573 ANDREW JACKSON[8] LYNN (*Eliza P.*,[7] *Josiah*,[6] *Nathaniel*,[5] *Dr. Anthony*,[4] *John*,[3] *Jonathan*,[2] *John*[1]), son of Andrew and Eliza P. (Emery) Lynn; married in Charlestown, Mass., July, 1860, Amanda H. Page (died Jan., 1861); second, Joan Eliz. Smith in Raymond, N. H., Jan., 1864. He died Sept., 1877.

Children:

   5185 i   EDITH BELL,[9] b. Feb., 1865, in Cambridgeport; d. in Portsmouth, N. H., July, 1865.
   5486 ii MYRA ELLEN, b. Sept., 1870, in Reading, Mass.
   5487 iii ANDREW CLARENCE, b. Jan., 1873, in Reading, Mass.
   5488 iv PERCY RAYMOND, b. Sept., 1874, in Reading, Mass.

3576 AURELIA EMERY[8] LYNN (*Eliza P.*,[7] *Josiah*,[6] *Nathaniel*,[5] *Dr. Anthony*,[4] *John*,[3] *Jonathan*,[2] *John*[1]), daughter of Andrew and Eliza P. (Emery) Lynn; married Jan., 1867, Washington Irving Leighton.

Children, born in Portsmouth:

   5489 i   T. SMITH,[9] b. May, 1868.
   5490 ii WASHINGTON IRVING, b. Oct., 1871.

3577 ALBERT CLARENCE[8] LYNN (*Eliza P.*,[7] *Josiah*,[6] *Nathaniel*,[5] *Dr. Anthony*,[4] *John*,[3] *Jonathan*,[2] *John*[1]), son of Andrew and Eliza P. (Emery) Lynn; married in Charlestown, Mass., Jan., 1874, Emma S. Titcomb.

Children:

   5491 i   CLARENCE ALBERT,[9] b. Jan., 1876; d. Feb., 1877.
   5492 ii MAY WHITING, b. Oct., 1878.
   5493 iii ETHEL EMERY, b. Sept., 1880; d. Aug., 1883.

3580 ELIZABETH F.[8] PAGE (*Shuah B.*,[7] *Josiah*,[6] *Nathaniel*,[5] *Dr. Anthony*,[4] *John*,[3] *Jonathan*,[2] *John*[1]), daughter of Horatio D. and Shuah B. (Emery) Page; married May, 1859, Phineas Sabine (died in Raymond, N. H., Aug. 18, 1861).

Children:

   5494 i   HARRIET ARABELLA,[9] b. Aug. 27, 1860; m. James Buchanan of Lowell, Mass., Sept. 15, 1881.

3582 SHUAH ELLEN[8] PAGE (*Shuah B.*,[7] *Josiah*,[6] *Nathaniel*,[5] *Dr. Anthony*,[4] *John*,[3] *Jonathan*,[2] *John*[1]), daughter of Horatio D. and Shuah B. (Emery) Page; married, 1864, Olney T. Brown of Raymond, N. H.

Children:

   5495 i   EDGAR T.,[9] b. Oct. 2, 1864; m. Addie Silver of Deerfield, N. H.
   5496 ii FANNIE E., b. Nov. 19, 1865; m. Charles Poore of Raymond, N. H., Dec. 25, 1884.
   5497 iii MILLIE P., b. Sept. 2, 1875.

3583 LAURA F.[8] PAGE (*Shuah B.*,[7] *Josiah*,[6] *Nathaniel*,[5] *Dr. Anthony*,[4] *John*,[3] *Jonathan*,[2] *John*[1]), daughter of Horatio D. and Shuah B. (Emery) Page; married Jan. 26, 1867, Charles E. Wason.

Child:

   5498 i   VERNA A.,[9] b. Sept. 15, 1878.

3587 AMELIA FRANCES[8] EMERY (*Josiah*,[7] *Josiah*,[6] *Nathaniel*,[5] *Dr.*

Anthony,[4] *John*,[3] *Jonathan*,[2] *John*[1]), daughter of Josiah and Louisa J. (Woodbury) Emery; married Sept. 1, 1868, George H Cook.
Children :

5499   i   FANNY AMBROSE,[9] b Oct 20. 1876.
5500   ii   LILIAN MARIE, b Sept 30, 1879.

3590 LOUISA FLORENCE[8] EMERY (*Josiah*,[7] *Josiah*,[6] *Nathaniel*,[5] *Dr. Anthony*,[4] *John*,[3] *Jonathan*,[2] *John*[1]), daughter of Josiah and Louisa J (Woodbury) Emery; married Oct. 8, 1882, Capt. Henry Osgood Marshall (born Jan. 7, 1845).
Children :

5501   i   HENRY PERRY,[9] b Sept 23, 1884.
5502   ii   LOUIS EMERY, b March 26, 1889.

3591 LAURENS C.[8] EMERY (*Josiah*,[7] *Josiah*,[6] *Nathaniel*,[5] *Dr Anthony*,[4] *John*,[3] *Jonathan*,[2] *John*[1]), son of Josiah and Louisa J. (Woodbury) Emery; married Oct. 29, 1879, Margaret Martin (born in Lawrence, Mass., March 12, 1856).
Children :

5503   i   LEROY LOMOND,[9] b Oct 12, 1882.
5504   ii   CARL CLINTON, b. Nov. 4, 1888.

3592 REV. WILLIAM FORBES[8] EMERY (*Josiah*,[7] *Josiah*,[6] *Nathaniel*,[5] *Dr. Anthony*,[4] *John*,[3] *Jonathan*,[2] *John*[1]), son of Josiah and Louisa J. (Woodbury) Emery. married Mabel Farnham of Georgetown, Mass. (born Jan. 29, 1857).
Child :

5505   i   CHILD,[9] d. in infancy

3614 DANIEL F.[8] EMERY (*David*,[7] *Daniel*,[6] *Caleb*,[5] *Caleb*,[4] *Jonathan*,[3] *Jonathan*.[2] *John*[1]), son of David and Lydia (Flint) Emery; married Sept 29, 1863, Clara A. Wilkins.
Child .

5506   i   MINNIE M ,[9] b Sept. 28, 1865.

3615 LEANDER[8] EMERY (*David*,[7] *Daniel*,[6] *Caleb*,[5] *Caleb*.[4] *Jonathan*,[3] *Jonathan*.[2] *John*[1]), son of David and Lydia (Flint) Emery; married, first, June 30, 1866, Sarah O McAllister, second, Aug. 6, 1885. Julia A. Hastings, in Antrim, N H. He was in the Seventh New Hampshire Regiment, from Oct , 1861, to June, 1865.
Child .

5507   i   SCOTT E ,[9] b Sept. 19, 1868.

3616 LOVILLA[8] EMERY (*Levi*,[7] *Daniel*.[6] *Caleb*,[5] *Caleb*.[4] *Jonathan*,[3] *Jonathan*,[2] *John*[1]), daughter of Levi and Sarah (Hildreth) Emery; married J. H. T. Newell, merchant; died April 9, 1876.
Children, born in Hillsboro :

5508   i   SARAH M ,[9] b March 29. 1841.
5509   ii   ROSA A , b. March 4, 1844
5510   iii   ALBERT C., b Nov 15, 1847.
5511   iv   EVA Z., b July 10, 1854
5512   v   AMY N., b. Feb. 17, 1857.

3622 AURELIA[8] EMERY (*John*,[7] *Daniel*,[6] *Caleb*,[5] *Caleb*,[4] *Jonathan*,[3] *Jonathan*,[2] *John*[1]), daughter of John and Jane (Sweetzer) Emery; married July 3, 1851, Samuel Robb of Stoddard, N. H.

Children :

5513   i   GUY S.,[9] b. March 22, 1852.
5514   ii   HELEN, b. April 1, 1856.
5515   iii OSCAR, b. Nov. 15, 1859.

3623 MARTHA J.[8] EMERY (*John*,[7] *Daniel*,[6] *Caleb*,[5] *Caleb*,[4] *Jonathan*,[3] *Jonathan*,[2] *John*[1]), daughter of John and Jane (Sweetzer) Emery; married Sept. 12, 1860, B. F. McIlvaine.

Children, born in Antrim, N. H. :

5516   i   NELLY S.,[9] b. Sept. 27, 1862.
5517   ii   MADISON P., b. Jan. 27, 1865.
5518   iii FILLEE B., b. Nov. 30, 1867.

3636 LEWIS F.[8] EMERY (*Mark*,[7] *Sylvanus*,[6] *Sylvanus*,[5] *Caleb*,[4] *Jonathan*,[3] *Jonathan*,[2] *John*[1]), son of Mark and Simena S. (Silver) Emery; married Nov. 28, 1867, Mary A. Collins of Goshen, N. H.

Child :

5519   i   GRACIE AMELIA,[9] b. May 24, 1871.

3639 SAMUEL F. P.[8] EMERY (*Mark*,[7] *Sylvanus*,[6] *Sylvanus*,[5] *Caleb*,[4] *Jonathan*,[3] *Jonathan*,[2] *John*[1]), son of Mark and Simena S. (Silver) Emery; married June 11, 1869, Minerva Fellows.

Child :

5520   i   NELLIE,[9] b. March 15, 1870.

3646 GEORGE H.[8] EMERY (*Solomon H.*,[7] *Caleb*,[6] *Amos*,[5] *Caleb*,[4] *Jonathan*,[3] *Jonathan*,[2] *John*[1]), son of Solomon H. and Fanny (Day) Emery; married, first, 1854. Marelia Newton (died in Monroe, N. H., Oct., 1858) ; second, April 6, 1859, Ellen M. Little.

Children :

5521   i   EMILY G.,[9] b. March, 1855, in Monroe.
5522   ii   GEORGE N., } b. May 3, 1858, in Monroe.
5523   iii   ALIA M.,   }
5524   iv   CARLOS P., b. Feb. 25, 1860 ; d. April 9, 1863, in Monroe.
5525   v   LEVI A., b. March 20, 1861, in Monroe.
5526   vi   ADELAIDE, b. July 24, 1863 ; d. Aug. 8, 1863, in Monroe.
5527   vii   JOHN C., b. Jan. 10, 1865, in Brighton, Ill.

3647 MARY F.[8] EMERY (*Solomon H.*,[7] *Caleb*,[6] *Amos*,[5] *Caleb*,[4] *Jonathan*,[3] *Jonathan*,[2] *John*[1]), daughter of Solomon H. and Fanny (Day) Emery; married in Monroe, N. H., March 2, 1848, C. C. Percival.

Child :

5528   i   NELLIE V.,[9] b. Dec. 25, 1861, in Brighton, Ill.

3649 ANN E.[8] EMERY (*Solomon H.*,[7] *Caleb*,[6] *Amos*,[5] *Caleb*,[4] *Jonathan*,[3] *Jonathan*,[2] *John*[1]), daughter of Solomon H. and Fanny (Day), Emery; married May 20, 1856, W. W. Nelson.

Children :

5529 i INFANT SON,[9] b. Jan. 8, 1858.
5530 ii LYMAN A., b. Oct. 17, 1861.
5531 iii JOHN CLAYTON, b. Aug. 20, 1862; d. June 1, 1863.
5532 iv JOHN CARLTON, b. May 30, 1864.
5533 v WILLIE W., b. Nov. 5, 1871.
5534 vi MARIETTA STUART, b. Jan. 13, 1874.

3663 ELIZABETH GERTRUDE[8] BERRY (*Mary C.,[7] Caleb,[6] Amos,[5] Caleb,[4] Jonathan,[3] Jonathan,[2] John[1]*), daughter of Asa M. and Mary C. (Emery) Berry; married Dec. 20, 1883, Ezekiel T. Johnson, of Oak Lawn, R. I.
Child:
5535 i EDITH GERTRUDE,[9] b. Sept. 26, 1885.

3664 REV. JOHN C.[8] EMERY (*Chellis,[7] Samuel,[6] Amos,[5] Caleb,[4] Jonathan,[3] Jonathan,[2] John[1]*), son of Chellis and Martha H. (Cross) Emery; married in Johnson, Vt., March 18, 1858, Mary E. Massure. He was educated as a physician and practised his profession at Waterbury, Vt.; Jan. 4, 1863, entered New Hampshire Literary and Theological Institute; in 1864, entered the Union army as volunteer surgeon; 1864, appointed acting assistant surgeon; later, as first assistant surgeon in the 13th N. H. Vols.; mustered out at Concord, N. H., June 30, 1865; began to preach as a licentiate at Hyde Park, Mass., Sept., 1865; ordained Sept., 1866; has had charges in Haverhill, Athol and Lowell, Mass., Amsterdam, N. Y., and Hartford, Conn. She died in Lowell, Mass., July 8, 1888.
Child:
5536 i MINNIE FRANCES,[9] b. Aug. 6, 1866, in Hyde Park, Mass.

3687 GARDNER[8] EMERY (*Isaac,[7] Joel,[6] Joel,[5] Caleb,[4] Jonathan,[3] Jonathan,[2] John[1]*), son of Isaac and Alice (Austin) Emery; married Dec. 24, 1880, Sarah Perkins.
Children:
5537 i ALICE MAY,[9] b. May 1, 1883.
5538 ii ROBERT, b. Nov. 3, 1885.

3688 ELLEN M.[8] EMERY (*Isaac,[7] Joel,[6] Joel,[5] Caleb,[4] Jonathan,[3] Jonathan,[2] John[1]*), daughter of Isaac and Alice (Austin) Emery; married March 9, 1881, Willis C. Lattimer.
Children:
5539 i AUSTIN,[9] b. July 4, 1884.
5540 ii SUSAN ALICE, b. Feb. 27, 1886.

3723 BETSEY[8] WILLEY (*Abigail,[7] Esther,[6] Humphrey,[5] Humphrey,[4] Jonathan,[3] Jonathan,[2] John[1]*), daughter of Curtis and Abigail (Emery) Willey; married Wells Heath.
Children:
5541 i GEORGE.[9]
5542 ii FRED.
5543 iii WILLIE.

3728 SARAH F.[8] EMERY (*Samuel F.,[7] Esther,[6] Humphrey,[5] Hum-*

phrey,[4] *Jonathan,*[3] *Jonathan,*[2] *John*[1]), daughter of Samuel F. and Almira (McCarter) Emery ; married in Berlin, N. H., Sept. 9, 1871, Thomas W. Haley of Fryeburg, Me. (born in Fryeburg, Aug. 24, 1847).

Children :

```
5544   i    MINNIE E.,⁹ b. April 7, 1872.
5545   ii   ARTHUR E., b. April 7, 1874.
5546   iii  W. RALPH, b. Mar. 14, 1876.
5547   iv   HARRY, b. Feb. 11, 1878.
5548   v    ERNEST, b. May 25, 1880.
5549   vi   WALTER, b. Feb. 10, 1883.
```

3729 ELLA[8] EMERY (*Samuel F.,*[7] *Esther,*[6] *Humphrey,*[5] *Humphrey,*[4] *Jonathan,*[3] *Jonathan,*[2] *John*[1]), daughter of Samuel F. and Almira (McCarter) Emery ; married April, 1877, William D. Farris of Oxford, Me.

Children :

```
5550   i    OSCAR H.⁹
5551   ii   MELVIN.
5552   iii  MAUD.
```

3748 ALMIRA[8] EMERY (*Noah,*[7] *Ruth,*[6] *Humphrey,*[5] *Humphrey,*[4] *Jonathan,*[3] *Jonathan,*[2] *John*[1]), daughter of Noah and Irene L. (Morgan) Emery ; married Sept. 18, 1854, Royal Putnam (died May 8, 1881).

Children :

```
5553   i    MURRAY,⁹ }
5554   ii   MERVIN,  } b. Dec. 6, 1856.
```

3749 ANGELINE[8] EMERY (*Noah,*[7] *Ruth,*[6] *Humphrey,*[5] *Humphrey,*[4] *Jonathan,*[3] *Jonathan,*[2] *John*[1]), daughter of Noah and Irene L. (Morgan) Emery ; married Feb. 22, 1844, Eliakim Crosby (born Sept. 13, 1806 ; died Aug. 13, 1880). She died Nov., 1887. He was a lumber merchant and farmer.

Children :

```
5555   i    WALTER SCOTT,⁹ b. Nov. 30, 1844.
5556   ii   ELLEN AMELIA, b. June 24, 1847.
5557   iii  FREEMAN HOPKINS, b. May 23, 1849.
5558   iv   KATE L., b. April 15, 1854: m. Sept. 23, 1887, Frank Hunt.
5559   v    ANNA MAKEPEACE, b. Oct. 9, 1856.
5560   vi   MABEL FLORENCE, b. April 18, 1864.
5561   vii  BENJAMIN F., d. in infancy.
5562   viii MAUD, d. in infancy.
```

3751 AMELIA[8] EMERY (*Noah,*[7] *Ruth,*[6] *Humphrey,*[5] *Humphrey,*[4] *Jonathan,*[3] *Jonathan,*[2] *John*[1]), daughter of Noah and Irene L. (Morgan) Emery ; married Dec. 19, 1843, Ephraim Davenport (born Feb. 4, 1819).

Children :

```
5563   i    MARTHA,⁹ b. Nov. 6, 1845.
5564   ii   EMERY M., b. June 2, 1847; d. April 18, 1887.
5565   iii  MARY, b. April 9, 1849.
5566   iv   OLIVIA ABBY, b. Feb. 16, 1856.
5567   v    IRENE AMELIA, b. Sept. 15, 1864; m. Nov. 15, 1882, Daniel
            Walker.
```

3753 ALVINA D.[8] EMERY (*Noah*,[7] *Ruth*,[6] *Humphrey*,[5] *Humphrey*,[4] *Jonathan*,[3] *Jonathan*,[2] *John*[1]), daughter of Noah and Irene L. (Morgan) Emery; married in Poland, Dec. 16, 1851, Bravity Taylor (born Dec. 17, 1820; died Oct. 23, 1867). She died May 10, 1889.

Children:

```
5568   i    FRANK H ,9 b Oct 29, 1852.
5569   ii   LAURENCE NORMAND, ⎫ b  Sept  9, 1856.
5570   iii  CLARENCE NORTON,  ⎭
```

3756 LODEMA[8] EMERY (*Noah*,[7] *Ruth*,[6] *Humphrey*,[5] *Humphrey*,[4] *Jonathan*,[3] *Jonathan*,[2] *John*[1]), daughter of Noah and Irene L (Morgan) Emery, married Nov. 30, 1858, Newton Taylor (born Aug. 15, 1831, died May 1, 1884). Miller.

Children.

```
5571   i    MINNIE,9 b  June 30, 1859.
5572   ii   BENNIE, b  Aug 19, 1866
5573   iii  FRANK F , b  Sept 4, 1869.
```

3757 SARAH SIBLEY[8] EMERY (*Noah*,[7] *Ruth*,[6] *Humphrey*,[5] *Humphrey*,[4] *Jonathan*,[3] *Jonathan*,[2] *John*[1]), daughter of Noah and Irene L. (Morgan) Emery, married at Jamestown, N. Y., Dec 26, 1860. Ransom W Wolcott, farmer.

Children

```
5574   i    MILTON FREEMAN,9 b  July 20, 1862.
5575   ii   LORAINE OFFTT, b  Aug 17, 1865
5576   iii  MORGAN EMERY, ⎫ b  July 27, 1871
5577   iv   MYRA EMERY,   ⎭
5578   v    MEAD D , b  Oct 10, 1873 ; d. Dec. 16, 1877
```

3758 ORETT JANE[8] EMERY (*Noah*,[7] *Ruth*,[6] *Humphrey*,[5] *Humphrey*,[4] *Jonathan*,[3] *Jonathan*,[2] *John*[1]), daughter of Noah and Irene L. (Morgan) Emery ; married Nov. 26, 1870, Joseph Knight, farmer.

Children.

```
5579   i    ARTHUR,9 b  Oct. 10, 1871
5580   ii   WALTER, b  July 14, 1873
5581   iii  LYNN, b  Dec. 31, 1875.
5582   iv   IRENE, b  Feb 9, 1877
5583   v    BESSIE, b. Aug 13, 1880
```

3762 THOMAS[8] EMERY (*Jonas*,[7] *Ruth*,[6] *Humphrey*,[5] *Humphrey*,[4] *Jonathan*,[3] *Jonathan*,[2] *John*[1]), son of Jonas and Lucett (Wood) Emery, married Jan. 1, 1851, Sarah M. Safford (born March 6, 1828).

Children:

```
5584   i    JAMES B ,9 b Dec 31  1851, in Pomfret, N  Y
5585   ii   LUCETTA J , b  Nov 4, 1854  in Pomfret, N  Y
5586   iii  BATTIA A., b  Oct 28, 1856, in Cherry Creek, N. Y.
5587   iv   CLARA S , b. Aug 22, 1858, in Cherry Creek, N  Y
5588   v    RUTH D , b  Sept 12, 1860, in Cherry Creek, N  Y , d May 1,
                 1862
5589   vi   CURTIS D , b  Feb  18, 1863, in Cherry Creek, N. Y.
5590   vii  MARY M , b  Jan 31, 1865, in Derry, N. H
```

3764 JAMES M.[8] EMERY (*Jonas*,[7] *Ruth*,[6] *Humphrey*,[5] *Humphrey*,[4]

Jonathan,[3] Jonathan,[2] John[1]), son of Jonas and Lucett (Wood) Emery; married Annett Baldwin.

Child :

   5591 i CARRIE B.[9]

3768 FRANKLIN F.[8] NORMAND (*Sarah,[7] Ruth.[6] Humphrey,[5] Humphrey,[4] Jonathan,[3] Jonathan,[2] John[1]*), son of Jabez Reed and Sarah Emery (Morgan) Normand : married, first, in Boston, Mass., Aug. 1, 1867, Mary J. Wells, who died May 31, 1877; second, March 7, 1884, Jennie Shepard (born April 25, 1852). Engineer.

Children, born in Boston, Mass. :

   5592 i JOHN FREEMAN,[9] b. Sept. 4, 1868.
   5593 ii THOMAS HOBART, b. Sept. 8, 1870; d. Sept. 25, 1876.
   5594 iii JAMES MORGAN, b. July 8, 1872; adopted by his aunt Kate E. Normand.
   5595 iv FRANK HENRY, b. Jan. 1, 1876.
   5596 v GEORGE ARNALDA, b. Jan. 15, 1886, in Boston.

3770 ESTHER[8] NORMAND (*Sarah,[7] Ruth.[6] Humphrey,[5] Humphrey,[4] Jonathan,[3] Jonathan,[2] John[1]*), daughter of Jabez Reed and Sarah Emery (Morgan) Normand; married in Westfield, N. Y., June 16, 1868, James W. Lucas (born Oct. 5, 1843).

Child adopted :

   i FRANK H.,[9] son of Franklin F. Normand (see No. 5595).

3771 HOBART[8] NORMAND (*Sarah,[7] Ruth.[6] Humphrey,[5] Humphrey,[4] Jonathan,[3] Jonathan,[2] John[1]*), son of Jabez Reed and Sarah Emery (Morgan) Normand; married at Salamanca, N. Y., Rose M. Velie (born March 8, 1851).

Child :

   5597 i KATHERINE J.,[9] b. Jan. 22, 1876.

3772 DAVID J.[8] FLETCHER (*Emily,[7] Ruth,[6] Humphrey,[5] Humphrey,[4] Jonathan,[3] Jonathan,[2] John[1]*), son of Daniel and Emily (Morgan) Fletcher : married Oct. 1, 1874, Polly S. Baker, of Hustisford, Wis.

Children :

   5598 i ROY MORGAN,[9] b. Jan. 11, 1876.
   5599 ii ANNA BELLE, b. July 31, 1879.
   5600 iii WALDO L., b. Sept. 29, 1881.
   5601 iv DANIEL BAKER, b. Dec. 30, 1884.

3773 SARAH KATHARINE[8] FLETCHER (*Emily[7], Ruth.[6] Humphrey,[5] Humphrey,[4] Jonathan,[3] Jonathan,[2] John[1]*), daughter of Daniel and Emily (Morgan) Fletcher; married in Oconomowoc, Wis., Oct. 5, 1875, William C. Lyman.

Child :

   5602 i CHARLES MORGAN,[9] b. Nov. 11, 1876.

3774 CHARLES NELSON[8] FLETCHER (*Emily,[7] Ruth,[6] Humphrey,[5] Humphrey,[4] Jonathan,[3] Jonathan,[2] John[1]*), son of Daniel and Emily (Morgan) Fletcher; married at Hustisford, Wis., Dec. 25, 1878, Abbie A. R.

Children :

5603   i   GRACE ARDEL,[9] b. Oct. 9, 1874.
5604   ii   HARRY ELTON, b. May 20, 1876.
5605   iii   FRANK DELAMONT, b. June 22, 1880.
5606   iv   ROBERT CHARLES, b. Oct. 17, 1885.

3776 NOAH R.[8] EMERY (*Peter,*[7] *Sarah,*[6] *Humphrey,*[5] *Humphrey,*[4] *Jonathan,*[3] *Jonathan,*[2] *John*[1]), son of Peter and Mrs. Hannah (Upton-Moore) Emery ; married Sept. 16, 1875, Lucy A. Wright.
Children, born in Albany, Me. :

5607   i   CARRIE F.,[9] b. Dec. 4, 1878.
5608   ii   OLLA M., b. May 20, 1883.

3782 JOHN PITMAN[8] EMERY (*Joshua,*[7] *Stephen,*[6] *Enoch,*[5] *Humphrey,*[4] *Jonathan,*[3] *Jonathan,*[2] *John*[1]), son of Joshua and Hannah (Wentworth) Emery ; married in Jan., 1853, Louisa Sanderson.
Children :

5609   i   ADELAIDE LOUISA,[9] b. Nov. 4, 1854.
5610   ii   LUELLA CORNELIA, b. Oct. 3, 1856.
5611   iii   NELLIE A., b. May 21, 1860.
5612   iv   GEORGE IRVING, b. Jan. 26, 1862.
5613   v   MAGGIE HANNAH, b. Aug. 10, 1869.
5614   vi   MERTIE MAUD, b. July 13, 1871.
5615   vii   MINNIE AGNES, b. July 13, 1873.

3784 STEPHEN WENTWORTH[8] EMERY (*Joshua,*[7] *Stephen,*[6] *Enoch,*[5] *Humphrey,*[4] *Jonathan,*[3] *Jonathan,*[2] *John*[1]), son of Joshua and Hannah (Wentworth) Emery ; married June 12, 1864, Betsey Amy.
Children :

5616   i   FLETCHER STEPHEN,[9] b. April 14, 1866.
5617   ii   ALBERT, b. April 14, 1873.

3785 LOUISA L.[8] EMERY (*Joshua,*[7] *Stephen,*[6] *Enoch,*[5] *Humphrey,*[4] *Jonathan,*[3] *Jonathan,*[2] *John*[1]), daughter of Joshua and Hannah (Wentworth) Emery ; married Jan. 1, 1867, Frank J. Hartshorn of Canaan, Vt. :
Child :

5618   i   FRANK M.,[9] b. Oct. 6, 1874.

3786 WARREN DANA[8] EMERY (*Joshua,*[7] *Stephen,*[6] *Enoch,*[5] *Humphrey,*[4] *Jonathan,*[3] *Jonathan,*[2] *John*[1]), son of Joshua and Hannah (Wentworth) Emery ; married Nov., 1870, Ruby Hendrick.
Children :

5619   i   EVERETT JOSHUA.[9]
5620   ii   HARRIET.
5621   iii   CHARLES.

3787 ELIZABETH HANNAH[8] EMERY (*Joshua,*[7] *Stephen,*[6] *Enoch,*[5] *Humphrey,*[4] *Jonathan,*[3] *Jonathan,*[2] *John*[1]), daughter of Joshua and Hannah (Wentworth) Emery ; married, first, Jan. 1, 1864, Marvin Fletcher of Canaan, Vt., who died Oct. 21, 1872 ; second, May 5, 1873, Charles H. Weeks of Canaan, Vt.

Children :

5622   i   JENNIE H.,[9] b. June 3, 1875.
5623   ii   GERTRUDE, b. 1877.

3788 ELSIE ANN[8] EMERY (*Joshua*,[7] *Stephen*,[6] *Enoch*,[5] *Humphrey*,[4] *Jonathan*,[3] *Jonathan*,[2] *John*[1]), daughter of Joshua and Hannah (Wentworth) Emery; married Aug. 15, 1863, John Carbe of Canaan, Vt.
Children :

5624   i   E. EUGENE,[9] b. 1864.
5625   ii   FRANK DANA, b. 1866.
5626   iii EVERETT IRVING, b. 1869.

3790 JEREMIAH B.[8] COPP (*Dolly*,[7] *Nathaniel*,[6] *Enoch*,[5] *Humphrey*,[4] *Jonathan*,[3] *Jonathan*,[2] *John*[1]), son of Hayes D. and Dolly (Emery) Copp; married Susan G. Rogers, Jan. 10, 1858.
Children :

5627   i   MARCELLA M.,[9] b. June 24, 1859; m. John W. Fuller, Jan. 23, 1883.
5628   ii   SUSAN J., b. April 29, 1862; m. Albert J. Hoyt, March 18, 1882. He d. Aug. 17, 1887.
5629   iii CHARLES B., b. Dec. 26, 1870.

3795 FANNY[8] VINING (*Martha B.*,[7] *Nathaniel*,[6] *Enoch*,[5] *Humphrey*,[4] *Jonathan*,[3] *Jonathan*,[2] *John*[1]), daughter of George and Martha B. (Emery) Vining; married in Fitchburg, Mass., Sept. 4, 1872, George F. Gould.
Children, except last, born in Templeton, Mass. :

5630   i   BENJAMIN ABBOT,[9] b. May 11, 1874.
5631   ii   FANNIE MAY, b. May 24, 1876.
5632   iii GEORGE LEROY, b. Dec. 16, 1878.
5633   iv   HERBERT WARREN, b. Nov. 27, 1881.
5634   v   EDGAR WALTON, b. Dec. 12, 1885, in Phillipston, Mass.

3796 MARTHA[8] VINING (*Martha B.*,[7] *Nathaniel*,[6] *Enoch*,[5] *Humphrey*,[4] *Jonathan*,[3] *Jonathan*,[2] *John*[1]), daughter of George and Martha B. (Emery) Vining; married June 15, 1868, in Templeton, Mass., Austin Curtis Drury.
Children :

5635   i   FREDERICK CURTIS,[9] b. Dec. 30, 1870, in Templeton, Mass.
5636   ii   ANNA MAY, b. Jan. 15, 1876, in Worcester, Mass.
5637   iii MARTHA EUNICE, b. Feb. 17, 1883, in Worcester, Mass.; d. Sept. 14, 1883.

3830 RICHARD H.[8] EMERY (*Theo. M.*,[7] *William*,[6] *Richardson*,[5] *Humphrey*,[4] *Jonathan*,[3] *Jonathan*,[2] *John*[1]), son of Theo. M. and Hannah Bruce (Coolidge) Emery; married Emeline L. Smith, April 4, 1855.
Children, born in Schuyler Falls, N. Y. :

5638   i   LEANDER M,[9] b. Dec. 16, 1856; d. May 4, 1872.
5639   ii   ALLEN S., b. July 25, 1858; d. Dec. 25, 1861.
5640   iii ELLA H., b. June 15, 1863; d. Feb. 11, 1864.
5641   iv   LOTTIE E., b. Jan. 25, 1866; d. Oct. 19, 1877.

5642 v VILLETTA A , b Nov 19, 1868, d Feb 24, 1871
5643 vi FLORENCE O., b. June 7, 1871, d Dec 24, 1871
5644 vii EDITH GRACE, b Jan 1, 1875
5645 viii STELLA V , b July 28, 1880, d Oct 25, 1880

3851 HANNAH[8] EMERY (*William*,[7] *William*,[6] *Richardson*,[5] *Humphrey*,[4] *Jonathan*,[3] *Jonathan*,[2] *John*[1]), daughter of William and Rosanna (Witherell) Emery , married in Nicholville, N. Y , March 9, 1866, Henry Barber She died Jan. 6. 1885.
Children, born in Brandon, N. Y. :

5646 i FRED,[9] b Jan 6, 1867, m Hannah Emery, daughter of Ezekiel Emery
5647 ii EDWIN, b Jan 5, 1868, m Mary McManus who was born in Brushton, N Y , 1869
5648 iii HENRY, b Oct 14, 1869
5649 iv FLORA, b Sept 12, 1871
5650 v CLARA, b Sept 18, 1873; d. May, 1875.
5651 vi ARTHUR, b March 11, 1875.
5652 vii FRANKLIN, b April 5, 1877.

3854 ALBERT W.[8] EMERY (*William*,[7] *William*,[6] *Richardson*,[5] *Humphrey*,[4] *Jonathan*,[3] *Jonathan*,[2] *John*[1]), son of William and Rosanna (Witherell) Emery ; married in Schuyler Falls, N. Y . June 9, 1878, Jane S. Bowles (born in Bangor, N. Y , June 3, 1848), daughter of William and Martha (Emery) Bowles.
Child :

5653 i CLAYTON,[9] b and d in Plattsburg, N. Y Feb 12, 1880

3856 PASCAL[8] EMERY (*William*,[7] *William*,[6] *Richardson*,[5] *Humphrey*,[4] *Jonathan*,[3] *Jonathan*,[2] *John*[1]), son of William and Rosanna (Witherell) Emery: married in Minnesota, April 1, 1884, Hattie E. Fuller (born in Blue Earth Co., Minn., Feb 9, 1862).
Child :

5654 A DAUGHTER,[9] b June 11, 1887; d Feb 25, 1888

3857 NEWELL[8] EMERY (*William*,[7] *William*,[6] *Richardson*,[5] *Humphrey*,[4] *Jonathan*,[3] *Jonathan*,[2] *John*[1]), son of William and Rosanna (Witherell) Emery , married in Zumbrota, Minn , March 31, 1886, Ida May Stoddard (born June 20, 1864).
Child :

5655 i WILLIAM H ,[9] b Nov 21, 1887

3861 ANNA[8] EMERY (*William*,[7] *William*,[6] *Richardson*,[5] *Humphrey*,[4] *Jonathan*,[3] *Jonathan*,[2] *John*[1]), daughter of William and Rosanna (Witherell) Emery ; married in Plattsburg, N. Y , April 13, 1876, John Rosman (born in Schuyler Falls, N. Y., Oct. 25, 1860).
Child .

5656 i BESSIE,[9] b Feb 27, 1878

3885 JOHN V. R [8] BOWLES (*Martha*,[7] *Nathaniel*,[6] *Richardson*,[5] *Humphrey*,[4] *Jonathan*,[3] *Jonathan*,[2] *John*[1]), son of William and

Martha (Emery) Bowles ; married in Bangor, N. Y., Mary Potter.   He died Oct. 19, 1887.
  Children :

    5657   i   HENRY.[9]
    5658   ii   JOHN.
    5659   iii BELLE.

3887 LYDIA BOWLES[8] (*Martha,*[7] *Nathaniel,*[6] *Richardson,*[5] *Humphrey,*[4] *Jonathan,*[3] *Jonathan,*[2] *John*[1]), daughter of William and Martha (Emery) Bowles ; married in Peasleyville, N. Y., 1848, Franklin Alford.   She died in 1886.
  Children :

    5660   i   GRATEY.[9]
    5661   ii   MYRON.

3889 BETSEY BOWLES[8] (*Martha,*[7] *Nathaniel,*[6] *Richardson,*[5] *Humphrey,*[4] *Jonathan,*[3] *Jonathan,*[2] *John*[1]), daughter of William and Martha (Emery) Bowles ; married in Bangor, N. Y., 1864, Bishop White.
  Child :

    5662   i   IMOGENE,[9] b. in Schuyler Falls, N. Y., 1865.

3890 SAMUEL BOWLES[8] (*Martha,*[7] *Nathaniel,*[6] *Richardson,*[5] *Humphrey,*[4] *Jonathan,*[3] *Jonathan,*[2] *John*[1]), son of William and Martha (Emery) Bowles ; married in Bangor, N. Y., 1866, Floretta Hinon.
  Children :

    5663   i   RUSSELL.[9]
    5664   ii   ETTIE.
    5665   iii HERBERT.

3894 EZEKIEL EMERY[8] (*Samuel,*[7] *Nathaniel,*[6] *Richardson,*[5] *Humphrey,*[4] *Jonathan,*[3] *Jonathan,*[2] *John*[1]), son of Samuel and —— (——) Emery ; married —— —— and is a farmer in Brandon, N. Y.
  Child :

    5666   i   HANNAH,[9] b. 1868 ; m. Fred Barber.

3904 CHARLES AUGUSTUS[8] EMERY (*Daniel,*[7] *Daniel,*[6] *John,*[5] *Stephen,*[4] *Stephen,*[3] *Jonathan,*[2] *John*[1]), son of Daniel and Susannah (Pierce) Emery ; married, June 20, 1854, Nancy C. Pierce of Lunenburg (born March 18, 1829).
  Children :

    5667   i   NELLIE FRANCES,[9] b. July 24, 1855 ; d. March 27, 1863.
    5668   ii   MINNIE LOUISA, b. March 20, 1859 ; d. April 9, 1863.
    5669   iii CHARLES LINCOLN, b. March 15, 1861 ; d. March 22, 1863.
    5670   iv   FRANK EUGENE, b. Jan. 19, 1866.
    5671   v   BERTRAM PIERCE, b. Aug. 26, 1868.

3905 SIDNEY PATTERSON[8] EMERY (*Daniel,*[7] *Daniel,*[6] *John,*[5] *Stephen,*[4] *Stephen,*[3] *Jonathan,*[2] *John*[1]), son of Daniel and Susannah (Pierce) Emery ; married, first, Feb. 24, 1863, Cynthia E. Osborn, daughter of Leonard Osborn ; second, Nov. 7, 1867, Sarah (Davis)

Newton (born March 21, 1837), widow of Dexter Newton and daughter of Winslow and Lydia (Learned) Davis of Templeton, Mass.
Children .

5672   1   WALTER OSBORN,[9] b March 31 1865, d June 26, 1865
5673   11 LOUIE PATTERSON, b. March 13, 1871, d May 29, 1871

3906 WILLIAM CHILDS[8] EMERY (*Daniel,[7] Daniel,[6] John,[5] Stephen,[4] Stephen,[3] Jonathan,[2] John[1]*), son of Daniel and Susannah (Pierce) Emery; married, June 9, 1859, Georgiana Frances Leavitt, daughter of James and Louisa (Lord) Leavitt of Lowell, Mass.
Children .

5674   1   WILLIE L ,[9] b May 5, 1864   d May 8, 1867
5675   11 WALTER L , b Nov 10, 1868

3908 EDWARD FRANKLIN[8] EMERY (*Daniel,[7] Daniel,[6] John,[5] Stephen,[4] Stephen,[3] Jonathan,[2] John[1]*), son of Daniel and Susannah (Pierce) Emery , married , Aug 29, 1860, Mary Mildred Colby, daughter of John and Sarah C. (Purington) Colby of Bath, Me.   He served three years in the 36th Massachusetts Volunteer Infantry ; Commissary Sergeant, July 17, 1862, to Aug. 1, 1863 ; 2nd Lieut., Aug. 1, 1863, to Feb. 21, 1864, then 1st Lieut. to June 8, 1865, expiration of service.
Children :

5676   1   CORA ALTHEA[9] b Dec 19, 1861, in Fitchburg Mass
5677   11 GERTRUDE SUSAN, b Jan 10, 1865, in Fitchburg, Mass
5678   111 FREDERICK LINCOLN, b April 9, 1867, in Lunenburg, Mass

3910 SARAH EMMA[8] EMERY (*Daniel,[7] Daniel,[6] John,[5] Stephen,[4] Stephen,[3] Jonathan,[2] John[1]*), daughter of Daniel and Susannah (Pierce) Emery , married, June 15, 1869, Henry D Yerxa, son of Isabella and Benjamin Yerxa.
Children .

5679   1   SADIE E ,[9] b Sept 6, 1871.
5680   11 HENRY D , b March 12, 1874

3916 GEORGE A [8] EMERY (*Derostus W ,[7] Stephen,[6] John,[5] Stephen,[4] Stephen [3] Jonathan,[2] John[1]*), son of Derostus W and Mary (Pierce) Emery ; married, first, May 20, 1854, Martha L Bass, daughter of David Bass of Sharon, N H (died June 21, 1863) ; second, June 5, 1864, Mary E Stearns of Jaffrey, N H.

3921 DEROSTUS P.[8] EMERY (*Derostus W.,[7] Stephen,[6] John,[5] Stephen,[4] Stephen,[3] Jonathan,[2] John[1]*), son of Derostus W. and Mary (Pierce) Emery , married, Nov , 1858, H. Augusta Davis, daughter of Joseph Davis.
Child :

5681   1   GEORGE E ,[9] b Feb 6, 1862

3943 EMILY R [8] KING (*Mary,[7] Stephen,[6] Jesse,[5] Stephen,[4] Stephen,[3] Jonathan,[2] John[1]*), daughter of Isaac and Mary (Emery) King ; married Stephen L. Etheredge.

18

Children :

5682 i   WILLIE.[9]
5683 ii   LIZZIE.

3944 DELPHINA A.[8] KING (*Mary*,[7] *Stephen*,[6] *Jesse*,[5] *Stephen*,[4] *Stephen*,[3] *Jonathan*,[2] *John*[1]), daughter of Isaac and Mary (Emery) King; married, first, Frank Merrow; second, Luther Prescott Holt.
Children :

5684 i   RENA ISAAC.[9]
5685 ii   LAWRENCE BERTRAM.

3945 SARAH ADELAIDE[8] KING (*Mary*,[7] *Stephen*,[6] *Jesse*,[5] *Stephen*,[4] *Stephen*,[3] *Jonathan*,[2] *John*[1]), daughter of Isaac and Mary (Emery) King; married, in Newry, Me., March 1, 1869, Willard Barker Wight.
Children :

5686 i   GEORGE KING.[9] b. May 9, 1871,
5687 ii   ARTHUR CLIFTON, b. Jan. 30, 1873.
5688 iii LOU EDSON, b. Oct. 27, 1880.
5689 iv   CARRIE MAY, b. April 3, 1884.
5690 v   FRED WILLARD, b. June 9, 1886.

3946 AMOS S.[8] KING (*Mary*,[7] *Stephen*,[6] *Jesse*,[5] *Stephen*,[4] *Stephen*,[3] *Jonathan*,[2] *John*[1]), son of Isaac and Mary (Emery) King; married Jennie Goodwin.
Children :

5691 i   HAROLD CHESTER.[9]
5692 ii   GRACE.
5693 iii BENJAMIN HARRISON.

3959 IDA L.[8] EMERY (*John*,[7] *Stephen*,[6] *Jesse*,[5] *Stephen*,[4] *Stephen*,[3] *Jonathan*,[2] *John*[1]), daughter of John and A. W. (Littlefield) Emery; married June 9, 1881, Ernest Rowe.
Child :

5694 i   ESMA A.,[9] b. March 9, 1882.

3960 ESMA L.[8] EMERY (*John*,[7] *Stephen*,[6] *Jesse*,[5] *Stephen*,[4] *Stephen*,[3] *Jonathan*,[2] *John*[1]), daughter of John and A. W. (Littlefield) Emery; married June 1, 1884, William F. Walker.
Child :

5695 i   ELLIE E.,[9] b. May 11, 1885.

4046 HARRIET FRANCES[8] EMERY (*Benjamin E.*,[7] *Jesse*,[6] *Moses*,[5] *Benjamin*,[4] *Stephen*,[3] *Jonathan*,[2] *John*[1]), daughter of Benjamin E. and Elizabeth H. (Poor) Emery; married Tristram G. Glines (born Jan. 1, 1846).
Children, born in Haverhill, Mass. :

5696 i   WILLIE CHENEY,[9] b. June 7, 1870.
5697 ii   FRANK MILTON, b. Dec. 5, 1872.
5698 iii LULU BELL, b. Nov. 12, 1879; d. March, 1880.
5699 iv   ALBERT EMERY, b. Jan. 3, 1882.

4047 Susan Perley[8] Emery (*Benjamin E.,*[7] *Jesse,*[6] *Moses,*[5] *Benjamin,*[4] *Stephen,*[3] *Jonathan,*[2] *John*[1]), daughter of Benjamin E and Elizabeth H. (Poor) Emery; married Dec. 26, 1881, Charles S. Towle (born in Danville, N H , June 17, 1848).

Children .

5700   i   Sumner Emery [9] b Sept 19, 1882.
5700a   ii   Irena Rovena, b. Sept. 20, 1884.

4092 Wilson C [8] Fitzgerald (*Orra,*[7] *Benjamin,*[6] *David,*[5] *Jonathan,*[4] *James,*[3] *Jonathan,*[2] *John*[1]), son of Benjamin and Orra (Emery) Fitzgerald, married Mary H Ganley at Brush Creek, California (born at sea on the Pacific Ocean, May 13, 1851). He was Corporal Co. "F," 7th Maine Infantry, during the rebellion.

Children ·

5701   i   Selden W ,[9] b. March 4, 1876, in Point Arenas, Cal.
5702   ii   Carl Pitt, b May 26, 1878, in Canaan. Me
5703   iii   Orra E , b Nov. 2, 1880, d Nov. 4, 1881
5704   iv   Benjamin O , b April 26, 1884

4093 Paulina N.[8] Fitzgerald (*Orra,*[7] *Benjamin,*[6] *David,*[5] *Jonathan,*[4] *James,*[3] *Jonathan,*[2] *John*[1]), daughter of Benjamin and Orra (Emery) Fitzgerald; married Jan. 1, 1867, Francis T. Shorey (born in Oakland, Me., 1833). She died in West Waterville, Me., Dec. 26, 1878.

Children, born in West Waterville :

5705   i   Blanch M ,[9] b Jan 28, 1868, m. June 30, 1888, William Sturdefant, and d June 17, 1889, in Fairfield, Me
5706   ii   Maud E , b Nov. 13, 1870
5707   iii   Caddie H , b July 6, 1875
5708   iv   Paulina B , b Dec. 15, 1878

4094 Mary E.[8] Fitzgerald (*Orra,*[7] *Benjamin,*[6] *David,*[5] *Jonathan,*[4] *James,*[3] *Jonathan,*[2] *John*[1]), daughter of Benjamin and Orra (Emery) Fitzgerald, married Nov 2, 1861, in Canaan, Me , Noah H. Burrill (born Nov. 19, 1836).

Children, born in Canaan :

5709   i   Ellsworth S.,[9] b Aug 8, 1862, noted rifleman; d , unm., Feb. 3, 1886
5710   ii   Schuyler C , b July 28, 1867.

4095 Ann Salome[8] Fitzgerald (*Orra,*[7] *Benjamin,*[6] *David,*[5] *Jonathan,*[4] *James,*[3] *Jonathan,*[2] *John*[1]), daughter of Benjamin and Orra (Emery) Fitzgerald, married May 2, 1866, George W Burrill (born in Fairfield, Me., Oct 7, 1843, died in Canaan, Me., July 13, 1875). Member of Co. "C." 24th Regt , Maine Infantry, in the war of the Rebellion. She died Sept 6, 1867.

Child, born in Canaan :

5711   i   Child,[9] b Aug 17, 1867, d. Sept 16, 1867

4096 Burke L [8] Fitzgerald (*Orra,*[7] *Benjamin,*[6] *David,*[5] *Jonathan,*[4] *James,*[3] *Jonathan,*[2] *John*[1]), son of Benjamin and Orra (Emery) Fitzgerald, married Oct. 3, 1874, Emma G. Cole (born in Burnham, Me., March 13, 1857).

Child :

5712   i   ELIZABETH ABBY,[9] b. July 14, 1875, in Skowhegan, Me.

4097 VARA ELLEN[8] FITZGERALD (*Orra*,[7] *Benjamin*,[6] *David*,[5] *Jonathan*,[4] *James*,[3] *Jonathan*,[2] *John*[1]), daughter of Benjamin and Orra (Emery) Fitzgerald; married Oct. 3, 1874, W. H. Richardson (born in Clinton, Me., June 10, 1848).

Child :

5713   i   EVA ESTELLE,[9] b. April 1, 1875, in Clinton, Me.

4098 BENJAMIN EMERY[8] LIBBY (*Rachel*,[7] *Benjamin*,[6] *David*,[5] *Jonathan*,[4] *James*,[3] *Jonathan*,[2] *John*[1]), son of William and Rachel (Emery) Libby; married April 27, 1863, Rebecca, daughter of Hiram and Mary Delameter Mirack.

Child :

5714   i   EDWIN WILSON,[9] b. Jan. 13, 1864.

4101 JOHN F.[8] LIBBY (*Rachel*,[7] *Benjamin*,[6] *David*,[5] *Jonathan*,[4] *James*,[3] *Jonathan*,[2] *John*[1]), son of William and Rachel (Emery) Libby; married Nov., 1874, Mary Ann Thompson (born in Vineland, Wis.). Farmer.

Children, born in Vineland, Wis. :

5715   i   CHARLES DELBERT,[9] b. Sept. 28, 1875.
5716   ii   CARRIE RACHEL, b. April 17, 1877.
5717   iii   WILLIAM FURNESS, b. Jan. 22, 1879.
5718   iv   NINA, b. Oct. 20, 1883.

4102 ESTHER[8] LIBBY (*Rachel*,[7] *Benjamin*,[6] *David*,[5] *Jonathan*,[4] *James*,[3] *Jonathan*,[2] *John*[1]), daughter of William and Rachel (Emery) Libby; married Dec. 19, 1865, William Courtney (died Nov. 4, 1874). She died Aug. 8, 1875.

Two children, Nos. 5719–5720.

4103 CHARLES H.[8] EMERY (*Harrison*,[7] *Benjamin*,[6] *David*,[5] *Jonathan*,[4] *James*,[3] *Jonathan*,[2] *John*[1]), son of Harrison and Nancy (Stiles) Emery; married in Bangor, Me., Oct. 6, 1869, Abbie H. Scripture (died Aug. 8, 1885).

Children, born in Glenburn, Me. :

5721   i   CHARLES M.,[9] b. Mar. 6, 1876.
5722   ii   MORRIS, d. young.
5723   iii   INFANT, d. young.

4106 MILES E.[8] EMERY (*Harrison*,[7] *Benjamin*,[6] *David*,[5] *Jonathan*,[4] *James*,[3] *Jonathan*,[2] *John*[1]), son of Harrison and Nancy (Stiles) Emery; married in Milo, Me., May 5, 1874, Frances A. Scripture niece of Abbie H. Scripture who married C. H. Emery No. 4103. She died in Bangor, Me., July 4, 1887.

Child :

5724   i   MINNIE F.,[9] b. in Milo, Me., Aug. 22, 1875.

4110 MARY E.[8] EMERY (*Harrison,*[7] *Benjamin,*[6] *David,*[5] *Jonathan,*[4] *James,*[3] *Jonathan,*[2] *John*[1]), daughter of Harrison and Nancy (Stiles) Emery, married April 12, 1877, in Bangor, Me., Walter F. Brown (born in Harmony, Me., Feb 15, 1856, market gardener).
Children.

    5725 i   BERNHARD H.,[9] b March 22, 1879, in Bangor, Me
    5726 ii GRACE M., b Aug. 28, 1881, in Dedham, Mass
    5727 iii WILLIS S., b. June 19 1884, in Jamaica Plains, Mass
    5728 iv DAVID S., b Jan 22 1886 in Roslindale, Mass
    5729 v   WALTER F., b May 27, 1887, in Winchester, Mass

4118 ANDREW MERRILL[8] EMERY (*Dr Samuel I,*[7] *Benjamin,*[6] *David,*[5] *Jonathan,*[4] *James,*[3] *Jonathan,*[2] *John*[1]), son of Dr. Samuel I. and Olive (Merrill) Emery; married Dec 11, 1879, in Lowell, Mass., Mary Jane Haseltine (born in Windham, N. H., Sept 9, 1854).
Child:

    5730 i   DORA FRANCES,[9] b Jan. 5, 1881, in Lowell, Mass.

4120 CHAPIN SAMUEL[8] EMERY (*Dr. Samuel I,*[7] *Benjamin,*[6] *David,*[5] *Jonathan,*[4] *James,*[3] *Jonathan,*[2] *John*[1]), son of Dr. Samuel I. and Olive (Merrill) Emery; married March 7, 1882, in Lowell, Mass., Kate Edith Haseltine (born in Windham, N. H., July 30, 1859), sister of Mary Jane (Haseltine) Emery.
Child:

    5731 i   CHARLES HASELTINE,[9] b Oct. 28, 1883, in Windham, N H

4125 BYRON WATSON[8] EMERY (*Benjamin W.,*[7] *Benjamin,*[6] *David,*[5] *Jonathan,*[4] *James,*[3] *Jonathan,*[2] *John*[1]), son of Benjamin W and Emily (Merrill) Emery, married July 24, 1887, in Grant Co., South Dakota, Lillie May Stroup (born in Hixton, Jackson Co., Wis., Dec. 1, 1869). Farmer in Sparta, Wis.
Child.

    5732 i   RUBY MAY,[9] b May 6, 1888.

4129 MARGIE ANNA H.[8] EMERY (*Lorenzo D,*[7] *Benjamin,*[6] *David,*[5] *Jonathan,*[4] *James,*[3] *Jonathan,*[2] *John*[1]), daughter of Lorenzo D and Mary A (Inman) Emery; married in Lewiston, Me., April 17, 1880, Austin S Woodman (born in Dayton, Me., May 19, 1854).
Children:

    5733 i   ETHEL MAY,[8] b Feb 16, 1881, in Auburn, Me ; d in Lewiston, Me , Jan 7, 1887
    5734 ii GEORGE AUSTIN, b Jan 21, 1883, d in Lewiston, Me , Feb. 5, 1883
    5735 iii MARY EMMA, b. May 24, 1885, d. in Lewiston, Me , Jan 7, 1887

4139 CHENEY H.[8] EMERY (*Columbus W.,*[7] *Jonathan,*[6] *David,*[5] *Jonathan,*[4] *James,*[3] *Jonathan,*[2] *John*[1]), son of Columbus W. and Sophia (Hutchins) Emery; married Feb 2, 1881, Phœbe G. Mitchell (born in China, Me., July 24, 1845). Agent of Elliott and Puzley's Publishing House, Philadelphia, Pa.

Children, born in Pittsfield, Me. :

5736 i MINNIE VESTA,[9] b. April 12, 1882.
5737 ii ANNIE BURGESS, b. Oct. 9, 1883.

4140 CYNTHIA P.[8] EMERY (*Columbus W.,*[7] *Jonathan,*[6] *David,*[5] *Jonathan,*[4] *James,*[3] *Jonathan,*[2] *John*[1]), daughter of Columbus W. and Sophia (Hutchins) Emery ; married in Burnham, Me., May 27, 1879, Rev. F. H. Osgood (born in Burnham, Jan. 22, 1850). Presiding Elder of Bangor District, E. Me. Conference, M. E. Church.
Children, born in Bangor :

5738 i LENA M.,[9] b. July 15, 1880.
5739 ii EARLE VICTOR, b. May 1, 1886.

4146 MARY A.[8] EMERY (*Jonathan E.,*[7] *Jonathan,*[6] *David,*[5] *Jonathan,*[4] *James,*[3] *Jonathan,*[2] *John*[1]), daughter of Jonathan E. and Mary E. (Leathers) Emery ; married in Dover, Me., March 30, 1866, Judson Briggs (born in Parkham, Me., March 18, 1832 ; mill owner).
Child :

5740 i MAUD ELLENA,[9] b. July 19, 1869, in Brownville, Me. ; graduate of Bradford, Me., Seminary, class of 1889.

4147 CORREN EVERETTE[8] EMERY (*Jonathan E.,*[7] *Jonathan,*[6] *David,*[5] *Jonathan,*[4] *James,*[3] *Jonathan,*[2] *John*[1]), son of Jonathan E. and Mary E. (Leathers) Emery ; married in Providence, R. I., April 29, 1880, Francis H. Mongovan (born in Boston, Mass., Sept. 16, 1854). Soldier in 3d Me. Light Art. ; enlisted Nov. 9, 1861 ; served to the close of war ; was at the 2d Bull Run, Petersburg, and other battles ; mustered out at Augusta, Me., June, 1865.
Children, born in Minneapolis, Minn. :

5741 i MINA FRANCES,[9] b. July 14, 1881.
5742 ii MARGARETTA, b. June 1, 1889.

4148 EMMA A.[8] EMERY (*Jonathan E.,*[7] *Jonathan,*[6] *David,*[5] *Jonathan,*[4] *James,*[3] *Jonathan,*[2] *John*[1]), daughter of Jonathan E. and Mary E. (Leathers) Emery ; married in Manchester, N. H., Aug. 27, 1867, Fred Hanson (born in Moultonboro, N. H., March 23, 1843 ; broker).
Child :

5743 i WILBUR NORTON,[9] b. Jan. 23, 1869, in Lowell, Mass.

4149 CARO ELIZABETH[8] EMERY (*Jonathan E.,*[7] *Jonathan,*[6] *David,*[5] *Jonathan,*[4] *James,*[3] *Jonathan,*[2] *John*[1]), daughter of Jonathan E. and Mary E. (Leathers) Emery ; married in Nashua, N. H., Aug. 15, 1872, Henry B. Flint (born in Monson, Me., Sept. 10, 1850), clerk of Judicial Courts of Piscataquis Co., Me., since Jan. 1, 1875.
Children, born in Dover :

5744 i ROBERT EMERY,[9] b. April 18, 1873 ; d. Jan. 21, 1876.
5745 ii EDGAR THOMPSON, b. June 2, 1877.
5746 iii CHARLOTTE MARION, b. Aug. 15, 1882.

4152 MARY ANN[8] WARMLIGHT (*Emily O.,[7] Jonathan,[6] David,[5] Jonathan,[4] James,[3] Jonathan,[2] John[1]*). daughter of John and Emily Ora (Emery) Warmlight; married in Lewiston, Me, March 5, 1877, George Elmer Ross (born in Farmingdale, Me, Sept. 3, 1854; superintendent of Chester Oil Co. of St. Paul, Minn).
Children:

  5747 i ALBERT HOWARD,[9] b March 20, 1878, in Lewiston, Me
  5748 ii FRED ARTHUR, b May 17, 1880. in Minneapolis, Minn
  5749 iii GEORGIA MAY, b March 6, 1884, in St. Paul, Minn

4155 FRANCIS A[8] CHAMBERLAIN (*Caroline Eliz .[7] Jonathan,[6] David,[5] Jonathan,[4] James,[3] Jonathan,[2] John[1]*), son of James F. and Caroline E (Emery) Chamberlain, married in Minneapolis, Minn, May 28, 1884, Fannie Foss, daughter of Rev. Bishop Foss of New York City. Cashier of Security Bank of Minneapolis.
Children, born in Minneapolis:

  5750 i RUTH,[9] b Aug 16, 1885
  5751 ii CARO, b May 7, 1887
  5752 iii CYRUS FOSS, b Feb 28, 1889.

4156 CARRIE LOUISE[8] CHAMBERLAIN (*Caroline E ,[7] Jonathan,[6] David,[5] Jonathan,[4] James,[3] Jonathan,[2] John[1]*), daughter of James F. and Caroline E (Emery) Chamberlain, married in Minneapolis, Minn, Oct. 8, 1880, A. J Dean (born May 31, 1853; banker.)
Children, born in Minneapolis ·

  5753 i AGNES L ,[9] b Nov 11, 1881
  5754 ii HELEN MARGERIE, b Jan 16, 1885
  5755 iii MARGARET E , b Jan 24, 1887.

4177 ELIZABETH[8] HAFFORD (*Louisa,[7] Miles,[6] David,[5] Jonathan,[4] James,[3] Jonathan,[2] John[1]*), daughter of William and Louisa (Emery) Hafford, married in Fort Kent, Me., Nov. 22, 1880, Taddie Violette (born Dec 15, 1840; farmer).
Children, born in Fort Kent:

  5756 i LOUISA MAY,[9] b Jan 3, 1882
  5757 ii ESTHER CORA, b April 15, 1883
  5758 iii MONDY ELLEN, b Jan 30, 1885. d Jan. 4, 1887
  5759 iv FRANK WILLIAM, b Feb 23, 1887, d Nov 15, 1889.
  5760 v MARK HERBERT, b. Jan 23, 1889

4183 ROSANNA[8] HAFFORD (*Louisa,[7] Miles,[6] David,[5] Jonathan,[4] James,[3] Jonathan,[2] John[1]*), daughter of William and Louisa (Emery) Hafford; married Oct. 5, 1885, George Pelletier (born July 15, 1861).
Child, born in Fort Kent, Me :

  5761 i MONDY,[9] b June 28, 1888

4190 CYNTHIA[8] PELLETIER (*Susan,[7] Miles,[6] David,[5] Jonathan,[4] James,[3] Jonathan,[2] John[1]*), daughter of Charles and Susan (Emery) Pelletier; married in Fort Kent, Me , Eli Carron. She died in Fort Kent.

Child :

5762 i   DAUGHTER,[9] d. young.

4240 ELLEN A.[8] EMERY (*Zeri J.*,[7] *Samuel*,[6] *Briggs H.*,[5] *Jonathan*,[4] *James*,[3] *Jonathan*,[2] *John*[1]), daughter of Zeri J. and Rosanna (Whitcomb) Emery ; married May 20, 1865, Lewis Marcia (born June 16, 1847 ; lumber surveyor.)

Children, born in Fairfield, Me. :

5763 i   ANNIE B.,[9] b. Feb. 28, 1869 ; m. Albert Brown, Nov. 9, 1884.
5764 ii MERTIA P., b. Sept. 25, 1877.

4248 FRANK EDWIN[8] EMERY (*Edwin A.*,[7] *Samuel*,[6] *Briggs H.*,[5] *Jonathan*,[4] *James*,[3] *Jonathan*,[2] *John*[1]), son of Edwin A. and Mary Ann (Ricker) Emery ; married by Rev. C. M. Emery, in Fairfield, Me., Feb. 20, 1885, to Clara A. Drew (born in Canaan, Me., Sept. 1, 1862). Superintendent of Farm at New York Agricultural Experiment Station, Geneva, N. Y.

Children :

5765 i   CLARA,[9] b. Nov. 9, 1887, in Pawling, N. Y.
5766 ii JEANETTE, b. Nov. 14, 1889, in Geneva, N. Y.

4249 LYDIA ABBY[8] EMERY (*Edwin A.*,[7] *Samuel*,[6] *Briggs H.*,[5] *Jonathan*,[4] *James*,[3] *Jonathan*,[2] *John*[1]), daughter of Edwin A. and Mary Ann (Ricker) Emery ; married in Skowhegan, Me., July 4, 1876, John H. Moore (born in Canaan, Me., May 27, 1848 ; farmer).

Children, born in Canaan, Me. :

5767 i   MAE,[9] b. Oct. 20, 1879.
5768 ii ALICE EMERY, b. July 30, 1884.

4250 HANNAH ABIAH[8] EMERY (*Edwin A.*,[7] *Samuel*,[6] *Briggs H.*,[5] *Jonathan*,[4] *James*,[3] *Jonathan*,[2] *John*[1]), daughter of Edwin A. and Mary A. (Ricker) Emery ; married in Canaan, Me., Oct. 30, 1880, Daniel Almon Ames (born Dec. 16, 1847).

Children, born in Fairfield :

5769 i   ALTON EDWIN,[9] b. Jan. 19, 1882.
5770 ii   NELLIE MAY, b. Jan. 21, 1884.
5771 iii ANNA ESTELLA, b. Aug. 13, 1887.

4251 WALTER S.[8] EMERY (*Edwin A.*,[7] *Samuel*,[6] *Briggs H.*,[5] *Jonathan*,[4] *James*,[3] *Jonathan*,[2] *John*[1]), son of Edwin A. and Mary A. (Ricker) Emery ; married in Valley City, North Dakota, March 27, 1884, Martha B. Beal (born in Fairfield, Me., Feb. 16, 1866).

Children, born in Valley City, North Dakota :

5772 i   EDWIN HENRY,[9] b. March 14, 1885.
5773 ii   AMOS MEAD, b. Oct. 12, 1886.
5774 iii VIOLA MAY, b. July 2, 1888.

4252 NELLIE G.[8] BROOKS (*Abigail J.*,[7] *Samuel*,[6] *Briggs H.*,[5] *Jonathan*,[4] *James*,[3] *Jonathan*,[2] *John*[1]), daughter of George W. and Abigail J. (Emery) Brooks : married in Bath, Me., Sept. 4, 1883, Charles H. Rogers (born in Vienna, Me., Nov. 17, 1860 ; carpenter).

Child :

5775   i   WALTER M.,[9] b. July 8, 1888, in Bath, Me

4271 WILLIAM H.[8] AGRY (*Mary Ann,[7] Joseph,[6] Briggs H.,[5] Jonathan,[4] James,[3] Jonathan,[2] John[1]*), son of Thomas and Mary A. (Emery) Agry, married in Charlestown, Mass, Oct. 8, 1872, Ella Louise Graves (born in Lynn, Mass., Dec. 19, 1853).   Grocer
    Children :

5776   i   MARY E ,[9] b Sept 15, 1873, in Boston, Mass.
5777   ii   CARLETON W , b March 22. 1875, in Melrose, Mass.
5778   iii GENEVA L , b April 19, 1876, d Nov 18, 1877, in Boston, Mass.

4275 SARAH H [8] AGRY (*Mary Ann,[7] Joseph,[6] Briggs H ,[5] Jonathan,[4] James,[3] Jonathan,[2] John[1]*), daughter of Thomas and Mary A. (Emery) Agry, married in Boston, Mass., March 3, 1880, James W. Gwinn (born at Cape North, Cape Breton, Sept. 16, 1852, grocer).
    Child .

5779   i   BERTHA,[9] b Dec. 27, 1881; d July, 1886, b and d in Revere, Mass

4277 CARRIE V.[8] AGRY (*Mary Ann,[7] Joseph,[6] Briggs H..[5] Jonathan,[4] James,[3] Jonathan,[2] John[1]*), daughter of Thomas and Mary A. (Emery) Agry, married in Amherst, Me., Aug. 25, 1881, John F. Collar (born in Great Pond, Me , March 14, 1859 , grocer).
    Child

5780   i   FLOSSIE E ,[9] b. Aug. 25, 1884, in Revere, Mass

4279 EMMA V.[8] DAVIS (*Susan J ,[7] Joseph,[6] Briggs H ,[5] Jonathan,[4] James,[3] Jonathan,[2] John[1]*), daughter of Lorenzo M. and Susan J. (Emery) Davis , married in Waterville, Me., Dec. 25, 1874, Horace L Moody of Livermore Falls, Me . carpenter.
    Children .

5781   i   NELLIE E ,[9] b Sept 11, 1875, in Waterville, Me.
5782   ii   CORA E , b Jan 1, 1877. in Winthrop, Me
5783   iii FLOSSIE, b Aug. 5, 1882, in Farmington, Me.

4327 WALTER HOWARD[8] EMERY (*Daniel W ,[7] William,[6] Samuel,[5] Jonathan,[4] James,[3] Jonathan,[2] John[1]*), son of Daniel W and Rose B. (Lawrence) Emery : married in Canaan, Vt., Aug. 25, 1886, Ella Maria Raymond (born in Stanstead, Canada, Aug. 1, 1866).   Mechanical engineer.
    Child .

5784   i   LAWRENCE RAYMOND,[9] b June 24, 1887, in Averill, Vt.

4350 CHARLES F [8] ATWOOD (*Zenora A.,[7] John J.,[6] Samuel.[5] Jonathan,[4] James,[3] Jonathan,[2] John[1]*), son of A. L. M and Zenora A. (Emery) Atwood , married in Chippewa Falls, Wis., Oct. 5. 1883, Mary Livingston (born May 3, 1850)
    Child .

5785   i   STELLA JOSEPHINE,[9] b. Dec. 29, 1884, in Lakeville, Wis.

4351 WALTER L.[8] ATWOOD (*Zenora A.,*[7] *John J.,*[6] *Samuel,*[5] *Jonathan,*[4] *James,*[3] *Jonathan,*[2] *John*[1]), son of A. L. M. and Zenora A. (Emery) Atwood ; married in Bloomer, Wis., Dec. 1, 1883, Nettie E. Little (born Jan. 19, 1868, in Wisconsin).

Children, born in Bloomer, Wis. :

5786 i   HOWARD LEROY,[9] b. Dec. 23, 1885.
5787 ii   CLARA BELLE, b. Dec. 25, 1887.

4352 MARY ALICE[8] LANPHERE (*Zenora A.,*[7] *John J.,*[6] *Samuel,*[5] *Jonathan,*[4] *James,*[3] *Jonathan,*[2] *John*[1]), daughter of Ezra and Mrs. Zenora A. (Emery-Atwood) Lanphere ; married in Bloomer, Wis., Sept. 15, 1883, Jesse O. Doers. She died Aug. 23,1887.

Child :

5788 i   FLORENCE JESSIE,[9] b. Oct. 30, 1884, in Bloomer, Wis.

4384 ABBIE J.[8] OLIVER (*Paulina D,*[7] *Samuel,*[6] *Samuel,*[5] *Jonathan,*[4] *James,*[3] *Jonathan,*[2] *John*[1]), daughter of Ezekiel and Paulina D. (Emery) Oliver ; married in Phippsburg, Me., Jan. 1, 1880, Alpheus Evans Purington (born March 8, 1854 ; mechanical engineer).

Child, born in Phippsburg :

5789 i   SILAS M.,[9] b. 1880.

4451 ARTHUR CLIFFORD[8] EMERY (*Oliver G.,*[7] *Lewis,*[6] *Samuel,*[5] *Anthony,*[4] *James,*[3] *Jonathan,*[2] *John*[1]), son of Oliver G. and Ellen (Stebbins) Emery ; married Ellen Bass.

Children, born in South Dakota :

5790 i   LULU,[9] b. April 7, 1878.
5791 ii   NELLIE.
5792 iii ARTHUR.
5793 iv BERYL.

4464 HELEN[8] KELSEY (*Margaret A.,*[7] *Jehu A.,*[6] *John,*[5] *Ambrose,*[4] *James,*[3] *Jonathan,*[2] *John*[1]), daughter of James A. and Margaret A. (Emrie) Kelsey ; married in Aurora, Ind., April 18, 1867, John S. Hope.   She died in Ridgeville, Ind., Dec. 29, 1874.

Child :

5794 i   MARGARET FRANCES.[9]

4467 ANNA[8] KELSEY (*Margaret A.,*[7] *Jehu A.,*[6] *John,*[5] *Ambrose,*[4] *James,*[3] *Jonathan,*[2] *John*[1]), daughter of James A. and Margaret A. (Emrie) Kelsey ; married in Hastings, Neb., June 15, 1886, George A. Sommers.

Child ;

5795 i   DAUGHTER;[9] d. young.

4468 CHARLES A.[8] KELSEY (*Margaret A.,*[7] *Jehu A.,*[6] *John,*[5] *Ambrose,*[4] *James,*[3] *Jonathan,*[2] *John*[1]), son of James A. and Margaret A. (Emrie) Kelsey ; married in Victor, Ia., Nov. 29, 1877, Frances Eva Brown.   Missionary of American Sunday School Union.

Children :

5796　i　PEARL FENTON,[9] b. Nov. 20, 1878, in Victor, Ia
5797　ii　LILLIL BROWN, b Feb 10, 1880, in Hastings, Neb.
5798　iii　CLARA B , b Feb 14, 1882, in Domphan, Neb

4469 HARRIET[8] KELSEY (*Margaret A* ,[7] *John A* ,[6] *John*,[5] *Ambrose*,[4] *James*,[3] *Jonathan*,[2] *John*[1]), daughter of James A. and Margaret A (Emire) Kelsey; married in Hamilton, O , 1884, John S Hope. husband of her deceased sister Helen.

Child:

5799　i　HARRY [9]

4520 EDWARD M [8] DAVIDSON (*Nancy E* ,[7] *Ambrose*,[6] *Samuel*,[5] *Ambrose*,[4] *James*,[3] *Jonathan*,[2] *John*[1]), son of Ellis and Nancy E. (Emery) Davidson; married Dec. 11, 1887, Owrie Wiggins.

Child:

5800　i　PEARLY LEE,[9] b. July 24, 1888, in Gibson City, Ill

4521 EVA L [8] DAVIDSON (*Nancy E* ,[7] *Ambrose*,[6] *Samuel* [5] *Ambrose*,[4] *James*,[3] *Jonathan*,[2] *John*[1]), daughter of Ellis and Nancy E. (Emery) Davidson , married in Winkle, O , Jan. 1, 1883, Noble Carrier.

Children:

5801　i　EMMA,[9] b Dec 24, 1883. in Wilmington, O
5802　ii　AMOS EDWARD, b Aug 13, 1887, in Wilmington, O.

4522 MARY M [8] DAVIDSON (*Nancy E.*,[7] *Ambrose*,[6] *Samuel*,[5] *Ambrose*,[4] *James*,[3] *Jonathan*,[2] *John*[1]), daughter of Ellis and Nancy E. (Emery) Davidson , married in Winkle, O , Jan. 25, 1885, Anthony Miller.

Children, born in Wilmington, O. :

5803　i　JOSEPHINE,[9] b Dec 2, 1886
5804　ii　EVA, b May 5, 1888.

4524 ELVIRA E [8] DAVIDSON (*Nancy E* ,[7] *Ambrose*,[6] *Samuel*,[5] *Ambrose*,[4] *James*,[3] *Jonathan*,[2] *John*[1]), daughter of Ellis and Nancy E. (Emery) Davidson; married June 4, 1888, Thomas Massais of Lafayette, Ind.

Child :

5805　i　GROVER CLEVELAND.[9] b. March 2, 1889, in Winkle, O.

4604 HARRIET R [8] HAYES (*Mary*,[7] *John*,[6] *Ambrose*,[5] *Ambrose*,[4] *James*,[3] *Jonathan*,[2] *John*[1]), daughter of Walter and Mary (Emery) Hayes; married Feb. 6, 1873, William W Edington (born Oct. 22, 1855).

Children, born in Greene Co , Ind. :

5806　i　ISADORE.[9] b Oct 11, 1874
5807　ii　PEARY E , b Sept 2, 1878, d Feb 16, 1879
5808　iii　IONA D , b. Dec 4, 1885.

4605 JOHN P.[8] HAYES (*Mary*,[7] *John*,[6] *Ambrose*,[5] *Ambrose*,[4]

James,[3] Jonathan,[2] John[1]), son of Walter and Mary (Emery) Hayes; married in Greene Co, Ind., March 20, 1879, Nancy Miller (born 1855, in Lawrence Co . Ind)

Children, born in Greene Co., Ind. ;

5809   i   MARY B ,[9] d July, 1880.
5810   ii   AIGIE, b Oct 25, 1880
5811   iii ALLEN, b Feb 16, 1882, d Sept 9, 1883.
5812   iv   JONAS, b Oct 27, 1886

4606 WILLIAM JONAS[8] HAYES (*Mary,[7] John,[6] Ambrose,[5] Ambrose,[4] James.[3] Jonathan,[2] John[1]*), son of Walter and Mary (Emery) Hayes, married June 12, 1887, Della Baker (born Feb. 4, 1871).

Child .

5813   i   BELLE,[9] b. Dec 16, 1887, in Greene Co , Ind

4614 URSULA ANN[8] AULT (*Sarah A D.,[7] John,[6] Ambrose,[5] Ambrose,[4] James,[3] Jonathan,[2] John[1]*), daughter of James and Sarah A. D (Emery) Ault; married in Greene Co , Ind., April 16, 1887, John F. Britten (born Oct. 19, 1862, in Shelby Co., Ind.).

Child .

5814   i   JAMES CLARENCE,[9] b Jan. 17, 1888

4618 ANNA A.[8] EMERY (*Charles A ,[7] John,[6] Ambrose,[5] Ambrose,[4] James,[3] Jonathan,[2] John[1]*), daughter of Charles A. and Sarah J. (Stalcup) Emery; married in Greene Co., Ind., in 1886, Hubbard Morton Dowden.

Children :

5815   i   EMERY,[9] d young
5816   ii   DAUGHTER

4672 NORA F [8] DAGLEY (*Catharine,[7] Ambrose,[6] Ambrose,[5] Ambrose,[4] James,[3] Jonathan,[2] John[1]*), daughter of Emit and Catharine (Emery) Dagley, married in Greene Co., Ind., Joseph H. Hutchins (born July 10, 1853 , farmer).

Children, born near Cincinnati, Ind. :

5817   i   EDGAR,[9] b Feb 14, 1886
5818   ii   KINSY C , b March 29, 1888

4778 WARREN A [8] EMERY (*Albert,[7] Hamilton,[6] Robert S ,[5] Edward,[4] James,[3] Jonathan,[2] John[1]*), son of Albert and Joanna (Bragg) Emery ; married April 26, 1885, Emma Scott of Wayne, Neb.

Children, born in Wakefield, Neb :

5819   i   INEZ E ,[9] b Sept 6, 1886
5820   ii   RALPH A , b Sept 19, 1888.

4782 LESTER M [8] EMERY (*John H.,[7] Hamilton,[6] Robert S ,[5] Edward,[4] James,[3] Jonathan,[2] John[1]*), son of John H. and Deborah (Bragg) Emery, married April 29, 1882, Ida Crowell.

Children, born in Vassalboro, Me :

5821   i   James B.,[9] b March 12 1889
5822   ii   Wilhelmina F., b Nov 4. 1884
5823   iii Maurice D., h. Dec 23, 1886

4784 Nettie F.[8] Emery (*John H.*,[7] *Hamilton*,[6] *Robert S.*,[5] *Edward*,[4] *James*,[3] *Jonathan*,[2] *John[1]*) daughter of John H and Deborah (Bragg) Emery; married Oct. 8, 1887, George L Pope of Vassalboro, Me., grocer.
  Child:

5824   i   Harold,[9] b in Vassalboro

4831 Lucinda Jerusha[9] Emery (*Robert G.*,[8] *Jonah E.*,[7] *John*,[6] *Daniel*,[5] *John*,[4] *John*,[3] *John*,[2] *John[1]*), daughter of Robert G and Jerusha E. (White) Emery, married March 3, 1872, Louis Carpenter. She died Oct 16, 1879
  Children.

5825   i   Eldora[10] b June 2 1873, in Ridgeville Centre, O
5826   ii   Emery L, b April 9, in Weston, Mich

4842 Anna M[9] Emery (*Joseph M.*,[8] *Joseph*,[7] *Joseph*[6] *Joseph*,[5] *Joseph*,[4] *Joseph*,[3] *John*,[2] *John[1]*), daughter of Joseph M. and Martha E. (Hall) Emery; married Nov. 24, 1881 George M. French, M.D., of Malden, Mass.
  Children ·

5827   i   Mary Harriet,[10] b July 13, 1888
Three sons died in infancy

5024 Henry[9] Rolfe (*Eliza Ann*,[8] *Enoch*,[7] *Enoch*[6] *Stephen*,[5] *Stephen*[4] *Stephen*,[3] *John*,[2] *John[1]*), son of Timothy C. and Eliza Ann (Emery) Rolfe; married in 1869, Nellie L Gleason.
  Children.

5828   i   Abbie E.,[10] b. April 19, 1870
5829   ii   Timothy P, b July 11, 1871
5830   iii Mattie E, b Nov 8, 1874
5831   iv   Henry, b March 25 1878

5027 Martha[9] Rolfe (*Eliza Ann*[8] *Enoch*,[7] *Enoch*,[6] *Stephen*,[5] *Stephen*,[4] *Stephen*,[3] *John*,[2] *John[1]*), daughter of Timothy C. and Eliza Ann (Emery) Rolfe, married Feb 6, 1873, Orilla J. Evans.
  Children

5832   i   Natt G.,[10] b Nov 28 1873
5833   ii   Mary E, b. Aug 8, 1875

5030 Abby[9] Emery (*Moses Moody*,[8] *Enoch*,[7] *Enoch*,[6] *Stephen*,[5] *Stephen*,[4] *Stephen*,[3] *John*,[2] *John[1]*), daughter of Moses Moody and Judith G. (Moore) Emery, married in Jan., 1869, George P Morrill.
  Children:

5834   i   Louis David,[10] b Nov, 1869
5835   ii   Bertha Ellen b May, 1871
5836   iii Charles Emery, b Nov, 1872
5837   iv   William George. b Feb, 1876
5838   v   Alice Wellington, b. Aug, 1877.

5031 Millard Fillmore[9] Emery (*Moses Moody,*[8] *Enoch,*[7] *Enoch,*[6] *Stephen,*[5] *Stephen,*[4] *Stephen,*[3] *John,*[2] *John*[1]), son of Moses M. and Judith G. (Moore) Emery ; married, Feb. 22, 1876, Elizabeth W. Tulloch.

Child :

5839 i   Mildred Elizabeth,[10] b. Aug., 1881.

5108 Rachel Evans[10] Emery (*Charles D.,*[9] *Josiah,*[8] *Nathan,*[7] *Josiah,*[6] *Moses,*[5] *John,*[4] *John,*[3] *John,*[2] *John*[1]), daughter of Charles D. and Lavinia D. (Evans) Emery ; married April 9, 1877, Judge Henry E. Hathaway of Seattle, Washington.

Children :

5840 i   Charles E.,[11] b. Feb. 11, 1878.
5841 ii   Laura Florence, b. Jan. 29, 1879.
5842 iii Henry M., b. March 27, 1880.

5204 Josephine[9] Emery (*Samuel B.,*[8] *Samuel,*[7] *John,*[6] *John,*[5] *Joshua,*[4] *John,*[3] *Jonathan,*[2] *John*[1]), daughter of Samuel B. and Sarah E. (Parkhurst) Emery ; married Sept. 30, 1868, Walker N. Hitchcock. She died March 28, 1874.

Children :

5843 i   Samuel,[10] b. 1869.
5844 ii   Nellie, b. 1871 : d. July, 1884.
5845 iii Walker, b. 1874.

5205 Ann Abiah[9] Emery (*Samuel B.,*[8] *Samuel,*[7] *John,*[6] *John,*[5] *Joshua,*[4] *John,*[3] *Jonathan,*[2] *John*[1]), daughter of Samuel B. and Sarah E. (Parkhurst) Emery ; married William J. Smith.

Child :

5846 i   Josephine E ,[10] b. 1887.

5207 Lavinia G.[9] Emery (*Samuel B.,*[8] *Samuel,*[7] *John,*[6] *John,*[5] *Joshua,*[4] *John,*[3] *Jonathan,*[2] *John*[1]), daughter of Samuel B. and Sarah E. (Parkhurst) Emery ; married Dec. 2, 1886, Henry L. Young.

Child :

5847 i   Lavinia E.,[10] b. 1887.

5298 Alice E.[9] Emery (*John D. P.,*[8] *Moses,*[7] *Joshua,*[6] *John,*[5] *Joshua,*[4] *John,*[3] *Jonathan,*[2] *John*[1]), daughter of John D. P. and Sarah H. (Morey) Emery ; married in East Bridgewater, Mass., Edmund E. Hill of Taunton, Mass.

Child :

5848 i   Edna Jane.[10]

5300 Edward Emery[9] Brown (*Lucy S.,*[8] *Moses,*[7] *Joshua,*[6] *John,*[5] *Joshua,*[4] *John,*[3] *Jonathan,*[2] *John*[1]), son of Edward and Lucy Stowell (Emery) Brown ; married in Pawtucket, R. I., April 16, 1873, Ella Annette Swift (born in Middleton, Mass., Sept. 27, 1856).

Children :

```
5849  i    CHARLES ELLSWORTH,¹⁰ b  June 3, 1875, in Lakeville, Mass
5850  ii   MABEL FLORENCE. b  Sept  26, 1877, in Lakeville, Mass.
5851  iii  LILLIE ANNETTE, b. March 17, 1879, in E. Bridgewater, Mass.
```

5556 ELLEN AMELIA⁹ CROSBY (*Angelina,*⁸ *Noah,*⁷ *Ruth,*⁶ *Humphrey,*⁵ *Humphrey,*⁴ *Jonathan,*³ *Jonathan,*² *John*¹), daughter of Eliakim and Angelina (Emery) Crosby ; married Aug , 1869, Wellington W. Seymour.
Children :

```
5852  i    ANABEL ¹⁰ b  Dec. 4, 1871, in Poland, Chautauqua Co , N  Y
5853  ii   FREEMAN H., b  Aug 23, 1874, in Poland, Chautauqua Co ,
           N  Y.
5554  iii  SUSA A , b  June 13, 1879, in Randolph, Catt  Co , N  Y.
5855  iv   FRANK W , b  Jan  1, 1884, in Randolph, Catt. Co., N. Y.
5856  v    WEBSTER W , b  Dec  29, 1885, in Kennedy, Chautauqua Co ,
           N. Y
```

5557 FREEMAN HOPKINS⁹ CROSBY (*Angelina,*⁸ *Noah,*⁷ *Ruth,*ᵇ *Humphrey,*⁵ *Humphrey,*⁴ *Jonathan,*³ *Jonathan,*² *John*¹), son of Eliakim and Angelina (Emery) Crosby , married Dec 18, 1884, Julie H. Halsey. Educated at the Naval Academy , graduated in 1870 and has been in service since ; was executive officer of "The Bear" which went to the Arctic region on the Greeley relief expedition in 1884 He is now in command of the U. S. steamer Gedney in the U. S Coast Survey.
Child :

```
5857  i    HALSEY EMERY,¹⁰ b  Aug 16, 1887, in Jamestown, N  Y.
```

5559 ANNA M ⁹ CROSBY (*Angelina,*⁸ *Noah,*⁷ *Ruth,*⁶ *Humphrey,*⁵ *Humphrey,*⁴ *Jonathan,*³ *Jonathan,*² *John*¹), daughter of Eliakim and Angelina (Emery) Crosby , married July 1, 1885, William B Webster
Children :

```
5858  i    CORNELIUS CROSBY,¹⁰ b  July 25, 1886, in Kennedy, N  Y
5859  ii   WILLIAM BURTON, b  Nov  29, 1887, in Binghamton, N  Y
```

5564 EMERY M.⁹ DAVENPORT (*Amelia,*⁸ *Noah,*⁷ *Ruth,*⁶ *Humphrey,*⁵ *Humphrey,*⁴ *Jonathan,*³ *Jonathan,*² *John*¹), son of Ephraim and Amelia (Emery) Davenport, married March 22, 1870, Ellen Thayer and died April 18, 1887.
Children

```
5860  i    CHARLES E ,¹⁰ b  Feb. 19, 1877.
5861  ii   HARRY T , b  Dec. 22, 1879.
5862  iii  MARY E , b  Sept 19, 1881
5863  iv   J  HERBERT, b  Dec 19, 1883.
```

5565 MARY⁹ DAVENPORT (*Amelia,*⁸ *Noah,*⁷ *Ruth,*⁶ *Humphrey,*⁵ *Humphrey,*⁴ *Jonathan,*³ *Jonathan,*² *John*¹), daughter of Ephraim and Amelia (Emery) Davenport; married March 22, 1870, Luther F. Shepard.
Children :

```
5864  i    HENRY,¹⁰ b  March 4, 1872.
5865  ii   LAURA.
```

5566 OLIVIA A.[9] DAVENPORT (*Amelia,*[8] *Noah,*[7] *Ruth,*[6] *Humphrey,*[5] *Humphrey,*[4] *Jonathan,*[3] *Jonathan,*[2] *John*[1]), daughter of Ephraim and Amelia (Emery) Davenport; married April 10, 1884, John H. Anderson.

Children :

    5866 i   MAUD.[10]
    5867 ii   MERRILL D.

5568 FRANK H.[9] TAYLOR (*Alvina D.,*[8] *Noah,*[7] *Ruth,*[6] *Humphrey,*[5] *Humphrey,*[4] *Jonathan,*[3] *Jonathan,*[2] *John*[1]), son of Bravity and Alvina D. (Emery) Taylor; married Feb. 2, 1879, Anna Pluth.

Children :

    5868 i   AROLINE A.,[10] b. Dec., 1879.
    5869 ii   FRANK BRAVITY, b. Sept. 13, 1882.
    5870 iii HARRY P., b. June 16, 1886.

5569 LAWRENCE N.[9] TAYLOR (*Alvina D.,*[8] *Noah,*[7] *Ruth,*[6] *Humphrey,*[5] *Humphrey,*[4] *Jonathan,*[3] *Jonathan,*[2] *John*[1]), son of Bravity and Alvina D. (Emery) Taylor; married Oct. 8, 1879, Florence A. Annis.

Children :

    5871 i   GLENDINE IDA,[10] b. May 17, 1881.
    5872 ii   GORDON L., b. March 10, 1883.

APPENDIX A.

569 NOAH[5] EMERY (*Humphrey,*[4] *Jonathan,*[3] *Jonathan,*[2] *John*[1]), son of Humphrey and Sarah (Heath) Emery; married Hannah Smith of Pembroke, N. H.; removed to Bartlett, N. H.

Children :

    5873 i   JOHN,[6] b July 16, 1766, in Pembroke, N. H.; d. in Portland,
                    Me., March 16, 1806.
    5874 ii   ENOCH.
    5875 iii NEHEMIAH, m. in Concord, N. H., Mary Henderson.
    5876 iv RUTH, m. Josiah Copp.
    5877 v   ROSANNAH, m. Jacob Emery, son of Enoch and Rachel Tyrrell,
                    her cousin.

5873 JOHN[6] EMERY (*Noah,*[5] *Humphrey,*[4] *Jonathan,*[3] *Jonathan,*[2] *John*[1]), son of Noah and Hannah (Smith) Emery; married March 28, 1793, Patience Cole of Somersworth, N. H. His widow married, second, Joshua Saunders, and died in Poland, Me., Nov. 12, 1842.

Children :

    5878 i   SARAH W.,[7] b. Sept. 24, 1794, in Sandwich, N. H.; d. in Calais,
                    Me., June 30, 1865.
    5879 ii   WILLIAM K., b. April 4, 1796, in Bartlett, N. H.; d. in Norway,
                    Me., May, 1852.
    5880 iii ELIAS C., b. July 9, 1799; d. Oct. 9, 1799.
    5881 iv JAMES OSGOOD, b. July 24, 1801, in Portland, Me.; d. Nov. 12,
                    1874.
    5882 v   MARY ANN, b. March 20, 1804; d. in Poland, Me.

5878 SARAH W.[7] EMERY (*John,*[6] *Noah,*[5] *Humphrey,*[4] *Jonathan,*[3]

Jonathan,[2] *John*[1]), daughter of John and Patience (Cole) Emery; married James Watson, of Calais, Me.

Children ·

    5883   i   DAUGHTER,[8] d in infancy.
    5884   ii SON, m., went to sea.

5879 WILLIAM KNOX[7] EMERY (*John,*[6] *Noah,*[5] *Humphrey*[4] *Jonathan,*[3] *Jonathan,*[2] *John*[1]), son of John and Patience (Cole) Emery; married Sarah Heath Emery (died in Turner, Me., April 5, 1888), daughter of Jacob (son of Enoch and Rachel (Tyrrell) Emery) and Rosannah (Emery) Emery, daughter of Noah and Hannah (Smith) Emery.

Children :

    5885   i   ONA CARPENTER,[8] b in Calais, Me , d , unm , in Turner, Me , Oct 9, 1888 A deaf mute
    5886   ii MARY ANN. m George Latham of Gray, Me , had three sons, Porter, Valentine and Leander. Valentine was killed in the Union army

5881 JAMES OSGOOD[7] EMERY (*John,*[6] *Noah,*[5] *Humphrey,*[4] *Jonathan,*[3] *Jonathan,*[2] *John*[1]), son of John and Patience (Cole) Emery , married March 12, 1826, Lydia Small of Lisbon, Me. (born Jan. 31, 1808). Universalist minister.

Children :

    5887   i   SUSAN ELIZABETH,[8] b Nov 5, 1827, in Lisbon, Me ; d in Hermon, Me , June 3, 1845.
    5888   ii GEORGE BATES, b July 7, 1829, in Lisbon, Me Went South.
    5889   iii LYDIA ELLEN, b. May 17, 1840, in Farmington, Me
    5890   iv NANCIE MEDORA, b July 26, 1842 in Carthage, Me.
    5891   v   FLAVILLA ADELAIDE, b May 13, 1845
    5892   vi FLORA LAVILLA, b April 2, 1849, in Guilford, Me
    5893   vii JAMES W., b Feb. 25, 1851, in Guilford, Me

5889 LYDIA ELLEN[8] EMERY (*James O ,*[7] *John,*[6] *Noah,*[5] *Humphrey,*[4] *Jonathan,*[3] *Jonathan,*[2] *John*[1]), daughter of Rev. James O and Lydia (Small) Emery , married Henri Rensselaer Foster of Albany, Me. Resides in Denver, Col.

Children :

    5894   i   HENRI REGINALD,[9] b Feb 15, 1866, d. June 16, 1869 in St. Louis, Mo.
    5895   ii HAROLD RENSSELAER, b. May 1, 1870.
    5896   iii FRANCIS AUBRIE, b Aug 28, 1873

5891 FLAVILLA A.[8] EMERY (*James O.,*[7] *John,*[6] *Noah,*[5] *Humphrey,*[4] *Jonathan,*[3] *Jonathan,*[2] *John*[1]), daughter of Rev. James O and Lydia (Small) Emery ; married Sept. 13, 1871, Henry Barnard Luce of Waltham, Mass. (died in Auburn, Me., Oct. 11, 1872).

Child :

    5897   i   EDIA LILLIAN,[9] b June 16, 1872, in Auburn, Me.

5892 FLORA L [8] EMERY (*James O ,*[7] *John,*[6] *Noah,*[5] *Humphrey,*[4] *Jonathan,*[3] *Jonathan,*[2] *John*[1]), daughter of Rev. James O and Lydia

19

(Small) Emery; married Dec. 7, 1873, Walter Harris Farnham of Rumford, Me.

Children:

5898   i   PERCY WALFRED,[9] b. Nov. 4, 1874, in Auburn, Me.
5899   ii HENRI BARNARD, b. Sept. 22, 1875, in Auburn, Me.

5893 JAMES WILLIAM[8] EMERY (*James O.*,[7] *John*,[6] *Noah*,[5] *Humphrey*,[4] *Jonathan*,[3] *Jonathan*,[2] *John*[1]), son of Rev. James O. and Lydia (Small) Emery; married Jan. 31, 1886, Mary McDonald.

Children, born in Malden, Mass.:

5900   i   WILLARD LESLIE,[9] b. Dec. 17, 1887.
5901   ii MARY ETHEL, b. Sept. 12, 1889.

APPENDIX B.

578 DAVID STILES[5] EMERY; supposed to be the son of Stephen and Deliverance (Stiles) Emery, and is said to have gone from Salisbury, N. H., or Mass., to Moultonboro, N. H.

Children:

5902   i   DAVID[6]
5903   ii   OTHNIEL.
5904   iii NATHANIEL, m. —— Sanborn.
5905   iv   REBECCA, m. Mark Clark.
5906   v   ABIGAIL, m. Jonathan Paine.
5907   vi   ELMIRA, m., 1st, —— Bailey; 2nd, James Ranney; 3rd, Enoch
            Blake; children by all.

5902 DAVID[6] EMERY (*David S.*[5]), son of David S.; married Mrs. Jane (Hall) Pierce, daughter of Ebenezer and Susannah (Young) Hall of Matanicus, and widow of David Pierce of Boothbay, Me.

Children, born in Boothbay, Me.:

5908   i   SARAH,[7]   } b. Oct. 7, 1791; { d. in Matanicus, Me., July 17,
5909   ii   JONATHAN,   }   {   1872.
5910   iii FANNY, b. July 12, 1793; d. in Lubeck, Me., April, 1866.
5911   iv   ROBERT, b. April 21, 1795; drowned in Portland harbor, Feb.
            21, 1829.
5912   v   HIRAM, b. Aug. 18, 1797.
5913   vi   GEORGE, b. Feb. 13, 1799.
5914   vii ESTHER, b. April 1, 1802; d. in Prospect, Me., Dec. 10, 1887.

5903 OTHNIEL[6] EMERY (*David S.*[5]), son of David S.; married —— Meloon.

Children:

5915   i   SALLY.[7]
5916   ii   CHARLOTTE.
5917   iii   REBECCA.
5918   iv   NATHANIEL.
5919   v   SAMUEL M.
5920   vi   MOSES, m. ——
5921   vii   DAVID S.
5922   viii ALBERT, m. and had a son Albert.
5923   ix   ALPHEUS.

5905 REBECCA[6] EMERY (*David S.*[5]), daughter of David S Emery; married, Dec. 20, 1789, Mark L Clark.

Children.

5924   i   DAVID,[7] unm.
5925   ii   JOANNA, m Eliphalet Richardson.
5926   iii REBECCA, m Samuel Richardson
5927   iv   CYNTHIA, m E Jones, had two children.
5928   v   JOSEPH, m —— Boardman
5929   vi   EBENEZER.
5930   vii ELMIRA, d young of spotted fever.

5906 ABIGAIL[6] EMERY (*David S* [5]), daughter of David S. Emery; married Jonathan M. Paine.

Children:

5931   i   HARRIET,[7] m David Crane
5932   ii   ELMIRA, m Josiah Beede
5933   iii CHARLES, m
5934   iv   JAMES, m , 1st, Sarah Towle, 2nd, Mrs —— Bailey
5935   v   SALLY m John Mudgett.
5936   vi   NATHANIEL E , m Priscilla Burleigh.
5937   vii GEORGE W
5938   viii JONATHAN R , unm.

5908 SARAH[7] EMERY (*David,*[6] *David S* [5]), daughter of David and Mrs. Jane (Hall-Pierce) Emery, married, May 23, 1813, Capt. John Cue, jr (died Aug 3, 1858)

Children born in Belfast, Me., and Matanicus :

5939   i   REUBEN LELAND,[8] b May 10, 1814, m. 1840, d Oct. 18, 1841. One child
5940   ii   OLIVE HALL, b Jan 24 1816, m 1844; d April, 1875
5941   iii MARY JANE, b June 5, 1818, d. Feb 19, 1830
5942   iv   WILLIAM b April 7, 1820, m 1844
5943   v   NANCY DILLOWAY, b April 11, 1822, m 1846
5944   vi   ORINDA FLETCHER, b. Dec. 5, 1823, m 1847, d 1878   Six children
5945   vii ROBERT FRANK, b Jan 11, 1826, m. 1848.
5946   viii EBEN, b May 24, 1828, m 1873
5947   ix   ISAAC HALL, b July 29, 1830, m 1857
5948   x   SARAH ELIZABETH, b Nov 2, 1832, m 1849, d Oct 11, 1879 Four children
5949   xi   ELVIRA JANE, b Sept 1, 1834, d Oct 9, 1834.

5910 FANNY[7] EMERY (*David,*[6] *David S* [5]), daughter of David and Mrs Jane (Hall Pierce) Emery ; married in Belfast, Me , 1809, Capt. John Wooster (died 1867).

Children.

5950   i   HENRY A ,[8] b in Belfast, Me , m , resides in Mt Desert, Me.
5951   ii   LUCY b in Belfast, Me ; m ; has ten children
5952   iii DAVID PIERCE, b 1815, in Belfast, Me ; m , has six children
5953   iv   JOHN EMERY, b 1817, in Eastport, Me , d in Portland, Me , 1876   Eight children
5954   v   HIRAM EMERY, b 1819, in Grand Manan, m , has six children
5955   vi   ROBERT EMERY, b 1822, in Grand Manan, d in N. Y. Three children.
5956   vii GEORGE WILLIAM, b 1824 in Grand Manan, d at sea, 1844
5957   viii ELIZABETH ANN, b. 1826, in Grand Manan, m , d six months after
5958   ix   JAMES EMERY, b 1830, in Grand Manan; m.; has eight children.

5959 x   OLIVER A., b. 1832, in Grand Manan; m.; has four children.
5960 xi JOSEPH THOMAS, b. 1834, in Grand Manan; d. 1854.
5961 xii MARY JANE, b. 1836, in Lubec, Me.; d. 1837.

5911 ROBERT[7] EMERY (*David,*[6] *David S.*[5]), son of David and Mrs. Jane (Hall-Pierce) Emery; married March 12, 1820, Martha Hopkins daughter of Geo. Hopkins of Belfast, Me. (died Oct. 31, 1830).
Children, born in Belfast, Me.:

5962 i   JAMES,[8] b. Dec. 14, 1820.
5963 ii ROBERT, JR., b. June 30, 1822.
5964 iii THOMAS, b. Dec. 19, 1825; d. Jan. 11, 1826.
5965 iv THOMAS BARTLETT, b. Jan. 9, 1827; m. Katharine Kimball Hanson in Belfast, Me., Oct. 22, 1853.
5966 v   RUFUS HOPKINS, b. April 29, 1829.

5914 ESTHER[7] EMERY (*David,*[6] *David S.*[5]), daughter of David and Mrs. Jane (Hall-Pierce) Emery; married, first, Jan. 1, 1820, Calvin Burden of Augusta, Me. (died March 29, 1827); second, Luther Calder Wood of Vinal Haven, Me., Dec. 3, 1832 (died Feb. 11, 1865).
Children, by first marriage:

5967 i   CALVIN,[8] b. July 5, 1823, in Knox, Me.; m.; had five children.
5968 ii HIRAM EMERY, b. Feb. 1, 1825, in Belfast, Me.; m.; had eight children.
5969 iii GEORGE WATSON, b. May 24, 1827, in Belfast, Me.; m.

By second marriage, born in Vinal Haven:

5970 iv   EMERY AMASA, b. Sept. 3, 1833; m.; had six children.
5971 v   JANE ELIZA, b. Sept. 12, 1835; m.; had nine children.
5972 vi   SARAH FRANCES, b. July 14, 1837; m.; had four children.
5973 vii LUTHER JAMES, b. March 31, 1839; m.; had six children.
5974 viii REBECCA ESTHER, b. Nov. 19, 1842; m.; had ten children; d. Oct. 29, 1864.

5915 SALLY[7] EMERY (*Othniel,*[6] *David S.*[5]), daughter of Othniel and —— Meloon; married Nathaniel Noyes.
Children:

5975 i   ALBERT.[8]
5976 ii JOHN B., m. Priscilla Hanford; had three children.
5977 iii MARY A., m. D. A. Cummings; had one child.
5978 iv ABBIE, m. George Cummings; had one child.
5979 v   CAROLINE E. G., m. P. S. Emmerson of Wilmont.

5916 CHARLOTTE[7] EMERY (*Othniel,*[6] *David S.*[5]), daughter of Othniel and ——Meloon; married Nathaniel Watson.
Children:

5980 i   ELBRIDGE,[8] m. —— Gliddon; had two children.
5981 ii ALONZO, m. Ellen Meloon; had three children.
5982 iii ANDREW J., m. Mary Berry.
5983 iv ADELINE, m. —— Osgood; 2nd, ——Felch; had one son.
5984 v   SARAH E., m., 1st, James Chase; 2nd, Charles Meloon; four daughters.
5985 vi EDWARD, unm.

5917 REBECCA[7] EMERY (*Othniel,*[6] *David S.*[5]), daughter of Othniel and —— Meloon; married Gilman Webster.

Children :

5986   i   ANGLLINE,[8] d young
5987   ii   EMILY, m. George Whidden.

5918 NATHANIEI[7] EMERY (*Othniel,*[6] *David S*[5]), son of Othniel and ——— Meloon ; married, first, Hannah Brown, second, Lucy Morse

Children, by first marriage :

5988   i   CHARLES N ,[8] m Grace Green
5989   ii   A DAUGHTER, m. John Scavey, had several children.

By second marriage :

5990   iii A DAUGHTER, m. George Cummings, had one son

5919 SAMUEL M[7] EMERY (*Othniel,*[6] *David S.*[5]), son of Othniel and ——— Meloon, married Olive Brown.

Children ·

5991   i   ALONZO[8]
5992   ii   CAROLINE, m. ——— Sanborn, had one dau. Kate

5920 MOSES[7] EMERY (*Othniel,*[6] *David S.*[5]), son of Othniel and ——— Meloon ; married ——— Straw.

Children :

5993   i   WILLIAM,[8] m. and had children
5994   ii   JOHN, d in the army.
5995   iii   CHARLES
5996   iv   JULIA

5921 DAVID S[7] EMERY (*Othniel,*[6] *David S.*[5]), son of Othniel and ——— (Meloon) Emery ; married Ruth S. Norris.

Children ·

5997   i   STEPHEN N ,[8] d
5998   ii   SARAH L , m. Dr. W. A. Page.
5999   iii   SMITH F.
6000   iv   DAVID N

5922 ALBERT[7] EMERY (*Othniel,*[6] *David S.*[5]), son of Othniel and ——— Meloon, married Eliza Brown.

Child :

6001   i   ALBERT S ,[8] m and has two children.

5923 ALPHEUS[7] EMERY (*Othniel,*[6] *David S.*[5]), son of Othniel and ——— Meloon, married Sally Brown.

Children :

6002   i   GEO N ,[8] m Lydia Ann Glines, have son, Wm A
6003   ii   OLIVE BEAN, d
6004   iii   ELLA C., m James A Proctor have son, Emery E
6005   iv   ALBERT E , m , 1st, Caroline F Jewett; 2nd, Julia W. Sturdevant.

5962 JAMES[8] EMERY (*Capt. Robert,*[7] *David,*[6] *David S.*[5]), son of

Captain Robert and Martha (Hopkins) Emery, married, first, in Bucksport, Me., June 1, 1844, Matilda Goodale Hervey (died July 3, 1852), second, Sept 2, 1853, Caroline Elliott Hervey, sister of first wife.

Children, by first marriage, born in Bucksport, Me :

    6006   i   CHARLES A ,⁹ b Feb 26, 1846, d Aug 20, 1846
    6007   ii   HARRY LINWOOD, b Nov 2, 1847, d. Oct 5, 1850
    6008   iii   ELIZABETH HERVEY, b June 26, 1852, d July 2, 1852.

By second marriage

    6009   iv   ALICE LINWOOD, b July 16, 1854, d Jan 11, 1886
    6010   v   ELIZABETH HERVEY, b May 11, 1856
    6011   vi   JAMES ROBERT, b Feb 22, 1858, m. in Everett, Mass , July 11,
                 1882, Jessie Benton Ross (b Dec 30, 1856)
    6012   vii   MARTHA CAROLINE, b March 18, 1861, d Dec 26, 1861.
    6013   viii   HORACE VERNEI, b July 24, 1863, d. Jan 30, 1864
    6014   ix   MARY LOUISA, b Feb 7, 1865, d March 31, 1865

5966 RUFUS HOPKINS⁸ EMERY (*Robert*,⁷ *David*,⁶ *David S* ⁵), son of Captain Robert and Martha (Hopkins) Emery, married in Bucksport, Me , Oct. 30, 1854, Harriet S Goodale (born Oct. 10, 1833).
    Child.

    6015   i   EFFIE HOWARD,⁹ b March 20, 1856, d Oct. 17, 1861.

5999 SMITH F ⁸ EMERY (*David S.*,⁷ *Othniel*,⁶ *David S* ⁵), son of David S and Ruth S. (Norris) Emery; married Susan H Moulton, a descendant of Dr. Anthony Emery of Hampton, N. H
    Children :

    6016   i   JOHN H ,⁹ d young
    6017   ii   CAROLINE P , m. W. V. Hill
    6018   iii   ALICE H , d young.

APPENDIX C

189 WILLIAM⁴ EMERY, SEN , (*Edward*,³ *Jonathan*,² *John*¹), son of Edward (one of the original proprietors of the Plantation of Contoocook, now Boscawen and Webster, N. H) and Sarah (Sibley) Emery, married Aug 4, 1749, Mary Chase, daughter of Nathan and Judith (Sawyer) Chase He was an energetic business man. In 1754 his cabin, which was about five miles outside the stockade at Contoocook, was attacked by the Indians He had notice in time to remove his wife (who was ill) and the rest of his family, but the cabin was sacked and a neighbor's wife and children carried off After his father was killed by the Indians about 1749, he purchased the rights of his brothers and sisters in the estate, sold the land in parcels from time to time, and in 1775 and afterward, he and his sons purchased land at Fishersfield (Newbury), N. H. His wife died Feb. 19, 1808.

Children, born in Contoocook, N. H.:

ERRATA

The names and arrangement of children of Wm Emery, No. 189, page 295, Appendix C, should be as follows :

6019 i   WILLIAM, b 1751, m Hannah Emerson

6020 ii SARAH, b abt 1753; m Jonathan Brown (For issue see Town Records, Newport, N H)

       iii JUDITH, b July 6, 1755, m Cutting Moulton.

6021 iv JOSIAH, b 1756-7, m Abigail Cutler

6022 v DAVID, b abt 1758

6022a vi PATIENCE, b Apr 14, 1760 m Dr Samuel Thompson (For issue see Town Records, Newport, N H)

Among descendants of Philip Emery, Appendix C, page 296, make

6049 iii JAMES, m Eliza Durgin, not Duryea

6019   i   WILLIAM, JR ,[5] b 1751.
6020   ii SARAH, b ab 1753 m , 1st, Nathan Brown of Unity, N H ;
           2nd, David Huntoon.
       iii JUDITH, b July 6, 1755   (See No. 594.)
6020a iv LYDIA, b ab 1757, m John Lattemore and settled in New-
           port N H
6021   v   JOSIAH, b ab 1759.
6022   vi DAVID, b ab 1761.

6019 WILLIAM[5] EMERY, JR (*William,*[1] *Edward,*[3] *Jonathan,*[2] *John*[1]),
son of William, sen , and Mary (Chase) Emery; married Sept. 17,
1778, Hannah Emerson of Derryfield (Manchester) , died at Fishersfield (Newbury), N. H , Jan. 27, 1829. The family afterwards removed to Croydon

Children, born in Fishersfield, N. H :

6023   i   WILLIAM,[6] 3RD, b March 29, 1780.
6024   ii   PHILIP, b. Aug. 13, 1781
6025   iii JUDITH, b July 3, 1783, m John Wadleigh Lived in Canada
6026   iv   RHODA, b April 2, 1785, m Sibley Melindy of Croydon,
            June 7, 1809   (Croydon Town Records).
6027   v   NATHAN, b Feb 7, 1787
6028   vi   SALLY, b. Jan. 14, 1789.
6029   vii HANNAH, b Jan 14, 1791, m Samuel Crowell, Newport N H
6030   viii MOLLEY, b May 5, 1793; m David Harden, Croydon, N. H.
6031   ix   AMOS, b May 31, 1795
6032   x   LYDIA, b May 26, 1797; m Benjamin Baker, in Newport, N H

6021 JOSIAH[5] EMERY, SEN (*William,*[4] *Edward,*[3] *Jonathan,*[2] *John*[1]),
son of William, sen., and Mary (Chase) Emery , married, about 1782,
Abigail Cutler.   He settled with his father and brothers at Fishersfield (Newbury), N. H , about 1775, and removed with his family to
Ludlow, Vt., before 1800, where he died May 18, 1813   His wife
died March 5, 1808.

Children :

6033   i   JOSIAH,[6] b July 1, 1784
6034   ii   RUTH, b Feb 5, 1786, m. Amos Wheeton, Jan 31, 1805.
6035   iii MARY, b Dec 4, 1787
6036   iv   SAMUEL, b Oct 31, 1789
6037   v   EDWARD, b April 7, 1792   Enlisted in the Army in 1812 for
            five years
6038   vi   ELIZABETH, b May 22, 1794
6039   vii JOHN CUTLER, b. July 11, 1796
6040   viii ABIGAIL, b April 16 1798, m , 1st, Michael Schmellzer, a well-
            to-do farmer of Lodi, Seneca Co , N Y., 2d, Mr Biggs, now
            deceased
6041   ix   RUSHA, b March 8, 1800.
6042   x   DAVID, b. May 3, 1802
6043   xi   LUCINDA, b Dec. 2, 1804
6044   xii WM. WATERS, b June 1, 1807

6022 DAVID[5] EMERY (*William,*[1] *Edward,*[3] *Jonathan,*[2] *John*[1]), son
of William, sen., and Mary (Chase) Emery, probably born in 1759, in
Contoocook. He settled with his father and brothers at Fishersfield
(Newbury), N H , about 1775 , married about 1801 and followed his
brother Josiah to Ludlow, Vt.

Children :

6044a i   RUTH,[6] b June 25, 1802
6044b ii REUBEN, b. April 18, 1804

6023 WILLIAM[6] EMERY, 3RD (*William,*[5] *William,*[4] *Edward,*[3] *Jonathan,*[2] *John*[1]), son of William, jr., and Hannah (Emerson) Emery; married Sept. 12, 1802, Polly Simons (Dunbarton Records). Moved from Fishersfield to Hatley, Canada, where he died.

Children :

6045   i   POLLY,[7] b. May 31, 1803.
6046   ii   JOHN, b. March 20, 1805.

William Emery has a large number of descendants in Canada, whose names are unknown.

6024 PHILIP[6] EMERY (*William,*[5] *William,*[4] *Edward,*[3] *Jonathan,*[2] *John*[1]), son of William, jr., and Hannah (Emerson) Emery; married Dec. 26, 1805, Sally Eaton of Goffstown, N. H. ; died May 20, 1870; she died Sept. 28, 1874, aged nearly 91 years.

Children :

6047   i   CLARISSA,[7] b. Oct. 14. 1806; m. T. F. Moore, in Bedford, N. H.;
              d. Oct. 14. 1885.   Had three children.
6048   ii   WILLIAM, b. May 4, 1808.   Lived in Rochester, N. Y.; m.; d.
6049   iii   JAMES, b. Oct. 4, 1810; m. Eliza Duryea, in Lexington, Mass.
              Had a dau.
6050   iv   AMES, b. July 8, 1811; d. Sept. 18, 1831.
6051   v   HANNAH, b. Jan. 9, 1813; m. R. Melven of Merrimac, N. H.
6052   vi   SAMUEL E., b. Dec. 21, 1814; m. Marrah Presby; d. in Me.
6053   vii   OBADIAH, b. Oct. 27, 1816; d. Jan. 24, 1817.
6054   viii ALICE E., b. Feb. 23, 1818; m. J. Plummer, of Henniker, N. H.
6055   ix   SARAH, b. Dec. 20, 1819; m. Charles Spears, in Woburn, Mass.
              Had a dau.
6056   x   OBADIAH W., b. May 26, 1822; m. Mary Ann Gregg, Nov. 20,
              1855. Lives in Goshen, N. H. Has a dau. b. Dec. 23, 1869.
6057   xi   HARVEY, b. Nov. 27, 1823.
6058   xii   URANA, b. April 19, 1825; m. J. Barnard. Lived first in New-
              port. now in Goshen.
6059   xiii POLLY F., b. Jan. 10, 1827; m. J. Haines, in Henniker, N. H.

6027 GEN. NATHAN[6] EMERY (*William,*[5] *William,*[4] *Edward,*[3] *Jonathan,*[2] *John*[1]), son of William, jr., and Hannah (Emerson) Emery; married Dec. 29, 1811, Esther Hager of Croydon. He was an active and successful farmer, noted for his public spirit and his zeal and interest in the militia, in which he rose to the position of Major-General. He died at Croydon Flat, Jan. 7, 1852. She died Aug. 10, 1858, aged 68 years.

Children all died in infancy. An adopted daughter married Wm. W. Hall, son of Edward Hall, jr., and Sally Emery.

6028 SALLY[6] EMERY (*William,*[5] *William,*[4] *Edward,*[3] *Jonathan,*[2] *John*[1]), daughter of William, jr., and Hannah (Emerson) Emery; married Feb. 12, 1811, Edward Hall, jr., of Croydon.

Child :

6060   i   WILLIAM W.,[7] m. adopted dau. of Gen. Nathan Emery, and
              now resides at Croydon Flat.

6031 AMOS[6] EMERY (*William,*[5] *William,*[4] *Edward,*[3] *Jonathan,*[2] *John*[1]), son of William, jr., and Hannah (Emerson) Emery; married Roxana Ayer. He died at Goshen, Oct. 12, 1856. She died March 1, 1865.

Children :

6061 i ELIJAH P ,⁷ b May 28 1824, at Newbury, N H , m Ruth M.
         Blodgett, dau of Nathaniel Dec 20, 1849. Removed to
         Newport, N H , in 1855. Has had two children who d.
         young
6062 ii WILLIAM, b Feb 15, 1826; d Aug 20, 1827
6063 iii SIMON A., b Sept 6, 1827; m , 1st, Feb , 1853, Elvira D Blod-
          gett, 2nd, a lady from Maine Had two children who d.
          young Lives in Newport, N H
6064 iv RANSOM, b Aug 24, 1829, m Belinda A Jones
6065 v LAURA ANN, b. May 14, 1831, m Dennis Lear
6066 vi LUCINDA C , b Aug 17, 1833
6067 vii MARY C , b Aug 18, 1837, m James M Blodget
6068 viii CAROLINE P , b May 19 1839, m John F. Jones
6069 ix WILLIAM H , b Sept 5, 1841
6070 x JOHN Q A , b Jan 29, 1845, m Eda V. Maxwell.

6033 JOSIAH⁶ EMERY, JR (*Josiah*,⁵ *William*,⁴ *Edward*,³ *Jonathan*,²
*John*¹), son of Josiah, sen , and Abigail (Cutler) Emery , married in
1809, Susannah Little, daughter of Lieut. Moses and Mary (Stevens)
Little of Goffstown, N H. He was a man of remarkable enterprise
and a representative pioneer whose life spanned the period from the
close of the Revolution to the end of the Rebellion. He was in business in Salem, Mass , in the year 1804, and a part owner in a saw
mill and store at Barre, Vt., in 1808. In January, 1811, he moved
his family and portable effects in a four-horse sleigh to western New
York, settling temporarily at Caledonia and permanently at Willink
(Aurora), south of Buffalo, then a wilderness near an Indian Reser-
vation. He was an influential man in his new home, was a lieutenant
in the war of 1812, engaged at Lundy's Lane and other battles and
later became a colonel in the state militia He died Aug. 14, 1873.
His wife died Feb. 5, 1861.

Children :

6071 i LUCIUS HARRISON,⁷ b. July 23, 1811
6072 ii MOSES LITTLE, b March 28, 1815
6073 iii JOHN CUTLER, 2D, b Dec 1, 1817
6074 iv JOSIAH, 3D, b Oct 29, 1819
6075 v ASHER BATES, b May 12, 1821, d Sept. 5, 1839
6076 vi MARY SUSAN, b March 2, 1824.

6039 DR. JOHN CUTLER⁶ EMERY (*Josiah*,⁵ *William*,⁴ *Edward*,³
Jonathan,² *John*¹), son of Josiah, sen , and Abigail (Cutler) Emery ,
married about 1822, Marinda Haines of Chester, N. J He enlisted
in the war of 1812, went to New Jersey about 1816, studied medicine,
and finally settled at Lansing, Mich , where he became a prominent
physician.

Children :

6077 i CORNELIA,⁷ b Aug 19, 1824, m Joseph Willoughby Crain
6078 ii JANETTE, b Sept 14, 1826
6079 iii JARED HAINES, b Sept 20, 1828
6080 iv HELEN SANDFORD, b Oct 6, 1830, m. J Smith Davison.
6081 v MARY ANN DEMOTT, b March 28, 1833, m. William R. Free-
         man Resides in Newark, N Y
6082 vi FRANKLIN, b Oct 31, 1835 Killed in the battle of Fredericks-
         burg, Va , Dec. 11, 1862.

6042 David[6] EMERY (*Josiah,[5] William,[4] Edward,[3] Jonathan,[2] John[1]*), son of Josiah and Abigail (Cutler) Emery ; married Diantha, daughter of James and Catharine (Chamberlin) Faxon of Washington, N. H., who died 1842 ; second, Lucy H., daughter of John and Sally (Jewell) Howe.

Children, born in Newport, N. H., except the last :

6083 i   MARY MATILDA,[7] b. Feb. 20, 1828; m. Stephen M. Bennett.
6084 ii WILLIAM JOSIAH, b. Jan. 13, 1829; m. Mary J. Moore.
6085 iii IRA P., b. Sept. 30, 1831; m. April 3, 1855, Charity A. McIntire.
6086 iv ALFRED D., b. March 18, 1838; res. in Chin Kiang, China.
6087 v   FRANCES E., b. June 2, 1842; m. Helen J. Buckman.

Child, by second wife :

6088 vi DIANTHA M., b. Aug. 10, 1856.

6043 Lucinda[6] EMERY (*Josiah,[5] William,[4] Edward,[3] Jonathan,[2] John[1]*), daughter of Josiah, sen., and Abigail (Cutler) Emery ; married William Kimball, farmer, of Aurora, N. Y. She died Jan. 13, 1844. He died in 1872.

Children :

6089 i   ABIGAIL A.,[7] b. 1828; res. at South Wales, Erie Co., N. Y.
6090 ii ORLANDO, b. 1832.
6091 iii WILLIAM HENRY, b. 1838.

6044b Reuben[6] EMERY (*David,[5] William,[4] Edward,[3] Jonathan,[2] John[1]*), son of David and ——— Emery ; born at Ludlow, Vt., April 18, 1804 ; married Roxana Adams who is now (1890) 88 years old and living at Ludlow, Vt. He died March 15, 1887.

Children :

6091*a* i   CHARLES P.,[7] d. Feb. 26, 1857.
6091*b* ii LEVI A., d. Sept. 10, 1852.
6091*c* iii LOUISA. d. March 6, 1843.
6091*d* iv FRANCES M., m. G. W. Hemenway; d. Feb. 29, 1856.
6091*e* v   ABBEY, m. Mr. Shattuck, of Ludlow, Vt.
6091*f* vi SARAH, m. Mr. Smith, of Rockingham, Vt.
6091*g* vii ANN, m. Mr. Chapman, of Ludlow, Vt.

6071 Lucius Harrison[7] EMERY (*Josiah,[6] Josiah,[5] William,[4] Edward,[3] Jonathan,[2] John[1]*), son of Josiah, jr., and Susannah (Little) Emery ; born at Aurora, N. Y. ; married Lorinda S. Brigham, daughter of Pierrepont Brigham, originally from St. Albans, Vt. Carriage maker and farmer. Both deceased.

Children :

6092 i   EDWIN FRANCIS,[8] b. March 29, 1843.
6093 ii JOHN RUSSELL, b. Dec. 26, 1846.

6072 Moses Little[7] EMERY (*Josiah,[6] Josiah,[5] William,[4] Edward,[3] Jonathan,[2] John[1]*), son of Josiah, jr., and Susannah(Little) Emery ; married Nov. 8. 1836, Minerva (born Sept., 1811), daughter of Jared and Betsey Prentiss, of Canandaigua, N. Y. Architect and builder. He died Aug. 2, 1840. She died March 20, 1882.

Children

6094 i   CHARLES EDWARD,[8] b March 29, 1838
6095 ii HENRY (Wm Henry Harrison), b May 16, 1840 He was in
         Rosencrans' cavalry early in the Civil War and connected
         afterward with the U S Military Telegraph

6073 JOHN CUTLER[7] EMERY, 2D (*Josiah,*[6] *Josiah,*[5] *William,*[4] *Edward,*[3] *Jonathan,*[2] *John*[1]), son of Josiah, jr., and Susannah (Little) Emery, born Dec 1, 1817, at Aurora, N Y , married, first, in 1840, Mary Yerkes, who died in March, 1851. Married, second, in Nov., 1851, Ellen Nevins He removed to Michigan in 1838 and died in 1885 at Northville, Mich. He was a builder early in life and a farmer later. Was a recruiting agent during the war and an internal revenue collector after

Children, by first wife.

6096 i   CHILD,[8] b in 1841, at Lyons, Mich ; d in infancy.
6097 ii ELLEN Y., b. in 1843 at Lyons
6098 iii JOSIAH, b Dec 26, 1844, at Lyons
6099 iv Z TAYLOR, b 1847, at Northville

Children, by second wife

6100 v   MARY, b 1852
6101 vi JOHN N , b 1854
6102 vii SUSIE L , b 1860; m in 1888, Wm Wooley, who d. in 1889.
6103 viii LUCY A , b Dec 5, 1862, d Sept 28, 1865
6104 ix BENJAMIN FRANKLIN, b 1867

6074 JOSIAH[7] EMERY, 3D (*Josiah,*[6] *Josiah.*[5] *William,*[4] *Edward,*[3] *Jonathan.*[2] *John*[1]), son of Josiah, jr , and Susannah (Little) Emery, married, July 11, 1847, Elizabeth, daughter of Alexander and Mary (Ingersoll) Kellogg (formerly of Bethlehem, Conn). He is a man of great intellectual power, who, while conducting the homestead farm at Aurora, N Y , has almost continually held a county office and is very frequently consulted in legal matters She died Dec. 12, 1884.

Children :

6105 i   ELLA FRANCES,[8] b Aug 31, 1849 d Oct 17, 1865
6106 ii EDWARD KELLOGG, b July 29, 1851.
6107 iii JOSIAH ALBERT, b. May 23, 1856. A rising criminal lawyer in
         the office of the district attorney of Erie Co , Buffalo, N Y.
6108 iv MARY ELIZABETH, b Sept 30, 1858.
6109 v   ASHER BAILS, b. Feb. 18, 1867

6076 MARY SUSAN[7] EMERY (*Josiah,*[6] *Josiah,*[5] *William,*[4] *Edward,*[3] *Jonathan,*[2] *John*[1]), daughter of Josiah, jr , and Susannah (Little) Emery; married John H. McMillan of Aurora, Erie Co., N. Y.

Children

6110 i   FRANK E ,[8] b Sept. 11, 1853, m in 1878, Mary Letson One
         child, Willie
6111 ii ARTHUR H , b Oct 16, 1858, m in 1880, Emily Dudley
6112 iii JOHN HOWARD, b. Jan. 11, 1861; m. in 1881, Nellie Burlingham.

6078 JANETTE[7] EMERY (*Dr. John C ,*[6] *Josiah,*[5] *William,*[4] *Edward,*[3] *Jonathan,*[2] *John*[1]), daughter of Dr. John C and Marinda (Haines) Emery ; married George Sprague, M.D. She is now a widow residing at St Elmo, Tenn.

Children :

6113　i　　Frank R.,[8] b. —— ; editor *Progressive Age*, 18 Broadway, N.Y.
6114　ii　William R., b. —— ; firm of Sprague, Warner & Co., Chicago, Ill.

6079 Jared Haines[7] Emery (*Dr. John C.*,[6] *Josiah*,[5] *William*,[4] *Edward*,[3] *Jonathan*,[2] *John*[1]), son of Dr. John C. and Marinda (Haines) Emery ; married Ann W. Wilson. Resides at Ashton, Dakota.
Children :

6115　i　　Charles S.[9]
6116　ii　Jared L.
6117　iii　Helen G.
6118　iv　John Franklin.
6119　v　　Oscar W.

6092 Edwin Francis[8] Emery (*Lucius H.*,[7] *Josiah*,[6] *Josiah*,[5] *William*,[4] *Edward*,[3] *Jonathan*,[2] *John*[1]), son of Lucius Harrison and Lorinda (Brigham) Emery ; married, May 29, 1869, Mary Fidelia, daughter of John Harrison and Mary C. Hodges. Foreman pattern maker, Frankfort, N. Y.
Children :

6120　i　　Albert Guy,[9] b. May 17, 1870.
6121　ii　Charles Vernon, b. Dec. 6, 1874.

6093 John Russell[8] Emery (*Lucius H.*,[7] *Josiah*,[6] *Josiah*,[5] *William*,[4] *Edward*,[3] *Jonathan*,[2] *John*[1]), son of Lucius Harrison and Lorinda (Brigham) Emery ; married Abbey B., daughter of William and Mary Cutler, formerly of Waterbury, Vt. Carriage-maker. He died Jan. 29, 1887. Widow living at South Wales, Erie Co., N. Y.
Children :

6122　i　　Maria T.[9]
6123　ii　Florence.

6094 Charles Edward[8] Emery, Ph.D. (*Moses L.*,[7] *Josiah*,[6] *Josiah*,[5] *William*,[4] *Edward*,[3] *Jonathan*,[2] *John*[1]), married Aug. 6, 1863, Susan S., daughter of Hon. E. R. Livingston of Brooklyn, N. Y. When studying law in Canandaigua, N. Y., early in 1861, he organized a military company which was disbanded when President Lincoln made the mistaken announcement that no more troops were needed. Soon after he entered the regular navy as an assistant engineer and participated on the U. S. steamer Richmond in the engagement at Fort Pickens, the capture of New Orleans and the naval attacks on Vicksburg and Port Hudson. Was afterward on the U. S. steamer Nipsic at Charleston, S. C. Before the close of the war, was ordered to New York and assisted in conducting U. S. experiments. Resigned Jan. 1, 1869. Appointed consulting engineer of the U. S. service and U. S. revenue marine in the same year and the latter appointment has continued to the present time. Made experiments with different types of machinery in U. S. revenue marine steamers which have been published in scientific literature all over the world. The degree of Doctor of Philosophy conferred upon him soon after. Was one of the judges at the Centennial Exhibition at Philadelphia. He built the plant of the

successful steam company in New York City at a cost of nearly
$2,000 000. Has been consulting engineer of the terminal facili-
ities of the New York and Brooklyn bridge and of several of the
principal plants of the Edison Electric Lighting Company. Is a
member of the principal scientific and engineering societies at home
and abroad. Has been a frequent contributor to the engineering
and scientific periodicals, receiving the Watt medal and Telford pre-
mium from the (British) Institution of Civil Engineers. Is a non-
resident professor and lectures at Cornell University. Is chairman
of the engineers' examining boards of the U. S. revenue marine and
lectures to the cadets on the U. S. revenue marine schoolship. Office, New York City.

Child :

6124   i   LIVINGSTON[9] b May 7, 1864. Two years in Cadet Corps of
23rd Regt., New York state militia, graduated at Adelphi
Academy, 1882, A B Columbia College, 1886; LL B Columbia College Law School 1888, admitted to the bar same
year ; now a practising lawyer in New York City.

6097 ELLEN Y.[8] EMERY (*John C ,*[7] *Josiah,*[6] *Josiah,*[5] *William,*[4] *Edward,*[3] *Jonathan,*[2] *John*[1]), daughter of John Cutler, 2nd, and Mary
(Yerkes) Emery, married July 19, 1865, Henry W. Holcomb. Resides in Northville, Mich.

Children :

6125   i   WILLIAM,[9] b. Oct. 1, 1866
6126   ii   MARY HESTER, b Aug 26,1868
6127   iii HENRY RAYMOND, b July 29, 1884

6098 JOSIAH[8] EMERY, 4TH (*John C ,*[7] *Josiah,*[6] *Josiah,*[5] *William,*[4]
Edward,[3] *Jonathan,*[2] *John*[1]), son of John Cutler and Mary (Yerkes)
Emery; married Aug 18, 1867, Cordelia J. P. R. Bradley (born
Aug. 24, 1842). Farmer in Waterford, Mich.

Children ·

6128   i   CLARENCE B .[9] b Nov. 28, 1869.
6129   ii   RALPH E , b Dec. 16, 1872, d Jan 23, 1877
6130   iii JAMES B , b Sept 16, 1875.
6131   iv   WILLIAM J , ⎫
6132   v   WALLER E , ⎭ b. Dec 19, 1879

6099 Z. TAYLOR[8] EMERY, M D (*John C ,*[7] *Josiah,*[6] *Josiah* [5] *Wil-
liam,*[4] *Edward,*[3] *Jonathan,*[2] *John*[1]), son of John Cutler and Mary
(Yerkes) Emery , married in 1889, Miss Georgina Colville of Glasgow,
Scotland Graduate of Detroit Medical College. *Ad eundem* degree
at Long Island College Hospital. A prominent physician in Brooklyn,
N. Y. Formerly secretary of King's County Medical Society.

6100 MARY[8] EMERY (*John C.,*[7] *Josiah,*[6] *Josiah,*[5] *William,*[4] *Ed-
ward,*[3] *Jonathan,*[2] *John*[1]), daughter of John Cutler, 2d, and Ellen
(Nevins) Emery, married Oct 13, 1875, Orion N. Bornhort of
Northville, Mich.

Child :

6133   i   ALBERT EMERY,[9] b. Aug 29, 1876.

6101 JOHN N.[8] EMERY (*John C.*,[7] *Josiah*,[6] *Josiah*,[5] *William*,[4] *Edward*,[3] *Jonathan*,[2] *John*[1]), son of John Cutler, 2d, and Ellen (Nevins) Emery ; married in 1882, Minney Withey ; resides in Northville, Mich.
  Child :

  6134 i LIZZIE,[9] b. 1884.

6106 EDWARD KELLOGG[8] EMERY (*Josiah*,[7] *Josiah*,[6] *Josiah*,[5] *William*,[4] *Edward*,[3] *Jonathan*,[2] *John*[1]), son of Josiah, 3d, and Elizabeth (Kellogg) Emery ; married Oct. 7, 1886, Clara B., daughter of Jedediah and Mary A. Darbee. He is a well-known lawyer of Buffalo, N. Y., and was a member of the New York State Assembly for two terms.
  Child :

  6135 i MARY ELIZABETH,[9] b. July 31, 1888.

6108 MARY ELIZABETH[8] EMERY (*Josiah*,[7] *Josiah*,[6] *Josiah*,[5] *William*,[4] *Edward*,[3] *Jonathan*,[2] *John*[1]), daughter of Josiah, 2d, and Elizabeth (Kellogg) Emery ; married Oct. 9, 1878, DeWitt C. Blakely, son of Ransom and Laura Blakely. Farmer. She died June 10, 1882.
  Child :

  6136 i ELLA F.,[9] b. Jan., 1882.

APPENDIX D.

178a* THOMAS[4] EMERY (*Jonathan*,[3] *Jonathan*,[2] *John*[1]), supposed son of Jonathan and Ruth (Richardson) Emery ; baptized in Newbury, Mass., Jan. 6, 1722 ; married Jan. 7, 1745-6, Mary Greenough of Haverhill district.
  Children :

  6137 i ELIPHALET,[5] settled in Bedford, N. H.
  6138 ii DAUGHTER, m. ——— Burroughs; lived in Hampstead, N. H.
  6139 iii THOMAS, b. in Plaistow, N. H., or Derry, about 1736.
  6140 iv JONATHAN.
  6141 v MOSES, lived in Bradford, N. H.

6139 THOMAS[5] EMERY (*Thomas*,[4] *Jonathan*,[3] *Jonathan*,[2] *John*[1]), son of Thomas and Mary (Greenough) Emery ; married ——— ——— ; removed to Rindge, N. H. ; was in the whole of the Revolntionary war ; was at the battle of Bunker Hill. He sold, it is said, six oxen to get a gun ; died at Rindge, N. H., aged 96.
  Children :

  6142 i ZIBA,[6] d. unm.
  6143 ii SAMUEL, d., unm., in Westminster, Mass.
  6144 iii WILLIAM.

* This should have appeared in the body of the work as a child of Jonathan,[3] but was not received in time. See p. 8.

6145 iv THOMAS, settled in New Ipswich, N H ; m. and had son
              Hiram
6146 v   POLLY.
6147 vi SARAH
6148 vii BETSEY
6149 viii HANNAH.
6150 ix MERCY
6151 x   JOHN.

6140 JONATHAN[5] EMERY (*Thomas,[4] Jonathan,[3] Jonathan,[2] John[1]*),
son of Thomas and Mary (Greenough) Emery, married Elizabeth
Gliddon.
   Children:

6152 i   DOLLY [6]
6153 ii   JOHN, m Rebecca, dau of Peter Aikin; was lost at sea
6154 iii DAVID, m Polly Porter; d 1809, had a son and dau
6155 iv   BETSEY, m Jacob Burrill
6156 v   THOMAS, lived in Sheldon, Vt
6157 vi   MOSES, m Lois Stebbins, had son, Kendrick Emery
6158 vii RICHARD, b Dec 17, 1786, in Chester, N. H (Auburn)
6159 viii JONATHAN
6160 ix   SAMUEL, m Abigail Noyes

6144 WILLIAM[6] EMERY (*Thomas,[5] Thomas,[4] Jonathan,[3] Jonathan,[2] John[1]*), son of Thomas and ——— ———.
   Children:

6161 i   WILLIAM J [7]
6162 ii   AMOS
6163 iii THOMAS.

6151 JOHN[6] EMERY (*Thomas,[5] Thomas,[4] Jonathan,[3] Jonathan,[2]
John[1]*), married and had one child.
   Child:

6164 i   SAMUEL,[7] b March 3, 1811, in Rindge, N H

6158 RICHARD[6] EMERY (*Jonathan,[5] Thomas,[4] Jonathan,[3] Jonathan,[2] John[1]*), son of Jonathan and Elizabeth (Gliddon) Emery; married Nov. 18, 1813. Polly Palmer (born Dec. 6, 1791, died April 7,
1854) He died May 28, 1837.
   Children

6165 i   RICHARD,[7] b. May 18, 1814.
6166 ii   JONATHAN, b Jan 9 1816
6167 iii STEPHEN, b March 5, 1818
6168 iv   AMHERST, b Dec 5, 1821
6169 v   MARIA, b Sept. 3, 1823
6170 vi   WILLIAM, b March 27, 1825.
6171 vii ALVAH, b. March 26, 1827, d Sept 11, 1834.

6159 JONATHAN[6] EMERY (*Jonathan,[5] Thomas,[4] Jonathan,[3] Jonathan,[2] John[1]*), son of Jonathan and Elizabeth (Gliddon) Emery;
married Nancy Eaton (born Aug. 16, 1793).
   Children:

6172 i   EATON,[7] b Dec. 28, 1815.
6173 ii   DAVID, b 1817.
6174 iii AMOS, b. March 27, 1820.

6175 iv CHARLES, b. June 6, 1822.
6176 v   ALPHEUS, b. Jan. 10, 1826.
6177 vi LOVE ANN, b. Feb. 13, 1828.
6178 vii BENJAMIN, b. June 14, 1830.
6179 viii FRANCES, b. June 25, 1835.

6164 SAMUEL[7] EMERY (*John*,[6] *Thomas*,[5] *Thomas*,[4] *Jonathan*,[3] *Jonathan*,[2] *John*[1]), son of John[6]; married, first, Thirza Weston; second, Mary Jane Wardwell (born in Maine).
Children :

6180 i   GEORGIANA E.,[8] d. young.
6181 ii LEVI LE FOREST, d. young.
6182 iii ABBIE, m. and has children.
6183 iv NATHANIEL, m. —— ——; res. in Lowell, Mass.
6184 v   ALONZO G., m. —— ——; res. in Dracut, Mass.

6165 RICHARD[7] EMERY (*Richard*,[6] *Jonathan*,[5] *Thomas*,[4] *Jonathan*,[3] *Jonathan*,[2] *John*[1]), son of Richard and Polly (Palmer) Emery ; married May 8. 1839, Mary Gray, daughter of Amos and Lucy (Lovejoy) Emery (born Oct. 16, 1876). He died March 26, 1874. Wheelwright.
Children :

6185 i   ALVAH TYLER,[8] b. June 1, 1841.
6186 ii GEORGE, b. 1842; d. 1847.
6187 iii LUCY ANN.
6188 iv HERMAN FRANKLIN, b. Aug. 14, 1847; m. April 6, 1872, Sarah Gibson.
6189 v   LUCY ANN, b. July 12, 1849.
6190 vi MARY ETTA, d. young, 1859.
6191 vii GEORGE AMOS, b. July 27, 1856.
6192 viii ALBERT HENRY, b. Feb., 1858.

6166 JONATHAN[7] EMERY (*Richard*,[6] *Jonathan*,[5] *Thomas*,[4] *Jonathan*,[3] *Jonathan*,[2] *John*[1]), son of Richard and Polly (Palmer) Emery ; married Sept. 5, 1839, in Charlestown, Mass., Nancy Raymond, daughter of Joel and Elizabeth (Bishpan) Raymond (born May 5, 1821; died Feb. 18, 1886).
Children :

6193 i   MARIA FRANCES,[8] b. Feb. 28, 1842.
6194 ii JONATHAN HENRY, b. Dec. 5, 1845.

6167 STEPHEN[7] EMERY (*Richard*,[6] *Jonathan*,[5] *Thomas*,[4] *Jonathan*,[3] *Jonathan*,[2] *John*[1]), son of Richard and Polly (Palmer) Emery ; married, first, in Malden, Mass., Mary Ann Holt (born Nov. 5, 1820 ; died Aug. 18, 1858) ; second, April 12, 1859, Sarah Robinson (born Aug. 25, 1824).

Child, by first marriage:

6195 i   ALFRED D.,[8] b. March 2, 1845.

6168 AMHERST[7] EMERY (*Richard*,[6] *Jonathan*,[5] *Thomas*,[4] *Jonathan*,[3] *Jonathan*,[2] *John*[1]), son of Richard and Polly (Palmer) Emery ; married Oct. 22, 1846, in Auburn, N. H., Mary M. Sawyer (born June 13, 1828; died Sept. 24, 1877).

Children :

6196 i   EUGENE HENRY,[8] b Sept 8. 1849; d. Nov. 14, 1874.
6197 ii PARK MORRIS, b. July 8, 1856, d in Lowell, Mass , Jan 4, 1884.
6198 iii FARNSWORTH BURNHAM, b Dec. 24, 1861.
6199 iv LYNDON EARL, b Nov 7, 1866
6200 v   ELVIRA R., b. Nov. 4, 1869, d May 31, 1870

6169 MARIA[7] EMERY (*Richard,[6] Jonathan,[5] Thomas,[4] Jonathan,[3] Jonathan,[2] John[1]*), daughter of Richard and Polly (Palmer) Emery; married Sept. 29, 1844, in Auburn, N. H., John Haselton (born Sept. 24, 1820, died March 24, 1885).

Children .

6201 i   WILLIAM ALVAH,[8] b Aug 21, 1845
6202 ii STEPHEN EMERY, b Dec 6, 1847, studied medicine, d. Nov. 29, 1829

6170 WILLIAM[7] EMERY (*Richard,[6] Jonathan,[5] Thomas,[4] Jonathan,[3] Jonathan,[2] John[1]*), son of Richard and Polly (Palmer) Emery, married in Auburn, N. H., Harriet H. Haselton (born April 7, 1831; died Jan. 20, 1874).

Children

6203 i   FRANK WILBUR,[8] b Sept 18, 1853
6204 ii ISABEL HATTIE, b Aug. 9, 1855
6205 iii CLARENCE WILLIAM, b. Oct 24, 1857.

6174 AMOS[7] EMERY (*Jonathan,[6] Jonathan,[5] Thomas,[4] Jonathan,[3] Jonathan,[2] John[1]*), son of Jonathan and Elizabeth (Gliddon) Emery, married, first, Almira Hibbard (born Jan. 13, 1822; died Nov. 29, 1856), second, Oct. 9, 1860, Sarah M. Hibbard (born Sept. 23, 1826, died Jan 25, 1883)

Children, by first marriage :

6206 i   GEORGE A ,[8] b Oct 6. 1844, m. March 20, 1867, Climena Allen, have Allen A., b Dec 25, 1867
6207 ii ALBERT E , b Aug 11, 1848, m , 1st, Luella L Corliss (d 1873), 2nd, Hattie Durkee. Had George A , b Dec 4, 1879.

Children, by second marriage

6208 iii CURTIS, b Nov 6, 1861; m May 12, 1884, Hattie M Ordway, have Sallie M , b. Aug 15, 1886
6209 iv WILSON S , b Nov. 9, 1863, m Bell Dudley, July 15, 1886

6185 ALVAH TYLER[8] EMERY (*Richard,[7] Richard,[6] Jonathan,[5] Thomas,[4] Jonathan,[3] Jonathan,[2] John[1]*), son of Richard and Mary (Gray) Emery; married March 6, 1860, Harriet Wason (born April 9, 1839).

Child :

6210 i   CELINDA,[9] b Jan 6, 1861, m July 15, 1877, James Brown, d. Feb 10, 1879

6187 LUCY ANN[8] EMERY (*Richard,[7] Richard,[6] Jonathan,[5] Thomas,[4] Jonathan,[3] Jonathan,[2] John[1]*), daughter of Richard and Mary (Gray) Emery, married March 13, 1869, Levi H. Putnam (died Jan 12, 1877).

20

Children :

6211 i   NELLIE JANE,[9] b. May 22, 1870.
6212 ii   ROSA ANN, b. Jan. 13, 1873.
6213 iii ANNIE BELL, b. Dec. 31, 1874.

6192 ALBERT HENRY[8] EMERY (*Richard*,[7] *Richard*,[6] *Jonathan*,[5] *Thomas*,[4] *Jonathan*,[3] *Jonathan*,[2] *John*[1]), son of Richard and Mary (Gray) Emery; married May 11, 1877, in Nashua, N. H., Abbie E. Draper (born April 29, 1860).

Children :

6214 i   ANSTIS ESTELLA,[9] b. March 23, 1881.
6215 ii   ELLA ASENATH, b. June 10, 1883.
6216 iii JAMES, b. Dec. 5, 1886.

6194 JONATHAN HENRY[8] EMERY (*Jonathan*,[7] *Richard*,[6] *Jonathan*,[5] *Thomas*,[4] *Jonathan*,[3] *Jonathan*,[2] *John*[1]), son of Jonathan and Nancy (Raymond) Emery; married Oct. 1, 1868, in Quincy, Mass., Ellen B. Churchill (born Oct. 15, 1845).

Children :

6217 i   ALICE JACOB,[9] b. July 5, 1871.
6218 ii   FLORENCE RAYMOND, b. Nov. 22, 1877.

6195 ALFRED D.[8] EMERY (*Stephen*,[7] *Richard*,[6] *Jonathan*,[5] *Thomas*,[4] *Jonathan*,[3] *Jonathan*,[2] *John*[1]), son of Stephen and Mary Ann (Holt) Emery; married April 17, 1864, in Auburn, N. H., Caroline F. Wood (born Sept. 16, 1844).

Children :

6219 i   SADIE FRANCES,[9] b. March 9, 1865; m. Nov. 15, 1885, Elmer E. French.
6220 ii   MARY CAROLINE, b. March 14, 1867.
6221 iii THOMAS STEPHEN, b. Feb. 21, 1869.
6222 iv   ELVIRA ROBINSON, b. Aug. 13, 1874.
6223 v   DANA ALFRED, b. July 28, 1877
6224 vi   WALTER PALMER, b. Dec. 19, 1879.

6201 WILLIAM ALVAH[8] EMERY (*Maria*,[7] *Richard*,[6] *Jonathan*,[5] *Thomas*,[4] *Jonathan*,[3] *Jonathan*,[2] *John*[1]), son of John and Maria (Haselton) Emery; married Feb. 26, 1870, Julia H. Harwood.

Children :

6225 i   SUSAN FRANCES,[8] b. Jan. 13, 1871; d. Nov. 15, 1886.
6226 ii   WILLIAM STEPHEN, b. Nov. 18, 1872.
6227 iii ALICE JENNIE, b. April 7, 1875.
6228 iv   SIDNEY HOMER, b. July 18, 1877.

APPENDIX E.

469 WILLARD[6] EMERY (*Willard*,[5] *Dr. Anthony*,[4] *John*,[3] *Jonathan*,[2] *John*[1]), son of Willard and Sarah (Perkins) Emery; married Nov. 11, 1811, Sally, daughter of Benjamin and Anna (Hoar) Morse. He died May 15, 1836. His widow married, second, July 15, 1844, Ezra Chase.

Children ·

6229 i ELIZA ANN [7]
6230 ii HARRIET H
6231 iii ALBIN
6232 iv DAVID.
6233 v MARY
6234 vi MARY ABBY
6235 vii SARAH DANA
6236 viii MARTHA VESTA.
6237 ix DAVID WILLARD, b July 12, 1836

6237 DAVID WILLARD[7] EMERY (*Willard*,[6] *Willard*,[5] *Dr Anthony*,[4] *John*,[3] *Jonathan*,[2] *John*[1]), son of Willard and Sally (Morse) Emery, married Abby Townsend Sanderson
Children .

6238 i MARION,[8] b Dec , 1872, d Aug. 20, 1873
6239 ii WILLARD, b Feb. 4, 1875.

PART II.

ANTHONY EMERY AND HIS DESCENDANTS

1 ANTHONY EMERY, second son of John and Agnes Emery, was born in Romsey, Hants, England; married Frances ———, and came to America in the ship "James," landing in Boston, June 3, 1635. He was probably in Ipswich, Mass., in the following August, and soon after settled in Newbury, where he lived until about 1640.

A court record of Dec. 22, 1637, shows that he was a brother of John, and a similar record of June 10, 1638, that he was then residing in Newbury.

He removed to Dover, New Hampshire, about 1640, and Oct. 22, of that year, signed the " Dover Combination " From that time until 1649, when he removed to Kittery, Maine, he was identified with the interests of that town. His house was at Dover Neck, about a mile from the present railroad station at Dover Point, and three or four miles from Major Richard Waldron's settlement on the Cocheco river. There he kept an ordinary, which was destroyed by fire, as appears from the following petition :

"Right worp com of the Massachusetts
The humble peticon of Anthony Emry of Dover
Humbly showeth
Unto your good worp that your poore peticonr was licenced b the towne abousd to keept an ordinary wh shd give Dyet & to sell beere & wine as was accustomed & sithence there was an order that non but one should sell wine upon which there hath beene complaint made to your worp as Mr Smyths saith & hee hath in a manner dischaiged your petr wch wilbe to your petr great damage haueing a wife & 8 children to maintain & not a house fitted for present to liue in haueing had his house & goods lately burnt downe to the ground " Humbly beseeching yor worp to bee pleased to grant to your peti that he may sell wine & that Mr Smyth may be certified thereof hee keeping good order in his house & he shall as hee is in Duty bound pray for your worps health & happyness."

This petition does not bear date, but it is known from other papers that Anthony Emery petitioned in 1648, for permission to keep an ordinary, and that March 7, 1643-4, he was "allowed whereby to draw out his wine." In that year and in 1648 also, he was one of the townsmen (selectmen) for the " prudentiall affaires " of Dover.

On November 15, 1648, he bought of John White, a house, field, and great barren marsh on Sturgeon Creek in Pischataqua, afterward Kittery, now Eliot, and two other marshes. He seems not to have taken possession, however, until the next year, for he served as grand juror in Dover, in 1649.

During his eleven years' (1649-1660) residence in Kittery, he was juryman several times, selectman in 1652 and 1659, and constable. He was one of the forty-one inhabitants of Kittery, who acknowledged themselves subject to the government of Massachusetts Bay, Nov. 16, 1652. At four different times he received grants of land from the town. He also bought of Joseph Austin of Pischataqua, July 15, 1650, " a little Marsh soe Commanly called aboue Sturgeon Cricke, with a little house & vpland yrunto belonging, as also one thousand fiue hundred foote of boards, for & in Consideration of Two stears Called by ye name of draggon and Benbow with a weeks worke of him selfe & other two oxen wch is to be done at Cutcheeha."

In 1656, he was fined £5 for mutinous courage in questioning the authority of the court at Kittery, and in 1660, again fined, for entertaining Quakers, and disfranchised.

May 12, 1660, he and Frances his wife, sold house and land at Cold Harbor to son James for £150 together with all other lands in Kittery, "with all & singular the houseing barne Garden orchards Commans profetts priviledges fences wood Tymber appurtenances & Haereditaments belonging, or in any way appitayning thereunto "

Deprived of the rights and privileges of a freeman in Kittery, he turned his footsteps toward a colony in which greater liberty was allowed, and was received as a free inhabitant of Portsmouth, Rhode Island, Sept 29, 1660.

It has been conjectured that he, prior to settling in Newbury, or removing to Dover, bought land in Portsmouth, and dwelt there awhile. This conjecture has its origin in the fact, that one "Good-man Emeres" owned land in Portsmouth in 1643, as is known from the records of a general town meeting held in Portsmouth, March 1, 1643.

Who "Goodman Emeres" was, or whence came the Little Compton, Rhode Island, family of Emerys, has been mere conjecture. We have been unable thus far to trace their genealogy, or to connect them with our ancestor, except in name and locality. We accept the Portsmouth records as evidence of Anthony Emery's first legal residence there until 1680, though he is designated " of Kittery," in a deed to his son James, Oct. 1, 1668

He served as juryman from Portsmouth on several occasions, was chosen constable, June 4, 1666, and deputy to the General Court, April 25, 1672   The last record that we find of him living is that of a deed of land in Portsmouth to Rebecca Sadler, his daughter, dated March 9, 1680   It is barely possible that he returned to Kittery, and that Anthony Emery who was representative from Kittery at York, March 30, 1680, was our ancestor, but it does not seem probable that he, an old man, disfranchised, would after twenty years' absence, be chosen to legislate for the " province of Mayne."

From the petition quoted, we know that he had three children, and from another paper, that James was his surviving son. We are thus enabled to give this list of children :

2   i   JAMES,² b in England about 1630, came to America with his
          father
3   ii   A SON, name unknown.
4   iii REBECCA

It is difficult to estimate the character of Anthony Emery. From
what little we know of him, however, we infer that he was a capable
business man, energetic, independent, resolute in purpose, bold in
action, severe in speech, jealous of his own rights, and willing to suffer for conscience' sake.   He did not hesitate to express his opinions,
though on one occasion it may have savored of "mutinous courage."
He recognized a higher law than statute-law, and with the courage of
his convictions, preferred to suffer the penalty of the latter rather than
disobey the former and violate his conscience.   In entertaining Quakers he obeyed the divine commandment . " Thou shalt love thy neighbor as thyself."

2 JAMES² EMERY, SEN. (*Anthony¹*), son of Anthony and Frances
Emery, came to America with his father in the ship "James ;" married, first, Elizabeth ——— She died after 1687. He married, second. Dec. 28, 1695, Mrs. Elizabeth Pidge (*née* Newcomb), widow
and second wife of John Pidge of Dedham, Mass   Administration
was granted in 1691 to Elizabeth, widow of John Pidge, who died in-
testate.   Inventory of the estate was filed June 19, 1691   "The account of Elizabeth Emery late Relict or widow and admin. of the
Estate of John Pigg deceased in Dedham," and on June 10. 1709,
James Emery presents the division of the estate. May 10, 1700,
"James Emery of Dedham in New England, the only surviving son of
Anthony Emery late of Portsmouth on Rhode Island and Providence
Plantations deceased, quitclaims to his sister Rebecca Sadler *alias*
Eaton, lands, estate Goods and Chattels of said Anthony Emery late
deceased." In 1713, James Emery gives a deed in which he describes
himself as of Berwick   It would seem that James Emery, after his
election as representative to the General Court, resided in Dedham, and
after the settlement of the estate of John Pidge or Pigg removed to Berwick. He had grants of land in Kittery, 1653, 1656, 1669, 1671 ; was selectman of Kittery, 1674, 1676, 1677, 1684, 1685. 1692, 1693, 1695 ;
elected representative to the General Court, 1693, 1695 ; grand juror
and constable, 1670.   It is related of him that when he went to Boston
his carriage was a chair placed in an ox cart drawn by a yoke of
steers.   This mode of conveyance was necessary as there was not in
Kittery a carriage large or strong enough to carry him safely.   He
was a large man weighing over three hundred and fifty pounds.   The
date of his death is unknown, but from a deed given in 1714 in which
his son James called himself James senior, it is evident it was before
1714
    Children, born in Kittery.

     5   i   JAMES,³ b ab 1658
     6   ii   ZACHARIAH, b ab 1660
     7   iii NOAH, b ab 1663
     8   iv   DANIEL, b Sept. 13, 1667.
     9   v   JOB, b in 1670.
    10   vi   ELIZABETH.
    11   vii SARAH.

3 A son[2] (*Anthony*[1]) of Anthony and Frances Emery. That there was a son is known by the fact that in 1643 Anthony Emery mentions having three children, and in 1700 James Emery of Kittery, but then of Dedham, gives his sister Rebecca Eaton *alias* Sadler a quitclaim to the estate of Anthony Emery late deceased In this he is described as the only surviving son of Anthony Emery, late of Portsmouth, Rhode Island, and in power of attorney given by Anthony Emery to his kinsman John Emery of Newbury he mentions sons. It is probable that the name of this son was Anthony.

4 REBECCA[2] EMERY (*Anthony*[1]), daughter of Anthony and Frances Emery; married, first, Thomas Sadler, second, Daniel Eaton, who died July 11, 1704. In 1714 she was a resident of Little Compton, R. I, and her son Anthony a resident of E. Greenwich, R. I.
Child:

    12 i ANTHONY,[3] m. Mary ———.

5 JAMES[3] EMERY (*James*,[2] *Anthony*[1]), son of James and Elizabeth Emery; married Dec. 18, 1685, Margaret Hitchcock, daughter of Richard Hitchcock. He made his will Dec. 28, 1724. In his will he mentions his wife Elizabeth, who was probably his second wife
Children, born in Berwick, Me. ·

    13 i MARGARET,[4] b Dec 18, 1686.
    14 ii JAMES, b Feb 18, 1688.
    15 iii LYDIA, b April 28, 1691
    16 iv FRANCES, b Dec 17, 1694
    17 v REBECCA, b March 7, 1697.
    18 vi SAMUEL, b Sept 2, 1700
    19 vii ELIZABETH, b March 7, 1703, d unm.
    20 viii THOMAS, b Dec 2, 1706
    21 ix LUCRETIA, b. March 6, 1709

6 ZACHARIAH[3] EMERY (*James*,[2] *Anthony*[1]), son of James and Elizabeth Emery, married Dec 9, 1686, Elizabeth Goodwin, daughter of Daniel Goodwin. He died prior to Dec. 22, 1692, when his widow married Philip Hubbard.
Children, born in Kittery, Me.:

    22 i ELIZABETH,[4] b Nov. 24, 1687.
    23 ii ZACHARIAH, b. Oct. 5, 1690.

7 NOAH[3] EMERY (*James*,[2] *Anthony*[1]), son of James and Elizabeth Emery, had a land grant from the town 1685; grand juror, 1723, 1724, selectman, 1725, 1726, 1727, 1728, 1729, trial juror, 1727; surveyor of land, 1728, 1729. The records of the first church in Kittery contain the notice of the baptism of three children of Noah and Elizabeth. The record is:

    24 i RICHARD, ⎫
    25 ii SAMUEL, ⎬ bapt Sept., 1722.
    26 iii ELIZABETH, ⎭

This record indicates that he was married and had children. He died before 1729.

8 Daniel[3] Emery (*James,*[2] *Anthony*[1]), son of James and Elizabeth Emery; married March 17, 1695. Margaret Gowen, *alias* Smith (born Nov. 15, 1678). He was a noted surveyor of land, having been elected surveyor of Kittery, 1706-1717; selectman, 1704-1712, 1718. In 1712 he was elected to attend the surveyors appointed by General Court to run the lines of the town, and in 1718 one of the Commissioners to mark the line between the common rights of Berwick and Kittery and to mark the division between Kittery and Berwick; moderator, 1707, 1718. He made his will April 5, 1722, proved Nov. 8, 1722. He died Oct. 15, 1722. He was chosen deacon of the Congregational Church, Berwick, Me , May, 1703, elder Nov 21, 1720, and was probably one of the original members or "foundation brethren" of that church. His wife died Nov 21, 1751.

Children, born in Berwick, Me .

27 i Daniel, b June 25, 1697.
28 ii Noah, b Dec 11, 1699
29 iii Simon, b Jan 6, 1702
30 iv Zachariah, b March 12, 1704-5.
31 v Margaret, b March 3, 1707, m Stephen Tobey, d s p , 1795
32 vi Caleb, b Oct 17, 1710
33 vii Ann b March 19 1712-13
34 viii Joshua, b June 30, 1715
35 ix Tirzah, b Sept 19, 1717.
36 x Huldah, b Aug 4, 1720

9 Job[3] Emery (*James,*[2] *Anthony*[1]), son of James and Elizabeth Emery, married April 6, 1696, Charity Nason. He was chosen deacon, 1721; ruling elder, 1735, tithing-man, 1715; petit juryman, 1716, 1720; grand juryman, 1717, 1730, 1731, 1735, juryman, 1724; selectman, 1719, 1720, 1726. Made his will Feb. 6, 1736-7; proved Dec 26, 1738; the amount of inventory, £519 10s. His wife made her will March 26, 1748, proved Jan 6, 1752; amount of inventory, £33 12s.

Children, born in Berwick ·

37 i Job,[4] b Jan 29, 1697.
38 ii Charity, b. April 24, 1699
39 iii Sarah, b Feb 4, 1700
40 iv Joslph, b Feb 24, 1702
41 v Benjamin, b May 25, 1704
42 vi Elizabeth, b Aug 27, 1705, d Feb 2, 1707
43 vii Jonathan, b Jan 31, 1707
44 viii Elizabeth, b July 2, 1710, m. ——— Pasen.
45 ix Mary, b. July 2, 1710
46 x Abigail, b Sept 20, 1713
47 xi Miriam, b. Feb 27, 1716 m John Andros
48 xii Jabez, bapt July 13, 1718
49 xiii Mercy, bapt Dec 4, 1720, probably m ——— Stone
50 xiv Olive, bapt Feb 9, 1724, in Joshua Andros.

10 Elizabeth[3] (*James,*[2] *Anthony*[1]), daughter of James and Elizabeth Emery, married Sylvanus Knock. She died June 6, 1704.

Children :

51 i Elizabeth [4] b Feb 12, 1678.
52 ii Mary, b May 4, 1680.

53　iii　SYLVANUS.
54　iv　THOMAS
55　v　JAMES
56　vi　ZACHARIAH.
57　vii　HENRY, b June 10, 1691

There were probably two more children, Mary and Sarah.

11 SARAH[3] (*James,*[2] *Anthony*[1]), daughter of James and Elizabeth Emery, probably born in Kittery ; married Gilbert Warren   The reason for giving James Emery a second daughter is found in the following sentence from a deed made March 17, 1767 ·

" We, James Emery, Daniel Emery, Job Emery and Gilbert Warren of ye town of Kittery in ye County of York in ye Province of ye Massachusetts Bay in New England and Sylvanus Knock of ye town of Dover in ye Province of New Hampshire in ye county aforesaid," give unto Zachariah Emery, son of our brother Zachariah Emery, a tract of land which was granted by the town of Kittery to our brother Noah Emery and to our brother Zachariah Emery   This deed contains the names of the sons of James Emery living at that date, for Zachariah Emery died before 1692, as his widow in that year married again and Noah Emery is mentioned on the Kittery records as deceased in the year 1729. From the language used it is evident that Sylvanus Knock and Gilbert Warren sustained the same relations towards James, Job and Daniel, and as Sylvanus Knock was a brother-in-law, so we conclude that Gilbert Warren was also a brother-in-law, and from the Alfred records we find that Gilbert Warren and his wife, Sarah, Feb. 19, 1706–7 sold land in Kittery, and on Dec 28, 1738, Sarah Warren, widow of Gilbert Warren, sold land in Kittery.

14 JAMES[4] EMERY (*James,*[3] *James,*[2] *Anthony*[1]), son of James and Margaret (Hitchcock) Emery ; married Elizabeth —— He died before July 6, 1724. His widow married Thomas Abbot, jr , son of Thomas and Eliza Abbot

Children, born in Berwick .

58　i　OBED,[5] b March 10, 1718.
59　ii　JOHN, b 1719; bapt Feb 28, 1719.
60　iii　MARGARET, bapt April 10, 1722
61　iv　ELIZABETH, bapt April 12, 1724

16 FRANCES[4] EMERY (*James,*[3] *James,*[2] *Anthony*[1]), daughter of James and Margaret (Hitchcock) Emery ; married John Roberts, May 17. 1720. They lived in Somersworth, N. H.

Children ·

62　i　EBENEZER,[5] b. Feb 5, 1721, m Sarah Miller
63　ii　ALEXANDER, b Jan 15, 1725, m Rebecca Garland.

17 REBECCA[4] EMERY (*James,*[3] *James,*[2] *Anthony*[1]), daughter of James and Margaret (Hitchcock) Emery, married Capt Daniel Smith of Saco, Jan. 1, 1719, who died in 1750. The widow married, second, Capt Nathaniel Ladd of Falmouth, Me , May 28 1755. Capt. Ladd died in 1776. Mrs. R. Ladd died in Biddeford, Me , Jan. 27, 1786, aged 88. She had "one hundred and forty-four descendants: ten children, forty-eight grandchildren, eighty-two great-grandchildren and four great-great-grandchildren." (Biddeford Records.)

Children, born in Biddeford:

64 i   THEOPHILUS,⁵ b Nov 25, 1720
65 ii   DANIEL, b. April 11, 1722
66 iii REBECCA, b Oct 12, 1724
67 iv   LYDIA, b Dec. 25, 1727, m. Benj Hooper in 1744
68 v   MARY, b June 26, 1729, m Jeremiah Hill, Aug 11, 1746
69 vi   NATHANIEL, b Jan 29, 1732.
70 vii ALEXANDER, b May 3, 1734, d May 28, 1734.
71 viii NOAH, b May 11, 1735, d July 25, 1738.

20 THOMAS⁴ EMERY (*James,³ James,² Anthony¹*), son of James and Margaret (Hitchcock) Emery; settled in Biddeford, married March 22, 1731, Susannah Hill, daughter of Deacon Ebenezer Hill; his will made May 9, 1781, mentions children, James, Ebenezer and Thomas. The other children probably died before the date of his will.

Children, born in Biddeford:

72 i   JAMES,⁵ b Nov 22, 1738
73 ii   JOSHUA, bapt Feb 19 1743-4.
74 iii EBENEZER, bapt. June 15, 1746.
75 iv   NATHAN
76 v   LOIS, bapt May 14, 1749
77 vi   THOMAS, b Sept 10, 1752
78 vii NATHANIEL, bapt July 20, 1755.
79 viii SUSANNAH, bapt. March 12, 1759

Some records give another child, Jonah or Jonathan.

21 LUCRETIA⁴ EMERY (*James,³ James,² Anthony¹*), daughter of James and Margaret (Hitchcock) Emery; married William Dyer and lived in Biddeford, Me.

Children, born in Biddeford.

80 i   JOHN,⁵ b Feb 27, 1742
81 ii   SAMUEL, b Oct. 12, 1746
82 iii HUMPHREY, b. June 2, 1749.

22 ELIZABETH⁴ EMERY (*Zachariah,³ James,² Anthony¹*) daughter of Zachariah and Elizabeth (Goodwin) Emery; married before 1709, Nathaniel Tarbox, who died before May 20, 1726. They had three sons and two daughters. The eldest son Joseph Tarbox lived in Biddeford.

23 ZACHARIAH⁴ EMERY (*Zachariah,³ James,² Anthony¹*), son of Zachariah and Elizabeth (Goodwin) Emery, married Sarah —— (died Oct. 8, 1732). He married, second, Rebecca Reddington, of Topsfield, Mass., May 20, 1733; married, third, Thankful Foster, June 26, 1744, who after the death of her husband, married Jona. Spaulding of Carlisle and died Aug. 31, 1785, aged 85.

Zachariah Emery resided in Chelmsford, Mass, enlisted June, 1745, in the Expedition against Cape Breton in Capt Gershom Davis' Company. In Oct., 1745, he was sent to Boston as the agent of his com-

pany to make up the muster roll and being taken sick did not return
to Cape Breton. After his recovery he petitioned the General Court
for remuneration for the loss of his gun and that of his son Samuel who
was in the same Expedition. He places the value of the two guns at
twenty-five pounds and ten shillings. The sum paid him for his loss
was three pounds and eighteen shillings.

Children, born in Chelmsford, Mass. :

83 i   SARAH,³ b Oct 20, 1713, probably d young.
84 ii   NOAH, b Oct 15, 1714, d July 18, 1718.
85 iii ZACHARIAH, b Aug 26, 1716.
86 iv   NOAH, b June 18, 1720
87 v   SAMUEL, b Aug 2, 1722, he enlisted in Capt Peter Hunt's
         Company, died subsequently to Oct , 1745, at Cape Breton.
88 vi   JOHN, b Jan 2, 1724-5
89 vii SARAH b Aug. 17, 1727.
90 viii DANIEL, b May 5, 1730.
91 ix   EBENEZER
92 x   ELIZABETH, b. Sept , 1732

Child, by second wife

93 xi   JAMES, b 1738 enlisted in Crown Point Expedition in Capt
         John Reed's Co of Woburn and was killed at Lake George,
         Sept 8, 1755, in a fight with the French and Indians.

Children, by third wife :

94 xii THANKFUL, b July 3, 1749; d Oct 9, 1757
95 xiii SAMUEL, b. June 3, 1753

27 ELDER DANIEL⁴ EMERY (*Daniel*,³ *James*,² *Anthony*¹), son of
Daniel and Margaret (Gowen) Emery, married June 16, 1720, Mary
Hodgdon. Made his will, Oct. 10, 1778 ; proved Oct. 4, 1779.

Children, born in Kittery :

96   i   MARTHA,³ b June 24, 1721, d Feb 27, 1777.
97   ii   MARGARET, bapt. Sept 2, 1722; probably d young
97a iii MARGARET, bapt Mar 31, 1724, m Alex Gould
98   iv   ELIZABETH, b Sept 24, 1725, m. Wm. Hooper, Oct 29, 1743.
99   v   SARAH, b Oct 1, 1727.
100 vi   DANIEL, b Aug 18, 1731.

28 NOAH⁴ EMERY (*Daniel*,³ *James*,² *Anthony*¹), son of Daniel and
Margaret (Gowen) Emery, married, first, Jan 22, 1722, Elizabeth
Chick, daughter of Richard Chick (died Jan. 15, 1739-40) ; second,
Oct. 30, 1740, Sarah Cooper, daughter of John and Sarah Cooper, resided in the northern part of Eliot, Me   He was bred to the trade
of a cooper, but as he grew to maturity turned his attention to the
law. In 1725 he was admitted to the bar by taking the required oath.
In a certain deed of record he styles himself "a practitioner in the
courts."

He thus attained the distinction of being, says Willis, "the first
lawyer who ever resided in the state of Maine " His great grandson
Nicholas, grandson of Noah of Exeter, it may be added in passing, became one of the Justices of the Supreme Court in the same state. The
subsequent career of Noah proved that he had not mistaken his calling. The writer already cited characterized him as a lawyer "pos-

sessed of much legal acumen and accuracy; a ready draftsman, of quick perceptions and considerable ability, which gave him an extensive practice. He was repeatedly commissioned as "King's Attorney" for the Province of Maine, Attorney General of the state, as he would now be described. A man of bookish tastes, he had an interest in the Portsmouth Social Library and also had a library of his own. To his sons he bequeathed his "books of law, physic, divinity and history." One of these old law books was a copy of the earliest extant edition of the Laws of the Colony of Massachusetts, the edition of 1660 It now belongs to the Massachusetts State Library where it is carefully kept under lock and key, being "worth its weight in gold," says the librarian, since there are only two or three others in existence. His autograph and the date of its purchase are on the title page.

Mr Emery was also a military man of local consequence, being captain of the "upper foot" company, in Kittery, in which there were nine other Emerys including the ensign This office brought him into personal relations with Sir William Pepperrell then in chief command of the military forces of the state. A note from Sir William directing Captain Emery to have a detail of his command at Boston by a certain time discloses this fact. He died Dec. 9, 1761.

Children, by first wife:

101 i   DANIEL,⁵ b. Sept 24, 1722; d Dec 24, 1722.
102 ii DANIEL, b Nov 19, 1723
103 iii NOAH, b Dec 23, 1725.
104 iv RICHARD, b May 9, 1728; m Mary Blunt, dau of Capt Jonathan Blunt of Chester, N H , 1765 He was captain of the Sixth Co in the Reg of five hundred men raised by N H , in 1757, for the Crown Point Expedition In 1760 he was major of a Reg raised by N H for the invasion of Canada.
105 v   MARY, b May 12, 1730, d Jan 14, 1736.
106 vi JAPHET, b. July 27, 1732
107 vii SARAH, b March 1, 1733–4, d Jan 15, 1736.
108 viii ELIZABETH, b Feb 1, 1735; d Jan 14, 1736
109 ix MARY, b April 6, 1737, d the same day
110 x   SHEM, b May 6, 1738 Was in Capt Thomas Bragdon's Co. to convey stores to Fort Halifax, May–June, 1755, enlisted in one of the Expeditions of 1758; was sergeant in Capt James Gowen's Co , in Col Jedediah Preble's Reg , April 14, 1758, and July 8, 1758, reported dead. An old record states that he died at Fort Edward, Hudson River, July 8, 1758. One record says he was in the Co of Ichabod Goodwin.
111 xi ELIZABETH, b Dec. 11, 1739; d May 21, 1744

By second wife:

112 xii JOHN, b. June 9, 1743, m. Mehitable ———. In his will proved Aug 29, 1799, he calls himself a schoolmaster on board the frigate "Constitution," but mentions no children.

29 SIMON⁴ EMERY (*Daniel,³ James,² Anthony¹*), son of Daniel and Margaret (Gowen) Emery, married Oct. 21, 1725, Martha Lord daughter of Nathan Lord, jun. He made his will Nov 8, 1760; proved Nov 22, 1760 He signed the Kittery Memorial, March 20, 1751, and was on the "Alarm List" 1757 Grand juror 1744–1750; surveyor of highways, 1745, 1746, 1748. He died Nov. 10, 1760. His wife died April 29, 1760.

Children, born in Kittery, Me.:

    113   i   MARTHA,[5] b Aug 6, 1726.
    114   ii   SIMON, b Nov 26, 1727
    115   iii   MARGARET, b July 1, 1729
    116   iv   STEPHEN, b March 21, 1730
    117   v   SAMUEL, b 1732
    118   vi   JOHN, b May 15, 1734.
    119   vii   MARY, b. Feb. 15, 1737–8; m Japhet Emery (see No. 106).
    120   viii MERIBAH, b March 20, 1740
    121   ix   SARAH, b Sept 3, 1742
    122   x   CHARLES, b Aug 16, 1745.

30 ZACHARIAH[4] EMERY (*Daniel,*[3] *James,*[2] *Anthony*[1]), son of Daniel
and Margaret (Gowen) Emery , married, first, Ann Hodgdon ; second,
Hannah Johnson ; administration was taken out on his estate, April
30, 1789   He lived in Kittery.

Children, by first wife .

    123   i   ANN,[5] b Feb. 26, 1728, m Daniel Emery (see No. 102).
    124   ii   JAMES, bapt. Nov 1, 1730
    125   iii   ZACHARIAH, bapt May 5, 1734.

By second wife:

    126   iv   PELATIAH, bapt. March 6, 1737, d July, 1756.
    127   v   HANNAH
    128   vi   JOSIAH, bapt Feb 4, 1738–9
    129   vii   HULDAH, bapt Feb 9, 1755, m.—— Frost.
    130   viii SARAH, prob m. Joseph Pillsbury.
    131   ix   BETSEY, m ——— Bowen
    132   x   SIMEON.

32 CALEB[4] EMERY (*Daniel,*[3] *James,*[2] *Anthony*[1]), son of Daniel and
Margaret (Gowen) Emery; married March 10, 1747–8, Jane Frost of
Berwick (died March 5, 1767).   King's Attorney, 1761 ; lawyer, farmer and tanner.   He read law with his brother Noah, and was admitted to the Court of Common Pleas in 1750.   He was a man of plain
manners, of strict integrity, of peaceful character, discouraging litiga-
tion among his neighbors, even after he had entered the legal profession.   He had the confidence of all with whom he came in contact,
and was highly esteemed by his relatives and clients.

Children :

    133   i   CALEB,[5] b April 6, 1741
    134   ii   SON, b and d March 10, 1748–9.
    135   iii   CALEB, b Feb 10, 1749–50, d Sept. 29, 1754.
    136   iv   JANE, b Oct 20, 1753, d Sept 30, 1754.
    137   v   JANE, b Nov 19, 1759.
    138   vi   CALEB, b July 27, 1763
    139   vii   DAUGHTER, b and d March 5, 1767.

33 ANN[4] EMERY (*Daniel,*[3] *James,*[2] *Anthony*[1]), daughter of Daniel
and Margaret (Gowen) Emery ; married Eleazar Ferguson.

Children :

    140   i   ELEAZAR,[5] b Dec. 15, 1734
    141   ii   MEHITABLE, b Jan 24, 1736
    142   iii   ANNA, b Jan 5, 1738
    143   iv   ABIGAIL, b Feb 3, 1740

144 v   Susannah, b Feb 19, 1742.
145 vi   Phinfas, b March 31, 1745.
146 vii Eunice, b July 19, 1747
147 viii William, b July 21, 1749
148 ix   Daniel, b Dec 14, 1751
149 x   Margarel, b June 5, 1755.

34 Rev. Joshua[4] Emery (*Daniel*,[3] *James*.[2] *Anthony*[1]), son of Daniel and Margaret (Gowen) Emery ; married Nov. 4, 1735, Adah Tidy (born Jan. 22, 1716), daughter of John and Hannah (Morrill) Tidy. In 1766 or 1767, Joshua Emery separated from the Congregational Church in Berwick, Me , and was called a " New Light." Through his influence, Elder (afterwards Doctor) Hezekiah Smith of Haverhill, Mass , came to Berwick and presented the Baptist cause, which resulted in the organization of the " First Baptist Church of Berwick," June 28, 1768, the first of that denomination in Maine Mr Emery's name stands first on the list of the seventeen original members and his wife Adah, the first of the six female members. He was elected elder at the First Church meeting. He was never ordained but preached most of the time in this church till his death. He built a fourth part of the meeting house and gave it to the church, and a parsonage also. In thought he was independent and in opinion stern and resolute He had some disagreements with his brethren but in the end he generally had the best of it. He died Feb., 1797. His wife died 1815.
Children :

150 i   Hannah," b March 19, 1737-8, probably d young
151 ii   Margaret, b. Oct 20, 1739.
152 iii Adah, b June 29, 1741, m John Emery (see No. 118)
153 iv   Keziah, b March 7, 1746, probably d young
154 v   William, bapt March 20, 1747, probably d young
155 vi   Joshua, bapt March 8 1748, probably d young
156 vii John, bapt Feb 13, 1750, probably d young.
157 viii Meribah, bapt Aug 20, 1754
158 ix   Mary, bapt. Aug 20, 1754, probably d young
159 x   Hannah, b. 1756

35 Tirzah[4] Emery (*Daniel*,[3] *James*,[2] *Anthony*[1]), daughter of Daniel and Margaret (Gowen) Emery; married July 12, 1753, Dudley James of Exeter, N. H., son of Francis and Elizabeth (Hall) James , (born Nov. 5, 1713 ; died Feb. 24, 1776), probably his second wife She died Dec. 2, 1759.
Children :

160 i   Tirzah,[5] }   { m ——— Brooks.
161 ii   Caleb,   } b May 15, 1755, { m Mary ———, lived in Kittery,
                                               Me
162 iii Joshua, b Aug 81, 1757; d Oct 4, 1825, lived in Exeter.
163 iv   Mary, b Dec 2, 1759, m Caleb Emery (see No 188)

36 Huldah[4] Emery (*Daniel*,[3] *James*,[2] *Anthony*[1]), daughter of Daniel and Margaret (Gowen) Emery, married John Bowden and died at the age of ninety-seven.
Children .

164 i   Michael,[5] d 1841, æt 80.
165 ii   Mary, m , Feb 20, 1777, James, son of James and Mary (Fogg) Emery.

37 Job[4] EMERY (*Job,* [3]*James,*[2] *Anthony*[1]), son of Job and Charity (Nason) Emery ; married Feb. 10, 1725, Phœbe Goodwin.
Child :

    166 i   ELEANOR,[5] bapt July 8, 1744 An adult

38 CHARITY[4] EMERY (*Job,*[3] *James,*[2] *Anthony*[1]), daughter of Job and Charity (Nason) Emery , married Samuel Lunt, lived in Falmouth, Me.
Children :

    167 i   DANIEL,[5] b. Sept 7, 1728
    168 ii   CHARITY, b July 17, 1730 , m. ——— Proctor
    169 iii MARY, b Aug 23, 1732
    170 iv ABRAHAM, b Oct. 22, 1734.
    171 v   JANE, b Oct 1, 1739
    172 vi SARAH, b July 30, 1742
    173 vii JOB.

39 SARAH[4] EMERY (*Job,*[3] *James,*[2] *Anthony*[1]), daughter of Job and Charity (Nason) Emery ; married, Aug. 16, 1720, Samuel Brackett, and lived in Berwick.
Children .

    174 i   JOHN,[5] bapt. Jan 21, 1728
    175 ii   ISAAC, bapt. Jan 21, 1728
    176 iii SAMUEL, bapt Jan 21, 1728.
    177 iv JAMES, bapt. Jan 21, 1728.
    178 v   JOSHUA, bapt Aug 25, 1729.
    179 vi MARY, bapt Oct 11 1730
    180 vii SARAH, bapt June 13, 1736.
    181 viii JACOB, bapt Nov 20, 1737
    182 ix JOSEPH, bapt. April 22, 1739.
    183 x   ELIZABETH.
    184 xi BATHSHEBA.

40 JOSEPH[4] EMERY (*Job,*[3] *James,*[2] *Anthony*[1]). son of Job and Charity (Nason) Emery ; married Oct 10, 1726, Mehitable Stacey who died in 1786.   He died July 1, 1793
Children :

    185 i   JAMES,[5] b Nov 6, 1728.
    186 ii   JOHN b Jan 22, 1730
    187 iii MARY, b Nov 25, 1732
    188 iv ESTHER, b May 31, 1734.
    189 v   MEHITABLE, b March 10, 1736 , m. James Emery (see No 124)
    190 vi STEPHEN, b March 21, 1738.
    191 vii ELIZABETH, b Feb 28, 1740
    192 viii JOSEPH, b. Aug 25, 1742 , m Rebecca Wakefield, Oct 30, 1767 ;
                       d *s p*   He was a Revolutionary soldier, lived in Kennebunkport
    193 ix JOB, b. Jan. 29, 1745
    194 x   WILLIAM, b Feb 6, 1747.
    195 xi JOSIAH, b. Sept 24, 1751

43 JONATHAN[4] EMERY (*Job,*[3] *James,*[2] *Anthony*[1]), son of Job and Charity (Nason) Emery , baptized Feb. 27, 1708. Probably removed to Biddeford and married Phœbe Bracey, daughter of William Bracey. Was on the " Alarm List," March 9, 1758.
Children :

196   i   JONATHAN,[5] b Aug 12, 1737.
197   ii   REBECCA, b Nov. 22, 1739
198   iii JOB, bapt. July 24, 1748.
199   iv   CHARITY, bap[t]. Oct 15, 1750; probably m. John Treworgy,
           Ap[r]il 23, 1781
200   v   JOHN, bapt. June 14, 1752.

46 ABIGAIL[4] EMERY (*Job,[3] James,[2] Anthony[1]*), daughter of Job and Charity (Nason) Emer[y], married Benjam[i]n Ta[r]box of Biddeford, Me. Children, born in Biddefo[r]d, Me. .

201   i   NATHANIEL,[5] bapt. Nov. 25, 1743
202   ii   HAVEN, bapt. Feb 24, 1744.
203   iii RUTH, bapt May 31, 1747

48 JABEZ[4] EMERY (*Job,[3] James,[2] Anthony[1]*), son of Job and Char[i]ty (Nason) Emer[y]; removed to that pa[r]t of Wells now called Kennebunk and ma[rr]ied Feb. 6, 1744–5, Elizabeth Butland. He died May 19, 1790.
Childr[e]n ·

204   i   JAB[E]Z,[5] bapt April 6, 1746.
205   ii   G[E]ORGE, b Aug 27, 1749
206   iii JOB, b 1751
207   iv   MARY, b 1754, m Jedediah Gooch.
208   v   ISAAC, b April 22, 1756
209   vi   BETSEY, b July, 1759, m Samuel Gooch, 1783

58 OB[E]D[5] EMERY (*James,[4] James,[3] James,[2] Anthony[1]*), son of James and Elizabeth (———) Emery; married Aug. 9, 1742, Sarah Dyer (bo[r]n Sept 29, 1721), removed f[r]om Be[r]wick to B[i]ddeford, M[e], about 1740. Su[r]veyor of h[i]ghways, 1747, fence viewer, 1750–52, tithing man, 1754, 1773, constable, 1757, selectman, 1771; member of committee on co[r]respondence, inspection and safety, 1777–80. Co[r]po[r]al Obed Emer[y] was in Capt. Thomas Bradbury's "Train-band," April 7, 1757, and on the "Alarm L[i]st," March 9, 1758 He died in Ma[r]ch, 1803
Childr[e]n, born in B[i]ddefo[r]d :

210   i   OBADIAH,[6] b June 16, 1743.
211   ii   SARAH, b Aug 7, 1745, m Benjam[i]n Hooper
212   iii MARGA[R]ET, b Nov 16, 1747; m Snell W[i]ngate
213   iv   PRISCILLA, b Jan 1, 1750, m Joseph Hale[y], Nov 12, 1806.
214   v   MARY, b March 2[6], 1752; m Jeremiah H[i]ll
215   vi   DA[N]ILL, b March 28, 1754, m Hannah Deshon
216   vii REBECCA, b May 19, 1756, d. Aug 23, 1756.
217   viii SAMUEL, b May 17, 1758, d. Aug 23, 1759.
218   ix   RA[L]PH, b Dec 8, 1759, m Oli[v]e Foss
219   x   LUCRETIA, b Jan 1, 1763, m. Ma[r]ch 22, 1786, Joseph Patter-
           so[n]
220   xi   PEACE, b. Oct. 21, 1765, m. Ma[r]ch, 1790, Franc[i]s Tucker.

64 THEOPHILUS[5] SMITH (*Rebecca,[4] James,[3] James,[2] Anthony[1]*), son of Daniel and Rebecca (Emer[y]) Smith, married Olive ———.
Childr[e]n ·

221   i   OL[I]VE,[6] bapt April 24, 1742
222   ii   MARGA[R]ET, b Oct 27, 1745
223   iii ANN[A], b May 25, 1757

21

66 REBECCA[5] SMITH (*Rebecca,*[4] *James,*[3] *James,*[2] *Anthony*[1]), daughter of Daniel and Rebecca (Emery) Smith ; married, 1741, Dominicus Scammon, son of Capt Humphrey Scammon. They both died of malignant fever, leaving two children.

Children :

    224 i DOMINICUS,[6] bapt June 19, 1743.
    225 ii ELIZABETH, b. March 7, 1745, m Aug 24 1762, Col Thomas
              Cutts of Indian Island, Saco; d Jan 11, 1803   Sarah, then
              seventh child, m Nov 26, 1793, Dr Thomas G Thornton

72 DEACON JAMES[5] EMERY (*Thomas,*[4] *James,*[3] *James,*[2] *Anthony*[1]), son of Thomas and Susannah (Hill) Emery, married, first, 1763, Mary Scammon of Pepperellboro (Saco), Me. (born April 29, 1745 ; died March 1, 1795) ; second, in 1795 or 96, Sarah Jenkins.   Lived in 1763 in Biddeford, Me., and known as Deacon James

Children, born in Biddeford :

    226 i LEVI,[6] b May 27, 1765 , d , unm , Oct 3, 1809
    227 ii SUSANNAH, b. Dec 28, 1767, m. in Biddeford 1789 Samuel Hill.
    228 iii MEHITABLE, b March 4, 1770 , m. William Smith, pub Sept.
            14, 1795
    229 iv JAMES, b March 31, 1772
    230 v JOSHUA, b April 7, 1774
    231 vi MARY, b Feb. 11, 1776
    232 vii SIMON, b Jan 11, 1778
    233 viii SAMUEL, b Jan 7, 1781.
    234 ix THOMAS, b Feb 7, 1783, d unm.
    235 x NATHANIEL, b. May 15, 1785.
    236 xi LYDIA, b May 23, 1787

74 EBENEZER[5] EMERY (*Thomas,*[4] *James,*[3] *James,*[2] *Anthony*[1]), son of Thomas and Susannah (Hill) Emery ; married, 1784, Alice (Polk) Spofford (born April 1, 1750 ; died Feb 19, 1843), widow of Joseph Spofford.   Lived in Biddeford.

Children :

    237 i SUSAN H ,[6] b Dec 24, 1785.
    238 ii JONAH, b Jan 8, 1788, lost at sea, unm.
    239 iii JOHN P., b. Aug. 25, 1791.

77 THOMAS[5] EMERY (*Thomas,*[4] *James,*[3] *James,*[2] *Anthony*[1]), son of Thomas and Susannah (Hill) Emery, married Nov 27, 1773, Hannah Harmon of Buxton, Me. (born April 26, 1754 ; died June 17, 1844) , removed to Buxton, May 28, 1774. He died Oct 31, 1827.

Children, born in Buxton .

    240 i SUSANNAH,[6] b Nov. 29 1774, d young
    241 ii NATHANIEL, b Feb 23, 1776
    242 iii THOMAS, b. Jan 26, 1779.
    243 iv HANNAH, b July 7, 1781, d July, 1783.
    244 v SUSANNAH, b Jan 22, 1784, d young
    245 vi SALLY, b. May 19, 1786
    246 vii JOHN, b Nov. 17, 1788
    247 viii JOSEPH D , b April 5, 1791.
    248 ix ISAAC, b March 31, 1793
    249 x PETER, }
    250 xi MARK, } b. Feb 24, 1796 { d Dec 24, 1813
    251 xii DORCAS, b. June 5, 1799 , d June 10, 1799.

85 ZACHARIAH[5] EMERY (*Zachariah,*[4] *Zachariah,*[3] *James,*[2] *Anthony*[1]), son of Zachariah and Sarah (———) Emery; married Dec. 2, 1741, Esther Stevens (died June 17, 1804) Lived in Townsend, Mass., selectman, 1754-6, 1761, 1763, 1772-3, 1776-7, nine years. He died May 3, 1804.

Children, born in Townsend :

- 252 i   ZACHARIAH,[6] } b. July 31, 1742; { d July 31, 1742.
- 253 ii   JAMES, }
- 254 iii AMOS, b Oct 29, 1744, d Nov 2, 1827.
- 255 iv   ESTHER, b Sept 12, 1746; m Feb 4, 1773, Nathan Conant
- 256 v   SARAH, b June 12, 1748, m. Aug 23, 1781, Levi Proctor
- 257 vi   ELIZABETH. b May 3, 1750, m July 10, 1771, Jonathan Robbins of Chelmsford
- 258 vii THANKFUL, b March 9, 1752, d Sept 25, 1753
- 259 viii JOHN, b Sept 21, 1753
- 260 ix   LUCY, b April 28, 1756
- 261 x   SAMUEL, } b. Oct 23, 1758, { d Jan 12, 1836
- 262 xi   WILLIAM, }   { d July 16, 1840
- 263 xii LEVI, b Nov 3, 1762, settled in Bloomfield, Me ; m and had children

86 NOAH[5] EMERY (*Zachariah,*[4] *Zachariah,*[3] *James,*[2] *Anthony*[1]), son of Zachariah and Sarah (———) Emery; married Dec. 22, 1743, Mary, daughter of Joseph and Mary (Taylor) Barrett. He lived in Townsend, Mass., and died in 1746.

Children.

- 264 i   DANIEL,[6] b Dec 19 1744, d Dec 23, 1744
- 265 ii   NOAH, b Dec 20, 1745

88 JOHN[5] EMERY (*Zachariah,*[4] *Zachariah,*[3] *James,*[2] *Anthony*[1]), son of Zachariah and Sarah (———) Emery; married April 24, 1745, Mary Munroe. He settled in Acton, Mass., where his children were born, afterwards he removed to the vicinity of Bloomfield, Me. He was a private in Capt. James Hosley's company in 1775.

Children.

- 266 i   MARY,[6] b May 4, 1746; d Feb. 12, 1750
- 267 ii   SAMUEL, b Feb 9, 1748, d April 20, 1754.
- 268 iii ELIZABETH b Dec. 25, 1749, m Jan 23, 1771, Jonathan Davis
- 269 iv   MARY, b Nov. 20, 1751, m —— Gould
- 270 v   JOHN, b Nov 20, 1753
- 271 vi   SAMUEL, b Feb 9, 1755.
- 272 vii JAMES, b. March 13, 1756, soldier in the Revolutionary war five months and twenty-five days. Killed in battle near Saratoga, N Y , Oct 8, 1777
- 273 viii JOSEPH, b Aug 3, 1757
- 274 ix   NOAH, b March 25, 1759, d Feb 8, 1760

89 SARAH[5] EMERY (*Zachariah,*[4] *Zachariah,*[3] *James,*[2] *Anthony*[1]), daughter of Zachariah and Sarah(———)Emery, married April 11, 1751, James Hayward.

Children.

- 275 i   BENJAMIN,[6] b Oct 22, 1753.
- 276 ii   JESSE, b Aug 3, 1755
- 277 iii JAMES, b. Oct 13, 1758, d young
- 278 iv   SARAH, b Sept 20, 1764, m. John Byam.
- 279 v   JAMES, b Jan 7, 1770.

Perhaps other children.

90 DANIEL[5] EMERY (*Zachariah*,[4] *Zachariah*,[3] *James*,[2] *Anthony*[1]),
son of Zachariah and Sarah (———) Emery; married, first, Jane
———, who died in Jaffrey, N. H., June 7, 1803, aged 71 years; married, second, Esther, widow of Ebenezer Jaquith, who died May 7,
1828, aged 87.   He was four years tithing man at Townsend, also
selectman and one of the committee of correspondence in 1775 ; removed from Townsend to Jaffrey in 1776, where he was selectman
1777 and 1781 ; one of the committee of inspection in 1778 and of
safety in 1779 ; and one of the original members of the church at
Jaffrey in 1780 and its first deacon
  Children, born in Townsend, Mass. :

    280 i   JANE,[6] b. Feb 1, 1755, m ——— Start
    281 ii   DANIEL, b Dec 6, 1756
    282 iii BRISLY, b April 9, 1759
    283 iv   NOAH, b. Sept 6, 1761
    284 v   JONATHAN, b July 25, 1763; m Hannah Jaquith, 1788. who d
                 Nov 19, 1840   He gave half of his real estate to the Con-
                 gregational Church in Jaffrey, N. H , d Nov. 19, 1824
    285 vi   ASA, b Sept. 9, 1769

  91 EBENEZER[5] EMERY (*Zachariah*,[4] *Zachariah*,[3] *James*,[2] *Anthony*[1]),
son of Zachariah and Sarah (———) Emery , married Jan. 16, 1769,
Agnes Proctor.   Lived in Jaffrey, N H.
    Children :

    286 i   EBENEZER,[6] b Nov 23, 1769, m April 16, 1795, Abigail Shat-
                 tuck (b Dec 25. 1766), dau of Benjamin and Abigail (Fains-
                 worth) Shattuck
    287 ii   SILAS, b March 14, 1773
    288 iii ZACHARIAH, removed to New York
    289 iv   JOSEPH, removed to Maine, m. Rachel Runnels, and had nine
                 children.

  92 ELIZABETH[5] EMERY (*Zachariah*,[4] *Zachariah*,[3] *James*,[2] *Anthony*[1]), daughter of Zachariah and Sarah (———) Emery ; married
Jan. 6, 1762, Ebenezer Butterfield, jr., of Dunstable (born Jan. 26,
1732 ; died April 2, 1821) ; removed to Farmington, Me.   She died
May 1, 1818   He was a Revolutionary soldier.
    Children, born in Dunstable :

    290 i   ELIZABETH,[5] b. Jan. 20, 1763; d. March 10, 1842
    291 ii   REUBEN, b Dec 29, 1764
    292 iii JOSEPH, b July 10, 1768
    293 iv   MARY, b Aug 8, 1770, d Jan 19, 1851
    294 v   SARAH, b Sept 17, 1772, d Feb 4, 1802.

  95 SAMUEL[5] EMERY (*Zachariah*,[4] *Zachariah*,[3] *James*,[2] *Anthony*[1]),
son of Zachariah and Thankful (Foster) Emery ; married, first, Mary
Green, May 31, 1774 ; removed to Jaffrey, N H , and subsequently
to Rockingham, Vt   She died Feb. 22, 1808.   He married, second,
April 22, 1809, Ruth Roundy.   He died Oct. 8. 1832.
    Children.

    295 i   MARY,[6] b April 1, 1775, in Chelmsford, Mass
    296 ii   THANKFUL, b Dec 8, 1777, removed to Jaffrey in 1778, and d
                 there
    297 iii SARAH, b. April 24, 1779, in Jaffrey, N. H.

298   iv   SAMUEL, b. June 3, 1782, m Jaffrey, N. H
299   v   ZACHARIAH, b March 4, 1785.
300   vi   JOSIAH, b Aug 30, 1787
301   vii THANKFUL, b Feb 27, 1790
302   viii ELIZABEIH, b March 7. 1792, d March 21, 1792
303   ix   BEISEY, b April 19, 1793, m. Samuel Raymenton
304   x   JOHN, b April 9, 1795
305   xi   ELEAZAR, b. May 27, 1797.

96 MARTHA[5] EMERY (*Daniel,[4] Daniel,[3] James,[2] Anthony[1]*). daughter of Elder Daniel and Mary (Hodgdon) Emery, married Richard Shackley, jr. (born Jan 1, 1716). She died Feb. 27, 1777.
Children :

306   i   DANIEL,[6] bapt Nov 23, 1740.
307   ii   SARAH, bapt Jan 8, 1742
308   iii MARTHA, bapt Nov 15, 1743.
309   iv   HANNAH, bapt Sept. 6, 1745.
310   v   RICHARD, bapt Oct 19, 1746
311   vi   HANNAH, bapt Sept 4, 1748
312   vii MARY, b July 20, 1750
313   viii THOMAS, bapt. April 21, 1752
314   ix   LOIS, bapt May 6, 1754
315   x   MARY, bapt Aug 23, 1759.
316   xi   LOIS, bapt June 1, 1760

99 SARAH[5] EMERY (*Daniel,[4] Daniel,[3] James,[2] Anthony[1]*), daughter of Elder Daniel and Mary (Hodgdon) Emery ; married Joseph Hubbard (bapt. June 11, 1721).
Children :

317   i   MERCY,[6] }
318   ii   JAMES,   } bapt. Nov. 8, 1747.
319   iii JOSEPH, bapt Feb. 19, 1749
320   iv   SAMUEL, bapt. April 14, 1751.
321   v   DANIEL, bapt June 3, 1753
322   vi   WILLIAM, bapt Aug 20 1758.
323   vii SARAH, bapt May 24, 1761
324   viii THOMAS, b April 10, 1763
325   ix   TIMOTHY, b Feb 19, 1769.

100 DANIEL[5] EMERY (*Daniel,[4] Daniel,[3] James,[2] Anthony[1]*), son of Daniel and Mary (Hodgdon) Emery ; married May 25, 1751, Sarah Shackley.
Children, born in Berwick :

326   i   DANIEL,[6] bapt. May 31 1752, d. young.
327   ii   SARAH, bapt Jan 20, 1754, d young.
328   iii MARY, bapt Aug. 10, 1755, probably d young
329   iv   SARAH, bapt. Aug 7, 1757, m Stephen Emery (see No 395).
330   v   DANIEL, bapt. March 25, 1759.
331   vi   NAHUM, bapt April 23, 1762
332   vii NATHAN, bapt Oct. 30, 1763
333   viii JOEL, bapt. Sept. 1, 1765
334   ix   HOSEA, bapt May 30, 1767.

102 DANIEL[5] EMERY (*Noah,[4] Daniel,[3] James,[2] Anthony[1]*), son of Noah and Elizabeth (Chick) Emery, married Oct 21, 1747, Anne daughter of Zachariah and Anne (Hodgdon) Emery. He was constable

of Kittery and clerk of the fourth foot company, of which Noah Emery was captain.   Cooper and lawyer.

Children ·

335   i   DANIEL,⁶ b Jan 31, 1741
336   ii   NOAH, b May 3, 1748
337   iii ELIZABETH, b Jan 1, 1749–50, m Nathaniel Bowen, Mar 18,
           1785
338   iv   ANNA, b Oct 29, 1751, d March 14, 1752
339   v   ANNA, b Feb 14, 1753
340   vi   RICHARD, b May 8, 1755
341   vii SARAH m Joseph Pillsbury, removed to S Thomaston, Me.
342   viii MARGARET
343   ix   GEORGE, b about 1763.
344   x   SHEM
345   xi   DENNIS
346   xii NATHANIEL, b April 20, 1772

103 NOAH⁵ EMERY (*Noah,*⁴ *Daniel,*³ *James,*² *Anthony¹*), son of
Noah and Elizabeth (Chick) Emery; married March 20, 1745, Joanna
Perryman, sole surviving child of Nicholas and Joanna (Dudley)
Perryman (born Nov. 14 1731 , died April 1, 1814).   She was a lineal descendant in the fifth generation of Thomas Dudley, second governor of Massachusetts.   Noah Emery, before the end of his minority,
became a resident of Exeter. N. H.   In 1746, he was already settled
there with his wife and child.   He studied his profession in the office
of Mr. Perryman and then entered upon the practice of law.   He
had inherited from his father large landed estates in New Hampshire,
among which were certain "proprietors' rights" in the township of
Dartmouth, now the town of Jefferson.   This property he conveyed
by deed of gift to Dartmouth College in 1769, the year of its foundation, " in consideration of the extensive Charity of the Design "

Mr Emery continued to lead a quiet life until the age of fifty when
the outbreak of the Revolution at once brought him to the front.   He
was made deputy secretary of the fourth and fifth provincial con-
gresses of New Hampshire and was a member of both   When the
new government was organized, he became the clerk of its house of
assembly and so continued through the greater part of the Revolutionary period.   His name appears on the records for the first time
under date of June 27, 1775, and for the last time under date of July
12, 1781.   Within this period he was placed on many important committees . one to "make a Draft of some Solemn obligation to be
entered into by the members" (a " New Hampshire Declaration of
Independence ") ; one " to draw up a Plan for the Government of the
Colony during the Contest with Great Britain ;" one to sign the bills
of credit and so make them into current money.   The earliest records,
now in the state house at Concord, are in his handwriting ; among
them that of the official copy of the Declaration of Independence, in
red ink.

In 1776, he had been appointed clerk of the courts and this office
he continued to hold till the close of his life.   His death took place
Jan. 17, 1788.   He was a stanch patriot, and had an important hand
in shaping the destinies of New Hampshire.

Children :

347. i   JOHN,[6] b March 25, 1745-6
348. ii   NOAH, b Nov 10, 1748
349. iii ELIZABETH, b. Jan 13, 1750
350. iv   NICHOLAS, b June 27, 1753, d, unm, Sept. 26, 1775
351. v   RICHARD, b June 20, 1756; d Nov 5, 1758
352. vi   JOANNA b Sept 20, 1758, m. Samuel B. Stevens, d Jan 5, 1827
353. vii THERESA, b April 4, 1761
354. viii RICHARD, b. Oct 24 1762
355. ix   MARGARET, b Oct 15, 1772, d, unm, at Exeter, Oct 25, 1862, æt 90

106 JAPHET[5] EMERY (*Noah*,[4] *Daniel*,[3] *James*,[2] *Anthony*[1]), son of Noah and Elizabeth (Chick) Emery; married Jan. 30, 1755, Mary Emery, daughter of Simon and Martha (Lord) Emery (born Feb 15, 1737, died July 29, 1824). He was in the "Blue Troop" in 1757, and lieutenant of the fourth Kittery Company in 1762 He died March 2, 1804
Children:

356. i   MARY,[6] b March 23, 1758; d, unm, Jan 12, 1797.
357. ii   SHEM, b Nov 6. 1760
358. iii JAPHET, b. Jan 11, 1763
359. iv   RHODA, b June 22, 1774, d July 3, 1774
360. v   RHODA, b Aug 13, 1775; d Feb 11, 1797.
361. vi   THEODORE, b. May 9, 1779.

113 MARTHA[5] EMERY (*Simon*,[4] *Daniel*,[3] *James*,[2] *Anthony*[1]), daughter of Simon and Martha (Lord) Emery; married Ebenezer, son of Capt Samuel and Martha (Wentworth) Lord (born in 1720 and died Feb 19, 1812); lived in Berwick, Me. She died May 5, 1773. He married, second, Jane Plaisted (*née* Hight) in 1774, and had two children
Children

362. i   EBENEZER,[6] b Sept 15, 1744, m, 1st, Sarah Hersom. d Nov 24, 1799, m, 2nd, Sarah Hodgdon He d March 12, 1819
363. ii   DORCAS, b. Sept 15, 1746; d Jan 19, 1838
364. iii   NOAH, b Aug 30, 1748, m, 1st, Keziah Brackett; 2nd, Alice (Farnum) Burrows
365. iv   SIMON, b Dec., 1750; m Mary Hansom, Aug 15, 1774.
366. v   GERSHOM b Jan. 18, 1752, m Esther Hanson, Sept 30, 1776.
367. vi   MARTHA, b Nov 14, 1754, d March 28, 1847.
368. vii   NATHAN, b Jan 26, 1756
369. viii SAMUEL, b. Sept 14. 1759, d. Feb 8, 1855
370. ix   WILLIAM WENTWORTH, b. Feb 18, 1761.
371. x   MARY, b Feb 28, 1763; d. 1766
372. xi   JOHN, b. April 18, 1765, d 1786
373. xii   MARY, b June 22, 1767, d 1862; m., 1st, Thomas Murray; 2nd, Stephen Hatch
374. xiii TIRZAH, b 1769, d Sept 19, 1863.

114 SIMON[5] EMERY (*Simon*,[4] *Daniel*,[3] *James*,[2] *Anthony*[1]), son of Simon and Martha (Lord) Emery, married Jan. 17, 1746, Elizabeth Bane or Bean He was at the siege of Louisburg in the first company of the first Massachusetts Reg. under Sir William Pepperell, June 3, 1745; settled in Shapleigh, 1772. He built the mills on Mousam river called Emery's Mills. *

Children :

375 i   MARY,[6] bapt March 13, 1748.
376 ii   SIMON bapt May 23, 1749
377 iii ELIZABETH, bapt July 9, 1750
378 iv   MARTHA, bapt Feb 2, 1752
379 v   SIMON, bapt Dec 9, 1753.
380 vi   JEREMIAH, bapt. Nov. 9, 1755
381 vii JACOB bapt Feb 9, 1758, drowned in 1774
382 viii MARTHA, bapt. July 6, 1760.
383 ix   SIMON, bapt. May 13, 1763
384 x   MOSES, bapt July 3, 1768, d Oct 16, 1827, æt 59 yrs.
385 xi   JOTHAM, bapt July 3, 1768, m Comfort Day, 1792
386 xii MARGARET, bapt March 18, 1770, m Josiah Trafton, 1787.

115 MARGARET[5] EMERY (*Simon,[4] Daniel,[3] James,[2] Anthony[1]*),
daughter of Simon and Martha (Lord) Emery, married Dec. 21, 1750,
Noah Ricker (baptized in Dover, N H , July 20, 1726), son of Joseph
Ricker   She died Jan , 1822.
    Children :

387 i   SIMON,[6] bapt in Berwick, Me., April 17, 1757
388 ii   PATTY, m Stephen James, removed to Vermont
389 iii NOAH, b 1762
390 iv   JOANNA, m Jonathan Ross, lived in Shapleigh, Me.
391 v   MARGARET, m Benj Stone.
392 vi   POLLY, d unm
393 vii JOSEPH, b 1771, removed to Acton, Me , afterward to Vermont.
394 viii GIDEON, b 1773

116 STEPHEN[5] EMERY (*Simon,[4] Daniel,[3] James,[2] Anthony[1]*), son
of Simon and Martha (Lord) Emery ; married March 6, 1753, Sarah Hodgdon. He was an Elder in the Free Will Baptist Church in
Kittery, Me.
    Children :

395 i   STEPHEN.[6] b Dec , 1753
396 ii   JOSHUA b 1755
397 iii JACOB, b 1757
398 iv   SIMON, b Feb , 1750
399 v   ABIGAIL, b 1761
400 vi   PRUDENCE, bapt May 22, 1763
401 vii GEORGE, b 1765
402 viii DOMINICUS, b 1767 ; m Hannah Goodwin, 1798, d at sea
403 ix   MARY, b 1768–9, d unm.
404 x   WILLIAM, b 1770, physician of repute in New Orleans, La
405 xi   ICHABOD, b 1784.

117 SAMUEL[5] EMERY (*Simon,[4] Daniel,[3] James,[2] Anthony[1]*), son of
Simon and Martha (Lord) Emery, married, first, April 15, 1756,
Abigail Shackley , second, Abigail Ferguson, daughter of Eleazar and
Ann (Emery) Ferguson (No. 38), Jan 29, 1785. Lived in Emery
Town, Kittery , died before June 25, 1811.
    Children :

406 i   SAMUEL,[6] b May 12, 1757.
407 ii   SIMON, b May 1, 1758
408 iii ISAAC, b June 9, 1760, d in Parsonsfield, Me , Nov 22, 1825
409 iv   ISRAEL, b May 18, 1763, m Prudence Emery (No 400)
410 v   JOTHAM, b Aug , 1764 ; d young.

118 JOHN[5] EMERY (*Simon*,[4] *Daniel*,[3] *James*,[2] *Anthony*[1]), son of
Simon and Martha (Lord) Emery; married Adah, daughter of Rev.
Joshua and Adah (Tidy) Emery (died before May 5, 1765); second,
Mary (Bragdon) Dunning (published Feb 10, 1778). He died April
10, 1810.

Children, born in York, except the first.

    411   i   KEZIAH,[6] b. May 6, 1759, in Berwick, m Shem Emery (see
                  No. 357).
    412   ii   MERIBAH, b Aug 4, 1763, m Nath'l Walker, Dec 5, 1785
    413   iii JOSHUA, b July 8. 1766.
    414   iv   POLLY, b Oct 6, 1768

By second wife ·

    415   v   LYDIA, b Feb 4, 1780, m John Follet of Kittery, 1806
    416   vi   ADAH, b. Dec 4, 1784, m Abiel Hamilton.

120 MERIBAH[5] EMERY (*Simon*,[4] *Daniel*,[3] *James*,[2] *Anthony*[1]), daughter of Simon and Martha (Lord) Emery, married Jabez Dame about
1760 (his second wife) He was a lawyer in Newington, N. H.
(born Aug. 24, 1732). She died Feb 24, 1838.

Children

    417   i   RICHARD,[6] b 1762, m Hannah McDuffee; d July 11, 1832
    418   ii   DANIEL, teacher, d., unm., Dec., 1842, in Rochester, N. H
    419   iii JOSHUA, d young
    420   iv   SIMON, b April 28, 1767, m. Marg Hayes, d June 2, 1847
    421   v   TIMOTHY, b 1770, m Feb 19, 1795, Betsey Locke, d Feb.
                  16, 1856
    422   vi   CALEB, b Sept, 1772, m, 1st, Abigail Guppy, 2nd, Fanny
                  Twombley, d May 29, 1864
    423   vii CHARITY, b Sept 1, 1775, m Joseph Hanson, d Feb 3, 1833.
    424   viii POLLY, b ———; d in Rochester, N. H, unm
    425   ix   JABEZ b 1782, m. Dec 8, 1811, Betsey Cushing, d Jan 26,
                  1850
    426   x   MERIBAH, b. 1785, m Rev. Harvey Morey, d Nov 15, 1856

121 SARAH[5] EMERY (*Simon*,[4] *Daniel*,[3] *James*,[2] *Anthony*[1]), daughter
of Simon and Martha (Lord) Emery, married May 18, 1762, Capt.
Jonathan Tibbetts of Berwick, Me. (died Dec 27, 1798) Removed
to Sanford, 1780. She died Jan. 25, 1825.

Children, born in Berwick, except last three:

    427   i   EDWARD,[6] b Feb 25, 1763.
    428   ii   CHARITY, b June 15, 1765.
    429   iii JONATHAN, b Dec 20, 1767.
    430   iv   SIMON, b April 30, 1770, m Tirzah Lord, Sept. 27, 1794 (see
                  No 374)
    431   v   MARTHA, b June 28, 1772
    432   vi   MOSES, b Nov 4, 1774
    433   vii JOSHUA, b Feb. 2, 1777
    434   viii MARY, b. June 10, 1779.
    435   ix   ENOCH, b Feb 26, 1782, in Sanford, Me.
    436   x   SARAH b July 15, 1785, in Sanford, Me.
    437   xi   PAUL, b Feb 25, 1788, in Sanford, Me

122 CHARLES[5] EMERY (*Simon*,[4] *Daniel*,[3] *James*,[2] *Anthony*[1]), son of
Simon and Martha (Lord) Emery; married, first, Ann Hodgdon (died

in Groton, Vt , July 14, 1803), second, Oct 11, 1803, Jane Vance
of Topsham, Vt (died Dec. 8, 1832) , removed with his brother Simon to Shapleigh (Emery's Mills) about 1790 and afterwards to Vermont   He died May 14, 1823
   Children, born in Kittery, Me.

   488   i   PATTY (MARTHA),[6] b 1761.
   489   ii   JOHN, b April 12, 1763.
   440   iii BETSEY, b May 10, 1767
   441   iv   TIMOTHY, b ——
   442   v   POLLY, b 1773
   443   vi   MERIBAH, b ——, m Noah Morrison; both d soon after mar-
              riage

   124 JAMES[5] EMERY (*Zachariah*,[4] *Daniel*,[3] *James*,[2] *Anthony*[1]), son
of Zachariah and Ann (Hodgdon) Emery , married July 4, 1752, Mary
Fogg, daughter of James and Elizabeth (Fernald) Fogg (born Feb.
21, 1734; died 1759) , second, Mehitable Emery, daughter of Joseph
and Mehitable (Stacey) Emery , third, Jan. 27, 1782, Catherine
(Frye) Jenkins, widow of Joseph Jenkins.
   Children, by first wife

   444   i   JAMES,[6] b 1754, m Mary Bowden, Feb 20, 1777 , enlisted
              April, 1775, in Captain Leighton s Co , Colonel Scammon's
              Regt and served eight months   In 1778 he again enlisted
              and was stationed at Fort Sullivan Portsmouth, N H , one
              year under Capt. Daniels.
   445   ii   ABIGAIL, b 1756, m Alexander Thompson, Nov. 10, 1772.

   Children, by second wife

   446   iii DANIEL, b 1758
   447   iv   WILLIAM, b May 10, 1767
   448   v   MARK, b May 22, 1769
   449   vi   JOSIAH
   450   vii MARY or MOLLY, m Stephen Andrews
   451   viii MEHITABLE
   452   ix   BETSEY
   453   x   EUNICE.

   Children, by his third wife

   454   xi   CATHARINE, m ——— Chick
   455   xii SIMEON, b Dec. 15, 1787

   125 ZACHARIAH[5] EMERY (*Zachariah*,[4] *Daniel*,[3] *James*,[2] *Anthony*[1]) ,
son of Zachariah and Ann (Hodgdon) Emery , married, 1753, Huldah
Bean of Berwick ; died in 1805. Joined the church in Berwick, Jan.
9, 1755. He died in 1820.
   Children :

   456   i   HULDAH,[6] bapt Feb. 9, 1755, m Samuel Parker, July 1, 1776
   457   ii   CALEB, bapt March 13, 1757.
   458   iii TIRZAH, bapt Nov. 18, 1759, m Joshua Emery, No 396, son of
              Stephen and Sarah (Hodgdon) Emery.
   459   iv   MARY, b 1761, m Jona Knox, had nine children
   460   v   HANNAH, } b 1764, { d with the Shakers in Alfred, Me
   461   vi   ANNA,   }   {
   462   vii OLIVE, b 1775, m Samuel Freeman , had four children
   463   viii REUBEN, b 1777, d 1796, at sea, at nineteen years of age
   464   ix   THOMAS, b 1778
   465   x   RICHARD, b Jan 17, 1779.

133 Col. Caleb[5] Emery (*Caleb,[4] Daniel,[3] James,[2] Anthony[1]*), son of Caleb and Mary Hambleton, married, 1764, Elizabeth Gowen (born Sept. 15, 1743; died Aug. 17, 1799), second, Feb. 21, 1802, Elizabeth Emery, daughter of Simon and Elizabeth (Bean) Emery (died Feb. 26, 1812); third, 1812 (published Nov. 14), Mrs. Hannah Gould, daughter of Rev. John and Susannah (Swett) Hovey and widow of James Gould of Kennebunkport, Me. (born 1746). He died at Sanford, Me., March 4, 1825.

At seventeen years of age he was a soldier in the French and Indian war at Lake George in 1758, probably in Capt. James Gowen's company, Col. Jedediah Preble's regiment, from April to September, in Sir William Pepperrell's expedition in 1759, corporal in Capt. Joshua Moody's company, from November, 1759, to Jan., 1761, sergeant in Capt. Simon Jefferds' company, Dec., 1761, to May, 1762. He removed from Berwick to Sanford, Me., about 1773, where he resided more than fifty years, a tanner, shoemaker, potash-manufacturer, trader, innholder, becoming one of its most prominent men, and holding many positions of honor and trust. He served in the Revolutionary war from May 19, to July 18, 1777, in Capt. Abel Moulton's company, Col. Jonathan Titcomb's regiment, when Rhode Island was threatened, in 1782, a member of the committee of safety; captain in the militia as early as 1785, major in 1786, and colonel in 1788, familiarly known as the "Old Colonel."

He was town clerk in 1780, selectman, 1780, 1785-6, 1791, 1801, representative, 1785-6, deputy sheriff, 1784-6, justice of the peace and of the peace and quorum, 1787-1820, postmaster, 1796-1804, one of the nine original members of the Congregational church, 1786, and its first deacon, in politics, a radical Federalist. He was one of the original grantees of Porter, Me., and in 1793 built the first mill in that town.

Colonel Emery was of humble birth, of indigent youth, of influential manhood, of venerable old age, endowed with good common sense, remarkable business capacity, keen discernment, rare judgment, austere in manner, unpolished, ofttimes severe in speech, yet of large heart and generous impulses —a man of honor and integrity, though shrewd and exacting, of Christian faith, but sometimes wanting in Christian charity.—a man, indeed, of many faults, of redeeming virtues more.

Children :

    466 i   William,[6] b. March 23, 1765.
    467 ii Elizabeth, b Oct 21, 1771.

137 Jane[5] Emery (*Caleb,[4] Daniel,[3] James,[2] Anthony[1]*), daughter of Caleb and Jane (Frost) Emery, married Simon Frost, jr., son of Judge Simon Frost of Kittery. He died, and she married, second, Peaslee Morrill, of Berwick, grandfather of Hons Anson P. and Lot M Morrill, former governors of Maine.

Children ·

    468 i   Jane.[6]
    469 ii Henry, b. in 1786, m Sophia Gilman, d. in Albion, Me, Oct 2, 1859, elder of the Christian denomination

138 CALEB[5] EMERY (*Caleb,*[4] *Daniel,*[3] *James,*[2] *Anthony*[1]), son of Caleb and Jane (Frost) Emery, lived in Eliot, Me., until 1807, when he removed to Sanford, and a few years later to Lebanon, Me.; married Dec. 3, 1782, Mary James, daughter of Dudley and Tuzah (Emery) James (born in Exeter, N. H, Dec 2, 1759).

Children.

    470   i   HENRY T.,[6] b. May 31, 1783.
    471   ii   CALEB, b. Sept 12 1785
    472   iii IVORY, b April 4, 1791, d in youth.
    473   iv   OLIVER, b May 25, 1795 d young
    474   v   MARY JANE, b May 21, 1798, m F P Marsh.
    475   vi   ADALINE, b June 11, 1802, m Leonard Wood; d Nov. 18,
              1848

151 MARGARET[5] EMERY (*Joshua,*[4] *Daniel,*[3] *James,*[2] *Anthony*[1]), daughter of Rev. Joshua and Adah (Tidy) Emery; married Jan. 24, 1777, David Blaisdell of York.

Child.

    476   i   EMERY.[6]

159 HANNAH[5] EMERY (*Joshua,*[4] *Daniel,*[3] *James,*[2] *Anthony*[1]), daughter of Rev Joshua and Adah (Tidy) Emery, married Oct. 7, 1771, Jedediah Goodwin, lived in Berwick, Me.

Children ·

    477   i   EMERY,[6] b Aug 4, 1772, d young.
    478   ii   HANNAH, b April 24. 1774, m Aug 21, 1788, Joshua Emery
    479   iii MARY, b. Nov 19, 1775
    480   iv   JAMES E , b. Dec. 26, 1777.
    481   v   EMERY, b Dec 27. 1780
    482   vi   JEDEDIAH, b Jan 17, 1782; m , 1st, Hannah Leavitt; 2nd, Isa-
              bella Goodwin, 3rd, Lucy Sawyer.
    483   vii MARGARET, b Dec 28, 1783, m., 1798, Thomas Teal, jr., of York
    484   viii JOHN, b. Oct 17, 1785.
    485   ix   JOSHUA, b May 10, 1787, m Sarah Neal
    486   x   SAMUEL, b June 10, 1789
    487   xi   JAMES, b Aug 8, 1791, m Sept 9, 1809, Mary Goodwin.
    488   xii EUNICE, b June 13, 1793 m. Benj. Chase
    489   xiii BETSEY, b Dec 23, 1795
    490   xiv HARRIET, b April 12, 1800 m Daniel Stone.

185 JAMES[5] EMERY (*Joseph,*[4] *Job,*[3] *James,*[2] *Anthony*[1]), son of Joseph and Mehitable (Stacey) Emery, married Aug. 24, 1750, Mercy Bean, daughter of Capt. Jonathan Bean of the Block House, Saco; resided in Buxton, where he removed about 1760, until 1816, when he removed to Hollis and died 1821, aged 93. She died Nov., 1813

He was a noted hunter and furnished the meat for the ordination dinner of Rev. Paul Coffin. He was in Captain Bean's company at Saco Block House in 1757, and in Capt. William Gerrish's company on the eastern frontier in 1760.

Children:

    491   i   MERCY,[6] b March 20, 1751.
    492   ii   DANIEL, b Nov 30, 1752
    493   iii ELIZABETH, b Jan , 1755, m Simeon Brown.
    494   iv   BENJAMIN, b. Oct , 1761

495 v   JAMES, b 1763
496 vi CHARLES, b June 9, 1766; d. June 29, 1766
497 vii JERUSHA, b Jan 7, 1768, m. May 21, 1787, Samuel Strout of
         Raymond
498 viii JOSHUA, b Sept 7, 1771.

186 JOHN[5] EMERY (*Joseph*,[4] *Job*,[3] *James*,[2] *Anthony*[1]), son of Joseph and Mehitable (Stacey) Emery; married Hannah Furbush of Kittery, published Sept. 22, 1753, died Oct. 12, 1805. Lived in Kittery till 1773, when they removed to what is now Brewer, Me, afterwards to Hampden where he died Feb. 24, 1795.

Children:

499 i   ANNA,[6] b July 17, 1755, m Goodwin Grant
500 ii SALLY, b. 1756, m ——— Craige
501 iii JOHN, b Oct 15, 1758
502 iv JAMES, b. 1761, drowned Sept 14, 1793.
503 v   NAHUM, b 1763.

188 ESTHER[5] EMERY (*Joseph*,[4] *Job*,[3] *James*,[2] *Anthony*[1]), daughter of Joseph and Mehitable (Stacey) Emery, married, 1767, Asa Burbank of Rowley, Mass., his second wife

Children, born in Kennebunkport, Me..

504 i   JOSEPH,[6] d. at sea.
505 ii CALEB, m. Sally Littlefield, removed to Parsonsfield, Me
506 iii DAVID, m Susannah Stowell, d *s p*
507 iv JOSHUA, m Sally Mitchell
508 v   JOHN, m. his brother David's widow

193 JOB[5] EMERY (*Joseph*,[4] *Job*,[3] *James*,[2] *Anthony*[1]), son of Joseph and Mehitable (Stacey) Emery, married, 1770 (certificate granted Sept. 3, 1770), Polly Hubbard (born Jan. 12, 1745). He died May, 1828.

Children, born in Berwick.

509 i   ICHABOD,[6] b April 21, 1771
510 ii POLLY, b Jan 7, 1773
511 iii JOSEPH, b Feb 15, 1775.

194 WILLIAM[5] EMERY (*Joseph*,[4] *Job*,[3] *James*,[2] *Anthony*[1]), son of Joseph and Mehitable (Stacey) Emery, married Jan. 16, 1772, Philomelia Webber (died Jan. 9, 1822). He died Jan. 30, 1816.

Children, born in South Berwick, Me :

512 i   PHILOMELIA,[6] b Dec. 26, 1772.
513 ii   BENJAMIN, b Nov. 30, 1774. ⎰ These two sons left home clandestinely about 1800 Shipped
514 iii ROBERT, b. April 17, 1777 ⎱ on a vessel bound from Portsmouth, N H, and were never heard from It is probable that they were captured by the Algerines and carried to Tripoli.
515 iv   WILLIAM, b May 3, 1779
516 v   JOEL, b Aug 17, 1781
517 vi   ANDREW, b May 28, 1784
518 vii HIRAM, b June 19, 1786
519 viii LUCY, b March 21, 1789
520 ix   MEHITABLE, b March 21, 1792

196 JONATHAN[5] EMERY (*Jonathan*,[4] *Job*,[3] *James*,[2] *Anthony*[1]), son of Jonathan and Phœbe (Bracey) Emery; married Oct. 15, 1772, Elizabeth Tarbox. Made his will Oct. 3, 1806.

Children :

    521 i   JOHN⁶ bapt. May 29, 1774.
    522 ii   HAVEN, bapt Oct 15, 1775.
    523 iii THOMAS
    524 iv   JONATHAN m and went South; had a son, Jonathan
    525 v   MARY ANN.

204 JABEZ⁵ EMERY (*Jabez,⁴ Job,³ James,² Anthony¹*), son of Jabez and Elizabeth (Butland) Emery; married Nov. 11, 1769, Anne Gowen

Children .

    526 i   SALLY,⁶ m Amos Towne
    527 ii   POLLY, m Amos Towne, his second wife.
    528 iii JAMES
    529 iv   ANNA, m James Mitchell
    530 v   LUCY, m David Lord
    531 vi   GEORGE, lost at sea in the Brig "Louisa," Capt Jere Paul
    532 vii SAMUEL, unm
    533 viii ASA, d at sea

206 JOB⁵ EMERY (*Jabez,⁴ Job,³ James,² Anthony¹*), son of Jabez and Elizabeth (Butland) Emery, married Keziah Webber In 1775 he was in Capt. Jas Hubbard's company, Col. Ephraim Doolittle's regiment, and from Dec , 1775, to Dec , 1776, in Capt. Woods' company, Col. Baldwin's regiment; was at Bunker Hill, discharged at Morristown, N J., Dec., 1776 He died July 31, 1832, she died April, 1831, aged 73 years.

Children :

    534 i   PHILIP⁶
    535 ii   DANIEL
    536 iii JACOB
    537 iv   JOSHUA, b April 26, 1792
    538 v   THOMAS, b Jan 27, 1795
    539 vi   KEZIAH, m Amaziah Noble. Moved East

208 ISAAC⁵ EMERY (*Jabez,⁴ Job,³ James,² Anthony¹*), son of Jabez and Elizabeth (Butland) Emery, married May 15, 1783, Eunice Perkins (born March 6, 1761; died Aug. 10, 1834) Merchant and importer. He died June 14. 1836.

Children, born in Kennebunk :

    540 i   LYDIA,⁵ b March 6, 1784, m Robert Patten, Jan. 24, 1802, s p
    541 ii   EUNICE, b Aug 15, 1786, m Edward White, Dec. 11, 1811.
    542 iii ELIZABETH, b Jan 28, 1789, d. Oct 15, 1789
    543 iv   JOHN, b Oct 23, 1790
    544 v   BENJAMIN, b Feb 25, 1793
    545 vi   ISAAC, b July 24, 1795.
    546 vii SETH, b Jan 19, 1798; d. at sea, unm , June 20, 1822; Capt of "Barque" America.
    547 viii ELIPHALET, b Feb 2, 1800, d , unm , Aug 18, 1822, at St Domingo.
    548 ix   MARY E , b Jan 15, 1803.
    549 x   LOUISA, b. Nov. 7, 1805, m George Davis, Feb. 5, 1827.

210 OBADIAH[6] EMERY (*Obed*,[5] *James*,[4] *James*,[3] *James*,[2] *Anthony*[1]), son of·Obed and Sarah (Dyer) Emery; married Nov. 1, 1768, Lydia Emery (died Jan. 17, 1778). He died Jan 23, 1782.

Children, born in Biddeford .

550 i   LYDIA,[7] b March 14, 1769, m William Cole, June 29, 1794, d 1847
551 ii   SAMUEL, b Aug 21, 1770
552 iii   ANNA, b Nov 12, 1771, m William Frost, of Topsham, Me (b Dec. 11, 1781, d Jan 17, 1857) He was a trader, president of First National Bank of Brunswick major of militia, Rep. to the Legislature.
553 iv   SARAH b. July 7, 1775.
554 v   ABIGAIL, b April 20, 1777. This dau and her mother d the same day, June 17, 1778

211 SARAH[6] EMERY (*Obed*,[5] *James*,[4] *James*,[3] *James*,[2] *Anthony*[1]), daughter of Obed and Sarah (Dyer) Emery, married Oct. 25, 1770. Benjamin Hooper, jr. (born Sept. 23, 1747, died April 14, 1802). She died July 10, 1829.

Children, born in Biddeford, Me. :

535 i   REBECCA [7] b March 25, 1772
556 ii   BENJAMIN, b Sept 18, 1774
557 iii   JOHN, b July 16, 1777
558 iv   OBED, b Nov 5, 1780
559 v   SIMON, b Jan 10, 1784
560 vi   DANIEL SMITH, b. May 17, 1788.

212 MARGARET[6] EMERY (*Obed*,[5] *James*,[4] *James*,[3] *James*,[2] *Anthony*[1]), daughter of Obed and Sarah (Dyer) Emery ; married Nov. 10, 1768, Snell Wingate.

Children :

561 i   MOLLY,[7] bapt April 2, 1770.
562 ii   SIMON, bapt Aug 25, 1771
563 iii   SAMUEL, bapt Aug 26, 1772.
564 iv   SNELL, bapt Aug 18, 1779
565 v   SIMON, bapt. April 29, 1781.
566 vi   OBADIAH, bapt Oct 30, 1783

214 MARY[6] EMERY (*Obed*,[5] *James*,[4] *James*,[3] *James*,[2] *Anthony*[1]), daughter of Obed and Sarah (Dyer) Emery, married May 10, 1772, Jeremiah Hill, jr. He is said to have raised a company for three years' service during the Revolutionary War His company joined the regiment of Col. Vose at West Point, and was at the surrender of Burgoyne, Oct., 1777. He resigned his commission at the end of a year and returned home. In 1779, he was appointed Adjutant General of the State forces on the Penobscot River, collector of customs for the district of Saco, 1799–1809, member of Massachusetts Legislature six consecutive terms, received the honorable degree of M.A. from Harvard College, 1787. It is said that he commanded a company at the battle of Bunker Hill He died in 1820

Children, born in Biddeford, Me :

567 i   MARY S ,[7] b June 10, 1773
568 ii   SARAH, b July 25, 1775
569 iii   SUSANNAH.
570 iv   REBECCA, b June 6, 1790.
571 v   MARGARET

215 Daniel[6] Emery (*Obed*,[5] *James*,[4] *James*,[3] *James*,[2] *Anthony*[1]), son of Obed and Sarah (Dyer) Emery, married Hannah Deshon. He died June 18, 1788.

 Child.

  572 i Hannah,[7] b——, d young.

218 Ralph[6] Emery (*Obed*,[5] *James*,[4] *James*,[3] *James*,[2] *Anthony*[1]), son of Obed and Sarah (Dyer) Emery, married Sept , 1786, Olive Foss (died April, 1838). He enlisted for twelve months in April, 1778, and joined at Fishkill, Capt. Lane's company, Col. Ichabod Alden's regiment. He died July 24, 1830

 Children, born in Biddeford, Me. :

  573 i Polly,[7] b. April, 1787, m. William Maxwell
  574 ii Lemuel, b July 12 1789, drowned Aug 7, 1827 , unm
  575 iii Obed, b June 2, 1792, unm
  576 iv Sally, b Dec 23, 1794, d , unm , July 23, 1883
  577 v Daniel, b Sept 20, 1796
  578 vi Olive,   { d unm , July 23, 1883.
  579 vii Priscilla, } b July 29, 1800; { d Nov. 12, 1815.
  580 viii Ralph, b May 16, 1803

229 James[6] Emery (*James*,[5] *Thomas*[4] *James*,[3] *James*,[2] *Anthony*[1]), son of James and Mary (Scammon) Emery ; married March 12, 1795, Catharine Freethy of York (born Oct. 17, 1771 , died Sept 9, 1855). He died in Buxton, March 6, 1840

 Children, born in Buxton

  581 i Mary,[7] b Nov 18, 1796; d. May 20, 1822.
  582 ii Samuel, b Jan 6, 1798
  583 iii Alexander J , b Dec 13, 1801
  584 iv Jonas, b Sept 10, 1803
  585 v Hannah, b May 10, 1805
  586 vi Thomas F , b Sept 23, 1807.
  587 vii James S , b June 14, 1813

230 Joshua[6] Emery (*James*,[5] *Thomas*,[4] *James*,[3] *James*,[2] *Anthony*[1]), son of James and Mary (Scammon) Emery ; married Martha Freeman. Lived in Portland, Me He died in 1858.

 Children, born in Portland

  588 i Mary,[7] b May 14, 1797.
  589 ii Martha, b Feb , 1800, d Sept , 1833
  590 iii Joseph, b Dec 28, 1801.
  591 iv Hannah, b Dec 23, 1803
  592 v Elizabeth, b Jan 17, 1806
  593 vi Daniel F , b Feb 4, 1808
  594 vii Hester A , b Nov 30, 1810
  595 viii Lydia, b. July 11, 1812, d April 8, 1823
  596 ix John Wesley, b May 28, 1816
  597 x Joshua T , b. Dec 12, 1819

231 Mary[6] Emery (*James*,[5] *Thomas*,[4] *James*,[3] *James*,[2] *Anthony*[1]), daughter of James and Mary (Scammon) Emery, married May 4, 1797, Joseph Haley (born Feb. 16, 1776 ; died May 10, 1866). Lived in Portland, Me. She died Sept. 10, 1833.

 Children :

598   i   JAMES,[7] b Oct. 19, 1799; d Oct 26, 1799
599   ii   JAMES E , b March 11, 1804; d March 18, 1816
600   iii MARY S , b July 30, 1806
601   iv   SAMUEL W , b Dec 31, 1808; m. Charlotte Gale, d Oct 6,
           1855, s p
602   v   ANN E., b. June 11, 1811, d. June 22, 1811
603   vi   MARTHA E , b. May 12, 1813.
604   vii MEHITABLE A , b March 29, 1816, d Feb 26, 1822
605   viii JOSEPH K , b Jan 30. 1821.

232 SIMON[6] EMERY (*James,[5] Thomas,[4] James,[3] James,[2] Anthony[1]*),
son of James and Mary (Scammon) Emery, married, first, July 1,
1803, Olive Staples (died Dec. 27, 1809) ; second, Eunice Scammon.
He died Oct. 29, 1825.
  Children.

606   i   JOSEPH,[7] b Nov 19, 1804, d. Dec 25, 1809
607   ii   MARY S , b April 30, 1807
608   iii MEHITABLE, b Nov 7, 1808, d 1808

  By second wife :

609   iv   JAMES FREEMAN, b July 22, 1811
610   v   OLIVE S , b Aug 16, 1813.
611   vi   LIZZIE, b March 4, 1815.
612   vii ASENATH, b Oct. 27, 1817, d. May 20, 1831
613   viii FREDERICK A., b Jan 19, 1820; d Oct 3, 1827

233 SAMUEL[6] EMERY (*James,[5] Thomas,[4] James,[3] James,[2] Anthony[1]*),
son of James and Mary (Scammon) Emery, married Dec 2, 1819,
Sophia Webster (born July 16, 1790 ; died Feb , 1877), daughter
of Rev Nathaniel Webster. He died Jan. 15, 1862.
  Children, born in Portland :

614   i   SAMUEL WEBSTER,[7] b. June 12, 1821
615   ii   EDWARDS WHIPPLE, b Nov 22, 1822, d. Aug 23, 1827
616   iii JAMES NATHANIEL, b Oct 29, 1824, d Feb 19, 1846
617   iv   EDWARDS WHIPPLE, b. May 8, 1827, d March 29, 1829   The
           second Edwards Whipple, though born before the death of
           the first of this name, was not named till after the death of
           the first, being baptized at the funeral of his brother

235 NATHANIEL[6] EMERY (*James,[5] Thomas,[4] James,[3] James,[2] Anthony[1]*), son of James and Mary (Scammon) Emery, married Dec 1,
1808, Philadelphia N Rankin (born in Wells, Me., June 28, 1789)
He died Oct 19, 1871.
  Children, born in Biddeford :

618   i   JAMES,[7] b June 23. 1810.
619   ii   EMILY J , b. May 12, 1812.
620   iii SARAH ANN, b June 4, 1814
621   iv   NATHANIEL WEBSTER, b Nov. 1, 1817
622   v   THOMAS DODGE, b Feb 6, 1820
623   vi   MARY ABIGAIL, b March 12, 1822
624   vii NARCISSA, b April 5, 1824

236 LYDIA[6] EMERY (*James,[5] Thomas,[4] James,[3] James,[2] Anthony[1]*),
daughter of James and Mary (Scammon) Emery ; married Thomas
Dodge. Lived in Portland

22

Child :

   625 i   THOMAS K.[7] ; m. Martha E. Haley, dau. of Joseph and Mary S.
           (Emery) Haley (see No. 603).

237 SUSAN H.[6] EMERY (*Ebenezer*,[5] *Thomas*,[4] *James*,[3] *James*,[2] *Anthony*[1]), daughter of Ebenezer and Mrs. Alice (Polk) Emery ; married William Fairfield.

   Child :

   626 i   HARRIET[7] ; d. April 14, 1830.

239 JOHN P.[6] EMERY (*Ebenezer*,[5] *Thomas*,[4] *James*,[3] *James*,[2] *Anthony*[1]), son of Ebenezer and Mrs. Alice (Polk) Emery ; married June 8, 1817, Polly Smith (born in Hollis, Me., April 10, 1795 ; died Nov. 3, 1881). He died April 18, 1861.

   Children :

   627 i   MIRANDA,[7] b. Aug. 22, 1818.
   628 ii JOSEPH S., b. Dec. 29, 1819 ; m. Olive Johnson.
   629 iii CHARLES E., b. Jan. 19, 1822.
   630 iv HENRY, b. Nov. 5, 1823.
   631 v   HARRIET C., b. Sept. 17, 1825.
   632 vi JONAS, b. April 30, 1829.
   633 vii SETH, b. Dec. 31, 1832.
   634 viii MARY C., b. Aug. 24, 1834.
   635 ix SUSAN E., b. Dec. 12, 1839 ; d. Oct. 8, 1852.

241 NATHANIEL[6] EMERY (*Thomas*,[5] *Thomas*,[4] *James*,[3] *James*,[2] *Anthony*[1]), son of Thomas and Hannah (Harmon) Emery ; married in Scarborough, Me., Feb. 14, 1800, Jane Harmon.

   Children, born in Buxton :

   636 i   BENJAMIN,[7] b. Dec. 1, 1800.
   637 ii DORCAS, b. Feb. 25, 1803
   638 iii JOHN H., b. Sept. 4, 1805 ; m. Sarah Jones ; d. 1878.
   639 iv ANN, b. Nov. 17, 1809.
   640 v   NATHANIEL, JR., b. July 3, 1814.
   641 vi THEODORE, b. March 31, 1818 ; d. July 12, 1819.
   642 vii REBECCA, b. May 27, 1819.
   643 viii ISAAC, b. July 8, 1821 ; d. April 9, 1827.
   644 ix THEODORE, b. March 15, 1827.
   644*a* x SON, b. Sept., 1829 ; d. Jan. 4, 1830.

242 THOMAS[6] EMERY (*Thomas*,[5] *Thomas*,[4] *James*,[3] *James*,[2] *Anthony*[1]), son of Thomas and Hannah (Harmon) Emery ; married Oct. 4, 1799, Mary Woodman. Farmer and lumberman ; a prominent citizen of his town ; selectman of Buxton and sheriff of York Co., Me. He died June 27, 1858.

   Children, born in Buxton :

   645 i   RUFUS,[7] b. April 29, 1800.
   646 ii HANNAH, b. April 3, 1802.
   647 iii MARY, b. Dec. 11, 1805.
   648 iv THOMAS J., b. Sept. 15, 1807.
   649 v   JAMES W., b. Aug. 24, 1809.
   650 vi HORACE, b. Jan. 1, 1812.
   651 vii ALEXANDER J., b. Oct. 6, 1814.

652 viii MARK P , b Feb 11, 1817; m Jan 1, 1846, Mary S Smith dau of Ezra and Maria (Burleigh) Smith   Prominent in business relations in Portland in shipping, in the lumber business, import trade and real estate, director of the First National Bank and trustee of Maine Savings Bank , director of the Maine Steamboat Company , alderman of the city and chairman of the committee of the fire department, an influential and universally respected citizen
653 ix ELIZA W , b July 27, 1820
654 x HARRIET F. B , b. March 17, 1825

245 SALLY[6] EMERY (*Thomas,*[5] *Thomas,*[4] *James,*[3] *James,*[2] *Anthony*[1]), daughter of Thomas and Hannah (Harmon) Emery, married May 14, 1807, Alexander Jose (born in Buxton, Me , Dec 11, 1780, died Sept. 22, 1868)   She died March 11, 1883.
Children, born in Buxton :

655 i HANNAH EMERY,[7] b April 4, 1808
656 ii ABIGAIL ANN, b April 23, 1810
657 iii MARK EMERY, b. April 15, 1814
658 iv CHARLES EDWIN, b Jan 25, 1817
659 v HORATIO NELSON, b March 18, 1819
660 vi SARAH EMERY, b. Feb 2, 1822, m Sam'l T Hooper, June 8, 1845, d. Jan 9, 1872
661 vii EMILY MOTLEY, b Dec 17, 1827.

246 JOHN[6] EMERY(*Thomas,*[5] *Thomas,*[4] *James,*[3] *James,*[2] *Anthony*[1]), son of Thomas and Hannah (Harmon) Emery; married June 10, 1813, Hannah Locke of Hollis, Me. (died May 29, 1849).   He was a citizen greatly respected in his town and regarded with deep affection in the church in which he was a leading member.   He died Dec. 19, 1868.
Children, born in Kennebunk :

662 i MARY LOCKE,[7] b. April 29, 1814.
663 ii ELIZA ELDEN, b Feb 25, 1816, d , unm , in Neponset, Mass , Nov 2, 1880
664 iii HANNAH, b Jan 4, 1818, d Feb 17, 1818.
665 iv STEPHEN LOCKE, b Sept 26, 1819
666 v HANNAH, b. Aug 3, 1821.
667 vi SUSAN H , b Jan 15, 1823.
668 vii ABBY M , b Nov. 17, 1824
669 viii JOHN WESLEY, b March 16, 1827, d March 14, 1832
670 ix CHARLES WESLEY, b April 12, 1829, unm

247 JOSEPH D [6] EMERY (*Thomas,*[5] *Thomas,*[4] *James,*[3] *James,*[2] *Anthony*[1]), son of Thomas and Hannah (Harmon) Emery ; married in Scarborough, Me., March 10, 1813, Abigail Moulton (born Jan 26, 1792)   He died Nov. 15, 1847   His widow married, second, May 5, 1851, Nathan D. Rice of Union, Me. (born Aug. 29, 1784 , died April 1, 1860).   She died Oct. 12, 1874
Children, born in Buxton :

671 i ALMIRA,[7] b. Dec. 24, 1813.
672 ii ABIGAIL, b Nov 12, 1816, d Dec 21, 1831.
673 iii AMELIA CATHARINE, b. Feb 6, 1819
674 iv MARY ADALINE, b Feb 6, 1821, m Danforth Prescott of Cal , 1867.
675 v SUSAN A , b. Feb. 18, 1823.

676   vi   Sarah Eliz., b. Nov. 5, 1824.
677   vii Joseph Henry, b. Oct. 23, 1826.
678   viii Ellen Maria, b. Sept. 3, 1828.
679   ix   George Robinson, b. March 5, 1833.

248 Isaac[6] Emery (*Thomas,[5] Thomas,[4] James,[3] James,[2] Anthony[1]*), son of Thomas and Hannah (Harmon) Emery ; married, first, July 15, 1819, Faith Savage Bigelow, daughter of Amos and Lucy (Savage) Bigelow (died Nov. 27, 1826) and granddaughter of Samuel Phillips Savage of Weston. Mass., who presided at the meeting held in the Old South Meeting House, Dec. 16, 1773, and was president of the Board of War during the Revolution. Isaac Emery married, second, May 2, 1827, Sarah Spring (died Feb., 1876). He died in Boston, July 3, 1875.

Children :

680   i   George Fred.,[7] b. May 20, 1820.
681   ii   William H., b. March 22, 1822.
682   iii Lucy Bigelow, b. Nov. 20, 1824 ; d. Oct. 14, 1834.

249 Peter[6] Emery (*Thomas,[5] Thomas,[4] James,[3] James,[2] Anthony[1]*), son of Thomas and Hannah (Harmon) Emery ; married Jan. 17, 1820, Eliza (born Feb. 15, 1800 ; died Nov. 14, 1882), daughter of Samuel and Mehitable Dunnell Sands of Buxton. He died March 2, 1877.

Children, born in Buxton :

683   i   Mark,[7] b. Apr. 25, 1821 ; d. Aug. 13, 1839.
684   ii   Joseph Dunnell, b. Feb. 13, 1823 ; d. Oct. 28, 1888.
685   iii John, b. March 31, 1825.
686   iv Susan B., b. Sept. 24, 1827 ; m. Alex. Brooks (d. 1876) of Hollis, Me., June 11, 1861 ; d. Sept. 20, 1879, s. p.
687   v   Almira S., b. Jan. 10, 1830 ; d. Feb. 13, 1870.
688   vi Thomas H., b. July 3, 1832 ; m. Ellen E. Hooper, dau. of John and Hannah H. Hooper of Biddeford, Me. Graduate of Bowdoin Medical College, 1860 ; assistant physician at the Insane Asylum, Augusta, Me., 1862 ; assistant surgeon 11th Me. Vols., 1863, and since a teacher in Biddeford, Me.
689   vii Samuel S., b. July 8, 1832 ; graduate of Dartmouth Medical College, 1859 ; practised medicine in Jacksonville, Fla. ; 1st Lieutenant in Co. " C," 40th Ill. Vols., during the Rebellion ; resigned from the army, 1863 ; d. in Buxton, Me., Dec. 13, 1866.
690   viii Sallie J., b. Jan. 26, 1835 ; d. June, 1887.
691   ix William H., b. Sept. 14, 1837 ; d. Feb. 15, 1838.
692   x   Jane E., b. June 9, 1839 ; d. Dec. 3, 1869.
693   xi Nancy M., b. Dec. 9, 1843.

252 Zachariah[6] Emery (*Zachariah,[5] Zachariah,[4] Zachariah,[3] James,[2] Anthony[1]*), son of Zachariah and Esther (Stevens) Emery ; married June 25, 1778, Mary Lemon ; resided in Temple, N. H. He marched from Temple to Cambridge on the alarm of April 19, 1775, and was gone fourteen days ; afterwards he enlisted for eight months' service in Captain Town's company, Col. J. Reed's regiment. In 1776 he went on an alarm to Ticonderoga ; signed the "Association Test," and 1780 he marched to Coos when Royalston was burnt ; selectman, 1771 ; constable, 1773.

Children, born in Townsend ·

694   i   POLLY,[7] b May 30, 1779, m ——— Bridge.
695   ii DAVID, b. April 26, 1781
696   iii Lucy, b. July 19, 1784
697   iv SAMUEL, b May 30 1786
698   v   BETSEY, b Sept 27, 1768
699   vi HORACE, b Jan 4, 1793
700   vii LUCRETIA, b Feb 5, 1795, m. Robert Corbet.
701   viii MELINDA, b March 21, 1797
701a ix CLEMENTINA b April 13, 1799, d Jan. 28, 1802

254 AMOS[6] EMERY (*Zachariah,[5] Zachariah,[4] Zachariah,[3] James,[2] Anthony[1]*), son of Zachariah and Esther (Stevens) Emery; married Lucretia Morse (born April 8, 1753; died May 15, 1821), daughter of Jonathan and Phœbe (Keyes) Morse. Removed from Temple to Dublin, March, 1778, signed the agreement to the Declaration of Independence, June 1, 1776, served in Capt. Abijah Smith's company, Col. Baldwin's regiment Sept. to Dec., 1776, in New York, member of the House for the sessions of 1779–80; delegate from Dublin to the Constitutional Convention, March 28, 1781, selectman, 1781 and 1784. He died in Dublin, N. H., Nov. 2, 1827.

Children, born in Dublin, except the first :

702   i   AMOS,[7] b. July 25, 1773, in Temple
703   ii   Lucy, b Oct 30, 1778
704   iii ESTHER, b Dec. 31, 1780.
705   iv   CYRUS, b 1783, d , unm , Jan 1, 1801
706   v   JONATHAN, b. 1785 m. Dec 30, 1819, Lucy Hoar, d. March 31, 1872, *s p*
707   vi   LEVI, b April 1, 1793, m , April 19, 1831, Elvira Mason (b Nov. 16, 1804), dau of Thaddeus, jr , and Lydia (Berry) Mason He d March 14, 1879, *s. p.*

259 JOHN[6] EMERY (*Zachariah,[5] Zachariah,[4] Zachariah,[3] James,[2] Anthony[1]*), son of Zachariah and Esther (Stevens) Emery, married (published Aug 19, 1780) in 1780, Ruth Sanders of Lunenburg, Mass. (died Feb. 1. 1857, aged ninety-two years) He was selectman of his town for nine years. He died in Townsend, March 13, 1828

Children, born in Townsend :

708   i   JOHN,[7] b March 5, 1782; m. Patty Stone, Dec 17, 1811, d. Oct 12. 1866, *s p*
709   ii   LEVI, b July 10, 1783
710   iii RUTH b Jan 5, 1787
711   iv   Lucy, b Sept. 19, 1788.
712   v   NANCY, b May 12, 1790
713   vi   JOEL, b March 27, 1792
714   vii POLLY b Feb 8, 1795, d July 11, 1801.
715   viii EZRA, b Sept. 29, 1796
716   ix   DARIUS, b May 17, 1800.

260 LUCY[6] EMERY (*Zachariah,[5] Zachariah,[4] Zachariah,[3] James,[2] Anthony[1]*), daughter of Zachariah and Esther (Stevens) Emery, married July 4, 1782, Daniel Campbell, second, Nov. 19, 1789, David Elliot (died Jan 4, 1793). David Elliot was at the battle of Bunker Hill in the hottest of the fight; his gun becoming hot, he threw it away and took the gun of one who had been killed and used up his ammunition. This gun he kept to the day of his death. Moderator and selectman, 1788; selectman again, 1790. She died Jan. 23, 1846.

Child, by first husband :

   717 i   Lucy,[7] b. May 28, 1783.

By second husband :

   718 ii David, b. Nov. 8, 1790; d. Aug. 20, 1798.
   719 iii Daniel, b. Oct. 1, 1792; graduate of Dartmouth College, 1813; m. Abby Grule; d. Mar. 30, 1868.

261 Samuel[6] Emery (*Zachariah,[5] Zachariah,[4] Zachariah,[3] James,[2] Anthony[1]*), son of Zachariah and Esther (Stevens) Emery ; married Jan. 31, 1789, Olive Jaquith (died Oct. 8, 1832). Lived near Gilmore Pond in Jaffrey, N. H. He died Jan. 12, 1826.

Children, born in Jaffrey :

   720 i Esther,[7] b. Nov. 24, 1792.
   721 ii Samuel, b. Sept. 7, 1794.
   722 iii Olive, b. May 29, 1799.

262 William[5] Emery (*Zachariah,[5] Zachariah,[4] Zachariah,[3] James,[2] Anthony[1]*), son of Zachariah and Esther (Stevens) Emery ; married, first, Mary Stanley (died June 2, 1827) ; second, Lucy ———. She died July 29, 1858. Settled in Jaffrey, N. H. He died July 16, 1840.

Children, born in Jaffrey :

   723 i Zachariah,[7] b. Feb. 1, 1790.
   724 ii Polly, b. March 27, 1792; d. March 4, 1865, unm.
   725 iii Sybil, b. March 25, 1794.
   726 iv Ralph, b. Sept. 26, 1796.
   727 v William, b. March 29, 1799; m. Lucy Downes, Dec. 10, 1826; d. May 8, 1864.
   728 vi Edward, b. May 3, 1801.
   729 vii Amasa, b. April 2, 1804.
   730 viii Nancy Ann, b. April 29, 1807.
   731 ix John S., b. March 1, 1810.
   732 x Laura A., b. May 31, 1815; d. July 23, 1855, unm.

270 John[6] Emery (*John,[5] Zachariah,[4] Zachariah,[3] James,[2] Anthony[1]*), son of John and Mary (Munroe) Emery ; married Jan. 9, 1786, Deborah Colburn of Dracut, Mass. (born 1763 ; died June 23, 1853). He was out during the Revolutionary war for eight months and afterwards for forty-three months and twenty-three days ; was at the battle of Bunker Hill, at the surrender of Burgoyne, Oct. 17, 1777, at the assault of General Wayne, at Stony Point, July 16, 1779, and at the surrender of Cornwallis at Yorktown ; prisoner in New York City ten months and ten days ; settled in Bloomfield or Canaan, Me., and died Feb. 26, 1848.

Children, born in Skowhegan, Me. :

   733 i Joseph,[7] b. 1790.
   734 ii John, d. at Oldtown, Me.; unm.
   735 iii Betsey, m. Benj. Prescott.

736   iv   HANNAH, m Levi Judkins.
737   v   SALLY, b 1799.
738   vi   ESTHER
739   vii MARY, b 1804, d. unm

271 SAMUEL[6] EMERY (*John,[5] Zachariah,[4] Zachariah,[3] James,[2] Anthony[1]*), son of John and Mary (Munroe) Emery, married, first, April 26, 1781, Rebecca Wheeler of Carlisle, Mass. (born March 6, 1752; died Sept 30, 1825), second, Oct. 4, 1826, Hannah Boston (died May 23, 1854, aged eighty-four years). He was one of the eight months' men in the Revolutionary war, was at the battle of Bunker Hill, under Colonel Nixon, and afterwards was forty-five months in the service in Captain Toogood's company, Colonel Thomas Nixon's regiment; sergeant, Aug 1, 1777, first tax gatherer in Canaan, Me., 1788, lived in Bloomfield and Ripley, Me. He died Oct. 2, 1836.

Children;

740   i   ASENATH,[7] b Aug 9, 1782; m John Davenport, Nov. 1801, d. April 25, 1850
741   ii   SUSAN, b April 19, 1784, m. Alvin Bigelow, Dec 3, 1803; d. May 25, 1855
742   iii   INFANT, b July 10, 1785; d. July 28, 1785.
743   iv   INFANT, b. 1786 d. 1786
744   v   LUCY, b Jan 13, 1787
745   vi   JOHN, b Feb 18, 1789
746   vii   OLIVE, b March 16, 1791, d. unm.
747   viii LUCINDA, b Feb 4, 1793
748   ix   RACHEL, b. Dec. 13, 1794, m. Edw Leavitt, d Aug 14, 1834
749   x   REBECCA, b April 1, 1797; m. Benj. Allen, July 21, 1817, d Aug. 12, 1871
750   xi   SAMUEL, b April 20, 1799
751   xii   JOANNA, b. March 27, 1801
752   xiii MARY, b. May 25, 1803; m Rufus Greely, April 1827, d Nov 21, 1874

273 JOSEPH[6] EMERY (*John,[5] Zachariah,[4] Zachariah,[3] James,[2] Anthony[1]*), son of John and Mary (Munroe) Emery; married Elizabeth Mason (died May 26, 1838, aged 80 years), went to Bloomfield, Me., and died March 17, 1842.

Children:

753   i   TILLY,[7] b Nov 1792, m 1815, Esther (b Dec. 18, 1789 d Feb 11, 1836), dau of William and Sarah (Russell) Spaulding
754   ii   BETSEY, b 1794
755   iii JOSEPH, b 1795.
756   iv   ARTEMAS, b. 1800, m. Naomi Western and had a large family.

280 JANE[6] EMERY (*Daniel,[5] Zachariah,[4] Zachariah,[3] James,[2] Anthony[1]*), daughter of Deacon Daniel and Jane (———) Emery, married, about 1778, John Stait of Temple, N. H. She died about 1824.

Children, born in Temple

757   i   JOHN,[7] b 1779
758   ii   WILLIAM, b 1782
759   iii SALLY, b March 28, 1784.
760   iv   NOAH, b 1785
761   v   LUCY, b 1788

762   vi   DANIEL, b. June 17, 1793.
763   vii GEORGE, b. ———; d. at eight years of age.
764   viii BETSEY, b. Sept., 1798.

281 CAPT. DANIEL[6] EMERY (*Daniel,[5] Zachariah,[4] Zachariah,[3] James,[2] Anthony[1]*), son of Deacon Daniel and Jane (————) Emery ; married, first, June 18, 1780, Elizabeth Farnsworth (died Oct. 23, 1783) ; second, June 6, 1786, Hannah Bates of Jaffrey (died in N. Y., 1852). He removed to Jaffrey, N. H., 1776, and afterwards to Walpole, N. H. ; was probably in Capt. James Hosley's Co. of Townsend, Mass., at the time of the battle of Lexington, and was in service from April 19 to 27, 1775, and was probably commissioned Lieut. in Capt. Thomas Warren's Co. of the Sixth Middlesex Regt. He died in Walpole, N. H., March 5, 1826.

Children, born in Walpole, except first two :

765   i   DANIEL,[7] b. Feb. 13, 1782, in Jaffrey.
766   ii   INFANT, b. 1783, and d. the same year, in Jaffrey.

By second wife :

767   iii STEPHEN, b. Dec. 23, 1786.
768   iv   BETSEY, b. April 15, 1788; m. Zach. Emery (see No. 299).
769   v   HANNAH, b. Oct. 10, 1789; m. ——— White; d. at Rockingham, Vt.
770   vi   SARAH, b. April 14, 1791; m. ——— Todd; had a son Ruel, living in Dundee, Ill., in 1882.
771   vii NANCY, b. Jan. 27, 1793.
772   viii JOSEPH, b. May 24, 1794; d. at Aurora, N. Y., Sept. 12, 1869.
773   ix   ABNER, b. April 27, 1796; m. and had son Frank.
774   x   JONATHAN, b. July 31, 1797.
775   xi   AARON, b. Feb. 24, 1799; d. July 11, 1883.
776   xii IRA, b. April 16, 1801; m., 1st, Julia Fisher (b. July 1, 1791) ; 2nd, Mrs. Sabrina Stearns; d. Jan. 19, 1864.
777   xiii ACHSAH, b. July 30, 1802; d. at Bodax, Mich., June 12, 1884.
778   xiv FRANKLIN, b. Feb. 7, 1807; d. at Walpole, N. H., Oct. 29, 1825.
779   xv   CYNTHIA, b. April 1, 1809.
780   xvi IRENE, b. June 16, 1810.

282 BETSEY[6] EMERY (*Daniel,[5] Zachariah,[4] Zachariah,[3] James,[2] Anthony[1]*), daughter of Deacon Daniel and Jane (————) Emery ; married Alexander Milliken (died Oct. 9, 1811), who kept a public house in Jaffrey, N. H., at the foot of the Monadnock Mountain. She died May 9, 1823.

Children :

781   i   JOHN,[7] b. Dec. 27, 1781; d. March 10, 1783.
782   ii   MOLLY, b. April 24, 1784; m. Moses Hill.
783   iii BETSEY, b. Nov. 29, 1786; m. May 30, 1803, Jonathan Gilmore; removed to Potsdam, N. Y.
784   iv   JOHN, b. Feb. 26, 1790; m. Sally Stevens, June, 1810.
785   v   AMASA, b. Oct. 20, 1792; m. Sophia Hill.
786   vi   ALEXANDER, b. 1796.
787   vii NABBY, d. in 1800.
788   viii NABBY, b. 1802.

283 NOAH[6] EMERY (*Daniel,[5] Zachariah,[4] Zachariah,[3] James,[2] An-*

thony[1]), son of Deacon Daniel and Jane (———) Emery, married, first, Elizabeth Philbrick (born July 18, 1762, died Feb. 13, 1813, of spotted fever) ; second, ——— ———. He died Aug. 9, 1837. Children, of the first marriage, fourteen ; of the second, ten.

789	i	JANE,[7] b May 23, 1784 ; m —— Walker and d 1852
790	ii	JAMES, b Aug 22, 1785 ; d at Spencer, N Y, 1861
791	iii	BETSEY, b Aug 5, 1787, m James Adams, 1803, d 1805.
792	iv	EUNICE, b Nov. 3, 1788, m. Samuel Hewett, d. 1813 of spotted fever.
793	v	ASA, b. Dec 16, 1789 ; d. 1830
794	vi	NATHAN, d young
795	vii	NATHAN, b May 12, 1793, d. July 23, 1825
796	viii	NOAH, b. Oct 27, 1794
797	ix	JOEL, b. Feb 18, 1796
798	x	WALTER, b July 7, 1797
799	xi	DAVID, b Dec 31, 1798, m. in Canada, d in Ill.
800	xii	JOHN, b. March 24, 1800, d. Jan 2, 1814
801	xiii	GRATIA, b Sept 29, 1801 ; d Sept 10, 1829
802	xiv	JONATHAN, b. Sept 9, 1803, d 1853
803	xv	BETSEY, m, 1st, James Adams, who d in 1865, 2nd, Marvin Marshall
804	xvi	LUCY.
805	xvii	WILLIAM
806	xviii	ORLANDO
807	xix	JOSIAH
808	xx	SARAH, m. —— Newcomb of Richmond, Me

Four children d in infancy.

285 ASA[6] EMERY (*Daniel,*[5] *Zachariah,*[4] *Zachariah,*[3] *James,*[2] *Anthony*[1]), son of Deacon Daniel and Jane (———) Emery ; married, 1793, Mary Rider of Grafton, Vt. (born Aug. 30, 1771, died in 1849), went to Pike, N. Y., made the first brick in the county ; assisted in starting the first Methodist church in Pike. He died April 14, 1860. Children :

809	i	JONATHAN,[7] b. June 29, 1794 ; d in Pike N Y, 1879
810	ii	ASA, b Aug 8, 1796 ; d in Belfast, N Y
811	iii	LIBA, b. April 24, 1798 ; m. Lucy Kelley in Pike, N. Y.
812	iv	MARY, b Feb 14, 1800, m William Bailey, 1820, d. Nov 23, 1846, in Wis.
813	v	SABRA, b March 4, 1802
814	vi	LOUISA, b Dec 20, 1803 ; d. 1809
815	vii	LABAN, b March 27, 1807
816	viii	DAN, b May 10, 1809, d 1880.
817	ix	EMELINE, b April 12, 1813
818	x	ORIN, b. July 13, 1815, m. Amanda Bostwick.
819	xi	LEVERETT, b Nov. 17, 1817, d 1841.

290 ELIZABETH[6] BUTTERFIELD (*Elizabeth,*[5] *Zachariah,*[4] *Zachariah,*[3] *James,*[2] *Anthony*[1]), daughter of Ebenezer and Elizabeth (Emery) Butterfield, married, 1784, Capt. Oliver Bailey of Dunstable, Mass. (born Sept. 17, 1763, died Sept. 24, 1829). She died March 10, 1842. Children :

820	i	LUTHER [7]
821	ii	OLIVER
822	iii	SALLY
823	iv	RUEL
824	v	OZIAS C.
825	vi	MARY
826	vii	BETSEY.

291 REUBEN[6] BUTTERFIELD (*Elizabeth*,[5] *Zachariah*,[4] *Zachariah*,[3] *James*,[2] *Anthony*[1]), son of Ebenezer and Elizabeth (Emery) Butterfield; married, first, Feb. 13, 1792, Jane Whitney of Dunstable, N. H.; second, Elizabeth Hardy (published Dec. 29, 1823). He died Dec. 1, 1857.

Children :

    827   i   JOSEPH,[7] b. Sept. 30, 1794; m.; d. June, 1879, *s. p.*
    828   ii   OLIVE, b. 1795; d. 1799.
    829   iii ASA, b. Nov. 1, 1797; m. and had children.
    830   iv   SARAH, b. April 3, 1799.
    831   v   HANNAH, b. March 7, 1803.
    832   vi   JANE W., b. Oct. 15, 1811.
    833   vii CHILD.

292 REV. JOSEPH[6] BUTTERFIELD (*Elizabeth*,[5] *Zachariah*,[4] *Zachariah*,[3] *James*,[2] *Anthony*[1]), son of Ebenezer and Elizabeth (Emery) Butterfield; married Mary Hastings. He was first a Baptist minister, then a physician, and afterwards a Universalist minister.

Children :

    834   i   MARY.[7]
    835   ii   MARCIA.
    836   iii MALVINA.
    837   iv   ELIZABETH.

293 MARY[6] BUTTERFIELD (*Elizabeth*,[5] *Zachariah*,[4] *Zachariah*,[3] *James*,[2] *Anthony*[1]) daughter of Ebenezer and Elizabeth (Emery) Butterfield; married Eliphalet Jennings. She died Jan. 19, 1851.

Children :

    838   i   JOSEPH.[7]
    839   ii   HANNAH.
    840   iii ASA.
    841   iv   RUFUS.
    842   v   DAVID.
    843   vi   GEORGE.
    844   vii MARY.
    845   viii BETSEY.
    846   ix   JOHN.
    847   x   REUBEN.
    848   xi   ELIPHALET.
    849   xii NANCY.

There were other children, names unknown, sixteen in all.

294 SARAH[6] BUTTERFIELD (*Elizabeth*,[5] *Zachariah*,[4] *Zachariah*,[3] *James*,[2] *Anthony*[1]), daughter of Ebenezer and Elizabeth (Emery) Butterfield; married Oliver Wright; published March 27, 1799; died Feb. 4, 1862.

Children :

    850   i   OLIVER, JR.[7]
    851   ii   SALLY.
    852   iii REUBEN.
    853   iv   JOTHAM.
    854   v   THOMAS.
    855   vi   BETSEY.

295 MARY[6] EMERY (*Samuel*,[5] *Zachariah*,[4] *Zachariah*,[3] *James*,[2]

Anthony[1]), daughter of Samuel and Mary (Green) Emery; married Benjamin Gowing of Dublin, N. H., went to Vermont and afterwards to New York.

Child:

858 i CURTIS [7]

297 SARAH[6] EMERY (*Samuel*,[5] *Zachariah*,[4] *Zachariah*,[3] *James*,[2] *Anthony*[1]), daughter of Samuel and Mary (Green) Emery, married Samuel Raymenton

Children.

857 i SARAH,[7] m Robert Finley, lived in Ackworth and Rockingham, N H ; d in 1872
858 ii MARY, b Dec., 1800.

299 ZACHARIAH[6] EMERY (*Samuel*,[5] *Zachariah*,[4] *Zachariah*,[3] *James*,[2] *Anthony*[1]), son of Samuel and Mary (Green) Emery, married Jan. 14, 1805, Betsey Emery, daughter of Daniel and Hannah (Bates) Emery of Jaffrey, N. H (died Jan. 13, 1860), removed to Rockingham, Vt., then to Belfast, N. Y, where he died March 28, 1853

Children, born in Rockingham, Vt..

859 i ELLIOT,[7] b. July 10, 1807, killed by the falling of a tree, Feb 10, 1874, in Belfast. N Y
860 ii DANIEL, b May 8, 1810, d in Belfast, N. Y., Jan 14, 1879
861 iii SARAH ANN, b Nov 9, 1812; m ——— Stewart; d Jan 20, 1837, s p
862 iv FREDERICK REED, b. March 8, 1815, d. Sept. 27, 1819
863 v HANNAH ZILPHA, b March 3, 1820.
864 vi JARVIS CHASE, b Jan 21, 1822
865 vii BETSEY MARIA, b Aug 24, 1827

300 JOSIAH[6] EMERY (*Samuel*,[5] *Zachariah*,[4] *Zachariah*,[3] *James*,[2] *Anthony*[1]), son of Samuel and Mary (Green) Emery ; married April 26, 1806, Esther Raymenton (died Oct. 13, 1844). He died Sept 29, 1843. Lived in Rockingham, Vt.

Children

866 i ELVIRA,[7] b June 23, 1807, m Quartus Durand, March 22, 1827, d Nov. 10, 1882
867 ii MARY, b Feb 25, 1809; d Jan 27, 1878
868 iii BETSEY, b. July 23, 1812, d April 15. 1871
869 iv LOUISA, b April 15, 1815, m H C Whitcomb, Aug 19, 1833, d June 5, 1843
870 v OSMAN BAKER, b April 21, 1817
871 vi HANNAH GREEN, b July 17, 1819
872 vii ESTHER ROSINA, b Sept 20, 1821
873 viii HARRIET CAMPBELL, b Feb 14, 1823, m. Solomon Wright, 1844, d July 18, 1855
874 ix SAMUEL H R, b June 20, 1825, m , 1st Achsa Woodward, 2nd, Eliza Sherman
875 x SARAH A , b Sept 20, 1827.

330 DANIEL[6] EMERY (*Daniel*,[5] *Daniel*,[4] *Daniel*,[3] *James*,[2] *Anthony*[1]), son of Daniel and Sarah (Shackley) Emery ; married, first, March 28. 1782, Olive Lord ; second, Nov. 12, 1789, Abigail Lord. Lived in Eliot , made his will Aug. 15, 1824.

Children:

876 I DAVID,[7] b 1790
877 II ENOCH, b 1796.
878 III ELIJAH, b 1802, d , unm , Dec. 26, 1825
879 IV SALLY.
880 V OLIVE, m. Mar. 23, 1826, Arthur Came of York, Me.
881 VI DANIEL, probably d young

331 NAHUM[6] EMERY (*Daniel,*[5] *Daniel,*[4] *Daniel,*[3] *James,*[2] *Anthony*[1]), son of Daniel and Sarah (Shackley) Emery ; married, first, July 5, 1795, Rhoda, daughter of Japhet and Mary (Emery) Emery; second, Nov. 29, 1798, Eunice Hodgdon ; third, Aug 16, 1800, Sarah Pickernell (born 1765 ; died May 9, 1852).

Children, a daughter by each wife .

882 I SERENA,[7] d. young
883 II RHODA, b ——, m William Pike.
884 III EUNICE, b. Oct 28, 1801, d June 2, 1855

332 NATHAN[6] EMERY (*Daniel,*[5] *Daniel,*[4] *Daniel,*[3] *James,*[2] *Anthony*[1]), son of Daniel and Sarah (Shackley) Emery , married Nov. 10, 1785, Hannah Kingsbury, daughter of Joseph Kingsbury and sister of Elizabeth, who married Isaac Emery, son of Samuel and Abigail (Shackley) Emery , died in 1821.

Children .

885 I RUFUS,[7] unm
886 II JOHN, d. in Eliot
887 III JOEL, b in 1784, m Betsey Emery (see No 896).
888 IV IVORY, unm
889 V HANNAH, m , 1st, —— Foss, 2nd, Eliot Emery, son of Israel and Prudence (Emery) Emery, Oct. 30, 1831
890 VI BETSEY, d., unm
891 VII MARY, m John Simpson

335 DANIEL[6] EMERY (*Daniel,*[5] *Noah,*[4] *Daniel,*[3] *James,*[2] *Anthony*[1]). son of Daniel and Elizabeth (Beatles) Emery ; married Elizabeth Crosby (published in York, Me., July 3, 1779).

Children :

892 I SARAH C ,[7] b. Dec 6, 1780; m Stephen Webber, May 13, 1819
893 II POLLY, b. July 8, 1782; m. Theodore Emery, son of Japhet. No 361.
894 III TIMOTHY, b Sept 7, 1785
895 IV DANIEL C., b. July 1, 1787
896 V ELIZABETH, b. Oct. 10, 1789; m , 1st, Joel Emery(see No. 887), 2nd, Nathan Grant
897 VI HANNAH, b Nov 5, 1792, m. John Goodwin of Lynn, Mass

336 NOAH[6] EMERY (*Daniel,*[5] *Noah,*[4] *Daniel,*[3] *James,*[2] *Anthony*[1]), son of Daniel and Ann (Emery) Emery ; married Dec 1, 1774, Elizabeth Gould (born March 19, 1749 , died May 24, 1811). He died June 29, 1821.

Children :

898 I NOAH,[7] b July 15, 1775
899 II LOVICY, b Aug 10, 1776
900 III SUSANNAH, b. Feb 13, 1778; d Jan. 30, 1785

901　iv　RICHARD, b Nov 27, 1779, d Jan 27, 1785
902 ꞏ v　SHEM, b Feb 14, 1781, d Feb 19, 1781
903　vi　ENOCH, b Feb 25, 1782, d Sept 16, 1832.
904　vii　SHEM, b Jan 20, 1785, d June 30, 1847.
905　viii　SUSANNAH, b Nov 1, 1786; m Benjamin Brown
906　ix　BLISEY, b Nov 4, 1789 (see No 1192); m Thos Salter Emery
907　x　RICHARD, b March 15, 1791, d the same day

343 GEORGE[6] EMERY (*Daniel,[5] Noah,[4] Daniel,[3] James,[2] Anthony[1]*), son of Daniel and Ann (Emery) Emery; married Sarah Dean. After the Revolution he removed to what is now South Thomaston, died in 1846.

Children.

908　i　SARAH W.[7]
909　ii　LOUISA (LOIS).
910　iii　JOHN b 1788
911　iv　DENNIS, b April 14, 1791
912　v　JONAS, b Jan 27, 1793
913　vi　GEORGE, b 1795.
914　vii　NATHANIEL, d unm
915　viii　DANIEL, b July 26, 1802.
916　ix　WILLIAM D., b June 15, 1804; d in Quincy, Mass, Oct 18, 1883
917　x　MARY m Joseph Pillsbury, 3d; lived in Rockland, Me
918　xi　LUCY, m , 1st, Archibald C Lowell, 2nd Jonathan Post
919　xii　EPHRAIM H , b July 6, 1806, d Aug 9, 1883.

346 NATHANIEL[6] EMERY (*Daniel,[5] Noah,[4] Daniel,[3] James,[2] Anthony[1]*), son of Daniel and Ann (Emery) Emery, married, first, Lucy Crockett (born Aug. 3, 1772; died June 20, 1832), second, 1832, Barbara Sidlinger Whittier (died July 10, 1852). He settled in South Thomaston and afterwards removed to Thorndike, Me , where he died May 21, 1865   He was a very prominent and leading citizen of this place, and held many important offices

Children:

920　i　ANNA,[7] b Nov 21, 1792
921　ii　ELONA, b Nov. 30, 1794, m David Packard; had son Alonzo.
922　iii　TRISTRAM, b April 26, 1796
923　iv　LEVI, b Sept 22, 1798
924　v　THOMAS, b. Sept. 22, 1802, d. April 1, 1803
925　vi　ASA, b Aug 29, 1806
926　vii　STILLMAN S b. Sept 8, 1833
927　viii　OLIVE, b June 24, 1835, d. Oct 12, 1857

347 JOHN[6] EMERY (*Noah,[5] Noah,[4] Daniel,[3] James,[2] Anthony[1]*), son of Noah and Joanna (Perryman) Emery; married Margaret Gookin (born Aug 11, 1745, died in 1788). daughter of Rev Nathaniel Gookin of Northwood, N. H   He died at sea in 1787.

Children, born in Exeter, N. H.:

928　i　HANNAH TRACY,[7] b March 7, 1771
929　ii　ROBERT, b. Sept 20, 1773

348 NOAH[6] EMERY (*Noah,[5] Noah,[4] Daniel,[3] James,[2] Anthony[1]*), son of Noah and Joanna (Perryman) Emery; married Dec 5, 1771, Jane Hale (born May 10, 1751, died June 19, 1813), daughter of

Dr. Eliphalet and Elizabeth (Jackson) Hale. He was conspicuously active in the Revolution and succeeded his father as clerk of the courts for Rockingham county. He died Jan. 6, 1817.

Children :

930 i MARY HALE,[7] b. Sept. 24, 1772; d. in Exeter, Sept. 20, 1856; unm.
931 ii ELIZABETH, b. Oct. 15, 1774; d. in 1779.
932 iii NICHOLAS, b. Sept. 4, 1776.
933 iv JOHN, b. Oct. 29, 1780.
934 v NOAH, b. Dec. 30, 1782; d. in Archangel, Russia, in 1813 (see No. 939).
935 vi JANE, b. Oct. 19, 1788; d. Jan. 19, 1802.
936 vii ELIZABETH PHILLIPS, b. Aug. 15, 1794; d. in Exeter, N. H., May 9, 1883.

349 ELIZABETH[6] EMERY (*Noah,[5] Noah,[4] Daniel,[3] James,[2] Anthony[1]*), daughter of Noah and Joanna (Perryman) Emery; married April 30, 1780, Col. Samuel Folsom, son of Jonathan and Ann (Ladd) Folsom (born Feb. 22, 1732; died May 22, 1790), his second wife. She died Sept. 1, 1805.

Children, born in Exeter :

937 i ANN,[7] b. Feb. 4, 1781; m. Joseph Tilton; d. March 10, 1837.
938 ii SAMUEL, b. June 7, 1783; d. at sea, 1804.
939 iii BETSEY, b. March 26, 1785 (see No. 934).
940 iv JOANNA, b. June 25, 1787; d. May 18, 1875.

353 THERESA[6] EMERY (*Noah,[5] Noah,[4] Daniel,[3] James,[2] Anthony[1]*), daughter of Noah and Joanna (Perryman) Emery; married Oct., 1781, Dr. Joseph Orne. He graduated at Harvard College in 1765; one of the founders of the American Academy of Arts and Sciences; died Jan. 28, 1786. His widow survived him fifty-seven years and died in Exeter, Nov. 14, 1843, aged 82.

Child :

941 i THERESA,[7] b. Aug. 16, 1782; m. Charles Norris of Exeter, N. H.

354 RICHARD[6] EMERY (*Noah,[5] Noah,[4] Daniel,[3] James,[2] Anthony[1]*), son of Noah and Joanna (Perryman) Emery; married Nov. 14, 1784, Liberty Hale, daughter of Eliphalet and Dorothy (Bartlett) Hale, (born April 14, 1766; died Feb. 22, 1829). He was educated at Phillips Exeter Academy, being a member in 1784, the second year of its opening. He was living in Exeter in Feb., 1786, with his wife and a daughter (Catherine Hale), then nearly a year old. Afterwards (year unknown) he sailed on a ship as supercargo; was wrecked, rescued and taken to London "where," he afterwards wrote, " I was pressed in March, 1793." Hard service on the continent, capture and imprisonment followed. A letter written by him on board "H. M. Ship *Triumph*, Portsmo' Harb' (Eng.)," dated Dec. 20, 1804, addressed to his brother Noah and asking his friends to take measures for his liberation, gave the last that was heard of him. Every effort was made in his behalf but in vain.

Child :

942 i CATHERINE HALE,[7] b. March 24, 1785; d. Sept. 7, 1864.

357 SHEM[6] EMERY (*Japhet*,[5] *Noah*,[4] *Daniel*,[3] *James*,[2] *Anthony*[1]),
son of Japhet and Mary (Emery) Emery; married, first, Oct. 19,
1782, Keziah, daughter of John and Adah (Emery) Emery (died
June 26, 1798) ; second, Dec. 23, 1798, Martha Tibbetts, daughter of
Jonathan and Sarah (Emery) Tibbetts of Sanford, Me. (died Dec.
20, 1859, aged 87)   He served more than seven months in 1780, in
Capt. Thomas Bragdon's company, Colonel Prince's regiment, for the
defence of the eastern coast.   There is a tradition in the family that
he was at the "taking of Burgoyne," Oct. 17, 1777.   He died Jan.
16, 1824.

Children :

    943 i   SHEM,[7] b 1783, d in Norfolk, Va
    944 ii   JOSEPH, b. April 21, 1796.

By second marriage :

    945 iii RHODA, b 1799; d , unm , Oct 31, 1822
    946 iv   SALLY, b Sept 5, 1801, m. Samuel Shaw of York, Me , March,
              1844.
    947 v   KEZIAH, b April 25, 1803; m Wright Wigglesworth of Great
              Falls, N H
    948 vi   MARY ANN, m Samuel Hussey of So Berwick, Me
    949 vii RALPH, m Abigail Stevens.
    950 viii SHEM, b Nov. 10, 1813, m Dorcas Witham.

358 JAPHET[6] EMERY (*Japhet*,[5] *Noah*,[4] *Daniel*,[3] *James*,[2] *Anthony*[1]),
son of Japhet and Mary (Emery) Emery , married Feb. 5, 1792, Molly
Shorey ; lived in Eliot, Me.   He died Dec. 21, 1796.
Children, born in Eliot :

    951 i   POLLY,[7] b Oct. 30, 1794.
    952 ii   LYDIA, b Aug 27, 1796, m Simeon Emery (see No 455)
    953 iii JAPHET, b June 17, 1797

361 THEODORE[6] EMERY (*Japhet*,[5] *Noah*,[4] *Daniel*,[3] *James*,[2] *Anthony*[1]),
son of Japhet and Mary (Emery) Emery ; married Polly (see No.
893), daughter of Daniel Emery, jr.   He and his wife were living in
Porter, Me , in 1842.

Children :

    954 i   AUGUSTUS,[7] b Sept 22, 1800; d., unm , Sept. 2, 1824
    955 ii   THEODORE, b Feb 8, 1803
    956 iii   SYRENA, b Dec 15, 1804; d young.
    957 iv   JOHN, b and d Sept 8, 1805
    958 v   MARY. b. Sept 10, 1806
    959 vi   BETSEY CROSBY, b Jan 18, 1809 , d , unm , Aug 18, 1874.
    960 vii   JAPHET, b March 22, 1811 , d. young.
    961 viii ALVAH C , b Sept 20, 1813
    962 ix   NOAH, b. Feb 26, 1816 , d in Sanford, Me , Feb. 27, 1816
    963 x   JOSIAH GILMAN, b Jan 26, 1817
    964 xi   STEPHEN WEBBER, b May 9, 1820
    965 xii   JAPHET, b Oct. 29, 1823.
    966 xiii RHODA AUGUSTA, b. Dec 13, 1826
    967 xiv   EDWIN AUGUSTUS, b April 13, 1830, d in Boston, Mass , Aug
              10, 1834

363 DORCAS[6] LORD (*Martha*,[5] *Simon*,[4] *Daniel*,[3] *James*,[2] *Anthony*[1]),
daughter of Ebenezer and Martha (Emery) Lord; married Moses
Hodsdon.   She died Jan. 19, 1838.

Child :

968 i Isaac,[7] b. Dec. 18, 1781; m. Polly Wentworth, Jan. 24. 1805; lived in Corinth, Me., Capt. U. S. A. 1813-1815 and Maj. Gen. in Maine Militia; Clerk of Courts in Penobscot Co. 1821-1837; d. *s. p.*

368 Nathan[6] Lord(*Martha,[5] Simon,[4] Daniel,[3] James,[2] Anthony[1]*), son of Ebenezer and Martha (Emery) Lord ; married, first, Mercy (Knox) Downs, widow of William Downs; second, Sarah Wingate. Child :

969 i Nathan,[7] m. March 23, 1846, Mary (Twombly) Wentworth.

369 Samuel[6] Lord (*Martha,[5] Simon,[4] Daniel,[3] James,[2] Anthony[1]*), son of Ebenezer and Martha (Emery) Lord ; married, first, March, 1781, Abigail Allen of Rochester, N.H. (died Oct. 25, 1825) ; second, Sept. 7, 1826, Mary (Roberts) Wentworth (born May 12, 1769 ; died May 1, 1858). He died Feb. 8, 1855.

Children :

970 i James,[7] b. Aug. 12, 1782; d. Nov. 30, 1846.
971 ii John, b. Sept. 26, 1785; m. Feb. 12, 1809, Abra Chadwick; d. Mar. 31, 1855.
972 iii Martha, b. Nov. 19, 1789; d. May 26, 1844.
973 iv Hannah, b. April 28, 1792.
974 v Susannah, b. May 28, 1796.
975 vi William Allen, b. March 20, 1801; m. Clarissa Allen, of Milton, N. H.
976 vii Abigail, b. March 1, 1803.
977 viii Samuel, b. Sept. 25, 1805.

370 William Wentworth[6] Lord (*Martha,[5] Simon,[4] Daniel,[3] James,[2] Anthony[1]*), son of Ebenezer and Martha (Emery) Lord ; married. first, Mary (Garland) Allen ; second, Mercy (Corson) Langdon. Children, by first marriage :

978 i Sally,[7] m. Jedediah Ricker.
979 ii Mary, m. Charles Ricker.

374 Tirzah[6] Lord (*Martha,[5] Simon,[4] Daniel,[3] James,[2] Anthony[1]*), daughter of Ebenezer and Martha (Emery) Lord ; married Sept. 24, 1794, Simon Tibbetts of Sanford, Me., son of Capt. Jonathan and Sarah (Emery) Tibbetts, who was daughter of Simon and Martha (Lord) Emery. She died Sept. 19, 1863, aged 94 years.

Child :

980 i Jane,[7] m. William Fernald.

380 Jeremiah[6] Emery (*Simon,[5] Simon,[4] Daniel,[3] James,[2] Anthony[1]*), son of Simon and Elizabeth (Bean) Emery ; married, first, April 10, 1776, Anna Pray (born May, 1754 ; died Sept. 17, 1812) ; second, Sept. 23, 1841, Mary Boothby of Limerick, Me. He was a prominent man in the early history of Shapleigh, Me. ; delegate to the Convention for adopting the Constitution of the United States, voting "nay ;" representative to the General Court, 1788, 1808, 1809, 1812. Selectman, 1796-1802, 1805-1806 and 1810. He died in Acton, Aug. 20, 1848.

Children, born in Shapleigh, Me :

981 i JACOB [7]
982 ii JEREMIAH, b 1789.
983 iii WILLIAM
984 iv SIMON.
985 v JAMES b Oct 11, 1793
986 vi ELIZABETH, b July 20. 1789, d July 19, 1868
987 vii MARTHA, b. Aug 3, 1797, d May, 1851, in Bangor, Me.

383 REV. SIMON[6] EMERY (*Simon,*[5] *Simon,*[4] *Daniel,*[3] *James,*[2] *Anthony*[1]), son of Simon and Elizabeth (Bean) Emery; married, first, Molly Hodskins; second, Mrs. Lydia Bickford, third, Mrs. Sarah Stubbs.

Children .

988 i LYDIA [7]
989 ii BETSEY.

384 MOSES[6] EMERY (*Simon,*[5] *Simon,*[4] *Daniel,*[3] *James,*[2] *Anthony*[1]), son of Simon and Elizabeth (Bean) Emery, married Dec. 14. 1785, Betsey Parsons (died Sept 25, 1852), daughter of William Parsons of Alfred, Me. He died Oct. 16, 1827, aged 59 years.

Children :

990 i JOHN,[7] left home for Norfolk, Va., and never was heard from.
991 ii HUMPHREY E , lost at sea
992 iii BETSEY E , b 1788; m Wm. Emery (see No 1193)
993 iv MARTHA E , m. William Greenleaf of Cambridge, Mass
994 v SIMON. b Feb. 5, 1790; m Mary Lord (b Sept 3, 1797)
995 vi EDWARD, b. Dec. 5, 1801.

394 GIDEON[6] RICKER (*Margaret,*[5] *Simon,*[4] *Daniel,*[3] *James,*[2] *Anthony*[1]), son of Noah and Margaret (Emery) Ricker; married Mary Buzzell; moved to Waterboro, Me , afterward to Vermont, 1839. Children, born in Berwick, Me. :

996 i RUTH [7] b May 4, 1796.
997 ii GIDEON, b April, 1798, d. young.
998 iii THOMAS, b Feb 9, 1801.
999 iv DAVID, b Aug 8, 1803
1000 v THEODOTE, b March, 1806, m Edmund Cole.
1001 vi PHŒBE, b Oct , 1808
1002 vii GIDEON, b July 25, 1811.

395 STEPHEN[6] EMERY (*Stephen,*[5] *Simon,*[4] *Daniel,*[3] *James,*[2] *Anthony*[1]), son of Elder Stephen and Sarah (Hodgdon) Emery, married, first, Sept. 8, 1775, Sarah, daughter of Daniel and Sarah (Shackley) Emery; second, March 6, 1783, Mary (Libby) Sharples (born in Portsmouth, N. H , 1759), widow of John Sharples He joined the Shakers at Alfred, left them, returned and again left them. He died in Gorham, Me , 1830.

Children, born in Kittery, Me :

1003 i HOSEA,[7] b Dec. 17, 1776
1004 ii DANIEL, bapt March 9, 1786
1005 iii SARAH, bapt March 9, 1786.

23

By second marriage :

1006 iv OLIVER, b. in Shapleigh, Me., removed to Ellisburg, Jefferson
           Co., N. Y.
1007   v MAY, b. in Alfred, Me., 1784; d. Sept. 8, 1845, among the Shak-
           ers.
1008 vi SOPHIA, b. in Alfred, Me., Aug. 28, 1785; d. among the Shakers,
           Oct. 16, 1834.
1009 vii HIRAM, b. in Alfred, Me., 1790; d. among the Alfred Shakers,
           Dec. 19, 1812.
1010 viii ROBERT, b. in Alfred, Me., May 10, 1799; d. among the Shak-
           ers, Feb. 5, 1826.
1011 ix CATHARINE, b. in Alfred, Me.; d. in Saco, 1878.
1012   x CALVIN, b. in Biddeford, Me., Dec. 3, 1806.

396 JOSHUA[6] EMERY (*Stephen,[5] Simon,[4] Daniel,[3] James,[2] Anthony[1]*),
son of Elder Stephen and Sarah (Hodgdon) Emery ; married, first,
Sept. 3, 1778, Tirzah, daughter of Zachariah and Huldah (Bean)
Emery ; second, —— Hall. Removed from Alfred to Windham, Me.,
1807. He had the first pottery in Alfred. Lived among the Shakers.
He was in Capt. Samuel Leighton's company, Col. James Scammon's
regiment in 1775, eight months. This is probably the Joshua, who
married Abigail Whitney in 1809, and died in Gorham, Me., April 6,
1827.

Children :

1013   i MARY.[7]
1014 ii JANE.
1015 iii HANNAH.
1016 iv SARAH.
1017   v JAMES.
1018 vi ELIJAH, b. Jan. 3, 1793, in Alfred.
1019 vii ELISHA.

By second marriage :

1020 viii LUCRETIA.
1021 ix HANNAH.

397 JACOB[6] EMERY (*Stephen,[5] Simon,[4] Daniel,[3] James,[2] Anthony[1]*),
son of Elder Stephen and Sarah (Hodgdon) Emery ; married Jan. 3,
1779, Huldah Thompson of York. He volunteered in Dec., 1775, to
serve one year under Capt. Silas Wilde in Col. Phinney's regiment.
He died in 1844.

Children, born in Waterboro, Me. :

1022   i SALLY,[7] b. Sept. 21, 1779.
1023 ii JOHN, b. June 30, 1782.
1024 iii HANNAH, b. 1784; a leading member among the Shakers; d.
           in Alfred, Me., Jan. 2, 1859.
1025 iv LUCY, b. June 16, 1786.
1026   v PATIENCE, b. 1788; d. at New Gloucester, Me., Dec. 23, 1848;
           an overseer among the Shakers, distinguished for piety and
           refinement.
1027 vi HULDAH, b. Oct. 21, 1791.
1028 vii POLLY, b. 1793.
1029 viii JACOB, b. April 6, 1796.
1030 ix THATCHER, b. April 10, 1800.

398 SIMON[6] EMERY (*Stephen,[5] Simon,[4] Daniel,[3] James,[2] Anthony[1]*),
son of Elder Stephen and Sarah (Hodgdon) Emery ; married March,

1785, Martha Nowell (died March 8, 1841, aged 80).   He died July 10, 1831

Children :

    1031   i   JOHN,[7] b 1793, in York.
    1032   ii   PETER, b. June 29, 1794.
    1033   iii   HENRY
    1034   iv   SOPHIA, lived in Salem, Mass ; unm.
    1035   v   MARTHA
    1036   vi   SALLY
    1037   vii   ALZINA

399 ABIGAIL[6] EMERY (*Stephen*,[5] *Simon*,[4] *Daniel*,[3] *James*,[2] *Anthony*[1]), daughter of Elder Stephen and Sarah (Hodgdon) Emery, married Ebenezer Nowell of York, Me. (published in Kittery, Me., June 29, 1793).

Children :

    1038   i   OLIVER [7]
    1039   ii   NATHANIEL
    1040   iii   FOXWELL.
    1041   iv   ROSWELL.
    1042   v   THOMAS
    1043   vi   JOSIAH
    1044   vii   MINDWELL

400 PRUDENCE[6] EMERY (*Stephen*,[5] *Simon*,[4] *Daniel*,[3] *James*,[2] *Anthony*[1]), daughter of Elder Stephen and Sarah (Hodgdon) Emery ; married March 18, 1791, Israel Emery, son of Samuel and Abigail (Shackley) Emery (died Oct. 29, 1829).   Lived in Emery Town, Eliot, Me.

Children :

    1045   i   THOMAS,[7] m. Abigail Caswell, Feb 24, 1822   Three sons
    1046   ii   DANIEL, m Dolly Hutchins, published Jan 2, 1824.   Four
                     children
    1047   iii   JOSHUA, b. July 12, 1792.
    1048   iv   ELIOT
    1049   v   ALVIN, b 1811
    1050   vi   JOSEPH.
    1051   vii   WILLIAM.
    1052   viii JANE
    1053   ix   CAROLINE
    1054   x   TIRZAH, unm
    1054a xi   HORATIO

401 GEORGE[6] EMERY (*Stephen*,[5] *Simon*,[4] *Daniel*,[3] *James*,[2] *Anthony*[1]), son of Elder Stephen and Sarah (Hodgdon) Emery ; married Betsey Pierce (born April 13, 1772), published in Kittery, Me., Sept. 26, 1794.

Children :

    1055   i   ALMIRA,[7] b about 1795
    1056   ii   MARY ANN L , b. May 25, 1800
    1057   iii   THATCHER, b Feb. 22, 1801.
    1058   iv   JAMES W., b. 1805; d July 27, 1876; m. Frances M. Tucker-
                     man.

405 ICHABOD[6] EMERY (*Stephen,[5] Simon,[4] Daniel,[3] James,[2] Anthony[1]*), son of Elder Stephen and Sarah (Hodgdon) Emery; married Nov. 25, 1804, Mary Tetherly (born, 1792; died in Portsmouth, N. H., Dec. 10, 1834). He died Oct. 21, 1825, in York, Me.

Children :

1059   i   ELIZA ANN,[7] b. Oct. 13, 1808; m. Nov. 3, 1833, William B. Sherburn; d. Oct. 10, 1845.
1060   ii   ALFRED, b. April 29, 1811; d. Nov. 15, 1870; m. Sarah Perry, May, 1833.
1061   iii   MARY JANE, b. Nov. 28, 1814; m., 1st, Samuel Sherburn; 2nd, Peter Emery (see No. 1032).
1062   iv   STEPHEN DECATUR, b. May 7, 1818. Went west among the Indians, 1849; afterwards to California.
1063   v   GEORGE ALEXANDER, b. Feb. 5, 1821.
1064   vi   CHARLES H., b. Aug. 3, 1824; m. Nov. 19, 1855, Mary Y. Holman; d. April 28, 1866.

406 SAMUEL[6] EMERY (*Samuel,[5] Simon,[4] Daniel,[3] James,[2] Anthony[1]*), son of Samuel and Abigail (Shackley) Emery; married Oct. 21, 1784, Eunice Ferguson, sister to his father's second wife. Lived in Eliot, Me.

Children :

1065   i   PEGGY (MARGARET);[7] m. James Warren of Eliot, Me.
1066   ii   HANNAH, d. unm.
1067   iii   LEVI, d. unm.

407 SIMON[6] EMERY (*Samuel,[5] Simon,[4] Daniel,[3] James,[2] Anthony[1]*), son of Samuel and Abigail (Shackley) Emery; married Dec. 23, 1781, Elizabeth Mendum. Lived in Eliot, Me.

Children :

1068   i   ABIGAIL,[7] m. Daniel Grant of South Berwick, March 13, 1821.
1069   ii   ANN, m. Benjamin Goodwin of South Berwick.
1070   iii   SOPHIA, m. Mark Spinney of Portsmouth, N. H.
1071   iv   LUCY, m. May 3, 1825, Mark Spinney; his second wife.
1072   v   JANE, m. James Crockett of Great Falls, N. H.
1073   vi   THOMAS, b. Sept. 29, 1797.
1074   vii   SAMUEL, m. Betsey Norton, pub. in Kittery, Me., Oct. 21, 1804.
1075   viii ROBERT.
1076   ix   WILLIAM.

408 ISAAC[6] EMERY (*Samuel,[5] Simon,[4] Daniel,[3] James,[2] Anthony[1]*), son of Samuel and Abigail (Shackley) Emery; married Dec. 19, 1782, Elizabeth, daughter of Joseph Kingsbury (by his first wife). Removed in 1802 to South Parsonsfield, Me. He died Nov. 22, 1825. Farmer. She died Feb. 15, 1846. All the children but the two youngest were born in what is now Eliot, Me., formerly Kittery.

Children :

1077   i   JOSEPH,[7] b. July 26, 1788; d. at sea Aug. 19, 1821, on the voyage from the West Indies to Boston; unm.
1078   ii   HANNAH, b. March 7, 1791; m. David Campbell of Wakefield, N. H; d. Aug., 1876. Had a son Joseph.
1079   iii   LOVEY, b. Sept. 26, 1792; d., unm., Feb. 3, 1883.
1080   iv   MARY, b. Jan. 11, 1795; d. Nov. 4, 1857.
1081   v   HIRAM, b. Oct. 25, 1796; d. in Falmouth, Me., Oct. 31, 1876.

1082 vi WILLIAM, b. April 2, 1799, d. Apr. 25, 1884, in South Parsons-
          field
1083 vii IVORY, b. Aug 19, 1802, d , nnm , March 4, 1890, in South
          Parsonsfield
1084 viii TEMPLE H . b Aug 19, 1804, m Sarah Weymouth

413 JOSHUA[6] EMERY (*John,[5] Simon,[4] Daniel,[3] James,[2] Anthony[1]*) ,
son of John and Adah (Emery) Emery; married Aug. 21, 1788, Hannah Goodwin, daughter of Jedediah and Hannah (Emery) Goodwin
(In the record at Alfred, Me., he is called Joshua, jr.)
Children :

1085 i   ADAH,[7] b Jan , 1789, m. Stephen Chase of Portland, Me , June
          10, 1810.
1086 ii   TIRZAH, b June, 1791, m. Jonathan Chase of Portland, Me ,
          Feb 3, 1811
1087 iii KEZIAH, b Mar., 1793, m Samuel Stone of York, Me , March
          16, 1820.
1088 iv   JOSHUA, d in infancy
1089 v   SOPHIA b Jan , 1796, m John Thurrell of Berwick, Me
1090 vi   HANNAH, b Feb , 1798
1091 vii CLARISSA, } b June, 1800, { m Joshua Chase, Feb. 16, 1819.
1092 viii SERENA,   }   { m Tho Hanscom, Nov. 19, 1819.
1093 ix   MARY, b. Sept , 1802, m. John Bartlett of Portsmouth, N. H.
1094 x   JOHN, b Oct 2, 1804; drowned March 30, 1824
1095 xi   ELIZA JANE, b April 5, 1809; m. Joseph Emery (see No. 944).

414 POLLY[6] EMERY (*John,[5] Simon,[4] Daniel,[3] James,[2] Anthony[1]*),
daughter of John and Adah (Emery) Emery, married Dec. 11, 1787,
Elijah Blaisdell, jr. He made his will Jan. 27, 1814, proved Aug. 9,
1824.
Children .

1096 i   DORCAS [7]
1097 ii   THEODORE.
1098 iii ELIJAH.
1099 iv   SAMUEL.
1100 v   JOSEPH
1101 vi   RUTH, m Jotham Blaisdell.

438 MARTHA[6] EMERY (*Charles,[5] Simon,[4] Daniel,[3] James,[2] An-
thony[1]*), daughter of Charles and Ann (Hodgdon) Emery , married
Aug 3, 1786, Jonathan Welch (born 1761 , died March 28, 1839).
She died in Groton, Vt , July 30, 1834.
Children, born in Groton, Vt., except first three :

1102 i   HOSEA,[7] b in Sanford, Me , April 26, 1787; m Sept. 8, 1808,
          Polly Gray of Groton. Vt.
1103 ii   BETSEY, b in Shapleigh, Me , Jan. 18, 1789, m Enoch Page;
          d in Groton, Vt
1104 iii ANNA, b. in Shapleigh, Me , May 20, 1791; m John Whitehill
          of Scotland; d April 14, 1826
1105 iv   MEDAD, b March 9, 1793, m. in Groton, Vt , March 9, 1815,
          Abigail Hosmer
1106 v   PATTY, b Jan 22, 1795; d Nov 3, 1799 in Groton, Vt
1107 vi   JOEL, b March 8, 1797; d Nov 10, 1800
1108 vii RUTH, b. Nov. 17, 1799, m in Groton, Vt., Aug 11, 1817,
          William Vance , d Dec. 5, 1869
1109 viii JOEL, b Feb. 19, 1802, m. in Groton, Vt , July 22, 1824, Eliz-
          abeth Lunt. Went west.

1110 ix JONATHAN, b April 12, 1803; m. Jan. 31, 1839, Martha Mor-
          rison; d. Nov. 16, 1871.
1111 x   DAVID, b. May 14, 1808; m. in Corinth, Vt., Dec. 24, 1829,
          Dolly Titus; d. June 10, 1879.

439 JOHN[6] EMERY (*Charles,[5] Simon,[4] Daniel,[3] James,[2] Anthony[1]*),
son of Charles and Ann (Hodgdon) Emery; married in Shapleigh,
Me., Feb. 4, 1788, Sally Parker (born Jan. 31, 1768). He died Dec.
13, 1857, in Groton, Vt.
  Children, born in Groton, Vt., except the first two :

1112 i   CALEB,[7] b. Jan. 13, 1789, in Shapleigh, Me.
1113 ii   NOAH, b. July 18, 1791, in Newbury, Vt.
1114 iii JOHN, b. Nov. 28, 1794; m.; d. Feb. 8, 1884; wife and children
          d. soon after marriage.
1115 iv   SIMON, b. Feb. 22, 1797.
1116 v   CHARLES, b. April 4, 1799.
1117 vi   BETSEY, b. Oct. 15, 1800; m. in Groton, March 14, 1827,
          John Whitehill, 3rd.
1118 vii SAMUEL P., b. June 30, 1803; d. in Topsham, Vt., Dec. 12,
          1884.
1119 viii ANNA, b. June 21, 1805.
1120 ix   SALLY, b. Sept. 26, 1807; d. Aug. 15, 1811, in Groton, Vt.
1121 x   JOSHUA, b. June 16, 1812; d. July 22, 1880, at Money Creek,
          Minn.

440 BETSEY[6] EMERY (*Charles,[5] Simon,[4] Daniel,[3] James,[2] Anthony[1]*), daughter of Charles and Ann (Hodgdon) Emery; married
Jan. 25, 1790, Bradbury Morrison of Sanford, Me. (born 1766; died
April 20, 1810). Removed from Sanford, Me., to Groton, Vt., about
1796. He died Nov. 13, 1844.
  Children, born in Sanford, Me., and Groton, Vt. :

1122 i   CHARLES,[7] b. Dec. 25, 1790; m., 1st, Sally Rhodes; 2nd, Eliza-
          beth Crown; 3rd, Sally Page; d. April 1, 1867.
1123 ii   BETSEY, b. Aug. 15, 1792; m. Jan. 16, 1816, Isaiah Frost; his
          second wife; d. Oct. 15, 1857.
1124 iii ABRAHAM, b. Aug. 2, 1794; m. March 6, 1819, Martha Town-
          send; d. July 23, 1875.
1125 iv   SALLY, b. Aug. 17, 1796; m. Dec. 4, 1817, Jacob Hatch; d. Dec.
          9, 1875.
1126 v   NANCY, b. Oct. 10, 1798; m. May, 1818, Samuel Plummer; d.
          Feb. 5, 1871.
1127 vi   JOSEPH,   } b. Oct. 10, 1801 ; { m. Sally Darling; d. Sept. 18, 1842.
1128 vii BRADLEY, }   { m. Jan. 13, 1830, Avis D. Jones; d.
                                           Nov. 30, 1879.
1129 viii TIMOTHY, b. Feb. 8, 1805; m., 1st, Olive Paul; 2nd, Sarah
          Rhodes; d. June 24, 1882.
1130 ix   MERIBAH, b. May 10, 1807; m. April 7, 1830, Joseph Ricker.
1131 x   MARTHA, b. Nov. 11, 1809; m. Jan. 31, 1839, Jonathan Welch
          (see No. 1110).

441 TIMOTHY[6] EMERY (*Charles,[5] Simon,[4] Daniel,[3] James,[2] Anthony[1]*), son of Charles and Ann (Hodgdon) Emery; married Dec.
6, 1792, Mary Wilson of Shapleigh, Me. (born Dec. 22, 1773). He
removed to Groton, Vt., with his father; died there Oct. 15, 1844.
  Children, born in Groton, except the first two :

1132 i   MARTHA,[7] b. March 22, 1793, in Sanford.
1133 ii   ANDREW, b. April 15, 1795, in Sanford.

1134　iii　Phœbe, b May 7, 1798
1135　iv　Timothy, b April 24, 1801, d Sept 17, 1806.
1136　v　Polly, b Jan 2, 1805, m Ross Parker; d. July, 1805.
1137　vi　Timothy, b April 24, 1807
1138　vii　Lydia, b July 12, 1809
1139　viii　Esther, b March 24 1812.
1140　ix　Isaiah, b. Dec. 6, 1814.

442 Polly[6] Emery (*Charles*,[5] *Simon*,[4] *Daniel*,[3] *James*,[2] *Anthony*[1]), daughter of Charles and Ann (Hodgdon) Emery; married (published Jan. 21, 1793) James Hooper (born March, 1770, died Sept. 16, 1848) She died in Groton, Vt., Dec. 28, 1828.
Children :

1141　i　Anna,[7] b July 31, 1793.
1142　ii　Polly, b. Nov 3, 1794, d , unm , July 4, 1873
1143　iii　Peggy, b June 15, 1796
1144　iv　Susannah, b July 24, 1798, m. Jona. Lund, June 30, 1835, d Jan 30, 1870
1145　v　Meribah, b March 11, 1801.
1146　vi　Betsey, b. May 17. 1803
1147　vii　James, b June 8, 1805, d Feb 16, 1811.
1148　viii　John, b. May 5, 1807, m Betsey Welch of Groton, May 5, 1836
1149　ix　Asenath b Sept 29, 1809.
1150　x　Lois, b May 9, 1811.
1151　xi　Elijah, b. Aug , 1814

447 William[6] Emery (*James*,[5] *Zachariah*,[4] *Daniel*,[3] *James*,[2] *Anthony*[1]), son of James and his second wife Mehitable (Emery) Emery; married in 1785, Sarah Maguire of New Gloucester, Me. , removed to Poland, Me.; died Mar. 19, 1862.
Children :

1152　i　Betsey,[7] b Jan. 14, 1787, in New Gloucester,
1153　ii　William, b March 15, 1789 in New Gloucester; m. Hannah Fernald, d Dec 9, 1831
1154　iii　Sally, b. Feb. 23 1791, in New Gloucester.
1155　iv　Polly, b Sept 28, 1792, in New Gloucester, m Joshua Lunt
1156　v　Eunice, b July 23, 1794, in New Gloucester , m Isaiah Dunn
1157　vi　Rachel, b. Aug 4, 1796, in Poland, d 1799.
1158　vii　Mehitable, b May 22, 1798, in Poland.
1159　viii　Thankful, b Jan 9, 1800, in Poland.
1160　ix　John, b March 5, 1802, in Poland
1161　x　Celia, b Aug 11, 1804, in Poland, d 1805
1162　xi　Eliphalet, b April 26, 1806, in Poland; m Elizabeth Stephens
1163　xii　Esther b July 14, 1808, in Poland, d 1815
1164　xiii　Rebecca, b Oct. 20, 1810, in Poland, m John Tenney of Raymond, Me
1165　xiv　Jane, b Jan 12, 1813, in Poland, m W. E Morton of Portland, Me.

448 Mark[6] Emery (*James*,[5] *Zachariah*,[4] *Daniel*,[3] *James*,[2] *Anthony*[1]), son of James and his second wife Mehitable (Emery) Emery; married May 17, 1789, Anne Maguire of New Gloucester, Me (died June 2, 1865). He removed to Poland, Me. , died May 18, 1814.
Children, born in Poland, Me. :

1166　i　Nancy,[7] b. 1789, m William Barton of Raymond, Me
1167　ii　Mark b March 24, 1791.

1168 iii JANE, b. April 3, 1794.
1169 iv SALLIE, b. June 26, 1795; m. Moses Hodgdon.
1170 v HANNAH, b. March 1, 1797.
1171 vi JAMES, b. June 6, 1799.
1172 vii RACHEL, b. April 18, 1802.
1173 viii CLARA, b. June 2, 1807; m. Nathan Dawes of New Gloucester, Me. Had three children.
1174 ix ELIZA, b. April 18, 1811; m. Jefferson Dawes of New Gloncester, Me. Had two children.

455 SIMEON[6] EMERY (*James,*[5] *Zachariah,*[4] *Daniel,*[3] *James,*[2] *Anthony*[1]), son of James and his third wife Catharine (Frye-Jenkins) Emery; married Oct. 13, 1811, Lydia Emery, daughter of Japhet and Molly (Shorey) Emery. Lived in Eliot, Me.; died July 30, 1867.
Children:

1175 i MARY JANE,[7] b. April 1, 1814; m. Asa Gowen, Oct. 30, 1836.
1176 ii WILLIAM H., b. March 24, 1816.
1177 iii LYDIA, b. Nov. 16, 1818.
1178 iv GEORGE W., b. Feb. 12, 1821.
1179 v OLIVER P., b. April 24, 1823.
1180 vi ALMIRA, b. March 9, 1825; d. Sept. 22, 1825.
1181 vii CATHARINE, b. Oct. 5, 1826; d. Jan. 9, 1856.
1182 viii JAMES, b. Nov. 9, 1829; d. Sept. 4, 1830.
1183 ix PAULINA, b. Nov. 29, 1830.
1184 x CHARLES A., b. July 24, 1833; d. in the army Aug. 29, 1863.

464 THOMAS[6] EMERY (*Zachariah,*[5] *Zachariah,*[4] *Daniel,*[3] *James,*[2] *Anthony*[1]), son of Zachariah and Huldah (Bean) Emery; married Sarah Knox. He died in 1802, from wounds received in the Revolutionary war.
Children:

1185 i REUBEN KNOX,[7] b. in 1800.
1186 ii HULDAH (see Appendix A).

465 REV. RICHARD[6] EMERY (*Zachariah,*[5] *Zachariah,*[4] *Daniel,*[3] *James,*[2] *Anthony*[1]), son of Zachariah and Huldah (Bean) Emery; married, first, May 19, 1803, Dorcas Card (born in Portsmouth, N. H., Aug. 28, 1777; died March 27, 1831); second, Aug. 21, 1831, Lucy Blaisdell (died May, 1860). He was a Free Baptist minister and preached in Alfred, Lyman and Waterborough, between 1821 and 1847. He died March 29, 1854, in Limerick, Me.
Children:

1187 i OLIVE,[7] b. Aug. 27, 1807; m. Henry H. McKenney of Saco, Me., 1839.
1188 ii ISAAC, b. Oct. 7, 1812.
1189 iii KEZIAH, b. Dec., 1814.
1190 iv REUBEN, b. Aug. 22, 1817 (see Appendix A).

466 WILLIAM[6] EMERY (*Caleb,*[5] *Caleb,*[4] *Daniel,*[3] *James,*[2] *Anthony*[1]), son of Caleb and Elizabeth (Gowen) Emery; married Dec. 3, 1786, Mary Salter (born March 8, 1761; died May 2, 1842), daughter of Capt. Titus Salter of Portsmouth, N. H. He died March 2, 1848.
Children, born in Sanford:

1191   ı   CALEB,[7] b June 17, 1787.
1192   ıı   THOMAS S , b May 13, 1789.
1193   ııı   WILLIAM, b. April 10, 1791
1194   ıv   JOHN S , b June 11, 1793
1195   v   ELIZABETH B., b Aug 1, 1795, m Oct 5, 1817, Henry Hamil-
      ton, jr (b. Nov 2, 1787; d Nov 25, 1825) She d April 2,
      1818
1196   vı   MARY A , b Nov 3, 1797, d Aug 29, 1882, unm
1197   vıı   HANNAH B., b Sept. 16, 1799
1198   vııı   SARAH, b Dec 10, 1801
1199   ıx   ABIGAIL, b March 31, 1804, d Oct. 1, 1825, unm
1200   x   SAMUEL B., b Aug. 29, 1806

467 ELIZABETH[6] EMERY(*Caleb,[5] Caleb,[4] Daniel,[3] James.[2] Anthony[1]*),
daughter of Caleb and Elizabeth (Gowen) Emery, married April 6,
1794, Jesse Colcord (born in New Market, N. H., Feb 9, 1769 ; died
April 3, 1835). She was his second wife. She died Dec. 6, 1829.
Children :
1201   ı   ELIZABETH,[7] b. Nov 30, 1794, in Sanford.
1202   ıı   DAVID, b. April 28, 1796, in Sanford
1203   ııı   MARY H., b April 27, 1798, in Sanford
1204   ıv   BETSEY, b. July 13, 1800, in Sanford; d Dec 8, 1800.
1205   v   RHODA E., b March 16, 1802, in Sanford, d April 27, 1802
1206   vı   JESSE, b April 8, 1803, in Sanford; d Nov 25, 1825, unm
1207   vıı   PHINEAS, b Feb 8, 1806, in Kennebunk, m Nancy Garland,
      d , *s p* , Aug. 21, 1846.
1208   vııı   SUSAN N , b. Dec. 4, 1808, in Porter, d , unm , July 18, 1832.
1209   ıx   ISABELLA, b June 5, 1811, in Porter.
1210   x   CALEB E , b March 4, 1814
1211   xı   CHARLOTTE, b. Feb 18, 1817.

468 JANE[6] FROST (*Jane,[5] Caleb,[4] Daniel,[3] James,[2] Anthony[1]*),
daughter of Simon, jr., and Jane (Emery) Frost ; married about 1796,
William Nason of Sanford (died in 1830, in Monmouth, Me.).
Children, born in Sanford, Me :
1212   ı   SAMUEL,[7] d. March 11, 1815
1213   ıı   MARY S., d. young.
1214   ııı   JANE E.
1215   ıv   SUSAN, d May, 1814.
1216   v   WILLIAM II , b. 1804, m. in 1828, Mary H Norris; began to
      preach in 1831, licensed, 1842, d in West Springfield, N. H.,
      March 28, 1877
1217   vı   LYDIA F
1218   vıı   NATHANIEL F , b in 1808, m M H Richardson, dau of An-
      drew Richardson of Clinton, Me , began to preach about
      1840 as a Christian Baptist, but in 1848 became an Adventist.
1219   vııı   SOPHIA F , b 1811, d. Oct 20, 1812
1220   ıx   JOSEPH F., lived in Hallowell, Me.
1221   x   HANNAH F
1222   xı   SAMUEL S., b in 1818, entered the ministry at 19 years of age ;
      d in Bangor, Me., July 3, 1865
1223   xıı   SIMON F.

470 HENRY T.[6] EMERY (*Caleb,[5] Caleb,[4] Daniel,[3] James,[2] Anthony[1]*),
son of Caleb and Mary (James) Emery, married, first, Jan. 1, 1808,
Elizabeth Morrill (died Nov., 1824), daughter of Isaac Morrill of
Berwick, second, 1825, Mercy E. Stover of Deer Island, N. B. Removed to Sanford, Me. ; engaged in the West Indies trade ; was cap-

tured by the British during the war of 1812 ; engaged in business in
Eastport, Me., in 1836 ; became a farmer.

Children, by first marriage :

   1224 i   HENRY,[7] b. Nov. 10, 1808, in Sanford.
   1225 ii   FRANKLIN, b. Aug 10, 1810, in Sanford; m., 1st, Sophia Jen-
              kins ; 2nd, Mary Elizabeth Emery ; d. *s. p.* Lawyer and writer.
   1226 iii ELIZABETH, b. March, 1816, in Berwick; d., unm., 1858, in
              Lowell.
   1227 iv ANN, b. 1818, in Eastport; m. James Kellan of Bangor, Me.
   1228 v   WILLIAM H., b. 1820, in Eastport; d., unm., 1847.
   1229 vi JOHN W., b. Nov. 15, 1822, in Eastport.

By second marriage :

   1230 vii ADELINE, b. Feb. 19, 1827, in Deer Island, N. B.
   1231 viii ROBERT S., b. Aug. 20, 1829.
   1232 ix MARY JANE, b. June 28, 1831; m. Sept. 14, 1851, Nathaniel
              McDonald.
   1233 x   CALEB JAMES, b. March 27, 1833, in Perry, Wash. Co., Me. ;
              m. March 29, 1883, Marion L. Leslie (b. in Baltimore,
              Md., July 22, 1858), dau. of Capt. John and Elnora (Little)
              Leslie (b. in Richmond, Va., May 30, 1836). Engaged in the
              printing business in Baltimore for thirty years.
   1234 xi SABINE, b. Feb. 28, 1835.
   1235 xii OLIVER, b. July 30, 1837.
   1236 xiii FRED AUGUSTUS, b. July 4, 1839.
   1237 xiv IVORY, b. May 9, 1843.

471 CALEB[6] EMERY (*Caleb,[5] Caleb,[4] Daniel,[3] James,[2] Anthony[1]*),
son of Caleb and Mary (James) Emery ; married Elizabeth Hurd
(born June 10, 1786 ; died in Hudson, N. Y., Sept. 20, 1877). Trader
in Sanford and Lebanon, Me. ; deputy sheriff.

Children :

   1238 i   MARY ELIZABETH,[7] b. July 23, 1814 ; unm.
   1239 ii   MARIA ANTONETTE, b. June 7, 1816 ; d. April 11, 1825.
   1240 iii LOUISA JANE, b. April 25, 1818 ; m. J. Dudley.
   1241 iv MARIA ANTONETTE, b. April 11, 1822 ; m. Charles Putney.
   1242 v   CALEB JAMES, b May 28, 1825.
   1243 vi HENRY L., b. June 9, 1824 ; d. Sept. 18, 1826.
   1244 vii CLARA AUGUSTA, b. June 9, 1827 ; m. Joseph Turner.
   1245 viii SARAH ADELINE, b. Oct. 12, 1830 ; d. May 25, 1845.

481 EMERY[6] GOODWIN (*Hannah,[5] Rev. Joshua,[4] Daniel,[3] James,[2]
Anthony[1]*), son of Jedediah and Hannah (Emery) Goodwin ; married Polly Hamilton.

Children :

   1246 i   GEORGE W.,[7] b. Feb. 12, 1799 ; m. June, 1824, Cyrena Hodsdon.
   1247 ii   FANNY, b. June 24, 1800 ; m. Aug. 11, 1822, Samuel Guptail.
   1248 iii IVORY, b. Dec. 28, 1803 ; m. Jan. 18, 1824, Jerusha Tannt ; d.
              Feb. 19, 1864.
   1249 iv JOHN W., b. July 15, 1804 ; m. Dec. 24, 1826, Sally Jenkins.

491 MERCY[6] EMERY (*James,[5] Joseph,[4] Job,[3] James,[2] Anthony[1]*),
daughter of James and Mercy (Bean) Emery ; married Thomas Meserve of Scarborough, Me.

Children :

   1250 i   MOSES,[7] d. young.
   1251 ii   LYDIA, b. 1775; d. 1816.

1252   iii   THOMAS
1253   iv   MERCY, b 1783, m Jacob McDaniel, who m her sister Lydia

492 DANIEL[6] EMERY (*James,[5] Joseph,[4] Job,[3] James,[2] Anthony[1]*), son of James and Mercy (Bean) Emery; married Sarah Moulton
  Children:

1254   i   JONATHAN,[7] b Nov 24, 1779
1255   ii   COMFORT, m June 21, 1804, George Strout
1256   iii MERCY, m Nathaniel Rice, jr, Aug 25, 1808
1257   iv   MARY DOW, m Phineas Harmon
1258   v   JOSIAH
Five other children, Nos. 1259-1263, who d. in infancy

494 BENJAMIN[6] EMERY (*James,[5] Joseph,[4] Job.[3] James,[2] Anthony[1]*), son of James and Mercy (Bean) Emery; married, first, Mary Moulton, sister of Sarah Moulton, wife of his brother Daniel, second,——— Milliken.
  Children:

1264   i   MERCY[7]
1265   ii   SALLY
1266   iii WILLIAM, b. Nov. 17, 1792, d. Sept. 16, 1876

495 JAMES[6] EMERY (*James,[5] Joseph,[4] Job,[3] James,[2] Anthony[1]*), son of James and Mercy (Bean) Emery, married, first, Hannah Dunn, of Cornish, Me.; second, Sarah Fogg (born June 20, 1768, died 1840), removed from Gorham to Limerick, Me., when Limerick was thinly settled, about 1783.   He died in 1844.
  Children:

1267   i   NATHANIEL,[7] b July, 1786; d 1803.
1268   ii   JOSHUA, b Sept 19, 1788, d Jan 16, 1858.
1269   iii HANNAH, d. young, 1790
1270   iv   JAMES, b Aug. 22, 1791, d Nov 22 1814, in Tamworth, N H.
1271   v   MARTHA, b. Nov 4, 1797; m Rev Nathaniel Strout, d Feb, 1838
1272   vi   HANNAH, b June 12 1804, d, unm, Jan 28, 1852
1273   vii SARAH, b May 13, 1806, d April 29, 1877
1274   viii JOSEPH, b July 4, 1808, d March 11, 1866.
1275   ix   JEREMIAH, b Aug 18 1812
1276   x   MARY, b Nov. 4, 1814, d, unm, Feb 16, 1848

501 JOHN[6] EMERY (*John,[5] Joseph.[4] Job,[3] James,[2] Anthony[1]*), son of John and Hannah (Furbush) Emery; married Abigail Wasgatt of Mount Desert, Me. (born July 17, 1762, died Sept. 1, 1834).   He died June 19, 1831.
  Children.

1277   i   CHARITY,[7] b Nov. 14, 1783, d Oct 21, 1854.
1278   ii   JOHN,   } b Sept 7, { drowned in Penobscot R, Jan 7, 1819
1279   iii THOMAS, } 1785,   { d in childhood
1280   iv   JOSEPH,   } b April 20, 1787, { went to sea and d in youth.
1281   v   BENJAMIN, }   { d Dec, 1835
1282   vi   SARAH, b Aug 27, 1789, d in New Orleans, La, Aug 20, 1870
1283   vii WILLIAM, b March 3, 1791, d young
1284   viii DANIEL, b. March 11, 1793, d in Abbot, Me., Aug 10, 1864

1285 ix WILLIAM, b. March 3, 1795; d. May 19, 1844, in Hampden, Me.
1286 x   THOMAS, b. Dec. 11, 1797; d. at Martinique, Jan. 18, 1848.
1287 xi JULIA ANN, b. March 18, 1801; d. Dec. 29, 1818.
1288 xii CYRUS, b. Feb. 1, 1804; d. Jan. 19, 1859, in Bangor, Me.

503 NAHUM[6] EMERY (*John,*[5] *Joseph,*[4] *Job,*[3] *James,*[2] *Anthony*[1]), son of John and Hannah (Furbush) Emery ; married, first, 1788, Hannah Arey (died 1808) ; second, Nov., 1808, Mrs. Betsey F. Barker. He died Feb. 14, 1846.
  Children :

1289 i   JOSEPH,[7] b. March 7, 1790; d. 1868.
1290 ii   NAHUM, b. July 13, 1792; d. July 23, 1870.
1291 iii HANNAH, b. May, 1794.
1292 iv   CYNTHIA, b. June 21, 1796.
1293 v   ANNA, b. June 22, 1798.
1294 vi   ABIGAIL, b. Sept. 6, 1800.
1295 vii DEMARIS, b. Feb. 10, 1802.
1296 viii MARIA, b. 1804.
1297 ix   JOHN, b. April, 1808; d. Oct. 7, 1870.

By second marriage :
1298 x   MARTHA A., b. 1809; d. 1849.
1299 xi   JAMES, b. 1811.
1300 xii ELIZA, b. 1812.
1301 xiii BARKER, b. Feb. 28, 1814.

509 ICHABOD[6] EMERY (*Job,*[5] *Joseph,*[4] *Job,*[3] *James,*[2] *Anthony*[1]), son of Job and Polly (Hubbard) Emery ; married June 8, 1794, Lois Stacey (born in Kittery, Me., April 9, 1774). Lived in No. Berwick, Me.
  Children :

1302 i   WILLIAM,[7] b. July 23, 1796.
1303 ii   JOB, b. April 12, 1798; d. Oct. 12, 1876.
1304 iii BETSEY, b. July 1, 1800.
1305 iv   JOSEPH, b. Aug. 31, 1802; d. Sept. 19, 1840.
1306 v   OLIVER H., b. Feb. 12, 1805; d. Sept. 9, 1870.
1307 vi   THOMAS C., b. June 20, 1808; d. 7 years of age.
1308 vii NATHAN N , b. Sept. 17, 1810; d. 1811.
1309 viii POLLY, b. May 2, 1813.
1310 ix   JACOB, b. Nov., 1815; d. young.
1311 x   LOIS, b. May 6, 1819.

510 POLLY[6] EMERY (*Job,*[5] *Joseph,*[4] *Job,*[3] *James,*[2] *Anthony*[1]), daughter of Job and Polly (Hubbard) Emery ; married July 19, 1792, Nathan Nason (born 1770 ; died Nov. 8, 1826).   Lived in South Berwick, Me.
  Children, born in South Berwick, Me. :

1312 i   MARY[7], b. Nov. 24, 1793; m. Daniel Goodwin of Eliot, Me.
1313 ii   MARTHA, b. July 7, 1795; d. unm.
1314 iii WILLIAM, b. Jan. 13, 1797; m. Betsey Nason; d. 1879.
1315 iv   LOIS, b. Jan. 24, 1799; m. Samuel Fox of Gt. Falls, N. H.
1316 v   KEZIAH, b. Feb. 26, 1801; m. George Fishley of Portsmouth, N. H.
1317 vi   NATHAN, b. Nov. 23, 1802; d. Nov. 29, 1802.
1318 vii ELIZABETH, b. Jan. 8, 1804; m. Daniel Thompson of Wells, Me.
1319 viii SARAH ANN, b. Dec. 6, 1805; m. Charles Dove of Gt. Falls, N. H.; d. Nov. 20, 1837.
1320 ix   ALMIRA, b. Jan. 18, 1808; d. Feb. 18, 1839.

1321 x   Susannah, b Sept 23, 1809, m. Nathan Record of Peoria, Ill.
1322 xi Frederick, b. Aug. 20, 1811, d May 30, 1821.
1323 xii Nathan, b March 9, 1813, d unm
1324 xiii Ann Maria, b Aug 8, 1815, d July 4, 1838

511 Joseph[6] Emery (*Job,*[5] *Joseph,*[4] *Job,*[3] *James,*[2] *Anthony*[1]). son of Joseph and Polly (Hubbard) Emery; married, first, Polly, daughter of John and Sarah Hubbard (born March 30, 1779; died May 24, 1814), second July 4, 1816, Matilda Nason (died Mar. 12, 1818); third, Sarah (Bragdon) Hubbard, Nov. 3, 1822 He died Oct. 16, 1848.

Children, all of the first marriage :

1325 i   Sarah [7] b July 3, 1800, d Nov 6, 1806.
1326 ii Molly b April 27, 1802 d Jan 24, 1810.
1327 iii John H , b April 17, 1804
1328 iv Joseph b April 12, 1806, d Feb. 6, 1816.
1329 v   Job, b March 20 1808
1330 vi Sarah, b. Feb. 26, 1810, d 1816
1331 vii Mary, b. Oct. 4, 1812, d. Jan 14, 1831

512 Philomelia[6] Emery (*William,*[5] *Joseph.*[4] *Job,*[3] *James,*[2] *Anthony*[1]), daughter of William and Philomelia (Webber) Emery, married, 1794–5, Edmund Lord (born 1775, died Jan. 28, 1852). She died June 3, 1851.

Children :

1332 i   Robert,[7] b 1796
1333 ii Jason, b March 1, 1799
1334 iii William, b 1801, d in Pelham N H
1335 iv Hannah J., b. Feb , 1809

515 William[6] Emery (*William,*[5] *Joseph,*[4] *Job,*[3] *James,*[2] *Anthony*[1]), son of William and Philomelia (Webber) Emery, married Jan 24, 1805, Sally Paine (died in Eden, Me , Aug., 1850) ; removed to Eden, 1804. He died June 21, 1857.

Children, born in Eden, Me. :

1336 i   Joel,[7] b Oct. 22, 1805, d April 10, 1880, at Mayaguez, P R
1337 ii   Philomelia, b Dec 16, 1806, d June 1, 1874
1338 iii Benjamin, b Feb 17, 1808, d. June 8, 1883.
1339 iv   Jedediah S., b Aug 20, 1809
1340 v   Pamelia, b Dec 25, 1810, d Jan 8, 1811.
1341 vi   William, b March 2, 1812, removed to Aroostook Co ; never heard from.
1342 vii Julia A , b June 16, 1813, m Isaac Fogg, May 1, 1836, d Oct 22, 1836, *s p*
1343 viii Clement, b April 13, 1815, moved to Cal , probably killed by Indians.
1344 ix   Sarah A , b Jan 5, 1817
1345 x   Lucetta, b. Nov 29, 1818, d March 27, 1819
1346 xi   Lucetta A , b March 22, 1820.
1347 xii Francis F , b Feb 28, 1822, d Nov. 19, 1839, at St Thomas on Brig Abigail
1348 xiii Mary R , b April 18, 1824, m. Freeman Sparrow of Bangor, Me , April 9, 1848
1349 xiv Ursula S , b Oct 1, 1825, d July 4, 1854, m Isaiah Gilpatrick of Trenton, Aug , 1842

1350 xv Thomas P., b. April 17, 1827.
1351 xvi Laura N., b. March 21, 1832.

516 Joel[6] Emery (*William,[5] Joseph,[4] Job,[3] James,[2] Anthony[1]*),
son of William and Philomelia (Webber) Emery; married, first, at
Eden, Me., Jan. 1, 1807, Hannah Thomas (born Oct. 30, 1782; died
Sept. 12, 1825); second, Oct. 6, 1826, Martha Mayo (born in Or-
leans, Mass., 1792; died Jan. 31, 1872). He died Feb. 19, 1867.
  Children, born in Eden, Me. :

1352 i   Alfred,[7] b. Oct. 6, 1807.
1353 ii   Adaline, b. April 19, 1809; m. Capt. John Thompson, Dec. 20,
           1827.
1354 iii Jared, b. March 25, 1811; d. in Eden, Me., June 4, 1883.
1355 iv   Mehitable, b. Sept. 12, 1813; d. in Oakland, Cal., March,
           1853.
1356 v   Samuel N., b. Aug. 25, 1816.
1357 vi   Edward W. W., b. June 4, 1819; m. Sally Hopkins, Feb. 5,
           1846; d. April 23, 1859.
1358 vii Hiram W., b. Dec. 18, 1821; m. Sarah F. Bartlett of Eliot, Me.,
           March 1, 1860. She died Jan., 1875.
1359 viii John T., b. July 9, 1825.

By second marriage :

1360 ix   Hannah T., b. Sept. 27, 1827.
1361 x   Joel, b. May 1, 1829; d. in Eden, Me., Dec. 31, 1866.
1362 xi   Josiah M., b. Feb. 15, 1831; d. Nov. 14, 1861; unm.
1363 xii Andrew, b. Jan. 5, 1833.
1364 xiii Simeon S., b. March 10, 1835.
1365 xiv Washington Irving, b. March 15, 1837.
1366 xv   Weston F., b. May 2, 1839.

517 Andrew[6] Emery (*William,[5] Joseph,[4] Job,[3] James,[2] Anthony[1]*),
son of William and Philomelia (Webber) Emery; married Feb. 1,
1810, Shuah Bartlett, of Kittery (born Jan. 30, 1785; died in New
Portland, Me., Jan. 30, 1844).
  Children, born in South Berwick, Me. :

1367 i   Alvan,[7] ⎫ b. Nov. 28, ⎧ d. in New Portland, Me., July 27, 1864.
1368 ii   Almira, ⎬   1810;   ⎨ d. in Somersworth, N. H., April, 1840.
1369 iii Hiram A., b. April 12, 1812.
1370 iv   Adeline, b. Feb. 22, 1814; m. Zacheus Roberts, Jan. 1, 1837;
           d. in Buffalo, N. Y.

518 Hiram[6] Emery (*William,[5] Joseph,[4] Job,[3] James,[2] Anthony[1]*),
son of William and Philomelia (Webber) Emery; married Nov. 15,
1815, Rachel S. Simpson (born April 22, 1793; died Sept. 2, 1844).
Went to Trenton in 1804 and to Sullivan, Me., in 1807. He died
Jan. 11, 1863. Hiram Emery was one of the leading citizens of
Sullivan from the time he moved there in 1807 till his death in 1863,
and being a justice of the peace he did about all the legal business
of the town, and held many town offices, was postmaster for several
years and acting deputy collector of customs for some four years.
  Children, born in Sullivan :

1371 i JOHN SIMPSON,[7] b Sept 13, 1816, m Prudence Simpson, Dec 1,
      ·   1850 (b in Sullivan, Me., Feb 5, 1819), removed from Sulli-
          van, Me , to Boston, Mass , where he has been engaged in
          business as ship broker for forty-one years being the princi-
          pal in the well known firm of John S Emery & Co , 168 State
          St , Boston, and with one exception is the oldest man en-
          gaged in ship brokerage business in Boston He is a man of
          broad sympathies, liberal in his opinions and means, a friend
          of the needy and distressed, devoted to the shipping inter-
          ests of his own country, and of wide influence and acknowl-
          edged integrity He is a director in the China Mutual In-
          surance Co of Boston, and also in the Boston Marine Insu-
          rance Co , and President of the East Boston Dry Dock Co.
1372 ii PHILOMELIA WEBBER, b April 22, 1818, d Aug 15. 1866
1373 iii ABIGAIL SULLIVAN, b Oct 8, 1820, d. in Sullivan, Me , April 4,
          1883, distinguished for gentleness and refinement, "with
          malice towards none, with charity towards all."
1374 iv CYRUS, b Oct 2, 1822
1375 v   WILLIAM DARIUS, b Aug 4, 1824
1376 vi RACHEL PRUDENCE S., b April 9, 1830, d May 21, 1850
1377 vii DANIEL SULLIVAN, b Dec. 29, 1833. He is a member of the
          firm of J S Emery & Co., a man of excellent judgment, ex-
          ceedingly cautious and of unwavering integrity, and has a
          large circle of friends wherever known
1378 viii ANN S., b. Dec 29, 1833, m Sylvester W. Cummings, Lieut
          in U. S A , Oct , 1863, who d at Morganzie, La , June 17,
          1864
1379 ix ERASTUS OSCAR, b. April 5, 1836, m. Ellen S. Niles, Dec 3,
          1864, d. from an accident Nov 15, 1882, in Boston, Mass.

519 LUCY[6] EMERY (*William*,[5] *Joseph*,[4] *Job*,[3] *James*,[2] *Anthony*[1]),
daughter of William and Philomelia (Webber) Emery; married
March 4, 1813, James Lord, of Lebanon, Me. (born Jan. 2, 1786;
died Oct. 29, 1856) , lived in Lebanon, Me. She died Aug. 8, 1870.
Children, born in Lebanon, Me. :

1380 i   EMILY,[7] b Oct. 14, 1814; d in Lebanon, Me , May 30, 1857.
1381 ii MARIA, b Oct 25, 1817.
1382 iii AUGUSTA, b Nov 8, 1819, m Benjamin F Horn, Nov 17,
          1864
1383 iv WILLIAM, b. March 8, 1821.
1384 v   PHILOMELIA, b March 28, 1826, m. Reuben Hanscom, Mar 20,
          1853
1385 vi HIRAM, b Jan 3, 1830.

520 MEHITABLE[6] EMERY (*William*,[5] *Joseph*,[4] *Job*,[3] *James*,[2] *Anthony*[1]), daughter of William and Philomelia (Webber) Emery; married Dec. 26. 1817, Nathan Bartlett (died Oct. 15, 1865). She died
Sept. 1, 1857.
Children, born in Eliot, Me. ·

1386 i   LUCINDA,[7] b May 24, 1819; d , unm , May 7, 1852
1387 ii   SYLVESTER, b July 4, 1822
1388 iii ELIZABETH S , b June 14, 1824, m. Ed. B. Farley, Nov. 11,
           1873, in Lockport, Ill
1389 iv   SARAH F , b. Aug 30, 1826, m Hiram W Emery, March 1,
           1860, d. in Lockport, Ill , Jan. 11, 1875.
1390 v   JAMES W , b July 1, 1828.
1391 vi   JUSTIN S , b Sept. 11, 1830; m. Emily D. Shorey, Jan. 12,
           1857, d. 1866.

521 John[6] Emery (*Jonathan,[5] Jonathan,[4] Job,[3] James,[2] Anthony[1]*), son of Jonathan and Elizabeth (Tarbox) Emery ; married, 1796, Elizabeth Haley (died Nov., 1845).

Children :

1392	i	Sarah Ann,[7] b. April 13, 1798.
1393	ii	John, b. July 13, 1800 : d. Feb. 11, 1811.
1394	iii	Thomas, b. Dec. 6, 1802.
1395	iv	Jotham, b. Oct. 11, 1804.
1396	v	Samuel, b. Nov. 2, 1806 ; m. Hannah Harper.
1397	vi	Elizabeth, b. Dec. 3, 1808.
1398	vii	Naomi, b. April 12, 1810 ; m. Nathaniel Abbot, May 21, 1830.
1399	viii	John, b. Feb. 1, 1812 ; probably d. young.

522 Haven[6] Emery (*Jonathan,[5] Jonathan,[4] Job,[3] James,[2] Anthony[1]*), son of Jonathan and Elizabeth (Tarbox) Emery ; married April 7, 1799, Deborah Murch.

Children, born in Biddford, Me. :

1400	i	William M.,[7] b. Oct. 12, 1799.
1401	ii	Sally Jenkins, b. April 17, 1801 ; m. William Smith, 1820.
1402	iii	Betsey Tarbox, b. Nov. 22, 1804.
1403	iv	Lydia Gilpatrick, b. April 6, 1807 ; m. —— McNelege.
1404	v	Jonathan, b. Jan. 30, 1809.
1405	vi	John, b. Jan. 27, 1811.
1406	vii	Susannah Fairfield, b. July 4, 1813.
1407	viii	Mary Ann, b. May 11, 1815 ; probably m. Samuel Hill.
1408	ix	Deborah, b. July 27, 1817 ; m. Daniel Johuson.
1409	x	Thomas, b. Feb. 8, 1822.

523 Thomas[6] Emery (*Jonathan,[5] Jonathan,[4] Job,[3] James,[2] Anthony[1]*), son of Jonathan and Elizabeth (Tarbox) Emery ; married, June 20, 1806, Mary Gray.

Children :

1410	i	Amaziah,[7] b. Nov. 10, 1807.
1411	ii	Mary Ann, b. June 8, 1811 ; m. Benj. Staples, May 21, 1830.
1412	iii	Elizabeth Moore, b. May 15, 1818 ; m. James W. Smith.
1413	iv	Isabella, b. July 1, 1820 ; m. Israel C. Russell.

525 Mary Ann[6] Emery (*Jonathan,[5] Jonathan,[4] Job,[3] James,[2] Anthony[1]*), daughter of Jonathan and Elizabeth (Tarbox) Emery ; married, 1806, Samuel Tarbox ; published in Biddeford, Me., Nov. 20, 1805.

Children :

1414	i	Jonathan.[7]
1415	ii	Samuel.
1416	iii	Thomas.
1417	iv	John.
1418	v	Clara.
1419	vi	Betsey.

528 James[6] Emery (*Jabez,[5] Jabez,[4] Job,[3] James,[2] Anthony[1]*), son of Jabez and Anne (Gowen) Emery ; married Abigail Harding.

Children :

1420	i	Betsey L.,[7] m. Joseph Adams.
1421	ii	Mary A., m. William Pitts.

1422 iii JAMES, d at sea, unm.
1423 iv STEPHEN, d unm
1424 v ABIGAIL, d unm
1425 vi MARTHA, b. Dec 5, 1820; m William Johnson.
1426 vii CATHARINE, b 1822, m —— Billings of Providence, R I.

534 PHILIP[6] EMERY (*Job*,[5] *Jabez*,[4] *Job*,[3] *James*,[2] *Anthony*[1]), son of Job and Keziah (Webber) Emery; married Sarah Kimball. Served in the war of 1812.
Children.

1427 i LOUISA,[7] b April, 1812, m Gardner Warren.
1428 ii ELEANOR, b May, 1813, m William White of Middleboro, Mass.
1429 iii BENJAMIN F , b. Aug. 16, 1816.

535 DANIEL[6] EMERY (*Job*,[5] *Jabez*,[4] *Job*,[3] *James*,[2] *Anthony*[1]), son of Jabez and Keziah (Webber) Emery, married Hannah Downing.
Children :

1430 i GEORGE,[7] b Sept 5, 1811, d. at sea May, 1834.
1431 ii DANIEL C , b June 17, 1817.

536 JACOB[6] EMERY (*Job*,[5] *Jabez*,[4] *Job*,[3] *James*,[2] *Anthony*[1]), son of Job and Keziah (Webber) Emery; married Polly Wormwood. He died at sea.
Children :

1432 i THOMAS W ,[7] m Martha Wormwood
1433 ii JOB, went from Kennebunk to Boston, where he m, and had children and d
1434 iii JACOB, lost at sea, m Victoria Wentworth
1435 iv NATHANIEL, killed in the army, 1864

537 JOSHUA[6] EMERY (*Job*,[5] *Jabez*,[4] *Job*,[3] *James*,[2] *Anthony*[1]), son of Job and Keziah (Webber) Emery, married Dec. 5, 1819, Sally Kimball of Lyman, Me. (born Feb. 28, 1794), daughter of Deacon Ezra and Lucretia Kimball.
Children :

1436 i JOSHUA S ,[7] b June 7, 1822
1437 ii LEONORA, b Jan 16, 1824 , d Dec 14, 1824
1438 iii SARAH, b Sept 8, 1825 , d Oct 6, 1860
1439 iv OLIVE, b Dec 20, 1831 , m —— Seaver.
1440 v GEORGE G , b July 12, 1834, removed west, m Helen Pierce, in Wisconsin

538 THOMAS[6] EMERY (*Job*,[5] *Jabez*,[4] *Job*,[3] *James*,[2] *Anthony*[1]), son of Job and Keziah (Webber) Emery; married Sept 27, 1818, Eunice Greenough.
Children :

1441 i JASON L ,[7] b June 10, 1819
1442 ii JOSHUA, b. Feb 5, 1821.
1443 iii JANE S , b. Feb 1, 1823, m Sept , 1841, in Kennebunkport, Me , Asa Leach
1444 iv LOUISA P , b Jan 7, 1825, m Charles Kimball of Portland, Me
1445 v ASENATH M , b. Feb. 2, 1827, d. Nov. 16, 1838

24

1446   vi   JACOB, b. May 8, 1829.
1447   vii THOMAS, b. June 13, 1831.
1448   viii BURLEIGH S., b. June 9, 1833.

543 JOHN[6] EMERY (*Isaac,[5] Jabez,[4] Job,[3] James,[2] Anthony[1]*), son of
Isaac and Eunice (Perkins) Emery; married Aug. 11, 1817, Eliz.
Morrill (born in Saco, Me., July 11, 1790; died in 1848), daughter
of Joseph and Mary (Jordan) Morrill. He was master of brig "Corsair"
and was lost on the passage from New Orleans to New York, 1830.
  Children :

1449   i   JOHN H.,[7] b. June 17, 1821.
1450   ii   MARY, b. 1823; d. 1825.

544 BENJAMIN[6] EMERY (*Isaac,[5] Jabez,[4] Job,[3] James,[2] Anthony[1]*), son
of Isaac and Eunice (Perkins) Emery; married Oct. 5, 1817, Sally
Towne. He died July 20, 1871.
  Children :

1451   i   WILLIAM B.,[7] b Nov. 23, 1818; drowned July 13, 1835.
1452   ii   ELIZABETH M., b. April 2, 1820; m. Aug., 1837, Richard Bur-
            gess.
1453   iii LUCINDA F., b. Nov. 28, 1822; m., 1st, Nathaniel Rankin; 2nd,
            Joseph M. Curtis.
1454   iv   BENJAMIN F., b. Sept. 20, 1824; d. March 2, 1881.
1455   v   ELIPHALET P., b. July 14, 1826.
1456   vi   SARAH F., b. April 25, 1828; m. Cornelius Wilson of Thorndike,
            Me.
1457   vii ISAAC M., b. March 25, 1830.
1458   viii JOHN A., b. Jan. 8, 1832.
1459   ix   JACOB T., b. Sept. 19, 1833; d. May 4, 1837.
1460   x   WILLIAM H., b. Dec. 15, 1835.
1461   xi   JULIA A., b. Jan. 30, 1838; m. Charles W. Gooch of Kenne-
            bunkport, Me.

545 ISAAC[6] EMERY (*Isaac,[5] Jabez,[4] Job,[3] James,[2] Anthony[1]*), son
of Isaac and Eunice (Perkins) Emery; married Aug. 11, 1823, Lucinda Fairfield; died at sea 1830. She married, second, 1837, Clement Perkins. They had five children.
  Children, born in Kennebunk, Me. :

1462   i   SUSAN D.,[7] b. Oct. 19, 1824.
1463   ii   MARY L., b. April 12, 1826.
1464   iii EUNICE P., b. April 17, 1828; m., 1st, Joseph Wheelwright; 2nd,
            H. Smart; had three children.
1465   iv   CHARLES ISAAC, b. Aug. 12, 1830.

548 MARY E.[6] EMERY (*Isaac,[5] Jabez,[4] Job,[3] James,[2] Anthony[1]*),
daughter of Isaac and Eunice (Perkins) Emery; married Aug. 17,
1823, William M. Bryant (born June 9, 1794; died Jan. 9, 1874).
She died Jan. 13, 1879.
  Children :

1466   i   SARAH P.,[7] b. Oct. 11, 1824; d. Oct. 26, 1825.
1467   ii   SETH E., b. March 14, 1826.
1468   iii WILLIAM A., b. March 26, 1828; d. Sept. 18, 1828.
1469   iv   ORVILLE D., b. Aug. 1, 1829.
1470   v   FREDERICK S., b. April 4, 1831.

1471 .vi JAMES A , b March 11, 1833; d Oct 8, 1834
1472 vii SARAH E. P , b March 28, 1835; d Nov 4, 1838.
1473 viii WILLIE, b Feb 3, 1837, d Feb 10, 1837.
1474 ix SUSAN L , b Dec 21. 1838
1475 x LOUISA D , b Jan 30, 1841.
1476 xi MARY E , b July 24, 1844, d Feb. 10, 1871.

551 SAMUEL[7] EMERY (*Obadiah,*[6] *Obed,*[5] *James,*[4] *James,*[3] *James,*[2]
Anthony[1]), son of Obadiah and Lydia (Emery) Emery; married July
24, 1816, Mary Smith Gilpatrick (died Sept 19, 1854), daughter of
Benjamin Gilpatrick, Esq. He died April 24, 1850. He became
master of a vessel on his first voyage, about 1790; retired after a successful career, in 1816; was selectman of Biddeford for many years;
Justice of the Peace, and Representative in the Legislature of Maine
both at Portland and Augusta; a man of sterling integrity and universally respected. "His word was as good as his bond."
Children, born in Biddeford, Me

1477 i SAMUEL,[7] b Aug. 23, 1817, m Mary Scammon; drowned at
Beals Bar, California, April 17, 1851
1478 ii MARY G , b. Aug 20, 1819
1479 iii OBADIAH, b Feb 27, 1822; d Jan 4, 1842
1480 iv REBECCA H , b July 23, 1826, d June 8, 1884
1481 v HANNAH, b. Sept. 9, 1828.

553 SARAH[7] EMERY (*Obadiah,*[6] *Obed,*[5] *James,*[4] *James,*[3] *James,*[2]
Anthony[1]), daughter of Obadiah and Lydia (Emery) Emery; mar-
ried Humphrey Purington of Topsham, Me. (died Dec. 31, 1841).
She died Sept. 20, 1855
Children, born in Topsham, Me ·

1482 i PRISCILLA,[8] b. Dec 10, 1800, d Sept 23, 1880
1483 ii ANN EMERY, b May 10, 1802, d Jan 1, 1873
1484 iii SAMUEL E , b March 6, 1804; d Nov. 16. 1821.
1485 iv SARAH P , b Aug 24, 1806, d Nov. 16 1844
1486 v HANNAH E , b. Dec 17, 1809, d Aug 25, 1850.
1487 vi FRANCIS T , b Feb 21, 1813, d May 21, 1857
1488 vii WOODBURY BRYANT, b Dec 24, 1814

580 RALPH[7] EMERY (*Ralph.*[6] *Obed,*[5] *James,*[4] *James,*[3] *James,*[2] *Anthony*[1]), son of Ralph and Olive (Foss) Emery; married Nov. 9,
1828, Happy Woodman (born Oct 20, 1801, died Oct. 16, 1873).
He died Dec 10, 1875.
Children, born in Biddeford, Me. :

1489 i ANN JEWETT,[8] b July 2, 1829
1490 ii GEORGE F , b July 11, 1831, d in Biddeford, Me , Oct 27, 1878
1491 iii OBED, b Aug 13, 1837, d Oct 6, 1888
1492 iv ALICE WOODMAN, b April 27, 1841, m June 15, 1869 Charles
Came Hodsdon (b Jan 27, 1840). He was 1st Lieut and
Adjt 80th U S C. Infantry, Brv't Capt , U S. Vols. Bookkeeper in the Saco and Biddeford Savings Institution.

582 SAMUEL[7] EMERY (*James,*[6] *James,*[5] *Thomas,*[4] *James,*[3] *James,*[2]
Anthony[1]), son of James and Catharine (Freethy) Emery; married
first, Ann Elwell, second, Nancy (Royce) Fairington. He died
July 6, 1864.

Children :

1493　i　JOHN E.,⁸ b. Feb. 20, 1823, in Buxton, Me.
1494　ii　CAROLINE A., b. April 21, 1825, in Buxton; d. Feb. 8, 1856, in
　　　　　Charlestown, Mass.
1495　iii　MARY E., b. March 10, 1827.
1496　iv　JAMES WALLACE, b. Feb. 7, 1829.
1497　v　MEHITABLE J., b. July 1, 1831, in Bridgton, Me.; d. in Was-
　　　　　toja, Minn.
1498　vi　LOIS B., b. June 25, 1833, in Bridgton, Me.
1499　vii　SAMUEL, b. Jan. 23, 1838, in Bridgton, Me.

583 ALEXANDER J. EMERY⁷ (*James*,⁶ *James*,⁵ *Thomas*,⁴ *James*,³
James,² *Anthony*¹), son of James and Catharine (Freethy) Emery ;
married Nov. 29, 1823, Mary S. Haley (born July 30, 1806).　He
died March 5, 1875.
　　Children :

1500　i　MARY CATHARINE,⁸ b. Jan. 29, 1825; d. March 20, 1827.
1501　ii　ANN ELIZABETH, b. May 22, 1827; d. May 19, 1839.
1502　iii　MARTHA ELLEN, b. April 18, 1829; m. C. F. Holt, Nov. 25, 1865.
1503　iv　JAMES H., b. June 29, 1830; d. July 1, 1830.
1504　v　JULIA SOPHIA, b. Sept. 20, 1832; m. O. H. Peck, Jan. 15, 1861.
1505　vi　LUCY C. BROOKE, b. Dec. 20, 1834; d. July 14, 1877.
1506　vii　MARY ELIZA, b. Nov. 22, 1844; d. Feb. 14, 1882.

584 JONAS⁷ EMERY (*James*,⁶ *James*,⁵ *Thomas*,⁴ *James*,³ *James*,²
*Anthony*¹), son of James and Catharine (Freethy) Emery ; married
June 20, 1833, Eliza Boynton of Buxton, Me.
　　Child :

1507　i　MARY C.,⁷ b. Dec. 18, 1836.

585 HANNAH⁷ EMERY (*James*,⁶ *James*,⁵ *Thomas*,⁴ *James*,³ *James*,²
*Anthony*¹), daughter of James and Catharine (Freethy) Emery ; mar-
ried Oct. 27, 1831, George Jewett (born in Gardiner, July 17, 1795).
Farmer in Pittston, Me.
　　Children, born in Pittston, Me. :

1508　i　ANN V.,⁷ b. Dec. 25, 1832.
1509　ii　GEORGE F., b. March 9, 1838; m. Lizzie L. Fuller in Pittston,
　　　　　Me., Jan. 9, 1877.
1510　iii　JAMES E., b. Dec. 21, 1841; m. Georgia Roundy of Benton, Me.,
　　　　　Sept. 14, 1882.

586 THOMAS F.⁷ EMERY (*James*,⁶ *James*,⁵ *Thomas*,⁴ *James*,³ *James*,²
*Anthony*¹), son of James and Catharine (Freethy) Emery ; married
July 1, 1834, Nancy M. Webster (born July 5, 1812).　Lived in
Biddeford, Me.
　　Children :

1511　i　CATHARINE W.,⁸ b. June 10, 1835; d. July, 1835.
1512　ii　JAMES W., b. July 9, 1836; d. May 30, 1861, at Saco, Me.;
　　　　　unm.
1513　iii　CHARLES P., b. Sept. 7, 1838.
1514　iv　THOMAS C., b. Jan. 27, 1841; d. Nov. 26, 1862.
1515　v　N. ELLEN, b. Dec. 31, 1843.
1516　vi　FRANK L., b. March 18, 1853; m. in Gorham, Me., Luella Ha-
　　　　　ley, Nov. 19, 1873; d. Jan. 6, 1879.

587 JAMES S.[7] EMERY (*James,*[6] *James,*[5] *Thomas,*[4] *James,*[3] *James,*[2] *Anthony*[1]), son of James and Catharine (Freethy) Emery ; married Eliza Ann (daughter of Aaron and Sylvina (Perry) Wing of Wayne, Me.; born June 22, 1811). He died May 24, 1868.

Children, born in Carmel .

    1517 i   LUCILIUS A.,[8] b July 27, 1840
    1518 ii   FLORENCE, b 1846
    1519 iii CHARLES, drowned

600 MARY S [7] HALEY (*Mary,*[6] *James,*[5] *Thomas,*[4] *James,*[3] *James,*[2] *Anthony*[1]), daughter of Joseph and Mary (Emery) Haley , married Nov. 29, 1823, A. J. Emery (born Dec. 3, 1801 ; died March 5, 1875). (See No. 583)

603 MARTHA E.[7] HALEY (*Mary,*[6] *James,*[5] *Thomas,*[4] *James,*[3] *James,*[2] *Anthony*[1]), daughter of Joseph and Mary (Emery) Haley; married Thomas K. Dodge, son of Thomas R. and Lydia (Emery) Dodge.

Child .

    1520 i   FRANK CUTLER,[8] b 1845, d. June 12, 1886.

605 JOSEPH K [7] HALEY (*Mary,*[6] *James,*[5] *Thomas,*[4] *James,*[3] *James,*[2] *Anthony*[1]), son of Joseph and Mary (Emery) Haley; married April 17, 1853, Lavinia L. Clark (born July 10, 1826).

Children ·

    1521 i   HATTIE E ,[8] b May 1 1854
    1522 ii   IDA J , b Oct 15, 1855
    1523 iii FANNIE E , b April 18, 1857
    1524 iv   MINNIE E , b March 1, 1863
    1525 v   M GERTRUDE, b. Oct 19, 1864.

607 MARY S.[7] EMERY (*Simon,*[6] *James,*[5] *Thomas,*[4] *James,*[3] *James,*[2] *Anthony*[1]), daughter of Simon and Olive (Staples) Emery ; married Jonathan Priest, died April 17, 1871.

Children

    1526 i   OLIVIA M ,[8] b Sept. 23, 1827.
    1527 ii   SOPHIA, b March 26, 1831.
    1528 iii LUCY, b June 9, 1835
    1529 iv   FRANCES, b Aug 31, 1849

609 JAMES FREEMAN[7] EMERY (*Simon,*[6] *James,*[5] *Thomas,*[4] *James,*[3] *James,*[2] *Anthony*[1]), son of Simon and his second wife, Eunice (Scammon) Emery ; married Mary Pike.

Children :

    1530 i   SIMON OTIS,[8] b March 2, 1836
    1531 ii   EDWARD F , b May 23, 1838
    1532 iii EDWARD O., b Aug. 4, 1840.

610 OLIVE S.[7] EMERY (*Simon,*[6] *James,*[5] *Thomas,*[4] *James,*[3] *James,*[2] *Anthony*[1]), daughter of Simon and his second wife, Eunice (Scammon) Emery , married Dec. 29, 1835, Moses Bradbury.

Children :

    1533   i   FREDERICK T.,[8] b. July 20, 1837.
    1534   ii   SARAH E., b. April 3, 1839.
    1535   iii EDWARD, b. June 7, 1841.
    1536   iv   AUGUSTUS F., b. July 6, 1843.

611 LIZZIE[7] EMERY (*Simon,[6] James,[5] Thomas,[4] James,[3] James,[2] Anthony[1]*), daughter of Simon and his second wife, Eunice (Scammon) Emery ; married John Pike, Oct. 6, 1841.
    Children :

    1537   i   ANNA M.,[8] b. Feb. 12, 1846.
    1538   ii   HARRIET, b. July 17, 1848.
    1539   iii LIZZIE O., b. July 7, 1857.

614 SAMUEL WEBSTER[7] EMERY (*Samuel,[6] James,[5] Thomas,[4] James,[3] James,[2] Anthony[1]*), son of Samuel and Sophia (Webster) Emery ; married Oct. 25, 1849, Lois Weeks of Portland.
    Children :

    1540   i   SOPHIA ELIZABETH,[8] b. Nov. 14, 1850; m. Eben. S. Emery of
                Portland, Oct. 25, 1884.
    1541   ii   ELLEN MARIA, b. May 18, 1855, in Cape Elizabeth, Me.
    1542   iii JOSHUA F. WEEKS, b. April 4, 1858, in Cape Elizabeth, Me.
    1543   iv   CHARLES A. BEARD, b. March 29, 1861, in Portland, Me.; d.
                Feb. 24, 1862.
    1544   v   LOIS WEEKS,   } b. Feb. 20, 1864, in Portland, Me.
    1545   vi   WEBSTER H. PRINCE. }
    1546   vii JENNIE SPEAR, b. Oct. 25, 1866, in Portland, Me.

618 JAMES[7] EMERY (*Nathaniel,[6] James,[5] Thomas,[4] James,[3] James,[2] Anthony[1]*), son of Nathaniel and Phila. N. (Rankin) Emery ; married Nov. 22, 1835, Maria Withington (born Oct. 8, 1816). Live in Charlestown, Mass.
    Children :

    1547   i   JAMES,[8] b. Nov. 13, 1836.
    1548   ii   NATHANIEL W., b. Jan. 11, 1838; d. Dec. 10, 1859.
    1549   iii THOMAS J., b. Nov. 22, 1840.
    1550   iv   FREEMAN, b. June 22, 1842.
    1551   v   CHARLES B., b. Nov. 16, 1851.

619 EMILY J.[7] EMERY (*Nathaniel,[6] James,[5] Thomas,[4] James,[3] James,[2] Anthony[1]*), daughter of Nathaniel and Phila. N. (Rankin) Emery ; married July 3, 1833, William Murch.
    Children :

    1552   i   ANNE M.,[8] b. May 25, 1835.
    1553   ii   CHARLES, b. May 22, 1837.
    1554   iii NATHANIEL E., b. July 4, 1843.
    1555   iv   PHILA, b. Jan., 1848.
    1556   v   SARAH, b. Dec. 1, 1853.

620 SARAH ANN[7] EMERY (*Nathaniel,[6] James,[5] Thomas,[4] James,[3] James,[2] Anthony[1]*), daughter of Nathaniel and Phila N. (Rankin) Emery ; married Nov. 12, 1834, John Whitcomb. She died Jan. 11, 1873.

Children, born in Wells, Me.

1557   i   NATHANIEL EMERY,⁸ b April 11, 1836.
1558   ii   JOHN, b. Nov. 19, 1838.
1559   iii   MARIA, b Oct 5, 1841, m. Charles E Smith of Holden, Mass ,
             May 1, 1867.
1560   iv   JAMES H , b April 24, 1847
1561   v   WILLIE GREEN, b March 9, 1853; d April 15, 1853

621 NATHANIEL WEBSTER⁷ EMERY (*Nathaniel,*⁶ *James,*⁵ *Thomas,*⁴ *James,*³ *James,*² *Anthony*¹), son of Nathaniel and Phila. N (Rankin) Emery, married Dec. 23, 1841, Phœbe Stevens (born Dec. 4, 1815; died Aug. 9, 1871). He died Oct. 19, 1871.

Child :

1562   i   JAMES,⁸ b. Sept 18, 1843, in Biddeford, Me.

622 THOMAS D.⁷ EMERY (*Nathaniel,*⁶ *James,*⁵ *Thomas,*⁴ *James,*³ *James ² Anthony*¹), son of Nathaniel and Phila N (Rankin) Emery, married Dec. 2, 1841, Lucy Ann Bunker (born Sept. 3, 1819). He died Sept 6, 1873.

Children, born in Biddeford :

1563   i   HENRIETTA,⁸ b Aug 22, 1842.
1564   ii   GEORGE L , b Dec 15, 1846; m July 11, 1868, Harriet O.
             Tarbox
1565   iii   ELIZABETH A , b March 31, 1856

623 MARY ABIGAIL⁷ EMERY (*Nathaniel,*⁶ *James,*⁵ *Thomas,*⁴ *James,*³ *James,*⁹ *Anthony*¹), daughter of Nathaniel and Phila. N. (Rankin) Emery : married Oct. 21, 1841, Samuel Hill, ship master (born Dec. 12, 1813).

Children, born in Biddeford, Me. :

1566   i   MARTHA ELLEN,⁸ b. July 23, 1842, m. Thomas J Emery
             (see No 1549).
1567   ii   MARY ABIGAIL, b Feb 11, 1846, d April 21, 1864.
1568   iii   NARCISSA EMERY, b Sept 17, 1848
1569   iv   EMILY FRANCES, b Jan 5, 1854
1570   v   SAMUEL HOWARD, b April 27, 1865

624 NARCISSA⁷ EMERY (*Nathaniel,*⁶ *James,*⁵ *Thomas,*⁴ *James,*³ *James,*² *Anthony*¹), daughter of Nathaniel and Phila. N. (Rankin) Emery ; married Aug 14, 1848, Anthony C. Campbell (born in Brunswick, Me., June 7, 1814).

Children :

1571   i   EDWIN EMERY,⁸ b Feb. 23, 1850, in East Boston. Mass.
1572   ii   HELEN AUGUSTA, b. May 28, 1854, in Biddeford, Me

627 MIRANDA⁷ EMERY (*John P.,*⁶ *Ebenezer,*⁵ *Thomas,*⁴ *James,*³ *James,*² *Anthony*¹), daughter of John P and Polly (Smith) Emery; married July 20, 1839, Beniah Clark. She died Dec. 23, 1866.

Children :

1573   i   LUCY G ,⁸ b. March 6, 1840.
1574   ii   GEORGE H , b Dec 12, 1848; d 1861
1575   iii   EMMA F , b Jan 2, 1851; d Dec 5, 1860
1576   iv   EMERY, b April 30, 1853; d Dec 13, 1860

629 CHARLES E.[7] EMERY (*John P.,*[6] *Ebenezer,*[5] *Thomas,*[4] *James,*[3] *James,*[2] *Anthony*[1]), son of John P. and Polly (Smith) Emery ; married Abbie Brown.   He died July 13, 1857.
Child :

    1577 i   ADELAIDE.[8]

630 HENRY[7] EMERY (*John P.,*[6] *Ebenezer,*[5] *Thomas,*[4] *James,*[3] *James,*[2] *Anthony*[1]), son of John P. and Polly (Smith) Emery ; married Miranda Emery.
Child :

    1578 i   HATTIE.[8]

631 HARRIET C.[7] EMERY (*John P.,*[6] *Ebenezer,*[5] *Thomas,*[4] *James,*[3] *James,*[2] *Anthony*[1]), daughter of John P. and Polly (Smith) Emery ; married William A. Abbot.   She died July 18, 1876.
Children :

    1579 i   CHARLES.[8]
    1580 ii   TRACY.

632 JONAS[7] EMERY (*John P.,*[6] *Ebenezer,*[5] *Thomas,*[4] *James,*[3] *James,*[2] *Anthony*[1]), son of John P. and Polly (Smith) Emery ; married Dec. 23, 1859, Sarah E. Langley.
Children :

    1581 i   WALTER S.,[8] b. Jan. 12, 1861.
    1582 ii   NELLIE S., b. April 26, 1863.
    1583 iii   JAMES H., b. May 22, 1865.
    1584 iv   SUSIE E., b. Dec. 22, 1867.
    1585 v   LIZZIE S., b. Oct. 24, 1872.
    1586 vi   WILLIAM E., b. Feb. 18, 1875.
    1587 vii   HATTIE M., b. Nov. 5, 1880; d. March 3, 1883.

633 SETH[7] EMERY (*John P.,*[6] *Ebenezer,*[5] *Thomas,*[4] *James,*[3] *James,*[2] *Anthony*[1]), son of John P. and Polly (Smith) Emery ; married Marilla Edgecomb (born Aug. 29, 1863).
Children :

    1588 i   EDDIE,[8] b. Dec. 26, 1869; d. April 9, 1888.
    1589 ii   ALICE, b. Aug. 1, 1872.

634 MARY C.[7] EMERY (*John P.,*[6] *Ebenezer,*[5] *Thomas,*[4] *James,*[3] *James,*[2] *Anthony*[1]), daughter of John P. and Polly (Smith) Emery ; married July 3, 1859, George M. Bickford.
Children :

    1590 i   EMERY,[8] b. Sept. 1, 1862; d. Oct. 3, 1868.
    1591 ii   CLARENCE O., b. July 9, 1870.

636 BENJAMIN[7] EMERY (*Nathaniel,*[6] *Thomas,*[5] *Thomas,*[4] *James,*[3] *James,*[2] *Anthony*[1]), son of Nathaniel and Jane (Harmon) Emery ; married Mary Davis : died June 26, 1877.
Children, born in Hartford, Me., except the first :

    1592 i   JAMES I.,[8] b. May 24, 1824, in Buxton, Me.
    1593 ii   JOSIAH D., b. April 1, 1826.

1594 iii MARTHA N , b Feb 10, 1828
1595 iv MARY J , b Oct 28, 1831
1596 v EMILY A , b April 1, 1834, m. Oct. 26, 1867, Ralph Jewett.
1597 vi ELIZABETH A , b Jan 21, 1836
1598 vii SARAH W , b. March 24, 1840, m James Jewett

637 DORCAS[7] EMERY (*Nathaniel,[6] Thomas,[5] Thomas,[4] James,[3] James,[2] Anthony[1]*), daughter of Nathaniel and Jane (Harmon) Emery; married May, 1830, James Hussey of Buckfield. Me , born Nov. 25, 1806. She died Sept. 4. 1865.

Children :

1599 i SIMEON,[8] b Dec 3, 1830
1600 ii SARAH JANE, b June 24, 1833, d May 24, 1837
1601 iii EMILY A , b. July 23, 1835, m March 9, 1872, William W. Bessey
1602 iv CAROLINE, b. 1836
1603 v SARAH JANE
1604 vi HENRIETTA
1605 vii REBECCA L.

640 NATHANIEL[7] EMERY, JR. (*Nathaniel,[6] Thomas,[5] Thomas,[4] James,[3] James,[2] Anthony[1]*), son of Nathaniel and Jane (Harmon) Emery , married Eliza Clary.

Children :

1606 i JENNIE,[8] b Sept 17, 1850, d Dec. 11, 1864.
1607 ii ISAAC, b Jan. 18, 1854, m Myra Thompson.
1608 iii FRANK, b Oct. 20, 1859

641 THEODORE[7] EMERY (*Nathaniel,[6] Thomas,[5] Thomas,[4] James,[3] James,[2] Anthony[1]*), son of Nathaniel and Jane (Harmon) Emery , married Charlotte J Lombard of Otisfield, Me. (born Aug. 16, 1831). He died Dec 17, 1866.

Children .

1609 i JENNIE N ,[8] b Dec 14, 1851, in Hartford, Me , d in Brockton, Mass , July 17, 1882
1610 ii ADDIE M., b June 10, 1853
1611 iii WALTER L , b April 1, 1855, in Buxton, Me
1612 iv CLARA B , b Feb 8, 1857, d at Otisfield, Me , Feb 2, 1869
1613 v WILLIAM A , b July 21, 1862

645 RUFUS[7] EMERY (*Thomas,[6] Thomas,[5] Thomas,[4] James,[3] James,[2] Anthony[1]*), son of Thomas and Mary (Woodman) Emery , married July 4, 1827, Sophia Fitch

Children, born in Buxton, Me.

1614 i FRANK C ,[8] b Sept 8, 1828.
1615 ii ISAAC, b June 15, 1832
1616 iii SARAH, b Dec 25, 1834, d Sept 24, 1861
1617 iv MARY, b Oct 19, 1841, m Oct. 6, 1878, Joseph B. Sherman
1618 v ALPHEUS, b May 5, 1845

646 HANNAH[7] EMERY (*Thomas,[6] Thomas,[5] Thomas,[4] James,[3] James,[2] Anthony[1]*), daughter of Thomas and Mary (Woodman) Emery , married Nov. 25, 1822, Richard Steele.

Children :

1619   i   RUFUS E ,[8] b Aug. 13, 1823 , d Oct 4, 1841.
1620   ii MARY JANE, b Feb 25, 1826.
1621   iii ELIZABETH, b Sept 30, 1828.
1622   iv AMANDA b April 14, 1832 , m. Feb 5, 1856, W. H Eaton, d.
           Feb 25, 1857

647 MARY[7] EMERY (*Thomas,[6] Thomas,[5] Thomas,[4] James.[3] James,[2] Anthony[1]*), daughter of Thomas and Mary (Woodman) Emery ; married Sept. 18, 1823, John Bradbury.
   Children, born in Buxton, Me. :

1623   i   HIRAM W ,[8] b July 12, 1826
1624   ii THOMAS, b Aug 10, 1830
1625   iii CHARLES H., b. April 7, 1836.
1626   iv MARY E , b April 5, 1842

648 THOMAS J.[7] EMERY (*Thomas,[6] Thomas,[5] Thomas,[4] James,[3] James,[2] Anthony[1]*), son of Thomas and Mary (Woodman) Emery ; married Nov. 14, 1830, Mary Ann Cobb
   Children ·

1627   i   ELIZABETH D ,[8] b Dec 31, 1833
1628   ii HATTIE J , b April 15, 1835 ; m Oren Marston, 1850
1629   iii HELEN B , b July 15, 1845 ; m March 30, 1864, John M.
           Stevens.

649 JAMES W[7] EMERY (*Thomas,[6] Thomas,[5] Thomas,[4] James,[3] James,[2] Anthony[1]*), son of Thomas and Mary (Woodman) Emery ; married in Boston, Mass., Oct. 20, 1830, Abigail E. Wood (born May 29, 1809 , died in Standish, Me., March 27, 1880).
   Children .

1630   i   JAMES KIRK,[8] b Feb 25, 1832, in Boston.
1631   ii GEO HENRY, b. May 5, 1834, in Boston
1632   iii THOMAS DILL, b May 25, 1838, in Standish, Me.
1633   iv ELLEN, b Sept. 13, 1845, d Oct. 15, 1865, in Standish, Me

650 HORACE[7] EMERY (*Thomas,[6] Thomas,[5] Thomas,[4] James,[3] James,[2] Anthony[1]*), son of Thomas and Mary (Woodman) Emery , married Nov. 25, 1835, Sarah Davis.
   Children, born in Buxton, Me. :

1634   i   GEORGE M ,[8] b Nov. 4, 1836, m. Eunice Sherman, Dec 1,
           1857
1635   ii HORACE B , b July 5, 1841, m Rebecca Berry, June 18, 1868
1636   iii JULIA A , b March 26, 1843
1637   iv JOHN E , b Aug 19, 1845 , d March 1, 1847.
1638   v   HATTIE A , b May 17, 1848
1639   vi WILLIAM F b March 27 1851
1640   vii HORATIO J., b Feb 1, 1854, unm

651 ALEXANDER J.[7] EMERY (*Thomas,[6] Thomas.[5] Thomas,[4] James,[3] James,[2] Anthony[1]*), son of Thomas and Mary (Woodman) Emery ; married Aug 1, 1838, Eliza Steele. He died Nov. 15, 1865.
   Children, born in Buxton :

1641   i   CHARLES E ,[8] b July 20, 1839
1642   ii JOHN S , b Jan 24, 1842, wounded at the second battle of
           Bull Run , d in hospital at Philadelphia, Pa., Sept. 28, 1862.

1643 iii MARCIA S., b. June 29, 1844, d Aug 4, 1845
1644 iv RUFUS S, b Jan. 4, 1847, m Amanda E Nokes, had four
         children
1645 v MARCIA S., b July 1, 1849, d Aug 10, 1883
1646 vi BARTLETT S, b June 7, 1851, m Ellamæ Sawyer, Oct. 30,
         1880
1647 vii CLARA S , b Dec 29, 1853, d Jan 1, 1856

653 ELIZA W.[7] EMERY (*Thomas,*[6] *Thomas,*[5] *Thomas,*[4] *James,*[3]
James,[2] *Anthony*[1]), daughter of Thomas and Mary (Woodman) Emery, married, first, Sept. 28, 1836, Washington Kimball, second,
Nov. 10, 1851, Joseph G. Steele.
Children, born in Buxton, Me. :

1648 i THOMAS K ,[8] b. Sept. 11, 1837 , m Ellen M. Tomlinson, April
         4, 1874
1649 ii MARK W , b June 20, 1839; died on board the U S S "Kear-
         sarge " at Brest, Aug 19, 1863

By an act of the Maine legislature the surnames of the above children were changed from Kimball to Emery.

654 HARRIET F. B.[7] EMERY (*Thomas,*[6] *Thomas,*[5] *Thomas,*[4] *James,*[3]
James,[2] *Anthony*[1]) daughter of Thomas and Mary (Woodman) Emery; married Nov. 17, 1858, Joseph Dunnell.
Children :

1650 i GEORGE E ,[8] b Aug 5, 1845
1651 ii MILLARD F , b May 6, 1851, d April 16, 1852
1652 iii MARY A , b. Nov. 17, 1858.

655 HANNAH E.[7] JOSE (*Sally,*[6] *Thomas,*[5] *Thomas,*[4] *James,*[3] *James,*[2]
Anthony[1]), daughter of Alexander and Sally (Emery) Jose , married
June 10, 1828, Moses Small of Limington, Me. (born May 24, 1804 ;
died Oct. 24, 1833).
Children, born in Limington :

1653 i ARVILLA WHARTON,[8] b April 5, 1829
1654 ii SARAH ELLEN, b Dec 23, 1830
1655 iii MOSES, b June 24, 1833; d July 23, 1833.

656 ABIGAIL A.[7] JOSE (*Sally,*[6] *Thomas,*[5] *Thomas,*[4] *James,*[3]
James,[2] *Anthony*[1]), daughter of Alexander and Sally (Emery) Jose ;
married April 29, 1834, Richard Small.
Children ·

1656 i MOSES,[8] b. Feb. 24, 1835; d Oct 15, 1842, in Limington, Me.
1657 ii SALLY EMERY, b Dec 26, 1836, in Limington, Me
1658 iii HORATIO NELSON b Nov. 10, 1839, in Buxton, Me
1659 iv JOHN CHASE, b Nov 5, 1841, in Buxton, Me.
1660 v ABBY ANN, b. Jan. 21, 1844, in Buxton, Me

657 MARK E [7] JOSE (*Sally,*[6] *Thomas,*[5] *Thomas,*[4] *James,*[3] *James,*[2]
Anthony[1]), son of Alexander and Sally (Emery) Jose , married Dec.
11, 1837, Dorcas Rebecca Hanson (born Oct. 17, 1816).
Children, born in Buxton :

1661 i MARY MORRIS,[8] b Aug 2, 1838
1662 ii SARAH ELIZABETH, b Jan 14, 1840
1663 iii ANN ELIZA, b. Feb. 28, 1846

658 CHARLES E [7] JOSE (*Sally,*[6] *Thomas,*[5] *Thomas,*[4] *James,*[3] *James,*[2] *Anthony*[1]), son of Alexander and Sally (Emery) Jose; married Sept. 20, 1852 Augusta Wood (born in Portland, Me , April 13, 1828).
    Child :

        1664   i   LOVEY,[8] b April 23, 1854; d Aug. 28, 1863

659 HORATIO N [7] JOSE (*Sally,*[6] *Thomas,*[5] *Thomas,*[4] *James,*[3] *James,*[2] *Anthony*[1]), son of Alexander and Sally (Emery) Jose , married Aug. 30, 1843, Nanny Brown Hooper (born April 17, 1820). He was an active business man, interested in the prosperity of his city and a supporter of all enterprises benefiting society.
    Children, born in Portland, Me. ·

        1665   i   HORATIO NELSON,[8] b March 27, 1845, d. Aug 4, 1853
        1666   ii   CARRIE HOOPER b May 18, 1848, d Sept 11, 1851
        1667   iii   HELEN NOYES, b Jan 25, 1853
        1668   iv   JESSIE HOOPER, b Nov 8, 1860

661 EMILY M.[7] JOSE (*Sally,*[6] *Thomas,*[5] *Thomas,*[4] *James,*[3] *James,*[2] *Anthony*[1]), daughter of Alexander and Sally (Emery) Jose; married, first, Sept 10, 1848, Oliver P Reynolds (died 1852); second, June 10, 1861, Elias Tarbox Milliken (born April 10, 1810).
    Children, born in Boston

        1669   i   EMILY JOSE,[8] b Nov 30, 1867
        1670   ii   EDITH BURNSIDE, b. Oct. 18, 1869.

662 MARY L.[7] EMERY (*John,*[6] *Thomas,*[5] *Thomas,*[4] *James,*[3] *James,*[2] *Anthony*[1]), daughter of John and Hannah (Locke) Emery; married July 29, 1839, Rev. Edward Cook, D.D. ; minister in the Methodist Episcopal Church, engaged in educational work in charge of Pennington Seminary, N. J , Laurence University, Wis , Wilbraham Seminary, Mass., Claflin Seminary, S. C ; received the degree of D.D. from Harvard University, 1855.
    Children .

        1671   i   JOSEPHINE EMERY,[8] b Sept 12, 1840, in Kennebunk, Me
        1672   ii   WILBUR FISK, b in Pennington, N. J., Feb. 17, 1842, d. in
                     Kennebunk, Me., Oct. 31. 1842
        1673   iii   MARY ELIZA, b July 21, 1845, in Pennington, N J ; m. in
                     Wilbraham, Mass., Robert R Wright

665 STEPHEN L.[7] EMERY (*John,*[6] *Thomas,*[5] *Thomas,*[4] *James,*[3] *James,*[2] *Anthony*[1]), son of John and Hannah (Locke) Emery; married Clara Gilman in Portland, Me
    Children :

        1674   i   ELLEN FRANCES,[8] b Dec 15, 1849, in Charlestown, Mass
        1675   ii   CLARA MARCIA, b. Oct 3, 1852, in Boston, Mass , m. Dec. 23,
                     1873, Charles C Dunbar.

666 HANNAH[7] EMERY (*John,*[6] *Thomas,*[5] *Thomas,*[4] *James,*[3] *James,*[2] *Anthony*[1]), daughter of John and Hannah (Locke) Emery; married Sept 4, 1845, James Neal (born July 3, 1817).
    Children, born in North Berwick, Me. :

1676 i CHARLES EDWARD,[9] b Nov. 11, 1847; m in Neponset, Mass ,
     .   Roselle Barker, Dec. 10, 1873, d Jan 25, 1877.
1677 ii CLARA ABBY, b April 2, 1851, m. in Neponset, Mass , July
          16, 1885, Geo. E. Curry.

667 SUSAN H [7] EMERY (*John*,[6] *Thomas*,[5] *Thomas*,[4] *James*,[3] *James*,[2] *Anthony*[1]), daughter of John and Hannah (Locke) Emery , married in Boston, Mass , March 17, 1851, Thomas J. Hobbs (born Sept., 1821).
Children, born in North Berwick, Me. ·

1678 i FRANK EMERY,[8] b Jan , 1855
1679 ii GEORGE SHELDEN, b. April, 1861; d in Washington, D. C.,
          Nov , 1884

668 ABBY M [7] EMERY (*John*,[6] *Thomas*,[5] *Thomas*,[4] *James*,[3] *James*,[2] *Anthony*[1]), daughter of John and Hannah (Locke) Emery; married, Oct. 19, 1854, William G. Perkins (born June 25, 1823).
Children :

1680 i WILLIE BABCOCK,[8] b Nov. 30, 1857, d in Kennebunkport,
          Me., Nov 21, 1862.
1681 ii HARRY FRENCH, b. Sept. 18, 1865.

671 ALMIRA[7] EMERY (*Joseph D* ,[6] *Thomas*,[5] *Thomas*,[4] *James*,[3] *James*,[2] *Anthony*[1]), daughter of Joseph D and Abigail (Moulton) Emery ; married, first, Sept. 18, 1833, George Robinson, a graduate of Bowdoin College, 1831, and lawyer of Augusta, Me. (died Feb. 25, 1840) ; second, Nov. 18, 1840, Hon. Richard Drury Rice; lawyer, appointed judge of the Court of Common Pleas, 1848 , associate justice of the Superior Court, 1852 : resigned, 1863 , died May 27, 1882.
Children, by first marriage :

1682 i GEORGE,[8] b. Aug. 6, 1834, grad at Bowdoin Coll , professor in
          Jefferson Coll , La , d June 21, 1867.
1683 ii SUSAN HOWARD, b Nov 26, 1836
1684 iii JOSEPH EMERY, b Sept 7, 1839, m Jan 18, 1872, Helen Ste-
          vens Cook of Rockland, Me., d Oct. 3, 1885

By second marriage :

1685 iv ABBY EMERY, b. May 18, 1842, d in San Francisco, Cal , Sept
          27, 1870

673 AMELIA CATHARINE[7] EMERY (*Joseph D.*,[6] *Thomas*,[5] *Thomas*,[4] *James*,[3] *James*,[2] *Anthony*[1]), daughter of Joseph D. and Abigail (Moulton) Emery ; married April 22, 1840, Rev. Ezekiel McLeod of St. John, N B (died in Fredericton, N. B., March 20, 1857).
Children

1686 i HARRIET,[8] b 1841
1687 ii EDWARD, b 1842; d 1844.
1688 iii JOSEPH EMERY
1689 iv GEORGE.
1690 v ABBIE
1691 vi ALBERT, d 1858
1692 vii EZEKIEL
1693 viii AMELIA
1694 ix REBECCA
1695 x IDA, d 1868.

675 SUSAN A.[7] EMERY (*Joseph D.,*[6] *Thomas,*[5] *Thomas,*[4] *James,*[3] *James,*[2] *Anthony*[1]), daughter of Joseph D. and Abigail (Moulton) Emery, married Nov. 30, 1846, William S. Badger of Augusta, Me. (born Feb. 23, 1820), son of Nathaniel and Jane (Owen) Badger Children.

    1696 i   ABBY JANE,[8] b Aug 30, 1847; d. Sept. 9, 1848.
    1697 ii WILLIAM S , b. Nov. 1, 1848
    1698 iii JOSEPH EMERY, b. March 19, 1851

676 SARAH ELIZABETH[7] EMERY (*Joseph D.,*[6] *Thomas,*[5] *Thomas,*[4] *James,*[3] *James,*[2] *Anthony*[1]), daughter of Joseph D. and Abigail (Moulton) Emery, married, first, March 11, 1849, Samuel C. Holman of Charlottetown, P. E. Island (d Oct. 6 1852) , second, May 1, 1855, Hester N Hope of St. Eleanors, P. E. Island (died June, 1867)
    Children, by first marriage:

    1699 i   SARAH AMANDA,[8] b May 13. 1850, d 1857
    1700 ii SUSAN MARIA, b Sept 13, 1852, d 1853

By second marriage:

    1701 iii SUSIE GOODWIN, b Feb 22, 1858; d June, 1867.

678 ELLEN M.[7] EMERY (*Joseph D.,*[6] *Thomas,*[5] *Thomas,*[4] *James,*[3] *James,*[2] *Anthony*[1]), daughter of Joseph D. and Abigail (Moulton) Emery, married April 26, 1853, John R. Larrabee of California
    Children :

    1702 i   EBEN FRANCIS,[8] b. March 19, 1854.
    1703 ii ABBY JOSEPHINE, b Jan 30, 1858
    1704 iii NELLIE EMERY, b Jan 31, 1860; d 1869
    1705 iv JULIA GAIL, b May 29, 1870
    1706 v   MARY ROBERTS, b. Aug. 20, 1872.

680 GEORGE FRED[7] EMERY (*Isaac,*[6] *Thomas,*[5] *Thomas,*[4] *James,*[3] *James,*[2] *Anthony*[1]), son of Isaac and Faith Savage (Bigelow) Emery; married, first, May 29, 1842, Elizabeth Marble (died Aug. 28, 1847) ; second, July 5, 1855, Imogene A. Farrar of Providence, R I. (died July 24, 1861) ; third, Feb. 2, 1869, Catharine H. Thorndike. He died suddenly Jan. 19, 1885, being stricken with apoplexy while attending the annual meeting of the Webster Historical Society in the Old South Meeting House, Boston.
    Children, by first wife:

    1707 i   LUCY BIGELOW,[8] b Feb 20, 1843, d. Sept 2, 1849.
    1708 ii WILLIAM H , b Oct 24, 1844

By second wife, born in Boston:

    1709 iii I WILL, b. March 30, 1856.
    1710 iv FLORENCE L , b. Nov. 19, 1858.
    1711 v   MARY J , b March 22, 1861

By third wife:

    1712 vi BEATRICE T , b March 1, 1870, in Boston.

681 WILLIAM H.[7] EMERY (*Isaac,*[6] *Thomas,*[5] *Thomas,*[4] *James,*[3]

James,[2] *Anthony*[1]), son of Isaac and Faith Savage (Bigelow) Emery ;
married, first. Oct 5, 1847, Sarah R Haviland (died Oct. 16, 1855) ;
second, Oct. 22, 1856, Eliza Bishop (born Aug. 12, 1833).
Children, by first wife :

    1713 i   MARY H ,[3] b Aug. 11, 1848.
    1714 ii   HELEN B , b Jan 31, 1851

By second wife .

    1715 iii ELIZA KATE, b Aug. 1, 1864
    1716 iv   WILLIAM BISHOP, b. Nov 18, 1867.
    1717 v   HEBER BISHOP, b March 12, 1870

684 JOSEPH D [7] EMERY (*Peter,*[6] *Thomas,*[5] *Thomas,*[4] *James,*[3] *James,*[2]
Anthony[1]), son of Peter and Eliza (Sands) Emery , married Dec. 17,
1851, Shuah (born in Standish, Me., July 30, 1826 ; died Jan 27,
1889), daughter of John and Ann (Hooper) Woodman.   Machinist.
Children

    1718 i   ANNIE E ,[8] b Nov 14, 1852, d Sept 1, 1869
    1719 ii   ESTELLA, b March 6, 1855 ; m Oct , 1887, C A Boothby of
               Kennebunk, Me
    1720 iii LUCY E , b Sept 20, 1861, m July, 1888, Bradbury S Gerold
               of Waltham, Mass.

685 JOHN[7] EMERY (*Peter,*[6] *Thomas,*[5] *Thomas,*[4] *James,*[3] *James,*[2]
Anthony[1]), son of Peter and Eliza (Sands) Emery , married Nov 11,
1862, Sarah J Redman, daughter of James and Agnes (Wilson) Redman of New Brunswick.   Farmer ; died April 19, 1890
Child .

    1721 i   ALICE C ,[8] b Dec 27, 1864, m Dec 31, 1885, S L. Libby of
               So Gorham, Me.

687 ALMIRA S [7] EMERY (*Peter,*[6] *Thomas,*[5] *Thomas,*[4] *James,*[3]
James,[2] *Anthony*[1]), daughter of Peter and Eliza (Sands) Emery ;
married Jan. 2, 1854, Israel Clifford, son of Israel and Rebecca (Gilpatrick) Clifford, of Biddeford, Me.
Children :

    1722 i   ELIZA REBECCA,[8] b Feb. 5, 1855, d Sept , 1869
    1723 ii   SARAH ELLEN, b April 1, 1858

690 SALLIE J.[7] EMERY (*Peter,*[6] *Thomas,*[5] *Thomas,*[4] *James,*[3] *James,*[2]
Anthony[1]). daughter of Peter and Eliza (Sands) Emery , married
Sept 22, 1854, Arthur Boothby (died Nov., 1887), son of Samuel and
Althea (Edgerly) Boothby of Buxton, Me.   She died June 23, 1887.
Children .

    1724 i   SAMUEL,[8] b. Oct 31, 1855 ; m. July 25, 1882, Ella Gertrude
               Hicks of Portland, Me
    1725 ii   MIRIAM M , b Feb 5, 1858
    1726 iii SUSAN E , b Jan 20, 1861, d April 16, 1884
    1727 iv   EILEEN H , b Sept 29, 1862

693 NANCY M.[7] EMERY (*Peter,*[6] *Thomas,*[5] *Thomas,*[4] *James,*[3] *James,*[2]
Anthony[1]), daughter of Peter and Eliza (Sands) Emery , married

Sept 23, 1866, George H Libby (born Sept 8, 1836), son of Richard J and Jane W (Merrill) Libby.
Children:

    1728 i   IRA FRAZIER,[8] b Oct 18, 1867
    1729 ii ELIZA SANDS, b Feb 1 1872
    1730 iii RICHARD JOSE, b Feb 9, 1881.

695 DAVID[7] EMERY (*Zachariah,*[6] *Zachariah,*[5] *Zachariah,*[4] *Zachariah,*[3] *James,*[2] *Anthony*[1]), son of Zachariah and Mary (Leeman) Emery, married Polly Corbet; settled in Winfield, Oneida Co., N. Y
Children:

    1731 i   CORBET[8]
    1732 ii LEEMAN
    1733 iii GEORGE
    1734 iv ORESTES A BRONSON
    1735 v   EMILY A.
    1736 vi CAROLINE, d at 20 years of age

696 LUCY[7] EMERY (*Zachariah,*[6] *Zachariah,*[5] *Zachariah,*[4] *Zachariah,*[3] *James,*[2] *Anthony*[1]), daughter of Zachariah and Mary (Leeman) Emery; married, Feb. 25, 1802 Joseph Ball, settled in Litchfield, Herkimer Co, N. Y.
Children:

    1737 I   HORACE[8]
    1738 ii WILBUR
    1739 iii HARTLEY.
    1740 iv JONATHAN
    1741 v   MARY ANN
    1742 vi LUCY
Two other children, Nos 1743–1744

697 SAMUEL[7] EMERY (*Zachariah,*[6] *Zachariah,*[5] *Zachariah,*[4] *Zachariah,*[3] *James,*[2] *Anthony*[1]), son of Zachariah and Mary (Leeman) Emery; married May 11, 1815, Nancy Gardner, daughter of Abel and Susannah (Bryant) Gardner of Hingham, Mass.; removed to Ohio in 1831.
Children ·

    1745 i   SAMUEL LEEMAN,[8] b March 1, 1816, in Temple, N H
    1746 ii CLEMENTINE, b May 6, 1817, in Temple, N H ; d April 22, 1884.
    1747 iii HOMER CHARLES, b April 4, 1820, in Temple, N. H. Lives in Union, Oregon
    1748 iv LUCY, b Oct 27, 1823, in Temple, N H , d. May 15, 1825
    1749 v   ABEL GARDNER, } b Dec. 25, 1826, {
    1750 vi SUSANNAH BRYANT, }   { d Oct 4, 1837

698 BETSEY[7] EMERY (*Zachariah,*[6] *Zachariah,*[5] *Zachariah,*[4] *Zachariah,*[3] *James,*[2] *Anthony*[1]), daughter of Zachariah and Mary (Leeman) Emery, married Jeremiah Everett, settled in Michigan previous to Hull's surrender, then went to what is now Fremont, Ohio He died Dec 30, 1830.
Child

    1751 i   HOMER EVERETT,[8] lawyer in Fremont, O.

699 HORACE[7] EMERY (*Zachariah,[6] Zachariah,[5] Zachariah,[4] Zachariah,[3] James,[2] Anthony[1]*), son of Zachariah and Mary (Leeman) Emery, married Nov. 4, 1821, Sally Beardsley (born Oct. 12, 1795; died in Chicago, Ill, March 27, 1869). He died at Albany, N Y., June 19, 1851.

Children :

1752	i	HORACE L ,[8] b Sept 21, 1822
1753	ii	WILLIAM B., b March 16, 1824.
1754	iii	HENRY D., b Feb. 12, 1826.
1755	iv	SARAH C., b. Dec. 17, 1827, m. Jan., 1850, John P Blood, d. May, 1856.
1756	v	GEORGE W , b May 8, 1830, d May, 1868.
1757	vi	ALBERT T , b April 27, 1832.
1758	vii	CHARLES, b July 20, 1834
1759	viii	LAURA L , b July 2, 1836.
1760	ix	CLARISSA A., b Oct 25, 1840.

701 MELINDA[7] EMERY(*Zachariah,[6] Zachariah,[5] Zachariah,[4] Zachariah,[3] James,[2] Anthony[1]*), daughter of Zachariah and Mary (Leeman) Emery; married June 16, 1823, Oliver Corbet (died Sept. 26, 1856); lived at Bridgewater, N. Y. She died Oct., 1861.

Children :

1761	i	OLIVER H. PERRY,[8] b. June 16, 1828, m April 12, 1851, Julia W Birdsey.
1762	ii	ELIZABETH M , b Nov 23, 1830
1763	iii	ULYSSES F , b. March 30, 1836, m. Salome L. Hibbard, Feb 28, 1856
1764	iv	WALLACE W , b Dec 23, 1838; m in Chicago, Ill., Mercy C. Johnson

702 AMOS[7] EMERY (*Amos,[6] Zachariah,[5] Zachariah,[4] Zachariah,[3] James,[2] Anthony[1]*), son of Amos and Lucretia (Morse) Emery; married Sept. 26, 1799, Hannah Elliot (born March 31, 1781, died Feb. 3, 1855), daughter of David and Hannah (Adams) Elliot He died Oct 11, 1857.

Children :

1765	i	DAVID ELLIOT,[8] b Sept 14, 1800, in Windham, Vt ; d in York, Wis , June 10, 1854.
1766	ii	EUNICE ADAMS, b June 30, 1802.
1767	iii	ELIZA, b Feb 14, 1804, d Feb 15, 1804
1768	iv	ELIJAH, b March 24, 1805, d April 11, 1805.
1769	v	HARRIET, b April 28, 1806, d. Oct 9, 1806
1770	vi	EMILY, b Feb 28, 1808 , d Sept. 27, 1810
1771	vii	ELVIRA, b April 10, 1810
1772	viii	HANNAH, b April 26, 1812, d Feb 5, 1821.
1773	ix	AMOS, b Jan 28, 1815, d Sept 23, 1831.
1774	x	LUCRETIA, b July 29, 1817.
1775	xi	AZRO, b Nov 18, 1819
1776	xii	HENRY EVERETT, b May 17, 1822; d at St James, Mo , Dec 22, 1871.
1777	xiii	HENRIETTA, b Oct 3, 1825, resides in Windham, Vt , unm.

703 LUCY[7] EMERY (*Amos,[6] Zachariah,[5] Zachariah,[4] Zachariah,[3] James,[2] Anthony[1]*), daughter of Amos and Lucretia (Morse) Emery; married Nov. 6, 1801, Samuel Buss of Jaffrey, N. H. (died July 29, 1837). She died Jan. 9, 1863.

25

Children, born in Jaffrey, N H. :

1778 i ARTEMAS [8] b Aug 24, 1802, d. Sept 13, 1802
1779 ii EMILY, b Sept 3, 1803, m. Dec 29, 1829, Dea. Liberty Mower of Jaffrey, N H , d. July 14, 1845
1780 iii CLARISSA, b. Sept 20, 1805, m Jabez Stearns, who d. Oct. 6, 1854
1781 iv LUCY EMERY, b March 31, 1807, d , unm , Dec. 19, 1870.
1782 v WILLIAM b Dec 20, 1809, m Oct 28, 1837, Ruth Frye Wolcott of Boston, Mass , d March 10, 1862
1783 vi AMOS EMERY, b Nov 27, 1812, m Aug. 5, 1841, Harriet Adams of Jaffrey, N H , went to Oneida, O , d. April 25, 1872.
1784 vii MARIA, b Jan 14, 1815, m June 8, 1842, Dwight Thompson of Ill , d Sept 18, 1870
1785 viii MARY ANN, b Aug 21, 1817.
1786 ix SAMUEL LINCOLN, b Aug 19, 1821; m March 10, 1846, Margaret Baker of Boston, d Aug. 10, 1868

704 ESTHER[7] EMERY (*Amos,*[6] *Zachariah,*[5] *Zachariah,*[4] *Zachariah,*[3] *James,*[2] *Anthony*[1]), daughter of Amos and Lucretia (Morse) Emery; married June 15, 1800, John Perry (born June 12, 1768, died Dec 1, 1863). She died Dec. 24, 1863 Lived in Dublin, N. H.
Children .

1787 i CAROLINE,[8] b April 1. 1801
1788 ii THOMAS, b Jan 3, 1803, m 1854
1789 iii LUCRETIA E , b June 28, 1805, m Calmer Harris, and had one child, Eunice; d. March 1, 1854
1790 iv JOHN, b. Aug. 29, 1807, m. Nov 16, 1837, Elmira Jewell of Jaffrey, N. H
1791 v ORPHA B , b June 7, 1809; d., unm , March 22, 1880.
1792 vi MARY A , b Oct 26, 1811.
1793 vii CATHARINE E , b. Oct. 16, 1813, d , unm., Aug 27, 1847.
1794 viii AMOS E., b May 5 1816, m Dec. 2, 1846, Sophia Mower of Jaffrey, N H
1795 ix MOSES K , b July 22, 1819, m April 18, 1848, Louisa A. Stanley of Jaffrey, N H

710 RUTH[7] EMERY (*John,*[6] *Zachariah,*[5] *Zachariah,*[4] *Zachariah,*[3] *James,*[2] *Anthony*[1]), daughter of John and Ruth (Sanders) Emery, married Feb. 14, 1805, Daniel Warner (died 1815).
Children :

1796 i DANIEL,[8] b June 17, 1807.
1797 ii NANCY, b July 24, 1809, m Artemas Hodgeman, d Jan 23, 1870
1798 iii ADELINE
1799 iv MARY, m. B. Patrick, removed west.
1800 v RUTH.

711 LUCY[7] EMERY (*John,*[6] *Zachariah,*[5] *Zachariah,*[4] *Zachariah,*[3] *James,*[2] *Anthony*[1]), daughter of John and Ruth (Sanders) Emery; married Feb. 21, 1805, Capt Isaac Spaulding (born Dec 24, 1779, died Dec 15, 1834), son of Lieut. Benj. and Mary (Heald) Spaulding. Lived in Townsend, Mass. She died Dec. 29, 1862.
Children :

1801 i POLLY,[8] b Jan 24, 1806, m Eli Baldwin, May 25, 1829; d Sept. 10, 1833
1802 ii ISAAC, b. Dec. 4, 1807.

1803 iii JOHN, b Oct 6, 1809; d at Townsend, Mass Oct 4, 1882
1804 iv LUCY, b Jan 12, 1812; m Flint Ball, May, 1833
1805 v DANIEL, b Feb 14, 1814.
1806 vi RUTH, b Sept 29, 1816.
1807 vii MILES, b. April 4, 1819.
1808 viii HARRIET N , b. Sept. 5, 1822, lives in Townsend, Mass., unm
1809 ix NANCY, b. Sept 15, 1826, m James Gibson, Sept., 1849.

712 NANCY[7] EMERY (*John,*[6] *Zachariah,*[5] *Zachariah,*[4] *Zachariah,*[3] *James,*[2] *Anthony*[1]), daughter of John and Ruth (Sanders) Emery; married Dec 1, 1814, John Scales (died March 23, 1879). She died March 29, 1874. Lived in Townsend, Mass.
Children :

1810 i JOHN,[8] b Feb. 9, 1818.
1811 ii RALPH, b. June 17, 1820; m Nov , 1856
1812 iii MARY, b. Aug 8, 1827, m June 10, 1856.
1813 iv JOEL, b June 28, 1831; m Dec , 1878

713 JOEL[7] EMERY (*John,*[6] *Zachariah,*[5] *Zachariah.*[4] *Zachariah,*[3] *James,*[2] *Anthony*[1]), son of John and Ruth (Sanders) Emery, married, first, June 27, 1819, Mary Sylvester, second, March 8, 1821, Fanny Gilchrist. He died July 13, 1875.
Children :

1814 i CHARLES,[8] b Dec 3, 1819; m Amanda Wolcott.
1815 ii SUSAN, b. April 10, 1822, m. Warren Wilson (d Nov. 23, 1881)

715 EZRA[7] EMERY (*John,*[6] *Zachariah,*[5] *Zachariah,*[4] *Zachariah,*[3] *James,*[2] *Anthony*[1]), son of John and Ruth (Sanders) Emery, married Oct. 5, 1824, Sally Warner (died Nov. 19, 1880) ; removed to Augusta, Me , the same year. He was an earnest advocate of the temperance cause and much respected in the community. He died Sept. 13, 1871.
Children :

1816 i MARY L.,[8] b Oct 7, 1825, res in Augusta, Me , unm
1817 ii CHARLES W , b. June 16, 1831, d in Boston, Mass , March 4, 1871.

716 DARIUS[7] EMERY (*John,*[6] *Zachariah,*[5] *Zachariah,*[4] *Zachariah,*[3] *James,*[2] *Anthony*[1]), son of John and Ruth (Sanders) Emery; married Lucy Longley. Lived in Shirley, Mass. He died in Springfield, Mass., Jan. 27, 1881.
Child :

1818 i HIRAM,[8] d in Springfield, Mass , m , had a dau now Mrs Fuller

717 LUCY EMERY[7] CAMPBELL (*Lucy,*[6] *Zachariah,*[5] *Zachariah,*[4] *Zachariah,*[3] *James,*[2] *Anthony*[1]), daughter of Daniel and Lucy (Emery) Campbell; married Dec. 31, 1801, Moses Marshall of Dublin, N. H. (born in Holliston, Me., Dec. 15, 1775).
Children ·

1819 i EVELINE,[8] b. Sept. 18, 1802.
1820 ii MOSES, b Jan. 16, 1804; d young.

1821   iii   ORLANDO, b Jan 28, 1805
1822   iv   LUCY E , b Aug 2, 1811
1823   v   SYBIL, d young
1824   vi   AUGUSTA M , b Feb 22, 1813
1825   vii   MARY ANN, b July 19, 1816.
1826   viii   GEORGE C , b May 28, 1818
1827   ix   SARAH J , b. Jan 3. 1820, d 1826.
1828   x   CHARLES B., b Sept. 26, 1824

720 ESTHER[7] EMERY (*Samuel*,[6] *Zachariah*,[5] *Zachariah*,[4] *Zachariah*,[3] *James*,[2] *Anthony*[1]), daughter of Samuel and Olive (Jaquith) Emery; married April, 1819, Stephen Knight of Rindge, N. H. (born Sept. 28, 1791, died Oct. 1, 1853); removed to Jaffrey, N. H. She died Nov. 27, 1859.

Children :

1829   i   STEPHEN EMERY,[8] b April 24, 1823
1830   ii   ESTHER ROSANNA, b Jan. 10, 1830.
1831   iii   SARAH M., b July 1, 1831, m Norman Boardman of Lynn, Iowa

721 SAMUEL[7] EMERY (*Samuel*,[6] *Zachariah*,[5] *Zachariah*,[4] *Zachariah*,[3] *James*,[2] *Anthony*[1]), son of Samuel and Olive (Jaquith) Emery; married July 11, 1821, Mary Bailey, daughter of Oliver and Polly (Perkins) Bailey (born May 8, 1794, died at Cleveland, O., March 26, 1883). He died July 27, 1860

Children :

1832   i   FREDERICK A.,[8] b. Feb. 13, 1823; d Nov 6, 1850.
1833   ii   MARY L , b Sept 15, 1824
1834   iii   AIMOND S , b March 21, 1830
1835   iv   CHRISTOPHER F., b April 10, 1832.
1836   v   ERMINA M., b March 25, 1835.
1837   vi   OLIVER B , b March 4, 1839, d Feb 17, 1840.
1838   vii   ELIZABETH, b 1841, d Feb 13, 1845

722 OLIVE[7] EMERY (*Samuel*,[6] *Zachariah*,[5] *Zachariah*,[4] *Zachariah*,[3] *James*,[2] *Anthony*[1]), daughter of Samuel and Olive (Jaquith) Emery; married David Howe, Feb. 20, 1821. She died July 13, 1871.

Children, born in Rindge, N. H. :

1839   i   JERUSHA A.,[8] b April 8, 1822, m John S Dutton, Sept. 8, 1843, d Jan 25, 1845
1840   ii   OLIVE M   b. Aug 17, 1823, m. Aaron Perkins of Jaffrey, N H , Dec 6, 1843
1841   iii   EMORANCY, b Jan 15, 1825, d in Jaffrey, N H , Oct. 16, 1846
1842   iv   MARY ANN, b Dec 18, 1826, d Jan 21, 1845
1843   v   NANCY R., b. Aug. 22, 1831; d. Nov. 26, 1848.

723 ZACHARIAH[7] EMERY (*William*,[6] *Zachariah*,[5] *Zachariah*,[4] *Zachariah*,[3] *James*,[2] *Anthony*[1]), son of William and Mary (Stanley) Emery, married Rebecca Mower, who after his death married June 11, 1831, Ithamel Lawrence of Jaffrey, N. H. He died March 26, 1830.

Children :

1844   i   MARY REBECCA,[9] b 1821, d. at Hudson, Mich , April 27, 1863
1845   ii   SARAH ELIZA, b. 1823, d. at Jaffrey, N. H., July 2, 1873.

725 Sybil[7] Emery (*William,[6] Zachariah,[5] Zachariah,[4] Zachariah,[3] James,[2] Anthony[1]*), daughter of William and Mary (Stanley) Emery; married April 27, 1820, Josiah Bemis (his second wife) son of James and Lois (Walker) Bemis (born Aug. 20, 1795; died March 6, 1852)

Children, born in Dublin, N. H :

1846 i Alvin J ,[8] b. Aug. 18, 1821, m Mary Greenwood, Mar. 20, 1842
1847 ii James Emery, b May 1, 1824, m. Sarah Lincoln of Jaffrey, N H , Nov 19, 1873

726 Ralph[7] Emery (*William,[6] Zachariah,[5] Zachariah,[4] Zachariah,[3] James,[2] Anthony[1]*), son of William and Mary (Stanley) Emery, married June 6, 1827, Susan Williams of Lynn, Mass. (born July 30, 1801 ; died May 29, 1883, in Orange, Mass.). He died May 8, 1864.

Children :

1848 i Henry W ,[8] b July 14, 1830
1849 ii Charles F , b. Nov 11, 1835
1850 iii Ralph L , b Nov 12, 1837, d Feb. 19, 1845.
1851 iv Amos E , b. Aug 27, 1840.

728 Edward[7] Emery (*William,[6] Zachariah,[5] Zachariah,[4] Zachariah,[3] James,[2] Anthony[1]*), son of William and Mary (Stanley) Emery, married March 1, 1836, Fanny Nutting (born June 13, 1816). He died June 9, 1848.

Children :

1852 i Mary C ,[8] b. March 7, 1838
1853 ii Willard A , b Nov. 28, 1844, d Sept. 17, 1847.

729 Amasa[7] Emery (*William,[6] Zachariah,[5] Zachariah,[4] Zachariah,[3] James,[2] Anthony[1]*), son of William and Mary (Stanley) Emery, married Dec. 25, 1828 Abigail Dutton (died Aug 23, 1871). He died May, 1887.

Children, born in Jaffrey :

1854 i Alonzo Amasa,[8] b Dec 18, 1829, m , 1st, Ellen Kennedy (d. Feb 6, 1864); 2nd, Jenny Wickoff
1855 ii George Dutton, b. Dec 4, 1831, m Oct 26, 1863, Theresa Vanaisdale of Somerville, N Y.
1856 iii Paulina, b Nov 2, 1836; d May 2, 1845.
1857 iv Eliza Ann, b July 4, 1840, d. Aug 26, 1858.
1858 v Ellen Adelaide, b. Sept 5, 1844, d Nov 1, 1845.
1859 vi Frederick W , } b Jan 26, 1847, { d April 12, 1872.
1860 vii Mary Frances, } { d March 27, 1879

730 Nancy Ann[7] Emery (*William,[6] Zachariah,[5] Zachariah,[4] Zachariah,[3] James,[2] Anthony[1]*), daughter of William and Mary (Stanley) Emery; married April 28, 1831, Hervey H Robbins (born Aug. 24, 1807, died Nov. 17, 1849). She died March 1, 1879.

Children, born in Jaffrey, N. H. :

1861 i Mary Stanley,[8] b. Jan 21, 1832
1862 ii Luther Gardner, b July 13, 1833; unm., res in Boston; Robbins & Rowell, Boston
1863 iii Susan Caroline, b July 27, 1835; d April 14, 1855.
1864 iv Elizabeth Carter, b. June 16, 1837, d April 14, 1839

1865   v   LAURA ANN, b. June 17, 1839; d. March 31, 1851.
1866   vi   LUCY ANN, b. Sept. 24, 1842.
1867   vii ALBERT EMERY, b. Dec. 21, 1845; d. Oct. 5, 1880.
1868   viii PAULINE ADELINE, b. April 9, 1847; m. Albert R. Whitney,
             Jan. 9, 1871; d. July 11, 1871.

731 JOHN STANLEY[7] EMERY (*William*,[6] *Zachariah*,[5] *Zachariah*,[4] *Zachariah*,[3] *James*,[2] *Anthony*[1]), son of William and Mary (Stanley) Emery; married Dec. 22, 1839, Abby Eddy of Warwick, Mass. (born Dec. 23, 1814). He died in Warwick, Mass., May 16, 1878.
  Children :

1869   i   ABBY STANLEY,[8] b. Sept. 18, 1840, in Hinsdale, N. Y.; d. Dec.
             13, 1845
1870   ii   WILLIAM STANLEY, b. July 8, 1844, in Newfane, Vt.
1871   iii MARY SUSAN, b. April 27, 1846, in Hinsdale, N. Y.
1872   iv   JAMES EDWARD, ⎰ b. May 18, 1853, ⎰ d. Aug. 25, 1853.
1873   v   JOHN WARREN, ⎱ in Orange, Mass.; ⎱ d. April 30, 1878, unm.
1874   vi   HARRIET JANE BEULAH, b. April 8, 1858.

733 JOSEPH[7] EMERY (*John*,[6] *John*,[5] *Zachariah*,[4] *Zachariah*,[3] *James*,[2] *Anthony*[1]), son of John and Deborah (Colburn) Emery; married Harriet Clapham.
  Children, born in Skowhegan, Me. :

1875   i   EMELINE P.,[8] b. 1817.
1876   ii   CHARLES C., b. 1821.
1877   iii HARRIET, b. 1825; m. Josiah B. Field, in Skowhegan, Me.,
             1847.
1878   iv   ABNER C., b. 1833; d. in Skowhegan, Me., 1875.

751 JOANNA[7] EMERY (*Samuel*,[6] *John*,[5] *Zachariah*,[4] *Zachariah*,[3] *James*,[2] *Anthony*[1]), daughter of Samuel and Rebecca (Wheeler) Emery; married in Ripley, Me., July 6, 1817, Joseph Butler (born June 6, 1792; died June 7, 1875). She died Aug. 16, 1880.
  Children, born in Ripley, Me. :

1879   i   REBECCA,[8] b. March 6, 1818.
1880   ii   SUSAN, b. Feb. 5, 1820.
1881   iii ASENATH, b. March 7, 1822; d. Aug. 30, 1826.
1882   iv   SARAH, b. July 30, 1824.
1883   v   SON, b. and d. Sept. 11, 1826.
1884   vi   ASENATH, b. Aug. 25, 1827.
1885   vii BENJAMIN F., b. Dec. 31, 1829; d. Oct. 28, 1847.
1886   viii JOANNA, b. Feb. 3, 1832.
1887   ix   JOHN BURLEIGH, b. Aug. 10, 1834.
1888   x   FREEMAN ALLEN, b. Aug. 8, 1836.
1889   xi   JOSEPH EMERY, b. May 4, 1839; m. Amanda Ransom, March
             19, 1865; d. April 18, 1872.
1890   xii CAROLINE A., b. June 24, 1841.
1891   xiii HENRY F., b. Nov. 30, 1844.

753 TILLY[7] EMERY (*Joseph*,[6] *John*,[5] *Zachariah*,[4] *Zachariah*,[3] *James*,[2] *Anthony*[1]), son of Joseph and Elizabeth (Mason) Emery; married, first, Esther Spaulding; second, in 1837, Celia N. Hinds. Removed to Fairfield, Me., 1815. Postmaster and magistrate; respected by all.
  Children :

1892 i ALBERT G ,[8] b July 14, 1838.
1893 ii MILTON F , b Nov 28, 1846, m. Nellie Stafford, res. in St.
Paul, Minn

754 BETSEY[7] EMERY (*Joseph*,[6] *John*,[5] *Zachariah*,[4] *Zachariah*,[3]
James,[2] *Anthony*[1]), daughter of Joseph and Elizabeth (Mason) Em-
ery; married Otis Spaulding of Norridgewock, Me.
Children.

1894 i JOSEPH.[8]
1895 ii HARRIET, m. William Lander
1896 iii FRANCIS, m. ——, settled in Beaver Dam, Wis.
1897 iv LIZZIE E , m Henry W Lander, lawyer in Beaver Dam, Wis
1898 v PHILANDER, m and lived in Oak Grove, Wis
1899 vi CAROLINE, m. David Barnes in Lowell, Mass.

755 JOSEPH[7] EMERY (*Joseph*,[6] *John*,[5] *Zachariah*,[4] *Zachariah*,[3]
James,[2] *Anthony*[1]), son of Joseph and Elizabeth (Mason) Emery;
married in Skowhegan, Me., Ruth Cushing.
Children:

1900 i JOHN H.,[8] b 1822, d. Aug 3, 1854.
1901 ii HORATIO C , b. 1828
1902 iii KEZIAH C , b 1829, d Dec 1, 1856
1903 iv ESTHER E , b, 1832; m William Edwards, Downer's Grove, Ill.
1904 v BENJAMIN C . b 1835, unm.
1905 vi MARIA P , b. 1837, m Samuel P C. Cleveland; d 1885

765 LIEUT. EMERY DANIEL[7] (*Daniel*,[6] *Daniel*,[5] *Zachariah*,[4] *Zachariah*,[3] *James*,[2] *Anthony*[1]), son of Capt Daniel and Elizabeth (Farnsworth) Emery; married April 3, 1804, Polly Felt (born Nov. 1, 1782;
died June 22, 1862), daughter of Peter and Lucy (Andrews) Felt.
Daniel Emery at the death of his mother, at her request, was adopted
by her sister, the wife of Lieut. Thomas Adams, by whom he was
brought up and inherited a half of the Adams' estate He died Aug.
24, 1828.
Children:

1906 i ADAMS,[8] b Dec 4, 1804, d. in Boston, Mass , July 13, 1841.
1907 ii ANDREWS, b May 12, 1806.
1908 iii DANIEL F , b Feb. 21, 1808; d. in Sebawa, Mich , July 12,
1876
1909 iv CAROLINE, b Jan 1, 1810, d. June 28, 1829
1910 v ELIZABETH, b Dec 6, 1813
1911 vi GEORGE b March 5, 1816, d. Dec 15, 1816.
1912 vii HARRIET, b Dec. 28, 1819, m April 1, 1847, Rev George F
Clark of Dublin, N H. (b Feb 24, 1817); son of Jonas and
Mary (Twitchell) Clark , educated at Exeter, N H , graduate
of Cambridge Divinity school, July 17, 1846, ordained Evan-
gelist at Charlemont, Mass , Aug 11 1847, installed at Warwick, Mass , May 14, 1848, and at Norton, Mass , Aug 11,
1852 Settled in Stow, Mendon and Hubbardston, Mass Author of the history of Norton and history of the temperance
cause in Mass
1913 viii SOPHRONIA, b Jan 11, 1821
1914 ix STEPHEN F , b. June 25, 1823; m Sarah Maria Pierce, Oct 5,
1847.

767 STEPHEN[7] EMERY (*Daniel*,[6] *Daniel*,[5] *Zachariah*,[4] *Zachariah*,[3]

James,[2] *Anthony*[1]), son of Capt. Daniel and his second wife, Hannah (Bates) Emery; married Sally Eddy of Wales, N. Y.

Children :

    1915 i   IRENE.[9]
    1916 ii JULIA.
    1917 iii DANIEL.
    1918 iv CYNTHIA.
    1919 v   SOPHIA, m., 1865, David Huntington of Marengo, Ill.
    1920 vi FRANKLIN.
    1921 vii STEPHEN.

771 NANCY[7] EMERY (*Daniel,*[6] *Daniel,*[5] *Zachariah,*[4] *Zachariah,*[3] *James,*[2] *Anthony*[1]), daughter of Daniel and his second wife, Hannah (Bates) Emery; married Hoxey Barbour (born at Mt. Holly, Vt., Dec. 6, 1791; died at Walpole, N. H., March 5, 1864). Lived at Rockingham, Vt. She died Aug. 17, 1850, at Walpole, N. H.

Children :

    1922 i   SAMUEL T.,[8] b. Sept. 11, 1815; m. Lorinda E. Parker of Wallingford, Vt.; he d. in U. S. hospital, Philadelphia, Pa., Jan. 11, 1862.
    1923 ii ANNA D., b. Dec. 30, 1817.
    1924 iii HOXEY E., b. Sept. 14, 1820; d. May 11. 1826.
    1925 iv ALVIN M., b. April 17, 1822; d. Feb. 1, 1829.
    1926 v   HANNAH A., b. Oct. 4, 1824; d. Jan. 11, 1878, in Wallingford, Vt.
    1927 vi RHODA S., b. Feb. 23, 1827.
    1928 vii FRANKLIN E., b. Jan. 8, 1829; d. March 16, 1830.
    1929 viii LOIS IRENE, b. Dec. 16, 1830.
    1930 ix CALEB L., b. April 14, 1833; d. Sept. 7, 1868.
    1931 x   LAWSON E., b. Jan. 16, 1836; m. Aurora Hatch. She d. Jan. 4, 1871.

772 JOSEPH[7] EMERY (*Daniel,*[6] *Daniel,*[5] *Zachariah,*[4] *Zachariah,*[3] *James,*[2] *Anthony*[1]), son of Daniel and his second wife, Hannah (Bates) Emery; married, 1814, Betsey Bowen (died June 25, 1872). Lived in Wales, N. Y.

Children :

    1932 i   LYMAN,[8] b. July 12, 1816.
    1933 ii MARY LEE, b July 19, 1820; m. Thomas Stokes, of Wales, N. Y., April 9, 1879.
    1934 iii MELINDA, b. Sept. 13. 1822.
    1935 iv CORDELIA, b. April 25, 1829.

Two other children d. in infancy.

774 JONATHAN[7] EMERY (*Daniel,*[6] *Daniel,*[5] *Zachariah,*[4] *Zachariah,*[3] *James,*[2] *Anthony*[1]), son of Daniel and his second wife Hannah (Bates) Emery; married Feb. 15, 1826, Fanny Dunshee, daughter of Hugh and Cynthia (Allen) Dunshee (born May 28, 1803). Lived in Stockholm, Vt.

Children :

    1936 i   CHARLES,[8] b. June 9, 1827.
    1937 ii GEORGE, b. Sept. 28, 1828.
    1938 iii EMILY S., b. April 27, 1830.
    1939 iv ALLEN, b. Oct. 26, 1831; d. Nov. 11, 1832.
    1940 v   LEVI A., b. April 23, 1833; d. Nov. 14, 1853.

1941 vi EDWIN, b Feb 27, 1835
1942 vii DIANTHA, b March 12, 1837 , d Sept 8, 1838
1943 viii CURTIS, b Oct 17, 1839
1944 ix DIANTHA, b. Sept. 25, 1841

775 AARON[7] EMERY (*Daniel,*[6] *Daniel,*[5] *Zachariah,*[4] *Zachariah,*[3] *James,*[2] *Anthony*[1]), son of Daniel and his second wife, Hannah (Bates) Emery; married April 20, 1824, Susan Martin of Walpole, N. H. (born Nov. 1, 1803 , died Aug. 24, 1888)   Removed to West Stockholm, N. Y.

Children :

1945 i   REBECCA,[8] b. Jan 25, 1825 , d Sept. 18, 1864.
1946 ii OLIVER M., b July 29, 1827.
1947 iii MARY, b Sept 13. 1828
1948 iv LYDIA A., b Oct 11 1830; d May 7, 1856
1949 v   LAURA, b Oct. 6, 1833
1950 vi FRANCIS A., b. Jan. 25, 1835; m. Feb 18, 1857, Esther Gurley.
1951 vii ELNORA, b Oct. 23, 1837
1952 viii JOHN, b July 1, 1839 , d. Nov 10, 1839
1953 ix JAMES, b. July 8, 1841, d Feb 12, 1842.
1954 x   ELLEN, b. May, 1843 , d Sept 18, 1844.

777 ACHSA[7] EMERY (*Daniel,*[6] *Daniel,*[5] *Zachariah,*[4] *Zachariah,*[3] *James,*[2] *Anthony*[1]), daughter of Daniel and his second wife, Hannah (Bates) Emery; married Roswell Russell. She died June 12, 1884, at Badox, Mich.

Children .

1955 i   JEREMIAH [8]
1956 ii JOHN.
1957 iii ALMIRA

779 CYNTHIA[7] EMERY (*Daniel,*[6] *Daniel,*[5] *Zachariah,*[4] *Zachariah,*[3] *James,*[2] *Anthony*[1]), daughter of Daniel and his second wife, Hannah (Bates) Emery ; married Abraham Johnson. Resides in Colorado.

Children :

1958 i   WILLIAM F [8]
1959 ii EMILY.

780 IRENE[7] EMERY (*Daniel,*[6] *Daniel,*[5] *Zachariah,*[4] *Zachariah,*[3] *James,*[2] *Anthony*[1]), daughter of Daniel and his second wife, Hannah (Bates) Emery , married Curtis Gowing, son of Benjamin and Mary (Emery) Gowing.

Children

1960 i   WILLIAM OSCAR[8] (see No 1935).
1961 ii AMANDA MALVINA, m John Van Campen

790 JAMES[7] EMERY (*Noah,*[6] *Daniel,*[5] *Zachariah,*[4] *Zachariah,*[3] *James,*[2] *Anthony*[1]), son of Noah and Elizabeth (Philbrick) Emery , married June 9, 1810, Elizabeth Wilder of Townsend, Mass.

Children, born in Grafton, Vt. :

1962 i   ELIZABETH,[8] b April 7, 1814
1963 ii JAMES C , b July 2, 1817
1964 iii JUSTIN W , b Sept 24, 1820.

1965 iv Rev. Isaac W., b. May 12, 1822.
1966 v   Selinda Agetis, b. Oct. 22, 1833.
1967 vi James E. Wheat, b. Oct. 8, 1836.
And seven other children d. in infancy.

793 Asa[7] Emery (*Noah*,[6] *Daniel*,[5] *Zachariah*,[4] *Zachariah*,[3] *James*,[2] *Anthony*[1]), son of Noah and Elizabeth (Philbrick) Emery ; married Orilla Thompson.
Children :

1968 i   Noah L.[8]
1969 ii Jared.

795 Nathan[7] Emery (*Noah*,[6] *Daniel*,[5] *Zachariah*,[4] *Zachariah*,[3] *James*,[2] *Anthony*[1]), son of Noah and Elizabeth (Philbrick) Emery ; married Betsey Pettingale (died in Middlebury, Vt., 1850).
Children :

1970 i   James P.,[8] b. March 10, 1821, in Wyoming, N. Y. ; d. May 28, 1858 ; m. Martha G. Newhall, Feb. 10, 1848.
1971 ii Electa L., d. unm., Apr. 14, 1855.
1972 iii Emeline M., m. Hosea Chapin ; d. Oct. 24, 1859.

796 Noah[7] Emery (*Noah*,[6] *Daniel*,[5] *Zachariah*,[4] *Zachariah*,[3] *James*,[2] *Anthony*[1]), son of Noah and Elizabeth (Philbrick) Emery ; married, first, 1818, Mary Martin ; second, 1833, Sophia Hugg.
Children :

1973 i   Chauncy W.,[8] b. March 8, 1819 ; d. Jan. 11, 1865.
1974 ii   William G., b. 1823.
1975 iii Mary Jane, b. Sept. 16, 1827 ; m. D. Billings ; d. 1862.
1976 iv   Nathan M., b. 1830.
1977 v   David H., b. Dec. 22, 1836.
1978 vi   Amanda M., b. March, 1839.
1979 vii Phœbe A., b. Nov. 1, 1841.

797 Joel[7] Emery (*Noah*,[6] *Daniel*,[5] *Zachariah*,[4] *Zachariah*,[3] *James*,[2] *Anthony*[1]), son of Noah and Elizabeth (Philbrick) Emery ; married, first, Nov. 18, 1818, Cynthia Smead (died 1823) ; second, Mrs. Nancy Johnson (died 1852) ; third, Margaret Ryan.
Children, by first marriage :

1980 i   Albert,[8] b. 1820, in Lockport, N. Y. ; m. Cynthia Smead, 1842.
1981 ii Charlotte, b. 1822, in Bethany, N. Y. ; m. Alvin Read, 1842.

By second marriage :

1982 iii Ellen, b. in Warsaw, N. Y. ; res. in California.
1983 iv   Walter, b. 1837.

By third marriage :

1984 v   David L., b. 1857.

798 Walter[7] Emery (*Noah*,[6] *Daniel*,[5] *Zachariah*,[4] *Zachariah*,[3] *James*,[2] *Anthony*[1]), son of Noah and Elizabeth (Philbrick) Emery ; married Matilda Goodrich (born June 17, 1815).
Children, born in Quincy, Ill. :

1985 i   CHARLOTTE.[8] b Sept 27, 1834
1986 ii DANIEL, b April 17, 1836, d Aug , 1836
1987 iii WALTER, b June 1, 1837, d. Sept. 6, 1837
1988 iv MARY CLARISSA, b Feb 23, 1841; d. Aug. 13, 1845.
1989 v   HENRY CLAY, b Jan. 25, 1843, d Dec. 30, 1849.
1990 vi EMILY ADELAIDE, b Feb 25, 1845
1991 vii JOHN FRANKLIN, b. Oct 28, 1847.
1992 viii JAMES L , b Aug 25, 1853.

801 GRATIA[7] EMERY (*Noah,*[6] *Daniel,*[5] *Zachariah,*[4] *Zachariah,*[3] *James,*[2] *Anthony*[1]), daughter of Noah and Elizabeth (Philbrick) Emery, married in Rockingham, Vt., July 10, 1821, Peter Nourse (died April 30, 1875).
Child :

1993 i   ABIGAIL,[8] b Oct 8, 1825.

802 JONATHAN[7] EMERY (*Noah,*[6] *Daniel,*[5] *Zachariah,*[4] *Zachariah,*[3] *James,*[2] *Anthony*[1]), son of Noah and Elizabeth (Philbrick) Emery ; married, 1829, Abigail Nourse (died March 15, 1879).
Children :

1994 i   HENRY P ,[8] b Dec 31, 1830, d In Vt
1995 ii EDWIN B , b Aug 11, 1833, d March, 1888
1996 iii ALLEN N , b Sept. 20, 1835, d Nov. 27, 1835.
1997 iv GEORGE F , b July 10, 1839, d Oct 24, 1850
1998 v   OSCAR P , b Aug 11, 1840; d May 12, 1862.
1999 vi ALBERT NOAH, b March 26, 1842

803 BETSEY[7] EMERY (*Noah,*[6] *Daniel,*[5] *Zachariah,*[4] *Zachariah,*[3] *James,*[2] *Anthony*[1]), daughter of Noah and Elizabeth (Philbrick) Emery, married in Pike, N Y., Dec. 7, 1832, Marvin Marshall. He died 1844
Child .

2000 i   BETSEY LOUISA,[8] b. Feb 14, 1839.

809 JONATHAN[7] EMERY (*Asa,*[6] *Daniel,*[5] *Zachariah,*[4] *Zachariah,*[3] *James,*[2] *Anthony*[1]). son of Asa and Mary (Rider) Emery, married, first, Emma L Hindman, daughter of Judge Hindman ; second, Mrs. Abigail A. Hindman (died June 13, 1833).
Children :

2001 i   HOMER H ,[8] b March 18, 1822, d in the army, April, 1863
2002 ii ORACE W , b April 8, 1834 m Kate Calligan, Sept 3 1869
2003 iii JONATHAN W , b July 21, 1838, m Cora Luther, June 7, 1879, d May 16, 1882, Union soldier
2004 iv EMERY N , b Aug 26, 1839, was in the Union army two years.
2005 v   LOUISA H., b. Feb. 6, 1848 , m. Henry B. Fairchild.

810 ASA[7] EMERY (*Asa,*[6] *Daniel,*[5] *Zachariah,*[4] *Zachariah,*[3] *James,*[2] *Anthony*[1]), son of Asa and Mary (Rider) Emery ; married, 1823, Betsey Johnson (died 1850) ; removed to Belfast, N. Y.
Children :

2006 i   LAURA [8]
2007 ii ALMOND.
2008 iii LORAINE.
2009 iv ORIN, d. in the army.

813 SABRA[7] EMERY(*Asa,*[6] *Daniel,*[5] *Zachariah,*[4] *Zachariah,*[3] *James,*[2] *Anthony*[1]), daughter of Asa and Mary (Rider) Emery; married, 1830, Simeon Heath.

Children:

2010 i EMERY.[8]
2011 ii CHARLES P.
Eight other children, names unknown.

815 LABAN[7] EMERY(*Asa,*[6] *Daniel,*[5] *Zachariah,*[4] *Zachariah,*[3] *James,*[2] *Anthony*[1]), son of Asa and Mary (Rider) Emery; married Feb. 15, 1837, Nancy Bemis (born Jan. 15, 1816; died Oct. 11, 1876).

Children:

2012 i SUELA ROSABELLE,[8] b. June 8, 1838; d. March 27, 1841.
2013 ii STOPPANI LA MOTTE, b. Nov. 8, 1839; d. March 20, 1841.
2014 iii RENWICK, b. Aug. 8, 1842; d. Oct. 5, 1842.
2015 iv HENRY CLAY, b. Aug. 8, 1843; Union soldier; clerk under Gen. Hooker; studied law.
2016 v AUGUSTA ANGELA, b. June 27, 1845.
2017 vi LABAN DAVID, b. April 14, 1847.
2018 vii CYRUS WRIGHT, b. April 12, 1849.
2019 viii ALICE MAY, b. May 16, 1851; m. David Barney, Oct. 15, 1867.
2020 ix NANCY EMELINE, b. May 20, 1855; m. John Crisp, Sept. 30, 1874.

816 DAN.[7] EMERY (*Asa,*[6] *Daniel,*[5] *Zachariah,*[4] *Zachariah,*[3] *James,*[2] *Anthony*[1]), son of Asa and Mary (Rider) Emery; married in Centreville, N. Y., Eliza Abby. He was a drummer in the army; died in Wisconsin.

Children:

2021 i BYRON.[8]
2022 ii EMELINE.

817 EMELINE[7] EMERY (*Asa,*[6] *Daniel,*[5] *Zachariah,*[4] *Zachariah,*[3] *James,*[2] *Anthony*[1]), daughter of Asa and Mary (Rider) Emery; married, 1833, George Merrill; had two sons and three daughters. One of the sons, Stanley Merrill, was in the army and in prison in Andersonville; returned home well. She lives in Avon, N. Y.

818 ORIN[7] EMERY(*Asa,*[6] *Daniel,*[5] *Zachariah,*[4] *Zachariah,*[3] *James,*[2] *Anthony*[1]), son of Asa and Mary (Rider) Emery; married Amanda Bostwick. Lives in Pike, N. Y.

Child:

2023 i JOHN B.[8]

858 MARY[7] RAYMENTON (*Sarah,*[6] *Samuel,*[5] *Zachariah,*[4] *Zachariah,*[3] *James,*[2] *Anthony*[1]), daughter of Samuel and Mary (Emery) Raymenton; married Samuel Gowing.

Children:

2024 i JOHN R.,[8] b. 1848.
2025 ii EDWIN F.
2026 iii NATHAN W.
2027 iv ARTHUR, b. Sept., 1864.

859 Elliot[7] Emery (*Zachariah,*[6] *Samuel,*[5] *Zachariah,*[4] *Zachariah,*[3] *James,*[2] *Anthony*[1]), son of Zachariah and Betsey (Emery) Emery; married, March 20, 1834, in Belfast, N. Y., Rosanna Cole.

Children.

2028	i	Martha Ann,[8] b Jan. 5, 1835; d March 16, 1842.
2029	ii	Miles Allen, b Jan 15, 1837; d. in the army July 6, 1862.
2030	iii	Sarah Jane, b July 9, 1839
2031	iv	David Elliot, b Aug 24, 1841.
2032	v	Zachariah, b March 17, 1847, d Nov 15, 1847.
2033	vi	Lillian Eudora, b. July 21, 1856.

860 Daniel[7] Emery (*Zachariah,*[6] *Samuel,*[5] *Zachariah,*[4] *Zachariah,*[3] *James,*[2] *Anthony*[1]), son of Zachariah and Betsey (Emery) Emery, married in Belfast, N. Y., Dec. 16, 1834, Elsie Stewart.

Children:

2034	i	Lewis Austin,[8] b March 21, 1837
2035	ii	Harriet, b June 6, 1838, d March 3, 1839
2036	iii	Oliver C P., b Dec 23, 1839
2037	iv	Melissa, b April 6, 1841, d March 12, 1872
2038	v	Chauncy, b Jan 10, 1843, d. March 12, 1845.
2039	vi	Romanzo Jarvis, b July 18, 1844
2040	vii	Rozeno Manlius, b Jan 18, 1846
2041	viii	Nancy Jane, b Sept. 6, 1847, d June 1, 1848.
2042	ix	Rosannah, b. March 5, 1849
2043	x	Mary Ellen, b Aug 18, 1854.
2044	xi	Alma, } b Nov. 22, 1858.
2045	xii	Alva,

863 Hannah Zilpha[7] Emery (*Zachariah,*[6] *Samuel,*[5] *Zachariah,*[4] *Zachariah,*[3] *James,*[2] *Anthony*[1]), daughter of Zachariah and Betsey (Emery) Emery, married in Belfast, N. Y., Jan. 14, 1846, David Dudley.

Children:

2046	i	Betsey Maria,[8] b Dec 13, 1847
2047	ii	John Emery, b March 18, 1850
2048	iii	Florence Mary, b Feb 18 1853.
2049	iv	Emily Sarah. b April 4, 1855
2050	v	Clara Frances, b Feb 11, 1859.

864 Jarvis Chase[7] Emery (*Zachariah,*[6] *Samuel,*[5] *Zachariah,*[4] *Zachariah,*[3] *James,*[2] *Anthony*[1]), son of Zachariah and Betsey (Emery) Emery, married, Sept. 16, 1852, in Allen, N. Y., Paulina Crane. Lives at Maple Grove, Mich.

Children:

2051	i	Zachariah,[8] b Oct 12 1854, d Sept. 14, 1856
2052	ii	Nellie N, b May 6, 1856
2053	iii	Willie Jarvis, b May 21, 1858.
2054	iv	Rosalie, b May 8, 1862

865 Betsey Maria[7] Emery (*Zachariah,*[6] *Samuel,*[5] *Zachariah,*[4] *Zachariah,*[3] *James,*[2] *Anthony*[1]), daughter of Zachariah and Betsey (Emery) Emery; married July 17, 1860, Harrison Madison.

Children:

2055	i	Harrison E ,[8] b Oct 29, 1867.
2056	ii	Jarvis A., b. July 16, 1869; d young.

867 MARY[7] EMERY (*Josiah,[6] Samuel,[5] Zachariah,[4] Zachariah,[3] James,[2] Anthony[1]*), daughter of Josiah and Esther (Raymenton) Emery, married April 18, 1828, Levi Gowing. Lives in Owanee, N. Y.
Children:

```
2057  i    NORMAN M ,8 b Feb 10, 1829, d. Oct 27, 1877.
2058  ii   ELVIRA D , b April 1, 1831, d  Dec , 1832
2059  iii  ACHSA, b  April 7, 1833, d  March 19, 1836
2060  iv   AMANDA, b  Nov 1, 1837, d. Sept 15, 1859.
2061  v    LEVI N , b  May 1, 1838;  d  May 19, 1862
2062  vi   MARY J , b  May 21, 1843 , m ——— Clark
2063  vii  LEWIS H , b  Feb 14, 1845, d  Sept 1, 1872
2064  viii CHARLES A , b. April 1, 1848, d  Dec 25, 1871.
```

868 BETSEY[7] EMERY (*Josiah,[6] Samuel,[5] Zachariah,[4] Zachariah,[3] James,[2] Anthony[1]*), daughter of Josiah and Esther (Raymenton) Emery, married George W. Morrison ; published March 19, 1843.
Children :

```
2065  i    GEORGE W ,8 b Sept 7, 1846
2066  ii   MARY J., b  Aug 7, 1849,  m May 31, 1871, George N Gould.
2067  iii  SHERBURN C., b. Sept. 1, 1850,  m  in Missouri, Dec 28, 1880.
```

869 LOUISA[7] EMERY (*Josiah,[6] Samuel,[5] Zachariah,[4] Zachariah,[3] James,[2] Anthony[1]*), daughter of Josiah and Esther (Raymenton) Emery, married Aug. 19 1833, Horace C. Whitcomb; died June 5, 1845.
Children :

```
2067a i    GEORGE T ,8 b  Jan 25, 1835
2067b ii   JOHN D . b. Sept 28, 1837
2067c iii  VERNON J , b. July 10, 1839.
2067d iv   HARRIET A , b  Jan 23, 1840,  m  Aaron Finnan (?), Oct. 11,
                1863.
2067e v    LOUISA, b  March 10, 1845;  d  Sept 25, 1845.
```

870 OSMAN B [7] EMERY (*Josiah,[6] Samuel,[5] Zachariah,[4] Zachariah,[3] James,[2] Anthony[1]*), son of Josiah and Esther (Raymenton) Emery ; married March 6, 1845, Lucy A. Barton.
Children ·

```
2068  i    JEREMIAH,8 b  May 13, 1848;  d  March 18, 1866.
2069  ii   ESTHER LOUISA, b  1849
2070  iii  LUCY ANN, b  Jan. 4, 1852, d March 20  1854
2071  iv   SARAH B., b. July 1, 1868;  d. Aug 28, 1868.
```

871 HANNAH G [7] EMERY(*Josiah,[6] Samuel,[5] Zachariah,[4] Zachariah,[3] James,[2] Anthony[1]*), daughter of Josiah and Esther (Raymenton) Emery ; married John Brown of Woodstock, Vt., April 12, 1842.
Child :

```
2072  i    JOSIAH ALLEN,8 b  Feb  16, 1843
```

872 ESTHER ROSINA[7] EMERY(*Josiah,[6] Samuel,[5] Zachariah,[4] Zachariah,[3] James,[2] Anthony[1]*), daughter of Josiah and Esther (Raymenton) Emery , married March 16, 1841, D. Barton.
Child :

```
2073  i    ETTA HARLOW,8 b. Sept. 12, 1840.
```

875 SARAH A.[7] EMERY(*Josiah,*[6] *Samuel,*[5] *Zachariah,*[4] *Zachariah,*[3] *James,*[2] *Anthony*[1])', daughter of Josiah and Esther (Raymenton) Emery, married Aug. 27, 1850, John W. Edson.
Children:

 2074 i JOSIAH EMERY,[8] b Aug 19, 1852, m Oct 3, 1875, Clara A Ellis.
 2075 ii QUARTUS D, b. Oct 19, 1854, m Oct. 1, 1875, Ida B Philips

876 DAVID[7] EMERY (*Daniel,*[6] *Daniel,*[5] *Daniel,*[4] *Daniel,*[3] *James,*[2] *Anthony*[1]). son of Daniel and Abigail (Lord) Emery; married in So. Berwick, Me, Feb. 18. 1814, Betsey Chase, died before Aug 15, 1827.
Children

 2076 i SIMEON,[8] b 1814, in the navy during the war, d. at the Soldiers' Home, Chelsea, Mass, June 9, 1884.
 2077 ii ELIZABETH, b Dec 25, 1823, d. Aug. 9, 1878.

877 ENOCH[7] EMERY (*Daniel,*[6] *Daniel,*[5] *Daniel,*[4] *Daniel,*[3] *James,*[2] *Anthony*[1]). son of Daniel and Abigail (Lord) Emery; married, 1824, Rhoda Staples (born 1799); lived in Eliot, Me.
Children:

 2078 i DAVID,[8] b Sept 2, 1825; m Oct. 15, 1848, Mary C. Hamilton, d Feb, 1854
 2079 ii ABBIE, b Aug. 23, 1828; no children, m Otis Rollins, Oct. 15, 1848; d May 19, 1855
 2080 iii JAMES, b Oct. 27, 1832
 2081 iv FRANCES, b June 25, 1834; d Sept 27, 1848
 2082 v LUCY, b Oct 25, 1836, m James York, March 12, 1854; d. April, 1857.
 2083 vi NANCIE, b March 20, 1838; m Dec 25, 1863, James Decoff.
 2084 vii ENOCH b April 5, 1840
 2085 viii HANNAH, b April 5, 1842.
 2086 ix MARY E
Two children d. in infancy.

884 EUNICE[7] EMERY (*Nahum,*[6] *Daniel,*[5] *Daniel,*[4] *Daniel,*[3] *James,*[2] *Anthony*[1]), daughter of Nahum and his third wife, Sarah (Pickernell) Emery, married, 1827, Ebenezer Plaisted (died Sept. 21, 1881).
Children:

 2087 i SARAH E, [8] b June 22, 1828, d Nov 8, 1884.
 2088 ii MARY A, b June 19, 1830
 2089 iii NAHUM E, b July 30, 1832.
 2090 iv WILLIAM, b Feb 17, 1835, d. April 22, 1882
 2091 v EBENEZER, b April 6, 1840, d Aug 16, 1843.

886 JOEL[7] EMERY (*Nathan,*[6] *Daniel,*[5] *Daniel,*[4] *Daniel,*[3] *James,*[2] *Anthony*[1]), son of Nathan and Hannah (Kingsbury) Emery; married Nov. 27. 1806, Betsey (born Oct. 10, 1789), daughter of Daniel and Elizabeth (Crosby) Emery. He died before 1825. His widow married, second, Nathan Grant, 1828. Lived in Berwick.
Children:

 2092 i TIMOTHY,[8] b 1807, m March 19, 1843, Lydia Ann Watson; d. 1856.
 2093 ii JULIA ANN, d Jan 15, 1827, æt 18 years.
 2094 iii ASA, b. Oct., 1814; d in Medford, Mass., 1849.

2095 iv CATHARINE m Alvin, son of Israel and Prudence (Emery) Emery, May 23, 1841
2096 v BETSEY, d 1832, æt 12 years
2097 vi RHODA, b Dec 12, 1820, d March 27, 1885.
2098 vii JOEL, d in San Francisco, Cal , 1850.

By second marriage :

2099 viii OLIVE, b Dec 14, 1828
2100 ix AIMIRA, b March 19, 1830; d Sept. 8, 1839.
2101 x BETSEY, b Jan 24, 1833; d May 9, 1851.

894 TIMOTHY[7] EMERY (*Daniel,*[6] *Daniel,*[5] *Noah,*[4] *Daniel,*[3] *James,*[2] *Anthony*[1]), son of Daniel and Elizabeth (Crosby) Emery, married Jan. 4, 1815, Olive Wentworth of Limington, Me. (died Aug. 13, 1851), daughter of William and Judith (Knight) Wentworth. He died July 16, 1860. Lived in Dover, N. H.
Children :

2102 i JULIA A ,[8] b April 1 1817; d June, 1845.
2103 ii NANCY S . b Feb 28, 1819
2104 iii HORACE W , b Aug , 1821
2105 iv DANIEL C , b Nov 19, 1824
2106 v TIMOTHY K , b June, 1827; d July, 1863, in the army
2107 vi OLIVE J , b Sept 21, 1829.

895 DANIEL C [7] EMERY (*Daniel,*[6] *Daniel,*[5] *Noah,*[4] *Daniel,*[3] *James,*[2] *Anthony*[1]), son of Daniel and Elizabeth (Crosby) Emery ; married, 1805, Hannah Goodwin (died in Great Falls, N H., Dec 12, 1878), sister of John Goodwin, who married Hannah, sister of D. C. Emery.
Children :

2108 i SON,[8] b Aug 24, 1805; d Aug 31, 1805
2109 ii CHARLES, b July 28, 1806; d previous to March 15, 1878.
2110 iii MARY, b. March 14 1809, d April 7, 1809.
2111 iv SALLY, b May 8, 1810, d Sept 10, 1818
2112 v JOHN, b Sept 28, 1812, d. Jan 14, 1814.
2113 vi DANIEL, b Oct. 19, 1814
2114 vii TIMOTHY, b Feb 19, 1817, d Feb 26, 1817
2115 viii HARRIET, b March 22, 1818, d Dec 28, 1875
2116 ix RUFUS, b Nov 10, 1820, m Julia A Fernald, lives in N. Y
2117 x JOEL, b. Jan 23, 1823, drowned in Portland Harbor, July 26, 1854.
2118 xi HANNAH, b. Oct. 31, 1825, m. April 29, 1843, George W., son of George and Abra (Pray) Young. and had three sons and one dau , lives in Great Falls, N H
2119 xii WILLIAM, b Feb 1, 1828, d Nov. 5, 1831.
2120 xiii SYLVIA, b May 11, 1833, d. Sept 11, 1834.

898 NOAH[7] EMERY (*Noah,*[6] *Daniel,*[5] *Noah,*[4] *Daniel,*[3] *James,*[2] *Anthony*[1]), son of Noah and Betsey (Gould) Emery ; married Sept 2, 1798, Sarah Gowen (born April 10, 1776). Lived in Eliot, Me.
Children ·

2121 i HARRIET,[8] b Jan 14, 1799; unm
2122 ii JOSEPH, b. Nov. 16, 1803; d Feb 23, 1867.
2123 iii JULIA ANN, b. Aug. 26, 1814, d. June, 1883 , unm

899 Lovicy[7] Emery (*Noah*,[6] *Daniel*,[5] *Noah*,[4] *Daniel*,[3] *James*,[2] *Anthony*[1]), daughter of Noah and Elizabeth (Gould) Emery; married, first, John Gowen, jr., second, Samuel Gould in 1807. Lived in Dixmont, Me.

Children:

2124 i John,[8] d at 5 years
2125 ii James, m, resides in Lynn, Mass., and had son Emery.[9]

Children, by second husband:

2126 iii John S , d young.
2127 iv Susan E , d Jan , 1814
2128 v Gilman.
2129 vi George, last one living.
2130 vii Lyman
2131 viii Susan, b Jan , 1814

903 Enoch[7] Emery (*Noah*,[6] *Daniel*,[5] *Noah*,[4] *Daniel*,[3] *James*,[2] *Anthony*[1]), son of Noah and Elizabeth (Gould) Emery, married Dec 18, 1808, Harriet (born March 15, 1786), daughter of Daniel Bradbury of York. Settled in Portsmouth, N. H. He died Sept. 16, 1832.

Children, born in Portsmouth, N. H. :

2132 i Olivia,[8] b Feb 27, 1810
2133 ii John, b June 7, 1812; d Aug 20, 1835
2134 iii Abby B , b. Jan 9, 1815, d Jan 13, 1872
2135 iv Caroline P , b. Jan 7, 1818
2136 v Hannah J , b Nov. 4, 1819

904 Shem[7] Emery (*Noah*,[6] *Daniel*,[5] *Noah*,[4] *Daniel*,[3] *James*,[2] *Anthony*[1]), son of Noah and Elizabeth (Gould) Emery, married Nov. 6, 1806, Mary Walker (born Feb. 16, 1785 ; died Nov. 5, 1862).

Children, born in Portsmouth, N. H :

2137 i Mary Eliz ,[8] b. June 30, 1807
2138 ii Daniel, b Sept 24, 1809 , d March 13, 1835
2139 iii Geo. Francis, b Feb 25, 1812, d April 14 1886. He was for many years one of the appraisers of the Boston Custom House, and during the war was a paymaster in the army, was for a time in Maryland and Virginia and afterwards with Gen Banks in New Orleans For more than twenty years he was treasurer of the " Union Institution for Savings " in Boston, which office he held at the time of his death.
2140 iv Ira, b May 14, 1814, d July 24, 1819
2141 v Nathaniel Stone, b March 18, 1818 , d March 10, 1872.
2142 vi Susan B , b Aug. 20, 1819 , d April 22, 1872
2143 vii Ira, b. Nov. 5, 1821, d. Aug., 1857.
2144 viii Woodbury, b Feb 12, 1821.
2145 ix Sophia Ladd, b Nov 7, 1826; m. William A Varney of Portsmouth, N. H.

908 Sarah W [7] Emery (*George*,[6] *Daniel*,[5] *Noah*,[4] *Daniel*,[3] *James*,[2] *Anthony*[1]), daughter of George and Sarah (Dean) Emery, married John Whitcher and removed to Belfast, Me

Children.

2146 i Joshua.[8]
2147 ii John

26

909 LOIS[7] EMERY (*George,[6] Daniel,[5] Noah.[4] Daniel,[3] James,[2] Anthony[1]*), daughter of George and Sarah (Dean) Emery, married, 1809, Nathaniel Graves. Removed to St. George, Me. She died Mar. 29 1852.

Children, born in St George :

2148   i   LYDIA,[8] b Dec 20, 1809; m Oliver Wheeler of St. George, Me ; d the same year of her marriage.
2149   ii GEORGE, b Feb, 1811, m Lucy Harrington, d March, 1857.
2150   iii ELIZABETH J., b Oct. 2, 1813, m , 1st, Capt Benj Thompson, 2nd, —— Waltz
2151   iv MARY S , b Feb 13, 1815, m Wm. A Graves of So. Thomaston, d. Feb , 1883
2152   v   DENNIS, b Oct 3 1816, d young in a foreign port
2153   vi MARGARET S , b June 2, 1818, m Oliver R Butler; d Aug. 24, 1883.
2154   vii SYLVINIA b Jan 11, 1820, m Henry Hopkins, d 1861.
2155   viii EDWARD S , b Oct. 21, 1822, m Oct 7, 1865, Mercy K Hathorne.
2156   ix HARRY, b June 30, 1825, d in infancy.
2157   x   JOSIAH,   } b March 27, 1826; { d in youth
2158   xi NATHANIEL
2159   xii SARAH, b Dec 7, 1827, d. in infancy.
2160   xiii SOPHIA E , b Nov 29, 1829, m Richard Realf, d. Oct , 1883, in Indiana
2161   xiv LOUISA M , b Nov 15, 1831, m Ed L Furness, Nov , 1863

910 JOHN[7] EMERY (*George.[6] Daniel,[5] Noah,[4] Daniel,[3] James,[2] Anthony[1]*), son of George and Sarah (Dean) Emery, married, first, Hannah Post (published Aug. 27, 1814) , second, Nov. 20, 1834, Mrs. Margaret (Crie) Bartlett. Resided in South Thomaston, Me.

Children, by first marriage :

2162   i   ELIZA H ,[8] b Nov 27, 1815
2163   ii   WILLIAM S , b Oct 10, 1817
2164   iii HANNAH, b Oct 4, 1819
2165   iv   EMILY A , b Jan 2, 1823, m Capt Elias Sleeper; d July 17, 1850
2166   v   SARAH M., b May 17, 1824, d Sept , 1826
2167   vi   AMANDA C , b. March, 1826
2168   vii JOHN A , b March 7, 1829, m Kate S Thorndike, June 21, 1856 Shipmaster   Resides in Rockland, Me
2169   viii MARY S , b June 27, 1831, m Nathan P. Webster, Jan. 1, 1852, d. Dec. 14, 1852
2170   ix   ALVAN S b. March 13, 1833, d 1849

By second marriage :

2171   x   SUSAN E , b Nov , 1835
2172   xi   RICHARD A , b Nov 18, 1837, d young
2173   xii RICHARD B , b 1839, soldier in 2nd Me Battery, d at Brooke's Station, Va , Nov 26, 1862.
2174   xiii BRADFORD ALDEN, b April 13, 1840
2175   xiv SAMUEL A., b 1843

911 DENNIS[7] EMERY (*George,[6] Daniel,[5] Noah.[4] Daniel,[3] James,[2] Anthony[1]*), son of George and Sarah (Dean) Emery, married in Digby, N S , Dec. 8, 1817, Jane Turnbull (born Aug. 6, 1796 , died May 2, 1880). He died Jan. 19, 1873, in Belfast, Me., where he lived.

Children, born in Belfast, Me , except the first:

2176 i ANN,[8] b June 6, 1819, in Digby, N S
2177 ii LYDIA JANE, b Jan. 26, 1821, m Jan. 24, 1864, Capt. W. O Alden , his second wife
2178 iii ROBERT T , b. May 9, 1823 , res in Belfast, Me , a retired shipmaster and has commanded some of the finest ships in eastern Maine
2179 iv KEZIAH, b June 26, 1825
2180 v ELIZABETH, b Sept 22, 1827, d Feb 9, 1862.
2181 vi JOHN H , b Aug 10, 1829; d March 25, 1885, in Belfast, Me
2182 vii HARRIET L , b March 3, 1832; d Oct 16, 1833
2183 viii RALPH M., b Oct 16, 1837, d June 19, 1861, at Havana, Cuba; mate of ship " Ocean Traveller "
2184 ix ISABELLA H , b Nov 16, 1839, d June 17, 1842

912 JONAS[7] EMERY (*George,[6] Daniel,[5] Noah,[4] Daniel,[3] James,[2] Anthony[1]*), son of George and Sarah (Dean) Emery, married, first, Oct 17, 1816, Abigail Sleeper; second, Mehitable Keller (born Mar. 14, 1800, died Feb 5, 1879). Lived in Belfast, Me.
Children of first marriage

2185 i NANCY,[8] b Nov. 14, 1817, m , Nov 8, 1835, Josiah Flagg (d Feb 15, 1837); d Feb 5, 1879
2186 ii GEORGE, b Dec 7, 1819, d in Baltimore, Md , March 6, 1887.

By second marriage:

2187 iii SARAH, b April 9, 1821; d May 25, 1828
2188 iv NATHANIEL, b Nov 15, 1822, d July 23, 1824
2189 v LUCY L , b Dec 9, 1824, d July 4, 1851
2190 vi MARY ABIGAIL, b July 20, 1826
2191 vii SARAH D , b April 13, 1828
2192 viii FRANCES JANE, b. Jan 19, 1830, d May 3. 1883.
2193 ix WILLIAM C., b Oct 15, 1831
2194 x JONAS D , b Aug 1, 1833.
2195 xi JOHN K , b Aug 3, 1835
2196 xii JAMES A , b Nov 15, 1836, m , July 30, 1860, Angeline Elkins , d in East Salisbury, Mass , Dec 31, 1885 He was Lieutenant in the 48th Mozart regiment
2197 xiii SUSAN E , b April 23, 1839
2198 xiv HELEN C , b March 3, 1845

913 GEORGE[7] EMERY (*George,[6] Daniel,[5] Noah,[4] Daniel,[3] James,[2] Anthony[1]*), son of George and Sarah (Dean) Emery , married, first, Dec. 17, 1820, Nancy Sleeper; second, 1826, Rebecca Maddocks. He died April 13, 1856
Children of first marriage :

2199 i EDWIN THOMAS,[8] b. April 27, 1823
2200 ii EVELINE, b. Oct 7, 1824; d. Aug. 18, 1843.

By second marriage :

2201 iii JOHN J , b Sept 1, 1827, res in Rockland, Me
2202 iv JOSEPH M., b. March 27, 1829, res in Rockland, Me.
2203 v GEORGE W , b Sept. 29, 1830, res in Cherryfield, Me
2204 vi NANCY ROSETTA, } b May 6, 1832; { d unm.
2205 vii HARRIET R , } { d unm.
2206 viii LUCY, b April 14, 1834, d June 3, 1852, unm

915 DANIEL[7] EMERY (*George,[6] Daniel,[5] Noah,[4] Daniel,[3] James,[2]*

Anthony[1]), son of George and Sarah (Dean) Emery ; married Sept. 6, 1827, Sophia Sleeper (born Aug. 2, 1807).

Children :

2207 i ABIGAIL,[8] b. April 18, 1833 ; d. July 25, 1842.
2208 ii SARAH, b. May 29. 1835 ; m., Aug. 3, 1873, A. J. McNutt ; d. Dec. 19, 1873.
2209 iii BETHIAH, b. July 31, 1837 ; m. Nov. 28, 1877, A. L. Rawson.
2210 iv DANIEL W., b. Jan. 9, 1839 ; d. in Mexico, July 30, 1860 ; mariner.
2211 v HARRISON, b. April 30, 1841 ; m. Oct. 16, 1876, Adelaide Moody. Mariner ; lives in South Thomaston, Me.
2212 vi CLARA, b. Oct. 24, 1843 ; lives in Minneapolis, Minn.
2213 vii SOPHIA, b. March 9, 1846 ; m. Dec. 7, 1880, Homer Dorman.
2214 viii KNOTT C., b. March 14, 1848.
2215 ix ABBIE S., b. Sept. 6, 1853 ; m. Joshua Bartlett.

916 WILLIAM D.[7] EMERY (*George,*[6] *Daniel,*[5] *Noah,*[4] *Daniel,*[3] *James,*[2] *Anthony*[1]), son of George and Sarah (Dean) Emery ; married June 23, 1826, Harriet E. Pratt of Dunstable, Mass. Lived in Boston and Quincy, Mass. He died Oct. 18, 1843.

Children :

2216 i HARRIET E.,[8] b. March 18, 1827, in Boston ; d. March 29, 1859.
2217 ii ALBERT T., b. Oct. 7, 1829 ; m. in Rockland, Me., March 31, 1856, Mary E. Andrews of Norfolk, Mass. Dentist in Boston, Mass.
2218 iii CATHARINE R., b. May 17, 1831, in South Thomaston, Me. ; d. in Boston, Nov. 14. 1878.
2219 iv MARY H., b. May 21, 1833, in South Thomaston, Me.
2220 v WILLIAM N., b. May 20, 1835, in South Thomaston, Me. ; d. in Boston, Mass., Dec. 1, 1873.
2221 vi ADONIRAM J., b. Aug. 10, 1838, in South Thomaston, Me.
2222 vii EDWARD C. T., b. April 21, 1840, in South Thomaston, Me. ; d. in Boston, Mass., March 5, 1882. Enlisted in 5th and 30th Mass. Vols., May 10, 1861 ; served through the war.
2223 viii FRANKLIN C. P., b. June 20, 1842, in South Thomaston, Me. ; m. Nov. 8, 1868, Marie Davis of Kennebunk, Me. Enlisted in the 44th Mass. Vol. ; discharged June, 1863.
2224 ix ISABEL F. T., b. May 18, 1844, in South Thomaston, Me. Teacher in Boston.
2225 x FANNIE W., b. June 13, 1850 ; d. Jan. 30, 1851.

919 REV. EPHRAIM H.[7] EMERY (*George,*[6] *Daniel,*[5] *Noah,*[4] *Daniel,*[3] *James,*[2] *Anthony*[1]), son of George and Sarah (Dean) Emery ; married at Ilesboro, Me., March 27, 1832, Mrs. Temperance Pruden (*née* Williams, born April 21, 1821 ; d. Aug. 9, 1883, at South Thomaston, Me.). He was a Baptist minister in Knox, 1837-41 ; in Unity, 1843.

Children :

2226 i SARAH J.,[8] b. Jan. 17, 1833 ; d. Sept. 28, 1835, in Northport, Me.
2227 ii FRANCES M., b. March 27, 1834 ; m. Sept. 30, 1854, John O'Meara.
2228 iii MARY E., b. Aug. 20, 1835 ; d. June 29, 1868.
2229 iv EPHRAIM, b. June 9, 1837 ; d. Jan. 14, 1863.
2230 v WASHBURN, b. Sept. 23, 1839.
2231 vi ACHSIE S., b. Oct. 15, 1841.

920 ANNA[7] EMERY (*Nathaniel,*[6] *Daniel,*[5] *Noah,*[4] *Daniel,*[3] *James,*[2]

Anthony[1]), daughter of Nathaniel and Lucy (Crockett) Emery, married Isaac Hall (born April 12, 1788). She died July 11, 1868.
Children :

2232   i   Lucy,[8] b March 9, 1810, d April 5, 1879.
2233   ii   Mehitable, b Oct. 4, 1811.
2234 iii William, b Sept 25, 1814
2235 iv Asa, b June 26, 1817
2236   v   Arnold, b. April 24, 1819; d. June 2, 1822
2237 vi   Nathaniel, b Sept 2, 1821
2238 vii Arnold, b April 29, 1823, d Aug 21, 1825
2239 viii Elona, b June 30, 1825, d Sept 26, 1826.
2240 ix Isaac, b June 24, 1827, d. Oct. 24, 1864
2241   x   Elvira, b Oct 2, 1829
2242 xi   Charles S , b Dec 20, 1831, d Dec 15, 1880
2243 xii Mary, b Aug 29, 1835
2244 xiii Lucinda, b. Nov. 2, 1837; d Nov 16, 1857

922 Tristram[7] Emery (*Nathaniel,*[6] *Daniel,*[5] *Noah,*[4] *Daniel,*[3] *James,*[2] *Anthony*[1]), son of Nathaniel and Lucy (Crockett) Emery; married Lydia W. Emery (born in Raymond, Me., July 21, 1796, died April 14, 1879). He died April 1, 1850.
Children .

2245   i   Irene[8] b Sept. 6, 1815
2246 ii   Caroline, b Jan 20, 1818, m Jesse Meade, lived in Middle-
             bury, Ind
2247 iii Horace, b Feb 4, 1821
2248 iv Rufus, b March 1, 1825
2249   v   Mary, b Aug 2, 1827, d Oct 23, 1848
2250 vi   James C , b Feb 5, 1830; m Sarah Martin
2251 vii Lucy, b Feb. 2, 1834, d April 12, 1875
2252 viii Josephine, b March 10, 1841; d July 5 1868

923 Levi[7] Emery (*Nathaniel,*[6] *Daniel,*[5] *Noah,*[4] *Daniel,*[3] *James,*[2] *Anthony*[1]), son of Nathaniel and Lucy (Crockett) Emery, married, May 23, 1819, Lois Keen (born June 24. 1798; died June 13, 1866).
Children, born in Montville, Me :

2253   i   Judson,[8] b July 9, 1820.
2254 ii   Elona, b June 15, 1822
2255 iii Enos, b Aug 6, 1824
2256 iv Ann H , b July 14, 1826
2257   v   Harriet N , b June 19, 1828
2258 vi   Nathaniel, b March 29, 1830, killed in battle, June 22, 1863,
             at Millikens' Bend, La
2259 vii Willard, b March 29, 1832.
2260 viii Alden C , b April 28, 1834
2261 ix Ellen, b March 16, 1836, m. June 20, 1878, Asa C. Senter
2262   x   Thomas B , b Feb 26, 1838

925 Asa[7] Emery (*Nathaniel,*[6] *Daniel,*[5] *Noah,*[4] *Daniel,*[3] *James,*[2] *Anthony*[1]), son of Nathaniel and Lucy (Crockett) Emery ; married Betsey Keen (born June 10, 1803, at Nobleboro, Me).
Children ·

2263   i   Phillyra,[8] b Feb 23, 1829, in Montville, Me.
2264 ii   Vibilia, b July 8, 1830 in Montville, Me
2265 iii Alphonso, b Sept 20, 1832, in Lagrange, Mich.
2266 iv Adelaide, b April 30, 1835, in Lagrange, Mich, d. Sept 21,
             1850

2267   v   ANGELO, b June 8, 1838, in Lagrange, Mich ; lives in Kansas.
2268   vi LORAINE, b. July 31, 1841. in Montville, Me.
2269   vii FLORENCE, b. April 12. 1844, in Montville. Me. ; lives in Kansas.
2270   viii OPHELIA, b. Aug. 1, 1846, in Adams, O. ; d. Dec. 23, 1849.
2271   ix VOLNEY, b. June 18, 1849, in Pleasant, O. ; d. Sept. 21, 1850.

926 STILLMAN S.[7] EMERY (*Nathaniel*,[6] *Daniel*,[5] *Noah*,[4] *Daniel*,[3] *James*,[2] *Anthony*[1]), son of Nathaniel and Lucy (Crockett) Emery ; married June 6, 1859, Mary F. Watts (born Aug. 20, 1833).   Live in Lowell, Mass.

Children :

2272   i   DANIEL F.,[8] b. April 25, 1863 ; d. Aug. 26, 1864.
2273   ii   EMMA W., b. July 8, 1869.
2274   iii J. FRANK, b. March 21, 1871 ; d. Dec. 11, 1874.

928 HANNAH TRACY[7] EMERY (*John*,[6] *Noah*,[5] *Noah*,[4] *Daniel*,[3] *James*,[2] *Anthony*[1]), daughter of John and Margaret (Gookin) Emery ; married Nov. 1, 1791, Dr. Benjamin Abbot, LL.D. (born Sept. 17, 1762), principal of Phillips (Exeter) Academy.   She died Dec. 6, 1793.   Dr. Abbot married, second, Mary Perkins who had three children.

Child :

2275   i   JOHN EMERY,[8] b. Aug. 6, 1793 ; grad. at Bowdoin Coll., 1810 ; pastor of the North Church, Salem, Mass., April 20, 1815 ; d., unm., at Exeter, N. H., Oct. 7, 1819.

929 CAPT. ROBERT[7] EMERY (*John*,[6] *Noah*,[5] *Noah*,[4] *Daniel*,[3] *James*,[2] *Anthony*[1]), son of John and Margaret (Gookin) Emery ; married, first, July 7, 1795, Eunice Orne of Salem, Mass. (d. ——— ——) ; second, Sarah (died Sept. 25, 1809), only daughter of Rev. Thomas Barnard ; third, Mary, daughter of Hon. Samuel Lyman of Springfield, Mass.   He entered Harvard College, but from loss of property did not graduate but went to sea and became shipmaster at twenty years of age.   He sailed from Newburyport, Salem and Boston, Mass. He died Aug. 1, 1841.

Child, by first marriage :

2276   i   MARGARET THERESA,[8] b. May 12, 1796 ; d., unm., in Hartford, Conn., Aug., 1865.

By second marriage there were six children, all of whom died in childhood.

By third marriage :

2277   ii   CHARLES, b. July 1, 1816 ; d. in Dorchester, Mass., Jan. 3, 1890.
2278   iii ROBERT, d. in infancy.
2279   iv   JOHN ABBOT, b. Sept. 20, 1818 ; d. in Exeter, N. H., Oct. 8, 1842, during his senior year in Harvard College.
2280   v   ROBERT, d. in infancy.
2281   vi   MARY LYMAN, b. Aug. 12, 1821.

932 NICHOLAS[7] EMERY (*Noah*,[6] *Noah*,[5] *Noah*,[4] *Daniel*,[3] *James*,[2] *Anthony*[1]), son of Noah and Jane (Hale) Emery ; married Nov. 12, 1807, Ann Taylor Gilman, daughter of Gov. John T. and Deborah

(Folsom) Gilman; graduated at Dartmouth College, 1795, studied law under Judge Livermore of Portsmouth, N H., assistant instructor in Exeter Academy in 1797, admitted to the bar in 1798; settled in Parsonsfield, Me ; removed to Portland, Me., 1807; appointed associate judge in the Supreme Court in 1834; member of the Brunswick convention, 1816, delegate to the convention which formed the present constitution of Maine, 1832, commissioner to settle the disputed territory under the treaty of 1783 He prepared the delivered opinions of the Supreme Court recorded in the Maine Reports, Vols XII to XIX, inclusive. "At the bar and on the bench he was honored; in private life, respected and trusted, prudent, sagacious, cautious." He died Aug. 24, 1861

Children, born in Portland :

| 2282 | i | NICHOLAS,[8] | } b Sept. 28, 1808, | { d. when 3 days old. |
| 2283 | ii | JOHN TAYLOR GILMAN, | | { d. in Malden, Mass. Feb 16, 1880 |

2284 iii MARY JANE, b. July 14, 1810. d Feb 8, 1841, unm
2285 iv THERESA ORNE b May 18 1813
2286 v ANN TAYLOR GILMAN, b May 15, 1815, d Jan 31, 1861.
2287 vi CHARLOTTE GILMAN, b March 2, 1817; unm
2288 vii NICHOLAS b Dec 2, 1821, d on a voyage to Calcutta for his health, March 8, 1842

933 JOHN[7] EMERY (*Noah,[6] Noah,[5] Noah,[4] Daniel,[3] James,[2] Anthony[1]*), son of Noah and Jane (Hale) Emery, married, first, Jan. 11, 1802, Deborah Webb; second, Mary Rand. He died March 15, 1874.

Children, by first marriage :

2289 i HENRIETTA O[8]
2290 ii ELIZABETH, m May 15, 1827, Joshua Holt, had one child d young.

By second marriage :

2291 iii MARY FRANCES, b. Feb 20, 1842.

936 ELIZABETH P.[7] EMERY (*Noah,[6] Noah,[5] Noah,[4] Daniel,[3] James,[2] Anthony[1]*), daughter of Noah and Jane (Hale) Emery ; married in Portland, Me., Aug 26, 1822, Gideon L Soule (born July 26, 1796, in Freeport, Me. ; died May 28. 1879) Mr. Soule graduated at Bowdoin College, 1818, became professor in Phillips Academy, 1822, principal, 1838; resigned, 1873, received the degree of LL D. from Harvard College, 1856. She died May 9, 1883.

Children ·

2292 i CHARLES EMERY,[8] b July 3, 1823, grad Bowdoin College 1842, d in New York City, Dec 12, 1887
2293 ii NICHOLAS EMERY, b June 3, 1825, grad Harvard University, 1845; M D in 1851, unm
2294 iii AUGUSTUS LORD, b April 19, 1827
2295 iv MARY E , b March 8, 1829, d Jan 11, 1833
2296 v MARTHA, b Aug 8, 1831, d Nov 5, 1831

939 ELIZABETH (BETSEY)[7] FOLSOM (*Elizabeth,[6] Noah.[5] Noah,[4] Daniel,[3] James,[2] Anthony[1]*), daughter of Col. Samuel and Elizabeth

(Emery) Folsom; married, first, 1811, Noah, son of Noah and Jane (Hale) Emery; second, March 16, 1819, Rev. Isaac Hurd (born Dec. 7, 1785; died Oct. 4, 1856; graduated at Harvard College, 1806).

Children :

2297 i   JOSEPH ORNE,[8] b. Oct. 12, 1812; d. Dec., 1812.

By second marriage :

2298 ii FRANCES PARKMAN, b. Feb. 22, 1820.
2299 iii AUGUSTUS EMERY, b. Jan. 27, 1824; d. June 2, 1825.

940 JOANNA[7] FOLSOM (*Elizabeth,*[6] *Noah,*[5] *Noah,*[4] *Daniel,*[3] *James,*[2] *Anthony*[1]), daughter of Col. Samuel and Elizabeth (Emery) Folsom; married Samuel B. Stevens (born Nov. 30, 1783; died Aug., 1826). She died May 18, 1875.

Children :

2300 i   SAMUEL FOLSOM,[8] b. Sept. 10, 1811; m. Harriet J. De Lacroix;
            d. in South America, Dec. 30, 1852.
2301 ii ELIZABETH, b. Feb. 5, 1816; m. Prof. William A. Norton,
            (b. Oct. 25, 1810; grad. West Point, professor in Sheffield
            Scientific School, New Haven, Conn.).
2302 iii ANNE, b. July 6, 1821; d., unm., Nov. 2, 1842.
2303 iv SOLON BINGHAM, b. April, 1825; d. Aug., 1825.

942 CATHERINE HALE[7] EMERY (*Richard,*[6] *Noah,*[5] *Noah,*[4] *Daniel,*[3] *James,*[2] *Anthony*[1]), only child of Richard and Liberty (Hale) Emery; married May 16, 1814, Boswell Stevens, judge of probate for Merrimack Co., N. H.; graduated at Dartmouth College, 1804 (died Jan. 13, 1836). She died Sept. 7, 1864.

Children :

2304 i   CHARLES EMERY,[8] b. March 24, 1815, in Pembroke, N. H.
2305 ii WILLIAM, b. Feb., 1817; d. Oct. 7, 1828.
2306 iii ELIZABETH EMERY HURD, b. Nov. 2, 1818; d. in Carlisle,
            Mass.
2307 iv IVAN STEVENS, b. in Pembroke, N. H., July 7, 1821; grad. at
            Dartmouth College, 1842; read law with Bell & Tuck, Exe-
            ter, N. H., and practised law in Lawrence, Mass.; d., unm.,
            in Lawrence, Mass., Oct. 6, 1880; buried in Worcester,
            Mass.

944 JOSEPH[7] EMERY (*Shem,*[6] *Japhet,*[5] *Noah,*[4] *Daniel,*[3] *James,*[2] *Anthony*[1]), son of Shem and Keziah (Emery) Emery; married Elizabeth Jane Emery, daughter of Joshua and Hannah (Goodwin) Emery.

Children :

2308 i   KEZIAH,[8] b. Oct. 17, 1830; m. in Wells, Me., Nov. 29, 1865,
             George E. Baston; d. 1867.
2309 ii   JOSHUA, b. Aug. 4, 1832; m. in South Berwick, Me., April 20,
             1865, Abbie A. Baston.
2310 iii JOSEPH, b. Feb. 15, 1834; m. Oct. 21, 1860, Celestia A. Nowell
             of South Berwick, Me.
2311 iv   HANNAH J., b. Feb. 8, 1836; m. Edwin Nowell of So. Berwick,
             Me.
2312 v   MARY E., b. Nov 27, 1838; m. George Bartlett of Eliot, Me. .
2313 vi   SHEM, b. Oct. 12, 1841; m. Sarah N. Goodwin.
2314 vii JOHN, b. Dec. 28, 1843; m. Ann Nichols of So. Berwick, Me.

2315 ʋɪɪ ALBERT H , b. April 4, 1847, m , 1st, Mary Baston, 2nd, C.
        Norman
2316 ʋɪɪɪ GEORGE O , b Feb 27, 1853.

950 SHEM⁷ EMERY (*Shem,⁶ Japhet,⁵ Noah,⁴ Daniel,³ James,² Anthony¹*), son of Shem and his second wife Martha (Tebbetts) Emery; married Dorcas Witham.
Children :

2317 ɪ   JOHN,⁸ res in Great Falls, N H.
2318 ɪɪ ORIN, res. in Great Falls, N H.

951 POLLY⁷ EMERY (*Japhet,⁶ Japhet,⁵ Noah,⁴ Daniel,³ James,² Anthony¹*), daughter of Japhet and Molly (Shorey) Emery, married Feb. 22, 1815, William Morrill.
Children ·

2319 ɪ   JANE,⁸ b. April 6, 1816.
2320 ɪɪ   ISAAC, b May 15, 1818, d. Jan 2, 1845
2321 ɪɪɪ JAPHET, b March 11, 1821, m Eliz Hanscom, d. Dec 30,
              1859.
2322 ɪʋ   SARAH A , b Feb 7, 1827.
2323 ʋ   MOSES, b June 16, 1830
2324 ʋɪ   ALONZO, b Nov 7, 1833, m Helen Hill.
2325 ʋɪɪ MARTHA, b. June 16, 1835; d. June 13, 1844

952 LYDIA⁷ EMERY (*Japhet,⁶ Japhet,⁵ Noah,⁴ Daniel,³ James,² Anthony¹*), daughter of Japhet and Molly (Shorey) Emery; married Oct. 11, 1811, Simeon Emery, son of James and Catharine (Frye-Jenkins) Emery. She died Jan. 25, 1849.

953 JAPHET⁷ EMERY (*Japhet,⁶ Japhet.⁵ Noah,⁴ Daniel,³ James,² Anthony¹*), son of Japhet and Molly (Shorey) Emery; married Hannah Leighton, lived in Eliot, Me.
Children ·

2326 ɪ   MARY ANN,⁸ b. Oct. 5, 1827, m in So Berwick, July 6, 1853,
              Geo Butler.
2327 ɪɪ   OLIVIA S , b Feb 13, 1829, m Jan 30, 1858, Jefferson Raitt.
2328 ɪɪɪ JOHN LEIGHTON b June 8, 1832
2329 ɪʋ   JANE T , b Dec. 21, 1837, d Sept 21, 1855

955 THEODORE⁷ EMERY (*Theodore,⁶ Japhet,⁵ Noah,⁴ Daniel,³ James,² Anthony¹*), son of Theodore and Polly (Emery) Emery; married Susan Storer, lived in Sanford, Me. He died April 29, 1826.
Children, born in Sanford, Me :

2330 ɪ   CYRENA A ,⁸ b Feb 24, 1824
2331 ɪɪ THEODORE A , b Nov 23, 1825

958 MARY⁷ EMERY (*Theodore,⁶ Japhet,⁵ Noah,⁴ Daniel,³ James,² Anthony¹*), daughter of Theodore and Polly (Emery) Emery, married Jedediah Storer, brother of Susan Storer, the wife of her brother Theodore. Lived in Porter, Me.
Children :

2332 ɪ   MELISSA,⁸ b. Oct. 3, 1827, m. John Walker. Live in Brownfield, Me.

2333 ii Francis Calvin, d Aug. 22, 1834.
2334 iii John, b. March 20, 1833; m. Ida J. Clapp; lives in Ossipee,
          N. H.

961 Alva Crosby[7] Emery (*Theodore,*[6] *Japhet,*[5] *Noah,*[4] *Daniel,*[3] *James,*[2] *Anthony*[1]), son of Japhet and Polly (Emery) Emery; married, first, Sept. 5, 1834, Lucinda Welch (born Dec. 27, 1813; died Aug. 22, 1838); second, Nov. 26, 1840, Priscilla L. Marsh (born June 5, 1823; died Sept. 19, 1875); lived in Biddeford, Me. She afterwards married Marquis L. Emery.

Children, by first marriage :

2335 i Alonzo,[5] b. March, 1835; d. young.
2336 ii Lucinda, b. April 6, 1838; m. Ivory C. Morrison.

By second marriage :

2337 i Daniel A., b. Dec. 20, 1841; m. July 2, 1866, Pamelia A. Emery, b. June 15, 1844, dau. of Marquis L. Emery; live in
          Reading, Mass.
2338 iv Mary E., b. Sept. 14, 1845; d. June 25, 1861.
2339 v Julia A., b. Feb. 24, 1847; d. Oct. 29, 1851.
2340 vi Ann M., b. June 2, 1849; d. Sept. 14, 1860.
2341 vii Theodore F., b. Dec. 23, 1851; m. Ella Stevens of Woburn,
          Mass.; lives in Stoneham, Mass.
2342 viii Ida Jane, b. Sept. 18. 1853.
2343 ix Clarence E., b. Oct. 15, 1856; d. Nov. 3, 1860.

963 Josiah Gilman[7] Emery (*Theodore,*[6] *Japhet,*[5] *Noah,*[4] *Daniel,*[3] *James,*[2] *Anthony*[1]), son of Theodore and Polly (Emery) Emery; married Jan. 2, 1848, Arvilla Head of Tamworth, N. H. Farmer. He died Oct. 29, 1871.

Children :

2344 i A son,[8] d. young.
2345 ii A daughter, d. young.
2346 iii Ida A.

964 Stephen W.[7] Emery (*Theodore,*[6] *Japhet,*[5] *John,*[4] *Daniel,*[3] *James,*[2] *Anthony*[1]), son of Theodore and Polly (Emery) Emery; married March 22, 1864, Susan E. Hunt. Farmer. Lived in Parsonsfield, Me.

Child :

2347 i Etta E.,[8] b. Jan. 28, 1865; m. May 23, 1883, LeRoy Patch of
          Newfield, Me.

965 Japhet[7] Emery (*Theodore,*[6] *Japhet,*[5] *Noah,*[4] *Daniel,*[3] *James,*[2] *Anthony*[1]), son of Theodore and Polly (Emery) Emery; married Mary E. Jenness of Eaton, N. H. He was a soldier in company "K," 12th Regt. N. H. Vols.; wounded at Chancellorsville and died, Jan. 27, 1864, of his wounds; lived in Bartlett and Wolfboro, N. H. Farmer.

Children :

2348 i Elizabeth,[9] b. June 13, 1855, in Bartlett, N. H.; d. July 1,
          1855.
2349 ii George E., b. Feb. 11, 1857, in Eaton, N. H.; mechanic; unm.

966 RHODA A.[7] EMERY (*Theodore*,[6] *Japhet*,[5] *Noah*,[4] *Daniel*,[3] *James*,[2] *Anthony*[1]), daughter of Theodore and Polly (Emery) Emery; married Dec 26, 1847, George E. Bennett, of Tamworth, N H. She died Feb. 20, 1875.

Children .

2350 i   JAMES M ,[8] b June 12, 1849
2351 ii GEORGE F., b July 20, 1865

982 JEREMIAH[7] EMERY (*Jeremiah*,[6] *Simon*,[5] *Simon*,[4] *Daniel*,[3] *James*,[2] *Anthony*[1]), son of Jeremiah and Anna (Pray) Emery, married, Agnes Huntress (born 1782, died July 12, 1844)   She was killed, and her daughter Elvira injured, by being thrown from a carriage. He died Oct , 1837   Lived in Shapleigh, Me.

Children :

2352 i   ROSA ANNA,[8] } b 1811. {
2353 ii   ELVIRA,   }   { d July 22, 1844, in Newfield, Me
2354 iii ALEXANDER, b Dec 18, 1815
2355 iv   ROSELLA, b 1817, m Asa Sweet, 1843, d in Acton, Me ,
            March, 1849.
2356 v   GILMORE, b Sept 1, 1823
2357 vi   JOSEPH H , b 1825, m Rebecca Hill, lives in Portsmouth
2358 vii MONTGOMERY HILL, b 1828, m Mary Langley, April 28, 1852
            live in Weymouth, Mass
2359 viii JEREMIAH W , b July 21, 1833.

985 DR JAMES[7] EMERY (*Jeremiah*,[6] *Simon*,[5] *Simon*,[4] *Daniel*[3] *James*,[2] *Anthony*[1]), son of Jeremiah and Anna (Pray) Emery, married Sally, daughter of Dr. Ephraim Rowe, an early settler of Acton, Mass ; removed to Frankfort, Me., 1828. Physician   Member of convention that framed the Constitution of Maine. He died Sept. 17, 1861.

Children :

2360 i   CELIA PRAY,[8] b Dec. 16, 1816 ┌d July 19, 1862, at Patten Me
2361 ii   MARY ADELAIDE, b Sept. 10, 1818. d. in Shapleigh, Me., 1825.
2362 iii ISABEL, b April 16, 1821, d April 2, 1853
2363 iv   ABIJAH FISK, b March 29, 1823, d April 16, 1871
2364 v   LEWELIN, b. Nov 26, 1826, in Shapleigh, Me
2365 vi   MARCELLUS, b July 28, 1830, d Feb. 22, 1879, in Bangor. Me
            Graduated from Bowdoin College in 1853, taught the High
            School in Gardiner, Me , and was private tutor in Woodville,
            Miss , admitted to the bar in 1856, and entered into copartner-
            ship with Abraham Sanborn, Esq , of Bangor, editor of the
            "*Daily Union*," and also of the "*Democrat*," established the
            Bangor "*Daily Commercial*;" alderman one year ; delegate
            to the Democratic convention in Chicago, 1868 , twice nomi-
            nated for Congress   "His gentle manner in private life, and
            simple, temperate habits were in vivid contrast with the bit-
            terness of his journalistic and political utterances "
2366 vii ADALINE S , b Aug 31, 1833
2367 viii JAMES ORLANDO, b April 3, 1838, d. at Montevideo, S A ,
            Feb 14, 1867
2368 ix   JOSEPHINE, b. Dec 9, 1840, m Capt Tyler Metcalf, 1876, lives
            in Waterford, Me

986 ELIZABETH[7] EMERY (*Jeremiah*,[6] *Simon*,[5] *Simon*,[4] *Daniel*,[3] *James*,[2] *Anthony*[1]), daughter of Jeremiah and Anna (Pray) Emery , married, 1812. James Tebbetts of Berwick, Me. (born May 23, 1781 ; died April 20, 1861). She died July 19, 1863.

Children :

2369 i JEREMIAH E.,⁸ b. Oct. 13, 1812.
2370 ii JAMES M., b. April 30, 1816.
2371 iii LUTHER C., b. June 26, 1820.
2372 iv SARAH A., b. July 25, 1818.
2373 v EBENEZER, b. Aug. 1, 1824.
2374 vi LYMAN, b. April 25, 1828 ; d. Nov. 28, 1863.

987 MARTHA⁷ EMERY (*Jeremiah,*⁶ *Simon,*⁵ *Simon,*⁴ *Daniel,*³ *James,*² *Anthony*¹), daughter of Jeremiah and Anna (Pray) Emery ; married Feb. 22, 1818, John Gowen of Sanford, Me. (born May 31, 1793 ; died Sept. 13, 1863). Lived in Shapleigh and Farmington, Me. She died, May, 1851.

Children :

2375 i ROXANNA,⁸ b. Oct. 10, 1818 ; m. Royal B. Smith, Nov. 30, 1840.
2376 ii MARY A., b. Aug. 26, 1820 ; m. Simon P. Bradley, Oct. 10, 1838.
2377 iii GEORGIANA, b. April 1, 1822 ; d. Dec. 22, 1822.
2378 iv LORENZO D., b. Jan. 2, 1824 ; m. Angelina M. Zimmerman, Feb. 10, 1861.
2379 v EDWIN L., b. May 28, 1826 ; m., 1st, Eliza J. Ford, 1845 ; 2nd, Mrs. Mary Haley, 1865 ; lives in Salford, Kansas.
2380 vi MARTHA E., b. April 27, 1836 ; m. Dighton Corson, Oct., 1855 ; lives in San Francisco.

988 LYDIA⁷ EMERY (*Rev. Simon,*⁶ *Simon,*⁵ *Simon,*⁴ *Daniel,*³ *James,*² *Anthony*¹), daughter of Rev. Simon and Molly (Hodgdon) Emery ; married in Shapleigh, Me., June 3, 1799, Joseph Jellison.

Children :

2381 i STEPHEN.⁸
2382 ii JOHN, d. in war 1812, at sea ; m. Sarah Bowen.
2383 iii NANCY, m. James Webb.
2384 iv OLIVE, m. Eli Webb.
2385 v MOSES, b. in Trenton, Me., Aug. 6, 1810.
2386 vi JANE, m. Josiah Roberts.
2387 vii MARY.
2388 viii SIMON.
2389 ix JOSEPH, m., 1st, ——— Bowen ; 2nd, ———Hall.
2390 x MARTHA, m. Edward Webb.

989 BETSEY⁷ EMERY (*Rev. Simon,*⁶ *Simon,*⁵ *Simon,*⁴ *Daniel,*³ *James,*² *Anthony*¹), daughter of Rev. Simon and Molly (Hodgdon) Emery ; married Daniel Ricker.

Children :

2391 i MARTHA,⁸ b. Feb. 15, 1800.
2392 ii ISAIAH.
2393 iii SIMON.
2394 iv GEORGE.
2395 v WILLIAM.
2396 vi DANIEL.
2397 vii BENJAMIN.
2398 viii STEPHEN.
2399 ix BETSEY.
2400 x ROBERT.

995 EDWARD[7] EMERY (*Moses,[6] Simon,[5] Simon,[4] Daniel,[3] James,[2] Anthony[1]*), son of Moses and Betsey (Parsons) Emery, married, first, Sept. 19, 1824, Mary Sherburn (died March 9, 1855); second, Sarah Tucker

Children, by first wife:

2401 i WILLIAM,[8] b July 15, 1825
2402 ii GEORGE W , b March 9, 1829, d April 9, 1868, on board the Seabird, on Lake Michigan.
2403 iii MOSES S., b Feb 24, 1831
2404 iv BETSEY A , b May 26, 1833.
2405 v ELSIE E , b Feb 5, 1836
2406 vi EDWARD D , b July 18, 1838
2407 vii FAIRFIELD E , b Oct 17, 1841
2408 viii CHARLES E , b. Aug 28, 1847.

1003 HOSEA[7] EMERY (*Stephen,[6] Stephen,[5] Simon,[4] Daniel,[3] James,[2] Anthony[1]*), son of Stephen and Sarah (Emery) Emery, married Dec 6, 1798, Hannah Bartlett (died in Milford, Me., June 2, 1859). He died in Monroe, Me., Dec. 26, 1836.

Children:

2409 i TEMPLE H ,[8] b. Feb 3, 1800, in Kittery, Me ; d. in Bradley, Me., June 21, 1839
2410 ii ROSWELL, b May 12, 1803, in Berwick, Me.; d in Monroe, Me., 1860
2411 iii EMELINE, b Dec. 26, 1805, in Monroe, Me., d in Monroe, Me , Dec 26, 1824
2412 iv LYDIA b July 6, 1810, in Monroe, Me , d. in Monroe, Me., Feb 10 1826
2413 v SARAH, b March 1, 1813, in Monroe, Me , m Daniel Billings, Apr. 11, 1831, d in Boston, Mass , 1868
2414 vi HOSEA B , b Aug. 1, 1815, in Monroe, Me ; d in Bangor, Me., April 20, 1868
2415 vii HIRAM, b Nov 20, 1817, in Monroe, Me , m Harriet G Godfrey in Orono, Me , Jan 1, 1844, lives in Boston, Mass.
2416 viii HANNAH B b April 30, 1820; m Nathan Hinckley, March 1, 1840, d. Oct 9, 1843, in Bradley

1005 SARAH[7] EMERY (*Stephen,[6] Stephen,[5] Simon,[4] Daniel,[3] James,[2] Anthony[1]*), daughter of Stephen and Sarah (Emery) Emery; married Matthew McDaniel; lived and died in Monroe, Me.

Children:

2417 i CYNTHIA,[8] d unm.
2418 ii ELIZA, m. Hosea B Emery, son of Hosea and Hannah (Bartlett) Emery
2419 iii HANNAH, m Andrew McCausland.
2420 iv MATTHEW.
2421 v SARAH
2422 vi MARY, m ———— Edgecomb.

1012 CALVIN[7] EMERY (*Stephen,[6] Stephen,[5] Simon,[4] Daniel,[3] James,[2] Anthony[1]*), son of Stephen and his second wife Mrs Mary (Sharples) Emery; married, 1830, Rebecca Warren, daughter of James and Rebecca Warren of Gorham, Me.

Children ·

2423 i ELIZABETH J ,[8] b Jan 6, 1831
2424 ii ALBERT, b Feb 7, 1833, went to sea 1852, never heard from

2425　iii　CHARLES F., b. Oct. 26, 1835; d. Dec. 6, 1835.
2426　iv　EMILY F., b. Aug. 22, 1841; d. Nov. 17, 1844.
2427　v　FRANK J., b. July 1, 1847.
2428　vi　CLARA A., b. Sept. 3, 1850.

1017 JAMES[7] EMERY (*Joshua*,[6] *Stephen*,[5] *Simon*,[4] *Daniel*,[3] *James*,[2] *Anthony*[1]), son of Joshua and Tirzah (Emery) Emery.
Children :

2429　i　OTIS.[8]
2430　ii　BAXTER.
2431　iii　WILLIAM.
2432　iv　JANE.
2433　v　MARTHA.
2434　vi　ELIZABETH.
2435　vii　FRANCIS.

1018 ELIJAH[7] EMERY (*Joshua*,[6] *Stephen*,[5] *Simon*,[4] *Daniel*,[3] *James*,[2] *Anthony*[1]), son of Joshua and Tirzah(Emery)Emery ; married, first, in 1817, Rhoda (died March 12, 1804), daughter of Samuel and Huldah Parker of Berwick, Me. ; second, Mrs. Miriam Leavitt (died Nov. 13, 1876).
Children :

2436　i　LYDIA,[8] b. March 17, 1818; d. Sept. 13, 1876.
2437　ii　ANN, b. March 6, 1822 ; d. Sept. 16, 1831.
2438　iii　MARY JANE, b. May 8, 1824; m. S. Thompson; d. Sept. 14, 1872.
2439　iv　HARRIET T., b. Jan. 13, 1827; d. March 12, 1831.
2440　v　OLIVE, b. April 8, 1832; m. Joshua S. Mayberry; d. Oct. 22, 1855.
2441　vi　ASENATH, b. April 8, 1832.

1022 SALLY[7] EMERY (*Jacob*,[6] *Stephen*,[5] *Simon*,[4] *Daniel*,[3] *James*,[2] *Anthony*[1]), daughter of Jacob and Huldah (Thompson) Emery ; married March 6, 1806, Noah Thompson (born in York, Me., Sept. 13, 1780). She died March 2, 1857.
Children :

2442　i　HANNAH,[8] b. 1807; d. 1814.
2443　ii　JACOB, b. June 11, 1810.
2444　iii　HIRAM,　} b. Oct. 12, 1815; { d. unm.
2445　iv　HANNAH,

1023 JOHN[7] EMERY (*Jacob*,[6] *Stephen*,[5] *Simon*,[4] *Daniel*,[3] *James*,[2] *Anthony*[1]), son of Jacob and Huldah (Thompson) Emery ; married, 1820, Rosannah Abbot (died Oct. 3, 1868). He died Sept. 1, 1864, in Waterboro, Me.
Children :

2446　i　MARY ANN,[8] b. 1821; d. young.
2447　ii　MONROE, b. Feb. 26, 1824.
2448　iii　MARY ANN, b. Nov. 5, 1828; m., 1st, Orin Pray (d. Aug. 23, 1869); 2nd, Amasa Smith.
2449　iv　HULDAH JANE, b. 1830.
2450　v　MOSES J., b. April 25, 1831.
2451　vi　JOHN F., b. May 10, 1833; d. 1882.
2452　vii　THATCHER, b. April, 1836; m., 1865, Louisa Driden of Worces-, ter, Mass. (b. 1841).
2453　viii　STEPHEN, b. 1839; went to Cal. Nothing known of him.

1025 LUCY[7] EMERY (*Jacob*,[6] *Stephen*,[5] *Simon*,[4] *Daniel*,[3] *James*,[2] *Anthony*[1]), daughter of Jacob and Huldah (Thompson) Emery; married March 7, 1810, Trueworthy Chase (born Dec 3, 1779; died Nov. 28, 1855)

Children.

2454　i　ABIGAIL,[8] b July 3, 1813, d Jan 16, 1856
2455　ii　JOHN E　b June 3, 1815; d Apr 13, 1886, in Chicopee, Mass.
2456　iii　GEORGE F, b April 16, 1817; m Sarah Drew, d. Feb 28, 1887
2457　iv　THATCHER T, b July 3, 1820
2458　v　NANCY JANE, b Feb 19, 1827

1027 HULDAH[7] EMERY (*Jacob*,[6] *Stephen*,[5] *Simon*,[4] *Daniel*,[3] *James*,[2] *Anthony*[1]), daughter of Jacob and Huldah (Thompson) Emery, married Jan 28, 1813, Simon Chase (died Dec 24, 1864). She died Apr. 11, 1878.

Children.

2459　i　JOHN,[8] b June 2, 1815, d Sept 17, 1821
2460　ii　MARY ANN, b Oct 16, 1817
2461　iii　ELIJAH G, b March 22, 1819, m 1844, Phœbe Butterfield
2462　iv　HULDAH, b Oct 14, 1822, m June, 1850, William Adams.
2463　v　SIMON, b March 21, 1824, d April 2, 1851
2464　vi　JOHN MORRISON, b July 9, 1826
2465　vii　TRUEWORTHY, b Sept 11, 1828.
2466　viii　AMASA H, b April 8, 1833

1029 JACOB[7] EMERY (*Jacob*,[6] *Stephen*,[5] *Simon*,[4] *Daniel*,[3] *James*,[2] *Anthony*[1]), son of Jacob and Huldah (Thompson) Emery; married, first, March 22, 1818, Betsey March of Londonderry, N. H. (born 1801; died Oct. 12, 1836); second, Dec. 29, 1836, Rhoda H Ripley (died May 1, 1876). He died Nov. 8, 1869, in Nashua, N H.

Children, all by first wife·

2467　i　MORRIS MARCH,[8] b March 22, 1821, in Londonderry, N H, d. March 11, 1886
2468　ii　ENVILLE JACOB, b March 31, 1823, in Londonderry, N. H. d
2469　iii　LYDIA ANN, b Dec 14, 1825
2470　iv　JOHN MARCH, b July 11, 1828
2471　v　ALICE G ,
2472　vi　MOODY G , } b Feb. 11, 1832 { d April 21 1832.
2473　vii　MARY ELIZABETH, b Jan 24, 1835, m May 1, 1854, Horace Wallace of Nashua, N. H., d Feb 1, 1856

1030 THATCHER[7] EMERY (*Jacob*,[6] *Stephen*,[5] *Simon*,[4] *Daniel*,[3] *James*,[2] *Anthony*[1]), son of Jacob and Huldah (Thompson) Emery, married in Waterboro, Me, 1825, Sally Thing (born July 3, 1807). He died Sept 2, 1869.

Children

2474　i　CATHARINE,[8] b Dec 20, 1825
2475　ii　SARAH T, b Feb 21, 1828
2476　iii　WILLIAM T, b Dec. 23, 1830, lives in Utah
2477　iv　JOHN C, b July 10, 1833; m Sarah J Jellison, lives in Winnemucca, Nev.
2478　v　JACOB P, b July 8, 1835
2479　vi　THATCHER G., b Nov. 12, 1838.

2480 vii CHARLES F., b. Sept. 9, 1840; m. Susan Carter; lives in Nova
              Scotia.
2481 viii MARK A., b. Oct. 11, 1842.
2482 ix MARY D., b. Sept. 24, 1845; m. Charles H. Foss; d. Oct. 13,
              1877.
2483 x   ROSE A., b. June 24. 1848.
2484 xi NETTIE C., b. Dec. 23, 1853; m. Joseph C. Bradley.

1031 JOHN[7] EMERY (*Simon*,[6] *Stephen*,[5] *Simon*,[4] *Daniel*,[3] *James*,[2] *Anthony*[1]), son of Simon and Martha (Nowell) Emery; married, first, April, 1818, Mary Pike (died 1823); second, 1825, Mary Thing. He died May, 1873.

Children, by his first wife:

2485 i   CYRUS,[8] b. July 4, 1819.
2486 ii JOHN P., b. Dec. 3, 1821.

1032 PETER[7] EMERY (*Simon*,[6] *Stephen*,[5] *Simon*,[4] *Daniel*,[3] *James*,[2] *Anthony*[1]), son of Simon and Martha (Nowell) Emery; married, first, Nov. 14, 1816, Elizabeth Herd (died April 22, 1817); second, Nov. 29, 1821, Lydia Sias (died Nov. 21, 1858); third, May 5, 1861, Mrs. Mary J. Sherburn.

Child by first wife:

2487 i   ANN ELIZABETH,[8] d. April 26, 1842.

By second wife:

2488 ii MARY ANN, b. Aug. 1, 1822.
2489 iii ALMIRA, b. May 1, 1824.
2490 iv SAMUEL H., b. April 25, 1825.
2491 v   CHARLES H., b. April 26, 1827; d. Dec. 9, 1829.
2492 vi FRANCES S., b. Nov. 18, 1829.
2493 vii CHARLES T., b. Oct. 11, 1823; d. Aug. 12, 1834.
2494 viii WILLIAM H., b. June 22, 1834; d. Nov. 12, 1840.

1033 HENRY[7] EMERY (*Simon*,[6] *Stephen*,[5] *Simon*,[4] *Daniel*,[3] *James*,[2] *Anthony*[1]), son of Simon and Martha (Nowell) Emery; married Deborah Meserve.

Children, born in Waterboro, Me.:

2495 i   GEORGE T.,[8] b. June 14, 1821; d. June 9, 1881.
2496 ii SARAH E., b. 1823.
2496a iii ELIZABETH.

1035 MARTHA[7] EMERY (*Simon*,[6] *Stephen*,[5] *Simon*,[4] *Daniel*,[3] *James*,[2] *Anthony*[1]), daughter of Simon and Martha (Nowell) Emery; married Morris Pike.

Children:

2497 i   SARAH.[8]
2498 ii ROSAMOND.
2499 iii RACHEL.

1036 SALLY[7] EMERY (*Simon*,[6] *Stephen*,[5] *Simon*,[4] *Daniel*,[3] *James*,[2] *Anthony*[1]), daughter of Simon and Martha (Nowell) Emery; married Richard Fifield, who died in Salem, Mass., Dec. 29, 1880.

Children:

2500 i CHARLES E [8]
2501 .II GEORGE W
2502 III ANN MARY
2503 iv SOPHIA ANN
2504 v SALLY

1037 ALZIRA[7] EMERY (*Simon,[6] Stephen,[5] Simon,[4] Daniel,[3] James,[2] Anthony[1]*), daughter of Simon and Martha (Nowell) Emery; married Orin Giles.

Children:

2505 i ANDREW,[8] m. and had eight children.
2506 II CHARLES
2507 III MARTIN VAN BUREN.
2508 IV HENRY
2509 V SIMON.
2510 VI JOHN G.
2511 VII MARTHA
2512 VIII FRANCES

1047 JOSHUA[7] EMERY (*Israel,[6] Samuel,[5] Simon,[4] Daniel,[3] James,[2] Anthony[1]*), son of Israel and Prudence (Emery) Emery; married Sarah (Ham) Jones (born in Portsmouth, N. H, Feb. 22, 1799, died in Eliot, Me., Dec. 4, 1881). He died Mar. 27, 1883.

Children, born in Eliot, Me :

2513 I JAMES W ,[8] b. Jan 15, 1836
2514 II REBECCA, b July 12, 1838, d. June 22, 1866.

1049 ALVIN[7] EMERY (*Israel,[6] Samuel,[5] Simon,[4] Daniel,[3] James,[2] Anthony[1]*), son of Israel and Prudence (Emery) Emery; married, first, Catharine Emery, daughter of Joel and Betsey (Emery) Emery; second, June 15, 1851, Rebecca Grant, daughter of Daniel and Abigail (Emery) Grant. Her mother was daughter of Simon and Elizabeth (Mendum) Emery.

Children.

2515 I GEORGE W ,[8] } b Dec 18, 1844, { ies in Medford, Mass
2516 II CHARLES,   }   { d in infancy
2517 III PAULINA, b May, 1848, d Oct, 1848
2518 IV ORIN, b Jan 11, 1852, res in So Berwick
2519 V HORTON W , b Dec. 4, 1854 d. Aug 5, 1855.
2520 VI HORTON W., b. Sept 15, 1856; lives in South Berwick

1055 ALMIRA[7] EMERY (*George,[6] Stephen,[5] Simon,[4] Daniel,[3] James,[2] Anthony[1]*), daughter of George and Betsey (Pierce) Emery; married Joshua Main.

Child.

2521 I CHARLES [8]

1056 MARY ANN L [7] EMERY (*George,[6] Stephen,[5] Simon.[4] Daniel,[3] James,[2] Anthony[1]*), daughter of George and Betsey (Pierce) Emery; married July 4, 1833, James E. Macy of Fall River, Mass.

Child:

2522 I CHARLES T.[8]

27

1057 THATCHER[7] EMERY (*George,*[6] *Stephen,*[5] *Simon,*[4] *Daniel,*[3] *James,*[2] *Anthony*[1]), son of George and Betsey (Pierce) Emery ; married Elizabeth Woods (born July 19, 1801 ; died April 23, 1885).
   Children :

   2523   i   ROBERT L.,[8] b. Jan. 8, 1826 ; m. Abbie R. Sanborn.
   2524   ii   CHARLES T., b. June 19, 1830 ; m. Mary E. Pickering ; d. Dec. 17, 1875.
   2525   iii ELIZABETH ANN, b. July 19, 1832 ; m., 1st, Frank C. Plummer ; 2nd, Joseph S. Parsons.
   2526   iv   ALMIRA, b. March 21, 1834 ; m. Washington Freeman.
   2527   v   ANN MARIA, b. Nov. 27, 1836.
   2528   vi   JAMES H., b. Dec. 21, 1838 ; m. Lizzie Gerrish ; d. Aug. 5, 1870.
   2529   vii ALBERT, b. July 11, 1840.
   2530   viii MARGARET ELLEN, b. March 25, 1843 ; m. David T. Ross.

1060 ALFRED[7] EMERY (*Ichabod,*[6] *Stephen,*[5] *Simon,*[4] *Daniel,*[3] *James,*[2] *Anthony*[1]), son of Ichabod and Mary (Tetherly) Emery ; married May 13, 1833, Sarah J. Perry (died Feb. 17, 1867) in Ossipee, N. H.
   Child :

   2531   i   SON,[8] b. Sept. and d. Dec. 30, 1842.

1063 GEORGE ALEXANDER[7] EMERY (*Ichabod,*[6] *Stephen,*[5] *Simon,*[4] *Daniel,*[3] *James,*[2] *Anthony*[1]), son of Ichabod and Mary (Tetherly) Emery ; married Feb. 18, 1856, Elizabeth L. Nash (born April 2, 1827 ; died June 1, 1880).
   Children :

   2532   i   SON,[8] b. and d. June 8, 1857.
   2533   ii   STEPHEN N., b. June 13, 1858 ; d. June 22, 1864.

1073 THOMAS[7] EMERY (*Simon,*[6] *Samuel,*[5] *Simon,*[4] *Daniel,*[3] *James,*[2] *Anthony*[1]), son of Simon and Elizabeth (Mendum) Emery ; married Nov. 27, 1823, Theodosia Grant (born in York, Nov. 12, 1796) ; lived in Kittery, York, Eliot, Me., and Somersworth, N. H.
   Children :

   2534   i   ROSWELL,[8] b. Dec. 16, 1825 ; d. Nov. 12, 1828, in Kittery, Me.
   2535   ii   JULIA, b. Sept. 28, 1828, in Kittery, Me.
   2536   iii ELIZABETH P., b. in Somersworth, N. H.
   2537   iv   SIMON, b. Aug. 25, 1833, in Somersworth, N. H.
   2538   v   MARY A., b. Feb. 8, 1837, in Kittery, Me.
   2539   vi   SOPHIA S., b. Aug. 23, 1839, in Kittery, Me.
   2540   vii LUCY, b. Sept. 10, 1841, in Kittery, Me.; d. Nov. 30, 1861.

1080 MARY[7] EMERY (*Isaac,*[6] *Samuel,*[5] *Simon,*[4] *Daniel,*[3] *James,*[2] *Anthony*[1]), daughter of Isaac and Elizabeth (Kingsbury) Emery ; married Jan. 15, 1826, Ira Haynes. He died Dec. 8, 1857. She died Nov. 4, 1857.
   Children, born in South Parsonsfield, Me. :

   2541   i   JOHN M.,[8] b. Sept. 9, 1828.
   2542   ii   MARY J., b. Sept. 22, 1830 ; d., unm., Sept. 19, 1861, at Hadley, Mass.
   2543   iii CAROLINE B., b. April 20, 1832 ; d. Feb. 3, 1848.
   2544   iv   HARRIET P., b. Aug. 19, 1833 ; m. Roscoe G. Smith of Saco, Me.; d. July 3, 1858.

2545   v   RHODA A. L , b Oct 20, 1836 , d , nnm , June 6, 1859
2546· vi JOSEPH E , b April 10, 1838 , m Oct. 23, 1877, Ada B Cald-
            well; lives on Isaac's homestead

1081 HIRAM[7] EMERY (*Isaac,[6] Samuel,[5] Simon,[4] Daniel,[3] James,[2]
Anthony[1]*), son of Isaac and Elizabeth (Kingsbury) Emery ; married
May 11, 1825, Margaret Young of Surry, Me (born Aug. 15, 1804),
daughter of Samuel and Betsey (Brown) Young   He was a carpenter and wheelwright , lived in Poland, Me , from 1828 to 1850, when
he moved to North Falmouth.   He died Oct 31, 1876.
   Children, born in Poland, Me. .

   2547   i   ELIZABETH A ,[8] b April 28, 1829 ; d Feb. 12, 1843.
   2548   ii   ESTHER E , b July 21, 1830.
   2549   iii   JOSEPH M , b Oct. 7, 1832 , d Sept. 15, 1837.
   2550   iv   MARTHA D , b. June 21, 1834.
   2551   v   ABBIE L , b April 2, 1836.
   2552   vi   JOSEPH H , b Aug 8, 1838
   2553   vii   GEORGE B , b Oct 12, 1844 , d April 2, 1845
   2554   viii THOMAS J., b Dec 26, 1845, lawyer; ies in Boston, Mass ;
                grad Bowdoin Coll., 1868, Boston University Law School,
                1876; member of City Council, 1881–3, school committee,
                1889
   2555   ix   HIRAM J , b. Nov 23, 1849 , d. Sept 7, 1850

1082 WILLIAM[7] EMERY (*Isaac,[6] Samuel,[5] Simon,[4] Daniel,[3] James,[2]
Anthony[1]*), son of Isaac and Elizabeth (Kingsbury) Emery ; married
Nov 29, 1827, Sabina (born in Newfield, Me., May 22, 1804 ; died
Feb. 12. 1866), daughter of Clement and Nancy (Tebbetts) Drew.
They lived in South Parsonsfield, Me.   Farmer.   He died April 25,
1884
   Children :

   2556   i   ALBION P ,[8] b Oct 13, 1828, in Newfield, Me , d Oct 9, 1848,
                in Berwick
   2557   ii   LORENZO W., b. Feb 5, 1834, in Newfield
   2558   iii   MELVIN A , b Oct 12, 1837, in So Parsonsfield, d Dec. 31,
                1864, in Ill ; grad Bowdoin Med School.
   2559   iv   NANCY J., b July 22, 1848, in So. Parsonsfield, d. Feb 9, 1853.

1084 TEMPLE H.[7] EMERY (*Isaac,[6] Samuel,[5] Simon,[4] Daniel,[3]
James,[2] Anthony[1]*), son of Isaac and Elizabeth (Kingsbury) Emery ;
married Oct. 7, 1831, Sarah Weymouth (died March 15, 1883), daughter of James and Phœbe (Jenkins) Weymouth.
   Children, born in Sangerville, Me. ·

   2560   i   PHŒBE E ,[8] b Jan. 20, 1833
   2561   ii   ALBERT G , b June 14, 1839, d. Jan 15, 1872.
   2562   iii   JAMES W., b Aug 12, 1841 , m Oct 26, 1871, Annie Lennon
                (b Nov 13, 1847) ; had one child, adopted, Carrie W , b. Feb
                8, 1879 , lives in Cambridge, Mass
   2563   iv   ZACHARY T , b Jan 28, 1847 , d Sept. 2, 1880, in Renovo, Pa.
   2564   v   MARY E , b Jan 29, 1851 , grad. Farmington Normal School,
                1881

1085 ADAH[7] EMERY (*Joshua,[6] John,[5] Simon,[4] Daniel,[3] James,[2]
Anthony[1]*), daughter of Joshua and Hannah (Goodwin) Emery , married June 10, 1810, Stephen Chase.

Children :

2565   i   STEPHEN,[8] d. at sea.
2566   ii WILLIAM.

1086 TIRZAH[7] EMERY (*Joshua,*[6] *John,*[5] *Simon,*[4] *Daniel,*[3] *James,*[2] *Anthony*[1]), daughter of Joshua and Hannah (Goodwin) Emery ; married Feb. 3, 1811, Jonathan Chase.
Children :

2567   i   JOSHUA.[8]   } twins.
2568   ii   BENJAMIN.
2569   iii AUGUSTUS.
2570   iv   TIRZAH.
2571   v   ADAH.
2572   vi   HANNAH.
2573   vii JOHN.
2574   viii SIMON.
2575   ix   EMILY.

1087 KEZIAH[7] EMERY (*Joshua,*[6] *John,*[5] *Simon,*[4] *Daniel,*[3] *James,*[2] *Anthony*[1]), daughter of Joshua and Hannah (Goodwin) Emery ; married March 16, 1820, Samuel Stone.
Children :

2576   i   GEORGE.[8]
2577   ii MARY ELIZABETH.

1089 SOPHIA[7] EMERY (*Joshua,*[6] *John,*[5] *Simon,*[4] *Daniel,*[3] *James,*[2] *Anthony*[1]), daughter of Joshua and Hannah (Goodwin) Emery ; married John Thurrell.
Children :

2578   i   EDWIN.[8]
2579   ii   SARAH A.
2580   iii JAMES.
2581   iv   JOHN.
2582   v   HANNAH.
2583   vi   OLIVE J.
2584   vii THEODOTE.
2585   viii SERENA.
2586   ix   CHARLES.

1090 HANNAH[7] EMERY (*Joshua,*[6] *John,*[5] *Simon,*[4] *Daniel,*[3] *James,*[2] *Anthony*[1]), daughter of Joshua and Hannah (Goodwin) Emery ; married Sept. 21, 1834, Thomas Hanscom.
Child :

2587   i   CHARLES,[8] b. June 2, 1840; lives in New York.

1091 CLARISSA[7] EMERY (*Joshua,*[6] *John,*[5] *Simon,*[4] *Daniel,*[3] *James,*[2] *Anthony*[1]), daughter of Joshua and Hannah (Goodwin) Emery ; married, Feb. 16, 1819, Joshua Chase.
Children :

2588   i   JONATHAN.[8]
2589   ii   STEPHEN.
2590   iii EDWARD.
2591   iv   CHARLES.

2592 v   MARY ELIZABETH.
2593 vi HANNAH.
2594 vii JOSHUA.

1092 SERENA[7] EMERY (*Joshua,[6] John,[5] Simon,[4] Daniel,[3] James,[2] Anthony[1]*), daughter of Joshua and Hannah (Goodwin) Emery; married Nov. 19, 1819, Thomas Hanscom.
Children

2595 i   STEPHEN.[8]
2596 ii   JACOB
2597 iii ELIZABETH.
2598 iv   SERENA
2599 v   SARAH A.
2600 vi   LYMAN

1093 MARY[7] EMERY (*Joshua,[6] John,[5] Simon,[4] Daniel,[3] James,[2] Anthony[1]*), daughter of Joshua and Hannah (Goodwin) Emery, married, 1827, John Bartlett of Portsmouth, N. H.
Children.

2601 i   THEODORE [8]
2602 ii   MARY.
2603 iii EMELINE
2604 iv   JOHN
2605 v   MARIA.

1112 CALEB[7] EMERY (*John,[6] Charles,[5] Simon,[4] Daniel,[3] James,[2] Anthony[1]*), son of John and Sally (Parker) Emery; married, Margaret Powers.
Children:

2606 i   JOHN,[8] m in Groton, Vt, Oct 20, 1836, Huldah Darling
2607 ii SARAH, m. Chester Darling.

1113 NOAH[7] EMERY (*John,[6] Charles,[5] Simon,[4] Daniel,[3] James,[2] Anthony[1]*), son of John and Sally (Parker) Emery; married Nov. 2, 1816, Polly Page of Groton, Vt.
Children, born in Groton, Vt.:

2608 i   EUNICE,[8] b Oct 4, 1817, m in Groton, Vt., March 5,1844, Henry H. Clark, d. Jan. 21, 1876
2609 ii   SALLY, b Sept 24, 1819, d in Groton, Vt, Jan 29, 1820.
2610 iii DOLLY, b Aug 1, 1821, m Ancil Foster, Dec 8, 1842, d Sept 2, 1876
2611 iv   ANNA, b Aug 11, 1823, d. in Ryegate, Vt., Sept. 19, 1843
2612 v   SALLY, b May 7, 1825, m in Morgan, Vt., March 15, 1849, John Arthur
2613 vi   MARY, b Oct. 21, 1827, m Dec. 12, 1844, George Scott of Groton
2614 vii VIRTUE, b Dec 24, 1829, d July 1, 1831, in Groton, Vt.
2615 viii LAVINA, b Oct 31, 1832, m. May 24, 1851, Clark Hatch of Groton
2616 ix   NOAH, b Jan 27, 1835, m. Nov. 22, 1856, Sarah Marsh of Island Pond Vt
2617 x   LUCY, b Aug. 21, 1837; m. in Brfton, Jan 26, 1854, Ephraim Danforth
2618 xi   EMILY J, b July 11, 1839; m . 1st, Peter Craigie, Aug 19, 1860, 2nd, James J Davis, Nov 9, 1879, lives at Island Pond, Vt.
2619 xii CATHARINE, b Sept. 15, 1842, d in Groton, Vt, Sept 15, 1842.

1115 Simon[7] Emery (*John*,[6] *Charles*,[5] *Simon*,[4] *Daniel*,[3] *James*,[2] *Anthony*[1]), son of John and Sally (Parker) Emery; married in Groton, Vt., Nancy Goodwin (born June 6, 1807; died Oct. 13, 1881). Children:

2620　i　Lucy M.,[8] b. Sept. 22, 1832; d. in Groton, Vt., Oct. 25, 1866.
2621　ii　Jeremiah, b. Feb. 19, 1834; m. May 5, 1862, Drusilla Emery, dau. of Timothy and Matilda (Goodwin) Emery.
2622　iii　Phœbe, b. Sept. 23, 1835; d. Jan., 1836.
2623　iv　Benjamin, b. Dec. 14, 1836; d. Dec. 18, 1861, in Alexandria, Va., in the army.
2624　v　Charles, b. March 27, 1838; m. Juliet La Valley in Fergus Falls, Minn., Nov. 22, 1873.
2625　vi　Betsey Ann, b. Nov. 12, 1840; d. Oct. 6, 1863, in Groton, Vt.
2626　vii　John, b. Dec. 14, 1842.
2627　viii　Caleb, b. Dec. 14, 1844; d. Sept., 1848, in Groton, Vt.
2628　ix　Simon, b. June 10. 1846.
2629　x　Mary Jane, b. May 8, 1848.

1116 Charles[7] Emery (*John*,[6] *Charles*,[5] *Simon*,[4] *Daniel*,[3] *James*,[2] *Anthony*[1]), son of John and Sally (Parker) Emery; married Sally ———. He died in Constantine, N. Y., July 6, 1855. Children:

2630　i　Sarah Ann,[8] b. 1830; m. Elias Wilson.
2631　ii　Jonathan, b. 1832; d. young.
2632　iii　Jane Maria, b. 1834.
2633　iv　John A., b. 1836; d. young.
2634　v　John, b. 1838
2635　vi　Charles A., b. 1840.
2636　vii　Harriet Eliza, b. 1842.
2637　viii　Mary Louisa, b. 1847.

1118 Samuel P.[7] Emery (*John*,[6] *Charles*,[5] *Simon*,[4] *Daniel*,[3] *James*,[2] *Anthony*[1]), son of John and Sally (Parker) Emery; married Aug. 19, 1824, Betsey Hooper (born in Groton, Vt., May 17, 1803), daughter of James and Polly (Emery) Hooper. He died Dec. 12, 1884, in Topsham, Vt. Children:

2638　i　Lois,[8] b. Jan. 12, 1825; m in Topsham, Vt., Lyman Mills.
2639　ii　Mary, b. Jan. 12, 1828; m. in Topsham, Vt., Lewis Avery.
2640　iii　Samuel, b. March 24, 1830; d. March 5, 1832.
2641　iv　Eliza, b. Jan. 19, 1832; m. in Topsham, Vt., Sept. 15, 1878, Orville Cunningham.
2642　v　Elijah, b. Nov. 26, 1835.

1119 Anna[7] Emery (*John*,[6] *Charles*,[5] *Simon*,[4] *Daniel*,[3] *James*,[2] *Anthony*[1]), daughter of John and Sally (Parker) Emery; married in Groton, Vt., March 12, 1837, Levi Wilson. He died July 22, 1883. Children, born in Groton, Vt.:

2643　i　William,[8] b. Jan. 16, 1838; m. Jan. 3, 1861, Mary Ann Whitehill.
2644　ii　Patience A., b. Nov. 29, 1841; m. in Groton, Vt., Jan. 21, 1867, George Mills.
2645　iii　John E., b. June 3, 1844; d. Jan. 2, 1845.
2646　iv　Isaac M., b. May 11, 1846; m. in Groton, Vt., Nov. 26, 1867. Caroline E. Heath.

1121 Joshua[7] Emery (*John*,[6] *Charles*,[5] *Simon*,[4] *Daniel*,[3] *James*,[2] *Anthony*[1]), son of John and Sally (Parker) Emery; married, first, March 4, 1838, Sally Hadley (born Sept 5, 1814; died Dec 27, 1871); second, in Winona, Minn., Dec. 27, 1872, Jane Coy (born April 7, 1816; died Aug, 1880), third, Nov. 18, 1880, Eliza Scott (born 1843, in East Farley, Vt.) He was one of the first settlers in Rushford, Minn., in 1856; helped to build the first church and school in that place; removed to Money Creek, Minn., 1861, where he also gave the same help His farm is known as the Emery farm. He died July 22, 1883.

Children, born in Morgan, Vt.:

2647   i   Martha,[8] b Dec 6, 1838, d in Rushford, Minn, Jan 22, 1864

2648   ii   Stephen, b Feb 2, 1841; Union soldier, d. at St Louis, Mo, Jan 17, 1862.

2649   iii   Sarah Ann, b Feb 9, 1843, physician in Chicago

2650   iv   Betsey, b Dec 15, 1844

2651   v   Moses, b April 10, 1817.

2652   vi   Mary, b March 11, 1849, m. July 6, 1876, Edwin A. Kellett of Zumbrota, Minn

2653   vii   Phœbe, b April 10, 1851

2654   viii   George Pierce, b March 22, 1854, m

2655   ix   Louise Angelia, b Jan 17, 1859, in Rushford, Minn.

2656   x   Bertha Bell, b. Oct 1, 1862, in Money Creek, Minn ; m.

1152 Betsey[7] Emery (*William*,[6] *James*,[5] *Zachariah*,[4] *Daniel*,[3] *James*,[2] *Anthony*[1]), daughter of William and Sarah (Maguire) Emery, married, 1808, John Stanton (born in Lebanon, Me., Sept 30, 1784), son of Paul and Joanna (Ricker) Stanton. Lived in Poland, Me.

Children:

2657   i   John E ,[8] b 1809.

2658   ii   Mary B , b 1811, d 1838.

2659   iii   Benj. L , b 1813.

2660   iv   Sarah M , b 1815

2661   v   William E , b 1817

2662   vi   Hannah M , b 1820.

2663   vii   Jabez Ricker, b 1821; d 1822.

2664   viii   Isaac, b 1822

2665   ix   Otis, b 1827, m , 1850, Ann C Ricker (b. 1832).

1154 Sally[7] Emery (*William*,[6] *James*,[5] *Zachariah*,[4] *Daniel*,[3] *James*,[2] *Anthony*[1]), daughter of William and Sarah (Maguire) Emery; married Reuben Blau.

Children, born in Poland, Me :

2666   i   Mary,[8] b Aug 11, 1813, d 1814.

2667   ii   Lovina, b. July 14, 1814, m Daniel C Herrick of Poland, Me.; d Oct 19, 1873

2668   iii   Mark E , b Jan. 1, 1817; m Mrs Nancy C Stowe of Grafton, Mass , d May 15, 1819

2669   iv   Emily J , m Jacob O Pollard of Limington, Me., live in Poland, Me

2670   v   Andrew J , b Sept 29, 1828; d July 11, 1829

2671   vi   Andrew J , b. May 28, 1830.

2672   vii   William E , b Oct 3, 1833, m. Lorana Hodgdon of Poland, Me.

1158 Mehitable[7] Emery (*William*,[6] *James*,[5] *Zachariah*,[4] *Daniel*,[3]

James,[2] *Anthony*[1]), daughter of William and Sarah (Maguire) Emery ; married in 1816, William E. Brooks. She died Feb. 14, 1870.
　Children :

```
2673  i    EUNICE E.,8 b. March 24, 1817.
2674  ii   CHARLES B., b. Dec. 24, 1818 ; d. Dec. 12, 1865.
2675  iii  WILLIAM E., b. Dec. 18, 1820 ; d. Dec. 24, 1856.
2676  iv   ANSIL F., b. Feb. 18, 1823.
2677  v    LUCY A., b. Jan. 1, 1826.
2678  vi   SARAH J., b. Feb. 14, 1830 ; d. Sept. 25, 1855.
2679  vii  MARY E., b. Jan. 21, 1833.
2680  viii REBECCA M., b  March 7, 1835 ; d. Dec. 1, 1868.
2681  ix   FREDERICK A., d. Dec. 14, 1872.
2682  x    FRANKLIN A., d. Nov. 28, 1872.
```

1159 THANKFUL[7] EMERY (*William,*[6] *James,*[5] *Zachariah,*[4] *Daniel,*[3] *James,*[2] *Anthony*[1]), daughter of William and Sarah (Maguire) Emery ; married in 1820, Paul (born in Poland, Me., Dec. 14, 1799 ; died 1824), son of Paul and Joanna (Ricker) Stanton. She died in 1843.
　Children :

```
2683  i    BETSEY,8 b. 1821.
2684  ii   MARK E., b. 1823 ; m. Mary B. Staples (b. in 1833).
```

1160 JOHN[7] EMERY (*William,*[6] *James,*[5] *Zachariah,*[4] *Daniel,*[3] *James,*[2] *Anthony*[1]), son of William and Sarah (Maguire) Emery ; married Betsey Johnson (died July 18, 1880).   Lives in Poland, Me.
　Children, born in Poland, Me. :

```
2685  i    JEREMY,8 b. Feb. 26, 1826.
2686  ii   HENRY, b. May 7, 1827.
2687  iii  EDWIN, b. Dec. 31, 1829.
2688  iv   GREENLEAF, b. July 20, 1831.
2689  v    SALOME, b. Aug. 20, 1833 ; m. Charles J. Pierce ; lives in Po-
            land, Me.
2690  vi   ELIZABETH, b. Aug. 17, 1835 ; m. William H. Merrill of New
            Gloucester, Me.
2691  vii  ELLEN, b. July 13, 1838 ; m. H. R. Lewis of Malden, Mass.
2692  viii WILLIAM, b. July 27, 1840 ; m., 1st, June 10, 1862, Elizabeth
            James ; 2nd, April 26, 1864, Mary Ann James ; 3rd, Feb. 3,
            1877, Mary Murtrie.
2693  ix   MARTHA, b. Aug. 15, 1843 ; d. 1853.
```

1167 MARK[7] EMERY (*Mark,*[6] *James,*[5] *Zachariah,*[4] *Daniel,*[3] *James,*[2] *Anthony*[1]), son of Mark and Anne (Maguire) Emery ; married Lydia Bessey of Paris, Me.
　Child :

```
2694  i    JAMES L.,8 b. March 4, 1820, in Raymond, Me.
```

1168 JANE[7] EMERY (*Mark,*[6] *James,*[5] *Zachariah,*[4] *Daniel,*[3] *James,*[2] *Anthony*[1]), daughter of Mark and Anne (Maguire) Emery ; married, first, in 1814, William Hodgdon ; second, —— Stubbs.
　Children :

```
2695  i    PHŒBE H.,9 b. Sept. 11, 1815 ; m. Oct. 3, 1835, Potter J. May-
            berry.
```

2696 ii   Darius, b April 17, 1817, d in Fremont, Mich , Sept 27, 1878.
2697 iii Nancy J , b April 19, 1819, m Aug 8, 1841, William H.
           Merrow , lives in Casco, Me
2698 iv   William H , b Feb 25, 1821, m 1844; res. in Lynn, Mass.
2699 v   Albion K. P , b. July 18, 1826, res unknown.

By second marriage

2700 vi   Charles E , b Sept 12, 1835; res in Goshen, N H

1170 Hannah[7] Emery (*Mark,[6] James,[5] Zachariah,[4] Daniel,[3]
James,[2] Anthony[1]*), daughter of Mark and Anne (Maguire) Emery;
married in 1818, Isaac Barton of New Gloucester, Me.
Children, born in New Gloucester, Me. ·

2701 i   Isaac,[8] b Nov 4, 1819; m May 4, 1840, Rebecca Trites of
           New Brunswick, res in Gray, Me.
2702 ii   Albion, b. March 24, 1821; m June 15, 1846, Sophia Lougee
           of Effingham, N. H , d June 15, 1863
2703 iii William, b. April 22, 1823, m Maria Coburn of Paris, Me.;
           res. in Roxbury, Essex Co , Va
2704 iv   Anna, b Jan 28, 1825, m Jan 14, 1849, James Mitchell of
           Phillips, Me , lives in Poland, Me
2705 v   Sarah, b. Sept. 26, 1826, m. April 26, 1863, Daniel Harris of
           Poland, Me.
2706 vi   Andrew, b Nov 6, 1828
2707 vii Willard, b Jan 2, 1831, d.
2708 viii Lorana, b Jan 12, 1834, d young
2709 ix   Franklin, b May 3, 1836, in Poland, Me , d
2710 x   Lorana, b May 4, 1840, in Poland, Me , m Smith G. Bailey;
           graduate of Tufts College, lives in Newport, N H

1171 James[7] Emery (*Mark,[6] James,[5] Zachariah,[4] Daniel,[3] James,[2]
Anthony[1]*), son of Mark and Anne (Maguire) Emery , married March
7, 1823, Mary Ann Snow of Poland, Me.
Children, born in Poland, Me. .

2711 i   Ruxby,[8] b. July 28, 1823
2712 ii   Alice W , b Dec 1, 1824, m Geo R Keen of Abington, Mass.
2713 iii James H , b Aug 6, 1826, m. Mary Ann Edgecomb, lives in
           Poland, Me
2714 iv   Franklin, b Nov 17, 1830, unm , res in Poland, Me
2715 v   Emeline H , b Nov. 5, 1832, m. William Storey; res. in Po-
           land, Me.
2716 vi   Elizabeth, b Oct 10, 1834
2717 vii George W., b Nov. 3, 1843, m Lorinda Fowler of Bridgton,
           Me
2718 viii William W , b July 13, 1848

1172 Rachel[7] Emery (*Mark,[6] James,[5] Zachariah,[4] Daniel,[3] James,[2]
Anthony[1]*), daughter of Mark and Anne (Maguire) Emery , married
Nov 30, 1826, James Johnson.
Children

2719 i   William H ,[8] b Aug 27, 1827.
2720 ii   Anna L , b Oct 11, 1833
2721 iii Hannah M., b. March 14, 1836, m O. S. Keen, March, 1855.

1176 William H.[7] Emery (*Simeon,[6] James,[5] Zachariah,[4] Daniel,[3]
James,[2] Anthony[1]*), son of Simeon and Lydia (Emery) Emery ; mar-

ried Oct. 18, 1845, Mary Ann Littlefield. Lives in Gloucester City, N. J.

Children :

2722   i   WILLIAM ALBERT,[8] b. Oct. 22, 1846; d. Jan. 21, 1851.
2723   ii   GEORGE R., b. Oct. 7, 1849.
2724   iii   WILLARD, b. May 9, 1852.
2725   iv   HERBERT, b. May 13, 1856.
2726   v   ANNIE, b. March 14, 1862.

1177 LYDIA[7] EMERY (*Simeon,*[6] *James,*[5] *Zachariah,*[4] *Daniel,*[3] *James,*[2] *Anthony*[1]), daughter of Simeon and Lydia (Emery) Emery ; married Nov. 18, 1841, Stephen Worster of Eliot, Me.

Children :

2727   i   MARY.[8]
2728   ii   ELLA.
2729   iii   LILLIE.
2730   iv   THOMAS.
2731   v   GEORGE.
2732   vi   FRANK.

1178 GEORGE W.[7] EMERY (*Simeon,*[6] *James,*[5] *Zachariah,*[4] *Daniel,*[3] *James,*[2] *Anthony*[1]), son of Simeon and Lydia (Emery) Emery ; married Jan. 1, 1845, Sarah Knowlton of Eliot, Me. Removed to California.

Children :

2733   i   HORACE.[8]
2734   ii   ALFRED, m. Emma Goodwin ; lives in Evansville, Ind.
2735   iii   CARROLL.
2736   iv   GRACE.

1179 OLIVER P.[7] EMERY (*Simeon,*[6] *James,*[5] *Zachariah,*[4] *Daniel,*[3] *James,*[2] *Anthony*[1]), son of Simeon and Lydia (Emery) Emery ; married Dec. 5, 1844, Eleanor Fernald. He died in Chicago, Ill.

Children :

2737   i   ELLEN AUGUSTA.[8] b. July 12, 1845.
2738   ii   MARY JANE GOWEN, b. March 5, 1847.
2739   iii   JOHN RICHARDSON, b. Sept. 4, 1849.
2740   iv   GEORGE ALBERT, b. Dec. 3, 1855; d. Dec. 4, 1855.
2741   v   SUSIE R., b. Aug. 11, 1857; d. Nov. 27, 1857.
2742   vi   SUSIE E., b. April 12, 1860; d. June 2, 1863.

1185 REUBEN KNOX[7] EMERY (*Thomas,*[6] *Zachariah,*[5] *Zachariah,*[4] *Daniel,*[3] *James,*[2] *Anthony*[1]), son of Thomas and Sarah (Knox) Emery ; married, first, Louisa Tebbetts of Vermont ; second, Aug. 19, 1847. Elmira Hemingway, daughter of Elder Hemingway of the Methodist Episcopal Church. Lived in Dundas, Canada, Albany, N. Y., and Ann Arbor, Mich., where he died June 9, 1861.

Children :

2743   i   WILLIAM TEBBETTS,[8] d. 1863, *s. p.,* his wife dying before him.

By second marriage :

2744   ii   JAMES H., b. Aug. 22, 1848.
2745   iii   THOMAS, b. Oct. 8, 1850; m. Sept. 18, 1879.
2746   iv   JOHN M., b. Aug. 2, 1855; m. Aug. 13, 1876.

1191 Dr Caleb[7] Emery (*William,*[6] *Caleb,*[5] *Caleb,*[4] *Daniel,*[3] *James,*[2] *Anthony*[1]), son of William and Mary (Salter) Emery, married Oct. 14, 1813, Mary Ann Chandler (born March 19, 1794, died Aug 8, 1872), daughter of Rev. Samuel Chandler of Eliot He died Feb. 16, 1831. Captain of militia at nineteen, member of the Massachusetts Medical Society, 1820, of the Governor's Council, 1830; had extensive practice; was highly respected and trusted, and his sudden death much lamented.

Children, born in Eliot, Me. :

```
2747   i    CHANDLER,8 b  July 25, 1814
2748   ii   SARAH S , b  Sept 16, 1816, d  in Malden, Mass , Feb 21, 1860
2749   iii  ELIZABETH S , b  April 9, 1818, d  July 5, 1849
2750   iv   CALEB, b  April 3, 1820, d  in Augusta, Ga , Dec  16, 1872.
2751'  v    LYDIA S ,  b  Oct 8, 1822;  unm , res. in Eliot, Me
2752   vi   WILLIAM H , b  Nov. 19, 1827.
```

1192 Thomas S [7] Emery (*William,*[6] *Caleb,*[5] *Caleb,*[4] *Daniel,*[3] *James,*[2] *Anthony*[1]), son of William and Mary (Salter) Emery ; married, first, in 1808, Betsey (died July 23, 1828), daughter of Noah and Elizabeth (Gould) Emery ; second, June 14, 1829, Hannah Willard (born March 14, 1773, died in Dover, N. H , May 14, 1877), daughter of Samuel, jr , and Sarah (Clough-Dudley) Willard.

Children, born in Sanford, Me., except the first .

```
2753   i     WILLIAM L ,9 b  in Kittery, Aug 22, 1808, d  Oct 2, 1876
2754   ii    CALEB S., b. Dec. 25, 1809, d. April 23, 1879.
2755   iii   SHEM, b  March 3, 1812, d  in North Berwick, Me , Nov 18,
             1882
2756   iv    MARY ELIZABETH, b  Aug 8, 1814; d  Aug. 22, 1814
2757   v     MARY E , b. April 7, 1816.
2758   vi    SALTER, b  Aug 23  1818
2759   vii   JOHN FROST, b. Nov. 5, 1820
2760   viii  HENRY. b  Dec 4, 1822, d  in New Orleans, May 5, 1860.
2761   ix    CYRUS KING, b  Oct. 9, 1824, d  March 22, 1826
2762   x     SUSAN A , b  June 13, 1827; d  July 26, 1832
```

By second marriage :

```
2763   xi    CYRUS, b  June 3, 1830
2764   xii   SARAH C , b  April 12, 1832
2765   xiii  CYNTHIA A , b  Dec 19, 1834.
```

1193 William[7] Emery (*William,*[6] *Caleb,*[5] *Caleb,*[4] *Daniel,*[3] *James,*[2] *Anthony*[1]), son of William and Mary (Salter) Emery ; married, first, in 1812. Elizabeth (died Aug 29, 1827), daughter of Moses and Elizabeth (Parsons) Emery , second, Nov. 17, 1829, Abigail Moulton (born May 16, 1809, died May 8, 1834) ; third, in Limerick, Me , Sept. 22, 1836, Mary J. Hill (born in 1807, died Feb 11, 1861), fourth, Oct 20, 1861, Mrs. Sarah A Gowen (died Dec 28, 1887, aged 74 years). He was a merchant, farmer, deputy sheriff; town treasurer, 1863, an active, energetic shrewd business man, and an honorable, sagacious, intelligent, far-sighted citizen. He died Nov. 23, 1877.

Children, born in Sanford, Me. :

```
2766   i    CALEB,8 b  March 18, 1813.
2767   ii   WILLIAM, b  March 3, 1815, d. Feb. 28, 1821
```

2768 iii MARY ANN, b. Jan. 7, 1817; d. April 28, 1821.
2769 iv ELIZABETH, b. Feb. 3, 1819.
2770 v   MARY ANN, b. April 5, 1821; d. Dec. 1, 1873, in Brookline, Mass.
2771 vi WILLIAM, b. March 15, 1823; d. in Alfred, Me., Aug. 31, 1889.
2772 vii TITUS S., b. March 3, 1825; m. Jan. 23, 1851, Annie, dau. of Benj. and Barbara (Kinport) Witmer of Lancaster, Pa.; res. in Philadelphia, Pa. Manufacturer of bar-iron and nails. Author of pamphlet on geology.
2773 viii MARTHA G., b. May 27, 1827; d. at Great Falls, N. H., Aug. 29, 1855.

By second wife :

2774 ix GEORGE, b. April 24, 1831; d. April 1, 1853, grad. of Philadelphia College of Medicine, 1852. A young man of remarkable abilities and great promise.
2775 x   HELEN B., b. Aug. 1, 1833; d. March 3, 1834.

By third wife :

2776 xi   EDWARD H., b. July 9, 1837.
2777 xii CHARLES OSCAR, b. Nov. 15, 1838.
2778 xiii HOWARD, b. July 9, 1845; d. in Sanford, Me., July 15, 1869.

1194 JOHN S.[7] EMERY (*William*,[6] *Caleb*,[5] *Caleb*,[4] *Daniel*,[3] *James*,[2] *Anthony*[1]), son of William and Mary (Salter) Emery; married in Parsonsfield, Me., Dec. 12, 1818, Anna M. Ramsdell (born Dec. 21, 1801; died in Uxbridge, Mass., Jan. 23, 1849). He died in Lowell, Dec. 21, 1846.
Children, born in Sanford, Me., except the first three :

2779 i   ELIZABETH ANN,[8] b. Aug. 3, 1820, in Brownfield, Me.; m. Thomas Whitaker; d. March 23, 1849.
2780 ii   ALFRED HUBBARD, b. June 30, 1821, in Brownfield, Me.; d. in Portland, Me., March 15, 1853.
2781 iii WILLIAM BOWLES, b. Aug. 2, 1822, in Brownfield, Me.
2782 iv   JOHN DOW, b. Sept. 6, 1823.
2783 v   MARY JANE, b. April 23, 1825.
2784 vi   ABIGAIL S., b. Sept. 6, 1826.
2785 vii CALEB C., b. Oct. 9, 1827; d. May 9, 1832.
2786 viii LUCY M., b. Nov. 6, 1828.
2787 ix   ALANSON MELLEN, b. Oct. 26, 1829; drowned in Mousam River, May 28, 1832.
2788 x   MELISSA MARDEN, b. March 17, 1831.
2789 xi   SARAH FRANCES, b. May 17, 1832.
2790 xii ALICE CLARK, b. Sept. 6, 1833; d. in Lowell, Mass., March 11, 1884.
2791 xiii CALEB JACKSON, b July 15, 1835; d. Aug. 4, 1835.
2792 xiv HELEN MAR, b. Nov. 15, 1840.

1197 HANNAH B.[7] EMERY (*William*,[6] *Caleb*,[5] *Caleb*,[4] *Daniel*,[3] *James*,[2] *Anthony*[1]), daughter of William and Mary (Salter) Emery; married Oct. 16, 1825, Nahum M. Thompson. He married, second, —— McLellan of Newfield, Me., and died in Shapleigh, Me., 1883.
Children :

2793 i   JOHN W.,[8] b. 1826.
2794 ii   CHRISTOPHER T., b. 1828; d., unm., Sept., 1855.
2795 iii CALEB EMERY, b. 1831.
2796 iv   NAHUM F., b. 1834; d. May 20, 1843, nine years of age.

1198 Sarah[7] Emery (*William*,[6] *Caleb*,[5] *Caleb*,[4] *Daniel*,[3] *James*,[2] *Anthony*[1]), daughter of William and Mary (Salter) Emery, married Nov. 21, 1823, Moses Garey, removed to Dover, Me., where he died Feb. 28, 1869.

Children:

2797	i	Leander,[8] b. Aug 27, 1827, in Kennebunk, Me , m Oct. 6, 1852, Betsey M Hawkins (b June 29, 1839)
2798	ii	Cyrus M., b July 12, 1829, in Sanford, Me ; in 1st Maine Cavalry, m Sept 14, 1856, d in Farmville, Va , April 15, 1865, from wounds Wife and children all dead
2799	iii	William E , b Nov 8, 1831, d , unm , in Chicago, Ill , March 30, 1857
2800	iv	Caleb E , b June 7, 1834, m June 7, 1865, Eunice C Hawkins of Seymour, Conn (b Feb 10, 1843) Five children; Mabel H , only one living, 1883
2801	v	Moses E , b March 29, 1837, unm ; resides in Dover, Me
2802	vi	Mary E , b June 3, 1843, in Dover, Me , m Aug. 25, 1873, and lives in Dover, Me.

1200 Samuel B [7] Emery (*William*,[6] *Caleb*,[5] *Caleb*,[4] *Daniel*,[3] *James*,[2] *Anthony*[1]), son of William and Mary (Salter) Emery, married Feb. 27, 1832, Alice (born June 3, 1803 , died Jan. 17, 1879), daughter of Moses and Rachel (Carroll) Pray of Sanford, Me. He was a merchant thirty-five years , cashier of the Mousam River Bank, 1856–7; president of Sanford Bank, 1860–1 , deputy sheriff; sheriff, 1856 , selectman, five years , town treasurer, three years ; died Sept. 25. 1880.

Children, born in Sanford, Me :

2803	i	Harriet A.,[8] b. Nov 1, 1832, unm ; resides in Washington, D C., clerk in the Treasury Department
2804	ii	Benjamin F , b June 16, 1834, d May 28, 1882, in Sanford, Me
2805	iii	Moses W , b April 1, 1836
2806	iv	Charlotte S , b July 25, 1838; d April 9, 1882, in Logan, Kansas
2807	v	Samuel Benton, b Oct 15, 1848.

1202 David[7] Colcord (*Elizabeth*,[6] *Caleb*,[5] *Caleb*,[4] *Daniel*,[3] *James*,[2] *Anthony*[1]), son of Jesse and Elizabeth (Emery) Colcord , married Sally Mason , lived in Porter, Me. Farmer and school teacher , conveyancer He died July 9, 1867.

Children .

2808	i	Washington.[8]
2809	ii	David A
2810	iii	Sally Jane
2811	iv	Jesse

1203 Mary H.[7] Colcord (*Elizabeth*,[6] *Caleb*,[5] *Caleb*,[4] *Daniel*,[3] *James*,[2] *Anthony*[1]), daughter of Jesse and Elizabeth (Emery) Colcord ; married John Pearl, farmer. She died Aug. 28, 1876.

Children :

2812	i	John E [8]
2813	ii	Jesse C
2814	iii	Mary E
2815	iv	George W.

1209 ISABELLA[7] COLCORD (*Elizabeth*,[6] *Caleb*,[5] *Caleb*,[4] *Daniel*,[3] *James*,[2] *Anthony*[1]), daughter of Jesse and Elizabeth (Emery) Colcord ; married Stephen C. Brooks, farmer. She died in Iowa, 1872 or 1873.
  Children :

    2816   i   SUSAN C.[8]
    2817   ii   ANN.
    2818   iii THOMAS.

1210 CALEB E.[7] COLCORD (*Elizabeth*,[6] *Caleb*,[5] *Caleb*,[4] *Daniel*,[3] *James*,[2] *Anthony*[1]), son of Jesse and Elizabeth (Emery) Colcord ; married Mary Kennard. He was a dwarf, forty-four inches in height, weighing from ninety to one hundred pounds. He died Aug. 20, 1853.
  Child :

    2819   i   CHARLOTTE.[8]

1211 CHARLOTTE[7] COLCORD (*Elizabeth*,[6] *Caleb*,[5] *Caleb*,[4] *Daniel*,[3] *James*,[2] *Anthony*[1]), daughter of Jesse and Elizabeth (Emery) Colcord ; married, first, in Honolulu, Sandwich Islands, Peter H. Hatch ; second, —— Taylor. Removed to Portland, Oregon.
  Children, by first marriage :

    2820   i   DAVID C.[8]
    2821   ii   SUSAN C.

1224 HENRY[7] EMERY (*Henry T.*,[6] *Caleb*,[5] *Caleb*,[4] *Daniel*,[3] *James*,[2] *Anthony*[1]), son of Henry T. and Elizabeth (Morrill) Emery ; married 1830, Rebecca McKinney. He was master of a vessel.
  Children :

    2822   i   ADDIE,[8] b. 1840; d. young.
    2823   ii   HENRY, b. 1842.

1229 JOHN W.[7] EMERY (*Henry T.*,[6] *Caleb*,[5] *Caleb*,[4] *Daniel*,[3] *James*,[2] *Anthony*[1]), son of Henry T. and Elizabeth (Morrill) Emery ; married, first, Arabella E. Close ; second, in Boston, Mass., Feb. 23, 1867, Mary Kimball of Belfast, Me.
  Children, born in Eastport, Me. :

    2824   i   IMOGENE E.,[8] b. Dec. 7, 1848.
    2825   ii   CORA, b. July, 1850; d. Sept. 4, 1851.
    2826   iii CELIA, b. Feb., 1852.
    2827   iv   PAULINA, b. July 4, 1855; m. Robert Porter of Stoughton,
                Mass., and has one child, a dau.

1230 ADELINE[7] EMERY (*Henry T.*,[6] *Caleb*,[5] *Caleb*,[4] *Daniel*,[3] *James*,[2] *Anthony*[1]), daughter of Henry T. and his second wife, Mercy E. (Stover) Emery ; married Oct. 3, 1849, George N. Morang of Eastport, Me. (born April 5, 1829).
  Children, born in Eastport, Me. :

    2828   i   WILLIAM E.,[8] b. July 21, 1850 ; d. June 30, 1881, in Nashville,
                Tenn. In early life he was a printer, later professor and
                president of the Roger Williams University, Nashville, Tenn.,
                holding the office but a few months.
    2829   ii   MARY ANN, b. May, 1853; d. March, 1878.

2830   iii   Cora B., b March, 1855; m March 13, 1888, E W Boss of
               Boston.
2831   iv   Frank S , b July, 1857
2832   v   Frances S , b July, 1859, d March 2, 1886.
2833   vi   George N , b March, 1860, unm
2834   vii Addie E , b April 20, 1863, unm

1231 Robert S.[7] Emery (*Henry T.*,[6] *Caleb*,[5] *Caleb*,[4] *Daniel*,[3] *James*,[2] *Anthony*[1]), son of Henry T. and his second wife, Mercy E (Stover) Emery ; married, first, May 17, 1849, Lydia Leland, of Eastport, Me ; second, ———

Children :

2835   i   Lissett,[8] b Nov 9, 1850; m Thomas Ray.
2836   ii   Rebecca, b. May 14, 1852
2837   iii Adeline.
2838   iv   Maud, b Aug , 1856
2839   v   Robert, b May 4, 1858, d young
2840   vi   Bertie, b. April, 1860
2841   vii James, b March 8, 1862

By second marriage .

2842   viii Oliver, d in infancy
2843   ix   Robert, d at four years of age.

1234 Sabine[7] Emery (*Henry T* ,[6] *Caleb*,[5] *Caleb*,[4] *Daniel*,[3] *James*,[2] *Anthony*[1]), son of Henry T. and his second wife, Mercy E. (Stover) Emery , married in Waterville, Me., Oct. 20, 1862, M L Flint. He was a graduate of Colby University, Waterville, Me ; studied law in Skowhegan, Me ; admitted to the Bar in Bangor, Me , and practised in Baltimore, Md   During the war he raised Co. "A," 9th Maine Vol , and was elected captain ; later he became by promotion major, lieutenant-colonel and colonel of his regiment. His regiment re-enlisted for a second term of three years   At the storming of Fort Wagner, he was severely wounded from the effects of which he died. "Col. Emery combined the cultured gentleman with the brave and efficient officer, displaying a personal fearlessness that made him a most daring and brilliant leader."

Children :

2844   i   Henry Tilton,[8] b Aug 5, 1863, in Portland, Me ; d Aug. 20,
              1872
2845   ii   Ethel Graham, b March 3, 1866, in Baltimore, Md

1235 Oliver[7] Emery (*Henry T* ,[6] *Caleb*,[5] *Caleb*,[4] *Daniel*,[3] *James*,[2] *Anthony*[1]), son of Henry T. and his second wife, Mercy E. (Stover) Emery , married Sept , 1864, Josephine Holmes.

Children, born in Eastport, Me. .

2846   i   Josephine,[8] b. Aug , 1866.
2847   ii   Tilton, b Sept , 1867.
2848   iii Minnie, b March, 1869
2849   iv   Lillian, b Aug , 1870
2850   v   Marian, b Feb , 1872
2851   vi   Robert, b May, 1873
2852   vii John W , b March, 1875
2853   viii William H , b Nov., 1876.

2854 ix   Eva H., b. Nov., 1879.
2855 x   Henry E., b. July, 1883.
2856 xi   A daughter, b. March 28, 1886.

1236 Fred Augustus[7] Emery (*Henry E.,*[6] *Caleb,*[5] *Caleb,*[4] *Daniel,*[3] *James,*[2] *Anthony*[1]), son of Henry T. and his second wife, Mercy E. (Stover) Emery; married Sept., 1861, in Eastport, Me, Sarah Ann McDonald.
Children:

2857 i   Eugene,[8] b. 1862.
2858 ii   Hilton, b. 1864.
2859 iii   Beatrice, b. 1866.
2860 iv   Edward, b. 1867.
2861 v   Augustus, b. 1869.
2862 vi   Annie L., d. young.
2863 vii   Sabine, d. young.
2864 viii Dannetta, b. April, 1873.
2865 ix   George.
2866 x   Sarah, b. Nov. 1, 1879.

1237 Ivory[7] Emery (*Henry T.,*[6] *Caleb,*[5] *Caleb,*[4] *Daniel,*[3] *James,*[2] *Anthony*[1]), son of Henry T. and his second wife, Mercy E. (Stover) Emery; married Nov., 1872, Mrs. Maria Daggett.
Children:

2867 i   Mercy E.,[8] b. Oct. 9, 1873.
2868 ii   Ivory, b. April 5, 1875.
2869 iii   Mary Jane,   } b. Jan. 19, 1879.
2870 iv   Susan M.,   }
2871 v   Fred. Augustus, b. Aug. 16, 1881.
2872 vi   Dolly, b. June 7, 1883.
2873 vii   Leonard, b. April 21, 1887.

1242 Caleb James[7] Emery (*Caleb,*[6] *Caleb,*[5] *Caleb,*[4] *Daniel,*[3] *James,*[2] *Anthony*[1]), son of Caleb and Elizabeth (Hurd) Emery; married Nov. 7, 1848, Anna Maria, daughter of Christopher Page. Served as captain during the Mexican war; entered the naval service, April 18, 1854, as paymaster; in 1863 was stationed at Portsmouth, N. H., and in 1873 at Boston, being in constant service till he was retired.
Child:

2874 i   Henry Leslie,[8] b. Aug. 20, 1849, in Nashua, N. H.

1251 Lydia[7] Meserve (*Mercy,*[6] *James,*[5] *Joseph,*[4] *Job,*[3] *James,*[2] *Anthony*[1]), daughter of Thomas and Mercy (Emery) Meserve; married Jacob McDaniel. He married, second, Mercy Meserve, sister of his first wife.
Children:

2875 i   Moses.[8]
2876 ii   Jacob.
2877 iii   Sewall.
2878 iv   Joseph.

1254 Jonathan[7] Emery (*Daniel,*[6] *James,*[5] *Joseph,*[4] *Job,*[3] *James,*[2] *Anthony*[1]), son of Daniel and Sarah (Moulton) Emery; married, first, Jennie Stevens (died March 23, 1839); second, Elizabeth Clark.

Children .

2879 i   DANIEL C ,³ b May 2, 1803, d in Gorham, Me , June 1, 1881
2880 ii   HARRIET, b. 1805
2881 iii MARTHA, b. 1807 , d , unm , March 24, 1881.
2882 iv   GEORGE, b 1809; d 1815.

1256 MERCY⁷ EMERY (*Daniel*,⁶ *James*,⁵ *Joseph*,⁴ *Job*,³ *James*,² *Anthony¹*). daughter of Daniel and Sarah (Moulton) Emery ; married, 1808, Nathaniel Rice, jr.

Children :

2883 i   ALVAN ⁸
2884 ii   WILLIAM
2885 iii ALGERNON SIDNEY
2886 iv   LUCY ANN
2887 v   DUDLEY GILMAN
2888 vi   A S. D GILMAN.
2889 vii HARTLEY BILLINGS.

1258 JOSIAH⁷ EMERY (*Daniel*,⁶ *James*,⁵ *Joseph*,⁴ *Job*,³ *James*,² *Anthony¹*), son of Daniel and Sarah (Moulton) Emery ; married Jane Flood.

Children :

2890 i ALMIRA S ,⁸ d Sept 13, 1871
Two other children

1266 WILLIAM⁷ EMERY (*Benjamin*,⁶ *James*,⁵ *Joseph*,⁴ *Job*,³ *James*,² *Anthony¹*), son of Benjamin and Mary (Moulton) Emery , married Jane Brown. He died Sept 16, 1876, in Parsonsfield, Me.

Children :

2891 i   MARY JANE,⁸ m. Dec 20, 1840, Irving Piper
2892 ii   MARQUIS L , d Oct 30, 1873
2893 iii ELIZA, m. James Berry, lives at Alton, N H.
2894 iv   DAVID

1268 JOSHUA⁷ EMERY (*James*,⁶ *James*,⁵ *Joseph*,⁴ *Job*,³ *James*,² *Anthony¹*), son of James and Hannah (Dunn) Emery ; married, first, 1809, Shuah Chick (born in Limington, Me., 1787; died Feb. 17, 1824) , second, 1826, Mary Clark (died in Sebago, Me., June, 1881). Farmer. He died Jan. 16, 1858. Lived in Limington, Me.

Children :

2895 i   NATHANIEL,⁸ b 1810 , d in Limington, Me , Feb 1831.
2896 ii   LOUISA, b March 8, 1812
2897 iii LUCINDA, b. May 18, 1819.
2898 iv   CHARLES, b Feb 15, 1824.
2899 v   AVILDA.

1270 REV. JAMES⁷ EMERY (*James*,⁶ *James*,⁵ *Joseph*,⁴ *Job*,³ *James*,² *Anthony¹*), son of James and Hannah (Dunn) Emery , married Hannah Leathers of Limington, Me (born Feb 11, 1798). Baptist minister , died in Tamworth, N. H.

Children :

2900 i SALLY,⁸ b Dec. 18, 1816; m. Stetson Blaisdell of Tamworth, N H.

23

2901 ii JAMES, b. April 11, 1818; d. 1888.
2902 iii JOHN, b. Dec. 13, 1821; d. Nov. 28, 1835.
2903 iv COLBY, b. Feb. 23, 1823; m. Ruth Blaisdell.
2904 v WILLIAM, b. Feb. 11, 1827; d. April 22, 1832.
2905 vi JOANNA E., b. Aug. 12, 1830; m. Enoch Bickford of Tamworth, N. H.

1273 SARAH⁷ EMERY (*James,⁶ James,⁵ Joseph,⁴ Job,³ James,² Anthony¹*), daughter of James and Hannah (Dunn) Emery; married George Staples (born in Limerick, Me., Oct. 28, 1799; died Aug. 5, 1853). She died April 9, 1877.

Children:

2906 i CLARINDA,⁸ b. Aug. 10, 1831; d. March 15, 1863.
2907 ii JULIA A., b. March 6, 1833; d. Jan. 8, 1882.
2908 iii MELINDA, b. July 10, 1835; d. Feb. 5, 1878.
2909 iv JOSEPH, b. Oct. 7, 1839; m. March 20, 1862, Mary A. Blake of Biddeford, Me.; d. Sept. 9, 1865.

1274 JOSEPH⁷ EMERY (*James,⁶ James,⁵ Joseph,⁴ Job,³ James,² Anthony¹*), son of James and Hannah (Dunn) Emery; married June 12, 1836, Sarah Ann Libby of Berwick, Me. (born in North Berwick, Sept. 19, 1815; died in Limington, Me., Sept. 5, 1873). He died March 11, 1866.

Children, born in Limington, Me., except the last:

2910 i JAMES IRA,⁸ b. June 7, 1839; unm.
2911 ii SARAH F., b. Jan. 21, 1843; unm.
2912 iii MARTHA E., b. Dec. 14, 1845; unm.
2913 iv JOHN W., b. Nov. 1, 1847; unm.
2914 v CALVIN J., b. Feb. 2, 1851, in Limerick, Me.; lives in Lynn, Mass.

1275 JEREMIAH⁷ EMERY (*James,⁶ James,⁵ Joseph,⁴ Job,³ James,² Anthony¹*), son of James and Hannah (Dunn) Emery; married Oct. 22, 1837, Susan Libby (born July 26, 1817), sister of his brother Joseph's wife.

Children, born in Berwick, Me.:

2915 i IRA L.,⁸ b. Feb. 20, 1840.
2916 ii GEORGE S., b. April 2, 1842; d. Dec. 26, 1878.
2917 iii ALBERT N., b. Feb. 18, 1848; m. Fanny Cole; d. July 2, 1882, in Cornish, Me.

1277 CHARITY⁷ EMERY (*John,⁶ John,⁵ Joseph,⁴ Job,³ James,² Anthony¹*), daughter of John and Abigail (Wasgatt) Emery; married May 6, 1814, Arad H. Pomeroy; lived in Hampden, Me. She died Oct. 24, 1854.

Children:

2918 i SARAH A.,⁸ b. Nov. 27, 1815.
2919 ii FRANCES H., b. Nov. 21, 1817.
2920 iii JULIA A., b, May 17, 1819.
2921 iv MARTHA J., b. Feb. 26, 1821; d. May 15, 1843.
2922 v ARAD H., b. July 25, 1823; d. Oct. 10, 1856, at Turk's Island. Master of the brig "Hampden" of Bangor, Me.
2923 vi MARGARET, b. Sept. 25, 1825; d. Feb. 22, 1865.
2924 vii LYDIA M., b. July 17, 1828.
2925 viii MARY ELLEN, b. March 26, 1830.

1278 JOHN[7] EMERY(*John*,[6] *John*,[5] *Joseph*,[4] *Job*,[3] *James*,[2] *Anthony*[1]), son of John and Abigail (Wasgatt) Emery, married Feb 14, 1808, Mary Smith; lived in Hampden, Me.; died Jan. 7, 1819.
Children :

```
2926   i    MARY,8 b May 6, 1809, d. Oct 26, 1835
2927   ii   JOHN, b Sept 2, 1810, d Aug 2, 1849.
2928   iii  STEPHEN S , b March 24, 1812, d Sept 22, 1826
2929   iv   ABBIE W , b Dec 11, 1813
2930   v    ALBERT G , b March 28, 1815, d July 12, 1816.
2931   vi   JULIA A , d. in infancy
```

1281 BENJAMIN[7] EMERY (*John*,[6] *John*,[5] *Joseph*,[4] *Job*,[3] *James*,[2] *Anthony*[1]), son of John and Abigail (Wasgatt) Emery; married July 28, 1809, Mira Jones, lived in Hampden, Me.; died Dec , 1835.
Children :

```
2932   i    REBECCA 8
2933   ii   JOSEPH.
2934   iii  SARAH
2935   iv   MIRA
2936   v    NANCY.
2937   vi   RACHEL
2938   vii  MARY ANN.
```

1282 SARAH[7] EMERY (*John*,[6] *John*,[5] *Joseph*,[4] *Job*,[3] *James*,[2] *Anthony*[1]), daughter of John and Abigail (Wasgatt) Emery; married, 1814, Rev. James A Seaman, a Baptist clergyman who died in Hampden, Me , in 1832. She died in New Orleans, Aug 20, 1870
Children ·

```
2939   i    JOHN E ,8 b Oct 10, 1815
2940   ii   SARAH, b 1817; d 1840
2941   iii  JULIA, b 1818 , d 1842
2942   iv   EMERY, b. 1820, m , d 1861, left one child, Alice; his wife
                 was a sister of Mrs N P Banks, wife of Nath P Banks,
                 Gov of Mass , Maj Gen U S V , Rep in Congress and
                 speaker of the House
2943   v    CYRUS, d unm
2944   vi   SYLVANUS P , d 1860
2945   vii  CHARLOTTE, d unm
2946   viii FRANKLIN, d unm
```

1284 DANIEL[7] EMERY (*John*,[6] *John*,[5] *Joseph*,[4] *Job*,[3] *James*,[2] *Anthony*[1]), son of John and Abigail (Wasgatt) Emery; married, first, 1820, Mrs. Hannah Sabine (died Feb. 27, 1825) ; second, 1827, Lydia McDonald (died 1828) , third, July 1, 1829, Elvira Crosby (died Dec. 18, 1883), daughter of Gen John Crosby. Col Daniel was born and resided in Hampden till his death, Aug , 1864. He was a prominent man, and in early life was largely engaged in shipping and the West India trade. He was for several years representative and senator in the Maine legislature, and for several years collector of the port of Bangor.
Children :

```
2947   i    HANNAH CLARK.8 b Jan. 17, 1821.
2948   ii   LOUISA MARIA, b Feb 16, 1823
2949   iii  DANIEL CLARK, b Feb. 27, 1825, d in New Orleans, La , 1868
```

By third marriage :

2950 iv JOHN CROSBY, b. April 12, 1830.
2951 v GEORGE AUGUSTUS, b. Nov. 2, 1831.
2952 vi FRANKLIN, b. May 19. 1833; lost at sea, Jan., 1856.
2953 vii CHARLES, b. June 4, 1835; unm. in Cal.
2954 viii SARAH CROSBY, b. June 19, 1837.
2955 ix ELMIRA C., b. July 20, 1839; d. at three years of age.
2956 x EDWIN E., b. Sept. 10, 1841; d. eleven months old.
2957 xi ANN ELIZA, b. May 15, 1843; d. five months old.
2958 xii LUCIUS, b. July 15, 1846; unm.; res. in the Black Hills.

1285 WILLIAM[7] EMERY (*John*,[5] *John*,[5] *Joseph*,[4] *Job*,[3] *James*,[2] *Anthony*[1]), son of John and Abigail (Wasgatt) Emery; married, first, June 12, 1823, Lucy Covil; second, June 15, 1834, Elizabeth Emerson; third, Jan. 17, 1839, Catharine R. Goodwin.

Children, born in Hampden, Me.:

2959 i ELIZA C.,[*] b. June 3, 1824; d. Aug. 23, 1867, unm.
2960 ii WILLIAM P., b. May 12, 1826.
2961 iii MARY ABBY, b. July 16, 1830.

By third marriage:

2962 iv HENRY L., b. July 12, 1840; d. Sept. 3, 1841.
2963 v EDWARD W., b. Feb. 6, 1842; d. June 16, 1842.
2964 vi WILLIS, b. Aug. 14, 1843; d. March 5, 1845.

1286 THOMAS[7] EMERY (*John*,[5] *John*,[5] *Joseph*,[4] *Job*,[3] *James*,[2] *Anthony*[1]), son of John and Abigail (Wasgatt) Emery; married, first, March 22, 1821, Mercy Wasgatt of Eden, Me. (died Oct. 1, 1833); second, 1834, Lucy G. Edgerly. He was in early life a shipmaster and at the time of his death was U. S. Consul at Martinique.

Children:

2965 i JULIA A.,[*] b. March 3, 1822.
2966 ii CHARLOTTE C., b. Aug. 16, 1823.
2967 iii NOAH, b. April 2, 1825; m. Aug. 11, 1853, Mary Ellen Pomeroy. He was a shipmaster of wide reputation and acknowledged ability and integrity; d. in Bangor, Me., Feb. 16, 1888.
2968 iv LUCINDA, b. March 10, 1828; d. July 9, 1830.
2969 v ELMIRA A., b. Oct. 7, 1829; d. May 3, 1832.
2970 vi MELINDA M., b. April 27, 1831; d. May 3, 1832.

By second marriage:

2971 vii LUCY A., b. Nov. 3, 1843; d. June 30, 1844.
2972 viii MARY FRANCES, b. June 14, 1848; d. April 28, 1873.

1288 CYRUS[7] EMERY (*John*,[5] *John*,[5] *Joseph*,[4] *Job*,[3] *James*,[2] *Anthony*[1]), son of John and Abigail (Wasgatt) Emery; married, first, June 17, 1829, Rebecca D. Brown (died April 22, 1830); second, Jan. 27, 1840, Mary K. Brown (died Aug. 5, 1848); third, March 17, 1852, Elizabeth D. Brown. Lives in Bangor, Me.

Children:

2973 i HENRY B.,[*] b. Nov. 19, 1840; d. May 26, 1880.
2974 ii ANNA R., b. Jan. 9, 1842; d. Sept. 24, 1844.
2975 iii RICHARD J., b. Sept. 20, 1844; d. Nov. 17, 1847.
2976 iv MARY, b. July 28, 1848; d. Oct. 1, 1848.
2977 v ISAIAH S., b. Dec. 2, 1852; m. June 4, 1874, Ada S. Wiswell. Educated in Bangor High School and Hebron Academy; entered Harvard Medical College, 1872; went West as correspondent of the *New York Morning Record* and the *Boston M . E . . . . business; has

been clerk, assistant passenger agent, general passenger agent, general freight and passenger agent, member of the executive committee, U S General Passenger Agents Association, chairman N Y State Passenger Association, general agent Waterloo and Ogdensburg R R , hospital steward, 2nd Maine Regt , Sept , 1881–2, prominent Mason of the 33rd degree , member of I O. O F , A. O. U N , Knights of Pythias and Sons of Malta

2978 vi AUGUSTUS J , b Aug 27, 1856.

1289 JOSEPH[7] EMERY (*Nahum*,[6] *John*,[5] *Joseph*,[4] *Job*,[3] *James*,[2] *Anthony*[1]), son of Nahum and Hannah (Arey) Emery ; married, first, Alliance Mayo, second, Pamela Arey   Lived in Dixmont, Me   He died, 1868.

Children ·

```
2979   i    LORENZO,8 b Nov 24 1815, d 1860
2980   ii   NAHUM, b Aug 23, 1817
2981   iii  ELIZABETH, b Jan 24, 1820.
2982   iv   ELISHA, b March 24, 1823
2983   v    FREDERICK, b July 19, 1825
2984   vi   JOHN, b July 13, 1827
2985   vii  ELMIRA C , b Dec 29, 1829.
2986   viii FRANKLIN, b. Nov. 29, 1832
2987   ix   BAKER, b. June 21, 1835
2988   x    MARTIN b 1841
2989   xi   OLIVER F , b 1844   d in infancy
2990   xii  JOSEPH, b 1846, d. in the army
```

1290 NAHUM[7] EMERY (*Nahum*,[6] *John*,[5] *Joseph*,[4] *Job*,[3] *James*,[2] *Anthony*[1]), son of Nahum and Hannah (Arey) Emery ; married Cordelia Wasgatt of Eden, Me   He died, 1870

Children :

```
2991   i    ANDREW J ,8 b May 20, 1832
2992   ii   JEANNETTE, b Jan 20, 1834
2993   iii  NAHUM, b Feb 28, 1837.
2994   iv   JAMES, b Dec 30, 1840
2995   v    MARY, b Nov 10, 1844.
2996   vi   FREEMAN, b May 12, 1847.
```

1297 JOHN[7] EMERY (*Nahum*,[6] *John*,[5] *Joseph*,[4] *Job*,[3] *James*,[2] *Anthony*[1]), son of Nahum and Hannah (Arey) Emery , married Sarah Fernald ; lived in Hampden, Me.   He died Oct. 7, 1870.

Children :

```
2997   i    HARRIET,8 b Dec 4, 1835.
2998   ii   ELIZA, b Feb 24, 1888
2999   iii  CORDELIA, b July 16, 1840
3000   iv   JOHN, b March 13, 1843
3001   v    GEORGE E , b July 4, 1845, d  from wounds at Appomattox
              April 10, 1865.
3002   vi   OLIVER H ,  }
3003   vii  DEMARIS H , }  b Feb 23, 1848
```

1299 JAMES[7] EMERY (*Nahum*,[6] *John*,[5] *Joseph*,[4] *Job*,[3] *James*,[2] *Anthony*[1]), son of Nahum and his second wife, Mrs Betsey F. (Barker) Emery ; married Feb 9, 1841, Mary P. Nickerson. Lives at Provincetown, Mass.

Children :

```
3004   i    JAMES,8 b May 24, 1843; d May 23, 1847.
```

3005   ii   JAMES, b. Feb. 24, 1847.
3006   iii ELLA, b. April 23, 1819.
3007   iv   PRISCILLA, b. Dec. 6, 1855.
3008   v   WILLIS, b. Sept. 23, 1857; d. Aug. 20, 1876.

1301 BARKER[7] EMERY (*Nahum,*[6] *John,*[5] *Joseph,*[4] *Job,*[3] *James,*[2] *Anthony*[1]), son of Nahum and his second wife, Mrs. Betsey F. (Barker) Emery; married, first, April, 1843, Elizabeth Miller (died Nov. 26, 1852); second, Dec. 14, 1854, Sarah B. Prescott.

Children:

3009   i   LIZZIE,[8] b. Feb. 3, 1844; d. 1868.
3010   ii   WILLARD B., b. July 15, 1846.
3011   iii MARY J., b. 1849; d. Sept. 20, 1852.
3012   iv   JOHN H., b. June 30, 1851; d. Oct. 6, 1878.
3013   v   WALTER, d. in infancy.

1302 WILLIAM[7] EMERY (*Ichabod,*[6] *Job,*[5] *Joseph,*[4] *Job,*[3] *James,*[2] *Anthony*[1]), son of Ichabod and Lois (Stacey) Emery; married Eliza ————.

Children:

3014   i   MARY S.,[8] b. Feb. 5, 1824.
3015   ii   LOWELL MARSTON, b. March 18, 1830.
3016   iii CLARISSA, b. March 6, 1832.
3017   iv   ELIZABETH, b. Sept. 18, 1834.
3018   v   WILLIAM HENRY, b. May 15, 1836.
3019   vi   HARRIET, b. Jan. 8, 1840.

1303 JOB[7] EMERY (*Ichabod,*[6] *Job,*[5] *Joseph,*[4] *Job,*[3] *James,*[2] *Anthony*[1]), son of Ichabod and Lois (Stacey) Emery; married Dec. 28, 1824, Abigail Horne of Dover, N. H. (born in Somersworth, N. H., March 9, 1796; died at Berwick, Me., Oct. 1, 1879). He died Oct. 12, 1876.

Children:

3020   i   LYDIA L.,[8] b. Sept. 6, 1825; d. Sept. 20, 1825.
3021   ii   THOMAS C., b. Sept. 12, 1826; d. June 6, 1861, in N. Y.
3022   iii MARY ELIZABETH, b. July 7, 1828.
3023   iv   JACOB K., b. July 10, 1831; d. March 12, 1859, in N. Y.
3024   v   LOIS ANN, b. March 12, 1834; d. Sept. 12, 1836.
3025   vi   MOULTON, b. Dec. 16, 1836; m. Annie C. Heyward, Feb. 27, 1870, dau. of Thomas Heyward, jr., of S. C., and great granddaughter of Thomas Heyward, a signer of the Declaration of Independence. She died at Charleston, S. C., Oct. 15, 1885; lives in Charleston, S. C.

1305 JOSEPH[7] EMERY (*Ichabod,*[6] *Job,*[5] *Joseph,*[4] *Job,*[3] *James,*[2] *Anthony*[1]), son of Ichabod and Lois (Stacey) Emery; married in Dover, N. H., May 20, 1826, Sophronia Moore (born Feb. 3, 1800; died Sept. 19, 1840).

Children:

3026   i   FRANKLIN,[8] b. March 9, 1827.
3027   ii   JOSEPH, b. April 26, 1829.
3028   iii SOPHIA, b. May 13, 1831; d. Aug. 25, 1874, in Chicago, Ill.
3029   iv   JOHN, b. Oct. 28, 1833.
3030   v   GEORGE H., b. May 12, 1836.

1306 OLIVER HUBBARD[7] EMERY (*Ichabod,*[6] *Job,*[5] *Joseph,*[4] *Job,*[3]

James,[2] Anthony[1]), son of Ichabod and Lois (Stacey) Emery, married, Oct., 1829, in Dover, N. H , Hannah O Potter (born May 14, 1802 , died Sept 9, 1870), daughter of Nathaniel and Sarah (Ingalls) Potter, a descendant of Eben Eastman, one of the first settlers of Concord, N. H

Children :

```
3031  i    GEORGE W ,[8] b  Aug 13, 1833, in Corinth, Me.
3032  ii   ANN M , b  Aug 14, 1834, in Corinth, Me.
3033  iii  EITEN P , b  June 3, 1836, in Corinth, Me
3034  iv   HANNAH A , b  May 20, 1840  in Berwick, Me ; d  Jan  1, 1841.
3035  v    MYRA C , b  April 8, 1842, in Berwick, Me.
3036  vi   HATTIE O , b  May 29, 1844, in Berwick, Me
```

1327 JOHN H [7] EMERY (*Joseph,[6] Job,[5] Joseph,[4] Job,[3] James,[2] Anthony[1]*), son of Joseph and Polly (Hubbard) Emery ; married April 21, 1837, Betsey (born March 26, 1814), daughter of Theophilus and Abigail (Goodwin) Simpson , lived in South Berwick, Me.

Children, born in South Berwick, Me. :

```
3037  i    JOSEPH,[8] b. June 13, 1838, m. Feb , 1869, Carrie Currier of
                Portsmouth, N. H , who d  Feb , 1872
3038  ii   ABBIE, b  June 27, 1840, d  July 29, 1843
3039  iii  SARAH, b  Sept 11, 1842
3040. iv   ABBIE J , b  June 6, 1844, m  George Johnson of York, May 8,
                1872
3041  v    JOSEPHINE, b. Dec. 13, 1845.
3042  vi   JOHN, b  Oct 12, 1847.
3043  vii  LIZZIE A , b  May 18, 1849
3044  viii WOODBURY, b  July 7, 1851
3045  ix   NETTIE P , b  Feb. 18, 1855, m  William Crockett of Boston,
                April 2, 1884
```

1329 JOB[7] EMERY (*Joseph,[6] Job,[5] Joseph,[4] Job,[3] James,[2] Anthony[1]*), son of Joseph and Polly (Hubbard) Emery , married July 25, 1839, Abigail (born March 21, 1821), daughter of Theophilus and Abigail (Goodwin) Simpson ; lived in South Berwick, Me.

Children

```
3046  i    MARY,[8] b  June 28, 1840
3047  ii   LAURA, b  March 13, 1842
3048  iii  GEORGE W., b. Dec. 12, 1843; res. in Challis, Custer Co ,
                Idaho
3049  iv   ALBION, b  June 22, 1846; m  Nov. 11, 1884, Susie E  Bradford,
                res in Park City, Utah
3050  v    OLIVER S , b. May 13, 1848.
3051  vi   NANCY, b  Dec 5, 1849
3052  vii  FRANK, b  July 7, 1851
3053  viii ROSE B , b  April 13, 1853, res. in So  Berwick, Me.
3054  ix   JANE T , b. Nov  11, 1855, res in So  Berwick, Me
```

1332 ROBERT[7] LORD (*Philomelia,[6] William,[5] Joseph,[4] Job,[3] James,[2] Anthony[1]*), son of Edmund and Philomelia (Emery) Lord ; married Rhoda Shackley of South Berwick, Me.

Children :

```
3055  i    EMELINE [8]
3056  ii   WILLIAM.
3057  iii  FRANCES.
3058  iv   HARRIET
3059  v    HENRY.
```

1333 JASON[7] LORD (*Philomelia*,[6] *William*,[5] *Joseph*,[4] *Job*,[3] *James*,[2] *Anthony*[1]), son of Edmund and Philomelia (Emery) Lord; married, 1823, Mary A. Simpson (born March 6, 1798; died April 19, 1868); moved to Sullivan, Me., 1817.

Children:

```
3060   i    MARY J.,[8] b. June 25, 1824; d. Dec. 27, 1851.
3061   ii   DELPHINA A., b. Sept. 5, 1827.
3062   iii  JASON E., b. May 1, 1830; d. May 25, 1841.
3063   iv   JAMES S., b. Nov. 3, 1832.
3064   v    WILLIAM J., b. June 24, 1835.
3065   vi   JOHN E., b. April 17, 1838; d. June 28, 1841.
3066   vii  HOWARD J.,  } b. March 25, 1841; { d. Oct. 20, 1863.
3067   viii FRANK H.,   }                    { d. Sept. 8, 1863.
```

1334 WILLIAM[7] LORD (*Philomelia*,[6] *William*,[5] *Joseph*,[4] *Job*,[3] *James*,[2] *Anthony*[1]), son of Edmund and Philomelia (Emery) Lord; married ———— Nevins of Pelham, N. H.

Children:

```
3068   i    FRANCES.[8]
3069   ii   BENJAMIN.
3070   iii  PHILOMELIA.
3071   iv   ELIZABETH.
3072   v    JOHN.
```

1335 HANNAH[7] LORD (*Philomelia*,[6] *William*,[5] *Joseph*,[4] *Job*,[3] *James*,[2] *Anthony*[1]), daughter of Edmund and Philomelia (Emery) Lord; married Isaac Merrill of Dover, N. H. (born in Amesbury, Mass.); live in Farmington, N. H.

Children:

```
3073   i    CHARLES A.,[8] b. Aug. 7, 1833.
3074   ii   ANNE, b. Sept. 23, 1835.
3075   iii  LYDIA M., b. Sept. 3, 1843.
```

1337 PHILOMELIA[7] EMERY (*William*,[6] *William*,[5] *Joseph*,[4] *Job*,[3] *James*,[2] *Anthony*[1]), daughter of William and Sally (Paine) Emery; married Nov. 29, 1830, Nathaniel Johnson of Sullivan (born Nov. 2, 1803; died June 11, 1886).

Children:

```
3076   i    CORDELIA,[8] b. Sept. 19, 1831; d. Dec. 14, 1860; unm.
3077   ii   CLARISSA B., b. Aug. 11, 1833; d.
3078   iii  THEODORE B., b. July 14, 1835.
3079   iv   JULIA A., b. July 11, 1837; unm.
3080   v    EMELINE S., b. June 10, 1839.
3081   vi   CHARLES NATHANIEL, b. May 15, 1841; d. Nov. 27, 1841.
3082   vii  PHILOMELIA E., b. Dec. 27, 1842.
3083   viii FRANCIS E., b. Nov. 26, 1848; unm.
3084   ix   HERBERT O., b. Aug. 19, 1854; m. Lelia Clark.
```

1338 BENJAMIN[7] EMERY (*William*,[6] *William*,[5] *Joseph*,[4] *Job*,[3] *James*,[2] *Anthony*[1]), son of William and Sally (Paine) Emery; married Aug. 13, 1829, Elmira Robbins of Eden, Me. (died May, 1864).

Children:

```
3085   i    AMANDA,[8] b. April 27, 1830.
3086   ii   RUFUS R., b. April 30, 1832.
3087   iii  HANNAH A., b. Jan. 24, 1835.
```

3088   iv   SARAH E , b May 10, 1837, m Henry Knowles, 1860
3089   v   JULIA F , b June 16, 1840, m Chesnell Desailes, Sept , 1864.
      He d a few days after marriage   She d 1869
3090   vi   LYDIA H , b Nov 20, 1842
3091   vii   FLORENCE, b Nov 16, 1846
3092   viii   MINERVA, b July 7, 1850
3093   ix   CELESTIA b Jan 11, 1853, d April 15, 1866
3094   x   WILLIE, b Dec. 6, 1853, d Sept 9, 1856.

1339 JEDIDAH S [7] EMERY (*William*,[6] *William*,[5] *Joseph*,[4] *Job*,[3] *James*,[2] *Anthony*[1]), daughter of William and Sally (Paine) Emery ; married, first,, Oct 23, 1828, John Thomas of Eden, Me. (died at St Pierre, Martinique , master of brig " Envoy" of Mt Desert, Me , July 17, 1843) ; second, 1850, Z. P Eastes of Bangor, Me.
Children :

3095   i   JOEL O.,[8] b July 1830, d , 1860, at Mauritius, Isle of France; officer on a New Bedford whale ship.
3096   ii   MELEDIAH O , b April 4 1832, d Oct. 27, 1837
3097   iii   AMORI T , b. May 27, 1834, m Loren Fletcher
3098   iv   GEORGE G., b July 2, 1841, res in St. Paul, Minn.

By second marriage

3099   v   WILLIS, b 1852, d 1853

1344 SARAH A.[7] EMERY (*William*,[6] *William*,[5] *Joseph*,[4] *Job*,[3] *James*,[2] *Anthony*[1]), daughter of William and Sally (Paine) Emery ; married Sept. 2, 1841. Samuel Hill of Sullivan, Me.
Children :

3100   i   EDWARD LANGDON,[8] b April 22, 1843, d Dec 21, 1843
3101   ii   MONTGOMERY, b Sept 21, 1845, m in Providence, R I , Nov. 30, 1874, Eliza C Merchant
3102   iii   OLIN, b June 18, 1848, m in Providence, R. I , Jan 1, 1880, Mary Pierce

1346 LUCETTA A.[7] EMERY (*William*,[6] *William*,[5] *Joseph*,[4] *Job*,[3] *James*,[2] *Anthony*[1]) daughter of William and Sally (Paine) Emery ; married May 13, 1849, George Hill of Gouldsboro, Me.
' Children :

3103   i   OLIVE RELENZA,[8] b March 12, 1852.
3104   ii   SARAH A., b Jan. 14, 1855, unm

1350 THOMAS P.[7] EMERY (*William*,[6] *William*,[5] *Joseph*,[4] *Job*,[3] *James*,[2] *Anthony*[1]), son of William and Sally (Paine) Emery , married in Eden, Me., Jan. 15, 1853, Lydia Hamor (died March 12, 1880).
Children :

3105   i   ADA L ,[8] b March 10, 1854, m Nov. 25, 1879, Albert Corthell of Millbridge, Me , d. Jan. 9, 1882.
3106   ii   FRANK O , b July 21, 1857; unm
3107   iii   EVA L., b. Sept 15, 1863; unm

1351 LAURA N [7] EMERY (*William*,[6] *William*,[5] *Joseph*,[4] *Job*,[3] *James*,[2] *Anthony*[1]), daughter of William and Sally (Paine) Emery , married Dec. 25, 1865, Charles Crane of Lowell, Mass
Children :

3108   i   CHARLS W.,[9] b Sept 21, 1866
3109   ii   LILLIAN C , b. July 11, 1868

1352 ALFRED[7] EMERY (*Joel*,[6] *William*,[5] *Joseph*,[4] *Job*,[3] *James*,[2] *Anthony*[1]), son of Joel and Hannah (Thomas) Emery ; married, first, Aug. 31, 1829, Eliza Hopkins (died in Eden, Me., 1849) ; second, Dec. 1, 1850, Jane Richardson. Shipmaster.

Children :

3110   i   JONATHAN H.,[8] b. Aug. 12, 1830 ; d. at sea.
3111   ii   MARTHA A., b. June 23, 1835.
3112   iii ISAAC H., b. Dec. 14, 1836.
3113   iv   ADALINE, b. April 24, 1840.
3114   v   ANGELINE, b. Sept. 9, 1842 ; m. George B. Wetherbee.
3115   vi   EMMA S., b. Aug. 20, 1844 ; d. Aug., 1876.
3116   vii MARY J., b. Sept. 6, 1846.
3117   viii ELIZA A., b. Dec. 25, 1848.

By second marriage :

3118   ix   DELIA H., b. Oct. 31, 1851.
3119   x   ARDELL T., b. July 10, 1853.

1353 ADALINE[7] EMERY (*Joel*,[6] *William*,[5] *Joseph*,[4] *Job*,[3] *James*,[2] *Anthony*[1]), daughter of Joel and Hannah (Thomas) Emery ; married Dec. 20, 1827, Capt. John Thompson.

Captain Thompson was a shipmaster and in command of the brig "Margaret Ann," was wrecked at Rum Key, Bahama Island, in Sept. or Oct., 1837 or 1838, and the vessel was totally lost. He took passage on the brig "Tom Cringle" bound for St. John, N. B. He had his wife, son John S. and daughter Margaret A. with him, and they were to have been landed at Eden, Maine. The "Tom Cringle" was never heard from and was supposed to have been lost in a hurricane soon after leaving Rum Key.

Children :

3120   i   MARGARET A.,[8] b. April 11, 1831.
3121   ii   LEWIS T., b. Aug. 17, 1833 ; d. Sept. 25, 1834.
3122   iii JOHN S., b. May 11, 1835.

1354 JARED[7] EMERY (*Joel*,[6] *William*,[5] *Joseph*,[4] *Job*,[3] *James*,[2] *Anthony*[1]), son of Joel and Hannah (Thomas) Emery ; married May 16, 1833, Sophia Hopkins (born Sept. 14, 1814).

Children :

3123   i   JANE H.,[8] b. May 22, 1834 ; d. Sept. 9, 1840.
3124   ii   SOPHIA A., b. April 26, 1836 ; d. Oct. 20, 1864.
3125   iii MARGARET J., b. Aug. 4, 1838 ; d. Sept. 20, 1840.
3126   iv   MARGARET J., b. Dec. 31, 1840.
3127   v   JOHN L., b. May 10, 1843 ; d. July 23, 1866.
3128   vi   EVERETT E., b. June 14, 1845 ; killed in battle June 17, 1864.
3129   vii MARY H., b. April 8, 1847.
3130   viii HIRAM J., b. Feb. 8, 1850.
3131   ix   ONSLOW T., b. Feb. 12, 1852 ; d. April 17, 1876.
3132   x   ARTHUR L., b. May 17, 1854 ; lost at sea Aug. 23, 1873.
3133   xi   HOWARD C., b. Aug. 16, 1856.

1356 SAMUEL N.[7] EMERY (*Joel*,[6] *William*,[5] *Joseph*,[4] *Job*,[3] *James*,[2] *Anthony*[1]), son of Joel and Hannah (Thomas) Emery ; married, first, Aug. 30, 1838, Mary H. Hopkins (born in Eden, Me., May 10, 1819 ; died Dec. 18, 1846) ; second, March 18, 1847, Eliza H. Ladd (born in Mount Desert, Me., Jan. 6, 1828).

Children

   3134   i   Isadore,[8] b June 6, 1840, unm.

By second marriage :

   3135   ii   Ernest M., b May 1, 1849.
   3136   iii   Osmond, b Nov. 1, 1856, m. ——— Harper, Nov , 1886
   3137   iv   Julian, } b Feb 21, 1859
   3138   v   Lillian, }

1359 John T [7] Emery (*Joel,*[6] *William,*[5] *Joseph,*[4] *Job,*[3] *James,*[2] *Anthony*[1]), son of Joel and Hannah (Thomas) Emery ; married April 12, 1860, Ann S. Young (born in Eden, Me , Dec. 30, 1838) ; lived in Eden, Me.
   Children :

   3139   i   Cora E .[8] b April 7, 1861
   3140   ii   George L , b March 20, 1863
   3141   iii   Edward H., b Dec 21, 1864.
   3142   iv   Mary J , b Jan 16, 1871

1360 Hannah T.[7] Emery (*Joel,*[6] *William,*[5] *Joseph,*[4] *Job,*[3] *James,*[2] *Anthony*[1]), daughter of Joel and his second wife, Martha (Mayo) Emery , married at Eden, Me , Aug 18, 1850, Uriah Goodridge (died April, 1880).
   Children

   3143   i   Etta M ,[8] b. May 16, 1851.
   3144   ii   Omar, b Oct 17, 1852, res in Minneapolis, Minn
   3145   iii   Irving, b May 19, 1862; res in Minneapolis, Minn

1361 Joel[7] Emery (*Joel,*[6] *William,*[5] *Joseph,*[4] *Job,*[3] *James,*[2] *Anthony*[1]), son of Joel and his second wife, Martha (Mayo) Emery ; married Nov. 21, 1849, Abbie M. Liscomb (born in Belfast, Me., July 12, 1834) ; lived in Eden, Me.
   Children :

   3146   i   Lorenzo J ,[8] b March 7, 1851, d March 14, 1855
   3147   ii   Herbert P., b Feb 28, 1853
   3148   iii   Maurice P., b. Dec 27, 1855.
   3149   iv   Lora M , b June 21. 1858, res in Lockport, Ill.
   3150   v   Olive B., b Dec 27, 1860, m Charles A Hanscomb, Dec 7, 1886.

1363 Andrew[7] Emery (*Joel,*[6] *William,*[5] *Joseph,*[4] *Job,*[3] *James,*[2] *Anthony*[1]), son of Joel and his second wife, Martha (Mayo) Emery ; married, 1871, Alice Williams (born 1853)
   Child

   3151   i   Mabel Alice,[8] b. April 20, 1872

1365 Washington I [7] Emery (*Joel,*[6] *William,*[5] *Joseph,*[4] *Job,*[3] *James,*[2] *Anthony*[1]), son of Joel and his second wife, Martha (Mayo) Emery , married Sept.. 1862, Amanda M Hodgman (born in Boston, Mass , Oct 24, 1839). Master builder, Mobile, Ala.
   Children :

3152 i GEORGE HILLMAN,[8] b. Oct. 13, 1864, in New Orleans, La.; d.
Oct. 12, 1876.
3153 ii IRVING BARTLETT, b May 17, 1869, in Mobile, Ala.
3154 iii ORLANDO F., b. April 14, 1871, in Mobile, Ala.
3155 iv CLANDRAN V., b. Dec. 17, 1874, in Mobile, Ala.
3156 v GEORGE S., b. July 3, 1876, in Mobile, Ala.

1366 WESTON F.[7] EMERY (*Joel*,[6] *William*,[5] *Joseph*,[4] *Job*,[3] *James*,[2]
Anthony[1]), son of Joel and his second wife, Martha (Mayo) Emery;
married May 25, 1860, Dianthe Theresa Gilman of Houlton, Me.;
lives in Alvarado, Cal.
Children:

3157 i ORMOND JOEL,[8] b. Sept. 30, 1861.
3158 ii CHARLES IRVING, b. Dec. 20, 1863; d. May, 1870.
3159 iii MAYBELL AUGUSTA, b Dec. 17, 1865; d. May, 1867.
3160 iv GUY CARLTON, b. Aug. 19, 1868.
3161 v BLANCHE AUGUSTA, b. July 7, 1871.
3162 vi LORA, b. Sept. 22, 1873.
3163 vii ROY WESTON, b. Nov. 19, 1876.
3164 viii INEZ DIANTHE, b. March 18, 1880.

1367 ALVAN[7] EMERY (*Andrew*,[6] *William*,[5] *Joseph*,[4] *Job*,[3] *James*,[2]
Anthony[1]), son of Andrew and Shuah (Bartlett) Emery; married Jan.
10, 1839, Susan B. Hanson (born Aug. 2, 1821).
Children:

3165 i FRANKLIN L.,[8] b. Dec. 28, 1839.
3166 ii MARSHALL, b. Nov. 8, 1841.
3167 iii FREDERICK, b. May 21, 1844; res. in Deer Tail Station, Wis.;
unm.
3168 iv WILLIAM H., b. Aug. 19, 1846.

1368 ALMIRA[7] EMERY (*Andrew*,[6] *William*,[5] *Joseph*,[4] *Job*,[3] *James*,[2]
Anthony[1]), daughter of Andrew and Shuah (Bartlett) Emery; mar-
ried June 23, 1833, Paul Roberts.
Child:

3169 i SUSAN,[8] d. April 27, 1838.

1369 HIRAM A.[7] EMERY (*Andrew*,[6] *William*,[5] *Joseph*,[4] *Job*,[3]
James,[2] *Anthony*[1]), son of Andrew and Shuah (Bartlett) Emery;
married Oct. 25, 1835, Mary A. Goodwin (born Nov. 4, 1810). He
was for many years a leading dentist in Boston; was later engaged
in the oil business in western Virginia, where he acquired a compe-
tency, retired from the business and now resides in Brooklyn, N. Y.
Children:

3170 i CHARLES G.,[8] b. July 20, 1836, in New Portland, Me. He com-
menced his business career as clerk in the employ of his
uncles, Messrs. Goodwin & Co., tobacco merchants in New
York. At their death he succeeded them in business, in
which he has been eminently successful. Recently his house
has been consolidated, with many others, into a large corporation, of which he is now treasurer. He is a man of
large business capacity.
3171 ii HIRAM A., b. Sept. 23, 1839; d. June 21, 1842.
3172 iii HIRAM A., b. Nov. 11, 1842; d. Aug. 4, 1848.
3173 iv WILLIAM G., b. Sept. 23, 1853, in Boston, Mass.

1372 Philomelia W.[7] Emery (*Hiram*,[6] *William*,[5] *Joseph*,[4] *Job*,[3] *James*,[2] *Anthony*[1]), daughter of Hiram and Rachel S. (Simpson) Emery; married Feb 29, 1844, Gowen Whitaker (born Dec 22, 1808). Lived in Gouldsboro, Me.

Children:

3174 i George,[8]
3175 ii Hiram E, } b Sept 21, 1846, { d. Aug 7, 1850
3176 iii George E, b Aug 13, 1853, d. April 4, 1866.

1374 Cyrus[7] Emery (*Hiram*,[6] *William*,[5] *Joseph*,[4] *Job*,[3] *James*,[2] *Anthony*[1]), son of Hiram and Rachel S. (Simpson) Emery; married Oct. 27, 1850, Hannah L. Chilcott (born in Gouldsboro, Me., Nov. 15, 1826) Lives in Sullivan, Me. He was a blacksmith by trade, and held the office of deputy collector under President Lincoln's administration.

Children:

3177 i Rachel P,[8] b May 30, 1852, d Dec 1, 1856
3178 ii Lydia E, b Jan 2, 1854, d. Nov 2, 1870
3179 iii George C, b Oct 16, 1855
3180 iv Herman D, b May 24, 1858, d Jan 17, 1879.
3181 v William O, b July 3, 1860

1375 William Darius[7] Emery (*Hiram*,[6] *William*,[5] *Joseph*,[4] *Job*,[3] *James*,[2] *Anthony*[1]), son of Hiram and Rachel S. (Simpson) Emery, married Nov. 23, 1851, Amelia A. White (born in Sullivan, Me, Sept. 29, 1829) Resides in East Boston, Mass.

Children:

3182 i Alice A,[8] b Feb 18, 1856.
3183 ii John E, b. Nov. 21, 1861.

1377 Daniel S[7] Emery (*Hiram*,[6] *William*,[5] *Joseph*,[4] *Job*,[3] *James*,[2] *Anthony*[1]), son of Hiram and Rachel S (Simpson) Emery, married Dec 25, 1860, Lydia S Hill (born in Sullivan, Me, Oct. 15, 1835); removed to Boston, Mass, in 1850 and in 1859 became a member of the firm of John S Emery & Co

Children:

3184 i Fred H,[8] b Dec 23, 1863; d July 12, 1871
3185 ii John S, b June 1, 1866, d Jan 25, 1868
3186 iii Daniel R, b May 16, 1869, d Jan 16, 1870
3187 iv Georgie, b Feb 25, 1871
3188 v Ralph C., b Jan. 23, 1876

1380 Emily[7] Lord (*Lucy*,[6] *William*,[5] *Joseph*,[4] *Job*,[3] *James*,[2] *Anthony*[1]), daughter of James and Lucy (Emery) Lord; married March 13, 1839, David T. Varney (born June 30, 1810). She died March 30, 1857

Children:

3189 i Melvin S,[8] b 1839
3190 ii Lucinda, b March 2, 1841.
3191 iii William H, b. March 22, 1843.
3192 iv Emily J, b Aug 22, 1845
3193 v David F, b March 18, 1848
3194 vi Mary A, b Dec. 25, 1850
3195 vii George R, b April 13, 1853.
3196 viii Hiram D, b. Jan. 21, 1856.

1381 MARIA[7] LORD (*Lucy,[6] William,[5] Joseph,[4] Job,[3] James,[2] Anthony[1]*), daughter of James and Lucy (Emery) Lord; married Nov. 25, 1854, James Roberts. Live in Lebanon, Me.

Children:

3197	i	JANE M.,[8] b. Nov. 20, 1855.
3198	ii	ELIZA, b. March 30, 1857.
3199	iii	MIRANDA, b. June 27, 1859.
3200	iv	HARRIET, b. June 3, 1861.

1383 WILLIAM[7] LORD (*Lucy,[6] William,[5] Joseph,[4] Job,[3] James,[2] Anthony[1]*), son of James and Lucy (Emery) Lord; married July 20, 1854, Elizabeth D. Johonot (born in Palmyra, Me., Nov. 6, 1835). Lived in Lebanon, Me.

Children:

3201	i	RODNEY J.,[8] b. July 20, 1855.
3202	ii	WILLIAM EMERY. b. March 3, 1857.
3203	iii	MARTHA H , b. June 21, 1859.
3204	iv	MARY F., b. Oct. 1, 1861.
3205	v	HORACE M., b. March 27, 1863.

1385 HIRAM[7] LORD (*Lucy,[6] William,[5] Joseph,[4] Job,[3] James,[2] Anthony[1]*), son of James and Lucy (Emery) Lord; married Nov. 17, 1853, Mary E. Fall (born in Lebanon, Me., Aug. 25, 1830). Lives in Lebanon, Me.

Children:

3206	i	JAMES,[8] b. Aug. 29, 1854.
3207	ii	JENNIE C., b. Oct. 3, 1864.
3208	iii	HERBERT, b. May 31, 1873.

1387 SYLVESTER[7] BARTLETT (*Mehitable,[6] William,[5] Joseph,[4] Job,[3] James,[2] Anthony[1]*), son of Nathan and Mehitable (Emery) Bartlett; married Dec. 30, 1855, Clementine Raitt (born May 10, 1830). Lived in Eliot, Me.

Children:

3209	i	LIZZIE N.,[8] b. Sept. 21, 1857.
3210	ii	J. HOWARD, b. Oct. 29, 1860; d. Feb. 5, 1863.
3211	iii	C. EDWARD, b. Jan. 19, 1863.
3212	iv	RALPH S., b. April 29, 1868.
3213	v	ROLLA, b. Sept. 2, 1869.
3214	vi	GRACE B., b. Feb. 14, 1871; d. April 28, 1874.

1390 JAMES W.[7] BARTLETT (*Mehitable,[6] William,[5] Joseph,[4] Job,[3] James,[3] Anthony[1]*), son of Nathan and Mehitable (Emery) Bartlett; married Oct. 24, 1860, Caroline A. Goodwin (died March 26, 1887). Lives in Eliot, Me.; married, second, Lillian Wooster, 1888.

Children:

3215	i	ABBIE G.,[8] b. April 30, 1863.
3216	ii	JOHN H., b. April 9, 1866.
3217	iii	ALFRED, b. June 15, 1870.

1394 CAPT. THOMAS[7] EMERY (*John,[6] Jonathan,[5] Jonathan,[4] Job,[3] James,[2] Anthony[1]*), son of John and Elizabeth (Tarbox) Emery; married Feb. 28, 1826, Myra Hill.

Children :

3218 *i   OLINDA,[8] b Jan. 29, 1828.
3219 ii   FRED, b Oct 11, 1829
3220 iii KEZIAH HILL, b May 4, 1836
3221 iv   MARY, b Sept 3 1839

1395 JOTHAM[7] EMERY (*John*,[6] *Jonathan*,[5] *Jonathan*,[4] *Job*,[3] *James*,[2] *Anthony*[1]), son of John and Elizabeth (Furbox) Emery, married Sarah Fenderson.   He died, 1847.
Children

3222 i   HENRY,[8] b May 11, 1836 unm
3223 ii   JONATHAN, b Feb 28, 1838, m. —— Snow of Saco
3224 iii JOTHAM, b April 8, 1840
3225 iv   RUFUS, b March 2, 1842, d æt. 18.
3226 v   SARAH ELIZ., b Dec 29, 1843, d young.

1400 WILLIAM MURCH[7] EMERY (*Haven*,[6] *Jonathan*,[5] *Jonathan*,[4] *Job*,[3] *James*,[2] *Anthony*[1]), son of Capt. Haven and Deborah (Murch) Emery; married Eliza Stackpole (published in Biddeford, Me , Jan. 18, 1823).   He died Oct. 31, 1886, aged 86
Children :

3227 i   WILLIAM T [8]
3228 ii   LOUISA M

1410 AMAZIAH[7] EMERY (*Thomas*,[6] *Jonathan*,[5] *Jonathan*,[4] *Job*,[3] *James*,[2] *Anthony*[1]), son of Thomas and Mary (Gray) Emery, married Dec. 30, 1830, Abigail Tappan.   Shipmaster , lived in Saco, Me.
Children ·

3229 i   MARY ABIGAIL,[8] b June 24, 1832, m 1st, Wm S Jordan; 2nd, Mark Googins
3230 ii   THOMAS b Oct 6, 1834; d June 1, 1838, m. A Maria Small.
3231 iii GIDEON TUCKER, b April 3, 1837, master of ship "Jack Frost" of Boston, lost at sea, Jan , 1864
3232 iv   AMAZIAH, b May 25, 1839 m Fannie S Pennel, he was a shipmaster
3233 v   SARAH ANN CUSHING, b. Oct 3, 1841, d Oct. 31, 1847.
3234 vi   SAMUEL TAPPAN, b Nov 27, 1843, lost at sea Jan , 1864.
3235 vii EMMA JANE b Jan 11, 1846, m Edwin B Hooper
3236 viii FREEMAN SNOW, b. Sept 4, 1848, m Lottie Anderson
3237 ix   ALBERT HENRY, b. May 14, 1852; m Hattie Jordan.

1429 BENJAMIN F [7] EMERY (*Philip*,[6] *Job*,[5] *Jabez*,[4] *Job* [3] *James*,[2] *Anthony*[1]), son of Philip and Sarah (Kimball) Emery, married at Centreville, Me., May 5, 1842, Eliza D. Allen   Lived in Addison, Me., till 1850, when he removed to Lewiston, Me
Children ·

3238 i   HERNANDO N.,[8] b. March 14, 1843, in Addison, Me
3239 ii   BENJ G. F , b April 24, 1845, d April 5, 1848, in Addison, Me
3240 iii ELIZA E , b Oct. 18, 1856, in Lewiston, Me.

1431 DANIEL C.[7] EMERY (*Daniel*,[6] *Job*,[5] *Jabez*,[4] *Job*,[3] *James*,[2]

Anthony[1]), son of Daniel and Hannah (Downing) Emery ; married Aug. 15, 1838, Orpha J. Butterfield.
Children :

 3241 i GEORGE H.,[8] b. Dec. 11, 1839; d. at sea, 1864.
 3242 ii EMMA J., b. June 11, 1843; m. in Providence, R. I., May 4, 1869, George R Smith.

1436 JOSHUA S.[7] EMERY (*Joshua,[6] Job,[5] Jabez,[4] Job,[3] James,[2] Anthony[1]*), son of Joshua and Sally (Kimball) Emery ; married Dec. 24, 1845, Miriam Peabody.
Children :

 3243 i MARY ELIZABETH,[8] b. April 16, 1847; m. June 11, 1885, Laban Heath of Boston.
 3244 ii FREDERICK O., b. Jan. 18, 1850; res. in Kennebunk, Me.
 3245 iii MIRIAM ORILLA, b. Nov. 9, 1854.
 3246 iv WILLIAM ALLEN, b. May 4, 1857, in Kennebunkport; m. Dec. 7, 1887, Sadie E. Perkins.

1441 JASON L.[7] EMERY (*Thomas,[6] Job,[5] Jabez,[4] Job,[3] James,[2] Anthony[1]*), son of Thomas and Emma (Greenough) Emery ; married Dec. 5, 1839, Hannah D. Emmons.
Children :

 3247 i ASENATH,[8] b. Nov. 21, 1840; d. March 2, 1841.
 3248 ii LEANDER, b. Feb. 5, 1842; m. Etta Rounds.
 3249 iii SARAH F., b. Nov. 27, 1843.
 3250 iv HANNAH, b. Nov. 7, 1845.
 3251 v JASON, b. March 18, 1848.
 3252 vi LORENZO E., b. March 3, 1850.
 3253 vii EVELYN W., b. March 4, 1852.
 3254 viii MARY E., b. March 6, 1854.

1442 JOSHUA[7] EMERY (*Thomas,[6] Job,[5] Jabez,[4] Job,[3] James,[2] Anthony[1]*), son of Thomas and Emma (Greenough) Emery ; married Nov. 25, 1841, Edith McKenney.
Children :

 3255 i LORENZO SULLIVAN,[8] b. April 29, 1843.
 3256 ii JOSHUA W., b. Nov. 5, 1847.
 3257 iii EMMA S., b. July 28, 1850.
 3258 iv ELVIRA P., b. April 5, 1854.
 3259 v SARAH A., b. Nov. 15, 1861.
 3260 vi NELLIE M., b. Nov. 13, 1865.

1446 JACOB[7] EMERY (*Thomas,[6] Job,[5] Jabez,[4] Job,[3] James,[2] Anthony[1]*), son of Thomas and Emma (Greenough) Emery ; married Oct. 16, 1850, Harriet Wildes. Lives in Kennebunkport, Me.
Children :

 3261 i EUNICE A.,[8] b. Aug. 30, 1851; m. Charles Clough.
 3262 ii ELLA J., b. June 28, 1855; m. William Robinson.
 3263 iii MARY L., b. Feb. 16, 1861.

1447 THOMAS[7] EMERY (*Thomas,[6] Job,[5] Jabez,[4] Job,[3] James,[2] Anthony[1]*), son of Thomas and Emma (Greenough) Emery ; married Dec. 9, 1853, Maria J. Lynds ; resides in Kennebunkport, Me.

Children :

3264 i CHARLES L.,³ b Jan. 8, 1856; d Feb. 17. 1856.
3265 ii WILLIE H , b May 11, 1857, d Aug 26, 1857
3266 iii MARY E , b. April 2, 1859; m in Kennebunk, Me , Romanzo Brown
3267 iv GEORGE W , b. Sept. 17, 1860, res. in Lynn, Mass.
3268 v ELZIRA C , b June 6, 1862
3269 vi CHARLES, b May 2, 1866, d Oct 9, 1874.
3270 vii EDWARD H., b. July 28, 1868

1448 BURLEIGH S.⁷ EMERY (*Thomas,*⁶ *Job,*⁵ *Jabez,*⁴ *Job,*³ *James,*² *Anthony*¹), son of Thomas and Emma (Greenough) Emery, married April 5, 1856, Hattie E. Boothby.
Child ·

3271 1 WALTER H ,⁸ b Nov 18, 1868, an adopted son.

1449 JOHN H.⁷ EMERY (*John,*⁶ *Isaac,*⁵ *Jabez,*⁴ *Job,*³ *James,*² *Anthony*¹) son of John and Elizabeth (Morrill) Emery ; married June 25, 1843, Hannah Knight.
Children :

3272 i JOHN F ,⁸ b. March 5, 1844.
3273 ii MARY E , b July 2, 1850, m. William M. York.

1454 BENJAMIN F.⁷ EMERY (*Benjamin,*⁶ *Isaac,*⁵ *Jabez,*⁴ *Job,*³ *James,*² *Anthony*¹), son of Benjamin and Sally (Towne) Emery, married, first, 1849, Olive J Bragdon ; second, Susan Gooch, Dec 6, 1854
Children :

3274 i DANIEL C ,⁸ b 1851; d. Feb 15, 1853

By second marriage :

3275 ii SYLVIA A , b. March 8, 1864.
3276 iii JOHN A , b. July 19, 1867
3277 iv WARWICK G , b March 6, 1870, d. May 9, 1871
3278 v SUSAN E., b. May 3, 1873, d June 18, 1874.

1455 ELIPHALET P.⁷ EMERY (*Benjamin,*⁶ *Isaac,*⁵ *Jabez,*⁴ *Job,*³ *James,*² *Anthony*¹), son of Benjamin and Sally (Towne) Emery ; married May 16, 1849, Cassandra Littlefield.
Children .

3279 i SETH B ,⁸ b Nov 27, 1850; d Jan 2, 1852, in Biddeford, Me.
3280 ii ALONZO L , b July 19, 1853, d July 3, 1854, in Biddeford, Me.
3281 iii SARAH, b Jan 2, 1855, d Jan 20, 1858, in Biddeford, Me.
3282 iv ELLEN A , b July 19, 1857; d Sept 28, 1857, in Biddeford, Me.
3283 v SARAH ABBIE, b July 21, 1858 , d Feb. 22, 1859, in Biddeford, Me.
3284 vi CELIA P , b Jan. 15, 1860, in Wells, Me ; m Walter Chase of Warren, R I.
3285 vii DANIEL L , b March 28, 1861, in Wells, Me
3286 viii WILLIAM E , b Jan. 5, 1864, in Wells, Me.

1457 ISAAC M ⁷ EMERY (*Benjamin,*⁶ *Isaac,*⁵ *Jabez,*⁴ *Job,*³ *James,*² *Anthony*¹), son of Benjamin and Sally (Towne) Emery ; married
29

first, Jan. 18, 1857, Sarah E Pike (died Jan. 29, 1882) ; second, Nov 18, 1883, Matilda M. Pinkham of Kennebunkport, Me.
Children :

   3287   i   ISAAC M ,[8] b July 18, 1858
   3288   ii   MARY ELLEN, b Feb 9, 1860
   3289   iii   BENJAMIN F , b Dec 17, 1862; m March, 1883, Sarah J Whipple of Palmer, Mass
   3290   iv   JOHN JABEZ, b June 21, 1865, d. Sept 12, 1866.
   3291   v   CHARLES H , b Jan 23, 1869

1458 JOHN A [7] EMERY (*Benjamin,*[6] *Isaac,*[5] *Jabez,*[4] *Job,*[3] *James,*[2] *Anthony*[1]), son of Benjamin and Sally (Towne) Emery . married May 10, 1856, Sarah J. Bridges. Resides in Warren, R I.
Child .

   3292   i   ELIZABETH W ,[8] b April 10, 1864, an adopted daughter.

1460 WILLIAM H [7] EMERY (*Benjamin,*[6] *Isaac,*[5] *Jabez,*[4] *Job,*[3] *James,*[2] *Anthony*[1]), son of Benjamin and Sally (Towne) Emery , married May 26, 1858, Frances A Merrill. Resides in Kennebunkport, Me.
Children, born in Kennebunk, Me. :

   3293   i   SARAH F ,[8] b April 18, 1859
   3294   ii   ELIPHALET WILLIAM, b Aug 20, 1864
   3295   iii   GEORGE H , b Dec 13, 1869
   3296   iv   BENJAMIN P , b Sept 8, 1871
   3297   v   JONAS M , b July 14, 1873.
   3298   vi   FRANKLIN M , b Sept 17, 1877

1462 SUSAN D.[7] EMERY (*Isaac,*[6] *Isaac,*[5] *Jabez,*[4] *Job,*[3] *James,*[2] *Anthony*[1]), daughter of Isaac and Lucinda (Fairfield) Emery ; married Robert W. Towne.
Children :

   3299   i   MARY S [8]
   3300   ii   CHARLES E.

1463 MARY L [7] EMERY (*Isaac,*[6] *Isaac,*[5] *Jabez,*[4] *Job,*[3] *James,*[2] *Anthony*[1]), daughter of Isaac and Lucinda (Fairfield) Emery , married Cyrus Fenderson.
Children :

   3301   i   LAURETTA [8]
   3302   ii   JOSEPHINE.

1465 CHARLES ISAAC[7] EMERY (*Isaac,*[6] *Isaac,*[5] *Jabez,*[4] *Job,*[3] *James,*[2] *Anthony*[1]), son of Isaac and Lucinda (Fairfield) Emery ; married April 25, 1854, Sarah Perkins.
Children :

   3303   i   ELLA G ,[8] b. April 9, 1856
   3304   ii   CHARLES W , b April 7, 1859.

1478 MARY GILPATRICK[8] EMERY (*Samuel,*[7] *Obadiah,*[6] *Obed,*[5] *James,*[4] *James,*[3] *James,*[2] *Anthony*[1]), daughter of Samuel and Mary

Smith (Gilpatrick) Emery; married Jan. 19, 1841, David B Cleaves (born Oct. 14, 1816, died June 22, 1872) of Saco, Me.
Children, born in Saco, Me :

3305　i　EMERY,[9] b Jan 30, 1843 —
3306　ii　MARY SCAMMON, b May 3. 1844.
3307　iii　REBECCA HILL EMERY, b. March 22, 1847, m. Henry Drake
3308　iv　HELEN PAULINA, b in Lawrence, Mass, Sept 2, 1849, unm.
3309　v　SARAH ANNA THOMPSON, b Dec 18, 1851, d Aug 23, 1870
3310　vi　ROBERT EUGENE, b July 12, 1857, d July 31, 1868.

1481 HANNAH[8] EMERY (*Samuel,*[7] *Obadiah,*[6] *Obed,*[5] *James.*[4] *James,*[3] *James,*[2] *Anthony*[1]), daughter of Samuel and Mary Smith (Gilpatrick) Emery; married Aug. 18, 1850, Ethan Earle Maxwell (born in Brunswick, Me, March 23, 1828).
Children ·

3311　i　MARY EMERY,[9] b June 11, 1851, m Oct. 15, 1878, William H Cooper.
3312　ii　ELLA ISABELLA, b. Oct. 24, 1855, m April 27, 1888, Charles F Palmer.
3313　iii　ALICE JENNIE, b Nov 8, 1860, m. Jan 7, 1881, Joseph H. Kinsman
3314　iv　SAMUEL HAMILTON, b March 28, 1863

1482 PRISCILLA[8] PURINGTON (*Sarah,*[7] *Obadiah,*[6] *Obed,*[5] *James,*[4] *James,*[3] *James,*[2] *Anthony*[1]), daughter of Humphrey and Sarah (Emery) Purington; married June 3, 1836, Watson Hallett of Augusta, Me
Child :

3315　i　WATSON W, b. 1842; d. March 9, 1853.

1483 ANN EMERY[8] PURINGTON (*Sarah,*[7] *Obadiah,*[6] *Obed,*[5] *James.*[4] *James.*[3] *James,*[2] *Anthony*[1]), daughter of Humphrey and Sarah (Emery) Purington; married May 14, 1821, Charles Thompson of Topsham, Me.
Children :

3316　i　EMERY P,[9] b Feb 26, 1822, d April 13, 1826.
3317　ii　CHARLES W, b. Jan. 14, 1824, d June 5, 1880.
3318　iii　SARAH A, b April 5, 1826.
3319　iv　EUGENE, b May 8, 1828, grad Bowdoin College, 1850, d Oct. 1, 1850
3320　v　EMERY P, b Aug 10, 1831; grad Bowdoin College, 1855, d. Aug. 11, 1876
3321　vi　HUMPHREY P, b June 15, 1838, m. Oct. 7, 1863, Anne Sprowle of New York
3322　vii　HARRY H., b June 30, 1841.

1485 SARAH P.[8] PURINGTON (*Sarah,*[7] *Obadiah,*[6] *Obed,*[5] *James,*[4] *James,*[3] *James,*[2] *Anthony*[1]), daughter of Humphrey and Sarah (Emery) Purington; married June, 1833, D. W. Thompson.
Children.

3323　i　SARAH P.,[9] b. July 2, 1837, m Nov 28, 1860, Charles Hamlin of Bangor, Me　(See Part I, No 8002)
3324　ii　WILLIE P, b May 14, 1840, d Nov 1, 1840
3325　iii　EDWARD H P, b July 23, 1844, m Sept. 14, 1866, Jane Murray of Brunswick, Me
3326　iv　DIXEY, b ——, d. Oct. 12, 1859.

1487 Francis T.[8] Purington (*Sarah,*[7] *Obadiah,*[6] *Obed,*[5] *James,*[4] *James,*[3] *James,*[2] *Anthony*[1]), son of Humphrey and Sarah (Emery) Purington, married Oct. 3, 1837, Susan Tebbetts of Lisbon, Me.
Children :

   3327 i   Francis G ,[9] b July 1, 1839; m May 18, 1870, Hannah Stet-
                 son.
   3328 ii   Sarah E , b. Dec. 12, 1841
   3329 iii Joanna T , b March 10, 1845.
   3330 iv Humphrey, b Feb. 24, 1847
   3331 v   Paul C , b Oct 6, 1851, m. Dec. 20, 1877, Eunice Fisher of
                 Fort Fairfield, Me
   3332 vi Lizzie A , b Sept 15, 1853
   3333 vii Hattie A., b March 9, 1856.
   3334 viii Woodbury W., b July 13, 1857

1488 Woodbury B.[8] Purington (*Sarah,*[7] *Obadiah,*[6] *Obed,*[5] *James,*[4] *James,*[3] *James,*[2] *Anthony*[1]), son of Humphrey and Sarah (Emery) Purington, married, first, July 1, 1840. Elizabeth J Walker of Topsham, Me. ; second, May 15, 1857, Rebecca King of Saco, Me.
Children :

   3335 i   Jane W.,[9] m. April 25, 1866, Webster King, of Boston, Mass
   3336 ii   Annie E

By second marriage :

   3337 iii Walker King, b Feb 25 1859.
   3338 iv Wildes W , b Sept 30, 1866.

1489 Ann Jewett[8] Emery (*Ralph,*[7] *Ralph,*[6] *Obed.*[5] *James,*[4] *James,*[3] *James,*[2] *Anthony*[1]). daughter of Ralph and Happy (Woodman) Emery ; married Feb. 2, 1860, Benjamin Hooper (born March 5, 1828 , died in Biddeford, Me , Feb. 23, 1886), son of Daniel S. and Miriam (Locke) Hooper. He was a grocer.
Children :

   3339 i   A son,[9] b. April 12, 1861; d in infancy.
   3340 ii   Alice M , b May 9, 1864

1490 George Ferdinand[8] Emery (*Ralph,*[7] *Ralph,*[6] *Obed,*[5] *James,*[4] *James,*[3] *James,*[2] *Anthony*[1]). son of Ralph and Happy (Woodman) Emery ; married Sept. 13, 1855, Lucy Thacher, daughter of Josiah and Jane Thacher.
Children :

   3341 i   Josiah Thacher,[9] b. Dec 30, 1858
   3342 ii   Henry R., b Nov. 22, 1861.
   3343 iii Kate Bigelow, b March 22, 1870

1491 Obed[8] Emery (*Ralph,*[7] *Ralph,*[6] *Obed,*[5] *James,*[4] *James,*[3] *James,*[2] *Anthony*[1]), son of Ralph and Happy (Woodman) Emery ; married Dec. 5, 1860, Mary Louisa, daughter of William H. and Hannah Cluff. Farmer .
Children :

   3344 i   Georgia,[9] b. July 25, 1864
   3345 ii   Maud H , b. June 28, 1869; d. April 17, 1874.

1493 John E.[8] Emery (*Samuel,*[7] *James,*[b] *James,*[5] *Thomas,*[4]

James,[3] *James,*[2] *Anthony*[1]), son of Samuel and Anna (Elwell) Emery, married in Charlestown, Mass , Oct 14, 1851, Hannah M Hobbs (born in Chatham, N H., Jan 14, 1823)   Resides in Lovell, Me.
Children, born in Lovell, Me :

3346 i   LOTTIE A ,[9] b Feb 12 1853
3347 ii   JAMES H , b July 1, 1854; d Jan. 29, 1874.
3348 iii FRANK E., b Aug 23, 1858

1495 MARY E.[8] EMERY (*Samuel,*[7] *James,*[6] *James,*[5] *Thomas,*[4] *James,*[3] *James,*[2] *Anthony*[1]), daughter of Samuel and Anna (Elwell) Emery; married June 17, 1862, Lauson A. Reinhardt (born in Lincolnston, N. C., June 20, 1815; died near Quitman, Tex., Nov. 17, 1872).   She lives in Minneola, Texas
Children :

3349 i   LAUSON EMERY,[9] b Sept 1 1865; d Oct 15, 1866
3350 ii   SUSIE MARIA, b Feb 16, 1869
3351 iii LOIS SMITH, b June 9, 1871, d in infancy.

1496 JAMES WALLACE[8] EMERY (*Samuel,*[7] *James,*[6] *James,*[5] *Thomas,*[4] *James,*[3] *James,*[2] *Anthony*[1]), son of Samuel and Anna (Elwell) Emery, married Jan. 19, 1860, Elizabeth Jane Brown of Bunker Hill, Tex. (born March 16, 1844)   He graduated at Bowdoin College, 1853 , teacher in Texas and Maine , farmer in Minnesota.
Children .

3352 i   MARY EFFIE,[9] b March 3, 1861, in Comanche, Tex
3353 ii   RUPERT, b. March 18, 1863, in Rusk Co , Tex ; d Nov 13, 1880
3354 iii   CID, b April 21, 1865, in Rusk Co , Tex.
3355 iv   LOIS, b March 25, 1867, in Rusk Co , Tex
3356 v   SYBIL, b April 1, 1869, in Rusk Co., Tex
3357 vi   ARTHUR MCARTHUR, b Dec 1 1870, in Rusk Co , Tex
3358 vii   SON unnamed, b Nov 18, 1872, in Kaufman Co , Tex., d March 5 1873
3359 viii SUE LOTTIE, b Nov 1, 1874, in Kaufman Co , Tex
3360 ix   DAISY, b Sept 5, 1876, in Kaufman Co , Tex
3361 x   ANNE BELL, b July 2, 1878, in Kaufman Co , Tex
3362 xi   BERTHA ELIZABETH, b. March 28, 1882, in Kaufman Co , Tex

1497 MEHITABLE J [8] EMERY (*Samuel,*[7] *James,*[6] *James,*[5] *Thomas,*[4] *James,*[3] *James,*[2] *Anthony*[1]), daughter of Samuel and Anna (Elwell) Emery; married in Charlestown, Mass , Nov. 30, 1852, Horatio J. Lathrop.   She died Oct. 10, 1868.   He resides in Suffield, Conn.
Children

3363 i   JENNIE A ,[9] b Sept 24, 1855, in Somerville, Mass , m., May 4, 1880, Herbert F. Stevens, res in Passaic, N J.
3364 ii CARRIE H., b Oct 4, 1858

1498 LOIS B [8] EMERY (*Samuel,*[7] *James,*[6] *James,*[5] *Thomas,*[4] *James,*[3] *James,*[2] *Anthony*[1]), daughter of Samuel and Anna (Elwell) Emery, married in Bangor, Me., Jan. 24, 1859, Charles F. Smith (born July 3, 1832). cashier of Continental Bank, Boston, Mass.
Children, born in Charlestown, Mass. :

3365 i   FRANCIS ALBERT,[9] b. July 11, 1860; d. Aug. 13, 1882, at Fort
           Popham, Me.; was in Harvard College, class of 1884; shot
           by U. S. sergeant at Fort Popham, while getting into the
           fort during his vacation.
3366 ii   ANNIE EMERY, b. Sept. 2, 1863.
3367 iii ARTHUR REINHARDT, b. Dec. 20, 1865.
3368 iv   MARIANA PAGE, b. May 8, 1868.
3369 v   BERTHA EFFIE, b. April 17, 1870.
3370 vi   MABEL, b. May 3, 1872.
3371 vii ALICE LOUISE, b. Oct. 12, 1873.
3372 viii CHARLES FRANCIS, b. Nov. 27, 1876.

1499 SAMUEL[8] EMERY (*Samuel,*[7] *James,*[6] *James,*[5] *Thomas,*[4]
James,[3] *James,*[2] *Anthony*[1]). son of Samuel and Anna (Elwell) Em-
ery; married in Bangor, Me., May 26, 1861, Ellen Rand (born in
East Knox, Me., Dec. 27, 1840). Resides in Webster, Mass.
  Child:

  3373 i TERA GERTRUDE,[9] b. June 6, 1865, in Bangor, Me.

1504 JULIA S.[8] EMERY (*Alexander J.,*[7] *James,*[6] *James,*[5] *Thomas,*[4]
James,[3] *James,*[2] *Anthony*[1]), daughter of Alexander J. and Mary S.
(Haley) Emery; married Orin H. Peck.
  Child:

  3374 i HERBERT E.,[9] b. Sept., 1882.

1506 MARY E.[8] EMERY (*Alexander J.,*[7] *James,*[6] *James,*[5] *Thomas,*[4]
James,[3] *James,*[2] *Anthony*[1]), daughter of Alexander J. and Mary S.
(Haley) Emery; married Nov. 28, 1865, Charles F. Holt.
  Children:

  3375 i   GRACE G.,[9] b. April 5, 1867.
  3376 ii   EDITH D., b. Jan. 24, 1869; d. Dec. 15, 1874.
  3377 iii EDNA F., b. Jan. 1, 1875
  3378 iv   ALEXANDER S., b. May 18, 1877.

1507 MARY C.[8] EMERY (*Jonas,*[7] *James,*[6] *James,*[5] *Thomas,*[4] *James,*[3]
James,[2] *Anthony*[1]), daughter of Jonas and Eliza (Boynton) Emery;
married Jan. 17, 1859, John Scott of Buxton, Me. Resides in Pittston, Me.
  Children:

  3379 i   EVA E.,[9] b. Dec. 28, 1859.
  3380 ii   FRED. E., b. Dec. 14, 1867.
  3381 iii WALTER, b. Dec. 1, 1869.
  3382 iv   BURTON W., b. July 15, 1871.

1508 ANN V.[8] JEWETT (*Hannah,*[7] *James,*[6] *James,*[5] *Thomas,*[4]
James,[3] *James,*[2] *Anthony*[1]), daughter of George and Hannah (Emery)
Jewett; married in Gardiner, Me., Sept. 30, 1860, Sylvester Powell.
Resides in Clinton, Me.
  Child:

  3383 i HANNAH J.,[9] b. Oct. 8, 1866.

1513 CHARLES P.[8] EMERY (*Thomas F.,*[7] *James,*[6] *James,*[5] *Thomas,*[4]

James,[3] James,[2] Anthony[1]), son of Thomas F. and Nancy M (Webster) Emery, married in Buxton, Me., May 6, 1866, Pamelia B. Johnson Shoe manufacturer; city councillor of Biddeford, Me.; state representative; state senator.

Children:

3384   i   CHARLES HOWARD,[9] b Nov 14, 1867, d Jan 8, 1868, in Buxton, Me

3385   ii GRACE MAY, b Jun 29, 1869, d. Sept 21, 1881, in Biddeford, Me

3386   iii JAMES ALBERT, b. Aug 20, 1872, in Biddeford, Me

1515 N. ELLEN[8] EMERY (*Thomas F.*,[7] *James*,[6] *James*,[5] *Thomas*,[4] *James*,[3] *James*,[2] *Anthony*[1]), daughter of Thomas F. and Nancy M. (Webster) Emery, married in Buxton, Me., March 25, 1867, W. W Marr.

Children:

3387   i   HELEN,[9] b Aug 25, 1876 d in infancy

3388   ii MABEL EMERY, b July 25, 1877

3389   iii HARRIET WEBSTER, b. April 19, 1881

1517 HON. LUCILIUS A.[8] EMERY (*James S.*,[7] *James*,[6] *James*,[5] *Thomas*,[4] *James*,[3] *James*,[2] *Anthony*[1]), son of James S and Eliza Ann (Wing) Emery; married Annie E, daughter of Maj. John Crosby of Hampden, Me, Nov 9, 1864   He graduated at Bowdoin College, 1861; studied law in Bangor, located in Ellsworth. Me, 1863, county attorney from 1867–71, state senator 1874–75, 1881–82, attorney general 1876–79; member of board of overseers of Bowdoin College; member of Maine Historical Society, judge of the Supreme Court of Maine, 1883

Children, born in Ellsworth, Me.:

3390   i   ANNIE CROSBY,[9] b Jun 1, 1871

3391   ii HARRY CROSBY, b Dec 21, 1872, student in Bowdoin College

1518 FLORENCE[8] EMERY (*James S.*,[7] *James*,[6] *James*,[5] *Thomas*,[4] *James*,[3] *James*,[2] *Anthony*[1]), daughter of James S. and Eliza Ann (Wing) Emery, married John W. Blake.

Children:

3392   i   LULU ALICE[9]

3393   ii FLORENCE EMERY.

1541 ELLEN MARIA[8] EMERY (*Samuel W.*,[7] *Samuel*,[6] *James*,[5] *Thomas*,[4] *James*,[3] *James*,[2] *Anthony*[1]), daughter of Samuel W and Lois (Weeks) Emery; married April 5, 1880, Frank F. Jordan, divorced April 12, 1887. She married Sept. 27, 1887, Edwin M. Partridge of Windham, Me.

Child:

3394   i   FREEMAN EMERY,[9] b Jan 1, 1881, in Limerick, Me

1542 JOSHUA FREEMAN[8] WEEKS EMERY (*Samuel W.*,[7] *Samuel*,[6] *James*,[5] *Thomas*,[4] *James*,[3] *James*,[2] *Anthony*[1]), son of Samuel W. and Lois (Weeks) Emery; married Sept. 27, 1882, Ida L. Chase of Portland, Me.

Children, born in Portland, Me. :

3395 i WARREN WOODBURY,[9] b. Sept. 25, 1883.
3396 ii FRANK AUGUSTUS, b. April 6, 1888.

1544 LOIS WEEKS[8] EMERY (*Samuel W.,*[7] *Samuel,*[6] *James,*[5] *Thomas,*[4] *James,*[3] *James,*[2] *Anthony*[1]), daughter of Samuel W. and Lois (Weeks) Emery ; married Jan. 4, 1884, Arthur W. Gray of Portland, Me.

Children, born in Portland, Me. :

3397 i CHARLES EMERY,[9] b. Oct. 12, 1884.
3398 ii NORMAN PRINCE, b. Dec. 27, 1886.

1546 JENNIE SPEAR[8] EMERY (*Samuel W.,*[7] *Samuel,*[6] *James,*[5] *Thomas,*[4] *James,*[3] *James,*[2] *Anthony*[1]), daughter of Samuel W., and Lois (Weeks) Emery ; married in Rochester, N. H., March 12, 1887, George G. Gilman.

Child :

3399 i TRACY HARDEN,[9] b. June 23, 1887, in Limerick, Me.

1547 JAMES[8] EMERY (*James,*[7] *Nathaniel,*[6] *James,*[5] *Thomas,*[4] *James,*[3] *James,*[2] *Anthony*[1]), son of James and Maria (Withington) Emery ; married May 7, 1861, Emma W. Brown (born Oct. 15, 1840).

Children, born in Charlestown, Mass. :

3400 i JAMES HERBERT,[9] b. March 3, 1862.
3401 ii EMMA FLORENCE, b. Dec. 31, 1864.

1549 THOMAS J.[8] EMERY (*James,*[7] *Nathaniel,*[6] *James,*[5] *Thomas,*[4] *James,*[3] *James,*[2] *Anthony*[1]), son of James and Maria (Withington) Emery ; married Sept. 17, 1868, Martha Ellen Hill (born in Biddeford, Me., July 23, 1842).

Children, born in Charlestown, Mass. :

3402 i MARY ELLEN,[9] b. Dec. 31, 1869.
3403 ii WALTER FREEMAN, b. Nov. 3, 1871.
3404 iii EMMA DARLING, b. Jan. 24, 1876.

1550 FREEMAN[8] EMERY (*James,*[7] *Nathaniel,*[6] *James,*[5] *Thomas,*[4] *James,*[3] *James,*[2] *Anthony*[1]), son of James and Maria (Withington) Emery ; married July 17, 1868, Martha Moore Tonge (born in Saco, Me., May 11, 1845).

Children, born in Boston, Mass. :

3405 i FRANK WHITTEMORE,[9] b. Jan. 27, 1870.
3406 ii EDITH, b. June 3, 1873.

1551 CHARLES B.[8] EMERY (*James,*[7] *Nathaniel,*[6] *James,*[5] *Thomas,*[4] *James,*[3] *James,*[2] *Anthony*[1]), son of James and Maria (Withington) Emery ; married July 26, 1876, Mary Ellen Carter (born in Rockland, Mass., Nov. 24, 1854).

Child :

3407 i GEORGE WEBSTER,[9] b. Sept. 5, 1877, in Somerville, Mass.

1552 ANNIE M.[8] MURCH (*Emily Jane,[7] Nathaniel,[6] James,[5] Thomas,[4] James,[3] James,[2] Anthony[1]*), daughter of William and Emily J (Emery) Murch; married, 1862, Algernon D. Pearson, of Topsfield, Mass.

Children, born in Charlestown, Mass. .

```
3408  i    ABBY J ,⁹ b  July 3, 1863
3409  ii   GRACE L , b  Dec. 17, 1867 , d. 1888
3410  iii  ALGERNON D  b  July 17, 1869, d  1870
3411  iv   WILLIE E , b  March 10. 1871, d  1873
3412  v    MAUD E , b  Dec  24, 1873
3413  vi   HATTIE E  b. Oct  6, 1875
3414  vii  CLARENCE L., b  March 21, 1878, d. 1878
```

1553 CHARLES[8] MURCH(*Emily Jane,[7] Nathaniel,[6] James,[5] Thomas,[4] James,[3] James,[2] Anthony[1]*), son of William and Emily Jane (Emery) Murch, married Nov. 23, 1859, Laura McKinney (born Jan. 6, 1839).

Children :

```
3415  i    WILLIAM F ,⁹ b  Dec  2, 1860
3416  ii   CHARLES H , b  Oct 17, 1862
3417  iii  EMMA F , b  Dec. 9  1866.
3418  iv   HATTIE M , b  Jan  27, 1870 , d. 1876.
3419  v    MARILLA H , b  Feb  2, 1874
3420  vi   FRANK G , b. Dec. 19, 1877.
```

1557 NATHANIEL EMERY[8] WHITCOMB (*Sarah Ann,[7] Nathaniel,[6] James,[5] Thomas,[4] James,[3] James,[2] Anthony[1]*), son of Col John and Sarah Ann (Emery) Whitcomb, married Oct. 17, 1861, Abbie Blanchard of Boxborough, Mass.

Children, born in Boxborough, Mass.

```
3421  i    WALDO EMERY,⁹ b. May 25, 1864
3422  ii   ARTHUR MYRON  b  March 14, 1869.
```

1558 JOHN[8] WHITCOMB, JR (*Sarah Ann,[7] Nathaniel,[6] James,[5] Thomas,[4] James.[3] James,[2] Anthony[1]*). son of Col. John and Sarah Ann (Emery) Whitcomb; married in Lunenburg, Mass., June 11, 1864, Nellie M Rand.

Children

```
3423  i    SARAH A ,⁹ b. Feb. 6, 1865, in Lunenburg, Mass , m  George C.
             Hall, Sept. 1, 1884
3424  ii   FRED E , b. April 14, 1868, in Fitchburg, Mass
3425  iii  WILLIAM G , b  June 11, 1870, in Fitchburg, Mass.
3426  iv   WALTER E , b  July 15, 1872  in Fitchburg, Mass
3427  v    CHARLES A , b. April 19, 1875, in Fitchburg, Mass
3428  vi   GEORGE O , b  July 25, 1877, in Fitchburg, Mass
```

1560 JAMES HAYWARD[8] WHITCOMB (*Sarah Ann,[7] Nathaniel,[6] James,[5] Thomas,[4] James,[3] James,[2] Anthony[1]*), son of Col. John and Sarah Ann (Emery) Whitcomb, married in Boxborough, Mass., April 4, 1870, Edna L. Whitcomb.

Child

```
3429  i    MARIAN RAYMOND,⁹ b  Sept 14, 1882.
```

1562 JAMES[8] EMERY (*Nathaniel Webster,[7] Nathaniel,[6] James,[5]*

Thomas,[4] *James,*[3] *James,*[2] *Anthony*[1]), son of Nathaniel Webster and Phœbe (Stevens) Emery; married Nov. 12, 1876, Jennie Bell (born in Boston, Mass., Aug. 17, 1858).

Children :

   3430 i   EMMA FRANCES,[9] b. Nov., 1878, in Medford, Mass.; d. Dec. 29,
               1885.
   3431 ii   SADIE JOSEPHINE, b. Sept. 2, 1880, in Biddeford, Me.
   3432 iii ALICE MAY, b. Dec. 16, 1885, in Biddeford, Me.

1563 HENRIETTA[8] EMERY (*Thomas D.,*[7] *Nathaniel,*[6] *James,*[5] *Thomas,*[4] *James,*[3] *James,*[2] *Anthony*[1]), daughter of Thomas D. and Lucy Ann (Bunker) Emery; married Oct. 6, 1869, Walter H. Durell of Boston, Mass.

Child :

   3433 i   LUCY FLORENCE,[9] b. July 17, 1870, in Charlestown, Mass.

1565 ELIZABETH A.[8] EMERY (*Thomas D.,*[7] *Nathaniel,*[6] *James,*[5] *Thomas,*[4] *James,*[3] *James,*[2] *Anthony*[1]), daughter of Thomas D. and Lucy Ann (Bunker) Emery; married Jan. 20, 1879, Edward H. Goldthwait of Biddeford, Me.

Child :

   3434 i   LILLIE EMERY,[9] b. Feb. 29, 1880.

1569 EMILY FRANCES[8] HILL (*Mary Abigail,*[7] *Nathaniel,*[6] *James,*[5] *Thomas,*[4] *James,*[3] *James,*[2] *Anthony*[1]), daughter of Samuel and Mary Abigail (Emery) Hill ; married Charles Babeuf (born in Boston, Mass., Dec. 25, 1848).

Child :

   3435 i   FLORENCE LOUISA,[9] b. Jan. 14, 1886.

1571 EDWIN EMERY[8] CAMPBELL (*Narcissa,*[7] *Nathaniel,*[6] *James,*[5] *Thomas,*[4] *James,*[3] *James,*[2] *Anthony*[1]), son of Anthony C. and Narcissa (Emery) Campbell; married Jan. 29, 1886, Cora Frances Bell (born in Boston, Mass., Oct. 1, 1860).

Child :

   3436 i   HERBERT EDWIN,[9] b. May 15, 1887, in Biddeford, Me.

1592 JAMES I.[8] EMERY (*Benj.,*[7] *Nathaniel,*[6] *Thomas,*[5] *Thomas,*[4] *James,*[3] *James,*[2] *Anthony*[1]), son of Benjamin and Mary (Davis) Emery ; married Aug. 17, 1847, in Abington, Mass., Clarinda C. Robbins (born Sept. 18, 1827). Resides in Boston, Mass.

Children :

   3437 i   HELEN C.,[9] b. July 5, 1850, in Abington, Mass.; m. Jan. 21,
               1871, Henry A. Owen.
   3438 ii   ANNIE N., b. July 19, 1853, in Abington, Mass.; m. Jan. 20,
               1877, Arthur R. Whitcomb.
   3439 iii SOPHRONIA, b. June 14, 1857, in Abington, Mass.
   3440 iv BETSEY F., b. Oct. 15, 1859, in Braintree, Mass.; d. Sept. 6,
               1860.
   3441 v   BENJ. F., b. Jan. 27, 1861, in Braintree, Mass.; d. Sept. 12,
               1861.
   3442 vi BENJ. B., b. March 12, 1863, in Braintree.
   3443 vii JAMES I.,   ⎫
                       ⎬ b. May 22, 1864, in Braintree, Mass.
   3444 viii JOSIAH D., ⎭

1593 Josiah D[5] Emery (*Benj.*,[7] *Nathaniel,*[6] *Thomas,*[5] *Thomas,*[4] *James,*[3] *James,*[2] *Anthony*[1]), son of Benjamin and Mary (Davis) Emery, married Susannah A. Tuttle of Abington, Mass., Nov. 17, 1848. Children.

    3445　i　William G.,[9] b. Aug 22, 1849, in Hartford, Me.
    3446　ii　Mary Davis, b Feb 10, 1855, in Stoughton, Mass , d Sept 11 1864
    3447　iii　Sarah I , b Jan 2, 1857, in Canton, Mass
    3448　iv　Wendall P , b Feb. 19, 1859
    3449　v　Electra b Feb 16, 1861, in Stoughton, Mass
    3450　vi　Lillian E , b June 12, 1863, in Stoughton, Mass
    3451　vii　Mary E , b July 1 1866, in Stoughton, Mass., m William S Cook, July 5, 1881

1594 Martha N[8] Emery (*Benj ,*[7] *Nathaniel,*[6] *Thomas,*[5] *Thomas,*[4] *James,*[3] *James,*[2] *Anthony*[1]), daughter of Benjamin and Mary (Davis) Emery; married Feb. 7, 1847, —— Spaulding of Buckfield, Me.
  Child :

    3452　i　Orlando H ,[9] b Feb 18, 1857.

1595 Mary J[8] Emery (*Benj ,*[7] *Nathaniel,*[6] *Thomas,*[5] *Thomas,*[4] *James,*[3] *James,*[2] *Anthony*[1]), daughter of Benj and Mary (Davis) Emery; married Oct. 8, 1854, Kimball N. Prince of Buckfield, Me.
  Child :

    3453　i　Leonard R ,[9] b. Dec 23, 1857, in New York.

1597 Elizabeth A[8] Emery (*Benj.*,[7] *Nathaniel,*[6] *Thomas,*[5] *Thomas,*[4] *James,*[3] *James,*[2] *Anthony*[1]), daughter of Benj. and Mary (Davis) Emery, married Nov. 17, 1853, Armstrong Gerrish of Sumner, Me.
  Children :

    3454　i　Lizzie Love,[9] b Nov. 4, 1855, m Dec 25, 1880, Preston L. Lathrop
    3455　ii　Charles A , b Dec 8, 1856, d. Sept. 29, 1875.
    3456　iii　Benj E , b Sept 9, 1863.
    3457　iv　John D b March 1, 1867
    3458　v　Martha S , b Sept 6, 1872, d Jan 1, 1874.

1599 Simeon[8] Hussey (*Dorcas,*[7] *Nathaniel,*[6] *Thomas,*[5] *Thomas*[4] *James,*[3] *James,*[2] *Anthony*[1]), son of James and Dorcas (Emery) Hussey, married, 1854, Roanna Farrar of Buckfield, Me.
  Children :

    3459　i　Edith,[9] d young
    3460　ii　Amy b 1866, m, June 9, 1887, Harry Kelso of Cincinnati, Ohio.
    3461　iii　Stacey, b 1870
    3462　iv　Maud, b 1873, d 1879.

1602 Caroline[8] Hussey (*Dorcas,*[7] *Nathaniel,*[6] *Thomas,*[5] *Thomas,*[4] *James,*[3] *James,*[2] *Anthony*[1]), daughter of James and Dorcas (Emery) Hussey ; married Nov. 30, 1856, Amial Jones of North Turner, Me.
  Children :

    3463　i　Carrie I ,[9] b. Sept. 10, 1857, m. William A. Seavy of Boston, Mass.

3464 ii HERMAN J., b. Oct. 23, 1869; m. Sept. 27, 1884, Susie Wentworth of Boston, Mass.
3465 iii GEORGE O., b. Aug. 1, 1873, in Lynnfield, Mass.
3466 iv JOHN P., b. May 21, 1875, in Medford, Mass.

1609 JENNIE N.[8] EMERY (*Theodore*,[7] *Nathaniel*,[6] *Thomas*,[5] *Thom-
as*,[4] *James*,[3] *James*,[2] *Anthony*[1]), daughter of Theodore and Charlotte
J. (Lombard) Emery; married in Harrison, Me., A. M. Bolster.
Children:

3467 i WALTER E.,[9] b. Jan. 2, 1870, in Harrison, Me.
3468 ii LOTTIE N., b. in Haverhill, Mass; d. Jan. 9, 1875.
3469 iii LOTTIE N., b. July 15, 1875, in Harrison, Me.
3470 iv LENA N., b. Oct. 17, 1881, in Brockton, Mass.; d. July 15,
1882.

1610 ADDIE M.[8] EMERY (*Theodore*,[7] *Nathaniel*,[6] *Thomas*,[5] *Thom-
as*,[4] *James*,[3] *James*,[2] *Anthony*[1]), daughter of Theodore and Charlotte
J. (Lombard) Emery; married in Otisfield, Me., —— Barker.
Child:

3470a i LAVIS, b. Sept. 19, 1876, in Portland, Me.

1611 WALTER L.[8] EMERY (*Theodore*,[7] *Nathaniel*,[6] *Thomas*,[5]
Thomas,[4] *James*,[3] *James*,[2] *Anthony*[1]), son of Theodore and Charlotte
J. (Lombard) Emery; married in Enfield, Mass., Dec. 25, 1874,
Hattie L. Foster.
Children:

3471 i LOTTIE M.,[9] b. April 21, 1876, in Haverhill, Mass.; d. Sept. 28,
1877, in Haverhill.
3472 ii ADDIE M., b. Feb. 27, 1878, in Haverhill, Mass.
3473 iii MAUD L., b. March 26, 1880, in Nelson, Neb.

1614 FRANK C.[8] EMERY (*Rufus*,[7] *Thomas*,[6] *Thomas*,[5] *Thomas*,[4]
James,[3] *James*,[2] *Anthony*[1]), son of Rufus and Sophia (Felch) Em-
ery); married in Portland, Me., May 25, 1851, Octavia C. Starbird.
Children:

3474 i HERBERT E.,[9] b. March 1, 1852.
3475 ii THOMAS S., b. April 5, 1855.
3476 iii HARRIET S., b. April 7, 1870.
3477 iv GRACIE O., b. Dec. 23, 1871.

1615 ISAAC[8] EMERY (*Rufus*,[7] *Thomas*,[6] *Thomas*,[5] *Thomas*,[4]
James,[3] *James*,[2] *Anthony*[1]), son of Rufus and Sophia (Felch) Em-
ery; married in Portland, Me., Dec. 20, 1862, Hattie S. Dyer.
Child:

3478 i HELEN S.,[9] b. Oct. 9, 1863.

1616 SARAH[8] EMERY (*Rufus*,[7] *Thomas*,[6] *Thomas*,[5] *Thomas*,[4]
James,[3] *James*,[2] *Anthony*[1]), daughter of Rufus and Sophia (Felch)
Emery; married April 13, 1856, Edward M. Berry. She died Sept.
24, 1861.
Child:

3479 i OCTAVIA,[9] b. Nov. 14, 1856; d. July 6, 1886.

1617 MARY[8] EMERY (*Rufus,*[7] *Thomas,*[6] *Thomas,*[5] *Thomas,*[4] *James,*[3] *James,*[2] *Anthony*[1]), daughter of Rufus and Sophia (Felch) Emery, married Oct 6, 1878, Joseph B. Sherman.
Child.

3480 i GRACIE H,[9] b Nov 19, 1879

1618 ALPHEUS[8] EMERY (*Rufus,*[7] *Thomas,*[6] *Thomas,*[5] *Thomas,*[4] *James,*[3] *James,*[2] *Anthony*[1]), son of Rufus and Sophia (Felch) Emery; married Dec. 18, 1869, Mary E. Smith.
Children:

3481 i HARRY,[9] b Jan 23, 1872
3482 ii ANNIE L., b. March 16, 1879

1620 MARY JANE[8] STEELE (*Hannah,*[7] *Thomas,*[6] *Thomas,*[5] *Thomas,*[4] *James,*[3] *James,*[2] *Anthony*[1]), daughter of Richard and Hannah (Emery) Steele, married Dec 6, 1843, Samuel W Johnston (died Nov 15, 1857) Both were buried on the same day.
Children.

3483 i PAMELIA B,[9] b. Sept 8 1845.
3484 ii MARCIA E, b May 21, 1848
3485 iii HARRIET M, b Dec 6, 1850
3486 iv RUFUS M, b Oct 1, 1853

1621 ELIZABETH[8] STEELE (*Hannah,*[7] *Thomas,*[6] *Thomas,*[5] *Thomas,*[4] *James,*[3] *James,*[2] *Anthony*[1]), daughter of Richard and Hannah (Emery) Steele; married Dec. 9, 1856, John C. Dearborn.
Children

3487 i JOSEPH H,[9] b Oct 22, 1857
3488 ii JOHN C, b Aug 14, 1859
3489 iii SON, b Dec. 5, 1861, d Dec 6, 1861
3490 iv MILLARD, b Feb 13, 1863.

1624 THOMAS[8] BRADBURY (*Mary,*[7] *Thomas,*[6] *Thomas,*[5] *Thomas,*[4] *James,*[3] *James,*[2] *Anthony*[1]), son of John and Mary (Emery) Bradbury, married July 12, 1858, Angelett Elwell.
Children ·

3491 i FRED C[9] b Dec 24, 1859
3492 ii JENNIE, b April 12, 1862
3493 iii GEORGIE, b May 6, 1864

1625 CHARLES H.[8] BRADBURY (*Mary,*[7] *Thomas,*[6] *Thomas,*[5] *Thomas,*[4] *James,*[3] *James,*[2] *Anthony*[1]), son of John and Mary (Emery) Bradbury; married Oct. 19, 1856, Caroline E Peabody.
Children

3494 i HATTIE C,[9] b Feb 10, 1858
3495 ii ELLA E, b Dec 23, 1861
3496 iii JENNIE A, b Sept. 18, 1870.

1626 MARY E.[8] BRADBURY (*Mary,*[7] *Thomas,*[6] *Thomas,*[5] *Thomas,*[4] *James,*[3] *James,*[2] *Anthony*[1]), daughter of John and Mary (Emery) Bradbury, married Albert Sawyer, July 12, 1867.

Children :

3497   i   GEORGE M.,[9] b. Feb. 18, 1868.
3498   ii   CARRIE M., b. June 3, 1879.

1627 ELIZABETH D.[8] EMERY (*Thomas J.,*[7] *Thomas,*[6] *Thomas,*[5] *Thomas,*[4] *James,*[3] *James,*[2] *Anthony*[1]), daughter of Thomas J. and Mary Ann (Cobb) Emery; married in Boston, Mass., July 5, 1871, W. H. Dow.

Child :

3499   i   HATTIE J.[9]

1630 JAMES K.[8] EMERY (*James W.,*[7] *Thomas,*[6] *Thomas,*[5] *Thomas,*[4] *James,*[3] *James,*[2] *Anthony*[1]), son of James W. and Abigail E. (Wood) Emery; married June 7, 1860, Olive Maria Goodwin (born Aug. 16, 1836).

Child :

3500   i   ALICE CHASE,[9] b. April 9, 1862, in Standish, Me.; m. Geo. C. Bearse, Oct. 17, 1883.

1631 GEORGE H.[8] EMERY (*James W.,*[7] *Thomas,*[6] *Thomas,*[5] *Thomas,*[4] *James,*[3] *James,*[2] *Anthony*[1]), son of James W. and Abigail E. (Wood) Emery; married Feb. 4, 1860, Georgiana Walker Smith (born Jan. 24, 1840). Resides in Lexington, Mass.

Children, born in Portland, Me. :

3501   i   EVERETT STEVENS,[9] b. Oct. 22, 1861.
3502   ii   FRED. LINCOLN, b. May 5, 1867.
3503   iii NELLIE MAY, b. Oct. 20, 1869; d. April 28, 1872, in Lexington, Mass.

1632 THOMAS DILL[8] EMERY (*James W.,*[7] *Thomas,*[6] *Thomas,*[5] *Thomas,*[4] *James,*[3] *James,*[2] *Anthony*[1]), son of James W. and Abigail E. (Wood) Emery; married, first, Sept. 22, 1866, Sarah E. Harmon (born Oct. 26, 1844; died April 9, 1881); second, May 31, 1882, Nellie Giddings. Resides in Harrison, Me. Manufacturer of clothing.

Child :

3504   i   HARRY HARMON, b. Feb. 17, 1867.

1636 JULIA A.[8] EMERY (*Horace,*[7] *Thomas,*[6] *Thomas,*[5] *Thomas,*[4] *James,*[3] *James,*[2] *Anthony*[1]), daughter of Horace and Sarah (Davis) Emery; married March 11, 1860, Robert P. Jewett.

Children :

3505   i   EUGENE S.,[9] b. Dec. 12, 1860.
3506   ii   CHARLES M., b. July 3, 1864.
3507   iii SARAH, b. June 25, 1872.
3508   iv   GEORGE, b. Oct. 18, 1877; d. April 20, 1879.
3509   v   HARRY S., b. March 20, 1881; d. Nov. 21, 1882.

1638 HATTIE A.[8] EMERY (*Horace,*[7] *Thomas,*[6] *Thomas,*[5] *Thomas,*[4] *James,*[3] *James,*[2] *Anthony*[1]), daughter of Horace and Sarah (Davis) Emery; married Nov. 26, 1872, Joseph H. Bradbury.

Childien:

3510 i NELSON H ,[9] b Sept 2. 1874.
3511 ii HARRY, b Aug. 24, 1883.

1639 WILLIAM F.[8] EMERY (*Horace,*[7] *Thomas,*[6] *Thomas,*[5] *Thomas,*[4] *James,*[3] *James,*[2] *Anthony*[1]). son of Horace and Sarah (Davis) Emery; married Jan 31, 1875, Melvina Smith
   Childien

3512 i ERNEST H ,[9] b Dec 6, 1876
3513 ii GEORGE M , b. June 26, 1880

1641 CHARLES E [8] EMERY(*Alex J ,*[7] *Thomas,*[6] *Thomas,*[5] *Thomas,*[4] *James,*[3] *James,*[2] *Anthony*[1]), son of Alex. J and Eliza (Steele) Emery; married Sept. 12, 1858, Elizabeth J. Buzzell. Reside in Buxton, Me
   Children, born in Buxton Centre, Me. :

3514 i CLARA L ,[9] b. Oct 15. 1859
3515 ii JENNIE A , b. Aug 21, 1861.
3516 iii JOHN H , b Oct 13, 1863
3517 iv MARK W , b Oct 25, 1865
3518 v M LILLIAN, b April 12, 1869.
3519 vi CARL S., b June 3, 1871
3520 vii MABEL A , b May 25, 1874.

1645 MARCIA S [8] EMERY (*Alex. J.,*[7] *Thomas,*[6] *Thomas,*[5] *Thomas,*[4] *James,*[3] *James,*[2] *Anthony*[1]), daughter of Alex. J and Eliza (Steele) Emery, married Nov. 10, 1868, F. Howard Hill.
   Childien :

3521 i ELMER H [9] b June 3, 1871
3522 ii MARY E , b Oct 10, 1872
3523 iii ANNIE M , b Dec 18, 1874
3524 iv HERBERT S., b. July 24, 1883.

1652 MARY E [8] DUNNELL (*Harriet F B.,*[7] *Thomas,*[6] *Thomas,*[5] *Thomas,*[4] *James,*[3] *James,*[2] *Anthony*[1]), daughter of Joseph and Harriet F. B. (Emery) Dunnell, married, first. June 26, 1878, Lewis H. C. Warren; second, Feb. 5, 1883, Albert H. Small.
   Childien :

3525 i MILDRED A ,[9] b May 4, 1879
3526 ii HENRY F , b. April 16, 1880.

Child, by second marriage :

3527 iii JOSEPH DUNNELL, b Oct 14, 1885

1671 JOSEPHINE EMERY[8] COOKE (*Mary L ,*[7] *John,*[6] *Thomas,*[5] *Thomas,*[4] *James,*[3] *James,*[2] *Anthony*[1]), daughter of Rev. Edward and Mary L. (Emery) Cooke; married in Boston, Mass., Sept. 19, 1864, Albert R. Dyer. Reside in Denver, Col.
   Childien ·

3528 i GEORGE E ,[9] b Feb 22, 1870, in Wilbraham, Mass.
3529 ii MAUD C., b. June 30, 1876, in Denver, Col.

1674 ELLEN FRANCES[8] EMERY (*Stephen L.,*[7] *John,*[6] *Thomas,*[5] *Thomas,*[4] *James,*[3] *James,*[2] *Anthony*[1]), daughter of Stephen L. and Clara (Gilman) Emery; married Oct. 20, 1870, Charles H. Reed of Boston, Mass. He was killed by falling down a hatchway July 31, 1882.

Children, born in Boston, Mass.:

3530 i CHARLES CUSHING,[9] b. June 29, 1873; d. Aug. 12, 1874.
3531 ii CLARA ELEANOR, b. Sept. 16, 1875.
3532 iii GEORGE STANLEY, b. Dec. 11, 1881.

1678 FRANK EMERY[8] HOBBS (*Susan H.,*[7] *John,*[6] *Thomas,*[5] *Thomas,*[4] *James,*[3] *James,*[2] *Anthony*[1]), son of Thomas J. and Susan H. (Emery) Hobbs; married Oct., 1883, Lydia Seaman Banks. Graduate of West Point; now first lieutenant in ordnance department, U. S. A.

Child:

3533 i ELEANOR MILDRED.[9]

1683 SUSAN H.[8] ROBINSON (*Almira,*[7] *Joseph D.,*[6] *Thomas,*[5] *Thomas,*[4] *James,*[3] *James,*[2] *Anthony*[1]), daughter of George and Almira (Emery) Robinson; married Oct. 27, 1857, Hon. John Noble Goodwin of South Berwick, Me. He graduated from Dartmouth College, 1844; representative to Congress, 1851–1852; governor of Arizona, 1860–1864; member of Congress, 1865–1866; lawyer.

Children:

3534 i SUSIE ROBINSON,[9] b. July 12, 1858.
3535 ii RICHARD EMERY, b. July 24, 1861.
3536 iii HOWARD ROBINSON, b. Nov. 10, 1863.

1685 ABBIE EMERY[8] RICE (*Almira,*[7] *Joseph D.,*[6] *Thomas,*[5] *Thomas,*[4] *James,*[3] *James,*[2] *Anthony*[1]), daughter of Hon. Richard Drury and Mrs. Almira (Emery-Robinson) Rice; married Sept. 17, 1863, Col. Samuel Dana, U. S. A.; died in San Francisco, Cal., Feb. 12, 1868.

Children:

3537 i ELSIE WINCHESTER,[9] b. July 5, 1864, in Augusta, Me.
3538 ii GEORGE MURRAY, b. Nov. 10, 1867, in San Francisco, Cal.

1697 WILLIAM S.[8] BADGER (*Susan A.,*[7] *Jos. D.,*[6] *Thomas,*[5] *Thomas,*[4] *James,*[3] *James,*[2] *Anthony*[1]), son of William S. and Susan A. (Emery) Badger; married Jan. 2, 1870, Mary A. Dickenson of Detroit, Kansas.

Children:

3539 i JOSEPH EMERY,[9] b. Oct. 28, 1872.
3540 ii MARY DICKENSON, b. Oct. 12, 1873; d. April 5, 1877.
3541 iii WILLIAM S., b. Nov., 1875.
3542 iv DAUGHTER, } b. Dec. 21, 1879.
3543 v DAUGHTER, }

1713 MARY H.[8] EMERY (*Wm. H.,*[7] *Isaac,*[6] *Thomas,*[5] *Thomas,*[4] *James,*[3] *James,*[2] *Anthony*[1]), daughter of William H. and Sarah R. (Haviland) Emery; married Feb. 1, 1876, John H. Brocklesby of Hartford, Conn.

Child :

3544 i   PHILIP HAVILAND,[9] b Feb 14, 1881.

1723 SARAH EILEN[8] CLIFFORD (*Almira S ,[7] Peter,[6] Thomas,[5] Thomas,[4] James,[3] James,[2] Anthony[1]*), daughter of Israel and Almira S. (Emery) Clifford, married Dec. 21, 1880, Daniel A. Hamilton.
Children :

3545 i   EMILY M ,[9] b March 16, 1882, d March 20, 1882
3546 ii EMILY E , b March 23, 1883

1726 SUSAN E [8] BOOTHBY (*Sallie J ,[7] Peter,[6] Thomas,[5] Thomas,[4] James,[3] James,[2] Anthony[1]*), daughter of Arthur and Sallie J (Emery) Boothby, married Jan 4, 1881, Dr. Walter H. Dinsmore, graduate of Bowdoin Medical College.
Child :

3547 i   MARION BOOTHBY,[9] b April 28, 1882.

1735 EMILY A [8] EMERY (*David,[7] Zachariah,[6] Zachariah,[5] Zachariah,[4] Zachariah,[3] James,[2] Anthony[1]*), daughter of David and Polly (Corbet) Emery; married Dec. 5, 1824, Benjamin Cushman (born June 17, 1791) Resides in Hamilton, N. Y.
Children ·

3548 i   ARVILLA E ,[9] b Sept 11, 1825 , m L F. Fay of Earlville, N Y , 1844
3549 ii DELIA ANN, b May 20, 1829
3550 iii EMERY D , b Oct 20, 1831.
3551 iv HERBERT BENJAMIN, b March 21, 1835.
3552 v CAROLINE E , b Feb 23, 1839
3553 vi LETITIA J , b Sept. 20, 1841

1745 SAMUEL LEEMAN[8] EMERY (*Samuel,[7] Zachariah,[6] Zachariah,[5] Zachariah,[4] Zachariah,[3] James,[2] Anthony[1]*), son of Samuel and Nancy (Gardner) Emery, married Dec 1, 1842, Caroline Lucina Powell (born Aug 16, 1822, in Lebanon, N. Y.; died Jan. 31, 1878). Resides in Chesterville, Ohio.
Children .

3554 i   HOMER POWELL,[9] b Oct 16, 1846, in Lincoln, Ohio
3555 ii EUNICE NANCY, b Dec 24, 1854, in Franklin, Ohio

1746 CLEMENTINA[8] EMERY (*Samuel,[7] Zachariah,[6] Zachariah,[5] Zachariah,[4] Zachariah,[3] James,[2] Anthony[1]*), daughter of Samuel and Nancy (Gardner) Emery, married June 4, 1835. Jabez Wood (born June 8, 1811).
Children ·

3556 i   EMILY MERILLA,[9] b June 12, 1836, m May 5, 1871, David Spear
3557 ii MARIA SUSANNAH, b Jan 29, 1838; d March 17, 1838
3558 iii WILLIAM HARRISON, b March 25, 1839, m March 22, 1871, Mary Ellen Gooley
3559 iv LUCY RICE, b Sept 6, 1841, d Nov 24, 1867
3560 v JAMES MADISON, b Aug 17, 1844, m Dec. 26, 1866, Elizabeth Stovenour.

30

3561   vi   GEORGE ORESTES, b. April 24, 1848, m. Nov. 6, 1870, Emily M
                Sands
3562   vii   WALTER, b July 27, 1854, d April 27, 1855
3563   viii NANCY CAROLINE, b Nov 14, 1857

1747 HOMER CHARLES[8] EMERY (*Samuel,*[7] *Zachariah,*[6] *Zachariah,*[5]
Zachariah,[4] *Zachariah,*[3] *James,*[2] *Anthony*[1]), son of Samuel and Nancy
(Gardner) Emery ; married Nov. 2, 1841, Mary Ann Waters (born
in Virginia, Aug. 29, 1823 ; died Sept. 10, 1889).
  Children :

3564   i   SARAH LOUISA,[9] b. Jan. 9, 1843; d. Dec 25, 1848, in Lincoln,
          Ohio
3565   ii   NANCY JANE, b. Jan 14, 1848; d Jan 24, 1851, in Lenana Co ,
          Mich
3566   iii LUCY FIDELIA, b July 13, 1851 , m Dec 16, 1868, Henry Run-
          yan of Vienna, Kan (b April, 1841).
3567   iv LUCRETIA CAROLINE, b Feb. 5, 1853
3568   v   MARY ANGELINA, b Nov 19, 1854.
3569   vi CLEMENTINA W , b Feb 5, 1857.
3570   vii FRANCIS M., b June 1, 1859.
3571   viii HORACE, b. June 6 1864, and d the same day in Jackson,
          Kansas

1749 ABEL GARDNER[8] EMERY (*Samuel,*[7] *Zachariah,*[6] *Zachariah,*[5]
Zachariah,[4] *Zachariah,*[3] *James,*[2] *Anthony*[1]), son of Samuel and Nancy
(Gardner) Emery , married Elsie Minerva Bates (born Jan. 31, 1826,
near Batavia, N. Y). Resides in Lincoln, Ohio.
  Children ·

3572   i   FRANCELIA,[9] b Feb 5, 1859
3573   ii   IDELLA, b Aug 26, 1860

1752 HORACE L.[8] EMERY (*Horace,*[7] *Zachariah,*[6] *Zachariah,*[5] *Zachariah,*[4] *Zachariah,*[3] *James,*[2] *Anthony*[1]), son of Horace and Sally
(Beardsley) Emery ; married Frances M Wood. Resides in Cleveland, O.
  Children :

3574   i   JOSEPHINE M ,[9] b 1846, m. Grenville W. Wilson (b 1846).
3575   ii   HORACE HERBERT
3576   iii CHARLES A , b. Aug , 1850.
3577   iv GEORGE W , b Nov , 1852.

1753 WILLIAM B.[8] EMERY (*Horace,*[7] *Zachariah,*[6] *Zachariah,*[5] *Zachariah,*[4] *Zachariah,*[3] *James,*[2] *Anthony*[1]), son of Horace and Sally
(Beardsley) Emery ; married, first, Nov., 1850, Mary Conant (died
s. p.) ; second, June 30, 1863, Miriam Lansing (born Sept. 1, 1833,
in Glen, N. Y.). Resides in Albany, N. Y. Engraver.
  Children, by second marriage :

3578   i   MARSHALL L ,[9] b March 19, 1866
3579   ii   HENRY GEORGE, b July 17, 1870.
3580   iii MIRIAM ANNA, b. March 23, 1880.

1754 HENRY D.[8] EMERY (*Horace.*[7] *Zachariah,*[6] *Zachariah,*[5] *Zachariah,*[4] *Zachariah,*[3] *James,*[2] *Anthony*[1]), son of Horace and Sally

(Beardsley) Emery; married, April 3, 1851, Freelove W. Johnson. He was vice president of the board of agriculture. Resides in Chicago, Ill.

Child:

    3581 1   ADELIA C.,[9] b Feb 28, 1854, m. June 20, 1878, William E Langley.

1756 GEORGE W.[8] EMERY (*Horace,*[7] *Zachariah,*[6] *Zachariah,*[5] *Zachariah,*[4] *Zachariah,*[3] *James,*[2] *Anthony*[1]), son of Horace and Sally (Beardsley) Emery; married April, 1861, Lizzy Storer.

Child:

    3582 1   WILLIAM,[9] b March, 1867

1757 ALBERT T [8] EMERY (*Horace,*[7] *Zachariah,*[6] *Zachariah,*[5] *Zachariah,*[4] *Zachariah,*[3] *James,*[2] *Anthony*[1]), son of Horace and Sally (Beardsley) Emery; married, first, 1861, Alice Hepinstall (died March 31, 1862); second, March 18, 1863, Adele DeLaynes. Lives in Chicago

Children:

    3583 i   MARY ALICE,[9] b Feb., 1862, d young.

By second marriage:

    3584 ii   ADELE M , b Nov 8, 1864
    3585 iii THEODORE B , b Aug 6, 1866.
    3586 iv GEORGE D , b Sept 28, 1870.

1765 DAVID ELLIOT[8] EMERY (*Amos,*[7] *Amos,*[6] *Zachariah,*[5] *Zachariah,*[4] *Zachariah,*[3] *James,*[2] *Anthony*[1]), son of Amos and Hannah (Elliot) Emery, married Sept. 14, 1829, in Windham, Vt , Sophia Burnap, died in York, Wis , June 10, 1854.

Children, born in New York City ·

    3587 1   ELVIRA ANN,[9] b Sept 30, 1830, d July 14, 1831
    3588 ii   MARY ANN, b March 8, 1832, m Oct. 30, 1851, Abner Petty, of Waterloo, Wis
    3589 iii LEVI, b May 18, 1834
    3590 iv JULIA, b Aug. 7, 1836, m. Jan 25, 1855, Jeremiah Baldwin, d in Columbus. Wis , March 13, 1857
    3591 v   EMMA SOPHIA, b Nov 11, 1837; d Sept 29, 1839
    3592 vi EMILY CORNELIA, b Oct 4, 1842, in Lake Mills, Wis ; m Jan 16, 1861, William Harrison Cole, of Beaver Dam, Wis.

1766 EUNICE ADAMS[8] EMERY (*Amos,*[7] *Amos,*[6] *Zachariah,*[5] *Zachariah,*[4] *Zachariah,*[3] *James,*[2] *Anthony*[1]), daughter of Amos and Hannah (Elliot) Emery, married Oct. 11, 1827, Gardner Upham.

Children:

    3593 1   JAMES H ,[9] b June 5, 1828, d July 17, 1856
    3594 ii   FRANCINA M , b. Dec 21, 1831.
    3595 iii HANNAH E., b. Dec 15, 1833.
    3595a iv SOPHIA M , b Mar 30, 1836
    3596 v   MARIA A , b June 11, 1838, d. Oct 19, 1853.
    3597 vi EUGENIA E , b March 4, 1843
    3598 vii EDWARD Y., b. Aug. 28, 1846; d. Nov 11, 1846.

1771 ELVIRA[8] EMERY (*Amos,*[7] *Amos,*[6] *Zachariah,*[5] *Zachariah,*[4] *Zachariah,*[3] *James,*[2] *Anthony*[1]), daughter of Amos and Hannah (Elliot) Emery ; married, first, Sept. 12, 1833, Henry Harris (died June 9, 1840) , second, Dec. 25, 1845, Jason D. Jones (died Dec. 11, 1882)   Lives in Windham, Vt.

Child, by second marriage :

   3599 1   EMERY H ,[9] b Aug 11, 1848, graduate of Dartmouth Coll.
                1878; entered Union Theo Sem ; left on account of ill health.

1774 LUCRETIA[8] EMERY (*Amos,*[7] *Amos,*[6] *Zachariah,*[5] *Zachariah,*[4] *Zachariah,*[3] *James,*[2] *Anthony*[1]), daughter of Amos and Hannah (Elliot) Emery ; married May 10, 1838, Clark Stearns. Resides in Windham, Vt

Children :

   3600 1   JAMES ADELBERT,[9] b April 28, 1841.
   3601 11   JANE ANGELINE, b April 18, 1844
   3602 111 AUGUSTUS CLARK, b Dec 3, 1847.
   3603 1v MARY EUNICE, b May 6, 1852.

1775 AZRO[8] EMERY (*Amos,*[7] *Amos,*[6] *Zachariah,*[5] *Zachariah,*[4] *Zachariah,*[3] *James,*[2] *Anthony*[1]), son of Amos and Hannah (Elliot) Emery , married, first, Nov 16, 1848, at Steubenville. Mo., Martha C. Hamilton (died Jan. 6, 1855) ; second, June 5, 1856, Mrs. Teresa M. Fisher

Children, by first marriage ·

   3604 1   HANNAH JANE,[9] b Dec 16, 1849.
   3605 11 AZRO F H., b. Nov. 19, 1852.

By second marriage :

   3606 111 HENRIETTA M , b Dec 1, 1857
   3607 1v DELLA T , b Dec 10, 1859
   3608 v   EUGENIA E , b Feb 20, 1862
   3609 v1 H EVERETT, b Dec 30, 1864.
   3610 v11 EMMETT, b Dec 3, 1870

1776 HENRY EVERETT[8] EMERY (*Amos,*[7] *Amos,*[6] *Zachariah,*[5] *Zachariah,*[4] *Zachariah,*[3] *James,*[2] *Anthony*[1]), son of Amos and Hannah (Elliot) Emery ; married Nov. 25, 1845, in Londonderry, Vt., Urania Putnam (born April 21, 1824).

Children :

   3611 1   ALBEN HENRY,[9] b Nov 3, 1847
   3612 11 OBED EVERETT, b Oct 17, 1849, d March 19, 1850.
   3613 111 URANIA, b and d March 6, 1854
   3614 1v EUGENE ELLIOT, b Aug 26, 1856, m Dec 28, 1882, Sadie Ray
              at St Louis, Mo
   3615 v   AMOS ABEL, b Sept. 28, 1859, d Nov 29, 1859
   3616 v1 CLARENCE ALBERT, b June 24, 1861, d June 3, 1870
   3617 v11 JOSEPHINE, b April 18, 1863, m Sept 19, 1882, at St Louis,
              Jacob Story

1785 MARY ANN[8] BUSS (*Lucy,*[7] *Amos,*[6] *Zachariah,*[5] *Zachariah,*[4] *Zachariah,*[3] *James,*[2] *Anthony*[1]), daughter of Samuel and Lucy (Em-

er)) Buss; married June 3, 1846, Deacon Liberty Mower (his second wife) husband of her sister Emily (see No 1779).
Children·

    3618   i   ELLEN E ,⁹ b May 16, 1847
    3919   ii   SAMUEL II., b. July 31, 1849.
    3620   iii WILLIAM J., b June 23, 1855.

1787 CAROLINE⁸ PERRY (*Esther,*⁷ *Amos,*⁶ *Zachariah,*⁵ *Zachariah,*⁴ *Zachariah,*³ *James,*² *Anthony*¹). daughter of John and Esther (Emery) Perry; married Dec 27, 1826 (as his second wife) John Snow, Esq., of Dublin, N H (died Jan. 28, 1841)
Children.

    3621   i   HARRIET LOUISA,⁹ b Aug 8, 1830
    3622   ii   ELBRIDGE, b March 17, 1835

1789 LUCRETIA E⁸ PERRY (*Esther,*⁷ *Amos,*⁶ *Zachariah,*⁵ *Zachariah,*⁴ *Zachariah,*³ *James,*² *Anthony*¹), daughter of John and Esther (Emery) Perry; married Oct. 16, 1833, Calmer Harris.
Child

    3623   i   ENRICO.⁹

1802 ISAAC⁸ SPALDING (*Lucy,*⁷ *John,*⁶ *Zachariah,*⁵ *Zachariah,*⁴ *Zachariah,*³ *James,*² *Anthony*¹), son of Isaac and Lucy (Emery) Spalding; married, first, Elmira Kibling of Chester, Vt. (died July 29, 1838); second, Oct. 24, 1839, Cynthia A. Matthews of Pittsburgh, Pa. Lives in Harmar, Ohio.
Children, by his second marriage:

    3624   i   ELMIRA,⁹ b July 24, 1840; m June 1, 1880, John A. Liversay
    3625   ii   CYNTHIA M , b Nov 26, 1842, d June 28, 1845.
    3626   iii   OSCAR, b Jan 16, 1845, d June 17, 1847.
    3627   iv   HANNAH NEWTON, b Jan 30, 1847, d Jan 3, 1848
    3628   v   ISAAC EMERY, b Nov 12, 1848; d April 24 1852
    3629   vi   ABBIE BARBOUR, b July 1, 1850, m July 25, 1857, Alex Selkirk Hale of Harmar, O
    3630   vii   MAY, b May 6, 1852.
    3631   viii ELLA, b Feb 22 1854; m June 23, 1870, Charles W. Jenny
    3632   ix   SARAH, b Nov. 28, 1855.
    3633   x   ISAAC, b Sept 11, 1857

1803 JOHN⁸ SPALDING (*Lucy,*⁷ *John* ⁶ *Zachariah,*⁵ *Zachariah,*⁴ *Zachariah.*³ *James,*² *Anthony*¹), son of Isaac and Lucy (Emery) Spalding; married Dec 12, 1832, Permelia Wright; died at Townsend. Mass , 1882.
Children:

    3634   i   MARTHA ANN,⁹ b July 4, 1833, m. Nov 13, 1858, Washlngton Bartlett of Lowell, Mass
    3635   ii   HARRIET ELIZABETH, b Feb 20, 1838, m April 29, 1863, Geo. Parker of Pepperell, Mass
    3636   iii   ABBIE, b June 6, 1841, d Nov 16, 1841
    3637   iv   SIMON DOLVER, b Aug 24, 1844
    3638   v   MARSHALL DE RAY, b Feb 28, 1846
    3639   vi   FRANCIS WELLINGTON, b. June 20, 1853.

1805 Daniel[8] Spalding (*Lucy,[7] John,[6] Zachariah,[5] Zachariah,[4] Zachariah,[3] James,[2] Anthony[1]*), son of Isaac and Lucy (Emery) Spalding ; married Oct., 1837, Lucy W. Clement of Townsend, Mass. Resides in Townsend, Mass.

Children :

    3640   i   Hannah Clement,[9] b. Nov. 11, 1848.
    3641   ii   Randall, b. Feb. 8, 1845.
    3642   iii Wayland, b. Sept. 26, 1850.
    3643   iv   Nancy A., b. Aug. 15, 1851 ; d. Jan. 30, 1852.

1807 Dr. Miles[8] Spalding (*Lucy,[7] John,[6] Zachariah,[5] Zachariah,[4] Zachariah,[3] James,[2] Anthony[1]*), son of Isaac and Lucy (Emery) Spalding ; married, first, Jan. 12, 1848, Sophia Louisa Miller of New Haven, Conn. (died Oct. 4, 1852) ; second, Aug. 27, 1863, Mary Mehitable Stickney. Resides in Groton, Mass.

Child :

    3644   1   Son,[9] b. and d. Oct. 2, 1852.

1814 Charles[8] Emery (*Joel,[7] John,[6] Zachariah,[5] Zachariah,[4] Zachariah,[3] James,[2] Anthony[1]*), son of Joel and Mary (Sylvester) Emery ; married July 2, 1846, Amanda M. Wolcot. He was postmaster at Townsend Harbor, Mass., 1843–50 ; 1855 to present time.

Children :

    3645   i   Amy M ,[9] } b. Oct. 9, 1862 ; { d. Feb. 23, 1863.
    3646   ii   Charles H., }   { d. Oct. 17, 1879.

1817 Charles W.[8] Emery (*Ezra,[7] John,[6] Zachariah,[5] Zachariah,[4] Zachariah,[3] James,[2] Anthony[1]*), son of Ezra and Sally (Warner) Emery ; married in Boston, Mass., Jan. 27, 1855, Jane Lebroke (died Aug. 9, 1862). He died March 4, 1871.

Child :

    3647   i   Ezra W.,[9] b. 1860.

1829 Stephen Emery[8] Knight (*Esther,[7] Samuel,[6] Zachariah,[5] Zachariah,[4] Zachariah,[3] James,[2] Anthony[1]*), son of Stephen and Esther (Emery) Knight ; married, first, Sept. 24, 1850, Sarah A. Moores of Jaffrey, N. H. (died Sept. 27, 1855) ; second, Dec. 8, 1859, Elmira B. Baldwin of Mason, N. H. (died 1861) ; third, May 8, 1864, Mrs. Lucy A. Adams of Jaffrey, N. H. Lives in W. Gardner, Mass.

Child, by first marriage :

    3648   i   Ida R.,[9] b. March 4, 1855 ; m. Aug. 10, 1875, William W. Buel,
                of Lyons, Iowa.

By third marriage :

    3649   ii   Flora, b. 1866.

1830 Esther Rosanna[8] Knight (*Esther,[7] Samuel,[6] Zachariah,[5] Zachariah,[4] Zachariah,[3] James,[2] Anthony[1]*), daughter of Stephen and Esther (Emery) Knight ; married Nov. 6, 1856, J. Minot Howe of South Gardner, Mass.

Child:

3650 i   EDITH M.,[9] b Jan 7, 1859, res in Gardner, Mass

1833 MARY L.[8] EMERY (*Samuel*,[7] *Samuel*,[6] *Zachariah*,[5] *Zachariah*,[4] *Zachariah*,[3] *James*,[2] *Anthony*[1]), daughter of Samuel and Mary (Bailey) Emery; married Sept 28, 1847, Samuel Bent (died Aug. 10, 1883). He was a chair manufacturer in South Gardner, Mass.
Children:

3651 i   ELIZABETH ESTELLE,[9] b. Nov 23, 1858, m Franklin Eaton
3652 ii   CHARLES LESLIE, b Oct 23 1860; m ——— Eaton.
3653 iii   ADDIE MABEL, b. Jan. 3, 1868

1844 MARY R [8] EMERY (*Zachariah*,[7] *William*,[6] *Zachariah*,[5] *Zachariah*,[4] *Zachariah*,[3] *James*,[2] *Anthony*[1]), daughter of Zachariah and Rebecca (Mower) Emery, married Sylvester B Lawrence of Jaffrey, N H (died in Hudson, Mich., Jan. 3, 1869) She died April 27, 1863.
Children, born in Jaffrey:

3654 i   HENRY SYLVESTER,[9] b Jan 24, 1840, d. May 6, 1863 from wounds received at Fredericksburgh Va , May 4 1863
3655 ii   ALBERT JEWELL, b. Sept 4, 1841, res. in Hudson, Mich
3656 iii   CALVIN ADOLPHUS, b July 31 1843; m Sept 6, 1882, Lizzy J Kingsley
3657 iv   CHARLES ZACHARIAH b June 26, 1845
3658 v   LOREN ARTEMAS, b Feb 5, 1847
3659 vi   CLARA ELIZABLTH, b Feb 3, 1849
3660 vii   SIDNEY EMERY, b March 30, 1851, res. in Hudson, Mich.
3661 viii   EFFIE BENJAMIN, b May 20, 1853
3662 ix   MARY REBECCA, b. Nov 7, 1856

1845 SARAH E [8] EMERY (*Zachariah*,[7] *William*,[6] *Zachariah*,[5] *Zachariah*,[4] *Zachariah*,[3] *James*,[2] *Anthony*[1]), daughter of Zachariah and Rebecca (Mower) Emery, married John J Lawrence (died in Jaffrey, N. H., April 9, 1876), brother of Sylvester B Lawrence; removed to Hudson, Mich. He died April 9, 1876, in Jaffrey, N H.
Children:

3663 i   CLARA E ,[9] b 1847
3664 ii   ELLA F , m Albert A French, Jan 31, 1872.
3665 iii   FREDERICK J , m. Clara A Cutler , have one child

1846 ALVIN J [8] BEMIS (*Sybil*,[7] *William*,[6] *Zachariah*,[5] *Zachariah*,[4] *Zachariah*,[3] *James*,[2] *Anthony*[1]), son of Josiah and Sybil (Emery) Bemis , married Mary Greenwood of Marlboro, N. H.
Child

3666 i   EMILY S ,[9] b 1854, res East Jaffrey, N H.

1848 HENRY W.[8] EMERY (*Ralph*,[7] *William*,[6] *Zachariah*,[5] *Zachariah*,[4] *Zachariah*,[3] *James*,[2] *Anthony*[1]), son of Ralph and Susan (Williams) Emery , married, first, Oct. 8, 1852, Mary L Miner (born Mar. 16, 1833 ; died Sept. 10, 1856) , second, Caroline E Robbins, June 2, 1857, daughter of Daniel L and Elizabeth (Emery) Robbins.

Children :

3667   i   GEORGE W.,[9] b. March 24, 1855.

By second marriage :

3668   ii   EUGENE W., b. Sept. 9, 1866; d. Sept. 3, 1867.
3669   iii   LULA MAZOLA, b. Oct. 21, 1874.

1849 CHARLES F.[8] EMERY (*Ralph*,[7] *William*,[6] *Zachariah*,[5] *Zachariah*,[4] *Zachariah*,[3] *James*,[2] *Anthony*[1]), son of Ralph and Susan (Williams) Emery ; married, first, Sept. 1, 1861, Caroline A. Spofford of Peterboro, N. H. (born Sept. 7, 1831 ; died Dec. 22, 1868) ; second, ————————.

Children, by first marriage :

3670   i   FRED C.,[9] b. Oct. 6, 1862; unm.
3671   ii   MINNIE C., b. Sept. 12, 1868.

1851 AMOS E.[8] EMERY (*Ralph*,[7] *William*,[6] *Zachariah*,[5] *Zachariah*,[4] *Zachariah*,[3] *James*,[2] *Anthony*[1]), son of Ralph and Susan (Williams) Emery ; married, first, March 28, 1865, Sarah A. Eddy (died April 28, 1865) ; second, Aug. 23, 1871, Mary S. Ballou (born Nov. 9, 1846 ; daughter of Rev. Levi Ballou of North Orange, Mass.).

Children, by second marriage :

3672   i   LEONORA A.,[9] b. Aug. 5, 1872.
3673   ii   SUSAN E., b. Oct. 4, 1874.
3674   iii   MARY L., b. Sept. 18, 1878.
3675   iv   SARAH K., b. Feb. 18, 1882.
3676   v   RALPH BALLOU, b. Oct. 22, 1889.

1852 MARY C.[8] EMERY (*Edward*,[7] *William*,[6] *Zachariah*,[5] *Zachariah*,[4] *Zachariah*,[3] *James*,[2] *Anthony*[1]), daughter of Edward and Fanny (Nutting) Emery ; married, first, Jan. 16, 1855, Charles Stanwood of Newburyport, Mass. ; member of city council and Massachusetts State Legislature. She married, second, Jan. 8, 1880, Geo. W. Wadsworth (born in Petersham, Mass., May 25, 1831). Resides in Roxbury, Mass.

Child :

3677   i   FANNIE E.,[9] b. May 26, 1856 ; d. July 26, 1866.

1859 FRED. W.[8] EMERY (*Amasa*,[7] *William*,[6] *Zachariah*,[5] *Zachariah*,[4] *Zachariah*,[3] *James*,[2] *Anthony*[1]), son of Amasa and Abigail (Dutton) Emery ; married Jan. 1, 1870, Frances J. Cressey. He died at Peterborough, N. H., April 12, 1872.

Child :

3678   i   ADA.[9]

1861 MARY STANLEY[8] ROBBINS (*Nancy Ann*,[7] *William*,[6] *Zachariah*,[5] *Zachariah*,[4] *Zachariah*,[3] *James*,[2] *Anthony*[1]), daughter of Hervey and Nancy Ann (Emery) Robbins ; married Oct. 26, 1854, Oliver H. Brown.

Children :

3679   ι   FRANK HEROY,[9] b Sept 17, 1856
3680   ii   MARY AUGUSTA, b April 18, 1859
3681   iii   LENA LOUISA, b March 12, 1862
3682   iv   ANNA LUCRETIA, b Aug 31, 1868

1866 LUCY ANN[8] ROBBINS (*Nancy Ann,*[7] *William,*[6] *Zachariah,*[5] *Zachariah,*[4] *Zachariah,*[3] *James,*[2] *Anthony*[1]), daughter of Hervey and Nancy Ann (Emery) Robbins, married Dec. 6, 1865, Henry A Turner (born in Jaffrey. N H , May 12, 1841). He was selectman, 1877, deputy sheriff in Gardner, Mass.
Children.

3683   ι   SUSIE LORA,[9] b Dec 27, 1866
3684   ii   EFFIE BLANCHE, b March 19, 1869

1870 WILLIAM STANLEY[8] EMERY (*John Stanley,*[7] *William,*[6] *Zachariah,*[5] *Zachariah,*[4] *Zachariah,*[3] *James,*[2] *Anthony*[1]), son of John Stanley and Abby (Eddy) Emery, married in Grand Rapids, Mich , March 17, 1867, Caroline Isabella Kinkle
Child :

3685   ι   AARON STANLEY,[9] b June 2, 1868, in Grand Rapids.

1871 MARY SUSAN[8] EMERY (*John S.,*[7] *William,*[6] *Zachariah,*[5] *Zachariah,*[4] *Zachariah,*[3] *James,*[2] *Anthony*[1]), daughter of John S and Abby (Eddy) Emery, married in Orange, Mass., April 24, 1867, William J. Barrus of Warwick, Mass.
Children ·

3686   ι   ERNEST G ,[9] b May 31, 1868. in Orange, Mass
3687   ii   STELLA A , b. Dec 22, 1871, in Warwick, Mass.
3688   iii   JOHN EDDY, b April 22, 1876, in Grand Rapids, Mich

1876 CHARLES C[8] EMERY (*Joseph,*[7] *John,*[6] *John,*[5] *Zachariah,*[4] *Zachariah,*[3] *James,*[2] *Anthony*[1]), son of Joseph and Harriet (Clapham) Emery , married in Sangerville, Me , in 1848, Hannah G. Clark.
Children :

3689   ι   CHARLES F ,[9] b 1849, in Skowhegan, Me., d. in Waldoboro, Me 1851
3690   ii   MARY H , b 1851, in Skowhegan, Me.
3691   iii   GEORGE F , b 1859, in Skowhegan, Me
3692   iv   ANNIE C , b 1869, in Waldoboro, Me ; d in Skowhegan, Me., 1869
3693   v   WALTER A , b 1875.

1878 ABNER C.[8] EMERY (*Joseph,*[7] *John,*[6] *John,*[5] *Zachariah,*[4] *Zachariah,*[3] *James,*[2] *Anthony*[1]), son of Joseph and Harriet (Clapham) Emery , married in Skowhegan. Me , 1863, Anne J. Clark. He was in the 1st Maine Cav , wounded in battle, transferred to 2nd Maine Cav., appointed lieutenant, discharged at the close of the war.
Children :

3694   ι   ALICE S ,[9] b 1864, res in Skowhegan, Me.
3695   ii   EDGAR H , b 1866.

1879 REBECCA[8] BUTLER (*Joanna,*[7] *Samuel,*[6] *John,*[5] *Zachariah,*[4] *Zachariah,*[3] *James,*[2] *Anthony*[1]), daughter of Joseph and Joanna (Emery) Butler; married Aug. 30, 1847, Edson Buker. He lives in St. Albans. Me.

Children:

3696	i	CLARA.⁹
3697	ii	HENRY.
3698	iii	FRANK.
3699	iv	ALBION.
3700	v	ALPHONSO.

1880 SUSAN⁸ BUTLER (*Joanna,*⁷ *Samuel,*⁶ *John,*⁵ *Zachariah,*⁴ *Zachariah,*³ *James,*² *Anthony*¹), daughter of Joseph and Joanna (Emery) Butler; married May 23, 1841, Hiram Bassett. Lives in Dexter, Me.

Children:

3701	i	CLARA.⁹
3702	ii	ELLEN.
3703	iii	CLARA.
3704	iv	CELIA.
3705	v	HARRY.

1882 SARAH⁸ BUTLER (*Joanna,*⁷ *Samuel,*⁶ *John,*⁵ *Zachariah,*⁴ *Zachariah,*³ *James,*² *Anthony,*¹) daughter of Joseph and Joanna (Emery) Butler; married May 28, 1843, Greenwood Safford.

Children:

3706	i	FLORA.⁹
3707	ii	HELEN.
3708	iii	IDA.
3709	iv	HOWARD.
3710	v	ORA.
3711	vi	JOHN.

Two other children, d. young.

1884 ASENATH⁸ BUTLER (*Joanna,*⁷ *Samuel,*⁶ *John,*⁵ *Zachariah,*⁴ *Zachariah,*³ *James,*² *Anthony*¹), daughter of Joseph and Joanna (Emery) Butler; married May 14, 1845, Myron B. Knowles. Lives in Greeley, Colo.

Children:

3712	i	ADELIA.⁹
3713	ii	EVA.
3714	iii	WILLIAM.
3715	iv	WALTER.
3716	v	ANNABEL.
3717	vi	CASSANDRA.
3718	vii	FRANK.

1886 JOANNA⁸ BUTLER (*Joanna,*⁷ *Samuel,*⁶ *John,*⁵ *Zachariah,*⁴ *Zachariah,*³ *James,*² *Anthony*¹), daughter of Joseph and Joanna (Emery) Butler; married Dec. 9, 1853, Edwin B. Ramsdell. Lives in St. Albans. Me.

Children:

3719	i	CARRIE.⁹
3720	ii	ELLA.
3721	iii	FLORA.

1887 JOHN BURLEIGH⁸ BUTLER (*Joanna,*⁷ *Samuel,*⁶ *John,*⁵ *Zachariah,*⁴ *Zachariah,*³ *James,*² *Anthony*¹), son of Joseph and Joanna(Emery) Butler, married April 26, 1866, Mary Haskell. Lives in Monson, Me.

Children

3722	i	CLARA [9]
3723	ii	JOHN
3724	iii	MARY
3724a	iv	ANNIE
3724b	v	CORA
3724c	vi	NETTIE.

1888 FREEMAN ALLEN[8] BUTLER (*Joanna,*[7] *Samuel,*[6] *John,*[5] *Zachariah,*[4] *Zachariah,*[3] *James,*[2] *Anthony*[1]), son of Joseph and Joanna (Emery) Butler; married Sept. 28, 1860, Drusilla M. Trafton. Lives in St. Albans, Me.

Children

3725	i	EUGENE [9]
3726	ii	EDNA
3727	iii	FANNIE

1890 CAROLINE A [8] BUTLER(*Joanna,*[7] *Samuel,*[6] *John,*[5] *Zachariah,*[4] *Zachariah,*[3] *James,*[2] *Anthony*[1]), daughter of Joseph and Joanna (Emery) Butler; married Nov. 23, 1859, Alfred Bigelow. Lives in St. Albans, Me.

Child

| 3728 | i | ISRAEL [9] |

1891 HENRY F.[8] BUTLER (*Joanna,*[7] *Samuel,*[6] *John,*[5] *Zachariah,*[4] *Zachariah,*[3] *James,*[2] *Anthony*[1]), son of Joseph and Joanna (Emery) Butler, married June 4, 1871, Ella J. Denning. Lives in Ripley, Me

Children :

3729	i	HARRY [9]
3730	ii	BESSIE
3731	iii	CARRIE

1892 ALBERT G [8] EMERY (*Tilly,*[7] *Joseph,*[6] *John,*[5] *Zachariah,*[4] *Zachariah,*[3] *James,*[2] *Anthony*[1]), son of Tilly and second wife Celia N. (Hinds) Emery, married Nancy E. Potter of Fairfield, Me. Clerk in war department at Washington during the war, clerk of courts for Somerset Co., Me.; registrar of deeds for Somerset Co to 1874; lawyer

Children

| 3732 | i | HATTIE M ,[9] b April 29, 1860 |
| 3733 | ii | NEAL F , b Aug. 28, 1867 |

1901 HORATIO C.[8] EMERY (*Joseph,*[7] *Joseph,*[6] *John,*[5] *Zachariah,*[4] *Zachariah,*[3] *James,*[2] *Anthony*[1]), son of Joseph and Ruth (Cushing) Emery; married Mary Wheeler.

Children :

3734	i	NETTIE,[9] m Dr W. P. Cleveland of Eastport, Me
3735	ii	ETTA, teacher.
3736	iii	ALICE

1906 ADAMS[2] EMERY (*Daniel*,[7] *Daniel*,[6] *Daniel*,[5] *Zachariah*,[4] *Zachariah*,[3] *James*,[2] *Anthony*[1]), son of Lieut. Daniel and Polly (Felt) Emery; married, March, 1833, at Fall River, Mass., Mrs. Dolly W. (Wiggin) Smith (died in Ludlow, Mass., Dec. 20, 1881).
Children :

3737　i　MARY CAROLINE.[9] b. 1833; d. 1835.
3738　ii　GEORGE, b. 1835; d. when six years of age.
3739　iii　A DAUGHTER; d. 1837.
3740　iv　CHARLES ALBERT, b. April 8, 1838; m. Oct. 19, 1870, Orianna Adella Bastis; draughtsman at the U. S. Armory, Springfield, Mass.

1907 DEA. ANDREWS[8] EMERY (*Daniel*,[7] *Daniel*,[6] *Daniel*,[5] *Zachariah*,[4] *Zachariah*,[3] *James*,[2] *Anthony*[1]), son of Lieut. Daniel and Polly (Felt) Emery; married, first, April 28, 1830, Lucy Powers (born Dec. 29, 1806; died Aug. 22, 1832), daughter of Asa and Rachel (Cutler) Powers; second, July 2, 1833, Mary Smith (born Oct. 18, 1808; died May 24, 1880), daughter of William and Olive (Gray) Smith. He died April 8, 1860.
Child, by first marriage :

3741　i　JEREMIAH A.,[9] b. Jan. 22, 1831.

Children, by second marriage :

3742　ii　GEORGE S., b. Dec. 9, 1835.
3743　iii　LUCY M., b. July 1, 1838.
3744　iv　CHARLES DANIEL, b. Dec. 14, 1841; d. in the army, Nov. 14, 1863; member of Co. G, 14th N. H. Vols.; thirteen years after his burial in Jaffrey, N. H., his body was removed and found to be petrified.

1908 DANIEL F.[8] EMERY (*Daniel*,[7] *Daniel*,[6] *Daniel*,[5] *Zachariah*,[4] *Zachariah*,[3] *James*,[2] *Anthony*[1]), son of Lieut. Daniel and Polly (Felt) Emery; married Dec. 1, 1831, Catherine B. Brown of Fall River, Mass. (died March 17, 1886). He died July 12, 1876.
Children :

3745　i　HANNAH J.,[9] b. Dec. 4, 1837, in Providence, R. I.; d. Dec. 21, 1839.
3746　ii　GEORGE DANIEL, b. Sept. 10, 1838, in Fall River, Mass.
3747　iii　ALBERT BUGBEE, b. June 27, 1841, in Buffalo, N. Y.; d. May, 1888.
3748　iv　JOHN BROWN, b. May 20, 1853, in Buffalo, N. Y.; d. June 17, 1882.
3749　v　A DAUGHTER, b. 1857; d. 1859.

1909 CAROLINE[8] EMERY (*Daniel*,[7] *Daniel*,[6] *Daniel*,[5] *Zachariah*,[4] *Zachariah*,[3] *James*,[2] *Anthony*[1]), daughter of Lieut. Daniel and Polly (Felt) Emery; married May 17, 1827, James R. French; died, 1829.
Children :

3750　i　A DAUGHTER,[9] b. Dec. 17 and d. Dec. 18, 1827.
3751　ii　JAMES A., b.———; d. Feb., 1829, seven weeks old.

1910 ELIZABETH[8] EMERY (*Daniel*,[7] *Daniel*,[6] *Daniel*,[5] *Zachariah*,[4] *Zachariah*,[3] *James*,[2] *Anthony*[1]), daughter of Lieut. Daniel and Polly

(Felt) Emery ; married April 17, 1834, Daniel Lyman Robbins (born Oct. 12, 1806)

Children

3752　i　CAROLINE ELIZABETH,[9] b April 17, 1836 (see No 1848).
3753　ii　MARY ADELINE, b March 23, 1838
3754　iii　EDWIN E , b May 13, 1845 , d April 3, 1863, at Baton Rouge, La , member of Co G, 53d Reg Mass Vols.
3755　iv　EMMA M , b May 9, 1848; d July 29, 1849

1913 SOPHRONIA[8] EMERY (*Daniel,*[7] *Daniel,*[6] *Daniel,*[5] *Zachariah,*[4] *Zachariah,*[3] *James,*[2] *Anthony*[1]), daughter of Lieut Daniel and Polly (Felt) Emery , married June 7, 1842. George Bullard (died in Jaffrey, N. H., Dec. 11, 1853). She lives in Gardner, Mass

Children :

3756　i　ELLEN S ,[9] b March 8, 1843, in Dublin, N H , d March 24, 1858.
3757　ii　ADELIA C , b Dec. 30, 1846, in Dublin, N. H
3758　iii　GEORGE WILLIS, b July 31, 1852 in Jaffrey, N H , lived with his uncle, Stephen F Emery of Mexico, N Y. In 1870 his name was changed to George W Emery

1923 ANNA D [8] BARBOUR (*Nancy,*[7] *Daniel,*[6] *Daniel,*[5] *Zachariah,*[4] *Zachariah,*[3] *James,*[2] *Anthony*[1]), daughter of Hoxey and Nancy (Emery) Barbour ; married, first, Oct 31, 1839, Joseph A. Rogers (died March 19, 1853) ; second, Nov., 1860, James T. Holmes of Mount Holly, Vt. She lives at East Wallingford, Vt.

Children, by first marriage ·

3759　i　HOXEY C ,[9] b April 18, 1843.
3760　ii　ALFRED H , b July 18, 1845
3761　iii　HANNAH Q P , b. Oct 31, 1848

By second marriage :

3762　iv　DANIEL M., b Feb 8, 1869, d Jan 30, 1875

1927 RHODA S [8] BARBOUR (*Nancy,*[7] *Daniel,*[6] *Daniel,*[5] *Zachariah,*[4] *Zachariah,*[3] *James,*[2] *Anthony*[1]), daughter of Hoxey and Nancy (Emery) Barbour , married Feb , 1847, at Ludlow, Vt., Perry A Dawley Resides at Mount Holly, Vt.

Children .

3763　i　GEORGE A ,[9] b Dec. 5, 1847, killed by the kick of a horse, July 7, 1855
3764　ii　JANE S . b Feb 1, 1849
3765　iii　FRANKLIN R , b. Jan 18, 1851
3766　iv　WILLIAM W , b Dec 4, 1852.
3767　v　MARION MARTHA, b Sept 10, 1854
3768　vi　HENRY ALLEN, b Oct 14 1856
3769　vii　PERRY G , b May 26, 1858
3770　viii　ALVINA NANCY, b Feb 6, 1863.
3771　ix　NORMAN B , b Jan 5, 1864
3772　x　MARY ALICE, b Aug 1, 1866
3773　xi　INFANT, b Dec 3, 1868, d young.

1929 LOIS I.[8] BARBOUR (*Nancy,*[7] *Daniel,*[6] *Daniel,*[5] *Zachariah,*[4] *Zachariah,*[3] *James,*[2] *Anthony*[1]), daughter of Hoxey and Nancy (Em-

ery) Barbour; married Aram Caryl at Mount Holly, Vt.; died in
U. S. Hospital at Baton Rouge, La., July 21, 1864.

Children, born at Mount Holly, Vt.:

    3774   i   EDA ISABELL,⁹ b. Oct. 3, 1853.
    3775   ii   BESSIE ANNA, b. Oct. 4, 1855.
    3776   iii HARVEY WARREN, b. June 26, 1858.
    3777   iv   CALVIN ARAM, b. Oct. 30, 1861.
    3778   v   DAUGHTER, b. and d. Sept. 21, 1863.
    3779   vi   HOXEY A., b. Oct. 9, 1864; d. Nov. 9, 1864.

1932 LYMAN⁸ EMERY (*Joseph,*⁷ *Daniel,*⁶ *Daniel,*⁵ *Zachariah,*⁴ *Zachariah,*³ *James,*² *Anthony*¹), son of Joseph and Betsey (Bowen) Emery;
married, first, April, 1839, Sarah Stratton (died Jan. 21, 1867); married a second time and had one child.

Children:

    3780   i   ANN,⁹ b. 1840; d. at seven years of age.
    3781   ii   OLIVE, b.———; d. when fifteen months old.
    3782   iii AMELIA, b. March 28, 1848; m. Charles Hatch, Nov. 21, 1868;
                had a dau., b. about 1873.
    3783   iv   GEORGE, b. March 18, 1851.

1934 MELINDA⁸ EMERY (*Joseph,*⁷ *Daniel,*⁶ *Daniel,*⁵ *Zachariah,*⁴
*Zachariah,*³ *James,*² *Anthony*¹), daughter of Joseph and Betsey (Bow-
en) Emery; married Eli Balkam.

Child:

    3784   i   LUCILLA,⁹ b. Aug., 1850.

1935 CORDELIA⁸ EMERY (*Joseph,*⁷ *Daniel,*⁶ *Daniel,*⁵ *Zachariah,*⁴
*Zachariah,*³ *James,*² *Anthony*¹), daughter of Joseph and Betsey (Bow-
en) Emery; married William O. Gowing (her cousin), son of Curtis
and Irene (Emery) Gowing.   Lives in Colorado.

Children:

    3785   i   MARY LEE,⁹ b. June 21, 1852.
    3786   ii   IRENE, b. Aug. 6, 1856; m. Geo. Willard, Aug. 26, 1881.
    3787   iii MINNIE, b. Sept. 19, 1858; m.

1936 CHARLES⁸ EMERY (*Jonathan,*⁷ *Daniel,*⁶ *Daniel,*⁵ *Zachariah,*⁴
*Zachariah,*³ *James,*² *Anthony*¹), son of Jonathan and Fanny (Dun-
shee) Emery; married Feb. 5, 1850, Hester Ann Coon of Stockholm,
N. Y.

Children:

    3788   i   FANNY E.⁹
    3789   ii   ALMA A.
    3790   iii ALICE E.
    3791   iv   AMELIA A.
    3792   v   DIANTHA F.
    3793   vi   ALLEN C.

1937 GEORGE⁸ EMERY (*Jonathan,*⁷ *Daniel,*⁶ *Daniel,*⁵ *Zachariah,*⁴
*Zachariah,*³ *James,*² *Anthony*¹), son of Jonathan and Fanny (Dun-
shee) Emery; married March 27, 1851, Phœbe Rice, of Stockholm,
N. Y.

Child .

3794 i LORENZO L.[9]

1938 EMILY S [8] EMERY (*Jonathan*,[7] *Daniel*,[6] *Daniel*,[5] *Zachariah*,[4] *Zachariah*,[3] *James*,[2] *Anthony*[1]), daughter of Jonathan and Fanny (Dunshee) Emery; married March 6, 1850, Henry A. Munson of Potsdam, N. Y.

Children

3795 i HOMER [9]
3796 ii NOBLE.
3797 iii DIANA.
3798 iv OLIVE
3799 v EMERY.
3800 vi MARY.

1943 CURTIS[8] EMERY (*Jonathan*,[7] *Daniel*,[6] *Daniel*,[5] *Zachariah*,[4] *Zachariah*,[3] *James*,[2] *Anthony*[1]), son of Jonathan and Fanny (Dunshee) Emery; married Mrs. Delia Aikens of Westmoreland, N. H.

Children :

3801 i GUY [9]
3802 ii MAC
3803 iii HUGH D.
3804 iv INA.

1944 DIANTHA[8] EMERY (*Jonathan*,[7] *Daniel*,[6] *Daniel*,[5] *Zachariah*,[4] *Zachariah*,[3] *James*,[2] *Anthony*[1]), daughter of Jonathan and Fanny (Dunshee) Emery, married Feb. 1860, Curtis J Fletcher of Walpole, N. H.

Children :

3805 i ADELINA F [9]
3806 ii CARLOS E.

1945 REBECCA[8] EMERY (*Aaron*,[7] *Daniel*,[6] *Daniel*,[5] *Zachariah*,[4] *Zachariah*,[3] *James*,[2] *Anthony*[1]), daughter of Aaron and Susan (Martin) Emery, married Dec. 18, 1812, Thomas McDonald of Stockholm, N. Y.

Children :

3807 i LUCIEN B.[9]
3808 ii MIRON H ; d. in the army.
3809 iii JOHN M.
3810 iv LYDIA J
3811 v JAMES M
3812 vi MAY E.
3813 vii IDA.
3814 viii CURTIS
3815 ix THOMAS

1946 OLIVER M.[8] EMERY (*Aaron*,[7] *Daniel*,[6] *Daniel*,[5] *Zachariah*,[4] *Zachariah*,[3] *James*,[2] *Anthony*[1]), son of Aaron and Susan (Martin) Emery ; married Jan. 23, 1850, Lucinda Gurley of Stockholm, N. Y. Resides in Stockholm. N. Y.

Children :

3816 i   James F.[9]
3817 ii   Miles J.
3818 iii Willis C.
3819 iv   Bell E.

1947 Mary[8] Emery (*Aaron*,[7] *Daniel*,[6] *Daniel*,[5] *Zachariah*,[4] *Zachariah*,[3] *James*,[2] *Anthony*[1]), daughter of Aaron and Susan (Martin) Emery ; married Nov. 15, 1846, Amos S. Ward of Stockholm, N. Y.
    Children :

3820 i   James.[9]
3821 ii   Charles.
3822 iii Alfred.
3823 iv   Curtis.
3824 v   Clarence.
3825 vi   Samuel.
3826 vii Nora.
3827 viii Susan.

1948 Lydia A.[8] Emery (*Aaron*,[7] *Daniel*,[6] *Daniel*,[5] *Zachariah*,[4] *Zachariah*,[3] *James*,[2] *Anthony*[1]), daughter of Aaron and Susan (Martin) Emery ; married May 15, 1853, George Easton of Brasher, N. Y.
    Children :

3828 i   Nettie.[9]
3829 ii   George.

1949 Laura[8] Emery (*Aaron*,[7] *Daniel*,[6] *Daniel*,[5] *Zachariah*,[4] *Zachariah*,[3] *James*,[2] *Anthony*[1]), daughter of Aaron and Susan (Martin) Emery ; married April 30, 1857, James S. Curtis of Stockholm, N. Y.
    Children :

3830 i   Hiram C.[9]
3831 ii   Susan A.
3832 iii Oliver A.
3833 iv   Nora M.
3834 v   Berdie M.
3835 vi   Bell F.
3836 vii Jennie S.

1951 Elnora[8] Emery (*Aaron*,[7] *Daniel*,[6] *Daniel*,[5] *Zachariah*,[4] *Zachariah*,[3] *James*,[2] *Anthony*[1]), daughter of Aaron and Susan (Martin) Emery ; married Dec. 25, 1860, Henry Dyke of Stockholm, N. Y.
    Children :

3837 i   Chloe.[9]
3838 ii   Warren.

1962 Elizabeth[8] Emery (*James*,[7] *Noah*,[6] *Daniel*,[5] *Zachariah*,[4] *Zachariah*,[3] *James*,[2] *Anthony*[1]), daughter of James and Elizabeth (Wilder) Emery ; married Lewis Wheat ; went to St. Johns, Mich., where he died in 1867. She died Oct. 6, 1882.
    Children :

3839 i   Selinda,[9] b. Oct. 22, 1833; d. in Windsor, Canada, Oct. 6, 1882.
3840 ii   James E., b. May 16, 1835.
3841 iii Chastena M., b. Aug. 24, 1837.

3842 iv SOLOMON, b Dec 10, 1839
3843 v   ORIN, b July 6, 1841, m Eliza Carr, 1880.
3844 vi EDWIN R , b. Sept 11, 1843.
      Two children d in infancy

1963 JAMES C.[8] EMERY (*James,*[7] *Noah,*[6] *Daniel,*[5] *Zachariah,*[4] *Zachariah,*[3] *James,*[2] *Anthony*[1]), son of James and Elizabeth (Wilder) Emery, married Jan. 27, 1841, Jane Letts. Resides in Spencer, N.Y.
  Children :

3845 i   LAURA J ,[9] b Aug. 24, 1846
3846 ii ELLEN AUGUSTA, b March 19, 1849

1964 JUSTIN W [8] EMERY (*James,*[7] *Noah,*[6] *Daniel,*[5] *Zachariah,*[4] *Zachariah,*[3] *James,*[2] *Anthony*[1]), son of James and Elizabeth (Wilder) Emery, married Sarah Billings. Resides in Webster, N. Y.
  Children :

3847 i   AGNES M ,[9] b April 8, 1854
3848 ii HERBERT B , b April 18, 1856; d March 16, 1859.
3849 iii DARIUS B , b Jan. 9, 1859
3850 iv HIRAM B , b July 5, 1864.
3851 v   ASA B , b. Sept 21, 1866.

1965 REV. ISAAC W [8] EMERY (*James,*[7] *Noah,*[6] *Daniel,*[5] *Zachariah,*[4] *Zachariah,*[3] *James,*[2] *Anthony*[1]), son of James and Elizabeth (Wilder) Emery; married, 1844, Elizabeth Benton. Resides in Groton, N. Y. Licensed, 1851 , ordained, 1852.
  Children, born in Spencer, N. Y. :

3852 i   ALVIN W ,[9] b Sept 29, 1845
3853 ii JUSTUS J , b July 1, 1847

1970 JAMES P [8] EMERY (*Nathan,*[7] *Noah,*[6] *Daniel,*[5] *Zachariah,*[4] *Zachariah,*[3] *James,*[2] *Anthony*[1]), son of Nathan and Betsey (Pettingall) Emery, married in Staceyville, Iowa, Feb. 10, 1848, Martha G Newhall. He died May 28, 1858.
  Children :

3854 i   HENRY P ,[9] b Nov 11, 1848
3855 ii GEORGE H , b July 3, 1850
3856 iii JAMES P , b Feb 25, 1854; d Oct 9, 1854.
3857 iv EDWARD F , b March 10, 1856.
3858 v   JAMES L , b Aug. 30, 1858, res in Eddy, Texas; unm.

1973 CHAUNCEY W.[8] EMERY (*Noah,*[7] *Noah,*[6] *Daniel,*[5] *Zachariah,*[4] *Zachariah,*[3] *James,*[2] *Anthony*[1]), son of Noah and Mary (Martin) Emery, married, 1844, Phœbe Baker.
  Children :

3859 i   WEALTHY,[9] b March 2, 1846, d. Nov 4, 1863.
3860 ii   MARY, b Aug 27, 1848
3861 iii CHAUNCEY N , b March 27, 1851.
3862 iv   LORINDA, b May 10, 1853
3863 v   LORETTA, b Jan 22, 1856.
3864 vi   NORMAN C , b Sept 11, 1858.
3865 vii ALMA, b Oct 18, 1861; d. June 9, 1862.
3866 viii CHILD, d. in infancy.

31

1976 NATHAN M.[8] EMERY (*Noah,*[7] *Noah,*[6] *Daniel,*[5] *Zachariah,*[4] *Zachariah,*[3] *James,*[2] *Anthony*[1]), son of Noah and Mary (Martin) Emery; married May 2, 1855, Marion R. Weeks.

Children :

3867 i   EVA,[9] b. Nov. 11, 1857, in Webster, N. Y.
3868 ii   LOTTIE J., b. July 31, 1869.

1977 DAVID H.[3] EMERY (*Noah,*[7] *Noah,*[6] *Daniel,*[5] *Zachariah,*[4] *Zachariah,*[3] *James,*[2] *Anthony*[1]), son of Noah and Mary (Martin) Emery; married in Spencer, N. Y., Aug. 26, 1867, Almira Getman.

Children :

3869 i   CORA E.,[9] b. Oct. 17, 1868.
3870 ii   BERTHA L., b. Oct. 15, 1869.
3871 iii ALMIRA, b. Aug. 25, 1874.
3872 iv   IDA, b. June 24, 1876.
3873 v   BLANCH, b. Dec. 3, 1878.
3874 vi   HARRIET N., b. Jan. 11, 1880.

1978 AMANDA M.[8] EMERY (*Noah,*[7] *Noah,*[6] *Daniel,*[5] *Zachariah,*[4] *Zachariah,*[3] *James,*[2] *Anthony*[1]), daughter of Noah and Mary (Martin) Emery; married in Spencer, N. Y., March 9, 1865, Gilbert G. White.

Children :

3875 i   GEORGE H.,[9] b. April 16, 1866; d. Feb. 5, 1867.
3876 ii   ROSE S., b. March 11, 1869.
3877 iii ELLEN J., b. Nov. 3, 1870.
3878 iv   FRED. D., b. April 16, 1872.
3879 v   MYSTIE, b. Oct. 18, 1880.

1979 PHŒBE A.[6] EMERY (*Noah,*[7] *Noah,*[6] *Daniel,*[5] *Zachariah,*[4] *Zachariah,*[3] *James,*[2] *Anthony*[1]), daughter of Noah and Mary (Martin) Emery; married Lorenzo C. Brooks.

Children :

3880 i   EMILY J.,[9] b. May, 1875; d. Jan. 25, 1877.
3881 ii   EMILY AMANDA, b. July 22, 1877; d. Oct. 13, 1881.

1993 ABIGAIL[8] NOURSE (*Gratia,*[7] *Noah,*[6] *Daniel,*[5] *Zachariah,*[4] *Zachariah,*[3] *James,*[2] *Anthony*[1]), daughter of Peter and Gratia (Emery) Nourse; married March 6, 1844, William Fisher (born March 25, 1815; died April 26, 1890). Resides in Benton, Kansas.

Children :

3882 i   ANNIS N.,[9] b. Nov. 5, 1845, in Ill. ; m. Oct. 10, 1866, Perry G. Drew; d. March 28, 1877.
3883 ii   GRATIA M., b. Aug. 29, 1848; m. in Mich., June 10, 1867, Robert T. W. Fletcher.
3884 iii EMERY W., b. Oct. 23, 1856; m. Sept. 17, 1881, Mary A. Bonduraut; res. in Kansas.

1999 ALBERT NOAH[8] EMERY (*Jonathan,*[7] *Noah,*[6] *Daniel,*[5] *Zachariah,*[4] *Zachariah,*[3] *James,*[2] *Anthony*[1]), son of Jonathan and Abigail (Nourse) Emery; married Aug. 31, 1879, Alice C. Seaton of Rushford, N. Y.

Child :

3885 i   BERTHA MAY,[9] b. Oct. 15, 1880.

2000 BETSEY LOUISA[8] MARSHALL (*Betsey,*[7] *Noah,*[6] *Daniel,*[5] *Zachariah,*[4] *Zachariah,*[3] *James,*[2] *Anthony*[1]), daughter of Marvin and Betsey (Emery) Marshall; married, 1862, —— Dunn.
Child:

 3886 i MARSHALL B ,[9] b Jan 1, 1864.

2017 LABAN DAVID[8] EMERY (*Laban,*[7] *Asa,*[6] *Daniel,*[5] *Zachariah,*[4] *Zachariah,*[3] *James,*[2] *Anthony*[1]), son of Laban and Nancy (Bemis) Emery, married Aug. 3, 1880, Martha Jane White (born April 10, 1857).
Child:

 3887 i NELLIE AMELIA,[9] b March 29, 1883, in Pine Grove, Van Buren Co , Mich

2018 CYRUS WRIGHT[8] EMERY (*Laban,*[7] *Asa,*[6] *Daniel,*[5] *Zachariah,*[4] *Zachariah,*[3] *James,*[2] *Anthony*[1]), son of Laban and Nancy (Bemis) Emery; married Aug. 3, 1880, Emma Jane Camp (born Aug. 26, 1861).
Children:

 3888 i CLARA BELL[9] b Dec 12, 1881
 3889 ii CLARENCE WILLARD, b Feb 11, 1884

2058 ELVIRA D.[8] GOWING (*Mary,*[7] *Josiah,*[6] *Samuel,*[5] *Zachariah,*[4] *Zachariah,*[3] *James,*[2] *Anthony*[1]), daughter of Levi and Mary (Emery) Gowing, married Daniel March. She died Dec. 12, 1882.
Children:

 3890 i BETSEY ELLA,[9] b July 12 1853, d. May 19, 1870
 3891 ii HATTIE W., b. Feb 25, 1855, d June 16, 1857.
 3892 iii HENRY, b. April 8, 1862, d. Aug. 7, 1865.
 3893 iv MARY A , b July 11, 1866; d Oct 16, 1867

2065 GEORGE W.[8] MORRISON (*Betsey,*[7] *Josiah,*[6] *Samuel,*[5] *Zachariah,*[4] *Zachariah,*[3] *James,*[2] *Anthony*[1]), son of George W and Betsey (Emery) Morrison; married March 10, 1870, Harriet B. Wetherbee.
Children:

 3894 i FRANK W ,[9] b. July 6, 1871
 3895 ii FRED S b Oct 19, 1874.
 3896 iii HUGH E , b. May 7, 1877.
 3897 iv HARRY R., b. May 9, 1881.

2069 ESTHER LOUISA[8] EMERY (*Osman B ,*[7] *Josiah,*[6] *Samuel,*[5] *Zachariah,*[4] *Zachariah,*[3] *James,*[2] *Anthony*[1]), daughter of Osman B. and Lucy A. (Barton) Emery; married Jan. 2, 1868, Joel L. Marble.
Children.

 3898 i ERNEST E ,[9] b 1868.
 3899 ii LILLIAN E , b Dec. 5, 1869.
 3900 iii MINNIE A , b March 15 1874
 3901 iv OSMAN J., b Aug. 17, 1876. d Sept 25, 1877.

2072 JOSIAH ALLEN[8] BROWN (*Hannah G.,*[7] *Josiah,*[6] *Samuel,*[5] *Zachariah,*[4] *Zachariah,*[3] *James,*[2] *Anthony*[1]), son of John and Hannah G. (Emery) Brown; married Jan. 1, 1867, M. Wood.

Children :

    3902 i   WILLIS ALLEN,[9] b. March 3, 1871.
    3903 ii LOUIS EDWIN, b. Feb. 25, 1875.

2073 ETTA HARLOW[8] BARTON (*Esther R.*,[7] *Josiah,*[6] *Samuel,*[5] *Zachariah,*[4] *Zachariah,*[3] *James,*[2] *Anthony*[1]), daughter of D. and Esther R. (Emery) Barton ; married May 6, 1869, Charles H. Richards.
    Children :

    3904 i   JENNIE H.,[9] b. May 4, 1874.
    3905 ii ETTIE, b. March 4, 1876.

2076 SIMEON[8] EMERY (*David,*[7] *Daniel,*[6] *Daniel,*[5] *Daniel,*[4] *Daniel,*[3] *James,*[2] *Anthony*[1]), son of David and Betsey (Chase) Emery ; married Betsey Adams of Barnstable, Mass. (born Aug. 15, 1817). Lives in Yarmouth, Mass.
    Children :

    3906 i   JOHN,[9] b. May 1, 1837; m. Sept. 15, 1860, Jane Bunker of Kittery, Me.
    3907 ii SIMEON, b. Aug. 1, 1839, in Yarmouth, Mass.
    3908 iii IRA, b. Oct. 22, 1841; d. Nov. 13, 1843.
    3909 iv IRA, b. Nov. 2, 1844; d. Sept. 3, 1845.
    3910 v   MARY F., b. Oct. 31, 1846. in Yarmouth, Mass.; d. Jan. 5, 1870.
    3911 vi CHARLES A., b. Jan. 20, 1849.
    3912 vii ENOCH. b. Jan. 8, 1851, in Yarmouth, Mass. Merchant in Nikolarivsk, on the Amoor river, in Siberia, Asia; unm.
    3913 viii GEORGE A., b. Sept. 3, 1853; m. April 26, 1882, Ella N. Procter; res. in Fitchburg, Mass.
    3914 ix OLIVER L., b. Aug. 31, 1854, in Gloucester, Mass.
    3915 x   ALBERT B., b. Jan. 24, 1858, in Gloucester, Mass.
    3916 xi WILLIS, b. Feb. 29, 1860, in South Berwick, Me.

2077 ELIZABETH[8] EMERY (*David,*[7] *Daniel,*[6] *Daniel,*[5] *Daniel,*[4] *Daniel,*[3] *James,*[2] *Anthony*[1]), daughter of David and Betsey (Chase) Emery ; married, first, May 31, 1843, Parker W. Chadwick ; second, David Gould.
    Children, by first marriage :

    3917 i   OLIVE,[9] b. Nov. 16, 1844; m. Nov. 16, 1864, Horace A. Bennett of Rollinsford, N. H.
    3918 ii DAVID, b. May 14, 1846; d. young.
    3919 iii ROSILLA, b. Nov. 13, 1847.
    3920 iv MARY E., b. Sept. 10, 1849; m. Edwin Bennett; d. 1867.
    3921 v   PARKER W., b. March 14, 1851; d. Jan. 5, 1877.
    3922 vi ROBERT W., b. Nov. 30, 1852; d. young.

    By second marriage :

    3923 vii CHARLES, b. June 5, 1857.
    3924 viii ALANSON, b. June 6, 1859.
    3925 ix FREDERICK H., b. April 4, 1861.

2079 ABBIE[8] EMERY (*Enoch,*[7] *Daniel,*[6] *Daniel,*[5] *Daniel,*[4] *Daniel,*[3] *James,*[2] *Anthony*[1]), daughter of Enoch and Rhoda (Staples) Emery ; married Oct. 15, 1848, Otis Rollins. She died May 19, 1855.
    Children :

    3926 i   FRANK.[9]
    3927 ii ALMON, b. March 14, 1855.

2080 JAMES[8] EMERY (*Enoch,[7] Daniel,[6] Daniel,[5] Daniel,[4] Daniel,[3] James,[2] Anthony[1]*), son of Enoch and Rhoda (Staples) Emery; married Dec 24, 1856, Frances Farnell.
Children .*

3928 i NANCY [9]
3929 ii ENOCH

2084 ENOCH[8] EMERY (*Enoch,[7] Daniel,[6] Daniel,[5] Daniel,[4] Daniel,[3] James,[2] Anthony[1]*), son of Enoch and Rhoda (Staples) Emery, married Oct 28, 1870, Maria Eastman.
Children :

3930 i FLORENCE,[9] b April 29, 1871
3931 ii FRANK, b June 28, 1873; d July 14, 1878
3932 iii JOHN L , b May 10, 1880
3933 iv LIZZIE, b April 13, 1884
3934 v CORA B , b Aug 10, 1887.

2094 ASA[8] EMERY (*Joel,[7] Nathan,[6] Daniel,[5] Daniel,[4] Daniel.[3] James.[2] Anthony[1]*), son of Joel and Betsey (Emery) Emery ; married Oct , 1841, Mrs. Sarah Rendall. Lives in Medford, Mass.
Children :

3935 i ASA,[9] b March 17, 1846
3936 ii EVERETT, b Dec 18, 1848, d May 13, 1872.

2097 RHODA[8] EMERY (*Joel,[7] Nathan,[6] Daniel,[5] Daniel,[4] Daniel,[3] James,[2] Anthony[1]*), daughter of Joel and Betsey (Emery) Emery , married May 1, 1842, John Lord of South Berwick (born April 11, 1812).
Children :

3937 i JOHN H ,[9] b Feb 26, 1843, d Aug 6, 1843
3938 ii MARTIN, b July 2, 1845
3939 iii JOHN A , b April 12, 1847.
3940 iv RHODA A , b April 1, 1851
3941 v CHARLES T , b Aug. 6, 1860.

2098 JOEL[8] EMERY (*Joel,[7] Nathan,[6] Daniel,[5] Daniel,[4] Daniel,[3] James,[2] Anthony[1]*), son of Joel and Betsey (Emery) Emery , married Sept 6, 1846, Lydia Moulton of Parsonsfield, Me.
Children :

3942 i JOEL,[9] d in infancy.
3943 ii CHARLES H , m and d.

2102 JULIA A [8] EMERY (*Timothy,[7] Daniel,[6] Daniel,[5] Noah,[4] Daniel,[3] James,[2] Anthony[1]*), daughter of Timothy and Olive (Wentworth) Emery , married, 1838, John Perkins of Parsonsfield, Me.
Child :

3944 i EDWARD A ,[9] b Jan , 1843.

2103 NANCY S [8] EMERY (*Timothy,[7] Daniel,[6] Daniel,[5] Noah,[4] Daniel,[3] James,[2] Anthony[1]*), daughter of Timothy and Olive (Went-

* A second list gives as correct
i LEONARD A b Nov 14, 1858, m. June 28 1884, Emma L. Bennett.
ii URANIE M , b Sept 10, 1861, d Jan 17, 1864
iii GRANVILLE N , b. Oct 10, 1864, d Oct 15, 1864.
iv AN INFANT, b. and d Nov 18, 1865

worth) Emery ; married Feb. 22, 1840, John Pinkham (died July 1, 1856).

Children :

    3945   i   MARY A.,⁹ b. July 9, 1841.
    3946   ii   JOHN H., b. Aug. 13, 1843.
    3947   iii   CHARLES E., b. March 13, 1848.
    3948   iv   WILLIAM S., b. Aug. 20, 1851.

2105 DANIEL C.⁸ EMERY (*Timothy,*⁷ *Daniel,*⁶ *Daniel,*⁵ *Noah,*⁴ *Daniel,*³ *James,*² *Anthony*¹), son of Timothy and Olive (Wentworth) Emery ; married Jan. 28, 1846, Abigail Whitehouse of Middleton, N. H. Resides in Milton, N. H.

Children :

    3949   i   EDWARD H.,⁹ b. Jan. 22, 1847; m. Nov. 7, 1867, Fannie L.
                  Jenkins.
    3950   ii   THOMAS D., b. July 26, 1849.
    3951   iii   LESTER, b. Nov. 12, 1852.
    3952   iv   IRA G., b. Dec. 28, 1856.
    3953   v   ASENATH J., b. April 19, 1858.
    3954   vi   KING D., b. Dec. 9, 1868.
    3955   vii   FREDERICK H., b. Aug. 3, 1866.

2106 TIMOTHY K.⁸ EMERY (*Timothy,*⁷ *Daniel,*⁶ *Daniel,*⁵ *Noah,*⁴ *Daniel,*³ *James,*² *Anthony*¹), son of Timothy and Olive (Wentworth) Emery ; married, first, Nov., 1849, Hannah E. Pinkham of Milton, N. H. (died Sept., 1851) ; second, Dec., 1855, Irene P. Morrow of Milton Mills.

Children :

    3956   i   LIZZIE H.,⁹ b. May 7, 1851.

By second marriage :

    3957   ii   JAMES S., b. June 24, 1856.
    3958   iii   JOHN H., b. Dec. 11, 1858.

2107 OLIVE J.⁸ EMERY (*Timothy,*⁷ *Daniel,*⁶ *Daniel,*⁵ *Noah,*⁴ *Daniel,*³ *James,*² *Anthony*¹), daughter of Timothy and Olive (Wentworth) Emery ; married Aug. 14, 1849, William S. Keay of Dover, N. H.

Child :

    3959   i   JAMES C.,⁹ b. Jan. 14, 1856.

2109 CHARLES⁸ EMERY (*Daniel C.,*⁷ *Daniel,*⁶ *Daniel,*⁵ *Noah,*⁴ *Daniel,*³ *James,*² *Anthony*¹), son of Daniel C. and Hannah (Goodwin) Emery ; married Mrs. Sarah (Goodwin) Heard (died March 15, 1878).

Children :

    3960   i   LOUISA.⁹ b. Oct. 10, 1832; m. Feb. 14, 1852, Chas. W. Caswell.
    3961   ii   SARAH, b. 1834; m. William Bragdon.
    3962   iii   SYLVIA, b. 1836; m., 1st, Ezra Rogers; 2nd, Jackson Rogers;
                  3d, Dinsmore Bodwell.
    3963   iv   JETHRO,   ⎫ b. Sept.,1839; ⎰ d. Jan., 1840.
    3964   v   CHARLES W., ⎭   ⎱ d. Feb., 1840.

2113 DANIEL⁸ EMERY (*Daniel C.,*⁷ *Daniel,*⁶ *Daniel,*⁵ *Noah,*⁴ *Daniel,*³ *James,*² *Anthony*¹), son of Daniel C. and Hannah (Goodwin) Emery ; married Nov. 29, 1839, Mary P. Young of Great Falls, N. H. (born Feb. 8, 1819).

Children :

   3965 i   LAURA,[9] b. June 3, 1841.
   3966 ii GEORGE E , b Oct. 24, 1846
   3967 iii DANIEL, b Oct 4, 1848
   3968 iv ADDIE MAY, b May 11, 1857.
   3969 v   WILLIE B , b Aug 4, 1860.

2122 JOSEPH[8] EMERY (*Noah,*[7] *Noah,*[6] *Daniel,*[5] *Noah,*[4] *Daniel,*[3] *James,*[2] *Anthony*[1]), son of Noah and Sarah (Gowen) Emery, married May 7, 1830, Mrs. Olive (Raitt) Odiorne (born Feb. 2, 1795 ; died Nov. 11, 1866), daughter of William and Sarah Raitt.
Children:

   3970 i   SARAH ELIZABETH,[9] b Sept 1, 1831.
   3971 ii WILLIAM GOWEN, b Feb. 22, 1833.
   3972 iii LYDIA A , b. June 29, 1834
   3973 iv OLIVE JANE, b Dec 7, 1835.

2134 ABBY B [8] EMERY (*Enoch,*[7] *Noah,*[6] *Daniel,*[5] *Noah,*[4] *Daniel,*[3] *James,*[2] *Anthony*[1]), daughter of Enoch and Harriet (Bradbury) Emery, married Nov. 3, 1846, Benning Haley (born July 29, 1818).
Children :

   3974 i   EDWIN,[9] b Oct. 4, 1848 , d Nov 6, 1862
   3975 ii FRANKLIN, b May 5, 1850.
   3976 iii MARY EUNICE, b May 23, 1853, d Oct 30, 1862

2137 MARY ELIZABETH[8] EMERY (*Shem,*[7] *Noah,*[6] *Daniel,*[5] *Noah,*[4] *Daniel,*[3] *James,*[2] *Anthony*[1]), daughter of Shem and Mary (Walker) Emery ; married, first, William G. Seaward ; second, George Dennett of Portsmouth, N. H.
Child of first marriage :

   3977 i   OLIVIA MARIA,[9] b Feb 13, 1826.

By second marriage ·

   3978 ii GEORGE WILLIAM, b Nov 4, 1831
   3979 iii DANIEL EMERY, b May 16, 1836, d about 1885
   3980 iv GIDEON WALKER, b 1839; d July, 1841
   3981 v   GIDEON WALKER, b July, 1841

2139 GEORGE F [8] EMERY (*Shem,*[7] *Noah,*[6] *Daniel,*[5] *Noah,*[4] *Daniel,*[3] *James,*[2] *Anthony*[1]), son of Shem and Mary (Walker) Emery ; married, first, Abby F. Lewis of Boston ; second, Mrs. Elizabeth F. Tillinghast.
Children :

   3982 i   CATHARINE LEWIS,[9] b April 10, 1837
   3983 ii ABBY FRANCES, b Nov 28, 1839
   3984 iii GEORGE VINCENT, b Sept 1 1842
   3985 iv HENRY, b. July 31, 1845, d May, 1847.
   3986 v   WILFRED AUGUSTINE, b April 8, 1847.
   3987 vi JOHN B F., b Aug 6, 1851.

2141 NATHANIEL STONE[8] EMERY (*Shem,*[7] *Noah,*[6] *Daniel,*[5] *Noah,*[4] *Daniel,*[3] *James,*[2] *Anthony*[1]), son of Shem and Mary (Walker) Emery ; married Ellen Shannon of Portsmouth, N. H.

Children :

3988 i   HORACE STONE,[9] b. Jan. 7, 1841; m. Julianna Blake.
3989 ii   ALBERT WALDON.
3990 iii GEORGE SHANNON.

2142 SUSAN B.[8] EMERY (*Shem,*[7] *Noah,*[6] *Daniel,*[5] *Noah,*[4] *Daniel,*[3] *James,*[2] *Anthony*[1]), daughter of Shem and Mary (Walker) Emery ; married Charles W. Cheever of Portsmouth, N. H. She died April 22, 1872.
Children :

3991 i   CHARLES HOWARD.[9]
3992 ii   MARY A.
3993 iii EMMA.

2143 IRA[8] EMERY(*Shem,*[7] *Noah,*[6] *Daniel,*[5] *Noah,*[4] *Daniel,*[3] *James,*[2] *Anthony*[1]), son of Shem and Mary (Walker) Emery ; married Elizabeth S. Nason of Portsmouth, N. H.
Children :

3994 i   WALLACE H.[8]
3995 ii   HENRY S.

2144 WOODBURY[8] EMERY (*Shem,*[7] *Noah,*[6] *Daniel,*[5] *Noah,*[4] *Daniel,*[3] *James,*[2] *Anthony*[1]), son of Shem and Mary (Walker) Emery ; married Mary A. Gould of Boston, Mass. ; resided in Washington, D. C., 1853-1865. Resides in Boston where he occupies a responsible position in the post office.
Children, born in Washington :

3996 i   MARTHA WALKER,[9] b. Oct. 4, 1853.
3997 ii   ELLA WOODBURY, b. Jan. 9, 1856.
3998 iii ALICE CORA, b. Feb. 21, 1859.
3999 iv   FRANK WOODBURY, b. Jan. 29, 1861; d. Oct. 24, 1862.
4000 v   CLARA MAY, b. May 31, 1863.

2162 ELIZA H.[8] EMERY (*John,*[7] *George,*[6] *Daniel,*[5] *Noah,*[4] *Daniel,*[3] *James,*[2] *Anthony*[1]), daughter of John and Hannah (Post) Emery ; married Benjamin Webster. Resides in South Thomaston, Me.
Children :

4001 i   HANNAH M.,[9] b. May 29, 1836 ; m. —— Kimball ; res. in Cal.
4002 ii   ANN ELIZA, b. April 15, 1838 ; m. Capt. Jeremiah Hooper ; res. in Rockland, Me.
4003 iii EMMA T., b. 1844 ; m. Capt. Horatio B. Hooper ; res. in N. J.
4004 iv   LYDIA E., b. 1846 ; m. Eugene Alden ; d. in Hammonton, N. J., May 29, 1884.
4005 v   EVELINE B., b. 1848 ; m. Capt. J. W. Hall.

2163 WILLIAM S.[8] EMERY (*John,*[7] *George,*[6] *Daniel,*[5] *Noah,*[4] *Daniel,*[3] *James,*[2] *Anthony*[1]), son of John and Hannah (Post) Emery ; married July 7, 1839, Lucy J. Spaulding ; removed to San Diego, Cal.
Children :

4006 i   ELEANOR S.,[9] b. Feb. 20, 1840, in Thomaston, Me. ; d. April 14, 1840.

4007　ii　WILLIAM E., b Feb 21, 1842, in Thomaston, Me.
4008　iii　HENRY N.,
4009　iv　HERBERT L , ⎱ b June 30, 1843, in Thomaston, Me.
4010　v　JOSIAH S , b July 4, 1845, in Thomaston, Me ; d Oct. 3, 1872
4011　vi　EDWARD, b June 7, 1847, in Thomaston, Me.; d Dec 12, 1852
4012　vii　LUCY E , b April 27, 1849, in Thomaston, Me.
4013　viii　MARY W , b May 30, 1852, in Sacramento, Cal ; d March 4, 1855
4014　ix　EDWARD C , b Jan 1, 1854, in Sacramento, Cal
4015　x　ANNE S., b Aug 4, 1855, in Sacramento, Cal
4016　xi　CHARLES F , b Aug 16, 1857, in Woodland, Cal
4017　xii　MARY G　b May 22, 1859
4018　xiii　LILLIAN, b March 8, 1861, d. Aug 16, 1862
4019　xiv　LILLIAN G., b. Sept. 23, 1863.

2164 HANNAH[8] EMERY (*John,*[7] *George,*[6] *Daniel,*[5] *Noah,*[4] *Daniel,*[3] *James,*[2] *Anthony*[1]), daughter of John and Hannah (Post) Emery; married, first, Alden B. Arey ; second, William Eliot.
Children, by second marriage :

4020　i　LAURA,[9] b 1845 , m Frederick Fisher
4021　ii　JOHN, b 1848 , d 1868
4022　iii　HENRY, b. 1857

2167 AMANDA C [8] EMERY (*John,*[7] *George,*[6] *Daniel,*[5] *Noah,*[4] *Daniel,*[3] *James,*[2] *Anthony*[1]), daughter of John and Hannah (Post) Emery , married Sept. 27, 1847, Isaac A. Hix.
Children .

4023　i　GEORGE B ,[9] b 1849.
4024　ii　ALVAH W , b 1853
4025　iii　ALTHEA, b 1854
4026　iv　FREDDIE, b 1859 , d 1880

2171 SUSAN E.[8] EMERY (*John,*[7] *George,*[6] *Daniel,*[5] *Noah,*[4] *Daniel,*[3] *James,*[2] *Anthony*[1]), daughter of John and his second wife, Mrs Hannah (Crie-Bartlett) Emery , married Nov. 25, 1856, Samuel G. Everett
Children .

4027　i　ADRIAN C ,[9] b Feb 23, 1858
4028　ii　MAGGIE J , b July 25, 1861.
4029　iii　GEORGE S , b April 19 1871
4030　iv　AMELIA E . b. Jan 22, 1877

2174 BRADFORD ALDEN[8] EMERY (*John,*[7] *George,*[6] *Daniel,*[5] *Noah,*[4] *Daniel,*[3] *James,*[2] *Anthony*[1]), son of John and his second wife, Mrs. Hannah (Crie-Bartlett) Emery; married March 8, 1864, Lizzy O. Maddocks (born Aug 19, 1839).
Children :

4031　i　SIDNEY P ,[9] b April 21. 1866
4032　ii　SUSIE E , b July 19, 1868
4033　iii　CYNTHIA A , b March 10, 1870
4034　iv　CHARLES H., b April 17, 1872.
4035　v　HATTIE C., b June 19, 1873
4036　vi　FAITH R , b April 23, 1875
4037　vii　ROBERT L , b. June 7, 1880.

2176 Ann[8] Emery (*Dennis,[7] George,[6] Daniel,[5] Noah,[4] Daniel,[3] James,[2] Anthony[1]*), daughter of Dennis and Jane (Turnbull) Emery; married Capt. Thomas Cottrell, Dec. 15, 1839. Resides in Belfast, Me.

Children :

```
4038   i    ANGELINE F ,⁹ b  Nov  28, 1840, d  when fifteen years old.
4039   ii   VERENA A , b  June 1, 1847, m  James C. Townsend
4040   iii  LIZZIE A , b  Dec  26, 1857, d  young
```

2178 Robert T [8] Emery (*Dennis,[7] George,[6] Daniel,[5] Noah,[4] Daniel,[3] James,[2] Anthony[1]*), son of Dennis and Jane (Turnbull) Emery, married, first, July 3, 1854, Lizzie S. Ross; second, Nov. 24, 1869, Eliza R. Ritchie. Shipmaster in Belfast, Me.

Child ·

```
4041   i    RALPH,⁹ b  Dec  17, 1860, m  June 10, 1890, Louisa W. Buxton
            of Detroit, Mich.
```

2179 Keziah[8] Emery (*Dennis,[7] George,[6] Daniel,[5] Noah,[4] Daniel,[3] James,[2] Anthony[1]*), daughter of Dennis and Jane (Turnbull) Emery; married July 9, 1848, Capt. J M. Boardman. Resides in Belfast, Me.

Child :

```
4042   i    EMERY,⁹ b  April 10, 1849; lawyer in Belfast, Me
```

2180 Elizabeth[8] Emery (*Dennis,[7] George,[6] Daniel,[5] Noah,[4] Daniel,[3] James,[2] Anthony[1]*), daughter of Dennis and Jane (Turnbull) Emery; married Capt William O. Alden. He married, second, Jan. 24, 1864, Lydia Jane Emery, sister of his first wife.

Children, by first wife :

```
4043   i    WILLIAM O.⁹
4044   ii   ROBERT E
```

2181 John H.[8] Emery (*Dennis,[7] George,[6] Daniel,[5] Noah,[4] Daniel,[3] James,[2] Anthony[1]*), son of Dennis and Jane (Turnbull) Emery; married Nancy Bassett. Lives in Belfast, Me.

Children :

```
4045   i    CHARLES A ,⁹ b  May 13, 1864, d. April 18, 1882.
4046   ii   BERTHA, b. Nov. 13, 1871.
```

2186 Capt. George[8] Emery (*Jonas,[7] George,[6] Daniel,[5] Noah,[4] Daniel,[3] James,[2] Anthony[1]*), son of Jonas and Abigail (Sleeper) Emery; married Susan D Graves (born Sept 24, 1821). Shipmaster of note and prominence. Lived in Baltimore, Md.

Children :

```
4047   i     EVA P ,⁹ b  July 4, 1847
4048   ii    EDWIN R , b  May 19, 1849
4049   iii   LIZZIE C , b  March 15, 1853
4050   iv    LILLIAN M , b  March 24, 1854; d  Sept. 18, 1856
4051   v     WALTER N , b  Sept 24, 1856
4052   vi    ARTHUR S , b  May 1, 1859.
4053   vii   NELLIE N , b. May 18, 1861.
4054   viii  GEORGE N , b  May 2, 1867.
```

2189 Lucy L [8] Emery (*Jonas*,[7] *George*,[6] *Daniel*,[5] *Noah*,[4] *Daniel*,[3] *James*,[2] *Anthony*[1]), daughter of Jonas and his second wife, Mehitable (Keller) Emery; married Sept 11, 1842, William H. Raymond. Resides in Belfast, Me.; died July 4, 1857.

Children ·

    4055 i   Lucy Ann,[9] m Albert Elms of Searsmont, Me., d 1869
    4056 ii William H
    4057 iii Charles E , d March, 1872, in Rockport, Me.
    4058 iv Mary E , m. —— Clark; d 1871

2190 Mary Abigail[8] Emery (*Jonas*,[7] *George*,[6] *Daniel*,[5] *Noah*,[4] *Daniel*,[3] *James*,[2] *Anthony*[1]), daughter of Jonas and his second wife, Mehitable (Keller) Emery; married May 30, 1850, Richard Smith Goodwin (born in Newburyport, Mass.). Lives in Lynn, Mass.

Children :

    4059 i   Richard S [9] b Nov 19, 1851, m July 1, 1875, Mary E Batchelder of Lynn, Mass
    4060 ii Mary Abby, b Dec 11, 1853
    4061 iii Anna Hoyt, b Aug 3, 1855
    4062 iv James Caldwell, b. June 1, 1857.
    4063 v   Charlotte Elizabeth, b July 15, 1859
    4064 vi Walter Everett, b July 22, 1862, m Dec. 24, 1883, Edith M. Oliver of Saugus, Mass.

2191 Sarah D [8] Emery (*Jonas*,[7] *George*,[6] *Daniel*,[5] *Noah*,[4] *Daniel*,[3] *James*,[2] *Anthony*[1]), daughter of Jonas and his second wife, Mehitable (Keller) Emery ; married, 1852, Nathaniel Noyes of Newbury, Mass., who died in the army at Baton Rouge, La., May 10, 1863. She died in Newbury, Mass., Dec. 19, 1866.

Children :

    4065 i   Woodbridge N ,[9] b July 20, 1854, d Jan 5, 1862.
    4066 ii Leslie J , b Nov 3, 1856, d Aug. 8, 1858
    4067 iii Willard F., b Feb 24, 1859.
    4068 iv Albert E., b. Dec 20, 1861.
    4069 v   Nathaniel E , b. Jan 6, 1863.

2192 Frances J [8] Emery (*Jonas*,[7] *George*,[6] *Daniel*,[5] *Noah*,[4] *Daniel*,[3] *James*,[2] *Anthony*[1]), daughter of Jonas and his second wife, Mehitable (Keller) Emery; married Dec 25, 1856, Charles Hunt of Newburyport, Mass. Lived in North Carpenter.

Children ·

    4070 i   Frank E ,[9] b Oct 16 1857.
    4071 ii Willard E., b Jan 20, 1860.
    4072 iii Andrew E , b May 4, 1865
    4073 iv Jennie F , b March 25, 1867, d Nov 13, 1869
    4074 v   Susie F., b. March 25, 1870, d Aug. 14, 1874.

2193 William C [8] Emery (*Jonas*,[7] *George*,[6] *Daniel*,[5] *Noah*,[4] *Daniel*,[3] *James*,[2] *Anthony*[1]), son of Jonas and his second wife, Mehitable (Keller) Emery, married, first, June 15, 1853, Mary C. Crosby of Belfast, Me (died Feb. 22, 1868), second, Oct. 15, 1882, Mrs. Eliza Moore at Shenandoah, Pa. Miner.

Children :

    4075 i   EVA D ,⁹ b April 10, 1855
    4076 ii   GEORGE E , b. May 15, 1857
    4077 iii WILLIAM O , b Sept 3, 1859
    4078 iv   CHARLES O , b Jan 15, 1861
    4079 v   HENRY H , b Dec. 8, 1863

2194 JONAS D ⁸ EMERY (*Jonas,⁷ George,⁶ Daniel,⁵ Noah,⁴ Daniel,³ James,² Anthony¹*), son of Jonas and his second wife, Mehitable (Keller) Emery ; married, first, Harriet Blood of Camden, Me. ; second, Aug 1, 1869, Rhoda A Brown of Vinal Haven, Me. Resides in Carver's Harbor, Me.
Children .

    4080 i   GEORGE A ,⁹ b Aug 24, 1870
    4081 ii   ROSETTA, b Sept 25 1872, d Jan. 14, 1885
    4082 iii JAMES W , b Sept 10 1874.
    4083 iv   HERBERI, b. Oct. 10, 1876.
    4084 v   FREEMAN, b Nov. 29, 1879.

2195 JOHN K ⁸ EMERY (*Jonas,⁷ George,⁶ Daniel,⁵ Noah,⁴ Daniel,³ James,² Anthony¹*), son of Jonas and his second wife, Mehitable (Keller) Emery, married Sept. 2, 1862, Mary A. Smith of Brooklyn, N. Y. Was in a New York regiment during the Rebellion ; sea-faring man ; mate at one time. Has not been heard from for ten years
Children :

    4085 i   ANNIE V ,⁹ b July 28, 1865
    4086 ii   IDA, b May 17, 1869

2197 SUSAN E ⁸ EMERY (*Jonas,⁷ George,⁶ Daniel,⁵ Noah,⁴ Daniel,³ James,² Anthony¹*), daughter of Jonas and his second wife, Mehitable (Keller) Emery ; married Dec. 23, 1867, Charles R. Todd of Rowley, Mass   Resides in Newburyport, Mass.
Children :

    4087 i   EDWARD M ,⁹ b Dec 25, 1877
    Two children, SUSIE E. and CLEMENT M , twins, adopted

2198 HELEN CLEMENTINE⁸ EMERY (*Jonas,⁷ George,⁶ Daniel,⁵ Noah,⁴ Daniel,³ James,² Anthony¹*), daughter of Jonas and his second wife, Mehitable (Keller) Emery ; married Nov 1, 1862, E. L. Buzzell of Searsmont, Me   Resides in Newburyport, Mass.
Children .

    4088 i   CORA L ,⁹ b June 10, 1863
    4089 ii   MAURICE A , b Oct 23, 1865
    4090 iii CHARLES A , b April 28, 1869
    4091 iv   CLEMENT M , ⎫ b March 30, 1873, ⎰ adopted by Susan E (Em-
    4092 v   SUSIE E ,   ⎭   ⎱ ery) Todd
    4093 vi   GEORGIE, b Sept 28, 1878

2199 EDWIN THOMAS⁸ EMERY (*George,⁷ George,⁶ Daniel,⁵ Noah,⁴ Daniel,³ James,² Anthony¹*), son of George and Nancy (Sleeper) Emery ; married Susan Perry. Resides in So. Thomaston, Me.

Child :

4094 ı⁺   EDWARD G ,⁹ b June 15, 1852.

2200 EVELINE⁸ EMERY (*George,*⁷ *George,*⁶ *Daniel,*⁵ *Noah,*⁴ *Daniel,*³ *James,*² *Anthony*¹), daughter of George and Nancy (Sleeper) Emery ; married Charles Sherman.

Child ·

4095 ı   ———

2201 JOHN J ⁸ EMERY (*George,*⁷ *George,*⁶ *Daniel,*⁵ *Noah,*⁴ *Daniel,*³ *James,*² *Anthony*¹), son of George and his second wife, Rebecca (Maddocks) Emery , married Melissa L Arey (born May 26, 1837) Shipmaster and trader in So. Thomaston, Me.

Children :

4096 ı   SETH A ,⁹ b June 25, 1860
4097 ıı   MARY R , b Feb 21, 1864, m June 20, 1883, Fred M Smith
4098 ııı   NELLIE R , b March 3, 1868
4099 ıv   GRACE C., b May 20, 1872
4100 v   MARIAN A , b March 18, 1876.

2202 JOSEPH M ⁸ EMERY (*George,*⁷ *George,*⁶ *Daniel,*⁵ *Noah,*⁴ *Daniel,*³ *James,*² *Anthony*¹), son of George and his second wife, Rebecca (Maddocks) Emery ; married, 1852, May A. Masters   Master shipbuilder and granite contractor   Lives in Rockland, Me

Children, born in Rockland, Me. ·

4101 ı   GEORGIE,⁹ b March 14, 1853
4102 ıı   CHARLES O , b Feb 28, 1855.
4103 ııı   JOSEPH W , b Nov 24, 1857, d April 10, 1881
4104 ıv   ALICE M., b. April 13, 1862, m Jan 9, 1884, Arthur Horton of N. Y.

2203 GEORGE W ⁸ EMERY (*George,*⁷ *George,*⁶ *Daniel,*⁵ *Noah,*⁴ *Daniel,*³ *James,*² *Anthony*¹), son of George and his second wife, Rebecca (Maddocks) Emery ; married Dec. 17, 1865, Caroline A. Ricker (born Feb. 28, 1839) of Cherryfield, Me.   Master ship-builder.

Children .

4105 ı   HELEN,⁹ b. Oct 22, 1866.
4106 ıı   LUCY, b March 16, 1868
4107 ııı   GLEASON R , b April 16, 1871.
4108 ıv   WILLIAM C., b. Nov. 26, 1873

2214 KNOTT C ⁸ EMERY (*Daniel,*⁷ *George,*⁶ *Daniel,*⁵ *Noah,*⁴ *Daniel,*³ *James,*² *Anthony*¹), son of Daniel and Sophia (Sleeper) Emery ; married Oct 2, 1880, Ada Snow (born Feb. 28, 1859).   Resides at Owl's Head, So. Thomaston, Me.   Ship-master.

Children :

4109 ı   EUGENE R ,⁹ b. April 30, 1884.
4110 ıı   EVA M , b. Sept 16, 1866

2215 ABBIE S ⁸ EMERY (*Daniel,*⁷ *George,*⁶ *Daniel,*⁵ *Noah,*⁴ *Daniel,*³ *James,*² *Anthony*¹), daughter of Daniel and Sophia (Sleeper) Emery , married Capt. Joshua Bartlett.

Child :

4111 i MATTIE S.,[9] b Jan. 12, 1881

2218 CATHARINE R.[8] EMERY (*William D.,[7] George,[6] Daniel,[5] Noah [4] Daniel,[3] James,[2] Anthony[1]*), daughter of William D. and Harriet E. (Pratt) Emery; married Dec. 7, 1851, Gardner Prescott. Resides in Boston, Mass , died Nov. 14, 1878.

Children :

4112 i FRANK W ,[9] b Oct 24, 1852
4113 ii FANNIE G., b Sept 15, 1856

2220 WILLIAM N [8] EMERY (*William D ,[7] George,[6] Daniel,[5] Noah,[4] Daniel,[3] James,[2] Anthony[1]*). son of William D. and Harriet E. (Pratt) Emery , married Nov. 15, 1860, Martha Dearborn (died, 1873).

Children :

4114 i GILMAN N ,[9] b Aug 25 1861; d Sept 3, 1863
4115 ii GRACE G , b Sept 11, 1864
4116 iii MARTHA J , b July 12, 1867.
4117 iv WALTER F , b Jan 24, 1869
4118 v EDITH S , b. Oct 15, 1873

2221 ADONIRAM J.[8] EMERY (*William D.,[7] George,[6] Daniel,[5] Noah,[4] Daniel,[3] James,[2] Anthony[1]*), son of William D and Harriet E (Pratt) Emery; married, first, May 6, 1865, Josephine Sylvester (died Dec. 22, 1888) ; second, —— Carpenter.

Children :

4119 i ALBERT S ,[9] b April 5, 1866.
4120 ii ANNA R , b Oct 27, 1872, d. April 20, 1875.

2230 WASHBURN[8] EMERY (*Rev. Ephraim H ,[7] George,[6] Daniel,[5] Noah,[4] Daniel,[3] James,[2] Anthony[1]*), son of Rev. Ephraim H. and Mrs. Temperance (Pruden) Emery , married, first, March 15. 1869, Emma De Brennar (born Nov 22, 1839 ; died March 17, 1877) ; second, May 2, 1881, Mrs. Mary L. Busted (*née* De Brennar) born May 2, 1849.

Children :

4121 i ERNEST W ,[9] b Jan 3, 1870
4122 ii ARTHUR L , b March 20, 1871, d Aug 25, 1871.
4123 iii WILLARD I , b. March 11, 1874; d May 2, 1874.

2231 ACHSIE S [8] EMERY (*Rev. Ephraim H.,[7] George,[6] Daniel,[5] Noah,[4] Daniel,[3] James,[2] Anthony[1]*), daughter of Rev Ephraim H. and Mrs. Temperance (Pruden) Emery , married Aug. 15, 1864, at Palermo, Me , Levi G. Perry (born Aug. 15, 1841).

Children :

4124 i GERTRUDE B ,[9] b July 16, 1865.
4125 ii WEBSTER E , b Dec 23, 1867.
4126 iii GRACE M., b July 17, 1869
4127 iv RALPH E., b. Oct. 23, 1870.

2237 NATHANIEL[8] HALL (*Anna,[7] Nathaniel,[6] Daniel,[5] Noah,[4] Daniel,[3] James,[2] Anthony[1]*), son of Isaac and Anna (Emery) Hall ; married Dec. 3, 1848, Elona (born June 15, 1822), daughter of Levi and Lois (Keen) Emery

Children :

```
4128    i    ARVILLA,⁹ b Sept 21. 1849, d. Nov 16, 1857.
4129   ii    JUDSON E , b  Dec 27, 1851
4130   iii   CHARLES, b  July 4, 1855, d  Oct 26, 1857
4131   iv    FRANK, b  Oct. 28, 1859, d  Nov 22, 1864
4132    v    ELMER E , b  March 2, 1862.
```

2245 IRENE⁸ EMERY (*Tristram,⁷ Nathaniel,⁶ Daniel,⁵ Noah,⁴ Daniel,³ James,² Anthony¹*), daughter of Tristram and Lydia W. (Emery) Emery , married Harper Senter. Lives in Harrison, Ohio.

Children :

```
4133    i    CAROLINE ⁹  (See No. 2260.)
4134   ii    ASA C.  (See No. 2261 )
```

2246 CAROLINE⁸ EMERY (*Tristram,⁷ Nathaniel,⁶ Daniel,⁵ Noah,⁴ Daniel,³ James,² Anthony¹*), daughter of Tristram and Lydia W. (Emery) Emery ; married, Dec , 1843, in Harrison, Ohio, Jesse Mead.

Children .

```
4135    i    JULIETT,⁹ b Sept , 1844
4136   ii    CLARENCE, b  March, 1846, d  1870
4137   iii   CORDELIA, b  March, 1848, d  1867.
4138   iv    ELLA, b  Sept , 1851
4139    v    ELWOOD,  }
4140   vi    ELMER,   }  b July, 1858.
```

2247 HORACE⁸ EMERY (*Tristram,⁷ Nathaniel,⁶ Daniel,⁵ Noah,⁴ Daniel,³ James,² Anthony¹*), son of Tristram and Lydia E (Emery) Emery ; married Nov. 18, 1843, Mary West (born Sept. 13, 1819) in Salem, Washington County, N. Y. Lives in Green Springs, Ohio

Children .

```
4141    i    CORDELIA,⁹ b June 20, 1845, d  Sept 30, 1845.
4142   ii    ELIZABETH A , b  Nov 18, 1846; d  April 25  1852.
4143   iii   SANDERS N , b  April 24, 1849, d  Feb. 25, 1852
4144   iv    ELMER E , b  Nov 7, 1851
4145    v    MABEL S , b  Feb 12, 1854
4146   vi    CHARLES N., b  Sept. 1, 1856; d  Feb 28, 1858
4147   vii   WILLIAM J., b  Dec 16, 1858, grad of Buchtel College, Akron,
                Ohio.
4148  viii   ELLA C , b  Dec 7, 1864
```

2248 RUFUS⁸ EMERY (*Tristram,⁷ Nathaniel,⁶ Daniel,⁵ Noah,⁴ Daniel,³ James,² Anthony¹*), son of Tristram and Lydia W. (Emery) Emery , married, first, July 4, 1850, Cynthia Mead (born July 4, 1832 ; died Oct. 5, 1855) ; second, Nov. 23, 1858, Phillgia Pettis. Resides in Plymouth, Ohio.

Children :

```
4149    i    MARY ⁹ b July 28, 1852 , m Bert Porter  Lives in Clyde, Ohio.
4150   ii    WILLIS, b. Sept 26, 1858.  Lives in Liberty, Ohio
4151   iii   STELLA, b  May 1, 1860, d  Oct 22, 1865.
4152   iv    STANTON, b  Aug. 1, 1861, d  Aug 24, 1865
4153    v    DORA, b  May 2, 1863, d  April 15, 1864.
4154   vi    ZILLA, b  March 11, 1865.
4155   vii   RAY, b  Dec 7, 1866
4156  viii   EARL, b  Dec. 7, 1868.
```

2253 Judson[8] Emery (*Levi,[7] Nathaniel,[6] Daniel,[5] Noah,[4] Daniel,[3] James,[2] Anthony[1]*), son of Levi and Lois (Keen) Emery, married June 9, 1848, Lucinda Mead (born in Grelton, Ohio, Nov. 20, 1823).
Children:

   4157 i   Ophlita,[9] b Jan 13, 1850, m Oliver Bogart, Aug 6, 1868
   4158 ii Erika, b Feb. 7, 1854

2255 Enos[8] Emery (*Levi,[7] Nathaniel,[6] Daniel,[5] Noah,[4] Daniel,[3] James,[2] Anthony[1]*), son of Levi and Lois (Keen) Emery; married March 1, 1856, Olive J. Decrow (born April 1, 1832). Resides in Montville, Me
  Child ·

   4159 i   Cora J ,[9] b May 11, 1862 d Sept 1, 1876

2256 Ann H [8] Emery (*Levi,[7] Nathaniel,[6] Daniel,[5] Noah,[4] Daniel,[3] James,[2] Anthony[1]*), daughter of Levi and Lois (Keen) Emery; married Nov. 17, 1859, William L Sisty. member of Co "C," 55 Ohio Vols., wounded at Averysboro or Averasboro, N. C , and was taken to David's Island, where he died
  Children .

   4160 i   Lois J.,[9] b. Jan 21, 1861; d June 26, 1868
   4161 ii George L , b April 23, 1863, lives in Neb

2257 Harriet N.[8] Emery (*Levi,[7] Nathaniel,[6] Daniel,[5] Noah,[4] Daniel,[3] James,[2] Anthony[1]*), daughter of Levi and Lois (Keen) Emery; married March 15, 1851, George Crockett (died Nov. 30, 1871).
  Children ·

   4162 i   Malcolm [9] b July 11, 1852 , lives in Monroe, Ohio.
   4163 ii Alice A , b Nov 2, 1857, m Martin Koller, lives in Bloomville, Ohio
   4164 iii Mary, b March 9, 1861, d March 30, 1862
   4165 iv Ernest N b March 31, 1863
   4166 v   Knott, b. March 7, 1865.

2259 Willard[8] Emery (*Levi,[7] Nathaniel,[6] Daniel,[5] Noah,[4] Daniel,[3] James,[2] Anthony[1]*), son of Levi and Lois (Keen) Emery; married July 4, 1860, Sarah Martin ; they were divorced and he married, second, Lucinda Howe.
  Child :

   4167 i   Eltheon L ,[9] b Oct. 26, 1861, lives in Damascus, Ohio.

2260 Alden C [8] Emery (*Levi,[7] Nathaniel,[6] Daniel,[5] Noah,[4] Daniel,[3] James,[2] Anthony[1]*), son of Levi and Lois (Keen) Emery , married Nov. 14, 1858, Caroline Senter (See No. 4133). Lives in Henry Co., Ohio.
  Child :

   4168 i   Vernon J.,[9] b April 11, 1861, in Harrison, Ohio. Grad of Ohio State University in 1886 , teacher of Latin and Mathematics in Neb. State University, Neb.

2262 Thomas B [8] Emery (*Levi,*[7] *Nathaniel,*[6] *Daniel,*[5] *Noah,*[4] *Daniel,*[3] *James,*[2] *Anthony*[1]), son of Levi and Lois (Keen) Emery, married April 9, 1862, Cynthia Shively. Resides in Grelton, Ohio.
Child :

4169 i Eva M ,[9] b June 19, 1864, in Montville, Me.

2277 Capt. Charles[8] Emery (*Robert,*[7] *John,*[6] *Noah,*[5] *Noah,*[4] *Daniel,*[3] *James,*[2] *Anthony*[1]), son of Capt Robert and his third wife, Mary (Lyman) Emery, married Nov. 1, 1840, Susan Hilton, daughter of Hon John Kelly of Exeter, N H Resided in Springfield, Mass., Portsmouth, R. I., and Dorchester, Mass. He went to sea when fifteen years of age, was in command of a ship at twenty. making the voyage around Cape Horn, followed the sea for some years, making voyages to South America, China and the West Indies. In 1878, he commanded an expedition up the River Amazon in search of valuable woods, carrying the United States flag where it had never been before Later he sailed again up the Amazon, going a thousand miles up this river into the heart of the rubber country. He was interested and engaged in mining. He was a veteran and member of the Boston Marine Society, having joined it in 1852 ; trustee for twenty-five years, and its president from 1887 to 1889. Capt. Emery was a typical sea-captain of the old Merchant Service
Children .

4170 i Mary Abbot,[9] b. Feb 23, 1843, in Springfield, Mass., m Rev. Alva T Twing, D D , agent of Foreign and Domestic Missions of the Episcopal Church
4171 ii Susan Lavina, b Sept 26, 1846, in Dorchester, Mass
4172 iii John Abbot, b Jan 24, 1848
4173 iv Margaret Therese, b Aug 3, 1849, in Dorchester, Mass.
4174 v Julia Chester, b Sept 24, 1852, in Dorchester, Mass
4175 vi Charles Robert, b March 10, 1854, in Dorchester, Mass., d Aug 18, 1880, in Westfield, Mass
4176 vii Edith Foote, b March 14, 1855, in Dorchester, Mass ; d. Aug 26, 1855
4177 viii Carrie Maria, b Oct 18, 1856, in Portsmouth, R I.
4178 ix William Stanley, b May 6, 1858, in Portsmouth, R I.
4179 x Alice Kelly, b. Sept 2, 1859, in Dorchester, Mass , d June 27 1873
4180 xi Helen Winthrop, b Sept 30, 1862, in Dorchester, Mass

2281 Mary Lyman[8] Emery (*Robert,*[7] *John,*[6] *Noah,*[5] *Noah,*[4] *Daniel,*[3] *James,*[2] *Anthony*[1]), daughter of Capt. Robert and his third wife, Mary (Lyman) Emery, married, June, 1846, Charles B Pierce of Dorchester, Mass.
Children

4181 i Elizabeth Emery,[9] b April 24, 1847.
4182 ii Charles Bates, b Sept 3, 1851, drowned Oct., 1877

2283 John T. G [8] Emery (*Nicholas,*[7] *Noah,*[6] *Noah,*[5] *Noah,*[4] *Daniel,*[3] *James,*[2] *Anthony*[1]), son of Judge Nicholas and Ann Taylor (Gilman) Emery, married Sarah H. Sawyer (died July 25, 1877).
Children .

4183 i Mary Jane,[9] b Oct 29, 1830
4184 ii Charlotte Ann, b Aug. 7, 1832.

32

4185   iii   JOHN, b June 15, 1834; d Aug 22, 1838
4186   iv   HARRIET ELIZABETH, b Aug 11, 1836
4187   v   NICHOLAS, b June 26, 1838
4188   vi   SARAH E ELLEN, b June 7, 1840; d Nov 28, 1865.
4189   vii   JOHN T. G , b Aug 9, 1842
4190   viii   LENDALL BOYD, b. April 10, 1845, d Sept 10, 1871
4191   ix   CHARLES EDWIN, b May 15, 1847, d Dec 5, 1887
4192   x   EUGENE, b Dec 2, 1851, d Dec 5, 1887

2285 THERESA ORNE[8] EMERY (*Nicholas*,[7] *Noah*,[6] *Noah*,[5] *Noah*,[4] *Daniel*,[3] *James*,[2] *Anthony*[1]), daughter of Judge Nicholas and Ann Taylor (Gilman) Emery ; married Aug. 17. 1835, Lendall G. S Boyd. Child :

4193   i   NICHOLAS EMERY,[9] b Aug 13 1837. Grad Bowdoin College, 1860 Private 25th Me Inf in 1862; studied Theology at Meadville, Pa , and Cambridge, Mass , settled in Canastota, N Y , resigned on account of ill health , m. Kate Perkins Scott, Aug. 29, 1862, had two children not now living, res in Cal.

2286 ANN T G [8] EMERY (*Nicholas*,[7] *Noah*,[6] *Noah*,[5] *Noah*,[4] *Daniel*,[3] *James*,[2] *Anthony*[1]), daughter of Judge Nicholas and Ann Taylor (Gilman) Emery , married Aug 30, 1841, George Jacob Abbot of Washington, D. C He was a graduate of Harvard College , successful educator of boys , private secretary of Daniel Webster while Secretary of State; U S Consul at Sheffield, England, for six years , Professor of Theological School, Meadville, Pa.; Consul at Goderich, Canada, where he died Jan , 1879.
Children .

4194   i   MARY J. C.,[9] b. Dec 30, 1842
4195   ii   AN INFANT SON.
4196   iii   ANNE THERESA, b Aug 15, 1846.
4197   iv   JULIA WEBSTER, b July 1, 1848 , m Edgar H Nichols
4198   v   ELIZABETH G , d 1852, aged nine months
4199   vi   CHARLOTTE E , b Oct 26, 1853 , d Oct. 20, 1880

2289 HENRIETTA O.[8] EMERY (*John*,[7] *Noah* [6] *Noah*,[5] *Noah*,[4] *Daniel*,[3] *James*,[2] *Anthony*[1]), daughter of John and Deborah (Webb) Emery; married, 1830, William Burleigh (born Apr 1, 1794 , died Aug. 25, 1844).
Children .

4200   i   EDWARD WILLIAM,[9] b July 5, 1831
4201   ii   FRANK G , b. July 9, 1839.
4202   iii   MARY EMERY

2292 CHARLES EMERY[8] SOULE (*Elizabeth P.*,[7] *Noah*,[6] *Noah*,[5] *Noah*,[4] *Daniel*,[3] *James*,[2] *Anthony*[1]), son of Gideon L and Elizabeth P. (Emery) Soule ; married, first, Arianna F. French of Chester, N H. (died 1865) ; second, 1866, Eliza A. S Murdock, of New York City He entered Exeter Academy, 1833 , graduate of Bowdoin College, 1842 , admitted to the Bar of Rockingham County, N H , 1845 , served as law assistant to the Surrogate of N. Y , President of the Alumni Association of Bowdoin College in N. Y.

Children :

4203 i CHARLES EMERY [9]
4204 ii HELEN
4205 iii EDMUND F.

2294 Augustus Lord[8] Soule(*Elizabeth P.*,[7] *Noah,*[6] *Noah,*[5] *Noah,*[4] *Daniel* [3] *James,*[2] *Anthony*[1]), son of Gideon L. and Elizabeth P (Emery) Soule; married Maria Gray of Exeter, N H   Graduate of Harvard College, 1846, studied law at the Harvard Law School; admitted to the Bar, 1846; Judge of Supreme Court of Mass , 1877–1881 , Corporation Counsel for Boston and Albany R R ; member of the Commission to revise the Judicial system of Mass , 1877 , died 1887.

Children :

4206 i   CORA [9]
4207 ii MARY E

2304 Charles Emery[8] Stevens(*Catherine H.*,[7] *Richard,*[6] *Noah,*[5] *Noah,*[4] *Daniel,*[3] *James,*[2] *Anthony*[1]), son of Boswell and Catherine Hale (Emery) Stevens, born in Pembroke, N H , married Sept. 7, 1852, Caroline Elizabeth Caldwell (born in Barre, Mass., Nov 14, 1830) ; graduated at Dartmouth College, 1835 , read law with his father, studied theology at Andover, Mass , taught in Worthington Academy, Barre, Fitchburg and elsewhere in Massachusetts.   Editor (in 1846) of " *New Hampshire Statesman,*" editor and proprietor of " *Barre Patriot,*" editor of " *Worcester Transcript,*" assistant editor of "*Colonial Records of Mass.*"(vol. 5), assistant Register of Probate and Insolvency for Worcester County (1859–69), Register of Probate and Insolvency for Worcester Co (1869–83).

Children :

4208 i   WILLIAM CALDWELL,[9] b Dec 16, 1854, grad. at Amherst Coll , 1876, and M D at Harv Med School, 1883   Physician at Worcester, Mass
4209 ii KATE GOODNOW , b March 16, 1859

2306 Elizabeth E H.[8] Stevens (*Catherine H* ,[7] *Richard,*[6] *Noah,*[5] *Noah,*[4] *Daniel,*[3] *James,*[2] *Anthony*[1]), daughter of Boswell and Catherine Hale (Emery) Stevens; married Oct 5, 1841, Rev. Seth Warriner Banister (born Jan. 15, 1811 , died Oct. 5, 1861), graduated at Amherst College, 1835.   Elizabeth and her last two children were buried at Carlisle, Mass.   She died in Carlisle, Mass., July 21, 1850.

Children :

4210 i   CHILD ,[9] d unnamed when one week old
4211 ii SARAH ELIZA, b Oct 20, 1847 , d Sept. 12, 1851
4212 iii WILLIAM STEVENS, b June 25, 1850, d Sept 29, 1851

2316 George O [8] Emery (*Joseph,*[7] *Shem,*[6] *Japhet,*[5] *Noah,*[4] *Daniel,*[3] *James,*[2] *Anthony*[1]), son of Joseph and Elizabeth Jane (Emery) Emery, married Emma Brooks.

Children :

4213 i   GRACE,[9] b. Dec. 19, 1874.
4214 ii GEORGE, b. May 13, 1877.

2323 Moses[8] Morrill (*Polly*,[7] *Japhet*,[6] *Japhet*,[5] *Noah*,[4] *Daniel*,[3] *James*,[2] *Anthony*[1]), son of William and Polly (Emery) Morrill, married April 25, 1854, Sarah E Emery, daughter of Joseph and Olive (Raitt Odiorne) Emery. Lived in Eliot, Me.

Child.

4215　ı　Charles,[9] b April 14, 1859

2328 John L[8] Emery (*Japhet*,[7] *Japhet*,[6] *Japhet*,[5] *Noah*,[4] *Daniel*,[3] *James*,[2] *Anthony*[1]), son of Japhet and Hannah (Leighton) Emery; married ———.

Children :

4216　Harry.[9]
4217　Abbie

2330 Cyrena[8] Emery (*Theodore*,[7] *Theodore*,[6] *Japhet*,[5] *Noah*,[4] *Daniel*,[3] *James*,[2] *Anthony*[1]), daughter of Theodore and Susanna (Storer) Emery; married Sept. 1, 1849, Rev. Ransom Dunn (born in Bakersfield, Vt., July 7, 1818). Professor in college in Hillsdale, Mich.

Children :

4218　ı　Cyrena Amanda,[9] b Oct 17 1851, in Wis , d Oct 20, 1851.
4219　ıı　Sarah Abby, b Aug 19, 1853, in Mich , m. Geo. A. Stayton.
4220　ııı　Helen A , b Dec 21 1854, in Mass , m L M Gates
4221　ıv　Lillie Ceoia, b Sept 8, 1859; d May 5, 1861
4222　v　Nettie, b. Nov 9, 1863, in Ill

2331 Theodore A [8] Emery (*Theodore*,[7] *Theodore*,[6] *Japhet*,[5] *Noah*,[4] *Daniel*,[3] *James*,[2] *Anthony*[1]) son of Theodore and Susannah (Storer) Emery, married June 17, 1847, Sarah A Maxwell of Alfred, Me.

Children :

4223　ı　Elizabeth C ,[9] b April 30. 1848 , d March 4, 1875
4224　ıı　George A , b March 11, 1850
4225　ııı　Seavey D., b April 24, 1852
4226　ıv　Lindsey N , b April 15, 1854; m Helen E Randall of Portland, Me , April 17, 1878.
4227　v　Eliza E , b Oct 27, 1856 , d July 31, 1859
4228　vı　Melville T , b April 21, 1859 , d Feb. 12, 1860
4229　vıı　Melville T , b July 24, 1861
4230　vııı　Susan A , b Sept 11, 1862
4231　ıx　Ermina S , b Feb 1, 1866
4232　x　Howard A , b May 13, 1867 , d Jan 10, 1869

2342 Ida Jane[8] Emery (*Alva C.*,[7] *Theodore*,[6] *Japhet*,[5] *Noah*,[4] *Daniel*,[3] *James*,[2] *Anthony*[1]), daughter of Alva C and his second wife, Priscilla L (Marsh) Emery ; married March 7, 1876, H. Lorin Merrill. Lives in Parsonsfield, Me.

Child

4233　ı　Wilbur,[9] b Nov 14, 1879

2346 Ida A [8] Emery (*Josiah G* ,[7] *Theodore*,[6] *Japhet*,[5] *Noah*,[4] *Daniel*,[3] *James*,[2] *Anthony*[1]), daughter of Josiah G. and Arvilla (Head) Emery , married Edward O. Lord of South Berwick. Me.

Children :

4234 i   MARY EMMA,[9] b Dec 16, 1853
4235 ii IDA, b April 25, 1857.

2354 ALEXANDER[8] EMERY (*Jeremiah,*[7] *Jeremiah,*[6] *Simon,*[5] *Simon,*[4] *Daniel,*[3] *James.*[2] *Anthony*[1]). son of Jeremiah and Agnes (Huntress) Emery, married April 22, 1845. Clara Lowe, in Newfield, Me.

Children, born in Shapleigh, Me ·

4236 i   THARON F,[9] b. May 14, 1846, d Sept 29, 1869, in Shapleigh, Me
4237 ii ORAVILLE P.. b. March 8 1848, d Aug 28, 1869, in Hollis, Me
4238 iii ROSE A , b Feb 17, 1851, d July 12, 1872
4239 iv MARY E , b March 25, 1853, m. Frank Leavitt, Nov. 30, 1876
4240 v JOHN W , b Aug 23, 1855
4241 vi LIZZIL, b Sept. 15, 1858

2356 GILMORE[8] EMERY (*Jeremiah,*[7] *Jeremiah,*[6] *Simon,*[5] *Simon,*[4] *Daniel,*[3] *James,*[2] *Anthony*[1]), son of Jeremiah and Agnes (Huntress) Emery; married in Newfield, Me., Feb 14, 1847, Lizzie Chellis. Enlisted in the Second Maine Cavalry, 1863 ; discharged at the close of the war at New Orleans, La.

Children, except the first, born in Newfield, Me :

4242 i   ELVIRA,[9] b June 14, 1848; d Aug 31, 1849, in Wolfboro.
4243 ii EUGENE, b Jan 24, 1850
4244 iii CHARLES W , b June 14, 1851
4245 iv GEORGE S , b July 23, 1853
4246 v FDITH ANN b April 27, 1855 , d June 17, 1862
4247 vi ELLSWORTH G , b April 27, 1857.
4248 vii IDA, b April 27, 1859
4249 viii ELIZABLTH ANN, b June 30, 1862.
4250 ix SADIE F , b Oct 7, 1864
4251 x NELLIE J , b Nov 26, 1866
4252 xi AGNES S , b. Oct. 10, 1868
4253 xii FRANK DELMORE, b Oct 6, 1870

2357 JOSEPH H [8] EMERY (*Jeremiah,*[7] *Jeremiah,*[6] *Simon,*[5] *Simon,*[4] *Daniel,*[3] *James,*[2] *Anthony*[1]), son of Jeremiah and Agnes (Huntress) Emery, married in Parsonsfield, Me , Sept. 9, 1849, Rebecca C. Hill.

Children :

4254 i   ELLA.[9]
4255 ii EDWARD W.
4256 iii JOSEPH H , JR
4257 iv ALFRED D.

2359 JEREMIAH W [8] EMERY (*Jeremiah,*[7] *Jeremiah,*[6] *Simon,*[5] *Simon,*[4] *Daniel,*[3] *James,*[2] *Anthony*[1]), son of Jeremiah and Agnes (Huntress) Emery, married in Wakefield, N H , Jan. 15, 1853, Caroline M Reed.

Children, born in Acton, Me. :

4258 i   CHANDLER W ,[9] b July 11, 1854.
4259 ii ANNIE H., b June 28, 1859
4260 iii JOHN W , b July 24, 1861
4261 iv JAMES E , b Jan 15, 1864.

2360 CECELIA PRAY[8] EMERY (*James*,[7] *Jeremiah*,[6] *Simon*,[5] *Simon*,[4] *Daniel*,[3] *James*,[2] *Anthony*[1]), daughter of James and Sally (Rowe) Emery; married Rev. Moses Palmer, Oct. 7, 1835, and died in Patten, Me., July 19, 1862.

Children :

    4262 i   EDWARD,[9] b. Nov. 10, 1839.
    4262*a* ii   MARY, b. March 27, 1842; d. July 23, 1842.
    4263 iii MOSES, b. June 1, 1843; d. July 12, 1871.
    4264 iv EMILY, b. Jan. 16, 1845.
    4265 v   OLIN, b. Feb. 28, 1848; d. Dec. 29, 1849.
    4265*a* vi SUSAN, b. Jan. 14, 1852; d. Jan. 29, 1852.
    4266 vii LOREN, b Jan. 3, 1853; d. July 8, 1879.
    4267 viii CHARLES, b. April 28, 1856.
    4268 ix ANNIE, b. June 14, 1860.

2362 ISABEL[8] EMERY (*James*,[7] *Jeremiah*,[6] *Simon*,[5] *Simon*,[4] *Daniel*,[3] *James*,[2] *Anthony*[1]), daughter of James and Sally (Rowe) Emery; married Oliver S. Nason of Kennebunk, Me.

Children :

    4269 i   FRED A.[9]
    4270 ii JOSEPHINE.
    4271 iii DANIEL.
    4272 iv JAMES O.

2363 ABIJAH FISK[8] EMERY (*James*,[7] *Jeremiah*,[6] *Simon*,[5] *Simon*,[4] *Daniel*,[3] *James*,[2] *Anthony*[1]), son of James and Sally (Rowe) Emery; married, first, Emeline T. Metcalf; second, Orissa Metcalf, half-sister of his first wife.

Children, born in Frankfort, Me. :

    4273 i   ROWE,[9] b. April 24, 1846.
    4274 ii CHARLES, b. March 24, 1848.
    4275 iii ANNIE, b. April 13, 1850; d. Oct. 4, 1859.
    4276 iv EVA, b. Aug. 14, 1852.
    4277 v   JUBAL, b. June 26, 1854.
    4278 vi ANNIE, b. Jan. 5, 1856.

By second marriage :

    4279 vii RALPH, b. July 23, 1860; d. Nov. 7, 1873.
    4280 viii HUBERT, b. June, 1862.
    4281 ix GENEVIEVE, b. June 8, 1864.
    4282 x   FISKE, b. June 2, 1866.
    4283 xi GRACE, b. Oct. 21, 1869.

2364 LEWELIN[8] EMERY (*James*,[7] *Jeremiah*,[6] *Simon*,[5] *Simon*,[4] *Daniel*,[3] *James*,[2] *Anthony*[1]), son of James and Sally (Rowe) Emery; married, Dec. 19, 1850, Adeline L. Shaw.

Children :

    4284 i   CECELIA A.,[9] b. Jan. 24, 1852; m. Ambrose Fogg; d. Nov. 23, 1877.
    4284*a* ii MARCELLUS LEWELIN, b. Dec. 12, 1856.

2366 ADALINE S.[8] EMERY (*James*,[7] *Jeremiah*,[6] *Simon*,[5] *Simon*,[4] *Daniel*,[3] *James*,[2] *Anthony*[1]), daughter of James and Sally (Rowe) Emery; married D. B. Newton.

Children
```
4285    i    SARAH A 9
4286    ii   LILIAN B
4287    iii  HENRY C
```

2391 MARTHA[8] RICKER (*Betsey*,[7] *Rev Simon*,[6] *Simon*,[5] *Simon*,[4] *Daniel*,[3] *James*,[2] *Anthony*[1]), daughter of Daniel and Betsey (Emery) Ricker; married, 1819, Levi Mudgett.
Children.
```
4288    i    LEVI,9 b July 12, 1820
4289    ii   BEN J FRANKLIN, b July 11, 1822, d. April 24, 1886    Lawyer
             in N Y
4290    iii  SIMON EMERY, b July 29, 1824    Deputy Sheriff of Penobscot
             Co , Me
4291    iv   ALBERT G , b Dec 9, 1826    Capt. of Co "K," 11th Me Vols.
4292    v    MARY EMERY, b April 6, 1829
4293    vi   MARTHA A , b Nov 25, 1832
4294    vii  WILLIAM PITT, b Jan 23, 1842.  Res in Greenleaf, Kansas.
```

2402 GEORGE W.[8] EMERY (*Edward*,[7] *Moses*,[6] *Simon*[5] *Simon*,[4] *Daniel*,[3] *James*,[2] *Anthony*[1]), son of Edward and Mary (Sherburn) Emery, married in Milford, Me., Nov. 19, 1854 Hannah J. Norris (born March 13, 1829).
Children:
```
4295    i    MARY E ,9 b Aug 31, 1855, d March 11, 1873
4296    ii   WILLIE, b Jan 12 1857, d Sept. 14, 1858
4297    iii  ALICE W., b Jan 12, 1864
4298    iv   LIZZIE E , b March 11, 1866, m J Stilwell Vilas, April 30,
             1888, in Wis.
```

2409 TEMPLE II [8] EMERY (*Hosea*,[7] *Stephen*,[6] *Stephen*,[5] *Simon*,[4] *Daniel*,[3] *James*,[2] *Anthony*[1]), son of Hosea and Hannah (Bartlett) Emery; married at Orono, Me , Aug. 16, 1827, Diana Godfrey (died 1871)
Children:
```
4299    i    JOHN G ,9 b May 20, 1828, in Orono, Me
4300    ii   NICHOLAS, b Dec 29, 1829, in Monroe, Me.
4301    iii  ARD G , b June 19, 1833, in Orono, Me
4302    iv   TEMPLE, b July 5, 1837, in Bradley, Me
4303    v    HIRAM A , b June 14, 1839, in Orono, Me.
```

2410 ROSWELL[8] EMERY (*Hosea*,[7] *Stephen*,[6] *Stephen*,[5] *Simon*,[4] *Daniel*,[3] *James*,[2] *Anthony*[1]), son of Hosea and Hannah (Bartlett) Emery, married in Monroe, Me., Dec. 23, 1825, Sally Jones (born Sept 30, 1804 ; died Dec. 24, 1862)
Children:
```
4304    i    EMELINE,9 b Aug 4, 1828
4305    ii   ALBERT, b Dec 12, 1829
4306    iii  LYDIA, b Sept 19, 1832
4307    iv   ROSWELL, b March 17, 1835
4308    v    LOUISA, b March 15, 1837
4309    vi   TEMPLE, b Sept 14, 1841
4310    vii  SARAH, b July 8, 1843.
```

2414 Hosea B.[8] Emery (*Hosea,*[7] *Stephen,*[6] *Stephen,*[5] *Simon,*[4] *Daniel,*[3] *James,*[2] *Anthony*[1]), son of Hosea and Hannah (Bartlett) Emery ; married, first, at Monroe, Me., Sept. 14, 1837, Eliza Mc-Daniel (died in Bradley, Me.) ; second, Jan. 28, 1850, Nancy J. White of Frankfort, Me. (died Jan., 1852) ; third, April 3, 1852, Lydia T. Tapley of West Brookville, Me.

Children, of first marriage, born in Monroe, Me. :

    4311   i   Helen A.,[9] b. Oct. 8, 1840.
    4312   ii   Cynthia, b. 1841 ; d. young.
    4313   iii   Roy, b. 1846 ; d. young.
    4314   iv   Hosea, b. March, 1849.

By second marriage :

    4315   v   Child, d. in infancy.

By third marriage :

    4316   vi   Charles H., b. June 22, 1853, in Milford, Me.
    4317   vii   Cora A., b. April 8, 1858, in Milford, Me. ; d. in Bangor, Me.,
                   Jan. 6, 1872.
    4318   viii Inez G., b. April 10, 1861.

2423 Elizabeth J.[8] Emery (*Calvin,*[7] *Stephen,*[6] *Stephen,*[5] *Simon,*[4] *Daniel,*[3] *James,*[2] *Anthony*[1]), daughter of Calvin and Rebecca (Warren) Emery ; married Oct. 15, 1859, Albert L. Matthews of Windham, Me.

Children :

    4319   i   Lizzie E.,[9] b. Sept. 17, 1864.
    4320   ii   Emily F., b. Jan. 14, 1867.
    4321   iii   Ethel J., b. Feb. 23, 1869.

2443 Jacob[8] Thompson (*Sally,*[7] *Jacob,*[6] *Stephen,*[5] *Simon,*[4] *Daniel,*[3] *James,*[2] *Anthony*[1]), son of Noah and Sally (Emery) Thompson ; married in 1839.

Children :

    4322   i   Jacob,[9] b. 1840.
    4323   ii   Hiram, b. 1842.
    4324   iii   William, b. 1844.
    4325   iv   Noah, b. 1846.
    4326   v   Hannah, d.
    4327   vi   Anna.

2444 Hiram[8] Thompson (*Sally,*[7] *Jacob,*[6] *Stephen,*[5] *Simon.*[4] *Daniel,*[3] *James,*[2] *Anthony*[1]), son of Noah and Sally (Emery) Thompson ; married ———— Worcester, 1858.

Children :

    4328   i   Frederick E.,[9] b. March 26, 1859.
    4329   ii   Hiram F., b. Nov. 8, 1861.
    4330   iii   Ida May, b. April 28, 1864.
    4331   iv   Sara, b. Feb. 6, 1868.
    4332   v   Ella D., b. Feb. 7, 1872.

2447 Monroe[8] Emery (*John,*[7] *Jacob,*[6] *Stephen,*[5] *Simon,*[4] *Daniel,*[3] *James,*[2] *Anthony*[1]), son of John and Rosannah (Abbot) Emery ; married July 13, 1850, Temperance Goodrich.

Children :

4333 i   SAMUEL,[9] b Feb 1, 1852; d June, 1866.
4334 ii   GEORGE H , b July 14 1854
4335 iii   FRANK A , b July 13, 1856.

2449 HULDAH JANE[b] EMERY (*John,*[7] *Jacob,*[6] *Stephen,*[5] *Simon,*[4] *Daniel.*[3] *James,*[2] *Anthony*[1]), daughter of John and Rosannah (Abbot) Emery , married, in 1850, Marquis Hodgman of Manchester, N H. She died in Bloomington, Ind.
Children :

4336 i   FRANCES E ,[9] b April 17, 1851, m Theo Phillips, Nov 1, 1876
4337 ii   EMMA A , b Sept 18, 1853, m Norman H Shackford; had one child, d young.
4338 iii   HULDAH E.

2450 MOSES J.[8] EMERY (*John,*[7] *Jacob,*[6] *Stephen,*[5] *Simon,*[4] *Daniel,*[3] *James,*[2] *Anthony*[1]), son of John and Rosannah (Abbot) Emery ; married Oct 23, 1864, Mary A Bean.
Children :

4339 i   JOSEPH A ,[9] b June 26, 1866
4340 ii   ROSANNA, b April 21, 1869

2451 JOHN F 8 EMERY (*John,*[7] *Jacob,*[6] *Stephen,*[5] *Simon,*[4] *Daniel,*[3] *James,*[2] *Anthony*[1]), son of John and Rosannah (Abbot) Emery , married April 6, 1861, Mrs. Nancy J. Patten (born 1841)
Child :

4341 i   ORIN A ,[9] b. Jan 23, 1862.

2454 ABIGAIL[8] CHASE (*Lucy,*[7] *Jacob,*[6] *Stephen,*[5] *Simon.*[4] *Daniel,*[3] *James,*[2] *Anthony*[1]), daughter of Trueworthy and Lucy (Emery) Chase ; married July 4, 1839, Henry March (born July 1, 1812 , died March 28, 1851). She died Jan 16, 1856
Children :

4342 i   MORRIS [9]
4343 ii   TRUEWORTHY.
4344 iii   ALBERT N
4345 iv   JAMES M
4346 v   ENVILIE L

2455 JOHN E 8 CHASE (*Lucy,*[7] *Jacob,*[6] *Stephen,*[5] *Simon,*[4] *Daniel,*[3] *James,*[2] *Anthony*[1]), son of Trueworthy and Lucy (Emery) Chase , married April 15, 1840, Ruth Ann Ward. He died April 13, 1886, in Chicopee, Mass.
Child :

4347 i   ELLEN [9]

2457 THATCHER T.[8] CHASE (*Lucy,*[7] *Jacob,*[6] *Stephen,*[5] *Simon,*[4] *Daniel,*[3] *James,*[2] *Anthony*[1]), son of Trueworthy and Lucy (Emery) Chase ; married, first, 1842, Mary Harrington (died 1847) ; second, 1849, Susan Hodgman.

Children :

4348 i JOSEPHINE,[9] b. 1843.
4349 ii NANCIE, b. 1850.

2458 NANCY JANE[8] CHASE (*Lucy,*[7] *Jacob,*[6] *Stephen,*[5] *Simon,*[4] *Daniel,*[3] *James,*[2] *Anthony*[1]), daughter of Trueworthy and Lucy (Emery) Chase; married May 7, 1848, John H. Burbank of Sandown, N. H.

Children :

4350 i LUCY JANE,[9] b. April 27, 1849; d. Sept., 1849.
4351 ii LUCY ELLA, b. Feb., 1851; m. Daniel E. Stimpson.
4352 iii WILLIS P., b. March 8, 1853; d. March 13, 1855.
4353 iv HATTIE J., b. Jan. 9, 1856; d. Feb. 10, 1871.
4354 v JOHN E., b. May 4, 1862.
4355 vi ALBERT F., b. April 7, 1864.

2460 MARY ANN[8] CHASE (*Huldah,*[7] *Jacob,*[6] *Stephen,*[5] *Simon,*[4] *Daniel,*[3] *James,*[2] *Anthony*[1]), daughter of Simon and Huldah (Emery) Chase; married Dec. 25, 1841, Charles Clark (born Jan. 28, 1818).

Children :

4356 i GEORGE W.,[9] b. Oct. 2, 1842.
4357 ii ORIN F., b. July 6, 1845.
4358 iii CHARLES A., b. Oct. 20, 1846; d. young.
4359 iv EVELINE, b. Aug. 4, 1849.
4360 v CHARLES G., b. Feb. 9, 1852; d. Dec. 25, 1854.
4361 vi WILLIAM G., b. Aug. 11, 1852; an adopted son.

2464 JOHN M.[8] CHASE (*Huldah,*[7] *Jacob,*[6] *Stephen,*[5] *Simon,*[4] *Daniel,*[3] *James,*[2] *Anthony*[1]), son of Simon and Huldah (Emery) Chase; married Nov. 9, 1852, Hannah F. Clark.

Children :

4362 i EMERY M.,[9] b. July 7, 1853.
4363 ii FREMONT, b. Oct. 3, 1856.
4364 iii ELIJAH G., b. Sept. 29, 1858.
4365 iv ADAM A., b. Nov. 15, 1861.
4366 v CORA M., b. Feb. 13, 1868.
4367 vi EUGENE M., b. April 29, 1870.
4368 vii GEORGE F., b. Feb. 4, 1874.
4369 viii FIDELIA A.

2465 TRUEWORTHY[8] CHASE (*Huldah,*[7] *Jacob,*[6] *Stephen,*[5] *Simon,*[4] *Daniel,*[3] *James,*[2] *Anthony*[1]), son of Simon and Huldah (Emery) Chase; married Nancy M. Pettingill. He died Feb. 24, 1872.

Children :

4370 i ELENORA M.[9]
4371 ii CLARA E.
4372 iii JULIA M.
4373 iv IDA C.
4374 v TRUEWORTHY D.
4375 vi FRANK E.

2466 AMASA H.[8] CHASE (*Huldah,*[7] *Jacob,*[6] *Stephen,*[5] *Simon,*[4] *Daniel,*[3] *James,*[2] *Anthony*[1]), son of Simon and Huldah (Emery) Chase; married July 10, 1856, Elizabeth Howe (died Aug. 15, 1867).

Children :

4376 i   SIMON A ,[9] b Dec 1, 1857
4377 ii FRANK W., b. May 12, 1859, d Feb. 10. 1862
4378 iii ELIZ M , b Aug 11, 1861, m Frank J Johnson, Feb 21, 1880.
4379 iv MILDRED D , b June 28, 1864

2467 MORRIS MARCH[8] EMERY (*Jacob,*[7] *Jacob,*[6] *Stephen,*[5] *Simon,*[4] *Daniel,*[3] *James,*[2] *Anthony*[1]), son of Jacob and Betsey (March) Emery, married May 31, 1841, Lois H. Heath of Nashua, N H. (died June 3, 1887) He was a sailor for many years and lived on Middle Brewster Island, Boston Harbor, Mass , and Lyndeboro, N H.

Children .

4380 i   ENVILLE J ,[9] b 1843, in Lowell, Mass ; d young
4381 ii }
4381a iii } TWINS, b. 1845, d in infancy

2468 REV. ENVILLE JACOB[8] EMERY (*Jacob,*[7] *Jacob,*[6] *Stephen,*[5] *Simon,*[4] *Daniel,*[3] *James,*[2] *Anthony*[1]), son of Jacob and Betsey (March) Emery ; married April 13, 1850, Anna Judson Hagget of Hollis, N. H. (died in Mason Village, N. H , April 22, 1867), second, April 22, 1868, Melissa Smith Emery, widow of Horace Emery (died Oct. 21, 1887) ; third, Sept , 1888, Mrs Fanny A. (Mason) Brooks. He was a Baptist minister, having charges in So Lyndeboro, N H., 1854, Warwick, Mass , 1858, Mason Village, N. H., 1862, Barre, Mass , 1865, Jaffrey, N. H , 1869, Swanzey, N H., 1873 ; resided in Greenville, N. H , until his death, April 7, 1889. He was a lecturer of note, correspondent of newspapers and preacher of reputation.

Child, by first wife :

4382 i PAMELIA MADELON,[9] b. March 22, 1851

2469 LYDIA ANN[8] EMERY (*Jacob,*[7] *Jacob,*[6] *Stephen,*[5] *Simon,*[4] *Daniel,*[3] *James,*[2] *Anthony*[1]), daughter of Jacob and Betsey (March) Emery , married March 9, 1847, Albion K. P. Dunning of Brunswick, Me   She died Aug. 10, 1848.

Child

4383 i ELIZABETH E ,[9] b Feb. 1, 1848, d Aug. 19, 1848

2470 JOHN MARCH[8] EMERY (*Jacob,*[7] *Jacob,*[6] *Stephen,*[5] *Simon,*[4] *Daniel,*[3] *James,*[2] *Anthony*[1]), son of Jacob and Betsey (March) Emery , married April 26, 1857, Ann Bradford of So Lyndeboro, N. H. He was a musician.

Children, born in Lyndeboro', N H. :

4384 i HARLAN EDSON,[9] b Jan 14, 1868.
4385 ii CHRISTA ANN, b. Sept 13, 1871

2471 ALICE G.[8] EMERY (*Jacob,*[7] *Jacob,*[6] *Stephen,*[5] *Simon,*[4] *Daniel,*[3] *James,*[2] *Anthony*[1]), daughter of Jacob and Betsey (March) Emery, married Feb. 16, 1855, William Young of Manchester, N. H.

Children :

4386 i   ELIZABETH I ,[9] b March 22, 1861.
4387 ii RHODA ELLA, b. Jan 14, 1864
4388 iii ERNEST E , b Oct 4, 1867, d
4389 iv WILLIE M., b March 14, 1870, d.

2474 CATHERINE[8] EMERY (*Thatcher,[7] Jacob,[6] Stephen,[5] Simon,[4] Daniel,[3] James,[2] Anthony[1]*), daughter of Thatcher and Sally (Thing) Emery; married Dec. 18, 1849, Charles Thing. Lives in Waterboro, Me.

Children :

    4390   i   BRADFORD,[9] b. May 2, 1851; d. young.
    4391   ii   INEZ, b. Oct. 7, 1856; d. young.
    4392   iii   INEZ, b. Sept. 13, 1864.

2475 SARAH T.[8] EMERY (*Thatcher,[7] Jacob,[6] Stephen,[5] Simon,[4] Daniel,[3] James,[2] Anthony[1]*), daughter of Thatcher and Sally (Thing) Emery; married, first, July 18, 1849, William A. Kelly (born April 22, 1825; died Nov. 10, 1856); second, Dec. 20, 1859, Charles Pray (born Nov. 10, 1823).

Children by first marriage :

    4393   i   WILLIAM W.,[9] b. Oct. 19, 1850.
    4394   ii   JOSEPH N., b. Feb. 10, 1853.
    4395   iii   JOHN H., b. Oct. 3, 1855.

By second marriage :

    4396   iv   GEORGE W., b. Feb. 10, 1861.
    4397   v   LUELLA O., b. July 30, 1864.
    4398   vi   ADDIE B., b. Aug. 17, 1872.

2478 JACOB P.[8] EMERY (*Thatcher,[7] Jacob,[6] Stephen,[5] Simon,[4] Daniel,[3] James,[2] Anthony,[1]*), son of Thatcher and Sally (Thing) Emery; married Susan E. Fall, Nov. 24, 1859.

Child :

    4399   i   WILLIE.[9]

2481 MARK A.[8] EMERY (*Thatcher,[7] Jacob,[6] Stephen,[5] Simon,[4] Daniel,[3] James,[2] Anthony[1]*), son of Thatcher and Sally (Thing) Emery; married Aug. 31, 1863, Mary J. Thing.

Child :

    4400   i   ALONZO B.,[9] b. May 31, 1864.

2483 ROSE A.[8] EMERY (*Thatcher,[7] Jacob,[6] Stephen,[5] Simon,[4] Daniel,[3] James,[2] Anthony[1]*), daughter of Thatcher and Sally (Thing) Emery; married Bion Roberts. Resides in Kelton, Utah.

Child :

    4401   i   NELSON D.,[9] b. April 18, 1873.

2485 CYRUS[8] EMERY (*John,[7] Simon,[6] Stephen,[5] Simon,[4] Daniel,[3] James,[2] Anthony[1]*), son of John and Mary (Pike) Emery; married, 1866, Sarah Fifield, daughter of Richard and Sally (Emery) Fifield. He died of cholera, two days out from Calcutta, on his return voyage.

Child :

    4402   i   ANNA,[9] b. 1867.

2486 JOHN P.[8] EMERY (*John,*[7] *Simon,*[6] *Stephen,*[5] *Simon,*[4] *Daniel,*[3] *James,*[2] *Anthony*[1]), son of John and Mary (Pike) Emery; married in Shapleigh, Me., 1849, Betsey Thing (born Aug 14, 1828).
Children·

4403   i   LUCY,[9] b Dec 21, 1849, d Sept 29, 1850
4404   ii   LIZZIE M , b Feb 8, 1852; m Dec. 25, 1872, Albert Fisk of Somerville, Mass
4405   iii   JOHN WESLEY, b Oct. 29, 1856.

2488 MARY ANN[8] EMERY (*Peter,*[7] *Simon,*[6] *Stephen,*[5] *Simon,*[4] *Daniel,*[3] *James.*[2] *Anthony*[1]), daughter of Peter and his second wife, Lydia (Sias) Emery; married Allen Greenough, and died Oct. 12, 1862.
Children·

4406   i   JOHN,[9] b. 1857
4407   ii   FRANK, b 1860

2490 SAMUEL H.[8] EMERY (*Peter,*[7] *Simon,*[6] *Stephen,*[5] *Simon,*[4] *Daniel,*[3] *James,*[2] *Anthony*[1]), son of Peter and his second wife, Lydia (Sias) Emery; married Dec. 23, 1861, Mary Emerson Sias (born Aug. 11, 1845).
Children :

4408   i   SAMUEL W ,[9] b March 30, 1863.
4409   ii   LYDIA, b 1864, d Aug 12, 1866
4410   iii   GRACE, b Nov. 20, 1866
4411   iv   MABEL b March 13, 1870; d. Jan 15, 1885.
4412   v   CAROLINE, b Aug 9, 1872
4413   vi   PETER S , b. Aug 11, 1874

2492 FRANCES S.[8] EMERY (*Peter,*[7] *Simon,*[6] *Stephen,*[5] *Simon,*[4] *Daniel,*[3] *James,*[2] *Anthony*[1]), daughter of Peter and his second wife, Lydia (Sias) Emery ; married Allen Greenough. She died Dec. 1, 1866.
Child.

4414   i   WILLIAM ALLEN,[9] b. 1863, d. Oct 1, 1865

2495 GEORGE T.[8] EMERY (*Henry,*[7] *Simon,*[6] *Stephen,*[5] *Simon,*[4] *Daniel,*[3] *James,*[2] *Anthony*[1]), son of Henry and Deborah (Meserve) Emery; married, first, Nov. 11, 1848, Tryphena Staples (born April 19, 1826) , second, July 5, 1856, Eliza Works (born in Boston, Mass. ; died June 14, 1878).
Children.

4415   i   ELIZABETH M ,[9] b Jan. 27, 1849
4416   ii   FLORA, b Dec. 16, 1850, d. Dec 12, 1865
4417   iii   GEORGE H , b June 29, 1855, m July 1, 1879, Rachel Palmer.
4418   iv   ANN T , b Sept 10, 1857, d Nov 1, 1858
4419   v   ANN L , b Feb. 25, 1861, d June 14, 1878
4420   vi   JAMES W., b March 17, 1863.

2496 SARAH E.[8] EMERY (*Henry,*[7] *Simon,*[6] *Stephen,*[5] *Simon,*[4] *Daniel,*[3] *James,*[2] *Anthony*[1]), daughter of Henry and Deborah (Meserve) Emery , married Calvin Stevens of Milan, N. H.

Children:

4421   i   SARAH.[9]
4422   ii   IDA.
4423   iii HENRY.
4424   iv   ROBERT.
4425   v   ELIZABETH.

2513 JAMES W.[8] EMERY (*Joshua,*[7] *Israel,*[6] *Samuel,*[5] *Simon,*[4] *Daniel,*[3] *James,*[2] *Anthony*[1]), son of Joshua and Sarah Ham (Jones) Emery; married in Portsmouth, N. H., Jan. 5, 1861, Martha Ann Moulton (born Jan. 8, 1843); removed to Eliot, Me., 1866.

Children:

4426   i   GEORGE W.,[9] b. Sept. 7, 1863, in Portsmouth, N. H.
4427   ii   ANNIE A., b. May 8, 1873, in Eliot, Me.

2514 REBECCA[8] EMERY (*Joshua,*[7] *Israel,*[6] *Samuel,*[5] *Simon,*[4] *Daniel,*[3] *James,*[2] *Anthony*[1]), daughter of Joshua and Sarah Ham (Jones) Emery; married in Kittery, Me., John W. Young (born May 10, 1839).

Children:

4428   i   EMMA,[9] b. Nov. 4, 1861.
4429   ii   CHARLES W., b. Aug. 31, 1866; d. Feb. 14, 1867.

2535 JULIA[6] EMERY (*Thomas,*[7] *Simon,*[6] *Samuel,*[5] *Simon,*[4] *Daniel,*[3] *James,*[2] *Anthony*[1]), daughter of Thomas and Theodosia (Grant) Emery; married, first, in Somersworth, N. H., June 12, 1858, Edward Dalton (born, 1826, in England and died at Hilton Head, S. C., Dec. 5, 1861; volunteer in 3d N. H. Regt.); second, in Portsmouth, N. H., Jan. 1, 1865, Capt. Andrew Frisbee (born May 27, 1818; died in Chelsea, Mass., Oct. 17, 1871); third, Sept. 17, 1873, Benjamin Tetherly (born in Eliot, Me., Jan. 22, 1821).

Child, by first marriage:

4430   i   CHARLES E.,[9] b. June 1, 1861, in Somersworth, N. H.

By second marriage:

4431   ii   ABBIE M., b. June 6, 1867, in Kittery, Me.

2536 ELIZABETH P.[8] EMERY (*Thomas,*[7] *Simon,*[6] *Samuel,*[5] *Simon,*[4] *Daniel,*[3] *James,*[2] *Anthony*[1]), daughter of Thomas and Theodosia (Grant) Emery; married May 16, 1851, John T. Hubbard (born April 4, 1829; died April 2, 1875); lived in Portsmouth, N. H.; removed to Somersworth, N. H., 1851.

Children, born in Somersworth:

4432   i   HARRY E.,[9] b. Aug. 11, 1860.
4433   ii   FRED S., b. Sept. 3, 1869.

2537 SIMON[8] EMERY (*Thomas,*[7] *Simon,*[6] *Samuel,*[5] *Simon,*[4] *Daniel,*[3] *James,*[2] *Anthony*[1]); son of Thomas and Theodosia (Grant) Emery; married Dec. 22, 1867, A. Fernald (born in Eliot, Me., Sept. 17, 1833). Selectman of Eliot, Me., 1882–84. Lived in Kittery and Eliot, Me.

Child :

4434 i̇ HERBERT,⁹ b Oct 18, 1872

2539 SOPHIA S⁸ EMERY (*Thomas,⁷ Simon,⁶ Samuel,⁵ Simon,⁴ Daniel,³ James,² Anthony¹*), daughter of Thomas and Theodosia (Grant) Emery; married, first, at Smithfield, R. I., Jan. 27, 1861, Samuel S Howe (born in Worcester, Mass, March 15, 1825, died Sept. 15, 1864) ; second, in Cumberland, R. 1, Nov. 26, 1867, W. A Hixon (born in Medway, Mass., July 12, 1819, died in Derry, N. H, April 30, 1882).

Child

4435 i FRANCES E ,⁹ b Nov 10, 1861, in Smithfield, R I

2541 JOHN M⁸ HAYNES (*Mary,⁷ Isaac,⁶ Samuel,⁵ Simon,⁴ Daniel,³ James,² Anthony¹*), son of Ira and Mary (Emery) Haynes, married April 28, 1855, Abbie (born Feb. 10, 1831, in Newfield, Me), daughter of Luther and Hannah (Burbank) Symmes. Lives in So. Parsonsfield, Me.

Children, born in South Parsonfield, Me. :

4436 i ALBERT E ,⁹ b Jan 27, 1861
4437 ii THOMAS W ,
4438 iii JENNIE W , } b April 5, 1862.

2551 ABBIE L⁸ EMERY (*Hiram,⁷ Isaac,⁶ Samuel,⁵ Simon,⁴ Daniel,³ James,² Anthony¹*), daughter of Hiram and Margaret (Young) Emery, married Nov 14, 1853, James Larry (born Feb. 2, 1826) of Windham, Me, who died in the army in Banks' Red River expedition. July 6, 1864 Lived in Maxfield, Me.

Children :

4439 i FRANK H ,⁹ b Oct 29, 1854, d Sept 22, 1864
4440 ii CHARLES A , b Dec 7, 1859
4441 iii EDDO, b May 6, 1861, d Sept 16, 1864

2552 JOSEPH H⁸ EMERY (*Hiram,⁷ Isaac,⁶ Samuel,⁵ Simon,¹ Daniel,³ James,² Anthony¹*), daughter of Hiram and Margaret (Young) Emery; married Oct. 14, 1863, Delia Flynn of Providence, R. I. Lived at Providence and then removed to St. Louis, Mo

Children ·

4442 i JAMES H ,⁹ b. Sept. 5, 1864
4443 ii ALBERT J , b Nov. 29, 1865
4444 iii FRANK I , b Apr 1, 1867
4445 iv ELIA, b Dec 31, 1870, d Oct 8, 1876
4446 v MARY, b Nov 25, 1875.

2557 LORENZO W⁸ EMERY (*William,⁷ Isaac,⁶ Samuel,⁵ Simon,⁴ Daniel,³ James,² Anthony¹*), son of William and Sabina (Tebbetts) Emery, married May 31, 1865, Margaret Ferriman of Albion, Ill. (born Feb 1, 1844). Went West in 1852; settled in Paducah, Ky., in 1865, superintendent of the city public schools; director of the city National Bank and Mechanics' Flouring Mills ; manager of the Hub and Spoke manufactory; commission merchant in the tobacco business and owner of the Seven Mile Island Stock Farm.

Children :

4447   i   CHARLES W.,[9] b. May 3, 1866.
4448   ii   GEORGE F., b. Aug. 14, 1867.
4449   iii MARY, b. Sept. 14, 1870; d. Sept. 27, 1879.
4450   iv   LORENZO M., b. Feb. 16, 1872.

2560 PHŒBE E.[8] EMERY (*Temple H.,*[7] *Isaac,*[6] *Samuel,*[5] *Simon,*[4] *Daniel,*[3] *James,*[2] *Anthony*[1]), daughter of Temple H. and Sarah (Weymouth) Emery; married in Sangerville, Me., Sept. 15, 1851, Charles W. Cross.

Children :

4451   i   JOSEPHINE M.,[9] b. Dec. 30, 1853; unm.
4452   ii   ANNIE E., b. June 21, 1855; d. July 6, 1861.
4453   iii CHARLES A., b. June 3, 1857.
4454   iv   MARION W., b. April 27, 1859; d. July 2, 1861.
4455   v   MAUD E., b. Aug. 10, 1863; m. Oct. 6, 1887, Sandy Dow.
4456   vi   ANNIE R., b. May 8, 1865; m. Oct. 11, 1881, Elmer I. McKechnie.
4457   vii ETHEL L., b. March 24, 1876; d. April 6, 1880.

2563 ZACHARY T.[8] EMERY (*Temple H.,*[7] *Isaac,*[6] *Samuel,*[5] *Simon,*[4] *Daniel,*[3] *James,*[2] *Anthony*[1]) son of Temple H. and Sarah (Weymouth) Emery; married Sept. 2, 1871, Carrie ——— in Waltham, Mass. He lived and died in Renovo, Pa.

Children :

4457a i   SARAH,[9] b. May 14, 1872, in Waltham; d. in infancy.
4457b ii   ALTON, b. Oct. 26, 1873, in Renovo, Pa.
4457c iii DANIEL, b. April 1, 1876, in Renovo, Pa.
4457d iv   CARRIE, b. Feb. 8, 1879, in Renovo, Pa.; adopted by his brother
           James (No. 2562).

2647 MARTHA[8] EMERY (*Joshua,*[7] *John,*[6] *Charles,*[5] *Simon,*[4] *Daniel,*[3] *James,*[2] *Anthony*[1]), daughter of Joshua and Sally (Hadley) Emery; married Oct. 15, 1857, Henry Stage.

Children :

4458   i   FRANK.[9]
4459   ii   MARY JANE.
4460   iii ORVILLE.
4461   iv   HENRY.

2650 BETSEY[8] EMERY (*Joshua,*[7] *John,*[6] *Charles,*[5] *Simon,*[4] *Daniel,*[3] *James,*[2] *Anthony*[1]), daughter of Joshua and Sally (Hadley) Emery; married, first, at Money Creek, Minn., May 8, 1862, Henry I. Airron; second, at St. Paul, Minn., June 17, 1885, A. H. Corey.

Children, by first marriage :

4462   i   EDITH LOUELLA,[9] b. March 9, 1863, in Jamestown, N. Y.
4463   ii   ERNEST OLIVER, b. Jan. 8, 1865, in Money Creek, Minn.
4464   iii GEORGE FREDERICK, b. Feb. 5, 1867, in Money Creek, Minn.

2651 MOSES[8] EMERY (*Joshua,*[7] *John,*[6] *Charles,*[5] *Simon,*[4] *Daniel,*[3] *James,*[2] *Anthony*[1]), son of Joshua and Sally (Hadley) Emery; married at La Crosse, Wis., Feb. 9, 1874, Anna Webster. Clerk of District

Court, Caledonia, Minn. Served in the Union army through the war of the Rebellion

Children :

   4465 i   LESLIE WEBSTER [9] b May 7, 1876
   4466 ii   GERTRUDE LOUISE, b Nov 10, 1882
   4467 iii MARTHA HAZEL, b April, 1885.

2653 PHŒBE[8] EMERY (*Joshua,*[7] *John,*[6] *Charles,*[5] *Simon.*[4] *Daniel,*[3] *James,*[2] *Anthony*[1]), daughter of Joshua and Sarah (Hadley) Emery ; married June 7, 1883, Samuel Cummings of St. Paul, Minn.

Children, born in St Paul, Minn ·

   4468 i   MARY FRANCES,[9] b Aug 3 1885
   4469 ii ROBERT EMERY, b March 4, 1889.

2657 JOHN E [8] STANTON (*Betsey,*[7] *William,*[6] *James.*[5] *Zachariah.*[4] *Daniel,*[3] *James* [2] *Anthony*[1]), son of John and Betsey (Emery) Stanton ; married, 1835, Elvira B. Stevens (born 1818).

Children :

   4470 i   EDWARD H ,[9] b 1836
   4471 ii MARY E , b 1837.
   4472 iii WILLIAM O , b 1839
   4473 iv NELSON V , b 1841, captain in the Union army in the Rebellion
   4474 v   PAULINA H , b. 1844

2659 BENJAMIN L [8] STANTON (*Betsey,*[7] *William,*[6] *James.*[5] *Zacharah,*[4] *Daniel.*[3] *James,*[2] *Anthony*[1]), son of John and Betsey (Emery) Stanton , married, 1841, Sophia Granger. Lived in Poland, Me.

Child :

   4475 i   JOHN EDWIN,[9] b 1846

2662 HANNAH M [8] STANTON (*Betsey,*[7] *William,*[6] *James.*[5] *Zachariah,*[4] *Daniel,*[3] *James,*[2] *Anthony*[1]), daughter of John and Betsey (Emery) Stanton , married, 1848, Joel W. Merrill (born 1825). Resides in Poland, Me

Child :

   4476 i   JOEL F ,[9] b 1849.

2683 BETSEY[8] STANTON (*Thankful,*[7] *William,*[6] *James,*[5] *Zachariah,*[4] *Daniel.*[3] *James,*[2] *Anthony*[1]), daughter of Paul and Thankful (Emery) Stanton ; married, 1841, Isaac McCann. Resides in Poland, Me.

Child :

   4477 i   MARY ELIZA,[9] b 1846

2685 JEREMY[8] EMERY (*John.*[7] *William,*[6] *James,*[5] *Zachariah,*[4] *Daniel,*[3] *James,*[2] *Anthony*[1]), son of John and Betsey (Johnson) Emery , married Nov. 12, 1859, Jane M. Bailey.

Child :

   4478 i   FRANK BERTRAM,[9] b. June 23, 1862, d May 19, 1880

2694 JAMES L [8] EMERY (*Mark,*[7] *Mark,*[6] *James,*[5] *Zachariah,*[4] *Dan-*

33

iel,[3] *James*,[2] *Anthony*[1]), son of Mark and Lydia (Bessey) Emery ; married, first, Feb. 3, 1850, Caroline E. Foss (born Dec. 18, 1825 ; died Sept. 15, 1869) ; second, Oct. 9, 1874, Mary S. Muirhead (born in Scotland, April 9, 1834).

Children, born in Saco, Me. :

    4479   i   FRANK L.,[9] b. Nov. 27, 1850.
    4480   ii   CHARLES S., b. Oct. 12, 1852.
    4481   iii JAMES M., b. Sept. 8, 1855.
    4482   iv   SUSIE JANE, b. April 12, 1859 ; d. Aug. 26, 1869.
    4483   v   CARRIE LOUISE, b. Dec. 6, 1863.
    4484   vi   SUSAN LYDIA, b. Dec. 23, 1865.

2711 RUXBY[8] EMERY (*James*,[7] *Mark*,[6] *James*,[5] *Zachariah*,[4] *Daniel*,[3] *James*,[2] *Anthony*[1]), daughter of James and Mary Ann (Snow) Emery ; married March 20, 1845, James M. Badger of Boston, Mass.
Children :

    4485   i   WALTER S.,[9] b. Jan. 8, 1846 ; m. Eliz. A. Tucker, Nov. 13,
                1873.
    4486   ii   ADELAIDE E., b. May 31, 1848.

2716 ELIZABETH[8] EMERY (*James*,[7] *Mark*,[6] *James*,[5] *Zachariah*,[4] *Daniel*,[3] *James*,[2] *Anthony*[1]), daughter of James and Mary Ann (Snow) Emery ; married Dec. 31, 1860, Oliver Welch of Saco, Me. She is dead.
Children :

    4487   i   LIZZIE.[9]
    4488   ii   FLORENCE.

2718 WILLIAM W.[8] EMERY (*James*,[7] *Mark*,[6] *James*,[5] *Zachariah*,[4] *Daniel*,[3] *James*,[2] *Anthony*[1]), son of James and Mary Ann (Snow) Emery ; married Nov. 5, 1868, Nellie M. Baker. Resides in Lawrence, Mass.
Children :

    4489   i   CARRIE,[9] b. July 2, 1872 ; d. July 30, 1872.
    4490   ii   LILLIE A., b. March 5, 1876.

2720 ANNA L.[8] JOHNSON (*Rachel*,[7] *Mark*,[6] *James*,[5] *Zachariah*,[4] *Daniel*,[3] *James*,[2] *Anthony*[1]), daughter of James and Rachel (Emery) Johnson ; married Erastus H. Jordan, son of Joshua and Eliza (Emery) Jordan of Raymond, Me.
Children :

    4491   i   HANNAH E.[9]
    4492   ii   ADDIE.
    4493   iii MARY ELIZA.
    4494   iv   ALBERT.
    4495   v   JENNY.

2744 JAMES H.[8] EMERY (*Reuben Knox*,[7] *Thomas*,[6] *Zachariah*,[5] *Zachariah*,[4] *Daniel*,[3] *James*,[2] *Anthony*[1]), son of Reuben Knox and his second wife, Elmira (Hemingway) Emery ; married June, 1870. He was a soldier in an Ohio regiment during the Rebellion.
Children :

4496 i· T A⁹ (a son), b Dec 14, 1871
4497 ii WILLIE, b Dec , 1873

2747 CHANDLER SPRING⁸ EMERY (*Caleb,⁷ William,⁶ Caleb,⁵ Caleb,⁴ Daniel,³ James,² Anthony¹*), son of Caleb and Mary Ann (Chandler) Emery; entered Bowdoin College but did not graduate, went to Florida, married, and settled there. Became judge of the municipal court of Jacksonville, where he died suddenly July 20, 1880.
  Children:

4498 i   CHANDLER S ,⁹ b in Williamsburg; physician in Florida.
4499 ii   CALEB J , b April 16, 1844, in Mandarin, Florida
4500 iii A S , res in Jacksonville, Florida
4501 iv A DAUGHTER.

2748 SARAH S.⁸ EMERY (*Caleb,⁷ William,⁶ Caleb,⁵ Caleb,⁴ Daniel,³ James,² Anthony¹*), daughter of Caleb and Mary Ann (Chandler) Emery, married June 13, 1834, William L. Hanscom, Naval Constructor, U S Navy. He was born in Eliot, Me , 1812, appointed Naval Constructor, 1853, which position he held, with the exception of a short time while travelling in Europe. until 1874, when he was retired according to law. He died in Malden, Mass , Sept 3, 1881. She died Feb. 21, 1860.
  Child .

4502 i   HELEN L ,⁹ b. Dec 19, 1836; m. E D Bell, a dry goods'-merchant of Boston , d Aug. 1, 1871.

2749 ELIZABETH S ⁸ EMERY (*Caleb,⁷ William,⁶ Caleb,⁵ Caleb,⁴ Daniel,³ James,² Anthony¹*), daughter of Caleb and Mary Ann (Chandler) Emery, married Sept 9, 1839, T. D. Vincent of Delevan, Ill.
  Children .

4503 i   FRANK,⁸ b. 1842
4504 ii   CHARLES B , b 1844.
4505 iii MARY A , b 1847.

2750 CALEB⁸ EMERY (*Caleb,⁷ William,⁶ Caleb,⁵ Caleb,⁴ Daniel,³ James,² Anthony¹*), son of Caleb and Mary Ann (Chandler) Emery; married, 1843, Abbie A. (born Oct 23, 1822 ; died Mar. 23, 1888), daughter of Joseph H and Hannah (Jacobs) Cutts of York, Me   He removed to Georgia, 1850 , engaged in the ice business. He died in Augusta, Ga., Dec. 16, 1872.
  Children :

4506 i   ALICE R.,⁹ b. Dec. 15, 1845
4507 ii   CALEB, b —— 1847, d young
4508 iii HENRY F , b Aug 31, 1848.
4509 iv   MARY G , b Dec 20, 1851.
4510 v   LIZZIE J , b Feb 4, 1853.
4511 vi   CALEBANNA, b Sept. 1, 1857.
4512 vii SARAH A , b Jan 8, 1860
4513 viii CHANDLER C., b Feb 7, 1861; physician in New Orleans.
4514 ix ROBERT LEE, b. July 20, 1864.

2752 WILLIAM H.⁸ EMERY (*Caleb,⁷ William,⁶ Caleb,⁵ Caleb,⁴*

Daniel,[3] *James,*[2] *Anthony*[1]), son of Caleb and Mary Ann (Chandler) Emery; married Jan. 13, 1855, Martha H. (born Jan. 1, 1833), daughter of Jonathan and Harriet (Pickett) Holmes of New Gloucester, Me. Draughtsman in Eliot, Me.

Children:

4515 i HELEN S.,[9] b. May 30, 1856; m. Jan. 27, 1879, Arthur C. Gould of Boston, Mass.

4516 ii LIZZIE C., } m. July 5, 1883, Dr. E. P. Adams of Castine, Me.
b. April 4, 1858; { d. Sept. 19, 1858.
4517 iii ANNIE H., }

4518 iv WILLIAM E., b. Oct. 4, 1859; M.D., 1885, Med. School Burlington, Vt.; practised in Boston; d. April 27, 1886; unm.

4519 v EDWARD B., b. July 6, 1861; d. Sept. 10, 1861.

4520 vi SARAH S., b. Aug. 18, 1862; d. Sept. 18, 1862.

4521 vii EDWIN A., b. Aug. 4, 1864; d. Aug. 24, 1865.

4522 viii CALEB, b. Nov. 25, 1866; d. Dec. 1, 1866.

4523 ix ALICE MAY, b. March 4, 1870; d. July 16, 1870.

2753 DEA. WILLIAM L.[8] EMERY (*Thomas S.,*[7] *William,*[6] *Caleb,*[5] *Caleb,*[4] *Daniel,*[3] *James,*[2] *Anthony*[1]), son of Thomas S. and Betsey (Emery) Emery; married March 10, 1834, Mary E. (born Oct. 31, 1810; died April 12, 1885), daughter of Ezekiel and Betsey (Worcester) Prescott. He died in Sanford, Me., Oct. 2, 1876. Tinware and stove dealer, 1834–1876. Deacon of Congregational church, 1842–1876.

Children, born in Sanford, Me.:

4524 i BETSEY,[9] b. March 26, 1835; d. May 25, 1846.

4525 ii EDWIN, b. Sept. 4, 1836.

4526 iii ELMIRA, b. Nov. 22, 1837.

4527 iv FRANCES A., b. April 15, 1839; d. Jan. 29, 1862.

4528 v GEORGE P., b. Dec. 21, 1840; d. Dec. 25, 1840.

4529 vi GEORGE A., b. Dec. 21, 1841.

4530 vii ELLEN M., b. July 24, 1843.

4531 viii PRESCOTT, b. Feb. 4, 1845.

4532 ix INFANT, b. April 1, 1847; d April 2, 1847.

4533 x WILLIS T., b. Sept. 14, 1848.

2754 CALEB S.[8] EMERY (*Thomas S.,*[7] *William,*[6] *Caleb,*[5] *Caleb,*[4] *Daniel,*[3] *James,*[2] *Anthony*[1]), son of Thomas S. and Betsey (Emery) Emery; married Sept. 10, 1835, Caroline (born May 23, 1810; died Feb. 1, 1874), daughter of Dr. Ebenezer and Olive (Chadbourn) Linscott. Resided in Boston Highlands (Roxbury), Mass. He died April 23, 1879.

Children, born in Sanford, Me.:

4534 i LAURA W.,[9] b. May 12, 1837.

4535 ii HELEN J., b. Feb. 11, 1839; m. Feb. 3, 1885, John F. Woodman; d. in Amesbury, Mass., Dec. 30, 1888, s. p.

4536 iii CYRUS C., b. March 24, 1840.

4537 iv OLIVE C., b. May 23, 1842.

4538 v HOWARD, b. Jan. 10, 1845; d. Dec. 22, 1851.

4539 vi HERBERT, b. Aug. 5, 1846; d. May 17, 1850.

4540 vii WILLIAM H., b. May 11, 1848; M.D., Harvard Med. School, 1870; practised in Woodstock, Conn., till 1872; since then in Boston Highlands. In 1864 was Corp. Co. "D," 42d Mass. Vols., 4 mos.

4541 viii HERBERT C., b. Oct. 12, 1850; d. Aug. 8, 1856.

2755 SHEM[8] EMERY (*Thomas S.,*[7] *William,*[6] *Caleb,*[5] *Caleb,*[4] *Dan-*

iel,[3] *James,*[2] *Anthony*[1]), son of Thomas S and Betsey (Emery) Emery, married May 18, 1840, Judith (born March 16, 1812), daughter of James and Anna (Smith) Junkins. He died in North Berwick, Me , Nov 18, 1882.

Child .

4542   ı   THOMAS SALTER,[8] b Oct 5, 1847, d Oct. 19, 1847.

2757 MARY E[8] EMERY (*Thomas S.,*[7] *William,*[6] *Caleb,*[5] *Caleb,*[4] *Daniel,*[3] *James,*[2] *Anthony*[1]), daughter of Thomas S and Betsey (Emery) Emery; married April 18, 1841, Lyman P Crown (born in Topsham, Vt., Jan 31, 1820, died in Charlestown, Mass., Aug 22, 1875).

Children .

4543   ı   GEORGE L ,[9] b May 2, 1842, in Nashua, N. H , d Dec , 1844
4544   ıı   GEORGE H , b May 9, 1845, in Topsham, Vt , d in Lowell, Mass
4545   ııı   EDWARD S , ⎱ b Oct 6, 1847, ⎱ d Sept 7, 1849
4546   ıv   WILLIAM S , ⎰ in Lowell, Mass , ⎰
4547   v   EDWARD H , b March 14, 1851, m Oct , 1874, Hannah A White (b Sept 24, 1856) he d in Charlestown, April 13, 1875 She m , 2nd, 1887, Charles Ladd and d. June 1888
4548   vı   CHARLES ARTHUR b in Lowell, May 15 1853
4549   vıı   GEORGE L , b March, 1855, in Somerville, Mass. , d May 25, 1857, in Chelsea, Mass

2758 SALTER[8] EMERY (*Thomas S ,*[7] *William.*[6] *Caleb.*[5] *Caleb,*[4] *Daniel,*[3] *James,*[2] *Anthony*[1]), son of Thomas S and Betsey (Emery) Emery; married Feb 24, 1842, Rebecca F (born in Alfred, Me , Jan. 6, 1819), daughter of Daniel and Nancy (Leighton) Kilham. Merchant in Sanford, postmaster, town clerk, dealer in stoves and tinware in Roxbury ; resides in Melrose, Mass.

Children :

4550   ı   SUSAN A ,[9] b July 27, 1842, d. April 18, 1843
4551   ıı   SUSAN A , b Oct 31, 1845
4552   ııı   MARY S , b Jan 29, 1847, d Jan 30, 1847

2759 JOHN FROST[8] EMERY (*Thomas S ,*[7] *William.*[6] *Caleb.*[5] *Caleb,*[4] *Daniel,*[3] *James* [2] *Anthony*[1]), son of Thomas S and Betsey (Emery) Emery; married Dec. 10, 1844, Nancy B. Churchill (born in Buckfield, Me., Feb. 8, 1824).

Children

4553   ı   LYMAN C ,[9] b April 16, 1846, in Alfred, Me , d. Sept 2, 1847, in Portland, Me
4554   ıı   INFANT SON, b July 10, 1848, in Portland, Me , d July 18, 1848.
4555   ııı   JOHN C , b Sept 16, 1850, in Saco, Me , d Oct 17, 1851
4556   ıv   HOWARD b Oct 3, 1853; m June 15, 1855, Elizabeth A (b May 9, 1853), dau of Thomas P and Amelia A (York) Sanborn Lieut Revenue Marine Service since 1880
4557   v   HERBERT, b Oct 10, 1856, in Saco, Me. , d. Dec. 17, 1868

2760 HENRY[8] EMERY (*Thomas S.,*[7] *William,*[6] *Caleb,*[5] *Caleb,*[4]

Daniel,[3] James,[2] Anthony[1]), son of Thomas S. and Betsey (Emery) Emery; married Harriet Berry (died in Philadelphia, Pa., Nov. 21, 1856). He died in New Orleans, La., May 5, 1860.

Children :

    4558 i   GRANVILLE H.,[9] b. Jan. 9, 1852. in Lowell, Mass.
    4559 ii ADA FRANCES, b. in 1854; d. æ. 11 months.

2763 CYRUS[8] EMERY (*Thomas S.,[7] William,[6] Caleb,[5] Caleb,[4] Daniel,[3] James,[2] Anthony[1]*), son of Thomas S. and his second wife, Hannah (Willard) Emery ; married, first, June 5, 1853, Caroline B. (born in Shapleigh, Me., June 16, 1833 ; died April 24, 1857), daughter of Col. John and Lucinda (Clark) Trafton ; second, July 19, 1857, Martha Ann (born June 14, 1832), daughter of Joseph and Sarah (Edgecomb) Rose, of Limington, Me. Has resided in Prophetstown, Ill., since 1854. Dealer in hardware and stoves ; farmer.

Children, born in Prophetstown :

    4560 i   EVA LUCINDA,[9] b. July 17, 1855.
    4561 ii CAROLINE ERNESTINA, b. Jan. 2, 1857.
    4562 iii CORA LILIAN, b. April 21, 1858; grad. Hahnemann Med. College 1887, and practises in Geneseo, Ill.
    4563 iv IROLIN MAY, b. Aug. 31, 1859 ; d. April 19, 1865.
    4564 v   CHARLES ELLSWORTH, b. Feb. 13. 1862.
    4565 vi FLORENCE MAY, b. March 16, 1867.
    4566 vii LAURA IROLIN, b. Aug. 26, 1869; d. Sept. 29, 1874.
    4567 viii LEONARD R., b. Sept. 30, 1873; d. Nov. 16, 1874.

2764 SARAH C.[8] EMERY (*Thomas S.,[7] William,[6] Caleb,[5] Caleb,[4] Daniel,[3] James,[2] Anthony[1]*), daughter of Thomas S. and his second wife, Hannah (Willard) Emery ; married Oct. 29, 1851, Robert Evans of Dover, N. H., blacksmith (born in Barrington, N. H., March 24, 1816).

Children, born in Dover, N. H. :

    4568 i   MARY JANE,[9] b. Aug. 8, 1852; m. Feb. 8, 1873, Mark S. Hutchins; d. April 24, 1880.
    4569 ii JOHN FLAGG, b. July 31, 1854.
    4570 iii SUSAN ANN, b. May 24, 1857.
    4571 iv SALTER EMERY, b. July 7, 1859 ; d. June 30, 1860.
    4572 v   GEORGE WILLIAM, b. April 1, 1861 ; d. Sept. 2, 1861.
    4573 vi CAROLINE TRAFTON, b. Sept. 16, 1863 ; d. March 16. 1868.
    4574 vii CHARLES EDWIN, b. Oct. 9, 1867 ; d. March 27. 1868.
    4575 viii NELLIE LOUISE, b. June 14, 1870; d. Mar. 5, 1888.
    4576 ix ALICE REBECCA, b. March 11, 1875.

2765 CYNTHIA ANN[8] EMERY (*Thomas S.,[7] William,[6] Caleb,[5] Caleb,[4] Daniel,[3] James,[2] Anthony[1]*), daughter of Thomas S. and his second wife, Hannah (Willard) Emery ; married in Dover, N. H., Oct. 29, 1856, Edwin L. Morse (born Feb. 8, 1832 ; died Oct. 19, 1883, in Lowell).

Children :

    4577 i   ANNAH E.,[9] b. Dec. 25, 1857, in Sanford, Me.; d. Jan. 27, 1864.
    4578 ii GEORGE S., b. Aug. 31, 1865, in Lowell, Mass.; m. Hattie O. Perley, June 4, 1889, and had one child, Edgar Norman Morse. b. May 19, 1890.
    4579 iii MARION J., b. Nov. 11, 1869, in Lowell, Mass. ; m. Feb. 6, 1889, Farnham C. Lorrey.

2766 CALEB[8] EMERY (*William,*[7] *William,*[6] *Caleb,*[5] *Caleb,*[4] *Daniel*[3] *James,*[2] *Anthony*[1]), son of William and Elizabeth (Emery) Emery; married Aug 16, 1848, Marcia C. (born May 23, 1827), daughter of Isaac P. and Eliza J. (Harper) Choate of Derry, N H He was a merchant in Sanford, Me.; graduated at Dartmouth College, 1842, teacher in Westboro, Mass., Nashua and Derry, N H (Pinkerton Academy); Charlestown, Mass, 1848–50, Boston, 1850–55, private school in Boston, 1855–63; Charlestown, 1863–85.

Children :

    4580   ı   WILLIAM[9] b Nov 23, 1849, d Dec 22, 1869
    4581   ıı   MARCIA, b Dec 11, 1854

2769 ELIZABETH[8] EMERY (*William,*[7] *William,*[6] *Caleb,*[5] *Caleb,*[4] *Daniel,*[3] *James,*[2] *Anthony*[1]), daughter of William and Elizabeth (Emery) Emery, married June 14, 1837, Timothy Shaw, jr. (born Oct. 12, 1817), son of Gen Timothy and Lucy Shaw. Mr Shaw has been county commissioner of York Co. Me., register of deeds, treasurer of Biddeford, Me , and postmaster of Biddeford, Me , 1885–9.

Children, born in Sanford, Me.

    4582   ı   WILLIAM G ,[9] b Aug 3, 1839, d in Alfred, Sept 30, 1857.
    4583   ıı   HOWARD M , b Sept 16, 1841, d Feb 21, 1842.
    4584   ııı   LUCY E., b Jan 16, 1843, unm
    4585   ıv   JEREMIAH G , b Feb 28, 1845 ; m. —— Grant
    4586   v   MARCIA A , b Jan 4, 1852, m —— Staples.

2770 MARY ANN[8] EMERY (*William,*[7] *William,*[6] *Caleb,*[5] *Caleb,*[4] *Daniel,*[3] *James,*[2] *Anthony*[1]), daughter of William and Elizabeth (Emery) Emery, married Aug. 9, 1843, Samuel Tompson (born July 9, 1816) ; lawyer in Sanford and Boston. She died Dec 1, 1873.

Children :

    4587   ı   SARAH M ,[9] b Feb 6 1846
    4588   ıı   EDWARD W E , b March 12, 1848.
    4589   ııı MARTHA H., b. Jan 12, 1858

2771 WILLIAM[8] EMERY (*William,*[7] *William,*[6] *Caleb,*[5] *Caleb,*[4] *Daniel,*[3] *James,*[2] *Anthony*[1]), son of William and Elizabeth (Emery) Emery , married May 26, 1852, Harriet W. Fall (born in Lebanon, Me , Feb 18, 1832). He was admitted to the bar in 1847; practised in Biddeford, Me , Aug , 1848; in Lebanon till 1871, and in Alfred since , selectman, town agent in Lebanon and Alfred; school committee in Sanford and Lebanon ; representative from Sanford and Lebanon 1854 ; county attorney, 1878 ; democratic candidate for Congress, 1888.

Children :

    4590   ı   MARTHA G ,[9] b Oct. 24 1853, d Dec 20, 1854.
    4591   ıı   ELLA H (adopted), b July 8, 1863, m. Oct , 1882, John B.
              Donovan, lawyer in Biddeford, Me.

2773 MARTHA G [8] EMERY (*William,*[7] *William,*[6] *Caleb,*[5] *Caleb,*[4] *Daniel,*[3] *James,*[2] *Anthony*[1]), daughter of William and Elizabeth (Emery) Emery ; married April 16, 1843, Jeremiah Goodwin (born in Kittery (Eliot), July 1, 1784; paymaster in the army in 1812; post-master at Alfred, 1816–36; register of deeds York Co., Me.; treas-urer of Maine; died in Great Falls, N. H., July 29, 1857).

Children, born in Sanford, Me.:

4592   i   ISABELLA S.,⁹ b. July 30, 1844; m. Nov. 5, 1866, A. B. N.
            Wentworth, and has several children.
4593   ii JEREMIAH J., b. July 30, 1846.

2776 EDWARD H.⁸ EMERY (*William*,⁷ *William*,⁶ *Caleb*,⁵ *Caleb*,⁴ *Daniel*,³ *James*,² *Anthony*¹), son of William and his third wife, Mary J. (Hill) Emery; married at Powhatan (now Wetmore,) Kansas, Jan. 28, 1864, Mary A. (born in Cynthiana, Kentucky, March 3, 1847), daughter of W. H. and Caroline (White) Piatt. He went to Cali-fornia in 1854; returned to Sanford, Me., in 1857, and removed to Kansas where he lives. Farmer.

Children:

4594   i   CAROLINE,⁹ b. Aug. 17, 1865.
4595   ii   WILLIAM H., b. March 11, 1868; d. same day.
4596   iii CHARLES O., b. May 22, 1870; d. Oct. 7, 1873.
4597   iv   FRANCES, b. April 24, 1873.
4598   v   MINNIE, b. Oct. 4, 1875; d. March 14, 1877.
4599   vi   EDWARD H. H., b. Nov. 2, 1879.
4600   vii HELEN, b. Aug. 25, 1883; d. March 24, 1884.

2777 CHARLES O.⁸ EMERY (*William*,⁷ *William*,⁶ *Caleb*,⁵ *Caleb*,⁴ *Daniel*,³ *James*,² *Anthony*¹), son of William and his third wife, Mary J. (Hill) Emery; married Feb. 2, 1862, Abigail (born May 2, 1840), daughter of Capt. Nathaniel and Abigail M. (Hanson) Bennett (then the wife of William B. Emery) (see No. 2781). Farmer; town treas-urer, 1876–82; school committee, 1865–9, 1877–9; supervisor of schools, 1882; deputy sheriff. Resides in Sanford.

Children:

4601   i   MARY J.,⁹ b. Aug. 25, 1862; d. May 11, 1865.
4602   ii   EDWARD H., b. Aug. 22, 1864; grocer in Sanford, Me.
4603   iii GEORGE G., b. Aug. 23, 1866; dry goods' merchant in Spring-
            vale, Me.
4604   iv   WILLIAM O., b. Feb. 7, 1874.
4605   v   NELLIE F., b. Aug. 6, 1880.

2780 ALFRED HUBBARD⁸ EMERY (*John S.*,⁷ *William*,⁶ *Caleb*,⁵ *Ca-leb*,⁴ *Daniel*,³ *James*,² *Anthony*¹), son of John S. and Anna M. (Rams-dell) Emery; married, first, April 27, 1845, Harriet B. Stockman (born in Danville, Me., Aug. 31, 1820; died Dec. 8, 1847); second, June 19, 1848, Anna L. Smith (born in Danville, Me., July 30, 1824). Merchant in Portland, Me.

Children:

4606   i   FRANKLIN E.,⁹ b. Jan. 21, 1846.
4607   ii   ANNA L., b. Sept. 14, 1849.
4608   iii HARRIET E., b. Feb. 19, 1851; a teacher; d. in Minneapolis,
            Minn., Oct. 10, 1883.
4609   iv   ALFRED H., b. Nov. 17, 1852.

2781 WILLIAM BOWLES⁸ EMERY (*John S.*,⁷ *William*,⁶ *Caleb*,⁵ *Ca-*

leb,[4] *Daniel*,[3] *James*,[2] *Anthony*[1]), son of John S. and Anna M.
(Ramsdell) Emery, married Dec. 26, 1848, Abigail (Hanson) Bennett (born Dec. 16, 1807, died Jan. 3, 1879).
Children, born in Sanford, Me. :

4610 i   WILLIAM P ,[3] b March 12, 1849
4611 ii   FLORENCE M , b Sept 15, 1850
4612 iii CHARLES OCTAVIUS, b Aug 1, 1853.

2782 JOHN DOW[8] EMERY (*John S* ,[7] *William*,[6] *Caleb*,[5] *Caleb*,[4]
Daniel,[3] *James*,[2] *Anthony*[1]), son of John S. and Anna M (Ramsdell)
Emery, married Susan A (born April 28, 1823 ; died Oct 27, 1885),
daughter of Dominicus and Rachel (Roberts) Kimball.   Tinman
and farmer, greenback candidate for railroad commissioner in New
Hampshire, 1880.
Children, born in Manchester, N. H :

4613 i   ANNETTE A.,[9] b. Nov 20 1847, m June 22, 1870, Byron M
           Corning (b Dec 19, 1847), son of B Warren and Achsa P
           (Chase) Corning
4614 ii   ALFARITTA, b May 28, 1849, d Aug 4, 1850
4615 iii   FRANK A , b Oct 29, 1850 m June 18, 1884, Mary Alice Dill
4616 iv   FRED A , b Nov 27, 1851, d Jan 14, 1865.
4617 v   JOHN A , b Jan 18, 1855.
4618 vi   IDA E , b March 5, 1856
4619 vii   ELLA F , b May 21, 1857
4620 viii CHARLES E , b Sept 21, 1858, d Sept. 14, 1859.
4621 ix   LIZZIE J , b April 23, 1860
4622 x   HORACE K , b Feb 11, 1862; m Mrs Grace M (Watson)
           Marsh, and lives in Northwood N H.
4622a xi   WILLIE, b May 6, 1863, d May 7, 1863.
4622b xii EDWIN C , b May 11, 1864, d July 22, 1865
4623 xiii EDNA L , b Dec 13, 1866, m Leonard C Page, Jan 19, 1887
4624 xiv   MABEL B , b May 18, 1869, m Aug 29, 1889, Frank W Kimball (b May 6, 1870, in Franklin, N H), son of Sylvanus T.
           and Elina (Hoyt) Kimball   Printer in Manchester, N. H.

2783 MARY JANE[8] EMERY (*John S* ,[7] *William*,[6] *Caleb*,[5] *Caleb*,[4]
Daniel,[3] *James*,[2] *Anthony*[1]), daughter of John S and Anna M (Ramsdell) Emery ; married in Lowell, Mass., March 31, 1845, Oliver Russ
(born in St. Johnsbury, Vt , March 5, 1816 ; died Feb. 15, 1887).
Children ·

4625 i   ALFRED M ,[9] b in Woonsocket, R I , Dec 31, 1845, d in
           Blackstone, Mass , July 5, 1847
4626 ii   HERMAN M , b in Blackstone, Mass , March 31, 1847, enlisted
           in Co " F," 8th Mich Cav , d in a rebel prison in Savannah, Ga , Oct. 25, 1864

2784 ABIGAIL S [8] EMERY (*John S* ,[7] *William*,[6] *Caleb*,[5] *Caleb*,[4]
Daniel,[3] *James*,[2] *Anthony*[1]), daughter of John S and Anna M (Ramsdell) Emery, married May 24, 1845, George W Dow (born Oct 21,
1825).
Children :

4627 i   GEORGE L ,[9] b June 21, 1846; d Oct 13 1858
4628 ii   FLORA J , b April 11, 1847, d May 2, 1848
4629 iii   DANIEL F , b March 25, 1849 , d June 3, 1852.
4630 iv   RINALDO H , b June 25, 1851; d Oct 23, 1859.
4631 v   ALICE L , b April 20, 1855, d June 28, 1880

2786 LUCY M.[8] EMERY (*John S.,*[7] *William,*[6] *Caleb,*[5] *Caleb,*[4] *Daniel,*[3] *James,*[2] *Anthony*[1]), daughter of John S. and Anna M. (Ramsdell) Emery ; married May 23, 1845, George Peavey of Farmington, N. H., teamster (born Sept. 25, 1823 ; died March 13, 1890). He was a member of Co. " B," 35th Regt. Mass. Vols.

Children :

    4632 i   MARY F.,[9] b. April 6, 1849 ; d. Aug. 28, 1849.
    4633 ii   GEORGE H. C., b. July 30, 1850.
    4634 iii ALFRED A.. b. May 23, 1852 ; d. Sept. 11, 1852.
    4635 iv   MARY, b. March 29, 1854 ; d. Oct. 11, 1854.
    4636 v   MYER C., b. Aug. 27, 1856 ; d. Sept. 9, 1857.
    4637 vi   ANNIE H., b. Aug. 1, 1858.
    4638 vii HENRIETTA S., b. March 4, 1860.
    4639 viii LAURA J., b. Dec. 3, 1866.
    4640 ix   LAURENCE L., b. Nov. 12, 1868.

2788 MELISSA MARDEN[8] EMERY (*John S.,*[7] *William,*[6] *Caleb,*[5] *Caleb,*[4] *Daniel,*[3] *James,*[2] *Anthony*[1]), daughter of John S. and Anna M. (Ramsdell) Emery ; married Oct. 27, 1859, James C. Blanchard. He served as private in the 12th Vt. Infantry. In 1880, they removed from Pomfret, Vt., to Ionia, Fla.

Children, born in Pomfret, Vt. :

    4641 i   WILBUR A.,[9] b. March 17, 1861 ; m. June 1, 1886, Lillian Acres
               of East Douglass, Mass., who d. March, 1887, leaving one
               child that d. June, 1887.
    4642 ii   WILLIE, b. March 17, 1861 ; m. June 16, 1887, Mrs. Agnes
               Gwinn, and has one dau., Amy E., b. Jan., 1890.
    4643 iii ALANSON, b. Jan. 25, 1864 ; m. June 8, 1887, Miss McLeod of
               Green Cove, Fla., and has one child, Erosa M., b. July 15,
               1888.
    4644 iv   LINCOLN B., b. Oct. 12. 1865.
    4645 v   RALPH E., b. April 24, 1869.

2789 SARAH F.[8] EMERY (*John S.,*[7] *William,*[6] *Caleb,*[5] *Caleb,*[4] *Daniel,*[3] *James,*[2] *Anthony*[1]), daughter of John S. and Anna M. (Ramsdell) Emery ; married, first, in Nashua, N. H., Dec. 31, 1849, Lewis O. Howard (died Sept. 25, 1864, in Pomfret, Vt.), by whom she had four children who died in infancy ; second, in Pomfret, in 1865, Norman Clifford (died April 10, 1887). They were both farmers.

2790 ALICE CLARK[8] EMERY (*John S.,*[7] *William,*[6] *Caleb,*[5] *Caleb,*[4] *Daniel,*[3] *James,*[2] *Anthony*[1]), daughter of John S. and Anna M. (Ramsdell) Emery ; married, Jan. 3, 1852, James Ramsdell of Woburn, Mass., and died in Lowell, March 11, 1884. He married, second, ―― ――.

Children :

    4646 i   CHARLES,[9] b. ―― ; d. Aug., 1861.
    4647 ii   A DAUGHTER, who m. Thomas Johnson, and d., leaving no
               children.
    4648 iii WILLIAM EMERY, b. ―― ; m., 1st, Lena Stover, and had one
               child, who d. at the age of 4 or 5 years ; 2nd, Mrs. ――.

2792 HELEN M.[8] EMERY (*John S.,*[7] *William,*[6] *Caleb,*[5] *Caleb,*[4] *Daniel,*[3] *James,*[2] *Anthony*[1]), daughter of John S. and Anna M. (Ramsdell) Emery; married in Berlin, Vt., Sept 5, 1866, Mason Knapp (born Feb. 22, 1823), son of Nathan and Louisa (Grinnell) Knapp. Child, born in Sharon, Vt :

4649 i HERMAN MELVILLE,[9] b. June 11, 1867; m April 28, 1890, Leray M. Fraser, b in Fort Fairfield, Me , June 5, 1868

2793 JOHN W[8] THOMPSON (*Hannah B*,[7] *William*,[6] *Caleb*,[5] *Caleb*,[4] *Daniel*,[3] *James*,[2] *Anthony*[1]), son of Nahum M and Hannah B. (Emery) Thompson, married May 5, 1856, Phileua A., daughter of Dr Whiting and Abigail Stevens of Shapleigh, Me. Farmer and stock raiser in Goddard, Kansas.

Children :

4650 i LIZZIE H ,[9] b Feb 5, 1857, in Springfield, Ill . d Sept 9, 1857.
4651 ii FRANKLIN W S , b April 4, 1858, in Springfield, Ill , d March 2, 1861
4652 iii LIZZIE A , b May 10, 1860. in Fulton City, Whiteside Co , Ill
4653 iv FRANKLIN W b Oct 8, 1861, in Fulton City, Whiteside Co., Ill , d 1886
4654 v FRED W , b. Oct 15, 1864, in Fulton City, Whiteside Co Ill
4655 vi CHARLES AMORY, b Jan 25, 1867, in Fulton City, Whiteside Co , Ill
4656 vii MARY B , b Oct 6, 1871, Cass Township in Hamilton Co., Iowa
4657 viii JOHN W , JR , b. Aug 20, 1871, and d the same day, in Cass Township, Iowa

2795 CALEB E[8] THOMPSON (*Hannah B*,[7] *William*,[6] *Caleb*,[5] *Caleb*,[4] *Daniel*[3] *James*,[2] *Anthony*[1]), son of Nahum M and Hannah B. (Emery) Thompson, married Cornelia T Tyson of Georgia in 1859. Stock raiser in Kansas.

Children :

4658 i A SON,[9] d young in South Park, Col
4659 ii A SON, d young
4660 iii BELLE, b 1863
4661 iv FREDONIA, b 1871
4662 v ADA, b 1874

2804 BENJAMIN F[8] EMERY (*Samuel B*,[7] *William*,[6] *Caleb*,[5] *Caleb*,[4] *Daniel*,[3] *James*,[2] *Anthony*[1]), son of Samuel B and Alice (Pray) Emery, married June 28, 1863, Augusta A Tebbetts (born March 14, 1843), daughter of Jonathan and Jane (Chadbourn) Tebbetts. He died May 28, 1882 Mrs Emery married, second, Dec. 25, 1887, Charles F. Moulton of Sanford.

Children, born in Sanford, Me :

4663 i FRED A ,[9] b Jan 23, 1864; d Aug. 18, 1873.
4664 ii ALICE J , b July 19 1866, d Dec. 17, 1883
4665 iii LIZZIE H , b June 9, 1868
4666 iv IDA A , b Aug 20, 1870, d Jan 21, 1871.
4667 v IDA L , b Aug 1, 1874

2805 MOSES W.[8] EMERY (*Samuel B*,[7] *William*,[6] *Caleb*,[5] *Caleb*,[4] *Daniel*,[3] *James*,[2] *Anthony*[1]), son of Samuel B. and Alice (Pray) Emery, married Sept 28, 1858, Miriam W. (born in Lebanon, Me , June 13, 1836), daughter of Hon. Increase S. and Miriam W. (Bodwell) Kimball. He was a merchant ; town clerk, 1861–65 ; treasurer, 1862, of Sanford ; farmer, and has been mayor of Logan, Kansas ; now in Harriman, Tenn.

Children, born in Sanford, Me. :

   4668 i   HELEN M.,[9] b. July 23, 1860; d. Dec. 31, 1875.
   4669 ii   FRANK S., b. Nov. 14, 1861 ; d. Feb. 10, 1862.
   4670 iii HERBERT S., b. Jan. 7, 1863.
   4671 iv DAUGHTER, b. July 25, 1864; d. Sept. 3, 1864.
   4672 v   SUMNER K., b Oct. 25, 1870.

2806 CHARLOTTE S.[8] EMERY (*Samuel B.,*[7] *William,*[6] *Caleb,*[5] *Caleb,*[4] *Daniel,*[3] *James,*[2] *Anthony*[1]), daughter of Samuel B. and Alice (Pray) Emery ; married July 19, 1862, John B. Bodwell (born Oct. 5, 1838), son of Col. Horace Bodwell of Acton, Me. He was a lawyer in Logan, Kansas, also in Georgia and Florida. She died in Logan, Kansas, April 9, 1882. He married, second, ———.

 Children, all born in Sanford, Me. :

   4673 i   ARGIE,[9] b. Feb. 26, 1865.
   4674 ii   NELLIE E., b. Jan. 13, 1867; d. Aug. 17, 1867.

2807 SAMUEL BENTON[8] EMERY (*Samuel B.,*[7] *William,*[6] *Caleb,*[5] *Caleb,*[4] *Daniel,*[3] *James,*[2] *Anthony*[1]), son of Samuel B. and Alice (Pray) Emery ; married Jan. 11, 1870, Elizabeth F. A. (born in Sanford, Me., Oct. 29, 1847), daughter of Hon. Increase S. and Miriam W. (Bodwell) Kimball. Furniture dealer in Sanford, Me.

  Children:

   4675 i   FRANK M.,[9] b. Dec. 9, 1870; m. Alice A. Spinney, Aug. 2, 1890.
   4676 ii   MIRIAM K., b. April 30, 1872 ; d. June 28, 1872.
   4677 iii WALTER K., b. March 26, 1873.
   4678 iv HERMAN B , b. June 9, 1877 ; d. Dec. 3, 1883.
   4679 v   FAITH ELIZABETH, b. Aug. 11, 1884.

2824 IMOGENE E.[8] EMERY (*John W.,*[7] *Henry T.,*[6] *Caleb,*[5] *Caleb,*[4] *Daniel,*[3] *James,*[2] *Anthony*[1]), daughter of John W. and Arabella E. (Close) Emery ; married, 1870, in Boston, Shepard Bradley.

  Child :

   4680 i   HARRY.[9]

2829 MARY ANN[8] MORANG (*Adeline,*[7] *Henry T.,*[6] *Caleb,*[5] *Caleb,*[4] *Daniel,*[3] *James,*[2] *Anthony*[1]), daughter of George N. and Adeline (Emery) Morang ; married George W. Davenport.

  Children, born in Eastport, Me. :

   4681 i   ADA P.,[9] b. May 19, 1873.
   4682 ii   ANNIE II., b. Aug. 10, 1876.
   4683 iii MAC A., b. Oct. 2, 1878.

2845 ETHEL GRAHAM[8] EMERY (*Sabine,*[7] *Henry T.,*[6] *Caleb,*[5] *Caleb,*[4] *Daniel,*[3] *James,*[2] *Anthony*[1]), daughter of Sabine and M. L. (Flint) Emery ; married Nov. 26, 1886, Philip Sidney Lindsay, M.D., son of Hon. St. D. Lindsay of Norridgewock, Me.

  Child :

   4684 i   PHYLLIS SABYNE,[9] b. Feb. 25, 1888.

2879 DANIEL C.[8] EMERY (*Jonathan*,[7] *Daniel*,[6] *James*,[5] *Joseph*,[4] *Job*,[3] *James*,[2] *Anthony*[1]), son of Jonathan and Jennie (Stevens) Emery, married, first, Lucia Jordan (born in 1798; died Sept 17, 1834), daughter of Elisha and Mary (Armstrong) Jordan, second, Mary Barrett, widow of William Fogg. He was educated at Gorham Academy, taught school for a while; at twenty years of age settled in Gorham Village. He was always identified with the best interests of the town, and a leader of public sentiment. Member of the State Legislature; high sheriff; trustee of Gorham Academy. His mind was strong, clear and discriminating, his sense of justice keen, and his knowledge of human instinct, motives and possibilities profound. He was a man of fire but never in a passion, large in his ideas and liberal in his benefactions to church and school. It has been said of him that he never did a mean thing.

Children ·

By first wife .

4685   i   JESSL' APPLETON,[9] b May 22, 1827, m Phœbe Brown, d. May 22, 1862. They had one child, not living.
4686   ii   SARAH ELLEN, b May 6, 1829, m David D Briggs, d Feb, 1850. They had one child, not living.
4687   iii   JOSEPH MELVILLE, b June 1, 1831, m Catherine Bartlett, d. July 24, 1855. They had one child.

By second wife.

4688   iv   ELIZA BARRETT, b Aug 15 1836
4689   v   GEORGE BARRETT, b June 28, 1838, grad Bowd College 1860, lawyer, in Gorham, Me
4690   vi   LUCIA ANN, b Oct 15, 1847

2880 HARRIET[8] EMERY (*Jonathan*,[7] *Daniel*,[6] *James*,[5] *Joseph*,[4] *Job*,[3] *James*,[2] *Anthony*[1]), daughter of Jonathan and ———— , married in Buxton, Me , Dec., 1836, Col. Daniel Parsons.

Children, born in Hartford, Me :

4691   i   EMERY,[9] b June 3 1837
4692   ii   MARTHA JANE, b April 26, 1839, d April 1, 1867, in Sumner, Me
4693   iii   HARRIET, b April 19, 1841
4694   iv   HENRY, b Oct 22 1843
4695   v   SYLVINA HALL, b Dec 13, 1845, d May 14, 1868
4696   vi   JULIA ANN, b. Jan 19, 1847

2890 ALMIRA S [8] EMERY (*Josiah*,[7] *Daniel*,[6] *James*,[5] *Joseph*,[4] *Job*,[3] *James*,[2] *Anthony*[1]), daughter of Josiah and Jane (Flood) Emery, married Rufus Libby (born July 26, 1823). She died Sept 13, 1871

Children ·

4697   i   ALTHEA MARETTA,[9] b May 7, 1849
4698   ii   ELIZABETH JANE, b Dec 24, 1850
4699   iii   FREDERICK EMERY, b Aug 29, 1852
4700   iv   JULIA ANN, b Sept 25, 1854
4701   v   JOSIAH EMERY, b Feb 1, 1858
4702   vi   ARTHUR BENJAMIN, b Oct 21, 1861.
4703   vii   GEORGE W . b Dec. 18, 1863, d. Jan 30, 1864.
4704   viii   SARAH ELLEN, b Nov , 1864.
4705   ix   DANIEL C , b March, 1867; d Aug. 31, 1870
4706   x   EDMUND BERRY,   ⎫
4707   xi   MARTHA PAMELIA, ⎬ b. Nov 28, 1870.

2892 Marquis L.[8] Emery (*William*,[7] *Benjamin*,[6] *James*,[5] *Joseph*,[4] *Job*,[3] *James*,[2] *Anthony*[1]), son of William and Jane (Brown) Emery; married, first, April 29, 1841, Lucy L. Ridlon; second, March 2, 1843, Ann Hanson of Saco, Me. (died June 20, 1844) ; third, May 27, 1846, Sarah G. Allen (died Aug. 18, 1860) ; fourth, July 3, 1862, Priscilla L. (Marsh) Emery (died Sept. 19, 1875), widow of Alvah C. Emery (see No. 961). He died Oct. 30, 1873.

Children :
By first wife :

    4708 i   Lucy,[9]———b. 1841; m., Nov. 15, 1862, Albert Lougee (d. April, 1870).

By second wife :

    4709 ii Pamelia A., b. June 15, 1844; m. July 2, 1866, Daniel A. Emery, son of Alvah C. and Priscilla (Marsh) Emery. (See 2337).

By third wife :

    4710 iii Henry Allen, b. Dec. 18, 1846.

2896 Louisa[8] Emery (*Joshua*,[7] *James*,[6] *James*,[5] *Joseph*,[4] *Job*,[3] *James*,[2] *Anthony*[1]), daughter of Joshua and Shuah (Chick) Emery; married Nathaniel Blake of Limington, Me. Lived in Great Falls, N. H.

Children, born in Great Falls :

    4711 i   Frances Ellen,[9] b. Jan. 26, 1836.
    4712 ii Sylvania A., b. June 13, 1837; d. Nov. 11, 1841.
    4713 iii Charles O., b. Feb. 6, 1839; d. Oct. 29, 1841.

2897 Lucinda[8] Emery (*Joshua*,[7] *James*,[6] *James*,[5] *Joseph*,[4] *Job*,[3] *James*,[2] *Anthony*[1]), daughter of Joshua and Shuah (Chick) Emery; married June 18, 1844, Edmund T. Boody (born in Limington, Me., April 4, 1823). He is a farmer and mechanic.

Children :

    4714 i   Edmund F.,[9] b. April 11, 1845, in Great Falls; d. in Limington, Dec. 1, 1855.
    4715 ii Everett W., b. April 17, 1848.
    4716 iii Sylvania A., b. Aug. 17, 1850.
    4717 iv Celesta, b. Oct. 10, 1859.

2898 Charles[8] Emery (*Joshua*,[7] *James*,[6] *James*,[5] *Joseph*,[4] *Job*,[3] *James*,[2] *Anthony*[1]), son of Joshua and Shuah (Chick) Emery; married June 18, 1844, Charity Fogg of Limington, Me. (born in Hollis, Me., 1824 ; died in Pittsfield, Mass., 1882). Machinist.

Children :

    4718 i   James,[9] b. April 1, 1845, in Hollis; d. in Saco, 1855.
    4719 ii Lenora, b. July, 1850, in Limington; m. Freeman Carter.

2901 James[8] Emery (*Rev. James*,[7] *James*,[6] *James*,[5] *Joseph*,[4] *Job*,[3] *James*,[2] *Anthony*[1]), son of Rev. James and Hannah (Leathers) Emery; married Mary N. Brown of Tamworth, N. H.

Children :

    4720 i   John B.,[9] b. Dec. 1, 1842; m. Rebecca Blaisdell; res. in Cambridge, Mass.

4721 ·ii HANNAH E , b 1847
4722 iii MARK B , b July 25, 1850; m Hattie Harding; res. in Tamworth, N H

2903 COLBY[8] EMERY (*Rev. James,[7] James,[6] James,[5] Joseph,[4] Job,[3] James,[2] Anthony[1]*), son of Rev. James and Hannah (Leathers) Emery; married in Tamworth, N. H , July 2, 1855, Ruth Blaisdell (died Jan. 7, 1875), daughter of Zenas and Susannah (Roberts) Blaisdell Children, born in Champlin, Minn .

    4723 i JAMES R ,[9] b April 18, 1856 , m Lizzie Studley, May 4, 1887.
    4724 ii CHARLES EDGAR, b Oct 19, 1857
    4725 iii ZENAS BLAISDELL, b Jan 25. 1863, d Jan. 9, 1867
    4726 iv ANNA GERTRUDE, b Aug 2, 1867 , m Albert A Stockton, June 27, 1858.

2907 JULIA A.[8] STAPLES (*Sarah,[7] James,[6] James.[5] Joseph,[4] Job,[3] James,[2] Anthony[1]*), daughter of George and Sarah (Emery) Staples; married in Limerick, Me., Oct 28, 1854, Albion K. P. Boody (born Jan., 1825). Children born in Limerick, Me , except first:

    4727 i IDA,[9] b 1855, in Livingston, Me.
    4728 ii CHARLES, b 1857.
    4729 iii MILLARD F , b 1860.
    4730 iv HATTIE B , b. 1862
    4731 v JENNIE V.

2908 MELINDA[8] STAPLES (*Sarah,[7] James,[6] James,[5] Joseph,[4] Job,[3] James,[2] Anthony[1]*), daughter of George and Sarah (Emery) Staples; married April 14, 1860, Stephen Walker. She died Feb. 5, 1878. Children .

    4732 i ARAVESTA,[9] b in Limerick, Me.
    4733 ii FANNY M , b in Limerick, Me

2915 IRA L [8] EMERY (*Jeremiah,[7] James,[6] James,[5] Joseph,[4] Job,[3] James,[2] Anthony[1]*), son of Jeremiah and Susan (Libby) Emery , married April 10, 1863, Susan Kelly (died July 8, 1876). Children, born in Limerick, Me :

    4734 i SALENA E.,[9] b Dec. 4, 1864
    4735 ii NELLIE C , b. Dec 21, 1866
    4736 iii CHARLES D , b Aug 19, 1868.
    4737 iv JERRY, b May 3, 1870
    4738 v JAMES B , b Dec 20, 1871.

2916 GEORGE S [8] EMERY (*Jeremiah,[7] James,[6] James,[5] Joseph,[4] Job,[3] James,[2] Anthony[1]*), son of Jeremiah and Susan (Libby) Emery , married April 16, 1864, Lizzie Clark of Limerick, Me.   He died Dec. 16, 1878. Children :

    4739 i HOWARD L ,[9] b March 2, 1865, d. July 21, 1867.
    4740 ii GEORGE F , b Aug 9, 1867
    4741 iii EDITH M., b. April 13, 1870
    4742 iv MARY L , b. April 13, 1876.

2939 JOHN EMERY[8] SEAMAN (*Sarah,[7] John,[6] John,[5] Joseph,[4] Job,[3]*

James,[2] *Anthony*[1]), son of Rev. James A. and Sarah (Emery) Seaman; married, first, Marcella McCormick (born in Dublin, Ireland; died, *s. p.*, Jan. 2, 1865); second, July 27, 1878, Kate M. Cooney. Principal of Boys' High School, New Orleans, La.

Child :

4743   i   JOHN HENRY,[9] b. Sept. 10, 1879.

2940 SARAH[8] SEAMAN (*Sarah,*[7] *John,*[6] *John,*[5] *Joseph,*[4] *Job,*[3] *James,*[2] *Anthony*[1]), daughter of Rev. James A. and Sarah (Emery) Seaman; married, 1838, in Richmond, Ky., Rev. James M. Putney (died 1841). She died in 1840.

Child :

4744   1   JAMES S.[9]

2941 JULIA[8] SEAMAN (*Sarah,*[7] *John,*[6] *John,*[5] *Joseph,*[4] *Job,*[3] *James,*[2] *Anthony*[1]), daughter of Rev. James A. and Sarah (Emery) Seaman; married (at the same time and place as her sister Sarah) Spencer Harding, a distinguished artist. She died in 1842.

Child :

4745   i   GEORGE,[9] d. young.

2944 SYLVANUS P.[8] SEAMAN (*Sarah,*[7] *John,*[6] *John,*[5] *Joseph,*[4] *Job,*[3] *James,*[2] *Anthony*[1]), son of Rev. James A. and Sarah (Emery) Seaman; married Clara Faxon. Editor of the "Boston Gazette" at one time.

Child :

4746   1   ELLA,[9] who m. a physician of Brockton, Mass.

2948 LOUISA MARIA[8] EMERY (*Daniel,*[7] *John,*[6] *John,*[5] *Joseph,*[4] *Job,*[3] *James,*[2] *Anthony*[1]), daughter of Daniel and Hannah (Sabine) Emery; married in Hampden, Me., Sept. 11, 1845, Capt. William H. Adams, shipmaster (died in Bangor, Me., Nov., 1868).

Children :

4747   i   ELLA LOUISA,[9] b. June 18, 1846, in Hampden.
4748   ii   WILLIAM HENRY, b. Aug. 8, 1850, in Hampden.
4749   iii GEORGE EMERY, b. March 20, 1856, in Bangor.

2950 JOHN CROSBY[8] EMERY (*Daniel,*[7] *John,*[6] *John,*[5] *Joseph,*[4] *Job,*[3] *James,*[2] *Anthony*[1]), son of Daniel and his third wife, Elvira (Crosby) Emery; married Helen Wilson. Graduate of West Point Military Academy. Shipmaster; was several years in China and Japan; died at sea, Sept., 1868, the night before arriving at Acapulco, where he was buried. Resided in Hampden till 1850.

Children, born in Bangor :

4750   i   WILSON CROSBY,[9] b. July 8, 1865.
4751   ii   HELEN P., b. Dec. 19, 1868.

2951 GEORGE AUGUSTUS[8] EMERY (*Daniel,*[7] *John,*[6] *John,*[5] *Joseph,*[4] *Job,*[3] *James,*[2] *Anthony*[1]), son of Daniel and his third wife, Elvira (Crosby) Emery; married Frances N. Snow of Troy, N. Y. Resided in Hampden till 1868, when he removed to Chicago, Ill.

Children ·

4752 I   FRANK WILLIAM,[9] b Jan 29, 1864, d. Dec 18, 1864, in Hampden
4753 II   MINNIE CROSBY, b Oct 20, 1865
4754 III FIELD ALBION, b April 14, 1868
4755 IV   SON, b Aug 30, 1870, in Chicago; d Aug. 30, 1870
4756 V   GEORGE FRANCIS, b Dec. 22, 1872.
4757 VI   WILLIS EDWARD, b Oct 16, 1875; d March 8, 1876
4758 VII HOWARD PARKER, b Oct 21, 1877, d Dec. 21, 1879.
4759 VIII LOUISE ADAMS, b Nov 2, 1880

2954 SARAH CROSBY[8] EMERY (*Daniel,[7] John,[6] John,[5] Joseph,[4] Job,[3] James,[2] Anthony[1]*), daughter of Daniel and third wife Elvira (Crosby) Emery, married Sept. 30, 1867, Edward G. Blanchard of Yarmouth, Me.

Children, born in Yarmouth :

4760 I   OLIVE LOUISA,[9] b Jan 7, 1871
4761 II GEORGE EMERY, b March 31, 1873.
4762 III ALICE EMERY, b May 31, 1876

2960 WILLIAM P.[8] EMERY (*William,[7] John,[6] John,[5] Joseph,[4] Job,[3] James,[2] Anthony[1]*), son of William and Lucy (Covill) Emery, married Susan Nickerson. Resided in Hampden, Me.

Child :

4763 I   KATE,[9] b. Dec 4, 1869

2965 JULIA A.[8] EMERY (*Thomas,[7] John,[6] John,[5] Joseph,[4] Job,[3] James,[2] Anthony[1]*), daughter of Thomas and Mercy (Wasgatt) Emery; married March 29, 1840, Fayette D. Buker (born in Castine, Me., Sept. 30, 1812). Resided in Yorkshire, N. Y. Died in Foxboro, Mass.

Children

4764 I   THOMAS E ,[9] b Nov 26, 1842, d in Tmk's Island, 1859
4765 II FAYETTE, b. Oct 31, 1844.
4766 III CARVER I , b Jan 13, 1846.
4767 IV NOAH E , b Feb 17, 1848; d
4768 V   ARTHUR, b Feb. 8, 1852
4769 VI JULIA D , b March 20, 1856; d in Chicago, 1877.
4770 VII ANNIE M , b March 21, 1859, d 1875

2966 CHARLOTTE C.[8] EMERY (*Thomas,[7] John,[6] John,[5] Joseph,[4] Job,[3] James,[2] Anthony[1]*), daughter of Thomas and Mercy (Wasgatt) Emery; married May 6, 1851, James H Sewell of Hampden, Me.

Child :

4771 I   CATHARINE R ,[9] b Feb. 10, 1852, m Capt. Horace Whitmore, Oct 30, 1877

2969 ELMIRA A [8] EMERY (*Thomas,[7] John,[6] John,[5] Joseph,[4] Job,[3] James,[2] Anthony[1]*), daughter of Thomas and Mercy (Wasgatt) Emery; married Jan. 1, 1849, Stephen H. Goddard of Pownal, Me. (born Dec 3, 1814)   Resides in Foxboro, Mass

Children :

4772 i   GALEN,[9] b. April 14. 1850; d. April 18, 1850.
4773 ii   CAROLINE b. Aug 3, 1851.
4774 iii CHARLOTTE S., b. July 26, 1854.
4775 iv   GRACE L., b. March 27, 1873.

2979 LORENZO[8] EMERY (*Joseph*,[7] *Nahum*,[6] *John*,[5] *Joseph*.[4] *Job*,[3] *James*,[2] *Anthony*[1]), son of Joseph and Alliance (Mayo) Emery; married, first, Mrs. —— Cobb in Dixmont, Me.; second, Lizzie Pomeroy (died 1846) ; third, Paulina Pomeroy.   Resides in Dixmont, Me.
  Child of first marriage :

4776 i   LIZZIE,[9] b. 1842; d. 1868.

  By second marriage :

4777 ii   AUGUSTA, b. 1846.

  Children by third marriage :

4778 iii JULIA, b. 1848.
4779 iv   SUSAN, b. 1850.
4780 v   WILLARD, b. 1852.

2980 NAHUM[8] EMERY (*Joseph*,[7] *Nahum*,[6] *John*,[5] *Joseph*,[4] *Job*,[3] *James*,[2] *Anthony*[1]), son of Joseph and Alliance (Mayo) Emery; married Maria Dodge ; resides in Munroe, Me.   He died July 9, 1870.
  Children :

4781 i   SANFORD,[9] b. April 17, 1845.
4782 ii   CHARLES R., b. Jan. 3, 1850.
4783 iii NETTIE, b. Nov. 27, 1854 ; d. Nov. 2, 1858.
4784 iv   ELIZA M., b. March 20, 1856.
4785 v   AMOSETTE, b. June 21, 1858.
4786 vi   FREMONT, b. June 20, 1862.
4787 vii FREDERICK, b. June 13, 1864.
4788 viii NELLIE, b. July 9, 1867.

2982 ELISHA[8] EMERY (*Joseph*,[7] *Nahum*,[6] *John*,[5] *Joseph*,[4] *Job*,[3] *James*,[2] *Anthony*[1]), son of Joseph and Alliance (Mayo) Emery ; married Emily Dexter.
  Children :

4789 i   EVIE,[9] b. 1848 ; d. 1864.
4790 ii   FRANK, b. 1852.
4791 iii HARRY, b. 1858.

2983 FREDERICK[8] EMERY (*Joseph*,[7] *Nahum*,[6] *John*,[5] *Joseph*,[4] *Job*,[3] *James*,[2] *Anthony*[1]), son of Joseph and Alliance (Mayo) Emery ; married Aurilla Dodge.
  Children :

4792 i   ADELINA,[9] b. Oct. 31, 1857.
4793 ii   EVELINA, b. Feb 10, 1859.
4794 iii FRANK A., b. Feb. 17, 1860.

2987 BAKER[8] EMERY (*Joseph*,[7] *Nahum*,[6] *John*,[5] *Joseph*,[4] *Job*,[9] *James*,[2] *Anthony*[1]), son of Joseph and Alliance (Mayo) Emery ; married Loretta Garland.
  Child :

4795 i   EDWARD EVERETT,[9] b. 1864.
Two children, d. in infancy.

2991 ANDREW J.[8] EMERY (*Nahum,*[7] *Nahum.*[6] *John,*[5] *Joseph,*[4] *Job,*[3] *James,*[2] *Anthony*[1]), son of Nahum and Cordelia (Wasgatt) Emery, married Hester Smith.

Children:

    4796 i   WILLIAM E ,[9] b Feb 28, 1859; m Feb 19, 1887, Lucy J. Curtis, grad Me State Coll and Bellevue Hospital Med Coll , N Y City. Resides in Surry, Me.

    4797 ii   JEANNETTE F., b Aug 30, 1861, m. Dec 24, 1883, Dr. E W. Temple.

    4798 iii ETTA G , b June 2, 1863.

2992 JEANNETTE[8] EMERY (*Nahum,*[7] *Nahum,*[6] *John,*[5] *Joseph,* [4] *Job,*[3] *James,*[2] *Anthony*[1]), daughter of Nahum and Cordelia (Wasgatt) Emery; married, first, April 6, 1852, George W. Flagg (died in Col , Oct 5, 1876) ; second, Sept 17, 1865, Col Frank G. Flagg, brother of her first husband (died Jan. 22, 1881) F. G. Flagg was colonel of the 2d Maine militia and adjutant of 22d Maine regiment in the Civil War, 1863–65.

Children, by first marriage.

    4799 i   GEORGE EMERY,[9] b. Dec 15, 1855; m. Oct. 7, 1883, Clara E. Ware.

By second marriage:

    4800 ii   EDWIN H , b Jan 20, 1869
    4801 iii ALBERT M , b. Nov 4, 1875.

2993 NAHUM[8] EMERY (*Nahum,*[7] *Nahum,*[6] *John,*[5] *Joseph.*[4] *Job,*[3] *James,*[2] *Anthony*[1]), son of Nahum and Cordelia (Wasgatt) Emery; married Francelia Garland.

Children:

    4802 i   NELLIE,[9] b. Sept. 18, 1868
    4803 ii   FREDERICK, b Dec 10, 1871.
    4804 iii EDGAR, b Nov. 9, 1874

2996 FREEMAN[8] EMERY (*Nahum,*[7] *Nahum,*[6] *John,*[5] *Joseph.*[4] *Job,*[3] *James,*[2] *Anthony*[1]), son of Nahum and Cordelia (Wasgatt) Emery; married Caroline Baker.

Children:

    4805 i   CORDELIA S ,[9] b March 28, 1875.
    4806 ii   AGNES CLARK, b July 30, 1876

3000 JOHN[8] EMERY (*John,*[7] *Nahum,*[6] *John,*[5] *Joseph,*[4] *Job,*[3] *James,*[2] *Anthony*[1]), son of John and Sarah (Fernald) Emery; married Lizzie Humphrey. Resides in Hampden, Me.

Child:

    4807 i   GEORGE E ,[9] b. April 16, 1868

3002 OLIVER H.[8] EMERY (*John,*[7] *Nahum.*[6] *John,*[5] *Joseph,*[4] *Job,*[3] *James* [2] *Anthony*[1]), son of John and Sarah (Fernald) Emery; married Ellen Maddocks.

Children:

4808   i   LENA,⁹ b. 1874.
4809   ii   CYNTHIA, b. 1876.

3021 THOMAS C.⁸ EMERY (*Job,⁷ Ichabod,⁶ Job,⁵ Joseph,⁴ Job,³ James,² Anthony¹*), son of Job and Abigail (Horne) Emery ; married May 26, 1849, Sophronia Dole.

Child :

4810   i   ADA JANE,⁹ b. Nov. 6, 1850.

3022 MARY ELIZABETH⁸ EMERY (*Job,⁷ Ichabod,⁶ Job,⁵ Joseph,⁴ Job,³ James,² Anthony¹*), daughter of Job and Abigail (Horne) Emery ; married Dec. 20, 1849, Paul Spinney (born Jan. 27, 1828). Resides in Ipswich, Mass.

Children :

4811   i   GEORGE F.,⁹ b. July 9, 1852, in Somersworth, N. H.
4812   ii   ISABELLA F., b. July 30, 1853, in Somersworth, N. H.

3026 FRANKLIN⁸ EMERY (*Joseph,⁷ Ichabod,⁶ Job,⁵ Joseph,⁴ Job,³ James,² Anthony¹*), son of Joseph and Sophronia (Moore) Emery ; married in Lowell, Mass., Feb. 3, 1850, Alice C. Waterhouse (born in Limington, Me., Nov. 24, 1829).

Children :

4813   i   JOSEPH F.,⁹ b. Oct. 17. 1851.
4814   ii   ELLA M., b. April 21, 1853.
4815   iii   GEORGE D., b. June 4, 1854 ; d. Aug. 9, 1854.
4816   iv   CHARLES H , b July 2, 1855 ; d. July 28, 1855.
4817   v   ANNIE A., b. July 30, 1856 ; d. Sept. 24, 1856.
4818   vi   NELLIE E., b. Aug. 13, 1858 ; d. Aug. 25, 1858.
4819   vii   WILLIE BELLE, b. Oct. 31, 1861.
4820   viii CARRIE MAY, b. Jan. 27, 1866.

3028 SOPHIA⁸ EMERY (*Joseph,⁷ Ichabod,⁶ Job,⁵ Joseph,⁴ Job,³ James,² Anthony¹*), daughter of Joseph and Sophronia (Moore) Emery ; married Oct. 25, 1853, David Hatch (born Nov. 5, 1829).

Children :

4821   i   CHARLES,⁹ b. Aug. 12, 1854 ; d. May 25, 1855.
4822   ii   LIZZIE, b. April 16, 1856.
4823   iii ADIN A., b. May 29, 1858.
4824   iv   WILL. T., b. Dec. 3, 1866.
4825   v   ALICE T., b. Aug. 5, 1868.

3029 JOHN⁸ EMERY (*Joseph,⁷ Ichabod,⁶ Job,⁵ Joseph,⁴ Job,³ James,² Anthony¹*), son of Joseph and Sophronia (Moore) Emery ; married in Stratham, N. H., Nov. 7, 1866, Mary E. Whidden.

Child :

4826   i   FRED,⁹ b. Aug. 19, 1869.

3030 GEORGE H.⁸ EMERY (*Joseph,⁷ Ichabod,⁶ Job,⁵ Joseph,⁴ Job,³ James,² Anthony¹*), son of Joseph and Sophronia (Moore) Emery ; married Sept. 22, 1861, Abbie W. Clark (born in Gilford, N. H., March 24, 1835). Studied medicine in Chicago. Tutor and professor in Bell's Commercial College. In 1865 became a partner in the firm of

James R. Hill & Co , Concord, N. H , and manager of this well-known firm which through his influence and exertions has attained a world-wide reputation in its Concord harness. He is a "sagacious business man of tireless energy and great executive ability," a good and public spirited citizen.

Children, born in Concord, N. H. :

4827 i   LIZZIE CYRENA,[9] b Sept 3, 1863
4828 ii   LILLIAN ABBIE, b. Nov 4, 1865
4829 iii HATTIE SOPHIA, b May 11, 1870

3031 GEORGE W.[8] EMERY (*Oliver H* ,[7] *Ichabod,*[6] *Job,*[5] *Joseph,*[4] *Job,*[3] *James,*[2] *Anthony*[1]), son of Oliver H and Hannah O (Porter) Emery , married in Boston, Mass , April 11, 1866, Marcia Ives Hall, daughter of Samuel* and Huldah Barstow Hall   Graduate of Dartmouth College, 1858, and the Albany Law University , read law with Gen. Benj. F. Butler and practised in Boston till 1868   Supervisor of Internal Revenue for Kentucky, Tennessee, Alabama, Missouri and Louisiana , chairman of Republican State Committee of Tennessee for several years , Governor of the Territory of Utah, 1875–1880.

Child .

4830 i   FRANK HALL,[9] b May 6, 1867, in Boston

3032 ANN M [8] EMERY (*Oliver H.,*[7] *Ichabod,*[6] *Job,*[5] *Joseph.*[4] *Job,*[3] *James,*[2] *Anthony*[1]), daughter of Oliver H and Hannah O (Porter) Emery ; married in Boston, Mass , Feb. 22, 1858, John B. Perkins.

Child ·

4831 i   ELLEN PORTER.[9]

3035 MYRA C.[8] EMERY (*Oliver H* ,[7] *Ichabod,*[6] *Job,*[5] *Joseph,*[4] *Job,*[3] *James,*[2] *Anthony*[1]), daughter of Oliver H and Hannah (Porter) Emery , married in Medford, Mass , June 11, 1868, John F. Frye   Resides in Woodfords, Me.

Child

4832 i   ISAIAH J ,[9] b Aug 24, 1877, d in infancy.

3036 HATTIE OSGOOD[8] EMERY (*Oliver H* ,[7] *Ichabod,*[6] *Job,*[5] *Joseph,*[4] *Job.*[3] *James,*[2] *Anthony*[1]), daughter of Oliver H. and Hannah (Porter) Emery ; married in Medford, Mass , June 13, 1866, Darius A. Green. Resides in Washington, D. C

Children

4833 i   WINTHROP D ,[9] b. March 3 1873
4834 ii   G EMERY, b. Nov 12, 1878

3039 SARAH[8] EMERY (*John H* ,[7] *Joseph,*[6] *Job,*[5] *Joseph,*[4] *Job,*[3] *James,*[2] *Anthony*[1]), daughter of John H. and Betsey (Simpson) Emery , married Dec. 25, 1862, John Jackson of Salem, Mass. He died ug 18, 1873

*Samuel Hall was the fifth generation from Peregrine White the first white child born New England

Children :

    4835   i   SUMMER,[9] b. May 22, 1865.
    4836   ii   WALTER, b. Aug. 14, 1870.

3042 JOHN[8] EMERY (*John H.,[7] Joseph,[6] Job,[5] Joseph,[4] Job,[3]
James,[2] Anthony[1]*), son of John H. and Betsey (Simpson) Emery;
married Sept. 20, 1871, Sophia Baker of Yarmouth, Nova Scotia.
    Child :

    4837   i   EDNA JOSEPHINE,[9] b. June 2, 1875.

3043 LIZZIE A.[8] EMERY (*John H.,[7] Joseph,[6] Job,[5] Joseph,[4] Job,[3]
James,[2] Anthony[1]*), daughter of John H. and Betsey (Simpson) Em-
ery ; married March, 1875, John William Gregg of South Berwick,
Me.
    Children :

    4838   i   FLORENCE,[9] b. Jan. 17, 1877.
    4839   ii   BERT, b. Nov. 11, 1879.
    4840   iii FREDDIE EMERY, b. Feb. 4, 1885.

3044 WOODBURY[8] EMERY (*John H.,[7] Joseph,[6] Job,[5] Joseph,[4] Job,[3]
James,[2] Anthony[1]*), son of John H. and Betsey (Simpson) Emery ; married Nov. 27, 1880, Luetta Edgerly of Dover, N. H.
    Children :

    4841   i   WOODBURY ARTHUR,[9] b. Oct., 1881.
    4842   ii   PHILIP, b. Feb., 1883.

3047 LAURA[8] EMERY (*Job,[7] Joseph,[6] Job,[5] Joseph,[4] Job,[3] James,[2]
Anthony[1]*), daughter of Job and Abigail (Simpson) Emery; married
Dec. 2, 1862, P. Bradford Trask.
    Child :

    4843   i   MABEL,[8] b. Aug. 26, 1863 ; res. in Beverly, Mass.

3051 NANCY[8] EMERY (*Job,[7] Joseph,[6] Job,[5] Joseph,[4] Job,[3] James,[2]
Anthony[1]*), daughter of Job and Abigail (Simpson) Emery ; married
Dec. 9, 1869, James W. White.   Resides in Beverly, Mass.
    Children :

    4844   i   GEORGE A.,[9] b. Oct. 23, 1870; d. May 28, 1872.
    4845   ii   EMERY W., b. Sept. 27, 1874.
    4846   iii EUGENE R., b. March 9, 1883; d. June 20, 1884.

3052 FRANK[8] EMERY (*Job,[7] Joseph,[6] Job,[5] Joseph,[4] Job,[3] James,[2]
Anthony[1]*), son of Job and Abigail (Simpson) Emery ; married Nov.
27, 1873, Abbie Newcomb.   Resides in Florence, Kansas.
    Children :

    4847   i   FRANK W.,[9] b. May 12, 1874.
    4848   ii   EDNA L., b. Aug. 25, 1876.
    4849   iii ALBERT, b. Oct. 23, 1877.
    4850   iv   EDITH, b. Aug. 30, 1882; d. July 24, 1885.

3077 CLARISSA B.[8] JOHNSON (*Philomelia,[7] William,[6] William,[5]

Joseph,[4] *Job,*[3] *James,*[2] *Anthony*[1]), daughter of Dr. Nathaniel and Philomelia (Emery) Johuson, married Nov 26, 1857, Benjamin Ordway. Resides in Poland, Me.

Child :

4851 1 GERTRUDE,[9] b June, 1859.

3078 THEODORE B [8] JOHNSON (*Philomelia,*[7] *William,*[6] *William,*[5] *Joseph,*[4] *Job,*[3] *James,*[2] *Anthony*[1]), son of Dr. Nathaniel and Philomelia (Emery) Johnson, married in Sullivan, Me , April 7, 1866, Amelia Lakeman.

Children, born in Sullivan, Me. .

4852 1   MILTON W ,[9] b Jan 24, 1868, m Nellie Bunker, Dec 25, 1889.
4853 ii   DELIA E , b March 10 1870 , m Fred Billings, Dec 14, 1889.
4854 iii CHESTER L , b July 26 1872
4855 iv   ERNEST. b Nov 26, 1874
4856 v   SADIE M., b June 7, 1877
4857 vi   CHARLES M , b Feb 15, 1879.
4857a vii HERBERT E , b Feb 6, 1882
4858 viii IRVING B , b April 30, 1884
4859 ix   BEATRICE, b July, 1886

3079 JULIA A [8] JOHNSON (*Philomelia,*[7] *William,*[6] *William,*[5] *Joseph,*[4] *Job,*[3] *James,*[2] *Anthony*[1]), daughter of Dr Nathaniel and Philomelia (Emery) Johnson ; married May 20, 1858, William Dyer.

Children :

4860 i   ELLIS L ,[9] b April 11, 1859 , d March 17, 1864
4861 ii   PHILA, } b. June 17, { m Jan 1, 1884, Marcus T. Richards, one child.
4862 iii ANNE, }   1863,   { m John Allen of East Boston, one child

3082 PHILOMELIA E [8] JOHNSON (*Philomelia.*[7] *William,*[6] *William,*[5] *Joseph,*[4] *Job,*[3] *James,*[2] *Anthony*[1]), daughter of Dr Nathaniel and Philomelia (Emery) Johnson ; married June 3, 1862, Frank Warren.

Children .

4863 1   EDDIE,[9] b 1865
4864 ii NETTIE, b 1868

3084 HERBERT O [8] JOHNSON (*Philomelia.*[7] *William,*[6] *William,*[5] *Joseph.*[4] *Job.*[3] *James,*[2] *Anthony*[1]), son of Dr. Nathaniel and Philomelia (Emery) Johnson ; married Lelia Clark of Steuben, Me.

Children :

4865 1   LEMONT [9] } b 1883
4866 ii LENA,   }

3085 AMANDA[8] EMERY (*Benjamin,*[7] *William,*[6] *William,*[5] *Joseph,* *Job,*[3] *James,*[2] *Anthony*[1]), daughter of Benjamin and Elmira (Robbins) Emery, married Dec. 25, 1845, Emery Higgins (died Aug. 1, 1857). Resides in Eden, Me.

Child :

4867 1   GENEVA A.,[9] b. Dec. 25, 1849

3086 RUFUS R.[8] EMERY (*Benjamin,*[7] *William,*[6] *William,*[5] *Joseph,*[4]

Job,³ *James*,² *Anthony*¹). son of Benjamin and Elmira (Robbins) Emery; married Dec. 25, 1852, Eleanor McFarland.   Resides in Eden, Me.

Children :

    4868   i   CLARENCE,⁹ b. 1853; d. Sept. 28, 1864.
    4869   ii   ATTAVELA, b. April 26, 1854.
    4870   iii   CLIFFORD, b. April 12, 1855; d. Oct. 5, 1877.
    4871   iv   IRA, b. Nov. 16, 1856.
    4872   v   ADELE, b. Feb. 6, 1859.
    4873   vi   CORA L., b. Feb. 5, 1861; m. Nov. 29, 1881, Chas. A. Ingalls.
    4874   vii   HOYT, b. Nov. 8, 1863.
    4875   viii LAWRENCE, b. Sept. 5, 1865.
    4876   ix   CEYLON, b. March 18, 1867.
    4877   x   SEDELIA, b. Jan. 7, 1868.
    4878   xi   RALPH, b. Dec. 9, 1869.
    4879   xii   FANNIE, b. Nov. 11, 1870; d. Sept. 10, 1875.
    4880   xiii RAYMOND, b. Dec. 12, 1872.
    4881   xiv   EVERETT, b. April 5, 1874.
    4882   xv   ROBBY, b. July 6, 1875; d. July 10, 1875.
    4883   xvi   JOSIE, b. June 7, 1877.

3087 HANNAH ANN⁸ EMERY (*Benjamin*,⁷ *William*,⁶ *William*,⁵ *Joseph*,⁴ *Job*,³ *James*,² *Anthony*¹), daughter of Benjamin and Elmira (Robbins) Emery ; married Nov. 21, 1862, Charles Boss.   Resides in Bathurst, N. B.

Child :

    4884   i   REGINALD,⁹ b. Sept. 21, 1864.

3090 LYDIA H.⁸ EMERY (*Benjamin*,⁷ *William*,⁶ *William*,⁵ *Joseph*,⁴ *Job*,³ *James*,² *Anthony*¹), daughter of Benjamin and Elmira (Robbins) Emery ; married April 10, 1869, Frederick Wilcomb (died 1873).

Child :

    4885   i   FLORENCE E.,⁹ b. June 20, 1871.

3092 MINERVA⁸ EMERY (*Benjamin*,⁷ *William*,⁶ *William*,⁵ *Joseph*,⁴ *Job*,³ *James*,² *Anthony*¹), daughter of Benjamin and Elmira (Robbins) Emery ; married Aug. 9, 1878, Leonard J. Franks.   Resides in Ellsworth, Me.

Children, born in Ellsworth :

    4886   i   EMERY M.,⁹ b. Jan. 21, 1879.
    4887   ii   IRA C., b. Feb. 24, 1882.
    4888   iii   MELVIN, b. Jan. 19, 1885.

3097 AMORET J.⁸ THOMAS (*Jedidah S.*,⁷ *William*,⁶ *William*,⁵ *Joseph*,⁴ *Job*,³ *James*,² *Anthony*¹), daughter of John and Jedidah S. (Emery) Thomas ; married Oct. 10, 1855, Loren Fletcher of Mount Vernon, Me.   He has been a member of Minnesota Legislature and speaker of same three times.   Resides in Minneapolis, Minn.

Child :

    4889   i   ALICE J.,⁹ b. June 10, 1866; d. Jan. 20, 1874.

3103 OLIVE R.⁸ HILL (*Lucetta A.*,⁷ *William*,⁶ *William*,⁵ *Joseph*,⁴

Job,[3] *James,*[2] *Anthony*[1]), daughter of George and Lucetta A. (Emery) Hill ; married June 10, 1877, Richard H. Archibald.
Child :

    4890   i   EDITH [9]

3111 MARTHA A [8] EMERY (*Alfred,*[7] *Joel,*[6] *William,*[5] *Joseph,*[4] *Job,*[3] *James,*[2] *Anthony*[1]), daughter of Alfred and Eliza (Hopkins) Emery ; married July 1, 1860, Lorenzo Mayo, who died April, 1877.
Children ·

    4891   i   HAMLIN,[9] b July 25, 1861
    4892   ii   ADDIE L , b Dec 25, 1862
    4893   iii HOWARD. b March 8, 1864.
    4894   iv WALTER, b Oct 9, 1866, d April, 1877.
    4895   v   LORENZO, b 1868

3112 ISAAC H [8] EMERY (*Alfred,*[7] *Joel,*[6] *William,*[5] *Joseph,*[4] *Job,*[3] *James,*[2] *Anthony*[1]) son of Alfred and Eliza (Hopkins) Emery ; married July 16, 1862, Clara H. Richardson.
Children :

    4896   i   ELVIA M ,[9] b July 28, 1867
    4897   ii   ALFRED G , b May 18, 1868
    4898   iii CLARENCE D , b March 17, 1870
    4899   iv MELORIN H , b April 19, 1874
    4900   v   ABDON C , b Dec 5, 1876
    4901   vi   MAYNARD P , b Sept 4, 1881

3117 ELIZA A [8] EMERY (*Alfred,*[7] *Joel,*[6] *William,*[5] *Joseph,*[4] *Job,*[3] *James,*[2] *Anthony*[1]), daughter of Alfred and Eliza (Hopkins) Emery ; married in N. Y., James Sherrick. Resides in Jersey City, N. J.
Child :

    4902   i   JOHN H ,[9] b Aug., 1875

3118 DELIA H [8] EMERY (*Alfred,*[7] *Joel,*[6] *William,*[5] *Joseph,*[4] *Job,*[3] *James,*[2] *Anthony*[1]), daughter of Alfred and his second wife, Jane (Richardson) Emery ; married Dec. 7, 1872, Almon Harden. Resides in Bar Harbor, Me.
Children .

    4903   i   MABEL G ,[9] b April 27, 1874
    4904   ii   EVA B , b Oct 9, 1875
    4905   iii FRED, b July 15, 1881.
    4906   iv ALION, } b Dec 20, 1883; { d. Sept 7, 1884.
    4907   v   ALICE, }

3119 ADEL T.[8] EMERY (*Alfred,*[7] *Joel,*[6] *William,*[5] *Joseph,*[4] *Job,*[3] *James,*[2] *Anthony*[1]), daughter of Alfred and his second wife, Jane (Richardson) Emery , married Sept. 12, 1874, Benjamin L Hadley.
Children :

    4908   i   LORA E ,[9] b July 18, 1875
    4909   ii   FLORENCE, b May 15, 1879

3124 SOPHIA A.[8] EMERY (*Jared,*[7] *Joel,*[6] *William,*[5] *Joseph,*[4] *Job,*[3] *James,*[2] *Anthony*[1]), daughter of Jared and Sophia (Hopkins) Emery ; married Dec. 6, 1857, Richard Paine ; died Oct. 20, 1864.

Children, born in Eden, Me. :

   4910 i   EDGAR M.,[9] b. Sept. 18, 1859.
   4911 ii WILLIS C., b. Sept. 16, 1861.
   4912 iii MAYNARD W., b. March 15, 1863.

3126 MARGARET J.[8] EMERY (*Jared*,[7] *Joel*,[6] *William*,[5] *Joseph*,[4] *Job*,[3] *James*,[2] *Anthony*[1]), daughter of Jared and Sophia (Hopkins) Emery ; married June 4, 1864, Maynard J. Whittaker. Resides in Ellsworth, Me.

Children, born in Ellsworth, Me. :

   4913 i   FRED P.,[9] b. Sept. 24, 1865.
   4914 ii LEWIS E., b. July 20, 1867.
   4915 iii ADDIE H., b. Dec. 17, 1868; d. Aug. 5, 1872.
   4916 iv ERWIN M., b. May 22, 1873.

3129 MARY H.[8] EMERY (*Jared*,[7] *Joel*,[6] *William*,[5] *Joseph*,[4] *Job*,[3] *James*,[2] *Anthony*[1]), daughter of Jared and Sophia (Hopkins) Emery ; married May 30, 1875, Abdon J. Coolidge of Lamoine, Me.

Children :

   4917 i ORVILLE,[9] } b. Sept. 20, 1881; { d.
   4918 ii OLIVE,

3130 HIRAM J.[8] EMERY (*Jared*,[7] *Joel*,[6] *William*,[5] *Joseph*,[4] *Job*,[3] *James*,[2] *Anthony*[1]), son of Jared and Sophia (Hopkins) Emery ; married March 11, 1874, Rose B. Higgins. Resides in Eden, Me.

Children :

   4919 i   CHARLES M.,[9] b. Aug. 26, 1875; d. July 29, 1876.
   4920 ii ADDIE M., b. July 28, 1877.
   4921 iii AGNES M., b. Aug. 21, 1879.
   4922 iv CARRIE G., b. Oct. 26, 1883.

3133 HOWARD C.[8] EMERY (*Jared*,[7] *Joel*,[6] *William*,[5] *Joseph*,[4] *Job*,[3] *James*,[2] *Anthony*[1]), son of Jared and Sophia (Hopkins) Emery ; married Dec., 1878, P. Alley.

Children :

   4923 i ARTHUR G.,[9] b. Dec. 26, 1882.

3135 ERNEST M.[8] EMERY (*Samuel N.*,[7] *Joel*,[6] *William*,[5] *Joseph*,[4] *Job*,[3] *James*,[2] *Anthony*[1]), son of Samuel N. and his second wife, Eliza H. (Ladd) Emery ; married Dec. 30, 1875, Sarah M. Clements of Mount Desert, Me.

Child :

   4924 i JAMES M.,[9] b. June 11, 1884.

3143 ETTA M.[8] GOODRIDGE (*Hannah T.*,[7] *Joel*,[6] *William*,[5] *Joseph*,[4] *Job*,[3] *James*,[2] *Anthony*[1]), daughter of Uriah and Hannah T. (Emery) Goodridge ; married Oct. 12, 1872, Capt. Peleg Young.

Children :

   4925 i   MINNIE W.,[9] b. Oct. 10, 1873.
   4926 ii ELLIS W., b. Jan. 5, 1877.
   4927 iii FOSSIL, b. May 28, 1879.
   4928 iv GEORGIA, b. Nov. 1, 1882.

3147 HERBERT P.[8] EMERY (*Joel*,[7] *Joel*,[6] *William*,[5] *Joseph*,[4] *Job*,[3] *James*,[2] *Anthony*[1]), son of Joel and Abbie M (Liscomb) Emery; married July 24, 1873, Nancy M Peach. Resides in Eden, Me
Children :

4929 i   BERTHA M ,[9] b. Aug 24, 1874.
4930 ii   JOEL A.. b. April 8, 1877.
4931 iii FRED O , b March 14, 1879.
4932 iv   WILLIE H , b Oct 19, 1881
4933 v   GEORGIA, b April 17, 1883
There are two other children

3165 FRANKLIN L.[8] EMERY (*Alvan*,[7] *Andrew*,[6] *William*,[5] *Joseph*,[4] *Job*,[3] *James*,[2] *Anthony*[1]), son of Alvan and Susan B (Hanson) Emery ; married May 7, 1864, Martha A Luce.
Children .

4934 i   HIRAM,[9] b Feb 3, 1865
4935 ii   FRANK G , b Oct 7. 1880
4936 iii SUSAN A , b May 30, 1884

3166 MARSHALL[8] EMERY (*Alvan*,[7] *Andrew*,[6] *William*,[5] *Joseph*,[4] *Job*,[3] *James*,[2] *Anthony*[1]), son of Alvan and Susan B (Hanson) Emery ; married June 15, 1870, Mary P. Elliot (died Sept., 1884). Resides in Lewiston, Me.
Children :

4937 i   ARTHUR H ,[9] b July 13, 1871, d Aug 11, 1871.
4938 ii   BERTHA M , b. June 3, 1875, d July 17, 1875
4939 iii WILLIAM H., b Jan. 7, 1877, d July 25, 1886.
4940 iv   JOHN M

3168 WILLIAM H.[8] EMERY (*Alvan*,[7] *Andrew*,[6] *William*,[5] *Joseph*,[4] *Job*,[3] *James*,[2] *Anthony*[1]), son of Alvan and Susan B (Hanson) Emery ; married Nov. 22, 1874, Mabel B. Tracy. Resides in Brooklyn, N Y.
Children :

4941 i   HARRY L ,[9] b Oct 20, 1875
4942 ii   GERTRUDE.
4943 iii FRED

3170 CHARLES G.[8] EMERY (*Hiram A* ,[7] *Andrew*,[6] *William*,[5] *Joseph*,[4] *Job*,[3] *James*,[2] *Anthony*[1]), son of Hiram A. and Mary A. (Goodwin) Emery ; married Dec. 21, 1863, Francena E. Libby (born Aug. 24, 1844)
Children :

4944 i   FRANK W ,[9] b. May 3, 1865.
4945 ii   CHARLES L., b. Sept 26, 1866, d May 1, 1869
4946 iii MABEL, b March 6, 1870.
4947 iv   GERTRUDE, b Oct 20, 1874; d. Feb. 13, 1875
4948 v   FRANCENA, b Oct 20, 1880

3173 WILLIAM G.[8] EMERY (*Hiram A.*,[7] *Andrew*,[6] *William*,[5] *Joseph*,[4] *Job*,[3] *James*,[2] *Anthony*[1]), son of Hiram A. and Mary A. (Goodwin) Emery, married Oct. 29, 1878, Sarah P. Peacock. Resides in Brooklyn, N. Y.
Children :

4949 i WILLIAM F.,⁹ b. Aug. 2, 1879.
4950 ii MAUD LITTLE, b. Oct. 20, 1880.

3175 HIRAM E.⁸ WHITTAKER (*Philomelia W.,*⁷ *Hiram,*⁶ *William,*⁵ *Joseph,*⁴ *Job,*³ *James,*² *Anthony*¹), son of Gowen and Philomelia W. (Emery) Whittaker; married Ophelia Fernald.
Children:

4951 i ERNEST.⁹
4952 ii JOHN E.
4953 iii CYRUS E.
4954 iv GOWEN.

3179 GEORGE C.⁸ EMERY (*Cyrus,*⁷ *Hiram,*⁶ *William,*⁵ *Joseph,*⁴ *Job,*³ *James,*² *Anthony*¹), son of Cyrus and Hannah L. (Chilcott) Emery; married Dec. 14, 1887, Lillie A. Stimson, daughter of John H. and Catherine A. Stimson, of Sullivan, Me. Resides in Kansas City, Mo.
Child, born in Kansas City, Mo.:

4955 i RICHARD STIMSON,⁹ b. April 13, 1890.

3228 LOUISA M.⁸ EMERY (*William M.,*⁷ *Haven,*⁶ *Jonathan,*⁵ *Jonathan,*⁴ *Job,*³ *James,*² *Anthony*¹), daughter of William M. and Eliza (Stackpole) Emery; married Ezra H. Burnham (died 1868).
Children:

4956 i JENNIE,⁹ b. 1848; d. 1865.
4957 ii JOSEPH W., b. 1860.

3229 MARY ABIGAIL⁸ EMERY (*Amaziah,*⁷ *Thomas,*⁶ *Jonathan,*⁵ *Jonathan,*⁴ *Job,*³ *James,*² *Anthony*¹), daughter of Amaziah and Abigail (Tappan) Emery; married, first, Oct., 1855, William S. Jordan; second, Mark Googins.
Children:

4958 i CARRIE,⁹ b. Feb., 1857; d. 1858.
4959 ii EMMA E., b. Dec., 1859.
4960 iii FANNIE M., b. Aug., 1862; d. Dec., 1865.
4661 iv WILLIE E., b. Aug., 1867.

3231 GIDEON TUCKER⁸ EMERY (*Amaziah,*⁷ *Thomas,*⁶ *Jonathan,*⁵ *Jonathan,*⁴ *Job,*³ *James,*² *Anthony*¹), son of Amaziah and Abigail (Tappan) Emery; married A. Maria Small.
Child:

4962 i HATTIE,⁸ b. April, 1857; m. Luther F. Harrington.

3232 AMAZIAH⁸ EMERY (*Amaziah,*⁷ *Thomas,*⁶ *Jonathan,*⁵ *Jonathan,*⁴ *Job,*³ *James,*²*Anthony*¹), son of Amaziah and Abigail (Tappan) Emery; married Feb. 21, 1863, Fannie E. Parnell of Buxton, Me.
Children:

4963 i MARY TAPPAN,⁹ b. July 30, 1867; d. 1870.
4964 ii SAMUEL H. T., b. July 15, 1869.
4965 iii FRANK D., b. Jan. 6, 1872.
4966 iv HARRY B., b. Feb. 13, 1874.

3235 EMMA JANE⁸ EMERY (*Amaziah,*⁷ *Thomas,*⁶ *Jonathan,*⁵ *Jonathan,*⁴ *Job,*³ *James,*² *Anthony*¹), daughter of Amaziah and Abigail (Tappan) Emery; married, 1866, Edwin B. Hooper.

Child :

    4967 1   FRED A ,[9] b 1867

3236 FREEMAN SNOW[8] EMERY (*Amaziah,[7] Thomas,[6] Jonathan,[5] Jonathan,[4] Job,[3] James,[2] Anthony[1]*), son of Amaziah and Abigail (Tappan) Emery ; married, 1872, Lottie Anderson.
    Children .

    4968 1   EVERETT CHASE,[9] b Sept 6, 1874
    4969 11   LESTER F , b Sept 21, 1876
    4970 111 FREEMAN D , b Aug 16, 1880

3237 ALBERT HENRY[8] EMERY (*Amaziah,[7] Thomas,[6] Jonathan,[5] Jonathan,[4] Job,[3] James,[2] Anthony[1]*), son of Amaziah and Abigail (Tappan) Emery , married, 1874, Hattie R. Jordan.
    Children :

    4971 1   FLORENCE J ,[9] b. July 21, 1876
    4972 11   GRACE J , b July 9, 1880.

3272 JOHN F [8] EMERY (*John H.,[7] John,[6] Isaac,[5] Jabez,[4] Job,[3] James,[2] Anthony[1]*), son of John H. and Hannah (Knight) Emery , married Nov. 8, 1877, Jane Roake
    Children :

    4973 1   WALTER H ,[9] b June 22, 1878
    4974 11   EDWARD L , b March 23, 1880

3287 ISAAC M [8] EMERY, JR.(*Isaac M ,[7] Benjamin,[6] Isaac,[5] Jabez,[4] Job,[3] James,[2] Anthony[1]*), son of Isaac M and Sarah E. (Pike) Emery ; married Sept. 7, 1882, Hattie Palmer, of Portland, Me
    Child .

    4975 1   SARAH P ,[9] b May 23, 1884.

3288 MARY ELLEN[8] EMERY (*Isaac M.,[7] Benjamin,[6] Isaac,[5] Jabez,[4] Job,[3] James,[2] Anthony[1]*), daughter of Isaac M. and Sarah E (Pike) Emery , married Jan. 8, 1882, Edward C. Miller, of Kennebunkport, Me.
    Child :

    4976 1   BENJAMIN F ,[9] b. Dec. 22, 1882.

3303 ELLA G.[8] EMERY (*Charles Isaac,[7] Isaac,[6] Isaac,[5] Jabez,[4] Job,[3] James,[2] Anthony[1]*), daughter of Charles Isaac and Sarah (Perkins) Emery ; married Winfield S. Carmick.
    Child :

    4977 1   WINFIELD EMERY,[9] b April 17, 1881.

3305 EMERY[9] CLEAVES (*Mary G.,[8] Samuel,[7] Obadiah,[6] Obed,[5] James,[4] James,[3] James,[2] Anthony[1]*), son of David B. and Mary Gilpatrick (Emery) Cleaves ; married Oct. 9, 1872, at Clifton, N. J , Elizabeth Groocock (born in Leicester, Eng , May 26, 1844) He was in the Union Army in Co E., 47th Mass. Vols., 1862–63. Bookseller. Resides in Lynn, Mass.

Children:

4978   i   FREDERICK EMERY,[10] b. April 8, 1874.
4979   ii   ARTHUR WORDSWORTH, b. March 20, 1876.
4980   iii   ALFRED EDWARD, b. Nov. 24, 1877.
4981   iv   ROBERT, b. Nov. 24, 1879.

3306 MARY S.[9] CLEAVES (*Mary G.*,[8] *Samuel*,[7] *Obadiah*,[6] *Obed*,[5] *James*,[4] *James*,[3] *James*,[2] *Anthony*[1]), daughter of David B. and Mary Gilpatrick (Emery) Cleaves; married March 15, 1865, Nathaniel D. Wiggin (born Jan. 20, 1839, died March 20, 1882).
   Child:

4982   i   RALPH,[10] b. Jan. 4, 1877.

3346 LOTTIE A.[9] EMERY (*John E.*,[8] *Samuel*,[7] *James*,[6] *James*,[5] *Thomas*,[4] *James*,[3] *James*,[2] *Anthony*[1]), daughter of John E. and Hannah M. (Hobbs) Emery; married Jan. 7, 1875, William E. Decrow.
   Child:

4983   i   JOHN W.,[10] b. Feb. 20, 1876, in Bangor, Me.

3352 MARY EFFIE[9] EMERY (*James W.*,[8] *Samuel*,[7] *James*,[6] *James*,[5] *Thomas*,[4] *James*,[3] *James*,[2] *Anthony*[1]), daughter of James Wallace and Elizabeth Jane (Brown) Emery; married Dec. 23, 1879, in Kaufman Co., Tex., Frank P. Previtt. Resides in Fort Worth, Tex.
   Child:

4984   i   OLLIE PEARL,[10] b. Dec. 18, 1880, in Forth Worth.

3445 WILLIAM G.[9] EMERY (*Josiah D.*,[8] *Benjamin*,[7] *Nathaniel*,[6] *Thomas*,[5] *Thomas*,[4] *James*,[3] *James*,[2] *Anthony*[1]), son of Josiah D. and Susannah A. (Tuttle) Emery; married July 2, 1876, Martha E. G—— of Riverside, Mich.
   Child:

4985   i   ELLEN A.,[10] b. Nov. 15, 1880; d. Sept. 17, 1881.

3447 SARAH I.[9] EMERY (*Josiah D.*,[8] *Benjamin*,[7] *Nathaniel*,[6] *Thomas*,[5] *Thomas*,[4] *James*,[3] *James*,[2] *Anthony*[1]), daughter of Josiah D. and Susannah A. (Tuttle) Emery; married Nov. 28, 1875, A. W. Bishop. Resides in Hagar, Mich.
   Children:

4986   i   RALPH E.,[10] b. June 12, 1877.
4987   ii   JOSIAH D., b. April 14, 1880.

3448 WENDALL P.[9] EMERY (*Josiah D.*,[8] *Benjamin*,[7] *Nathaniel*,[6] *Thomas*,[5] *Thomas*,[4] *James*,[3] *James*,[2] *Anthony*[1]), son of Josiah D. and Susannah A. (Tuttle) Emery; married Dec. 5, 1880, Sarah E. Fuller. Resides in Hagar, Mich.
   Child:

4988   i   ROLAND G.,[10] b. Jan. 9, 1882, in Hagar, Mich.

3449 ELECTRA[9] EMERY (*Josiah D.*,[8] *Benjamin*,[7] *Nathaniel*,[6] *Thomas*,[5] *Thomas*,[4] *James*,[3] *James*,[2] *Anthony*[1]), daughter of Josiah D. and Susannah A. (Tuttle) Emery; married Nov. 19, 1879, Albert J. Jackson. Resides in Hagar, Mich.

Child :

4989 *1   Erving N.,[10] b. 1860.

3554 Homer Powell[9] Emery (*Samuel L.,[8] Samuel,[7] Zachariah,[6] Zachariah,[5] Zachariah,[4] Zachariah,[3] James,[2] Anthony[1]*), son of Samuel Leeman and Caroline L. (Powell) Emery ; married Nov. 27, 1879, Fanny Detwiles.

Child :

4990 1   Charles Bascom,[10] b. Nov. 2, 1880.

3567 Lucretia Caroline[9] Emery (*Homer C.,[8] Samuel,[7] Zachariah,[6] Zachariah,[5] Zachariah,[4] Zachariah,[3] James,[2] Anthony[1]*), daughter of Homer Charles and Mary Ann (Waters) Emery ; married Sept. 25, 1870, William Code (born June 12, 1839 ; died Nov., 1873, in Vienna, Kansas).

Child :

4991 1   Lillian Isabel,[10] b. Dec. 30, 1871, in Kansas City ; d. in Baker City, Oregon, April 2, 1886.

3568 Mary Angelina[9] Emery (*Homer C.,[8] Samuel,[7] Zachariah,[6] Zachariah,[5] Zachariah,[4] Zachariah,[3] James,[2] Anthony[1]*), daughter of Homer Charles and Mary Ann (Waters) Emery ; married Jan. 15, 1876, in Union, Oregon, Henry C. Edwards.

Children :

4992 i   Joseph F.,[10] b. Nov. 22, 1876 ; d. Feb. 21, 1883.
4993 ii Lucy Ellen, b. Aug. 16, 1878.
4994 iii Charlotte May, b. May 1, 1880.
4995 iv Katie Myrtle, b. March 16, 1882.
4996 v   Esther Aneta, b. April 12, 1885.
4997 vi Henry Clayton, b. Feb. 10, 1886.

3569 Clementina W.[9] Emery (*Homer C.,[8] Samuel,[7] Zachariah,[6] Zachariah,[5] Zachariah,[4] Zachariah,[3] James,[2] Anthony[1]*), daughter of Homer Charles and Mary Ann (Waters) Emery ; married March 31, 1880, in La Grande, Oregon, Edward Remillard (born July 6, 1843, in Ca.).

Children, born in Union Co., Oregon.

4998 i   Edna E.,[10] b. Oct. 10, 1880.
4999 ii Zoah Annetta, b. April 12, 1885.

3570 Francis M.[9] Emery (*Homer C.,[8] Samuel,[7] Zachariah,[6] Zachariah,[5] Zachariah,[4] Zachariah,[3] James,[2] Anthony[1]*), son of Homer Charles and Mary Ann (Waters) Emery ; married Oct. 1, 1882, near Pocahontas, Baker Co., Oregon, Martha Platte McQuowen (pronounced McKeen). She was born near the North Platte River when her parents were moving from Iowa to Oregon.

Children :

5000 i   Mary Annetta,[10] b. Feb. 16, 1884, near Baker City.
5001 ii Elsie Elva, b. Nov. 18, 1885, near Pocahontas.

3572 Francelia[9] Emery (*Abel G.,[8] Samuel,[7] Zachariah,[6] Zachariah,[5] Zachariah,[4] Zachariah,[3] James,[2] Anthony[1]*), daughter of Abel Gardner and Elsie M. (Bates) Emery ; married Charles Barry.

Child:

5002 i   DELLAH MAUD,[10] b. Aug. 9, 1881.

3573 IDELLA[9] EMERY (*Abel G.*,[8] *Samuel*,[7] *Zachariah*,[6] *Zachariah*,[5] *Zachariah*,[4] *Zachariah*,[3] *James*,[2] *Anthony*[1]), daughter of Abel Gardner and Elsie M. (Bates) Emery; married Jeremiah M. Hathaway.
Child:

5003 i   MELISSA ESTELLA,[10] b. Aug. 23, 1881.

3589 LEVI[9] EMERY (*David E.*,[8] *Amos*,[7] *Amos*,[6] *Zachariah*,[5] *Zachariah*,[4] *Zachariah*,[3] *James*,[2] *Anthony*[1]), son of David Elliot and Sophia (Burnap) Emery; married Jan. 1, 1864, at Whitewater Falls, Minn., Ursula M. Metcalf. Resides in Highland, Minn.
Children, born in Highland, Minn.:

5004 i   EDWIN LEVI,[10] b. Sept. 4, 1864.
5005 ii   SUMNER, b. Nov. 6, 1866.
5006 iii EVERETT, b. Nov. 14, 1868.
5007 iv   IRVING, b. Jan. 26, 1870.
5008 v   A SON, b. Nov. 26, 1872; d. Dec. 1, 1872.
5009 vi   CLEON,   } b. Dec. 9, 1873; { d. Aug. 19, 1874.
5010 vii CLAYTON,
5011 viii MARY SOPHIA, b. Aug. 24, 1875.
5012 ix   URSULA, b. May 6, 1878.
5013 x   JULIA, b. Jan. 29, 1883.

3611 ALBIN HENRY[9] EMERY (*Henry E.*,[8] *Amos*,[7] *Amos*,[6] *Zachariah*,[5] *Zachariah*,[4] *Zachariah*,[3] *James*,[2] *Anthony*[1]), son of Henry E. and Urania (Putnam) Emery; married June 4, 1874, at St. James, Mo., Annie M. Stimson.
Children:

5014 i   WILLIAM EVERETT,[10] b. May 2, 1875.
5015 ii WALTER GREGORY, b. Oct. 7, 1876; d. Dec. 30, 1877.

3654 HENRY S.[9] LAWRENCE (*Mary R.*,[8] *Zachariah*,[7] *William*,[6] *Zachariah*,[5] *Zachariah*,[4] *Zachariah*,[3] *James*,[2] *Anthony*[1]), son of Sylvester B. and Mary R. (Emery) Lawrence; married Dec. 31, 1862, Ellen L. Ackley. She resides in Hudson, Mich. He died May 6, 1863, from wounds received at Fredericksburg, Va., May 4, 1863.
Children:

5016 i   HENRY SYLVESTER,[10] b. Nov. 14, 1863.

3657 CHARLES Z.[9] LAWRENCE (*Mary R.*,[8] *Zachariah*,[7] *William*,[6] *Zachariah*,[5] *Zachariah*,[4] *Zachariah*,[3] *James*,[2] *Anthony*[1]), son of Sylvester B. and Mary R. (Emery) Lawrence; married Oct. 1, 1873, Kate Earskine. Resides in Elliston, Ohio.
Children:

5017 i   FREDERICK S.,[10] b. Oct. 31, 1878.
5018 ii HERBERT A., b. Dec. 25, 1881.

3658 LOREN A.[9] LAWRENCE (*Mary R.*,[8] *Zachariah*,[7] *William*,[6] *Zachariah*,[5] *Zachariah*,[4] *Zachariah*,[3] *James*,[2] *Anthony*[1]), son of Sylvester B. and Mary R. (Emery) Lawrence; married Oct. 30, 1878, Lilla J. Hotchkiss. Resides in Hudson, Mich.
Child:

5019 i   HELENA A.,[10] b. Sept. 15, 1881.

3659 CLARA E.[9] LAWRENCE (*Mary R ,*[8] *Zachariah,*[7] *William,*[6] *Zachariah,*[5] *Zachariah,*[4] *Zachariah,*[3] *James,*[2] *Anthony*[1]), daughter of Sylvester B. and Mary R (Emery) Lawrence, married Jan. 14, 1880, George W Burdick.   Resides in Hudson, Mich.
Children:

5020 i   LOREN A ,[10] b Nov 24. 1880
5021 ii MAUD E , b June 13, 1882.

3661 EFFIE BENJAMIN[9] LAWRENCE (*Mary R ,*[8] *Zachariah,*[7] *William,*[6] *Zachariah,*[5] *Zachariah,*[4] *Zachariah,*[3] *James,*[2] *Anthony*[1]), daughter of Sylvester B and Mary R (Emery) Lawrence, married Oct. 10, 1877, George D Moore. Resides in Hudson, Mich.
Children:

5022 i   MABEL L ,[10] b Sept 23, 1878
5023 ii WILLIAM A , b Nov 25, 1880

3662 MARY R.[9] LAWRENCE (*Mary R ,*[8] *Zachariah,*[7] *William,*[6] *Zachariah,*[5] *Zachariah,*[4] *Zachariah,*[3] *James.*[2] *Anthony*[1]), daughter of Sylvester B and Mary R. (Emery) Lawrence, married Sept. 19, 1876, John Dillon. Resides in Hudson, Mich

Child:

5024 i   PERRY S ,[10] b April 15, 1881.

3663 CLARA E [9] LAWRENCE (*Sarah E ,*[8] *Zachariah,*[7] *William,*[6] *Zachariah,*[5] *Zachariah,*[4] *Zachariah,*[3] *James.*[2] *Anthony*[1]), daughter of John J. and Sarah E. (Emery) Lawrence ; married Lucius A Cutter, of Jaffrey, N. H. (born Dec. 30, 1835).
Child :

5025 i   LUCIUS B.,[10] b 1872

3667 GEORGE H W [9] EMERY (*Henry W.,*[8] *Ralph,*[7] *William,*[6] *Zachariah,*[5] *Zachariah,*[4] *Zachariah,*[3] *James,*[2] *Anthony*[1]), son of Henry W. and Mary L. (Miner) Emery, married Aug. 25, 1879, Augusta Ellen Spencer (born May 4, 1859).
Child .

5026 i   BLANCH E.,[10] b May 2, 1880

3741 JEREMIAH A.[9] EMERY (*Deacon Andrews,*[8] *Daniel,*[7] *Daniel,*[6] *Daniel,*[5] *Zachariah,*[4] *Zachariah,*[3] *James,*[2] *Anthony*[1]), son of Deacon Andrews and Lucy (Powers) Emery, married March 6, 1856 Melinda A. Benson.
Child :

5027 i   THURSTINE A ,[10] b. April 24, 1861, in Windhall, Vt

3742 GEORGE S [9] EMERY (*Deacon Andrews,*[8] *Daniel,*[7] *Daniel,*[6] *Daniel,*[5] *Zachariah,*[4] *Zachariah,*[3] *James,*[2] *Anthony*[1]), son of Deacon Andrews and his second wife, Mary (Smith) Emery, married Nov. 9, 1864, Sarah Nutting. Resides in E. Jaffrey, N. H.
Children:

5028 i GEORGE S.[10]
5029 ii GERTRUDE, b. June 8, 1867.
5030 iii CHARLES H., b. Oct. 17, 1871.

3743 LUCY M.[9] EMERY (*Deacon Andrews,*[8] *Daniel,*[7] *Daniel,*[6] *Daniel,*[5] *Zachariah,*[4] *Zachariah,*[3] *James,*[2] *Anthony*[1]), daughter of Deacon Andrews and his second wife, Mary (Smith) Emery; married Jan. 19, 1869, Oliver W. Mead, of Acton, Mass. He is in business in Boston.
Children:
5031 i HOBART E.,[10] b. July 4, 1870
5032 ii LOUIS GUY, b. Oct. 3, 1873.

3746 GEORGE DANIEL[9] EMERY (*Daniel F.,*[8] *Daniel,*[7] *Daniel,*[6] *Daniel,*[5] *Zachariah,*[4] *Zachariah,*[3] *James,*[2] *Anthony*[1]), son of Daniel F. and Catherine B. (Brown) Emery; married Sarah Emeline Gowing of Batavia, N. Y. (born May 20, 1838; died in Cambridge, Aug., 1890). Importer and manufacturer of mahogany lumber. Resides in Cambridge, Mass.
Children:
5033 i HERBERT CLARK,[10] b. July 30, 1860, in Kendallville, Ind.
5034 ii MARY GOWING, b. Aug. 22, 1865, in Kendallville, Ind.
5035 iii DANIEL GEORGE, b. Nov. 22, 1872, in Indianapolis, Ind.
5036 iv SARAH LOTTA, b. Jan. 18, 1878, in Indianapolis, Ind.

3747 ALBERT BUGBEE[9] EMERY (*Daniel F.,*[8] *Daniel,*[7] *Daniel,*[6] *Daniel,*[5] *Zachariah,*[4] *Zachariah,*[3] *James,*[2] *Anthony*[1]), son of Daniel F. and Catherine B. (Brown) Emery; married March 23, 1865, Sarah M. Edwards of Albion, Ind. Resides in Sebewa, Mich.
Child:
5037 i MINNIE,[10] b. June 28, 1866, at Sebewa, Mich.; m.

3748 JOHN BROWN[9] EMERY (*Daniel F.,*[8] *Daniel,*[7] *Daniel,*[6] *Daniel,*[5] *Zachariah,*[4] *Zachariah,*[3] *James,*[2] *Anthony*[1]), son of Daniel F. and Catherine B. (Brown) Emery; married Nov. 10, 1874, Kate L. Baker. Resides in Reed City, Mich.
Children:
5038 i KATE F.,[10] b. May 20, 1876.
5039 ii HERBERT T., b. Nov. 21, 1879.

3753 MARY ADELINE[9] ROBBINS (*Elizabeth,*[6] *Daniel,*[7] *Daniel,*[6] *Daniel,*[5] *Zachariah,*[4] *Zachariah,*[3] *James,*[2] *Anthony*[1]), daughter of Daniel L. and Elizabeth (Emery) Robbins; married Nov. 13, 1860, Walter Hogen of So. Gardner, Mass. Resides in New York City.
Children:
5040 i FRANK G.,[10] } b. Aug. 5, 1875; { d. Aug. 1, 1876.
5041 ii FRED. R., } { d. Aug. 23, 1875.

3757 ADELIA C.[9] BULLARD (*Sophronia,*[8] *Daniel,*[7] *Daniel,*[6] *Daniel,*[5] *Zachariah,*[4] *Zachariah,*[3] *James,*[2] *Anthony*[1]), daughter of George and Sophronia (Emery) Bullard; married May 30, 1864, Warren P. Allen. Resides in Gardner, Mass.
Child:
5042 i NELLIE,[10] b. Jan. 14, 1870.

3758 GEORGE WILLIS[9] BULLARD (*Sophronia,*[8] *Daniel,*[7] *Daniel,*[6] *Daniel,*[5] *Zachariah,*[4] *Zachariah,*[3] *James,*[2] *Anthony*[1]), son of George and Sophronia (Emery) Bullard; married, first, July 1, 1874, Jane McQueen of Oswego, N. Y. (died Nov 6, 1878) ; second, in Potts-dam, N. Y, Sept. 16, 1880, Mrs. Mary E. Tripp. He lived with his uncle, Stephen F. Emery, of Mexico, N Y. His name was changed in 1874 to Geo. W. Emery.
Child:

5043 i WILLIAM EDWARD,[10] b Nov. 12, 1875, at Oswego, N. Y.

3783 GEORGE[9] EMERY (*Lyman,*[8] *Joseph,*[7] *Daniel,*[6] *Daniel,*[5] *Zachariah,*[4] *Zachariah,*[3] *James,*[2] *Anthony*[1]), son of Lyman and Sarah (Stratton) Emery; married Nov. 11, 1877, Addie Page.
Children :

5044 i LYMAN JOSEPH,[10] b Sept 15, 1878
5045 ii ANNA MARIA, b Feb 13, 1880

3784 LUCILLA[9] BALKAM (*Melinda,*[8] *Joseph,*[7] *Daniel,*[6] *Daniel,*[5] *Zachariah,*[4] *Zachariah,*[3] *James,*[2] *Anthony*[1]), daughter of Eli and Melinda (Emery) Balkam, married Dennis Sullivan.
Child ·

5046 i FRANK C ,[10] b. Nov. 6, 1873.

3785 MARY LEE[9] GOWING (*Cordelia,*[8] *Joseph,*[7] *Daniel,*[6] *Daniel,*[5] *Zachariah,*[4] *Zachariah,*[3] *James,*[2] *Anthony*[1]), daughter of William O. and Cordelia (Emery) Gowing; married Peter Rines or Kines.
Children .

5047 i MARY,[10] b 1869
5048 ii LUCILLA, b Sept 6, 1873
5049 iii EMMER, b Aug 11, 1876
5050 iv ADELIA, b May 24, 1878.
5051 v A SON, b. Feb. 5, 1882

3839 SELINDA[9] WHEAT (*Elizabeth,*[8] *James,*[7] *Noah,*[6] *Daniel,*[5] *Zachariah,*[4] *Zachariah*[3] *James,*[2] *Anthony*[1]), daughter of Lewis and Elizabeth (Emery) Wheat; married, 1852, Charles Ackles.
Children :

5052 i JOSEPH.[10]
5053 ii CHASTENA
5054 iii SARAH ANN
5055 iv JAMES
5056 v ABIGAIL.
5057 vi ROBERT.
5058 vii AGNES
5059 viii HATTIE

3840 JAMES E[9] WHEAT (*Elizabeth,*[8] *James,*[7] *Noah,*[6] *Daniel,*[5] *Zachariah,*[4] *Zachariah,*[3] *James,*[2] *Anthony*[1]), son of Lewis and Elizabeth (Emery) Wheat; married, 1863, Cornelia Davidson.
Child :

5060 i NETTIE [10]

3841 CHASTENA M.[9] WHEAT (*Elizabeth,*[8] *James,*[7] *Noah,*[6] *Daniel,*[5] *Zachariah,*[4] *Zachariah,*[3] *James,*[2] *Anthony*[1]), daughter of Lewis and Elizabeth (Emery) Wheat; married, 1871, George Welch.

Children :

  5061 i   CATHARINE C.[10]
  5062 ii ELIZABETH S.
  5063 iii GEORGE, b. in Webster, N. Y.

3842 SOLOMON[9] WHEAT (*Elizabeth,*[8] *James,*[7] *Noah,*[6] *Daniel,*[5] *Zachariah,*[4] *Zachariah,*[3] *James,*[2] *Anthony*[1]), son of Lewis and Elizabeth (Emery) Wheat; married, 1867, Mary Brown.

Child :

  5064 i   CORA,[10] b. in Webster, N. Y.

3844 EDWIN R.[9] WHEAT (*Elizabeth,*[8] *James,*[7] *Noah,*[6] *Daniel,*[5] *Zachariah,*[4] *Zachariah,*[3] *James,*[2] *Anthony*[1]), son of Lewis and Elizabeth (Emery) Wheat; married, 1868, Amelia Sage. Resides in Windsor, Canada.

Children :

  5065 i   NETTIE.[10]
  5066 ii FRANCES.

3845 LAURA J.[9] EMERY (*James C.,*[8] *James,*[7] *Noah,*[6] *Daniel,*[5] *Zachariah,*[4] *Zachariah,*[3] *James,*[2] *Anthony*[1]), daughter of James C. and Jane (Letts) Emery ; married Feb. 21, 1867, Frederick Barton.

Child :

  5067 i   ALMON E.,[10] b. March 1, 1875.

3846 ELLEN AUGUSTA[9] EMERY (*James C.,*[8] *James,*[7] *Noah,*[6] *Daniel,*[5] *Zachariah,*[4] *Zachariah,*[3] *James,*[2] *Anthony*[1]), daughter of James C. and Jane (Letts) Emery ; married April 14, 1868, Charles M. Ferris.

Child :

  5068 i   FRANK M.,[10] b. Dec. 1, 1872, in Spencer, N. Y.

3847 AGNES M.[9] EMERY (*Justus W.,*[8] *James,*[7] *Noah,*[6] *Daniel,*[5] *Zachariah,*[4] *Zachariah,*[3] *James,*[2] *Anthony*[1]), daughter of Justus W. and Sarah (Billings) Emery ; married Nov. 30, 1874, Henry Stoddard.

Children :

  5069 i   EMILY,[10] b. July 11, 1876.
  5070 ii GLEN W., b. March 16, 1879.
  5071 iii MARION, b. Nov. 26, 1881.

3852 ALVIN W.[9] EMERY (*Rev. Isaac W.,*[8] *James,*[7] *Noah,*[6] *Daniel,*[5] *Zachariah,*[4] *Zachariah,*[3] *James,*[2] *Anthony*[1]), son of Rev. Isaac W. and Elizabeth (Benton) Emery ; married Oct. 27, 1870, Milla E. Camp of Lenox, N. Y.

Children :

  5072 i   LENA,[10] } b. March 13, 1872; { d. Aug. 8, 1874.
  5073 ii RENA,   { d. Aug. 5, 1872.
  5074 iii LILLA MAY, b. June 11, 1874; d. the same day.
  5075 iv ISAAC C.
  5076 v   JOHN O.

3853 JUSTUS J.[9] EMERY (*Rev. Isaac W.*,[8] *James*,[7] *Noah*,[6] *Daniel*,[5] *Zachariah*,[4] *Zachariah*,[3] *James*,[2] *Anthony*[1]), son of Rev Isaac W. and Elizabeth (Benton) Emery, married Dec. 30, 1874, Julia E Harvey.
Child ·

5077   i   JESSE JAMES,[10] b July 25, 1878

3854 HENRY P.[9] EMERY (*James P.*,[8] *Nathan*,[7] *Noah*,[6] *Daniel*,[5] *Zachariah*,[4] *Zachariah*,[3] *James*,[2] *Anthony*[1]), son of James P and Martha G. (Newhall) Emery; married Elnora R. Houghton   Resides in Quincy, Ill
Children ·

5078   i   HATTIE P.,[10] b Aug 5, 1873.
5079   ii   EBEN G., b. Aug. 1, 1881

3855 GEORGE H.[9] EMERY (*James P.*,[8] *Nathan*,[7] *Noah*,[6] *Daniel*,[5] *Zachariah*,[4] *Zachariah*,[3] *James*,[2] *Anthony*[1]), son of James P. and Martha G (Newhall) Emery; married Dec. 25, 1879, Frances E. Ross. Resides in Indianapolis, Ind.
Child

5080   i   HENRY H.,[10] b. Sept. 19, 1880.

3857 EDWARD T.[9] EMERY (*James P.*,[8] *Nathan*,[7] *Noah*,[6] *Daniel*,[5] *Zachariah*,[4] *Zachariah*,[3] *James*,[2] *Anthony*[1]), son of James P and Martha G (Newhall) Emery, married Dec. 1, 1877, Annie Turpin   Resides in Archie, Mo.
Children:

5081   i   HATTIE,[10] b Dec 29, 1878
5082   ii   JAMES L, b June 3, 1881

3861 CHAUNCEY N.[9] EMERY (*Chauncey W.*,[8] *Noah*,[7] *Noah*,[6] *Daniel*,[5] *Zachariah*,[4] *Zachariah*,[3] *James*,[2] *Anthony*[1]), son of Chauncey W. and Phoebe (Baker) Emery, married Emma A. Leavins.
Child:

5083   i   GEORGE L.,[10] b. 1878.

3862 LORINDA[9] EMERY (*Chauncey W.*,[8] *Noah*,[7] *Noah*,[6] *Daniel*,[5] *Zachariah*,[4] *Zachariah*,[3] *James*,[2] *Anthony*[1]), daughter of Chauncey W. and Phoebe (Baker) Emery, married Aug. 29, 1877, William Ganning.
Children:

5084   i   MARY L.,[10] b Jan 21, 1880
5085   ii   NORMAN E., } b June 20, 1881
5086   iii   HERMAN E., }

3907 SIMEON[9] EMERY (*Simeon*,[8] *David*,[7] *Daniel*,[6] *Daniel*,[5] *Daniel*,[4] *Daniel*,[3] *James*,[2] *Anthony*[1]), son of Simeon and Betsey (Adams) Emery; married Dec. 24, 1868, Rose Oliver.
Child

5087   i   EDWARD [10]

3911 CHARLES A.[9] EMERY (*Simeon*,[8] *David*,[7] *Daniel*,[6] *Daniel*,[5]

Daniel,[4] Daniel,[3] James,[2] Anthony[1]), son of Simeon and Betsey (Adams) Emery; married June 26, 1872, Mercy Lothrop Thatcher. Resides in Dennis, Mass.

Child:

5088   i   MABEL E.[10]

3919 ROSALIA[9] CHADWICK (*Elizabeth,[8] David,[7] Daniel,[6] Daniel,[5] Daniel,[4] Daniel,[3] James,[2] Anthony[1]*), daughter of Parker W. and Elizabeth (Emery) Chadwick; married Aug. 3, 1871, George E. Stackpole.

Child:

5089   i   ANNIE ETTA,[10] b. March 18, 1872.

3921 PARKER W.[9] CHADWICK (*Elizabeth,[8] David,[7] Daniel,[6] Daniel,[5] Daniel,[4] Daniel,[3] James,[2] Anthony[1]*), son of Parker W. and Elizabeth (Emery) Chadwick; married Francena Knox; died Jan. 5, 1877.

Child:

5090   i   CORA,[10] b. Sept. 13, 1876.

3923 CHARLES[9] GOULD (*Elizabeth,[8] David,[7] Daniel,[6] Daniel,[5] Daniel,[4] Daniel,[3] James,[2] Anthony[1]*), son of David and Elizabeth (Emery-Chadwick) Gould; married Harriet Morgan.

Child:

5091   i   LIZZIE.[10]

3925 FREDERICK H.[9] GOULD (*Elizabeth,[8] David,[7] Daniel,[6] Daniel,[5] Daniel,[4] Daniel,[3] James,[2] Anthony[1]*), son of David and Elizabeth (Emery-Chadwick) Gould; married —— ——.

Children:

5092   i   FRED EVERETT,[10] b. April 27, 1885.
5093   ii   LILA DELANO, b. July 25, 1887.

3935 ASA[9] EMERY (*Asa,[8] Joel,[7] Nathan,[6] Daniel,[5] Daniel,[4] Daniel,[3] James,[2] Anthony[1]*), son of Asa and Sarah (Rendall) Emery; married Bell Godfrey. Resides in Medford, Mass.

Child:

5094   i   NELLIE,[10] b. May 18, 1868.

3938 MARTIN[9] LORD (*Rhoda A.,[8] Joel,[7] Nathan,[6] Daniel,[5] Daniel,[4] Daniel,[3] James,[2] Anthony[1]*), son of John and Rhoda A. (Emery) Lord; married Sept., 1880, Mrs. Mary E. Hansell.

Child:

5095   i   GROVER C.,[10] b. Aug. 31, 1884.

3939 JOHN A.[9] LORD (*Rhoda A.,[8] Joel,[7] Nathan,[6] Daniel,[5] Daniel,[4] Daniel,[3] James,[2] Anthony[1]*) son of John and Rhoda A. (Emery) Lord; married Dec. 14, 1870, Ruth M. Newton, of Medford, Mass.

Child:

5096   i   GRACIE J.,[10] b. May 4, 1872; d. Oct. 2, 1886.

3940 RHODA A.[9] LORD (*Rhoda A.,*[8] *Joel,*[7] *Nathan,*[6] *Daniel,*[5] *Daniel,*[4] *Daniel,*[3] *James,*[2] *Anthony*[1]), daughter of John and Rhoda A. (Emery) Lord; married July 7, 1875, George H. Rendall of Medford, Mass.

Child :

   5097 i   EDITH M.,[10] b. Aug. 6, 1877.

3965 LAURA[9] EMERY (*Daniel,*[8] *Daniel C.,*[7] *Daniel.*[6] *Daniel.*[5] *Noah,*[4] *Daniel,*[3] *James,*[2] *Anthony*[1]), daughter of Daniel and Mary P. (Young) Emery; married April 27, 1868, John Hunter of Brooklyn, N. Y.

Children :

   5098 i   JOHN,[10] d. young.
   5099 ii FREDERICK T.

3966 GEORGE EDGAR[9] EMERY (*Daniel,*[8] *Daniel C.,*[7] *Daniel,*[6] *Daniel,*[5] *Noah,*[4] *Daniel,*[3] *James,*[2] *Anthony*[1]), son of Daniel and Mary P. (Young) Emery; married, first, Oct. 24, 1866, Mary (died Jan. 27, 1869, aged about twenty-one years), daughter of Theodore and Rhoda Ricker; second, March 12, 1870, Clara M. (born Feb. 18, 1851), daughter of Mark M. and Mehitable (Wiggin) Sibley, of Wakefield, N. H. He was in Co. A, 1st Mass. Cavalry, 1864-5.

Children :

   5100 i   GEORGE F.,[10] b. Jan. 14, 1869.
   5101 ii EDGAR C., b. in Wakefield, Jan. 6, 1871.
   5102 iii ARCHIE C., b. in South Berwick, Me., June 30, 1872; d. in Sanford, Me., Jan. 10, 1879.
   5103 iv FRANK S., b. in Sanford. Dec. 6, 1874.
   5104 v   BERTHOLD L., b. in Sanford, Oct. 6, 1877.
   5105 vi ADDIE MAY, b. in Sanford, Jan. 24, 1880.

3967 DANIEL[9] EMERY(*Daniel,*[8] *Daniel C.,*[7] *Daniel,*[6] *Daniel,*[5] *Noah,*[4] *Daniel,*[3] *James,*[2] *Anthony*[1]), son of Daniel and Mary P. (Young) Emery; married April, 1876, Jennie Littlefield.

Child :

   5106 i   OLIVE MAY,[10] b. April, 1881.

3970 SARAH ELIZABETH[9] EMERY (*Joseph,*[8] *Noah,*[7] *Noah,*[6] *Daniel,*[5] *Noah,*[4] *Daniel,*[3] *James,*[2] *Anthony*[1]), daughter of Joseph and Olive (Raitt-Odiorne) Emery : married April 25, 1854, Moses Morrill, son of William and Polly (Emery) Morrill (see No. 2323). Resides in Eliot, Me.

Child :

   5107 i   CHARLES W.,[10] b. April 25, 1859.

3971 WILLIAM GOWEN[9] EMERY (*Joseph,*[8] *Noah,*[7] *Noah,*[6] *Daniel,*[5] *Noah,*[4] *Daniel,*[3] *James,*[2] *Anthony*[1]), son of Joseph and Olive (Raitt-Odiorne) Emery ; married June, 1869, Sarah A. Shaw of Middleton, Mass., daughter of Alfred and Sally Shaw. Builder in Boston, Mass., since 1869, Asst. Inspector of buildings 1874-78, Asst. Assessor 1883 ; he recently built a Hall and presented to his native town, Eliot, Me.

Child :

    5108 i   DAUGHTER,[10] d. in infancy.

3972 LYDIA ANN[9] EMERY (*Joseph,*[8] *Noah,*[7] *Noah,*[6] *Daniel,*[5] *Noah,*[4] *Daniel,*[3] *James,*[2] *Anthony*[1]), daughter of Joseph and Olive (Raitt-Odiorne) Emery ; married June 29, 1866, Oliver C. Stacey, son of Jonathan and Jane Stacey. Resides in Eliot, Me.

Child :

    5109 i   ELLA WENTWORTH,[10] b. Oct. 5, 1873.

3973 OLIVE JANE[9] EMERY (*Joseph,*[8] *Noah,*[7] *Noah,*[6] *Daniel,*[5] *Noah,*[4] *Daniel,*[3] *James,*[2] *Anthony*[1]), daughter of Joseph and Oliver (Raitt-Odiorne) Emery ; married Aug. 27, 1864, Nathaniel Frost. Resides in Eliot, Me.

Children :

    5110 i   NELLIE OLIVE,[10] b. Jan. 22, 1866.
    5111 ii   CHESTER EMERY, b. March 25, 1869.
    5112 iii GEORGIA ETTA, b. March 7, 1871; d. Aug. 19, 1871.

3975 FRANKLIN[9] HALEY (*Abby B.,*[8] *Enoch,*[7] *Noah,*[6] *Daniel,*[5] *Noah,*[4] *Daniel,*[3] *James,*[2] *Anthony*[1]), son of Benning and Abby B. (Emery) Haley ; married March 4, 1879, Oraville M. Manson.

Children :

    5113 i   EDWIN W., [10] d. Feb. 7, 1881.
    5114 ii   LUCY F , b. Jan. 25, 1884.
    5115 iii BESSIE C., b. July 25, 1886.

3977 OLIVIA M.[9] SEAWARD (*Mary E.,*[8] *Shem,*[7] *Noah,*[6] *Daniel,*[5] *Noah,*[4] *Daniel,*[3] *James,*[2] *Anthony*[1]), daughter of William H. and Mary E. (Emery) Seaward ; married Philip A. Butler.

Child :

    5116 i   MARY GRAVES,[10] b. June 2, 1859 ; d. March 17, 1872.

3981 GIDEON WALKER[9] DENNETT (*Mary E.,*[8] *Shem,*[7] *Noah,*[6] *Daniel,*[5] *Noah,*[4] *Daniel,*[3] *James,*[2] *Anthony*[1]), son of George and Mary E. (Emery-Seaward) Dennett ; married Elizabeth Marcus of New York City.

Child :

    5117 i   WALKER.[10]

3987 JOHN B. F.[9] EMERY (*Geo. F.,*[8] *Shem,*[7] *Noah,*[6] *Daniel,*[5] *Noah,*[4] *Daniel,*[3] *James,*[2] *Anthony*[1]), son of Geo. F. and Abby F. (Lewis) Emery ; married Sarah Ellen Greenish.

Child :

    5118 i   FRANCIS JOSEPH,[10] b. Dec. 11, 1886.

3996 MARTHA WALKER[9] EMERY (*Woodbury,*[8] *Shem,*[7] *Noah,*[6] *Daniel,*[5] *Noah,*[4] *Daniel,*[3] *James,*[2] *Anthony*[1]), daughter of Woodbury and Mary A. (Gould) Emery ; married Frank Carter of Woburn, Mass.

Child :
 5119 i FANNIE HARRISON.[10]

3998 ALICE CORA[9] EMERY (*Woodbury*,[8] *Shem*,[7] *Noah*,[6] *Daniel*,[5] *Noah*,[4] *Daniel*,[3] *James*,[2] *Anthony*[1]), daughter of Woodbury and Mary A. (Gould) Emery ; married Ellison B. Cushing of Boston.
 Children :

 5120 i ELLISON B.,[10] b. Jan. 15, 1880 ; d. Jan. 16, 1880.
 5121 ii ALICE ELLISON, b. May 3, 1885.

4002 ANN ELIZA[9] WEBSTER (*Eliza H.*,[8] *John*,[7] *George*,[6] *Daniel*,[5] *Noah*,[4] *Daniel*,[3] *James*,[2] *Anthony*[1]), daughter of Benjamin and Eliza H. (Emery) Webster ; married at Owl's Head, Me., Dec. 21, 1854, Capt. Jeremiah Hooper.
 Children :

 5122 i LOIS,[10] b. Feb. 16, 1862 ; d. Feb. 18, 1862.
 5123 ii MABEL E., b. Oct. 20, 1863 ; m. June 20, 1877, Washington R. Prescott.

4004 LYDIA E.[9] WEBSTER (*Eliza H.*,[8] *John*,[7] *George*,[6] *Daniel*,[5] *Noah*,[4] *Daniel*,[3] *James*,[2] *Anthony*[1]), daughter of Benjamin and Eliza H. (Emery) Webster ; married in Sacramento, Cal., Oct. 12, 1870, Eugene Alden.
 Children :

 5124 i BERTRAM FRANCIS,[10] b. Jan. 4, 1873.
There were two other children, daughters.

4005 EVELINE B.[9] WEBSTER (*Eliza H.*,[8] *John*,[7] *George*,[6] *Daniel*,[5] *Noah*,[4] *Daniel*,[3] *James*,[2] *Anthony*[1]), daughter of Benj. and Eliza H. (Emery) Webster ; married in Rockland, Me., Oct. 31, 1872, Capt. J. W. Hall.
 Children :

 5125 i BESSIE,[10] b. Sept. 3, 1873.
 5126 ii MABEL F., b. May 7, 1879.
 5127 iii JOSEPH, JR., b. May 21, 1885.

4007 WILLIAM E.[9] EMERY (*William S.*,[8] *John*,[7] *George*,[6] *Samuel*,[5] *Noah*,[4] *Daniel*,[3] *James*,[2] *Anthony*[1]), son of William S. and Lucy J. (Spaulding) Emery ; married, first, May 13, 1866, Mary A. Duncan (died March 17, 1881) ; second, Oct. 3, 1883, Anna Jeffrey of San Francisco, Cal.
 Children :

 5128 i MAY,[10] b. June 2, 1867, in San Francisco.
 5129 ii WILLIAM W., b. Feb. 26, 1869, in Gilroy, Cal.
 5130 iii LEWIS L., b. Feb. 26, 1871.
 5131 iv ALFRED A., b. Jan. 17, 1873, in San Francisco.
 5132 v BELLE, b. March 15, 1875, in San Francisco ; d. March 30, 1875.
 5133 vi DONALD D., b. June 21, 1876, in San Francisco.

4012 LUCY E.[9] EMERY (*William S.*,[8] *John*,[7] *George*,[6] *Daniel*,[5] *Noah*,[4] *Daniel*,[3] *James*,[2] *Anthony*[1]), daughter of William S. and Lucy

J. (Spaulding) Emery; married Oct. 1, 1868, Samuel H. Wheeler of Eastport, Me. (died in Berkeley, Cal., Aug. 22, 1882).

Children, born in San Francisco, Cal. :

5134   i   GERTRUDE R.,[10] b. July 24, 1869.
5135   ii   EDGAR T., b. May 3, 1870.
5136   iii   LUCY E., b. May 23, 1872.
5137   iv   AMY, b. Oct. 20, 1875.

4014 EDWARD C.[9] EMERY (*William S.*,[8] *John,*[7] *George,*[6] *Daniel,*[5] *Noah,*[4] *Daniel,*[3] *James,*[2] *Anthony*[1]), son of William S. and Lucy J. (Spaulding) Emery; married in San Diego, Cal., Aug. 28, 1877, Margaret E. Moore of New York City.

Children :

5138   i   GRACE E.,[10] b. June 15, 1878, in San Diego, Cal.
5139   ii   EDWARD E., b. July 16, 1879, in San Diego, Cal.
5140   iii   HARRIET S., b. Sept. 12, 1880, in San Diego, Cal.
5141   iv   PEARL, b. Feb. 22, 1882, in National, Cal.
5142   v   ADELAIDE, b. July 3, 1884, in San Diego, Cal.

4017 MARY G.[9] EMERY (*William S.*,[8] *John,*[7] *George,*[6] *Daniel,*[5] *Noah,*[4] *Daniel,*[3] *James,*[2] *Anthony*[1]), daughter of William S. and Lucy J. (Spaulding) Emery ; married in San Diego, Cal., May 10, 1877, John E. Rich of N. Y.

Children, born in San Diego, Cal. :

5143   i   ERNEST P.,[10] b. Feb. 9, 1878.
5144   ii   ARTHUR E., b. Feb. 3, 1879.
5145   iii   CHARLES E., b. Dec. 20, 1880.

4094 EDWARD G.[9] EMERY (*Edwin T.*,[8] *George,*[7] *George,*[6] *Daniel,*[5] *Noah,*[4] *Daniel,*[3] *James,*[2] *Anthony*[1]), son of Edwin Thomas and Susan (Perry) Emery ; married Elida Green, 1882.

Children :

5146   i   EVA B.,[10] b. July, 1873.
5147   ii   GEORGE W., b Nov., 1875.
5148   iii   CATHARINE, b. Oct., 1877.
5149   iv   MARY, b. Feb., 1884.

4101 GEORGIE[9] EMERY (*Joseph M.*,[8] *George,*[7] *George,*[6] *Daniel,*[5] *Noah,*[4] *Daniel,*[3] *James,*[2] *Anthony*[1]), daughter of Joseph M. and Mary A. (Masters) Emery ; married, 1870, Charles H. Berry.

Child :

5150   i   JOHN T.[10]

4102 CHARLES O.[9] EMERY (*Joseph M.*,[8] *George,*[7] *George,*[6] *Daniel,*[5] *Noah,*[4] *Daniel,*[3] *James,*[2] *Anthony*[1]), son of Joseph M. and Mary A. (Masters) Emery ; married Feb. 28, 1870, ——— Elms.

Children :

5151   i   HELEN W.[10]
5152   ii   MARY G.
5153   iii   CHARLES.

4135 JULIETT[9] MEAD (*Caroline,*[8] *Tristram,*[7] *Nathaniel,*[6] *Daniel,*[5]

Noah,[4] *Daniel*,[3] *James*,[2] *Anthony*[1]), daughter of Jesse and Caroline (Emery) Mead; married Jan , 1872, William Mead.
Children:

5154   i   JAMFS EDDY,[10] b. Feb., 1875.
5155   ii   ARTHUR RAYMOND, b April, 1880
5156   iii INA LEONA, b Sept , 1884
5157   iv   CLYDE LAVERNE, b June, 1886

4138 ELLA[9] MEAD (*Caroline*,[8] *Tristram*,[7] *Nathaniel*,[6] *Daniel*,[5] *Noah*,[4] *Daniel*,[3] *James*,[2] *Anthony*[1]), daughter of Jesse and Caroline (Emery) Mead; married Nov., 1875. Abijah Cornell.
Children:

5158   i   ROY,[10] b Aug , 1877
5159   ii   JESSE CARL, b Feb , 1882
5160   iii WARREN, b March, 1887

4140 ELMER[9] MEAD (*Caroline*,[8] *Tristram*,[7] *Nathaniel*,[6] *Daniel*,[5] *Noah*,[4] *Daniel*,[3] *James*,[2] *Anthony*[1]), son of Jesse and Caroline (Emery) Mead; married Sept., 1880, Jennie Bellows.
Children:

5161   i   L B EMERY,[10] b July, 1884
5162   ii   ALTON OSBORN, b. Feb , 1886

4144 ELMER E [9] EMERY (*Horace*,[8] *Tristram*,[7] *Nathaniel*,[6] *Daniel*,[5] *Noah*,[4] *Daniel*,[3] *James*,[2] *Anthony*[1]), son of Horace and Mary (West) Emery; married in Green Spring, Ohio, Dec. 6, 1876, Mary E Jopp. Resides in Seneca, O.
Children:

5163   i   CHARLES IRWIN,[10] b Dec 28, 1877
5164   ii   ASAHEL WESI, b April 9, 1880.
5165   iii ELBERT CARL, b. Jan 3, 1883.
5166   iv   GEORGE NORTON, b Sept. 6, 1885
5167   v   CHILD, b July 27, 1888

4145 MABEL S [9] EMERY (*Horace*,[8] *Tristram*,[7] *Nathaniel*,[6] *Daniel*,[5] *Noah*,[4] *Daniel*,[3] *James*,[2] *Anthony*[1]), daughter of Horace and Mary (West) Emery; married June 22, 1882, M. William Drown, M D., of Whitesville, Mo.
Child:

5168   i   EARL EMERY,[10] b. April 22, 1883

4158 ERIKA[9] EMERY (*Judson*,[8] *Levi*,[7] *Nathaniel*,[6] *Daniel*,[5] *Noah*,[4] *Daniel*,[3] *James*,[2] *Anthony*[1]), daughter of Judson and Lucinda (Mead) Emery; married March 22, 1877, Solomon P. Murray. Resides in Damascus, O.
Children:

5169   i   NORTON [10]
5170   ii   LOIS M

4172 REV JOHN ABBOT[9] EMERY (*Charles*,[8] *Robert*,[7] *John*,[6] *Noah*,[5] *Noah*,[4] *Daniel*,[3] *James*,[2] *Anthony*[1]), son of Capt. Charles and Susan

Hilton (Kelly) Emery ; married July 21, 1875, in Arizona, S. Frances Wiseman ; engaged in business in San Francisco and Nevada City, Cal. He was engaged in mining in various places ; superintendent of the Grass Valley Manufacturing Company ; book-keeper in Rutland, Vt. ; went west in 1871 ; in 1875 had a ferry on the Colorado River ; his health failing, he removed to San Francisco ; on the recovery of his health studied for the ministry of the Protestant Episcopal Church ; was ordained Deacon, May, 1880, and had charge of St. Michael's Church, Anaheim, Cal. Now Rector at St. Andrews, Oakland, Cal.

Children :

5171   i   CHARLES ABBOT,[10] b. June 22, 1876, in St. Thomas, Nevada.
5172   ii   MAXWELL WINTHROP, b. May 13, 1878, in The Oaks, Los Angeles Co., Cal. ; d. in Oakland, Cal., Aug. 30, 1886.
5173   iii   MARY ALICE, b. Nov. 11, 1880, in Anaheim, Cal. ; d. July 31, 1882.

4178 REV. WILLIAM STANLEY[9] EMERY (*Charles,*[8] *Robert,*[7] *John,*[6] *Noah,*[5] *Noah,*[4] *Daniel,*[3] *James,*[2] *Anthony*[1]), son of Capt. Charles and Susan Hilton (Kelly) Emery ; married Jan. 18, 1887, in Dorchester, Mass., Ethel N. Julien of St. Andrews, N. B. He was a graduate of Trinity College, Hartford, Conn. and of the General Theological Seminary of the Episcopal Church, New York City. Minister in charge of St. John Baptist's Church, Wolfboro Junction, N. H.

Child :

5174   i   MARGARET THERESE,[10] b. April 27, 1888.

4194 MARY J. C.[9] ABBOT (*Ann T. G.,*[8] *Nicholas,*[7] *Noah,*[6] *Noah,*[5] *Noah,*[4] *Daniel,*[3] *James,*[2] *Anthony*[1]), daughter of George J. and Ann T. G. (Emery) Abbot ; married April 8, 1868, Everett S. Throop, lawyer in Cincinnati, O.

Children :

5175   i   ANNA A.,[10] b. Oct. 17, 1869.
5176   ii   LUCY A., b. June 10, 1871.
5177   iii   MARY S. E., b. Dec. 12, 1872.
5178   iv   GEORGE W., b. Nov. 9, 1875.
5179   v   EVERETT A., b. Aug. 23, 1878.

4196 ANNE T.[9] ABBOT (*Ann T. G.,*[8] *Nicholas,*[7] *Noah,*[6] *Noah,*[5] *Noah,*[4] *Daniel,*[3] *James,*[2] *Anthony*[1]), daughter of George J. and Ann T. G. (Emery) Abbot ; married Feb. 21, 1877, Rev. Robert Swain Morrison (born in Milton, Mass., Oct. 13, 1847).

Children :

5180   i   RUTH.[10]
5181   ii   GEORGE A.

4200 EDWARD W.[9] BURLEIGH (*Henrietta O.,*[8] *John,*[7] *Noah,*[6] *Noah,*[5] *Noah,*[4] *Daniel,*[3] *James,*[2] *Anthony*[1]), son of William and Henrietta O. (Emery) Burleigh ; married Elizabeth Bristol, daughter of Johnson and Elizabeth (Davidson) Bristol.

Children :

5182   i   CLARENCE EMERY,[10] b. July 31, 1871.
5183   ii   MAUD MIRIAM, b. Feb. 24, 1875.

4223 ELIZABETH C.[9] EMERY (*Theodore A.,*[8] *Theodore,*[7] *Theodore,*[6] *Japhet,*[5] *Noah,*[4] *Daniel,*[3] *James,*[2] *Anthony*[1]), daughter of Theodore A. and Sarah A. (Maxwell) Emery; married July 16, 1871, Albert P Witham of Alfred, Me.

Child :

    5184   i   FREDDIE A ,[10] b July 13, 1875

4224 GEORGE A [9] EMERY (*Theodore A.,*[8] *Theodore,*[7] *Theodore,*[6] *Japhet,*[5] *Noah,*[4] *Daniel,*[3] *James,*[2] *Anthony*[1]), son of Theodore A. and Sarah A (Maxwell) Emery ; married Oct. 7, 1875, Minetta Florence Merritt of Pownal, Me. Resides in Boston, Mass.

Children :

    5185   i   ERNEST THEODORE,[10] b Oct 11. 1878
    5186   ii   FLORENCE ASHTON, b March 22, 1880.

4225 SEAVEY D [9] EMERY (*Theodore A.,*[8] *Theodore,*[7] *Theodore,*[6] *Japhet,*[5] *Noah,*[4] *Daniel,*[3] *James,*[2] *Anthony*[1]), son of Theodore A and Sarah A (Maxwell) Emery ; married Nov 29, 1877, Clara E. Merritt of Boston, sister of his brother George A s wife Resides in Boston, Mass.

Child :

    5187   i   WALTER CURTIS,[10] b Sept 12, 1878.

4299 JOHN G [9] EMERY (*Temple H ,*[8] *Hosea,*[7] *Stephen,*[6] *Stephen,*[5] *Simon,*[4] *Daniel,*[3] *James,*[2] *Anthony*[1]) son of Temple H. and Diana (Godfrey) Emery, married Oct. 7, 1855, Martha H. Waterhouse of Gardiner, Me. Resides in Minneapolis, Minn.

Children, born in Peshtigo, Wis :

    5188   i   JOHN G ,[10] b Aug 20, 1858
    5189   ii   CAROLINE A , b Sept 24, 1860.
    5190   iii HELEN L , b May 22, 1863

4300 NICHOLAS[9] EMERY (*Temple H ,*[8] *Hosea,*[7] *Stephen,*[6] *Stephen,*[5] *Simon,*[4] *Daniel,*[3] *James,*[2] *Anthony*[1]), son of Temple H. and Diana (Godfrey) Emery; married, 1852, Louisa Oaks. Resides in West Bay City, Mich.

Children :

    5191   i   CHARLES L ,[10] b. Dec 21, 1855, in Bradley, Me
    5192   ii   JAMES S , b Sept 25, 1857, in Orono, Me.

4301 ARD G.[9] EMERY (*Temple H ,*[8] *Hosea,*[7] *Stephen,*[6] *Stephen,*[5] *Simon,*[4] *Daniel,*[3] *James,*[2] *Anthony*[1]), son of Temple H. and Diana (Godfrey) Emery, married Feb. 16, 1865, Agnes Cole of Wales, N Y Resides in Kansas.

Children, born in Marquette, Mich. :

    5193   i   DIANA G ,[10] b Dec 12, 1865
    5194   ii   LILLIE B , b June 13, 1866, in Ishpeming, d Aug 31, 1868
    5195   iii EDWIN A , b Nov 3, 1868
    5196   iv   ARTHUR L , b March 6, 1873.

4302 TEMPLE[9] EMERY (*Temple H.,*[8] *Hosea,*[7] *Stephen,*[6] *Stephen,*[5]

Simon,[4] *Daniel,*[3] *James,*[2] *Anthony*[1]), son of Temple H. and Diana (Godfrey) Emery ; married Agnes Elizabeth Ogden of Delhi, **N. Y.** Resides in Bay City, Mich.

Children, born in Peshtigo, Mich. :

5197　i　WILLIAM OGDEN,[10] b. Oct. 2, 1862.
5198　ii　CORA ANN, b. Sept. 14, 1866.
5199　iii　TEMPLE J., b. Dec. 26, 1872.
5200　iv　JULIA, b. Oct. 29, 1876.

4303 HIRAM A.[9] EMERY (*Temple H.,*[8] *Hosea,*[7] *Stephen,*[6] *Stephen,*[5] *Simon,*[4] *Daniel,*[3] *James,*[2] *Anthony*[1]), son of Temple H. and Diana (Godfrey) Emery ; married July 27, 1869, Eunice W. Anderson of Kennebunk. Resides in West Bay City, Mich.

Children :

5201　i　HATTIE G.,[10] b. Oct. 5, 1870, in West Bay City, Mich.
5202　ii　HIRAM A., b. May 25, 1872.
5203　iii　EUNICE A., b. Dec. 22, 1873, in Eau Claire, Wis. ; d. March 18, 1878.
5204　iv　LIZZIE, b. Nov. 12, 1875, in West Bay City.
5205　v　ALBERT C., b. March 28, 1880.

4311 HELEN A.[9] EMERY (*Hosea B.,*[8] *Hosea,*[7] *Stephen,*[6] *Stephen,*[5] *Simon,*[4] *Daniel,*[3] *James,*[2] *Anthony*[1]), daughter of Hosea B. and Eliza (McDaniel) Emery ; married Dec. 1, 1865, George Bowen in Bangor, Me.

Children, born in Bangor, Me. :

5206　i　GEORGE H.,[10] b. June 17, 1866.
5207　ii　HOSEA E., b. Oct. 30, 1868.

4318 INEZ G.[9] EMERY (*Hosea B.,*[8] *Hosea,*[7] *Stephen,*[6] *Stephen,*[5] *Simon,*[4] *Daniel,*[3] *James,*[2] *Anthony*[1]), daughter of Hosea B. and Lydia T. (Tapley) Emery ; married Aug. 7, 1885, Frederick A. Eddy (born in Bradley, Me., Aug. 23, 1846).

Child :

5208　i　HAROLD FREDERICK.[10] b. May 17, 1886, in Bangor, Me.
5208a ii　HAZEL, b. Jan. 23, 1888.
5208b iii　MILDRED, b. July 23, 1890.

4334 GEORGE H.[9] EMERY (*Monroe,*[8] *John,*[7] *Jacob,*[6] *Stephen,*[5] *Simon,*[4] *Daniel,*[3] *James,*[2] *Anthony*[1]), son of Monroe and Temperance (Goodrich) Emery ; married Aug. 19, 1878, Ella M. Patten.

Child :

5209　i　FLORENCE M.,[10] b. Jan. 23, 1880.

4382 PAMELIA MADELON[9] EMERY (*Rev. E. J.,*[8] *Jacob,*[7] *Jacob,*[6] *Stephen,*[5] *Simon,*[4] *Daniel,*[3] *James,*[2] *Anthony*[1]), daughter of Rev. Enville J. and Anna J. (Hagget) Emery ; married Sept. 3, 1872, James Albert Wheeler of Jaffrey, N. H.

Children :

5210　i　ALBERT F.,[10] b. Oct., 1874.
5211　ii　JOHN E., b. Sept. 20, 1876.
5212　iii　EDWIN E., b. Sept. 6, 1879.
5213　iv　MORRIS J., b. Sept. 16, 1880.

5214 v   ANNA M , b Oct 31, 1881
5215 ·vi CHARLES A , b March 24, 1884
5216 vii ALFRED N , b Jun 9, 1887.

4386 ELIZABETH J [9] YOUNG (*Alice G ,*[8] *Jacob,*[7] *Jacob,*[6] *Stephen,*[5] *Simon,*[4] *Daniel,*[3] *James,*[2] *Anthony*[1]), daughter of William and Alice G. (Emery) Young; married, 1882, Harry Titus
Children :

5217 i   ALICE A ,[10] b Nov. 18, 1883
5218 ii HARRY E , b Feb 12, 1886.
5219 iii CHILD, b March 2, 1889.

4405 JOHN WESLEY[9] EMERY (*John P.,*[8] *John,*[7] *Simon,*[6] *Stephen,*[5] *Simon,*[4] *Daniel,*[3] *James,*[2] *Anthony*[1]), son of John P. and Betsey (Thing) Emery; married July 18, 1881, Bessie Linaberry of Waterboro, Me.
Children :

5220 i   WESLEY M ,[10] b Feb 18, 1883
5221 ii PAUL ALVA, b. May 8, 1887.
5222 iii SAMUEL B , b July 13, 1889

4408 SAMUEL W [9] EMERY (*Samuel H ,*[8] *Peter ,*[7] *Simon,*[6] *Stephen,*[5] *Simon,*[4] *Daniel,*[3] *James,*[2] *Anthony*[1]), son of Samuel H and Mary Emerson (Sias) Emery , married July 25, 1882, Lydia J. Hunt. Attorney-at law, Portsmouth, N. H.
Children :

5223 i SAMUEL P ,[10] b Dec. 2, 1883
5224 ii MABEL, b June 23, 1885

4431 ABBIE M.[9] FRISBEE (*Julia,*[8] *Thomas,*[7] *Simon,*[6] *Samuel,*[5] *Simon,*[4] *Daniel,*[3] *James,*[2] *Anthony*[1]), daughter of Capt. Andrew and Julia (Emery-Dalton) Frisbee ; married. 1882, Wilbra H. Spinney.
Child :

5225 i EVA M ,[10] b April 8, 1883, in Eliot, Me

4440 CHARLES A.[9] LARRY (*Abbie L ,*[8] *Hiram,*[7] *Isaac,*[6] *Samuel,*[5] *Simon,*[4] *Daniel,*[3] *James,*[2] *Anthony*[1]), son of James and Abbie L. (Emery) Larry ; married, Sept 12, 1882, Bertha (born in So Abington, Mass , Sept 23, 1860), daughter of Benjamin F. and Mary W. Hutchinson. Live in Whitman, Mass.
Child :

5225a i EDITH MAY,[10] b April 19, 1884

4447 CHARLES W [9] EMERY (*Lorenzo W.,*[8] *William,*[7] *Isaac,*[6] *Samuel,*[5] *Simon,*[4] *Daniel,*[3] *James,*[2] *Anthony*[1]), son of Lorenzo W. and Margaret (Ferriman) Emery ; married Oct., 1888, Ollie Coleman (born March, 1872).
Child :

5226 i LORENZO W.,[10] b. Oct., 1889.

4499 DR CALEB JOSEPH[9] EMERY (*Chandler S.,*[8] *Caleb,*[7] *William,*[6] *Caleb,*[5] *Caleb,*[4] *Daniel,*[3] *James,*[2] *Anthony*[1]), son of Chandler S and

—— (——) Emery; married Aug. 6, 1876, Llewella D. Bassick (born April 15, 1844). Graduate of Maine Medical School, 1871. Physician in Biddeford; in the Navy during the Rebellion as Surgeon's Steward.

Child:

5227 i GRACE CHANDLER,[10] b. April 14, 1879, in Biddeford, Me.

4508 HENRY F.[9] EMERY (*Caleb,*[8] *Caleb,*[7] *William,*[6] *Caleb,*[5] *Caleb,*[4] *Daniel,*[3] *James,*[2] *Anthony*[1]), son of Caleb and Abbie A. (Cutts) Emery; married Dec. 24, 1874, Lizzie, daughter of Rev. Walter and Lizzie Branham of Oxford, Ga.

Children:

5228 i WALTER B.,[10] b. March, 1876.
5229 ii ANNIE, b. June 7, 1877.
5230 iii JULIA J., b. Oct., 1879.

4510 LIZZIE J.[9] EMERY (*Caleb,*[8] *Caleb.*[7] *William,*[6] *Caleb,*[5] *Caleb,*[4] *Daniel,*[3] *James,*[2] *Anthony*[1]), daughter of Caleb and Abbie A. (Cutts) Emery; married Sept. 27, 1876, George W. Fernald, of Eliot, Me.

Children:

5231 i LEE EMERY,[10] b. July 7, 1877.
5232 ii ALICE A., b. Jan. 12, 1881.
5232a iii WILLIAM S., b. in Atlanta, Ga., May 1, 1883.

4525 EDWIN[9] EMERY (*William L.,*[8] *Thomas S.,*[7] *William,*[6] *Caleb,*[5] *Caleb,*[4] *Daniel,*[3] *James,*[2] *Anthony*[1]), son of Dea. W. L. and Mary E. (Prescott) Emery; married Oct. 27, 1864, Louisa F. (born in Brunswick, Me., April 20, 1841), daughter of Samuel S. and Mary (Cook) Wing. He was a graduate of Bowdoin College, 1861; private, sergeant, color-sergeant Co. "F" 17th Maine Infantry, Sept., 1863, to June, 1864, and 2nd Lieut. June, 1864, to June, 1865, in Company "A" same regiment; twice wounded at Spottsylvania Court House May 12, 1864. Teacher of High Schools in Gardiner and Belfast, Me., Great Falls, N. H., Southbridge and Northbridge, Mass.; instructor of cadets, U. S. Revenue Marine, 1877–90; insurance business.

Children:

5233 i WILLIAM MORRELL,[10] b. Oct. 2, 1866, in Brunswick, Me.; grad. Bowd. Coll., 1889; journalist, "Evening and Sunday Telegram," Providence, R. I., City Editor New Bedford "Evening Journal."
5234 ii HORACE FRANK, b. June 30, 1871; d. same day in Southbridge, Mass.
5235 iii FRED HAROLD, b. March 4, 1873; d. July 11, 1873, in Southbridge, Mass.
5236 iv CLARENCE PERCY, b. July 28, 1874, in Southbridge, Mass.
5237 v EDWIN PRESCOTT, b. Aug. 16, 1876, in Northbridge, Mass.
5238 vi MABEL LOUISE, b. June 15, 1880; d. Nov. 1, 1881, in New Bedford, Mass.

4526 ELMIRA[9] EMERY (*William L.,*[8] *Thomas S.,*[7] *William,*[6] *Caleb,*[5] *Caleb,*[4] *Daniel,*[3] *James,*[2] *Anthony*[1]), daughter of Dea. W. L. and Mary E. (Prescott) Emery; married July 15, 1860, John Colbath of Lebanon, Me. He is a farmer.

Children, born in Lebanon ·

5239 i HERBERT EMERY,[10] b May 23, 1866, d Aug 3, 1867
5240 ii WILLIAM L EMERY, b Sept. 14, 1878

4529 GEORGE ALBERT[9] EMERY (*William L ,[8] Thomas S.,[7] William [6] Caleb,[5] Caleb,[4] Daniel,[3] James,[2] Anthony[1]*), son of Dea W. L and Mary E (Prescott) Emery , married Feb. 18, 1865, Susan Ellen (born April 10, 1845), daughter of Alpheus and Rebecca (Hatch) Leavett of York, Me
Children, born in Boston, except the first .

5241 i MINNIE LAURA,[10] b Aug 8, 1866, in York, Me , m. Feb. 18, 1890, Charles E Moore of Providence, R. I
5242 ii FRED ALBERT, b Nov 22, 1869
5243 iii ARTHUR WILLIS, b Sept. 25 1875
5244 iv GEORGE ALBERT, JR , b Dec 20, 1884, d Dec 26, 1884

4531 PRESCOTT[9] EMERY (*William L ,[8] Thomas S.,[7] William,[6] Caleb.[5] Caleb,[4] Daniel,[3] James,[2] Anthony[1]*), son of Dea W. L and Mary E (Prescott) Emery , married, first, June 16, 1871, Alma Olivia Cleaves, adopted daughter of Dea Thomas H and Elizabeth (Hooper) Cole of Biddeford, Me (born Nov. 8, 1843 , died Oct 16, 1872) , second, April 15, 1878, Harriet L (born in Huddersfield, Yorkshire, Eng , Nov. 25, 1835), daughter of John and Harriet (Wordsworth) Clayton Trader in Sanford, Me
Child .

5245 i ALMA OLIVIA,[10] b May 10, 1872

4533 WILLIS TAPPAN[9] EMERY (*William L ,[8] Thomas S ,[7] William,[6] Caleb.[5] Caleb,[4] Daniel,[3] James,[2] Anthony[1]*), son of Dea W. L. and Mary E (Prescott) Emery , married Sept 9, 1875, Mary Elizabeth (born in Woodstock, Me., July 22, 1845), daughter of Orsamus and Emma (Stevens) Nute
Children, born in Boston :

5246 i AMY ETHEL,[10] b Aug 19, 1876
5247 ii INFANT SON, b March 23 1878 , d same day
5248 iii MARION M., b May 15, 1882 (adopted)

4534 LAURA W [9] EMERY (*Caleb S.,[8] Thomas S.,[7] William,[6] Caleb,[5] Caleb,[4] Daniel [3] James,[2] Anthony[1]*). daughter of Caleb S and Caroline (Linscott) Emery , married. first, Aug 30, 1855, William W. Silsby , second, W H. Young. Resides in Pueblo, Colorado.
Children :

5249 i EMERY L [10]
5250 ii WILLIAM
5251 iii HERBA
5252 iv ROY.

4536 CYRUS CHADBOURN[9] EMERY (*Caleb S ,[8] Thomas S ,[7] William,[6] Caleb,[5] Caleb,[4] Daniel,[3] James,[2] Anthony[1]*), son of Caleb S and Caroline (Linscott) Emery , married Dec 13, 1864, Martha Bampton of Roxbury (Boston), Mass ; enlisted in Co "F" 5th U S Cav , Oct 17, 1857 ; corporal on account of wounds and gallantry , dis-

charged July 15, 1862 ; sergeant and 2nd Lieut. Co. "C," 2nd Mass.
Cav., 1862-3 ; 1st Lieut., Capt., Major, 5th Mass. Cav., 1864-5 ; pri-
vate, corporal, 1st sergeant, 2nd Lieut., 1st Lieut., Capt., Co. "A"
(National Lancers), 1st Bat. Cav., Mass. Vol. Militia 1868-1874 ;
Custom Officer, Boston, 1867———.
Children, born in Boston :

5253   i   HERBERT Q.,[10] b Nov. 4, 1865.
5254   ii   HOWARD B., b. June 18, 1872.

4537 OLIVE CAROLINE[9] EMERY (*Caleb S.*,[8] *Thomas S.*,[7] *William*,[6]
Caleb,[5] *Caleb*,[4] *Daniel*,[3] *James*,[2] *Anthony*[1]), daughter of Caleb S. and
Caroline (Linscott) Emery ; married Jan. 1, 1868, Charles M. Hap-
good (born March 3, 1845).
Children, born in Boston :

5255   i   HERBERT JACKSON,[10] b. July 5, 1870.
5256   ii   HELEN E., b Aug. 3, 1873.

4546 WILLIAM SALTER[9] CROWN (*Mary E.*,[8] *Thomas S.*,[7] *William*,[6] *Caleb*,[5] *Caleb*,[4] *Daniel*,[3] *James*,[2] *Anthony*[1]), son of Lyman P.
and Mary E. (Emery) Crown ; married Sept. 9, 1875, Louise J.,
daughter of John and Sarah (Jones) Southwick. Union soldier in a
Mass. Regt., 1865.
Children :

5257   i   GERTRUDE E.,[10] b. Aug. 9, 1876 ; d. June 28, 1877.
5258   ii   WILLIAM S., b. April 9, 1878.
5259   iii   EDITH L., b. May 14, 1881.

4548 CHARLES ARTHUR[9] CROWN (*Mary E.*,[8] *Thomas S.*,[7] *William*,[6] *Caleb*,[5] *Caleb*,[4] *Daniel*,[3] *James*,[2] *Anthony*[1]), son of Lyman P.
and Mary E. (Emery) Crown ; married in Malden, Dec. 7, 1876,
Elizabeth (born Sept. 13, 1857), daughter of John and Annie L. Pur-
sell. Clerk.
Children, born in Charlestown, except the first :

5260   i   EDWARD LYMAN,[10] b. Feb. 6, 1878, in Malden.
5261   ii   ANNIE L., b. June 10, 1879.
5262   iii   CHARLES A., JR , b. Feb. 14, 1881.
5263   iv   ROBERT A., b. July 26, 1886.
5264   v   HOWARD E., b. June 3, 1890.

4550 SUSAN ANN[9] EMERY (*Salter*,[8] *Thomas S.*,[7] *William*,[6] *Caleb*,[5]
Caleb,[4] *Daniel*,[3] *James*,[2] *Anthony*[1]), daughter of Salter and Rebecca
F. (Kilham) Emery ; married June 3, 1868, Albert Nowell of Bos-
ton (born in York, Me.). Resides in Melrose, Mass.
Children :

5265   i   EFFIE SALTER,[10] b. April 27, 1870 ; d. June 7, 1870.
5266   ii   EDITH MAY, b. Dec. 4, 1871.

4560 EVA LUCINDA[9] EMERY (*Cyrus*,[8] *Thomas S.*,[7] *William*,[6] *Caleb*,[5] *Caleb*,[4] *Daniel*,[3] *James*,[2] *Anthony*[1]), daughter of Cyrus and Caroline B (Trafton) Emery, married July 13, 1882, Charles H. Dye of
Fort Madison, Iowa. Both graduated at Oberlin in 1882, and taught

in Franklin, Neb. He read law and was admitted to the Bar in 1887. She is a poetess. He is now a lawyer in Oregon City, Oregon.
Children:

5267 i   CHARLES EMERY,[10] b June 23, 1884
5268 ii TRAFTON MICKLEWAII, b Jan. 11, 1886

4561 CAROLINE E [9] EMERY (*Cyrus*,[8] *Thomas S* ,[7] *William*,[6] *Caleb*,[5] *Caleb*,[4] *Daniel*,[3] *James*,[2] *Anthony*[1]), daughter of Cyrus and Caroline (Trafton) Emery, married April 12, 1876, James O R Carley. He is a physician in Winchester, Kansas
Children:

5269 i   MAUD E ,[10] b Jan 19, 1877, d. Aug 29, 1880
5270 ii   MYRTLE TRAFTON, b. Jan. 4 1882, in Prophetstown, Ill
5271 iii IRENE EMERY, b Nov 9, 1889, in Winchester, Kansas.

4587 SARAH M [9] TOMPSON (*Mary A* ,[8] *William*,[7] *William*,[6] *Caleb*,[5] *Caleb*,[4] *Daniel*,[3] *James*,[2] *Anthony*[1]), daughter of Samuel and Mary Ann (Emery) Tompson, married March, 1869, Emery B. Moore of Brookline, Mass.

Children, born in Brookline, Mass :

5272 i   FREDERIC CLINTON,[10] b Feb 5, 1870
5273 ii ISABELLE TOMPSON, b June 29, 1874

4588 EDWARD W E [9] TOMPSON (*Mary A* ,[8] *William*,[7] *William*,[6] *Caleb*,[5] *Caleb*,[4] *Daniel*,[3] *James*,[2] *Anthony*[1]), son of Samuel and Mary Ann (Emery) Tompson; married Oct 16, 1870, Ruth H Ward of Boston Graduate of Harvard Law School, was admitted to the Bar in 1871, a lawyer in Boston
Children, born in Brookline

5274 i   ANNE WARD,[10] b June 18, 1874
5275 ii EDWARD SAMUEL b June 13, 1877
5276 iii NAHUM WARD, b May 29, 1879

4606 FRANKLIN E [9] EMERY (*Alfred H* ,[8] *John S* ,[7] *William*,[6] *Caleb*,[5] *Caleb*,[4] *Daniel*,[3] *James*,[2] *Anthony*[1]), son of Alfred H and Harriet B (Stockman) Emery, married, first, Helen M Merrill of Washington, Me. (born July 23, 1851, died Dec 11, 1874), second, Lydia S. Mann of Auburn, Mass (born Sept 10, 1849)
Children:

5277 i   CORA E ,[10] b June 17, 1870
5278 ii HELEN M., b June 17, 1877.

4609 ALFRED H [9] EMERY (*Alfred H* ,[8] *John S*.,[7] *William*,[6] *Caleb*,[5] *Caleb* [4] *Daniel*,[3] *James* [2] *Anthony*[1]), son of Alfred H and Anna L (Smith) Emery, married June 20, 1876, Ada L P (born June 24, 1856) daughter of Eben C and Fannie (Crawford) Snell of Waterville, Me, and Fresno, Cal He is a book keeper in Lewiston, Me.
Children .

5279 i   ALFRED LAWRENCE,[10] b Jan 19, 1877; d Nov 4, 1877.
5280 ii   MARY FRANCES b Jan. 14, 1880
5281 iii WILLIAM DEMPSEY, b Nov 19, 1881, d Aug 9, 1882
5281a iv HATTIE ELIZABETH, b Jan 18, 1887; d July 24, 1887

4610 WILLIAM P.[9] EMERY (*William B.*,[8] *John S.*,[7] *William*,[6] *Caleb*,[5] *Caleb*,[4] *Daniel*,[3] *James*,[2] *Anthony*[1]), son of William B. and Abigail M. (Hanson-Bennett) Emery ; married, first, Nov. 20, 1873, in Boxford, Mass., Sarah Lois M. (born Feb. 5, 1851 ; died March 28, 1875) daughter of Elbridge and Sarah (Kimball) Perley ; second, May 15, 1878, Lilla B. (born Sept. 20, 1858) daughter of Wentworth and Miranda J. (Perkins) Ricker. Resides in Lynn, Mass.

Children :

```
5282   i     VERNIE BLANCHE,[10] b. Aug. 18, 1879; d. Aug. 30, 1880.
5283   ii    A SON  }
5284   iii   A SON  } b. Jan. 13, 1883; { lived six hours.
```

4611 FLORENCE M.[9] EMERY (*William B.*,[8] *John S.*,[7] *Caleb*,[6] *William*,[5] *Caleb*,[4] *Daniel*,[3] *James*,[2] *Anthony*[1]), daughter of William B. and Abigail M. (Hanson-Bennett) Emery ; married Oct. 20, 1868, Bradford S. Bennett (born March 12, 1844 ; died June 25, 1880).

Child, born in Sanford, Me. :

```
5285   i     ELMER D.[10] b. Feb. 12, 1869; m. Aug. 17, 1889, Mary O. Cousins of Old Orchard, Me.
```

4612 CHARLES OCTAVIUS[9] EMERY (*William B.*,[8] *John S.*,[7] *William*,[6] *Caleb*,[5] *Caleb*,[4] *Daniel*,[3] *James*,[2] *Anthony*[1]). son of William B. and Abigail M. (Hanson-Bennett) Emery ; married Oct. 1, 1881, Nellie J. (born in North Vassalboro, Me., July 8, 1864) daughter of Joseph and Cynthia (Shaw) Moore. Selectman of Sanford, 1884–5, 1890——; U. S. Railway Postal Clerk, Sept. 7, 1885, to May 22, 1889.

Children :

```
5286   i     LINWOOD J.,[10] b. June 23, 1883.
5287   ii    LEE R., b. Dec. 8, 1885; d. Feb. 14, 1887.
```

4617 JOHN A.[9] EMERY (*John D.*,[8] *John S.*,[7] *William*,[6] *Caleb*,[5] *Caleb*,[4] *Daniel*,[3] *James*,[2] *Anthony*[1]), son of John D. and Susan A. (Kimball) Emery ; married Aug. 2, 1878, Lavinia Nutter (born April 23, 1860). Resides in Manchester, N. H.

Children :

```
5288   i     MABEL A.,[10] b. Dec. 26, 1879.
5289   ii    FRED A., b. June 2, 1881.
5289a  iii   JOHN R. b. Jan. 21, 1883.
5289b  iv    EDWARD E. b. Oct. 4, 1884.
```

4619 ELLA F.[9] EMERY (*John D.*,[8] *John S.*,[7] *William*,[6] *Caleb*,[5] *Caleb*,[4] *Daniel*,[3] *James*,[2] *Anthony*[1]), daughter of John D. and Susan A. (Kimball) Emery ; married Dec. 5, 1888, David A. (born Oct. 6, 1859) son of William and Cynthia (Drew) Woodbury. He is a blacksmith at Northwood Centre, N. H.

Child :

```
5290   i     WALTER ALFRED,[10] b. Feb. 3, 1890.
```

4621 LIZZIE J.[9] EMERY (*John D.*,[8] *John S.*,[7] *William*,[6] *Caleb*,[5] *Caleb*,[4] *Daniel*,[3] *James*,[2] *Anthony*[1]), daughter of John D. and Susan

A. (Kimball) Emery, married April 14, 1886, J. Francis (born May 7, 1843) son of John and Lucy (Gay) Baker He is a farmer in Derry, N. H.

Children :

5291 i   JOSEPHINE A.,[10] b. Feb 23 1887
5292 ii   GRACE L B b. April 16, 1889

4633 GEORGE H C [9] PEAVEY (*Lucy M*,[8] *John S* ,[7] *William*,[6] *Caleb*,[5] *Caleb*,[4] *Daniel*,[3] *James*,[2] *Anthony*[1]), son of George and Lucy M. (Emery) Peavey , married July 30, 1870, Maggie Cahill.

Children :

5293 i   HENRY M ,[10] b June 10, 1871
5294 ii   JOHN A , b Dec 27, 1873
5295 iii LUCY M , b Aug 10, 1876
5296 iv   ANNIE, b Jan 27 1879
5297 v   GEORGE W , b May 27 1888
5298 vi   FRED, b April 23, 1890

4637 ANNIE H.[9] PEAVEY (*Lucy M*,[8] *John S* ,[7] *William*,[6] *Caleb*,[5] *Caleb*,[4] *Daniel*,[3] *James*,[2] *Anthony*[1]), daughter of George and Lucy M. (Emery) Peavey , married March 8, 1877, George W. L Norton.

Children :

5299 i   ALFRED E ,[10] b May 14, 1878
5300 ii   GEORGE W , b Aug 10, 1879, d Dec 16, 1881.
5301 iii HENRY S , b Feb. 16, 1881, d July 8, 1881
5302 iv   EDWARD G , b June 1, 1882
5303 v   LUELLA D , b May 21, 1884
5304 vi   ANNIE L , b Aug 21, 1886, d June 21, 1887.
5305 vii CHARLOTTE J., b April 12, 1888
5306 viii CHARLES C , b April 22, 1890.

4638 HENRIETTA S.[9] PEAVEY (*Lucy M* ,[8] *John S* ,[7] *William*,[6] *Caleb*,[5] *Caleb*,[4] *Daniel*,[3] *James*,[2] *Anthony*[1]), daughter of George and Lucy M (Emery) Peavey; married July 3, 1882, Walter D Ellery (born March 17, 1861).

Children :

5307 i   HENRIETTA S ,[10] b May 6, 1883, d Sept 15, 1883
5308 ii   WALTER L , b July 7, 1884
5309 iii GEORGE W , b Oct. 8, 1885, d Aug 5 1886
5310 iv   HERBERT H , b Oct 25, 1886, d. Aug. 4, 1887.
5311 v   OLIVE G , b. Jan 26, 1890

4639 LAURA J [9] PEAVEY (*Lucy M* ,[8] *John S* ,[7] *William*,[6] *Caleb*,[5] *Caleb*,[4] *Daniel*,[3] *James*,[2] *Anthony*[1]), daughter of George and Lucy M. (Emery) Peavey ; married Feb 22, 1886, Orrin J Welch.

Children .

5312 i   ETHEL R ,[10] b July 17, 1886
5313 ii   ORRIN T. b Dec. 25, 1888

4670 HERBERT S [9] EMERY (*Moses W.*,[8] *Samuel B* ,[7] *William*,[6] *Caleb*,[5] *Caleb*,[4] *Daniel*,[3] *James*,[2] *Anthony*[1]), son of Moses W and Miriam W. (Kimball) Emery ; married in Logan, Kansas, 1886, Lora Dye.

Children :

5314 i   WALTER KIMBALL,[10] b. Oct. 13, 1886.
5315 ii   LEVERNE W., b. July, 1889; d. in infancy.

4691 EMERY[9] PARSONS (*Harriet,*[8] *Jonathan,*[7] *Daniel,*[6] *James,*[5] *Joseph,*[4] *Job,*[3] *James,*[2] *Anthony*[1]), son of Col. Daniel and Harriet (Emery) Parsons; married, first, March 4, 1865, Victoria Allen of Hartford, Me. (died Aug., 1866) ; second, Jan. 15, 1870, Abbie A. Mitchell.

Children, born in Hartford, Me. :

5316 i   BERTHA E.,[10] b. Jan. 23, 1871.
5317 ii   EDITH M., b. July 7, 1874.
5318 iii ADDIE L., b. May 23, 1882.
5319 iv   DANIEL EMERY, b. June 28, 1888.

4692 MARTHA JANE[9] PARSONS (*Harriet,*[8] *Jonathan,*[7] *Daniel,*[6] *James,*[5] *Joseph,*[4] *Job,*[3] *James,*[2] *Anthony*[1]), daughter of Col. Daniel and Harriet (Emery) Parsons; married in Canton, Me., Jan. 4, 1857, Sylvester Bisbee.

Children, born in Sumner, Me. :

5320 i   LUETTA JANE,[10] b. May 10, 1859; m. March 8, 1879, Levi G. Robinson.
5321 ii   HATTIE EMERY, b. Aug. 11, 1861; m. July 31, 1886, Austin F. Hollis.
5322 iii HIRAM SYLVESTER, b. Sept. 13, 1866.

4693 HARRIET[9] PARSONS (*Harriet,*[8] *Jonathan,*[7] *Daniel,*[6] *James,*[5] *Joseph,*[4] *Job,*[3] *James,*[2] *Anthony*[1]), daughter of Col. Daniel and Harriet (Emery) Parsons; married, first, June 3, 1856, Silas Ryerson of Roxbury, Mass.; second, George H. Fuller.

Children, born in Roxbury, Mass. :

5323 i   MARIA LOUISA,[10] b. July 10, 1857; m. Jan. 1, 1881, Charles M. Stetson.
5324 ii   CLINTON E., b. May 6, 1868.

4694 HENRY[9] PARSONS (*Harriet,*[8] *Jonathan,*[7] *Daniel,*[6] *James,*[5] *Joseph,*[4] *Job,*[3] *James,*[2] *Anthony*[1]), son of Col. Daniel and Harriet (Emery) Parsons; married April 9, 1864, Celia A. Russell of Hartford, Me.

Children :

5325 i   ADELLA A.,[10] b July 25, 1865.
5326 ii   ADELBERT E., b. Nov. 9, 1873.

4711 FRANCES ELLEN[9] BLAKE (*Louisa,*[8] *Joshua,*[7] *James,*[6] *James,*[5] *Joseph,*[4] *Job,*[3] *James,*[2] *Anthony*[1]), daughter of Nathaniel and Louisa (Emery) Blake; married William P. Moses of Great Falls, N. H.; where they live.

Children :

5327 i   WALTER G.[10]
5328 ii   LOUISA.

4715 EVERETT W.[9] BOODY (*Lucinda,*[8] *Joshua,*[7] *James,*[6] *James,*[5] *Joseph,*[4] *Job,*[3] *James,*[2] *Anthony*[1]), son of Edmund T and Lucinda (Emery) Boody; married Oct , 1871, Lizzie Gilpatrick (born 1848 in Hiram, Me). Live in Boston, Mass.

Child :

5329 ı LORANA,[10] b Oct., 1874

4716 SYLVANIA A [9] BOODY (*Lucinda,*[8] *Joshua,*[7] *James,*[6] *James,*[5] *Joseph* [4] *Job,*[3] *James,*[2] *Anthony*[1]), daughter of Edmund T. and Lucinda (Emery) Boody; married Oct 1870, Robert T. Boynton of Limington, Me

Children .

5330 ı LILLIAN L ,[10] b Feb 22, 1872
5331 ıı EDMUND T., b 1878.

4720 JOHN B [9] EMERY (*James,*[8] *Rev James,*[7] *James,*[6] *James,*[5] *Joseph,*[4] *Job,*[3] *James,*[2] *Anthony*[1]), son of James and Mary N (Brown) Emery ; married in Tamworth, N. H., April 13, 1871, Rebecca Blaisdell Resides in Cambridge, Mass

Child :

5332 ı HELEN MAUD,[10] b March 30, 1882

4721 HANNAH E [9] EMERY (*James,*[8] *Rev. James,*[7] *James,*[6] *James,*[5] *Joseph.*[4] *Job,*[3] *James,*[2] *Anthony*[1]), daughter of James and Mary N. (Brown) Emery, married April 15, 1865, George W. Roberts of Tamworth, N. H.

Children .

5333 ı MARY E ,[10] b July 12, 1868.
5334 ıı EDWIN J , b Jan 13, 1872
5335 ııı HENRY P C , b Feb 12, 1877

4769 JULIA D [9] BUKER (*Julia A ,*[8] *Thomas,*[7] *John,*[6] *John,*[5] *Joseph,*[4] *Job,*[3] *James.*[2] *Anthony*[1]), daughter of Fayette D and Julia A. (Emery) Buker , married ——— Perkins (died May, 1884).

Child :

5336 ı MERRILL D ,[10] b July 22, 1875

4773 CAROLINE A [9] GODDARD (*Elmira A ,*[8] *Thomas,*[7] *John,*[6] *John,*[5] *Joseph,*[4] *Job,*[3] *James,*[2] *Anthony*[1]), daughter of Stephen H. and Elmira A. (Emery) Goddard , married April 1, 1878, Herman R. Bennett.

Children .

5337 ı HARRY CLIFFORD,[10] b Nov 14, 1878
5338 ıı CHAUNCEY HANSON, b April 11, 1881, d young.
5339 ııı BATEMAN RUDOLPH, b May 20, 1882.

4774 CHARLOTTE S [9] GODDARD (*Elmira A.,*[8] *Thomas,*[7] *John,*[6] *John,*[5] *Joseph,*[4] *Job,*[3] *James,*[2] *Anthony*[1]), daughter of Stephen H and

Elmira A. (Emery) Goddard; married, first, Dec. 31, 1874, Leonidas H. Andrews; second, April 7, 1877, Henry T. Lally. Resides in Chicago, Ill.

Children :

5340 i   HENRY T.,[10] b. Dec. 14, 1877.
5341 ii   ELMIRA, b. Dec. 9, 1879.
5342 iii EVANS, b. July 19, 1881.
5343 iv   LOTTIE, b. April 9, 1883.

4944 FRANK W.[9] EMERY (*Charles G.*,[8] *Hiram A.*,[7] *Andrew*,[6] *William*,[5] *Joseph*,[4] *Job*,[3] *James*,[2] *Anthony*[1]), son of Charles G. and Franceua E. (Libby) Emery; married Nov. 17, 1886, Katherine Sinclair Hill.

Child :

5344 i   HELEN KENT,[10] b. Sept. 13, 1887.

5029 GERTRUDE[10] EMERY (*George S.*,[9] *Dea. Andrews*,[8] *Daniel*,[7] *Daniel*,[6] *Daniel*,[5] *Zachariah*,[4] *Zochariah*,[3] *James*,[2] *Anthony*[1]), daughter of George S. and Sarah (Nutting) Emery; married June 8, 1887, Jesse B. Twiss of Jaffrey, N. H.

Child :

5345 i   PAUL EMERY,[11] b. April 8, 1888.

APPENDIX A.   PART II.

464 THOMAS[6] EMERY (*Zachariah*,[5] *Zachariah*,[4] *Daniel*,[3] *James*,[2] *Anthony*[1]), son of Zachariah and Huldah (Bean) Emery; had a brother Reuben lost at sea. He had a cousin Reuben who was drowned near Albany or Troy, N. Y., 1830, married Huldah Warner and left two children, a son and a daughter.

Children :

5346 i   ABIGAIL A.[7] b. March 16, 1824.
5347 ii   JOSEPH B. KEWLEY, b. March 1, 1826, assumed the name of his guardian Sloan; d. in Goshen, Ind., April 7, 1884.

5346 A. A.[7] EMERY, born March 16, 1824, married Dec. 23, 1841, William C. Kewley. He enlisted in the 68th Ohio Vol. Infantry, Oct. 14, 1861, and was mortally wounded May 16, 1863, at Champion Hills and died in Memphis, Tenn., July 11, 1863.

Children :

5348 i   WILLIAM A.,[8] b. Aug. 26, 1843; d. in St. Clair, Mich., Sept. 17, 1843.
5349 ii   OTIS W., b. July 4, 1846; d. June 13, 1848, in St. Clair, Mich.

5350　iii　CHARLES L , b Sept 15 1848, in Lexington, Mich. , m in Cincinnati, O . Mary B Williamson.
5351　iv　SILAS D , b March 7, 1852, in Bay City, Mich , d Sept 23, 1852 in East Saginaw. Mich.
5352　v　JOSEPH B , b Sept. 8, 1853, in Saginaw, Mich , m in Cincinnati, O , Feb 27, 1878, Beulah C Bryan

APPENDIX B.

737 SALLY[7] EMERY (*John*,[6] *John*,[5] *Zachariah*,[4] *Zachariah*,[3] *James*,[2] *Anthony*[1]), daughter of John and Deborah (Colburn) Emery, married William F Pitts.

Children :

5353　i　SYLVANUS,[8] b 1822
5354　ii　SARAH F , b 1824.
5355　iii　LYDIA A , b 1826; d 1883
5356　iv　ELIZA B., b 1829, d 1867
5357　v　MARY E , b 1831, d. 1887
5358　vi　EMILY A , b 1833
5359　vii　ELVIRA C , b 1836, d. 1854
5360　viii　WILLIAM A , b 1838
5361　ix　DEBORAH L , b. 1841, d 1842

738 ESTHER[7] EMERY (*John*,[6] *John*,[5] *Zachariah*,[4] *Zachariah*,[3] *James*,[2] *Anthony*[1]), daughter of John and Deborah (Colburn) Emery ; married David Wheeler.
Children :

5362　i　AMOS,[8] m Abby Snell in Winthrop. Me.
5363　ii　MARTHA, m Horatio Cushing in Waterville, Me.
5364　iii　DAVID.
5365　iv　ESTHER, m Jonas Hammond in Waterville, Me
5366　v　JOHN, d unm
5367　vi　MARY. m Horatio C Emery (No 1895) in Skowhegan, Me.
5368　vii　WILLIAM, m Annie Garfield in Skowhegan, Me.
5369　viii　DELIA, m. James Lord in Skowhegan, Me

5354 SARAH F.[6] PITTS (*Sally*,[7] *John*,[6] *John*,[5] *Zachariah*,[4] *Zachariah*,[3] *James*,[2] *Anthony*[1]), daughter of William F. and Sally (Emery) Pitts , married Nahum C Steward.
Children :

5370　i　ASA S ,[9] b 1848　d 1851.
5371　ii　WILLIE P., b 1854; d 1860.
5372　iii　PHILO S , b 1856.

APPENDIX C.

JOHN EMERY (origin unknown), settled in Cape Elizabeth in that part of the town known as the Point , married, first, ——— ——— ;

second, April 30, 1778, Mrs. Rachel (?) Cobb. He died in 1803.
 Child, by first marriage :

 5373 i ELIZABETH,² m. Samuel Robinson, Sept. 17, 1781.

 By second marriage :

 5374 ii JOHN.²
 5375 iii EBENEZER, m. —— ——; had children who followed the sea.
 5376 iv SAMUEL, unm.; Grand Master Mason in Plattsburgh, N. Y.
 5377 v HANNAH.
 5378 vi MARY.

5374 JOHN² EMERY (*John¹*), son of John and Mrs. Rachel (Cobb)
Emery ; married ——— ———.
 Children :

 5379 i SHIRLEY.³
 5380 ii WILLIAM.
 5381 iii ELIZABETH.
 5382 iv ARTHUR.
 5383 v FRANKLIN.
 5384 vi JOHN.
 5385 vii RUSSELL.
 5386 viii SARAH.

5378 MARY² EMERY (*John¹*), daughter of John and Mrs. Rachel
(Cobb) Emery ; married Samuel Tyler. She died in 1875, aged 85.
 Children :

 5387 i MARIANA.³
 5388 ii ELIZABETH.
 5389 iii FRANCIS.

5384 JOHN³ EMERY (*John,² John¹*), son of John and ——— ———;
married ——— ———.
 Child :

 5390 i ALVAN.⁴

5390 ALVAN⁴ EMERY (*John,³ John,² John¹*), son of John and———
——— ; went to Quincy, Ill., about 1829 ; married Patience Authur-
ton ; lived in Falmouth where his house was burnt in 1849. Afterwards he removed to Portland and in 1854 went to Cape Elizabeth
and lived at Knightville.
 Children :

 5391 i JOHN A.⁵
 5392 ii HENRY F., lives in Minneapolis, Minn.

APPENDIX D.

2317 JOHN M.⁸ EMERY (*Shem,⁷ Shem,⁶ Japhet,⁵ Noah,⁴ Daniel,³
James,² Anthony¹*), son of Shem and Dorcas (Witham) Emery ; married ——— ———, July 19, 1867 (born July 17, 1839).

Children:

5393 i   GRACE HUBBARD,[9] b April 3, 1868
5394 ii ORIN SHEM, b May 30, 1869, d Aug 4, 1869
5395 iii LUCY GERTRUDE, b Oct 12 1870
5396 iv OLIN SHEM, b Aug 20, 1873
5397 v EDITH BELLE, b March 28 1876
5398 vi FRANK WARREN b. Feb 28, 1879
5399 vii ALICE MAY, b Sept. 2, 1882

APPENDIX E.[*]

5400 CLARA EMERY, daughter of William and Elizabeth (Ramsdell) Emery of York, Me ; married Benjamin F. Wilson, died April 4, 1883.

Children:

5401 i JOHN AUGUSTUS, b Sept 21, 1857.
5402 ii MARY ELIZABETH, b May 4, 1862
5403 iii EDWARD FRANKLIN, b Sept 25, 1864.

INDEX TO PART I.

NAMES OTHER THAN EMERY.

INDEX TO PART II.

CPSIA information can be obtained
at www.ICGtesting.com
Printed in the USA
LVHW081508140820
663196LV00012B/102